NOVELL'S

Guide to NetWare® 5 Networks

NOVELL'S

Guide to NetWare® 5 Networks

JEFFREY F. HUGHES AND BLAIR W. THOMAS

Novell Press, San Jose

Novell's Guide to NetWare® 5 Networks

Published by
Novell Press
2211 North First Street
San Jose, CA 95131

Library of Congress Catalog Card Number: 98-71854

ISBN: 0-7645-4544-2

Printed in the United States of America

10 9 8 7 6 5 4

1W/SQ/QR/ZZ/IN

Distributed in the United States by IDG Books Worldwide, Inc.

Distributed by Macmillan Canada for Canada; by Transworld Publishers Limited in the United Kingdom; by IDG Norge Books for Norway; by IDG Sweden Books for Sweden; by Woodslane Pty. Ltd. for Australia; by Woodslane (NZ) Ltd. for New Zealand; by Addison Wesley Longman Singapore Pte Ltd. for Singapore, Malaysia, Thailand, Indonesia, and Korea; by Norma Comunicaciones S.A. for Colombia; by Intersoft for South Africa; by International Thomson Publishing for Germany, Austria, and Switzerland; by Toppan Company Ltd. for Japan; by Distribuidora Cuspide for Argentina; by Livraria Cultura for Brazil; by Ediciencia S.A. for Ecuador; by Ediciones ZETA S.C.R. Ltda. for Peru; by WS Computer Publishing Corporation, Inc., for the Philippines; by Unalis Corporation for Taiwan; by Contemporanea de Ediciones for Venezuela; by Computer Book & Magazine Store for Puerto Rico; by Express Computer Distributors for the Caribbean and West Indies. Authorized Sales Agent: Anthony Rudkin Associates for the Middle East and North Africa.

For general information on IDG Books Worldwide's books in the U.S., please call our Consumer Customer Service department at 800-762-2974. For reseller information, including discounts and premium sales, please call our Reseller Customer Service department at 800-434-3422.

For information on where to purchase IDG Books Worldwide's books outside the U.S., please contact our International Sales department at 317-596-5530 or fax 317-596-5692.

For consumer information on foreign language translations, please contact our Customer Service department at 800-434-3422, fax 317-596-5692, or e-mail rights@idgbooks.com.

For information on licensing foreign or domestic rights, please phone +1-650-655-3109.

For sales inquiries and special prices for bulk quantities, please contact our Sales department at 650-655-3200 or write to IDG Books Worldwide, 919 E. Hillsdale Blvd., Suite 400, Foster City, CA 94404.

For information on using IDG Books Worldwide's books in the classroom or for ordering examination copies, please contact our Educational Sales department at 800-434-2086 or fax 317-596-5499.

For press review copies, author interviews, or other publicity information, please contact our Public Relations department at 650-655-3000 or fax 650-655-3299.

For authorization to photocopy items for corporate, personal, or educational use, please contact Novell, Inc., Copyright Permission, 1555 North Technology Way, Mail Stop ORM-C-311, Orem, UT 84097-2395; or fax 801-228-7077.

For general information on Novell Press books in the U.S., including information on discounts and premiums, contact IDG Books Worldwide at 800-434-3422 or 650-655-3200. For information on where to purchase Novell Press books outside the U.S., contact IDG Books International at 650-655-3021 or fax 650-655-3295.

John Kilcullen, *CEO, IDG Books Worldwide, Inc.*
Steven Berkowitz, *President, IDG Books Worldwide, Inc.*
Brenda McLaughlin, *Senior Vice President & Group Publisher, IDG Books Worldwide, Inc.*

The IDG Books Worldwide logo is a trademark under exclusive license to IDG Books Worldwide, Inc., from International Data Group, Inc.

Marcy Shanti, *Publisher, Novell Press, Novell, Inc.*

Novell Press and the Novell Press logo are trademarks of Novell, Inc.

Welcome to Novell Press

Novell Press, the world's leading provider of networking books, is the premier source for the most timely and useful information in the networking industry. Novell Press books cover fundamental networking issues as they emerge — from today's Novell and third-party products to the concepts and strategies that will guide the industry's future. The result is a broad spectrum of titles for the benefit of those involved in networking at any level: end user, department administrator, developer, systems manager, or network architect.

Novell Press books are written by experts with the full participation of Novell's technical, managerial, and marketing staff. The books are exhaustively reviewed by Novell's own technicians and are published only on the basis of final released software, never on prereleased versions.

Novell Press at IDG Books Worldwide is an exciting partnership between two companies at the forefront of the knowledge and communications revolution. The Press is implementing an ambitious publishing program to develop new networking titles centered on the current version of NetWare, GroupWise, BorderManager, ManageWise, and networking integration products.

Novell Press books are translated into several languages and sold throughout the world.

Marcy Shanti
Publisher
Novell Press, Novell, Inc.

Novell Press

Publisher
Marcy Shanti

Administrator
Diana Aviles

IDG Books Worldwide

Acquisitions Editor
Jim Sumser

Development Editors
Kurt Stephan
Valerie Perry
BC Crandall
Ellen Dendy

Technical Editor
Ken Neff

Copy Editors
Michael D. Welch
Robert Campbell
Brian MacDonald
Larisa North

Project Coordinator
Tom Missler

Graphics and Production Specialists
Angela F. Hunckler
Jane E. Martin
Brent Savage
Kathie S. Schutte
Janet Seib
Kate Snell

Proofreaders
Christine Berman
Nancy Price
Rebecca Senninger
Ethel M. Winslow
Janet M. Withers

Indexer
York Graphic Services

About the Authors

Jeffrey F. Hughes, Master Certified Novell Engineer, joined Novell in 1993. **Blair W. Thomas**, Master Certified Novell Engineer, joined Novell in 1986. Both authors are senior consultants for Novell Consulting Services and have designed and implemented NetWare 4 and NetWare 5 production sites around the globe. They have over 25 years of combined networking experience. Jeffrey Hughes holds a B.S. degree in marketing from Brigham Young University. Blair Thomas holds a B.S. degree in computer science and an MBA from Brigham Young University. For additional information regarding directory design and NetWare 5 implementation, you can also visit them at `www.directorydesign.com`.

For Wendy, Laurin, and McKenna.
Thanks for your constant support and understanding.
JFH

To Pam and Jessa, for the time and support you've given me while writing this book.
BWT

Foreword

An exciting time is upon us. Networks are at the heart of everything corporate and are quickly taking their rightful place as the communications connector to everything personal, yet external to your home. Virtually every business wants to look and act bigger than it is but is limited to the resources available. As corporations become more virtual, eventually a day will come when there is no such thing as a small business — if it's connected.

This is also a challenging time because your network requirements change as the competitive landscape around you changes; and the landscape is changing quickly. Because vendors are creatively adding value to differentiate their offerings, it's difficult to build a detailed technology plan for growth and maintain it. Your organization must take advantage of new technologies that improve efficiencies and allow your business to pursue new opportunities. Networks are becoming more, not less, diverse, and this trend will continue as critical business processes extend from the walls of your own company to your partners and customers around the world.

The one hope for keeping your budget stable (and your sanity intact) lies in building a network foundation that allows for growth and change with the least amount of disruption. This is a major objective for Novell. With the delivery of NetWare 5 and enhancements to Novell's Directory Services, Novell is providing a foundation for the continued growth of your network. Of course, the values of unsurpassed performance for network services on low-cost hardware are still there, but now with the delivery of NetWare 5 much more has been added. This foundation now also delivers Internet standards such as pure IP, DNS, DHCP, Java, and a Public Key Infrastructure (PKI). NetWare 5 is unique in offering integration of these standards with the world's leading directory service, NDS. The NetWare 5 and NDS foundation is what allows you to evolve your network at your own pace, with the least amount of disruption possible. You don't have to wait to deploy these services.

With new Internet technologies from Novell, enhancements to the core NetWare services you've been using for years, and guidance from the leading NetWare experts in the industry, your speed of deployment will be increased considerably. Jeff Hughes and Blair Thomas have made a name for themselves over the years, and their *Novell's Guide to NetWare 5 Networks* is another winner. Read and reread this text to soak up all the new exciting technologies in NetWare 5 and NDS through their tips and practical experience with these products. The value of a guide like this is not measured in a one-time read, but in the confidence you gain from putting into practice the lessons it teaches.

Michael L. Simpson
Director of Marketing, Novell, Inc.

Preface

NetWare 5 is Novell's latest flagship product, based on all the best features of NetWare 4, adding significant enhancements including native TCP/IP protocol support, a multiprocessor kernel, Java capability, PKI services, DNS and DHCP integration, and NDPS enhanced printing. NetWare 5 already is making inroads in the industry as a powerful network platform coupled with a powerful directory to provide a secure, scalable, and flexible infrastructure that fulfills the needs of any size environment.

Among its many exciting features, NetWare 5 once again offers enhancements to Novell Directory Services (NDS), including increased management capabilities, improved performance, and a powerful name service, as well as security, routing, messaging, Web publishing, and file and print services. Novell Directory Services is one of the most widely used directories in the industry. The Directory allows you to organize network resources, provide easy access to those network resources, and centralize the administration of your network.

NetWare 5 also offers integration with third-party products including the Novonyx FastTrack Server, Oracle8 for NetWare 5, and the Btrieve Database. The FastTrack Server allows you to deploy a Netscape Web server on NetWare 5. Oracle8 is a five-user version that runs on a NetWare 5 server. The Btrieve Database product provides a record manager that is used by many commercial applications.

This book is your comprehensive design and implementation guide for NetWare 5. If you are moving from NetWare 3 or NetWare 4, you'll find this book a rich source of information as you make the transition. If you're moving from IPX to IP, this book will help you install and configure native IP on your servers and clients. Topics covered in this book range from the fundamentals of NetWare 5 and its new features, to installation and maintenance, to managing the internal operations of Novell Directory Services. The information presented in this book will help you design, implement, maintain, and troubleshoot all aspects of NetWare 5 and related applications.

What You'll Learn from Reading This Book

This book is written for all LAN administrators, system administrators, consultants, resellers, and any others who design, implement, and support NetWare 5 networks.

Using this book, you will learn basic to complex concepts and rules on the aspects of NetWare 5. Whether your interest lies solely in designing a NetWare 5 tree or in understanding the requirements for conversion of your IPX protocol to IP, you will find this book to be the definitive source.

How This Book Is Organized

This book is organized into five conceptual parts: "The Basics of NetWare 5," "Designing Novell Directory Services," "NetWare 5 Operations and Maintenance," "NetWare 5 Administration," and "Integrating Additional Services with NetWare 5."

Part I, "The Basics of NetWare 5," includes information on the NetWare 5 operating system, Novell Directory Services, installation of NetWare 5, and other new features. Novell's NetWare 5 installation and management utilities are covered so that readers can quickly install and configure NetWare 5. Part I also provides readers with a comprehensive look at NDS objects and how these objects are used to build the Directory tree. An understanding of NDS objects is a prerequisite to utilizing the full potential of NDS. NDS naming conventions are covered in the last chapter of Part I.

Part II, "Designing Novell Directory Services," describes in great detail the steps required to design an NDS tree and covers design options for NDS trees, with many examples based on the fictitious ACME company. In addition, the design topics include a thorough discussion of partitioning and replicating your NDS tree. The last chapter of Part II provides clear explanations and examples of how to design your NDS tree for time synchronization.

Part III, "NetWare 5 Operations and Maintenance," provides a much-needed look at the internal operations of Novell Directory Services. We discuss NDS server operations that include partitioning operations, as well as managing NDS in a complex network environment. This section provides a thorough discussion on troubleshooting Novell Directory Services. Effective troubleshooting requires an understanding of NDS internal processes and the tools you can use to make adjustments to NDS. Refer to Chapter 9 for a detailed description on how to use the DSREPAIR and DSTRACE utilities during troubleshooting operations.

In addition, this section covers the new operating system features, security, NDS enhancements, hardware support, licensing, and third-party support. We conclude this section by discussing the tuning parameters you can use to maximize stability and performance of your NetWare 5 network.

Part IV, "NetWare 5 Administration," rounds out the many day-to-day aspects of NetWare 5 that you will need to know in order to upgrade, manage, and support your network. Topics include designing login scripts and access for NetWare 5, and providing a comprehensive security plan for your network.

In addition, Part IV discusses NetWare Distributed Print Services and how to set up and configure printing for a NetWare 4 and NetWare 5 network. This part presents valuable information on preparing for a NetWare 5 upgrade, including creating an implementation schedule, gaining lab experience, and readying your NetWare 4 servers. Also covered are the upgrade options available to you, and the advantages and disadvantages of these options. The options include the NetWare 5 Installation program, the Upgrade Wizard, and the Rexxware Migration Toolkit. Client migration options are also discussed in terms of the different approaches that are available to move workstations to Novell's latest Client 32 software.

Part V, "Integrating Additional Services with NetWare 5," discusses how you can integrate additional products with NetWare 5. These products include Z.E.N.works, NDS for NT, FastTrack, Internet Access/FTP services, and pure IP. Z.E.N.works allows you to manage desktops, distribute applications via NDS to your users, and remotely control desktops. Pure IP allows you to run IP as your standard protocol instead of IPX.

The four **Appendixes** include valuable information that you can use as a handy reference, as follows:

- Appendix A describes the contents of the three CD-ROMs that accompany this book and explains their installation and use.
- Appendix B covers the NDS error codes. This listing of error codes helps you identify problems and determine resolution steps.

- Appendix C provides information on the server console commands. This listing shows all the NetWare 5 utilities that run at the server console.
- Appendix D provides information on Novell's internal debugger and can be used to diagnose NetWare 5 operating system problems.

Special Features in This Book

Throughout this book, we use a fictitious company by the name of ACME, which serves as the basis for many of the examples illustrated in the book. We chose as an NDS tree a large, worldwide company with wide area network (WAN) connections. Our intent is not to preclude smaller companies, but to demonstrate as realistically as possible the many concepts of NetWare 5. Regardless of the size of your NetWare 5 installation, the design and installation strategies are the same. You may have fewer wide area connections or no WAN at all. As you read through the chapters (especially the design chapters), you will understand how to design a tree that meets your particular needs.

We have also, where appropriate, included Consulting Experience sidebars based on actual consulting visits with our customers. These Consulting Experience sidebars emphasize particular points or examples that demonstrate concepts and approaches to Novell Directory Services design.

The CD-ROM Set Accompanying This Book

Finally, this book includes three value-packed CD-ROMs: one containing a three-user version of the NetWare 5 operating system, another containing the NetWare Client Software, and another containing NetWare 5 online documentation, as well the Solution Pack for NDS and the Professional 5.0 Test Drive demo from Visio. If you are new to NetWare 5, we encourage you to install the NetWare 5 CD-ROM to learn and gain experience as you read through the book. The Visio Solution Pack for NDS allows you to quickly put into practice the design guidelines to create an NDS tree. You can then use your copy of Visio

Professional with the Solution Pack for NDS to design your tree. Quick installation instructions for NetWare 5 are found in Appendix A, with comprehensive installation instructions detailed in Chapter 2.

Sources

In the process of researching this book, we gratefully acknowledge the following Novell sources:

- "Migrating to Pure IP with NetWare 5" (*Novell AppNotes*, September 1998, Corey Plett)
- "Compatibility Mode Installation and Configuration" (*Novell AppNotes*, September 1998, Harinath Subramaniam)
- "DNS/DHCP Services Design Issues and Troubleshooting" (Novell White Paper, August 1998, Amitabh Sinha)
- "Novell Distributed Print Services" (Novell White Paper, August 1998, Hugo Parra)
- Novell's NetWare 5 Online Documentation

Acknowledgments

This book reflects the experience and information gathered from the members of Novell Consulting Services group and Novell as a whole. We wish to thank in particular Ed Liebing, Ed McGarr, Ed Shropshire, Michael Simpson, Steve Bearnson, Robb Perry, Alexander Adam, Deanne Higley, Howard Shapiro, Matt Keller, Kevin Prior, J. D. Nyland, Dave Beus, Bill Reiske, Kyrt Nay, Paul Reiner, Carl Seaver, Sally Specker, Jim Sorenson, Todd Powell, Todd Hogan, Richard Keil, Mark Farr, and Cindy Comstock. All have been contributors in one way or another to this effort.

Thanks to all those in Novell Documentation, Novell Technical Support, and the NDS Engineering team for their knowledge of NetWare 5.

Thank you to Marcy Shanti of Novell Press, who has been our constant advocate in producing this book and in making Novell information available to our readers.

We thank Kurt Stephan from IDG Books Worldwide, who diligently worked with us to edit and reedit this manuscript. Thanks for keeping up with all the little details of this book and keeping everything moving through production. Your help and experience have been invaluable. We also would like to thank all others from the IDG Books team, including Valerie Perry, Michael Welch, Robert Campbell, and Tom Missler, who have been very instrumental with many editorial and production aspects of this book. We appreciate your support and encouragement.

Also, thanks to Jim Sumser at IDG Books, who always supports us. His sense of humor, wit, and words of encouragement keep us going.

We also would like to thank Ken Neff, who provided a careful technical review of this work. Thanks for spending so much time working with us on this project.

Finally, as always, we thank our NetWare customers around the world who believe in NetWare and push Novell's products to their limits. We continually press forward with your help to make these products the very best in the industry.

Contents at a Glance

Contents

PART I

The Basics of NetWare 5

CHAPTER 1

Introduction to NetWare 5

"The only way round is through." — Robert Frost

NetWare is one of the world's most popular network operating systems. With NetWare 5, Novell has incorporated all the advantages of previous versions of NetWare and has added new features that build on the foundation to provide a distributed computing infrastructure. NetWare 5 increases productivity, reduces costs, and simplifies installing and maintaining your network.

Key to NetWare 5 is Novell Directory Services (NDS), which is a special-purpose name service that enables you to find and use network resources and data as a single integrated system. NDS provides this powerful operating system with the same speed and reliability that you've come to expect with NetWare 3 and NetWare 4. With NDS you can control your entire heterogeneous networking environment including the multiple protocols IP and IPX. You can also manage NT servers and desktops with NDS. Other enhancements include DNS and DHCP integration with NDS for easy IP management and workstation administration tools with Z.E.N.works, Novell's Zero Effort Networking initiative.

Many corporations have embraced and implemented NetWare as an integral part of everyday business computing solutions. Today, local and wide area networks are running business-critical applications once considered the sole domain of mainframe computers. More and more businesses are finding that they can operate more efficiently and cost-effectively on NetWare networks and still receive the same security and administrative benefits of larger systems.

With the advent of NetWare 5, NetWare has become even more powerful, scalable, and flexible, widening its lead over any other network operating system available. Before understanding what NetWare 5 is, it helps to understand the purpose and function of a network operating system. From this starting point we will begin an extremely comprehensive look at the NetWare 5 operating system and its many features.

Network Operating Systems

A network consists of resources such as servers, workstations, printers, bridges, routers, gateways, and other peripheral computer equipment (CD-ROMs or jukeboxes, modems, and so on).

The network operating system (NOS) is software that communicates with each of these devices to form an integrated system. Some of the resources tied together by Novell Directory Services are shown in Figure 1.1.

FIGURE 1.1

Novell Directory Services ties together the network resources from a central device called the server.

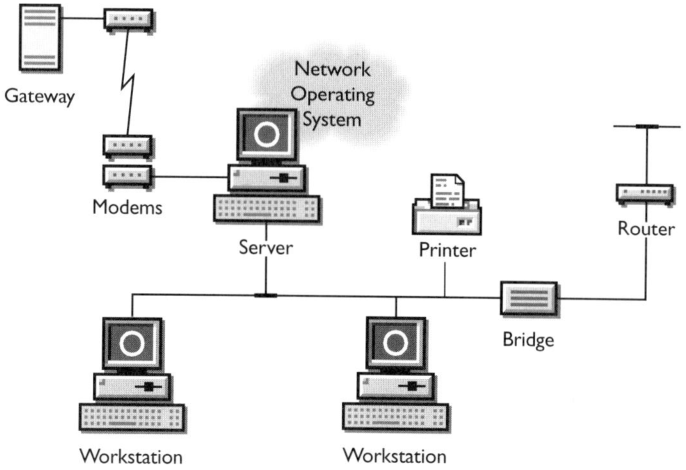

The primary goal of the NOS and all the other resources on the network is to build an infrastructure that distributes the processing power among all the network devices. The major network components or devices are the server and the client. The architecture that distributes the processing between these machines is called *distributed processing*. The following sections describe the server, then the client, and finally how processing can be distributed between each.

Servers

The server is the major component in the distributed processing model. The server is the physical hardware device or machine that runs the network operating system. In turn, the network operating system (NOS) is the software program that enables the local resources of the server to be shared among all the network users. The NOS controls the following resources of the server machine:

- Memory
- File system (disk drives)

- CPU scheduling
- Input/output to shared network devices (CD-ROM, modems, and so on)
- Workstation connectivity and access to file system resources
- Loading and distributing application programs

Figure 1.2 shows the local server resources that are managed by the NOS.

FIGURE 1.2

The NOS manages the sharing of the server's local resources.

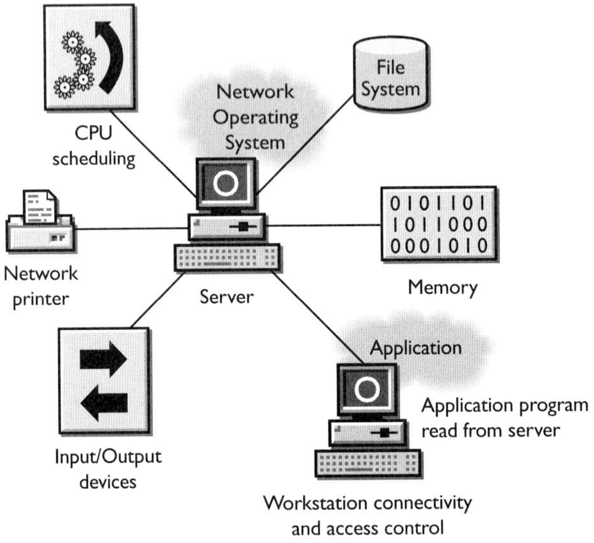

The NOS software either runs as a dedicated machine or can be distributed equally across all nodes on the network. An NOS that is distributed among all network nodes is called a peer-to-peer NOS. NetWare Lite is an example of a peer-to-peer NOS. A NOS whose major portion runs on a hardware platform is a *centralized NOS*. NetWare 5 is an example of a dedicated NOS in which the central node is called the server.

Clients

The portion of the NOS that connects the workstations to the server is called the *client software*. The client software runs on the workstations and is the consumer of services provided by the NetWare server. It also enables the workstation to load applications or share resources from the server. Figure 1.3 illustrates the relationship between the NOS running at the server and the client software running at the workstation.

Workstations that load the client portion of the network operating system are often referred to as clients. NDS servers also act as clients of other NDS servers in the tree, but not in the same way as a workstation. For example, an NDS server may communicate with other NDS servers during a login process.

FIGURE 1.3

Client software loads on the workstation and enables it to connect to the server.

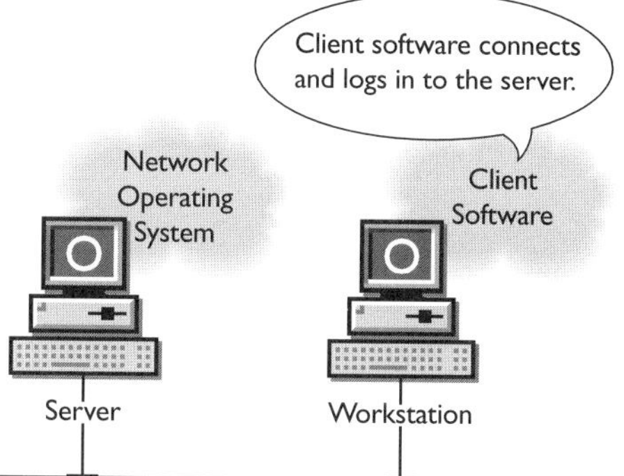

NOTE

In this book, we will use the terms "workstation" and "client" interchangeably. Technically, though, only the workstations that load the client software and make use of the services provided by the servers should be called clients.

Distributed Processing

Distributed processing occurs when the NOS coordinates the processing in a decentralized fashion. Applications running on the network are a type of distributed processing. For example, each workstation requests its own copy of an application from the operating system. The application is then loaded and run entirely on the workstation. The workstation runs the application independently, and the network operating system simply coordinates access to the shared resources. In the network, application processing can be distributed (client-based) or centralized (server-based) or both (client/server-based). Each of these methods offers advantages and disadvantages that make them right for certain applications and wrong for others.

Client-Based Applications

The types of applications that run entirely on the workstation are called *client-based applications.* For example, all the clients may use the same word processing application, but separate copies of the application are executed in each workstation. A copy of the application is transmitted from the server to the client but is executed at the client workstation. In general, applications that are keyboard and display intensive with minimal disk I/O are well suited for the client.

Spreadsheets and word processing programs are examples of client-based applications because they are heavy users of the display and keyboard with infrequent disk or file access. There is no benefit in running any part of these applications outside the workstation once the program has been loaded into workstation memory from the server. Figure 1.4 illustrates client-based application processing in which the application is loaded from the server.

FIGURE 1.4

Client-based application processing. The application is loaded from the server.

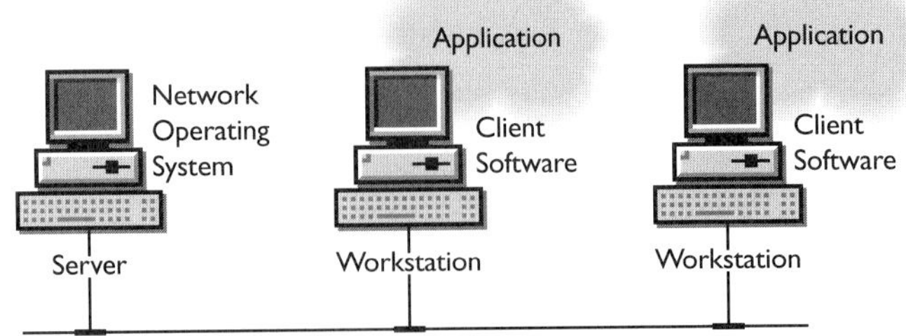

Server-Based Applications

Applications that do all the processing locally at the server are known as *server-based applications.* These applications are usually specialized applications that execute only on the server. For example, backup/restore software needs to read the file system and write it to the local tape device (on the server) and may not need to transfer data across the network. Other types of backup software run as clients on a server and transfer files from other servers. Another example is network management software that controls or monitors the operation of the operating system. In addition, NetWare Loadable Modules are primarily server-based applications, although some have a client counterpart that does some of the processing. Figure 1.5 illustrates server-based application processing.

FIGURE 1.5

Server-based application processing

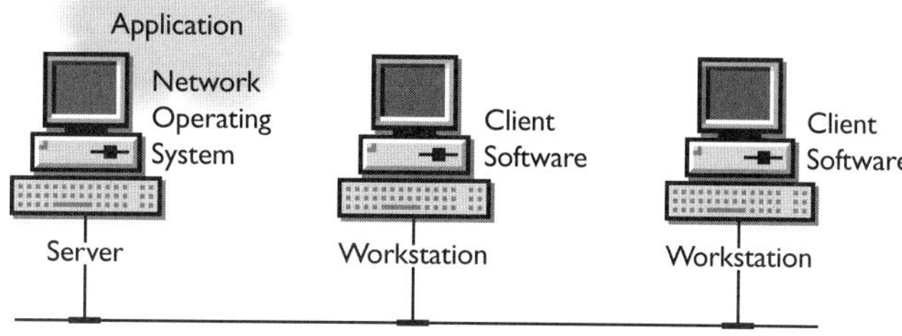

Client/Server-Based Applications

Client/server-based applications split the responsibility of the processing between the client and the server. The client and server work together to execute the application even though it is running on different machines. The fact that the parts of the application are running on different machines is entirely transparent to the user. The software that runs on the server is called the *back end* and manages the shared information. The client portion of the application is called the *front end* and allows communication and access to the server (or back end). Figure 1.6 illustrates client/server application processing.

FIGURE 1.6

Client/server application processing

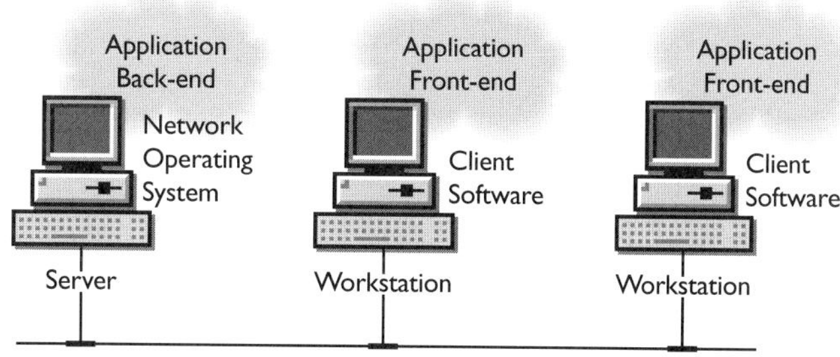

What Is NetWare 5?

NetWare 5 offers the widest range of distributed applications or network services in the industry. In Figure 1.7, you can see that NetWare 5 provides file, print, directory service, database, communication (includes host connectivity), messaging, network management, software distribution, imaging, and telephony.

FIGURE 1.7

NetWare 5 is defined as a complete range of network services.

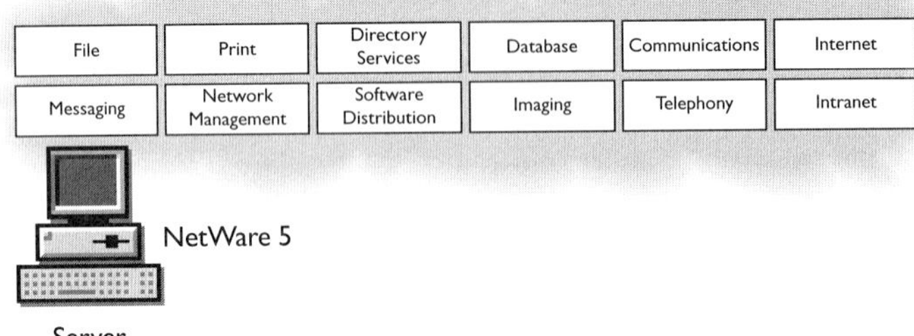

These network services are provided to the users regardless of their type of desktop. The goal of NetWare 5 is to tie users running DOS, MS Windows, OS/2, Macintosh, UNIX, or Windows NT into a distributed information system, as shown in Figure 1.8.

NetWare 5 allows these diverse workstations to access NetWare services and perform distributed processing in their native environments. Figure 1.9 shows how users can choose the desktop system that best fits their needs and still share services and information with other network users using different platforms.

In addition to the integration of desktops, NetWare 5 also integrates larger host computers from vendors such as IBM, Digital, and Hewlett-Packard. Regardless of where information is located on the network, users can access host-based resources and information from their desktops.

Applications that can benefit from client/server-based implementation are database, communications, and transactional applications that require frequent access to disk storage. Consider a database that searches, sorts, generates reports, and so forth. The database will perform better if you place the database engine on the server (where disk I/O is intensive) and process the data entry and user interface at the client. The client simply passes the data request to the database engine, which performs the action and responds accordingly.

FIGURE 1.8

NetWare 5 connects desktops running DOS, Windows, OS/2, Macintosh, UNIX, and Windows NT operating systems.

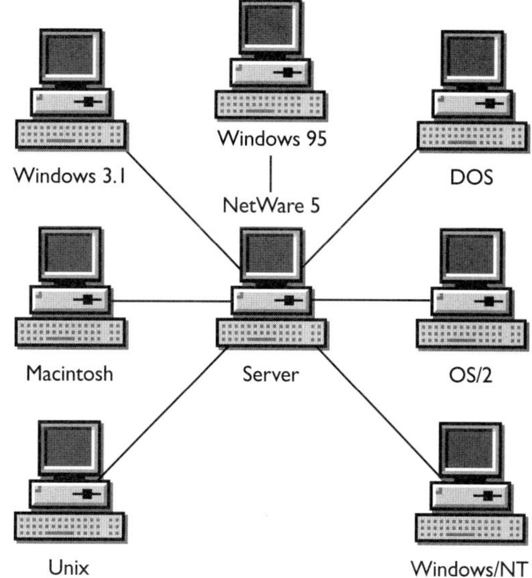

FIGURE 1.9

NetWare 5 offers distributed processing among workstations running the DOS, Windows, OS/2, Macintosh, UNIX, and Windows NT operating systems.

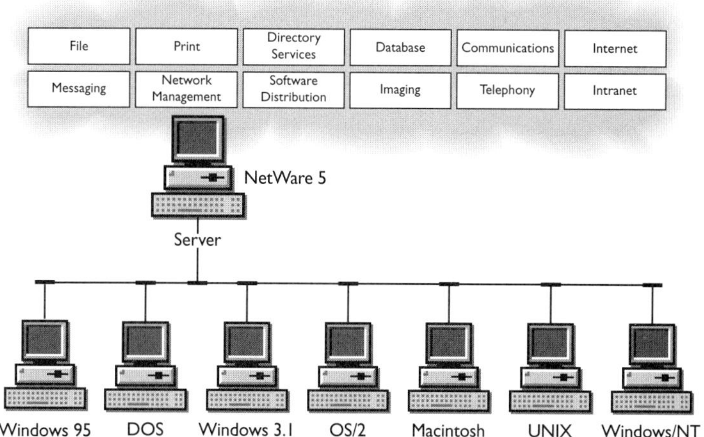

Another example would be an e-mail system in which the user reads and composes mail messages at the client and then passes the responsibility for delivery to a server process. Thus, while the server is delivering the messages to the other mail users, the client (or sender) can continue other activities.

Novell Directory Services

One of the major features that NetWare 5 offers is a true directory service called Novell Directory Services (NDS). NDS is an information name service that organizes network resources—users, groups, printers, servers, volumes, and other physical network devices—into a hierarchical tree structure. Figure 1.10 illustrates the structure of an NDS tree. We will use many examples of NDS trees in this book.

FIGURE 1.10

The structure of an NDS tree

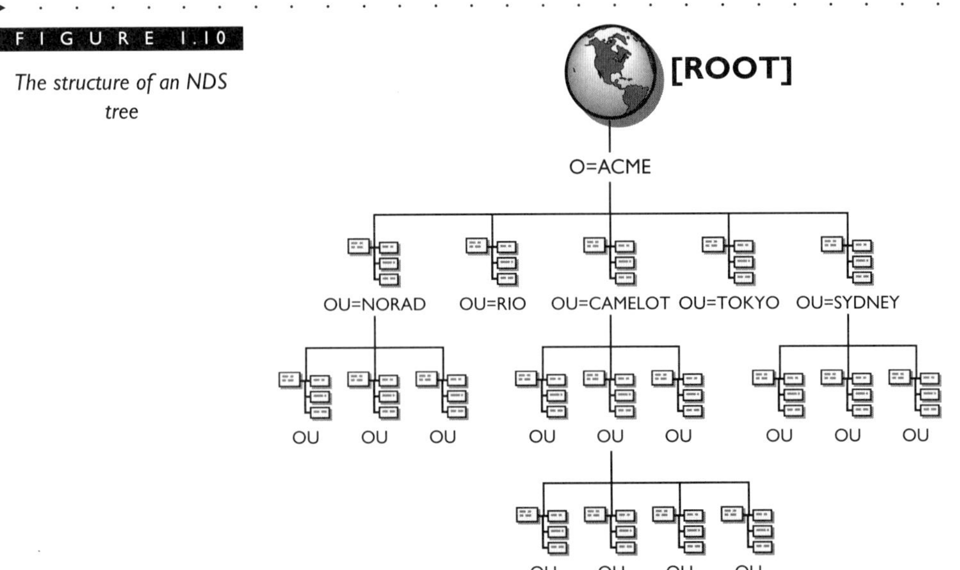

The NDS tree, also known as the Directory tree, allows resources to be managed and displayed as a single view. By contrast, NetWare 3 provides only a server-centric view. You can manage the tree including objects and their various properties by providing varying degrees of security access, giving your network enormous flexibility as it expands and changes.

NDS replaces the bindery found in NetWare 3 networks. A major difference between the two methods is that the Directory is distributed and can be replicated on multiple servers for increased fault tolerance and performance. The bindery in NetWare 3 is a flat structure in which resources belong to a single server. Compatibility with the bindery is available in NetWare 5 for applications requiring bindery services. This feature in NetWare 5 is known as *bindery services* and is discussed in great detail in subsequent chapters.

NDS provides capabilities unique to NetWare 5. These capabilities are single login, easy administration, and scalability.

NDS Provides a Single Point of Login

Users log into the network once using one username and password to access all authorized network resources. This means that users log into the network, and NDS will process other connections to NetWare 3 and NetWare 5 servers if the username and password are the same.

By contrast, NetWare 3 bindery users had to log into each network server individually with a username and password. This could mean that the users would have to provide a different ID and password for each additional server connection. Single-user login also makes your job easier as an administrator. You create each user account only once for all NetWare 5 servers in the Directory tree. Multiple user accounts on multiple servers are no longer needed in NetWare 5. This feature alone can save you hours of work. As you will see, NDS serves as the central point of management, eliminating tedious duplication and increased administrative costs.

NDS Provides Easy Administration

NetWare 5 consolidates most NDS administrative functions into a single, easy-to-use utility with a graphic interface that greatly reduces the time you spend on network administration. The Novell utility, called NWADMIN.EXE, is a Windows-based utility that enables you to make changes to the Directory with an easy point and click of the mouse. You can get information about a particular object by clicking on its icon. The icon will bring up a dialog box that displays object details that can be modified.

This object-oriented view of the NDS tree is what lets you perform many routine administrative functions easily. NDS objects, files, directories, and server functions can be controlled through the NWADMIN utility. When users change departments, for example, you simply drag and drop the users to a new location to give them appropriate directory rights, or move users with the move command. Adding file system directory rights for a user in previous versions of NetWare requires a multilayered menu and a somewhat tedious process of adding each new user. With NetWare 5 all that is required to add directory rights is to drag the user's icon to the specific directory or object; the NWADMIN utility will ask you for a confirmation prior to completing the request.

NDS Is Scalable

NDS is an object hierarchy that can be divided into smaller sections to be distributed to any number of network servers. We say it is "scalable" because one server does not need to contain all Directory information. With NDS, the information can be distributed and also replicated on multiple servers to provide increased accessibility and reliability. Figure 1.11 shows how NDS can be distributed across the servers in the network.

The feature that divides the hierarchy into smaller pieces is called *partitioning*. *Replication* is the mechanism that makes the partition redundant. The partitions and replicas are completely transparent to users and can be scattered across multiple NetWare 5 servers. These features make NDS a powerful facility for storing, accessing, managing, and using information about the network resources regardless of where they are physically located. This means that your NDS tree can easily grow to meet the demands of your environment. Another benefit is that your NDS tree design can be easily modified to reflect both organizational and functional changes in your company.

FIGURE 1.11

NDS provides distribution of the information across the network servers.

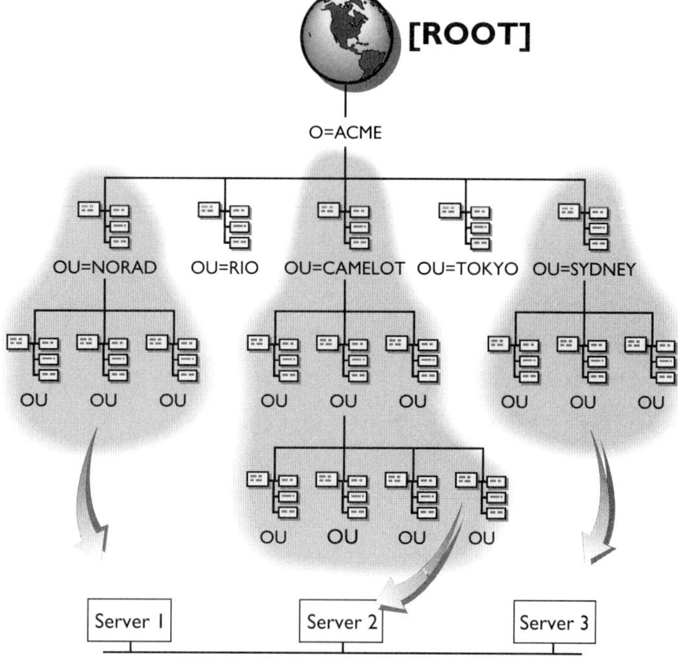

New NetWare 5 Features

NetWare 5 is the next generation of the NetWare operating system and thus inherits features from previous versions, namely those from NetWare 4 and some from NetWare 3. This section of the chapter examines the many new and enhanced features of NetWare 5. The descriptions given in this chapter will be brief, presenting only introductory information about each feature. More in-depth information will be offered in the later chapters. The new NetWare 5 features are categorized into the following sections:

- Operating system
- File and print systems
- Novell Directory Services (NDS)

- Network services
- Security
- Installation and upgrade
- Developer support
- Third-party add-ons
- Workstation/client support

Changes to the NetWare Operating System

NetWare 5 offers many new changes to the core NetWare operating system. This section describes the changes made to the operating system, which include a new multiprocessor kernel, virtual memory, memory protection, the GUI console, Year 2000 readiness, and support for Hot Plug and I_2O hardware.

The NetWare 5 Multiprocessor Kernel

The core of the NetWare 5 operating system is a new kernel that supports multiple processors out of the box. The new NetWare 5 kernel is called the NetWare multiprocessor kernel (MPK). The obvious benefit of having a multiprocessor kernel is the fact that it automatically supports machines that have more than one processor. In fact, it supports single and multiple processors from the same kernel. This means that you can make better use of existing processors in your servers or add processors as needed to help speed up specific services.

The NetWare MPK can support a machine with as many as 32 processors. During installation, NetWare 5 automatically detects the number of processors by reading the multiple processor table in the machine's BIOS. It then determines which of the NetWare 5 Platform Support Modules (PSMs) matches the hardware platform. The PSM is a hardware abstraction layer or interface that NetWare 5 uses to support different hardware dependencies.

In addition, the new multiprocessor kernel provides many new services and offers support for Java applications. The NetWare 5 operating system kernel adds these functions: memory protection, virtual memory, preemption, and application prioritization.

Memory Protection

The memory protection in NetWare 5 allows you to load any server applications in their own protected address space. The applications are then shielded from other applications and the operating system itself. The result is that failure of one application does not affect any of the other applications or processing of the operating system. You can use protected address spaces to run untried or troublesome applications. Any program or module loaded into a protected address space can't corrupt the operating system or cause server abends. The protected address space provides a safe place to run applications. All protected address spaces use virtual memory.

As mentioned, each application can be loaded into its own protected address space. A protected address space is a portion of cache server memory that has controlled communication with the server operating system. The protected address space is only a portion of cache memory that can be set aside, sometimes called user address spaces or ring 3. In contrast, the NetWare operating system does not run in a protected address space. The operating system address space is sometimes called ring 0 or the kernel address space.

In the first release of NetWare 5, only a few NLMs or applications can be loaded into the protected memory space. NetWare 5 loads Java-based applications in protected mode by default. In addition, you can optionally load GroupWise 5.2, Lotus Notes 4.6 (except for the debugging module), Oracle 7.3, and Oracle 8. However, certain types of modules and programs cannot run in protected addresses. The protected address spaces run in ring 3; others must be loaded at ring 0 instead. Here is a list of common NLM programs and executables that cannot be loaded into a protected address space:

- SERVER.EXE
- LAN drivers
- Disk drivers
- MONITOR.NLM
- Novell Storage Services (NSS)

Virtual Memory

Virtual memory is a memory management scheme that provides the NetWare 5 operating system the ability to allocate more than the actual physical memory of the server machine. It does this by using the disk as an extension of memory and by swapping code and data between physical memory and disk as necessary. When the data on disk is needed again, it is moved back into the physical memory. Because data is swapped in and out of disk, the available memory can be used for a larger amount of data than its actual physical capacity would allow. Virtual memory provides NetWare 5 with a more efficient use of memory and lessens the likelihood that low memory conditions will cause an abend condition.

NetWare 5 moves the data out of physical memory to swap files on the hard drive if the data has not been used frequently. More specifically, the available memory is assessed to see which data items have been used less recently than the rest. How recently data has been used is determined by a bit in each field of the translation table that indicates whether the address space has been used since the last time it was checked. Data that has not been used for some time can be moved from memory to disk, thus freeing memory for other uses.

As mentioned earlier, protected memory uses virtual memory. The reason is the memory management subsystem can allocate to each process a unique protected virtual address available to run the threads of the process. Thus, each process has a separate address space, so a thread in one process cannot view or modify the memory of another process. This architecture provides the protected memory for NetWare 5.

NetWare 5 will load a few applications or modules into virtual memory by default. One of those is the Java Virtual Machine (JVM). Any other modules that are loaded by the JVM will run in virtual memory. On the other hand, any modules and programs that cannot run in virtual memory can also not use protected memory, since protected memory uses virtual memory. Here is a list of common NLM programs and executables that cannot be loaded into virtual memory:

- SERVER.EXE
- LAN drivers
- Disk drivers

- MONITOR.NLM
- Novell Storage Services (NSS)

As an example, the server operating system (SERVER.EXE) cannot run in virtual memory because it must always be resident in memory and cannot be swapped to disk. The same condition exists for all the other modules.

Preemption

The NetWare 5 kernel has also been developed to support preemption. *Preemption* eliminates the problems associated with applications running on the server as NLMs that have been written poorly and monopolize the processor. In order to take advantage of preemption in NetWare 5, the application must be explicitly written or enabled by the developers to support the kernel's preemption.

Application Prioritization

As previously mentioned, MPK allows you to support *application prioritization* or *load balancing*, which ensures optimal application distribution among processors. Application prioritization is implemented as part of the new NetWare 5 kernel, and the system administrator decides how to prioritize the applications running on your servers. You can specify the level of processor use that you want to dedicate to each application.

By adjusting the amount of processor time dedicated to each application, you can tune the quality of service provided. In addition, both single-processor and multiple-processor machines can benefit from the flexibility of application prioritization. Thus, if a single processor machine has multiple applications, you can allow one application to have more CPU cycles than the others.

The NetWare 5 GUI Console (ConsoleOne)

NetWare 5 allows the server console to appear in a graphical user interface (GUI) environment. Its appearance and operation are similar to those for programs in the X Window environment found on UNIX platforms. A GUI server environment permits use of a graphical interface to programs such as installation and Java applications at the server console. To use ConsoleOne, the server must have a VGA or higher video adapter board and a VGA or higher display monitor, along with a mouse.

NOTE

The GUI environment requires additional server RAM. It is not recommended to run the GUI environment on servers with less than 64MB of RAM.

The Year 2000

Like NetWare 4 and NetWare 3.2, NetWare 5 is Year 2000 ready. For more information regarding Year 2000 compliance, visit Novell's Project 2000 Web site at `www.novell.com/p2000`.

Hot Plug PCI

NetWare 5 supports the ability to upgrade or replace network interface cards while the server is up and running, easing server expansion and providing longer server uptime.

I_2O Support

I_2O (Intelligent I/O) is a relatively new technology that improves I/O throughput and server performance by relieving the CPU of interrupt-intensive tasks such as memory calls and system interrupts. I_2O is an industry-driven software specification designed to provide a standards-based solution to offload input/output traffic from the central processing unit and allow hardware vendors to develop a single driver to work with all networking platforms. NetWare 5 provides I_2O support for Ethernet- and SCSI-class devices and block storage, making server management easier while increasing application processing efficiency.

Changes to the File and Print Systems

In addition to the changes that have been made to the operating system in NetWare 5, the file system has had significant changes. This section describes the changes made to the file system, including those to the Novell Storage Services (NSS) and Storage Management Services (SMS).

Novell Storage Services

Novell Storage Services (NSS) is the new NetWare 5 file system designed to mount large server volumes in seconds, virtually eliminating the limits on the number or size of files that can be stored in volumes and directories. You can use NSS to quickly open and update large files, such as those found in databases.

NSS cannot be used with the SYS volume. In addition, NSS cannot be used on servers running older versions of NetWare; however, use of NSS is optional. Also, NSS maintains compatibility with NetWare's traditional file system.

NSS is a 64-bit indexed storage system that allows for billions of volumes and directories. It allows up to 8-terabyte file sizes and 64-bit addressing with an extremely small memory footprint. Even more spectacular is the speed at which a volume can be remounted. Virtually any size volume can be mounted in seconds.

Novell Storage Services (NSS) eliminates several limitations that currently exist in the NetWare file system. NSS provides object-oriented storage with 64-bit internal and external interfaces. Without NSS, the NetWare file system only supports a 32-bit interface that limits file sizes to 2GB, maximum directory entries per volume to 16 million, and volumes per server to 64. With NSS, the NetWare file system can host a single 8TB (terabyte) file. This would be extremely useful for database applications. In addition, the NSS file system can support virtually unlimited directory entries (or number of files) per volume. During testing, a volume with a billion files was successfully created with three name spaces loaded. This demonstrates that the file system can support three billion directory entries on a single NetWare volume. Thousands of volumes can be created per server; however, the current NCP interface only supports 127 volumes per server.

In addition to larger volumes and more files, NSS supports very much faster volume mount times. A normal NSS volume will mount in less than one second regardless of size or number of files stored. If the NetWare 5 server crashes and a volume is not dismounted cleanly, then when the server is brought back up, the volume is restored and mounted in 15 seconds to one minute. This is the case for all NSS volumes on the server. By contrast, the older FAT-based file system is organized so that volume mount time increases with number and size of files.

These NSS features are available with NetWare 5:

- Up to 8-terabyte file sizes (a terabyte is equivalent to 8,192 gigabytes)
- Capability to create and access trillions of files in a single directory

- Faster volume mounting and repair
- Lower server memory requirements for mounting any size volume

NSS does not fully replace the default NetWare file system because of some current limitations. Future releases of NSS will address these issues. For example, NSS currently does not have the capability to create its own SYS volume and does not support the transaction tracking system (TTS), disk striping, disk mirroring, hierarchical storage management (HSM), or real time data migration (RTDM).

Storage Management Services (SMS)

Novell Storage Management Services (SMS) lets you back up, restore, and verify data stored on the network and on network clients. NetWare 5 SMS includes Enhanced SBACKUP, ensuring regular and complete backups of all the data on your network, including the NDS database, bindery data, GroupWise data, and client and server file systems.

An Improved Backup Utility

NetWare 5 introduces a new GUI-based backup utility that allows for multiple and repetitive scheduling. This new backup utility is a replacement version of the SBACKUP utility. Using this utility, network administrators can now perform backups across the network.

Novell Distributed Print Services (NDPS)

Novell Distributed Print Services (NDPS) is the next generation of print services. NDPS is designed to simplify access and administration of network print services. Novell Distributed Print Services (NDPS) is a distributed service that consists of client, server, and connectivity software components to seamlessly connect the applications to the network printers.

NDPS provides bidirectional communication between users and printers by downloading drivers for plug-and-print installation of new devices. NDPS allows users to easily locate network printers and can provide information such as printer and job status.

In the past, the Novell Distributed Print Services product has been offered as an add-on product that could be integrated into your existing NetWare 4 networks. In NetWare 5, NDPS is included as the regular print services for the operating system. If you are satisfied with your current NetWare printing infrastructure, however, NetWare 5 will continue to support it. Then you can incrementally deploy NDPS at your own pace to gain the features and benefits.

NDPS gives users and administrators greater control over their printing. Features such as bidirectional feedback, print job status, automatic driver downloading, and event notification for printer status help simplify and streamline the usability and administration of network printing. NDPS provides these major benefits, features, and printing capabilities:

- NDPS allows the network administrator to centrally manage printing services from a single location.
- Users submit print jobs directly to the printers; no print queues need to be created.
- NDPS supports bidirectional communications with the printers.
- Administrators can move, copy, delete, prioritize, and pause print jobs.
- Network administrators are able to monitor and control print jobs, and they can receive print alerts or event notifications through e-mail, pop-up windows, event logs, and other methods, such as beepers and faxes.
- Users can determine whether a printer is available or busy and can copy or move print jobs between network printers as necessary.
- A plug-and-print option allows you to quickly install printers that can be immediately used by everyone with setup rights.
- NDPS reduces the network traffic associated with SAP broadcast because direct-connect printer devices no longer require SAP.
- Any NDPS printer can be managed through a standard SNMP console using the standard printer management information base (MIB).
- NDPS completely supports the current NetWare queue-based printing environment and thus allows you to upgrade to NDPS as quickly or slowly as necessary.

Changes to Novell Directory Services

Several new enhancements make NDS more scalable, manageable, flexible, and secure. The new NDS features include transitive synchronization, transitive vector, caching the replica changes, multiple objects per packet, randomized replica lists, distributive reference links, and WAN Traffic Manager. In addition, new NDS features enable you to assign role-based administration using the inheritable ACLs, or the Password Administrator property.

NDS also enables you to more easily access the information that is stored in the tree. Using new features such as Catalog Services and LDAP, users have several different ways to view or edit the NDS tree structure.

Transitive Synchronization and Transitive Vectors

The replica synchronization process in NetWare 5 uses *transitive synchronization,* which is the method of using transitive vectors while synchronizing two NetWare 5 servers. Transitive synchronization uses the transitive vector instead of the synchronized up to property that was used in NetWare 4.

With NetWare 5, server replication no longer happens within a replica ring or list as it has in the past. Transitive synchronization works through the transitive vector. If a source server's transitive vector is more recent than a target server's vector, the source server does not need to synchronize with that target server. This procedure reduces synchronization traffic, freeing up bandwidth. It employs either the IPX or IP protocol.

The *transitive vector* is a new structure that has been added to the partition root object for each partition. It is essentially a group of modification timestamps representing the values held by each replica. There is one transitive vector for each replica. The transitive vector differs from the synchronized up to property in that it holds a group of timestamps for each replica, where synchronized up to only holds one value for each replica in the partition. Another major difference between the transitive vector and the synchronized up to property is that the transitive vector is synchronized between servers where synchronized up to is not synchronized.

Each time that the replica synchronization process is scheduled to run on the NetWare 5 server, transitive synchronization reads the transitive vector to determine which replicas it needs to synchronize with. Since each NetWare 5 server has a transitive vector, the process can immediately determine how up to date each of the other replicas are. Using transitive synchronization, a specific server does not have to contact each of the other servers in the partition to complete the replica synchronization process. After a successful synchronization, the target or destination server merges the transitive vector with that of the source server. In addition, the changes are guaranteed to converge across all replicas of a partition over time.

The Replica Ring Is Randomized

In NetWare 4, when the replica synchronization starts, it contacts and updates each of the replicas in the replica ring in a sequential order. Therefore, the first replica in the replica ring is updated first, followed by the second one, and so on. Since the replica ring is identical on all the servers holding copies of this partition, the synchronization process updates all the replicas for each partition in the same order. This may have an undesirable effect if multiple servers are trying to synchronize with the same replica on the same server simultaneously. Since only one inbound synchronization is supported per partition (not per server), one of the synchronization processes will have to back off and make the attempt again at a later time. This situation only arises if the synchronization process tends to execute at approximately the same time on multiple servers.

To help alleviate this situation, NetWare 5 changes the sequence in which replicas are processed by randomizing the replica ring list before attempting to contact the first server. This greatly reduces the possibility that one of the servers will have to back off and attempt to resynchronize with a replica. By randomizing which replica receives the first update, transitive synchronization will more quickly converge the data for each partition. As previously mentioned, the transitive synchronization process can converge the NDS data among all the replicas of a partition without having each replica talk to every other replica.

Cache Object Changes

A new feature that caches changes to the NDS objects enhances the performance of the replica synchronization process. Remember that the changes or updates that affect the NDS objects include adding, deleting, moving, or renaming an object, as well as changing the properties or attributes of the object.

Using NetWare 4, NDS sequentially searched the entire object file, comparing timestamps to find the objects that have been updated since the last successful synchronization. Sequential searching effectively limited the size of the NDS partitions. When describing implementation of the NDS tree in NetWare 4, we gave you a practical recommendation of 1000–1500 objects. In order to overcome this limitation, NetWare 5 eliminates the sequential search time by caching all changes to the objects. The capability to cache the objects in the NDS database greatly increases the speed of searching for and updating each replica and partition.

The object cache maintains a set of object IDs that have been modified since the last synchronization. The cache is populated by placing object IDs in the cache that have been modified as a result of client requests as well as inbound synchronization. Each cache entry has the modification time relative to the last synchronization. The cache that NDS maintains is for each partition that is stored on a server. The cache has a start time associated with it that identifies when the cache was built. Changes only need to be sent out if the transitive vector for the remote server is less than or equal to the transitive vector for the local server. The Janitor process cleans up the cache periodically by removing the object IDs that have already been sent to all the replicas.

Multiple Objects per Synchronization Packet

In order to help synchronize individual replicas faster, NetWare 5 supports more than one object in each communication packet. Formerly, NetWare 4 only allowed changes for one object in a single communication packet. By allowing multiple changes to different objects in a single packet, NetWare 5 reduces the total number of packets needed to synchronize replicas. If the number of changes between two replicas is small, all the updates between them can be accomplished in a single packet. Basically, this means that a partition can be synchronized in a minimum of one packet.

Distributed Reference Links

NetWare 5 includes a new method for maintaining external references, called *distributed reference links* (DRLs). These links are more efficient than backlinks for renaming, moving, and deleting external references. The distributed reference links are more efficient because unlike backlinks they are not tied to a specific NetWare server but instead reference the partition that stores the external reference object. By contrast, when a backlink is created it stores the NetWare server name and object ID for each external reference object.

As mentioned, the major downside to using backlinks is that they are tied to specific NetWare servers and not tied to the external reference object's location in the NDS tree. Backlinks result in each NetWare server's tending to have a connection to every other server in the NDS tree. In order to alleviate this problem, distributed reference links store the partition name and object ID where each external reference object exists. By storing the partition name, the individual NetWare servers can resolve the DRLs by using the NDS tree structure.

Inheritable ACLs

Using the inheritable ACLs, you can provide role-based assignments by assigning supervisor rights to operators or help desk staff to manage specific types of objects or resources. For example, you can assign rights to a group to manage only the printers, servers, or users. Using the new Password Administrator property, you can specify a help desk group to reset only the user's password.

Another new feature in NetWare 5 is the ability to see all the schema-defined properties in a single list in NWADMIN anywhere in the NDS tree. The properties that are shown are for all the objects in the schema. This gives you the ability to select any property at any level in the NDS tree. For example, you can give a group the rights to manage all users' telephone numbers at the O=Organizational level.

The WAN Traffic Manager

WAN Traffic Manager allows you to manage NDS traffic across WAN links, reducing network costs and increasing performance benefits. WAN Traffic Manager (WTM) is a policy-based tool for managing the cost and congestion of WAN traffic. Its clients (such as NDS) request a policy decision before initiating WAN traffic. WTM, as a policy evaluator, checks administrator-supplied policies and attempts to match input criteria to one of them. If it finds a match, it runs the rest of the policy to see whether to allow the WAN traffic to proceed or to delay it. WTM is a valuable tool for networks that have significant congestion on their WAN links (for example, with ISDN or slow dial-up links), allowing administrators to control and manage bandwidth use and congestion.

Catalog Services

NDS Catalog Services provides a method to store directory data in a nonpartitioned format, indexed for rapid access. Directory information stored in catalog or index format is easily customized for searching, sorting, and reporting purposes. Distribution and replication of these indexes allow administrators to quickly access a "snap shot" of the complete network directory as opposed to performing a query across the entire network.

Catalog Services enables the development of applications, which need rapid access to directory data in a centralized repository. These applications might include Contextless Login, NDS White Pages, fast lookup for LDAP gateways, and many others. One of these new Catalog Services applications, called Contextless Login, leverages the NDS catalog and allows users to authenticate from any point on the network simply by typing their login name and password, removing the need to know the location of their user object in the NDS tree.

Catalogs are stored as FLAIM databases within stream attributes in the NDS directory. Catalog databases can be scoped to include data from the entire directory tree or from one or more subtrees. The attributes stored in the catalog can be filtered according to user requirements. Catalog Services includes a dredger that reads the directory to build catalogs; an NWADMIN snap-in that controls the scope, filtering, time interval, and other aspects of catalog creation; and a set of query APIs that support development of applications to find catalogs and read data from them.

LDAP

NetWare 5 supports Lightweight Directory Access Protocol (LDAP) version 3, an industry-standard protocol that allows users to easily access X.500-based directories such as NDS. LDAP Services for NDS is a server-based interface between NDS and LDAP-compliant applications running optionally under Secure Sockets Layer (SSL). In NetWare 5, the performance of LDAP access to NDS has also been significantly enhanced, allowing unlimited scalability through NDS's advanced replication and management of back-end directory functions.

Changes to the Network Services

Several new enhancements make the basic network services in NetWare 5 more flexible, manageable, and secure. The new network services included in NetWare 5 are pure IP, Service Location Protocol (SLP), DNS/DHCP integration, the Z.E.N.works Starter Pack, NetWare Licensing Services, and Internet Connectivity.

Pure IP

New in NetWare 5 is pure IP, which enables NetWare to support TCP/IP in a pure sense. It does not encapsulate or tunnel IPX/SPX communications. Pure IP enables the servers and clients to make the NetWare Core Protocol (NCP) calls directly over the TCP/IP stack to be routed by any IP router on the network. Although NetWare 5 maintains support for IPX/SPX protocols, you now have the option of implementing a pure TCP/IP environment or using IPX/SPX alone or as part of a mixed TCP/IP and IPX/SPX environment. This is advantageous for customers who require a pure IP environment because it eliminates multiple protocols and frees up valuable network bandwidth, while allowing them to control IP implementation at their own pace.

Novell has severed the operating system's dependence on IPX/SPX and has rewritten the IPX-only applications and utilities to support TCP/IP. As a result, the NetWare 5 servers and workstations can use TCP/IP, IPX/SPX, or both. The major advantages of supporting pure IP in NetWare are as follows:

- Consolidation to one protocol in your network
- More efficient use of your LAN and WAN bandwidth
- A wider range of opportunities for remote user connectivity

Although there are major advantages to pure IP, Novell is committed to retain backward compatibility to IPX/SPX. NetWare 5 will ship with features that provide a seamless compatibility between IPX and IP-based technologies. NetWare 5's Compatibility Mode enables customers to move to an IP-only environment without having to replace valuable IPX-based applications and without having to introduce disruptions to their network operations. In addition, NetWare 5 ships an IP Compatibility Mode Migration Gateway that allows you to move to an IP-only network, incrementally if desired.

In essence, it is your choice whether to use IPX/SPX or TCP/IP as your network protocols. In order to install pure IP, you use the standard NetWare 5 installation program. During the installation process, you select the protocols that you want your server to support. If you enable IPX/SPX, you must select an internal IPX address for the server, as you normally would. If you enable TCP/IP, you must select an IP address for the server.

Service Location Protocol

Service Location Protocol (SLP) provides automatic resource discovery and registration over TCP/IP connections. Network resources such as servers and printers use SLP. SLP is more efficient than Service Advertisement Protocol (SAP) because it creates less ongoing network traffic than SAP. In addition, SLP allows network resources to carry extended description attributes. For example, a printer could be categorized as a "PostScript printer loaded with legal-sized paper used by Consulting."

DNS/DHCP Integration

With NetWare 5 you can store DHCP and DNS information in the NDS database and can easily manage IP addresses. This feature provides centralized management of your IP addresses, replication, and fault tolerance of these addresses. You can easily import DNS and DHCP data, automate IP address assignments, and eliminate network problems associated with duplicate IP addresses. Dynamic DNS is also supported.

Domain Name Service (DNS) converts domain names (such as "www.novell.com") to numerical IP addresses (such as 137.65.2.5). Since NetWare 5 integrates DNS with NDS, each user can automatically be assigned an appropriate DNS server upon login. For example, a mobile user in a distant location might be assigned a DNS server with a faster response time than for a desktop user in a local office.

Dynamic Host Configuration Protocol (DHCP) provides unique IP addresses upon request to users and network devices. Since NetWare 5 uses NDS to help automate DHCP services, you can store IP address in NDS. When the user logs into the network, DHCP consults NDS and provides an appropriate IP address to that user. DHCP eliminates the older methods of manually tracking and assigning IP addresses, and NDS ensures that DHCP provides managed IP addresses throughout the enterprise.

The Z.E.N.works Starter Pack

NetWare 5 ships with the Z.E.N.works Starter Pack, which includes Novell Application Launcher (NAL) and Workstation Manager as part of the NetWare 5 installation. NAL delivers applications to the user's desktop via NDS. Workstation Manager allows you to remotely manage and upgrade Windows 3.1, Windows 95/98, and Windows NT workstations. Z.E.N.works, which stands for Zero Effort

Networking, is a bundle of management utilities that assist you in managing individual workstations in an enterprise.

The components of Z.E.N.works allow administrators to solve a user's workstation problems without visiting the user's workstation. By adding workstation objects and workstation group objects to the NDS tree, administrators can manage the desktop configuration, distribute applications, and perform maintenance on the workstation through NDS.

With Z.E.N.works installed, workstations are registered with NDS each time a user logs into the network. Registration enables administrators to look at a workstation object's details and centrally manage workstations through NDS.

Features Available in the Full Z.E.N.works Product Additional Z.E.N.works functionality can be obtained by purchasing the full-featured product. Once you install Z.E.N.works and the Novell Client provided on the Z.E.N.works CD, you can take advantage of these additional features:

- **The Help Requester** — This application lets users send a message about a workstation problem to the administrator or Help Desk. The message automatically includes the workstation object's details stored in NDS. You can use the message and the workstation object in NWAdmin to solve the problem. This saves time and effort, especially when problem workstations are located on a WAN.
- **Workstation inventory** — Z.E.N.works allows you to easily inventory and track all the configuration data for Windows workstations on the network.
- **Remote control of workstations** — By enabling remote control access on the network's workstations, you can connect to a workstation remotely and navigate the desktop to troubleshoot workstation problems without having to visit the workstation.

The full Z.E.N.works product requires an additional purchase. For pricing and details check out the Z.E.N.works Web page at the following location:

`www.novell.com/products/nds/zenworks`

Both the starter pack and the full version of the Z.E.N.works product are discussed in detail in Chapter 19.

NetWare Licensing Services

These two services simplify installation and licensing of new Novell products. Each works on the server to reduce the time and effort you must spend on installing and licensing. Common utilities and interfaces now standardize each of these tasks. NLS provides a single utility you can use to license all future NetWare products; ensures consistent, efficient, and rapid licensing for NetWare products; and permits licensing for all products conforming to NLS requirements.

Internet Connectivity

NetWare 5 ships with the Novell Internet Access Server (NIAS) 4.1. NIAS provides routing between local and remote LANs, remote access to all company network resources (including e-mail and Internet access) through a modem or other connection, and remote service management of all connectivity services and servers from your workstation.

Changes to Security

Several new security features come with NetWare 5, which builds upon NetWare 4's existing security features. The new features have been integrated with Novell Directory Services (NDS) and help simplify administration of each new feature. They also provide security for improved Internet data integrity and privacy across public networks. The new security features include Public Key Infrastructure Services (PKIS), Novell International Cryptographic Infrastructure (NICI), Secure Authentication Services (SAS), and the audit system. This section discusses these new features and explains why they are important and how they provide NetWare 5 with advanced security services.

Public Key Infrastructure Services (PKIS)

NetWare 5 includes PKIS, which supports public key cryptography and digital certificates in a NetWare 5 environment. Digital certificates provide a method for checking the authenticity of keys used in a public key cryptographic session. In NetWare 5, PKIS allows you either to act as your own certificate authority or to use the services of third-party certificate authorities. Through PKIS, you can generate and sign various types of digital certificates and store and manage these certificates within NDS.

PKIS allows any designated NetWare 5 administrators to establish a Certificate Authority (CA) management domain within NDS. PKIS allows administrators to manage certificates and keys for Secure Sockets Layer (SSL) security for LDAP servers.

Certificate management includes services such as establishment of a CA local to your organization, certificate renewal, simplified certificate revocation with certificate suspension (without complex certificate revocation lists), creation of certificate signing requests (for use with external CAs), unlimited certificate minting services for applications, and using SSL in the NetWare environment (such as Novell LDAP Services for NDS).

Using PKIS, you can control the costs associated with obtaining key pairs and managing public key certificates. PKIS helps you create a local CA based on NDS that signs certificates for other services on the network. With PKIS you can also generate unlimited key pairs and issue unlimited public key certificates through the local CA at no charge.

NDS stores all keys and certificates that are generated by PKIS or obtained from external CAs. NDS's trusted directory features mean that public keys can be openly published while private keys are securely protected.

Novell International Cryptographic Infrastructure (NICI)

NetWare 5 includes cryptographic services named Novell International Cryptographic Infrastructure (NICI). NICI allows developers to use the Controlled Cryptography Service (CCS) API to integrate cryptographic schemes with their applications. NICI also allows developers to write a single application that can be used in several countries, regardless of the differences in countries' cryptographic laws. For example, a developer could write a single application that uses 128-bit cryptographic keys when used within the United States and 40-bit cryptographic keys when used within countries that allow only keys of that length.

NICI is an infrastructure of network cryptographic services for worldwide consumption that will support strong cryptography and multiple cryptographic technologies. The NICI infrastructure has been developed in response to customer and internal Novell needs while complying with various national policies on the shipment and use of cryptography. Cryptography services on the NetWare platform provide fundamental security features such as confidentiality, integrity, authentication, and nonrepudiation.

The services are modular in nature, which will allow new cryptographic engines, libraries, and policy managers to be dynamically added. The infrastructure is also tightly controlled, enforced through an integral OS loader that verifies modules before loading and controls access to modules only via standardized interfaces. Available cryptographic services will be provided via a Novell SDK.

NICI is the foundation for future network cryptographic services. It ensures that your product complies with international cryptography import and export laws through enforced region-specific cryptographic policies. NICI also provides for single, worldwide commodity vendor products and supports extensible, application-specific cryptographic libraries and interchangeable cryptographic technologies.

Secure Authentication Services

NetWare 5 includes Secure Authentication Services (SAS), an infrastructure for supporting both existing and emerging authentication mechanisms, such as biometric and token-authentication systems. Through SAS, NetWare 5 also supports SSL version 3. Developers can use the SAS API to write applications that can establish encrypted SSL connections. (Developers can then use NICI to ensure that these SSL connections conform to the laws of each country in which the applications are used.)

Authentication is a fundamental component of a robust network service — it is how you identify yourself. Without authentication, you cannot secure a network. Novell's Secure Authentication Services (SAS) provides next generation authentication services, as well as an evolving industry authentication mechanism for the future. In NetWare 5, SAS provides Secure Sockets Layer (SSL) support. Server applications use the SAS API set to establish encrypted SSL connections.

SAS is built entirely on NICI. This means that the SAS service itself is based on a single executable file. Because no cryptography is included in the SAS NLM, you can ship a single NLM worldwide for easy administrator management and tracking. Also, any applications written to the SAS API can also be based on a single executable file.

In addition, applications written to the SAS application can go through a one-time and usually expedited export approval process. Novell has already received export approval for SAS and NICI. This means that application developers benefit from expedited export procedures.

PKIS also provides key management for the SSL services. Any application written to the SAS interface inherits the ability to have PKIS manage its certificates. NDS access control lists (ACLs) manage access to the private key that enables SSL. Because SAS is a network service, it has its own network identity. ACLs are set up on the SSL key object in such a way that only the SAS identity can read the private key. This guarantees that nonauthorized entities such as users, other server applications, and even the application built on top of SAS cannot gain access to and expose or subvert the private key.

Auditing Services

NetWare 5 includes auditing services, which allow administrators to monitor users' access to an organization's network and to record this monitoring information in audit log files. You can create NDS objects to represent audit log files, and you can then manage these objects just as you manage other objects in the NDS tree. You can also grant rights to the NDS objects representing audit log files, just as you grant rights to other objects in the NDS tree. As a result, you can assign administrators to view and manage audit log files.

The audit system now takes advantage of exposed NDS audit services in the following ways:

- Audit log files are represented and managed as NDS objects.
- The access to the audit information and configuration is controlled by the standard NDS rights.
- Auditing is configured at the container and volume levels.
- The audit policy for a container or volume specifies what is audited within the volume or container and which users are audited.

The audit system is an essential element of the total NetWare security environment. You must have network audit integrity to ensure that the network is secure. Additionally, some industries such as banking require auditing to be done as part of business operations. The NetWare auditing system can monitor and record every relevant network transaction, which user performed the transaction, and when the transaction occurred.

NetWare provides the highest level of audit data granularity. This includes which events are audited, control of audit configuration, and access to audit data.

Changes to Installation and Upgrades

Several new installation or upgrade utilities are available in NetWare, including new upgrade utilities that easily move your NetWare 3 or NetWare 4 server to NetWare 5. In addition, there are utilities to help you upgrade your clients. These new installation and upgrade tools allow you to chose the option that best reflects your organization's network structure or design.

The NetWare 5 Installation Program (INSTALL.EXE and .NLM)

The NetWare 5 installation program is used either to install a new NetWare 5 server or to upgrade an existing NetWare 4 server to NetWare 5. Upgrading an existing NetWare 4 server to NetWare is often called an *in-place upgrade*.

The Novell Upgrade Wizard

New in NetWare 5 is the Novell Upgrade Wizard, which moves the NetWare 3 source server's bindery (including print information) and file system to destination NetWare 5 server. The utility is a wizard-based interface, which ensures ease of use for across-the-wire upgrades. The wizard can also detect potential conflicts and provide options to resolve them before the upgrade begins.

The Rexxware Migration Toolkit (RMT)

The Rexxware Migration Toolkit (RMT) is a batch-oriented, server-based tool with an unlimited capacity for migration and consolidation of servers, users, and data. This utility moves files and network bindery information from NetWare 3 source servers to NetWare 5 destination servers. RMT includes capabilities designed specifically for enhanced performance and customization during the upgrade.

The Rexxware Migration Toolkit (RMT) is provided free of charge to existing NetWare 3 customers who wish to upgrade to either NetWare 5 or NetWare 4. The utility is created by Simware, Inc., and can be downloaded from their Web site at `www.simware.com`.

Automatic Client Update

The Automated Client Update (ACU) ships with NetWare 5. This utility is used to upgrade all variety NetWare clients. For example, you can upgrade NetWare 3 clients to NetWare 5 clients automatically from a central location.

Changes to Developer Support

NetWare 5 caters to network developers by providing the world's fastest Java Virtual Machine (JVM) for running server-based Java applications and services. Listed here are several additional enhancements made to the NetWare 5 system.

Java Support in NetWare 5

NetWare 5 supports Java applications running on the server. Java Virtual Machine (JVM), which is part of the NetWare 5 kernel, allows a wide range of Java-developed applications to serve your network and users. You can now develop Java-based applications for the Internet using Java and Java scripting.

This means that the Java support on NetWare 5 allows you to run Java applets on the server console, display Java applications in X Window–style formats—with full mouse and graphic support—and run multiple Java applications on the server while the server performs other tasks.

Java support in NetWare 5 is provided by JAVA.NLM. This NLM starts the Java engine, which enables Java applications to run. You can load Java support by calling JAVA.NLM at the server console prompt, and you can run Java applications using the APPLET console command.

Scripting

NetWare 5 scripting and component services offer you choice, compatibility, and speed. NetWare 5 supports the major scripting languages available, including Perl 5, NetBasic 6.0, NetBasic 7.0, and JavaScript. In addition, NetWare 5 also ships with and supports the Common Object Request Broker Architecture (CORBA), ORB, JavaBeans for NetWare, and JavaScript.

Third-Party Add-Ons

Several third-party products are included at no cost in NetWare 5. Novell is including these third-party products as part of the NetWare 5 package software in order to integrate them with NDS and take advantage of the security and services of NetWare 5. The third-party products are listed in the sections that follow.

Oracle 8 for NetWare

NetWare 5 includes a five-user license of Oracle 8 for NetWare. This version of Oracle (specifically Oracle 8) has been integrated with NDS. As a result, you can use NDS to control access to your company's Oracle database.

NetScape FastTrack Server

NetWare 5 provides a fully integrated version of the Netscape FastTrack server. This Web server uses Netscape Web server code specifically adapted for maximum performance on NetWare 5 and integration with NDS. This integration with NDS makes the Web server easier to administer and more secure by restricting who can administer the Web server and what content users can publish. The Netscape FastTrack server supports these Web enhancing technologies: NDS, LDAP, Common Gateway Interface (CGI), PERL, and NetBasic.

BTRIEVE

The BTRIEVE key-indexed record management system is designed for high-performance data handling and improved programming productivity. BTRIEVE allows an application to retrieve, insert, update, or delete records either by key value or by sequential or random access methods.

Changes to Workstation/Client Support

Several new enhancements to the workstation or client appear in NetWare 5. Most notable is the support for Pure IP for each of the new clients that ship with NetWare 5. In addition Novell's new clients are all based on the new and advanced NetWare Client 32 architecture, which departs from the NetWare DOS Requester software (the VLM-based client). Client 32 enables client software to run in protected mode and in addition requires less than 5KB of conventional memory while providing a larger cache. The Client 32 architecture, designed for robust connectivity and easy maintenance, provides these features:

- Client 32 detects changes in a workstation's network environment and restores connections to the network when the relevant network service is restored. This makes Client 32 the most reliable NetWare client available.

And when a computer loses its connection to the network, the computer continues to run without having to reboot.

- Client 32 caches frequently used data, such as file content and network information, resulting in less traffic on the network and faster response times on the client.

- Client 32 supports multiple Directory tree access and complete Novell Directory Services access.

The new clients based on this Client 32 code are NetWare Client 32 for DOS/Windows 3.*x*, NetWare Client 32 for Windows 95/98, NetWare Client 32 for Windows NT, and NetWare Client for Macintosh.

NetWare Client 32 for DOS/Windows 3.x

In addition to all the benefits of the Client 32 architecture, the NetWare Client 32 for DOS/Windows 3.*x* software provides these capabilities:

- The familiar graphical NetWare User Tools utility is available in Windows to enable network users to manage their network environment.

- Support for Novell's 32-bit Pure IP transport is included.

- The same Target Service Agent used to enable backup and restore on workstations using the NetWare DOS Requester software works on workstations using the Client 32 for DOS/Windows 3.*x* software.

NetWare Client 32 for DOS/Windows 3.*x* differs from the NetWare Client 32 for Windows 95/98 software in these ways:

- The core Client 32 component, NIOS, runs as an executable file rather than as a virtual device driver (VXD).

- NIOS uses a text configuration file (NET.CFG) rather than the registry.

- There is no graphical interface for changing configuration parameters. You have to edit the NET.CFG file manually and restart the client software to implement the changes.

NetWare Client 32 for Windows 95/98

NetWare Client 32 for Windows 95/98 differs from the NetWare DOS Requester and the NetWare Client32 for DOS/Windows 3.*x* software in these ways:

- The core Client 32 component, NIOS, runs as a virtual device driver (VXD) rather than as an executable file.
- There is usually no STARTNET.BAT file. Windows 95/98 loads the client at startup.
- There is no NET.CFG file. Configuration settings are saved in the Windows 95/98 registry. Because configuration settings are saved in the registry, you can manage Client 32 parameters using the Windows 95/98 System Policies Editor.
- You can upgrade Windows 3.1*x* workstations to Windows 95/98 and NetWare Client 32 for Windows 95/98 in one installation process, called the Batch Install.
- Client 32 for Windows 95/98 is fully integrated into the Explorer and Network Neighborhood utilities. In addition, you can log into NetWare networks and run login scripts from the Windows 95 desktop environment.
- Client 32 for Windows 95/98 supports long filenames.
- Client 32 for Windows 95/98 supports the following industry standard protocols:
  - Windows 95/98 implementations of TCP/IP, Winsock, Named Pipes, and NetBIOS

- The Windows 95/98 WSOCK32.DLL (supported by the Client 32 IPX protocol stack)
- Simple Network Management Protocol (SNMP)
- The Microsoft Client for Microsoft Networks

NetWare Client 32 for Windows NT

The NetWare Client for Windows NT brings the full power, ease of use, manageability, and security of NetWare 4, intraNetWare, and NetWare 5 to Windows NT workstations. It allows organizations to get the most from their NetWare networks through NT workstations.

With the NetWare Client for Windows NT, you can take full advantage of NetWare services, such as NDS, and realize the performance of the NetWare Core Protocols (NCPs).

NetWare Client for Macintosh

The NetWare Client for Macintosh does not ship directly on the NetWare CD-ROMs. This client, the NetWare Client for Macintosh, is being provided for NetWare by a third-party vendor.

For detailed information about each of the NetWare clients and their installation and configuration instructions, please see Chapter 17 of this book.

Summary

This chapter has provided you with brief descriptions of the features of NetWare 5, including the many new features that greatly enhance NetWare 5 as a superior network management system. NetWare 5 is more friendly and flexible for users, while offering the most secure and cost-effective network operating system available. For installation and configuration information refer to the rest of the chapters found in this book.

CHAPTER 2

Installation and Management Utilities for NetWare 5

"The question of common sense is always 'What is it good for?'—a question which would abolish the rose and be answered triumphantly by the cabbage."—J. R. Lowell

The NetWare 5 operating system provides you with many utilities that will help you install and manage the NetWare 5 server. Your job as an administrator is made easier by being familiar with the utilities and their functions. This chapter will focus on just the installation and management utilities that are available in NetWare 5, and it will not attempt to cover all the utilities. For information on the other utilities please refer to Novell's NetWare 5 documentation. These are the installation and management utilities that this chapter covers:

- INSTALL (INSTALL.BAT and INSTALL.EXE)
- NWCONFIG (formerly called INSTALL.NLM)
- NWADMIN
- NDS MANAGER
- MONITOR
- DSREPAIR
- DSTRACE
- DSMERGE
- CX
- UIMPORT
- NLIST
- NETBASIC
- Miscellaneous server utilities
- Miscellaneous workstation utilities

NetWare 5 Installation

The first utility that you need to become familiar with is the NetWare 5 INSTALL.BAT installation program. This installation program loads the server INSTALL.NLM program. Both of these installation programs are found on the NetWare 5 CD-ROM.

Before you install the NetWare 5 software, however, you need to make sure that the server meets the hardware requirements. Next, you need to prepare the server hardware by creating the proper disk partitions. Finally, you need to update NDS running on any existing NetWare 4.11 servers to the proper version. This is the case only if you are installing the NetWare 5 server into an existing NDS tree.

If the NetWare 5 server being installed is the first NetWare server on the network, then you will want to take a moment and consider how to plan or design the NDS tree. We have found that well-designed trees, including partitions, replicas, and time synchronization design, are by far the easiest to manage and support. The design decisions you make before installation will affect how users interact with the network resources.

Server Hardware Requirements for NetWare 5

The most important item in preparing for a NetWare 5 installation is to make sure that you have the proper server hardware. The server hardware needs to meet or exceed the minimum hardware requirements as given in the Novell manuals. Novell recommends the following minimum hardware configuration:

- A PC with a Pentium or higher processor
- 64MB RAM
- 400MB of hard disk space (50MB for the boot partition and 350MB for the NetWare partition)
- A CD-ROM drive
- A 3.5-inch drive
- One network board

- A VGA monitor and card
- Network cabling

Preparing the Server Hardware for NetWare 5

NetWare 5 requires a boot partition of at least 50MB to start the computer and load NetWare. The boot partition contains the NetWare startup and server files. To create and format a boot partition, complete these steps.

1. If the computer already has an operating system installed, such as Windows, you should completely remove the operating system.
2. Boot your computer with DOS 3.3 or later. If needed, you can boot from the NetWare 5 License disk. DOS 7 and all required DOS utilities are included on the floppy disk. Do not use the version of DOS that ships with the Windows 95, Windows 98, or Windows NT operating system.
3. Use FDISK to create at least a 50MB active DOS partition: Type **FDISK**, create a primary DOS partition, and make it the active partition. The computer will restart.
4. Format and transfer DOS system files to the partition by changing to A: and typing **FORMAT C: /S**.
5. If installing from the NetWare 5 CD-ROM, make sure that the CONFIG.SYS file contains the settings of at least FILES=40 and BUFFERS=30.

Your computer should now have an active boot partition of at least 50MB. Continue the installation by accessing the installation files.

Consulting Experience

The following recommendations for the server hardware are based on a more realistic configuration for running NetWare 5 in your production network. Our recommendations are:

- A Pentium II class PC
- 128MB of RAM
- 4GB of hard disk space
- A 500MB partition for DOS
- A 24X speed CD-ROM drive
- A 3.5-inch drive
- A network card that is at least a 32-bit card
- An SVGA monitor and card
- Network cabling

In addition to the preceding server hardware requirements, there are a few software requirements. The list of software needed to install NetWare 5 on the server hardware is as follows:

- DOS 3.3 or higher (Novell DOS 7 is included on the NetWare 5 license disk)
- DOS CD-ROM drivers
- The NetWare 5 Operating System CD-ROM
- The NetWare 5 License disk
- The Novell Client for DOS 3.1*x* (if you want to install from a network)

Using this software, you can install NetWare 5 directly from the local CD-ROM or from installation files located on the network. To access the NetWare 5 installation files, complete the steps that follow.

Preparing Your Existing Network for NetWare 5

If the new NetWare 5 server is going to be installed into an existing NetWare 4.10 or NetWare 4.11 network, then you must upgrade NDS (DS.NLM) on each server first. You must upgrade NDS before installing your first NetWare 5 server. NetWare 5 will not synchronize with older versions of the NetWare 4 DS.NLM. The versions of DS.NLM that will work correctly with NetWare 5 are found in Table 2.1.

TABLE 2.1

Necessary DS.NLM Upgrades for NetWare 4 Versions

NETWARE 4 VERSION	DS.NLM VERSION REQUIRED
NetWare 4.10	5.13 or later
NetWare 4.11	5.99a or later

As of this writing, the only DS.NLM version available is version 5.99a. The NDS version 5.99a is available in the file DS411L.EXE, which can be downloaded from the Novell support Web site at `www.support.novell.com`.

IMPORTANT

It is extremely important that you upgrade the NDS on your existing NetWare 4 servers before installing any new NetWare 5 servers. Do not attempt to install a NetWare 5 server into an existing NDS tree unless the proper DS.NLM version requirements for NetWare 4.10 and NetWare 4.11 have been met. You can check the NDS versions on all your servers by going to DSREPAIR and running the Check Time Synchronization screen.

As mentioned, DS411L.EXE is the self-extracting file that is available from `support.novell.com`. It not only contains the latest changes to NDS but also includes all the latest NDS support tools. Specifically, it contains:

- DS.NLM v5.99a
- DSREPAIR.NLM v4.56.
- DSMERGE.NLM v1.63
- DSMAINT.NLM v4.96

- NDSMGR.EXE v1.25
- DSVIEW.NLM v1.05
- ROLLCALL.NLM v4.10

Once your servers are at DS 5.99a, it is important that you are using these latest NDS support tools and not the older versions, since these older versions are not supported with the updated DS.

The following information outlines the prerequisites and steps for upgrading your existing NetWare 4.11 servers to the newer NDS version 5.99a. These steps are as follows:

1. Ensure all NetWare 4.11 servers are at service pack IWSP5B before upgrading to DS 5.99a.
2. Ensure time is synchronized across all servers.
3. Ensure that NDS is healthy, which means that there are no NDS errors (–6*xx* errors) on the DSTRACE screen.
4. Ensure you have NDS ADMIN access rights to all areas of the NDS tree.
5. Ensure all communication links are up.
6. Ensure all servers remain up during this process.

After you have performed all the prerequisite steps, you will want to manually upgrade NDS to version 5.99a on the server that houses the master replica of the [ROOT] partition in the NDS tree. After this has been done, follow these steps for all other servers:

1. Create a batch file to copy all the files from DS411L.EXE to the appropriate directory on each NetWare 4.11 server. Please see the README file (from DS411L.EXE) for instructions on where the files should be placed. Since the upgrade will require unloading the old DS and reloading the new DS, you need to ensure that the DS.NLM 5.99a (and supporting NDS tools) are copied to all servers before this process is completed.

You may want to consider creating a batch file to revert to the old files, in the unlikely event of a problem.

2. Start the process of unloading and reloading DS.NLM on servers that have replicas on them first, and then move on to the ones that don't have replicas.

   This unloading and reloading process can be accomplished with NDS Manager 1.25 (which is part of DS411L.EXE). This utility will automate the update process so that you don't have to physically visit each server or RCONSOLE into the server. This will make the update process faster, with the goal of completing the unloading and reloading process before the next replication cycle.

3. After reloading the newer DS.NLM, run DSREPAIR to check for proper synchronization between replicas.

NOTE

Due to the older version of DS (5.73) running on your NetWare 4.11 servers, we recommend the entire process be completed within a 48-hour window. This upgrade is very simple and can be completed within a 4-hour window, assuming the prerequisites just described are met.

Installing a New NetWare 5 Server

The following sections describe in detail the step-by-step instructions for installing a new NetWare 5 server. These sections assume that you have completed the preparatory steps of acquiring the proper server hardware requirements, preparing the hardware, and updating NDS on any existing NetWare 4.10 or 4.11 servers. In addition, these sections only discuss how to install the NetWare 5 server from the NetWare 5 CD-ROM.

Begin the Installation

1. Insert the NetWare 5 CD-ROM into a CD-ROM drive installed as a DOS device or a network device. For information on setting up your CD-ROM refer to your CD-ROM vendor documentation.

2. Change to the root of the CD-ROM drive and run the NetWare 5 INSTALL program by typing **INSTALL** at the root. The first screen is the License Agreement. Please read and accept.

3. Select the type of NetWare Server Installation from the main menu as shown in Figure 2.1. NetWare 5 can be installed either on a new computer or as an upgrade on an existing server. If you are performing a new server installation, select New Server. You also have the option to specify the destination of the server startup files. The startup directory is the directory on the DOS boot partition that contains the files to launch the NetWare 5 server.

FIGURE 2.1

The NetWare Server Installation main menu screen

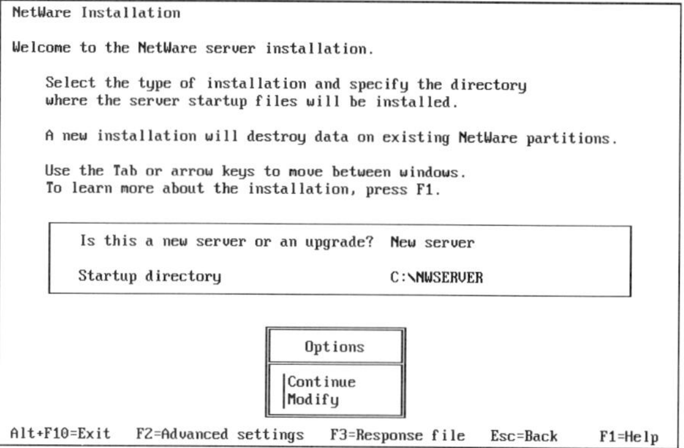
NetWare Installation
Welcome to the NetWare server installation.
Select the type of installation and specify the directory
where the server startup files will be installed.
A new installation will destroy data on existing NetWare partitions.
Use the Tab or arrow keys to move between windows.
To learn more about the installation, press F1.
Is this a new server or an upgrade? New server
Startup directory C:\NWSERVER
Options
Continue
Modify
Alt+F10=Exit F2=Advanced settings F3=Response file Esc=Back F1=Help

NOTE

If there is an existing NetWare partition, the new server installation automatically detects the existing volume and asks if you want to save it or not. The new server installation will delete the detected NetWare partition containing volume SYS and any other volumes that are part of that NetWare partition. If you want to keep volumes that are part of that NetWare partition, select Upgrade.

4. If you are upgrading from a previous version of NetWare, select the option Upgrade from NetWare 3.1*x* or 4.1*x*. An upgrade will preserve all server data including files, directory structures, partitions, and volumes. Figure 2.2 illustrates the selection for Upgrading from NetWare 3.1*x* or 4.1*x*.

FIGURE 2.2

You can select Upgrade from NetWare 3.1x or 4.1x instead of installing a new NetWare 5 server, in order to retain all of your server's data. Choosing this option will keep all the files, directories, NDS partitions, and replicas.

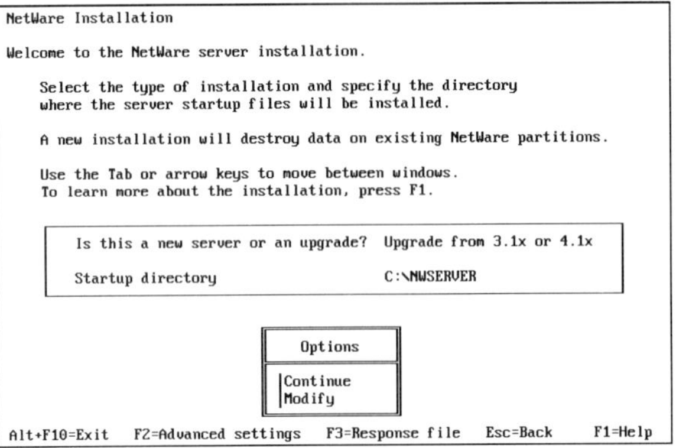
NetWare Installation
Welcome to the NetWare server installation.
Select the type of installation and specify the directory where the server startup files will be installed.
A new installation will destroy data on existing NetWare partitions.
Use the Tab or arrow keys to move between windows.
To learn more about the installation, press F1.
Is this a new server or an upgrade? Upgrade from 3.1x or 4.1x
Startup directory C:\NWSERVER
Options
Continue
Modify
Alt+F10=Exit F2=Advanced settings F3=Response file Esc=Back F1=Help

The NetWare installation program guides you through a basic server installation using default values. Although the default settings work for most configurations, you can change or specify new settings for the server ID number, numbering scheme, server reboot options, and SET parameters. In order to customize or change the default settings during the installation, simply press F2=Advanced Settings to access the advanced options.

The server ID number is a unique server identification number (up to eight hexadecimal digits) that identifies the server on the network. The server ID number functions like an internal IPX number. Although a server ID number is automatically created, you might want to enter a specific server ID number if you are installing in either of the following conditions:

- **The numbering scheme can be used to establish a predetermined numbering scheme to identify servers in particular locations or organizations.** For example, all servers in building A might begin with 0101, and all servers in building B might begin with 0102.

- **The Load Server at Reboot option defaults to Yes.** This means that the proper command to start up the NetWare 5 server during reboot is added to AUTOEXEC.BAT and CONFIG.SYS. The old files are renamed and saved with a .00*X* extension. You can select No to prevent the commands from being added to each file.

The server SET parameters option can be modified to include specific device drivers needed during the server startup process. Any modifications to these commands will be saved in the STARTUP.NCF file.

Select the Regional or Country Settings

After selecting the type of server installation that you want and setting or changing any of the default parameters, you will be prompted to choose the appropriate country, code page, and keyboard mapping for your language and computer hardware. Selecting the regional or country setting is shown in Figure 2.3.

FIGURE 2.3

During the server installation, you will need to choose the appropriate country, code page, and keyboard mapping for your language and computer hardware.

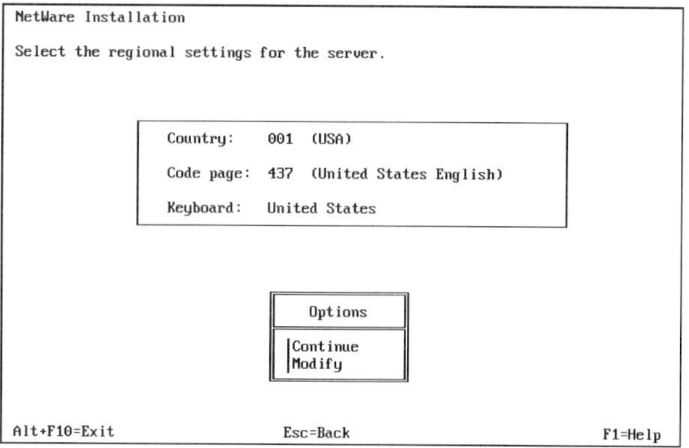

Next, select the mouse and video display type for your computer's hardware. The mouse type and video display are not automatically detected by the installation program. If the default settings for each do not match your computer hardware, you will need to identify the correct settings for each item. Please note that, although the NetWare 5 server supports either a PS/2 or serial mouse, no mouse is required.

You can select the mouse and video display using the information as displayed in Figure 2.4.

FIGURE 2.4

Select the mouse and video display types.

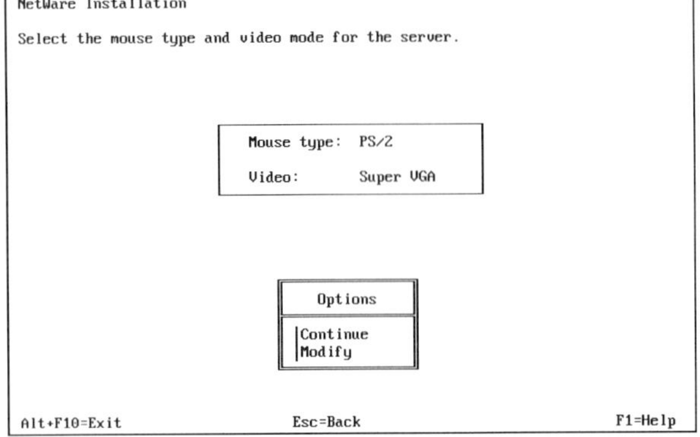

As mentioned, the installation program does not automatically detect the type of video display installed with your computer system. However, the installation program is optimized to display with video display hardware that is VESA 2 compliant. Choose Standard VGA only if your video board does not support 256 colors.

Select a Platform Support Module

The installation program will next automatically detect the device drivers that match the device types in your computer hardware. The different device types that the installation program supports include Platform Support Module (PSM), HotPlug PCI, and other storage adapters. You also have the option to change any of the selections manually. Figure 2.5 illustrates the screen in the installation program that enables you to provide hardware device driver support.

A Platform Support Module (PSM) provides increased performance for multiprocessor computers. As mentioned, the installation program will automatically detect PSM device drivers. If the install software does not detect a PSM, this means that the server does not have or need a PSM driver. Some server hardware supports the HotPlug PCI feature available in NetWare 5. If your computer does, the install program will detect it. HotPlug allows you to insert and remove an adapter card while the server is powered on.

FIGURE 2.5

The installation program automatically detects the appropriate device drivers for the Platform Support Module, HotPlug PCI, and Storage adapters. If you need to, you can easily change the drivers loaded.

```
NetWare Installation

The following device drivers were detected for this server.  Add, change, or
delete device drivers as needed.

  Device types                  Driver names
  Platform Support Module:      (optional)
  HotPlug Support Module:       (optional)
  Storage adapters:             AHA2940

                     Options
                     Continue
                     Modify

Alt+F10=Exit  Esc=Back                                              F1=Help
```

In addition to the PSM and HotPlug PCI, the installation will automatically detect and configure most storage adapters. The storage adapter requires a software driver called a disk driver to support the physical device. In previous versions of NetWare disk drivers had .DSK file extensions. In NetWare 5, the .DSK device drivers are no longer supported. Instead, NetWare 5 uses the NetWare Peripheral Architecture (NWPA), which replaces the .DSK with the Custom Device Module (CDM) and the Host Adapter Module (HAM).The storage adapter uses the HAM (.HAM file extension) as the interface between the computer and adapter card. The individual storage devices or drives use the CDM (.CDM file extension) as the interface between the drive and the HAM.

NOTE

The disk drivers with the .DSK drivers are no longer supported in NetWare 5. Instead, NetWare 5 uses the capabilities of the NetWare Peripheral Architecture (NWPA). NWPA uses a host adapter module (HAM) and a custom device module (CDM).

The installation program automatically detects many types of storage adapters, such as IDE and SCSI adapters. If your particular storage adapter is not detected, choose the appropriate driver from the drop-down list or copy it from a floppy disk. The CDMs and HAMs are obtained from the storage device or storage adapter manufacturer.

Select a Storage Device and Network Board

The install program automatically detects many type of storage devices such as IDE drives, SCSI drives, CD-ROM drives, and tape drives. You will want to make sure that the devices installed in your server have been properly detected. If one or more of your devices have not been detected, choose the appropriate driver from the list provided or insert the driver from a floppy disk. To add a driver, select Modify in the Options box shown in Figure 2.6.

FIGURE 2.6

Device drivers for your server's hardware have been automatically detected. In order to add any missing drivers to your configuration, select Modify and choose the driver from a list.

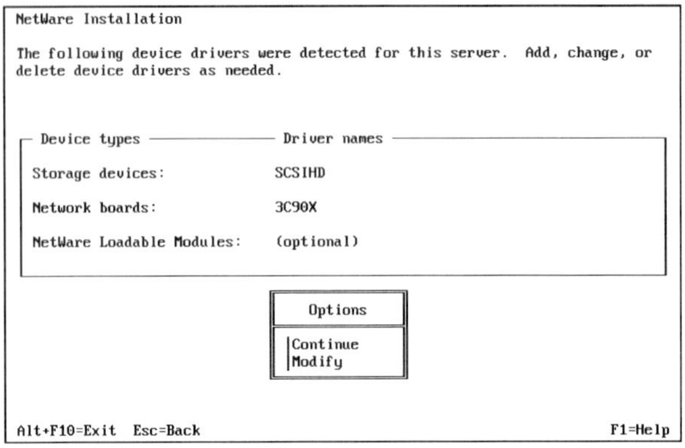

```
NetWare Installation

The following device drivers were detected for this server.  Add, change, or
delete device drivers as needed.

 Device types                Driver names
 Storage devices:            SCSIHD
 Network boards:             3C90X
 NetWare Loadable Modules:   (optional)

                          Options
                          Continue
                          Modify

Alt+F10=Exit  Esc=Back                                        F1=Help
```

Create a NetWare Partition and SYS Volume

After the device drivers have been installed, you next need to set up the NetWare partitions and volumes. You will want to use the volumes to divide NetWare partitions into smaller sections. During the installation, NetWare will automatically create the first NetWare volume on your server as volume SYS. NetWare 5 requires a minimum SYS volume of 350MB. You can modify the partition size by entering the desired size in megabytes. If you plan to have additional volumes on the NetWare partition, do not allocate the entire partition to the SYS volume. In order to create NetWare partitions and volume SYS for your server, follow these directions:

1. If volume SYS already exists on the server, you must replace volume SYS when doing a new server installation. Removing an existing volume SYS is optional. When removing volume SYS during a new server installation, you must choose either to replace just the SYS volume and its partition or to remove all NetWare volumes and NetWare/NSS partitions. Either option

will remove only NetWare partitions. Other types of partitions, such as DOS, Unix, and system/utility partitions, will not be removed. Figure 2.7 shows the installation screen for removing existing NetWare volumes and partitions.

FIGURE 2.7

The installation program will detect an existing NetWare volume. You have the option to replace just the SYS volume or all volumes.

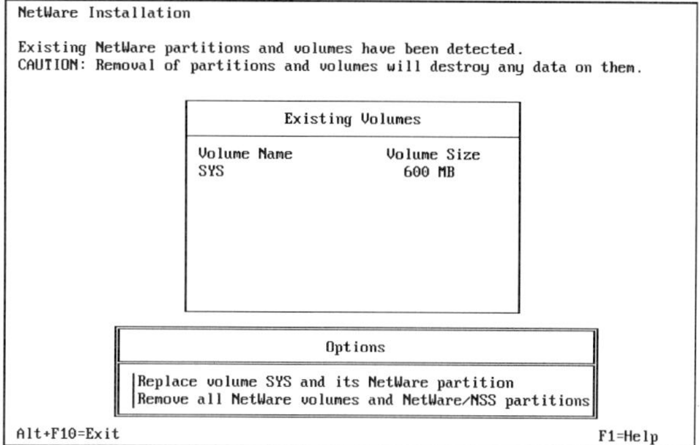
NetWare Installation

Existing NetWare partitions and volumes have been detected.
CAUTION: Removal of partitions and volumes will destroy any data on them.

Existing Volumes

Volume Name	Volume Size
SYS	600 MB

Options

Replace volume SYS and its NetWare partition
Remove all NetWare volumes and NetWare/NSS partitions

Alt+F10=Exit F1=Help

2. If there is no existing SYS volume, the installation program will guide you through creating one. First you must create the NetWare partition that will host the volume. By default, NetWare will try to take all available space on the storage device and allocate it to the NetWare partition, unless you change the size. To modify the NetWare partition size, select the Modify option as shown in Figure 2.8. Select the device, and backspace over the current size. Type the new size and press Enter. Press F10 to save the settings and continue.

NOTE

NSS volumes use disk space outside the NetWare partition. If you want to create NSS volumes, remember to reduce the size of the NetWare partition so that the appropriate amount of disk space is available for NSS volumes. The volume SYS must be a traditional volume. It cannot be an NSS volume.

FIGURE 2.8

The NetWare installation program will try to take all available space on the device and allocate it to the partition and volume. You can modify the size using the Modify option.

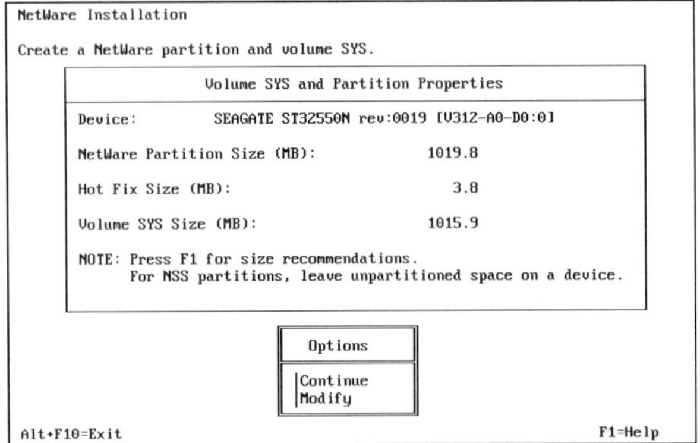

In order to know how big the SYS volume is, we should start with the minimum requirement for the NetWare 5 operating system. As previously mentioned, the operating system requires a SYS volume of at least 350MB. Although the NetWare operating system requires only 350MB, volume SYS must be large enough to accommodate all of the NetWare products that will be installed. Table 2.2 outlines the absolute minimum requirements for the SYS volume. In addition to the minimum sizes in the table, you should add as much as 200–300MB to the volume SYS size. This should prove optimal for most system operations.

TABLE 2.2

Minimum Recommendations for SYS Volume Size

NETWARE 5 PRODUCTS	MINIMUM VOLUME SYS SIZE
NetWare 5 operating system	350MB
NetWare 5 with default products	450MB
NetWare 5 with all products	550MB
NetWare 5 with all products and documentation	700MB

Although default settings work for most installations, you might need to modify volume properties such as block size, file compression, data migration, and suballocation. To modify the properties of the SYS volume, press F3=Volume Properties. A new screen will appear, which allows you to change the block size and change or display status (mounted or unmounted), file compression, block suballocation, and data migration. Figure 2.9 shows an example of the volume properties screen.

FIGURE 2.9

The installation program allows you to modify the properties of the volumes.

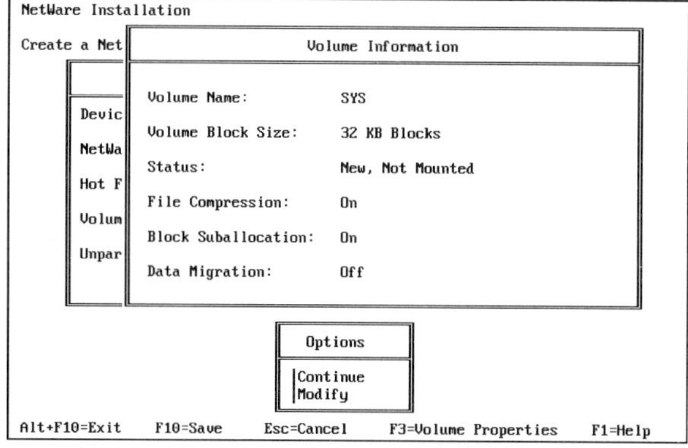

Although you can change the volume block size using the volume properties screen, the volume block size is automatically optimized for your server on the basis of the size of the volume. Typically, a larger block size optimizes the volume for large files.

File compression, by default, is automatically enabled. Enabling the compression feature maximizes disk space in NetWare 5. The only negative is that the file access for files that have been compressed is increased. Also note that some backup programs cannot back up compressed files.

Suballocation is also automatically enabled in NetWare 5. Suballocation allows more efficient use of disk space because it allows blocks to contain data from more than one file.

Data migration is automatically disabled. Data migration is used to identify inactive files and move them to near-line storage systems, such as optical disks. Inactive files are files that have not been opened for a specified amount of time.

Choose Graphical Mode for the Installation Program

After you have set up all the initial hardware features, the NetWare 5 system files will be copied to the SYS volume. If you are installing from the network, you will be prompted to reconnect to the network. To continue the installation, enter the password for the user that originally logged in. After the initial copy, the NetWare 5 installation program will continue in graphical display mode.

Although a mouse is recommended to navigate the graphical display, you can use the keyboard commands shown in Table 2.3. In general you will use the arrow keys on the numeric keypad for cursor movements. Before trying to use these keys, make sure that the NumLock (number lock) key is on to enable cursor movement from the keypad.

TABLE 2.3
Graphical Keyboard Actions

KEYSTROKE	ACTION
Tab	Move focus to next element.
Shift+Tab	Move focus to previous element.
Enter	Select.
Up-arrow (keypad 8)	Move cursor up.
Down-arrow (keypad 2)	Move cursor down.
Right-arrow (keypad 6)	Move cursor right.
Left-arrow (keypad 4)	Move cursor left.
Hold Shift while pressing keypad	Accelerate cursor movement.
Keypad 5	Select or click an object.
Keypad 0	Lock a selected object (for dragging).
Keypad . (period)	Unlock a selected object (to drop).
Keypad + (plus)	Double-click an object.
Alt+F7	Move to next window.
Alt+F8	Move to previous window.

Name the NetWare 5 Server

The first dialog box that appears in the NetWare 5 graphical display of the installation program names the NetWare 5 server. The NetWare 5 server must be unique among all other servers in the NDS tree. The server name can have from 2 to 47 alphanumeric characters and can contain underscores and dashes, but no spaces. The first character cannot be a period. Figure 2.10 shows this dialog box.

FIGURE 2.10

The NetWare 5 server is named using the graphical display mode in the installation program.

Install the NetWare File System

After giving the NetWare 5 server a name, you are now ready to create volumes in addition to the SYS volume, which has already been created. You can create either traditional volumes or NSS volumes. Additional volumes can be created from available disk space on your hard drive.

The traditional NetWare volume supports all the normal NetWare 5 features including suballocation, compression, data migration, and the transaction tracking system (TTS).

Novell Storage Services (NSS) is a new file system in NetWare 5 that offers increased flexibility with large files, name spaces, and storage devices. Although NSS volumes currently do not support data migration, data duplexing, disk mirroring, disk striping, file compression, TTS, FTP, VREPAIR, NFS, or filename lock in NetWare 5, these features are being developed.

The dialog box shown in Figure 2.11 is used to create NetWare volumes from free space on disk drives. Notice that the SYS volume already exists because it was created in an earlier process.

As mentioned, additional volumes can be created from any available free space on a storage device. Volume names can have between 2 and 15 characters. Valid characters include A through Z, 0 through 9, and the following characters: ! - @ # $ % & ( ). The volume name cannot begin with an underscore or have two or more consecutive underscores.

FIGURE 2.11

You can create volumes from free space on disk drives. Using this utility, you can create either traditional NetWare volumes or NSS volumes. The NSS volumes are new in NetWare 5.

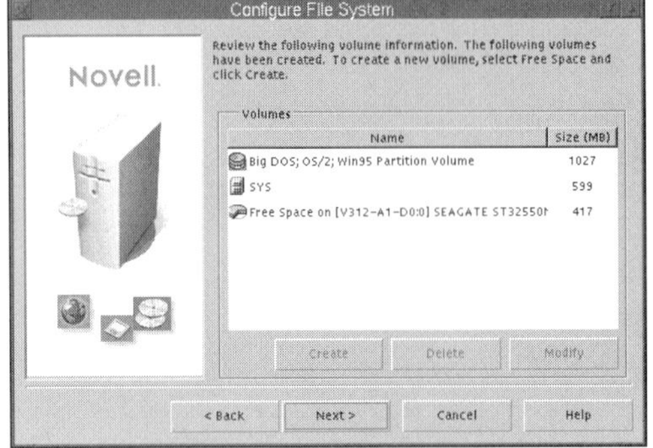

In NetWare 5, a large disk drive installed in the server can be divided into several volumes during installation. Conversely, a volume can be distributed over multiple physical disk drives. Be aware, however, that creating a volume that spans two or more storage devices is never recommended. If a volume spans disk devices and one of the devices fails, all data on the entire volume could be lost. We typically recommend that you create volumes that match the physical size of the disk device.

Traditional volumes can be created from either traditional or unpartitioned free space as shown in Figure 2.12. In this example we are creating a volume called VOL1.

FIGURE 2.12

The NetWare 5 installation program allows you to create volumes on the server. The volume called VOL1 is created as a traditional volume from the free space on the disk device.

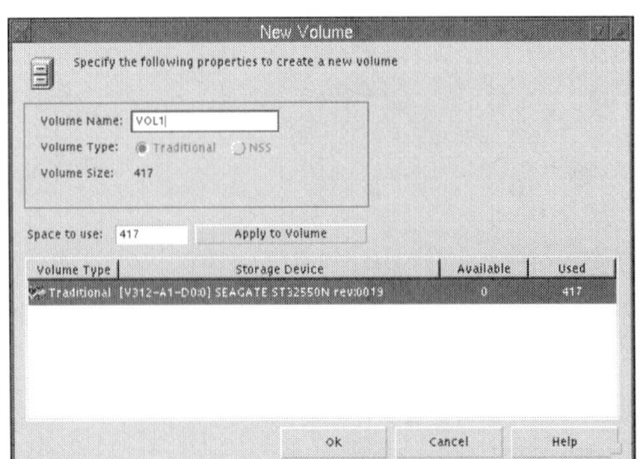

To create a traditional volume, you simply select free space on the appropriate disk drive, select the volume type, and click the Create button. Next, type the name of the volume that you desire and click the OK button. To allocate only a portion of the free disk space to the volume, type the amount of space to use, and click the Apply to Volume button.

If you want to add more space to the volume, first make the volume include additional free space by selecting any additional free space on any disk device, then type the amount of space to use on that device, and finally click the Apply to Volume button.

In addition to the traditional volumes, you can also create NSS volumes using this utility. In order to create the NSS volume, select the appropriate free space and click the Create button. Next select the Volume Type NSS option, type the name of the volume, and click OK.

If while creating the NSS volume you find that the Volume Type NSS option is not available, then the selected free space is not available for NSS. This means that the disk device will not support the NSS file system. To continue, you need to go back to the previous screen and select another area of free space.

Figure 2.13 shows an example in the NetWare 5 installation program of creating an NSS volume.

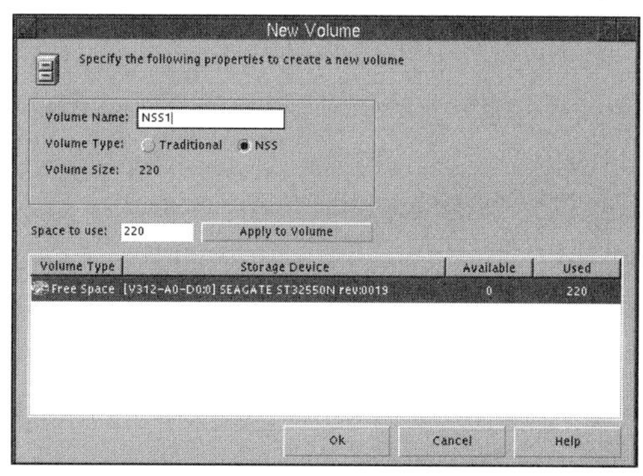

FIGURE 2.13

You can create an NSS volume using the installation program. In order to create the NSS volume, select the appropriate free space and click the Create button. Next select the Volume Type NSS option, type the name of the volume, and click OK.

In addition to creating new volumes for the NetWare 5 server, you can also modify the size of existing volumes, delete a volume, or mount volumes. When modifying the size of any existing volume, you can either increase or decrease it. To reduce the size of an existing volume, however, you must delete and recreate the volume. You can delete any volume you have created, except volume SYS. When a volume is deleted, all data on the volume is lost.

In order for volumes to be accessed by NetWare 5, they must be mounted. Volumes can be mounted immediately or at the end of installation. If you created a traditional NetWare volume, then the mounting time depends on its size. Figure 2.14 illustrates how new volumes can be mounted during the installation process. We recommend you mount the volumes now if you plan to install additional products and services, such as the NetWare 5 documentation, on a volume other than volume SYS. You can also wait to mount volumes after the installation program completes, if you are installing products and services on volume SYS only.

FIGURE 2.14

The new volumes that you have created can be mounted either immediately or after the installation completes.

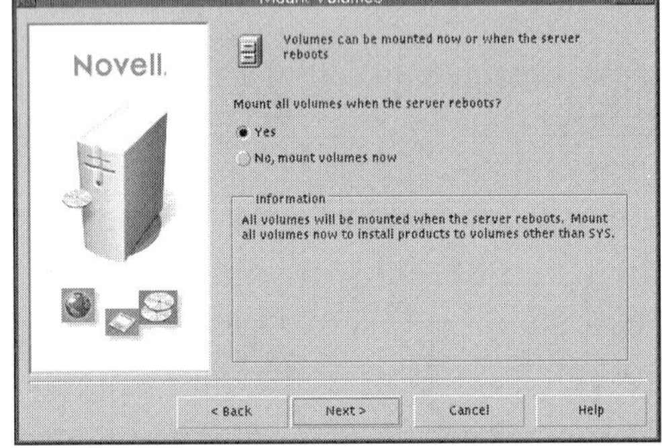

Install the Networking Protocols

The NetWare 5 server can be installed to support several different network protocol configurations. For example the server can process pure IP packets or IPX packets. In some cases you may want to mix and match IP and IPX. If you are moving from NetWare 4 and IPX to NetWare 5 and pure IP, then you will want the compatibility of both protocols during the transition period. Therefore, you can set up your NetWare 5 server to install IP only, IPX only, or both protocols.

NetWare 5 provides the NCPs to run on either IPX or IP. In a dual-stack environment, the NCP engine will select an IP connection before an IPX connection. If an IP connection is made, then all of the NCP packets will use the TCP transport for communication. One of the advantages of a protocol-independent system is that the system can support IP, IPX, or both concurrently. Thus, there is significant opportunity for mixing and matching the multiple protocols to achieve migration goals.

In the NetWare 5 installation program, the protocols are assigned to network boards. Both the IPX and IP protocols can be assigned to a single network board, a fact that allows the server to communicate using IP and IPX. Figure 2.15 illustrates how you select the protocols to use during the installation process.

FIGURE 2.15

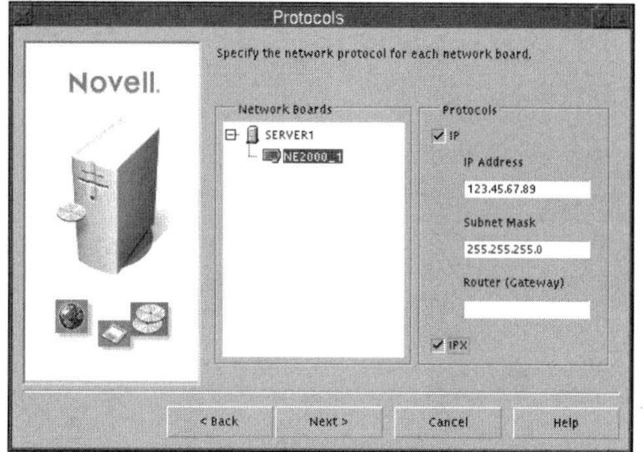

The network protocols are assigned directly to the network boards. Both the IPX and IP protocols can be assigned to a single network board, a fact that allows the server to communicate using IP and IPX.

For IP only, you must have a unique IP address, a subnet mask, and a router or gateway address. Follow the install instructions on the screen. NetWare 5 will automatically load and bind the appropriate IP frame type for your network board. Passive support for IPX is still provided. The server will respond to IPX requests but will not broadcast its service using IPX. For IPX only follow the instructions on the screen. NetWare will automatically load and bind the appropriate IPX frame types for your network board. For IPX and IP together likewise follow the instructions on the screen. Both protocols can be bound to a single network board. The server will process IP requests using pure IP. The server will also broadcast and reply to IPX requests using IPX.

Set the Server's Time Zone

After you have selected the specific protocols that you want the server to use, you need to set the server's time zone in preparation for installing Novell Directory Services (NDS). In order to set the server's time zone, select the appropriate location where the server will reside, as shown in Figure 2.16.

The server time and time zone are important in order to synchronize network events. Advanced time synchronization settings are available during the Customize section of the installation.

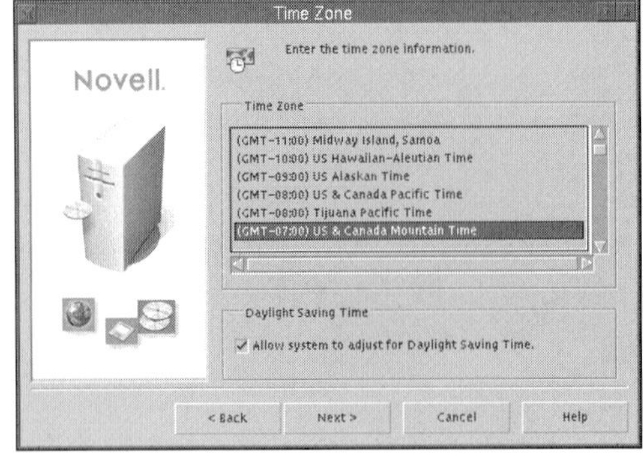

FIGURE 2.16

The NetWare 5 installation program allows you to set the server's time zone by selecting the appropriate location where the server will reside physically.

Set Up or Install Novell Directory Services (NDS)

Novell Directory Services (NDS) is Novell's directory technology, which provides global access to all networking resources. Network resources such as servers and printers are presented hierarchically in an NDS tree. Users log into the NDS tree with a single login name and password instead of logging into specific servers. NDS allows users with the proper access rights to log into the network and view and access network resources.

One of the most important steps during the installation of the NetWare 5 server is to set up NDS. We recommend that, in order to complete this step, you understand the basic concepts relating to NDS. These concepts include the NDS tree itself, NDS containers, and context. The NDS tree name is the top level of the available network resources and must be unique among other NDS tree names on the network. NDS container objects, much like subdirectories, contain network objects. The server can be installed into two types of container objects: Organization (O) and Organizational Unit (OU). The context, much like DOS directory paths, denotes the full path of a network object in the NDS tree. For example, a NetWare server might be installed into an Organizational Unit (OU) named Sales under the organization (O) named ACME. The context would be denoted as OU=SALES.O=ACME or SALES.ACME.

In order to install NDS, you will be offered the choice either to install the server into an existing NDS tree or to create a new NDS tree, as shown in Figure 2.17.

If you select an existing tree, the server will be installed into an Organization or Organizational Unit object. You must have Supervisor rights to a particular level in the tree in order to install the server there.

FIGURE 2.17

During the installation process, you have a choice either to install the server into an existing NDS tree or to create a new NDS tree.

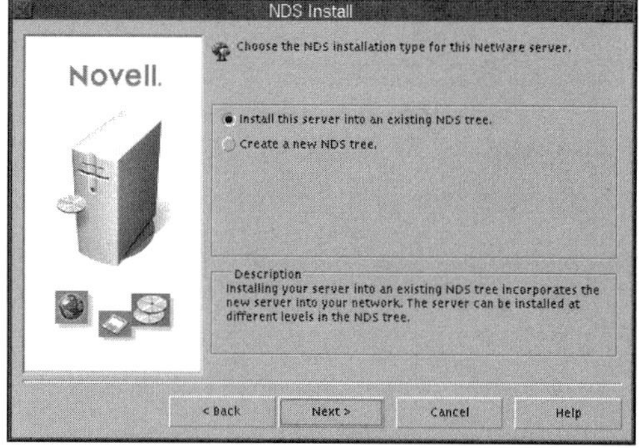

In addition, if the NetWare 5 server being installed is going into an existing NetWare 4.1*x* tree, it will cause the schema to be updated with the latest NetWare 5 schema. Since the schema is being modified, you must have Supervisor rights at the [ROOT] of the existing NDS tree. You will be prompted to enter the administrator name and password for the entire NDS tree.

Figure 2.18 shows what is needed to install the new NetWare 5 server into an existing NDS tree. Notice that you are required to provide the name and password for the user with administrator rights to the [ROOT] object of the tree.

FIGURE 2.18

If you have chosen to install the NetWare 5 server into an existing NDS tree, you are required to provide the tree name, the context for the server object, and the name and password for the user with administrative rights to the [ROOT] object of the tree.

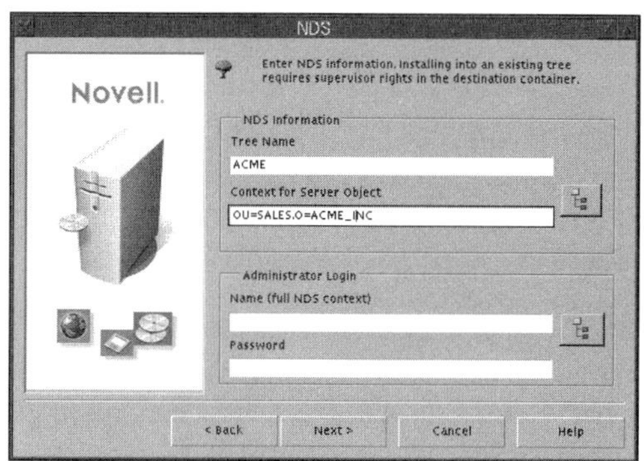

If you install the new NetWare 5 server into a new NDS tree, the installation will prompt you to enter several pieces of information, as shown in Figure 2.19. For example, you must enter a new NDS tree name (in this case the name is ACME_INC). The new NDS tree name must be unique in your network. Next, you will enter the context or location for placement of the server object. Finally, you will need to enter the name and password for a user with Supervisor rights at the O or OU that the server object will be installed in.

FIGURE 2.19

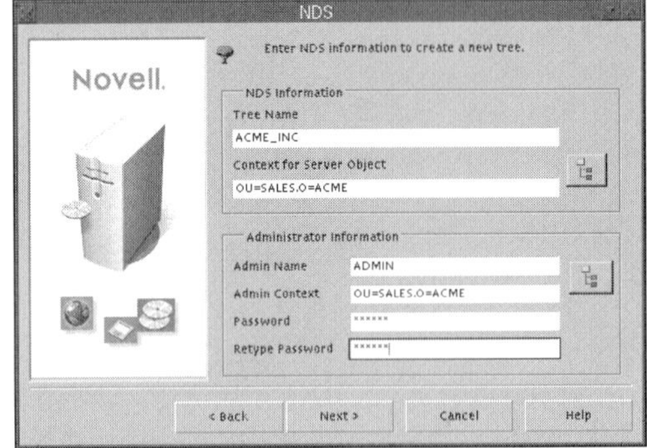

ACME_INC is the name of the new NDS tree in this example. In addition to the name, you will be prompted to enter the context of the server object and the name and password for a user with Supervisor rights at the O or OU where the server object will be installed.

When setting up a new NDS tree, be aware that the top level of the tree is the most important functionally because it serves as the foundation for the rest of the tree. The top of the tree is considered to be the first several levels of the tree and should be based on the network infrastructure. For more information on NDS tree design please refer to Chapter 5.

After you have entered the appropriate information, the new server will be added to either the new or existing NDS tree. A message informs you that the install of NDS has been successful, as seen in Figure 2.20. The message also informs you that the new NDS tree has been created or the server has been installed.

FIGURE 2.20

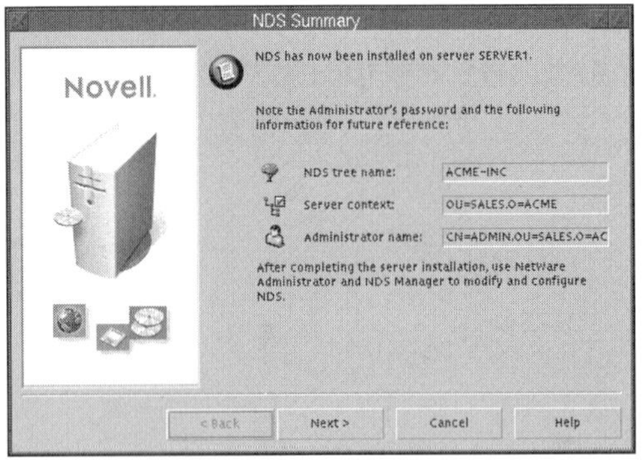

After you have entered and accepted the appropriate information to install the new server, an NDS summary screen is displayed. This is the case whether you installed the server using the new or existing NDS tree options.

The NetWare 5 server object and volume objects have been installed in the container you specified. If you have created a new NDS tree, a user (default name ADMIN) with Supervisor rights to the NDS tree will be created in the O or Organizational container. It is important that you remember or record the administrator password and other relevant information before future events.

License the NetWare 5 Server

The new NetWare 5 server must have a valid license in order to function properly. You can install the license from the NetWare 5 License disk or browse to a directory that contains NetWare 5 licenses. Figure 2.21 illustrates how the license file can be installed for NetWare 5 server.

FIGURE 2.21

The NetWare 5 server license is installed from the NetWare 5 License disk that comes with the server software.

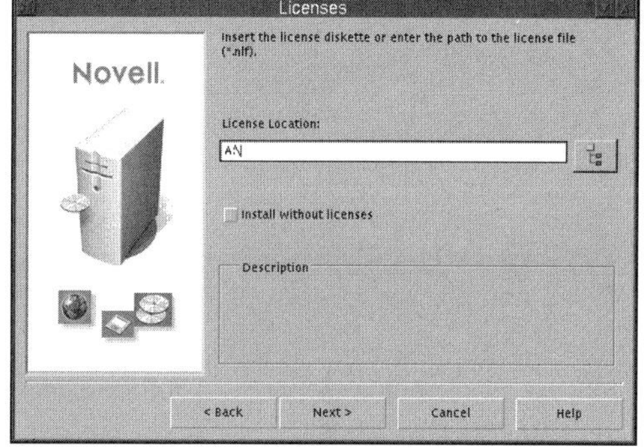

Although the server can be installed without a license, the unlicensed server will allow only two user connections. If you choose to initially install the NetWare 5 server without the license, you can use the NetWare Administrator (NWADMIN) utility to install licenses at a later date.

Install Other Networking Products

After you complete installation of the main server component, the NetWare 5 server installation is basically complete. However, you now have the option to select other networking products to install. The other networking products provide enhanced functionality, such as network management and Internet access, to NetWare 5. In order to install any of the optional networking products, select the appropriate check boxes next to the products you want to be installed, as seen in Figure 2.22.

FIGURE 2.22

The NetWare 5 installation program allows you to install additional networking products after the main server components have been installed. Although you can choose which products to install, installing the products that are already selected by default will ensure that you include the features recommended for NetWare.

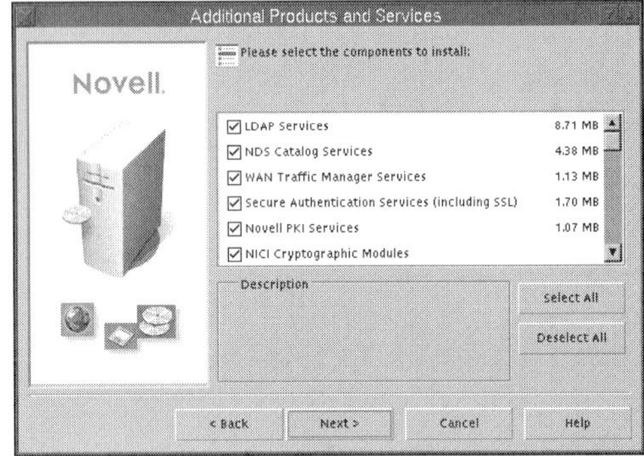

After you have selected and accepted the additional networking products, a summary dialog box is presented giving you the required space needed to install the products, as shown in Figure 2.23.

FIGURE 2.23

The installation program shows you a summary dialog box for the additional networking products. This dialog box shows you the space requirements to install the products.

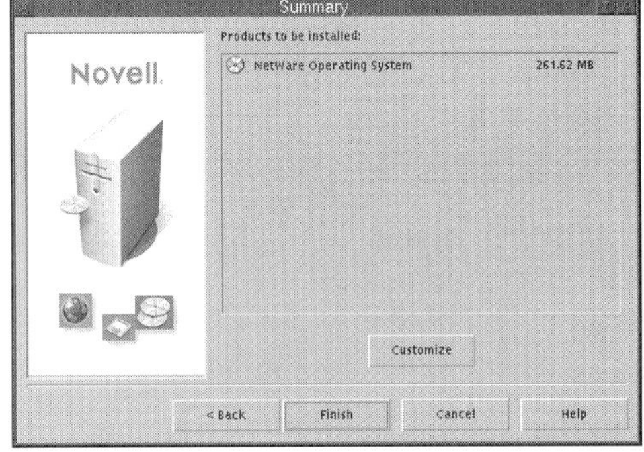

You can customize installation of many of the networking products for your networking environment. To customize the products and components, click the Customize button. For more information on customizing the additional networking products refer to the later section, "Customizing the NetWare 5 Installation."

Complete the Server Installation

If you do not want or need to customize the additional networking products, then basic server installation is now complete. Depending on which additional products you are installing, you may be prompted to insert additional CD-ROMs.

From the summary screen (shown in Figure 2.23), click the Finish button to begin installing NetWare 5 and additional products. After all files are copied, installation is completed, and a message is displayed. Figure 2.24 shows the Installation Complete dialog box.

FIGURE 2.24

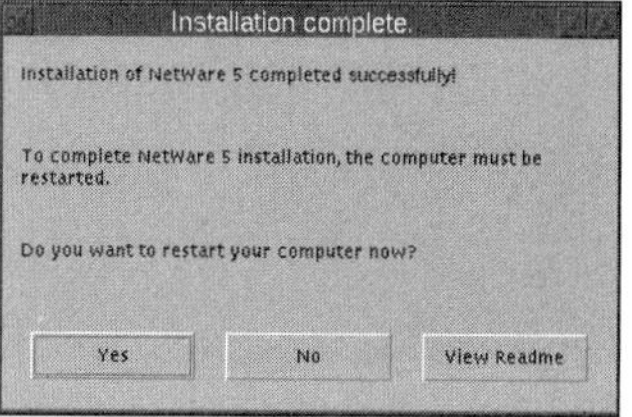

The NetWare 5 server installation is complete after it copies all the files for the additional networking products. You will need to reboot the server in order for the settings to take effect.

After the files are copied, you will need to reboot the NetWare 5 server by simply selecting or clicking the Yes button. NetWare 5 is automatically loaded when the computer reboots, or you can load it manually. To load the server manually, reboot the server by clicking Yes, change to the startup directory containing the NetWare server files (C:\NWSERVER), and finally type **SERVER**.

Customizing the NetWare 5 Installation

This section of the chapter describes how to set advanced options and customize installation of your new NetWare 5 server. Advanced options are available throughout the installation, and customization is available from the summary dialog box at the end of the installation program.

After you select the additional networking products and services to install, the installation program provides a summary dialog box with a Customize button. You will need to select this button if you want to customize the installation of each product and service for your networking environment.

The products and services are contained in several major categories that are presented to you as shown in Figure 2.25. The customization options categories are as follows:

- The NetWare operating system
- The file system
- Network protocols
- NDS
- Novell Distributed Print Services (NDPS)

FIGURE 2.25

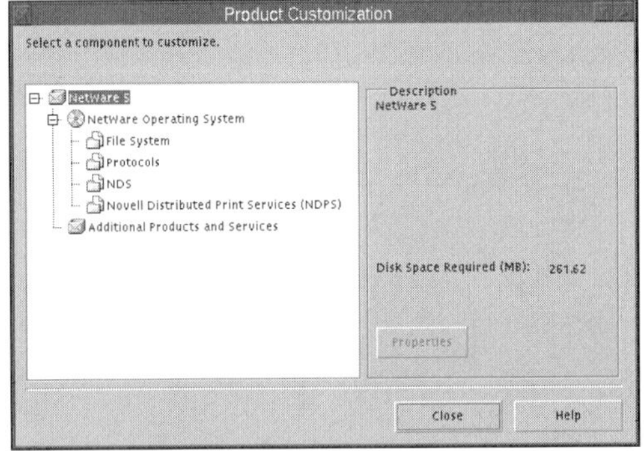

The installation program allows you to customize the additional products and services. In order to customize a product, select it and click the Properties button.

NetWare Operating System Properties

NetWare operating system properties include server, language, ConsoleOne, license, and component properties. Each property can be accessed by selecting the appropriate tab.

For example, the server property (not shown) that can be changed is the Server ID Number. The Server ID Number requires a unique identification number. Changing the server ID number during customization will place the new server ID number in the AUTOEXEC.NCF file. The new server ID number will take effect only after you reboot the server.

Using the Language tab, you can customize NetWare 5 to function in several different languages, as shown in Figure 2.26.

FIGURE 2.26

The Language tab is used to customize NetWare 5 to function in several different languages.

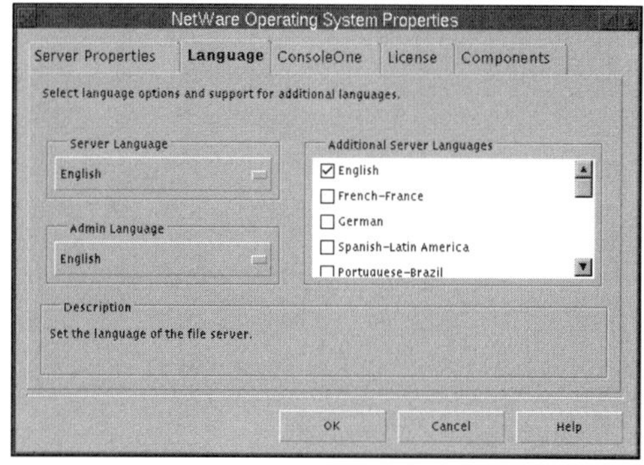

The server language settings determine which languages are supported by the server console and error messages. The messages will appear on the server console in the selected language(s). Although you can customize the language using this utility, the language on the server console can be changed using the LANGUAGE command. For more information, enter **LANGUAGE /?** at the server console.

In addition to setting the server language, you have the flexibility to set a language specifically for use by the Administrators of the server. This setting is called the admin language and determines which language the network administrator user object will use to log into the network. When additional NDS objects are created by the administrator, they will use the same language as the admin language.

For information on changing the language of the network client, see the client operating system's documentation.

In addition to the language settings, you can provide settings for the ConsoleOne management utility. ConsoleOne is a graphical network management utility that runs on the server and can be customized for your networking environment. Figure 2.27 illustrates how you can specify whether to load ConsoleOne when the server reboots.

NetWare 5 licenses consist of a server license and a connection license. Connection licenses determine how many connections can be maintained. Licenses for additional NetWare 5 products may be provided as part of your installation or can be purchased from your NetWare reseller.

FIGURE 2.27

Using this utility, you can decide whether or not to automatically load ConsoleOne, which is the graphical management utility for the server, every time you reboot. Checking this box will launch the ConsoleOne utility when the server loads.

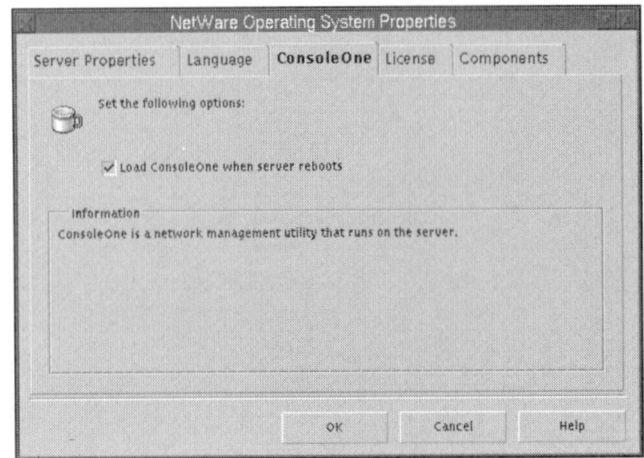

Licenses for servers and other products can be installed after installation using the NetWare Administrator (NWADMIN) utility or NLS Manager utility. However, a tab in the Properties dialog box allows you to view (but not modify) installed licenses, as shown in Figure 2.28.

FIGURE 2.28

The License tab in the NetWare Operating System Properties dialog box provides information about licenses that have been installed on the NetWare 5 server. The information here cannot be modified.

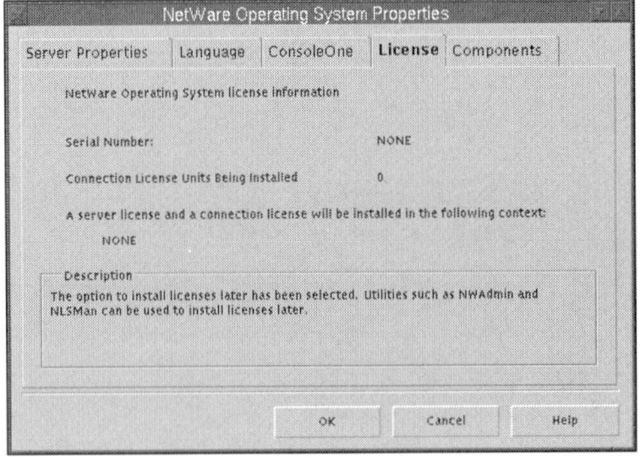

Some of the properties that relate directly to the licensing information on your NetWare 5 server include the serial number, connection licenses, and license context. The serial number uniquely identifies each license. Upgrades beyond NetWare 5 can require you to provide the license serial number. Serial numbers for licenses can also be viewed after installation using NetWare Administrator (NWADMIN) or NWCONFIG utilities. Connection licenses are valid for a specific level of operation. For example, a license with one server and 100 connections allows a single server to have 100 users. The license context indicates the location that the individual license objects that have been placed in the NDS tree. This setting means that the license object will be placed in the same the context as the server.

The final tab for the NetWare Operating System Properties is the Component tab. This tab lists the products and services that will be installed for each component. As shown in Figure 2.29, checking a box will add the entire component to the list of products and services to install. Unchecking a box removes the entire component from the list of products and services to be installed.

FIGURE 2.29

The Component tab in NetWare Operating System Properties enables you to control which products and services will be installed for each component.

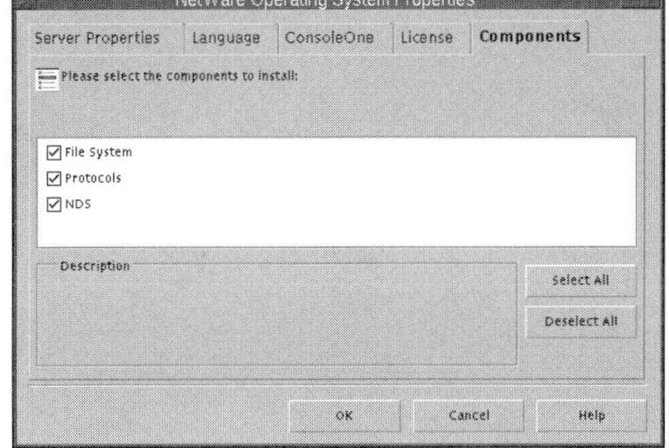

File System Properties

You are able to customize the NetWare file system, the physical and logical aspects of storing files on storage devices such as a disk drive. The file system consists of partitions, volumes, and free space. You can customize the NetWare file system by performing these tasks:

- Viewing available free space
- Creating, modifying, and deleting partitions
- Creating, modifying, and deleting volumes
- Mounting volumes

Figure 2.30 shows the File System Properties dialog box.

FIGURE 2.30

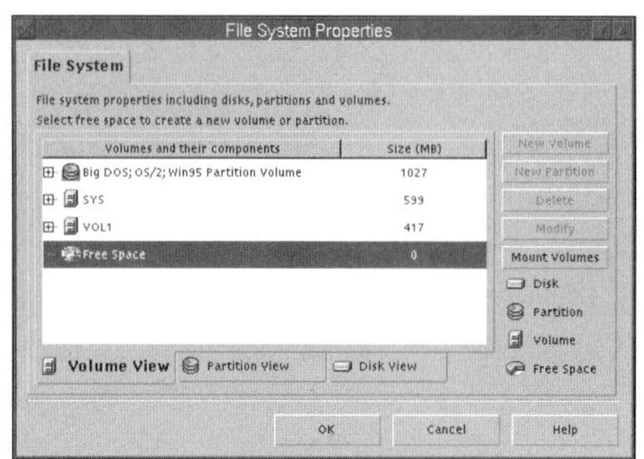

You are able to customize the NetWare file system, the physical and logical aspects of storing files on storage devices such as a disk drive. The file system consists of partitions, volumes, and free space.

Free space represents space available on storage devices for creating partitions and volumes. Several different types of free space can exist in NetWare. These include free space, NetWare partition free space, unpartitioned free space, and not partitioned free space. To create a traditional volume, you can use either free space or NetWare partition free space. To create an NSS volume, you can use free space, unpartitioned free space, or not partitioned free space.

As you know, partitions subdivide a physical storage device. Several types of server hardware can exist. For example, the server boot partition is typically formatted with DOS. The boot partition contains the files that load the NetWare operating system. In addition, the server will always contain at least one traditional partition that holds the SYS volume. This partition cannot be modified or deleted. The main purpose of the SYS volume is to contain server system setup information.

Besides the boot partition and the partition used by the SYS volume, you can create other partitions from any available free space on the server. You can create either standard (traditional) partitions or NSS partitions. The volumes in NetWare subdivide a partition. This means that the volumes are created within a partition. You can create two types of volumes:

- **Traditional volumes** — Traditional volumes can be created within NetWare (or NetWare traditional) partitions.
- **NSS volumes** — NSS volumes can be created within NetWare NSS partitions.

Once you have created either a traditional or NSS partition, you will then need to establish or create the NetWare volume from the partition. Traditional partitions can only contain traditional volumes. Likewise, NSS partitions can only contain NSS volumes. To create a traditional volume from a traditional partition, select the NetWare partition or traditional partition listed. Continue the process by clicking the New Volume button and naming the volume. Figure 2.31 gives you an example of creating traditional NetWare volumes from a partition.

FIGURE 2.31

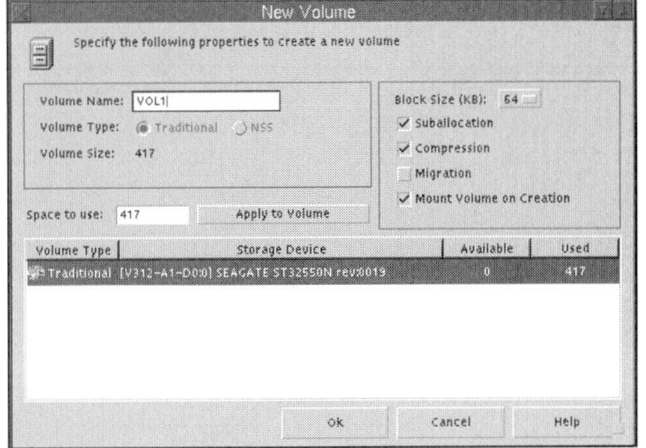

You can create a traditional volume from a traditional partition by first selecting the partition. You will need to give the new volume a name.

You can accept the default size of the volume or change the volume size by entering the amount of disk space. If required, increase the size of the volume by selecting another free space and clicking the Apply to Volume button.

In order to create an NSS volume, select the NetWare NSS free space and click New Volume. You will need to give a name to the volume. The installation program will attempt to take all the available free space and make it the volume. You can decide to accept the default size of the volume or change the volume size by entering the amount of disk space. Finish the process by clicking the Apply to Volume button. In addition, you can increase the size of the volume by selecting another free space and applying it to the volume. Figure 2.32 illustrates an example creating an NSS volume from the free space available on the server.

As always, in order for volumes to be accessed by NetWare, they must be mounted. Volumes can be mounted immediately or at the end of the customization or installation process.

FIGURE 2.32

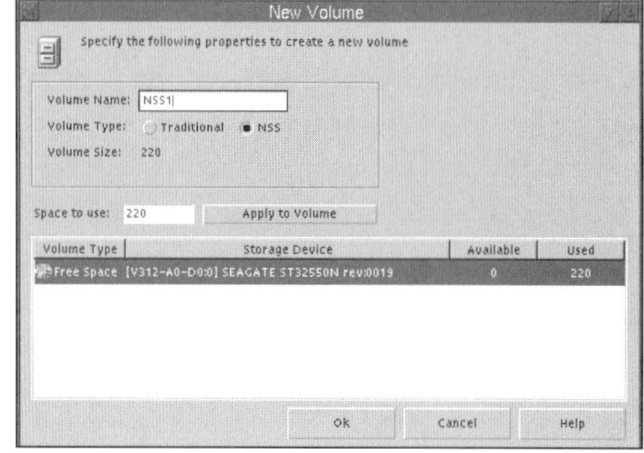

You can create an NSS volume by selecting the available free space on the server.

Network Protocols

NetWare 5 provides support for Internet Protocol (IP) and the Internetwork Packet Exchange (IPX) protocol. Figure 2.33 shows an example of configuring the network protocols. You can bind and configure either IPX or IP for the server.

FIGURE 2.33

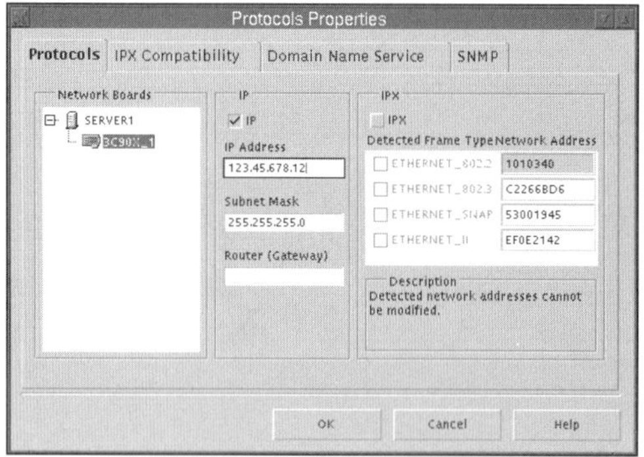

The installation program uses the Protocols Properties dialog box to customize the configuration of the IPX and IP network protocols.

Although the basic installation selects the default IPX frame types for your network, you can decide which frame types the server will support. Each frame type that is used on the network is treated as a logical network segment and requires its own IPX network address, even though each frame type is using the same network board and physical cable segment. To add IPX frame types from the Protocols Properties dialog box, check the box of the desired frame type and enter the network address. This is the IPX address, which is a hexadecimal number of one to eight digits (1 to FFFFFFFE) that identifies a specific network cable segment.

In addition, you can customize the IP configuration by specifying an IP address, which identifies each device on the network. The address consists of 32 bits, which are represented as decimal values separated by periods, such as 145.45.67.89. If your server will connect to the Internet, you must obtain a unique IP address. For information on receiving an IP address, contact your Internet service provider (ISP). IP addressing typically requires you to provide the subnet mask and router addresses.

Subnet masks allow you to break up your network into smaller networks. Your network could have too many nodes or could be too geographically diverse to manage as a single network. Dividing your network into smaller networks with their own addresses allows the network routers to filter and reduce the network activity seen by any of the nodes. However, this approach might not be appropriate on a large network that needs to appear to network administrators as a single network.

The router (gateway) is the address of the router that connects two different environments such as a LAN and the Internet. You can enter a specific router (gateway) address, or you can rely on the network to automatically find the nearest router. If you specify the address, remember that the router must exist on your network segment.

IPX Compatibility NetWare 5 allows you to provide compatibility between legacy IPX services and new pure IP services. This compatibility option, called IPX compatibility, is essential to an upgrade or migration process. It is also key in supporting a mixture of both IPX and IP services on the same wire. IPX compatibility, often called Compatibility Mode, consists of redirectors, a protocol Migration Agent (MA), a bindery population agent, and the Service Location Protocol (SLP). The combined use of these components creates the on-demand virtual IPX network within the IP network while allowing only IP packets to cross the wire. Moreover, Compatibility Mode provides continuity of communication between IP-based networks and IPX-based networks, and it supports SAP and RIP using SLP.

In order to enable IPX compatibility, you need to use the dialog box shown in Figure 2.34. When the appropriate box is checked, IPX compatibility is enabled to provide support for applications requiring IPX. Although the server does not broadcast services using RIP and SAP, NetWare 5 will process any IPX request that arrives at the server.

FIGURE 2.34

The installation program provides IPX compatibility through the Protocols Properties dialog box. IPX compatibility provides a virtual IPX network within the IP network while allowing only IP packets to cross the wire.

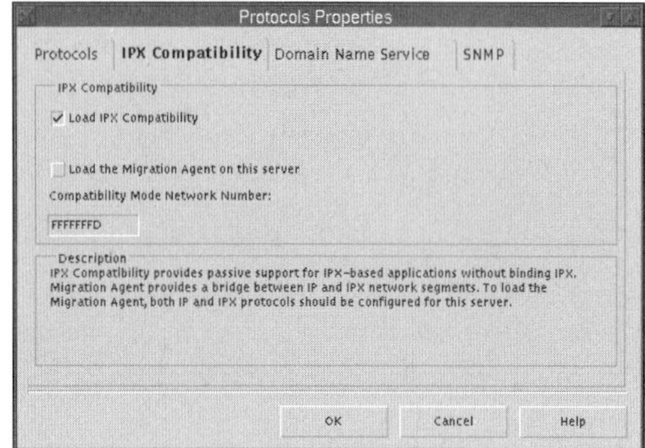

IPX compatibility uses a Compatibility Mode network number and allows you to load the Migration Agent on the server. The Compatibility Mode network number is an eight-digit hexadecimal number that identifies the IPX compatibility mode network. It functions as a virtual IPX network number. All compatibility devices, such as clients, servers, and Migration Agents, must use the same compatibility mode network number in order to communicate. The number must be unique among other numbers, such as the server ID number and the IPX network number. The default compatibility mode network number is FFFFFFFD.

NetWare 5 provides the capability to regulate IP and IPX protocols using a Migration Agent. A Migration Agent regulates the protocol function on different network segments. If a Migration Agent is not enabled, packets will not be forwarded onto network segments communicating with a different protocol. There are two different configurations for the Migration Agent depending on the number of network boards in the server:

- **One network board** — If your server contains only a single network board, enabling Migration Agent causes IPX packets destined for other networks to be "tunneled" in IP packets.

- **Two network boards** — If your server contains two network boards, enabling Migration Agent causes the server to function as a gateway that filters or forwards the packets in each network environment. For example, a server acting as a Migration Agent can have one network board communicating with the IP network and another network board communicating with IPX. IPX requests destined to travel across the IP network are tunneled in IP packets. IP packets destined to travel across the IPX network segment are tunneled in IPX packets. Separating the protocols on network segments reduces the traffic on both segments. IPX packets such as RIP and SAP are kept on the IPX segment, while IP packets remain on the IP segment.

Domain Name Service (DNS) NetWare 5 has added support for Domain Name Service (DNS), which provides the functionality that matches text names, such as "novell.com," with numbers used by computers, such as 145.45.67.89. For example, a workstation on a TCP/IP network uses the DNS to find the addresses to locate a NetWare server or other network resources. If you have an existing domain naming system already installed on your network, you will want to enter its domain name and name server(s) in the setup screen shown in Figure 2.35. If you want to install Novell's DNS on your network, you must return to the Summary dialog box and install Novell DNS/DHCP Services in Other Products and Services.

FIGURE 2.35

The NetWare Installation program allows you to set up and customize the DNS setting for the server.

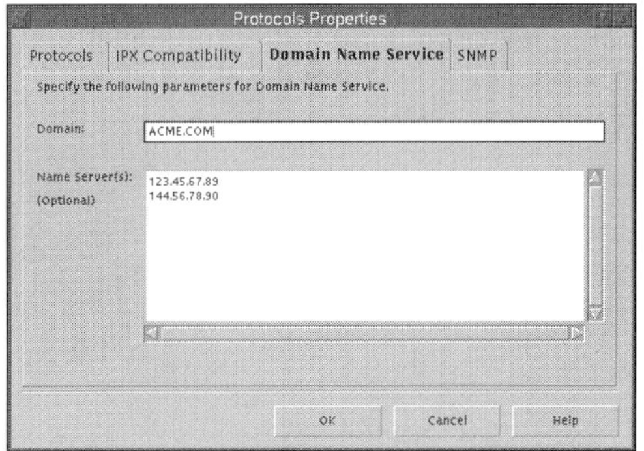

During setup of DNS you are asked to supply the domain name. A *domain name* divides the Internet into functional categories. The top-level domains identify types of organizations such as commercial (com), educational (edu), government (gov), international entities (int), U.S. military agencies (mil), network providers (net), and other organizations (org). Domain names can also use two-letter country codes to specify geographical locations such as United States (us) or United Kingdom (uk). Domain names are separated into individual levels with periods, such as sales.acme.com or norad.acme.co.us.

In addition to domain names, DNS manages domain name servers. A *name server* is a computer that translates names into IP addresses for other devices, such as workstations on the network. To obtain the name, NetWare 5 will search the IP address of each name server in the sequence entered into the Name Server field.

The Simple Network Management Protocol (SNMP) Network management utilities such as Novell's ManageWise utility use the Simple Network Management Protocol (SNMP) to record and communicate information about network devices. Using an SNMP-compatible utility, you can set and monitor threshold levels and specific events such as packets per second or error rates. When an event occurs, information such as event type, hardware description, server name, server location, and network administrator name is recorded. The information is then sent to the destination address of the workstation running the SNMP-compatible management utility. To configure SNMP, you can use the Protocols Properties dialog box shown in Figure 2.36.

FIGURE 2.36

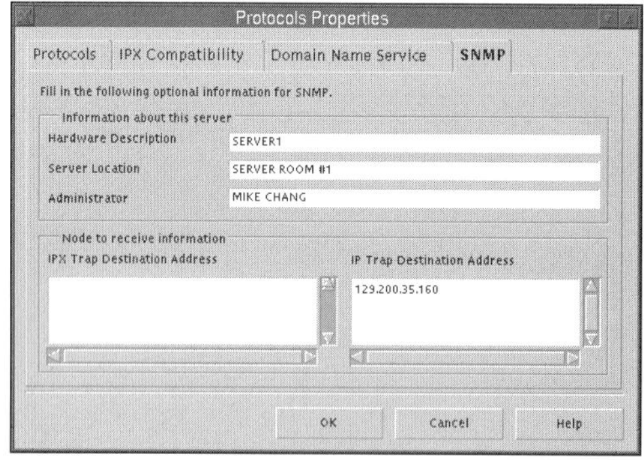

The Simple Network Management Protocol (SNMP) can be set up for your server to record and communicate information about network devices.

The information to be sent when an event occurs can include the server name, hardware description, server location, and administrator name. Any or all of this information will be recorded when an event occurs. You can also specify where to send the SNMP information, that is, which devices will receive the information when an SNMP event occurs. Each device should be running an SNMP-compatible management utility such as the ManageWise utility.

You can specify IPX and IP destination addresses for the devices to receive the information, for example, the IPX or IP trap destination address. A device's IPX trap destination address includes the network and node numbers separated by a colon, such as 01010340:1233456789. The IP trap destination address is the IP address of the destination device in standard notation, such as 145.45.67.89.

NDS Properties The first dialog box that appears when you select NDS Properties is an NDS summary page that details the current NDS installation (Figure 2.37). It lists the NDS tree name, server context, and administrator name and context. This page is for informational purposes only; nothing can be changed or modified using it.

FIGURE 2.37

The NDS Properties dialog box includes an informational summary detailing the current NDS installation. It lists the NDS tree name, server context, and administrator name and context. You cannot change or modify any of the NDS setting from this screen.

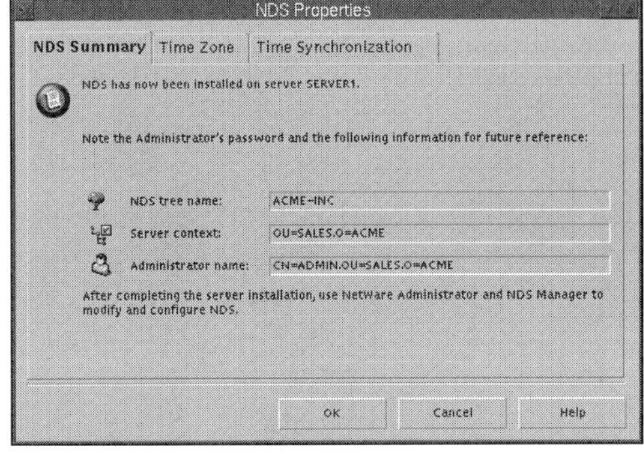

The next tab is the Time Zone setting. Although selecting the time zone will automatically configure the time zone properties, you might need to change some properties for your network environment. Figure 2.38 illustrates what you can set with the time zone page.

FIGURE 2.38

You can use the time zone page in NDS Properties to help you customize the time zone setting for the server.

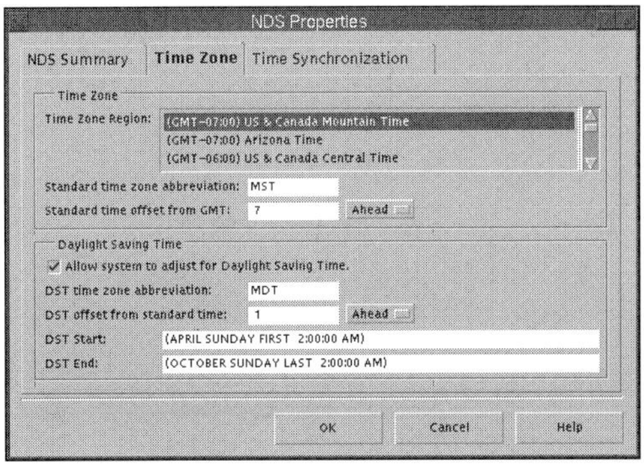

The settings that are available to you in the Time Zone page include the Time Zone Region, Standard Time Zone Abbreviation, Standard Time Offset from GMT, and Daylight Saving Time. The Time Zone Region is the time zone where the server is physically located. The Standard Time Zone Abbreviation is used by the operating system code running on the NetWare server to indicate the time zone where the server is located. The Difference in the Standard Time Zone Abbreviation defines, in number of hours, the deviation between Greenwich Mean Time (GMT) and the time zone where the server is located. GMT is equivalent to Universal Coordinated Time (UTC).

Using this screen, you can also set many daylight saving values. For example, the Allow System to Adjust for Daylight Saving Time parameter indicates whether daylight saving time is in effect. The DST Time Zone Abbreviation is used by the operating system for the daylight saving time zone where the server is located. The DST Offset from Standard Time indicates the difference, in number of hours, between standard time and daylight saving time. And finally, DST Start and DST End are the parameters that establish the beginning and ending dates for daylight saving time.

Time Synchronization The NetWare installation program allows you to specify the type of time server you want the server to be. The purpose of a time server is to synchronize the reported time across the network and provide expiration dates and time stamps to establish the order of events taking place in NDS. Figure 2.39 shows an example of how you can establish the proper time server type for your server.

FIGURE 2.39

The NetWare installation program allows you to specify the type of time server you want the server to be.

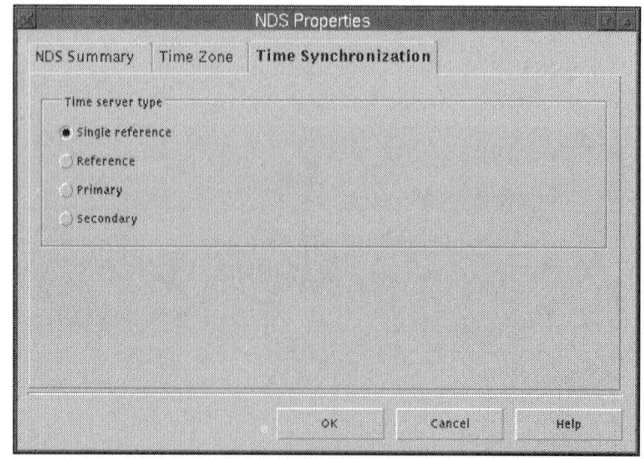

NetWare 5 distinguishes three types of time servers that provide network time: single-reference, reference, and primary. All other servers are called secondary time servers because they receive their time from the time providers. A single-reference time server is typically the first server in a network. The installation program will automatically designate the first NetWare 5 server installed as a single-reference time server. The single-reference time server will then be able to provide time to the entire network.

A primary time server is responsible for determining and setting the network time. A primary time server will poll other primary and reference servers to determine the "average network time," which is then distributed to other requesting servers.

A network usually has only one reference time server. A reference time server provides a network time for all primary time servers to migrate to. It is used on larger networks where primary time servers are required.

By default, all servers except the first server are designated as secondary time servers. The installation process of a typical NetWare 5 server will automatically set the server to be a secondary time server. The secondary time servers rely on other sources such as a single-reference time server to provide them with network time. A secondary time server can get the network time from another secondary time server or from a single-reference, reference, or primary time server.

Novell Distributed Print Services (NDPS) Novell Distributed Print Services (NDPS) is installed by default on each NetWare 5 server. An NDPS resource database (in the SYS:NDPS\REDIR directory) used by the NDPS Resource Management Service (RMS) is copied automatically to that server. The RMS is a central repository for network resources and services. It contains printer drivers, banners, printer definition (NPD) files, and possibly fonts.

If you choose to customize NDPS, you will be asked whether you want to create a new Broker object on this server and whether you want the different brokered services enabled. In general, you will want these services, including the resource database for the Resource Management Service, available for each broker that you create. If disk space is an issue on a specific server and you do not intend to create a Broker object on that server, be sure the Copy Resource Files box is not checked. This will save approximately 60MB of disk space on that server.

The NWCONFIG Utility

The NWCONFIG utility allows you to perform many routine tasks on your NetWare 5 servers ranging from loading and unloading drivers to removing and reinstalling NDS. The NWCONFIG utility is the former INSTALL utility found on NetWare 4.*x* versions. NWCONFIG includes all the functionality of INSTALL and additional functionality. In this section we primarily highlight what is new to this utility and do not discuss every option it includes.

You can initiate the NWCONFIG utility by typing **NWCONFIG** at any NetWare 5 server console or through the RCONSOLE utility. An example of the main screen for NWCONFIG is shown in Figure 2.40.

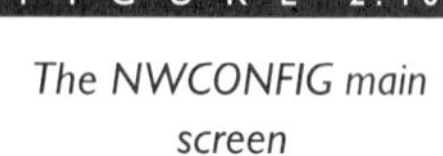
FIGURE 2.40

The NWCONFIG main screen

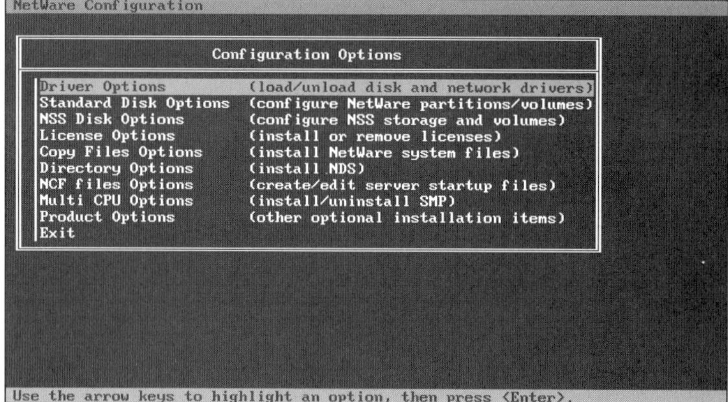

Novell Storage Services

Novell Storage Services (NSS) is a new product that runs on your NetWare 5 server. In addition to the traditional NetWare file system, administrators and users can now take advantage of Novell Storage Services, which offers more flexibility for storage and file management than previous versions of NetWare. Here are some of the advantages:

- NSS is ideal for systems with large files and volumes, or large numbers of volumes, directories, and files. NSS allows up to an 8 terabyte file size and holds up to 8 trillion files in an NSS volume. You can also mount up to 255

NSS volumes on a server. You no longer need to worry about file or volume limitations; you are limited only by the capacity of your storage devices.

- With NSS, hard disk space can be fully utilized. Unused free space on all hard drives in unpartitioned space attached to your server or in NetWare volumes (including SYS) can be combined into a storage pool and used to create NSS volumes.
- NSS volumes mount rapidly and with less RAM than ever before. You can mount any number of NSS volumes and any size NSS volume with as little as 1MB RAM.
- NSS is now the default method for mounting CD-ROMs as volumes, offering much faster access to multiple CD-ROM drives installed in towers.

As future storage device types appear on the market, new NSS modules can be developed to recognize the devices for the pool. This means that no matter what type of device you have attached to your server, NSS will recognize it and be able to use the available free space for NSS volumes if the device can be written to.

NSS and the traditional NetWare file system run side by side. You can create up to 64 NetWare volumes or 256 NSS and NetWare volumes combined, including volume SYS. The choice is yours as long as you have at least one NetWare volume, SYS, on each server.

Before creating an NSS volume, make sure you have met these requirements:

- A server running NetWare 5.
- A minimum of 10MB space free for an NSS volume. If you only have one hard drive and you did not allocate enough free space in your NetWare partition and NetWare volume for NSS, reconfigure your drive to allow the required 10MB space.
- 1.5MB RAM (300 cache buffers) for loading the modules.
- 2MB memory (500 cache buffers) for running NSS.

NOTE

The current version of NSS does not support TTS. Therefore, you must run your SYS volume as a traditional NetWare volume until that support is provided by Novell.

You can then follow these instructions after loading the NWCONFIG utility on your NetWare 5 server.

1. Select NSS Disk Options in the NWCONFIG utility. An example of this screen is shown in Figure 2.41.

FIGURE 2.41

The NSS Configuration screen

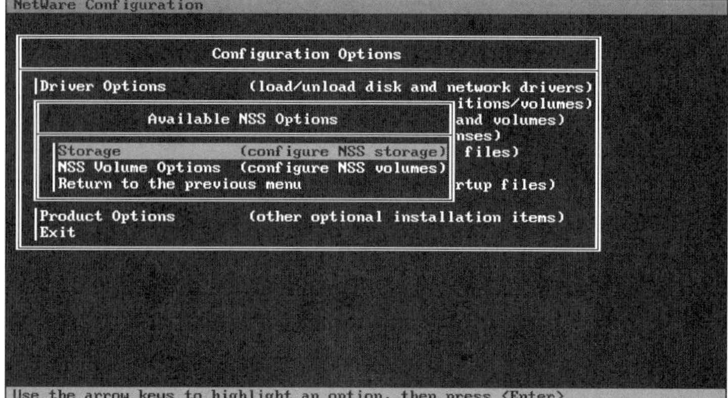

2. Select the Storage option. This option allows you to view and prepare free space for NSS configuration. It contains these options: Update Provider Information, Assign Ownership, Release Ownership, View Free Space, and Return to the Previous Menu.

   NSS will scan your devices to find free space for NSS to use, and it will list the free space on each device as a separate storage deposit object. You can also view free space. Once NSS has taken free space, you can create your storage groups and NSS volumes.

3. Select NSS Volume Options. Before you enter the options, you must authenticate to NDS using Administrator rights. NSS Volume Options allows you to create one or more NSS volumes. The volume options are Create, Modify, Delete, View Volumes, and Return to the Previous Menu.

   To create a single NSS volume from a single device, you select Create → NSS Volume, select a managed object marked Single, select a name for your volume, and then confirm your choice.

   To create multiple NSS volumes in one storage group, first create the storage group by selecting Create → Storage Group and confirm your choice. You then select Create → NSS Volume, select a managed object marked Group, select the volume size, select the name, and confirm your choice. For additional NSS volumes, you select NSS Volume again and repeat the steps, segmenting your volumes according to how much space you have in your storage group.

4. At the server console prompt, mount the newly created NSS volume by entering this command:

   ```
   mount volume_name
   ```

   where the *volume_name* is the name of the new NSS volume. You can use the mount all command if you prefer.

When you enter NSS volumes from the command line, you see the new NSS volume and an additional NSS_Admin volume — a read-only volume that contains configuration information describing NSS objects.

NOTE

CD-ROMs recognized by NSS are mounted automatically. In NetWare 5, this happens when the NetWare 5 version of the CDROM.NLM is loaded. The CD and CD-ROM utilities used in previous releases of NetWare are no longer supported.

Installing NetWare 5 Licenses

Novell License Services allows you to easily install additional licenses to your NetWare 5 server. After loading NWCONFIG at your NetWare 5 server, follow these steps to install NetWare 5 licenses:

1. Select License Options → Install Licenses.

2. Select a path to the .NLF file that has the license. The default path is SYS:\LICENSE. However, your license may be on a floppy disk or CD-ROM.

3. Log in by entering the administrator's complete name and password.

4. At the Installable Licenses screen, select an envelope file. An envelope file contains one or more licenses. A sample envelope file is 42c1f1d.nlf.

5. Exit NWCONFIG.

You can now view the installed licenses by using NLS Manager's Tree View or NetWare Administrator. An example of the NLS screen in NWCONFIG is shown in Figure 2.42.

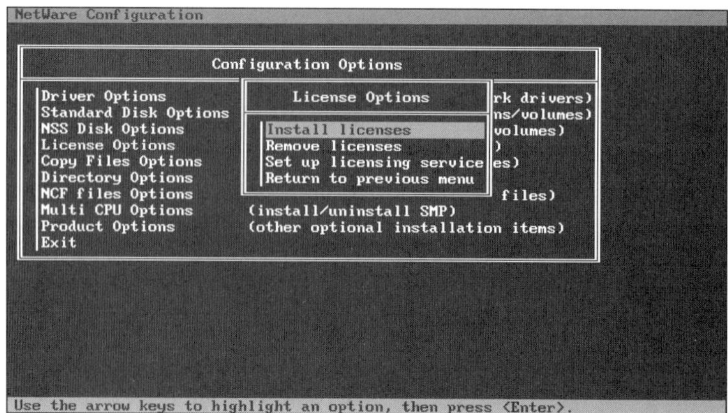

FIGURE 2.42

NetWare Licensing Services

Novell Directory Services

This option under NWCONFIG allows you to perform many NDS operations such as the installation and removal of Directory Services. It also allows you to move NetWare 3.*x* bindery information to the Directory and upgrade mounted volumes to the Directory. An example of this screen is shown in Figure 2.43.

FIGURE 2.43

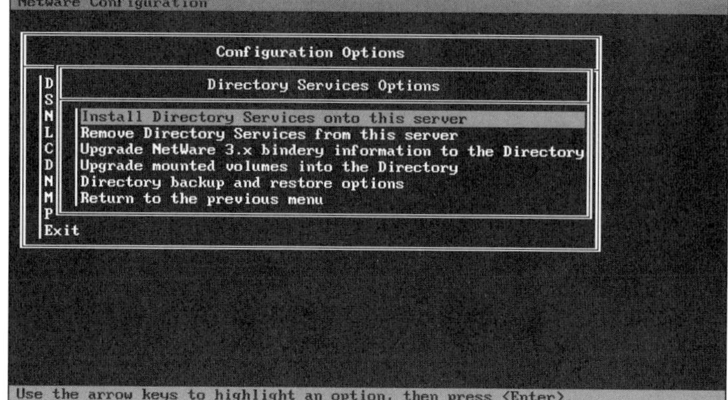

The Directory Services Options screen

NDS Backup and Restore

An important feature of the Directory Services screen is that of performing NDS maintenance. With this feature you can back up and restore the NDS data files that are stored on your NetWare 5 server. This is helpful whenever you need to perform a hardware upgrade on a NetWare 5 server. Keep in mind that this is a separate process additional to doing a full backup of your NetWare 5 server. For more information on backup and restore through Novell's enhanced SBACKUP utility, see Chapter 18.

NOTE

This functionality was provided in NetWare 4.11 through the DSBACKER utility. That product has basically been moved into the NWCONFIG utility.

To initiate a backup of your NDS files before a hardware upgrade, you need to select the option that says Save Local DS Information Prior to Hardware Upgrade, as shown in Figure 2.44.

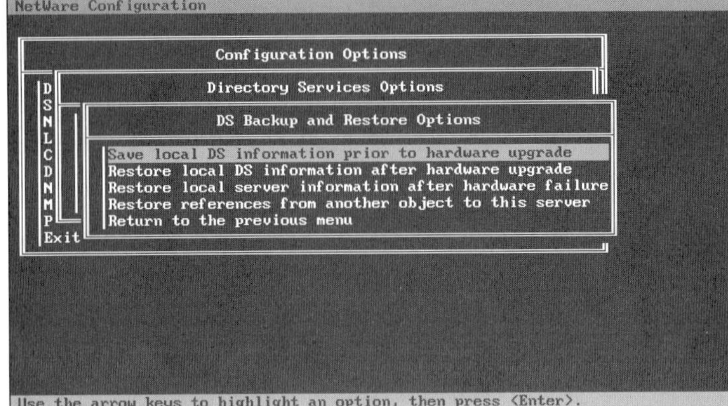

FIGURE 2.44

The NDS backup and restore options

After selecting this screen, you will be prompted to perform a backup of the NDS files on this server. Doing so creates a temporary file called BACKUP.NDS that stores all NDS and replica information in that server's SYS:SYSTEM directory as well as disables NDS on this system until you perform your hardware upgrade and do a restore of the backup file. This screen is displayed in Figure 2.45.

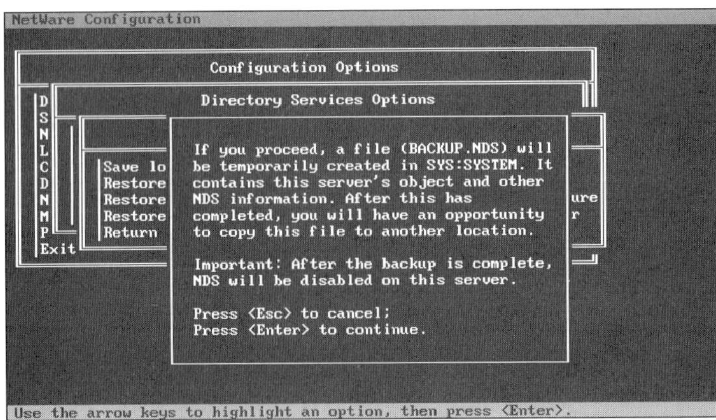

FIGURE 2.45

Getting ready to back up NDS data

You will then be prompted to log in to the Directory Services Login/Authentication screen. Enter the administrator name and password; the system will log you into the Directory and create the BACKUP.NDS file.

You can then exit the NWCONFIG utility and bring the NetWare 5 server down.

Once the changes have been made to the hardware (or you've installed a new NetWare 5 server), you can load NWCONFIG again. Go to the Directory Services options and select the option that says Restore Local DS Information after Hardware Upgrade, as shown in Figure 2.46. You can then specify the path to restore the information from.

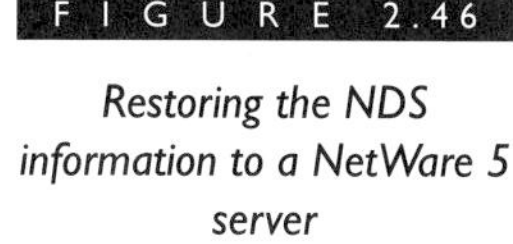

FIGURE 2.46

Restoring the NDS information to a NetWare 5 server

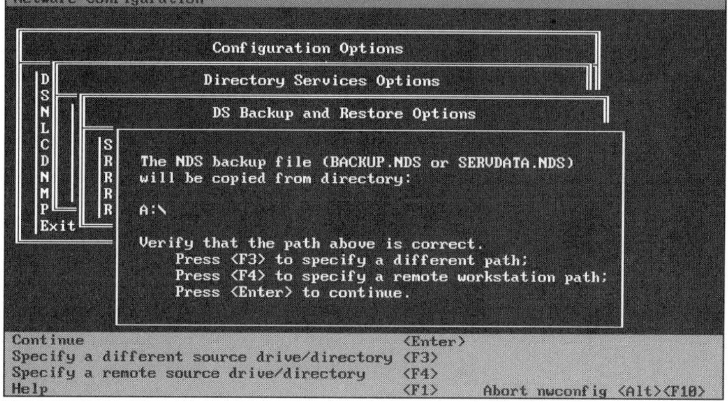

NOTE

You can also use this utility to perform a backup and restore after a hardware failure. Obviously, this requires that you have run the backup procedure beforehand and have stored the BACKUP.NDS file on another machine elsewhere.

Product Options

The last screen in the NWCONFIG utility is the Product Options screen. This option enables you to install new products to your NetWare 5 server. An example of this screen is shown in Figure 2.47.

FIGURE 2.47

Installing other products on a NetWare 5 server

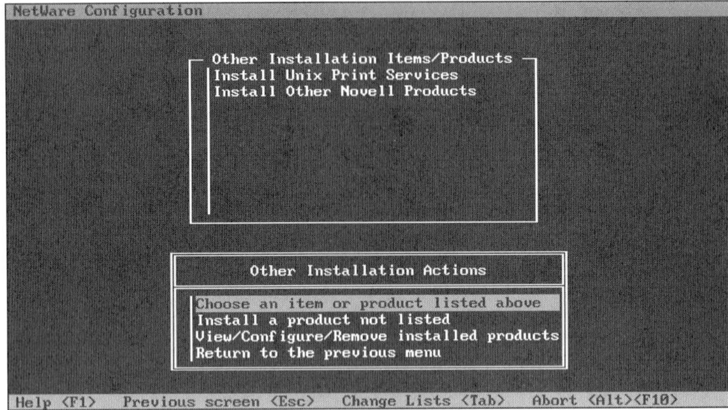

The NetWare Administrator (NWADMN32.EXE) Utility

NetWare 5 consolidates many of the NDS administrative functions into a graphical, easy-to-use new 32-bit utility that greatly reduces the time you spend administering the network. The NetWare Administrator utility, or NWADMN32.EXE, is a Windows-based utility that makes changes to the Directory as easy as a point and click of a mouse. This utility is used by system administrators to manage objects in the NDS tree. Figure 2.48 shows the main window for the 32-bit NWADMIN utility, which has an executable filename of NWADMN32.EXE.

Because NWADMN32.EXE is a Windows-based utility, it enables you to graphically manage all objects and properties in the NDS tree, which you can create, change, or browse by selecting or clicking the individual NDS objects.

The NWADMIN utility is executed at a client workstation from Windows. With this utility you can view, create, move, delete, and assign rights to the individual objects in the NDS tree. Typically, the individuals using NWADMIN will be system administrators with Supervisor rights over their container objects.

FIGURE 2.48

The main window for the 32-bit NWADMIN utility (called NWADMN32.EXE)

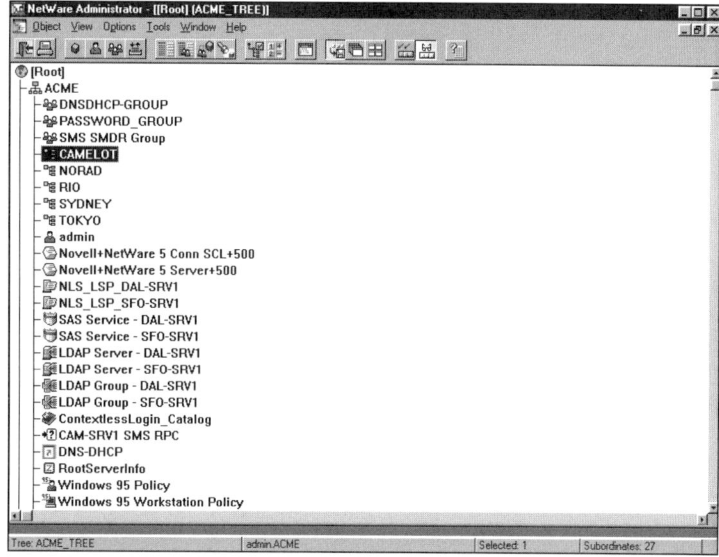

TIP

You may limit access to the NWADMIN utility by moving the utility from the SYS:\PUBLIC subdirectory to another subdirectory that only administrators have access to. Most of your users will not need to use this utility.

In order to execute this utility, you must have the NetWare DOS Requester, VLMs, or Client 32 software running on the workstation. Make sure that you have loaded the appropriate client software, or the NWADMIN utility will not load. (For more information on client software, see Chapter 18.) The 32-bit NWADMIN works with Novell's Client 32 for DOS/Windows and Windows 95/98.

You can use this utility to organize, manage, and browse the NDS objects that are contained in the tree by performing any of these functions:

- Create and manage NDS objects:
  - Assign rights in the NDS tree and file system.
  - Set up the print services.
- Display or browse object and property information stored in the tree.

- Set up and manage the NDS partitions and replicas through NDS Manager as a snap-in utility.

Using NWADMIN to Create and Manage NDS Objects

You can use NWADMIN to create, delete, modify, rename, move, and get detailed information about NDS objects. In order to create an NDS object, you must first be logged into the tree as an individual who has rights, such as the ADMIN (or other administrative) user at the container where you want to create the object.

For example, in order to create the user CN=GWASHINGTON in the container OU=RIO.O=ACME, move to that container in the tree and select the Create option from the Object menu. Figure 2.49 illustrates the New Object dialog box that is displayed after the Create option is selected.

FIGURE 2.49

The New Object dialog box in NWADMIN is displayed after the Create option is selected.

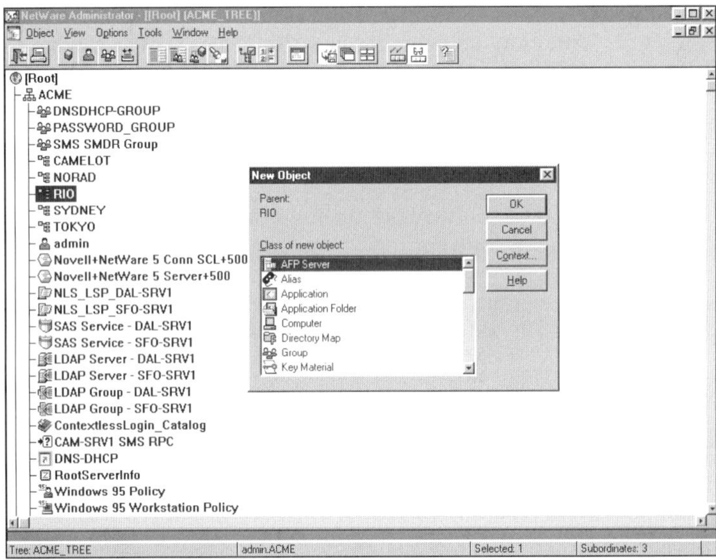

You can then select the User object from the list of objects, and you will be presented with the Create User dialog box to fill out. Figure 2.50 displays the Create User dialog box for the user GWASHINGTON in the container RIO.ACME.

You can also use this utility to delete or rename any of the NDS objects. You can also move a selected NDS object from one location in the NDS tree to another. Figure 2.51 shows how the move operation for ALINCOLN might look. In this figure we are moving CN=ALINCOLN from the ADMIN.RIO.ACME to AUDIT.ADMIN.RIO.O=ACME.

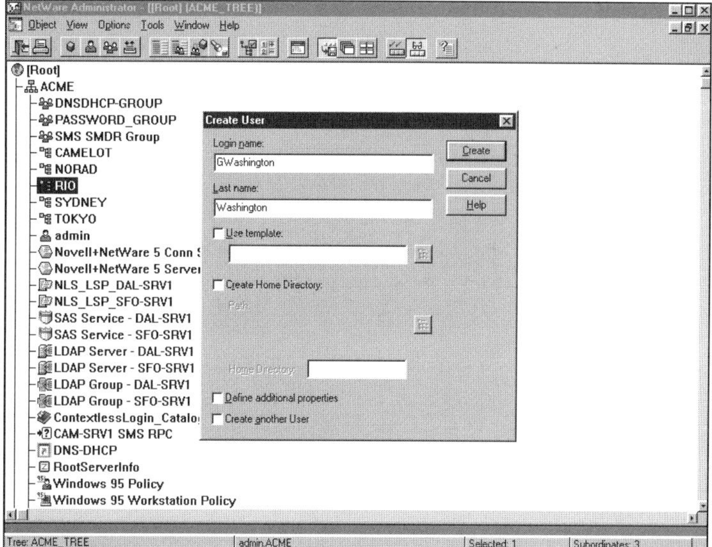

FIGURE 2.50

The Create User dialog box in NWADMIN for the user GWASHINGTON.RIO.ACME

Using NWADMIN to Assign Rights to the NDS Tree and File System

This object-oriented look of the utility makes the assignment of rights much easier. Rights to users, groups, containers (OUs), files, and directories can be assigned by simply dragging and dropping one icon onto another.

For example, when a user changes departments, you simply drag and drop the user to give that user the appropriate rights or move the user with the move command. Figure 2.52 shows the operation of dragging and dropping one object onto another to give it rights.

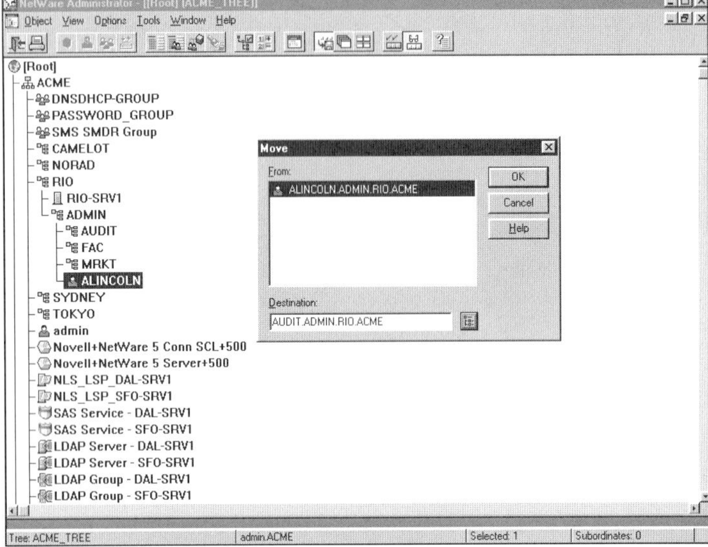

FIGURE 2.51

The NWADMIN screen for moving CN=ALINCOLN from the ADMIN.RIO.ACME to AUDIT.ADMIN.RIO.ACME

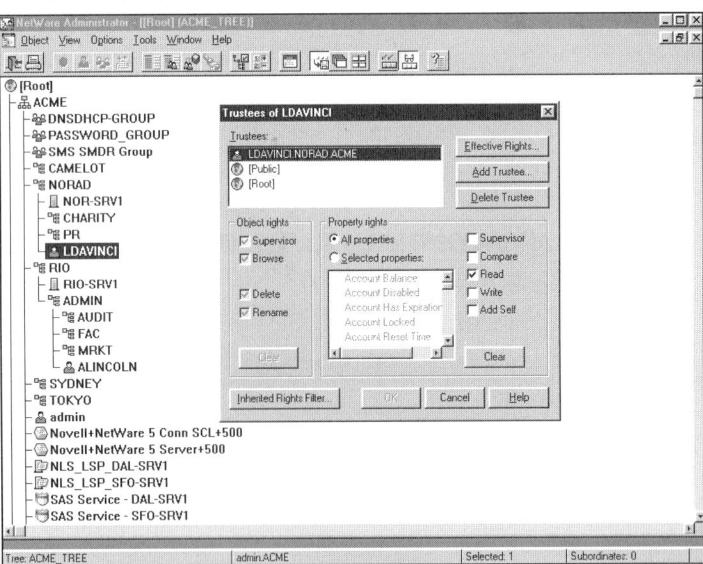

FIGURE 2.52

The NWADMIN windows associated with the operation of dragging and dropping one object onto another to give it rights

The operation of dragging and dropping is also used to assign rights to the files and directories in the file system. You can bring up the Details dialog box for an object and assign file and directories rights there. For example, in Figure 2.53, the NDS group object called CN=COMMON in the container ADMIN.RIO.ACME is granted rights to the COMMON subdirectory stored on the server CAM-SRV1.

FIGURE 2.53

The NDS group object called CN=COMMON in the container ADMIN.RIO.ACME is granted rights to the COMMON subdirectory stored on the server CAM-SRV1.

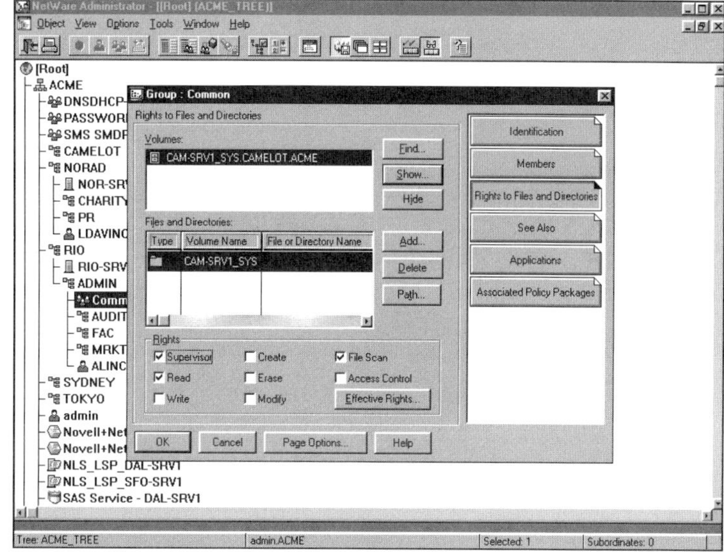

Adding file system directory or object rights in previous versions of NetWare required a multilayered menu utility and a tedious process of adding each user. Now all that is needed to add file system directory rights is to drag the user's icon over to the specific directory or object, and NetWare will simply ask you for a confirmation.

Because all the network resources in the NDS tree are represented by NWADMIN, managing multiple NetWare 5 servers is greatly simplified. Instead of managing a single server, you can focus your management efforts on a group of servers.

For more information on assigning rights, refer to Chapter 13.

Using NWADMIN to Set Up the Print Services

The NWADMIN utility can also be used to set up and manage the printing environment. NWADMIN is a functional equivalent to the PCONSOLE utility in DOS. For example, in order to create a printer, select the desired container where the printer will be located. Select Create from the Option menu and then select Printer as the object to create. Figure 2.54 shows the dialog box that appears.

FIGURE 2.54

Creating a printer object in NWADMIN

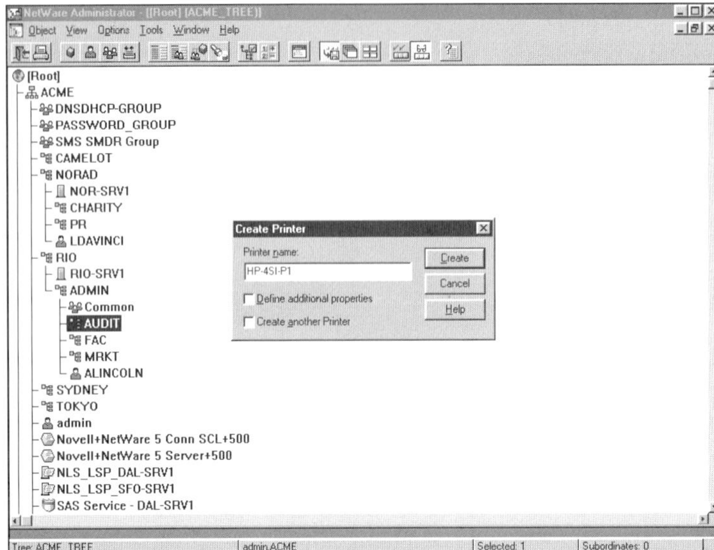

From the screen shown in Figure 2.54, you can click the Define Additional Properties button to define characteristics of the printer. If you select the additional properties, the Printer dialog box appears.

In order to create a print queue and print server object, you follow the same steps that you used to create the printer object. However, you select Print Queue and Print Server as the objects to create instead of Printer. The dialog boxes that are presented are very similar.

TIP

For the print queues, NetWare 5 creates a subdirectory immediately under the root of the volume called QUEUES. Under this subdirectory, the operating system creates a numbered directory that matches the ID number of the queue. If the directory is created remotely, it does not use the ID of the queue object at all.

Once all the corresponding print objects are created (printer, print queue, and print server), you can use NWADMIN to link them together. You perform this operation in a two-step process. First, you assign the print server to the print queue as shown in Figure 2.55. Second, you assign the printer to the print queue as shown in Figure 2.56.

FIGURE 2.55

Using NWADMIN to assign the print server to the print queue

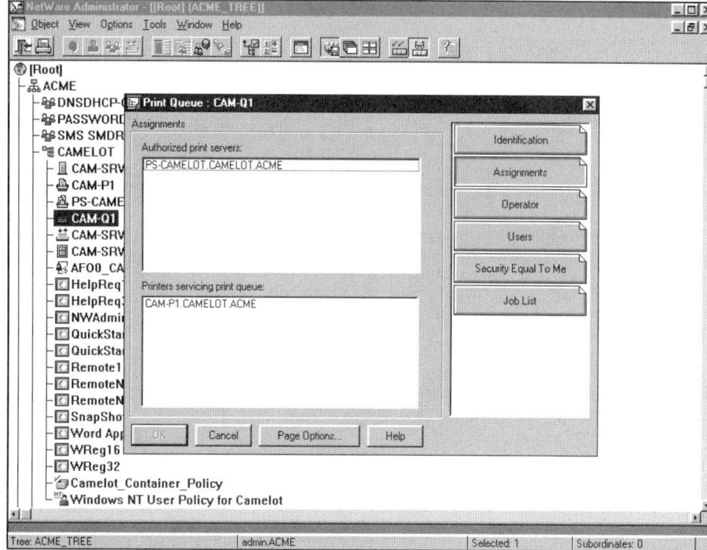

FIGURE 2.56

Using NWADMIN to assign the printer to the print queue

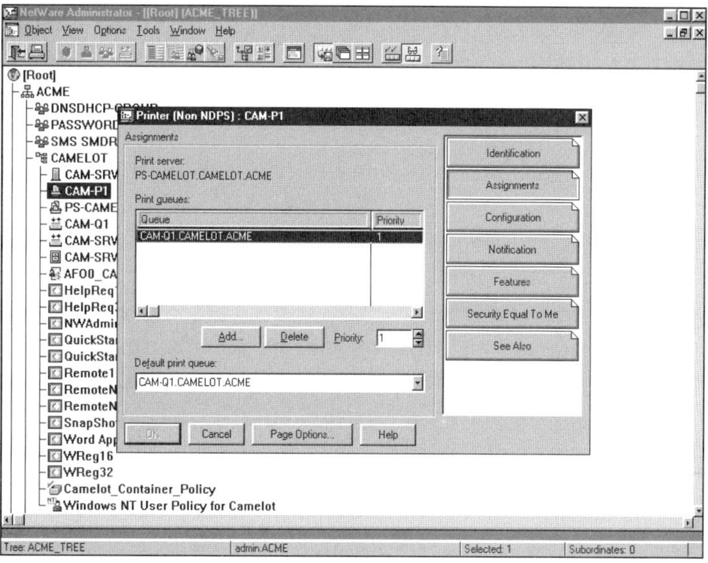

You can check the status of the printing setup using a new feature of NetWare 5 that displays the print layout. This feature is called Print Layout Page and is illustrated in Figure 2.57.

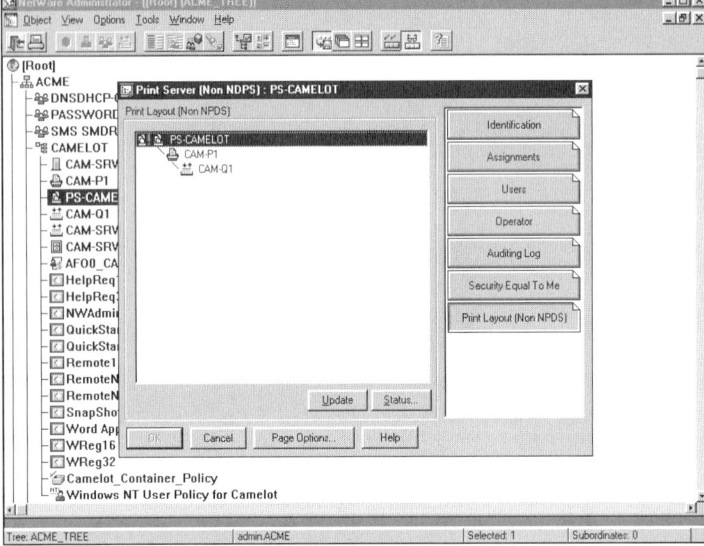

FIGURE 2.57

Using NWADMIN to display the Print Layout page

Using NWADMIN to Manage the NDS Partitions and Replicas

In order to manage your NDS partitions and replicas properly, you need to be able to perform several types of operations. These operations are Create Partition, Merge Partition, Move Subtree, Add Replica, Remove Replicas, Change Replica Type, and Abort Partition. You can also delete a server object after removing the replicas from the tree. All these operations can be performed using the NWADMIN.EXE utility and the new NDS Manager utility.

NOTE

Be sure to review Chapter 9 before performing any partitioning operations. Chapter 9 gives specific detailed instructions on how to check and verify partition operations and their states. It is important not to start an additional partition operation before the first partition operation has completed.

In the Tools menu of the NWADMIN.EXE utility, an option may appear known as the NDS Manager. For NDS Manager to appear in NWADMIN, you need to enable the snap-in for this utility. This option enables you to control partitioning and replica placement of the NDS database. Figure 2.58 shows you the NDS Manager utility, which can be run as a stand-alone utility under Tools in the main menu of NWADMIN. For more information, see the "NDS Manager Utility" section later in this chapter.

FIGURE 2.58

The NDS Manager option under Tools in the main menu of NWADMIN controls the partitioning and replica placement of the NDS database.

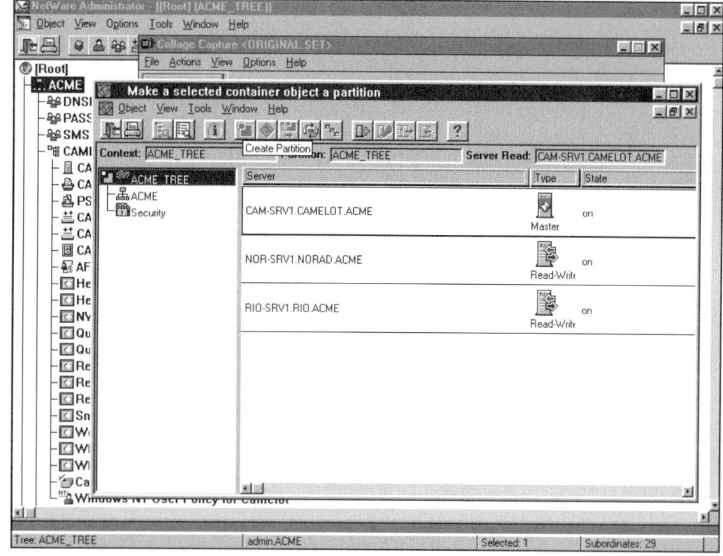

In Figure 2.59 you can see that the partitions are denoted with a small box icon to the left of the OU container object. In this example, OU=NORAD and OU=CAMELOT are partitions.

Using NWADMIN to Browse the NDS Tree

The NetWare Administrator utility runs as a multiple-document interface (MDI) application, which enables you to display up to nine different browsing windows at one time. The primary window illustrated in Figure 2.60 provides a background for viewing one or more secondary windows. The secondary windows support that browsing feature.

FIGURE 2.59

Using the NDS Manager in NWADMIN, you can see the partitions denoted with a small box icon to the left of the OU container. OU=NORAD and OU=CAMELOT are shown as partitions.

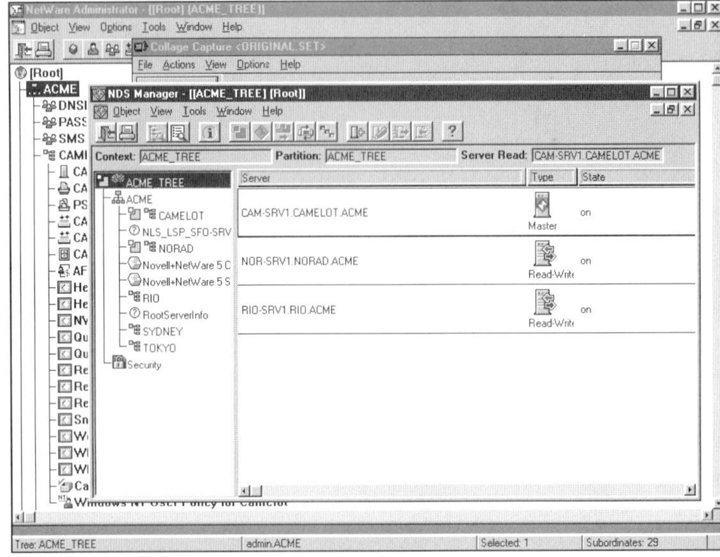

FIGURE 2.60

The main window for the NWADMIN utility

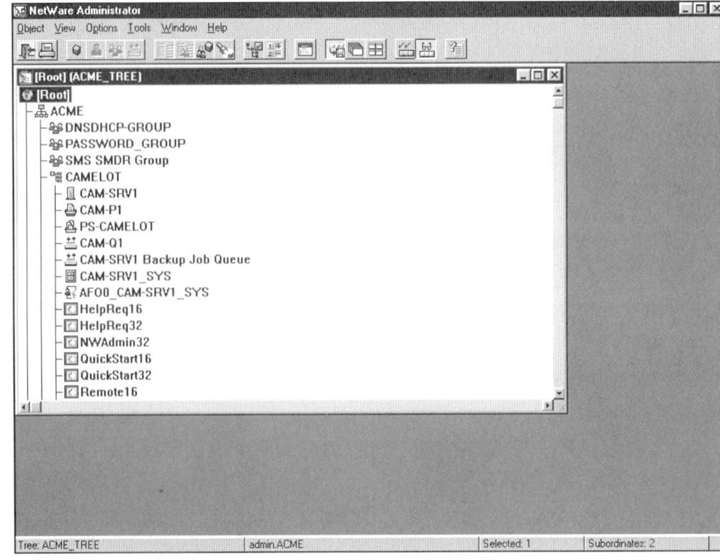

The browsers in NWADMIN are the secondary windows that appear in the utility. To open or enable a browser window, you need to select a container object from the primary window and then select the Browse option from the Tools menu.

The new window is the browser window that displays the NDS objects from the selected container or current context. You can then select objects, directories, and files to perform the administrative tasks. Figure 2.61 shows an example of a browser window for the objects in the ACME tree.

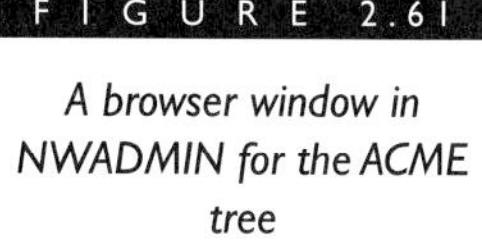

FIGURE 2.61

A browser window in NWADMIN for the ACME tree

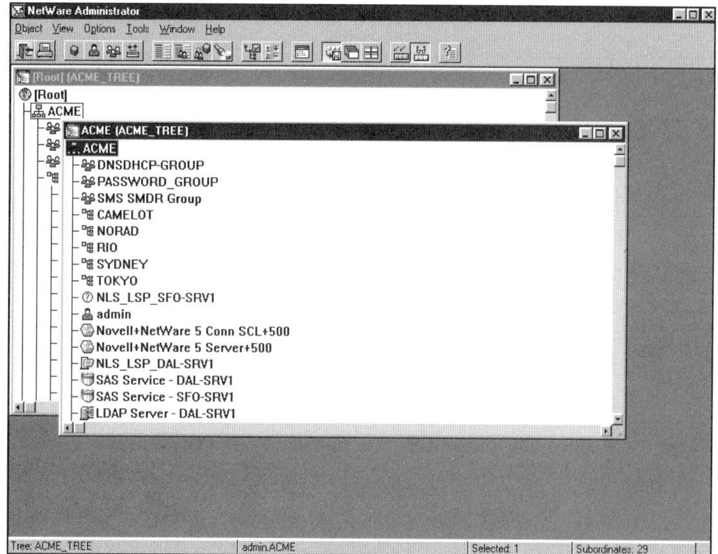

You can open up to nine browser windows to view the individual container objects. To view multiple browser windows at the same time, select the Tile option from the Windows menu. Figure 2.62 shows three browser windows tiled for the objects in the ACME tree.

The title for each of the browser windows displays the context of the container where the browser window is set. These will help you remember and organize the browser window on your screen.

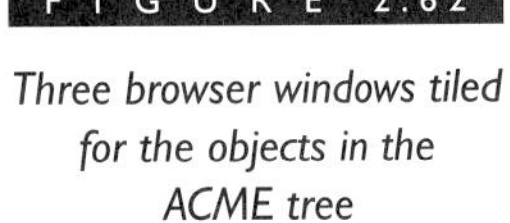

FIGURE 2.62

Three browser windows tiled for the objects in the ACME tree

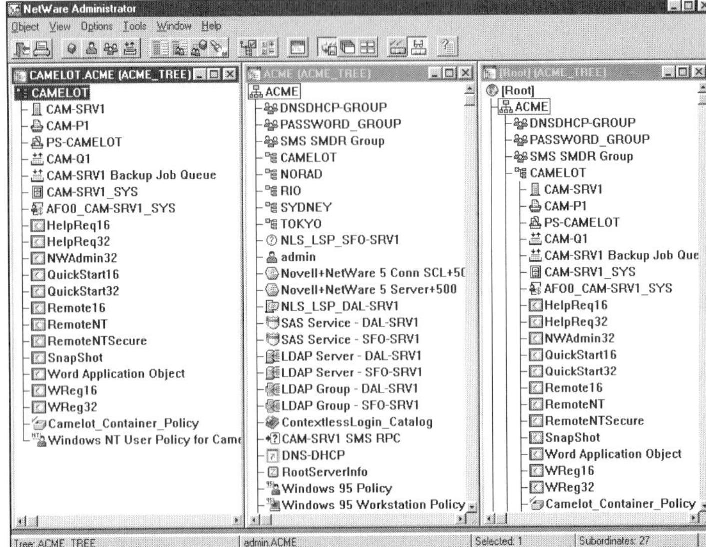

Browsing the NDS Tree Using the Container Objects in NWADMIN

You can browse the NDS tree by walking through the container objects. The container objects can be browsed by expanding or opening them and displaying their contents. There are several ways to expand the container objects within the NWADMIN utility:

- Double-click the object to expand the container to show its contents and the subordinate objects. If the container is expanded, you can collapse the container by double-clicking again.

- Select a container object in the tree and choose the Expand option from the View menu to expand the contents of the container. You can collapse the container using the Collapse option from the same menu.

- Select a container object and press the + key on the keypad of the keyboard. The container object will expand and show its contents. (The key with the + above the equal sign on your keyboard will not work for this operation.) You can collapse the container by pressing the – key on the keypad.

- Select a container object and press the right mouse button (or right-click). Select the Browse option from the short menu that appears. This option launches a new browser window with the contents of the container object. Figure 2.63 shows the short menu that appears after you press the right mouse button.

FIGURE 2.63

A short menu appears when the right mouse button is pressed.

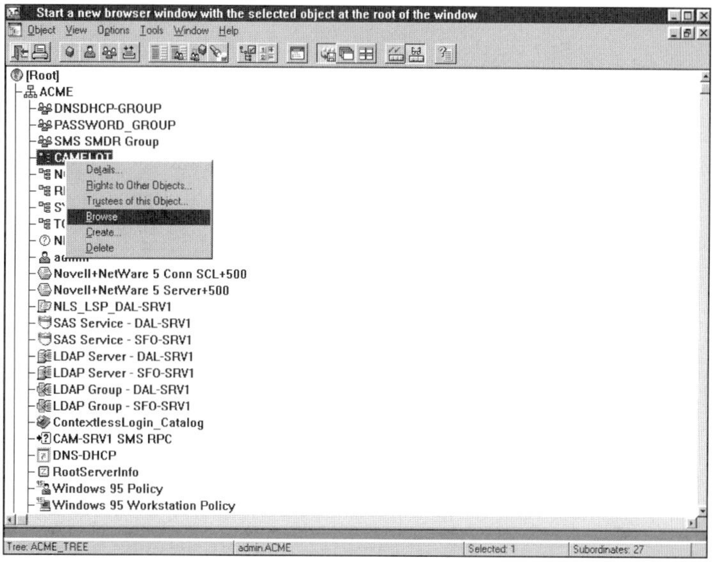

Figure 2.64 illustrates several container objects that have been expanded for the ACME tree.

Browsing the Properties in NWADMIN

You can browse the properties for the individual object by opening the Object dialog box or selecting the Details option from the Object menu. You can open the Object dialog box using any of these methods:

- Double-click the object.
- Select the object and then choose the Details option from the Object menu.

- Select the object and press the right mouse button. Choose Details from the short menu that appears.

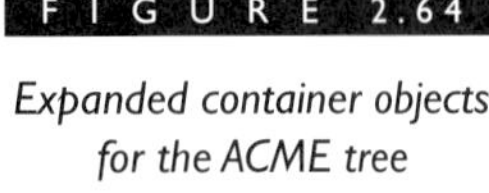

FIGURE 2.64

Expanded container objects for the ACME tree

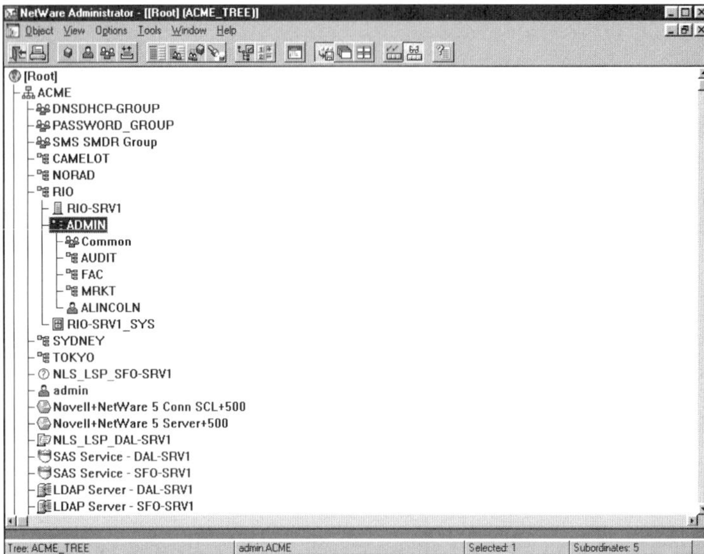

The Object dialog box is organized or divided into pages that you select individually. The Identification page is the default or first page shown. Figure 2.65 shows the dialog box for an object in the ACME tree.

You can browse the specific information for an object by selecting the corresponding page. The page icons are located on the right-hand side of the Object dialog box and are specific to the type of object being displayed.

The pages in the Object dialog box are all part of the same dialog box. When you select a different page, you are still in the same dialog box. If you press OK or Cancel on any page, you are affecting the entire dialog box, not just the individual page. Pressing OK will save modifications to all the pages, and pressing Cancel will exit the dialog box without saving any changes to any page. In order to move between pages of the dialog box, select the desired page.

FIGURE 2.65

The Object or Details dialog box for an object in the ACME tree

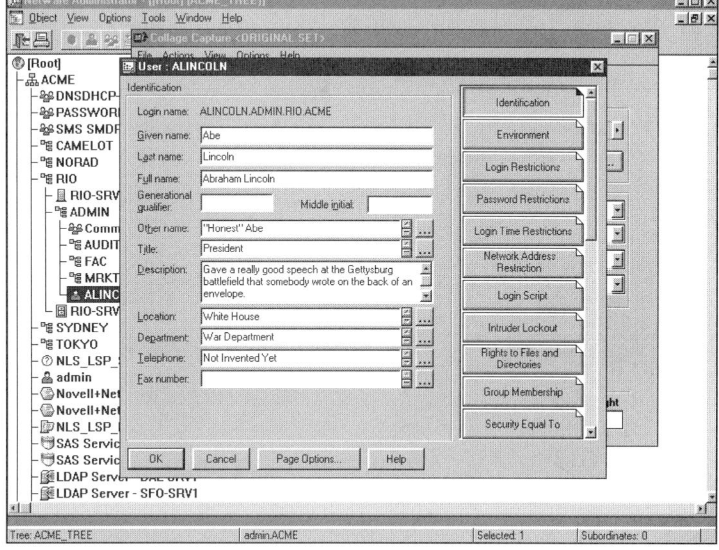

Searching for Objects and Properties in NWADMIN

You can find object and property information in the NDS tree using the Search feature. You can perform this function without having to expand each of the container objects. The search operation will check each of the objects in the tree unless you restrict or narrow the search criteria.

For example, in Figure 2.66, the search criteria are set up to find all the users in the ACME tree that have the department property equal to OU=CHARITY.

NDS MANAGER (NDSMGR32.EXE) Utility The NDS Manager (NDSMGR32.EXE) utility is available in NetWare 5 to allow you to manage and monitor the NDS tree, NDS partitions, and replicas.

NDS Manager is a graphical hierarchical browser that offers many new features. These feature include these capabilities:

- Can run as a stand-alone application or as an integrated part of the NetWare Administrator utility (NWADMIN).
- Provides partitioning and replication capabilities for Novell's Directory Services.

- Provides the capability to repair the Directory from a client workstation running NDS Manager.
- Includes a version update capability so that any or all NetWare servers in a network can be updated to a newer version of the DS.NLM file.
- Provides context-sensitive help for synchronization errors detected by the Partition Continuity option.

FIGURE 2.66

The search criteria are set up to find all the users in the ACME tree that have the department property equal to OU=CHARITY.

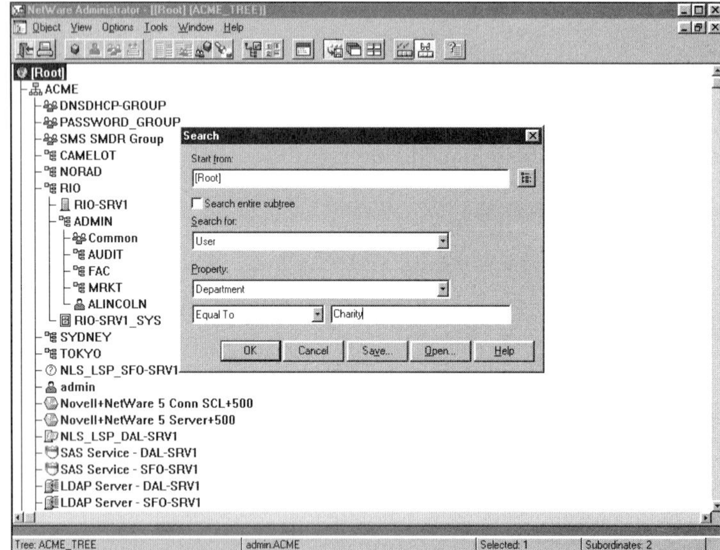

As shown in Figure 2.67, NDS Manager is part of Novell's NetWare 5 product. This utility can be run as a stand-alone utility or snapped into the NWADMIN utility. In order to snap the NDS Manager into NWADMIN, you need to copy the NWSNAP32.DLL from the server's SYS:PUBLIC\WIN32 directory to SYS:\PUBLIC\WIN32\SNAPINS. The next time that the NWADMIN utility is executed, the NDS Manager utility becomes available from the TOOLS menu.

If you receive an Access Deny error while copying NWSNAP.DLL, you will need to remove the read-only file attribute.

FIGURE 2.67

NDS Manager can be run as a stand-alone utility or snapped into the NWADMIN Tools menu.

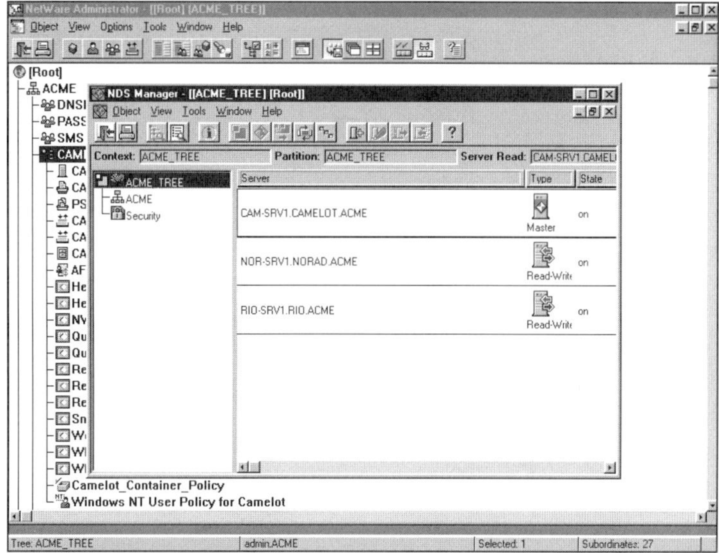

Most operations can be performed from either the hierarchical Tree view or the list of partitions and servers. They are represented on the button bar by icons so that you can toggle between views of partitions and servers and of the NDS trees.

The other view from which you work in NDS Manager is the Partition Continuity view, which allows you to view the condition of your tree and perform repair operations if necessary. Before using NDS Manager, you should access these views and become familiar with their features and options. An example of a server and partition view is shown in Figure 2.68.

As shown in Figure 2.69, after you select a particular partition, you can right-click the mouse or select the icons from the toolbar to pull up a series of options. The options shown in Figure 2.69 include these:

- **Information** — Displays information about the partition such as where the master replica is stored, the number of read/write replicas, and the time of the last replica synchronization (see Figure 2.70).

- **Check Synchronization** — Reads the partition synchronization status of the selected partition or partition list (see Figure 2.71).

- **Merge** — Merges the selected partition with its parent partition.

FIGURE 2.68

Your NDS tree can be viewed from two vantage points: partitions and the servers they are stored on, or servers and the partitions they contain.

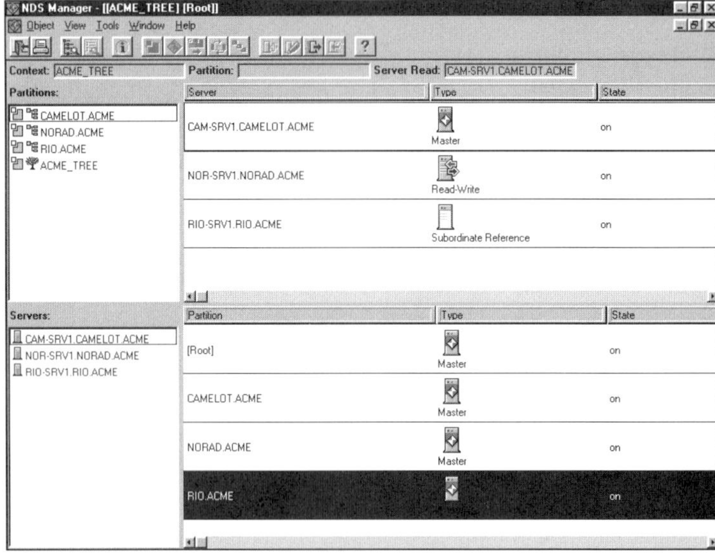

FIGURE 2.69

Selecting an individual partition lets you query the partition for information or make changes to it, such as moves and merges.

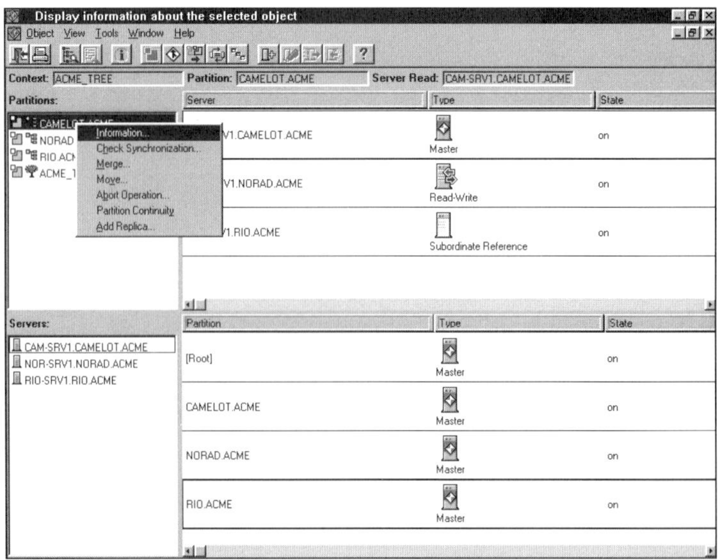

FIGURE 2.70

Selecting the information option on a partition will give you useful information such as the last time the partition was synchronized.

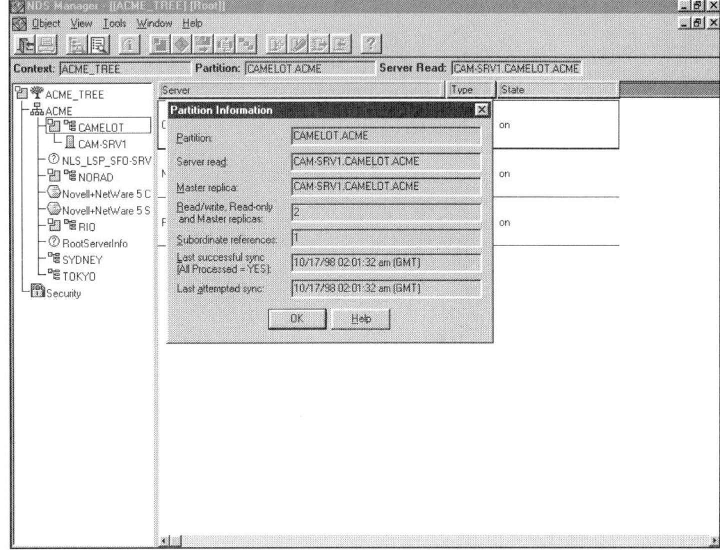

FIGURE 2.71

You can easily check the synchronization status of a partition before starting any type of partitioning operation.

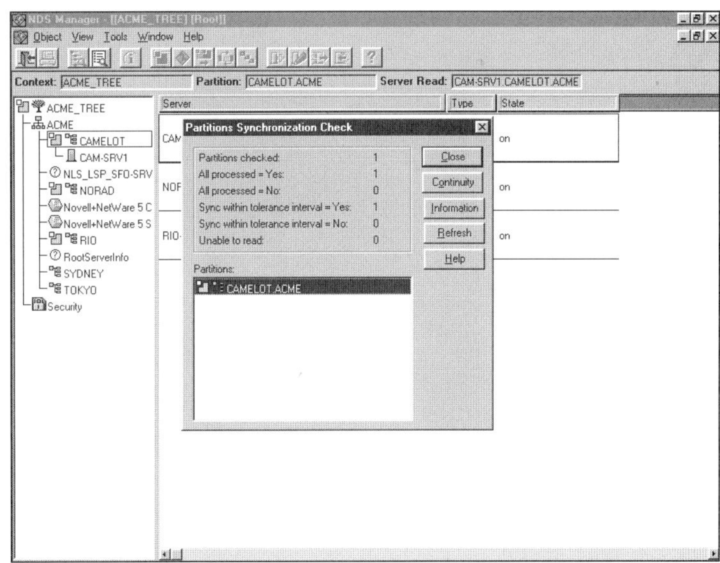

- **Move** — Moves the selected container (partition) to a new context that you specify.
- **Abort Operation** — Attempts to abort a partition operation that has been initiated on the selected partition.
- **Partition Continuity** — Helps you identify whether any of a partition's replicas are experiencing synchronization errors. This operation is also known as "walking the replica ring" as shown in Figure 2.72.
- **Add Replica** — Allows you to create and add additional replicas for the partition. When adding a new replica, you need to select the server where the replica will be held.

FIGURE 2.72

The Partition Continuity check will show you the state of partitions stored on servers in your tree.

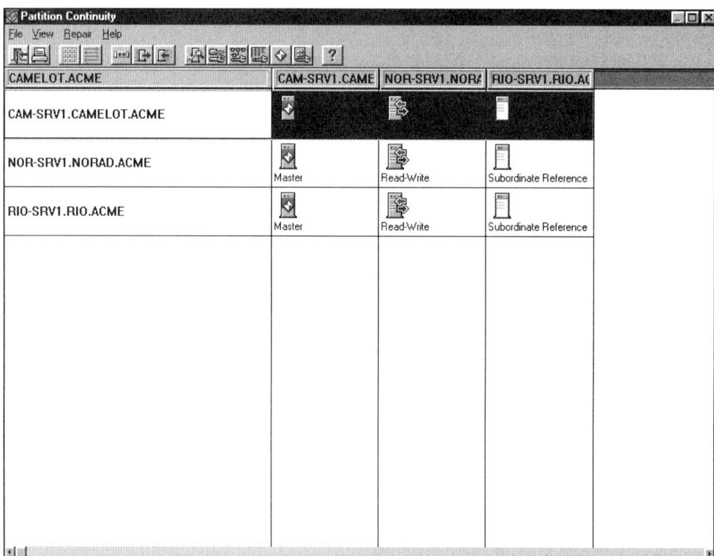

After you run the Partition Continuity option, you will be presented with the results of the check, mainly if all servers were able to "talk" in the replica list. This screen also provides another menu bar with the Repair option. Before running DSREPAIR, the utility will prompt you as shown in Figure 2.73.

FIGURE 2.73

The REPAIR option runs DSREPAIR on the local server's NDS database and issues a warning before performing the operation.

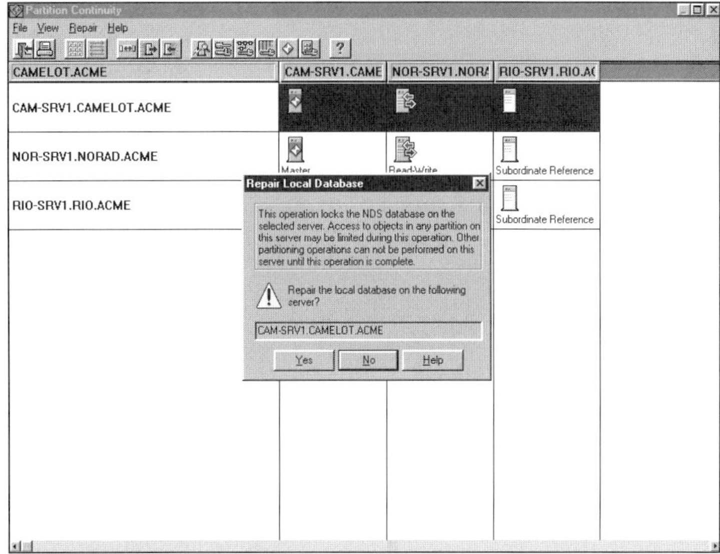

The REPAIR menu option allows you to perform the following DSREPAIR functions on your servers:

- **Synchronize Immediately** — Performs an immediate synchronization on every server that contains a copy of the replica selected for synchronization.
- **Receive Updates** — Deletes the Directory data of a replica and replaces it with data from the master replica of the partition. Choose this option if the replica is corrupted or has not received updated data for an extended period of time.
- **Send Updates** — Sends updates from one replica to another on the partition. When you send updates from a replica, the Directory data in that replica is broadcast from the server it resides on to all the other replicas of the partition, including the master replica. The other replicas combine the new information you sent with the data they already have. If the replicas have data besides the data sent to them, they will retain that data.

- **Information** — Provides information on partitions, replicas, servers, and synchronization errors.
- **Verify Remote Server IDs** — This operation verifies:
  - The remote server's name
  - The remote server's ID in a server's database
  - The remote ID, which is this server's ID as it is found in the remote server's database

  If any errors are detected, this operation will attempt to repair the server IDs.
- **Repair Replica** — Repairs a replica on a server. Repairing a replica consists of checking the replica ring information on each server that contains a replica and validating the remote ID. This operation repairs only the chosen replica on the server you select.
- **Repair Network Addresses** — Repairs network addresses to ensure that the servers in your network are broadcasting correct addresses.
- **Repair Local Database** — Repairs local database records when your NDS database is corrupted. This operation resolves inconsistencies in the local Directory database so that it can be opened and accessed.
- **Assign New Master** — A repair feature that should be used only when the current master replica is corrupted, when the server on which the current master replica resides has lost data integrity, or when the server on which the current master replica resides has had an unrecoverable hard disk failure. Do not use this feature to change a replica type.
- **Remove Server** — Removes a server from an NDS tree.

Misuse of the Remove Server operation can cause irrevocable damage to the NDS tree. If a server that is no longer in the tree appears in the replica ring, instead of using the Remove Server operation, perform a Delete Server operation to delete the server's object.

- **Repair Volume Objects** — Checks the association of all the mounted volumes with Volume objects in the Directory. If the volume is not associated with a Volume object, this operation looks for one in the context of the NetWare Server object. If the volume is found, the Volume object is attached to the volume. If the volume is not found, this operation attempts to create one.
- **Abort Operation** — Attempts to abort a partition operation that has been initiated on the selected partition.

NDS Manager allows you as an administrator to perform the operations just listed from a single utility. After running DSREPAIR, you can view the error log for any synchronization errors or other errors that may have occurred during the repair. An example of the log file is shown in Figure 2.74.

FIGURE 2.74

After running DSREPAIR from the NDS Manager utility, you can view the error log file generated by DSREPAIR.

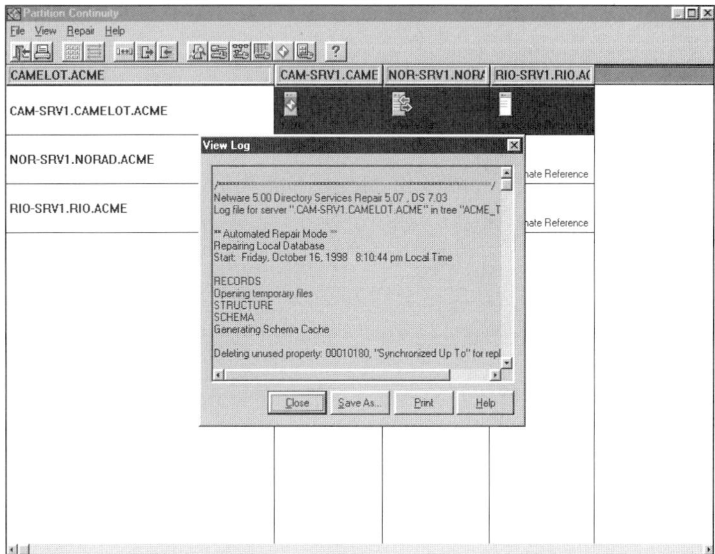

One other useful feature of the NDS Manager utility checks versions of the DS.NLM and then updates the server with a later version if necessary. An example of viewing the DS.NLM version is shown in Figure 2.75.

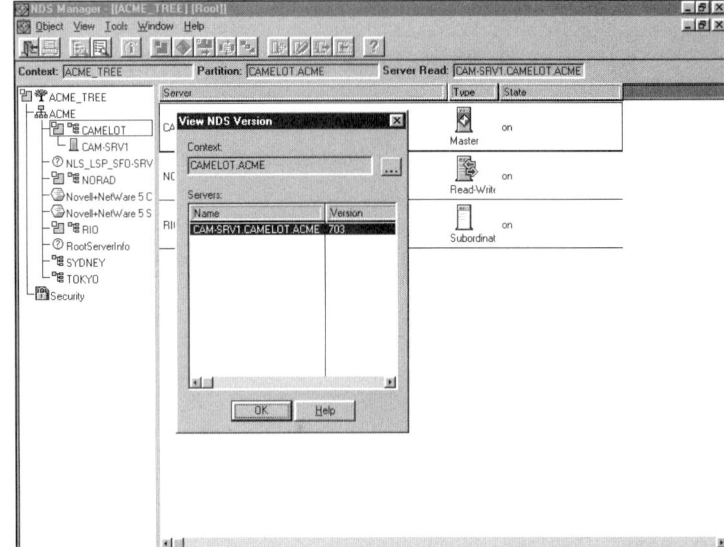

FIGURE 2.75

Prior to updating your servers to a newer version of the DS.NLM, you can check the version number through NDS Manager.

General Recommendations for Using NDS Manager

Keep in mind the following guidelines when using the NDS Manager utility:

- The NetWare Client 32 for DOS/Windows or Windows 95/98 is recommended when running NDS Manager.
- NDS Manager fully supports NDS v4.89a and above as well as DSREPAIR.NLM v4.31 and above.
- NDS Manager does not support DSREPAIR.NLM versions prior to 4.31.
- Partition and replica information will not display information for some fields if the information for the partition or replica is read from a server running NDS versions prior to 4.89a.
- The Partition Continuity Grid will not show any synchronization errors (even if they exist) for replicas stored on servers running NDS versions prior to 4.89a.

- When running NDS Manager on VLMs, be aware that VLMs default to a maximum of eight simultaneous connections to servers. This default can cause "Unable to attach" and "Unable to read" error messages (often in the form of statuses –321, x8801, and x8809) in NDS Manager. You can avoid this problem by upgrading to Client 32.

The MONITOR Utility

The MONITOR utility (MONITOR.NLM) is a server-based utility that helps you easily manage and configure much of the system as well as observe network performance statistics. This utility uses a C-Worthy menu interface. New in the MONITOR utility in NetWare 5 is the ability to view and change each of the server's SET parameters.

The MONITOR utility's main startup screen is called the General Information screen. Figure 2.76 shows an example of the MONITOR's main screen, which includes general information about server performance. At the top of the General Information screen you can view processor utilization, server up time, processor speed, server processes, and connections used (which typically represents the number of users logged in).

FIGURE 2.76

The MONITOR main screen includes general information about server performance.

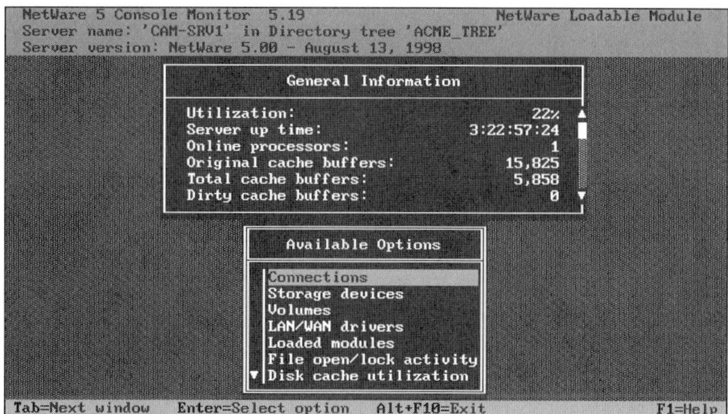

As mentioned, the main menu in MONITOR provides you with a menu-driven interface to the system SET parameters available on the server. MONITOR has replaced the SERVMAN utility that shipped with previous versions of NetWare 4. Thus, SERVMAN is not included with the NetWare 5 operating system.

To get to the SET parameters, select the menu item called Server Parameters from the main menu. Other options from the main menu cover connection information, LAN configuration, storage information, volume information, and network information. Once you have selected the Server Parameters, a list of categories (similar to the one displayed if you type SET at the server console) is displayed. At this point you can select a specific category or area to view and edit. Figure 2.77 shows the Server Parameters screen, which allows you to select the category of SET parameters.

FIGURE 2.77

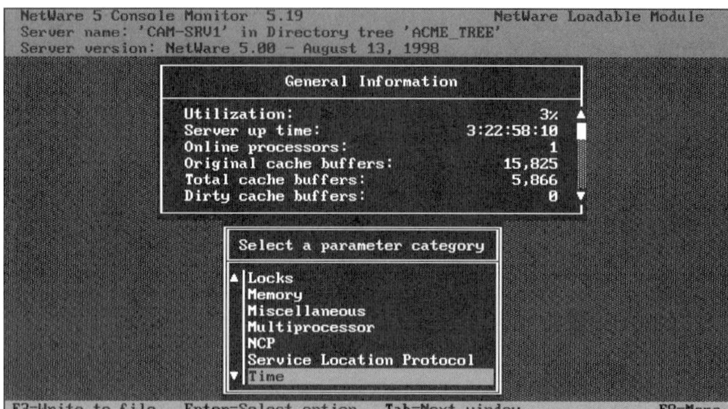

The Server Parameters main screen allows you to select the categories of SET parameters. In this example, the Time category has been selected.

An example of using the SET parameter in the MONITOR utility is shown in Figure 2.78. As shown, NetWare 5 includes a rich set of settable parameters governing time and time synchronization.

Using this section, you can configure the time on your NetWare 5 servers. Most changes and configurations with the SET parameters can be accomplished by using the MONITOR utility. The SET parameters will rarely need changing. However, some environments may require that you adjust some of them.

FIGURE 2.78

The time parameters can be found in the Server section of MONITOR.

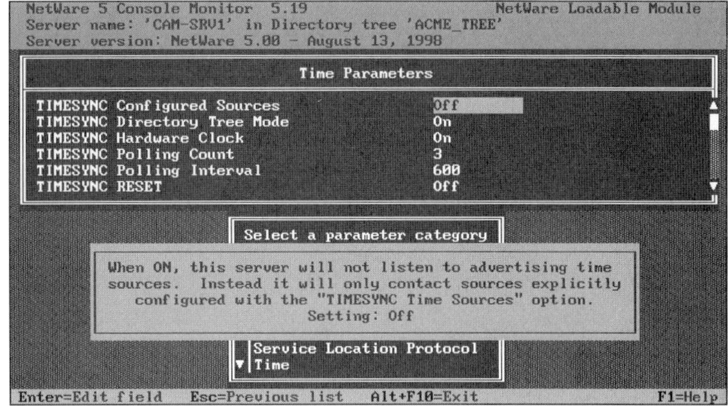

The DSREPAIR Utility

The DSREPAIR utility enables you to monitor NDS, check for errors, and correct problems in the name service on an individual server basis. The utility runs as a NetWare Loadable Module (NLM) at the server console. The utility is menu-driven and is written with the well-known C-worthy user interface.

You can run the DSREPAIR utility on any NetWare 5 server in the Directory tree. Additionally, the utility can either be loaded while at the server console or through access to a server via the RCONSOLE utility.

The DSREPAIR utility provides these options:

- **Unattended Full Repair** — This feature automatically performs repair operations on the local NDS name service without operator assistance.

- **Time Synchronization** — This option checks the time synchronization for all servers that are known to the local server. You must monitor and correct time synchronization problems before performing any repair operation. A replica of the [ROOT] partition must be on the local server running DSREPAIR for this feature to contact all servers in the tree.

- **Report Synchronization Status** — This option lets you check the synchronization status of any partition on the server and the servers holding the association replicas.

- **View Repair Log File** — This option lets you view all the operations of the DSREPAIR utility by consulting a log file stored on your server. The default log file is SYS:SYSTEM\DSREPAIR.LOG. You should always view the log file after running the utility.

- **Advanced Options Menu** — The advanced options on this menu give you greater flexibility to manually control the repair of your NDS tree.

For more complete information or detailed instructions on the many options available in the DSREPAIR utility, please refer to Chapter 9, "Novell Directory Services Objects and Properties."

The DSTRACE Utility

In previous versions of NetWare 4, DSTRACE referred to a group of SET commands available at the server console. In NetWare 5, DSTRACE is a utility that executes as a NetWare Loadable Module (NLM) and that provides expanded monitoring capabilities over its predecessor. Once it is loaded, you can use DSTRACE (also called the Novell Directory Services Trace Event Monitor) to monitor synchronization status and errors. DSTRACE is primarily used to determine and track the health of NDS as it communicates with the other NetWare 5 servers in the network.

You can use DSTRACE commands to:

- Monitor the status of NDS synchronization processes.

- View errors that occur during NDS synchronization.

The basic functions of DSTRACE are to view the status of the Directory Services trace screen in NetWare 5 and initiate limited synchronization processes. For more complete information or detailed instructions on how to establish the proper setting for the DSTRACE utility, please refer to Chapter 9, "Novell Directory Services Objects and Properties."

The DSMERGE Utility

The DSMERGE utility enables you to merge NDS trees into the same tree. DSMERGE.NLM provides the mechanism for combining two trees through four basic functions:

- Checks status of NetWare 5 servers in the Directory Tree before the merge.
- Checks time synchronization status of NetWare 5 servers before the merge.
- Renames a directory tree when necessary.
- Performs the merge of two trees when the previous criteria are satisfied.

The main screen of DSMERGE enables you to perform these operations; it is displayed in Figure 2.79.

FIGURE 2.79

The main DSMERGE screen

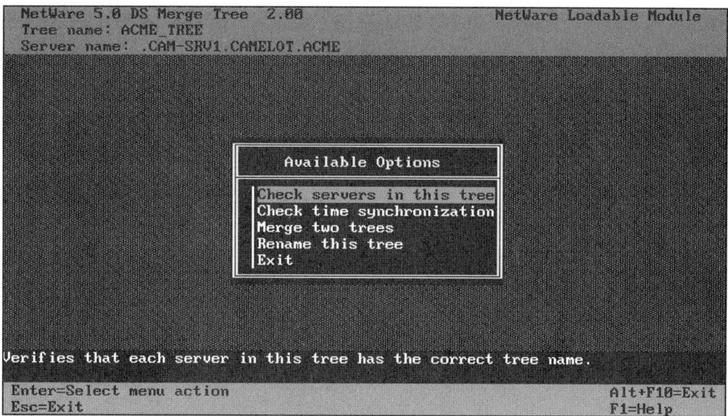

Checking the Status of NetWare 5 Servers

Before and after the merge of two trees it is important to check the status of your NetWare 5 servers. Before the merge, you want to check the versions of each NetWare 5 server and its current status. Table 2.4 lists the possible statuses and brief descriptions.

TABLE 2.4

NetWare 5 Server Statuses

STATUS	DESCRIPTION
DS Locked	The server responds with an error message indicating that the NDS name service is locked and not accessible.
Inaccessible/Down	The server does not respond and is considered to be inaccessible.
Error <–N>	N is the Directory Services error code number. This status indicates that the server is not responding because of the error condition listed in the value N.
Wrong Tree	The server is responding with a tree name that does not match the tree name of the local server containing the master replica of [ROOT].
UP	The server is up and functioning.

The check phase of DSMERGE also ensures that the current server on which you are running this utility holds a replica of the [ROOT] partition. If it cannot find a replica of [ROOT], the operation will abort.

Next, the DSMERGE utility will attempt to find all NetWare 5 servers in the tree by searching a list of servers to collect the server name, version of NDS, and tree name. If a server in the list cannot be found or has an incorrect tree name, the utility will issue an error message. Once all the servers have been contacted, the operation will display the list of servers on the screen and their statuses. An example of checking the servers before a DSMERGE operation is shown in Figure 2.80.

FIGURE 2.80

DSMERGE will check the status of servers before the merge operation begins.

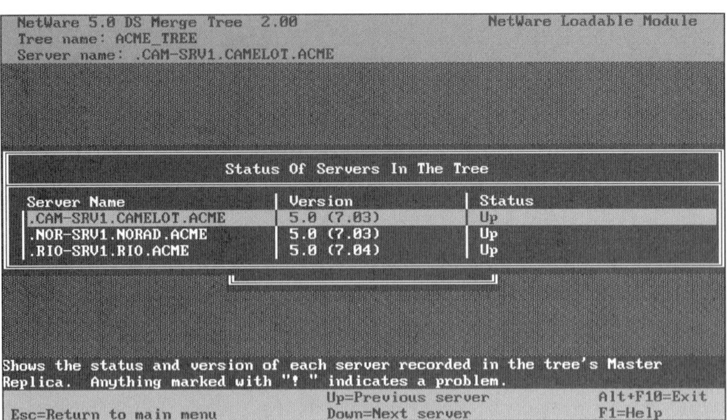

Checking Time Synchronization

Another important check that the DSMERGE utility performs is the status of time synchronization on all servers to be merged. Both trees must be synchronized, and they must refer to the same time source. Once DSMERGE is loaded on a server containing a replica of the [ROOT] partition, you can initiate the time synchronization command as shown in Figure 2.81.

FIGURE 2.81

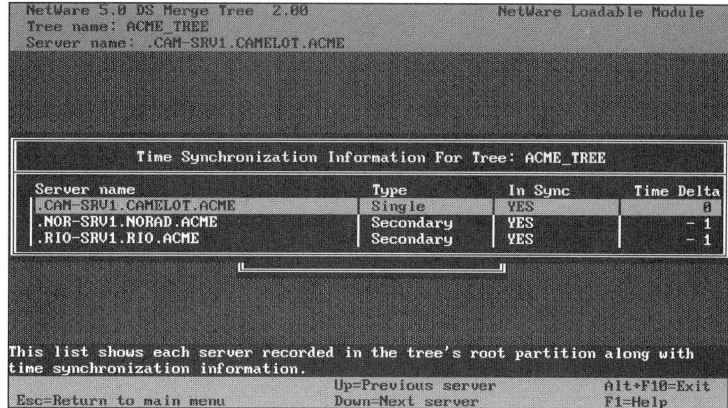

The time synchronization status screen in the DSMERGE utility

The option will check the time status of all servers for server name, NDS version, and the time synchronization status. If there is a time delta between a NetWare 5 server and the local server running DSMERGE, the difference is displayed as shown in Figure 2.82.

Your merged Directory tree must only have one reference or single-reference time source. If the two trees you are merging both have a reference or a single-reference server, you must assign one of them as a secondary server prior to initiating the merge.

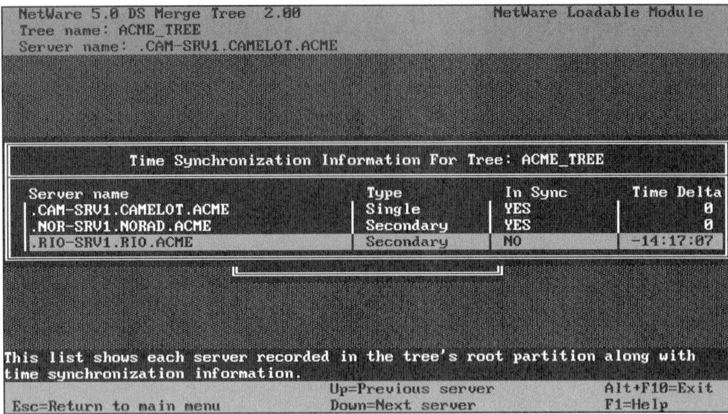

FIGURE 2.82

If time synchronization differs, the DSMERGE utility will show the time delta between servers.

Renaming a Directory Tree

Another useful feature found in the DSMERGE utility is the capability to rename an NDS tree. You must use this option if you are merging two trees that have the same name. Keep in mind that currently this is the only Novell utility that will enable you to change the name of your NDS tree. You must load DSMERGE.NLM on the server that contains the master replica of the [ROOT] partition. The utility will first verify that you are running on the server containing the master replica of [ROOT].The master replica can calculate a list of servers that the utility can contact to change the names of servers holding a replica of [ROOT].

If a server in the list cannot be contacted, a warning message will be issued. You can proceed to rename the tree if servers are unavailable, but you must enter a confirmation to continue the operation.

The operation actually begins by changing the name of the local tree's [ROOT] object to the new tree name. If an error should occur during this process, the operation is aborted. After the local server has changed the name of the [ROOT] object, a command is issued to change all servers in the local tree to the new tree name. Keep in mind that once this process has completed there are many more synchronization activities being performed in the background. Once initiated, this process is irrevocable. After completion of the operation, you should check the status of the servers once again to verify that all servers have received the new name.

Performing the Merge Operation

Once you have checked and verified the status of your NetWare 5 servers, along with time synchronization, you are ready to perform the merge operation. After the completion of DSMERGE, you will have a single tree with a common [ROOT]. The operation merges the selected source tree with a target tree. The end result is a tree with the target tree's name of [ROOT].

DSMERGE.NLM must be loaded on a server containing the master replica of [ROOT] of the source tree. The operation occurs in four phases:

Phase 1: Merge Check

This check ensures that your source server running DSMERGE.NLM contains the master replica of the [ROOT] partition. If this check is successful, you will see a screen similar to the one shown in Figure 2.83. This screen asks for the tree names of both the source and target trees along with their administrative names and passwords.

FIGURE 2.83

The Merge Trees Information screen

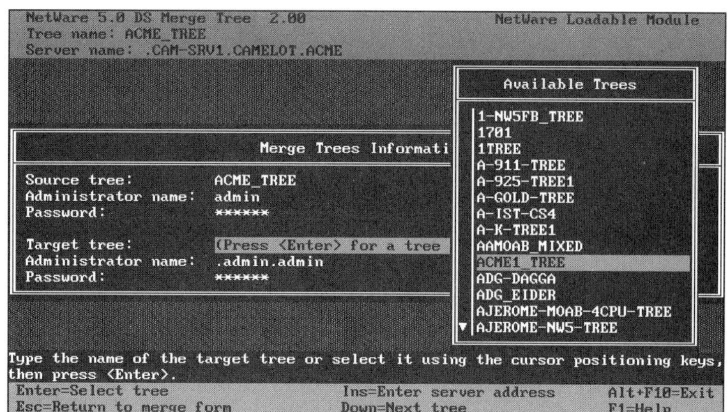

Phase 2: Merge Preparation

This phase modifies the source tree partitions. The utility will do a schema comparison. If the schemas do not match, you will need to use DSREPAIR to import a remote schema from the other tree. It will also split the [ROOT] partition from all other objects in the tree, making a partition that contains only the [ROOT] object. All other read/write or read-only replicas of [ROOT] will also be removed from any servers in the tree. Once this operation is completed, the utility can actually merge the trees. Keep in mind that the partitioning operations mentioned here could also be performed beforehand with the Partition Manager or PARTMGR utilities. The first two phases are displayed in the utility before you continue, as shown in Figure 2.84.

FIGURE 2.84

The first phases of the DSMERGE process are displayed for information purposes and are followed by another screen showing the next two phases.

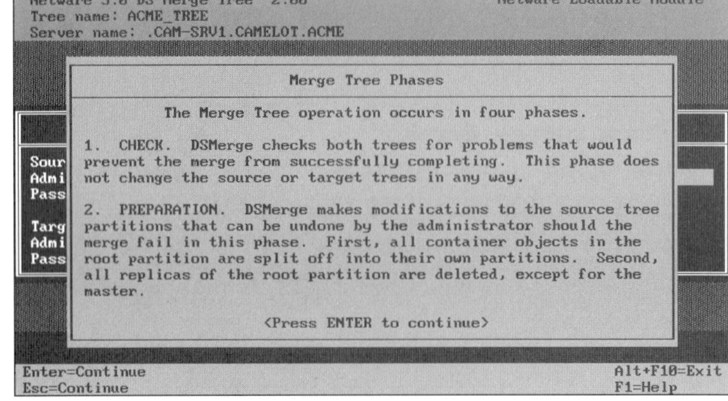

Phase 3: Merge Trees

Once the first two phases are completed, the merge operation will begin. Once again, the operation will gather the list of servers known by the source server. Each server in the source tree will be contacted to obtain its server address and distinguished name in preparation for merging the source tree to the target tree.

The merge operation actually changes the name of the source tree [ROOT] object to that of the [ROOT] in the target tree. Once this process occurs, the source server receives a new name and issues a command to change the tree names of all servers in the source tree.

Phase 4: Merge Completion

The merge completion phase includes the continuation of renaming the tree and servers in the source tree. A copy of the target tree's [ROOT] replica will then be copied over to the source server. This operation may take some time depending on the size of the target's [ROOT] replica. Any objects that are no longer needed will be removed by the background synchronization processes.

Some manual tasks may have to be completed after the two trees are merged. These tasks would include placing copies of the [ROOT] replica where needed in your tree. You may have to restore any objects that were deleted before the DSMERGE utility was run. Because the source tree has had significant changes to the partitions below [ROOT], you will have to use the Partition Manager or PARTMGR utilities to place partitions back again. Follow the guidelines discussed in Chapter 6 of this book.

Finally, you may have to check workstations that have the PREFERRED TREE statement set in their NET.CFG. Each workstation with the source tree name will have to be changed to reflect the target tree name. This can be accomplished through the use of batch files or an update program, such as the UCUPDATE utility, contained in the user's container login script.

The CX Utility

Change conteXt (CX) is a DOS-based utility that helps the user set the current context in the NDS tree. You can use this utility only to view the container hierarchy and leaf objects in the tree or to change to a new context. This utility is placed in the SYS:LOGIN subdirectory so that it can be executed before users are logged in. Figure 2.85 displays the help screen for the CX utility.

FIGURE 2.85

The CX help screen shows the options available to browse the NDS tree.

```
CX                          Options Help                          4.20
Syntax:  CX [new context | /VER] [/R] [/[T | CONT] [/A]] [/C] [/?]
To:                                                    Use:
  View all container objects below the                   /T
    current or specified context.
  View container objects at the current                  /CONT
    or specified level.
  Modify /T or /CONT to view All objects                 /A
    at or below the context
  Change context or view objects relative to root        /R
  Display version information                            /VER
  Scroll continuously                                    /C
For example, to:                                    Type:
  View directory tree below the current context       CX /T
  View containers within a specific context           CX .O=Novell /CONT

>>> Enter = More    C = Continuous    Esc = Cancel
```

This section will not discuss how to set the context using CX but will focus instead on the options available to you to browse the NDS tree. The browse options that display the tree information are:

- **/CONT** — Lists just the container objects at the current context.
- **/R** — Lists objects relative to the [ROOT] object. This option also can change the context to the [ROOT].
- **/T** — Lists all the container objects below the current context.
- **/A** — Lists all the objects, including all the leaf objects.
- **/VER** — Displays the version information.
- **/C** — Scrolls continuously.

Figure 2.86 displays the output of the CX /CONT command for the ACME tree when the current context is set to [ROOT].

FIGURE 2.86

The output of the CX /CONT command for the ACME tree when the current context is set to [ROOT]

```
*** Directory Services Mapping ***

ACME
   ├CAMELOT
   ├NORAD
   ├SYDNEY
   ├RIO
   └TOKYO
C:\>
```

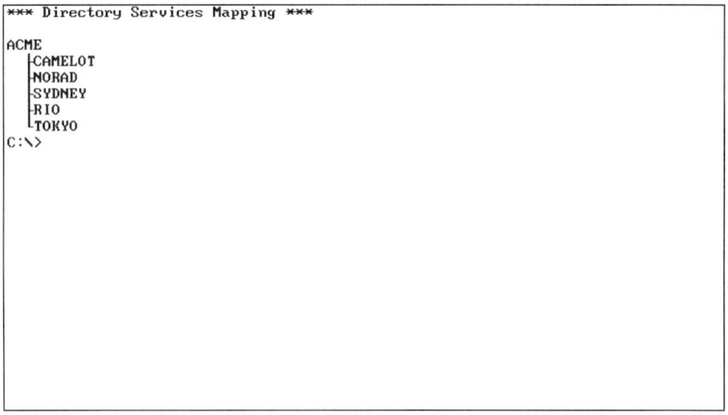

Figure 2.87 displays the output of the CX /T command for the ACME tree when the current context is set to [ROOT].

FIGURE 2.87

The output of the CX /T command for the ACME tree when the current context is set to [ROOT]

```
*** Directory Services Mapping ***

[ROOT]
  └ACME
     ├CAMELOT
     │  ├CHARITY
     │  ├PR
     │  └OPS
     │     ├FIN
     │     └DIST
     ├NORAD
     │  ├CHARITY
     │  ├PR
     │  └LABS
     │     ├R&D
     │     └WHI
     ├SYDNEY
     │  ├CHARITY
     │  ├PR
     │  └HR
     │     ├MEDICAL
     │     ├FOOD
     │     └SHELTER
     ├RIO
>>> Enter = More    C = Continuous    Esc = Cancel
```

The UIMPORT Utility

The UIMPORT utility enables you to import users from a database application to NDS. This utility can also create, delete, and update user objects and their existing properties. If you are using a database that has the capability to convert records to a comma-separated ASCII file, you can use UIMPORT to migrate this data to the NetWare Directory.

This utility is used primarily to create NDS user objects using records from another database, typically a database application that may contain lists of users. The process of using UIMPORT occurs in three phases:

1. Create a data file based on your existing database.
2. Create a control file to interpret and act on the data file.
3. Import the records into NDS.

The UIMPORT utility consists of two files, the data file and the import control file. The creation of your data file is simply the generation of your ASCII comma-separated file from your previous database. The control file consists of some control parameters and field definitions to define where in NDS the information should be placed.

The Data File

A data file is created by your database application when you save the information in a comma-separated ASCII file. A comma in the data file indicates a separation of fields in the NDS database. When a record is read through UIMPORT, a comma indicates a new property to be added in the user object. An example of the structure of your database might be as follows:

- Last Name:
- First Name:
- Local Address:
  - Street:
  - City:
  - State/Country:
  - Zip Code:
- Description:
- Job Title:

After you have created a data file in delimited ASCII format with any DOS editor, you will have a file with records that look like these:

```
Madison,James,"111 Calle de Carnival","Rio de
Janeiro",Brazil,56665,Facilities,Administrator
```

We named our file ACMEDATA as we exited and saved from our DOS editor.

The Import Control File

The next file you need to create is the import control file, which actually controls how the data file information will be written to NDS. The control file can be written using any DOS text editor. You will enter a set of control parameters first, followed by a list of field definitions. Control parameters define how the information in the data file is separated. The field parameters define how the information is to be written to NDS. Table 2.5 lists the control parameters and their functions.

TABLE 2.5

Control Parameters

PARAMETER	FUNCTION
Separator	Defines the type of separator used in the data file, such as a comma or a semicolon.
Quote	Defines the character used for string data in the data file.
Name Context	Defines the NDS context where the users will be created.
Replace Value	Enables you to overwrite or add data to multivalue fields, such as overwrite an existing telephone number in a user object.
User Template	Specifies the use of a user template in the creation of your NDS user objects.
Import Mode	Defines how user objects will be created. C = Create, B = Create and Update, and U = update data for existing objects.
Delete Property	Enables you to delete a property from a user object in NDS.
Create Home Directory	Enables the creation of a home directory for user objects.
Home Directory Path	Required if you create a home directory for users. The volume name is not necessary in the inclusion.
Home Directory Volume	Required if you create a home directory for users.

The field definitions define which fields should be used in NDS with the incoming data. The following fields can be selected as your particular needs warrant:

- Name
- Last Name
- Other Name

- Postal Address
- E-mail Address
- Telephone
- Fax Number
- Job Title
- Description
- Department
- Location
- Group Membership
- See Also
- Skip
- Login Script

Using our previous data file as an example, we would have an import control file that could appear as in this list created with any DOS editor utility (note that the Name Context is in the correct order):

```
Import Control
Name Context="O=ACME.OU=RIO.OU=ADMIN.OU=FAC"
User Template=y
Fields
Last Name
Other Name
```

```
Postal Address
Postal Address
Postal Address
Postal Address
Department
Job Title
```

We named our file ACMECTRL as we exited and saved from our DOS editor.

Importing Records into NDS

Once you have created a data file and a control file, you are ready to run the UIMPORT utility. At the DOS prompt of your workstation you simply type this:

```
UIMPORT control_file data_file <enter>
```

In our example we type:

```
UIMPORT ACMECTRL ACMEDATA <enter>
```

The process will then initiate. Keep in mind that you must have Supervisor rights to the container of the context you have specified in the utility. Supervisor rights are necessary for security purposes and will prevent someone from creating objects and then populating them to the NDS database with approval.

If errors should occur during the process, you will receive error messages on your DOS workstation. You can use the > filename command to pipe error messages to a file. Thus, in our example we could type:

```
UIMPORT ACMECTRL ACMEDATA >LOGFILE
```

The NLIST Utility

The NLIST utility in NetWare 5 enables you to browse the information in the NDS tree; it replaces a number of NetWare 3 utilities, including USERLIST, SLIST, SECURITY, and others.

The NLIST utility enables any user to search and view information for most of the NDS objects, such as these:

- AFP Server
- Alias
- Computer
- Directory Map
- Group
- Organization
- Organizational Unit
- Print Queue
- Print Server
- Printer
- Profile
- Server
- User
- Volume

You have several options for searching the Directory tree. Figure 2.88 displays one of the help screens for NLIST, which lists the display options for the objects in the tree.

FIGURE 2.88

The NLIST help screen that lists the display options for the objects in the tree

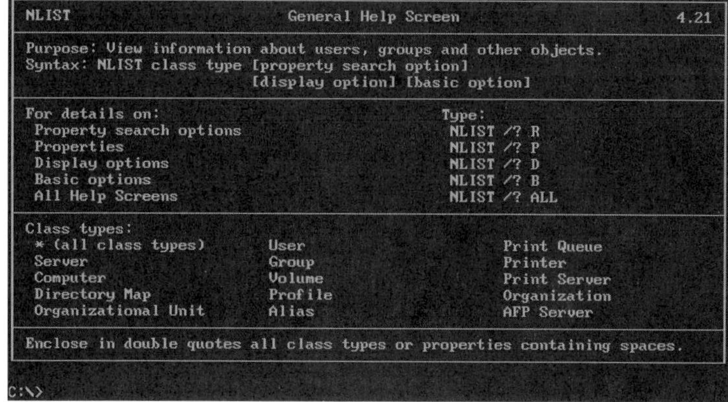

```
NLIST                       General Help Screen                          4.21
Purpose: View information about users, groups and other objects.
Syntax: NLIST class type [property search option]
                         [display option] [basic option]
For details on:                                   Type:
 Property search options                           NLIST /? R
 Properties                                        NLIST /? P
 Display options                                   NLIST /? D
 Basic options                                     NLIST /? B
 All Help Screens                                  NLIST /? ALL
Class types:
 * (all class types)       User                   Print Queue
 Server                    Group                  Printer
 Computer                  Volume                 Print Server
 Directory Map             Profile                Organization
 Organizational Unit       Alias                  AFP Server
Enclose in double quotes all class types or properties containing spaces.
C:\>
```

The proper syntax must be entered for the NLIST utility to execute. The syntax is as follows:

```
NLIST [object type] [=object name] [/options]
```

Examples:

- **NLIST User /R /S** — Searches for all user objects in the tree starting at [ROOT].
- **NLIST Server /B** — Displays all the servers using bindery calls just like the NetWare 3 SLIST command.

You can also use NLIST to search for and display information about the properties for each of the objects. You will use the WHERE and SHOW options in the command line to accomplish the browsing. For example, the syntax for the WHERE and SHOW options for an object is as follows:

```
NLIST object class [=object name] [WHERE

[property]operator [value]]

[SHOW property[,property . . .]]
```

Examples:

- **NLIST user=AEINSTEIN /D** — Displays all properties for the user AEINSTEIN in the ACME tree.
- **NLIST user WHERE "Security Equal To" EQ CAMELOT_ADMIN** — Shows all the users that are security equivalent to the CAMELOT_ADMIN organizational role relative to the current context in the ACME tree.

NETBASIC

NETBASIC is a scripting language specifically designed for the NetWare 5 environment. It creates BASIC language scripts that can be run on your server platform as interpreted BASIC programs and also compiled as NetWare Loadable Modules (NLMs) for server execution. NETBASIC ships with a suite of utility scripts and example programs demonstrating how the language is used. NETBASIC scripts can be written to query information from NDS as well as perform various management functions on your NetWare 5 servers. In fact, any Open Systems Architecture (OSA)–compliant component APIs are accessible, including the NetWare and Novell Directory Services APIs.

NETBASIC is licensed from HiTecSoft, Inc., and offers three basic features:

- The Network Management Extensions engine. This tool loads and unloads components such as NLMs and BASIC scripts from an operational server on demand.
- A BASIC script interpreter for NetWare 5 compatible with Visual Basic that allows an administrator to easily and quickly develop scripts for your servers, such as new utilities and automated tasks.
- BASIC scripting APIs for the Internet. With these APIs, an administrator can develop advanced Internet and intranet services, such as dynamic HTML pages and sites that access Novell services or Oracle databases.

NETBASIC provides the capability to create Web pages to output HTML source code. The output from a BASIC script is written to the Web server, which then routes the data back to the Web browser.

NETBASIC also provides a document management component known as DOC.NLM that allows you to write BASIC language scripts to generate HTML documents quickly and easily on the fly. You can then link a NETBASIC script to an HTML document.

Miscellaneous Server Utilities

By way of reference, the NetWare 5 utilities can be separated into two categories: the server utilities and the workstation utilities. The server utilities enable you to change server parameters, monitor the load on the server, and control its allocation of resources. A server utility runs on the server console and executes as either a NetWare Loadable Module (NLM) or a Java program. In contrast, the workstation utilities for NetWare 5 are generally run from a DOS, Windows 3.*x*, Windows 95/98, Windows NT, or OS/2 workstation. There are both menu-driven and graphical utilities. Like the server utilities, they allow you to manage the NetWare 5 server environment.

Typically the server utilities can be run directly from the NetWare 5 server console using the LOAD <utility name> command. However, one of the major changes that NetWare 5 offers is the ability to execute a server utility without having to use the LOAD command. In NetWare 5, the LOAD command is completely optional.

Table 2.6 lists several but not all of the server utilities for NetWare 5 server. For a complete description of the server console commands, see Appendix C.

TABLE 2.6

Server Utilities

UTILITY	DESCRIPTION
ACTIVATE SERVER	Loads the MSEngine for the NetWare 5 SFT III system, synchronizes the memory of both SFT III servers, and executes the MSSTART.NCF and MSAUTO.NCF scripts.

Continued

TABLE 2.6

Continued

UTILITY	DESCRIPTION
ATCON	Monitors the activity of AppleTalk network segments.
ATCONFIG	Configures NetWare for Macintosh after installation.
ATXRP	Works with PSERVER to send a print job to an AppleTalk network printer from a NetWare print queue.
BRGCON	Views bridge configuration information for a NetWare server for an OS/2 bridge.
CONLOG	Captures console messages generated by modules during system initialization and writes the messages to the default file, SYS:\ETC\CONSOLE.LOG, or to another file.
DSMERGE	Renames and merges Novell Directory Services (NDS) trees.
DSREPAIR	Maintains and repairs the NDS database on a server.
FILTCFG	Defines filters for the Internetwork Packet Exchange (IPX), TCP/IP, and AppleTalk protocols.
HALT	Used at a NetWare 5 SFT III server console to bring down an IOEngine on one SFT III server while leaving the other IOEngine running.
INETCFG	Defines an internetworking configuration for the IPX, TCP/IP, and AppleTalk protocols, simplifying the process of configuring local area networks using network and routing protocols supported by NetWare 5.
IPXCON	Monitors and troubleshoots IPX routers and network segments.
IPXPING	Sends an IPX ping packet to an IPX server or workstation to determine whether the node is reachable.
NPRINTER	Enables a printer attached to any server to be a network printer.

UTILITY	DESCRIPTION
NUT	Used with NetWare 3.11 NLMs that require NUT's library.
NWSNUT	(NLM utility user interface) Provides a library of routines used by certain NLM programs, such as MONITOR or SERVMAN.
PING	Determines whether an IP node on the network is reachable and provides statistics about the route between nodes. PING sends an Internet Control Message Protocol echo request packet to an IP node and notifies you when it receives a reply.
RPL	(Remote Program Load) Enables remote booting of IBM PC–compatible diskless workstations that have network boards installed.
RTDM	(Real Time Data Migration) Enables data migration at the server console.
SBACKUP	Used to back up and restore specified NDS and file system data on a server, workstation, or service that you select.
TCPCON	Enables you to monitor activity in the TCP/IP segments of the network.
TIMESYNC	Controls time synchronization on servers running NDS.
TPING	(Trivial PING) Enables you to determine whether an IP node on the network is reachable. TPING requires a hostname parameter.
UNICON	Used at the server console to manage certain NetWare/IP products installed on a server, such as the NetWare Domain Name System (DNS) and the NetWare/IP Domain SAP/RIP Service (DSS).

Miscellaneous Workstation Utilities

As mentioned, the workstation utilities for NetWare 5 are generally run from a DOS, Windows 3.*x*, Windows 95/98, Windows NT, or OS/2 workstation. For example, the 32-bit NetWare Administrator utility (NWADMN32.EXE) enables you to manage your NDS tree by creating, moving, deleting, changing, and renaming objects and containers. In addition, the NDS Manager utility allows you to easily view and manipulate the NDS partition and replicas.

Table 2.7 lists many of the NetWare 5 workstation utilities. All of the workstation utilities are executed from a workstation that is logged into the NetWare 5 network. Some utilities (for example, CX and LOGIN) only require an attachment to a NetWare 5 server.

TABLE 2.7

NetWare 5 Workstation Utilities

UTILITY	DESCRIPTION
AUDITCON	Audits file system and NDS events on the network.
ATOTAL	Used to total the accounting charges on your network.
CX	Allows you to change your context in the Directory tree.
NCUPDATE	Updates any number of users' NET.CFG files with a new name context after a container object has been moved or renamed.
NDS Manager	Allows you to create, manage, and repair Directory partitions and replicas. This utility includes a superset of the features in the menu-based DSREPAIR utility and replaces the graphical Partition Manager utility available with previous releases of NetWare 4.

UTILITY	DESCRIPTION
NetWare Administrator (NWADMIN)	A graphical utility that enables you to create and manage Directory objects, set up and manage network printing, manage partitions and replicas (via the integrated NDS Manager utility), and manage licensing services (via the integrated NLS Manager utility). NetWare Administrator incorporates all the functions available in FILER, NETADMIN, PARTMGR, and PCONSOLE. Includes the DSMigrate utility.
NetWare File Migration	A graphical utility that enables you to migrate files from NetWare 3.1*x* servers to NetWare 5 servers. The NetWare File Migration utility should be used after the NetWare 3.1*x* bindery has been migrated using DS Migrate.
NetWare Login	Used at a Windows 3.1*x* or Windows 95/98 workstation to access a NetWare Directory tree or server or to run a login script.
NetWare Print	Used at a Mac OS–based workstation to choose (Chooser Mac OS) and configure a Novell Directory Services printer or print queue.
NetWare Tools (OS/2)	Used to access network resources from an OS/2 workstation. NetWare Tools enable you to perform tasks such as mapping drives, managing printer connections, managing the Directory tree, managing server connections, displaying network users, and sending messages.
NetWare User Tools	Enables users to manage their network environment, including drive mappings, printing, sending broadcasts, and Directory access.

Continued

TABLE 2.7

Continued

UTILITY	DESCRIPTION
NetWare Volume Mounter (Mac OS)	Used at a Mac OS–based workstation to mount a NetWare volume.
NLIST	Enables you to view information about files, directories, users, groups, volumes, servers, and queues.
NLS Manager	Used to manage NetWare Licensing Services (NLS).
NPATH	Enables you to determine the search sequence that NetWare uses to find message files so that you can troubleshoot why a user's workstation can't find a particular file, why the workstation is finding an incorrect version of a file, or why the workstation is displaying a foreign language.
NPRINTER	Enables a printer attached to a DOS, Windows 3.1*x*, or OS/2 workstation to be a network printer.
NPTWIN95	Enables a printer attached to a Windows 95/98 workstation to be a network printer.
NWSTART (OS/2)	Starts NetWare Client for OS/2 on an OS/2 workstation if the DISCONNECT ON parameter is included in the NET.CFG file. The DISCONNECT ON parameter prevents NetWare Client for OS/2 from making a network connection when the workstation is started.
NWSTOP (OS/2)	Disconnects NetWare Client for OS/2 without turning off your computer.
NWXTRACT	Used to extract and copy files from the NetWare Installation CD-ROM to the network or to local drives.
Remote Console (Mac OS)	Used to view and control one or more server consoles from a Mac OS–based workstation.

UTILITY	DESCRIPTION
SETUPDOC	Used at a Windows 3.1*x* workstation to install and delete document collections and DynaText viewers, configure viewers to access document collections in various ways, and create viewer icons at individual workstations.
UIMPORT	Enables you to import data from an existing database into the NDS database.
/VER	Enables you to view the version number of a utility and the files the utility requires.
WSUPGRADE	Enables you to upgrade the IPX LAN driver on the workstation to the corresponding Open Data-Link Interface (ODI) driver.
Z.E.N.works	Enables you to manage and access network applications as Directory objects, providing advanced application control and access by network users. Also allows you to remotely manage desktops and take inventory.

There have been several changes to the DOS utilities. Table 2.8 lists the traditional DOS utilities that have been supported by previous versions of NetWare. The list indicates whether the DOS utility is currently supported in NetWare 5. Please refer to the Novell documentation for specific information about each of the supported DOS utilities.

TABLE 2.8

DOS Utilities Supported by NetWare 5

DOS UTILITY	SUPPORTED IN NETWARE 5
ADDICON	NO
ALLOW.BAT	NO
ATOTAL	YES
ATTACH.BAT	NO
AUDITCON	YES

Continued

TABLE 2.8

Continued

DOS UTILITY	SUPPORTED IN NETWARE 5
BREQUEST	YES
BREQUTIL	YES
BROADCAST	YES
BROLLFWD	YES
CAPTURE	YES
CASTOFF.BAT	NO
CASTON.BAT	NO
CHKDIR.BAT	NO
CHKVOL.BAT	NO
COLORPAL	NO
CX	YES
DOSGEN	YES
DSPACE.BAT	NO
ENDCAP.BAT	NO
FILER	YES
FLAG	YES
FLAGDIR.BAT	NO
GRANT.BAT	NO
LISTDIR.BAT	NO
LOGIN	YES
LOGOUT	YES
MAP	YES
MIGPRINT	NO
MIGRATE	NO
MENU_X.BAT	NO
MENUCNVT	NO
MENUEXE	NO
MENUMAKE	NO
MENURSET	NO

DOS UTILITY	SUPPORTED IN NETWARE 5
NCOPY	YES
NCUPDATE	YES
NDIR	YES
NETADMIN	NO
NETUSER	NO
NLIST	YES
NMENU.BAT	NO
NPATH	YES
NPRINT	YES
NPRINTER	YES
NVER	YES
NWDETECT	YES
NWLOG	YES
NWSTAMP	YES
NWXTRACT	YES
PARTMGR	NO
PCONSOLE	NO
PRINTCON	NO
PRINTDEF	NO
PSC	NO
PURGE	YES
PUPGRADE	NO
RCONSOLE	YES
REBOOT.COM	YES
REMOVE.BAT	NO
RENDIR	YES
REVOKE.BAT	NO
RIGHTS	YES

Continued

TABLE 2.8
Continued

DOS UTILITY	SUPPORTED IN NETWARE 5
SALVAGE.BAT	NO
SEND	YES
SESSION.BAT	NO
SETPASS	YES
SETTTS	YES
SLIST.BAT	NO
SMODE.BAT	NO
SYSCON.BAT	NO
SYSTIME	YES
TLIST.BAT	NO
TYPEMSG	YES
UIMPORT	YES
USERLIST.BAT	NO
VERSION.BAT	NO
VOLINFO.BAT	NO
WBROLL	YES
WHOAMI	YES
WNDBCNVT	YES
WSUPDATE	NO
WSUPGRD	NO

Summary

The first job of a network administrator is to understand the tools that are available for his or her use. The NetWare 5 operating system provides you with many utilities that will help you install and manage the NetWare 5 server. Your job is made easier when you are familiar with the utilities and their functions.

CHAPTER 3

Novell Directory Services Objects and Properties

"If two objects have the same logical form, the only distinction between them, apart from their external properties, is that they are different." —Wittgenstein

Novell Directory Services (NDS) consists of a collection of objects that follow a set of rules regarding how they are created and used. Familiarity with NDS objects and properties and the ways in which they are used to build the NDS tree structure will enhance your use of NetWare 5. Understanding the structure of the NDS schema will enable you to include additional objects by installing add-on or third-party applications. In addition, understanding the internal structure of NDS objects and the NDS schema will give you greater flexibility in managing and designing your NetWare 5 network.

This chapter begins with a discussion of NDS objects and properties (also referred to as attributes). We next explain the NDS schema, including its components and rules and how NDS objects are created. We discuss schema extensions to help you understand how additional object classes or properties can be added, and how you can modify existing classes. We then explore the purpose and use of many individual NDS objects with examples of how you can use them effectively in your tree. The end of the chapter provides a discussion on the Schema Manager utility and its use. Where pertinent, we also include notes from our consulting experience to help you understand how different objects are used in actual customer environments.

Introduction to NDS Objects and Properties

As a network administrator, your primary responsibility is to maintain the servers, volumes, users, groups, printers, and other resources in the network. To help with this task, NDS enables you to view all network resources as objects within a distributed or networkwide name service known as the NDS tree. You decide which network resources are created and placed as objects in the name service. These objects can include users, groups, printers, servers, volumes, computers, and so on.

Each entry in the NDS tree consists of an object and its properties, or of data stored as a property. For example, the User object can have up to 75 properties, some of which have multiple values. Table 3.1 shows an example of a User object.

This User object does not have all 75 properties, but notice that some of its properties have multiple values.

TABLE 3.1

Example of a User object

OBJECT	PROPERTY	VALUE(S)
User	Login Name	GWASHINGTON
	Given Name	George
	Last Name	Washington
	Title	President, Statesman, Farmer, Cherry Tree Killer
	Location	Washington, D.C., Mount Vernon
	Telephone	(not invented)
	Fax Number	(not invented)
	Description	President of the United States

NDS Objects

NDS objects are the entities that store the information or data about each network resource. NDS objects represent both physical and logical entities on the network. Table 3.2 presents examples of both logical and physical network resources that can be represented by NDS.

TABLE 3.2

Examples of logical and physical entities

LOGICAL ENTITIES	PHYSICAL ENTITIES
User	Printer
Group	NetWare Server
Print Queue	Volume
Alias	Computer/Workstation

Because there can be many NDS objects in a network, the objects are organized into a hierarchical structure called the NDS tree. A good analogy here is a file system. A file system is a hierarchy of subdirectories and files. A hierarchy is used because files are easier to manage in this structure, rather than storing them all at the same level. The same is true with NDS.

NDS classifies all objects as either container or leaf objects (noncontainer objects). Container objects are analogous to subdirectories in a file system, and leaf objects are analogous to files. Both are discussed below.

Container Objects

The container objects are objects that are allowed subordinate objects. Container objects form the hierarchy of the NDS tree and are typically named after the locations, divisions, departments, and workgroups in your company. Container objects enable you to group other NDS objects together into a tree. A branch or subtree of the NDS tree consists of a container object and all the objects it holds, which can include other container objects.

Several types of container objects are defined for your use. The container object base classes are as follows:

- **TOP [ROOT].** A special object at the top of the NDS tree.
- **Organization (O=).** Represents the name of your company.
- **Organizational Unit (OU=).** Represents locations, departments, divisions, or workgroups.
- **Country (C=).** Represents a country with a two-letter country code.
- **State (S=).** Represents a state. Not currently enabled.
- **Locality (L=).** Represents a locality. Not currently enabled.

Although the NetWare 5 Directory defines five container objects, the current utilities display only the Organization (O=), Organizational Unit (OU=), Locality (L=), and C=Country. The TOP [ROOT] class is supported but only the NDS system can create it. Both the State and Locality containers are supported in the

NDS schema but they are not displayed in the NWADMIN utility. The OU serves the same purpose.

Figure 3.1 illustrates how container objects are the building blocks of the NDS tree. Container objects also help you organize and manage the leaf objects or noncontainer objects.

FIGURE 3.1

The container objects are organized into a hierarchical structure called the NDS tree.

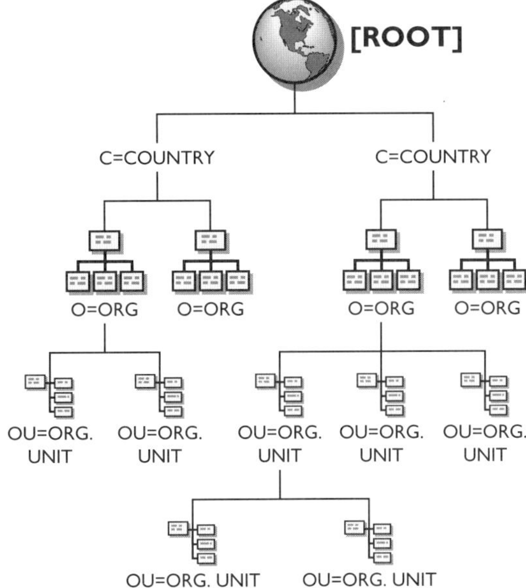

Leaf Objects (Noncontainer Objects)

Leaf objects are located at the ends of the NDS tree branches and don't contain any other subordinate objects. Leaf objects are used to represent network resources. Leaf objects for NetWare 5 include the following:

- AFP Server
- Application Object
- Alias
- Bindery Object
- Bindery Queue
- Computer
- Directory Map
- Group
- NCP Server
- CommExec
- External Entity
- Organization Role
- Queue
- Print Server
- Printer
- Profile
- User
- Unknown
- Volume
- Messaging Server
- Message Routing Group
- List

You can place container objects and leaf objects in different arrangements in your NDS tree, according to your company's needs. Figure 3.2 illustrates how container objects organize the leaf objects.

NDS Properties or Attributes

The *properties* or *attributes* of an object specify the type of information that object can store. Different types of objects have different types of properties. Thus, it can be said that the properties define or describe the object. For example, a User object has, among many others, the following properties: Login Name, Last Name, Group Membership, Telephone, and Fax Number. On the other hand, a Printer object can have the following properties: Name, Network Address, Location, Print Server, and so on.

There are two categories of properties for an object: mandatory and optional. *Mandatory properties* are required during the object creation and cannot be circumvented or removed. NDS utilities enforce data entry for properties that are mandatory. Typically, these are properties necessary for operation. Many of the properties that are mandatory are used to comply with the X.500 standard. For example, the last name of a User object is mandatory. Also, the host server property is mandatory when creating a Volume object.

NOTE

The X.500 standard defines the basic structure for a directory tree and the inheritance classes. Novell's implementation of X.500 is very similar to the 1988 and 1992 RFPs for directory trees.

FIGURE 3.2

Container objects organize leaf objects in the NDS tree.

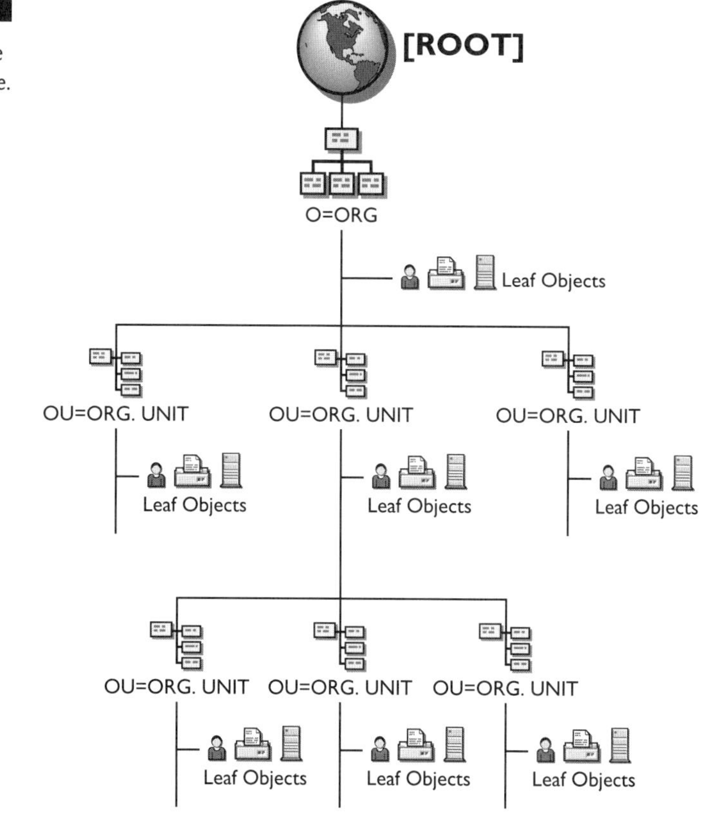

An object's *optional properties* can be entered as the network administrator deems appropriate.

The value of a property is the data stored in that property. In most cases, users can read and write an object's properties, although some properties are not readable or writable by the client. One property type may have a single value, whereas another may have multiple values. For example, the Telephone property of a User object can hold several different telephone numbers.

There is a specific syntax for the value of each property. One use of the syntax is to define the acceptable characters for the value field(s). See the next section for more details on the syntax (data types) for each property.

The NDS Schema

The NDS schema contains the rules used to create and maintain each object and property in the Directory. The schema rules dictate the requirements, limits, and relationships of all objects and properties that can exist in the Directory. NDS enforces those rules for each client request to change (add, delete, modify, and so on) an object or property.

The NDS schema is automatically stored on every NetWare 5 server you install, even if you don't have administrator-defined NDS replicas stored on that server. The NetWare 5 installation automatically places the schema on the server because:

- The schema enables each server to create and maintain all NDS objects and properties.
- The administration utilities require access to the schema during the creation of an object or objects.

The schema consists of three major components: object classes, property type definitions, and property syntaxes. Together, these three components establish the rules that control the creation of each particular object type in the Directory. In Figure 3.3, you can see the relationship between these components. For instance, each object class is defined in terms of attribute or property definitions. The property types, in turn, are defined in terms of the property syntaxes. The property syntaxes are the data type of the values or information that can be stored in the property.

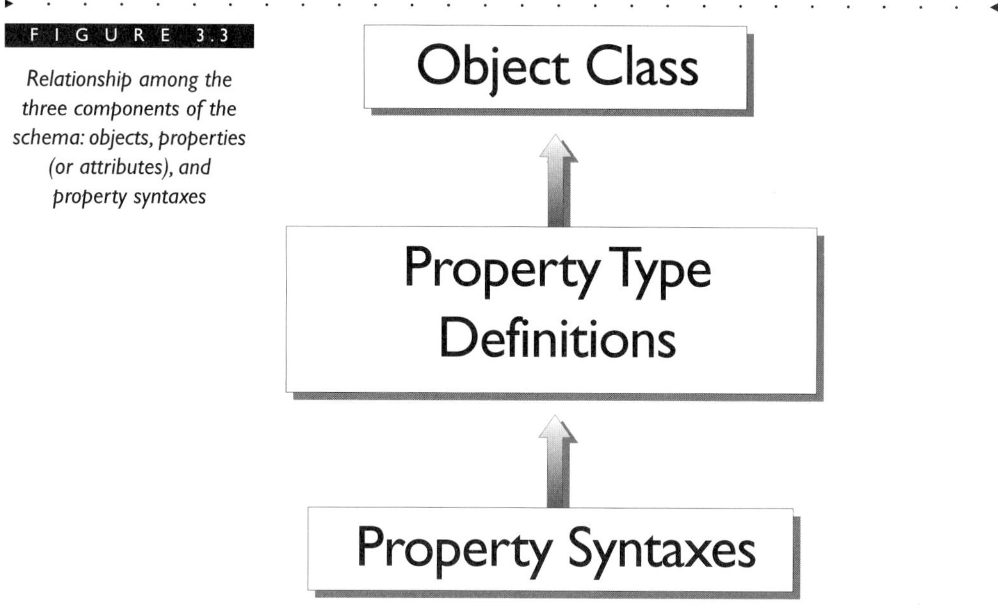

FIGURE 3.3

Relationship among the three components of the schema: objects, properties (or attributes), and property syntaxes

For the most part, the objects defined in the base schema for NetWare 5 are taken from the X.500 specifications for appropriate objects in a directory service. NetWare 5 defines additional objects that describe existing NetWare 3 bindery objects. You can also install other products, such as NDS for NT, that will create new object classes, thereby extending your network's schema. Some objects in the schema currently have little use and are intended for future enhancements to the Directory.

Object Classes

The *object class* defines the types of NDS objects that can be created and stored in the Directory. A set of object class rules are used to create individual objects and to determine its characteristics. This means that every object in a tree belongs to an object class that specifies which properties can be used, or must be used, as well as where objects can be created in relation to other objects. Figure 3.3

illustrates how object classes are constructed from property types. Keep in mind that object classes can refer to other object classes as well.

The base schema that ships with NetWare 5 contains approximately 34 object classes. These object classes cannot be removed or deleted. The following is a list of some of the object classes stored in the schema.

- AFP Server
- Alias
- Application
- Bindery Object
- Bindery Queue
- CommExec
- Computer
- Country
- Device
- Directory Map
- External Entity
- Group
- List
- Locality
- Message Routing Group
- Messaging Server
- NCP Server
- Organization
- Organizational Person
- Organizational Role
- Organizational Unit
- Partition
- Person
- Printer
- Print Server
- Profile
- Queue
- Resource
- Server
- Top
- Unknown
- User
- Volume

Each object class in the schema is determined by the distinctive information held in five components. The five components or type of information that make up an object class definition are as follows:

- **Structure Rules.** Defines the relationship of the objects in the Directory tree. The relationship is constructed based on two items: Naming Properties (how the object is named) and Containment Class (which object classes the object can be subordinate to).
- **Super Classes.** Builds the internal structure of the schema by relating the object classes to each other. Some object classes are simply the building blocks for the other object classes, or are classes from which the object class inherits its definition.
- **Mandatory Properties.** The properties listed in the mandatory property list for the object class are the properties required during the object's creation and throughout the life of the object.
- **Optional Properties.** The properties listed in the optional property list for the object class are the properties that are not required but may be added.
- **Object Class Flags.** There are five object class flags that are either set to ON or OFF. The three remaining object class flags include the container flag, effective status, and nonremovable flag.

For example, the following is the definition of the Group object class:

Object Class:	GROUP
Class Flags:	Effective Class
Super Classes:	Top
Named By:	CN (Common Name)
Containment:	Organization
	Organizational Unit

Mandatory Properties:	CN
Optional Properties:	Description
	Full Name
	GID
	Locality Name
	Member
	(and so forth)

The following is the definition of the Organization object class:

Object Class:	ORGANIZATION
Class Flags:	Effective Class, Container Class
Super Classes:	Top
Named By:	O (Organization Name)
Containment:	Country
	Locality
	Top
Mandatory Properties:	O
Optional Properties:	Description
	Detect Intruder
	E-mail Address
	Facsimile Telephone Number
	(and so forth)

Structure Rules

The *structure rules* for an object define the relationship between the objects in the NDS tree. The relationship between object classes is determined by two items: Naming Properties and Containment Class. The *naming properties* determine how the object is named. The *containment class* determines where the object may appear in the Directory tree relative to the other object classes. Both are discussed below.

Naming Properties The naming properties (or attributes) determine how an object is named in the NDS tree. An object is identified in the tree by its common name and also by the names of all its parent containers. An object's name includes the object name type and a value, connected together with an equal (=) sign. Some object classes are container objects, whereas other objects are the leaf objects (or noncontainer objects). Table 3.3 lists the object name types that are currently used in the naming property of the object class definition.

TABLE 3.3

List of the object name types that are available for use in object name type definitions

NAME TYPE	NAME VALUE
C	Country Name
L	Locality Name
S	State or Province Name
O	Organization Name
OU	Organizational Unit Name
CN	Common Name
BT	Bindery Type

The first four name types—C=Country Name, L=Locality Name (S=State or Province), O=Organization Name, and OU=Organizational Unit Name—are all the container objects. The CN=Common Name and BT=Bindery Type are used for the leaf objects.

An object's leaf-most name is referred to as its partial name or Relative Distinguished Name (RDN). For example, the user MTERESA in the ACME tree has an RDN of CN=MTERESA. If we refer to the user's distinguished name or full name, it would be defined as the RDN, MTERESA, plus the names of all the parent containers above the user MTERESA. The distinguished name would be written as follows:

```
CN=MTERESA.OU=FOOD.OU=SYDNEY.O=ACME
```

Therefore, the structure rules effectively control the formation of the distinguished names and relative distinguished names for each of the objects created in the NDS tree.

Nearly every object class will have one or more object name types defined in the Naming portion of the object class definition, unless inherited by a super class. For example, the Organization object class is named by the "O" name type. The naming property of the Organizational Unit object class is defined as an "OU" name type. The Country object class has the "C" name type. It is mandatory that at least one naming property be defined or inherited.

The Named By property is not always a reflection of the class to which an object belongs. For example, leaf objects such as User or Printer are named by the Common Name (CN). The CN= name property does not by itself give you any indication to which class the object belongs.

An object class can allow for multiple object name types in the Named By property in the definition. In these cases, any one of the object name types can be used to name the object. For classes having multiple naming properties, any combination of the naming properties can be used. The property values are connected together using the plus (+) sign.

A common occurrence of this peculiar naming convention occurs in the case of Bindery Objects. In the definition of the bindery object class, there are two object name type properties called Bindery Type (BT) and Common Name (CN). A bindery object would then be defined as:

```
CN=ATPSUSER+BINDERY TYPE=83
```

The Locality object class definition also has a multivalued Named By property definition. It is named by either the name type L=Locality Name, or S=State or Province Name. Therefore, the RDN for a Locality object could appear as:

```
L=NORAD+S=COLORADO
```

Containment Classes As we mentioned earlier in this chapter, some object classes are designed to contain other objects. The containment class list specifies where the individual object classes may appear in the NDS tree. Each object class has a definition or list of the container objects that it may be created in or subordinate to. This list, called the *containment class list*, builds the relationship between the object classes in the NDS tree.

An individual object can only reside or be created directly in a container that is found in its containment class list. For example, the Group object class can only be placed in or created subordinate to an Organization or Organizational Unit object. The containment class list for the Group object lists this relationship as illustrated in the list of Group object classes shown above. The following example for the Group object class is taken from the list of Group object classes:

Object Class: GROUP
Named By: CN (Common Name)

Containment: Organization
Organizational Unit

The containment class list simply specifies that the Group objects can be placed under either the Organization or Organizational Unit objects in the tree. Therefore, the containment class specifies where an individual object may appear in the Directory tree. The schema prohibits objects from being created directly below or subordinate to container objects whose class definition is not in the new object's containment list.

The following is a list of the container objects that are used in the containment class lists for each of the object class definitions:

- Top
- Country
- Locality
- Organization
- Organizational Unit

The containment class dictates the structure of the NDS tree and changes as the tree expands toward the bottom. For example, the Organization and Country object classes are the only object definitions that have Top in their containment class list. The Top object class is implemented as the [ROOT] object in the tree. This means that only Organization and Country objects can be subordinate objects to [ROOT]. The Organization and Locality object class definitions are the only object classes that have the Country object listed in their containment class. Thus, Organization and Locality objects can only be subordinate objects to Country. Continuing down the tree, the Organizational Unit has the Organization, Locality, and Organizational Unit (itself) defined in its containment class.

As the tree expands toward the bottom, most of the leaf object class definitions have the containment class for both Organization and Organizational Unit. This means that most leaf objects will reside either within the Organization or Organizational Unit container objects.

Super Classes

The internal structure of the schema is built using the super classes specification for the object class. The super classes help designate the structure of the schema internally and do not dictate the hierarchical structure for the NDS tree. As stated above, the NDS tree structure is dictated by each object's definition of the containment class.

The super classes are the object class definitions in the schema from which other object classes may be constructed. A complete definition for an object class is derived from the components of the object class itself plus all the components of its super class objects. An example of the super class structure for a User object class is illustrated in Figure 3.4.

The NDS Directory allows for classes to inherit from other class objects in a unidirectional manner. This means that object class B can inherit from object class A, but object class A cannot inherit from object class B. The concept of inheritance among objects in the schema stipulates that an object class inherits the features of its super classes. This means that all the definitions of the super class objects are inherited in the new object class. If object class B inherits from object class A, B must receive all the definitions from A. The Directory does not have the capability to inherit only parts of the super class definition. A class may inherit from multiple super classes.

Mandatory Properties

The properties listed in the mandatory property list for the object class are the properties that are required. If a property is mandatory, every object created from the class must have at least one assigned value for each mandatory property.

Optional Properties

The properties listed in the optional property list for the object class are the properties that are not required. If a property is listed as optional, that property may or may not be created when the object is created.

Object Class Flags

Several object class flags are set to either ON or OFF. These object class flags include the container flag, effective and noneffective status, and nonremovable flag, among others. All of these are discussed in this section.

FIGURE 3.4

Super class structure for the User object class as defined in the schema

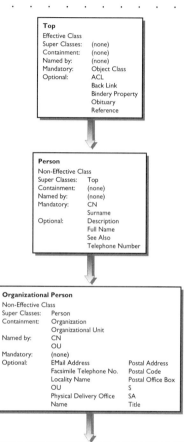

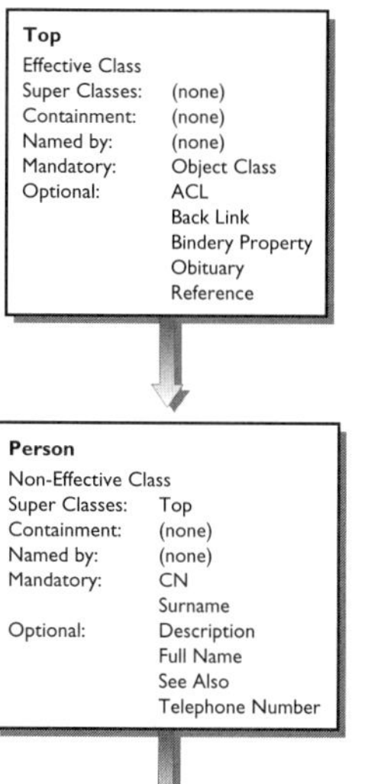

Organizational Person
Non-Effective Class
Super Classes: Person
Containment: Organization
Organizational Unit
Named by: CN
OU
Mandatory: (none)
Optional: EMail Address, Facsimile Telephone No., Locality Name, OU, Physical Delivery Office Name, Postal Address, Postal Code, Postal Office Box, S, SA, Title

Organizational User
Effective Class
Super Classes: Organizational Person
Containment: (none)
Named by: (none)
Mandatory: (none)
Optional: Account Balance, Allow Unlimited Credit, Group Membership, Higher Privileges, Home Directory, Language, Last Login Time, Locked By Intruder, Login Allowed Time Map, Login Disabled, Login Expiration Time, Login Grace Limit, Login Grace Remaining, Login Intruder Address, Login Intruder Attempts, Login Intruder Reset Time, Login Maximum Simultaneous, Login Script, Login Time, Message Server, Minimum Account Balance, Network Address, Network Address Restriction, Password Allow Change, Password Allow Interval, Password Expiration Time, Password Minimum Length, Password Required, Password Unique Required, Password Used, Print Job Configuration, Private Key, Profile, Public Key, Security Equals, Server Holds, Type Creator Map, UID

Container Flags The container flag is set to ON only for the object classes that are designated as the container object classes in the Directory tree. The container flag would be set to ON for the following object classes: Top, Country, Locality, Organization, and Organizational Unit.

The container flag is set to OFF for all the object classes that are the leaf objects in the schema or noneffective classes.

Effective and Noneffective Status Each object class is categorized as an effective or noneffective class. Effective classes are visible in the utilities and are used to create new objects in your NDS tree.

Noneffective object classes are used as super classes to build the other object class information. Therefore, noneffective classes are used only in the definition of other objects and not to create objects in the Directory tree. The noneffective object classes are not visible using the management utilities, however; they are visible as effective classes. Noneffective object classes in the schema are used to create other object classes in the Directory tree. (Later in this section, each object is listed along with a notation of its effective or noneffective class.)

Nonremovable Flag The nonremovable flag determines whether the object class can be removed from the schema definitions. The nonremovable flag is set to ON for all the object classes that are defined in the base schema that is shipped with NetWare 5. The object classes added later to extend the schema have the nonremovable set to OFF.

Property or Attribute Type Definitions

All the properties or attributes found in the Directory consist of a property type and a property value. The property identifies the nature of the information that will be stored by the property and dictates the syntax used to enter the value.

A property definition is based on special constraints and on a specific property syntax that determines the values the property can store. There is a one-to-one relationship between properties and their syntaxes. Approximately 142 available properties are defined in the base NDS schema that ships with NetWare 5. Various combinations of these properties apply to all object classes. You can view some of the available attributes or properties for each object through the use of the NWADMIN utility. You can also use the Schema Manager utility that is discussed at the end of this chapter.

The following is a list of some of the properties defined for the Group object class:

- Access Control List
- Authority Revocation
- Auto Start
- Back Link
- Bindery Property
- CA Public Key
- Certificate Validity Interval
- Common Name
- Default Queue
- Department
- Description
- Desktop
- E-mail Address
- Equivalent To Me
- Full Name
- GID
- Last Referenced Time
- Location
- Mailbox ID
- Mailbox Location
- Member
- Object Class
- Obituary
- Organization
- Other Name (other values of common name)
- Owner
- Reference
- Revision
- See Also

The property type definition consists of Property Syntax and Property Constraints, which are both discussed next.

Property Syntax

The *property syntaxes* are predefined data types for values that will be stored in the Directory. The NDS schema is *extensible*, as discussed in the next section, meaning that you can create new object classes and properties based on the property syntaxes. You can also add properties to existing class definitions. Although the schema is extensible, the property syntaxes cannot be alternated. There are currently 28 static property syntaxes defined in the schema. To view the syntax for a particular object, use the Schema Manager utility. The following is a list of some of the property syntaxes defined in the schema:

- Back Link
- Boolean
- Case Exact String
- Case Ignore List
- Case Ignore String
- Class Name
- Counter
- Distinguished Name
- E-mail Address
- Facsimile Telephone Number
- Hold
- Integer
- Interval
- Net Address
- Numeric String
- Object ACL
- Octet List
- Octet String
- Path
- Postal Address
- Printable String
- Replica Pointer
- Stream
- Telephone Number
- Time
- Timestamp
- Typed Name
- Unknown

Property Constraints

Property constraints are all restrictions that affect the property values for each of the properties. These constraints include whether the property values can have a single value or multiple values, whether the property values are immediately synchronized between replicas, or whether the property is hidden or nonremovable. The constraints also manage access control to the property value. For example, a property can be constrained to allow only someone with sufficient rights to the object to add a property.

The property constraint also dictates the matching rules that are used when comparing two values of the same syntax. The primary matching rules are equality, substrings, and ordering. The equality checks for equal values of the property values and only applies if the property types are the same. The equality check can't compare unless the property is the same. Therefore, the syntax would be the same. The substring compares two string property values where a wildcard "*" can be used. The ordering rules compare for "less than," "equal to," and "greater than."

For a complete definition of the property syntax IDs, data formats, and matching rules, please refer to Novell's Software Developer's Kit (SDK) or the Schema Manager utility, which is discussed at the end of this chapter.

Schema Structure

The NDS Base Schema consists of each object class along with its properties or attributes and the property syntaxes. As shown in Figure 3.5, the schema structure can be represented as a pyramid in which the foundation consists of the property syntaxes. These property syntaxes are used to define a property; in turn, the property defines the object classes, and the object classes determine the schema structure.

FIGURE 3.5

The schema structure is represented as a pyramid in which the foundation is the property syntaxes, which define the properties. The properties define the object classes, and the object classes determine the schema structure.

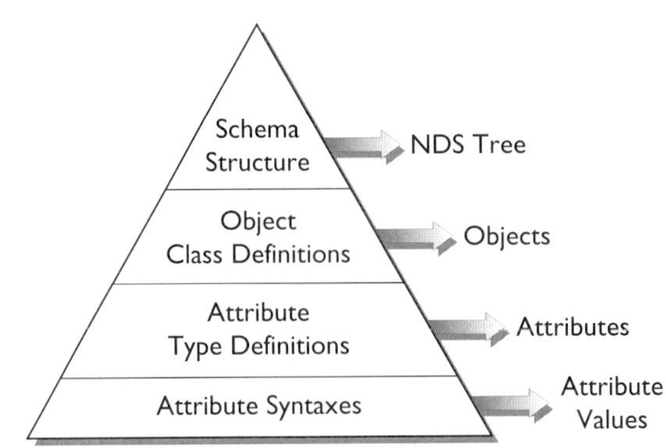

The Extensibility of the NDS Schema

NDS provides a mechanism for making changes or extensions to the schema. The purpose of this section is to give an overview of how this can be accomplished in your NetWare 5 environment. For specific information on API functions and making API (Application Programming Interface) calls, see the NDS API Reference Manual from Novell. By using the client API, the schema can be expanded beyond the base schema, which Novell provides. Properties can be added to existing object classes, or new object classes or properties can be created.

The first step to extending the schema is to create new property definitions and/or new object class definitions. The extensions to the schema can be accomplished through the use of programming, with Novell's API calls designed for this purpose. After completing this task, you have modified the schema. All changes or extensions are automatically replicated on all NetWare 5 servers in the Directory tree.

Third-party applications also provide a means for extending the schema. Novell's NetWare Application Launcher, for example, makes an extension to the schema to define an Application icon. Prefixes for schema extensions can be registered with Novell Developer Support. This registry ensures that schema prefixes among vendors are not duplicated on the schema.

Any user performing modifications to the schema must have write rights (Supervisor rights) on the [ROOT] object. Before you create a new property or object class, determine first if the property or object class already exists in the schema. If you cannot find the property or object class you need or if the class is missing a property, you can then take the steps necessary to extend the schema.

Each time there are modifications to the schema, these changes will be synchronized on all NetWare 5 servers in the tree. The synchronization process requires no administrator intervention because it is part of the NDS background processes that occur. The schema synchronization occurs through the use of the trickle-down algorithm because the synchronization occurs from the top and proceeds downward.

Therefore, the schema updates will propagate across replicas of the same partition and downward in the tree structure from the [ROOT].

The trickle-down method causes a NetWare 5 server receiving an updated schema to build a distribution list in order to update servers that it knows about. It then checks all servers in its distribution list to determine if they have received an updated copy of the schema. If they have not received a copy, that server sends an updated copy of the latest schema to other servers. This process extends only down and across, not up. The Schema Manager utility (discussed at the end of this chapter) enables you to make extensions to the NDS schema.

NDS Objects and Their Uses

You will discover, if you haven't already, that some NDS objects will be used much more than others. Obviously, the User object will be the most commonly used object in your tree. Some other leaf objects may never be used in your tree. That's okay. It's unlikely that any NetWare 5 networks will have a need for all the objects defined in NDS. However, they are in the schema for a general audience that may need them at some point.

To make your job easier, we have first grouped the objects in the following sections according to how they are used.

- **Required objects.** These are the objects that either you must define or are defined for you during the installation of NetWare 5.

- **Commonly used objects.** These objects include both the container and noncontainer objects along with examples of how the objects can be used. These examples are based on actual consulting experiences.
- **Less commonly used objects.** These are the objects that may have less importance for you. Where appropriate, we have listed consulting recommendations with these objects as well.

Required Objects

The following objects are required in your NDS tree. When you install your first NetWare 5 server, these objects are present in your NDS tree. All of these objects require you to name them at some point in the NetWare 5 installation.

As shown in Figure 3.6 of Novell's installation utility called NetWare Configuration (NWConfig), you are prompted for the name of the tree, organization, and organizational units. You can also create a Country object, which is not mandatory.

FIGURE 3.6

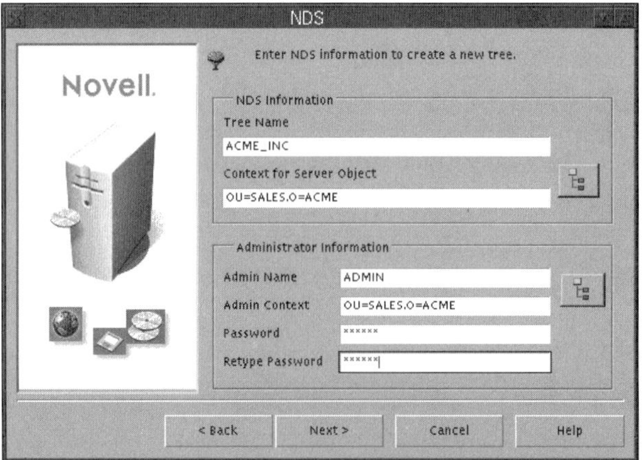

Novell's NetWare Configuration requires that you name all required objects during the installation.

Top and [ROOT] (Effective Class)

Purpose The Top object class is the super class of all other object classes in the schema. This object is also the container object for all other objects in the Directory hierarchy. The Top class is an effective class object. The only instance of the Top object is the [ROOT] object.

The [ROOT] object is at the top of your inverted tree structure. The [ROOT], from a visual standpoint in the utilities, is the starting point of your tree and branches downward as shown in Figure 3.7. The name of the [ROOT] object is your tree name, although this name is not indicated or displayed in the utilities. When you install the first NetWare 5 server in a tree, you are prompted for a tree name, which means that you actually assign a name to the [ROOT] object. Each tree will contain one and only one [ROOT] object.

FIGURE 3.7

ACME tree structure shows the [ROOT] object at the top of the inverted tree structure.

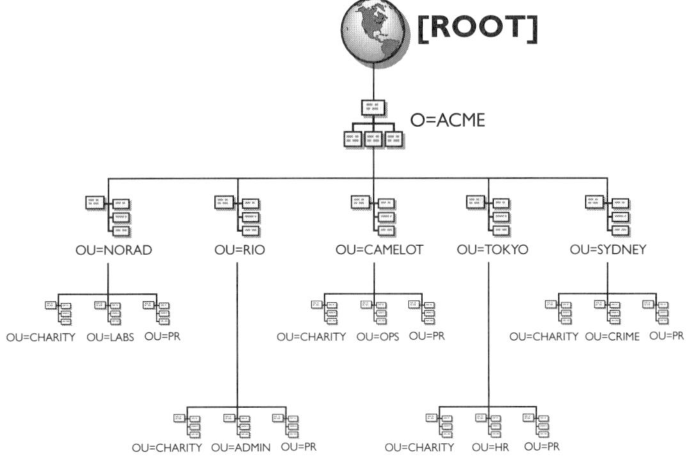

The [ROOT] object's name, which is the tree name, is broadcast on your network using the Service Advertising Protocol. If you have multiple trees running on the same network infrastructure, you must ensure that the names are unique.

Sample Uses Choose a name for [ROOT] that will clearly identify the organization or company for the tree. Keep in mind that renaming the [ROOT] object or tree name can only be done with the DSMERGE.

Consulting Experience

Most companies simply use the same name as their company or Organization object and add a _TREE. For example, our tree name for ACME is ACME_TREE. The organization name is O=ACME. You want to choose a name that you can recognize as the tree name if you are using software analysis tools on your network and looking at server-to-server communications. Figure 3.8 illustrates how the NDS tree for ACME has been named.

FIGURE 3.8

The NDS tree for ACME is named ACME_TREE.

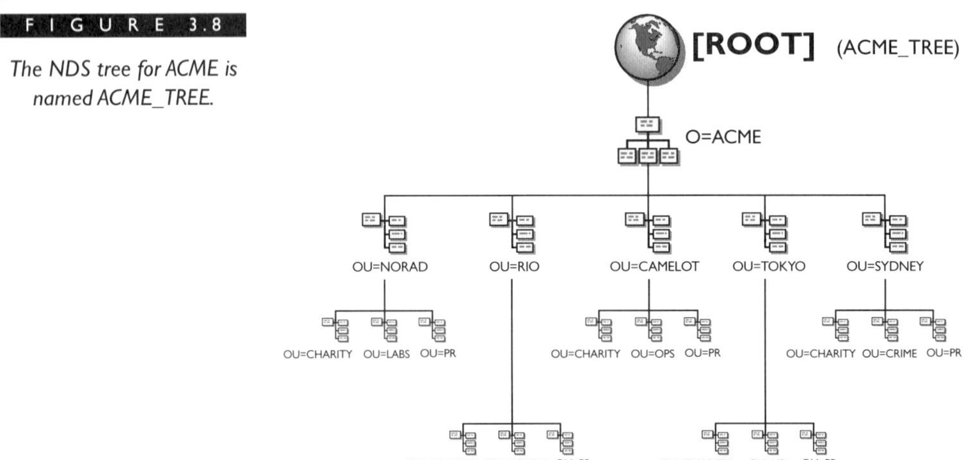

[ROOT] is the only instance of the Top object class in the NDS tree. However, in the schema, all object classes must have the super class of Top defined, including any new classes created by extending the schema. Top is the only object that has no super class. All object classes inherit from the class Top. All object classes that you may define through schema extensions must contain the Top class.

Organization (Effective Class)

Purpose This object class is used to define organization objects in the tree. An organization is located directly under the [ROOT] object or C=Country object. This object is used to define the name of a company, and you are required to define at least one organization in your NDS tree. Multiple O=Organization objects may be used directly below [ROOT] or Country as shown in Figure 3.9.

FIGURE 3.9

Multiple O=Organization objects defined for a large conglomerate company

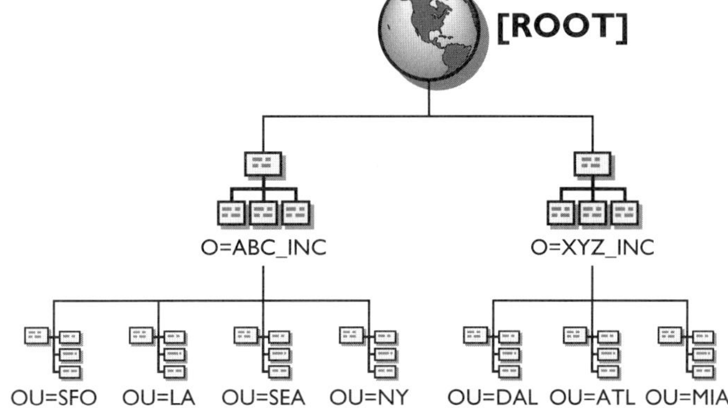

Sample Uses The ACME tree is defined as the name of its organization, O=ACME. The organization represents the name of your company or organization and should be an overall descriptor of the business. If you are a member of a nonprofit group or university, the name of your Organization object can be the same name as your university or group.

Consulting Experience

Most companies typically define only one Organization object in their NDS tree. If all your business units are connected with the same network, then a single Organization object more accurately represents your network. Our guideline for using multiple Organization objects is based on the network infrastructure in which you operate. For example, if you are a large conglomerate with varied businesses that have decided to communicate information together using NetWare 5 for the exchange of information, you can use multiple Organization objects as shown in Figure 3.9. If each company is separately managed with a separate network infrastructure, you can create multiple Organization objects for each business unit under the [ROOT] object. You can also use the Organizational Unit objects to represent your business units.

For more information on designing multiple Organization objects, see Chapter 5, "Novell Directory Services Tree."

User (Effective Class)

Purpose Obviously, the most common object in your tree, the User object, represents every user that is part of your NetWare 5 network. The User object is similar to the user object found in NetWare 3 environments but contains more properties.

Sample Uses During the installation of your first NetWare 5 server, you are prompted to assign a password for the first user ADMIN created on the network. This user, named ADMIN, has object Supervisor rights assigned to the [ROOT] object of your tree. Initially, the ADMIN user has all rights (NDS and File System) to the entire tree. At this point in your installation, it is the only object with such complete and extensive access to your network. The importance of maintaining the ADMIN user or another object with the same rights at [ROOT] is well known. If you should delete this object without making other rights assignments, say to an organizational role, your access to the tree is lost. Your options in this situation would be to reinstall NDS or call Novell Technical Support to provide you reentrance into your tree.

Consulting Experience

After you have installed the first couple of NetWare 5 servers, ensure that the ADMIN password is protected. Following these steps will diminish the likelihood of losing access to your tree:

1. Your first NetWare 5 server installation prompts you for a password for the ADMIN user. Remember that the first password you assign to the NDS for ADMIN is also assigned to the bindery Supervisor object created by the NetWare Configuration utility. If you are doing a bindery upgrade, the supervisor's password is taken from the bindery. If the bindery supervisor's password does not exist, then the NDS ADMIN password is used. If you later change the ADMIN user's password, the bindery Supervisor password does not change. Choose a password that will not easily be guessed. Change your passwords periodically for greater security. The ADMIN user password is changed through NWADMIN utilities. The bindery Supervisor password can be changed through the NetWare 3 SYSCON utility.
2. Create an organizational role in the O=Organization level of your tree and assign this role object Supervisor rights at the [ROOT] object of your tree.
3. Do not make this organizational role object a security equivalent to the original ADMIN user. If the original ADMIN were to be deleted, your organizational role would have no access to the tree because the security equivalency would be lost. For more information on how to define security for organizational roles, refer to Chapter 13, "Managing NetWare Security."

NCP Server (Effective Class)

Purpose A NetWare (NCP) server object is automatically created for any NetWare 5 server being installed or upgraded to NetWare 5. The server object holds key information such as the network address and the version of NetWare you are running on that machine. This object type is used to represent any server that provides NCP (NetWare Core Protocol) transport and session services and can represent either bindery or NDS-based NCP servers. This subclass of the Server object provides further definition of NCP services available on a particular server.

Sample Uses The supported Services property can be used to list NCP-based features and services available for this network address. As part of an NDS search engine, you can search for available NCP services.

Another useful feature is the Operator property, which is used by an NCP server as an access control list. If a particular object is part of this access control list, that object can perform remote console operations. These remote operations do not mean using RCONSOLE; they have the capability to exercise the console APIs, which RCONSOLE does not use.

The server object is basically managed by NDS and requires little attention from the administrator.

Volume (Effective Class)

Purpose The server volume object is automatically created when you install a NetWare 5 server into the tree. A file server must have at least one volume called the SYS volume. The server may have additional volumes that are defined during the installation of NetWare 5. A volume object is created for each mounted volume during the installation. The naming convention is *<file server name>* _ *<volume name>*.

Sample Uses This object type exists primarily to differentiate it from other types of resource objects and to allow greater flexibility for volume management if needed. It is also used in MAP commands and is required by the FILER utility to grant file system rights.

Consulting Experience

Be sure to follow the naming standards presented in Chapter 4, "Directory Services Naming Conventions." This is a resource on which you will no doubt want to perform Directory queries. Consistent and appropriate naming help this process considerably.

Consulting Experience

NetWare 5 gives you flexibility to place print queues on any NetWare 5 volume. We recommend that you always create at least one other volume in addition to the SYS volume, so your print queue doesn't fill up the SYS volume and cause NDS to become disabled.

Use the volume restrictions to limit the size of your volumes before they fill up completely. You can also limit the disk space used on the Home Directory if you are short on space or want to limit each user on the volume.

Commonly Used Objects

Following is a list of the most commonly used NDS objects. Most, if not all, of these objects will be used in your NDS tree. Small sites with perhaps one server may not use all of these objects. In fact, it is only necessary to make use of the objects that will best serve the purposes of your network environment.

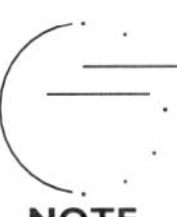

The following objects are schema extensions for the NetWare Application Launcher (NAL) version 1.0. These extensions occur during the installation of NetWare 5 automatically.

Application Object (Effective Class)

Purpose The purpose of this object is to define the application objects for the Novell Application Launcher. This object has changed since the introduction of NetWare 4, when there used to be a different application object for each workstation operating system. For example, there was an application object for DOS, Windows 3.1, Windows 95, and Windows NT. Now there is just one application object that represents programs that can be executed on all workstations.

Sample Uses You may want to create an application object for the application programs stored on a central server where all network users can access them. These applications can be DOS, Windows 3.1, Windows 95, or Windows NT. In addition, you can create application objects that represent application programs loaded on each user's local drives or desktops. For more information on using the Novell Application Launcher, refer to Chapter 20, "NDS for NT."

Bindery Object (Effective Class)

B

Purpose This leaf object represents any object other than user, group, queue, profile, and print server created through bindery services. The bindery object has the format of Common Name + Object Type and is used to provide backward compatibility for bindery-oriented applications or utilities.

Sample Uses You will see bindery objects appear after a migration from NetWare 3 to NetWare 5 if an object is not identifiable by NDS. Some applications create bindery objects to suit their particular purposes. For applications that still require the bindery services, a bindery object could exist in the tree. Although these objects appear in utilities such as NWADMIN, they are nonmanageable from NWADMIN and are present only for information purposes.

Organizational Unit (Effective Class)

Purpose Nearly all NDS trees, except environments with a single NetWare 5 server, use Organizational Units. They are, however, optional. Organizational Units subdivide the tree into either locations or organizations, which could be departments, divisions, or workgroups. The Organizational Unit is also referred to as a container and contains the login script property, also known as the container login script. All users in a container will execute that container's script if it is available.

Sample Uses As shown in Figure 3.10, the ACME tree uses containers to make logical divisions in the tree. Notice that the first level of OUs represent geographic sites based on the network infrastructure, and the subsequent levels represent the departments of ACME. Many trees will be designed in this fashion with several levels of nested organizational units. For more information on designing a NetWare 5 tree, see Chapter 5, "Novell Directory Services Tree."

Consulting Experience

Do not delete any bindery object until you verify its purpose in the Directory. Some installation utilities create a bindery object that, if removed, will cause problems for the application. Always check first before deleting bindery objects that appear in your containers.

FIGURE 3.10

The use of organizational units makes NDS tree subdivision clear and logical.

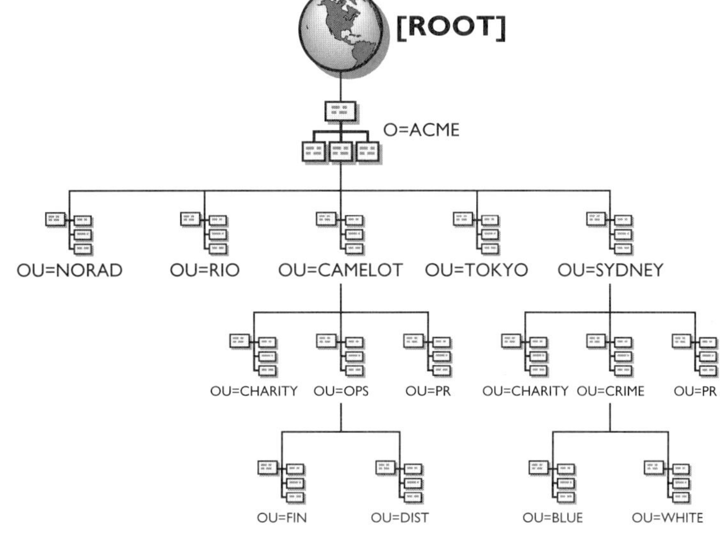

Organizational Role (Effective Class)

Purpose An Organizational Role object is typically used to define a role or position within an organization object or container object. The role is extremely useful because the object or file rights are granted to the role itself and not to the occupants who may belong to the role.

NOTE

This rule is different for object creation. For example, an object is created by a user assigned to the organizational role. The object creation rights to the new object go to the user creating the object, not to the organizational role.

Sample Uses Organizational Roles are especially useful in maintaining sub-administrators. The occupant can be moved in and out of the role quickly to facilitate short-term assignments. For example, if the regular administrator is absent for any length of time, another user can be moved into the role temporarily to manage the network. The implementation of this object is just like a group. The organizational role occupants derive their rights through security equivalence to the role object.

Consulting Experience

Most companies use the Organizational Unit to represent geographic locations, divisions, and workgroups. You generally use an Organizational Unit to group common users and resources in the same container. Organizational Units should not be created to represent a single person or a single resource. They are used to provide access to a group of users in a particular part of the tree. NetWare 5 does provide the capability to move containers to new locations in the tree should your needs change.

As shown in Figure 3.11, we have created an organizational role for each city contained in the ACME tree. This administrator will have rights to manage the entire container, such as adding and deleting users or servers.

FIGURE 3.11

Organizational Roles created for the ACME tree

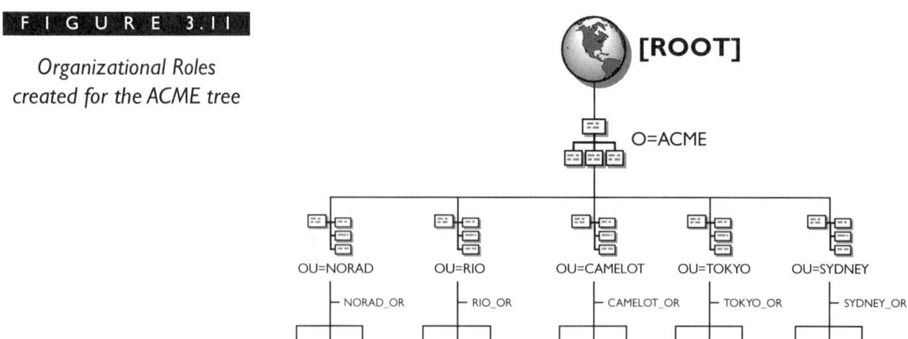

Group (Effective Class)

Purpose This class is used to represent a set of users from any part of the NDS tree. The membership of the group is static and is only modified by your administrative action.

Groups function the same way they did in NetWare 3. There is very little difference between using group objects and organizational unit (OU) objects. Both have the same function, which is to place common users close together. It is true that users who are members of both objects receive rights by security equivalence, but there are some differences. Because of security equivalence, any member of an OU will receive whatever rights the OU possesses. Users inside groups also receive whatever rights the group possesses — and as with a container, there is no IRF provision. For more information on NDS security refer to Chapter 13, "Managing NetWare Security."

Groups are used to differentiate rights within a particular Organizational Unit. Rather than create multiple subcontainers, you can simply use groups within a container for users who need a specific environment created.

Sample Use In order to provide rights to a smaller subset of users in the CHARITY.SYDNEY.ACME OU, you can use a group. Figure 3.12 shows an organizational unit called OU=Charity and is populated with users and resources. Within this OU are two sets of users. Each group is accessing different software on the server and needs different rights assignments. Within the container or OU login script (known as the system login script in NetWare 3), the IF MEMBER OF GROUP statements are used to determine which group a user belongs to for rights assignments. When each user logs into the network, the login script determines whether a user is a member of a group and sets the appropriate environment variables.

Consulting Experience

The use of an organizational role is highly recommended as a way to administer rights in your network to various administrators in your network. You can more easily track who has received rights as administrators in your tree by checking who has been made an occupant of a role. Assigning rights to individuals through means other than the organizational role is not recommended because it is more difficult to track which individuals have been granted rights in your tree. After a few months or even weeks, you'll forget who has been assigned rights. For more details on setting up an organizational role for your tree, see Chapter 13, "Managing NetWare Security."

FIGURE 3.12

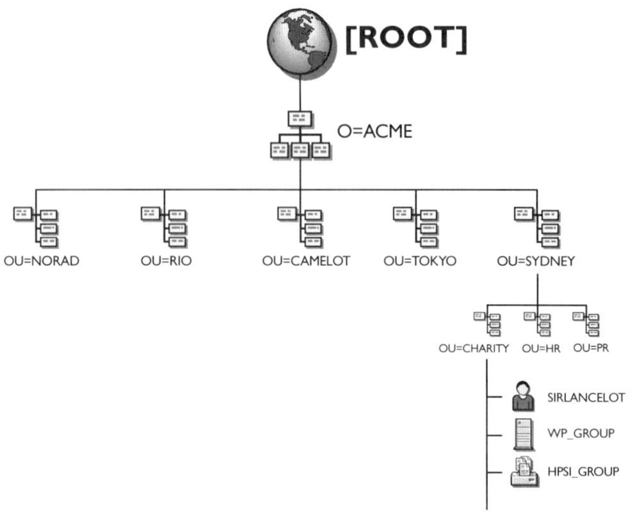

The Organizational Unit OU=Charity with two groups created to differentiate users within the same container

Directory Map (Effective Class)

Purpose The Directory Map object is a pointer that refers to a file system directory on a NetWare volume. It is used in login scripts or by the MAP command to point to a directory that contains a particular application.

Consulting Experience

Groups are great to use in a container to provide further differentiation of rights to a subset of users. We recommend that groups be used in a container instead of creating more containers. Additional containers would require the use of additional container login scripts. Limit the number of groups to fewer than 15 in a container login script, if possible. The more groups there are, the longer the container login script will be, and a slower login will occur. If you have 15 or more groups, however, you should create additional containers because the login script must check your users against each group membership list. Groups should be contained locally. Avoid the use of groups that contain users from multiple organizational units.

Sample Use Let's assume you have WordPerfect installed in a directory called WP60. If you were to upgrade your software to WordPerfect 6.1, you could choose to rename the subdirectory to WP61. You would also have to change every login script to reflect this change for the new subdirectory. Through the use of a directory map, you can eliminate making changes to your login scripts. Your directory map object is used in your login scripts and points to a subdirectory on a NetWare volume. Your only change is to have the directory map point to WP61. All container login scripts are left intact.

Alias (Effective Class)

Purpose An alias is another name for an object. An *alias* is an object that points to another object you specify in the Directory tree. An alias can point to either a container object (an object that holds other containers) or a noncontainer object (one that does not have any other containers).

Sample Uses An alias is a name containing at least one Relative Distinguished Name. As a network administrator, you may grant users access to a particular resource contained in another OU, such as a printer. You can create an alias to reference that printer, for example. The alias can be considered a relay to another object in a different part of the tree.

Consulting Experience

Directory map objects are useful for providing a standard container login script on multiple servers. We recommend that you have standard file structures for all your NetWare 5 file servers so you can facilitate easier use of directory maps. If you maintain a directory map for an application, you can make a change to the directory map pointer and have it be effective for many servers. The directory map requires that the administrator make each user security equivalent to the map object and for containers with large numbers of users. This could be a drawback, from an administration standpoint. You can, however, grant rights on the directory pointed to by the directory map to the container, to simplify this situation.

Consulting Experience

The alias object is very useful in moving subtrees or renaming containers so you can easily make the transition. The alias can assist you in this migration path. In addition, the alias can be useful for some companies wanting to create mobile users who do not want to remember their user context. The alias can be created at the top of the tree below the Organization object, for example, to shorten the user's context. If user DAVID wants to log in to the network, he only needs to remember that his context is DAVID.Acme, because that alias points to his actual context in the tree. This example is shown in Figure 3.13. Keep in mind that this example refers to a very limited number of users, such as mobile users. We are not implying that you should alias every user in your tree.

FIGURE 3.13

Mobile user DAVID has a shortened context through the use of aliasing.

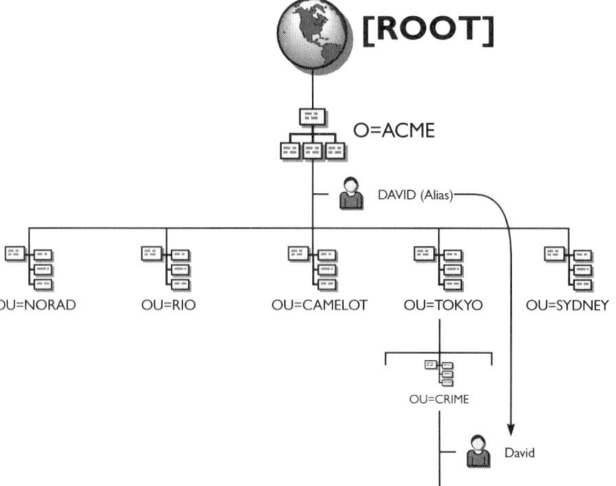

You can also alias one OU to another OU, giving one OU to the other OU's resources. It appears as though the alias places the alias's container inside the other container.

The object being aliased is known as the *primary object*. When you create an alias object, you may or may not name it with some indication that it is an alias to another object. For example, the name might include the word "alias," as in Alias_Blair.

Print Server (Effective Class)

Purpose The print server leaf object represents a server that takes print jobs out of a print queue and sends them to a network printer. This object is used in conjunction with the Printer and Print Queue objects. A print server object must be created for every actual print server that exists on the NetWare 5 network.

Sample Uses All NetWare 5 networks using printers will have at least one print server object. You can use this object to define which printers to assign to users, based on their position or location in the NDS tree. You can also define the print server operators.

Printer (Effective Class)

Purpose The Printer object is used in conjunction with the print server object. You use this object to manage a printer. The assignment for a print queue can be made within the object.

Sample Uses You can attach printers to the network in several different ways—namely, directly to the network, to a printer port of a NetWare server, or to a printer port of a PC.

Consulting Experience

You can place the Printer object along with the Print Queue object as high as possible in your NDS tree to support many users. If your printer is for only your container, then place the printer in your container. If more containers need access to the printer, place the object in the next highest level in your tree. Keep in mind that the placement of printers higher in the tree also adds overhead to NDS in terms of name resolution. We also recommend that you configure printers as network-direct printers in queue server mode as explained in Chapter 14, "NetWare 5 Print Services."

Queue (Effective Class)

Purpose This object represents a print queue defined on a NetWare 5 server. The queue actually represents the directories where the print jobs are sent to be serviced by a printer.

Sample Uses Place the Print Queue object along with the Print object at the highest level possible in your tree to service the most users.

Profile (Effective Class)

Purpose The Profile object is used as a special purpose scripting object that is executed by LOGIN.EXE and is a shared login script after the execution of your container login script. The profile script can contain special drive mappings or environment settings you want a select group of people to receive.

One of the properties of a user object is the profile. When a user is first created using the NWADMIN utility, you can specify that the user be part of a profile. You can also add a user to a profile anytime after by going back and adding the profile to a user object's properties.

Sample Uses There are three notable uses for a profile script:

- Creating a global login script
- Creating a location login script
- Creating a special function login script

Consulting Experience

All NetWare 5 print queues should be placed on a volume other than the SYS volume for greater fault tolerance of the server. A queue object must be created for NetWare 5 printing. A Print Queue object is assigned to a printer.

Creating Global Login Scripts NetWare 4 does not use a global system login script. Each Organizational Unit created will have its own login script, referred to as the OU login script. The order of execution of login scripts is as follows:

1. OU login script
2. Profile login script, if used
3. User login script
4. Default login script if no other script is available

Therefore, if you want to create a more global login script and include multiple Organizational Units, you could employ the profile object to set up a specific environment for a group of users. Keep in mind that this type of solution is expensive in terms of NDS overhead that will be created on your network.

Location Login Scripts A profile can also be used for determining allocation of resources based on location. For example, each department of a company may have three printers and three print queues. A profile enables you to assign a particular group of users to a specific print queue. You can use a profile login script to capture to a particular print queue, and the users will automatically capture to that print queue.

Special Function Scripts A profile can be used as a special function script to assign users access for applications. For example, you can create a profile script that will be used only by administrators. This script may give these users a specific drive assignment to a help desk utility. In this scenario, you would move the help desk utility out of the SYS:Public directory into a new subdirectory you create called HELPDESK. When a user logs into the network, the admin Profile object is executed, and the user is assigned a drive mapping to the HELPDESK directory. Only users who execute the profile script will be assigned rights to access the help desk utility.

Consulting Experience

Typically, the profile object is used as a global login script for a workgroup or organization. Keep in mind that the profile object will execute from one container, although users may be participating from other containers and may see some performance issues if the script is executing over a wide-area connection. In addition, you will notice increased overhead of NDS traffic as NDS searches the tree to locate a particular object.

Unknown (Effective Class)

Purpose This object class represents any object created by the server to restore any object whose base class is currently undefined in the schema. Objects of this class type are created by only the server, not the client, and usually occur when a mandatory property of an object has been lost.

Unknown objects are created during synchronization of objects as placeholders, when a mandatory property of an object has been lost, and when an object class has been deleted and the server had an object of that class.

Sample Uses NDS automatically creates this object. If an unknown object appears in your tree, check to see if some other object has been deleted. In the case of a deleted server object, the server's volume objects will appear as unknown objects and must be deleted by an administrator. In other circumstances, an unknown object may appear temporarily as the NDS background processes work through a synchronization process.

Consulting Experience

Before deleting an unknown object, first check to make sure it is not needed. When you have verified that the object is not needed, then remove it from your tree. There is no point in maintaining unknown and unused objects.

Less Commonly Used Objects

AFP Server (Effective Class)

Purpose The AFP Server object represents an AppleTalk Filing Protocol-based server that is part of your NetWare 5 network as a server node or router for connected Macintosh workstations.

Sample Use This object serves only as a descriptor object and does not provide any management capability for your AFP server in a NetWare 5 environment. You can use this object for informational purposes about AppleTalk in your NetWare 5 environment.

Bindery Queue (Effective Class)

Purpose The Bindery Queue object represents a leaf object queue that has been placed in the Directory through an upgrade or migration to NetWare 5.

Sample Use A bindery queue is used to support other queues upgraded from NetWare 3.

Country (Effective Class)

Purpose This object is used to define country entries in your NDS tree. The Country Name property is restricted to two characters as defined by the ISO3166 standard. Directory Services does not check to see if characters are correctly defined; it only determines whether there are two of them.

Sample Uses For companies desiring to use the Country object, there are several considerations. First, the object must be placed directly below the [ROOT] object. Specifying this option during installation of NetWare 5 is shown in Chapter 16, "Upgrading to NetWare 5." Second, consider the ramifications of adding the Country object to your tree in terms of adding another layer to your tree and lengthening your users' context. Also, carefully plan your tree design so your users' context will be logical and will make sense. For example, let's assume we added the Country object to the ACME tree under [ROOT]. Since our company is global in nature, which country do we choose? If we say that C=US, notice what the context would be for users not reporting under the US region. This example is shown in Figure 3.14.

FIGURE 3.14

The Country object can cause your users' context to look different from the context you are actually trying to represent.

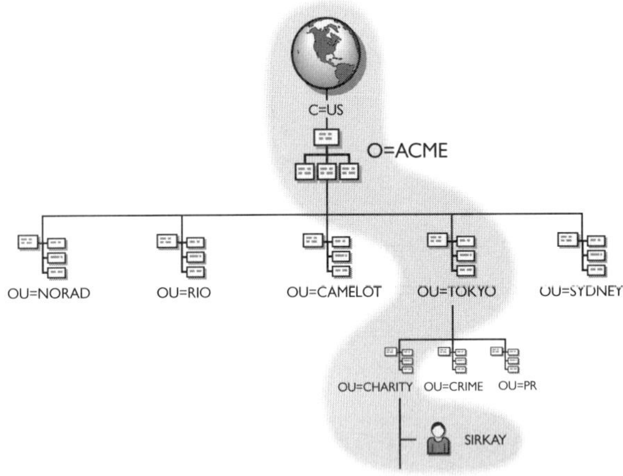

CommExec (Effective Class)

Purpose The CommExec object is used to manage Novell's NetWare for SAA NetWare Loadable Module on a NetWare 5 Server.

Sample Use This object is used only with NetWare SAA and provides management capabilities and rights privileges for the [ROOT] level of your NDS tree.

Consulting Experience

Our recommendation is to avoid using the Country object in your tree. Even with emerging gateway technology to interconnect disparate directory databases, the gateway will handle the distinction between databases using and not using the Country object. The Country object is also not necessary for companies wanting to connect to a public data provider for Directory Services.

Locality (Effective Class)

Purpose The Locality object is used to define geographic locations in the NDS tree, such as states, regions, or counties. The Locality object is currently not enabled by Novell's NWADMIN or NDS Manager utilities and therefore is not visible through the current utilities. Programs are available to define and view this object class.

Sample Uses This object must be named by one or both of its properties, L=Locality Name or S=State or Province Name. Most companies will not need to use this object. Some Directory Services that provide connection services through NDS will use the Locality object.

Computer (Effective Class)

Purpose This object class can represent both computers used as NetWare servers and computers used as client workstations.

Sample Use A key property of this object is the Operator, which can be used to identify individuals or groups that typically handle the daily hardware maintenance of this computer.

Consulting Experience

Although the Locality or State objects exist in the NDS schema, we do not recommend that you use them in the implementation of your NDS tree. The main reason is that these objects are not supported by the administrative utilities. For example, the current versions of NWADMN95 and NWADMNNT are not able to create new objects or manage the Locality or State objects. We feel the O and OU objects will meet your needs as containers in the NDS tree.

The Locality and State objects were primarily developed for implementation by the telecommunication providers into their NDS trees.

Device (Noneffective Class)

Purpose This object subclass is used to represent a physical device such as a modem or printer that you want to have defined in your tree.

Sample Uses One property contained in this object is the Locality Name, which can be used to identify the physical location of a device. In addition, as more devices become NDS enabled, the Device object may come into greater use for managing those objects.

External Entity (Effective Class)

Purpose This object is used to store information about nonnative NDS objects in the Directory tree.

Sample Use Some situations may require that an NDS object have information about another object that does not exist on the Directory Tree. A messaging service, for example, can use the External Entity class to store information about e-mail users who exist on other systems outside of the NetWare 5 tree.

List (Effective Class)

Purpose This object is used to represent an unordered set of object names in the Directory. It could be a list of leaf objects or other objects that you want to group together logically, based on some type of search criteria.

Sample Use The Member property is used to define the objects that are members of the list. The members can be any individual objects, even including Group objects. However, the key difference between this object and a group object is that membership in a list does not imply security equivalence as it does in a group. This object can be used to list objects logically for NDS searches.

Message Routing Group (Effective Class)

Purpose Closely related to the Messaging Server, the Message Routing Group object is used to represent a group of messaging servers that communicate with each other to transfer messages.

Sample Use The Member property is used to define the messaging servers that belong to the Message Routing Group.

Messaging Server (Effective Class)

Purpose This object is used to represent messaging servers, such as Novell's MHS servers, that may exist in the Directory tree.

Sample Uses If you are using Novell's MHS services for NetWare 5, you will use this object. Important properties such as the Message Routing Group, Messaging Server Type, and Supported Gateway will be configured to define the types of services provided for e-mail communications on your network.

Organizational Person (Noneffective Class)

Purpose This object defines anyone who either represents or is in some way associated with a particular organization, such as an employee. This object is part of two subclasses defined in the X.500 standard: Organizational Person and Residential Person.

Sample Use The User object is a subclass of the Organizational Person. The user class inherits from the organizational person.

Person (Noneffective Class)

Purpose This object contains the more common properties of the Organizational Person and Residential Person objects.

Sample Uses The X.500 specification defines two subclasses of Person: Organizational Person and Residential Person. The current NetWare 5 schema does not include Residential Person. The separation of Person from Organizational Person has been done for future compatibility with X.500.

Resource (Noneffective Class)

Purpose This object class is used to identify the logical resources available on your network. The resource class is similar to the device class in that a device is a physical unit, and a resource is a nonphysical or logical unit.

Sample Uses A very useful property in this object is the Host Resource Name, which can be used if a host's local identification differs from a more global resource identification. If a resource is being used by multiple localities, you can define a Locality name, Organization name, and Organizational Unit name as separate identifiers. If you define appropriate values, you can initiate NDS searches for a particular resource name, locality, or organization.

The Schema Manager Utility

The Schema Manager utility is found within the NDS Manager Utility from the Object pull-down menu. Schema Manager is an enhancement to NDS Manager. For more information on how to use NDS Manager, refer to Chapter 2, "Installation and Management Utilities for NetWare 5 Server Utilities." Schema Manager allows those with Supervisor rights to the [Root] of a tree to view and customize all aspects of the schema of that tree.

You can use Schema Manager to do the following:

- View a list of all classes and properties in the schema
- View information on a property, such as its syntax and flags
- Extend the schema by adding a class or a property to the existing schema
- Create a new class by naming it and specifying applicable properties, flags, containers to which it can be added, and parent classes from which it can inherit properties
- Create a property by naming it and specifying its syntax and flags
- Add a property to an existing class
- Compare the schemas of two trees and print the results
- View or print a report on a selected class or property, or on the entire schema
- View or print the extensions to the schema
- Delete a class that is not in use or that has become obsolete
- Delete a property that is not in use or that has become obsolete
- Identify and resolve potential problems

WARNING

Schema Manager is extremely powerful. An inexperienced user can cause serious damage to an NDS tree with this utility. Schema Manager requires Supervisor rights at the [Root] of the tree. Care should be taken when providing access to this utility.

As shown in Figure 3.15, the Schema Manager utility shows the existing object classes and properties for that tree. The object classes are shown on the left of the screen, and the properties on the right.

For example, if you double-click or right-click the User object, you will activate the Class Manager screen. This screen enables you to view all aspects of the User object including mandatory properties, optional properties, naming properties, containment classes, and class flags. An example of this screen is shown in Figure 3.16. To view class inheritance, click the Class Inheritance button within the Class Manager screen as shown in Figure 3.17.

FIGURE 3.15

The main screen of the Schema Manager utility shows the object classes and properties for that tree.

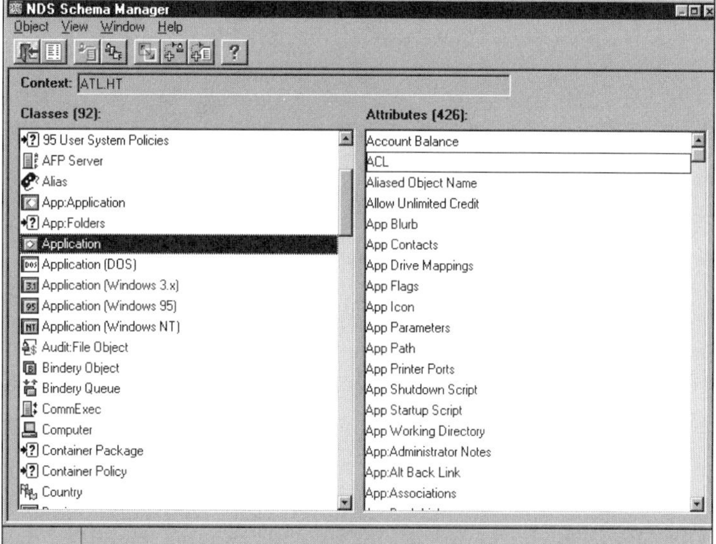

FIGURE 3.16

The Class Manager option shows you all property aspects of the object and enables you to add new properties.

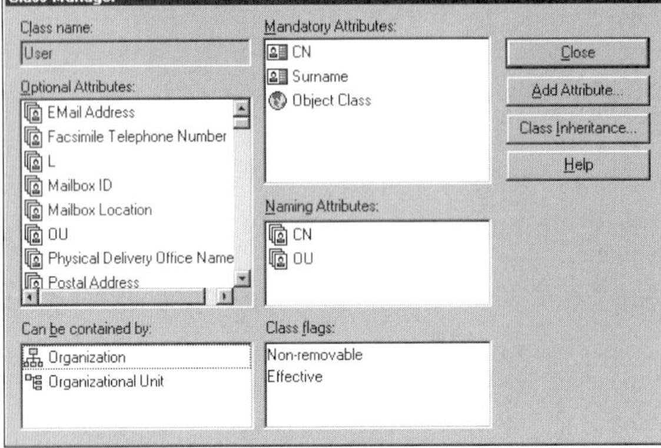

FIGURE 3.17

An example of the Class Inheritance for the user class

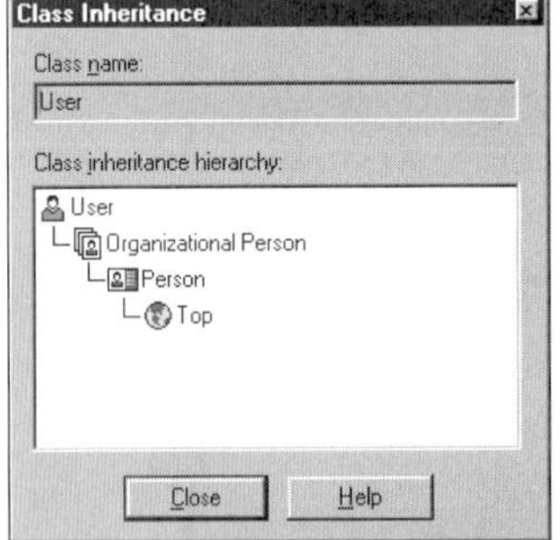

To add a new attribute (or property) to the object class, select the Add Attribute button in the Class Manager screen. As shown in Figure 3.18, a list of available attributes to select from appears, along with the object's current attributes. You simply select the attribute you wish to add to the object class and click OK. Doing so adds the attribute to the object class you have selected.

With Schema Manager, you also have the capability to add a completely new object class and/or attributes to your schema. You'll want to add a new class or attributes if you currently don't have such a class in your schema and want to represent that particular resource or property within NDS. The Schema Manager provides two wizards that walk you through the creation of a new object class and the creation of a new property. We will discuss the creation of a new object class using the wizard. The creation of a new property is basically the same process.

FIGURE 3.18

Adding optional attributes to an existing object class

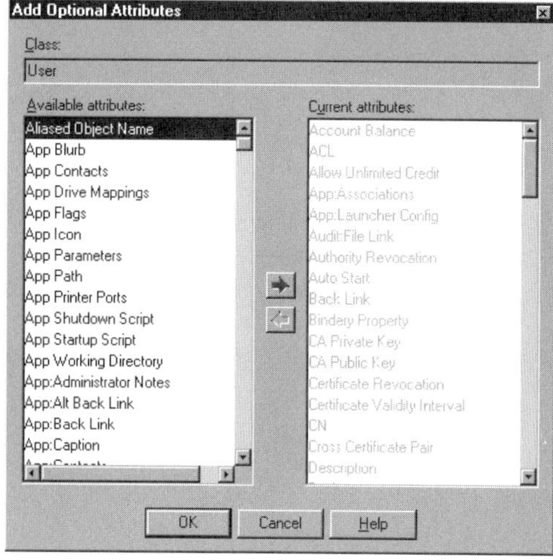

To enable the Create Class Wizard, select Object → Create New Class. The wizard appears, as shown in Figure 3.19.

FIGURE 3.19

Enabling the Create Class Wizard

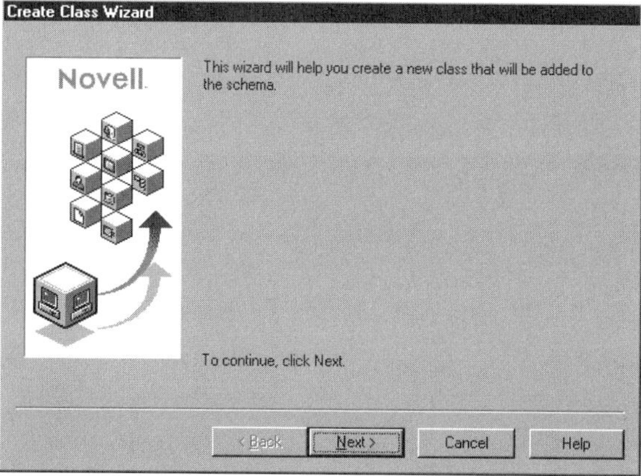

The first step in creating a new class is to select a name for your new object, as shown in Figure 3.20.

FIGURE 3.20

The first step in creating a new object class is to provide a name for the new object.

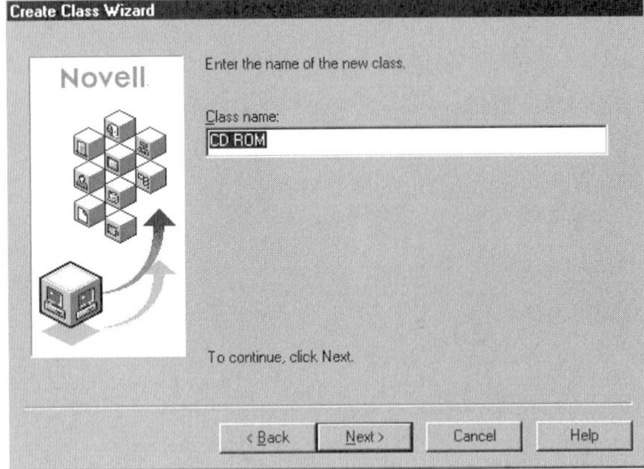

The next step is to select which class or classes the new class will inherit from. This basically means you are defining which attributes the object will receive through inheritance of other classes. When you move a class into the Available classes box as shown in Figure 3.21, the new class is automatically assigned the same attributes as the class specified. You can then add attributes as needed to customize the new class.

FIGURE 3.21

Selecting other classes from which you want the new class to inherit attributes

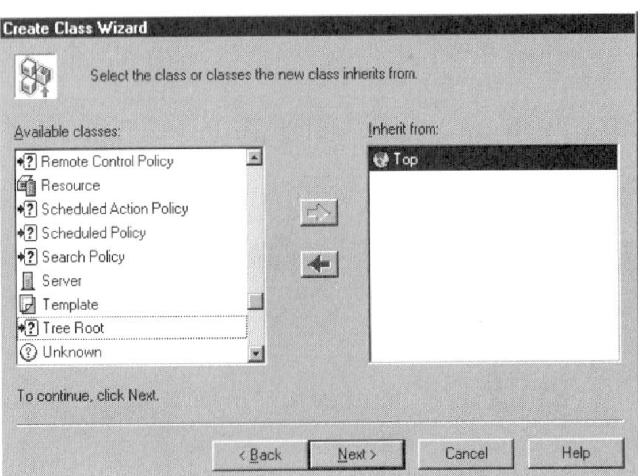

Figure 3.22 shows where you select the class flags for this new class. You can select either Effective Class, Container Class, or both. These class flags control how this class is used. There are five class flags, but only two of them are user defined. Check this flag when you want to create an effective class, which can be used to create objects.

FIGURE 3.22

Specifying the class flags for either effective class or container class

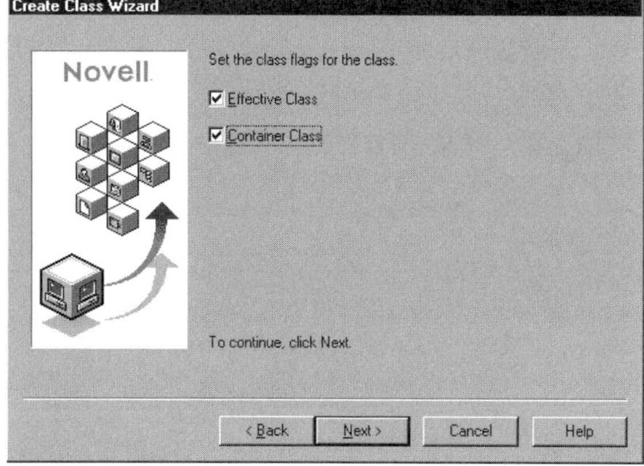

Uncheck this flag when you want to create a noneffective class, which can be used as a placeholder for a group of attributes. A noneffective class cannot be used to create objects but can be specified as a class from which other classes can inherit attributes.

Check the container class flag when you want to make this a container class. When it is used to create objects, those objects will become container objects (such as "OU"). Do not check this flag for a leaf object.

The wizard then asks you to select the mandatory and optional attributes for this new class. Mandatory attributes are required at the time the user object is created. An example of selecting the mandatory attributes is shown in Figure 3.23. An example of selecting the optional attributes for a new class is shown in Figure 3.24.

FIGURE 3.23

You can specify mandatory attributes (properties) for a new object class.

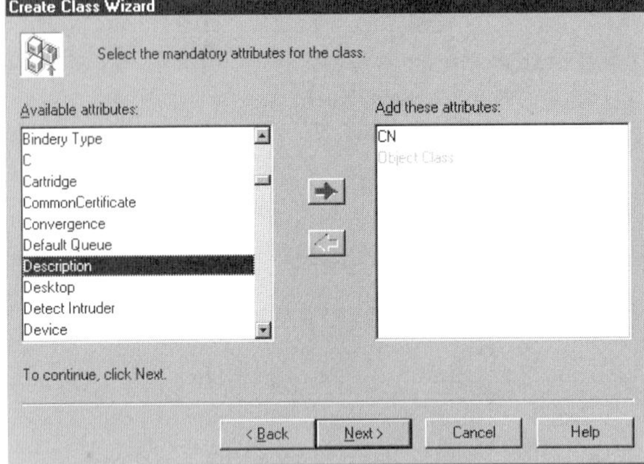

FIGURE 3.24

Selecting optional attributes (properties) for a new object class.

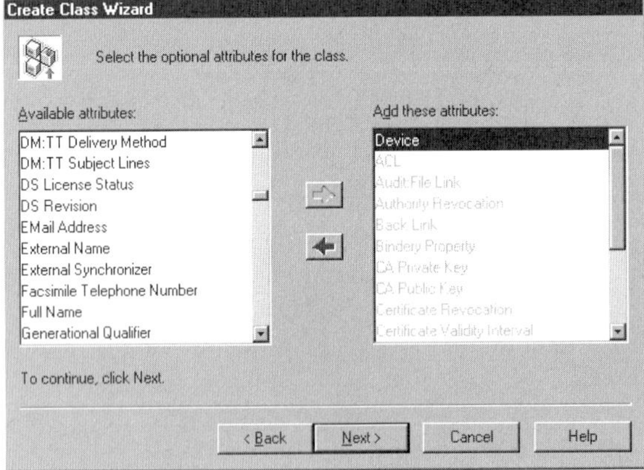

The last step in the creation of a new object class is to specify the containment classes for this object. This option enables you to specify to which containers the new object can be placed. An example of this screen is shown in Figure 3.25.

FIGURE 3.25

Selecting the container classes for the new object class

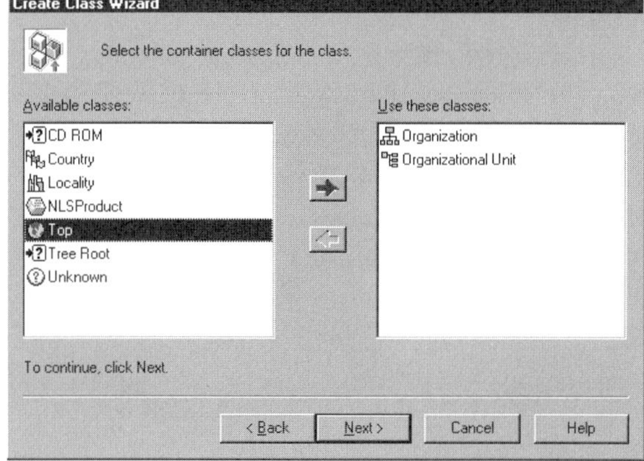

The last screen of the wizard shows a summary of the new object class (see Figure 3.26). Be sure to check carefully the specifications of this new object before writing it to your NDS schema. If any part of the new object needs modification, you can go back through the screens to make changes. Once you select the Finish button, the new object class is created in your NDS schema, providing there are no syntax violations. If such errors do occur, you need to go back through the wizard screens to determine why the object cannot be created.

FIGURE 3.26

Be sure to check the summary of the new class to be created.

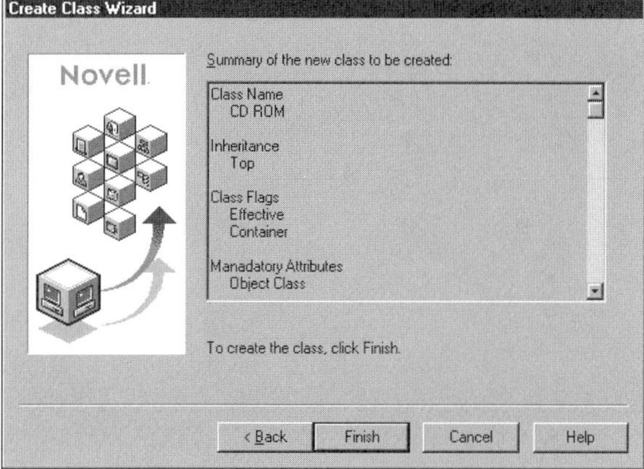

Summary

This chapter has presented a basis for understanding and using NDS objects in your tree along with the schema structure, which is the foundation of NDS. Extensions can be made to the schema to add new object classes or to add properties to existing object classes.

With this information, you will be able to create a useful naming standard and to define appropriate objects for use within your tree.

CHAPTER 4

Directory Services Naming Conventions

"It is impossible that every particular thing should have a distinct peculiar name." —John Locke

The concept of naming is closely tied to the Novell Directory Services (NDS) structure. Object naming is fundamental to the Directory because it provides a definition of the objects in the tree as well as their relationship to the other objects in the tree. In addition, resource searching, a key function of the NDS name service, is provided through the use of object naming within the Directory. Good naming implies improved search capabilities now and in the future as more applications take advantage of NDS capabilities.

NetWare 5 uses a set of rules known as the Directory *schema* to define the naming hierarchy for the entire NetWare 5 network. The schema is replicated across all NetWare 5 servers that exist in the same tree. By contrast, the NetWare 3 *bindery* is a flat naming structure that is defined by the individual NetWare 3 server and does not provide a hierarchy of bindery objects. This concept is depicted in Figure 4.1.

This section will first consider the basic elements provided within NDS for searching and locating objects within the Directory. These elements include the concepts of name types, distinguished names, relative distinguished names, contexts, typeful and typeless naming, and other methods of naming.

Next we will discuss how to create a naming standard for your particular needs, including sample standards that can be implemented at your organization.

NDS Naming Rules

NDS is a collection of objects that follow a set of rules regarding their creation, naming, and use. You can improve your NDS tree design by becoming familiar with how each of the NDS objects and properties are used in building the NDS tree structure and how they should be named.

Understanding the schema will help you to understand the internal rules of the objects, including the name types. Understanding the schema will also help you to determine the necessity of creating additional objects through schema extensions or through the use of existing NDS objects and properties.

FIGURE 4.1

A comparison between the NetWare 3 bindery and the NetWare 5 Directory

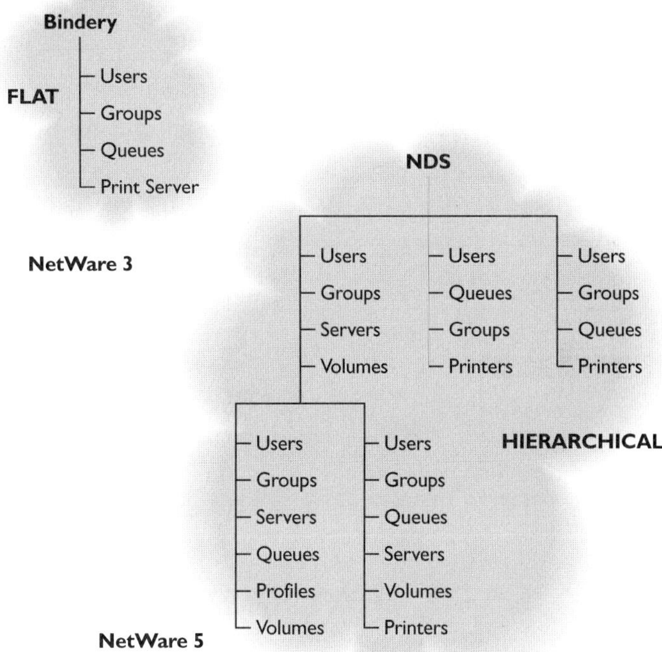

Next, we will explain briefly the NDS schema—its components, rules, and how the NDS objects are created. For a more detailed understanding of the NDS schema refer to Chapter 3, "Novell Directory Services Objects and Properties."

The NDS Schema

NDS consists of objects and properties that are defined by a set of rules in the Directory called the schema. The schema rules dictate the naming and relationship of the objects and properties that can exist in the Directory.

The NDS schema is automatically stored on every NetWare 5 server you install, and any updates to the schema are automatically synchronized to all NetWare 5 servers.

The schema consists of three major components: the object class, the property definitions, and the property syntaxes. These three components work together to establish the rules that control the creation of a particular object type in the Directory. For example, each object is defined in terms of the property definitions and other class definitions. The property definitions, in turn, are defined in terms of the property syntaxes. The property syntaxes are the data types of the property values and define the type and length of data. Figure 4.2 illustrates the relationship between the components of the schema. See Chapter 3, "Novell Directory Services Objects and Properties," for additional information on property classes and syntaxes.

FIGURE 4.2

Relationship between the three components of the schema: property syntaxes, property definitions, and objects

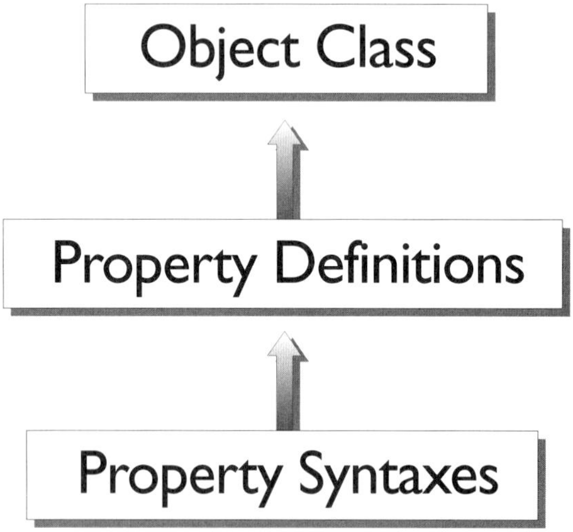

The *object class* defines the types of NDS objects that can be stored in the Directory. The object class comprises the rules for creating the individual objects and determining that object's set of characteristics. This means that every object in the tree belongs to an object class that specifies what properties are used.

The base schema that ships with NetWare 5 contains 34 object classes. These object classes cannot be removed or deleted from the schema.

Novell's INSTALL Utility also makes extensions to the schema to add additional objects. See Chapter 3, "Novell Directory Services Objects and Properties," for a complete listing of the schema extensions. Each of the object classes in the schema is defined by the relationship of the object's containment in the Directory tree. This relationship is constructed on the basis of the containment class rules.

Object Name Types

Each object consists of a naming attribute and its value. The value is assigned by the administrator during the object creation in the Directory tree. An equals (=) sign connects the naming attribute to the value.. The naming attribute determines how the object will be used in the Directory tree. Some objects are container objects, and other objects are leaf objects (or non-container objects). Table 4.1 lists the object name attributes that are assigned to each of the NDS objects. Generally, they are abbreviated.

TABLE 4.1

List of the object name types that are assigned to each of the NDS objects

NAME ATTRIBUTE	NAME DESCRIPTION
C	Country Name
L	Locality Name
S	State or Province Name
O	Organization Name
OU	Organizational Unit Name
CN	Common Name (includes all leaf objects)
BT	Bindery Type

The name types C=Country Name, L=Locality Name, O=Organization Name, and OU=Organizational Unit Name are naming attributes of container objects. The TOP class is also a container object (containing [ROOT]), although it is not visible to the Novell utilities. S=State or Province Name is not a base class. Bindery Type is a naming type for bindery objects that are migrated from NetWare 3 to NetWare 4 or NetWare 5.

Consulting Experience

As you may have noticed from the Novell utilities, not all of the object class attributes of the container objects are available to you when building your NDS tree. For example, the class L=Locality Name and the S=State or Province Name do not show up in the current versions of the Novell utilities. These object classes are found in the NDS schema, but have not been exposed by the utilities. The L=Locality class was placed in the schema for compatibility with the X.500 standard. When building the structure of your NDS tree, you can use the O=Organization and OU=Organizational Unit container classes, which provide you with the same functionality. The Locality container can be enabled through utilities such as the Preferred Systems' DS Standard utility.

The name type CN=Common Name includes all the leaf objects or non-container objects. Therefore, if the object is a user, printer, server, or any other leaf object, it is named by the type CN. The following is a list of all the leaf objects you may use to represent the network resources in your NDS tree. These objects are all named with the "CN=".

- Auditor
- AFP Server
- Bindery
- Bindery Queue
- Computer
- Directory Map
- Group
- NetWare Server
- NLS
- Organization Role
- Print Queue
- Print Server
- Printer
- Profile
- User
- Volume

Alias is not shown in this list because it is actually named by the object that it is referencing, such as an Organization, Organizational Unit, or Common Name.

Distinguished Names

Each object in the tree is given a distinguished name during its creation. An object's *distinguished name* consists of the name of the object plus the names of each of the container objects between itself and the [ROOT] object of the NDS tree. The naming of the object determines the location or position of the object in the tree. The object name attribute, mentioned in the previous section, can be used to help define the distinguished name by specifying the object type for the distinguished name. The distinguished name, therefore, provides a global, complete, and unique name in the Directory tree.

For example, in Figure 4.3 in the ACME tree, the distinguished name for the user Abraham Lincoln is the user object name plus the names of all the containers in which he is a member. It can be viewed as a path back to the top or [ROOT] of the tree. Thus, the distinguished name for the user Abraham Lincoln begins with his common name, CN=ALINCOLN, followed by each of the containers in which he is a member, OU=AUDIT.OU=ADMIN.OU=RIO.O=ACME, back to the [ROOT] object. Therefore, the distinguished name is read from left (lowest level in the tree Common Name) to right (highest level [ROOT]).

The sequence for writing or displaying the distinguished name of an object is as follows:

```
CN=ALINCOLN.OU=AUDIT.OU=ADMIN.OU=RIO.O=ACME
```

The distinguished name can be separated into segments, and each segment of the object's name is separated by periods. Each segment of an object's name consists of two parts: the object name type and the name value. The first segment in the example given above is CN=ALINCOLN where CN is the object name type (abbreviated CN for Common Name) and ALINCOLN is the object name value.

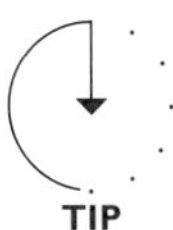
TIP

The proper order for writing an object's distinguished name is the least-significant (object deepest in the tree) to the most-significant (object closest to the [ROOT]). The distinguished name is always written left to right.

FIGURE 4.3

Each object in the ACME tree has a complete or distinguished name that is unique based on its object name plus the names of each of the container objects all the way back to [ROOT]. For example, CN=ALINCOLN.OU=AUDIT OU=ADMIN.OU=RIO.O= ACME.

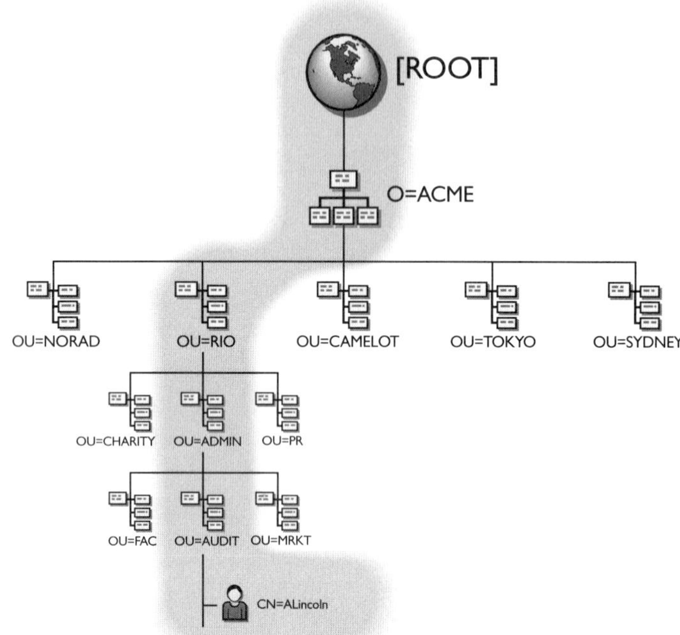

NDS will resolve the distinguished names regardless of their character case. For example, ALINCOLN's distinguished name could also be written as follows:

```
cn=alincoln.ou=audit.ou=admin.ou=rio.o=acme
```

as well as:

```
CN=ALincoln.OU=Audit.OU=Admin.OU=Rio.O=Acme
```

The above distinguished names for the user ALINCOLN are equivalent.

Another example of a distinguished name in the ACME tree is for the print queue object known as HP4SI-PQ1. The HP4SI-PQ1 is found in the NDS tree in the container MEDICAL, which is in the container HR, which is in the container SYDNEY, which, in turn, is in container ACME. Figure 4.4 illustrates the distinguished name for this print queue object.

FIGURE 4.4

The distinguished name for a print queue object in the ACME organization is CN=HP4SI-PQ1.OU=MEDICAL.OU=HR.OU=SYDNEY.O=ACME.

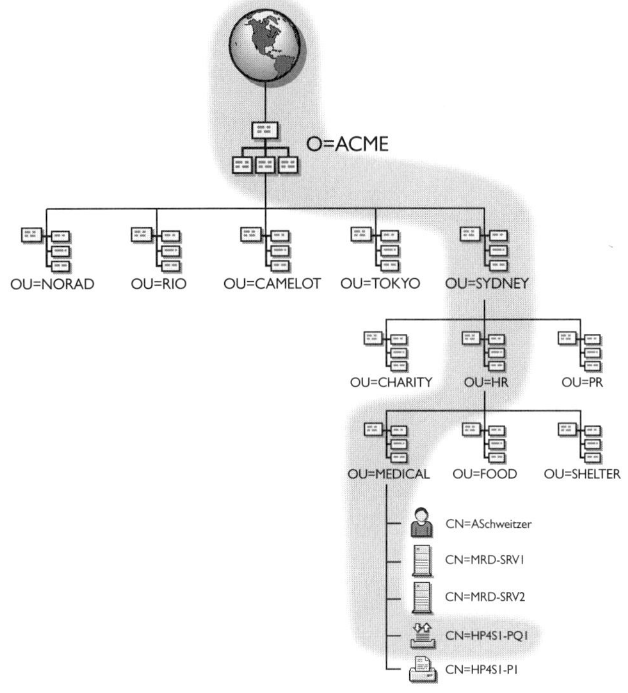

Figure 4.5 shows the distinguished name for two NDS server objects. These server objects are as follows:

`CN=LABS-SRV1.OU=LABS.OU=NORAD.O=ACME` and

`CN=WHITE-SRV1.OU=WHITE.OU=CRIME.OU=TOKYO.O=ACME`

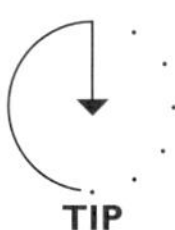

Notice that the object [ROOT] is not used in any of the distinguished names. The [ROOT] object is always implied by the NDS system. Therefore, you are not required to supply a [ROOT] object when entering a distinguished name.

FIGURE 4.5

The distinguished names for the server object CN=LABS-SRV1.OU=LABS.OU=NORAD.O=ACME and the server object CN=WHITE-SRV1.OU=WHITE.OU=CRIME.OU=TOKYO.O=ACME

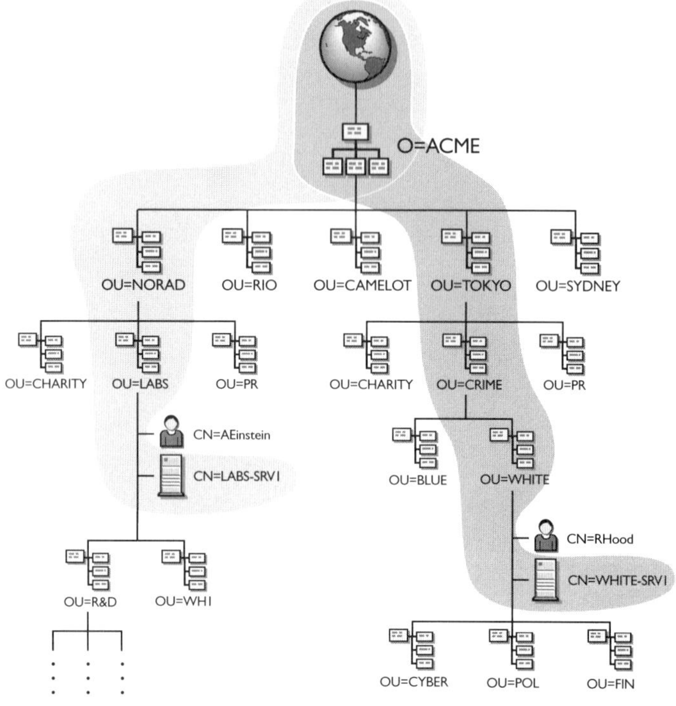

Consulting Experience

It can be cumbersome to use the distinguished name when referring to the NDS objects. You should become familiar with the use of the *relative distinguished name*, which is defined as the leaf-most portion of the name in relation to its parent container. A *partial name* is another commonly used term and is defined as the name in relation to a container. For example, referring back to Figure 4.5, LABS-SRV1.LABS is a partial name in relation to the container NORAD.ACME. The server object LABS-SRV1 is the relative distinguished name in relation to the container LABS.

Relative Distinguished Names

A *relative distinguished name* (RDN) is the individual name assigned to an object, otherwise known as the value plus the object naming attribute. The relative distinguished name must be unique only in relation to its parent object. This means that there cannot be two objects in the same container using the same name.

In Figure 4.6 objects in the R&D department in the NORAD location of the ACME tree have relative distinguished names that are unique in relation to their parent object OU=R&D. The objects are CN=LDAVINCI (user), CN=R&D-SRV1 (server), CN=R&D-SRV1_SYS (volume), and CN=R&D-PSI.

FIGURE 4.6

The objects in the R&D container of the ACME tree have unique relative distinguished names.

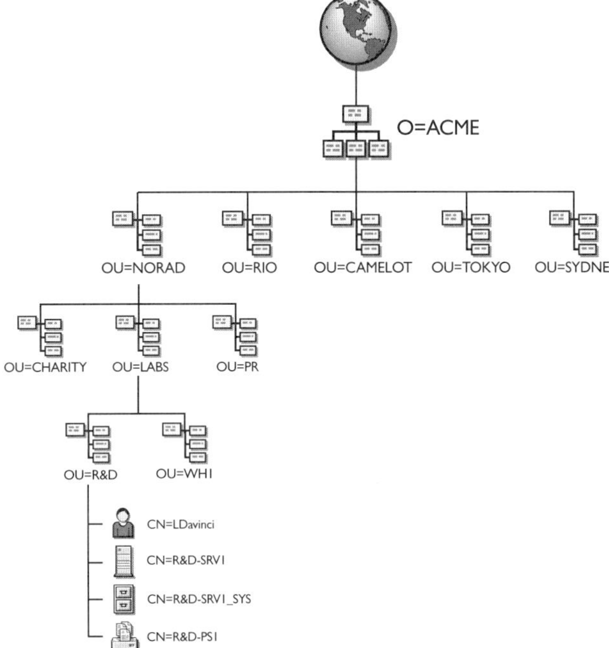

You can see in Figure 4.7 that you cannot create a second user object named CN=LDAVINCI in the same container R&D.LABS.NORAD.ACME. NDS naming does not permit duplicate object names in the same container, regardless of the object type.

FIGURE 4.7

Two objects within the same container cannot have the same relative distinguished name. There cannot be two objects named CN=LDAVINCI in the container R&D.LABS.NORAD.ACME.

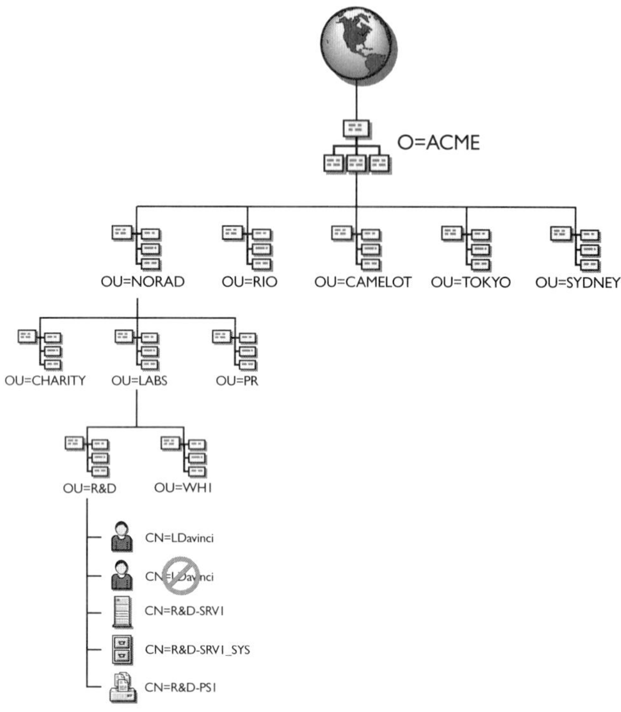

It may not always be obvious that objects of different types still need unique relative distinguished names in the container. For example, a print queue object and a group object cannot have the same relative distinguished name in the same container for the same reasons we just discussed.

The relative distinguished name only has to be unique in the parent container. The same object name can exist in the tree if the objects are located in different containers because the parent object has a different name, which causes the object to have a unique distinguished name. Thus, the objects with the same name in different containers have unique relative distinguished names in relation to their parents.

Figure 4.8 illustrates how two different printer objects in the ACME tree can have the same relative distinguished name but still have a unique distinguished name in the Directory. The two printer objects are as follows:

```
CN=HP4SI-P1 (in container OU=PR.OU=NORAD.O=ACME)

CN=HP4SI-P1 (in container OU=CHARITY.OU=TOKYO.O=ACME)
```

Consulting Experience

If you are migrating from NetWare 3, be aware that you will need to have a unique relative distinguished name for each of the objects that you will be moving to NetWare 5 and NDS. The NetWare 3 bindery permits you to create objects with the same name as long as the object types are different. This rule does not apply to NetWare 5 and NDS.

For example, it is very common for an administrator in NetWare 3 to create a print queue object and the group that will use the print queue with the same name. This is an easy method to administer the printing setup as this form of naming is legal in the NetWare 3 bindery. However, in NetWare 5 each object in the container must have a unique relative distinguished name.

When preparing to migrate from NetWare 3 to NetWare 5, you must resolve any of these duplicate names. If you do not resolve the naming conflicts, the NetWare 5 migration utility will migrate the first object but not the second object with the same name.

Both the printer objects named HP4SI-P1 are relative distinguished names in relation to their parent containers OU=PR.OU=NORAD.O=ACME and OU=CHARITY.OU=TOKYO.O=ACME, respectively.

Consulting Experience

Although the relative distinguished names for user objects must be unique within one container in the tree, we highly recommend that you create a unique naming standard across the entire NDS tree for users. Having a global naming standard for users reduces name conflicts when users are created and subsequently moved to another container for any reason. Keep in mind that e-mail systems also require unique names as well.

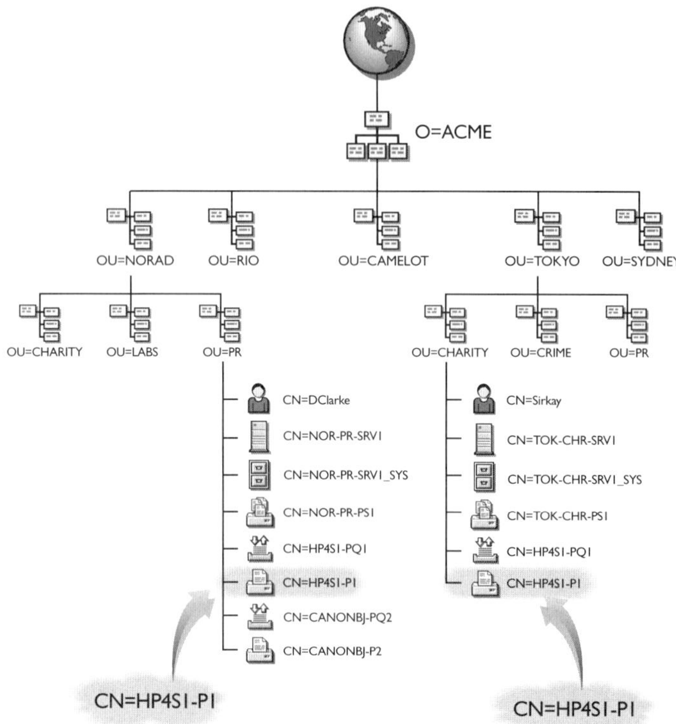

FIGURE 4.8

Two separate printer objects in the ACME tree can have the same relative distinguished name only if the printers are in different containers in the tree.

Relative distinguished names are not just reserved for the leaf objects. All objects in the NDS tree have relative distinguished names in relation to their parent containers. For example, in the ACME tree, two OU=NORAD containers cannot exist under the O=ACME. However, in Figure 4.9, notice that two containers called CHARITY and PR are under each of the locations. This is acceptable to NDS because each instance of the OU=CHARITY and OU=PR containers is unique in relation to its parent container.

Remember, combining each of the relative distinguished names with its parent object back to [ROOT] creates a distinguished name for the Directory object. Also, both the relative distinguished name and the distinguished name can be entered as *typeful* or *typeless* names.

FIGURE 4.9

Each of the OU=CHARITY and OU=PR containers under each of the location OUs have relative distinguished names because they are unique under each of the locations.

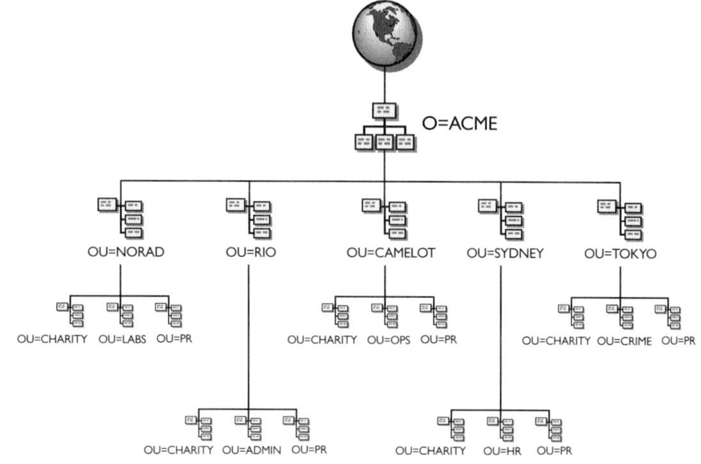

Typeful Names

Using or placing the object name types in an object's distinguished name is referred to as *typeful naming*. A couple of examples of typeful names in the ACME tree are as follows:

```
CN=SIRKAY.OU=CHARITY.OU=TOKYO.O=ACME
```

or

```
CN=TOK-CHR-PS1.OU=CHARITY.OU=TOKYO.O=ACME
```

where the user SIRKAY and print server TOK-CHR-PS1 are in the Charity OU in the Tokyo location.

You can also refer to each of these objects independently as CN=SIRKAY, CN=TOK-CHR-PS1, OU=CHARITY, OU=TOKYO, and O=ACME.

Each of these objects has its object name type plus the object name; hence, the definition of typeful naming. Typeful names, such as the CN designator, help define the object's location in the hierarchy. The CN designator always indicates a leaf object and is the lowest object in the NDS hierarchy.

Consulting Experience

Using typeful names can obviously be a lengthy method for indicating an object's distinguished name. Thus, this form of naming is not required or recommended for use with the command line utilities, especially LOGIN.EXE. It is cumbersome for the user to learn and use typeful naming. The user should only need to use typeless naming for the NDS objects.

Typeful names are not required by the Novell utilities or NDS to indicate an object's complete name because you can also use typeless names to write the complete name without using the object types. The Novell client software allows you to use typeless names because it parses the entered name with the appropriate name type.

The typeful naming method is not case sensitive. The following names from the earlier example are equivalent:

```
cn=sirkay.ou=charity.ou=tokyo.o=acme
```

is equivalent to

```
CN=SIRKAY.OU=CHARITY.OU=TOKYO.O=ACME
```

and

```
cn=tok-chr-ps1.ou=charity.ou=tokyo.o=acme
```

is equivalent to

```
CN=TOK-CHR-PS1.OU=CHARITY.OU=TOKYO.O=ACME
```

Typeless Names

Typeless names are object names that do not include the object name type in each segment. The typeless names for the examples mentioned ealier would be as follows:

```
SIRKAY.CHARITY.TOKYO.ACME
```

and

```
TOK-CHR-PS1.CHARITY.TOKYO.ACME
```

where the user SIRKAY and print server TOK-CHR-PS1 are in the Charity OU in the Tokyo location.

Notice that we have removed the object name type from each of the segments in the object. You can now refer to the objects as simply SIRKAY (where the CN= has been removed), TOK-CHR-PS1, CHARITY, TOKYO, and ACME. All the object name types have been removed.

Like the typeful naming method, typeless naming is not case sensitive. Again, using the examples given above, the following names are equivalent:

```
sirkay.charity.tokyo.acme
```

is equivalent to

```
SIRKAY.CHARITY.TOKYO.ACME
```

and

```
tok-chr-ps1.charity.tokyo.acme
```

is resolved in the same way as

```
TOK-CHR-PS1.CHARITY.TOKYO.ACME
```

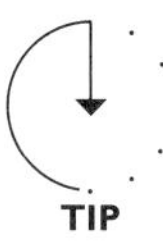
TIP

Typeless names are easier to use for both administrators and users because they are shorter and more intuitive. You will use the typeless naming more during your day-to-day operations. You should become very familiar with it. You can also use this method of typeless naming for indicating either a relative distinguished name or a distinguished name.

Context

An object is identified in the Directory by its distinguished name, which provides the dual benefits of uniqueness and location within the tree. An object's *context* is its position or location in the NDS tree. If two objects are in the same container, they have the same context because their parent container is identical. In NDS tree terms, the context can be defined as the name of the parent object.

For simplicity, NetWare 5 enables the client to shorten or abbreviate a complete object name through the use of a user context.

Figure 4.10 shows CDARWIN's context or location in the ACME tree. CDARWIN is in part of the Pollution department organizational unit (OU=POLL), in the R&D department (OU=R&D), in the LABS division (OU=LABS), in the NORAD office (OU=NORAD), under the ACME tree (O=ACME). The context for CDARWIN is OU=POLL.OU=R&D.OU=LABS.OU=NORAD.O=ACME.

FIGURE 4.10

The context in the ACME tree for the user CN=CDARWIN is OU=POLL.OU=R&D.OU=LABS.OU=NORAD.O=ACME.

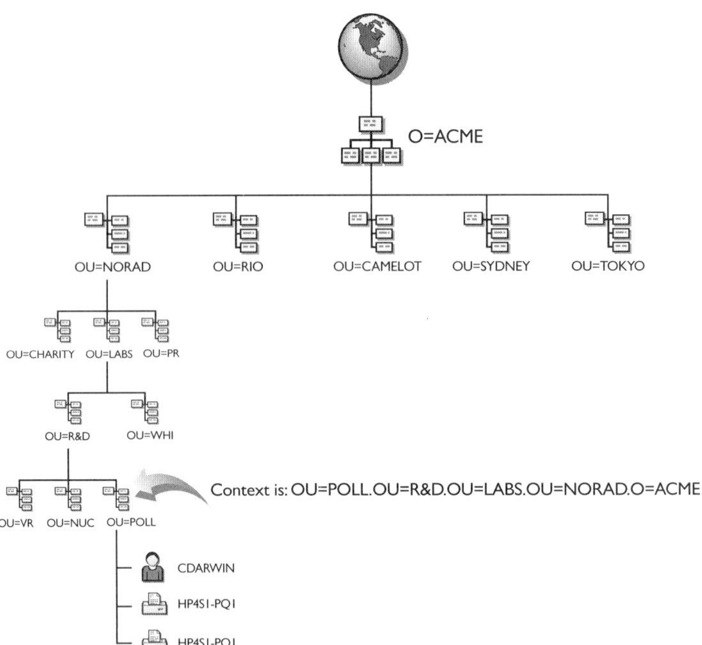

The best analogy for the context in NDS is the "path" in the DOS file system. The path statement in DOS helps you quickly and automatically find files stored in specific subdirectories. In the same fashion, the context in NDS helps you find resources in specific NDS containers.

Setting a context helps the user and administrator access NDS objects in the tree more easily. If a context is set, the user and administrator simply have to enter the relative distinguished name for the resource in the container where the context has been set. Figure 4.11 shows several contexts that exist on the ACME tree:

```
OU=OPS.OU=CAMELOT.O=ACME
OU=FIN.OU=OPS.OU=CAMELOT.O=ACME
OU=DIST.OU=OPS.OU=CAMELOT.O=ACME
```

A context can only be set to a container object. This means that you can set a context to point to either an Organizational Unit (OU=), an Organization (O=), or the [ROOT] object. You cannot set a context to a leaf object.

A user can more easily identify an object in the tree if his or her context is set to the appropriate container in the tree. For example, if the user MERLIN wants to search for all printers in the OU=DIST in the OPS division in CAMELOT, he can set his context to OU=DIST.OU=OPS.OU=CAMELOT.O=ACME and search only there for the desired printer using the NWUSER utility.

The name context in NDS enables you to navigate the NDS naming service more easily. The bindery context (discussed next) enables you to browse the same information as a bindery naming service, which is an entirely different context.

Bindery Context

NDS provides compatibility with NetWare 2 and NetWare 3 using a feature called bindery services. This feature allows bindery versions of NetWare and other bindery-based applications to access the NDS tree as if it were the bindery. Bindery services is accomplished by setting a bindery context on the server, which specifies the name of the NDS tree container(s) to search as the bindery.

FIGURE 4.11

Several contexts at different levels are shown in the ACME tree.

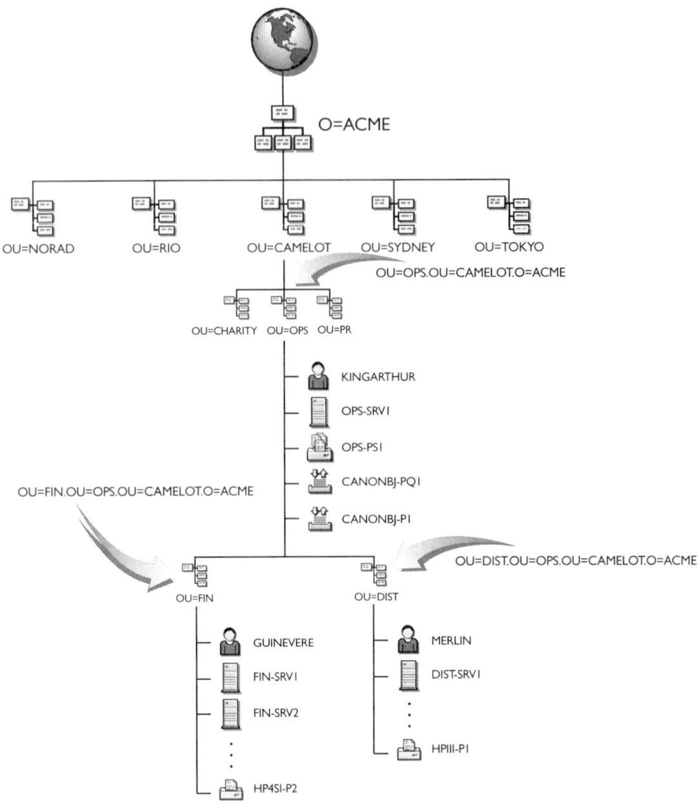

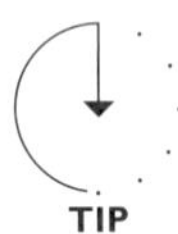

TIP

In order to set the bindery context on a server, you can, for example, enter `SET BINDERY CONTEXT = OPS.CAMELOT.ACME` **at the server console. The server bindery context can also be set using the server-based SERVMAN utility.**

Before the release of NetWare 4 and NetWare 5, object information was not available from a distributed directory. A NetWare 3 server stored only information related to its own server in the bindery. Therefore, applications were written that accessed each NetWare 3 server's bindery for a user name or other information. NDS provides bindery services that enable objects in a container to be accessed by bindery-based clients as well as by NDS objects. When a bindery-based application makes bindery calls to the server, the server sees the objects in the container where the server bindery context is set.

Simpler Log-Ins

Using the information in Figure 4.11, in order for the user KINGARTHUR to log in using just the command syntax

```
LOGIN KINGARTHUR
```

he should set the name context variable in the workstation file NET.CFG to

```
Name Context = "OU=OPS.OU=CAMELOT.O=ACME"
```

The user KINGARTHUR could also use the Novell CX (Change ConteXt) utility to manually select the same context. Keep in mind that the CX command is valid only during the current session. By selecting the correct context, he can simply enter his user name at the LOGIN.EXE command line and NDS will look in the OU=OPS container for his name.

The alternative is not having a context set. This means that the user would have to know his distinguished name and be able to enter it in order to log in. For example, if the user KINGARTHUR did not set a context, he would have to enter the following during login:

```
LOGIN CN=KINGARTHUR.OU=OPS.OU=CAMELOT.O=ACME
```

or

```
LOGIN KINGARTHUR.OPS.CAMELOT.ACME
```

NOTE

In terms of bindery context on the server, NDS will see only the objects that previously existed in a NetWare 3 bindery as the bindery objects. These objects are limited to user, group, print queue, print server. In addition, NetWare 4 and NetWare 5 have added the profile object to assist with migrations from NetWare Name Services (NNS).

The default server bindery context is set to the container where the server was installed. You can change the context to another container or OU if you want. Previous versions of NetWare 4, up to and including NetWare 4.02, only permitted you to set a single context for your server. NetWare 5 enables you to set up to 16 contexts for a single server.

You can set multiple contexts by using the MONITOR utility as shown in Figure 4.12. This utility allows you to separate each context using a semicolon or a space as shown in this example.

FIGURE 4.12

Use the MONITOR utility to set multiple bindery contexts.

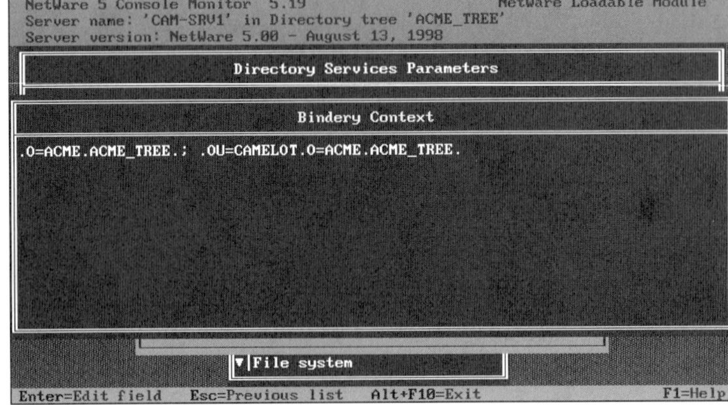

Leading Periods

The period (.) separates the individual name segments in distinguished names, relative distinguished names, and user contexts. Through the use of leading and trailing periods in the name sequence, you can quickly navigate to any object in the tree. This is useful for referencing objects located in other portions of the tree from a workstation console.

A name with a leading period instructs the client software to ignore the current context and start the search at the [ROOT] object. This means that any object name with a leading period will be treated as a distinguished name starting at the [ROOT] object.

For example, in Figure 4.13, the current context for a user is set to the following:

```
OU=R&D.OU=LABS.OU=NORAD.O=ACME
```

FIGURE 4.13

A view of the ACME tree and changing the context

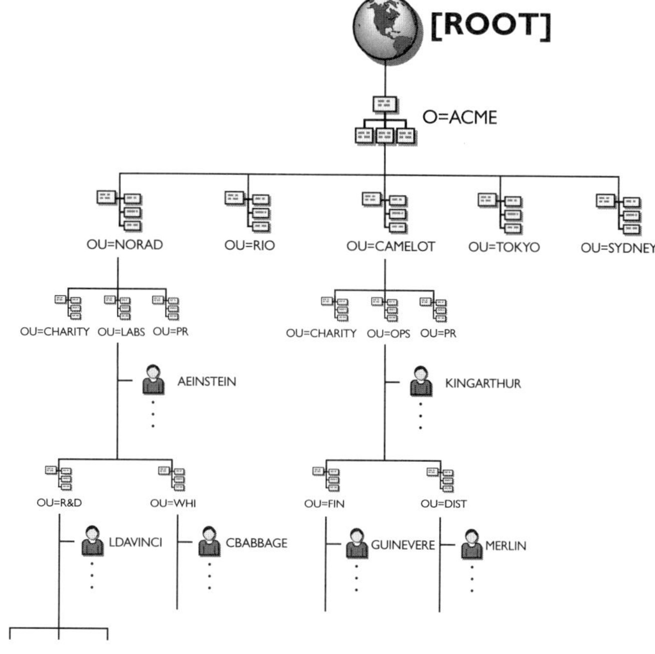

Using the Novell CX utility, you type the following command (notice the leading period at the beginning of the distinguished name):

```
CX .DIST.OPS.CAMELOT.ACME
```

which will be resolved to the container OU=DIST.OU=OPS.OU=CAMELOT.O=ACME by the NDS client. The leading period causes the name to be treated as a whole name, not a partial name. In other words, start at the [ROOT] and work down.

Using the leading period is simply a shortcut for navigating the tree from the command line utility of your workstation. There can be only one leading period in the object name on the command line.

Trailing Periods

A period after an object name (known as a *trailing period*) can be used to select a new context. The use of a single trailing period will move the current context up by one container in the tree. For instance, you can use the Novell CX (Change ConteXt) utility and type the following command at the DOS prompt (notice the single trailing period):

```
CX.
```

This command will automatically move you up one layer or container in the tree. Unlike leading periods, you can have as many trailing periods up to the number of relative distinguished names (RDNs) in the current context. If you want to move the current context up two layers in the tree, simply supply two trailing periods. You change the context in the tree one layer for every trailing period you supply at the end of the name.

In Figure 4.14, assume that the current context is

```
OU=DIST.OU=OPS.OU=CAMELOT.O=ACME
```

and you want to change the context to O=ACME. You simply type the following command (notice the three trailing periods):

```
CX...
```

Trailing periods can be used with relative distinguished names to indicate segments of the context to be replaced. The replacement occurs during the resolution of the full distinguished name.

In Figure 4.14, for example, assume that the current context is the following:

```
OU=DIST.OU=OPS.OU=CAMELOT.O=ACME
```

If you wanted to change your context to the OU=FIN container, which is under OU=OPS, you would simply type the following command (notice the trailing period):

```
CX OU=FIN.
```

FIGURE 4.14

Changing the context by using trailing periods

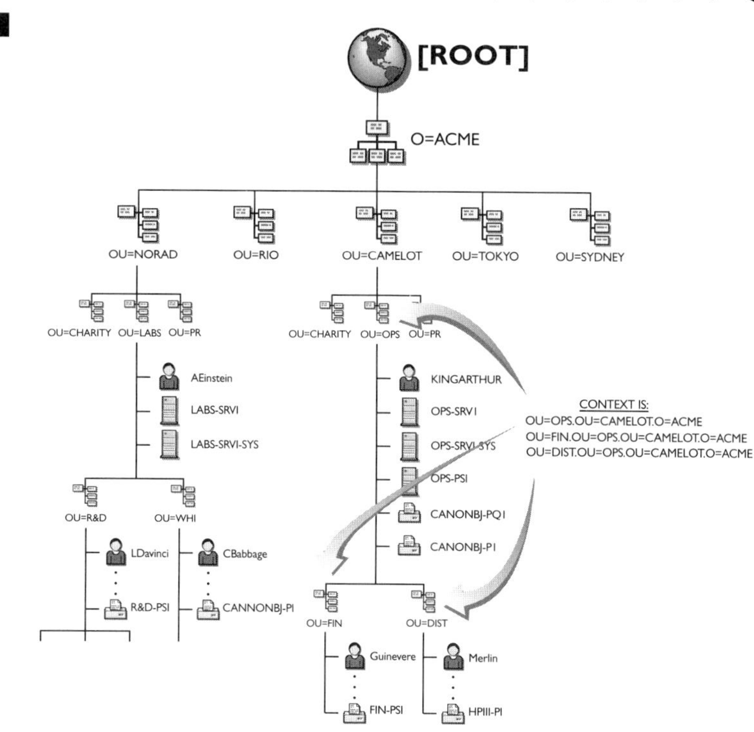

For each trailing period in the RDN, one segment of the context is ignored. This starts at the least-significant segment (deepest in the tree) and proceeds to the most-significant segment or until the trailing periods are exhausted.

Again in Figure 4.14, assume the current context is as follows:

```
OU=DIST.OU=OPS.OU=CAMELOT.O=ACME
```

If you wanted to change your context to the OU=WHI container, which is under OU=LABS in the NORAD location, you would need to type the following command:

```
CX OU=WHI.OU=LABS.OU=NORAD...
```

A Naming Standards Document

Creating a naming standards document need not be difficult or time consuming. The first step is to determine why such a standard should be created. The preceding sections of this chapter have demonstrated that naming is the structure of the Directory tree. As a basis or purpose for why the standard is important, consider the following:

- How can you provide a Directory structure for your employees that is flexible, easy to use, and meets today's business needs?
- How can you ensure that you provide a consistent Directory structure within all divisions, locations, and even operating companies?
- How can you communicate and implement a consistent standard that everyone will follow across an entire company?

The answers to these questions lie in creating a naming standards document that will force you to devise clear and easy-to-remember names and thus make the NDS database a more useful resource.

Naming Guidelines

Create some naming guidelines before installing your first NetWare 5 server. Once an installation has begun, it becomes more difficult to implement a standard. At a minimum, you should determine how Organizational Units, Servers, and User objects will be defined. These will be the most widely created objects along with your printing objects.

If you have already implemented some existing naming standards, that's the place to start your review. Many companies already have some guidelines in place for defining their users' names. These guidelines are usually based on an e-mail standard. Review the standard and make modifications where necessary. If your company's network is small, you should still create naming guidelines because the network will most likely grow to include more users and resources, which will make naming more important. It's also easier to support a network with consistent naming.

Your naming guidelines need to be global in nature. You should strive to implement your naming guidelines consistently across the entire network so that all users and departments can readily and easily access resources anywhere on the LAN. Global naming guidelines can also help your administrators understand the purpose and use of all objects in the tree.

Most likely you will need input from others in your company in order to create some naming guidelines. You should gather information from the organizations within your company that must participate in forming the naming standard. This information may include input from e-mail administrators, network administrators, and mainframe personnel.

Usually an established host environment will have user naming standards in place. Review these standards as a basis for your NetWare 5 user naming guidelines. Some customers prefer to maintain their host user IDs on the LAN rather than create a new standard at the network level. Others can't wait to change their host user IDs!

Consider all other naming guidelines that you may already have in place from a NetWare 3 environment to determine how well they might fit into the NetWare 5 environment. Your NetWare 3 printers and servers may already have names defined that will work just fine after migration to a NetWare 5 tree. If your organization has sufficient or acceptable guidelines, there is no need to change them.

As mentioned previously, many sites already have e-mail addresses set up that require a user naming convention, such as the first initial and last name of the user (for example, TJEFFERSON for Thomas Jefferson).

Naming guidelines provide consistency across your network. If your naming standard is already consistent and firmly in place, you are in great shape and can move on to the next phase of designing your NDS tree. If you do not have an existing naming standard, you should consider establishing naming guidelines that meet the following goals:

- Make browsing and navigation of the NDS tree easier for the users
- Make maintenance of the NDS tree easier for the administration staff

- Make merging separate NDS trees easier
- Keep the NDS object names unique, as required by certain services
- Avoid special characters reserved by the operating systems

Each of these guidelines is discussed in the following sections.

Improve NDS Browsing and Navigation

Your primary objective for creating the naming guidelines is to provide the network user with a simple view of the network resources contained in the tree. You may not see the immediate need for good naming guidelines, but as more applications are written to take advantage of NDS and its searching capabilities, an uncomplicated naming standard will be needed.

Objects named with purpose and consistency will eventually provide you with a solid foundation that benefits your administrators as well as your users. You will see that the system is much more efficient if users can quickly identify the network resources available to them and minimize the impact on searching NDS across multiple locations.

You should keep the names of all the objects short and simple, yet descriptive enough that the user knows what the object is and the services it provides from its name. For example, the object name HP4SI-P1 is short yet descriptive and lets the user know that this object is an HP4si laser printer. The object name HP4SI-PQ1 is another example of a short name, but is different from the previous example. The PQ1 suffix lets the user know that the object is the print queue that supports the printer (P1).

As you can see, there are many instances throughout the book where we have benefited from using the names of containers and network resources from the ACME tree. It has been helpful to have clear and simple names. Some examples of the naming guidelines for ACME are shown in Table 4.2.

TABLE 4.2

Examples of the naming guidelines for ACME

OBJECT	ENTITY	STANDARD
[ROOT]	Tree Name	ACME_TREE
O=Organization	A Cure for Mother Earth	ACME
OU=Organizational Unit	Rio de Janeiro, Brazil	RIO
	Tokyo, Japan	TOKYO
	Sydney, Australia	SYDNEY
	Research and Development	R&D
	World Health Index	WHI
	Facilities	FAC
	Public Relations	PR
Users	George Washington	GWASHINGTON
	Thomas Jefferson	TJEFFERSON
	Leonardo DaVinci	LDAVINCI
	Albert Einstein	AEINSTEIN
Servers	Server in Labs	LABS-SRV1
	Server in White	WHITE-SRV1
	Server in NORAD/PR	NOR-PR-SRV1
Printers	HP4si in NORAD/PR	HP4SI-P1
Print Queues	Queue in NORAD/PR	HP4SI-PQ1

Maintain Networks and NDS

Consistent naming provides a framework for the network administrators to monitor and maintain the network and NDS. The administrators will be installing file servers, creating users and printers, modifying existing objects, and moving objects within the tree. The administrators will also set up all the user configuration files at the workstation to connect to NDS in the predetermined fashion. The administrator's job will be much easier if naming guidelines are in place.

Merge NDS trees

The capability to merge multiple NDS trees is a feature introduced in NetWare 4.1. However, merging two trees within the company will be much easier if the trees are based on the same naming standards for container and leaf objects. The tree merge will be seamless to users because their workstation configuration files will not have to be modified, even though the NDS trees are merged.

Keep NDS Object Names Unique

Some of the NDS tree objects are required to have unique object names in order for the network to work properly. For instance, the file server and print server objects stored in NDS broadcast their services using the Service Advertising Protocol (SAP). Although the file server and print server objects are not required to have unique names on the network, it is highly recommended in order to avoid confusion for users and administrators.

Establishing the naming guidelines and dictating them to all the network administrators in the network will help keep the NDS objects unique. As stated previously, it is recommended that the user objects have unique names throughout the network. This way users can be moved or new users added without conflict.

Not all the objects in the NDS tree will need unique names throughout the network. You decide which NDS objects have unique names. The SAP requires that file server object names be unique on the network.

Consulting Experience

All network devices on the network that communicate using the SAP (Service Advertising Protocol) should have unique object names in the entire network. Therefore, all file servers and print servers should have unique names on the wire. The maximum length of the names of the objects that use SAP is 47 characters. The space character is illegal for server names.

Avoid Special or Reserved Characters

NDS requires the use of the escape character with some characters and therefore we recommend you avoid using them in your naming guidelines. The characters are as follows:

- **Period (.)** — The period is used by NDS to separate the name segments of distinguished names. For example, the distinguished name for the user George Washington is:

  ```
  CN=GWASHINGTON.OU=ADMIN.OU=RIO.O=ACME
  ```

- **Commas (,)** — The comma is allowed by NDS naming rules. However, it is very confusing and generally should be avoided.

- **Plus (+)** — The plus sign is used by NDS to represent objects with multiple naming attributes, such as the bindery objects. A common use of the plus sign is for bindery objects placed in the NDS database. For example, a bindery object with the plus sign in the name is seen as CN=BinderyObject +Name. In the case of an Appletalk print server, it might appear as:

  ```
  CN=AtpsQuser+83
  ```

- **Equals (=)** — The equals sign is used by NDS to tie together name types and object names. For example, the object type O=Organization would appear as:

  ```
  O=ACME
  ```

- **Backslash (\)** — The backslash precedes the special characters above if they are used as part of an object name. For example, suppose you want to use the name *ACME Inc.*, which has a period at the end. In order to make it a legal NDS name, you would need to enter:

  ```
  ACME Inc\.
  ```

It is also recommended that you understand the following guidelines if you use spaces in any of the object names; you may want to use the underscore character instead. Spaces are used as delimiters for all the command line parameters. If you use spaces in the NDS object names and need to use the name with a command line utility, you will need to enclose the name in quotes.

For example, the user George Washington is named "George Washington" in NDS with a space separating the first and last name. In order to use the relative distinguished name with the LOGIN.EXE program, the name would have to be entered with quotes around it:

```
LOGIN "George Washington"
```

and not

```
LOGIN George Washington
```

If you were required to provide the full distinguished name during login, the name would then appear as follows:

```
LOGIN "GEORGE WASHINGTON.ADMIN.RIO.ACME"
```

You can also use the underscore character as a replacement for the space character because NDS interprets the space and underscore in the same way. In the example of the user George Washington, his name would appear as follows:

```
George_Washington
```

When the name is used during login, it would be entered without the quotes:

```
LOGIN George_Washington
```

You should also avoid the use of the forward slash (/) in your naming of any container or leaf object. Some Windows-based utilities will fail if you map permanent drives or capture a print queue. This is a Windows issue that does not permit the use of the forward slash in any object name.

Producing a Naming Standards Document

Producing a naming standards document is not very glamorous, but it shouldn't require a great deal of time to complete, either. Here are some steps you can take to produce your naming standards document as quickly and efficiently as possible:

- Document the naming standard for each object to be used in the NDS tree
- Provide an example for each object used
- Specify properties for each of the objects selected

These steps are discussed in detail below.

Determining Object Naming Standards

In order to create the naming guidelines, review which NDS objects you will use in your NDS tree. Typically, these objects include organizational units, servers, users, printers, print queues, groups, organizational roles, directory maps, and profiles.

Other possible areas for naming consistency include the properties associated with each object you define in the NDS tree. In short, any information you plan on using to search the NDS database needs a naming standard for consistency.

The naming standard for each of the objects used in the ACME tree is included in Table 4.3.

TABLE 4.3

NDS object naming standard for the ACME tree

NDS OBJECTS	STANDARD
Users	First character of the first name plus the entire last name. All titles are spelled out.
Organization	Abbreviation of the company name.
Organizational Unit	Location, division, or department name. Abbreviate the names if they are over eight characters long.

Continued

TABLE 4.3

Continued

NDS OBJECTS	STANDARD
NetWare Server	Department-SRV#. Exception is the Location-Department-SRV#, which is for the CHARITY and PR departments. The difference is because of the duplication of container names for all locations of CHARITY and PR.
Volumes	ServerName_VolumeName.
Print Server	Department-PS#. Exception is the Location-Department-PS#, which is for the CHARITY and PR departments.
Printer	PrinterType-P#.
Print Queue	PrinterType-PQ#.
Computer	No standard because it is not used.

Providing Example Objects

You may have noticed when reading Table 4.3 that there were no examples of the object naming standards. Remember, a picture is worth a thousand words. An example can convey the meaning of an entire written page. Therefore, include some brief examples in your naming guidelines document. As shown in Table 4.4, you can convey your meaning more quickly and easily by providing an example. Table 4.4 is simply a reprint of Table 4.3, but examples for each of the object's naming standard have been added for clarity.

TABLE 4.4

NDS object naming standard for the ACME tree

NDS OBJECTS	STANDARD
Users	First character of the first name plus the entire last name. All titles are spelled out. Examples: GWASHINGTON, SIRGAWAIN
Organization	Abbreviation of the company name, which is "A Cure for Mother Earth." Example: ACME
Organizational Unit	Location, division, or department name. Abbreviate the names if they are over eight characters long. Example: NORAD, R&D, ADMIN

NDS OBJECTS	STANDARD
NetWare Server	Department-SRV#. Exception is Location-Department-SRV#, which is for the CHARITY and PR departments. Examples: LABS-SRV1, NOR-CHR-SRV1
Volumes	ServerName_VolumeName. Examples: LABS-SRV1_SYS, NOR-CHR-SRV1_SYS
Print Server	Department-PS#. Exception for the CHARITY and PR departments, which is Location-Department-PS#. Examples: FAC-PS1, TOK-PR-PS1
Printer	PrinterType-P#. Examples: HP4SI-P1, CANONBJ-P2
Print Queue	PrinterType-PQ#. Examples: HP4SI-PQ1, CANONBJ-PQ2
Computer	No standard because it is not used.

Specifying Object Class Properties

For some installations, you may need to determine which properties will be required for the selected objects. Some properties are mandated by the NDS schema when you create the object. This means that if the mandatory properties are not filled in, the NDS utilities will not create the object. For example, during the creation of a user object, you are required to specify the Login Name and Last Name properties.

You may have additional properties that you would like all your administrators to include when they create a new object. This type of information might include addresses, fax numbers, department names, and so on. Table 4.5 illustrates the naming standards for a user object with additional properties you want filled in when the users are created. Not all the properties for the user are represented in the table. Some properties are required and a value must be entered at creation, while other properties are optional and are left up to you to determine if they should be used. System properties are those properties that NDS automatically populates during the creation of the object.

TABLE 4.5

NDS property naming standards for a user object in the ACME tree

PROPERTY	REQ/OPT/SYSTEM	STANDARDS
Login Name	Required	First character of the first name plus the entire last name. Add a middle initial to resolve name conflicts.
Given Name	Optional	First name of the user.
Last Name	Required	Last name of the user.
Full Name	Optional	First and last name of the user.
Generational Qualifier	Optional	SR, JR
Middle Initial	Optional	Middle initial of the user, if known.
Other Name	Optional	
Title	Optional	Job title.
Description	Optional	
Location	Optional	City or site location (NORAD, RIO).
Department	Optional	
Telephone	Optional	Business phone number with area code.
Fax Number	Optional	Fax phone number with area code.
Language	Optional	Preferred language of the user.
Network Address	System	
Default Server	Optional	Enter the same server as the home directory.
Home Directory	Optional	Enter the volume/subdirectory/user path.
Require Password	Optional	Force the user to have a password.
Account Balance	Optional	
Login Script	Optional	Determined by the site administrators.

PROPERTY	REQ/OPT/SYSTEM	STANDARDS
Print Job Configuration	Optional	Determined by site administrators.
Post Office Box	Optional	
Street	Optional	
City	Optional	
State or Province	Optional	
Zip Code	Optional	
See Also	Optional	

More Naming Standards Ideas

User Accounts

When you create a naming standard, one of the first steps is to decide how to standardize your usernames. NetWare 5 allows usernames to be up to 64 characters long. However, a 64-character username is a very long name and not easy to use.

In the example of ACME, the username was limited to the first character of the first name plus the entire last name. If there are duplicate names within a single container, the middle initial is added to resolve the name conflict. This type of username may not be used globally because of the number of username conflicts.

Consulting Experience

Currently the Novell utilities do not enforce additional required properties that you define as an administrator. However, we recommend a well-documented guideline in which you explain your reason for including a particular property. Your administrators will be more likely to adhere to the guideline if they understand the reasoning behind the inclusion of an object's attribute.

Some companies have limited the length of the username to eight characters. This naming convention for the user accounts matches the naming of the user's DOS home directory. Because DOS is limited to just eight characters for subdirectory names, limiting the usernames to eight characters will automatically match the name of the DOS subdirectory assigned to the user. For example, if you use eight characters for the user Thomas Jefferson, his name could be defined as follows:

```
TJEFFERS
```

which is the first character of his first name and the first seven characters of his last name.

Another way to represent a user is to take the first six characters of his last name and the first two characters of his first name. This name would appear as follows:

```
JEFFERTH
```

Duplicate names can be handled by specifying a middle initial in one of the two names such as the following:

```
TQJEFFER
```

(Thomas Q. Jefferson)
or

```
QJEFFETH
```

(Q. Jefferson Thomas)

TIP

Remember, object names within the same container must be unique. Duplicate names are allowed only if the objects are in different containers. However, it is still recommended that you keep object names unique across the entire tree.

Organization and Organizational Unit Names

Your organization name should reflect your company name. The company name "A Cure for Mother Earth" is abbreviated to ACME. Thus, the O=Organization is called O=ACME. For the Organizational Units, the locations and departments with short but descriptive names are used. For instance, OU=SYDNEY and OU=TOKYO are examples of the location OUs. They could have been abbreviated to SYD and TOK, but their names are already short.

Examples of the division and department Organizational Units are OU=R&D for the Research and Development department and OU=MRKT for the Marketing department.

NOTE

The tree name can be named with the company name plus _TREE. We have chosen ACME_TREE as our tree name for the ACME company and O=ACME for the organization. Notice the difference between tree name and the organization name is simply the addition of the "_TREE."

Server Names

Server names should be unique on the entire network because each server name is broadcast through the SAP (Service Advertising Protocol). You may wish to consider a server name that signifies a location and department.

For ACME, a NetWare server in the CHARITY department of NORAD is called NOR-CHR-SRV1, and a print server is called NOR-CHR-PS1. A server in the R&D department in NORAD is called SRV1. You may wonder why the naming standards seem different for different departments. Notice that the R&D department is a unique department within the ACME tree and that there is no need for the location name in the server name. However, the CHARITY and PR departments are not unique departments within the ACME tree. These two departments are placed as OUs beneath every location, and the servers in those containers should have the location name in order to be unique.

Printer and Print Queue Names

Printers and print queue names do not have to be unique on the network. The department and location information is obtained by where the printer and print queue are placed in the tree. The distinguished name of the printer or print queue object is used to discover the location and department in which the printer is placed. Thus, the individual object name for the printer and print queue should show the function of the printer.

For example, in the ACME tree an HP4si printer is named HP4SI-P1, and the print queue that supports the printer is called HP4SI-PQ1. A Canon Bubble Jet printer is named CANONBJ-P2, and the print queue is named CANONBJ-PQ2. This type of naming provides users with fundamental information about the printer they will be using.

The user can obtain the location and department in which the printer has been placed from the distinguished name or location in the ACME tree. For example, a Canon Bubble Jet printer (CANONBJ-P1) in the Operations (OPS) department in Camelot (CAMELOT) has a distinguished name of CANONBJ-P1.OPS. CAMELOT.ACME.

The difference between the printer object and the print queue object is defined by the object suffix. For instance, the "P" is for the printer object and the "PQ" is for print queue object.

NOTE

A printer that connects directly to the network and services a print queue on the file server is called a *queue server.* A queue server is a special-purpose print server that needs to have a unique name to broadcast using SAP. All queue servers use SAP to advertise their services on the network.

A Sample Naming Standard

The following table provides another example of how you can create a naming standard document that is simple but very useful. Table 4.6 shows the document with the object type, the naming syntax, and an example. Keep in mind that, although we have already demonstrated our naming standard in previous sections of this chapter, the following naming standard is another one for your review.

TABLE 4.6

Sample of a Basic Naming Standard

OBJECT TYPE	SYNTAX	EXAMPLE
[ROOT] or Tree Name	AAAA_TREE	ACME_TREE
Organization	AAAA = Company Name	O=ACME
Organizational Units	XXXXXX,YYYYYY	OU=RIO, OU=FIN
	XXXXX = Location	
	YYYYY = Department	
NetWare Servers	XXXYYZ##	RIO-ADM-F01

OBJECT TYPE	SYNTAX	EXAMPLE
Print Servers	XXXYYZ##	NOR-CHR-P04
Volume Names	Server_Volume	RIO-ADM-F01_SYS
	XXX = Location (NOR, RIO, CAM, TOK, SYD)	
	YYY = Department (LAB, CHR, PR, ADM, OPS, FIN)	
	Z = Server type where:	
	F=File Server, T=Test Server, P=Print Server, C=Comm Server, etc. ## = Quantity (01, 02, 03, . . . , 99)	
	Volumes are SYS, APPS, DATA, USERS, SHARE	
Printers	YYYTTLL##P	FIN-LJPS01-P
Queues	YYYTTLL##Q	FIN-LJPS01-Q
Queue Server	YYYTTLL##QS	FIN-LJPS01-QS
	YY = Department (LAB, CHR, PR, ADM, OPS, FIN, HR)	
	TT = Type of printer (LJ for LaserJet, BJ for BubbleJet, PL for plotter)	
	LL = Language (PS for PostScript, PC for PCL, and so on)	
	## = Number of printer, queue, or queue server (01, 02, 03, . . . , and so on)	
	P = Printer	
	Q = Queue	
	QS = Queue Server	

Continued

TABLE 4.6
Continued

OBJECT TYPE	SYNTAX	EXAMPLE
Group Help Desk	Function	WP_Group
	Function (the activity that the group will perform)	
Organizational Roles	Name_Function	RIO_Admin_OR
	Function (the administrative activity or role that the Organizational Role performs)	
Profiles	Name_P	Mobile_P
	Name (the purpose of the Profile object)	
Directory Maps	Directory Name	WP61
	Directory Name (the DOS directory name in which the application has been installed)	

Network Addressing Standards

Network addresses are another important area of naming. Having a defined standard for internal network addresses and IP addresses is as important as NDS naming. This section provides some brief examples on defining standards for internal network addresses and IP addresses for your network.

Server Internal Network Address

The IPX cable address defines the physical cable segment for your file servers. The cable segment may be your entire network, or you may have many segments based on locations in your network infrastructure. If you do not already have a standard for cable segments, you should implement one. A brief example of a cable segment standard is as follows:

```
XXXSSSSN
```

For example, 20025451 represents the Norad (200) facility building 2545, segment number 1, where:

- XXX = Numeric value that represents a location such as NOR, CAM, TOK.
- SSSS = Numeric identifier for a wiring closet or building.
- N = Numeric value that represents a number for the specific segment. This value is useful if you have more than one segment in that location.

IPX Network Address

Most sites using NetWare 3 will have an IPX network address in place for the existing NetWare 3 servers. If you have an IPX network address, you can continue to use the same standard in NetWare 5. The important point is to maintain unique network addresses for all your NetWare servers because duplicate addresses will obviously cause great difficulties for your network. The IPX network address must be unique for the cable segment address as well.

A sample network address may appear as the following convention:

```
ARRSSSSN
```

where:

- A = Indicates that this is an internal IPX number
- RR = Indicates a numeric value designating a state or other region
- SSSS = Indicates a location
- N = Indicates the server number such as 1 to 10

IP Addressing

One of the new features in NetWare 5 is native support for network connectivity and access in a "Pure IP" environment. This is accomplished by enabling the NetWare Core Protocol (NCP), which drives NetWare connectivity and access to be passed through the network via IP.

Implementing IP connectivity in a LAN environment can be a daunting task for most administrators. The variety of network devices using IP, such as LAN-to-host connectivity, printing, and Internet browsers, increases the complexity. Thus an addressing standard is a requirement for implementing IP on your network.

The workstations, servers, host systems, gateways, and other network devices each must have a unique IP address to communicate. The IP addresses are 32-bit numbers that are structured and represented as twelve-digit numbers organized into four three-digit decimal numbers with the following format:

```
AAA.BBB.CCC.DDD
```

The first three fields have a possible range of numbers from 0 to 255, with the fourth ranging from 1 to 254. The numbers in the IP address represent two parts: the network number and the host number. In IP terminology, *host* refers to a node on your network. The IP address class determines where in the address IP splits between the network and host numbers. There are three IP classes that deal with network and host numbers, class A, B, and C. Each class has different rules for how it assigns the network and node numbers.

Table 4.7 illustrates how the different IP address classes split the network and host numbers for IP.

TABLE 4.7

The different IP address classes split the network and node numbers for IP.

IP ADDRESS CLASS	IP ADDRESS	NETWORK	#OST
Class A	A.B.C.D	A	B.C.D
Class B	A.B.C.D	A.B	C.D
Class C	A.B.C.D	A.B.C	D

The IP address class can be determined by the value of the first digits (that is, the A digits). Class A addresses begin with 1–127. Class B addresses begin with a value from 128 through 191. Class C addresses begin with a number equal to or greater than 192. For example, the following IP address is a class C address because its first number is greater than 192:

```
195.001.001.187
```

In this example, the first three numbers form the network number:

```
195.001.001
```

The last number forms the host node number:

187

These variations of the IP addressing classes create a variety of possible configurations for the network and host numbers. Table 4.8 illustrates the range for both the network numbers and host numbers.

TABLE 4.8

The IP classes create a variety of network and node addresses.

	CLASS A	CLASS B	CLASS C
Maximum number of networks	127	16,384	2,097,152
Maximum number of computers per network	16,777,214	65,534	254
Network number part	A	A.B	A.B.C
Network number range	001–127	128.0–191.255	192.0.0–223.255.255
Node number part	B.C.D	C.D	D
Node number range	0.0.1–255.255.254	0.1.255.254	0–254
Subnet mask	255.0.0.0	255.255.0.0	255.255.255.0

Subnet Masks

If your large network is large enough to use class A or B addresses, the network may be divided into subnets. A *subnet* is a segment of a network used to divide a network into more manageable groups. When using class A and B addresses, there are typically too many addresses for networks and not enough for the nodes or computers. You can eliminate this problem by using subnets to divide the number of computers that can be placed on a network.

NOTE

IPv6 is currently in progress to address the issue of creating additional IP addresses. NetWare 5 will support both the current IPv4 and IPv6 standards.

IP Addressing Standards

Because IP addresses are unique, they must be assigned according to the type and class of your network. You should create an address standard accordingly. The basic addressing standards should include addresses for the company's backbone and major network infrastructure. A range of network addresses should be reserved for growth. You can develop standard IP addresses for departments, type of network media connecting the computers, and so on.

For workstations, as you assign node (host) numbers, it is a good idea to begin with the low end of the node number range and work up. You should reserve the number 0 and the number 255 and not use them as node assignments because they are sometimes used by TCP/IP. This means that you should start at 1 and go up to 254 when addressing all your workstations.

NOTE

Novell is providing with NetWare 5 a DHCP capability that allows workstations to be assigned an IP address dynamically from a pool of available addresses. See Chapter 10 for more information.

If you connect your network to the Internet, you must get a DARPA Internet address from the Internet Network Information Center, called InterNIC. They can be contacted at WWW.INTERNIC.COM.

With a naming standard in place, you are ready to begin the design of your NDS tree. Remember that your naming standard will make administration of your tree easier and will provide you with consistent naming across your entire organization.

Summary

We have reviewed the fundamentals of creating a naming standard for NDS, network addresses, and IP addresses. If you don't have a standard in place for these aspects of your network, now is the time create one. With a naming standard in place, you are now ready to move on to the more challenging (and exciting) aspect of designing your NDS tree.

PART II

Designing Novell Directory Services

CHAPTER 5

Novell Directory Services Tree

"He that plants trees loves others beside himself."
—Thomas Fuller (Gnomolgia 1732)

After you are familiar with NDS objects and have devised a naming standard, you are ready to design your NetWare 5 tree. This section outlines the steps involved in the design of your NDS tree and explores different design options. Once you have a design that meets your needs, you can begin the installation or upgrade to NetWare 5. Although you can always make changes to your tree later, a properly designed tree will almost never need significant changes. Modifications may be necessary at some point to meet the needs of your changing organization.

NDS Tree Design

When designing your NDS tree, the following three goals should drive the design decisions you make:

- Organize the network resources in your company for ease of access
- Provide a blueprint for a consistent rollout of NetWare 5
- Provide flexibility to the design to reflect corporate changes

Organize Network Resources

The primary objective for designing the NDS tree is to organize the network resources in your company. The NDS tree should be arranged to reflect the location and placement of the network resources in the network. The network resources should also be placed in the tree to provide easy access to both users and administrators. The goal of the NDS tree design then is not to reproduce the organization chart of the company but to represent all users and resources in a way that enables them to work efficiently and easily. Notice in Figure 5.1 how users and resources are grouped together for ease of access. Some users need access to a particular printer or server, while a larger group may need access to an e-mail server. The e-mail server can be placed higher in the tree so that all users needing that resource have easier access to it.

FIGURE 5.1

Resources and users are grouped near each other in the ACME tree. The OPS division has a NetWare 5 server dedicated for e-mail.

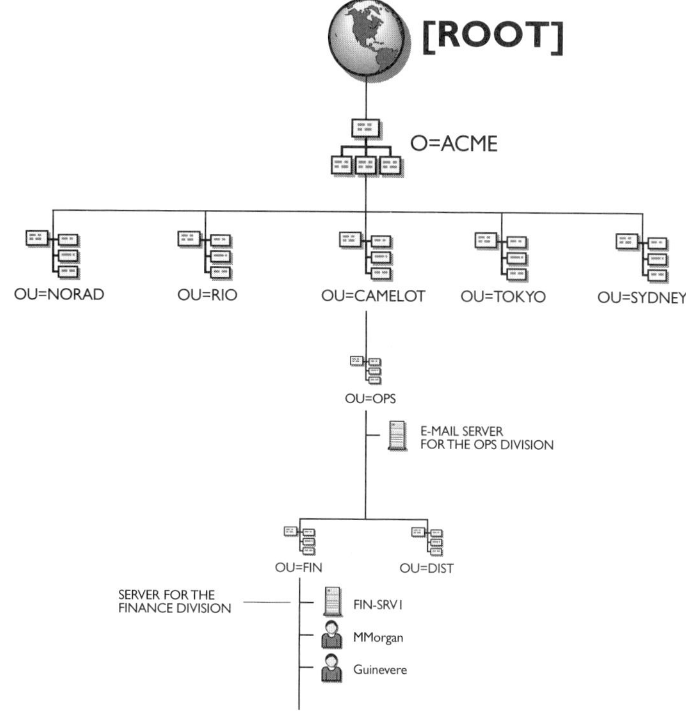

Provide a Blueprint for Consistent Rollout

Your blueprint for NDS installation includes naming standards, tree design, and upgrade strategies. With this information in hand, you will have a guide for the installation of all your NetWare 5 servers. For example, the tree design gives you the location where an NDS server should be installed. An administrator can review the naming standards and know exactly how a server should be named. During the rollout of NetWare 5, some companies may be forced to implement more than one NDS tree on the network, with the intent to merge them together in the future. Creating more than one NDS tree is much easier if the multiple trees are based on a similar NDS tree design.

In addition, your blueprint gives you a clear map of how to upgrade an entire corporation to NetWare 5. Initially, your upgrade will begin with a few servers and may eventually involve hundreds. Your design can be the master plan for upgrading all your servers to NetWare 5.

Allow for Corporate Changes

Another objective of the NDS tree design is to provide flexibility for both users and administrators. This simply means that as the corporation changes, both organizationally and physically, you will be able to facilitate those changes easily without making large modifications to your tree structure. For example, you may want a design that allows for easy moves of users and containers. This objective can be met by designing the NDS tree as described in the following sections.

These goals seem trivial, but they become very important when you are considering all the NDS design issues. One classic example that always seems to come up is that different groups or individuals in your organization will want the NDS tree designed to meet their specific needs or situation. These political issues can best be handled by referring to your design goals. For example, how does a particular design approach help you organize your network resources? In other words, if you have specific goals to fall back on, you can deal with the political issues by applying each issue against your design goals. Keep in mind that the network is installed to serve a business purpose and your job as an administrator is to see that that purpose is being met. If you design your NDS tree with this in mind, many of the political issues can be removed from this process.

Consulting Experience

Politics should not get in the way of your tree design, but sometimes it does. Not long ago an agency was in the process of designing its NetWare 5 tree. During the design process, some individuals insisted that they be represented as their own organizational units in the tree because of where they appeared organizationally in their agency. They incorrectly assumed that managerial positions or positions of authority should receive special attention in the design of the tree. As important as these individuals may be, they do not function as their own organizational units in the tree. Regardless of their titles, they are users and, thus, share resources with other individuals on the same floor or building.

NDS Tree Design Tasks

This section introduces the tasks associated with the NDS tree design. The tasks or steps provide an easy-to-understand and effective method for designing your NDS tree. The tree design consists of five steps:

1. Gather your network and company documents
2. Design your tree in the shape of a pyramid
3. Design the top level of your tree
4. Design the bottom level of your tree
5. Make modifications to the tree based on your needs

NOTE

Modifications to your tree may include any new products that you wish to add to NDS such as Novell's Z.E.N.works product. For more information on Z.E.N.works, see chapter 19. See also the section "NDS Design for Z.E.N.works" found later in this chapter.

While there is no absolute or exact way to design an NDS tree, some methods are definitely more efficient than others. Efficiency is achieved when the tree is stable, and the design provides for the least amount of NDS traffic possible.

These methods are presented in the following sections to help you design an efficient NDS tree. The methods presented here have been developed by Novell Consulting and have been successfully implemented by hundreds of their large and small customers. The design guidelines presented here work for small and large companies regardless of any unique requirements.

It is important to define what we mean by small and large companies. For the purposes of the examples given in this chapter, a small company consists of five or fewer servers (with no wide area network [WAN] connections) and fewer than 500 users. Certainly, there is no written law that this definition is always true; however, a network of this size has fewer design ramifications than a network with thousands of users and a very complicated network infrastructure.

A large network then is anything with more than five servers with a WAN connection and more than 500 users. As you read through this chapter, you will be able to determine which category (small or large) you fall into. So, let's begin the design.

Gather Corporate Documents

Some company information or documentation is necessary to help you initiate an NDS tree design for your corporation. Typically, the most difficult task in designing the NDS tree is gathering all these corporate documents. However, trying to design the tree without them is an even more difficult task. These documents are the inputs into the NDS tree design process; try to obtain as many of them as you can. Each of the documents is used during a different phase of the design process, and some documents are more important than others. The following documents are listed and discussed below in order of importance.

Wide Area Network Diagrams

The most important company document is the Wide Area Network (WAN) layout or map. The WAN map is required before starting the NDS design for your company because it is used to design the top of the NDS tree. If your company has campus networks at one or more locations, documentation of the physical campus network is also needed.

Figure 5.2 shows the ACME WAN layout map. The WAN layout or physical layout usually consists of all your major hub locations that are interconnected with routers and bridges. Notice in ACME's WAN layout map that all five main sites are shown with their router connections and the speed of these links in kilobits per second. Your WAN layout map may look similar or it may include the link speeds of your satellite offices.

Your WAN documentation may consist of more than one compact diagram. Don't worry if your documentation consists of many pages of information. The key here is to understand how your infrastructure is organized and where the major hub locations exist. These documents are necessary for the upper layer design of your tree, as we will explain. Most large companies have some sort of wide area network diagrams available. We recognize that a WAN network diagram is a document always in flux at most companies. However, try to obtain the latest WAN map from the staff that manages your network infrastructure.

FIGURE 5.2

The ACME Physical WAN layout map includes important information such as the major hub locations of its network as well as router connections and link speeds.

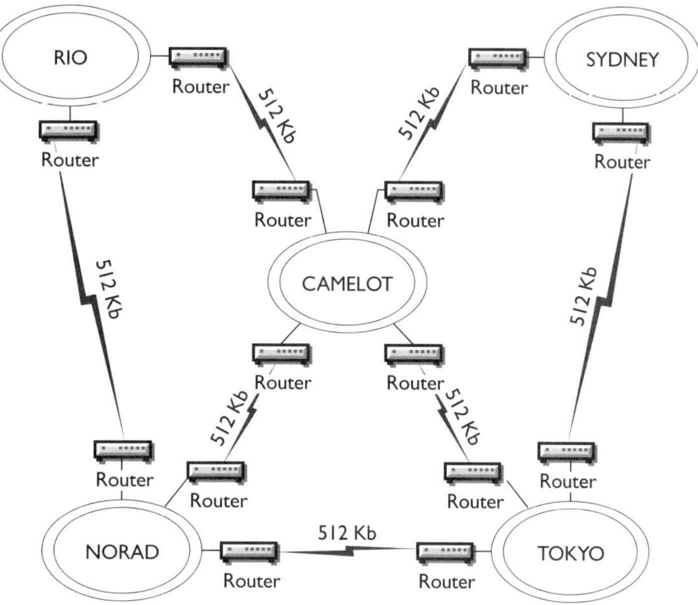

If you have a small network (no WAN, five or fewer servers, fewer than 500 users), you may not have a WAN map, but you will probably have an organizational chart. Organizational charts are discussed at the end of this section.

Campus Network Maps

Along with your WAN layout maps, campus diagrams will provide a further breakout of locations of your hub sites. This type of documentation varies from company to company. Some companies show the entire hub and campus diagrams together; others separate the information because of the size of their network. A campus network map may show you a campus, such as the NORAD campus shown in Figure 5.3.

The ACME campus map for NORAD shows information such as an FDDI ring and routers connecting this site's buildings. The campus diagram may also show buildings and their interconnections. Again, this information, along with the physical WAN map, describes your WAN/LAN infrastructure. This preliminary information is necessary to build the foundation for your NetWare 5 environment.

FIGURE 5.3

The campus diagrams show a continuation of your physical WAN diagrams. Information can include connection types between buildings, such as FDDI, bridged token rings, 10baseT, fiber, and so on.

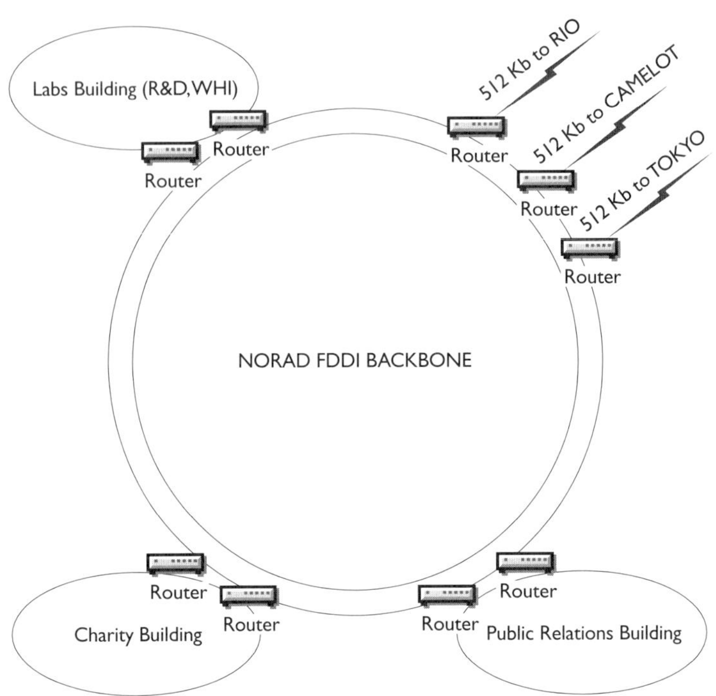

Site Lists

The next item to obtain for your tree design is a list of sites or locations of your network. Sometimes this information is included with your other documentation discussed previously. In large companies, there is usually a list of sites with their locations. For example, the ACME network has a site known as CAMELOT, which is shown as a single site on the WAN map for ACME. Further documentation, however, shows sites within the CAMELOT area, such as an operations center (OPS) located at the south end of the city and a public relations office (PR) center located in the downtown district. An office for charitable contributions (CHARITY) is also found at the downtown location. Figure 5.4 shows an example of the sites for the CAMELOT location.

Resource Lists (File Servers, Printers, and Other Resources)

A resource list may be included with your LAN maps for each site. This list gives important information about the servers and printers found in each region, site, building, or department. Table 5.1 shows the resource list for ACME with its servers, printers, and print queues. This information is later used in your tree design for the placement of these resources.

FIGURE 5.4

The CAMELOT site includes three buildings under its designation: Operations (OPS), Public Relations (PR), and CHARITY.

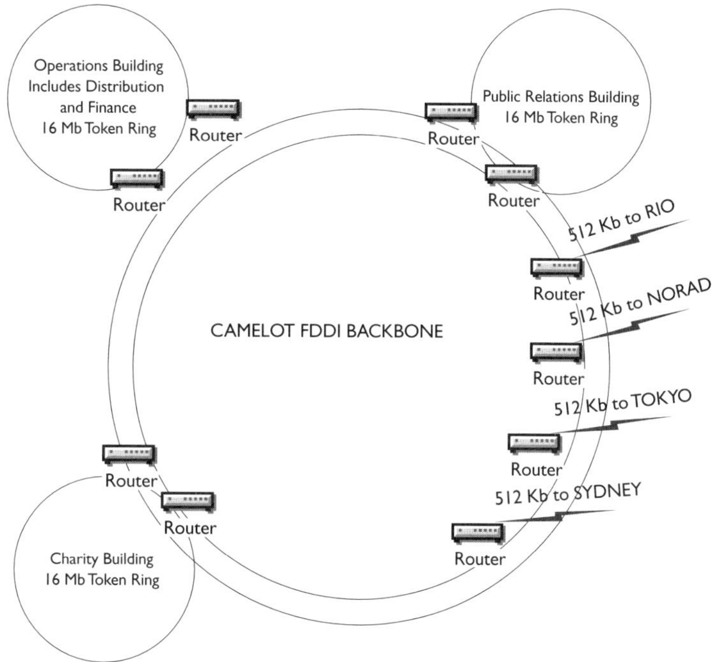

Keep in mind that the information we are referring to in this resource list will be either NetWare 3 server information or other operating systems that will be upgraded to NetWare 5. This list enables you to know beforehand where objects need to be created in the NDS tree. Notice also that some of the naming standards shown in the list can be used in your NetWare 5 environment while others may need some slight changes.

TABLE 5.1

ACME Resource List

LOC/DIV	SERVER NAME	PRINTERS/QUEUES
NORAD	NOR-SRV1	
CHARITY	NOR-CHR-SRV1	HP4SI-PQ1
		HP4SI-P1

Continued

TABLE 5.1
Continued

LOC/DIV	SERVER NAME	PRINTERS/QUEUES
LABS	LABS-SRV1	
R&D.LABS	R&D-SRV1	HP4S1-PQ1
	R&D-PS1	HP4S1-P1
POLL.R&D.LABS		HP4S1-PQ2
		HP4S1-P2
NUC.R&D.LABS		HP4S1-PQ3
		HP4S1-P3
VR.R&D.LABS		HP4S1-PQ2
		HP4S1-P2
WHI.LABS	WHI-SRV1	CANONBJ-PQ1
	WHI-SRV2	CANONBJ-P1
WHI.LABS	WHI-SRV3	
	WHI-PS1	
PR	NOR-PR-SRV1	HP4S1-PQ1
	NOR-PR-PS1	HP4S1-P1
		CANONBJ-PQ2
		CANONBJ-P2
RIO	RIO-SRV1	
CHARITY	RIO-CHR-SRV1	HP4S1-PQ1
	RIO-CHR-PS1	HP4S1-P1
ADMIN	ADMIN-SRV1	CANONBJ-PQ1
	ADMIN-SRV2	CANONBJ-P1
	ADMIN-ADM-PS1	
FAC.ADMIN	FAC-SRV1	HP4S1-PQ1
	FAC-PS1	HP4S1-P1
AUDIT.ADMIN	AUDIT-SRV1	HP4S1-PQ1
		HP4S1-P2

LOC/DIV	SERVER NAME	PRINTERS/QUEUES
MRKT.ADMIN	MRKT-SRV1	HPIII-PQ1
		HPIII-P2
PR	RIO-PR-SRV1	HP4S1-PQ1
	RIO-PR-PS1	HP4S1-P1
		CANONBJ-PQ2
		CANONBJ-P2
CAMELOT	CAM-SRV1	
CHARITY	CAM-CHR-SRV1	HP4S1-PQ1
	CAM-CHR-PS1	HP4S1-P1
OPS	OPS-SRV1	CANONBJ-PQ1
	OPS-PS1	CANONBJ-P1
FIN.OPS	FIN-SRV1	HP4SI-PQ1
	FIN-SRV2	HP4S1-PQ2
	FIN-SRV3	HP4SI-P1
	FIN-PS1	HP4S1-P2
	FIN-PS2	
DIST.OPS	DIST-SRV1	HPIII-PS1
	DIST-SRV2	HPIII-PQ1
		HPIII-P1
PR	CAM-PR-SRV1	HP4S1-PQ1
	CAM-PR-PS1	HP4S1-P1
SYDNEY	SYD-SRV1	
CHARITY	SYD-CHR-SRV1	HP4S1-PQ1
	SYD-CHR-SRV1	HP4S1-P1
	SYD-CHR-PS1	
HR	HR-SRV1	HP4S1-PQ1
	HR-SRV2	HP4S1-P1
	HR-PS1	

Continued

TABLE 5.1 *Continued*

LOC/DIV	SERVER NAME	PRINTERS/QUEUES
MEDICAL.HR	MED-SRV1	HP4SI-PQ1
	MED-SRV2	HP4S1-P1
FOOD.HR	FOOD-SRV1	HP4SI-PQ2
	FOOD-SRV2	HP4S1-P2
SHELTER.HR	SHELT-SRV1	HP4SI-PQ3
	SHELT-SRV2	HP4S1-P3
PEACE.HR	PEACE-SRV1	HPIII-PQ4
		HPIII-P4
PR	SYD-PR-SRV1	HP4S1-PQ1
	SYD-PR-PS1	HP4S1-P1
TOKYO	TOK-SRV1	
CHARITY	TOK-CHR-SRV1	HP4S1-PQ1
	TOK-CHR-SRV1	HP4S1-P1
	TOK-CHR-PS1	
CRIME	CRIMEI-SRV1	HP5-PQ1
	CRIME1-SRV2	HP5-PQ1
	CRIMEI-PS1	HP4FI-P2
BLUE.CRIME	BLUE-SRV1	HPIII-PQ1
	BLUE-PS1	HPIII-P1
VIO.BLUE.CRIME	VIO-SRV1	HP4SI-PQ2
	VIO-SRV2	HP4S1-P2
ENV.BLUE.CRIME	ENV-SRV1	HP4S1-PQ3
		HP4S1-P3
THEFT.BLUE.CRIME	THEFT-SRV1	HP4SI-PQ4
		HP4SI-P4
WHITE.CRIME	WHITE-SRV1	CANONBJ-PQ1
	WHITE-SRV2	CANONBJ-P1
	WHITE-PS1	

LOC/DIV	SERVER NAME	PRINTERS/QUEUES
CYBER.WHITE.CRIME	CYBER-SRV1	HPIII-PQ2
		HPIII-P1
POL.WHITE.CRIME	POL-SRV1	HP4SI-PQ3
		HP4SI-P3
FIN.WHITE.CRIME	CRIMEI-FIN-SRV1	HP4SI-PQ4
		HP4SI-P4
		HP4SI-P5
PR	TOK-PR-SRV1	HP4S1-PQ1
	TOK-PR-PS1	HP4S1-P1

Company Organizational Chart

The organizational chart is also an important document. It is the last piece of information that is helpful in designing your tree. Your company may have many pages of organizational charts or a single chart. Your main purpose in obtaining the organization chart is to determine what divisions, departments, or other groups need to be created at the bottom layer of your tree. Figure 5.5 shows ACME's organizational structure. It is the input from this structure that will determine the lower layers of the NDS trees.

FIGURE 5.5

The organizational structure for ACME provides information about departments, divisions, and workgroups that may need to be represented in your NDS tree structure.

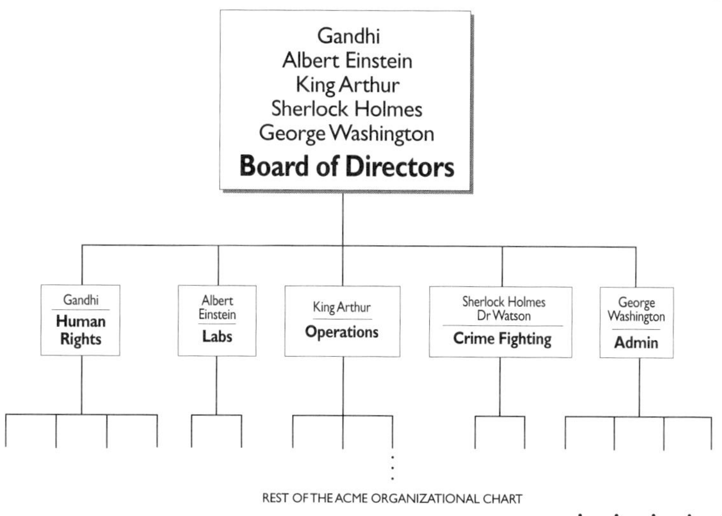

As you will see, the organizational chart is used only during the design of the bottom of the tree. After you have gathered the corporate documents, you are ready to start the planning of the NDS tree.

Design Tree in the Shape of a Pyramid

The design of the NDS tree should take the shape of a pyramid or inverted tree. The pyramid design implies that you place most of the containers and objects at the bottom of the structure with fewer containers at the top. The pyramid design shape of the tree is logically split into two sections. First you will design the top of the tree, with its appropriate containers, and then you will design the bottom of the tree. Figure 5.6 illustrates how the pyramid design is split into the top and bottom sections of the tree.

FIGURE 5.6

The NDS tree should be designed like a pyramid with a top and bottom portion of the tree.

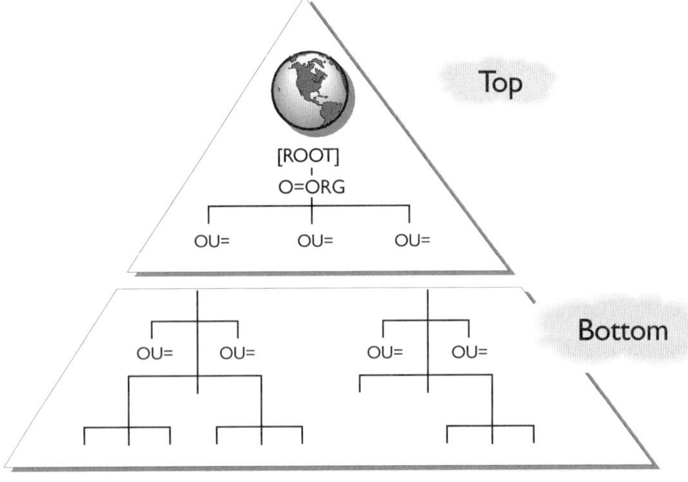

The advantage of a pyramid-shaped tree layout is that the top layers become the foundation (or static layers) upon which the bottom layers can be established. The bottom layers of the tree will be more dynamic, allowing for greater flexibility to change when your company changes. This design approach enables you to more easily make changes, such as moving users or subtrees.

Another advantage of the pyramid tree design is that the partitioning of the NDS database is more natural. The alternative to the pyramid design is to create a flat tree layout or structure that places all the objects in the top layers of the tree. As shown in Figure 5.7, a very flat and wide tree is not an efficient design approach because of how NDS communicates with its subordinate levels.

FIGURE 5.7

A very flat and wide tree is not as efficient as designing an NDS tree with the pyramid shape. The design in this figure is not recommended because it shows 150 locations at one level.

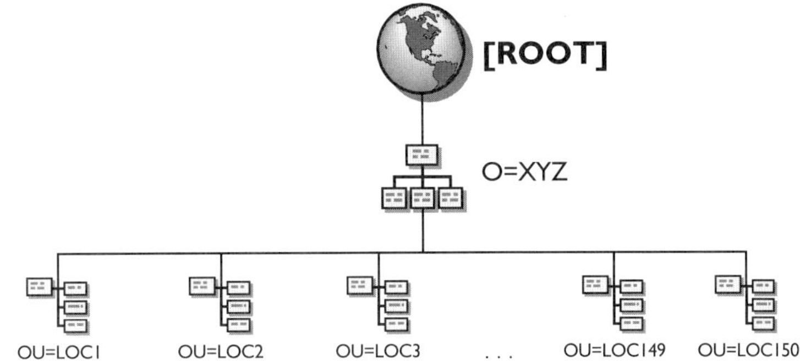

An efficient NDS tree will have more organizational units at the bottom and less at the top. Our recommendation is to have only 10 to 15 OUs per level in the tree. Even the largest companies with many branch offices will usually meet this requirement as explained later in this chapter.

Having all the objects in the top of the tree also makes the tree rigid and inefficient for most large companies. A flat tree is not recommended primarily because of the way it has to be partitioned and replicated. Synchronization traffic of NDS on all servers in the tree is increased considerably with this type of approach. The tree partition and replica layout becomes extremely flat, which could cause many subordinate reference replicas to be created. Subordinate references are pointers between partitions and subordinate partitions and are automatically created by NDS. For more information about subordinate reference replicas, refer to the "NDS Partitions and Replicas" section later in this chapter.

As seen in Figure 5.8, the tree begins with the [ROOT] object at the top followed by the O=Organization object. After the O=Organization object(s), the next level is a layer of OU=Organization Unit(s). Typically, only a selected set of users and network resources is located in the top layers of the tree. For example, the ADMIN user object is located in the O=Organization object because the installation program automatically creates it.

FIGURE 5.8

The top of the tree includes the [ROOT] object, O=Organization, and the first layer of OUs. The first layer of OUs should be based on the network infrastructure.

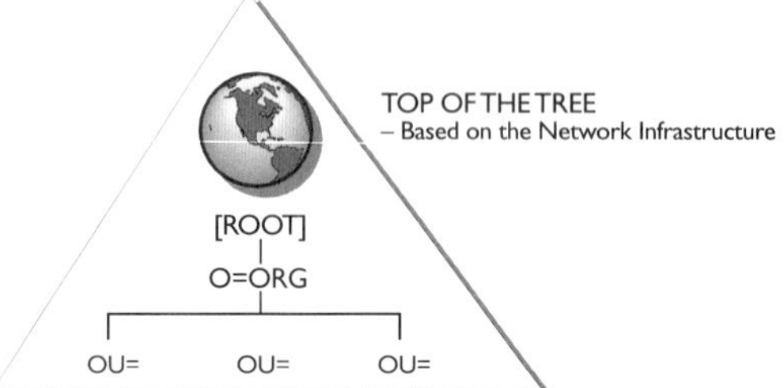

The bottom of the tree is defined by the local area network (LAN) and is based on the actual organization of your company from a departmental or divisional standpoint. In Figure 5.9, the bottom layers in the tree are most flexible if they represent the organizational structure of your company. This can be accomplished by using the divisions, departments, and workgroups in the corporation. The bottom layer OUs will hold the majority of your leaf objects such as the users, file servers, printers, queues, and other network resources. This approach provides the greatest flexibility because when you make changes to a department you will only affect the container(s) of that department. The rest of the tree is left unchanged. In contrast, if you have organizations represented at the top of your tree, and you make changes to an organization, these changes can possibly affect containers that are subordinate to the container you initially changed.

FIGURE 5.9

The bottom of the tree is based on the organization of the company. These lower layers offer flexibility to the tree design for moves and other changes.

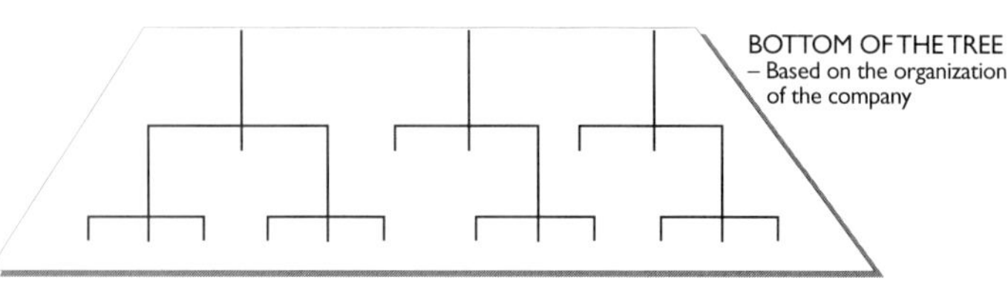

Both the top and the bottom of the tree are illustrated in Figure 5.10 and will be discussed in the following sections in greater detail.

FIGURE 5.10

The top of the NDS tree is based on the WAN or locations of your company and becomes the static portion of the tree. The bottom of the tree is based on the LAN and organization of your company and gives you the flexibility to make moves and other changes.

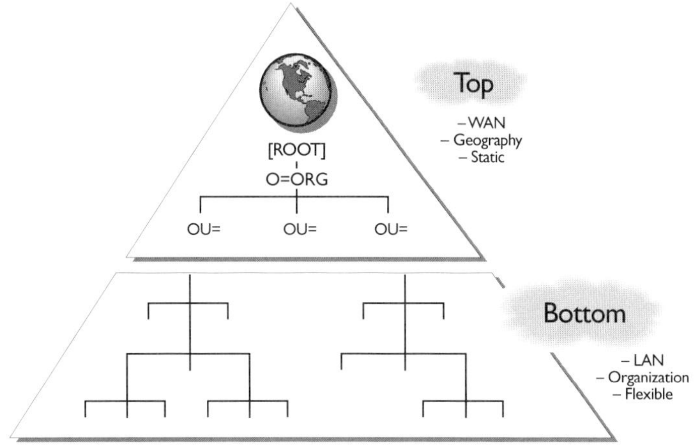

Design Top Level of the Tree

The design of the top of the NDS tree is the most important because it is the foundation of the NDS tree. The rest of the tree will branch downward from the top. As we mentioned earlier in this chapter, the top level of the tree includes the tree name, which is the [ROOT] object, the O=Organization object, and the first layer of OU=Organization Units which, for most companies, will be based on your WAN infrastructure and locations. Figure 5.11 illustrates how we are taking the information from the WAN diagrams and designing the upper layer of the tree.

As shown in Figure 5.12, a guideline for the maximum number of containers at each level is 50. Although this number is not a strict rule, we have found that most companies can maintain greater efficiency for NDS synchronization if they stay at or below this range. For companies with many branch offices exceeding this value, try to insert a level of regional organizational units one level above to distribute the load of branch offices under these regional containers.

Most companies will be able to work within this guideline. However, for exceptionally large companies with thousands of branch offices, you may have no choice but to exceed this recommendation. If you must, pay special attention to partitioning and replication guidelines as presented in Chapter 6, "Designing and Using NDS Partitions and Replicas."

FIGURE 5.11

For the upper layer of the tree, match the major hub locations of your network to the first level of organizational units in your tree.

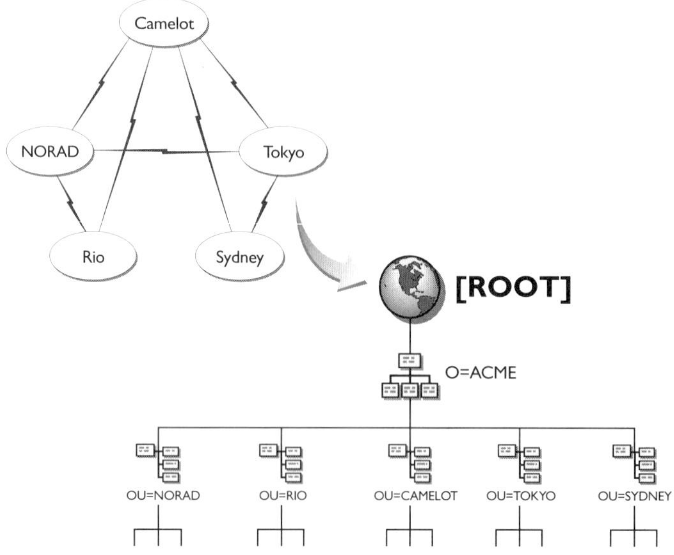

FIGURE 5.12

The appropriate number of subordinate containers is 10 to 15 at each level in the tree. Beyond this number you should consider adding another level in your tree to distribute your containers.

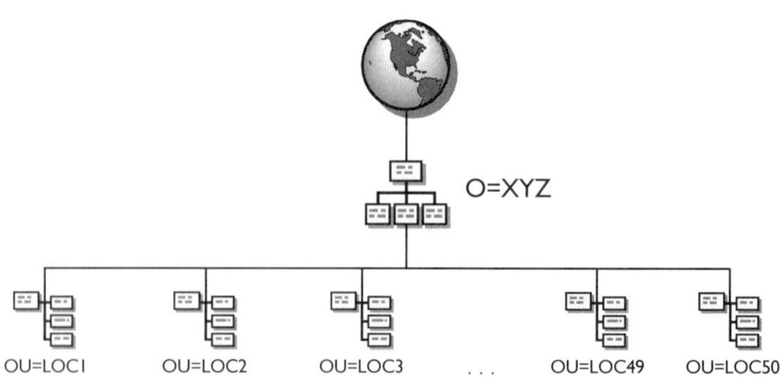

For synchronization efficiency do not exceed 10 to15 containers at each level in the tree.

Tree Name or [ROOT] Object

The first entity that needs to be named in NDS is the tree itself. The tree name is also the name of the [ROOT] object, which is placed as the top-most object in your tree. The NDS tree name is displayed in many of the current NetWare utilities such as MONITOR and INSTALL. The tree name you choose can represent the company name plus _TREE. For example, our company is called ACME, so we chose to name the tree ACME_TREE, as shown in Figure 5.13.

FIGURE 5.13

Another name for the [ROOT] object is ACME_TREE.

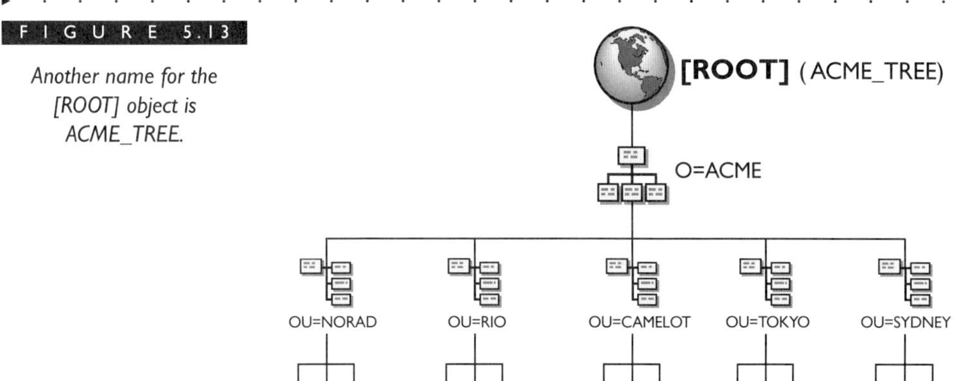

The name of the tree should be a unique value on the network wire because the tree uses SAP to broadcast to the client or workstations where the tree can be found. SAP bootstraps clients and all applications requiring NDS to find the NDS database very efficiently. If you need to install more than one physical NDS tree, make sure that the trees have different names. An example of this important point is illustrated in Figure 5.14.

The company name plus _TREE is recommended because it clearly identifies the tree SAP as an NDS tree when you DISPLAY SERVERS at a console. Be careful not to make this name too long. Also, the SAP does not support spaces in the name, which is advertised via SAP, and the NetWare 5 installation utility (NWCONFIG) will not let you place spaces in the tree name.

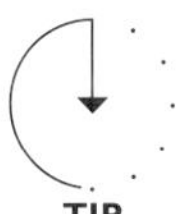

The NDS tree always starts with the [ROOT] container object. In most discussions, however, the [ROOT] object is not counted as a layer in the tree.

The object class definition in the schema that defines the [ROOT] is the object class TOP. The [ROOT] object is the only instance of the object class TOP and for this reason TOP is known as an effective class.

FIGURE 5.14

You may have multiple trees on your network. Each NDS tree must have a unique name such as ACME_TREE1 on Server1 and ACME_TREE2 on Server2.

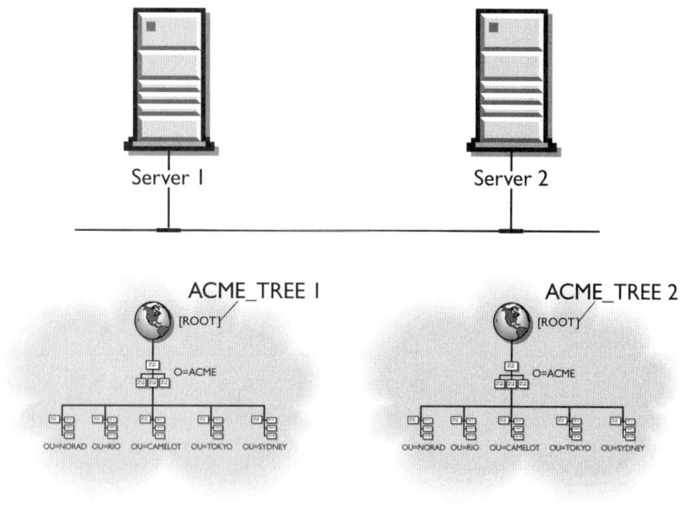

The [ROOT] object is parent to either the C=Country and/or O=Organization. Novell Consulting recommends that you use the O=Organization below [ROOT] rather than the C=Country object.

To Use or Not to Use Country Objects

The C=Country designator is used to specify a particular country code based on the X.500 standard. Public network providers, such as NetWare Connect Services (NCS) being offered with the cooperation of Novell, will make use of the Country object in their trees. The question often asked is, "If a company wants to connect to a public service provider, is it required to use the C=Country code in the NDS tree?" Most companies are not required to use the country object for their corporate trees. Instead, they can create a separate tree used for connecting to the public data network or through a 32-bit client that can connect to multiple trees.

If you choose to use the Country object, keep in mind that it will add an additional layer to your NDS tree and it will also create some rather odd distinguished names for your objects. Consider the example in Figure 5.15. If we were to add the Country object to the ACME tree, which country do we choose? Do we use multiple country codes? For our example, ACME is headquartered primarily in CAMELOT; therefore, our Country object will be C=UK for England in this example.

FIGURE 5.15

The use of the Country object can create some odd contexts in your tree.

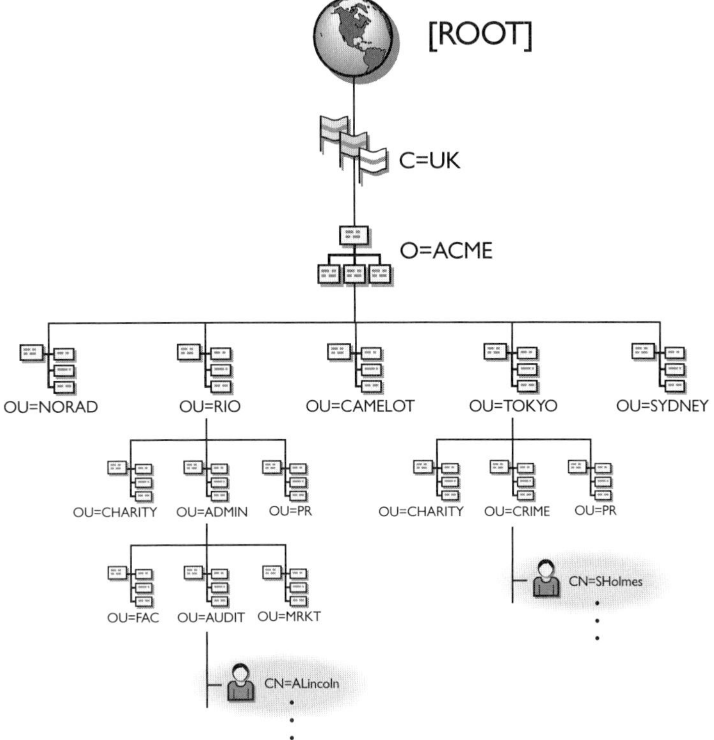

Let's look at some of the user's contexts that would be created in other locations if we used only the C-UK COUNTRY designator. Abe Lincoln resides in the RIO location and so his context would be as follows:

```
CN=ALINCOLN.OU=AUDIT.OU=ADMIN.OU=RIO.O=ACME.C=UK
```

User Sherlock Holmes in the TOKYO location would have the following context:

```
CN=SHOLMES.OU=CRIME.OU=TOKYO.O=ACME.C=UK
```

Now, if your names are supposed to adequately describe and identify a user's location in the tree, these examples are a little confusing and add more length to the context. Also, for some users who work in both the UK and the United States, it is difficult, if not impossible, to determine where in the tree they belong.

If you have already implemented the Country object in your tree, not to worry. It does not cause any serious consequences, but keep in mind the considerations just discussed.

Organization Names

After the [ROOT] object at the top, you will provide the NDS tree with at least one O=Organization. At least one O=Organization object is required for all NDS trees. The subsequent layers in the tree (the OUs) will be placed directly below the O=Organization.

We recommend that you name the O=Organization the same name as your company or use an abbreviation. Most companies use an abbreviation for the company name because it is easier when you are typing an object's context. For example, our company is named A Cure for Mother Earth, which is abbreviated to ACME. In almost every case, the Organization layer in the tree contains only one O=Organization, which gives you a single object to represent the entire company. Figure 5.16 shows how we have named our organization to represent our company name ACME.

FIGURE 5.16

ACME is representative of our entire company and is used as our organization name in our NDS tree.

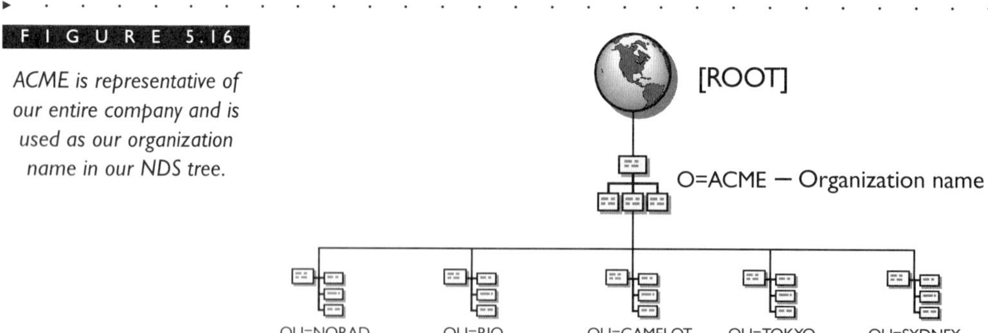

Your company may want to use more than one O=Organization if your corporation has multiple companies that do not share the same network infrastructure. For example, the large conglomerate shown in Figure 5.17 uses multiple O=Organization objects because there are two separate companies (separate network infrastructures) included in a single NDS tree.

FIGURE 5.17

A large conglomerate company with multiple O=Organization objects

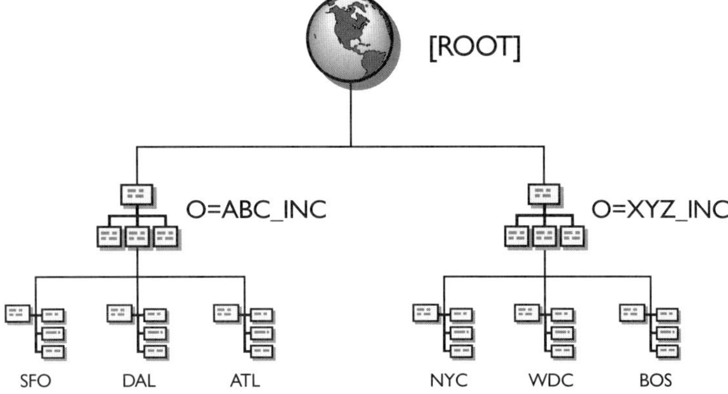

Consulting Experience

We recommend that you not name the O=Organization the same name that you used for the NDS tree. For troubleshooting purposes, the NDS tree should be named with the company name plus _TREE, and the O=Organization should be named with just the company name or an abbreviated company name. The ACME corporation would therefore be named O=ACME, with a tree name ACME_TREE.

Small Companies

In some cases the tree design can be finished very easily for small companies at this point because most servers, users, and other resources can be placed in the Organization container without creating any more containers. If you are the network manager responsible for all users, printers, and servers, you can simply group everyone in the same container, which can be the Organization container.

Figure 5.18 shows how a tree design can be very simple for a small company. If ACME had only a few servers in a single location, its tree could appear as shown in the figure. You may still want to subdivide the tree a little more if you have separate groups.

FIGURE 5.18

Small companies can group all their resources in the organization container if they have only a single network administrator managing all resources.

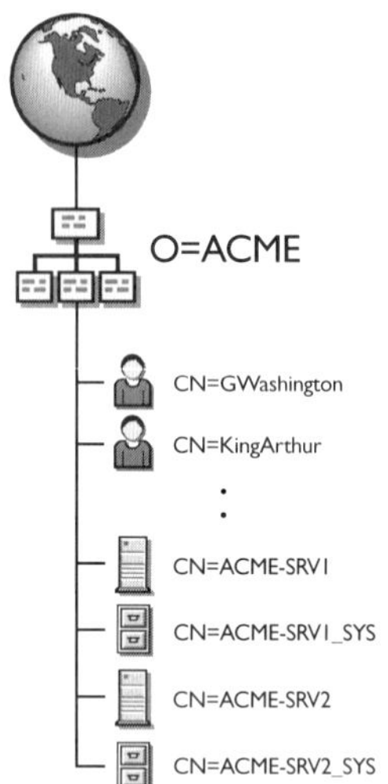

Consulting Experience

A single NDS tree with two or more O=Organization objects is rarely used and is not usually recommended. This configuration is not often used because one of the design goals is to represent the entire corporation in the single tree with the same organization name. NDS will operate either way without difficulty, however.

Geographic Design

As mentioned previously, the layer below the O=Organization is the first layer of OU=Organizational Units in the NDS tree. This layer of OUs is the most important layer of the NDS tree because it represents the geographical locations of your company. You can use your company WAN maps or WAN documentation to carefully design the contents of this layer, which becomes the foundation for the entire tree. This method is often referred to as the geographical design approach because you use your company's geographic or location information for the design at the top of the tree.

The key to designing the top of the tree is to match the WAN infrastructure or locations of your company with the first OU layers or containers. Based on our experience at many sites, the design of the top of the tree should be completely based on the WAN infrastructure. You will have a successful NDS tree design if you follow the guideline of representing the sites of your company with the top-most OUs. Figure 5.19 and Figure 5.20 illustrate how the top layer of the ACME tree is designed based on the physical WAN layout of the company.

FIGURE 5.19

Physical WAN layout for ACME

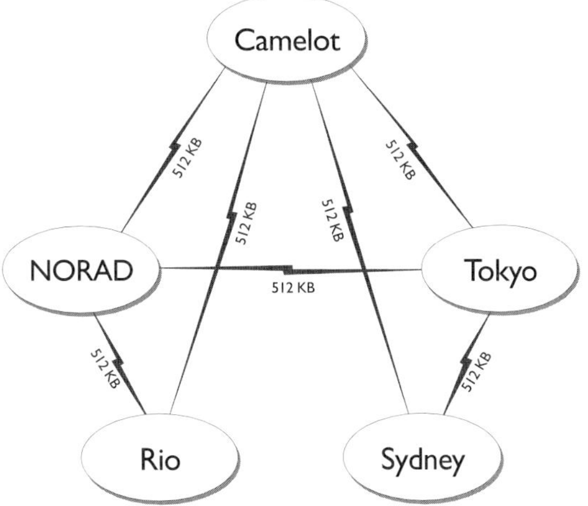

FIGURE 5.20

Top layer of the tree design for ACME, which is based on the physical or geographical WAN sites

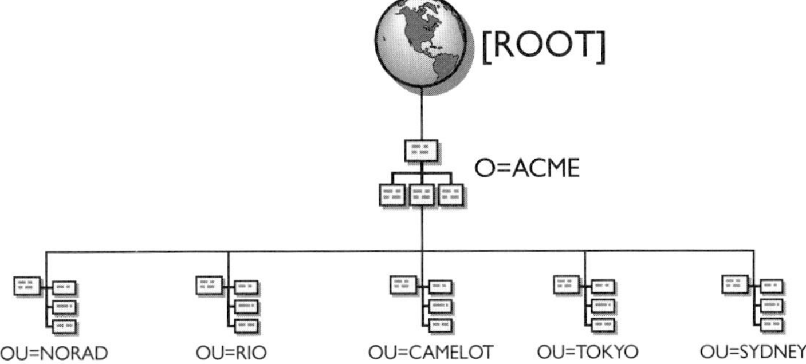

If you are a small company (no WAN, 5 servers or fewer, fewer than 500 users), you can simply use the first Organization container you created to name your company. This container will hold all your objects including printers, servers, and users. Administration of a single container is very easy and requires very little maintenance. You can also create a container beneath the Organization container and place the resources there.

In general, if your company has multiple geographic sites or locations, you should represent the locations in the NDS tree at the top of your tree. The organizational structure of departments, divisions, and workgroups will be placed under each of these locations. Keep in mind that one of our design goals is to design a flexible tree in which changes are easily made. As you might expect, there are a few exceptions to the practice of designing geographically:

- Companies with a single site or campus-connected network are not dependent upon the geographic design approach. Since this configuration does not have physical locations that can be placed under or created as OUs, you will skip the geographical design approach at the top of the tree and proceed directly to the departmental design approach. Some companies with few servers and users may not need to create additional containers. Rather, they can place all the NDS objects under the single O=Organization.

- For companies with WAN sites or locations connected with very high speed links, such as T-3 or greater, the location OUs are less important because the limitation of the WAN has been removed. This is because WAN speeds are approaching LAN speeds. For the purpose of NDS tree design, the high-speed WAN connections really represent LAN bandwidths. However, we still recommend that you use the geographic design approach. See the section "Design the Bottom Level of the Tree" later in this chapter.

When considering a campus network layout, such as a research park or university, consider first the speed of the links between the buildings or floors of the campus network. The locations in the campus network, such as buildings, could be used to represent minor sites in the network infrastructure and in the NDS tree. The buildings in the campus network can be useful container objects if they help organize your network resources and the NDS tree. The ability to effectively organize network resources is one of your design goals. The ACME tree

NORAD location as shown in Figure 5.21 has used buildings named by function as its organizational units. Either design approach is acceptable. You must determine which one provides the best description of your environment.

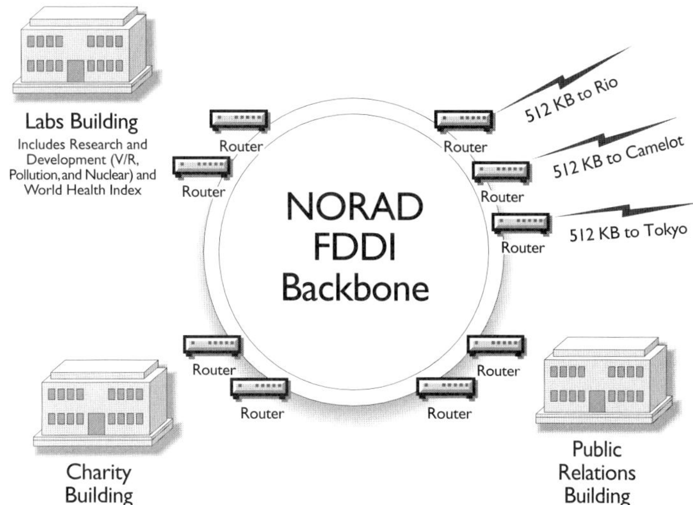

FIGURE 5.21

The ACME NORAD organization units are named based on their functions, which are also the building names, such as OU=CHARITY, OU=LABS, and OU=PR.

If your company does not have a WAN infrastructure but only a LAN network, then you can skip the geographical design approach and go directly to the departmental design discussed later in this section.

Consulting Experience

Many companies still choose to use geographic containers even though they have very high speed WAN links. One company, for example, has a metropolitan area network (MAN) running FDDI to connect 12 buildings together across a city. The basis for the company's decision to use geographic sites at the top of the tree was twofold. First, for administrative purposes, the company wanted a single administrator to support each site. The sites gave the tree a good place to break out security administration. Second, the company was installing an e-mail application on its servers at each geographic location. So, even though the company has high-speed links, it still chose to design geographically.

Regional Layers

In some cases, it will be necessary to place regional containers directly below the O=Organization in the NDS tree to more fully distribute the total number of locations or geographical sites. Placing regional OUs under the O=Organization, but before the actual location OUs, will increase NDS operating efficiency and give the tree a closer pyramid shape.

As an example, consider the company ACME as we change the WAN layout to include more offices or cities around the world. We are changing ACME's WAN infrastructure only for this example. Figure 5.22 illustrates the offices or cities that are connected together via 56K links. Each of the cities added to the WAN layout is connected to its appropriate regional hub. Using the WAN infrastructure, we have designed a new tree, which includes regional OUs named North America (NA), South America (SA), Europe (EUR), Asia (ASIA), and Australia (AUST). These regional OUs group the appropriate cities and help keep the NDS tree design closer to a pyramid shape. See Figure 5.23 for the new ACME tree based on regional containers. Notice how the physical WAN layout in Figure 5.22 is driving the tree design in Figure 5.23.

FIGURE 5.22

Example of ACME with regions and cities. This is typically called a "hub and spoke" WAN infrastructure.

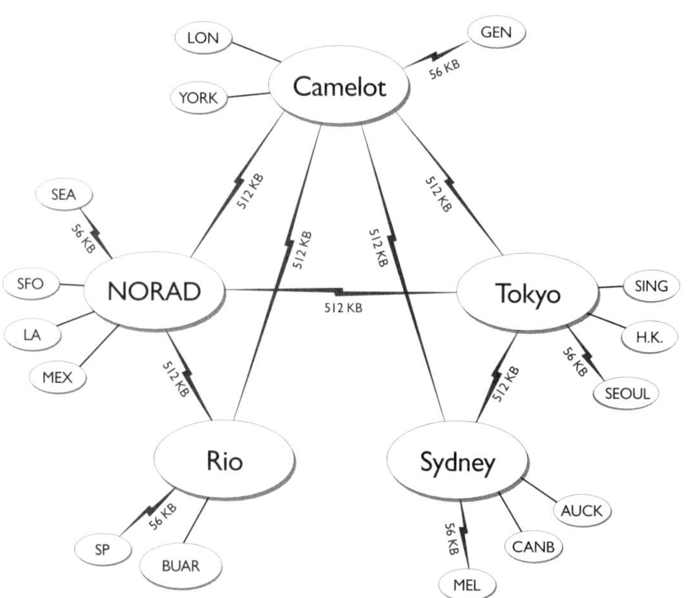

FIGURE 5.23

Example of ACME tree with the regions and cities as the top layers

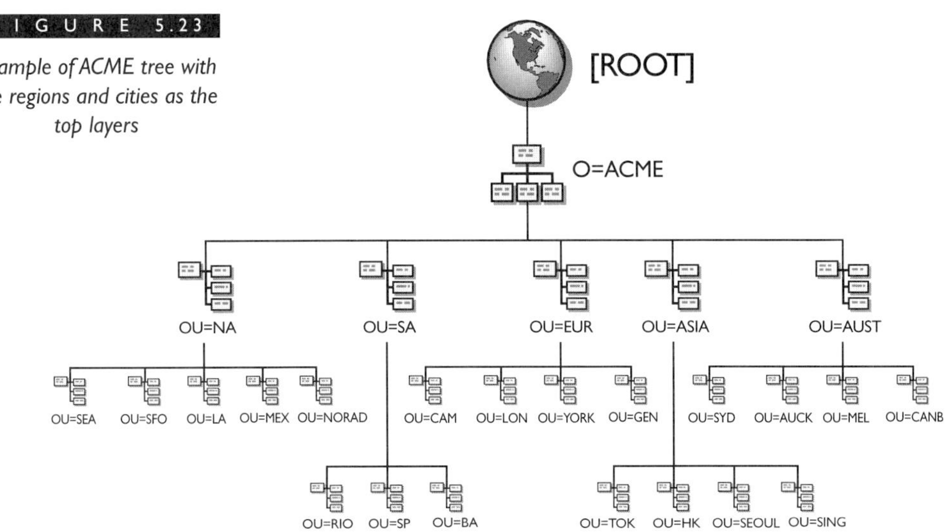

If your network uses a WAN infrastructure with a number of physical sites or offices, you may want to create regional containers based on those WAN sites at the top layer, which will help distribute the individual offices. Having the regional OUs helps the NDS tree operate more efficiently during all phases of operation.

Departmental Design Not Based on Your WAN

The departmental design approach can be used most efficiently at the top of the tree only if your company does not have a WAN infrastructure or other locations to consider. If your company has only a LAN-based network, you can skip the design of the top layers and go directly to the bottom layer design, which is based solely on the organization of the company.

If you have WAN links, you may consider designing your NDS tree by placing the departments, divisions, and workgroups at the top of the tree and placing the physical locations at the bottom. This method is often called the departmental design approach and is not recommended for a company with a WAN infrastructure. Having the organizations placed at the top of the tree is a less efficient tree design because any change to the top organizations will ripple down the entire structure, including the site locations below.

Consider the example in Figure 5.24 in which we have designed the top of the tree organizationally with locations at the bottom. The first question you need to ask is, "Where do most network changes occur?" Most changes will occur in your organization. That's not to say that changes don't occur in geographic sites as well, but they are less frequent. Therefore, when you make changes to the tree, you want to impact as few people as possible. This is the third design goal of building flexibility into the tree design. In terms of other design elements, such as administration, partitions, replicas, network resource placement, login scripts, and bindery services, it is apparent that the organization layers at the bottom of the NDS tree more adequately address these factors.

FIGURE 5.24

The ACME tree with organizations at the top and geographic sites on the bottom is a less flexible way to design a tree in a network with WAN links and multiple locations. This is not a good tree design.

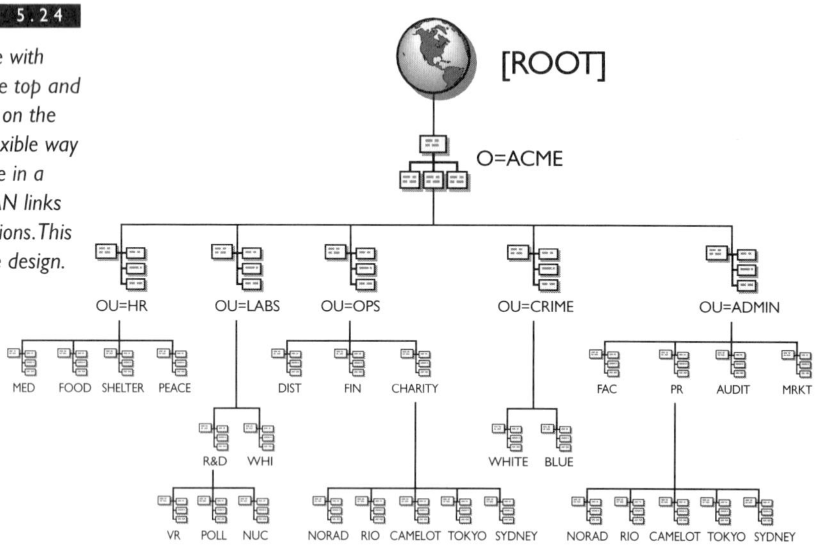

Design Bottom Levels of the Tree

You should design the bottom levels of the NDS tree along the organizational lines of your company by using your company's organizational charts or similar documents. The bottom layers of the tree are made up of OU containers, which are based on the divisions, departments, workgroups, and teams under each of the various locations defined at the top of the tree. Figure 5.25 shows the ACME organization chart that we will use in our tree.

FIGURE 5.25

The ACME organization chart used in our NDS tree

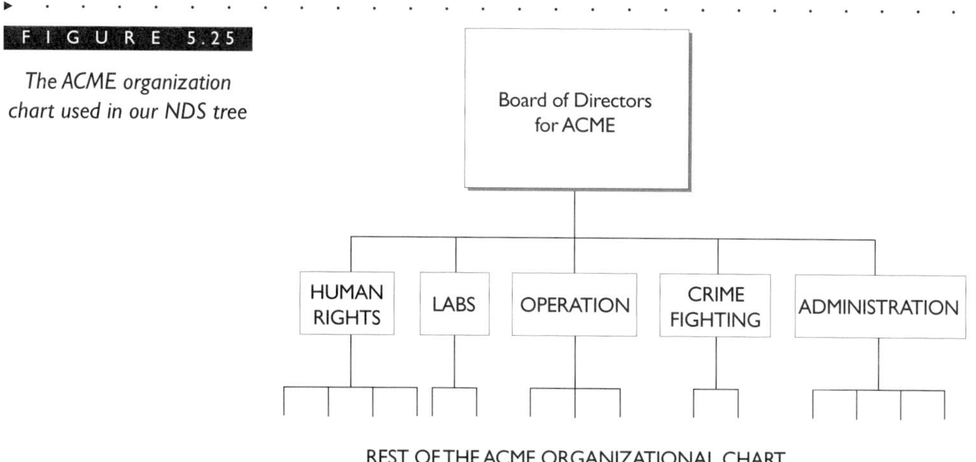

The bottom layers of the tree should represent the network resources located in the LAN network of the location or site. Since the LAN supports a greater bandwidth or throughput of information than the WAN, the design of the bottom layers is extremely flexible. You, as the designer and administrator, can shape the bottom of the tree to meet your specific needs.

We recommend that you design the bottom of the tree based on the organizational chart documents because the users and administrators are already familiar with that type of layout. Remember that the bottom section is flexible if it is designed around organizations. You will discover through experience that a tree designed with the organizations at the bottom of the tree can more easily adapt to the changing requirements of the corporation. Figure 5.26 shows the bottom layers of the ACME tree based on the organizational charts for each ACME site.

During the design of the bottom of the NDS tree, ensure that there is a place for every user and network resource currently in your company. Remember that the primary goal in designing the NDS tree is to organize the network resources, including the users. If you do not have a place for all the users or network resources then you need to adjust your tree design. The bottom layers are typically the only ones affected. Refer back to Table 5.1 for the ACME resource list. This list has information on servers and printers and provides you with helpful information for placing resources in your tree.

FIGURE 5.26

The ACME tree with the bottom layers of OUs based on the organizational charts of the company

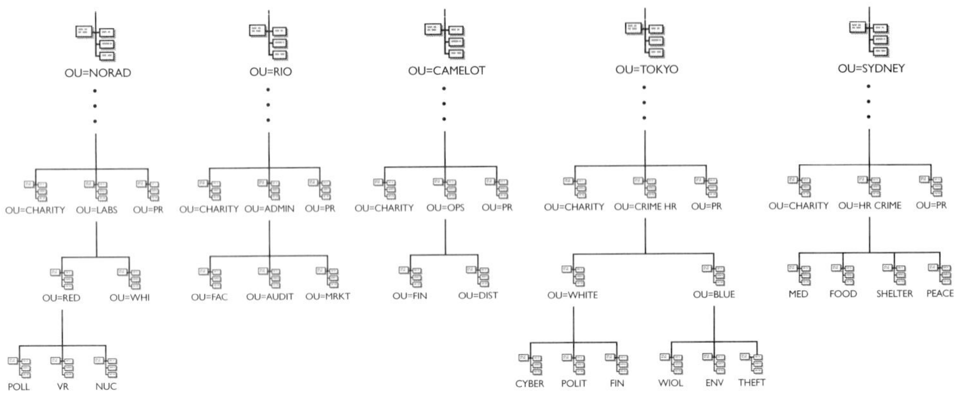

As mentioned earlier, the bottom containers or OUs in the tree are typically the divisions, departments, workgroups, and teams of your company. Do not include as containers any individuals that appear as division or department heads in your company's organizational charts. You simply want to identify the functional groups or departments; the individuals become the users in each container.

The ACME Tree Design

Notice in Figure 5.27 that the top layers of the ACME tree are based solely on the WAN infrastructure and will remain fairly stable or constant. Once the WAN infrastructure for ACME is considered in the design, the design effort shifts to the bottom of the tree. The bottom of the tree is based on the organizational chart for ACME. Most of the network resources will be placed in the bottom of the tree. Figure 5.27 illustrates a clear division between the top and bottom of the tree design phases in which the top is based on locations in the WAN and the bottom is based on the company's organizational information after crossing into the LAN infrastructure.

FIGURE 5.27

The ACME tree has been designed and consists of two phases: the top and bottom of the tree.

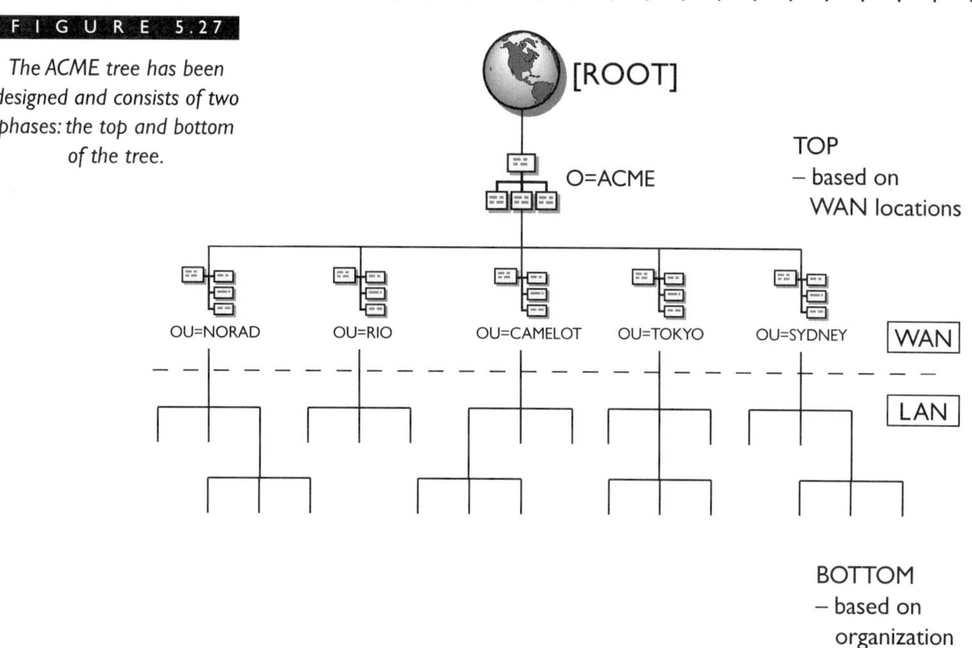

Placement of Network Resources

The placement of the network resources, such as servers or printers, in the tree can affect how you design the bottom layers. As you decide where to place the physical network resources in the tree, you should consider the needs of the users who will share these resources. If the network resources are organized according to divisions, departments, and workgroups, they should be placed in the same container with the users. However, if the network resources offer services to multiple departments in one site or location, you should place the resources in the location OU.

The placement of the network resources is an important design consideration for the bottom of the tree because the appropriate containers need to exist to place resources. If the OUs or containers do not exist, they will need to be created. Remember that one of the primary goals for designing the NDS tree is to organize your network resources.

With your resource list in hand, you can place your resources in their appropriate locations in the NDS tree. In the rest of this section, we display illustrations of the ACME tree's five main sites. Included with each of these illustrations are some examples of how objects can be used in the ACME tree for the greatest impact and efficiency. Figure 5.28 shows the NORAD subtree with its resources.

FIGURE 5.28

ACME NORAD Site

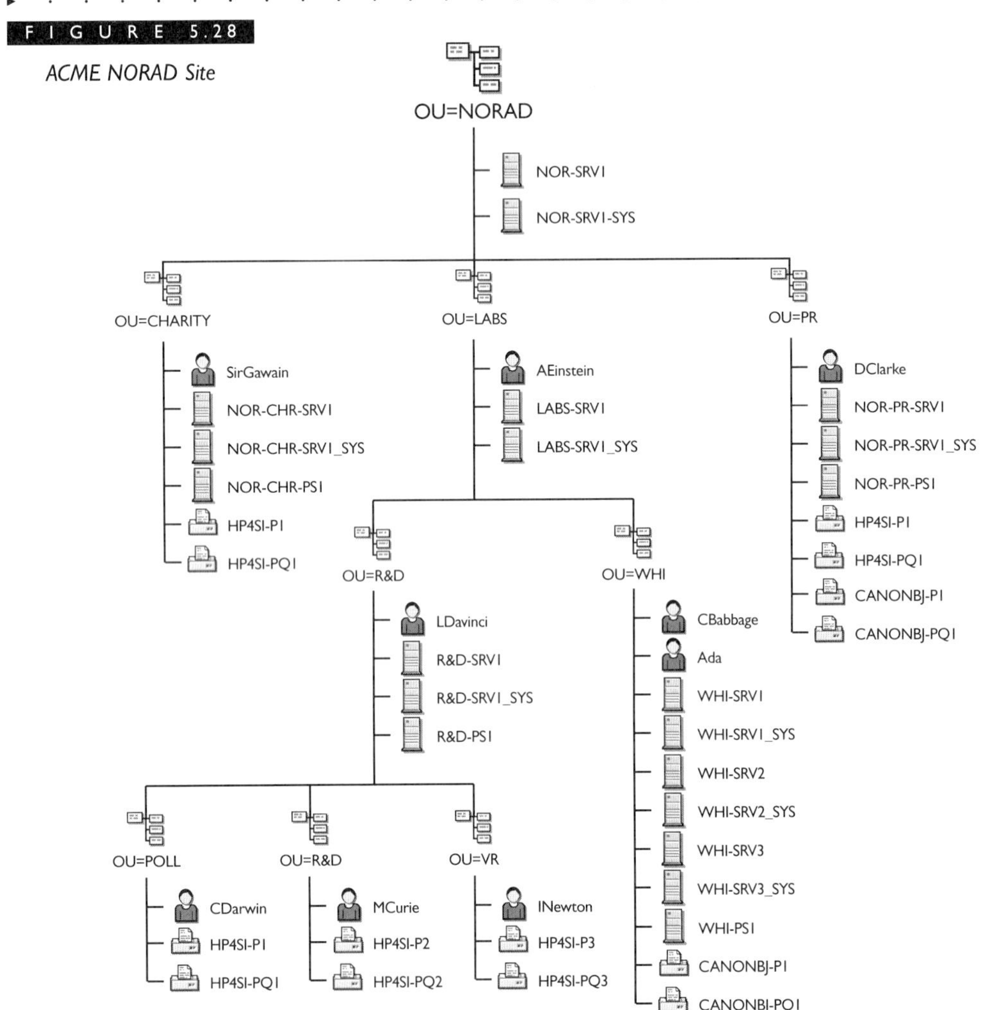

At the NORAD site, as well as all other sites, we have placed a central server at the top OU=NORAD. This server will hold the master replica of the NORAD partition and can also function as an e-mail server for this location. The same process is repeated at all five sites.

Notice that the naming standards follow a very simple pattern based on our naming standards document. Servers are always defined by unique names across the entire tree because of the SAP requirement. Printers and print queues, however, can have the same name as long as they reside in different containers, such as HP4SI-P1, found in both OU=CHARITY and OU=POLL containers.

In Figure 5.29, the RIO location shows the placement of resources in each of the departments. It is not necessary to place all users in your tree using drawings such as these. We have included a user in each location as an example. The primary purpose in placing objects in this fashion is to determine their general placement in the tree. This will give you a better understanding of organizations and their resources.

In addition to creating user and server objects, you will want to create some other objects as well. For the RIO location, as well as all major locations, you should consider creating an organizational role object as the site administrator. Grant supervisor rights at the site location, such as RIO, to the organizational role object. For example, create a role called ADMIN_RIO. You can then move a user or two in as occupants of the role. If you have multiple administrators managing organizations at the same site, you may want to create separate roles for each department.

Since CAMELOT is basically the center of activity for the ACME tree, you may want to maintain control over the ADMIN user object from this location. Change the password frequently and limit the number of users who know the password. An example of the CAMELOT site is shown in Figure 5.30.

You can also use directory map objects to simplify the administration of your users. For example, the SYDNEY office uses directory maps in all their container login scripts. As versions of their specialized software change, the SYDNEY site administrator changes only the pointer of the directory map object to the new software version. This automatically enables all users in SYDNEY to see the new version of software because all container login scripts use the same directory map. An example of this site is shown in Figure 5.31.

FIGURE 5.29

ACME RIO Site

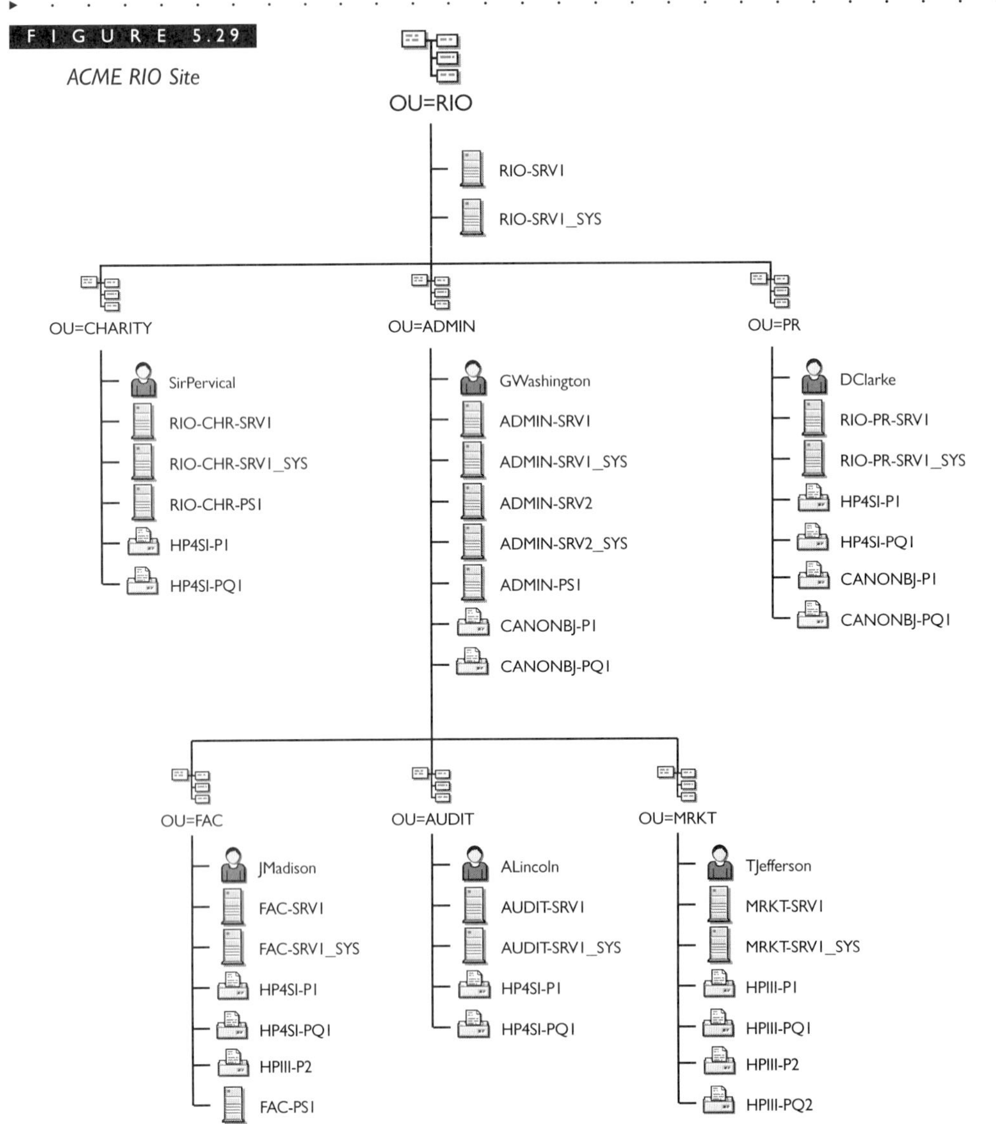

FIGURE 5.30

ACME CAMELOT Site

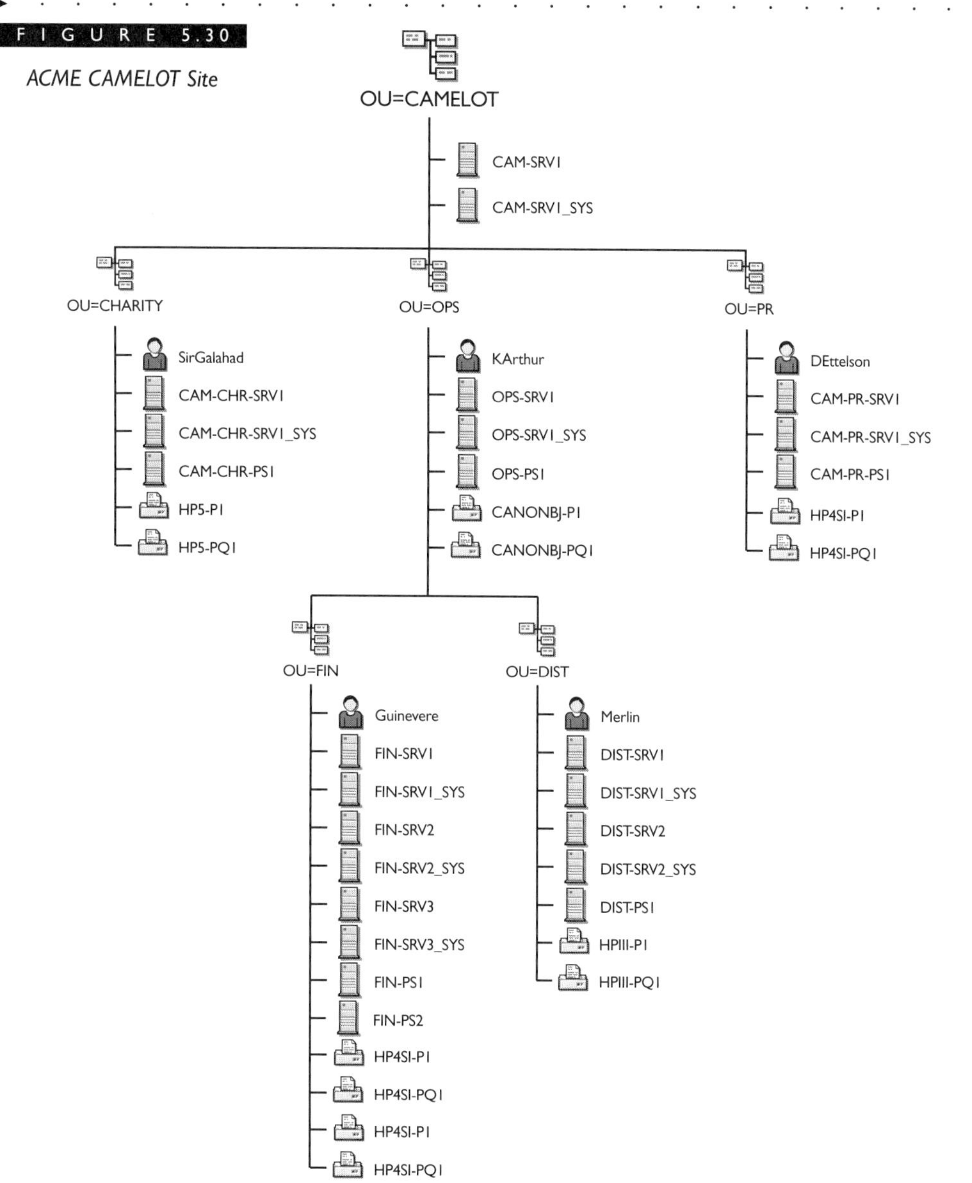

FIGURE 5.31

ACME SYDNEY Site

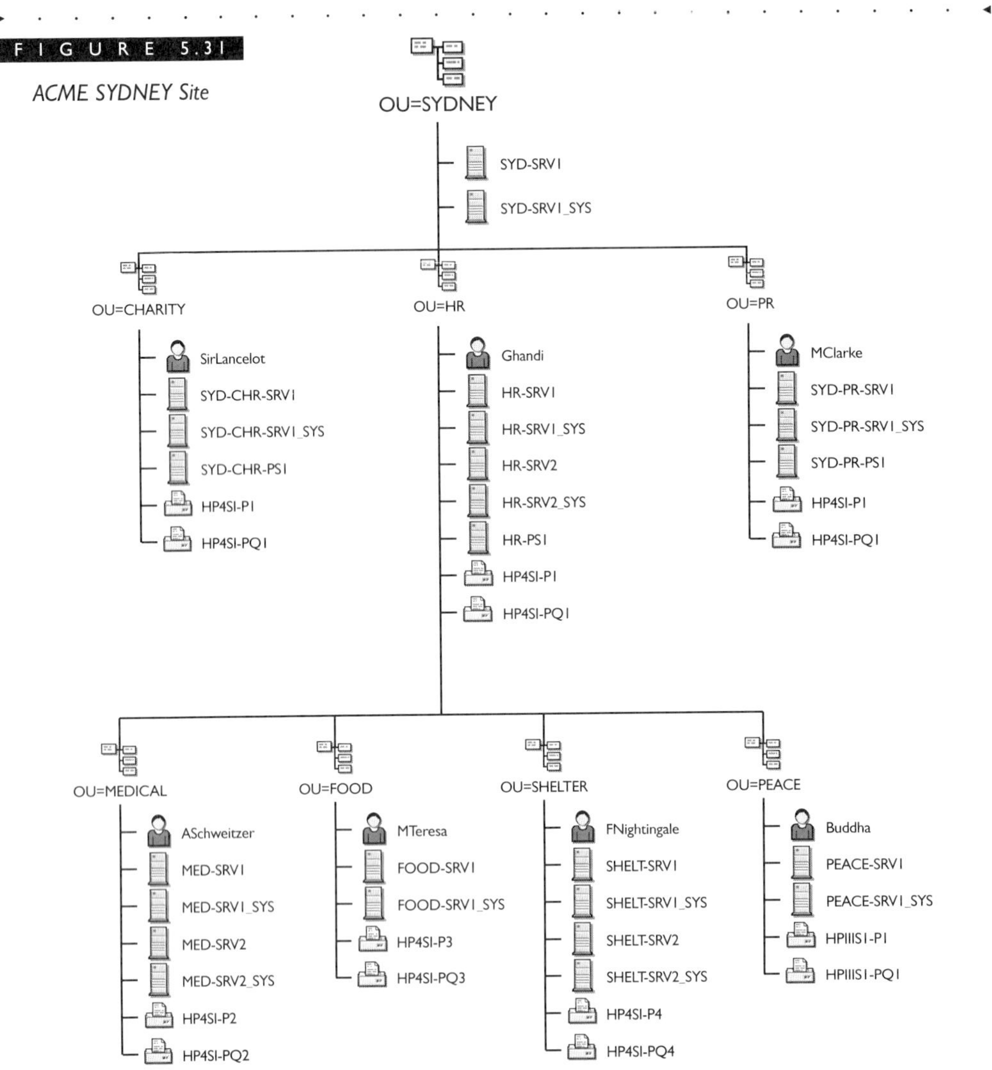

The TOKYO office has traveling users as shown in Figure 5.32. We will create an alias for these users at the top of the tree at O=ACME. With the alias in place, a traveling user such as DHOLIDAY in the OU=THEFT only has to remember to log in as DHOLIDAY.ACME. This makes the login process much easier for users who travel but do not carry their own laptops.

FIGURE 5.32

ACME TOKYO Site

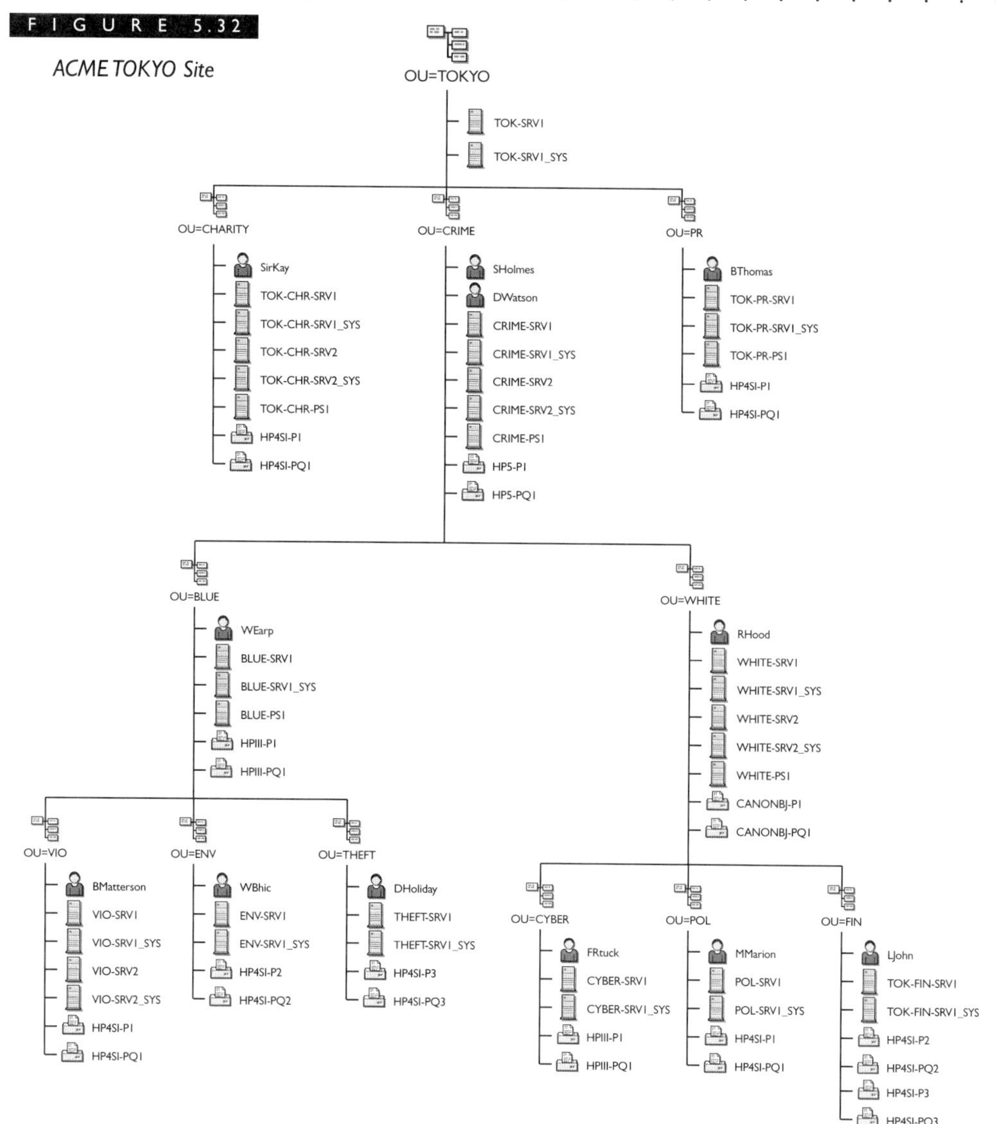

Creating Common Resource Containers

Some companies prefer to group similar resources in the same containers, such as a container for all servers, printers, and users. Keep in mind that this approach may work for smaller companies that do not have to group thousands of users in the same container or hundreds of servers together. This design approach works best with smaller companies that want to provide a simple grouping of resources.

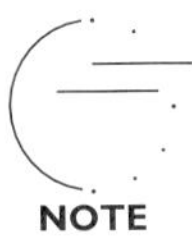
NOTE

Universities may also need to use this approach to designing an NDS tree because of the location of servers and users. If you are designing a tree for a university, create containers based on students' last names (that is, A-C, D-F) rather than lumping them all into one container. You will get better performance with this approach.

NDS Design for Z.E.N.works

This section describes how you can fine-tune the design guidelines to efficiently accommodate the additional objects created by the Zero Effort Networks (Z.E.N.works) software. The specific design guidelines do not require you to redesign your tree, but simply add objects to containers in the existing design. If you designed your NDS tree correctly (according to the recommendations given previously) it should be flexible enough at the bottom of the tree to handle the increase of objects that Z.E.N.works creates.

Z.E.N.works is made up of several important features: Novell Application Launcher (NAL), Workstation Manager, Inventory, and Remote Control. Z.E.N.works allows you to create the following objects:

- Application objects
- Application folders
- Policy Packages
- Workstations (not Computer object)
- Workstation Groups

In order to design your NDS tree with these objects, we recommend that you continue to follow the NDS guidelines as described above. Nothing in your design should change. The only issue should be where to place the objects and the number of new objects you will create. If the container or partition does not have room to accommodate the increase in new objects (based on our recommendations) you will need to create new containers and partitions appropriately. These changes will only affect the bottom of the tree.

Therefore, the main issues are as follows:

- Where do I place the new objects?
- Do I use existing department containers or the same container for each workstation user?
- Do I use containers called OU=APPLICATIONS, OU=WORKSTATIONS, OU=USERS, and so on to separate out these new objects?

To answer each of these questions, let's consider each product feature individually.

Novell Application Launcher

Novell Application Launcher (NAL), with accompanying Application and Application Folder objects, enables you to quickly and easily distribute applications to users' workstations and manage those applications as objects in the NDS tree. Users access the applications that you assign to them using the Application Launcher Window and Application Launcher Explorer components. Place or create the application objects and the supporting group objects close to the users who will be accessing them.

The application folders are only used by the network administrators. The user never accesses an application folder object. Therefore, you can place the application folder objects in the most convenient location for the administrators. The information in the application folder is cached in each of the application objects that are linked to the application folder. This method reduces that NDS traffic needed to maintain the application folders with their enclosed applications. An example of where to place the application object folder using NWADMIN is shown in Figure 5.33. This example shows placement of the folders near the network administrator.

FIGURE 5.33

The user does not need to access the application folder, so place it in the same container with the network administrator.

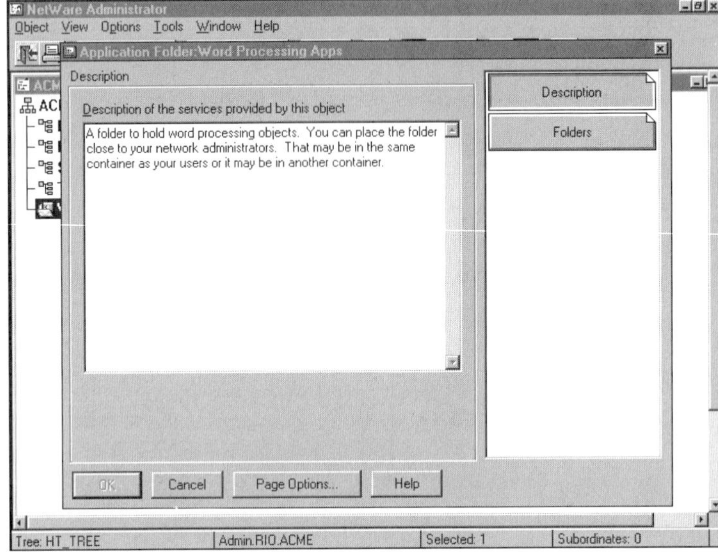

For networks with multiple locations across a WAN, you should create the application objects in the NDS container that represents the physical site or location. For example, the application objects would be placed in the OU=SFO and OU=ATL containers if you had two locations. The reason for creating new application objects for each location is to achieve better scalability across the network. By following this approach, the users are associated with an application object that is local to them.

NOTE

We recommend that you avoid designing Z.E.N.works so that the users have to access the application objects across the WAN in remote partitions. Do not create one application for your entire network if it will be accessed from multiple locations across the WAN. A better approach is to create application objects in the same containers as the users. This approach keeps users going to a local object rather than increasing traffic across your WAN links.

On the other hand, if your network is contained in a single LAN infrastructure, you could create just one application object per application program. In addition, you should create a different application object to reference each application server that is installed. If you have multiple application servers at one location or site, we recommend that you create a Z.E.N.works application object for each different application object on each server. For example, if you have three servers holding applications that will be used by your users, create a Z.E.N.works application for each program on each server. An example of this design approach is shown in Figure 5.34. You can use the following format to name the Z.E.N.works application object:

```
<PROGRAM_NAME>-<SERVER_NAME>
```

FIGURE 5.34

An example of three servers holding application objects for each application on each server

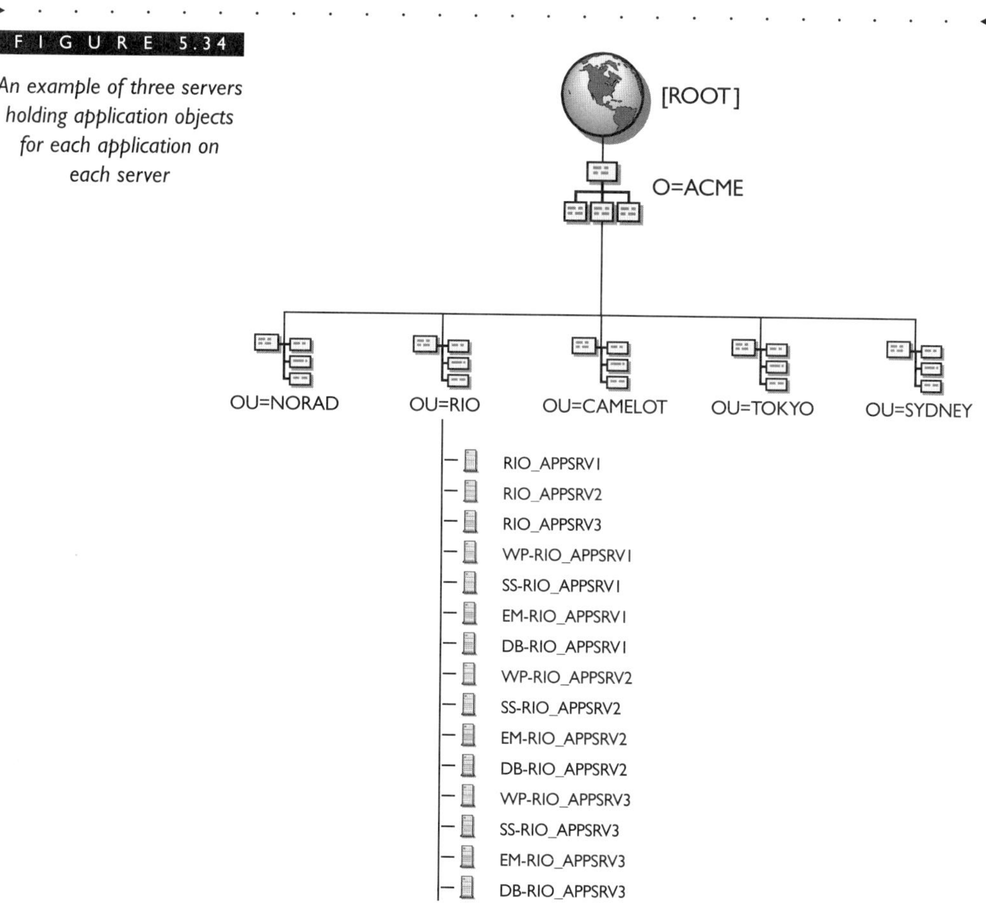

Table 5.2 illustrates how you can create individual applications objects that represent the programs installed on each NetWare server.

TABLE 5.2

Example of how to create individual application objects in your NDS tree to represent the programs installed on each NetWare Application Server

	NETWARE SERVER HOLDING APPLICATIONS	MATCHING APPLICATION OBJECTS
RIO_APPSRV1	Word Processing application	WP-RIO_APPSRV1
	Spread Sheet application	SS-RIO_APPSRV1
	E-mail application	EM-RIO_APPSRV1
	Database application	DB-RIO_APPSRV1
RIO_APPSRV2	Word Processing application	WP-RIO_APPSRV2
	Spread Sheet application	SS-RIO_APPSRV2
	E-mail application	EM-RIO_APPSRV2
	Database application	DB-RIO_APPSRV2
RIO_APPSRV3	Word Processing application	WP-RIO_APPSRV3
	Spread Sheet application	SS-RIO_APPSRV3
	E-mail application	EM-RIO_APPSRV3
	Database application	DB-RIO_APPSRV3

This configuration enables you to set up and effectively use the fault tolerance and load balancing features built into the Z.E.N.works product.

In order to manage these similar application objects pointing to different servers, use the new application object copy feature that is available in Z.E.N.works. When creating a new application object, you are given the option to create it from an existing application object in the tree. After copying an application object, you will need to change the source server, path, drive mapping, and others (as necessary). An example of creating an application object from an existing application object is shown in Figure 5.35

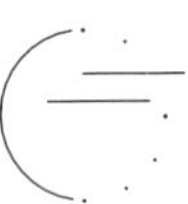
NOTE

We recommend that you *do not* use a generic NDS object copy utility to create new application objects. Instead, always use the application object copy feature in Z.E.N.works.

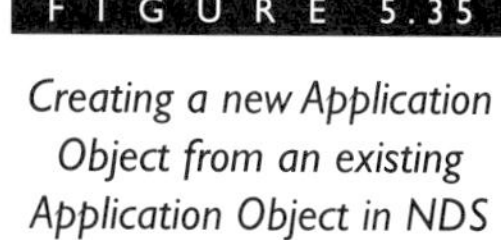

Creating a new Application Object from an existing Application Object in NDS

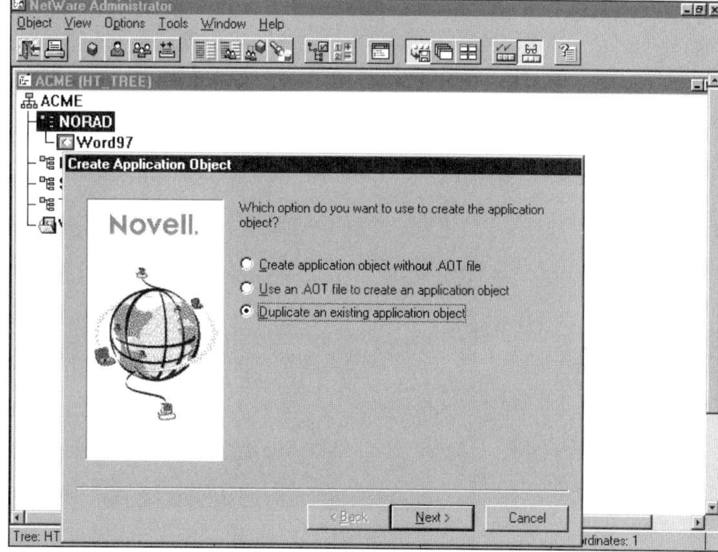

Group Objects

Group objects in NDS are used for many different purposes. One use is to grant users rights to other resources. With Z.E.N.works, groups are often created to grant multiple users rights and associate them to application objects. The group objects used to grant rights to the Z.E.N.works application objects need to follow the same design guidelines as the application and application folder objects themselves. Place the group objects in the same container with the associated application object. Try to avoid creating a global group with user objects that contains members from multiple physical locations in different partitions.

Consider the following design rules for group objects:

- Create the group object in the same container as the associated application.
- Limit the number of members in the membership list to 1,000–1,500.
- Never span group membership across a WAN network.
- If possible, keep the users in the group in the same partition. The result is that you minimize external references and its associated network traffic.

An example of creating a group local to the users is shown in Figure 5.36.

FIGURE 5.36

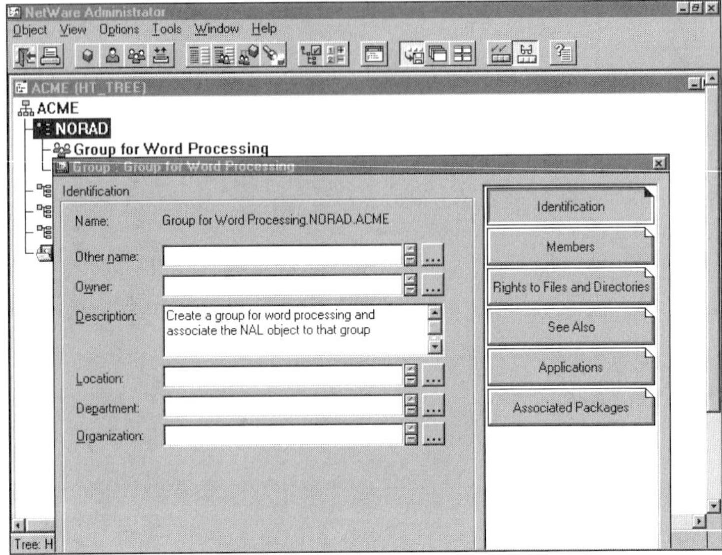

Create groups that are close to users for the best NDS performance.

Application Object Associations

For ease of administration, you can associate or assign the application objects to a user, group, or container. When the Application Launcher Window or Application Launcher Explorer starts up, it searches for all associated applications from the user object. It next searches for application objects associated to groups to which the user is a member. And finally, depending on the Container Levels setting in the launcher configuration (known as the up-context), it searches for applications associated to the user object's parent containers. The up-context settings are as follows:

- –1 Reads all parent containers to the top of the tree for associated applications
- 0 Does not read any parent, searching is turned off
- 1 Only reads the immediate parent container for associated applications
- 2 Reads only two levels up; parent and parent's parent associated applications

You can control the searching criteria used by changing the configuration in the Launcher Configuration property page in Configuration/Current Settings/Inherit Container Applications. An example of this configuration setting is shown in Figure 5.37.

FIGURE 5.37

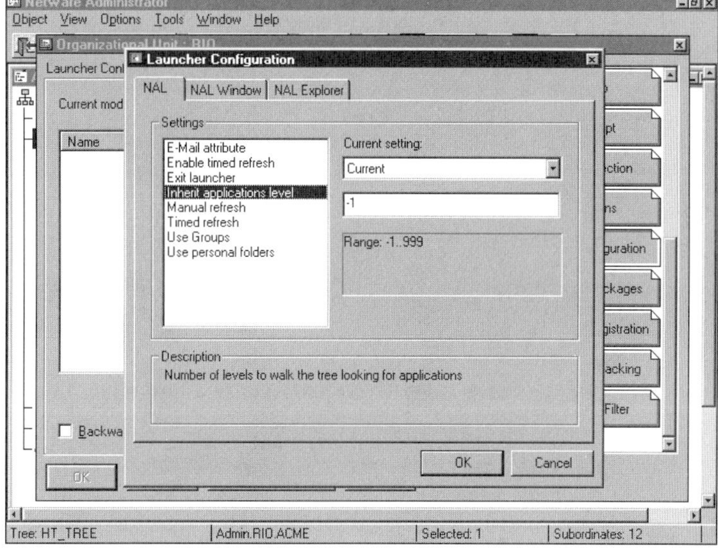

Setting the search criteria for application associations in the Novell Application Launcher

We recommend that for the best performance you use the following guidelines for establishing the associations to application objects:

- Set the searching to 0 or 1, which turns off searching or localizes the search just to the users' local container.
- You can set the searching to 2, if the parent and parent's parent are local to the user. Local means in the containers on the same LAN, not across the WAN network.
- Use the –1 (search to top of tree) setting sparingly; it should only be used on LAN-only networks.
- If user access is across the WAN, restrict the searching of groups. The group searching can be turned off.

Another design consideration is using the Application object's Schedule property page to let you control when users are delivered applications. This is useful in the scenario where you want to distribute a large Service Pack to all users. For example, you do not want a large update to occur at 8:00 a.m. when all network users are logging in to the network. In addition, you may not want this distribution to occur on weekends when there are no technical support people on-site.

For these reasons, we recommend that you make the Application object available Monday through Friday, spreading the network traffic load throughout the day. This can be accomplished by configuring the system to download the Service Pack at 8:00 a.m. during user login; however, make sure to set the "Spread from Start Time" to 180 minutes. The application then becomes available on a random basis between the hours of 8:00 a.m. through 11:00 a.m. For more information, refer to context-sensitive Help on the Application object's Schedule property page and to Chapter 21, "Novell Replication Services."

Workstations and Workstation Groups

As previously mentioned, the advent of Z.E.N.works and the use of the Workstation objects could potentially double the total number of objects in your tree. How does this impact the current NDS tree design guidelines? The answer is that the new objects should not impact any of the current design guidelines. However, when creating the Workstations and Workstation Groups you should make sure that each container (Organization or Organizational Unit) has enough room (based on our recommendations) to accommodate the new objects that you plan to add. More importantly, make sure that each partition still has fewer than 1,500 objects per partition. These changes may require you to create new containers and partitions to accommodate the addition of new objects.

It is also extremely important that your NDS is healthy (functioning without errors) before you add the additional objects that Z.E.N.works offers. In addition, make sure that each of your servers has the latest patches loaded.

Since the Workstation Import Policy defines where the Workstation objects are created in your NDS tree, consider the following guidelines:

- Create the Workstation objects in the same container as the user object
- Create the Workstation in a single-purpose container (OU= WORKSTATIONS), but this has limitations

As a general rule, we recommend that you place the Workstation and Workstation Group objects with the accompanying users. Placing the Workstation objects with the users enables you to keep the NDS design flexible and efficient.

However, we recognize the fact that the Workstation objects are not going to be accessed by the users, but instead by the client component itself. Therefore, the speed of access depends on the proximity of the physical workstation to the NDS partition and not the location of the user in the NDS tree.

Another aspect to consider is that the administrative staff will use the Workstation object to store the inventory for the physical machine. If your administrative staff is decentralized, with different groups handling different functions, you may want to create a separate container called OU= WORKSTATIONS to place the objects in. This type of design enables you to assign certain network administrators access to manage just the Workstation objects.

As the number of objects in the current partition grows, you can partition off just the OU=WORKSTATIONS container as its own partition. The use of OU= WORKSTATIONS may be appropriate for some NDS trees only because the workstation objects are used exclusively by the network administrators and not the users. An example of using a container solely for Workstations is shown in Figure 5.38.

We typically *do not* recommend that you create resource specific containers to place similar resources together for the other network resources. For example, we *do not* recommend creating a separate container for all servers, users, printers, groups, organizational roles, applications, policies, and others. Figure 5.39 illustrates the bottom of the NDS tree using resource specific containers. This is typically not recommended except for the Workstation objects because eventually you may end up with all your users in one partition and their resources in another partition on another server. This reduces the efficiency of NDS.

Consulting Experience

Please keep in mind that we are recommending a separate container for workstation objects because these objects are used almost solely by the administrator. For all other resources (user objects, servers, and so on), we don't recommend the use of separate containers as explained in further detail next.

FIGURE 5.38

Using a resource-specific container for OU=WORKSTATIONS

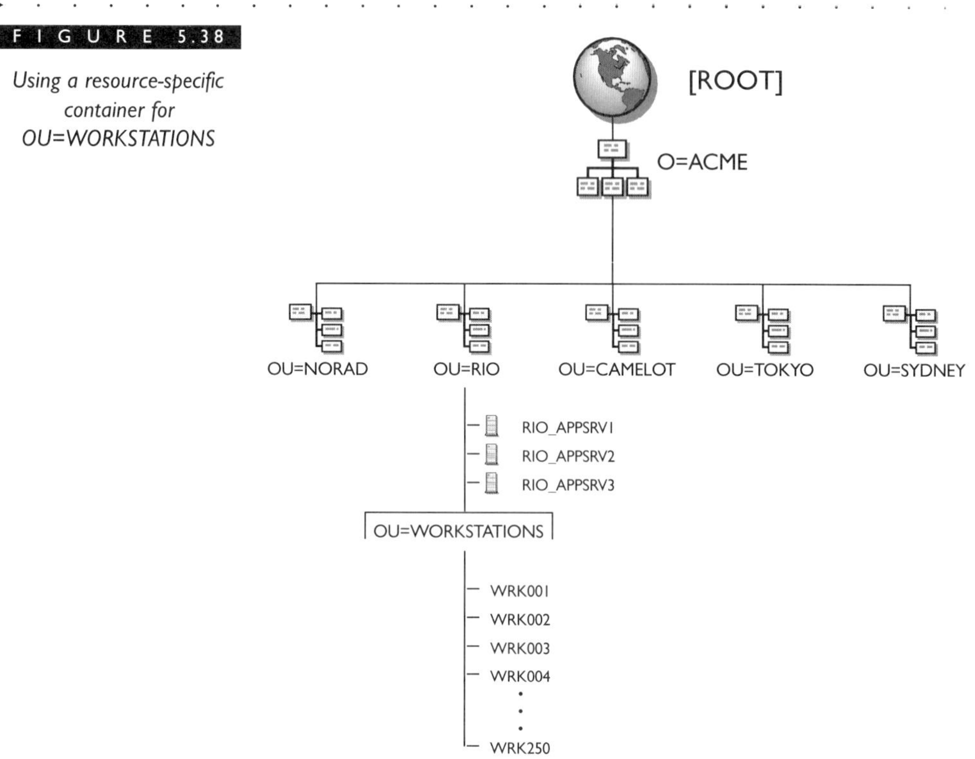

FIGURE 5.39

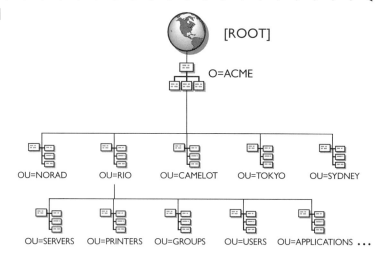

An example of resource-specific containers at the bottom of the tree

[ROOT]
O=ACME
OU=NORAD
OU=RIO
OU=CAMELOT
OU=TOKYO
OU=SYDNEY
OU=SERVERS
OU=PRINTERS
OU=GROUPS
OU=USERS
OU=APPLICATIONS ...

Keep in mind that this design may seem to work if all the containers are in the same partition. However, we do not recommend designing your NDS tree using these single-purpose containers for the following reasons:

- Reduces user speed of access
- Bottom of the tree becomes more inflexible
- Scalability at the bottom of the tree is limited
- Further partitioning of containers reduces performance
- Designed for the administrators and not users

These problems are magnified if the site or location has thousands of users, workstations, and so on. As each OU is partitioned off, the performance and access is greatly reduced. Partitions are created to help NDS scale across the servers, which typically means that each partition will reside on different servers. As the replicas are moved off each server, the user's resources (servers, printers, groups, applications, policies) become dispersed, reducing the speed of access.

In addition to the reduced access and flexibility, the network performance can be adversely affected with the higher number of external references that are created to track all the objects not physically residing on each server.

Policy Packages

There are several new objects offered by Z.E.N.works known as Policy Packages that enable you to manage users' workstations remotely and in a consistent fashion. There are several different types of Policy Packages that can be created:

- Container Package
- WIN31 User Package
- WIN31 Workstation Package
- WIN95 User Package

- WIN95 Workstation Package
- WINNT User Package
- WINNT Workstation Package

The Container Package is used to define how the client component searches in NDS for associated Policy Packages. The User Policy Packages are associated to either users, groups or containers. The Workstation Policy Packages can be associated to either Workstations, Workstation Groups, or containers. It is not possible to assign several Policy Packages to the same user object.

We recommend that you place the Policy Package objects closest to the users or workstations that will be accessing it. For Policy Packages consider the following guidelines:

- Create the Container Policy Package at the highest level of the tree as needed. It should never exceed the location or site container.
- Create the User Policy Package in the same container as the users that will access it.
- Create the Workstation Policy Package in the same container as the workstations that will access it. If you have defined a single-purpose container for workstations (OU=WORKSTATIONS), place the policies in the same container.

If user access to the Policy Package is across the WAN, restrict the searching of groups. The group searching can be turned off using the Search Policy. Examples of where to place the policy packages are shown in Figures 5.40, 5.41, and 5.42.

For more information about installation and configuration of these policy packages, refer to Chapter 21, "Integrating Novell Replication Services."

FIGURE 5.40

Create the Container Policy Package at the highest level needed in your NDS tree.

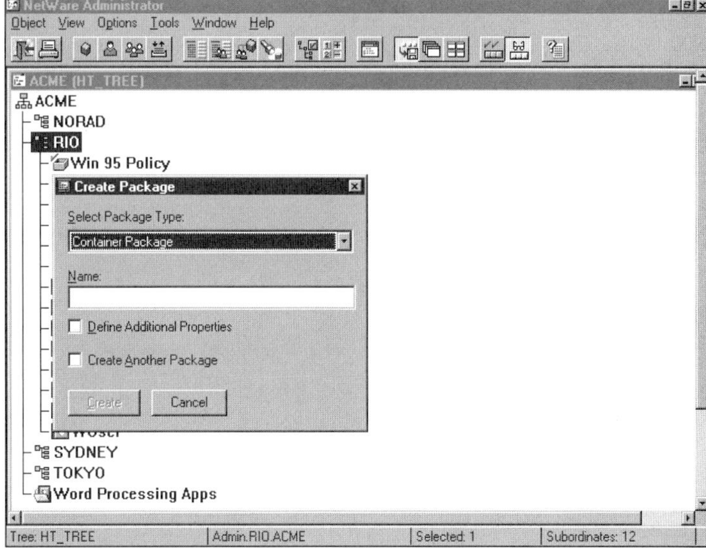

FIGURE 5.41

Create the User Policy Package local to the users that will use it.

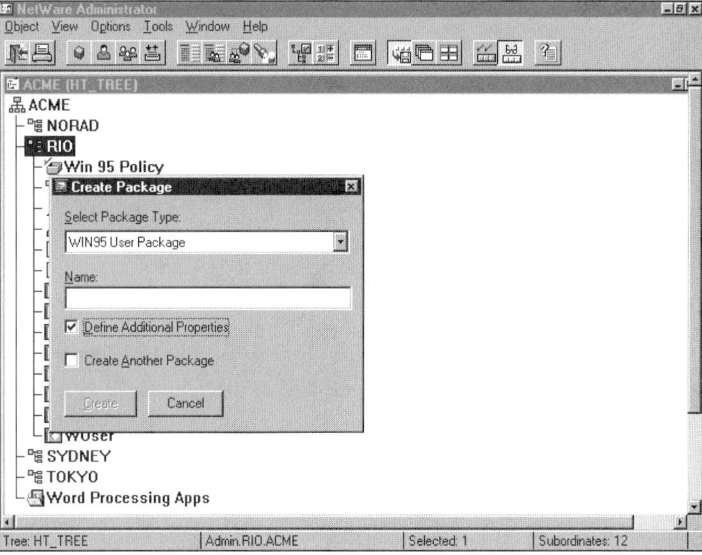

FIGURE 5.42

Create the Workstation Policy Package in the same container where the users will access it.

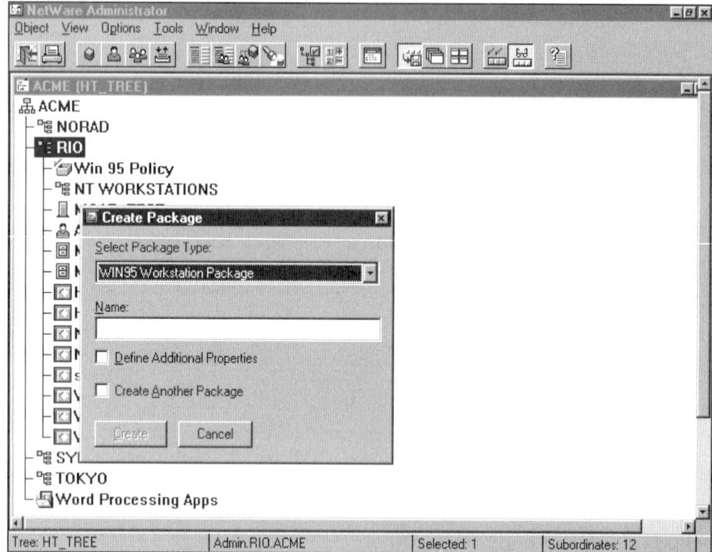

Using NDS with Windows NT

Since NDS for NT gives you the ability to integrate Windows NT domains directly into your NDS tree, it requires you to design your NDS tree to accommodate the new objects. New topics that we need to cover include how to design NDS trees with NT domains in them to support the NDS for NT product and also the best way to design domains.

Because the NT domain object in NDS acts as a group with a list of domain members, it takes on the NDS design characteristics of an NDS Group object. However, it is also a special NDS container object that holds NDS for NT Local Group objects, NDS for NT Global Group objects, and NDS for NT Workstation objects that are migrated from the original NT domain.

One of the unique design characteristics is the fact that you can create an NDS partition at the domain object. In other words, the NT domain object in the tree can become its own partition. The information that is stored in the partition created from the domain object is just the objects found under the domain. These objects are NDS for NT Local Group objects, NDS for NT Global Group objects,

NDS for NT Workstation objects, and alias objects. The users that were migrated from the original NT domain cannot be part of a partition created from the NT domain object in NDS.

The domain object in NDS can only partition using NDS Manager. NDS Manager version 1.25 (and later) is the only version that will let you make this change. Versions of NDS Manager shipped with NetWare 4 will not let you perform the operation. Version 1.25 of NDS Manager comes with the NDS for NT product and is installed automatically on the server where you install NDS for NT. Make sure that you are using the correct version of NDS Manager before trying to do the partition operation. To help reduce the confusion, you can copy the latest NDS Manager version (1.25 or later) to all of your NetWare 4 servers.

Because the domain object represents the original NT domain, one of the first design decisions is where to create or place the domain object in the NDS tree. We recommend that the object be placed in a container that is local to the domain users. For example, if there is a Windows NT domain in a specific site or location then the NT domain object in NDS should be created within the same location container of the NDS tree. In addition, the user objects should be migrated to the appropriate department containers under the same container as the domain object. You want to place the users in the container with the network resources that they use.

After you have decided where in the NDS tree the domain object and users will be placed, consider the following design rules for NDS for NT:

- Limit the number of members in the membership list of the NT domain object to 3,000. This implies that you limit the number of users in the original NT domains to fewer than 3,000 users.

- If possible, keep the users associated with the NT domain in the same partition. The result is that you minimize external references and the associated traffic.

- If you have multiple NT domains in your NDS tree, place each NT domain and its associated users in separate partitions.

- Create the NT domain object as its own partition when the number of objects contained is greater than 1,000.

- Always have NDS for NT running on all PDCs and BDCs supporting the Windows NT domain.
- The NT domain PDC or BDC must be in the same SAP domain as the NDS domains supporting the user objects.

An example of the placement of an NDS for NT domain object is shown in Figure 5.43.

FIGURE 5.43

The NT Domain object should be placed close to the users that are associated with the domain.

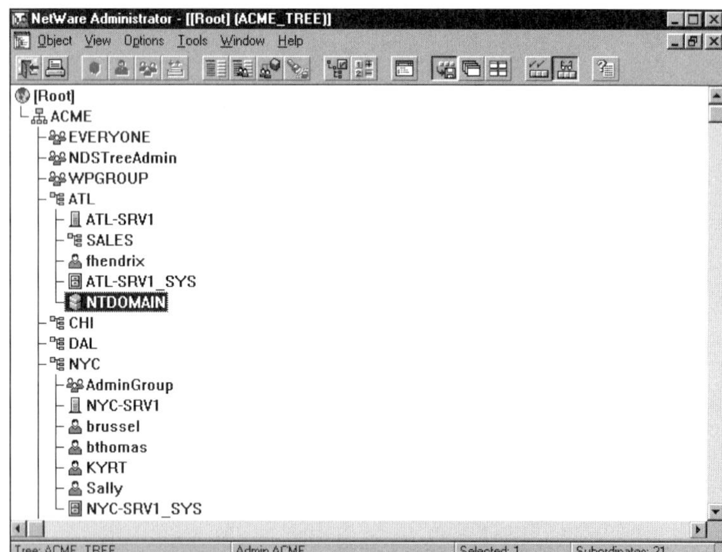

Additional Design Considerations

Some LAN administrators may try to design the NDS tree and simultaneously consider all the external factors that may affect the design of the tree. Considering all the factors at once is difficult because the tree will shift and change as you attempt to consider all the design inputs. Some of the most popular distractions are bindery services, partitioning, replication, and login scripts.

Experience has shown that designing the tree is simple if you base the top layers of the tree solely on the WAN infrastructure and the bottom layers according to your organizational information.

When you have completed your first draft design of the NDS tree, you are ready to apply some other design considerations as needed. This process greatly simplifies the tree design effort. It is interesting to note that the design considerations affect primarily the design of the bottom of the tree, not the top of the tree. This is acceptable because the greatest flexibility for changes in the design is supported at the bottom of the tree.

Again, our approach is to design the bottom level of the NDS tree aligned entirely to the organizations of your company. You can then apply the design considerations as needed. The following design considerations affect the bottom of the tree:

- Administration
- NDS partitions and replicas
- Login scripts
- Bindery services

Remember that these design considerations apply only to the bottom of the tree; they do not alter the top layers in the tree design. By reviewing each design consideration, you will see how these considerations apply only to the users and other network resources that are contained in the bottom layers.

Administration

One of the most important design considerations is how the NDS tree is going to be managed at your company. Are you going to manage the NDS tree as one Information System (IS) group (the centralized approach) or by several different IS groups (the decentralized approach)?

Centralized Management

The entire NDS tree is controlled by one group in the company. This group manages all the additions and deletions of the NDS objects, partitioning, replication, and everything else related to the NDS database. Figure 5.44 shows how you can centrally manage your tree with one IS group having rights to the top of your tree and down. For more information regarding rights assignments, refer to Chapter 13, "Managing NetWare Security."

FIGURE 5.44

A centralized management approach with a single group having rights to the entire tree

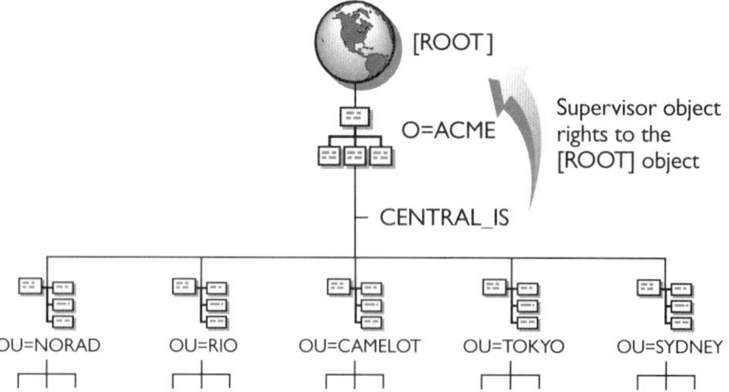

Decentralized Management

Portions of the NDS tree are delegated to individuals or independent groups in the company for management. These individuals or groups may be administrators for each department or site administrators responsible for all the network resources in a particular location. All subadministrators should, however, adhere to your previously defined naming standards. Figure 5.45 illustrates how you can set up administration for the lower containers in your group. You will have a central IS staff managing the upper layers of the tree, with other administrators being responsible for their respective containers.

If the NDS tree is going to be centrally managed, it makes sense to further the tree design to the bottom layers. The central team that provides administration has control of all the objects in the tree from top to bottom.

However, if the tree is going to be decentrally managed, each department administrator or site administrator will decide independently how the tree is organized in that portion of the tree. The top administrators have full responsibility to create the tree down to the department or site and then relinquish control at that layer to each of the independent LAN administrators. Top administrators of the tree will still want to give design guidelines and suggestions to the bottom administrators on organizing the lower containers and grouping network resources. The following is a list of suggestions that you can give your administrators as guidelines. These ideas can also be mandated through the use of access controls as explained in Chapter 13, "Managing NetWare Security."

FIGURE 5.45

Creating a distributed administration approach by creating container administrators. Each subadministrator has rights to his or her own organizational unit.

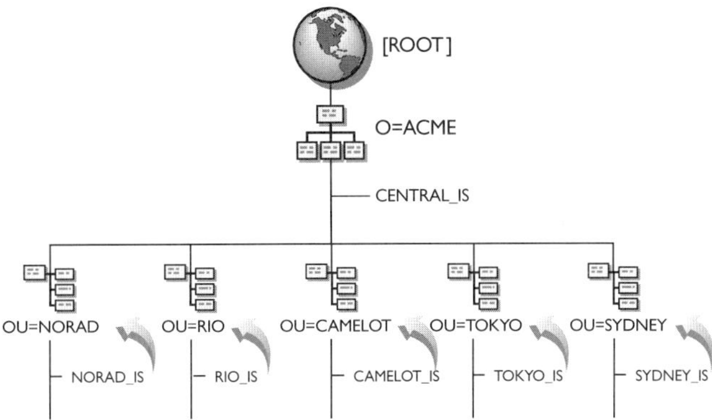

Guidelines for Subadministrators

Here are some rules of thumb for subadministrators:

- Subadministrators should have sufficient security and access rights over their container(s) to create, delete, or change all objects within their subcontainer.
- Each subadministrator will carefully determine if more levels need to be created beneath their container before making changes.
- Subadministrators should maintain the naming standards as defined by the corporation at all levels in the NDS tree.
- Subadministrators should not further partition their OUs without the assistance of the central IS department. In some cases, the subadministrator will not be granted rights to do so.
- Subadministrators will inform the central IS staff before adding a new server into the corporate tree.

The depth of the tree or number of layers in the tree may be affected by whether your administration is centralized or decentralized. Remember, the recommendation is to build the NDS tree like a pyramid with fewer containers at the top and more containers at the bottom. Centralized administration may imply that a tree designed flat and wide would be easier to administer. If your company has only a few servers and users, you can build a shallow tree that is suited to centralized administration.

This may not be possible if your company is large with many servers, users, and geographic sites. In this case you will need to design the NDS tree with more layers, which means a deeper tree.

For decentralized management of NDS trees, individual administrators along with central administrators can determine the depth of their portion of the tree. Although there is no hard and fast rule regarding the total number of layers in the tree, the NDS tree is more flexible and easier for the user to find information if the tree has three to five layers. Typically, even the largest companies can design a very useful tree with five layers or fewer. Notice in Figure 5.46 that the ACME tree consists of five layers, not including [ROOT].

FIGURE 5.46

The ACME tree consists of five layers, not including [ROOT].

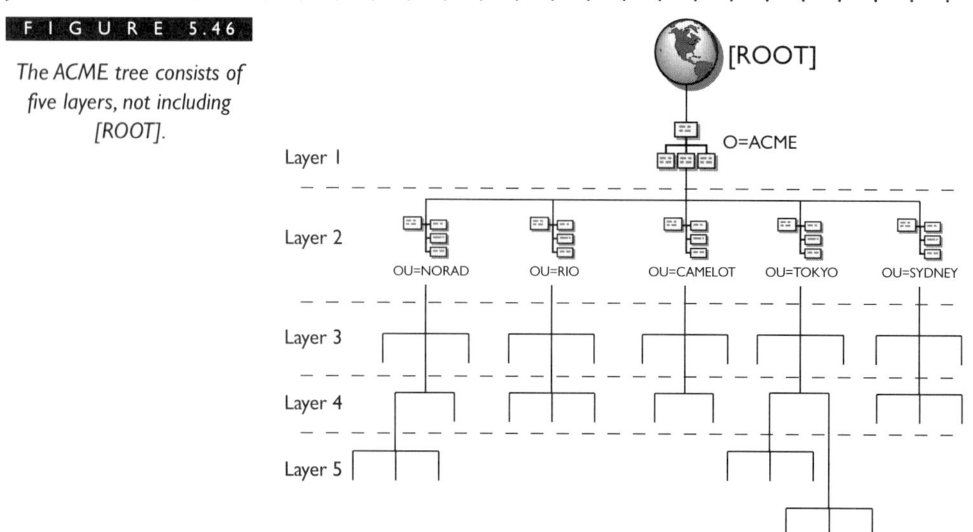

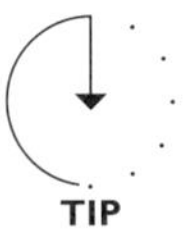

TIP

There is a logical limit to the total number of layers in the tree you can access. For example, NDS has a limit of 255 characters for a distinguished name. Thus, the actual limit for the number of layers is dependent on the number of characters in the names of your objects. If your OU names are long, your tree will not be able to have as many layers as it would with shorter OU names. For example, if all the OU names were just two characters, you would be able to have 51 layers (OU=US, 256/5 = 51). We recommend that you give the OUs in your tree short, descriptive names. For more information on naming standards, see Chapter 4, "Directory Services Naming Conventions."

NDS Partitions and Replicas

The next design consideration you need to address is how you will split the NDS database into partitions. For this discussion, we will consider the size of the partition (total number of objects), the total number of replicas, and where in the tree the partition is to be created. A container object is required for the creation of a partition and is designated the root-most object of the partition. Figure 5.47 shows a partition root called NORAD in the NORAD facility. The partition root is named NORAD because that is the starting point of that partition.

FIGURE 5.47

A partition root object is named NORAD in the ACME tree.

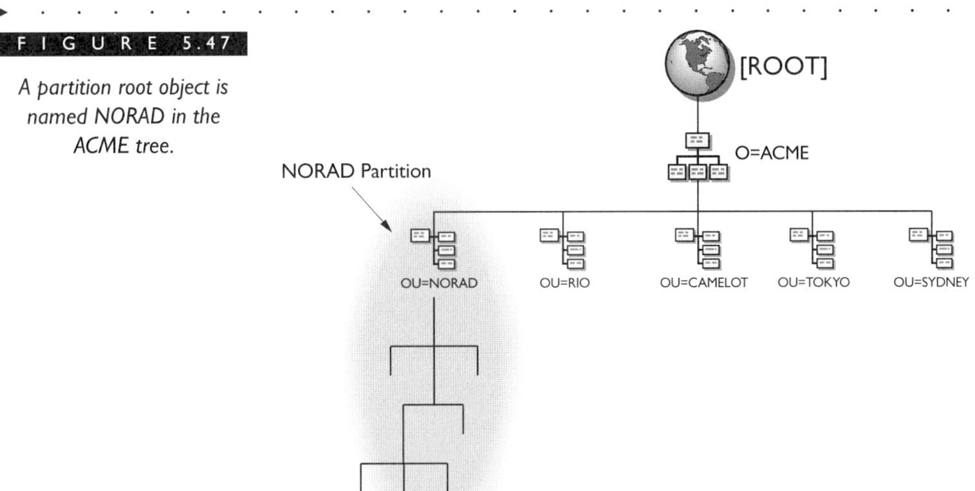

When deciding where to create a partition, you should follow the physical network infrastructure. Like the top layer of the tree, the partitions of the tree should represent the WAN, making each site or location its own partition. The benefit of partitioning the NDS database according to the WAN is that the information needed by the local users stays inside that location. We have partitioned each of the location organizational units by site as illustrated in Figure 5.48.

FIGURE 5.48

Each site is its own partition and maintains its portion of the NDS database on its own servers within the site.

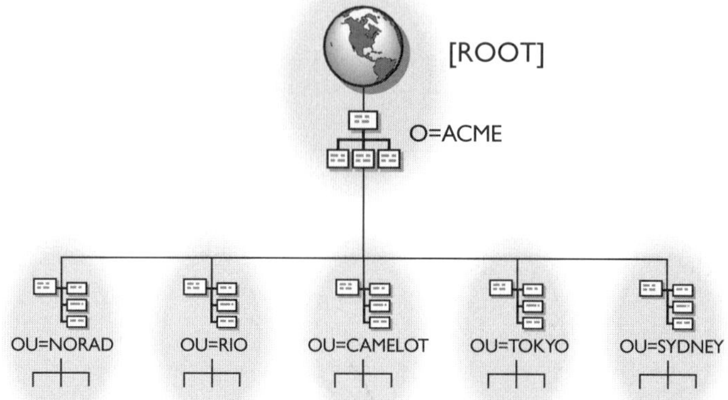

The size of your partitions and the total number of replicas is a design consideration for the bottom of the tree. Typically, partitions consist of fewer than 1,500 objects. If the partition grows to be significantly larger than 1,500 objects, you should split the partition. Therefore, in Figure 5.49 we have created a new partition called OPS under CAMELOT because that location's partition has grown beyond 1,500 objects. More partitions in the right places provide greater efficiency in your tree design. Remember, a partition contains all the objects in a defined subtree, not just the objects in a single container.

FIGURE 5.49

A new partition is created in the OPS department. It is now a child partition of its parent named CAMELOT.

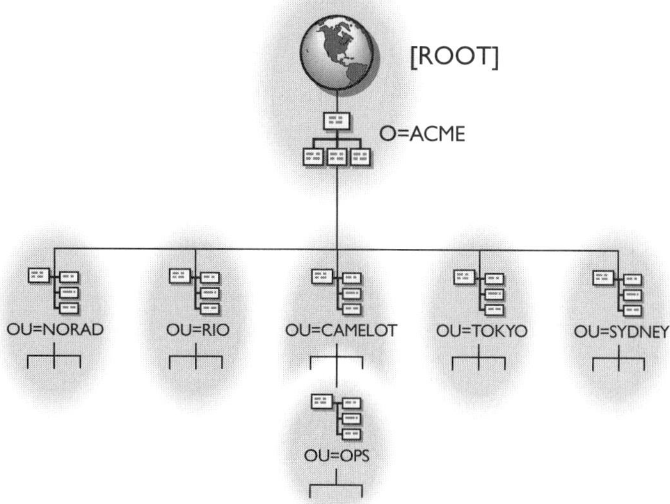

The next consideration is the total number of replicas of a partition. If the number of replicas is greater than 10, consider creating additional partitions to reduce the total number of replicas. Novell recommends three replicas for each partition. The primary reason you would need more than three replicas of any partition is for bindery services. Bindery services requires a writable copy of the replica. Refer to the "Bindery Services" section later in this chapter.

Consulting Experience

We are suggesting that NDS is more efficient using partitions of fewer than 1,500 objects. Therefore, when your partitions reach this size, you can begin to assess the need to split the partitions. Check your user and synchronization performance and use that as a guide. These recommendations are dependent upon the speed of your server hardware. We recommend that your server hardware be a Pentium class machine with 128MB of RAM if you exceed 1,500 objects.

Decide who is responsible for the partitioning of the NDS tree. If you manage the tree centrally, all the partitioning decisions are made by the central IS department. If the tree is decentralized, you may turn over the rights of partitioning the tree to each of the local site or facility administrators. Whichever way you decide to handle partitioning, make sure you decide before installation of NetWare 5 begins, and make a company policy stating who will handle the partitioning.

Login Scripts

Another design consideration for the bottom of the tree is designing how the users will access the information in the tree. The users will primarily access NDS through the use of login scripts. Remember, the users need login scripts to map network drives and applications, capture to print queues, and set other variables. Thus, the login scripts become a very important design consideration. Typically, the users needing the same login script will be grouped together in the same OU container. You can then use the OU login script to provide users access to the NDS tree. Figure 5.50 shows a container login script that will be used by everyone in the container.

FIGURE 5.50

All users execute the login script in the container where they reside.

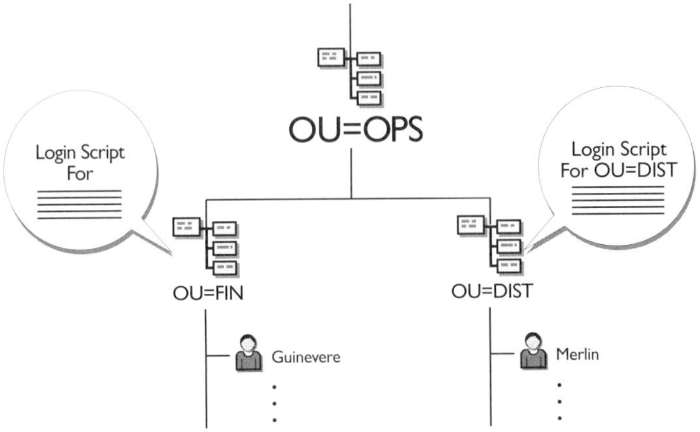

You will separate the users that need different login scripts for the same reason. As you design the login scripts for your users, you are in fact designing the organization of the bottom level of the tree.

Another strategy for organizing the login scripts is to have the same login script for all users and copy it to multiple containers. In this manner, the user placement in the tree is not affected. However, this strategy requires that the network administrator be responsible for keeping all copies of the login script the same.

It is recommended that you use the OU container login script to replace the functionality of the NetWare 3 system login script. This will help you organize the bottom layers and containers in your tree.

You can also make use of the profile login script whenever possible for configuring the users for access to resources that are more global in nature. The profile login script enables you to span a single login script across multiple OU containers and assign it to specific users. For example, the container SYDNEY has a profile script created for the HR department, and its subordinate departments of MEDICAL, FOOD, and SHELTER as shown in Figure 5.51 all use the script. The script can reside in any container, and users from any container can execute it.

FIGURE 5.51

A profile script used by users from MEDICAL, FOOD, and SHELTER

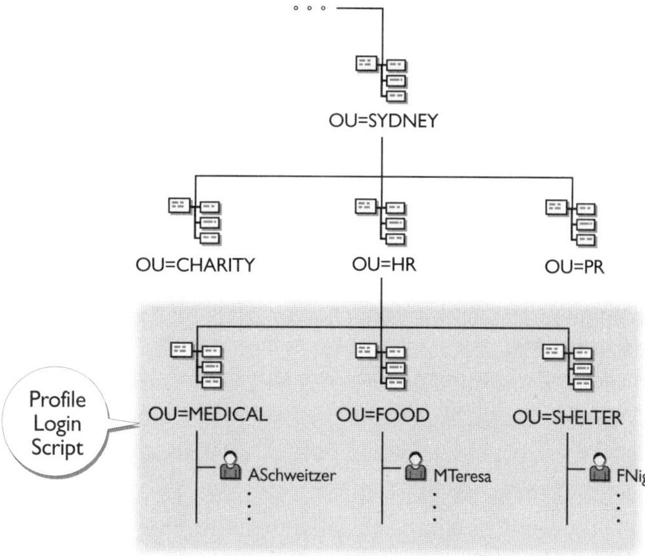

Through the login script, each user maps network drives to the appropriate network server and establishes access to specific network applications and services. Most login scripts depend on groups and directory map objects for these drive mappings. These groups and directory map objects must be accessible so that any users needing them can find them during the login process.

In order to simplify the mapping to generic network applications (ones needed by all network users), it is appropriate to place the applications in the same subdirectory structure on all the servers. In other words, use the same file structure for all servers. Then when a user maps the drive, he or she does not care which server responds.

For example, assume that each network user needs to have drive mappings to both a word processor and spreadsheet software. These two software packages are installed on all file servers in the same place on the file system (SYS:APPS\WP and SYS:APPS\QPRO). All servers that have a generic file system structure enable the users to map these applications regardless of their location or the server to which they are physically attached. An example of how you can standardize your file system is shown in Figure 5.52.

FIGURE 5.52

A standard file system on all your NetWare 5 servers will make administration of your network easier.

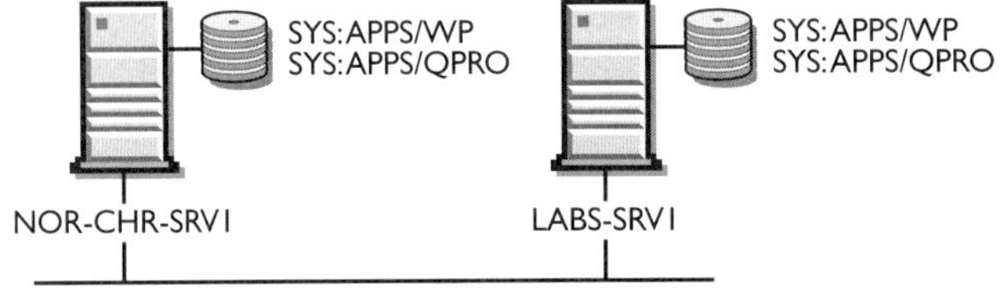

Bindery Services

NDS provides compatibility with NetWare 2 and NetWare 3 using a feature called bindery services. This feature allows bindery versions of NetWare applications and other third-party software that requires the bindery to access the NDS database as if it were the bindery. For example, a client can use the NETX shell (NetWare 3 client) to log in to a NetWare 5 server and run any bindery-based application that may exist on the NetWare 5 server.

Bindery services can be enabled through the server SET Server Bindery Context command. The server can select one OU, Organization, or Locality container, or many containers, as the bindery context. The server bindery context is simply the containers the server sees as the bindery. All the leaf objects in the NDS container(s) that are also objects in the NetWare 3 bindery (for example, users, groups, queues, print servers, and profiles) are seen as objects through the bindery application programming interfaces (APIs). The following figures show how you can set a server's bindery context(s). Figure 5.53 shows how you can use the MONITOR utility to set the bindery context(s). Figure 5.54 shows how you can verify that the bindery context(s) have been set on a server.

FIGURE 5.53

Using the MONITOR utility to set the server context at OU=CRIME. OU=TOKYO. O=ACME. This setting implies that the container "CRIME" is set as the bindery context.

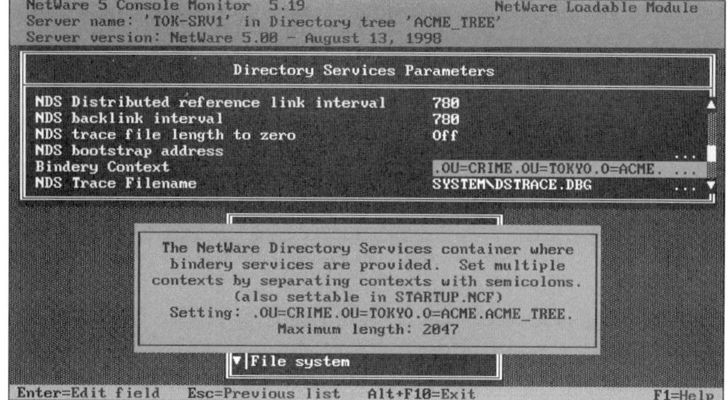

FIGURE 5.54

Typing SET BINDERY CONTEXT at a NetWare 5 server console will display a server's bindery context(s) if the context has been set.

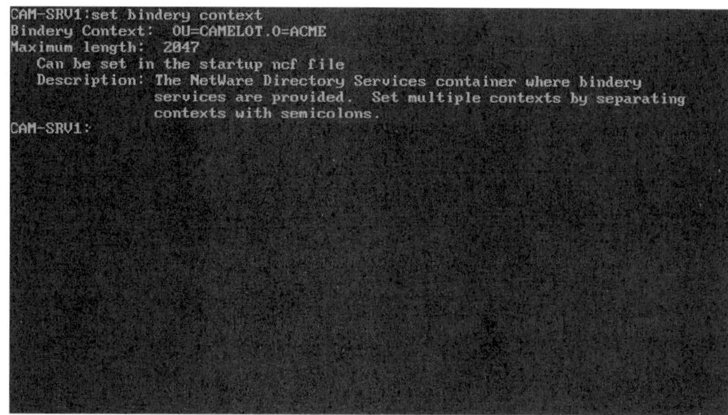

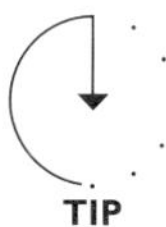

Typing Set Bindery Context at a server shows the string of contexts as valid or invalid. If you want to see only the valid (effective and active) contexts, you must type CONFIG at the server console.

Bindery services in NetWare 5 lets you select up to 16 containers as the server bindery context. The major requirement for bindery services is that the server must store at least a read/write replica of the partition where the bindery context is set. If a server has the maximum 16 bindery contexts set, the server would have to store 16 separate replicas just to support bindery services on all contexts. Figure 5.55 shows how we have set multiple bindery contexts on a server in TOKYO to search the organizational units of CRIME, BLUE, and WHITE when a bindery request is made.

FIGURE 5.55

Multiple bindery contexts are separated by semicolons on a server in TOKYO, which will view the CRIME, BLUE, and WHITE containers as its bindery.

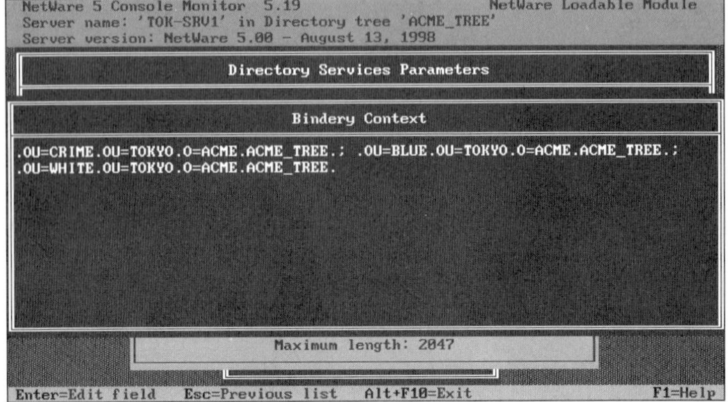

As you can see, placing replicas on servers to support bindery services will increase the total number of replicas for each partition. This will affect the tree design because you may be forced to split a partition to reduce the number of replicas. Bindery services is the principal reason for maintaining more than a few replicas of any partition. Refer back to the section "NDS Partitions and Replicas" earlier in this chapter.

Another design consideration is that you should place all the clients or users requiring bindery services from a particular file server in the OU container where you have set the server bindery context. This consideration can affect the NDS tree design at the bottom level because it may require you to combine users and resources of multiple departments or workgroups into one OU. You may need to separate users from the resources they don't use for the same reason. In any event, the organization of the bottom layers of the tree may be affected because the users and resources need to be arranged for bindery services.

Consulting Experience

Here is a brief list of some of the applications you may encounter that make bindery calls. Although this list is brief, you need to check all your applications to determine if they require the bindery.

- NetWare 3 Print Services
- Backup Utilities
- Host Connectivity Products
- Menuing Systems
- Network Management Utilities
- Other NetWare 3-Based Applications and Utilities

Before you change the bottom of the tree design to accommodate bindery services, determine whether you even need bindery services for the servers. Remember, bindery services is an optional feature that does not have to be enabled at each server. You should determine if the clients are using NETX or applications that require bindery services. You could also identify the users and key applications and force them to use bindery services on specific servers.

With an NDS tree design roughed out, you are now ready to design for partitioning and replication.

Summary

This chapter presented the basics of NDS tree design for any size environment regardless of the size of the network. Once you have your WAN information and other corporate documents in hand, you can design the top level of your NDS tree. Then you can move on to designing the bottom level of your tree by considering the effects of administration, partitions and replicas, login scripts, and bindery services. By following the guidelines presented here, you will have an NDS tree that is flexible enough to meet the changing needs of your company.

CHAPTER 6

Designing and Using NDS Partitions and Replicas

"The beginning is the most important part of the work." — Plato

The NDS tree information is stored on the servers in data files. These data files may either be centralized on one or two network servers or be distributed across all the network servers in the company. Although the NDS tree can be distributed to servers across the network, users are provided a single view of its resources. With NDS, the information is not only distributed but also replicated on multiple servers to provide increased reliability. Figure 6.1 shows how NDS might be distributed across a few servers in the network for the ACME company while still providing the user with a single view of the network resources.

FIGURE 6.1

NDS provides distribution of the information across a few of the network servers for ACME while still providing the user with a single view of the network resources.

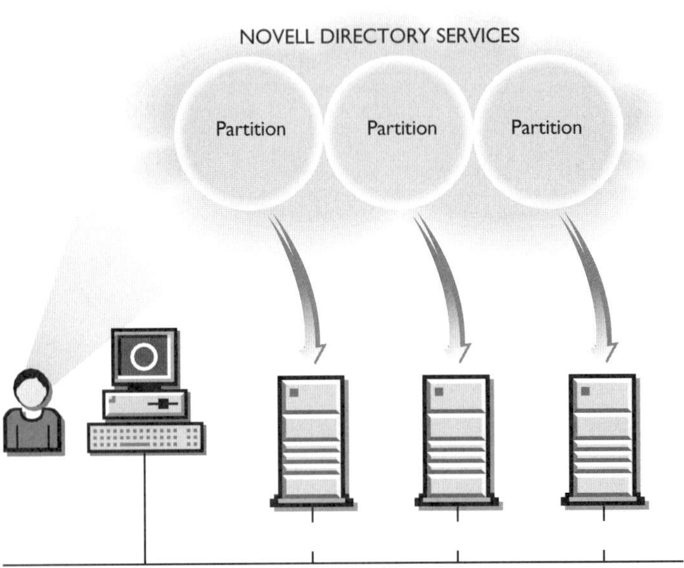

In a company with a small number of servers, the NDS tree information could be centralized with all the information residing on one or two network servers. The benefit of having the data files centralized on just a couple of servers is that administration is easier. The NDS tree will perform efficiently as long as the total number of users and network resources for the entire company remains small.

Consulting Experience

In a small company, you can place all of its resources into a single O=Organization in the NDS tree structure for simplicity or create an OU under the O=Organization.

Companies that have large networks with a large number of servers should split the NDS tree (or object hierarchy) into sections and distribute them to the appropriate network servers.

NDS Partitions

NDS is represented as a hierarchical structure called a tree into which all the network resources are placed. Figure 6.2 illustrates how the NDS database is viewed as a hierarchical tree. The NDS partitions are also hierarchical and follow the same structure as the tree.

FIGURE 6.2

NDS for ACME is viewed as a hierarchical structure called a tree.

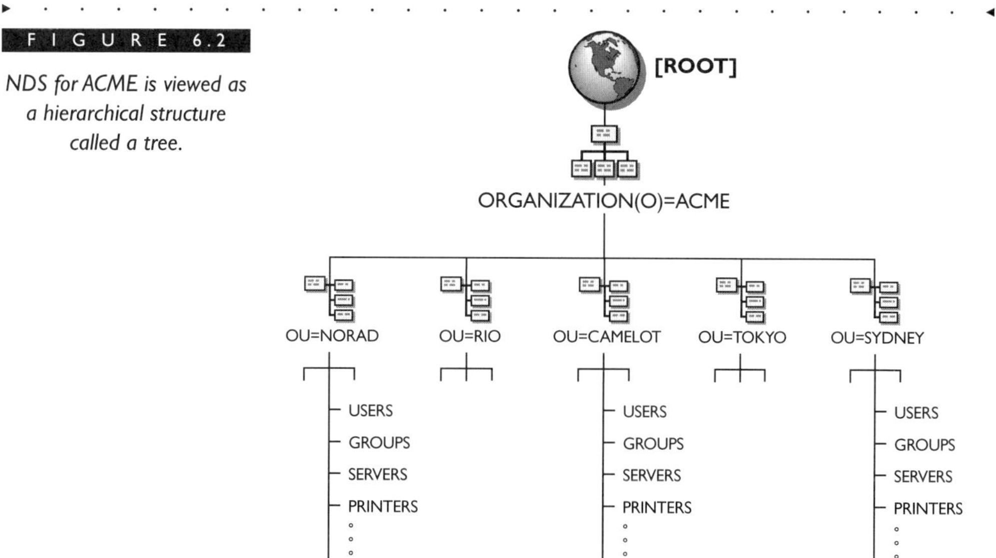

NDS partitions are logical sections of the NDS tree and are based on the same structure as the NDS tree. *Partitioning* is the process of splitting the NDS hierarchy or tree into smaller parts or subtrees. These subtrees can then be physically stored on your network servers as replicas of the partition. Partitioning the NDS tree enables you to selectively distribute the NDS tree information to the areas in the network that need the information. Figure 6.3 illustrates how the NDS hierarchy or tree for ACME can be split into partitions and placed on or copied to the network servers.

FIGURE 6.3

The NDS tree for ACME has been partitioned and placed on or copied to the network servers.

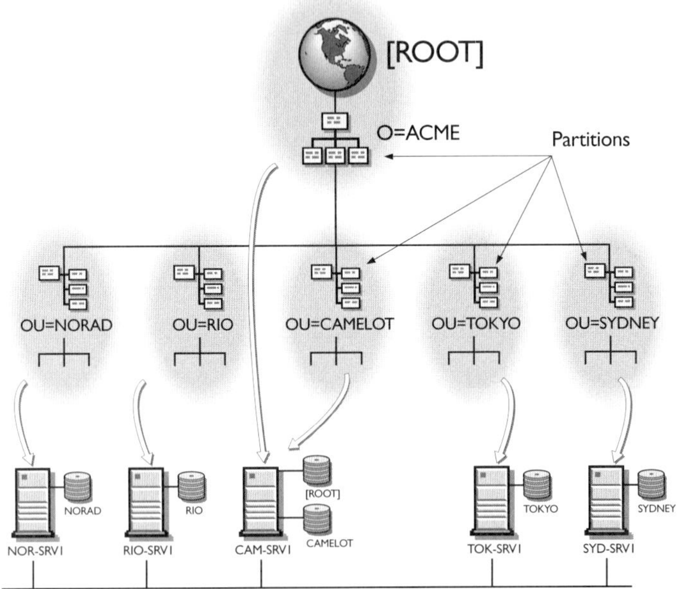

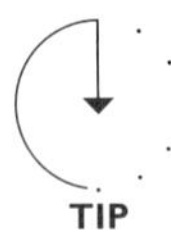

When NDS partitions are mentioned and described, you should not confuse them with file system partitions. An *NDS partition* is a portion of the NDS tree and does not contain any file system information. A *file system partition*, on the other hand, has the capability to split a hard drive into logical segments for use by the operating system.

NDS partitions and file system partitions serve different purposes and are not related in any way.

Partitioning gives you the ability to scale the NDS tree across the network servers. Splitting up the NDS tree into partitions and storing them on separate network servers will distribute the workload for each of the servers. In addition, the NetWare utilities enable you to select the servers in the network where you want to store the different NDS partitions.

As mentioned earlier, the layout of the NDS partitions is hierarchical, meaning that one partition is parent to subordinate or child partitions. When all partitions (parents and children) are connected together via NDS, they form a hierarchical map back to the [ROOT] object. Figure 6.4 illustrates how the individual partitions form a hierarchical map, often called a *partition map*.

FIGURE 6.4

Individual partitions for the ACME tree form a hierarchical partition map.

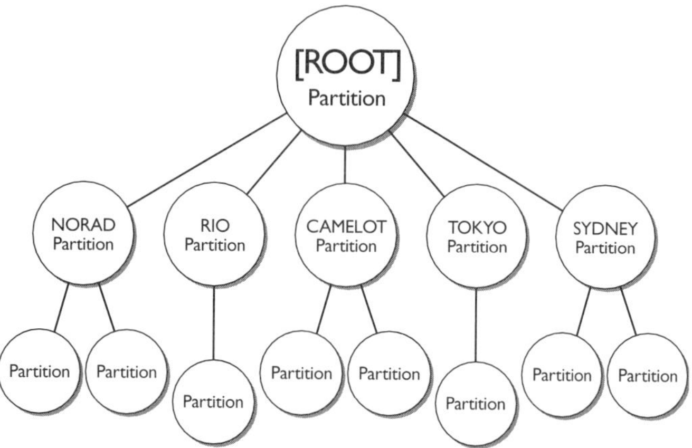

The Parent-Child Relationship between Partitions

The relationship between the individual partitions in the tree is a *parent-child relationship*. Where the boundaries between the partitions meet, the partition closer to the [ROOT] is considered the parent and the one farther away is the child.

The parent-child relationship is also described in terms of subordinate and superior partitions. A subordinate partition (or child) is the partition that is down the tree or farther from the [ROOT]. The superior partition (or parent) is the partition that is closer to the top of the tree than its subordinate partition.

In the ACME partition map, the parent-child relationship between partitions is illustrated in Figure 6.5. In this example, the OU containers that have been partitioned at NORAD, RIO, CAMELOT, TOKYO, and SYDNEY are child partitions to the partition [ROOT], which is the parent. In the case of the CAMELOT partition, it is also a parent partition with the three subordinate partitions as the child partitions.

FIGURE 6.5

The parent-child relationship between the partitions in the ACME tree

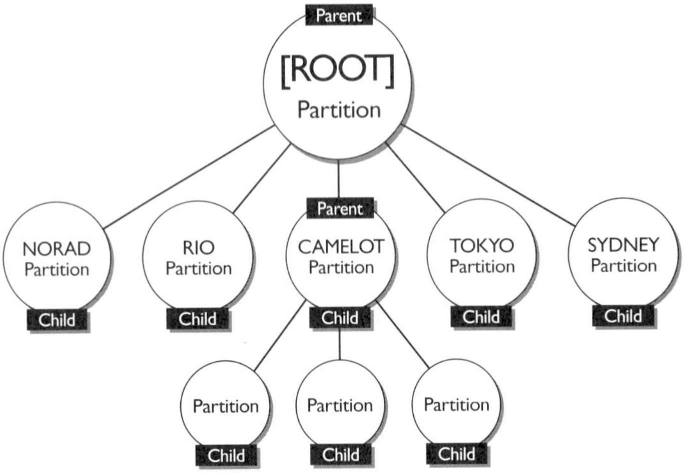

Partitioning can be compared to the responsibility of parents for keeping track of their children. When child partitions are created, their parent must maintain their locations. If the server does not hold both the parent and its child partitions, NDS will create a subordinate reference replica for each of the child partitions and place it on the server.

NDS requires that the location of the subordinate partitions be linked with their parent to form a common set of NDS information. The tree can then be traversed by the users. The parent only needs to know the location of its child partitions if the child partitions are not stored on the same server as the parent. The mechanism that maintains the relationship is called a subordinate reference replica. This topic will be discussed in more detail in the "Subordinate Reference Replicas" section later in this chapter.

If you should create new partitions below the CAMELOT partition as illustrated in Figure 6.6, then CAMELOT becomes a parent partition to the newly formed partitions. Although CAMELOT is a new parent, it is still a child partition of [ROOT]. However, there is no grandparent relationship, in which a grandparent must know about grandchild partitions. Only the parent-child relationship exists among partitions in NDS.

FIGURE 6.6

New partitions created below the CAMELOT partition

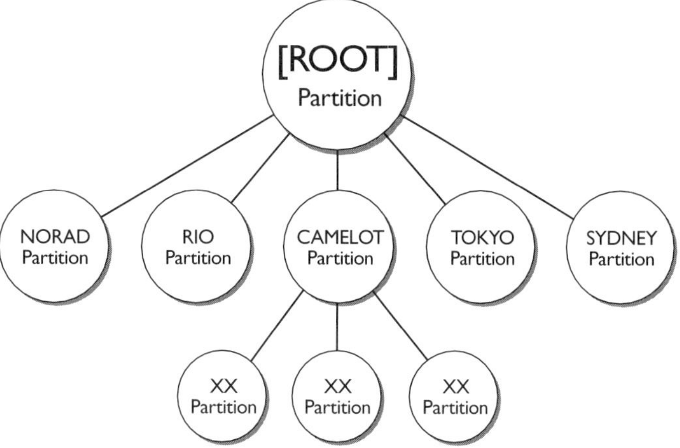

TIP

NDS maintains the relationship between the parent and child partitions. If a server is holding a parent partition and is not storing the child partition, NDS creates a subordinate reference replica pointing to the child partition. This replica maintains the links in the NDS tree. Again, the subordinate reference replicas are placed on servers where the parent partition is and the child partition is not. Therefore, any server holding a parent partition can end up storing subordinate reference replicas to child partitions.

Servers can also end up holding a large number of subordinate reference replicas depending on how you design the partitions for your NDS tree—for example, creating or partitioning each of the organizational units beneath the [ROOT] partition. If you have too many partitioned organizational units that are immediately below the [ROOT], NDS creates subordinate reference replicas automatically for any servers holding a copy of the [ROOT] partition.

Design your tree so that you minimize the degree to which each server holds subordinate reference replicas. More on this topic later.

Partitioning Is Transparent to Users

Partitioning of the NDS database is completely transparent to users, who can access the entire NDS tree regardless of which server they are connected to. For example, a user sitting at a single workstation on the network sees the NDS tree as a single logical entity, even though the NDS tree has been partitioned and distributed across the servers.

Although a specific server may not contain the complete set of NDS data files for the network, users still have the ability to get the information they request through background processes that NDS establishes and maintains between the separate partitions.

Partitioning Rules

The NDS partitions will follow these rules:

- The partition is named and requires a single container object at the top (or root) of the partition (not to be confused with the [ROOT] partition). The container object that is used as the start of the partition is called the *partition root object*. Only one partition root object exists for each partition, and it is the topmost container object. An example of partition root objects is shown in Figure 6.7.

- Two organizational unit containers at the same level cannot exist as a partition without a parent container. This rule is very similar to the first rule. Figure 6.8 illustrates how two peer OUs in the ACME tree cannot be contained in the same partition.

- The partitions cannot overlap with any other part of the NDS tree, meaning that one object will never reside in two partitions as illustrated in Figure 6.9.

- The partition contains all of the information for the connected subtree. Each partition may be thought of as a section or subtree of the entire NDS tree.

FIGURE 6.7

Several partition root objects in the ACME tree

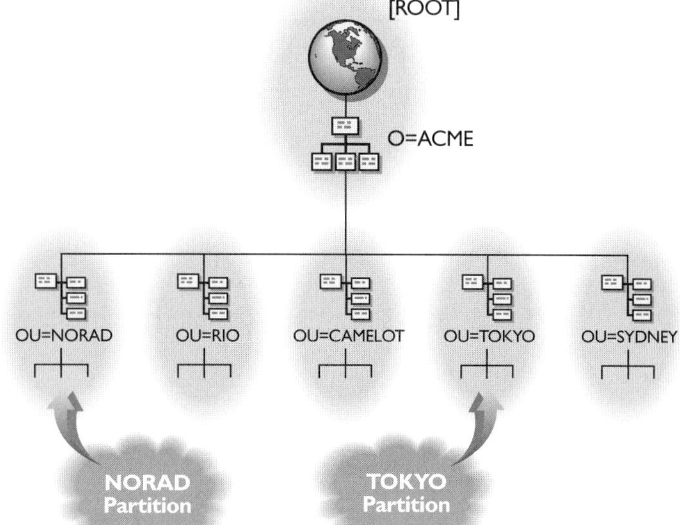

FIGURE 6.8

Two peer OUs in the ACME tree, such as OU=NOR and OU=RIO, cannot be contained in the same partition. A partition must have a single container object to define the top of the partition.

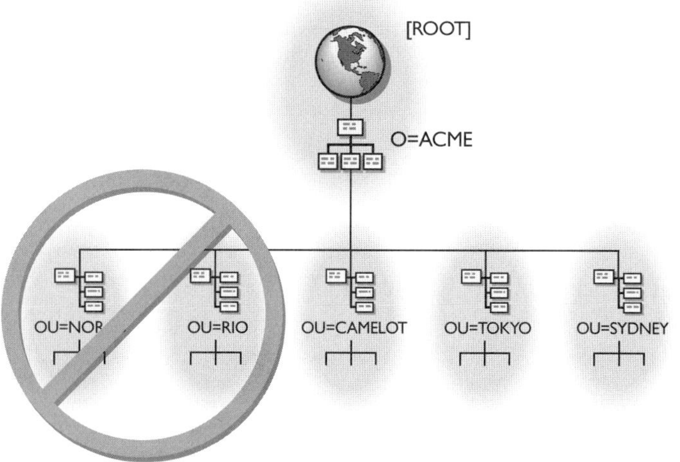

FIGURE 6.9

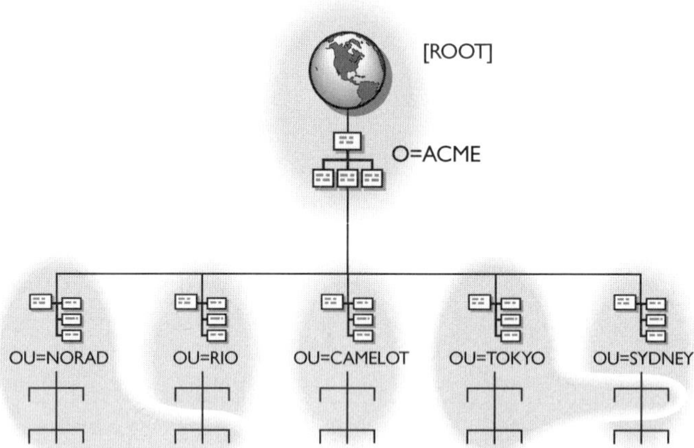

Partition information cannot overlap as shown in this figure. For example, the NORAD and TOKYO partitions cannot contain information that is subordinate to OU=RIO and OU=SYDNEY, respectively. An object can exist in only one partition.

The [ROOT] Partition

During the installation of the first NDS server, the [ROOT] partition for the tree is created automatically and placed on the NetWare 5 server. A copy (replica) of [ROOT] is placed on this server. In NetWare 5, the [ROOT] partition is the only partition that the installation program will create. Figure 6.10 illustrates the point at which the [ROOT] partition is created during the installation of NDS on the first NetWare 5 server. All other partitioning of the NDS database must be created by you or other system administrators. The [ROOT] partition cannot be removed unless you remove NDS from all the NetWare 5 servers, which is really removing the entire tree.

After the first server has been installed, you can add the objects necessary to build the tree structure for your company. In Figure 6.11, the ACME tree has been constructed using the NWADMIN utility to add the necessary container objects.

All the objects that have been added to the ACME tree are initially held by a single partition called the [ROOT] partition. Figure 6.12 illustrates how the [ROOT] partition is holding all the objects in the NDS tree until further partitioning can take place. After installation this partition resides only on the first NetWare 5 server installed.

Since there is only one copy of the [ROOT] partition, you should place the partition on other servers as they are installed in the system. The Novell Installation Program automatically creates additional copies of the partition as you add servers. For example, server NOR-SRV1 is installed into the tree and receives a read/write copy of the partition. Figure 6.13 shows that you will have two copies of the [ROOT] partition placed on the servers, NOR-SRV1 and CAM-SRV1.

FIGURE 6.10

The [ROOT] partition is created automatically when the first NetWare 5 server is installed. In this example, the first server is the CAM-SRV1 server in CAMELOT, which holds the master replica of [ROOT].

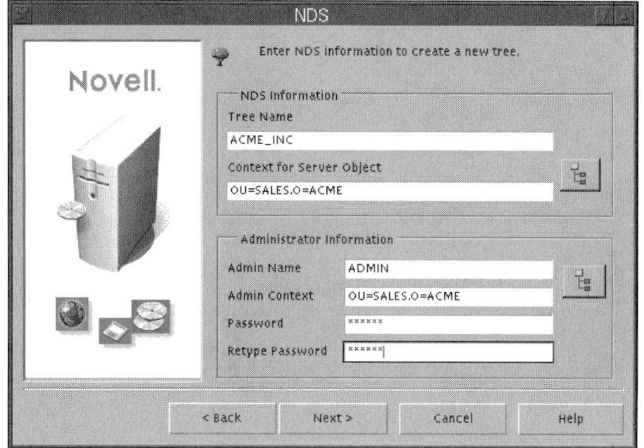

FIGURE 6.11

The ACME tree has been constructed by adding the necessary objects.

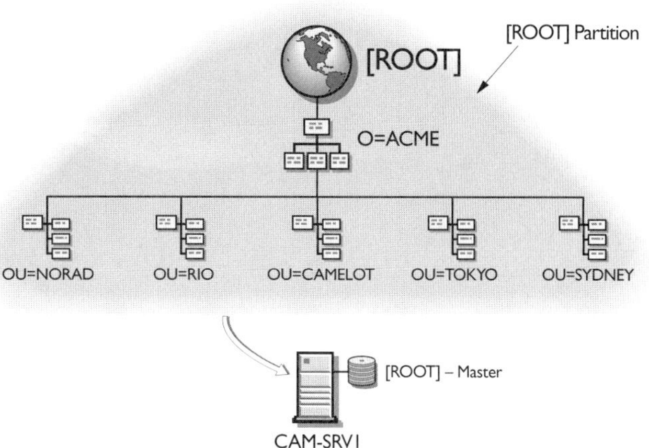

Child partitions can be created from the [ROOT] partition by selecting a subordinate container object, typically an OU, as the top of the partition. A partition can have only one topmost container object (referred to as the *partition root object*).

FIGURE 6.12

The [ROOT] partition holds all the objects in the tree until further partitioning takes place.

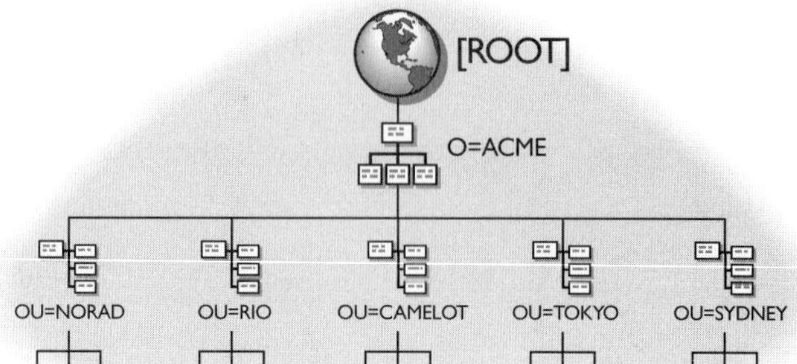

FIGURE 6.13

Using the NDS Manager utility, you can see two copies of the [ROOT] partition, NOR-SRV1 and CAM-SRV1, that have been placed on the servers for the ACME tree.

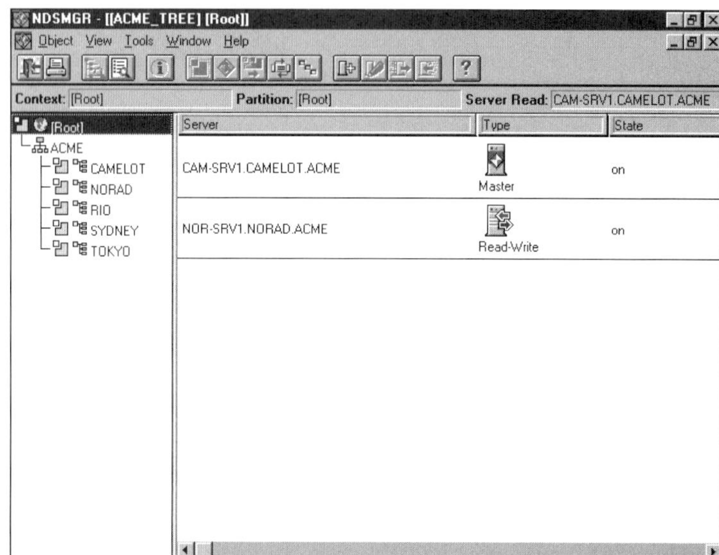

When the partition is created, it takes its name from the topmost container object (partition root object). All the objects in the tree that are under the container object comprise the contents of the new partition. Creating a partition does not affect the child partition boundaries. Figure 6.14 shows the creation of the NORAD partition for the ACME tree. All the objects in the subtree under NORAD are included in the partition.

FIGURE 6.14

A new partition called NORAD is created for the ACME tree.

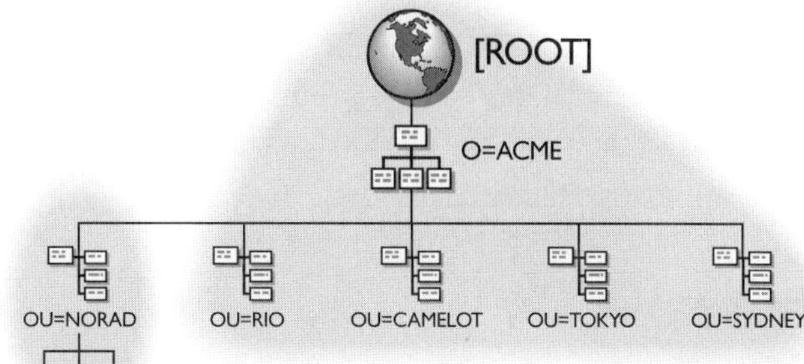

Creating a child partition from the parent partition is an operation called create partition in the NetWare utilities. The operation is fast and in most cases does not generate a lot of traffic on your network unless you have many replicas of the partition. The operation simply divides one partition into two with all the information staying on the same server that contained the original partition. This create partition operation will make a new child partition on all the servers that had a copy of the parent partition. Figure 6.15 shows the NORAD partition being created from the [ROOT] partition.

FIGURE 6.15

A conceptual view of a create partition operation to create the NORAD partition. This operation affects both original copies of the [ROOT] partition, which are stored on CAM-SRV1 and NOR-SRV1.

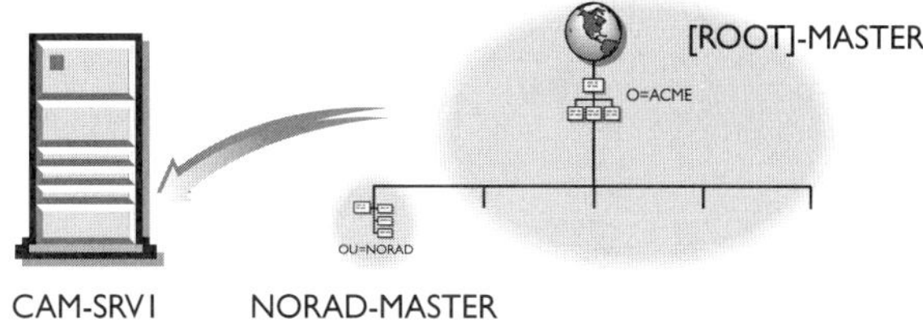

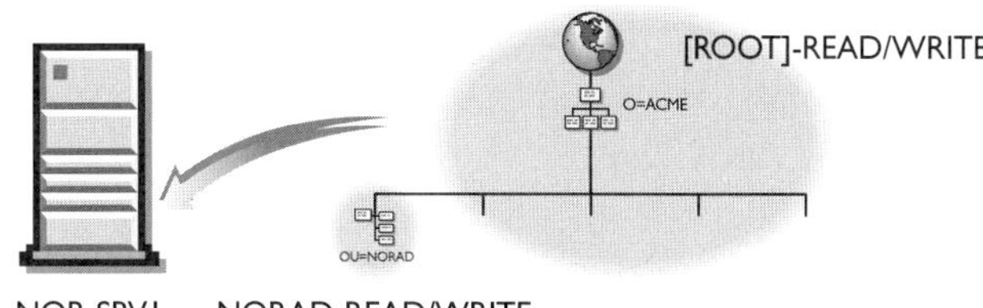

It is recommended that the [ROOT] partition be kept small with only the [ROOT] object and O=Organization containers and a few objects if necessary. For example, in order to keep the [ROOT] partition small for ACME, further partitioning needs to take place. As illustrated in Figure 6.16, if more partitions are created directly under the [ROOT] partition, then the [ROOT] partition holds only the topmost portions of the tree.

FIGURE 6.16

The [ROOT] partition for the ACME tree should hold only the topmost portion of the tree.

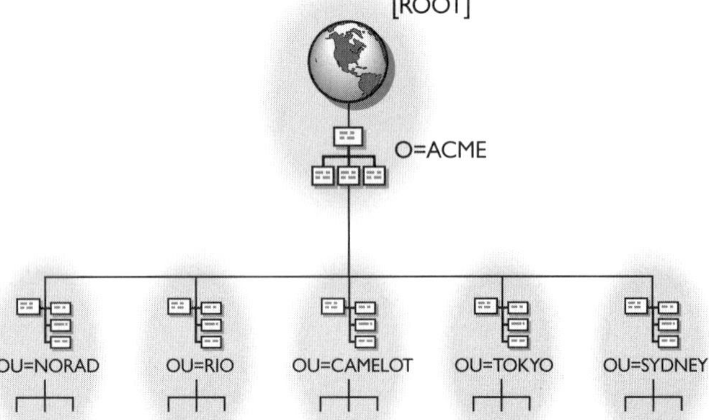

Partition Design

Designing the partitioning of your NDS tree can be very simple if you remember why you create a partition. You create a partition to scale NDS across your network servers. If your network is very small, then you do not need to partition your NDS tree.

The number one design criterion for partitioning is the physical layout of your network infrastructure: the WAN links and the network servers. Using this criterion, your main task is to partition the NDS tree to localize the information. This means that you want to partition the Directory to keep the NORAD information in NORAD, the RIO information in RIO, and so on. Figure 6.17

illustrates the physical WAN layout for the ACME company. Figure 6.18 shows how the ACME tree has been partitioned to support the physical WAN layout. Note that in our example the [ROOT] partition is very small and includes only the [ROOT] and organization container objects. Keeping the [ROOT] partition small is recommended and will be discussed later when we address replication.

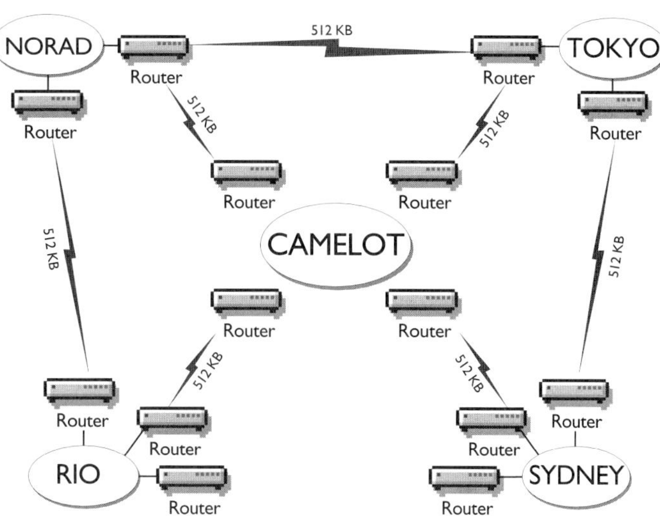

FIGURE 6.17

The physical WAN network layout for the ACME company

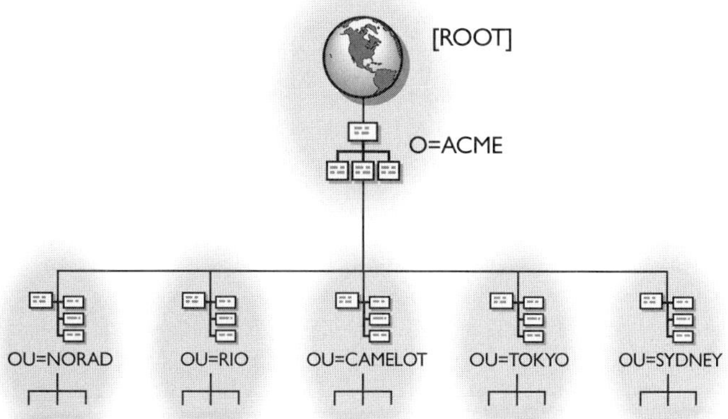

FIGURE 6.18

The ACME tree has been partitioned according to the WAN infrastructure.

As illustrated in Figure 6.19, you can see that the NORAD partition and its object information have been be placed on the server in NORAD. The same is true for all the locations. By partitioning the NDS tree based on your WAN network layout, you can keep the information local to each location and yet still find and use the resources throughout the entire NDS tree.

FIGURE 6.19

NDS distributes the information across the network servers for ACME. The NORAD partition is stored locally on the NORAD server. Each of the partitions is stored on its local server.

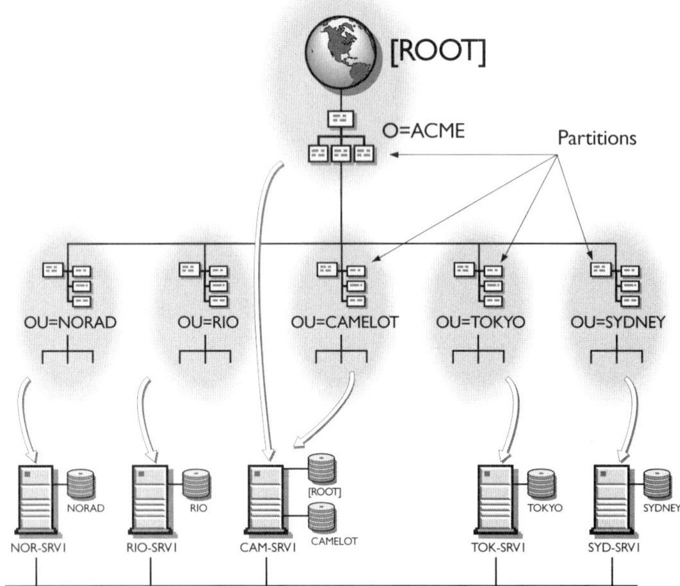

Guidelines for Creating Partitions

The following guidelines were developed to assist network administrators when designing a plan for partitioning and replication that provides a stable and efficient network.

Consulting Experience

The guidelines presented here assume that your server hardware is fast, meaning Pentium-class PCs operating at 300 MHz or better. Keep in mind that the slowest server in the replica list tends to affect all synchronization activities of even the faster servers in the same partition. If you are operating on slower hardware, you should carefully read the recommendations throughout this section for partitioning guidelines.

The specific guidelines and recommendations for designing your NDS partitions are as follows:

- Do not span a WAN link or physical locations with a partition. This design rule is very important and should not be ignored. The reason we don't recommend spanning with the WAN link is that unnecessary NDS traffic will travel between two locations and across your WAN infrastructure. This extra traffic will occur during each of the normal synchronization operations. Spanning a partition across the WAN link as shown in Figure 6.20 generally should be avoided.

FIGURE 6.20

Do not span the WAN link as shown in this example of the [ROOT] partition spanning the CAMELOT, RIO, and TOKYO sites.

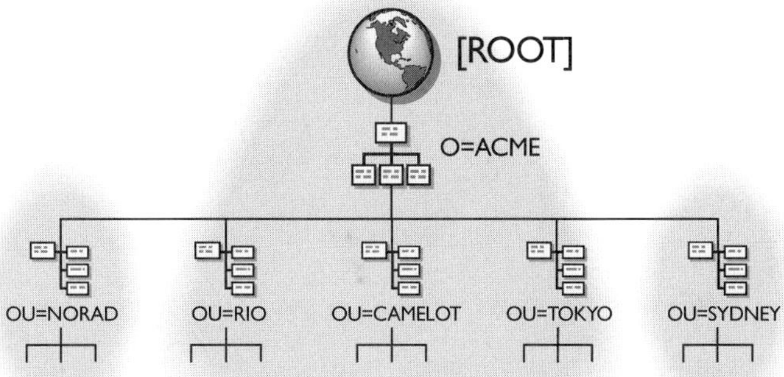

- Keep the [ROOT] partition small. The [ROOT] partition should include only the [ROOT] object and the O=Organization object. Do not include additional containers in the [ROOT] partition other than the [ROOT] object and Organization=ACME object as shown in Figure 6.21. This means that you should not include any other subordinate container OUs in the partition with the [ROOT] partition. As illustrated in Figure 6.21, you should avoid partitioning an individual location within the [ROOT] partition.
- The top layers of the tree should be partitioned according to the locations in your company. Again, do not span a WAN link with the same partition. Partition locally wherever possible.

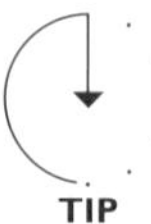

These guidelines do not suggest that you partition every organizational unit in your tree. Partition locally, and partition further at that site only if necessary.

FIGURE 6.21

Do not include additional containers in the [ROOT] partition other than [ROOT] object and Organization=ACME as shown in this example. We recommend that you not leave the individual location information in the [ROOT] partition.

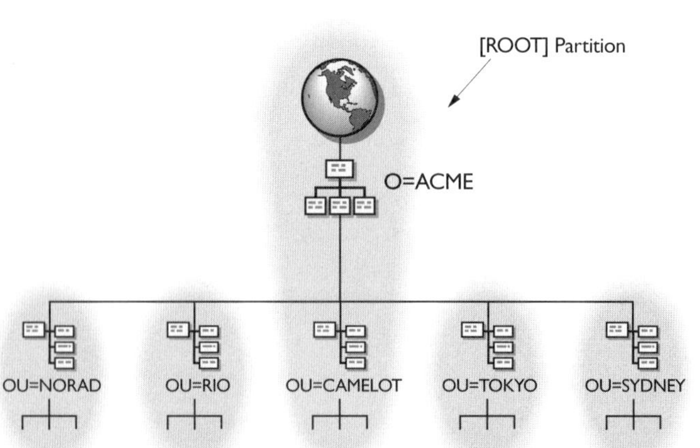

- The bottom layers of the tree should be split off into additional partitions only if there are special requirements. The special requirements are either a large partition (total number of objects is greater than 5,000), more than ten replicas of the same partition, or the need to break out an administrative subtree.

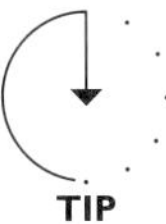
TIP

The previous partitioning thresholds assume you are operating on high-end server hardware. For some servers the thresholds may be 10,000 objects per partition and 20 replicas.

- You will want a small number of partitions at the top layers of the tree and possibly more partitions as you move toward the bottom. If you have designed the tree based on a pyramid shape, as recommended in Chapter 5, "Novell Directory Services Tree," then your partition design will naturally follow the tree design.
- Do not create a partition for a location (even if it is across a WAN link) if there is no local server to store it on. This situation is common only with small remote offices that do not have servers at their local site. The users in this situation would currently access all the network services across the WAN infrastructure. Access to NDS is no different. Figure 6.22 shows how these users at OU=DIST would still be part of a partition contained on a server in OU=DIST because they do not have their own server.

FIGURE 6.22

Users will be part of a partition stored on another server if they do not have a local server in their office.

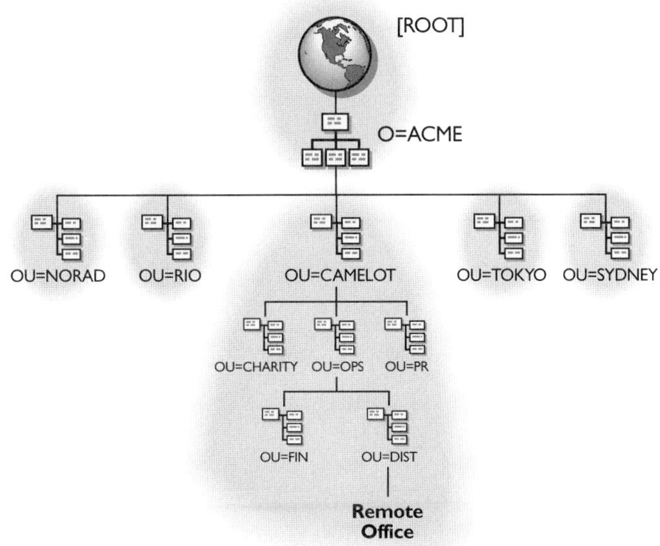

Partitioning the Top Layers

As mentioned earlier, the top layers in the tree should be partitioned according to the WAN infrastructure as shown in Figure 6.23. Since the top layers of the tree should already be designed according to the WAN links, then partitioning will naturally follow these boundaries.

FIGURE 6.23

The top layers of the ACME tree partitioned according to the WAN infrastructure

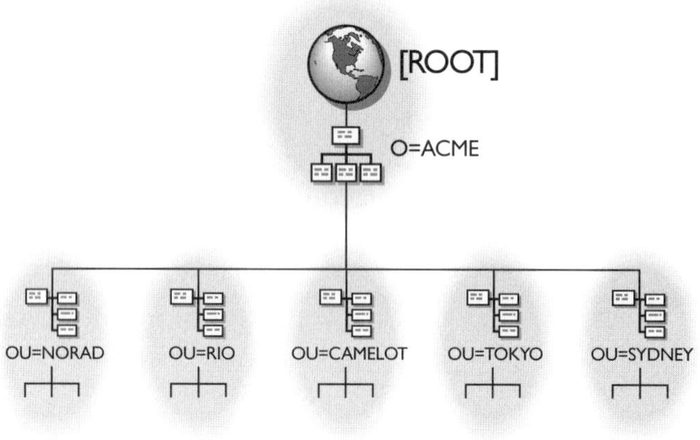

The NDS database will not scale as well if you try to combine multiple geographical sites into one partition. If you try to span more than one location in a partition, then the information in the partition will synchronize with the other copies across the slower WAN links. This reduces the efficiencies of the network and destroys the purpose of trying to create a partition in the first place.

If you have implemented regional OU containers in your tree, then you should create a partition for each of the regional OUs and store that partition on a server separate from its parent partition. After the region partitions are defined in your tree, you will need to create partitions at the locations under each of the regions and store them on separate servers from their parents in order to distribute the subordinate references to multiple servers.

Partitioning the Bottom Layers

Because the design of the bottom of the tree is based on the divisions, departments, and workgroups within each location of the WAN, the tree should already be partitioned at the WAN site or location. Further partitioning may not be needed. Follow the partitioning guidelines presented earlier regarding the number of objects in a partition and the number of replicas. The bottom layers of the tree can be partitioned only if there is a special requirement. The special requirements include the following:

- Partition size
- Number of replicas
- Partition administration

Partition Size

As the partition size grows, you should consider creating another partition to help distribute the workload that any one server or set of servers has to handle. A larger partition is approximately 5,000 objects on a high-end PC. So as the partition grows larger, you should then split the partition by creating a new child partition. Remember, a partition contains all the objects in a defined subtree, not just the objects in a single container.

Figure 6.24 depicts the CAMELOT partition being split into two partitions. The OU=OPS container object becomes a new child partition to CAMELOT. It is assumed that this new partition was created because the CAMELOT partition became larger than 5,000 objects and was running on a Pentium-class PC. The OU=OPS container and subtree hold a large number of the objects and were split off as a new partition.

Number of Replicas

Another consideration is the total number of replicas of a single partition. If the total number of replicas for the same partition goes beyond 20, then you should consider splitting the partition just to reduce the total number of replicas for that partition. The primary reason you will need more than three replicas of any partition is to support bindery services at NetWare 5 servers for backup and other utilities that need the bindery.

FIGURE 6.24

The OU=OPS container object is created as a new partition because the CAMELOT partition became too large.

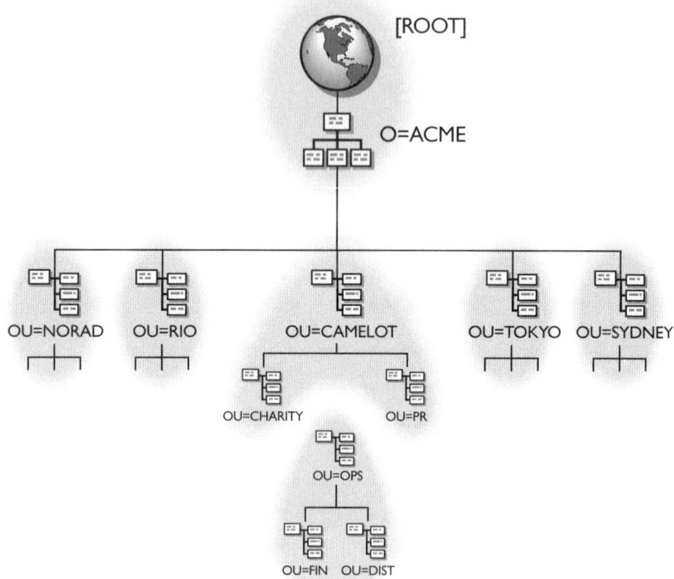

Also, keep in mind that more replicas means more management if a partition should need repairing. Using Novell's utilities to make repairs becomes a bigger task if you have many replicas. Each server holding a replica (and the subordinate replicas) may need to be repaired if you encounter problems. Obviously, the more replicas, the larger the task of repair for you, your administrators, or outside support personnel.

Partition Administration

NDS enables several different administrators to be responsible for partitioning the NDS tree. If a departmental or site manager wants the responsibility to manage his or her own partitioning, then you need to plan the parent partitions accordingly. For example, the rights needed to partition the NDS tree are effective write rights to the access control list (ACL) of the top container object of the partition. There are several ways to receive this privilege. One way is through the Supervisor object right to the container object that defines the partition. You can also grant explicit write rights to its ACL. Also, if there is a need to create a new partition from the parent partition, then the administrator creating the child needs full rights to the parent.

In order to perform other partition operations such as add/remove replica and change replica type, you are required to have rights to the server object that is being affected. For more information on security and rights, see Chapter 13, "Managing NetWare Security."

A Pyramid Shape for the Partitions

The pyramid-shaped design for the partitions is recommended because it automatically distributes the subordinate reference replicas. Having a smaller number of partitions at the top of the tree with more at the bottom of the tree satisfies the requirement of fewer subordinate reference replicas per server and minimizes the supportability and repairability of your tree if problems should occur.

The pyramid-shaped design can be accomplished if you always create partitions at the top layers according to the WAN infrastructure and then create the bottom layer partitions as specified in the previous guidelines. For example, as illustrated in Figure 6.25, the ACME tree has been partitioned according to the WAN infrastructure with some further partitioning at the lower layers. The partitioning for the ACME tree is in the shape of a pyramid.

By following the partitioning guidelines for both the top and bottom layers of your tree, you ensure that the NDS information will always remain close to the user and other leaf objects because the partitions have been based on the locations. An exception would be the [ROOT] partition, which is created automatically during installation of the first NetWare 5 server.

Partitioning the NT Domain Object

NDS for NT is an add-on software product to NetWare 5 that makes it easier to manage the resources in both your NetWare and Windows NT networks. It alleviates the dual administration necessary in managing NT domains and an NDS tree. With NDS for NT, all administration is done from a single point using NWADMIN. NDS for NT will store all information necessary in the NDS tree, and all NT requests to the domain are redirected to NDS. This provides a single point of administration for both worlds. The result is that you can manage all aspects of the NT Server domain through NDS.

FIGURE 6.25

The ACME tree has been partitioned according to the WAN infrastructure, which naturally takes the shape of a pyramid.

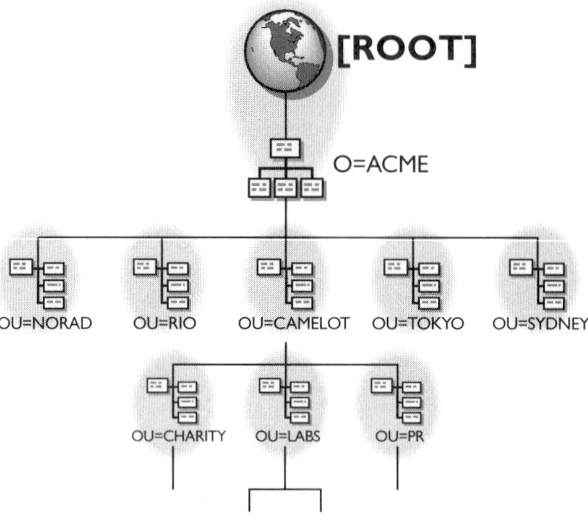

Hierarchical partitions in the map

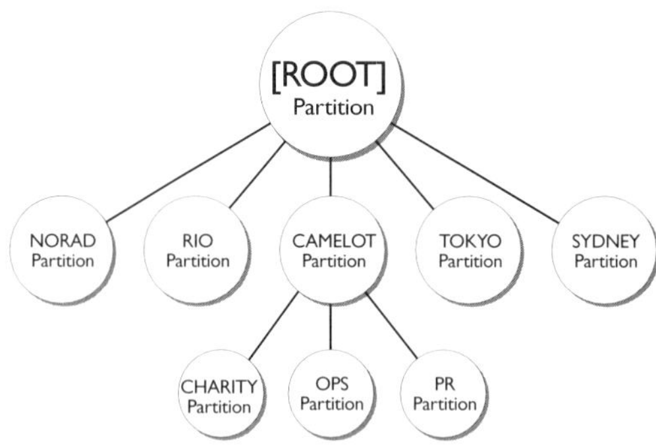

Pyramid-shaped partition map

When you configure the NDS for NT software, you select a specific context in the tree where the current NT domain objects will be migrated. The migration is performed using the Domain Object Wizard. During the execution of the Wizard, you are asked to provide a name for the NT domain object that is created in the selected context. This domain object in NDS represents the NT domain. This object behaves similarly to a Group object or a Container object in that it holds information about the domain and users that are members of the domain, but it also contains member objects such as computers and groups just as an actual domain does. Figure 6.26 illustrates how the domain object placed in the NDS tree represents the NT domain.

FIGURE 6.26

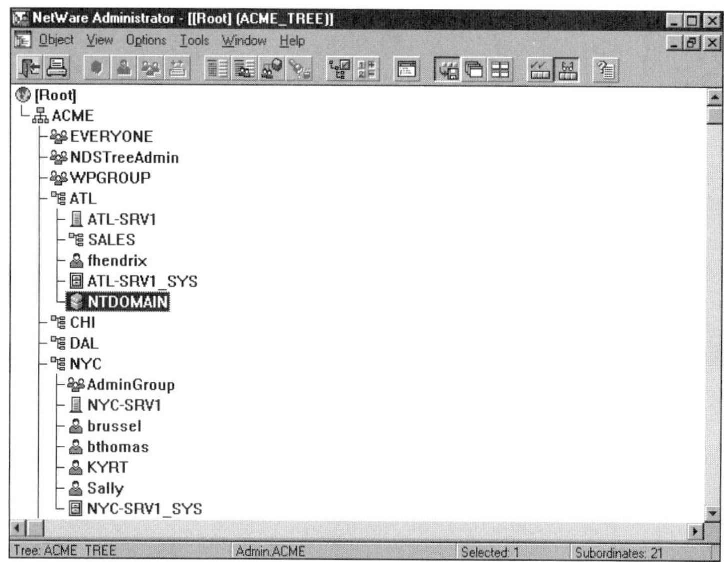

The domain object (in this case, NTDOMAIN) is created in the NDS tree, which represents the NT domain. Users added to the domain object in NDS are immediately visible to the NT Server domain.

Since the NT domain object in NDS acts as a group with a list of domain members, it takes on the NDS design characteristics of an NDS Group object. However, it is also a special NDS container object that holds NDS for NT Local Group objects, NDS for NT Global Group objects, and NDS for NT Workstation objects that are migrated from the original NT domain. Figure 6.27 illustrates how the NTDOMAIN object contains the NDS for NT Local Group objects, NDS for NT Global Group objects, and NDS for NT Workstation objects that have been migrated.

Since this new NDS object called the NT Domain object acts as both a group and a container, it has unique design characteristics. One of these characteristics is its ability to create an NDS partition at the domain object. In other words, the NT domain object in the tree can become its own partition. Figure 6.28 illustrates how a domain object can be partitioned using the NDS Manager utility. In this case, the NT domain object called NTDOMAIN in ATL.ACME is being created as an NDS partition.

FIGURE 6.27

The NTDOMAIN object in the NDS tree contains the NDS for NT Local Group objects, NDS for NT Global Group objects, and NDS for NT Workstation objects that have been migrated.

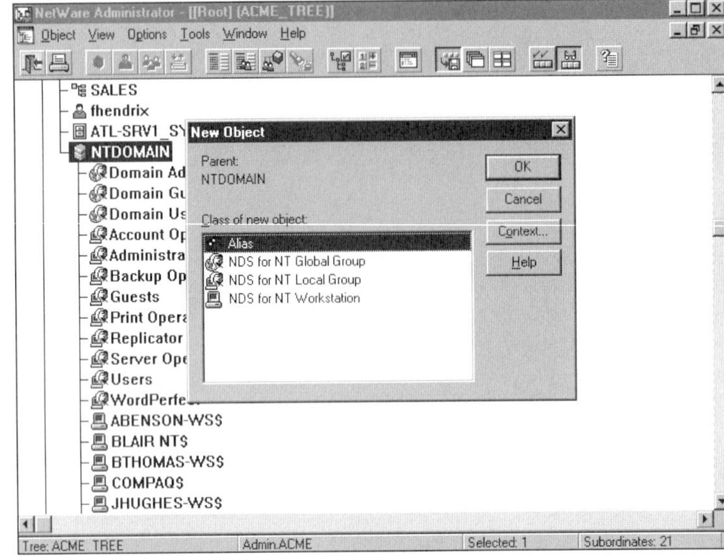

FIGURE 6.28

The NT domain object, NTDOMAIN.ATL.ACME, is being partitioned using the NDS Manager utility.

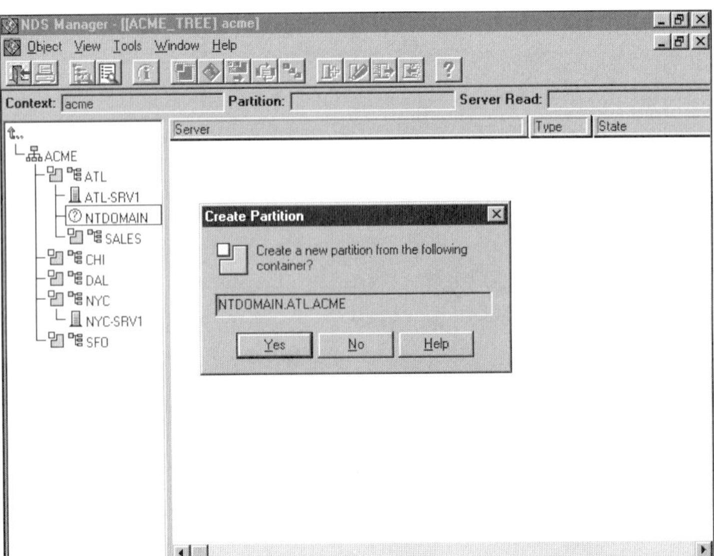

The information that is stored in the partition created from the domain object consists of the objects found under the domain. These objects are NDS for NT Local Group objects, NDS for NT Global Group objects, NDS for NT Workstation objects, and Alias objects. The users that were migrated from the original NT domain are not included as part of a partition created from the NT domain object in NDS.

NOTE

The domain object in NDS can only be partitioned using NDS Manager. Also, NDS Manager version 1.25 (or later) is the only version that will let you make this change. Make sure that you are using the correct version of NDS Manager before trying to do the partitioning operation.

NDS Replicas

As mentioned earlier, NDS is a global name service; it can be split into partitions and then distributed to any number of network servers. The feature that distributes NDS is called *partitioning*, and the characteristic that makes it redundant is called *replication*. An NDS replica is the physical copy of a partition that is stored on a network server. An NDS partition can have multiple replicas or copies stored on different network servers. The group of replicas that exist for a particular partition is called a *replica list*.

It is important to remember that a partition is a logical structure, whereas the replica is a physical copy of the partition, as illustrated in Figure 6.29, where the [ROOT] partition for ACME is placed on servers NOR-SRV1, CAM-SRV1, and TOK-SRV1.

The fact that an NDS tree can be partitioned and replicated makes NDS a powerful facility for storing, accessing, managing, and using information about network resources regardless of where they are physically located. Replication increases the availability of NDS, so that any number of servers can be down and the users can still log in and access the network services.

FIGURE 6.29

NDS replicas for the [ROOT] partition are stored on different servers throughout the network. In this case, the [ROOT] partition for ACME is placed on servers NOR-SRV1, CAM-SRV1, and TOK-SRV1.

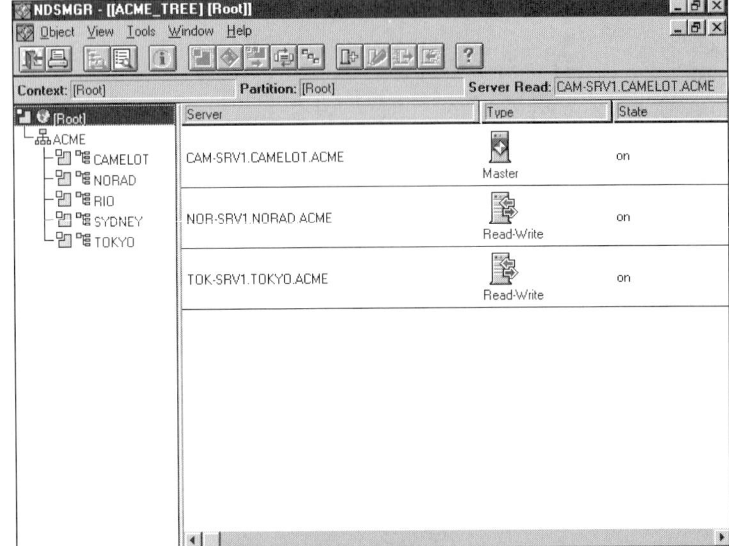

The Purpose of NDS Replicas

Replication is a major feature and advantage of NDS. Replication of the NDS tree serves three primary purposes:

- **Fault tolerance** — Replication increases the availability of a partition (a section of the NDS tree) to the users because the partition now has more than one copy of its information. For example, if a server holding a replica of the partition becomes unavailable, then the users can use another copy or replica for authentication and updates.

- **Performance** — You can increase the performance of NDS access by proper physical placement of the replicas. Replication enables you to have multiple replicas of the partition and to place those replicas local to the users that need the information. Having a local replica will decrease the time needed to authenticate, make changes, do searches, and extract NDS information.

- **Name resolution** — The mechanism that NDS uses to locate the proper server is *name resolution* or *tree walking*. Users requesting NDS information have to first locate the server that stores the information. If the requested information is not found on the server that the user is already connected to, then NDS will automatically connect the user to the proper server.

The primary goal of replication is to eliminate the single point of failure for an NDS partition. Having multiple replicas of a partition protects you against most outages in the network infrastructure such as downed servers, routers, or WAN links.

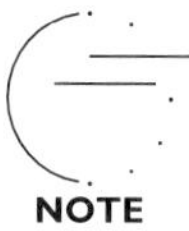

NOTE

NDS replication does not provide fault tolerance for the file system stored on the NetWare 5 servers. Replication only increases the availability of the NDS object and property information stored in the NDS partition.

The NetWare 5 installation program will help you replicate the NDS partitions for fault tolerance during installation of the server. When you are installing additional servers into the tree, the installation program will try to place up to three replicas for a partition. For example, the partition where you are installing the server has less than three total replicas. The installation will place a read/write replica on the new server. Automatic replication applies only to the partition where the server object is being installed and does not affect other partitions in the tree. The purpose for doing this automatic replication is to support fault tolerance of the NDS database. If you are comfortable with the three automatic replicas placed during installation, then you may not need to change the replication of a partition for fault tolerance.

Replica Types

Proper placement of replicas on the network servers is important to ensure proper operation of the Directory. A server may contain a number of replicas if they are from different partitions. A server also does not have to contain any replicas. In order to understand where and when to place the replicas, you must understand the different types of replicas and their characteristics.

As stated earlier, each partition can have multiple replicas. And each replica will be one of the following four replica types: master, read/write, read-only, and subordinate reference.

The Master Replica

The master (M) replica of a partition is always the first replica that is created; it can be changed as other replicas are added. Only one master replica can exist for each partition. The master replica provides these features:

- **Accepts client updates to the NDS object and attributes.** This is the ability to add, delete, and modify the objects in the partition.
- **Controls all partitioning operations.** These operations include splitting and joining partitions, moving objects and subtrees, adding and removing replicas, and repairing the replicas.
- **Conforms to the X.500 model.** This model enables clients to request the use of only the master replica.

NDS permits only one master replica per partition because the master replica controls all the partitioning operations. The master replica essentially locks the partition during any partition operation, thus ensuring that only one operation is performed at a time. This mechanism provides the NDS database integrity.

For example, in order to change the partition structure of the tree through either a create or merge partition operation, you must be able to contact the master for that partition. The master then works with the other replicas to complete the operation. If you are the system administrator, you must have sufficient rights to the partition before NDS will let you do the partitioning.

In addition, the master replica is equal to all other replicas during replica synchronization. Replica synchronization is a peer-to-peer mechanism, not a master-slave device.

The master replica provides complete access to the object and property information in the partition. This means that users can log in through this replica and make changes to the information in the replica. Changes include adding, deleting, and renaming NDS objects or modifying the objects and the properties.

Figure 6.30 shows the master replicas for the [ROOT], CAMELOT, NORAD, RIO, TOKYO, and SYDNEY partitions of the ACME tree. The master replicas are stored on the server CAM-SRV1.

FIGURE 6.30

The master replicas for the [ROOT], CAMELOT, NORAD, RIO, TOKYO, and SYDNEY partitions of the ACME tree are stored on the server CAM-SRV1.

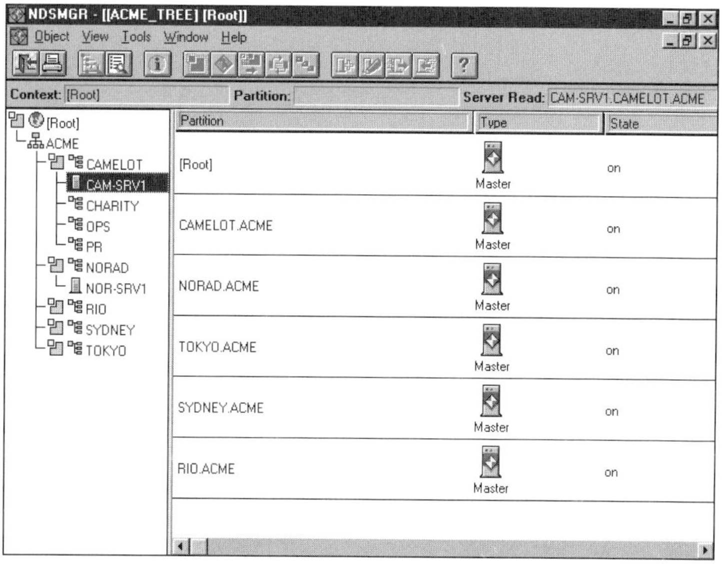

The Read/Write Replica

The purpose of the read/write (R/W) replica is to distribute the NDS partition information across the NetWare 5 servers on the network for fault tolerance and performance. The read/write replica is used most often (especially in large networks with many servers) because any number of them can exist for any given partition. Although there is no limit to the number of read/write replicas per partition, we do recommend that you keep the number small and create a new read/write replica only when needed.

A read/write replica provides these features:

- **Accepts client updates to the NDS objects and properties.** Client updates include adding, deleting, and modifying the objects in the partitions.
- **Provides fault tolerance for the partition.** This means that the read/write replicas improve availability of the information stored in the partition.

- **Increases performance of the NDS access by the physical placement of the read/write replicas.** The read/write replica enables you to have multiple replicas of the partition and to place those replicas local to the users who need the information.

Like the master replica, the read/write replica provides users complete access to the object and property information in the partition. A read/write replica also allows clients to make modifications. Since updates can be made to a read/write replica, users of the network can use the read/write replica to log in and make authentication requests.

In some of the other documentation on NetWare 5 the read/write replica is often referred to as a secondary replica.

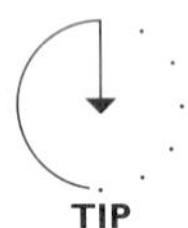
TIP

The bindery services feature in NetWare 5 requires that at least a read/write or master replica of the partition containing the bindery context exist on the server where the services are needed.

Figure 6.31 shows the read/write replicas for the [ROOT] partition of the ACME tree. There are several read/write replicas, which are stored on the servers, CAM-SRV1, and TOK-SRV1.

FIGURE 6.31

The read/write replicas for the [ROOT] partition of the ACME tree are stored on the servers NOR-SRV1 and TOK-SRV1.

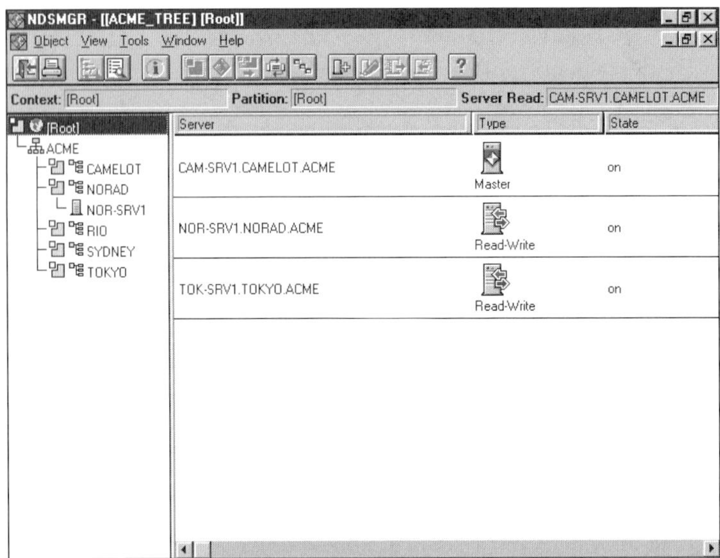

The Read-Only Replica

The read-only (RO) replica, as the name implies, will not accept changes from users. The only way that a read-only replica discovers changes is through synchronization with the other replicas (read/write and master).

The read-only replica has these features:

- **Provides access to the NDS objects and attributes in the partition**. This replica does not accept client updates but does accept read requests from the clients.
- **Provides fault tolerance for the partition**. This means that the read-only replicas improve availability of the information stored in the partition.
- **Increases performance of the NDS access through its physical placement.** You can make these replicas local to the users who need the information.

Because a read-only replica cannot be updated, it cannot support login or authentication requests from the users. For this reason, read-only replicas are seldom used or implemented into production. There are currently very few reasons to implement read-only partitions.

NOTE

When a network user logs into NDS, three properties of the user object are updated: Network Address, Login Time, and Last Login Time. In order for users to change or update these three properties, they must log into at least a read/write or master replica. The read-only replica cannot accept user logins because these properties cannot be updated. When a network user logs out of the Directory, the Network Address property for the user object is modified.

One possible use of a read-only replica is when you are trying to provide users read access to the NDS information but no update activity. For example, if you want to build an off-site disaster recovery center for your servers, you can implement a read-only replica, which will maintain itself through replica synchronization but not let any users connect to those servers.

NOTE

Be aware that if you disable the login on a NetWare 5 server (in this case a server with a read-only replica), then the other NetWare 5 servers will not be able to connect to the server to perform replica synchronization. Disabling logins on a server with any replicas should be avoided because it will discontinue the replica synchronization for that server.

The Subordinate Reference Replica

A subordinate reference (SR) replica contains only one object—the topmost container object in the partition. The topmost object in the partition defines the partition and is called the *partition root object*. This container object stores partition information that links together the partitions in the tree. Subordinate reference replicas connect the parent partitions with their child partitions.

Subordinate references replicas are created and managed by NDS and the servers. You do not need to manage them. The NDS system will place a subordinate reference replica on a server that contains a replica of the parent but does not have the child replica. NDS places a subordinate reference replica for each child of the parent on that server. Figure 6.32 illustrates a partitioned tree and its subsequent replica placement on the network servers. Some of the servers have subordinate reference replicas.

Some of the servers in Figure 6.32 are storing subordinate reference replicas because the servers are holding the parent partition, but not the corresponding child partition. For example, TOK-SRV1 holds a copy of the [ROOT] partition but not the NORAD, CAMELOT, or RIO partitions. So subordinate references are established on TOK-SRV1 to link the parent partition with its child partitions.

The subordinate reference replicas that connect the tree together are visible in Novell's NDS Manager utility and also the DSREPAIR utility. Figure 6.33 displays all the replicas on the server NOR-SRV1. Notice the subordinate reference replica for the CAMELOT partition.

Because a subordinate reference replica does not contain all of the information for each of the objects in the partition, it cannot provide users access to the object and property information. A user cannot log in through this replica because there is no NDS object information to access.

FIGURE 6.32

The ACME tree is partitioned, and subordinate reference replicas are created whenever a parent partition exists on a server without a copy of a child partition.

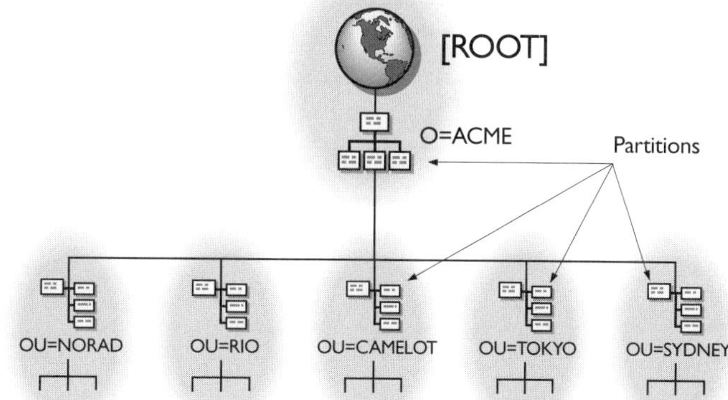

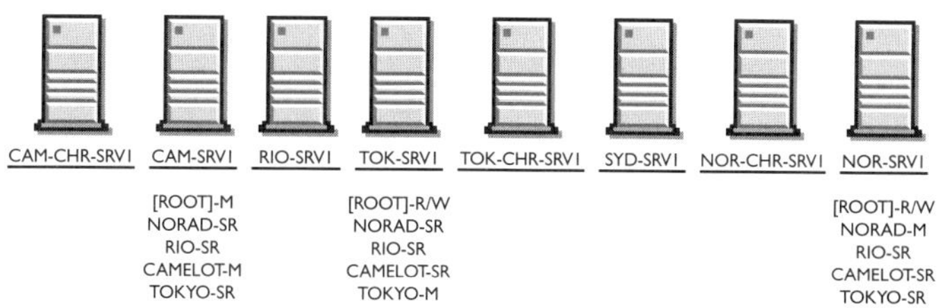

NDS Replication Design

One of the most important responsibilities of an NDS administrator is to design the placement of the NDS replicas. The replication design includes the distribution and placement of replicas to the specific network servers for each of the partitions. Your replica design should provide fault tolerance for each partition.

Before you complete your replication design, you will need to know some basic rules, as follows. These rules apply to all replicas and will help you understand how replicas are implemented or placed throughout the servers on the network.

FIGURE 6.33

NDS Manager displays all of the read/write replicas on the server NOR-SVR1.

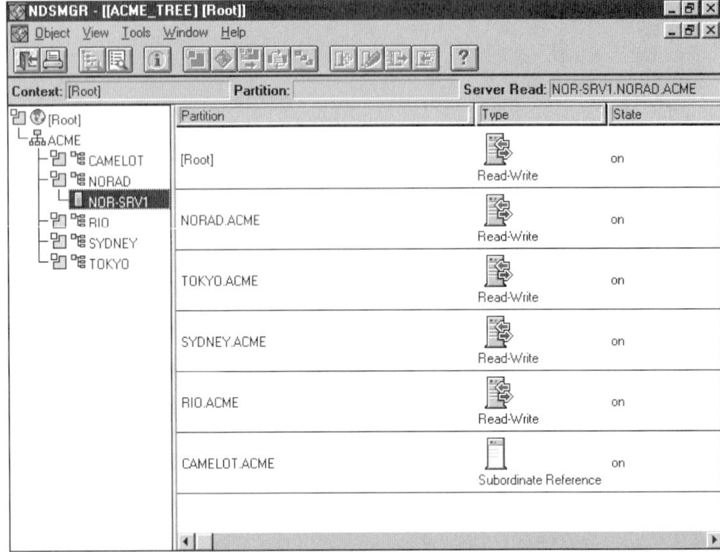

- A partition can have multiple replicas, which are copies of a partition that can be stored on separate servers across your network as explained in previous sections.
- A partition can only have one replica designated as the master. The other partitions will be read/write replicas or in some rare cases read-only replicas.
- Only one replica of a partition can be stored on any given server. A NetWare 5 server can hold multiple replicas from different partitions. It cannot hold two replicas of the same partition.
- All replicas will participate in the replica synchronization for a partition. All replicas are part of synchronization operations regardless of replica type.

These rules are important because they describe the characteristics of replication. Knowing these rules will help you efficiently design the replica placement during implementation of your NetWare 5 network.

Guidelines for Replica Placement

These are the design guidelines for replica placement for any partition:

- Replicate for fault tolerance
- Replicate locally
- Replicate for bindery services
- Replicate for improved name resolution

We will discuss each of these design considerations in detail in the following sections.

Replicate for Fault Tolerance

A primary goal of replication is to eliminate the single point of failure for an NDS partition. Having multiple replicas of a partition on separate servers increases the availability of object information if one of the servers should become unavailable. In Figure 6.34, the NORAD and CAMELOT partitions have been replicated to multiple servers at their respective sites to provide fault tolerance for each partition. If one of the servers in the partition becomes unavailable, NDS will respond from the other server.

The NetWare 5 installation program will automatically create up to three NDS replicas for fault tolerance. When you install additional servers into the tree, the installation program will place up to three replicas of the partition where the server is going to be located in the tree. If the partition where you are installing the server has fewer than three total replicas, the installation will place a read/write replica on the new server in that partition.

If the server being installed is upgraded or has an existing bindery, such as a NetWare 3.12 server, then the installation program will automatically convert the bindery to an NDS replica of the partition where the server is being installed. A NetWare 3.12 server being upgraded will receive at least a read/write replica of the partition even if three other replicas already exist for that partition.

FIGURE 6.34

The NORAD and CAMELOT partitions have been replicated to multiple servers on the network to provide fault tolerance for NDS.

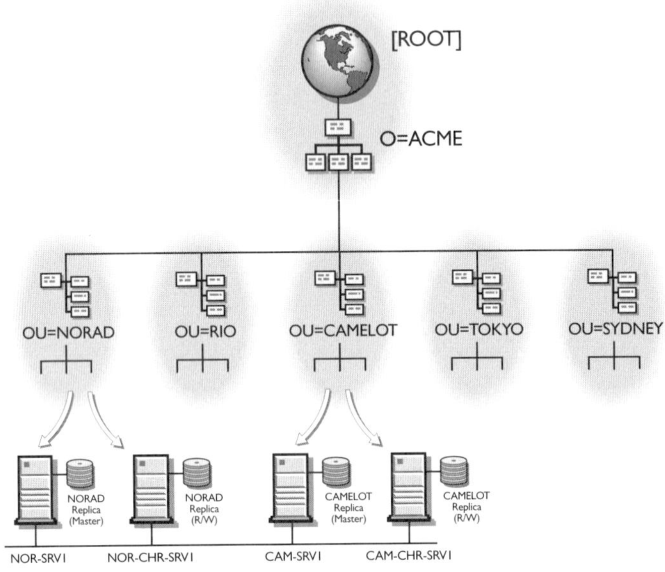

In Figure 6.35 the NORAD partition has been replicated automatically to the servers NOR-SRV1, NOR-CHR-SRV1, and LABS-SRV1 by the installation program. Because NOR-SRV1 contains the master replica of the [ROOT] partition, it will also receive the master replica for the NORAD partition. The other servers will receive read/write replicas until there are at least three replicas for the NORAD partition. Notice that a fourth server (R&D-SRV1) has been installed into the partition but did not automatically receive a replica. The installation program assumes that the R&D-SRV1 is a new server that was not upgraded from NetWare 3.12 (meaning there was no bindery to convert to a replica).

Automatic replication applies only to the partition where the server object is being installed and does not affect other partitions in the tree. The purpose of automatic replication is to support fault tolerance of the NDS tree information. If you are comfortable with where the three automatic replicas were placed during installation, then you need not change the replicas of a partition for fault tolerance.

FIGURE 6.35

The installation program automatically replicates the NORAD partition to the first three servers NOR-SRV1, NOR-CHR-SRV1, and LABS-SRV1. A fourth server (R&D-SRV1) was installed into the partition but did not receive an automatic replica.

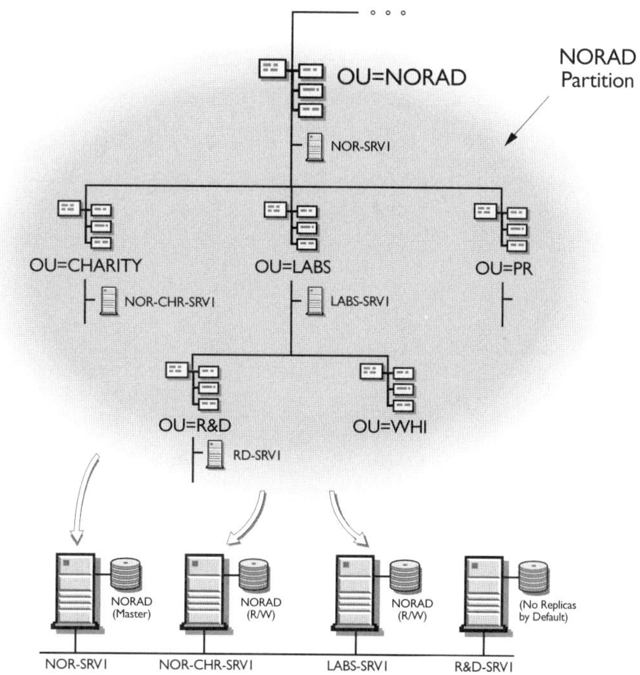

As a general guideline, you should always have both a master and two read/write replicas for every partition. At a minimum, we recommend two replicas, and three replicas are even better. Again, having two or three replicas eliminates any single point of failure in your network. By placing multiple replicas locally, you ensure that any NetWare 5 server with the same replica can fail without affecting NDS availability for your users.

Replicate Locally

The best method to guarantee efficiency in the replication design is to replicate locally. This means placing all the replicas of a partition on local servers. You should not place a replica across a WAN link if you have servers available locally, meaning on the same side of your WAN link. If you follow this guideline, you can guarantee that users will retrieve their object information from the nearest available server. Figure 6.36 is an example of placing a replica that is not local to that partition.

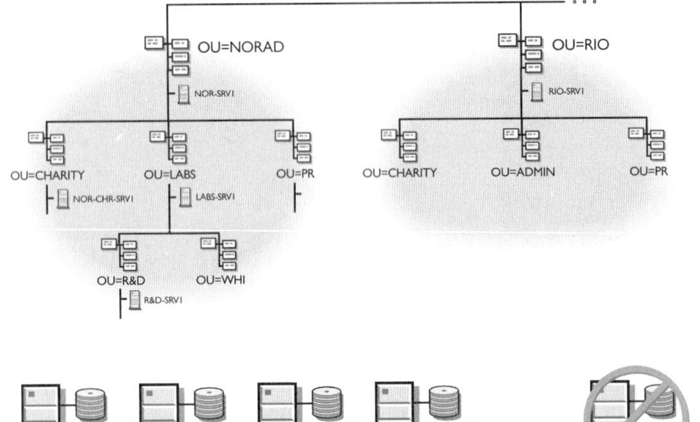

FIGURE 6.36

You should always try to replicate locally by placing replicas of a partition on the servers at that location or site. Do not place a replica across a WAN link from the original partition.

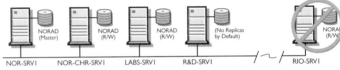

Ideally, you should place the replica containing a user's information on the server that stores the user's home directory. This may not always be possible, but it does improve the users' access to NDS objects and properties. For example, during the login process the user will map drives to volumes, capture to print queues, and access several of the user objects and properties. NDS will execute each of these requests regardless of where the replicas are stored. However, the login speed for the user will be increased if the user finds the requested information on his or her preferred server.

Again, the primary design consideration is that you replicate the NDS partition locally. For example, a partition is created for a specific location, and a master replica is placed on a server in that location. We recommend that you place your read/write replicas of the partition on different servers in the same physical location as the master replica. If you are forced to place the third replica across a WAN link because there are only two servers at the location, then we recommend that you not create the third replica if it is placed across the WAN link. This choice depends upon the level of fault tolerance you want to maintain.

The question is often asked, "What happens if the location or site has only one server? Do I still partition and replicate locally? How do I replicate for fault tolerance?" In the case of a remote site with just one server, you should still partition at that site and place the master replica on that server. A second replica of the partition can be placed on the nearest location for purposes of fault tolerance. Typically, the remote site with just one server contains a small number of user objects. Therefore, although we do not recommend replicating across your WAN, a small replica across your WAN in this case is your only alternative for replication. It is better to replicate a small partition across a WAN than to lose the NDS information if the server ever goes down.

Figure 6.37 illustrates how a small remote office in the ACME tree should be replicated. Assume that a small remote site called OU=SLC is connected to the NORAD hub. There is only one server (SLC1) in the remote site of SLC. You should create a small partition and replicate it to SLC1. You should also place a replica in the NORAD location on the server NOR-SRV1.

FIGURE 6.37

There is only one server (SLC-SRV1) in the remote site of SLC. You should create a small partition called SLC and replicate it to the SLC-SRV1 and NOR-SRV1 servers in the NORAD location. It is more important to replicate for fault tolerance than to not replicate across the WAN links.

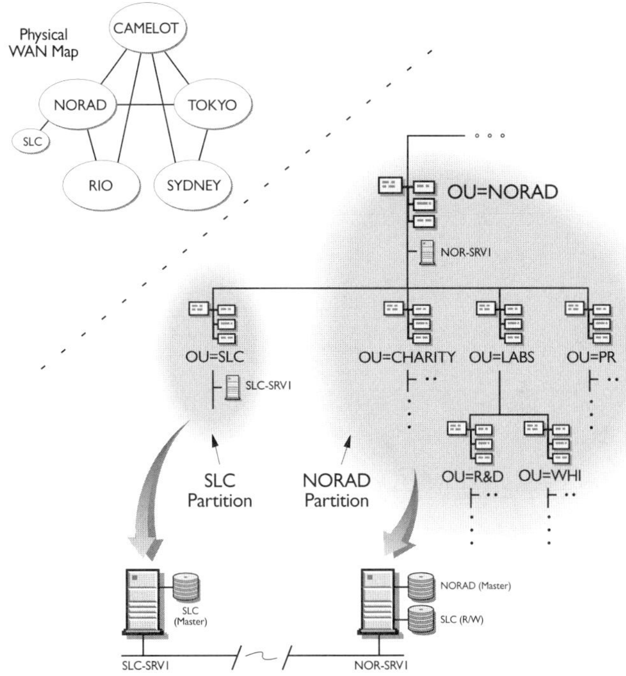

Place Replicas to Support Bindery Services

As mentioned earlier, bindery services does require the placement of a read/write or master replica on the server that sets the bindery context. The bindery context set at the server is officially known as the *server bindery context*.

Figure 6.38 illustrates how the NOR-SRV1 server needs to hold a read/write replica in order to set the server bindery context at OU=NORAD.

FIGURE 6.38

Setting the bindery services for partition NORAD requires that a read/write or master replica be stored on the NOR-SRV1 server, which is where the server sets the server bindery context.

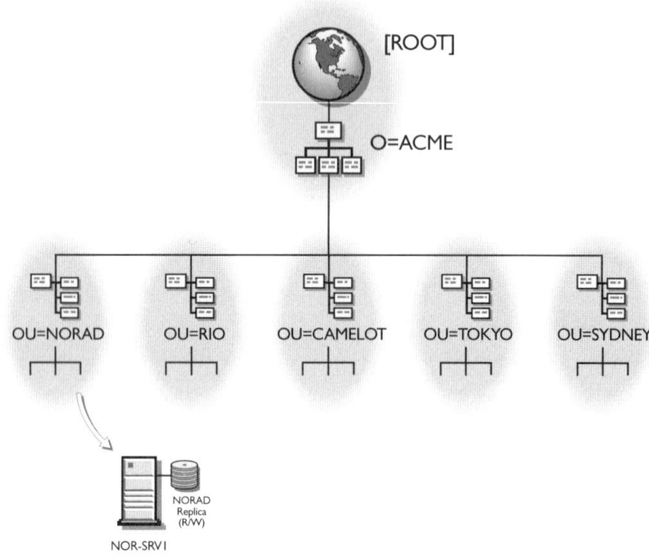

The server bindery context can be set at the server console by typing this command:

```
SET SERVER BINDERY CONTEXT = "OU=NORAD.O=ACME"
```

In Figure 6.39, all the objects in the NORAD container that are NetWare 3 bindery objects are viewed and accessed as if they are in a bindery. The NDS objects available through bindery services include the user, group, print queue, print server, profile, and bindery type objects. This list is included because these are the only objects that were defined in the NetWare 3 bindery. The new NDS objects such as directory map, organizational role, computer, and alias will not show up as bindery objects in your Directory.

In order for a NetWare 5 server to support bindery services, it must hold either a read/write or master replica of a partition where the server is installed. You will need to place read/write replicas on the network servers to support bindery services.

FIGURE 6.39

Server NOR-PR-SRV1 has a bindery context set to "OU=PR.OU=NORAD.O=ACME."

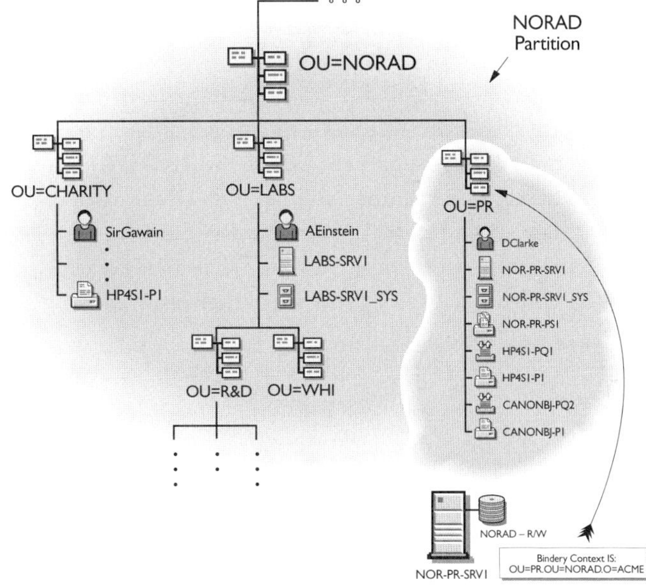

The NetWare 5 feature known as bindery services enables the NetWare 5 server to respond to the bindery calls made by the bindery-based utilities and applications. Bindery services lets these applications run on NetWare 5 and NDS without modifications.

Bindery services is also required during a NetWare 3 to NetWare 5 server upgrade. For example, if you are upgrading a NetWare 3 server, a read/write replica of the partition is placed on the upgraded NetWare 5 server. The read/write replica is placed on the server regardless of whether there are already three replicas, as described in the earlier "Replicate for Fault Tolerance" section. The system assumes that since the server is being upgraded from NetWare 3, bindery services in NetWare 5 will be needed.

Place Replicas for Improved Name Resolution

The mechanism NDS uses to find the object location is referred to as *name resolution*. If the object information is not stored locally, the server must search the directory tree to find the other servers that have the object information. Every replica maintains a set of pointers to all the other replicas in the same partition.

NDS uses these pointers to locate the partitions that are above and below in the Directory tree. With the name resolution mechanism, NDS can follow these pointers to locate the servers holding the requested data.

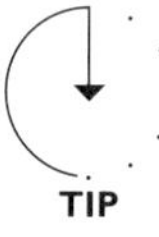

For improved speed of name resolution from one side of the tree to the other, you can replicate the [ROOT] partition in a couple of strategic locations, such as hub sites, so that users can search the tree faster. The [ROOT] partition should be small to keep NDS traffic to a minimum. However, unlike with other partitions, you should not replicate [ROOT] more than three times.

To speed access to the appropriate server, you can place replicas closer to that server to help the user find the requested information. For example, if you are trying to locate information from one side of the tree to the other, the partition that will help you is the [ROOT] partition. In this case, you can replicate the [ROOT] partition to that major hub site in your company. Replicating the [ROOT] partition is recommended only if it is set up as a small partition and you only replicate it a couple of times. "Small" means the [ROOT] partition should include just the [ROOT] object and the O=ACME object. See Figure 6.40 for an illustration of a small [ROOT] partition that is replicated across a WAN link.

FIGURE 6.40

The [ROOT] partition can be replicated across the WAN links if it is created as a small partition containing just the [ROOT] object and O=ACME object.

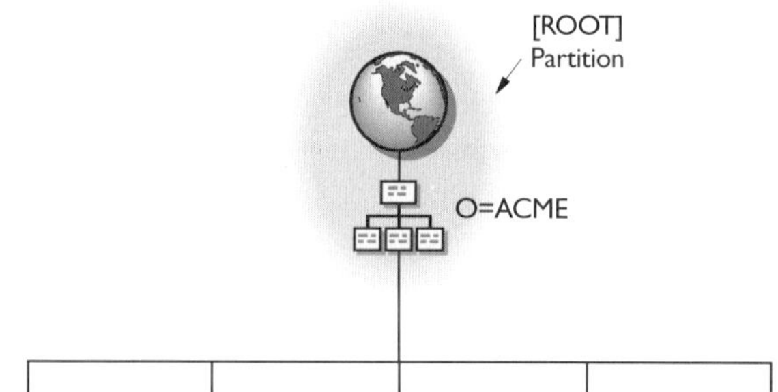

Consulting Experience

Do not replicate [ROOT] more than three times. Keep in mind your understanding of subordinate reference replicas. Each replica of [ROOT] you create will also create subordinate reference replicas. Spreading around more copies of a partition will increase the number of subordinate references. For example, let's assume you have 10 child partitions created directly below [ROOT] because you have 10 locations. When you replicate [ROOT] three times, you will have 10 subordinate reference replicas on 3 separate servers for a total of 30 subordinate reference replicas. Add two more replicas of [ROOT] and you have 50 servers holding subordinate reference replicas.

Figure 6.41 illustrates how the [ROOT] partition can be replicated to a few strategic locations in the WAN infrastructure to facilitate improved name resolution. In this case, we have placed a copy of [ROOT] in NORAD on the NOR-SRV1 server, in CAMELOT on the CAM-SRV1 server, and in TOKYO on the TOK-SRV1 server.

FIGURE 6.41

NDS replicas for the [ROOT] partition are stored on different servers throughout the network to improve name resolution.

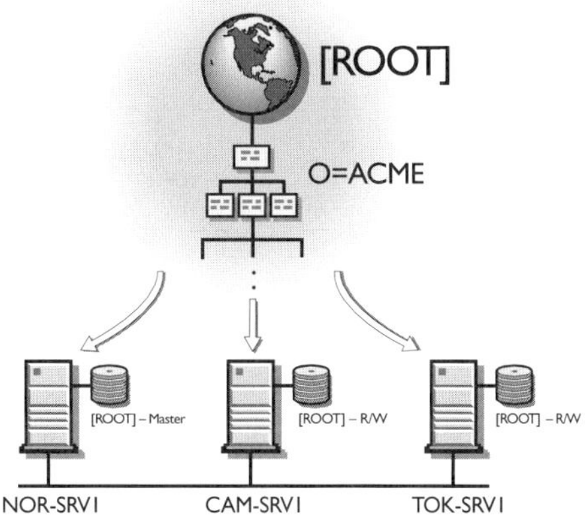

The small [ROOT] partition (containing very few objects) is also fairly static, so [ROOT] may be replicated across the WAN links. However, do not go overboard on replicating this partition. Three replicas of the [ROOT] partition are usually sufficient.

We do not recommend that you replicate any other partition across the WAN infrastructure for the purpose of name resolution. Because [ROOT] is at the top of your tree and a lot of name resolution must traverse the [ROOT] partition, it makes sense to replicate [ROOT] only at key hub locations in your tree.

Summary of NDS Partition and Replica Design Guidelines

The specific design rules for partitioning and replication of Novell Directory Services can be separated into two different categories depending on your specific implementation requirements, your hardware, and your staff's knowledge level. The two categories defined for the partition and replica design rules are Quick Design and Advanced Design.

Quick Design

The Quick Design rules for partitions and replicas are simple, basic rules that can be implemented in all companies and applied to almost every situation regardless of the WAN or LAN infrastructure. Quick Design is highly recommended for designers and customers who want to operate their NDS tree structures as effectively as possible. These design rules will minimize the impact of replica synchronization and will provide a good foundation for overall performance.

The Quick Design rules provide everyone with an easy and safe method to design and implement NDS in their network environments. If you follow the recommendations that follow, you will be successful in designing Novell Directory Services. The system will also be much easier to service and maintain.

Here are the specific Quick Design rules for partitioning and replication of NDS:

- Partition size — 5,000 objects
- Number of child partitions per parent — 30 partitions
- Number of replicas per partition — 10 replicas (typically 3)
- Number or replicas per server — 20 replicas

- Number of replicas per Replica Server — 60 replicas (see the next "Consulting Experience" sidebar)

- Minimum server hardware — Pentium 300+ MHz with 128MB of RAM

Only a few situations will arise in which the Quick Design rules will not apply. In the few portions of the tree where these rules cannot be followed, we introduce the more costly Advanced Design rules.

Advanced Design

The Advanced Design rules are simply greater numbers for each of the partition and replica areas. Because these rules will exceed the numbers given in the Quick Design rules, they are going to be more costly in terms of the efficiency of the replica synchronization process on the servers. For this reason, we strongly recommend, if not require, that you or your staff completely understand the effect or impact of the larger numbers. It is safe to say that the Advanced Design rules require the individuals maintaining the system to have a greater in-depth knowledge of NDS and NetWare 5.

For the most part, the Advanced Design rules are targeted at the consultant or administrator who understands the impacts or ramifications of moving past the Quick Design rules to the larger numbers.

The specific Advanced Design rules for partitioning and replication of NDS, shown in the following list, are the maximum values for each area and should never be exceeded. The Advanced Design rules are as follows:

- Partition size — 10,000 objects

- Number of child partitions per parent — 75 partitions

- Number of replicas per partition — 20 replicas (typically 3)

- Number or replicas per server — 40 replicas

- Number of replicas per Replica Server — 120 replicas (see the next "Consulting Experience" sidebar)

- Minimum server hardware — Pentium 400+ MHz with 256MB of RAM

Consulting Experience

A *replica server* is a dedicated NetWare 5 server that just stores NDS replicas. This type of server is sometimes referred to as a "DSMASTER server." This configuration has become popular with some companies that have many single server remote offices. The replica server provides a place for you to store additional replicas for the partition of a remote office location.

The ultimate limiting factor for the number of replicas on any server is that the replica synchronization process on the server must be able to complete in 30 minutes or less. The factors that affect the time it takes to complete the synchronization include the following:

- CPU speed of the replica server
- Number of replicas
- Number of objects in each replica
- Size of each replica ring
- Location of replicas in the replica ring (local or remote)
- Speed of the WAN links connecting remote replicas
- RAM on replica server
- Frequency of inbound replica synchronizations

Managing NDS Partitions and Replicas

In order to manage your NDS partitions and replicas properly, you need to understand and use several types of operations. The NDS partition and replica operations are as follows: create partition, merge partition, move partition (subtree), add replica, remove replica, change replica type, and abort partition operation. These operations are discussed later in this section. A new utility in NetWare 5, called NDS Manager, enables you to perform NDS partition and replica operations on the NDS tree.

The NDS Manager utility is the Windows-based administration program. This program is used by the system administrators to manage all the NDS partitions and replicas. Figure 6.42 shows the NDS Manager main window.

FIGURE 6.42

The NDS Manager utility controls the partitioning and replication of the NDS database.

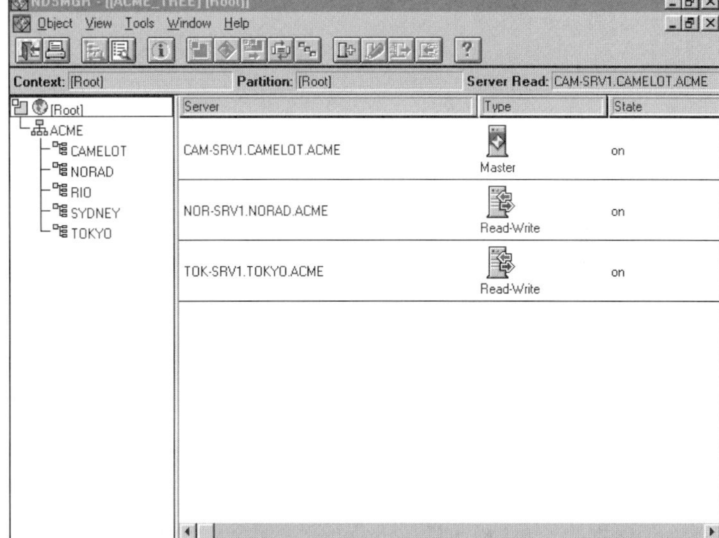

In Figure 6.43 you can see that the partitions are denoted with small box icons to the left of the OU container object. In this example, OU=CAMELOT and OU=NORAD are partitions.

NDS Partition and Replica Operations

All partition and replica operations require that the master replica for the partition be available. As mentioned earlier, the master replica locks the partition before it starts the operation. The only partition operations that do not require the master replica to lock the partition are the add replica and remove replica operations.

All the replicas for a specific partition must be available in order to complete the operation. If a replica is not reachable, the NDS system will wait until it is available.

If you are performing a merge partition operation, then you need to check the status of both the parent and child partitions involved in the merge. Again, you should check the status of the partitions before you start the merge operation.

FIGURE 6.43

In the NDS Manager, the partitions are denoted with a small box icon to the left of the OU container. OU=CAMELOT and OU=NORAD are shown as partitions.

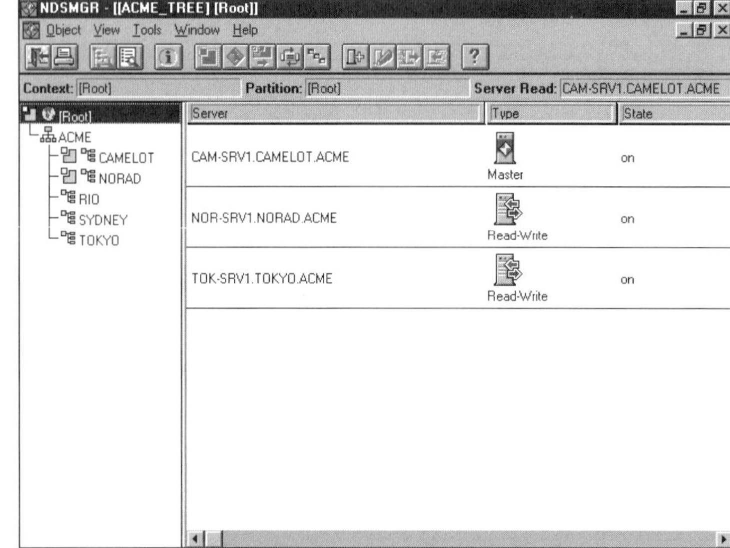

Another operational guideline is that after you have started a partition operation, you should be very patient and wait for all the synchronization work to complete. As we've mentioned, NDS is a distributed and replicated system that is loosely consistent, and it takes time for the partition changes to be reflected across the network. The synchronization process for a partition with many objects and replicas will naturally take longer than one with just a few objects.

Consulting Experience

Before you start a partition operation, you should *always* check the status of the replicas of the partition. You can avoid many problems if you check the synchronization status of the replicas before you perform any partition operation. You can use DSREPAIR to check the status of the replicas and synchronization. Make sure that the synchronization process is complete before starting a new operation on that partition. Figure 6.44 displays a status check of the replicas in DSREPAIR. For more information on specific interpretation of each of the items shown, you can refer to our discussion of the DSREPAIR utility in Chapter 10, "NetWare 5 Features."

FIGURE 6.44

Use DSREPAIR to check the status of the replicas before starting a partition operation.

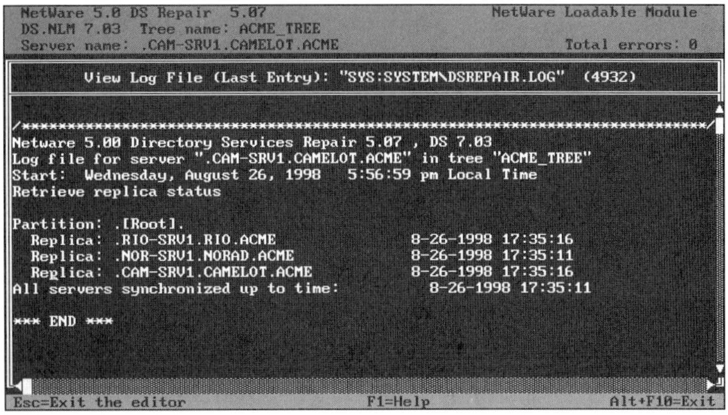

```
NetWare 5.0 DS Repair  5.07                              NetWare Loadable Module
DS.NLM 7.03  Tree name: ACME_TREE
Server name: .CAM-SRV1.CAMELOT.ACME                              Total errors: 0

     View Log File (Last Entry): "SYS:SYSTEM\DSREPAIR.LOG"  (4932)

/****************************************************************************/
Netware 5.00 Directory Services Repair 5.07 , DS 7.03
Log file for server ".CAM-SRV1.CAMELOT.ACME" in tree "ACME_TREE"
Start:  Wednesday, August 26, 1998  5:56:59 pm Local Time
Retrieve replica status

Partition: .[Root].
  Replica: .RIO-SRV1.RIO.ACME                  8-26-1998 17:35:16
  Replica: .NOR-SRV1.NORAD.ACME                8-26-1998 17:35:11
  Replica: .CAM-SRV1.CAMELOT.ACME              8-26-1998 17:35:16
All servers synchronized up to time:             8-26-1998 17:35:11

*** END ***

Esc=Exit the editor                F1=Help                      Alt+F10=Exit
```

Consulting Experience

If your NetWare 5 servers are running the code release of DS.NLM (Version 595 or greater), then you can use DSREPAIR to read the partition status after the partition operation. It will be more accurate than previous releases of DSREPAIR, which often generated the "partition busy" error message.

In addition to checking the partition status through the DSREPAIR utility, you can use the DSTRACE utility. Figure 6.45 shows the screen in DSTRACE to check when the synchronization process is completed. If the synchronization process has errors they will be displayed as shown in this example.

If possible, we recommend that you centralize partition operations management. Only one person or a small group of people should be responsible for all of the partitioning and replication for your company. You might decide that only one workstation on the network should start the partition operations. In this way, you can eliminate the possibility that two people or two different workstations are making changes to the partitions simultaneously.

The next several sections discuss each of the partition and replica operations that can be performed. These operations include create new partition, merge partition, move partition or subtree, add replica, remove replica, change replica type, rebuild replicas, and abort partition operations.

FIGURE 6.45

The Replica screen in DSTRACE shows you when the synchronization process has been completed for a partition.

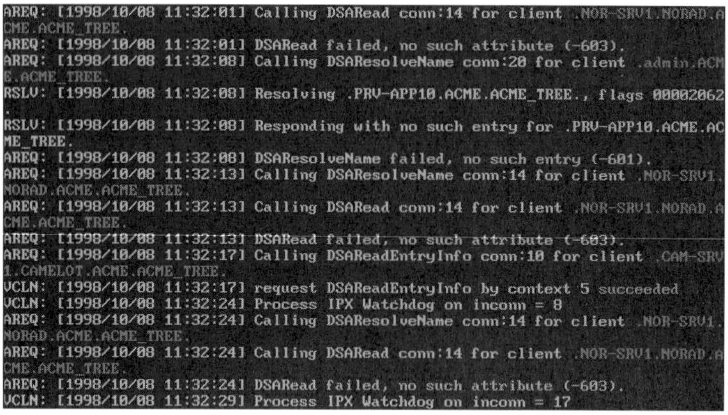

```
AREQ: [1998/10/08 11:32:01] Calling DSARead conn:14 for client .NOR-SRV1.NORAD.A
CME.ACME_TREE.
AREQ: [1998/10/08 11:32:01] DSARead failed, no such attribute (-603).
AREQ: [1998/10/08 11:32:08] Calling DSAResolveName conn:20 for client .admin.ACM
E.ACME_TREE.
RSLV: [1998/10/08 11:32:08] Resolving .PRV-APP10.ACME.ACME_TREE., flags 00002062
.
RSLV: [1998/10/08 11:32:08] Responding with no such entry for .PRV-APP10.ACME.AC
ME_TREE.
AREQ: [1998/10/08 11:32:08] DSAResolveName failed, no such entry (-601).
AREQ: [1998/10/08 11:32:13] Calling DSAResolveName conn:14 for client .NOR-SRV1.
NORAD.ACME.ACME_TREE.
AREQ: [1998/10/08 11:32:13] Calling DSARead conn:14 for client .NOR-SRV1.NORAD.A
CME.ACME_TREE.
AREQ: [1998/10/08 11:32:13] DSARead failed, no such attribute (-603).
AREQ: [1998/10/08 11:32:17] Calling DSAReadEntryInfo conn:10 for client .CAM-SRV
1.CAMELOT.ACME.ACME_TREE.
VCLN: [1998/10/08 11:32:17] request DSAReadEntryInfo by context 5 succeeded
VCLN: [1998/10/08 11:32:24] Process IPX Watchdog on inconn = 8
AREQ: [1998/10/08 11:32:24] Calling DSAResolveName conn:14 for client .NOR-SRV1.
NORAD.ACME.ACME_TREE.
AREQ: [1998/10/08 11:32:24] Calling DSARead conn:14 for client .NOR-SRV1.NORAD.A
CME.ACME_TREE.
AREQ: [1998/10/08 11:32:24] DSARead failed, no such attribute (-603).
VCLN: [1998/10/08 11:32:29] Process IPX Watchdog on inconn = 17
```

The Create Partition Operation

Creating a new partition is the same as creating a child partition from the parent partition. This operation is sometimes called a *partition split*. The terms "create" and "split" are used interchangeably. The operation is generally fast because it generates less network traffic than do other partition operations. The traffic is limited to changes to the replica pointers, synchronization, and partitioning control. Once again, however, if you have many replicas of the partition before the split, NDS must contact each server holding a replica in order to perform the operation there as well.

The operation simply divides the partition into two, with all the information staying on the same servers where the operation originally started. This split operation will create a new child partition on all the servers that had a copy of the parent partition.

When the partition is created, the partition takes its name from the topmost container object (partition root object). All the objects in the tree that are under the container object form the contents of the new partition.

In the following examples, we have installed a third server in the tree, called TOK-SRV1. The result of installing the TOK-SRV1 server into the tree is that it will receive a read/write copy of the [ROOT] partition. Figure 6.46 shows how you can use the NDS Manager utility to create a new partition called the TOKYO partition for the ACME company. All the objects in the subtree under TOKYO are included in the partition.

FIGURE 6.46

The OU=TOKYO container is created as a new partition for the ACME tree.

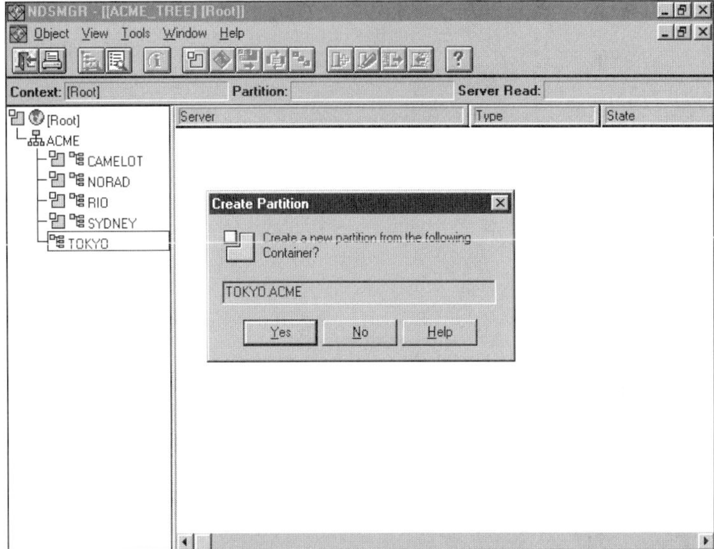

Notice in Figure 6.47 that the create partition operation for TOKYO places copies of the new TOKYO partition on all the servers that originally had copies of the parent partition [ROOT]. You can remove the additional copies if they are not placed on the servers you want.

In Figure 6.47 you can see that the TOKYO partition and its information can be placed on the servers in TOKYO. The same is true for all the locations. By partitioning the NDS tree, you can keep the location information in each location and still find and use the resources throughout the entire NDS tree.

In order to perform the create partition operation, you must have rights to the top of the partition or the OU container that defines the partition. The effective rights needed are write rights to the ACL of the top container object that defines the partition. There are several ways to receive this privilege. You can be granted either the Supervisor object right or the explicit write property right to the ACL. Either of these two rights will enable you to perform the create partition operations on the tree.

Figure 6.48 illustrates the rights needed to perform the future partition operation for the NORAD partition in the ACME tree. Notice that the user, AEinstein, has been given the Supervisor object right to the OU=NORAD. The

OU=NORAD is the top of the partition and is referred to as the partition root object of the NORAD partition.

FIGURE 6.47

The create partition operation placed copies of the new TOKYO partition on all the servers that originally had copies of the [ROOT] partition. These servers are NOR-SRV1, CAM-SRV1, TOK-SRV1.

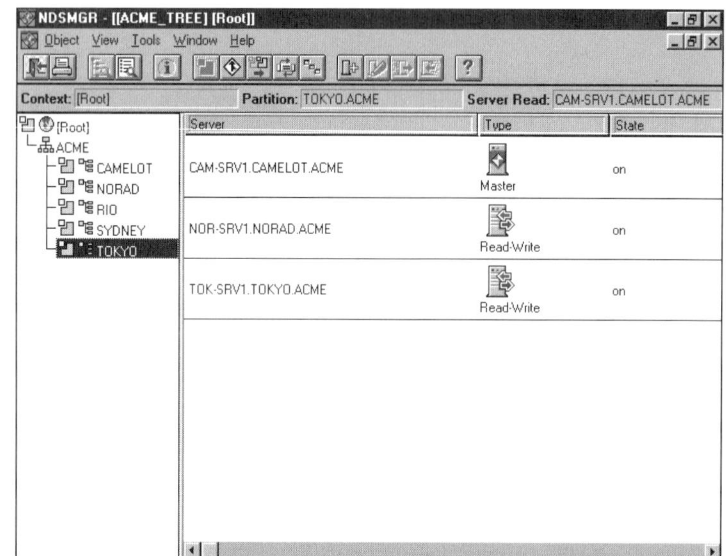

FIGURE 6.48

The user AEinstein has been assigned the rights needed to perform the create partition operation for the NORAD partition.

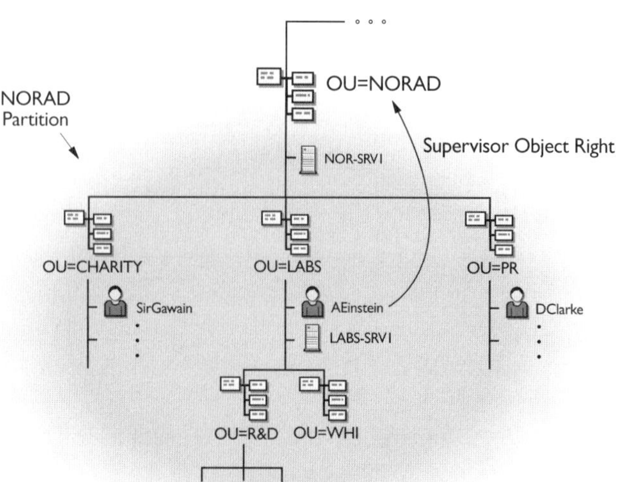

The Merge Partition Operation

The operation used to combine a child partition with its parent is called a *merge*. This operation is also sometimes called a *partition join*. The terms "merge" and "join" are used interchangeably. This operation takes varying amounts of time and could generate network traffic depending on which servers originally held the partitions.

The merge operation requires that each server holding a copy of the parent partition receive a copy of the child partition before the merge can take place. In return, each server holding a copy of the child partition must receive a copy of the parent before the merge can be completed. The merge operation will attempt to move copies of either the parent or child partition to the appropriate servers as needed. After the copies have been successfully moved, the merge operation then joins the partitions together.

It is strongly recommended that you manually place copies of the parent partition on all the servers with a child partition before you initiate the merge operation. In turn, you should place copies of each of the child partitions on the servers holding the parent partitions before you start the merge operation.

You will have greater success merging partitions if you manually place copies of the parent and child partitions on appropriate servers. In order to accomplish this task, you must know where each of the copies of the partitions is located. Refer to the "Partition and Replica Matrix" section later in this chapter.

If all the servers have copies of both the child and parent partitions before the merge operation is started, the merge will be quicker and encounter fewer problems, thus enabling the operation to complete. Copies of both child and parent partitions also prevent large amounts of NDS data moving across the network during the operation. Network traffic occurs when you prepare for the merge by placing the appropriate replicas on the servers.

An example of a merge partition operation is illustrated in Figure 6.49, where the OPS partition is merged back with its parent partition CAMELOT. The utility will ask you to confirm the merge operation as shown.

In order to perform the merge partition operation, you must have rights to only the child partitions. The effective rights needed are the write rights to the ACL of the child partitions. There are several ways to receive these privileges. You can be granted either the Supervisor object right or the explicit write property right to the ACL property.

Consulting Experience

Check the synchronization status of all replicas in the partition with DSREPAIR before initiating any partition operation. All replicas must be available and functioning properly before you proceed with the partitioning.

FIGURE 6.49

The OPS partition is merged back with its parent partition CAMELOT.

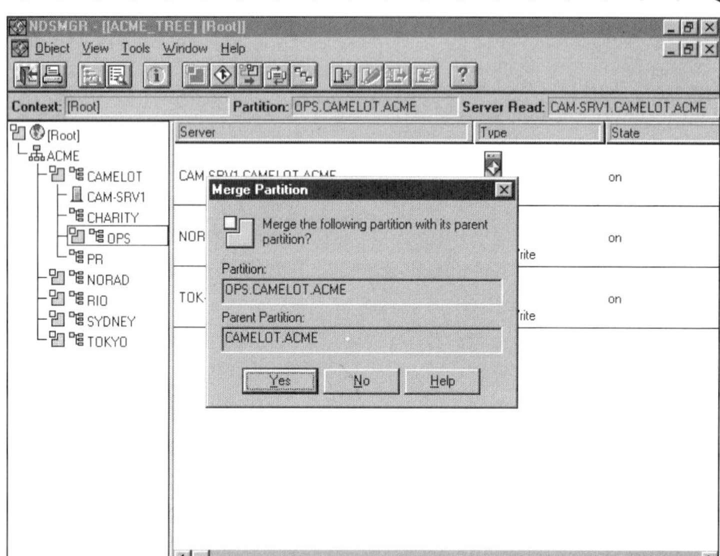

Figure 6.50 illustrates the rights needed to perform the merge partition operation for the CAMELOT and OPS partitions in the ACME tree. Notice that the user, KingArthur, has been given the Supervisor object right to the OU=OPS container.

FIGURE 6.50

The user, KingArthur, has been assigned the rights needed to perform the merge partition operation for the OPS and CAMELOT partitions.

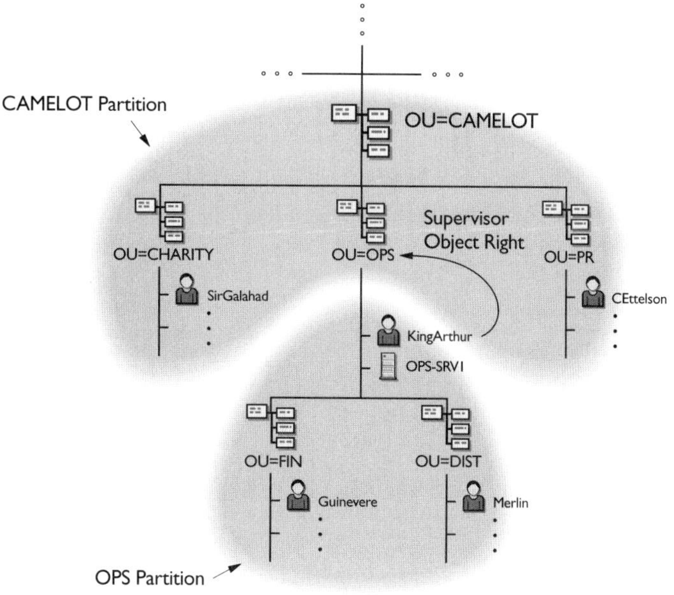

The Move Subtree Partition Operation

The operation used to move an OU container and its entire contents or subtree from one location in the NDS tree to another is called a *move subtree*. This operation is very important when you reorganize the information in your NDS tree because it enables you to move the container objects in the NDS tree. In order for you to move an OU container, two conditions must exist. The two conditions are as follows:

- The OU container object being moved must be a partition. This means that the OU container object must be a partition root object. You will need to create a partition from the OU container before moving it if one does not exist.

- The partition or subtree you want to move cannot have any child partitions. You may be forced to merge child partitions with their parent in order to move the subtree.

This operation is essentially moving a partition from one location in the NDS tree to another location. This operation can generate network traffic depending on the servers on which the parent partitions were originally placed.

In Figure 6.51 we have assumed that the join operation did not occur or was aborted. The NDS Manager Move Partition screen for the OPS partition under the CAMELOT location is moved to another location in the NDS tree, in this case, under the NORAD.ACME container.

FIGURE 6.51

The OPS partition is moved to another location (under the NORAD.ACME) in the NDS tree.

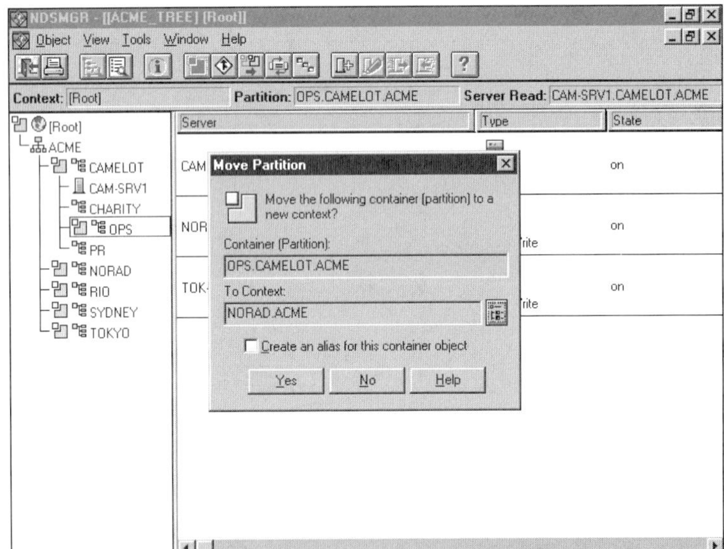

In order to perform the move partition (subtree) operation, you must have rights to all the partitions involved. The effective rights needed are the write rights to the ACL of the top container object that defines the partition. There are several ways to receive this privilege. You can be granted either the Supervisor object right or the explicit write property right to the ACL property.

The Add Replica Operation

The *add replica* operation is used to create a new copy of the partition information and store it on another server. Adding replicas to other network servers requires that all the data in the partition be copied to the new servers across the network. This operation will cause network traffic. Because the amount of traffic is dependent on the number of objects in the partition, it is a good idea to schedule this operation during a low-use time in the network.

Figure 6.52 shows the NDS Manager dialog box used to perform an add replica operation. You first select a partition to which you want to add a replica. In this case the [ROOT] partition is selected. You then select the server on which the new replica will be placed.

FIGURE 6.52

Using the NDS Manager utility to add a new replica to the [ROOT] partition

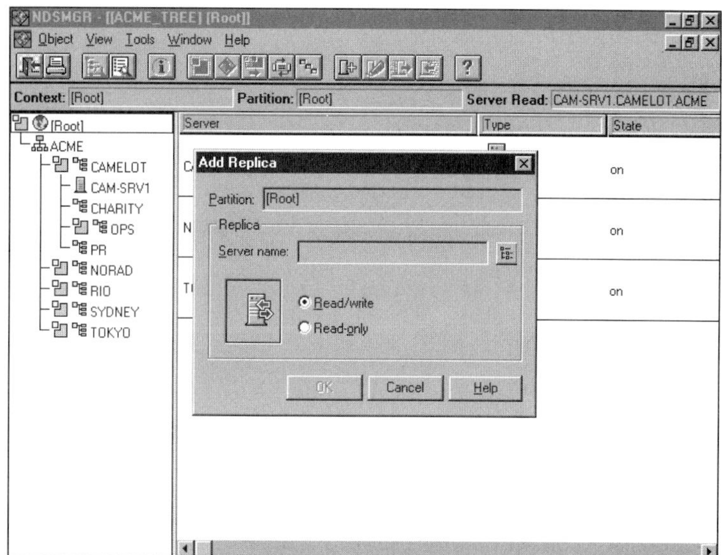

The Remove Replica Operation

The *remove replica* partition operation is used to delete a copy of the partition information from a specific server. You might think this operation to delete the replica happens very quickly because it simply marks the information to be removed from the server. However, every object in the replica must now be set up as an external reference, that is, as a pointer to the real object in another replica on another server. With the creation of the external references, *backlinks*, which are pointers back to the external references, are established. Even though the backlinks are checked in the background process, the initial setup will take time. For a complete discussion on external references and backlinks see Chapter 8, "NDS Internals Operations."

Figure 6.53 shows the NDS Manager dialog box that is used to remove a replica of a partition. You first select a partition from which you want to remove the replica. In this case the [ROOT] partition is selected. You then select the server from which to remove the replica. In this example, we have selected the TOK-SRV1 as the replica to remove. The result is that there are only two replicas left on the servers, CAM-SRV1 and NOR-SRV1.

FIGURE 6.53

Using the NDS Manager utility to remove the TOK-SRV1 replica from the [ROOT] partition

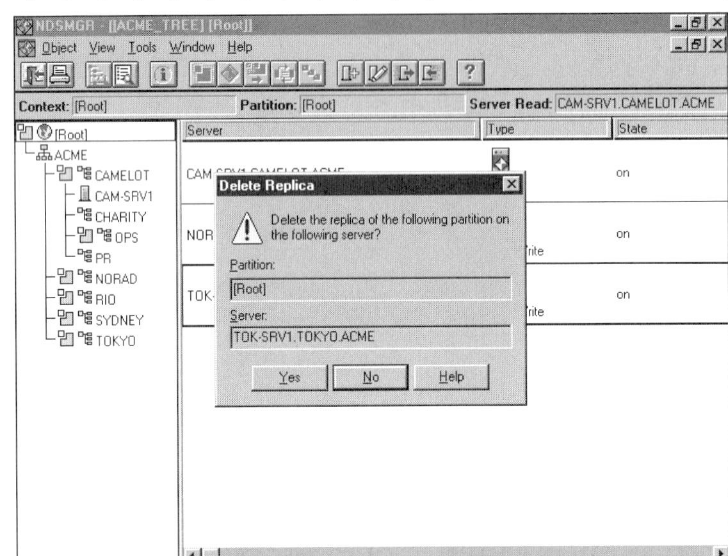

The Change Replica Type Operation

The *change replica type* operation can be performed when a specific type of replica needs to be changed. For example, if you want a different replica to be the master replica for the partition, you highlight which replica you want to be the new master and NDS will change the type and propagate the change to the other replicas. In order to change the master replica, the target server must have a read/write or read-only replica.

Figure 6.54 shows the NDS Manager dialog box used to change the replica type for a partition. You first select a partition for which you want to perform the change replica type operation. In this case the [ROOT] partition is selected. You then select the server on which to change the replica type. We have selected the read/write replica on NOR-SRV1. We can now change its type to master. The result is that the master replica on CAM-SRV1 will change to a read/write replica.

FIGURE 6.54

Using the NDS Manager utility to change the replica type for the [ROOT] partition

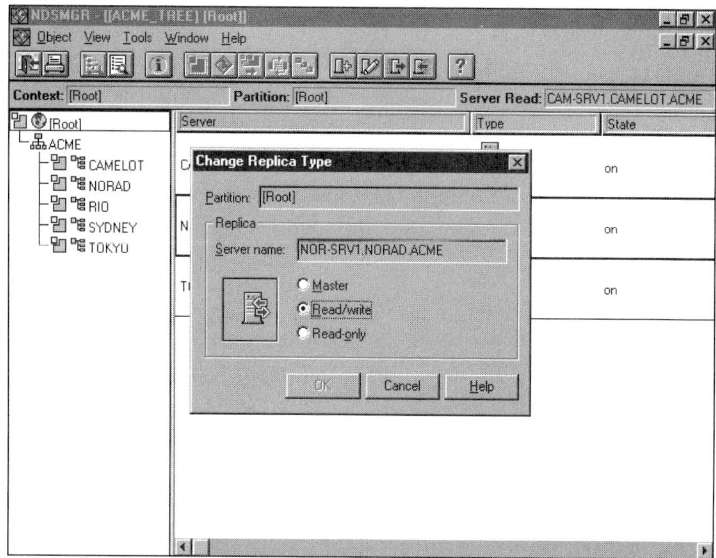

You are not allowed to change a master replica to read/write or read-only by selecting the server holding the master replica. The utility requires you to select either a read/write or read-only replica on another server and change it to the master replica.

The Rebuild Replica Operation

There are a couple of ways you can rebuild the replica information for each of the partitions. The *rebuild replica* operation is used when the NDS information on the current server is not completely accurate or has become corrupt.

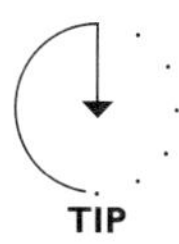

The current rebuild replica operation in NetWare 5 should not be confused with the older rebuild replicas from previous versions of NetWare 4 (specifically NetWare 4.0 and 4.01). The current rebuild replica operation does not destroy the partition information; instead, it sends all information to all the other replicas.

The previous versions of NetWare 4 used the rebuild replica operation to rebuild the timestamps for each object in the partition. The operation to rebuild timestamps is a very aggressive troubleshooting technique and will not be discussed here.

From the NDS Manager utility, there are two ways to update replica information. These two operations are called send updates and receive updates. Both of these functions are network intensive because they move all the partition data across the network to the servers. They are discussed in the sections that follow.

Send Updates The *send updates* operation tries to send all the object information to all the other replicas in the ring. This operation synchronizes all the other replicas for the partition with the replica you have selected. You would perform this operation when the partition information on some of the servers is not complete or has become corrupted. By selecting the most current replica or the replica that has the best information, you can send its information to all the other replicas in the partition. You can use either NDS Manager (Send Updates) or DSREPAIR (Send all objects to every replica in the ring).

Figure 6.55 shows an example of using NDS Manager to perform the send updates operation. In this example, the server CAM-SRV1, which is the master replica of the [ROOT] partition, is selected as the sending replica. The Send Updates operation will send the contents of the selected replica to all the other replicas in the partition.

FIGURE 6.55

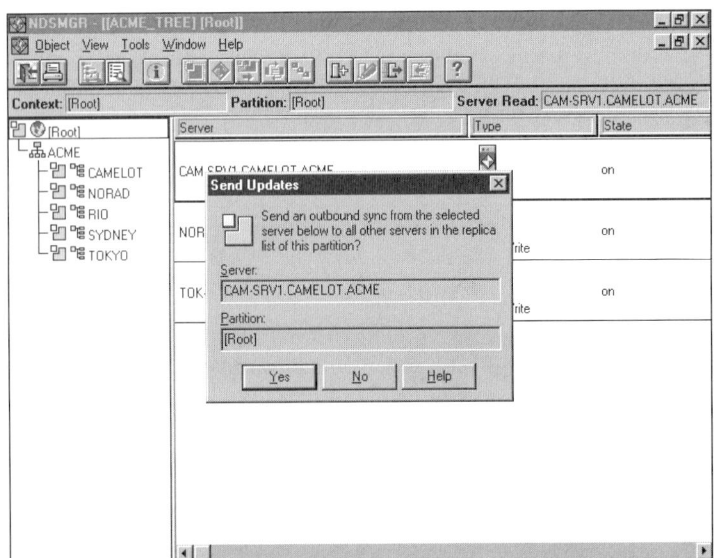

The send updates replica operation. The CAM-SRV1 server, which holds the master replica of the [ROOT] partition, is selected as the sending replica. This operation will send the contents of the selected replica to all the other replicas in the partition.

The receive updates operation synchronizes selected replica with the information from the master replica. You would perform this operation when the partition information on one of the servers is not as complete as the master replica. This operation can be performed using both the NDS Manager and DSREPAIR utilities.

Receive Updates The *receive updates* operation essentially marks the affected replica as a new replica. The operation begins the process of adding the partition information to the replica again. Figure 6.56 shows an example of the receive updates operation using the DSREPAIR utility. In this example, the server named NOR-SRV1 receives the replica information from the master replica of the [ROOT] partition. (Notice that the "Send all objects to every replica in the ring" message is the send updates operation mentioned earlier.)

FIGURE 6.56

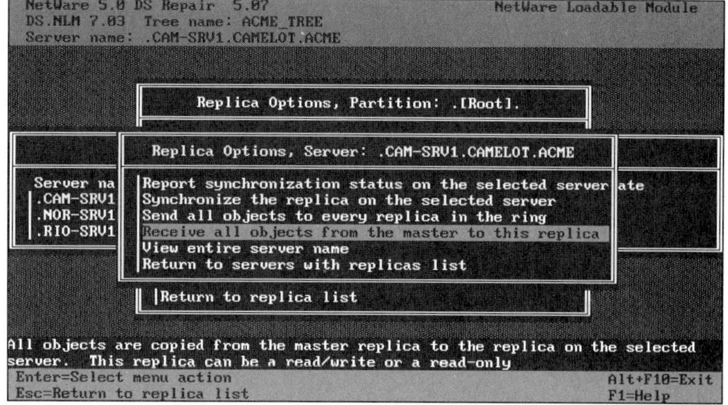

The receive updates replica operation. The server named NOR-SRV1 receives the replica information from the master replica of the [ROOT] partition. This operation will send the contents of the master replica to the server holding the selected replica.

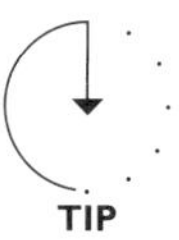
TIP

Check the synchronization status of all replicas in the partition with DSREPAIR before initiating any partition operation. All replicas must be available and functioning properly before you proceed with the partitioning.

The Abort Partition Operation

You have the ability to abort a partition operation that was previously started. The *abort partition* operation is valid only for certain partition operations, including create, merge, move subtree, and change replica type. The abort partition operation cannot be used on add replica or remove replica.

This feature is valuable not as an undo function but as a way to back out of partition operations that do not complete. For example, only one partition operation can take place at a time. So if a partition operation starts and does not complete, no other partition operations can be started. A partition operation will wait indefinitely if one of the servers in the replica list of the partition becomes unavailable because of either a downed server or an unavailable communication link. This problem is manifested by the "master replica state is not on for the selected partition" message if you try to start another partition operation (see Figure 6.57). You can also check the status of the replicas using the NDS Manager utility.

FIGURE 6.57

The message displayed from NDS Manager if another partition operation is requested before the first partition operation is completed

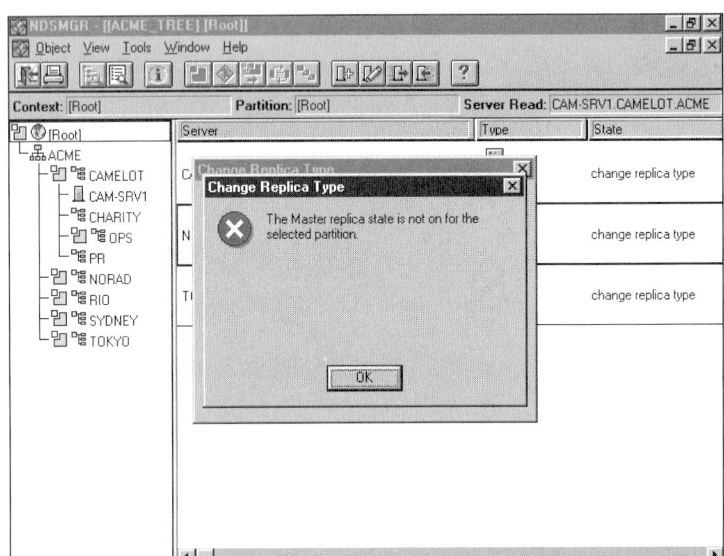

If you suspect that a partition operation is having difficulty completing, then either you can wait until the situation causing the problem is cleared up or you can abort the operation. To abort the partition operation, you can go to NDS Manager, select the partition, and press the Abort button. Figure 6.58 displays the abort partition operation in NDS Manager. In this example, the operation that has not completed is the change replica type operation because the replica state information shows each replica with Change Type 0. This means that the current change state of the replicas is 0. For more information and a complete list of the replica change states, see Chapter 8, "NDS Internals Operations."

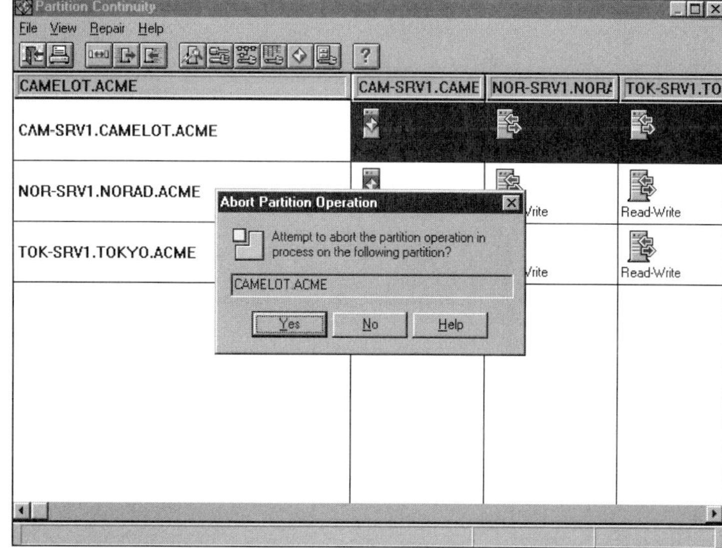

FIGURE 6.58

The Abort Partition Operation dialog box in NDS Manager

To execute the abort operation, click Yes at the bottom of the dialog box.

After the partition operation has been aborted, the replicas involved will be turned back on as illustrated in Figure 6.59. In this example, each replica state has been set to ON, meaning that the partition is ready once again.

You can also abort a partition operation within the DSREPAIR utility. From the DSREPAIR main menu select the Advanced Options menu. From the Advanced Option menu select the Replica and Partition Operations menu. A list of all the partitions and replicas stored on the server is displayed. After you select the partition that is having problems, the Replica Options menu is displayed (see Figure 6.60). Down the menu is the Cancel Partition Operation selection. When you select this item, you will be asked to log into Directory Services as someone who has rights over the partition.

FIGURE 6.59

The replica states are turned back to ON after the partition operation is aborted.

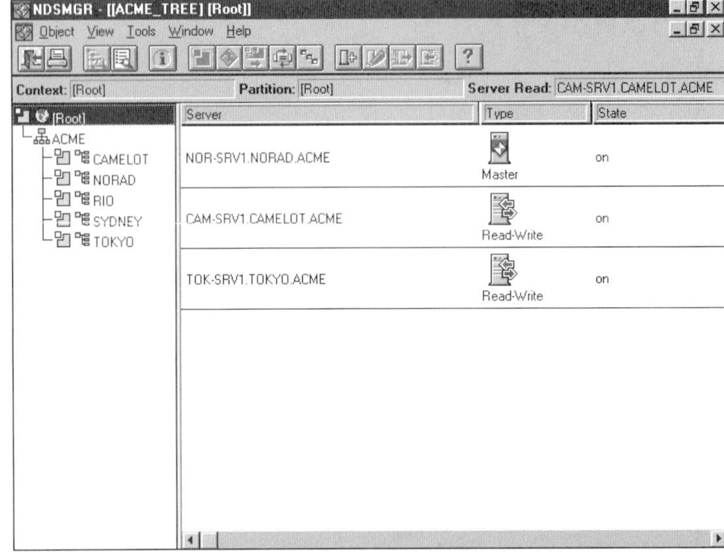

FIGURE 6.60

You can use DSREPAIR to abort or cancel a partition operation.

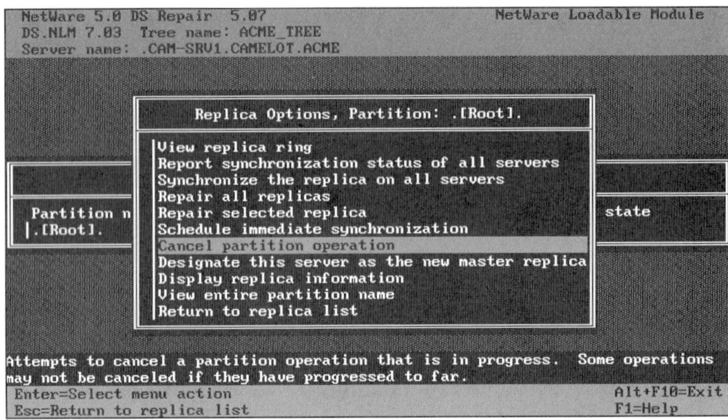

The Partition and Replica Matrix

The best method for keeping track of where partitions and replicas are stored in the NDS is to create a partition and replica matrix. The matrix, as shown in Figure 6.61, helps you document the creation and replication of partitions. The matrix will help you design and implement the partitions and replicas more efficiently. If you need to perform any partition operation, you have a quick and easy tool available.

FIGURE 6.61

You should document your NDS partitions and replicas using a partition and replica matrix.

M - MASTER R/W - READ/WRITE	RO - READ ONLY SR - SUBORDINATE REF.		PARTITIONS					
DESCRIPTION OF THE SERVER			[ROOT]	NORAD	RIO	CAMELOT	TOKYO	SYDNEY
NAME	LOCATION	NETWORK ADDRESS						
	CAMELOT	ØBØØFADE						
	NORAD	ØFFØBBØØ						
	NORAD	ØFFØBBØØ						
	RIO	ØØØØ1ØØØ						
	TOKYO	ØØ22ØØØ1						
	SYDNEY	21ØØ1ØØØ						

Replica Synchronization

Replication of the NDS database is one of the major features of NDS. Because a partition can be distributed, however, any changes or updates to that partition will take place on an individual replica, which in turn must pass the latest changes to all the other replicas of that partition. This process of ensuring that all the latest changes or updates to a particular partition are reflected in each of its replicas is called *synchronization*.

When updates and modifications are made to NDS, the fact that one of the replicas in a partition will change while the other replicas will not receive the updated information is known as *loose consistency*. Loose consistency simply means that all the replicas are not instantaneously changed as updates to NDS are made. So as NDS receives updates from users and administrators, all the replicas for the partition are not guaranteed to be completely converged or synchronized at any one time. However, to ensure the integrity of the database, NDS automatically synchronizes all the replicas for a specific partition. Figure 6.62 illustrates how the replicas for the [ROOT] partition will stay synchronized among the servers. This figure should be viewed only as a conceptual illustration. For a complete discussion on how the replicas send and receive data for the partition, see Chapter 9, "Troubleshooting Novell Directory Services."

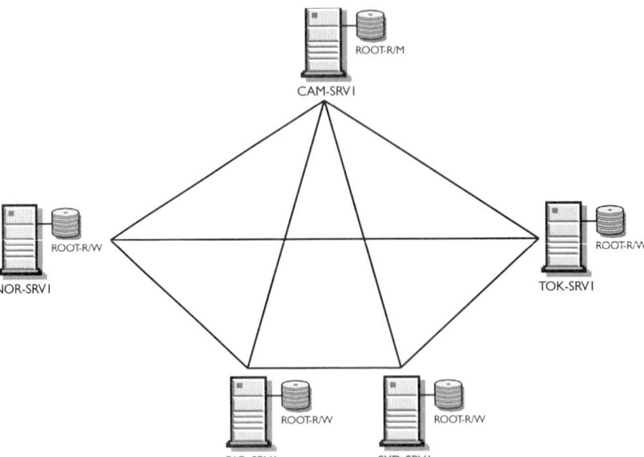

FIGURE 6.62

The NDS replicas synchronize with each other to maintain consistency of the [ROOT] partition information. The synchronization is loosely consistent because of the timing during the process.

This synchronization process, which runs in the background, introduces a new level of complexity to the network and the traffic it could generate. The information passed between the replicas during the synchronization exchange is limited to just the updates, thus reducing the total amount of network traffic.

Because the synchronization process between replicas could impact the traffic on both the local LAN and WAN networks, you should decide where to place the replicas. You can also control which replicas in the partition will accept client updates by choosing the type of replica to place in service.

Traffic Efficiency Based on Replication Synchronization

The process that synchronizes the data between the replicas needs to be considered during the placement of the replicas. Your goal is to minimize the impact of the synchronization between replicas. In general, you should avoid having too many replicas on a single server and too many total replicas per partition. These two factors go hand in hand to help you reduce the workload of the servers and the network traffic.

We will discuss three issues that you need to consider when organizing the replicas to minimize replica synchronization. The three issues are total number of replicas per partition, total number of replicas per server, and subordinate reference replicas.

Total Number of Replicas per Partition

The synchronization of information between all the replicas in a partition varies according to several factors. The amount of replica synchronization for one partition depends on the size of the partition (number of objects), the number of updates or changes to the object information, the number of replicas or servers participating in the synchronization, and the speed of the network (LAN and WAN links).

We encourage you to keep the size of the partitions small. We recommend that a partition hold no more than 5,000 objects so that the synchronization process can efficiently update all the replicas. If a partition grows larger, you should split the partition to reduce the total number of objects in the partition. Again, this recommendation assumes high-end Pentium hardware. Scale back to a smaller partition (2,000 objects) if you have slower hardware.

If the object information changes in one of the replicas, it needs to change in all the other replicas for that partition. Remember, the NDS database is loosely consistent, which means that not all the replicas are instantaneously updated. For example, each user object's information changes when the user logs into NDS. The change is written to the replica on the server that logged the user in. These changes are then synchronized to each of the other replicas in the partition. You can see that replica synchronization increases by simply having more objects in the partition and more replicas per partition.

The installation program will try to create up to three replicas per partition for fault tolerance. (You may, however, need to create more replicas simply to support bindery services on more servers. We recommend that you not have more than 10 to 20 full replicas.) These are the master, read/write, and read-only replicas, and do not include the subordinate reference replicas. If you need to have more than 10 to 20 replicas, then consider creating another partition to reduce the total number of replicas per partition and decrease the load for the NDS synchronization process. Keep in mind supportability and repairability of these partitions.

Number of Replicas per Server

Another consideration is the total number of replicas per server. A server cannot hold two replicas from the same partition. A server can hold multiple replicas only if the replicas are from different partitions in the NDS tree.

We always recommend that you place the NDS replicas on high-end servers that can keep up with the other servers on the network. The synchronization process between all the replicas is only as fast and efficient as the weakest link. Do not place replicas on a low-performance server, because it will impact the entire process.

The number of total replicas per server varies depending on the application or the server that is in use. For example, a home directory server is not recommended for holding more than 10 replicas. An application or e-mail server could hold 20 more replicas. A dedicated NDS replica server could hold up to 120 replicas per server. Again, the other network services that each server provides could affect the total number of replicas per server. We are also assuming a high-end server in all cases.

An extreme case, for example, is one in which a super-server is brought in just to maintain the NDS replicas. This server could possibly maintain up to 120 replicas of different partitions. This example assumes a very large NDS tree that has at least 120 separate NDS partitions. Such a case would include an NDS tree with many geographically dispersed locations.

Subordinate Reference Replicas

A special consideration applies to the distribution of subordinate reference replicas. The subordinate reference replicas participate in the synchronization process as much as the other types of replicas for the partition. However, the amount of information for the subordinate reference replicas is very little. Nonetheless, the subordinate reference replicas change timestamps with the other replicas, and no object data is passed.

If you have done a careful job of designing your tree and partitions like a pyramid, then a good distribution of the subordinate references will be automatically handled by the NDS system. If you have created only a few replicas per partition, then the subordinate references have been optimized and there is very little else that you need to change.

Remember, the subordinate reference replicas are needed because they provide tree connectivity by linking the parent partitions with their child partitions. A subordinate reference replica is essentially a pointer down the tree to the next layer of partitions. Using the subordinate reference mechanism, NDS operates more efficiently because it does not have to place a full replica (master, read/write, and read only) to provide the tree connectivity. The NDS system will place a subordinate reference replica on a server that contains a replica of the parent but does not have the child replica. Again, subordinate reference replicas are useful because NDS does not require you to connect the tree manually by placing full replicas.

Because the NDS system is responsible for maintaining the subordinate reference replicas, you, as administrators, need to be aware (not beware) of their placement and impact on the synchronization process. Again, keep in mind that supportability and repairability play heavily into this equation. The more subordinate references, the more servers need to be contacted during a repair procedure.

A subordinate reference replica contains only one object, which is the topmost container object in the partition (typically an OU). This top container object, which is called the *partition root object*, stores the partition information that links the tree together. The partition root object holds a list of all the replicas in the partition (master, read/write, read only, and subordinate references) that participate in the replica synchronization process. The greater the number of subordinate reference replicas, the larger their impact on the synchronization process. You should ascertain where the subordinate references are being created and, if possible, try to reduce them. By reducing the number of subordinate reference replicas, you will increase the performance of the synchronization process for each server. One way to reduce subordinate references is to reduce the number of replicas of the parent partition by reducing the number of servers that contain a copy of the parent partition. Another way to reduce subordinate reference replicas is to place the child partitions on the same servers as their parents. The second option is not always feasible.

An Example of Subordinate References

A good example with which to illustrate subordinate reference replicas is the [ROOT] partition, which is at the top of the tree. The ACME tree is partitioned as shown in Figure 6.63. In this example, we have 200 cities or locations, each partitioned under the [ROOT] partition.

FIGURE 6.63

The ACME tree has over 200 cities, each partitioned under the [ROOT] partition.

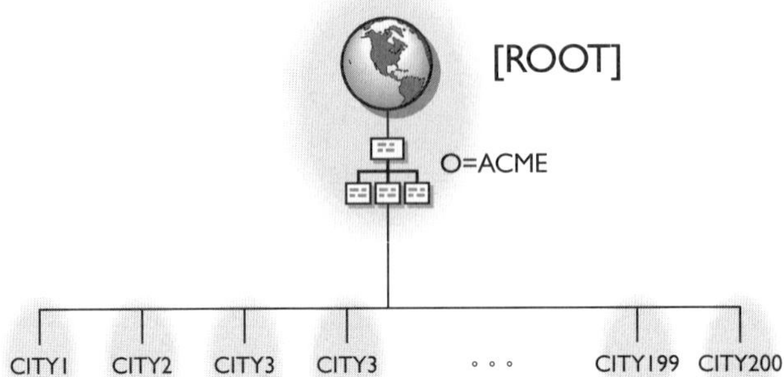

Consider what would happen each time you place a replica of the [ROOT] partition on a server. The NDS system would be forced to create 200 subordinate references replicas on that server, one for each of the child partitions. From the server's perspective, it now has to participate in each one of the 200 partitions' synchronization processes. This amount of work will probably overload the one server, and as a result, the server will not be able to keep up with all the changes in the network. You can see the problem, especially as you add more replicas of the [ROOT] partition to other servers in the network.

Consulting Experience

In the example of 200 cities being partitioned off the [ROOT], the issue is not just the traffic between the replicas, because very little data is passed between a subordinate reference replica and the other replicas. The bigger concern is the effect that the large number of subordinate reference replicas has on partition operations and completion of partition operations. Remember, each replica of a partition must be contacted before a partition operation can be successfully completed. The other issue, once again, is supportability and repairability.

The simplest way to eliminate this problem is to design your tree and partitions like a pyramid, which naturally distributes the subordinate references accordingly. For example, to fix the problem with the ACME tree in Figure 6.63, you simply need to change the design of the tree. By adding another layer of partitions or OUs directly under the [ROOT] partition, you can help distribute the subordinate reference replicas across more network servers. In Figure 6.64 we have added regional layer OUs and partitions in the ACME tree to help distribute the subordinate reference replicas. Each regional OU is its own partition.

FIGURE 6.64

Adding a layer of regional OUs and partitions in the ACME tree design will help distribute the subordinate reference replicas.

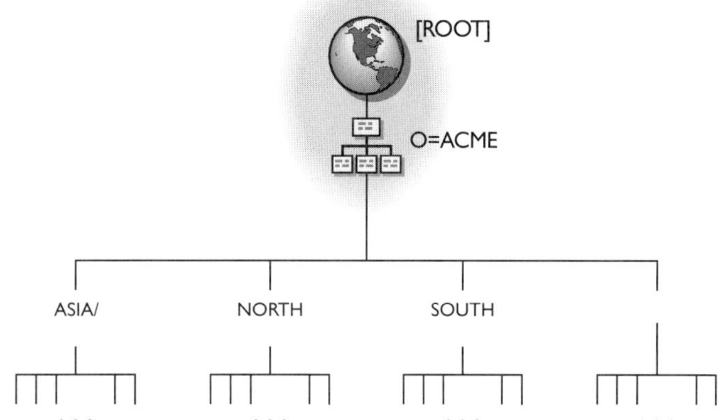

The Effect of Subordinate References on Partitioning Operations

Partitioning operations constitute another issue that could affect the placement of the subordinate reference replicas. During any partitioning operation all the replicas in the replica list, including the subordinate reference replicas, must be contacted in order for the partitioning operation to complete. If, for any reason, the server with a replica is not available, then the partitioning operation will not complete. The operation will try to contact the replicas that are unavailable until they can be reached. The total number of subordinate references could affect the efficiency of the partitioning operation.

One design consideration discussed earlier is to distribute the number of subordinate references among more servers, thus reducing the chance that a server containing subordinate references may not be up during partitioning operations.

You may be wondering why the subordinate reference replicas are contacted during a partition operation. Even though subordinate references do not contain all the partition information, they do contain the partition root object, which could change during the operation.

Summary

Now with these partitioning and replication guidelines in place you can move to the last step in the NDS design process. This step is NDS time synchronization, which is the topic of the next chapter.

CHAPTER 7

NDS Time Synchronization

"Nothing puzzles me more than time or space; and yet nothing troubles me less, as I never think about them." — Charles Lamb

A step in your NDS tree design is to determine the time synchronization configuration for your NetWare 5 servers. *Time synchronization* is the capability of NetWare 5 servers to coordinate and maintain consistent time among all servers in the NDS tree. Time synchronization is necessary to ensure that each Novell Directory Service event receives an accurate timestamp.

A time synchronization configuration can be easily and quickly designed for a NetWare 5 network of any size. For single-server or small-network environments you can accept the defaults provided by NetWare 5's installation utility. This configuration is commonly referred to as the *single reference configuration* or *default configuration*. No steps are required of the LAN administrator because the setup is handled completely by the NetWare 5 installation utility.

For larger networks with more servers or multiple sites, a configuration known as a time provider group is recommended. The *time provider group* is designed to provide greater fault tolerance and efficiency for communicating the time across multiple servers and wide area networks. Both of these approaches are discussed in this chapter.

Once NetWare time has been configured, very little additional activity is required to maintain this function. Time synchronization is both stable and dependable once it has been configured. Both the single reference and the time provider group design options are explained in this section, and background information about how time synchronization functions in a NetWare environment is provided. In addition, the SET commands that relate to time synchronization are discussed here.

NDS Time Synchronization

Time synchronization services provided in NetWare 5 is the mechanism by which network time is maintained on all NetWare 5 servers. If you are migrating from NetWare 4.*x*, you will already have time synchronization configured and will not need to change the configuration when migrating to NetWare 5. NetWare 5 uses the TIMESYNC NetWare Loadable Module (NLM) to coordinate the time between servers on the network. TIMESYNC.NLM will maintain each server's time to Universal Coordinated Time (UTC), which is the world time standard. The local time is used as a reference from which servers can calculate their UTC value. Local time will either be ahead of or behind the UTC value depending on your geographical location. Each time zone has an offset (+ or –) in relation to the UTC. For example, the United States time zones are behind UTC, and most of Europe's time zones are ahead of UTC.

TIMESYNC.NLM is automatically loaded each time the server is started. Time synchronization is active only when TIMESYNC.NLM is loaded. Do not unload this module or you will create problems with resolutions of duplicate event collisions of NDS timestamps (discussed later).

A strict relationship applies between local time and UTC. Each server uses this relationship to maintain both UTC and local time counters. To the extent that an accurate time signal is available, both UTC and local time will be accurate, but TIMESYNC does not guarantee accuracy, only consistency. The difference between local time and UTC depends on the time zone and daylight saving time (DST) status of the server, as illustrated in this equation:

```
UTC = LOCAL TIME + (timezone offset) - (current daylight
adjustment)
```

For example, consider a server located in Provo, Utah. Provo uses mountain standard time during part of the year and mountain daylight time the rest of the year. Mountain standard time is behind UTC by seven hours. When mountain daylight time takes effect, local time is adjusted forward by one hour from mountain standard time. So local time for the server in Provo is behind UTC by seven hours when daylight saving time is not in effect and six hours when it is.

```
UTC = LOCAL TIME + (7 hours) - (0 hours) [when DST is not in
effect]
```

```
UTC = LOCAL TIME + (7 hours) - (1 hour) [when DST is in
effect]
```

If you want to view time at a server's console, you can type TIME to display its status. Figure 7.1 shows how you can see the time information from the server, which displays the local server's time as well as the UTC value.

FIGURE 7.1

Time information is displayed at the server console by entering TIME.

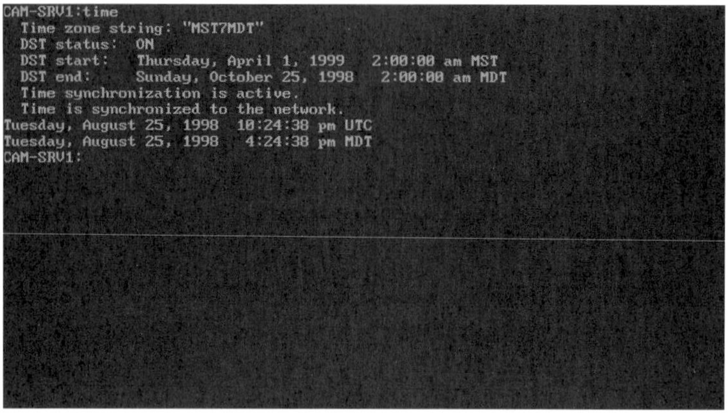

```
CAM-SRV1:time
  Time zone string: "MST7MDT"
  DST status:  ON
  DST start:    Thursday, April 1, 1999   2:00:00 am MST
  DST end:      Sunday, October 25, 1998   2:00:00 am MDT
  Time synchronization is active.
  Time is synchronized to the network.
Tuesday, August 25, 1998  10:24:38 pm UTC
Tuesday, August 25, 1998   4:24:38 pm MDT
CAM-SRV1:
```

The time information displayed includes the time zone string, the status of daylight saving time (including when it starts and ends), the UTC value, the local time, whether time synchronization is active, and whether the server's time is synchronized to the network. Using this information, you can easily detect whether the server is synchronized to the network time.

Once time is synchronized on all NetWare 5 servers, the Directory can accurately timestamp any network event; for example, adding a new user or assigning rights to a new administrator are both considered events. The timestamp ensures that as the Directory tree replicas are synchronized, the correct order of events will be applied during replica synchronization. Timestamps are discussed in detail in the next section.

NDS Timestamps

Each event that occurs in NDS is marked with a timestamp, a unique value within an NDS partition. The timestamps are used to order the events or changes that occur on multiple servers. Timestamping events keeps all NDS changes in their proper order. For more information regarding timestamps, refer to Chapter 8, "NDS Internals Operations."

Timestamps within all the replicas of any partition are unique. As shown in Figure 7.2, the left portion of the timestamp shows the seconds since 1970 of the change based on UTC. This ensures that there are unique timestamps for any changes that are at least 1 second apart. The second portion of the timestamp shows the replica number. The replica number will create unique timestamps for changes occurring within the same second on different replicas. The last portion of the timestamp is called the *event counter*. The event counter is set to zero at the beginning of each second. It is incremented with each change on a particular replica when changes occur within the same second. This event counter further enables a unique timestamp for events occurring in rapid succession on the same replica within the same second.

FIGURE 7.2

The components of an NDS timestamp

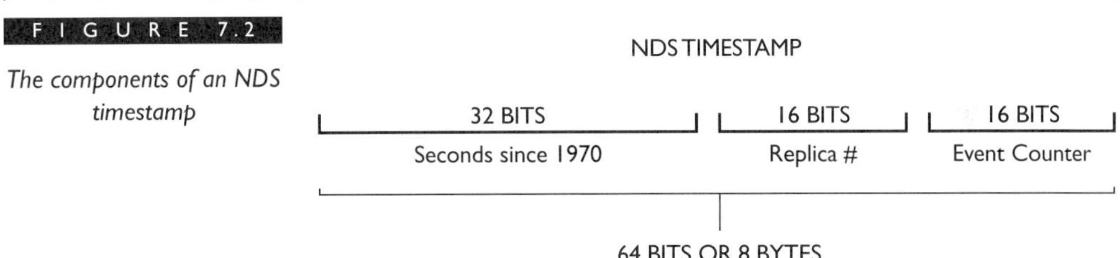

The timestamp is a critical component in the replica synchronization process. When NDS updates a replica, it requests the timestamps from that replica to identify the data. The timestamp provides a unique value for the object and properties that identifies the time and place of where the event originated. If the same object or property is updated on different replicas (or servers) at exactly the same second and event ID, the replica number between the servers would be different. NDS will make the updates using the greater or latest timestamp. When compared, timestamps are treated as 32-bit, 16-bit, 16-bit unsigned with seconds as the most significant.

An example of an object being deleted will help explain how timestamps work. While the actual procedures and processes for deleting objects are more complex than described here, this simplified explanation should provide a sufficient understanding for our purposes. In general terms, whenever a client or workstation deletes an object or property from a replica on a server, the server does not immediately purge it from its local database. Instead, it issues a timestamp for the object or property and marks the object or property value as "not present" or deleted. After the replica synchronization process propagates the change to all other replicas, the Janitor process purges the object or property. The Janitor process is simply an NDS process that periodically scans the Directory for deleted objects and purges them.

NOTE

To support accurate timestamps, the servers must maintain accurate time and that time must be synchronized between the servers. Time synchronization provides the mechanism to ensure that each server is synchronized to the network time. You want accurate timestamps so that the order of modification is accurate. This means that the last modification timestamp is the winner.

External Time Sources

An accurate and automated time of day can also be provided by attaching your NetWare 5 server (reference or single reference) to an external time source service such as a radio clock, an atomic clock, or the Internet (a time source provided by connecting to the Internet). Although not mandatory for the operation of a NetWare 5 network, the use of an external time source in larger network installations is highly recommended, as it eliminates the manual task for a network administrator to verify time. In addition, the external time source provides an accurate time of day for your network, which is required by some NLMs or backup devices. The use of an external time source is shown in Figure 7.3.

FIGURE 7.3

Attach your time server to an external source for automatic time updates.

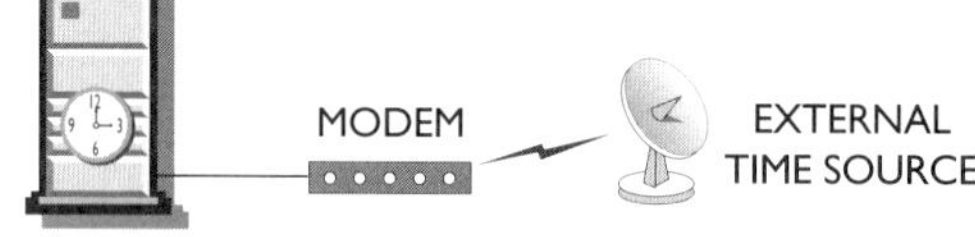

Time Server Types

Each NetWare 5 server is configured as a specific type of time server during installation. All NetWare 5 servers perform the same basic time functions, including the following:

- Providing UTC information to any client or NLM making the request
- Providing status information on time synchronization
- Making adjustments to correct discrepancies when time synchronization is active

A NetWare 5 server will provide time to any client or NLM making a request for network time. For example, your backup or archival software may require accurate network time to know when to initiate a particular process or function. Client utilities may also query time from a NetWare 5 server of any type.

Regardless of the configuration, all NetWare 5 servers will provide time status information. Through time synchronization, each NetWare 5 server knows the status of its clock with respect to the network.

All NetWare 5 servers are time servers and participate as either providers of time or consumers of time. The internal mechanism for querying the time is the same for all types of servers. There are three types of time providers: primary server, reference server, and single reference server. Time providers coordinate time among themselves to determine the "official" network time. Time consumers are known as secondary servers and can request time from any of the three types of time providers. Time consumers will constitute the majority of your NetWare 5 servers. Figure 7.4 shows the categories of the time servers.

FIGURE 7.4

Time servers are categorized into one of two classes: the time providers and the time consumers.

TIME PROVIDERS	TIME CONSUMERS
Primary	Secondary
Reference	
Single Reference	

Functionally, all NetWare 5 servers are very similar in terms of how they are configured for time. In fact, reference and single reference servers are just special cases of primary servers. Each NetWare 5 server on the network is responsible for its own synchronization and status. This means that each server will, at periodic intervals, poll other servers for time, make any necessary adjustments, and wait for the next interval to repeat the process.

Since time synchronization is a server-centric operation, each server determines if its time is within an acceptable limit, known as the *synchronization radius*. A server is synchronized to the time on the network when its time is within the synchronization radius. If the server determines that its time is within the radius, it raises a time synchronization flag. This synchronization flag indicates that this server has a UTC value that can be used by NDS to accurately timestamp events on the network.

Secondary servers are the most common type of server, as they will synchronize to either a time provider or another secondary server.

Secondary Time Servers

Secondary time servers rely on other sources to provide them with network time. A secondary server can query another secondary, single reference, reference, or primary time server for the network time.

The secondary server will be the most prevalent type of server on your network because most of your servers do not need to participate in determining network time. During the installation of your file servers, all servers except the first server are designated as secondary servers. The first server is automatically designated a single reference time server as explained later in this section.

During installation of your file servers, all servers except the first server are designated as secondary servers. The first server is automatically designated a single reference time server as shown in Figure 7.5. This is the default configuration. If the UTC value on the secondary time servers is within the synchronization radius, the synchronization flag can be raised.

FIGURE 7.5

The secondary time servers will attempt to get their network time from the time providers. In this case, all the secondary time servers are communicating with a single time provider called a single reference time server.

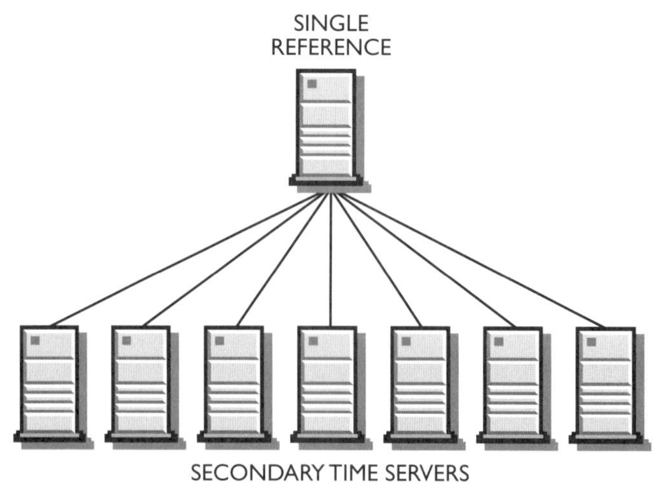

The secondary server adjusts its clock to make up any difference in the time it receives from the network. The network time will be provided by another server or servers during each polling interval. Therefore, any discrepancies in the secondary server's time will be resolved during each polling interval. The secondary servers can and do provide time to requesting client or server applications.

The secondary time servers do not participate in determining network time. These servers do not negotiate time with any other time servers. They simply get the network time from another source on the network and make the appropriate adjustments to their own clock during each polling interval. The secondary server will raise its synchronization flag once its time discrepancy is less than the synchronization radius set for that server.

Primary Time Servers

The *primary time servers* are responsible for determining and setting the network time. The primary time servers are classified as time providers because they distribute the network time to other requesting servers. The secondary servers will constitute the majority of the requesting servers needing network time.

In order to determine the network time, the primary server will poll other primary and reference servers from its list of servers. This process determines the "official time" for the network as each primary server polls other primary servers to determine any discrepancies between its local clock and the calculated network time. If there is a difference, the primary server will try to adjust its clock to remedy the discrepancy.

Figure 7.6 illustrates how a primary time server polls the other time providers. In this case, the other time providers are primary servers. Each primary time server wakes up (at default ten-minute intervals) and polls the other time providers on the network during its polling process. In this example, time is requested from all other primary time servers and the reference server.

Like all time servers, a primary server will determine if its time is within its synchronization radius. If the server is within the radius, it raises its synchronization flag to indicate that synchronization has occurred.

During the polling process, each primary time server has a weighting factor of one. This weighting factor means that all other primary servers will be given equal consideration during the polling interval. Each primary server will "wake up" on its polling interval and begin checking its time against other time providers.

FIGURE 7.6

A primary time server polls other time providers.

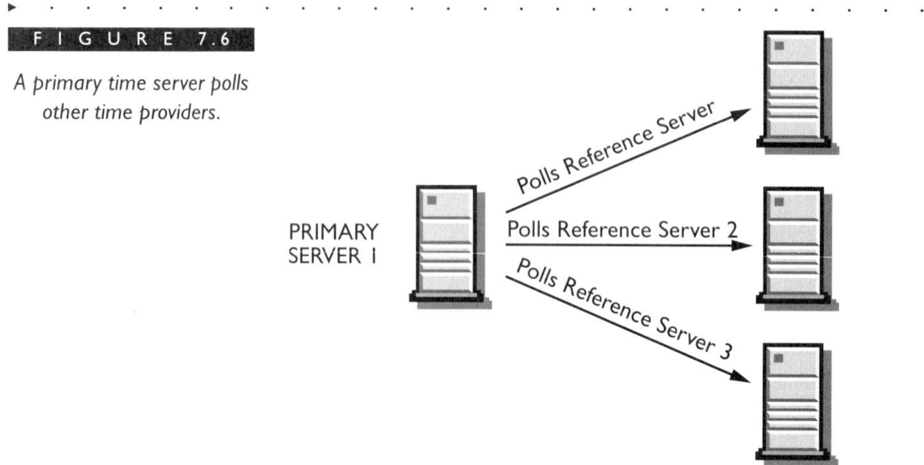

For example, primary server A begins a polling process of the other primary servers in the group. Its current network time is 10:15 A.M. After polling begins, primary server B returns a time of 10:20 A.M. and primary server C returns a time of 10:10 A.M. Because each server has a weighting factor of one, they are treated equally and the two times are averaged together to produce a time of 10:15 A.M. An example of this process is shown in Figure 7.7.

FIGURE 7.7

Each primary time server wakes up and begins polling the other time providers during its polling process.

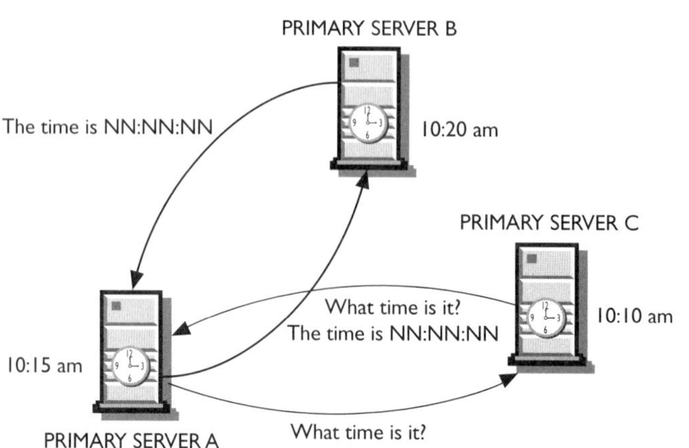

The polling process is unique and operates independently for all time servers, as each server is responsible for its own network time. Although your servers may have the default polling interval of every ten minutes, each server will most likely be polling at different ten-minute intervals as each primary server checks its time against other time providers in the tree.

While primary servers alone can achieve network time, they need the help of a consistent time provider that never makes adjustments to its clock after polling. A special case of the primary server is the reference server, which sets time for the entire network.

Reference Time Servers

A *reference time server* is a time provider that adds additional capability to a primary time server. The reference server works with other time providers, such as primary servers, to provide the network time. The difference between the reference server and a primary server is that the reference server will always believe that it has network time and will not adjust its internal clock. Therefore, you should place a reference server where you set network time and force all other primary servers to adjust their time to the reference server. The reference server participates in polling intervals just like the primary servers, but it does not adjust its clock.

The best configuration is to have one reference server with a few primary servers to provide accurate time. Figure 7.8 illustrates the configuration of one reference server and multiple primary time servers on the network.

Over time all NetWare 5 servers will converge their internal clocks to the time of the reference server. On the other hand, the reference server will never adjust its clock. This naturally makes the reference server over time the point of reference for convergence.

During the polling process, the reference server has a weighting factor of 16. This means that all primary servers will converge their time to that of the reference server because it has the greatest weighting in terms of time. You will typically want to have only one reference server on your network, as it is the definitive time source. The best configuration is to have one reference server with a few primary servers to provide accurate time. Design configuration options are discussed in the following section.

FIGURE 7.8

The configuration of one reference server and multiple primary time servers on the network

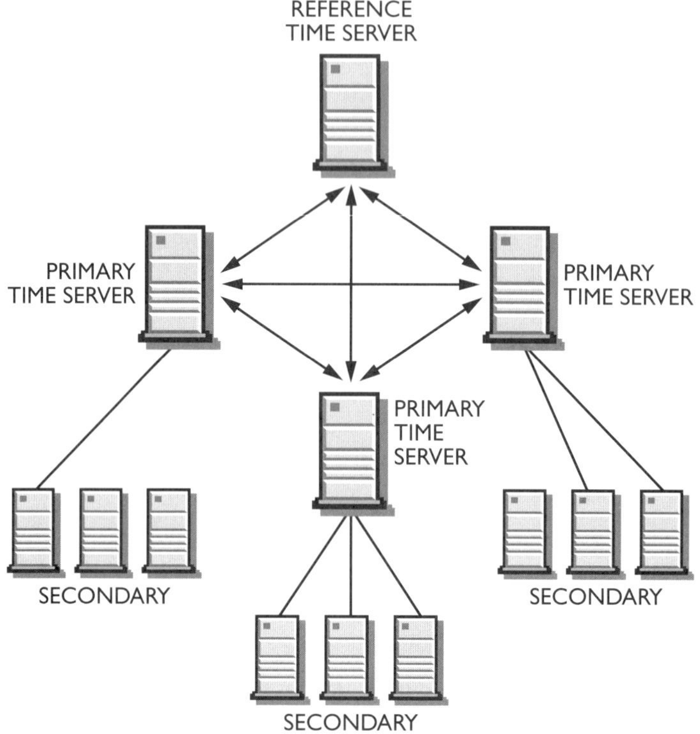

Primary servers work with the reference server to provide fault tolerance and multiple sources for time. The reference server must, like other primary servers, contact another source during the polling process in order to raise its synchronization flag. In addition, if the reference server should fail, multiple primary servers can still provide consistent network time to requesting servers and clients until you restore another reference server. Therefore, the reference server is the supreme authority for time, except when it is not accessible.

Like all time servers, a reference server will determine if its time is within the synchronization radius. If the server is within the radius, then it raises its time synchronization flag, which indicates that its time is acceptable for timestamping events.

Because the reference server does not make an adjustment to its internal clock, you can connect it to an external source. Having an external clock accomplishes several important things. First, it provides an accurate and automated mechanism to check time. Some of your applications may require accurate time of day if they initiate a process, such as a backup, in the middle of the night. Second, an automated time source will help ensure that the reference server's clock is not drifting and consequently is keeping all other servers in your network with accurate time.

The server's own clock can be used as a time source, but time must be verified manually by an administrator to ensure that it is staying accurate and not drifting. Ideally, the reference server can be connected to an external clock source to provide highly accurate time. Products are available that connect PCs to external time sources, such as a radio clock or modem, which can contact an outside source.

TIP

For more information on external clock solutions you can contact Novell's NetWire or Web server to download the TIMESG.TXT file. This file contains companies and their product names that support the external time source solution.

Only one reference server should be used on the network. Multiple reference servers could be placed on the network, but they will not synchronize with each other.

Single Reference Time Servers

The *single reference time server* is a stand-alone time provider for the entire network. The single reference is the default configuration and is established automatically during installation. The main difference between a reference server and a single reference server is that the single reference server can raise its synchronization flag without confirming its time with any other time providers. It does, however, go through the polling process like all NetWare 5 servers. In this case, the polling does not expect a response from any server. A response from another server would indicate that another time provider has been erroneously placed on the network. This condition would cause the single reference server to report an error to the console screen.

A single reference server should be the only time provider on the network. The rest of the time servers should be secondary servers. The secondary servers simply contact the single reference to get the network time. Figure 7.9 illustrates a single reference time server, with the others being secondary time servers.

FIGURE 7.9

A single reference time server provides time to the secondary time servers.

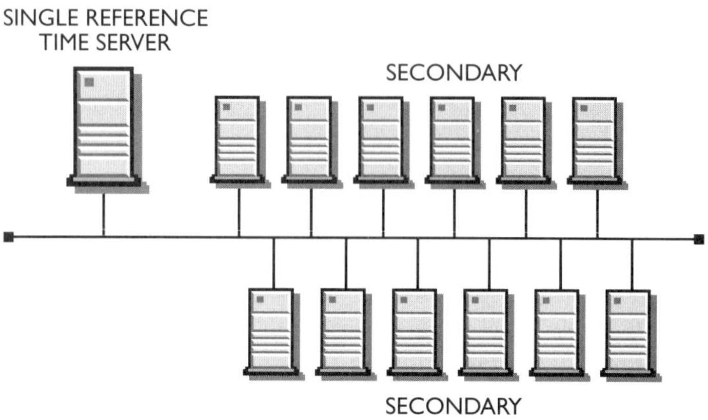

A single reference server enables you to have all other servers remain as secondary servers, which will adjust their times to the single reference time during each polling cycle. Like the reference server, a single reference server can be connected to an external source to feed the network accurate time of day.

In addition, the single reference server's own clock, instead of an external source, can be used as the time source. Occasionally, it may be necessary to check the server's time against a reliable source because some of your applications, such as backup or archiving software programs, may require accurate network time.

Time Synchronization Design

Once you understand the different types of time servers, you are ready to look at which design option best suits your particular needs. This section provides you with the options available to design NDS time synchronization.

Time Synchronization Configuration Options

Your NetWare 5 network may use two basic time server configurations for single reference (the default) or a time provider group. All other available configurations are variations of these two. As part of your NDS design, evaluate the time synchronization configurations and choose the one that best meets the needs of your company. Here are two important factors to consider:

- Is your network multisite-connected by a WAN? If it is, then we recommend always using the second option, that of a time provider group. A time provider group gives your network greater fault tolerance in a wide area network configuration by distributing the time providers to multiple locations.
- If your site consists of 30 or fewer NetWare 5 servers and is not connected by a WAN, the default option of single reference server will work extremely well. The LAN environment can easily contact a single reference server without crossing a WAN link. In addition, your servers can easily contact the single reference server without burdening the server.

Consider the configuration options discussed in the sections that follow in making your decision, and use the MONITOR utility to make the necessary changes. This utility is run from a NetWare 5 server console by typing LOADMONITOR. From the menu select Server Parameters and then select the Time option as shown in Figure 7.10.

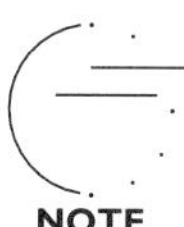
NOTE

NetWare 5 has moved the SERVMAN utility found in NetWare 4 to the Monitor utility for greater consolidation of utilities. You get the same functionality as you have with SERVMAN from NetWare 4.

FIGURE 7.10

The main screen of the MONITOR utility with the Time option selected

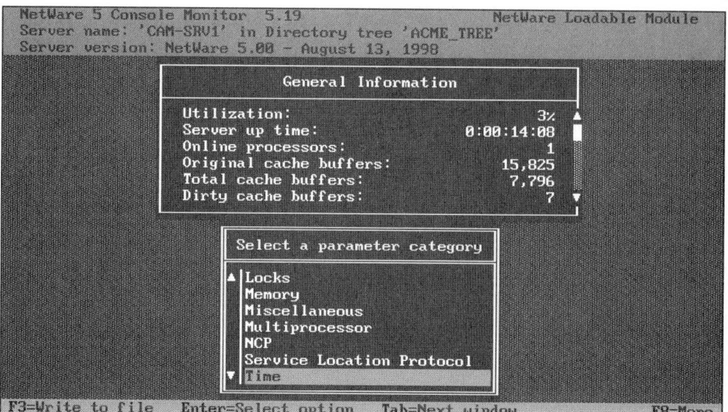

The Default Option: a Single Reference Time Server

When the first NetWare 5 server is installed in the NDS tree, it is automatically configured as a single reference server. All additional NetWare 5 servers installed in the same tree are automatically configured as secondary servers. The Novell installation utility assumes that your installation will initially consist of two levels of servers: A single reference at the first level and secondary servers at the second level provide you with a default installation.

The advantages of the default configuration are that it is easy to understand and requires absolutely no advanced planning. In addition, no configuration files are needed, and the possibility of errors during time synchronization is considerably minimized.

In the default configuration, select a central file server that can be easily contacted by the other NetWare 5 servers in your network. Remember, the first NetWare 5 server you install is automatically configured as the single reference server as shown in Figure 7.11. You can always designate another server as the single reference by using the MONITOR utility. Figure 7.12 shows an example of a single reference time server configuration setup.

FIGURE 7.11

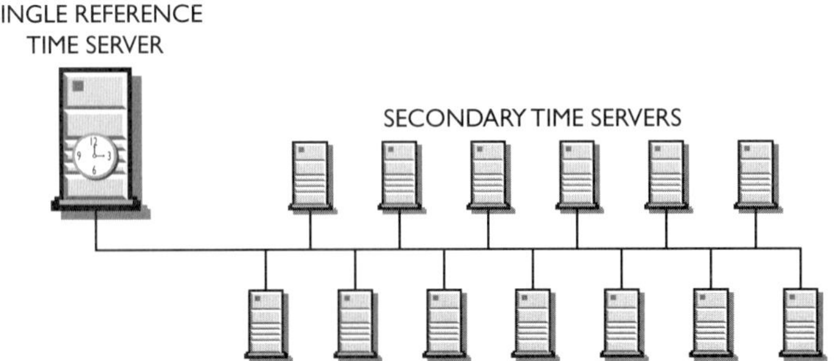

A single reference time configuration with only one server providing time to the entire network. This configuration is suitable for a network that has fewer than 30 servers and is situated in one geographical location.

A potential drawback of the default configuration is that if the single reference server should fail, the network has lost its only time provider. If this happens for only a short period of time (a day or less), however, there is little problem with the timestamping of events. All NetWare 5 servers should continue to maintain their time and continue to stamp NDS events. If your single reference is down for prolonged periods, we recommend that you designate a new server as the single reference to ensure that there is a source for time on your network. In order to designate a new server as the single reference, simply go to the server and make the change using MONITOR.

FIGURE 7.12

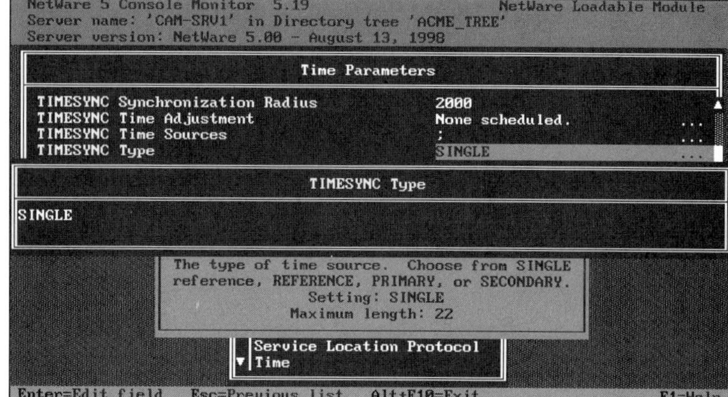

Use the MONITOR utility to designate another server as your single reference or to make other configuration changes.

The Custom Option: a Time Provider Group

The time provider group offers another design option. The time provider group requires one reference server and a minimum of two primary servers that will participate in the synchronization process to coordinate the network time. These time source servers form a time provider group that in turn provides time to the rest of the NetWare 5 servers.

Consulting Experience

Regardless of the size of your network, you can initially accept the single reference default until your installation grows beyond 30 servers or unless you immediately begin with NetWare 5 on both sides of a WAN. Also, if you choose the single reference server option, do not use any other time provider, such as a primary or a reference. A single reference is the only time source required on the entire network under this configuration.

The time provider group configuration works well for networks that have more than 30 NetWare 5 servers or are situated in several locations in a wide area configuration. Figure 7.13 illustrates the placement of the time providers in the major hub sites of the ACME tree.

FIGURE 7.13

The placement of the time providers in the major hub sites of the ACME tree

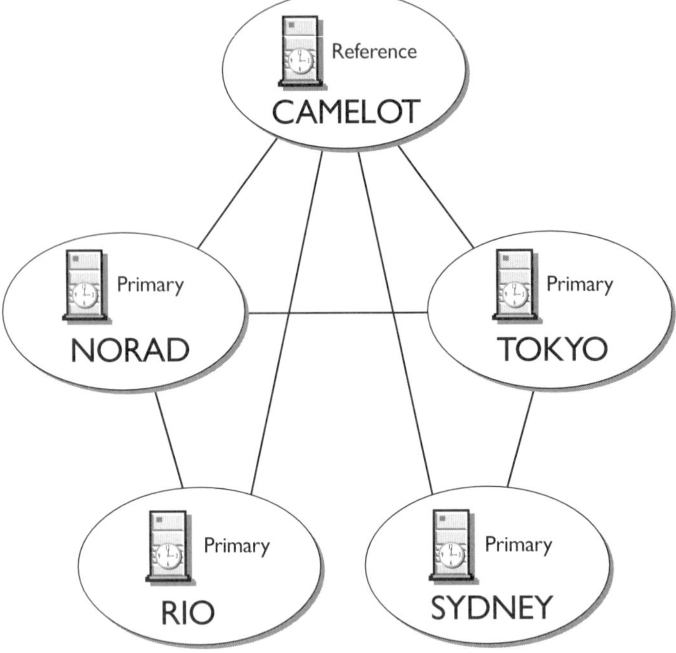

The time provider group configuration option requires simple configuration adjustments for the few servers you want to designate as participants in the time provider group. One server will be designated as the reference, and a recommended two to seven servers may be designated as primary servers. Primary servers may be designated by using the MONITOR utility's Time Parameters screen as shown in Figure 7.14.

In selecting your reference server, look for a centralized location in your network infrastructure. For example, if your WAN is designed like the ACME WAN with a hub-and-spoke design, your reference server should be centrally placed at the hub location. The primary servers should be distributed across your wide area links to the other hub locations. If your network is a large WAN, place your primary servers in just a few strategic locations. The rest of the installed file servers will be secondary servers. Figure 7.15 shows where the reference server and primary servers should be placed for network efficiency in the ACME tree.

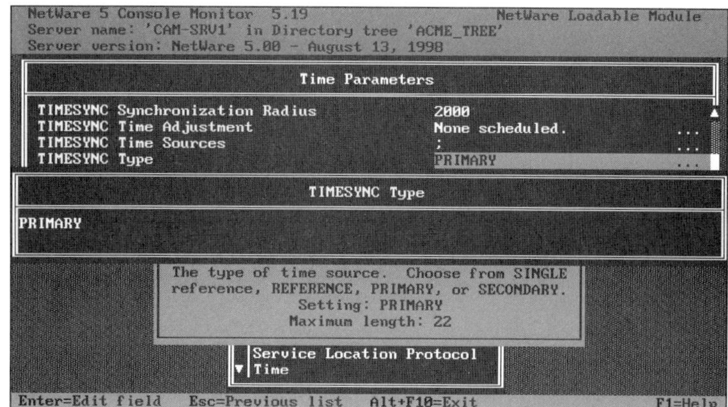

FIGURE 7.14

Using the MONITOR utility to designate a primary server

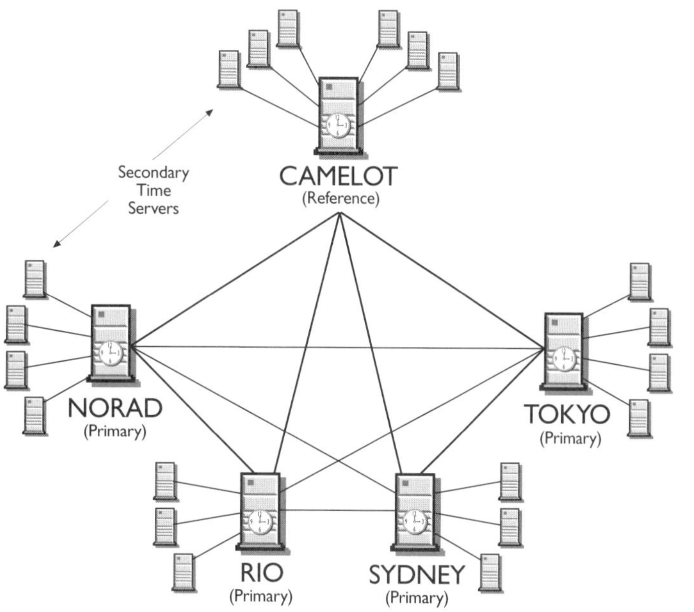

FIGURE 7.15

An example of time server designations for a hub-and-spoke infrastructure in the ACME tree

It is highly recommended that you connect the reference server to an external time source to provide highly accurate time. Figure 7.16 shows an example of a time provider group in the ACME tree that is connected to an external time source. The ACME time provider group contains one reference server located in CAMELOT and four other primary servers located in NORAD, RIO, TOKYO, and SYDNEY. This configuration offers redundancy and the capability to balance the requests for the time.

FIGURE 7.16

This time provider group configuration offers redundancy and the means to balance requests for the time.

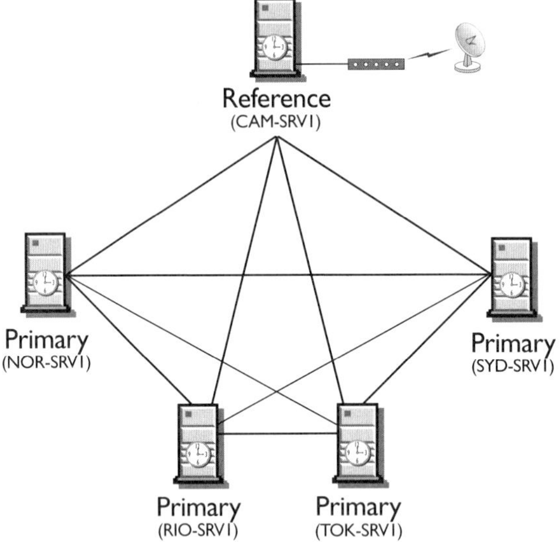

Multiple Time Provider Groups

Some companies may need to use multiple time provider groups for redundancy in worldwide corporations. For example, we could create a time provider group at NORAD and also at CAMELOT so that time is distributed from each area rather than traversing a WAN. Multiple time provider groups require that your reference servers be connected to external clocks to converge their times. An example of multiple time provider groups is shown in Figure 7.17. Each reference is connected to an external source to provide accurate and automated time, thus ensuring that both groups are distributing the same time (or very close to it) for the entire tree.

FIGURE 7.17

An example of multiple time provider groups in the ACME tree

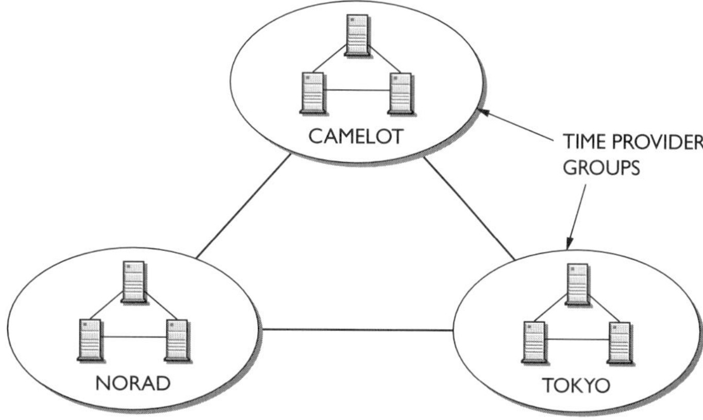

Time Synchronization Communication Options

Secondary time servers will periodically request the time and will need to communicate with time sources on the network. Time providers also need to find other time providers in order to determine the correct UTC.

NetWare 5 servers communicate time information using one of two methods: the Service Advertising Protocol (SAP) or configured lists. The following two sections discuss these two methods.

Time Synchronization Using the Service Advertising Protocol

The SAP method is the default at installation and requires no intervention. As new NetWare 5 servers are designated primary providers, no custom configurations to the existing time servers or to new servers are required for time communication. Time providers such as a primary, reference, or single reference servers advertise their presence on the network using SAP by default.

SAP can cause a small amount of additional traffic on your network. Also, because SAP is self-configuring, a new time server that is unintentionally configured as a wrong type in the same tree could disrupt your time synchronization.

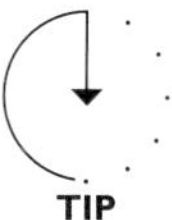

The time synchronization SAP type is 0x026B. If you have decided to use SAP for your time communication, you must not filter this packet type on any routers that connect your NetWare 5 servers together.

Time Synchronization Using Configured Lists

The use of a configured list enables you to specify exactly which servers should be contacted for a time provider group and to make requests for time consumers as well. For all implementations using time provider groups, we recommend that you use a configured list instead of SAP as your communication option. The configured list option will keep time synchronization traffic to a minimum and also prohibit anyone from placing other time providers on your network that might cause problems with the network time. A server must obtain the configured list if it is to participate in network time for your tree. For the ACME tree we have chosen to use a time provider group along with a configured list that specifies the time servers in the time provider group. After the list is created, it is then distributed to all time servers in the group through the file called TIMESYNC.CFG.

The configured list is created by using the MONITOR utility, selecting the Time option, and making the entries for each server name that you want to contact in your time provider group. The first step is to enable the configured list option as shown in Figure 7.18. Once it is set to ON, you are able to begin creating your configured list.

FIGURE 7.18

Using MONITOR to enable the configured list option for time communication

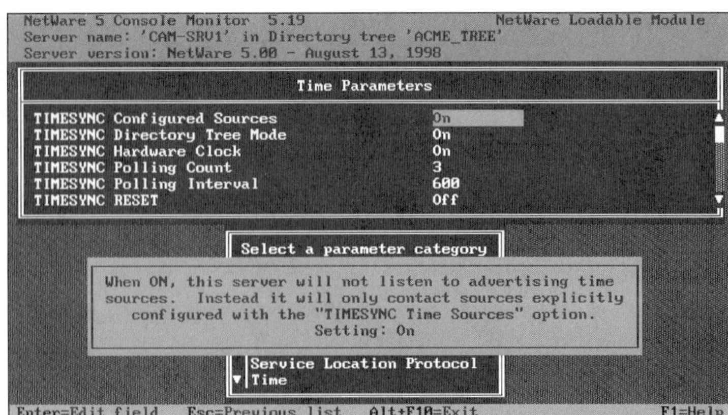

The configured list entries use the server names separated by spaces, as shown in Figure 7.19 for the ACME tree. We have designated CAMELOT as their reference server location. All other major sites in our tree will contain one primary server to communicate with the reference server in CAMELOT.

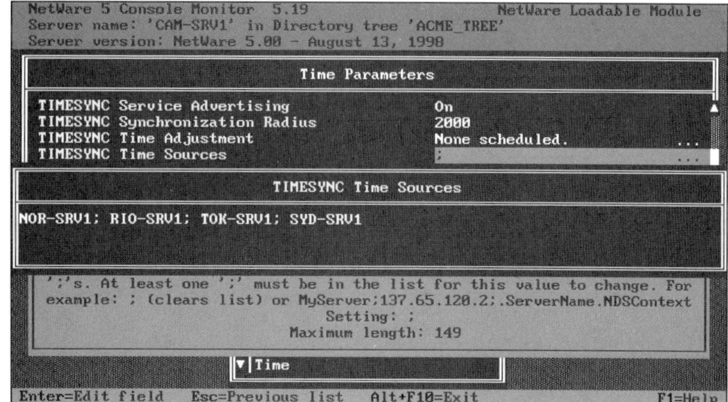

FIGURE 7.19

A configured list for the ACME time provider group. This list is stored on each file server in the time provider group.

Configured lists give you complete control of the time synchronization hierarchy. The configured list also reduces the SAP traffic on your network because SAP broadcasts are not used. Instead, the configured list specifies the source server by name to contact.

A proposed time synchronization configuration is found in the example that follows. In this example the corporate office is located in CAMELOT. The reference server in CAMELOT is linked to an external time source. This source server sets both the NetWare server clock and the hardware time-of-day clock. Primary servers are located in RIO, NORAD, SYDNEY, and TOKYO. These time sources will work together to determine the actual network time during each polling interval. The ACME tree is using the configured sources list so that all the servers can contact each other to determine the network time. In the example that follows, the TIMESYNC.CFG file is shown with its configured list.

TIMESYNC.CFG for reference server in CAMELOT # Configuration parameters for server CAM-SRV1

```
Configured Sources = ON

Directory Tree Mode = ON

Hardware Clock = ON

Polling Count = 3

Polling Interval = 10
```

```
Service Advertising = OFF
Synchronization Radius = 2000
Type = REFERENCE
# Configured time source list server CAM-SRV1
Time Source = RIO-SRV1
Time Source = TOK-SRV1
Time Source = SYD-SRV1
Time Source = NOR-SRV1
Time Source = CAM-SRV1
```

TIMESYNC.CFG for primary servers in RIO, TOKYO, NORAD, AND SYDNEY

```
# Configuration parameters for server TOK-SRV1
Configured Sources = ON
Directory Tree Mode = ON
Hardware Clock = ON
Polling Count = 3
Polling Interval = 10
Service Advertising = OFF
Synchronization Radius = 2000
Type = PRIMARY
# Configured time source list from server TOK-SRV1
Time Source = CAM-SRV1
Time Source = RIO-SRV1
Time Source = SYD-SRV1
Time Source = NOR-SRV1
Time Source = TOK-SRV1
```

The secondary servers located in each geographical region would use the following TIMESYNC.CFG file. The server *xxxxx* indicates any secondary server located in the ACME tree:

TIMESYNC.CFG for secondary servers # Configuration parameters from server *xxxxx*

```
Configured Sources = ON

Directory Tree Mode = ON

Hardware Clock = ON

Polling Count = 3

Polling Interval = 10

Service Advertising = OFF

Synchronization Radius = 2000

Type = SECONDARY
```

Configured time source list from server *xxxxx*

```
Time Source = CAM-SRV1

Time Source = RIO-SRV1

Time Source = TOK-SRV1

Time Source = NOR-SRV1

Time Source = SYD-SRV1
```

In each geographical region, the time source list should be reordered to place the closest time provider first on the list. Next, place the lowest-cost (time and hops) providers, and finally the rest of the providers. This will enable the secondary server to initially contact the closest available server to obtain the correct network time.

Other Design Considerations

This section describes some time configurations that are less frequently implemented but are used mostly by corporations that have multiple offices around the world.

Configuring Secondary Servers to Follow Other Secondary Servers

In some cases it may be necessary for secondary servers to receive their time from other secondary servers. For large companies this situation may occur as you try to limit the number of primary servers spread across your WAN network as time providers. Therefore, if you use the configured list option, you can configure secondary servers to obtain their time from other secondary servers that are obtaining their time from a primary server elsewhere. As shown in Figure 7.20, the ACME tree has secondary servers that follow other secondary servers.

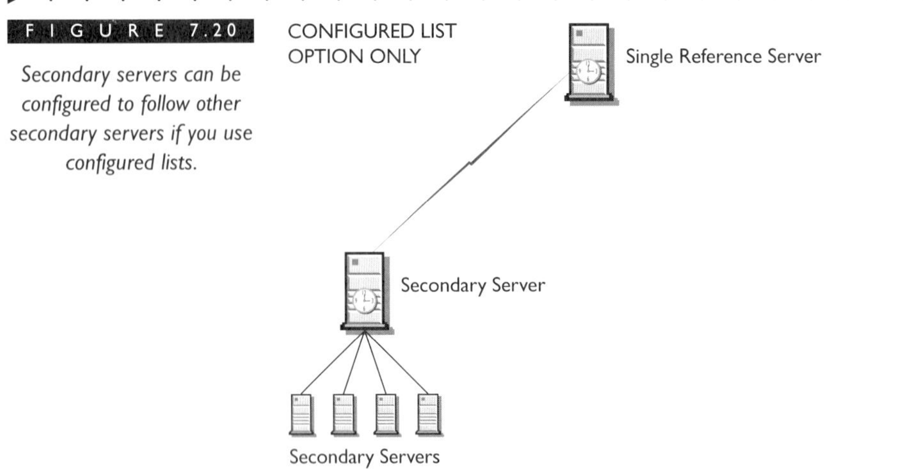

FIGURE 7.20

Secondary servers can be configured to follow other secondary servers if you use configured lists.

Time providers such as primary servers will not follow a secondary server. You can only configure a secondary server to follow another secondary server. If your company has many sites, you should consider placing a primary server at a hub location with your secondary servers contacting the hub. If your SPOKE or REMOTE locations have multiple servers, you may want to designate one secondary server to contact the primary server for time on behalf of the other secondary servers. An example of this arrangement is shown in Figure 7.21.

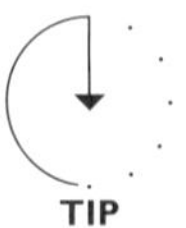

The total allowable time radius for the entire system is ten seconds. Therefore, keep the number of secondary servers following each secondary to a depth of only two to three servers. Any depth greater than two to three servers may lead to time synchronization errors, which are unacceptable for NDS.

FIGURE 7.21

A hub-and-spoke arrangement with primary and secondary servers. At the remote or spoke locations, the secondary servers contact other secondary servers for their time.

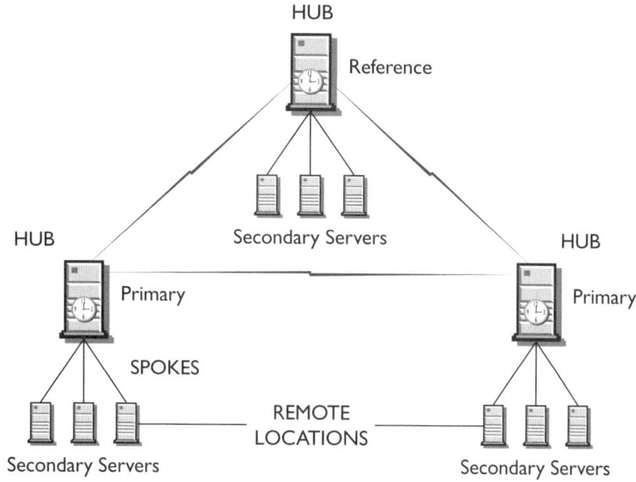

Having More Than One Reference Server

Some organizations may require more than one reference server because of their company's dispersed locations. For example, you may want to have a time provider group in two different countries, rather than having time traffic cross over expensive or extremely busy wide area connections. As shown in Figure 7.22, you can have multiple reference servers as long as they are each connected to an external source. The external source is needed so that these reference servers can maintain the same time and not drift.

FIGURE 7.22

Multiple reference servers can be used as long as they are connected to external time sources.

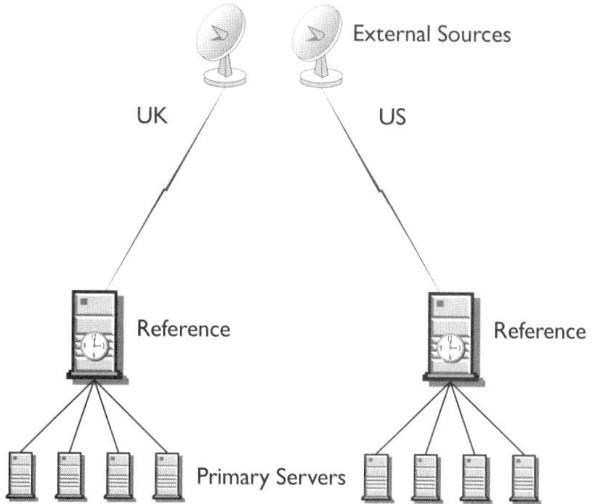

Time Synchronization Traffic Considerations

Although the amount of time traffic is generally small, it may be useful to know what kind of a network load is generated by time synchronization. The actual workload is controlled by the number of time exchanges during each polling loop. You can take steps to further minimize the workload if you have bandwidth constraints on your network. The actual traffic load is determined by how many time exchanges you have configured for each polling loop.

The default is to make three time exchanges, each of which involves an NCP send/receive pair totaling 332 bytes of data. Thus, the default three exchanges involve six packets totaling 996 bytes of data.

Therefore, you can calculate the amount of traffic for each server during a specific polling interval with this equation:

```
NDS Traffic = (N - 1) * (Polling Count) * 332
```

where N = the number of providers to contact.

For example, let's assume that a network has five time providers in its group (one reference and four primary servers) and is using the default intervals of three send/receive exchanges every ten minutes for each server. You can determine the amount of traffic generated in this way:

```
(5 - 1) * (3) * (332) = 3,984 bytes/10 minutes/per time
source server
```

Each time source server would, at its own ten-minute interval, generate 3,984 bytes of traffic on your network. Obviously, the more primary servers you have, the more traffic will be generated on your network.

It is also possible, but not recommended, to change the polling interval to cut down on network traffic. The default polling interval is ten minutes. But as long as the server clock is not drifting and synchronization is maintained, that polling interval may be extended.

In situations where perhaps dozens of secondary servers would poll a single primary server across a slow LAN or WAN segment, it may be helpful to increase the polling period to even one or two hours. This would cut back on the network traffic and probably have little or no effect on synchronization, unless the server clocks drift by several seconds a day.

In fact, once a server has reached a stable state, the amount of network traffic attributed to time synchronization will probably be minuscule compared to the normal everyday traffic.

Checking Time Synchronization Status

You can easily check the time synchronization status of all servers by using the DSREPAIR utility as shown in Figure 7.23. After typing LOAD DSREPAIR at the server's console, you can select Time Synchronization to check the status. Keep in mind that if you are running DSREPAIR on a server containing a copy of the [ROOT] partition, the Time Synchronization option will search all NetWare 5 servers in the entire tree beginning at ([ROOT]) and searching downward. If you do not want this to happen, run DSREPAIR on a server that does not hold a copy of the [ROOT] partition.

FIGURE 7.23

Using DSREPAIR to obtain a status of time synchronization

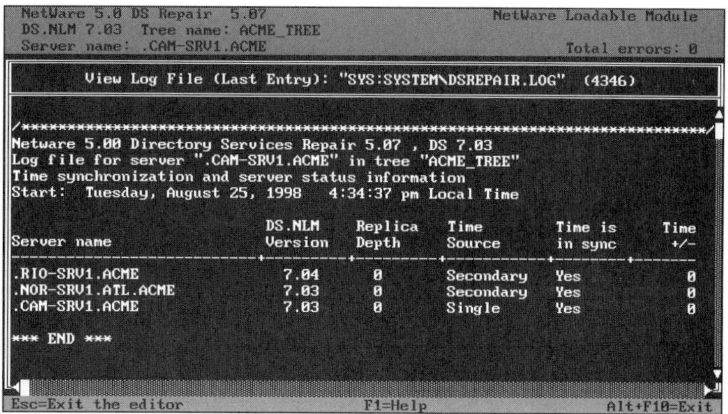

Adding New Time Servers

When you add a new server to an already synchronized network, time synchronization acts on two basic premises. First, it works from the notion that adding a server should not disrupt the network's time synchronization. Second, it assumes that if the new server's time doesn't agree with network time, the network time is more likely to be correct.

Therefore, the first act of time synchronization (for any server type) during boot-up is to set the server time to the time reported by the first time provider contacted. This is true even for reference and single reference servers that do not normally adjust their clocks.

When you bring up a server, make sure that time synchronizes properly and, if necessary, reset the time on reference and single reference servers manually. It is always a good idea to check the time after bringing up a server just to make sure that all the time parameters are set correctly and that the time is synchronized.

If you are currently using the default option of a single reference server and all other servers secondary, you can continue reading this section to make the change to a time provider group. This configuration requires you to change the time type on the server you want to designate as a reference server by using the MONITOR utility. An example of this is shown in Figure 7.24. Only one server will be designated as the reference server in our example.

FIGURE 7.24

An example of a server being designated as the reference time server

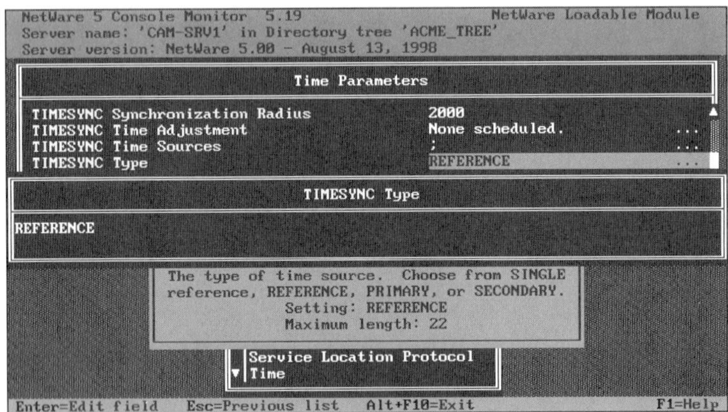

The next step is to designate some server as a primary time server. Using the MONITOR utility again, you will change your selected server's type to primary. Repeat this procedure for all appropriate servers, but for no more than seven servers. You can have more than seven primary servers, but keep in mind that the more primary servers, the greater the amount of traffic on your network during each polling interval for time.

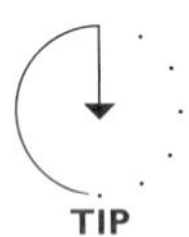

Experience has shown that most companies can have very stable time by using only three or four primary servers in the entire network. Only a few servers need to work with the reference server to determine time for the entire network. Also, consider that there should be only one server designated as the primary time provider per hub location.

After you have made configuration changes for both the reference server and the primary servers, save the changes when prompted before exiting the MONITOR utility. An example of how this screen appears is shown in Figure 7.25.

FIGURE 7.25

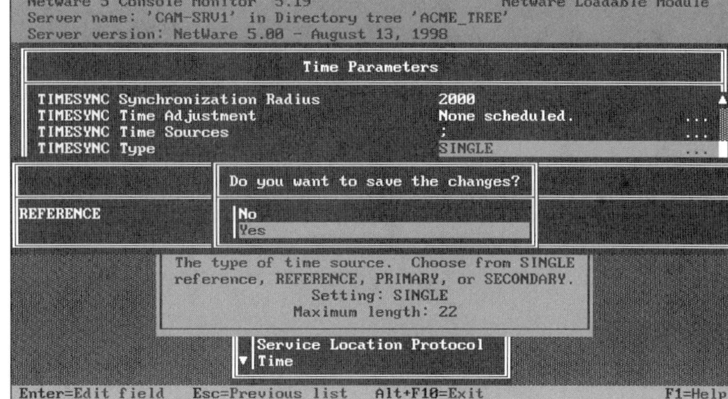

Be sure to save changes to the TIMESYNC.CFG file before exiting the MONITOR utility.

Time Synchronization Operations

This section discusses how you can configure the time on your NetWare 5 servers and explains how to use the various SET parameters that are provided. In addition, you will learn the commands found in the MONITOR utility for adjusting the time parameters. Most changes and configurations with time can be accomplished by using the MONITOR utility, which is discussed in this section. The SET parameters will rarely need changing. However, some environments may require that you adjust some of them.

Using the SET Parameters for Time Synchronization

NetWare 5 includes a rich set of settable parameters governing time synchronization. The time synchronization parameters can be set from the server console using the SET commands or through the menu-driven MONITOR utility. In addition, your current time synchronization SET parameters can be viewed from the server console by typing SET and then selecting the Time option as shown in Figures 7.26 and 7.27. The setting for time synchronization can be stored in a special configuration file called TIMESYNC.CFG. This file is located in the SYS:SYSTEM subdirectory of your NetWare 5 servers.

FIGURE 7.26

To view SET parameters at the server console, type SET.

```
CAM-SRV1:set
Settable configuration parameter categories
   1. Communications
   2. Memory
   3. File caching
   4. Directory caching
   5. File system
   6. Locks
   7. Transaction tracking
   8. Disk
   9. Time
   10. NCP
   11. Miscellaneous
   12. Error Handling
   13. Directory Services
   14. Multiprocessor
   15. Service Location Protocol
   16. Licensing Services
Which category do you want to view:
```

FIGURE 7.27

To view the current settings for time synchronization, select the Time option. This figure is only a partial view of the time SET parameters.

```
TIMESYNC ADD Time Source:  NOR-SRV1,TOK-SRV1
Maximum length:  47
   Description: Add the name of a server to contact to the configured list.

TIMESYNC Configuration File:  SYS:SYSTEM\TIMESYNC.CFG
Maximum length:  254
   Description: Sets a new path for operations involving the configuration
                file.

TIMESYNC Configured Sources:  ON
   Description: When ON, this server will not listen to advertising time
                sources.  Instead it will only contact sources explicitly
                configured with the "TIMESYNC Time Source" option.

TIMESYNC Directory Tree Mode:  ON
   Description: Controls the use of SAP packets in conjuction with the
                directory services tree structure.  The default, ON, causes
                time synchronization to ignore SAP packets which do not
                originate from within the tree to which this server belongs.
                The default installation puts a SINGLE time source at the root
                of every directory tree, which causes confusion since there
                should only be one SINGLE time source on the entire network.
                Setting this parameter to OFF allows this server to receive
                SAP packets from any time source on the network.
<Press ESC to terminate or any other key to continue>
```

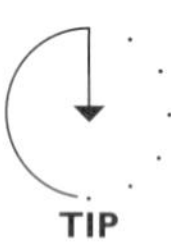
TIP

Do not place TIMESYNC parameters in the AUTOEXEC.NCF file, because they will not work from that file. Only time synchronization parameters that start with the TIMESYNC label can be placed in the TIMESYNC.CFG file. Figure 7.28 illustrates an example of a TIMESYNC.CFG file.

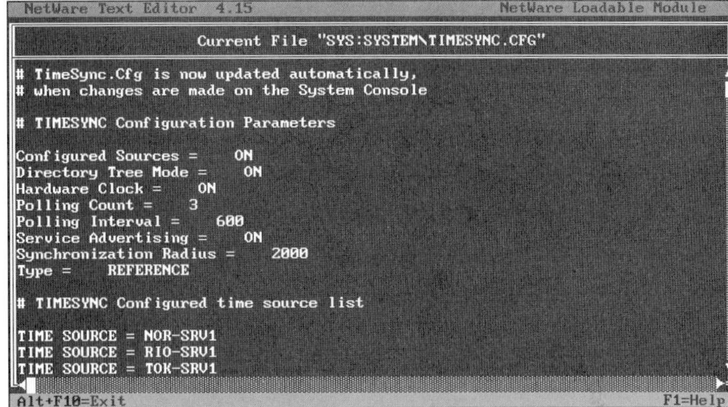

FIGURE 7.28

A sample TIMESYNC.CFG file

The easiest way to modify the time synchronization parameters is to use the MONITOR utility. After you load MONITOR from the server console select Server Parameters and then the Time option. The screen for the time synchronization parameters is shown in Figure 7.29.

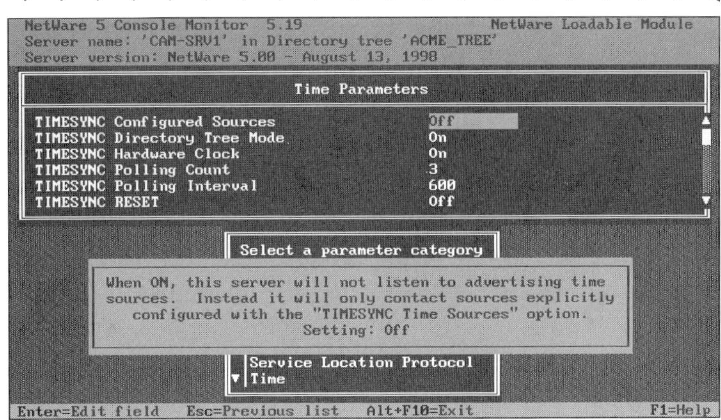

FIGURE 7.29

An example of the MONITOR utility as it is displayed after you select the Time option from Server Parameters. The Time Parameters screen enables you to modify many aspects of time.

The function and use of each of the settable time synchronization parameters are discussed in the text that follows.

TIMESYNC Add Time Source = <server name>
Default: Empty

This option enables you to add the name of a particular NetWare 5 server or servers as potential time providers to your configured list. The server name that you enter here will be stored in the TIMESYNC.CFG configuration file. The TIMESYNC.CFG configuration file is updated if you choose the Update TIMESYNC.CFG option after exiting the time parameter screen. Duplicate entries are not accepted in the time sources list and will be ignored.

You will use this option only if you are using a configured list and want to add a new server to the configured list as a time provider.

The name of the NetWare 5 server is not the distinguished name. Instead, it is the least significant segment of its name. For example, a NetWare 5 server in the ACME tree has a distinguished name of CN=NOR-SRV1.OU=NORAD.O=ACME. The name entered in this field is simply NOR-SRV1.

To add the servers NOR-SRV1, CAM-SRV1, and TOK-SRV1 to the list of time sources in the TIMESYNC.CFG files, enter these lines:

```
SET TIMESYNC ADD TIME Source = NOR-SRV1

SET TIMESYNC ADD TIME Source = CAM-SRV1

SET TIMESYNC ADD TIME Source = TOK-SRV1
```

TIMESYNC Configuration File = <volume:subdirectory\file>
Default: SYS:SYSTEM\TIMESYNC.CFG

This parameter defines the path or location of the configuration file used by time synchronization. TIMESYNC.CFG is the default name for the configuration file that stores all the settings for time on your NetWare 5 server. There is little if any need to change the name of this file, and we recommend that you accept the default, TIMESYNC.CFG. This file can easily be copied to multiple NetWare 5 servers if needed.

If you want to store the TIMESYNC.CFG file in the SYS:SYSTEM\TIME subdirectory, issue this command:

```
SET TIMESYNC CONFIGURATION FILE = SYS:SYSTEM\TIME
```

TIMESYNC Configured Sources = ON/OFF
Default: OFF

This parameter determines whether the NetWare 5 server finds the time providers on the network using SAP or an existing configured list. A setting of OFF tells the server to listen to any time providers that are sending out SAP. A setting of ON tells the server to ignore SAP and rely only on the configured lists set up in the TIMESYNC.CFG file. The server will only try to contact the time providers that are in its configured list. This parameter must be set to ON in order to support custom configured lists.

We recommend that, when you are using configured lists, each one of the secondary servers have a primary or reference server as the first member of its list. However, secondary servers may also be entered in the configured lists. This option enables a secondary server to get the time from other secondary servers in the event that the primary and reference time providers do not respond.

TIP

If you want to view the list of servers that have been established as the time providers in the configured list on a particular server, you can type this command from that server's console: SET TIMESYNC TIME SOURCE =. Notice that the equal sign is required with no following parameters.

TIMESYNC Directory Tree Mode = ON/OFF
Default: ON

This parameter controls the use of SAP in the NDS tree. A setting of ON, which is the default, tells the time server to ignore the SAP packets from servers that are not part of your NDS tree. A value of OFF enables the server to listen to all time SAP packets from any time provider on the network even if it is outside the same Directory Services tree.

When you leave this setting to ON, you maintain tighter control over the NDS tree of this server.

TIMESYNC Hardware Clock = ON/OFF
Default: ON

This parameter controls hardware clock synchronization to the software clock, which is maintained by NetWare 5 servers. A value of ON, which is the default, has a different meaning depending on the type of time server that is being used.

The value of ON for the single and reference servers enables them to read their hardware clocks at the beginning of each polling loop and to set the software clocks accordingly. The capability of the single and reference time servers to read their hardware clocks and reset the software clocks provides the network with a basic external clock synchronization. In this case the hardware clock acts as an external time source. This is kind of a poor man's radio clock.

Set this parameter to OFF only if the single or reference servers use an external time source, such as an atomic or radio clock.

The value of ON for the primary and secondary servers means that the hardware clock is set to the time of the software clock after each polling process. This setting is useful because corrections made to the software clock during the polling process can be written to the hardware clock. Thus, the network time is reflected the next time the server is brought down and back up. Each time the server is booted, it reads the hardware clock.

All primary and secondary servers in the same Directory tree should use the same setting for this parameter.

TIMESYNC Polling Count = <number (1 to 1,000)>
Default: 3

This parameter determines how many time packets to exchange during the polling process. Increasing the number of packets adds more traffic to the network. We recommend that you leave the default value of 3, which works well in most cases. The only time you may want to change this value is when you have unreliable or erratic network communication links between the time servers.

The higher the value is set, the greater the amount of network traffic introduced. The lower the value, the less accurate the time information exchanged. Again, the default value of 3 is highly recommended.

TIMESYNC Polling Interval = <number (10 to 2,678,400)>
Default: 600 seconds (or 10 minutes)

This parameter determines the length of time between each polling process. In the case of the default, every 600 seconds (or 10 minutes) the server will poll the other time servers in the tree. After the initial installation of your NetWare 5 servers, you may want to increase this value to reduce the total number of polling traffic on the network. Just remember that the time polling process does not generate an inordinate amount of traffic on your network. We recommend that you leave the default setting if you keep the total number of time providers under ten. We also recommend that all the time servers in the same NDS tree have the same setting for this parameter.

Decreasing this parameter creates an increase in network traffic but higher time synchronization accuracy. Increasing this interval is recommended when the time servers have to cross a WAN link to get time.

TIMESYNC Remove Time Source = <server name>
Default: Empty

This option enables you to specify a server or servers to be removed from the time source list. The server name entered in this field will be removed from the configuration file if you exit and choose YES to update TIMESYNC.CFG option after updating and exiting the time parameter screen. This field will return a blank screen after you have specified a value in this field. If you try to delete an entry from the time sources list, which does not exist, the request will be ignored.

This option is the reverse of the TIMESYNC Add Time Source option. Here, too, the name of the NetWare 5 server is not the distinguished name. Instead, it is the least significant segment of its name. For example, a NetWare 5 server in the ACME tree has a distinguished name of CN=NOR-SRV1.OU=NORAD.O=ACME. The name entered in this field is simply NOR-SRV1.

This command is primarily used at the server console to remove a time provider that has gone down or become unavailable for any reason.

If you are trying to add or remove a time source permanently, using either the TIMESYNC Add Time Source and TIMESYNC Remove Time Source parameters can be difficult because they do not give you any feedback on whether the instructions were successful. An alternative to using these fields is to edit the configuration file directly using any text editor.

TIMESYNC Reset = ON/OFF
Default: OFF

This parameter resets all time parameters to the default values and clears the configured lists. A value of ON resets the time parameters and writes the configuration file after exiting from the MONITOR screen. Be careful — any changes you have made previously to the TIMESYNC.CFG file will be lost. For example, all the configured server lists are cleared and set back to the internal defaults. If you set the parameter to ON and press Enter, the values are reset and the parameter automatically returns to the default OFF value.

You should never have to reset the time parameters on a production server. This option is valuable for restoring the parameters as you experiment with them in a lab situation.

TIMESYNC Restart Flag = ON/OFF
Default: OFF

This parameter controls restart time synchronization. You can use this feature to restart time synchronization after you have created or changed the configuration parameters in the file. After this command is issued from the file server console, the parameter automatically resets to OFF.

TIMESYNC Service Advertising = ON/OFF
Default: ON

This parameter controls the time servers that are time providers advertising through SAP. When the parameter is ON, the single reference and primary time primary servers send out or advertise using SAP. Setting the value to OFF means that the time provider servers will not send out SAP. You will want to set this parameter to OFF when you use configured lists. Turning SAP off will reduce the traffic on the network.

TIMESYNC Synchronization Radius = <milliseconds (0 to 2,147,483,647)>
Default: 2,000 (or 2 seconds)

This parameter controls the maximum time a server's clock is allowed to vary from network time and still be considered synchronized. The default of 2,000 milliseconds works well for most installations. This time parameter can be adjusted or increased to enable a wider margin of error for time synchronization between servers. However, increasing this value reduces the collision resolution occurring in NDS. A lower value causes the server to maintain tighter time synchronization. Because the tighter synchronization radius may be difficult or impossible to achieve, the time servers lose time synchronization. We recommend that you never set the synchronization radius under the 2,000 millisecond value.

If you need to change this parameter, you can do so through the MONITOR utility as shown in Figure 7.30.

FIGURE 7.30

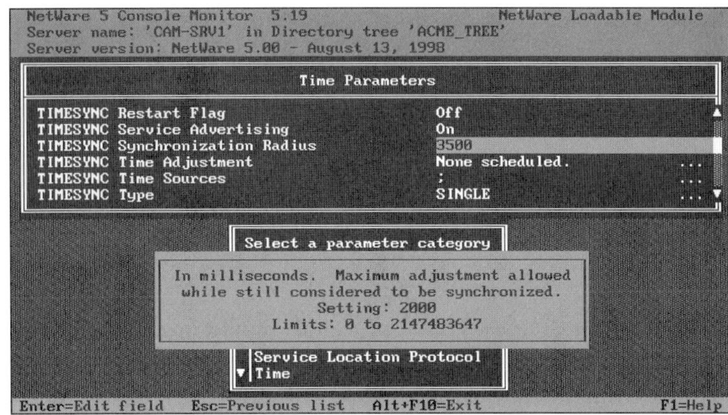

Changes to the synchronization radius can be made through the MONITOR utility.

TIMESYNC Time Adjustment = [+ | –] hour:minutes:seconds [AT month/day/year hour:minutes:seconds [AM | PM] | [CANCEL]]
Default: One hour from the current time or six polling intervals, whichever is longer

This parameter enables time adjustments to be made to the network time. You should use this feature sparingly. Misuse of this parameter will affect the servers networkwide and could change the order of the NDS events. You should also use this parameter during the day, when it will not be excessively disruptive to the network operation.

You can use the optional AT parameters to schedule the time adjustment to take place in the future. For example, the command for a time adjustment schedule in the future might look like this:

```
SET TIMESYNC TIME ADJUSTMENT = +00:01:30 AT 4/6/99
```

11:00:00 PM The command will adjust network time ahead one minute and thirty seconds on April 6, 1999, at 11:00 PM. Use the CANCEL command to remove a previously scheduled time adjustment from taking place. For example, in order to cancel the time adjustment of +00:01:30, enter the following:

```
SET TIMESYNC TIME ADJUSTMENT = +00:01:30 CANCEL
```

If you do not use the optional AM or PM parameters, then NetWare 5 assumes a 24-hour (military time) clock. Use a plus sign (+) to indicate a time adjustment forward and a minus sign (–) to indicate a time adjustment backward.

This command would not normally be used in a time server configuration that is receiving its time from an external source. We recommend that you use this option only when a significant one-time correction must be made to the network time. You should perform the time adjustment operation on either reference or single reference time servers.

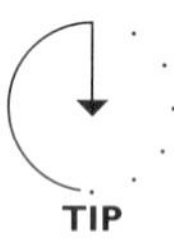
TIP

The TIMESYNC Time Adjustment parameter can modify the network time only on primary, reference, and single reference time providers because they can affect the network time. This parameter should not be used with a secondary time server.

TIMESYNC Time Source = <server name>
Default: None

This parameter is the same as the TIMESYNC Add Time Source parameter discussed previously. You can specify a server to be added to the configuration list. So you may ask, why are there two parameters that perform the same function? This option makes more sense and is easier to enter at the server console command line. For example, you simply type the following:

```
SET TIMESYNC TIME SOURCE = <server name>
```

By entering this command at the server console, you are adding the server to your configuration list. Use the TIMESYNC Remove Time Server parameter to remove the servers from the configured list.

To reduce the confusion, we recommend that you use this parameter only at the server console and use the TIMESYNC Add Time Source parameter in the MONITOR utility.

TIP

You can display the current list of time servers that has been established in the configuration list by entering the TIMESYNC Time Source = command at the server console. Notice that there is no server name entered.

TIMESYNC Type = <time server type>
Default: Single (during the first installation of NetWare 5)
Secondary (during all subsequent installations)

This parameter sets the time server type for the NetWare 5 server. The possible values are SECONDARY, PRIMARY, REFERENCE, and SINGLE (for single reference). You can use this parameter to change the time server type for the NetWare 5 server on the fly. This value is placed in the TIMESYNC.CFG configuration file and is used when TIMESYNC.NLM is initialized as the server is booted or when the restart flag is used.

TIMESYNC Write Parameters = ON/OFF
Default: OFF

This parameter writes all the current time synchronization parameters to the TIMESYNC.CFG configuration file. The value of ON writes the parameters; the value of OFF does not write the parameters. This SET parameter is a trigger and automatically resets to OFF.

TIMESYNC Write Value = <number>
Default: 3

This parameter controls which parameters are written to the TIMESYNC.CFG configuration file by the Write Parameter ON/OFF action. The possible values are as follows:

1. Write only the internal parameters
2. Write only the parameters for TIMESYNC Add Time Source
3. Write both internal and time source server parameters

Default Time Server Type = <time server type>
Default: Secondary

This parameter is used when the server first initializes because it is placed in the AUTOEXEC.NCF file. The value of this parameter is overridden by the TIMESYNC type parameter found in the configuration file. The default server type is used if the TIMESYNC configuration file is not present or is invalid. We recommend that you set the default time server type to the same value as the TIMESYNC Type value given previously. This will reduce confusion and the potential for problems if the configuration file is lost for some reason.

Time ZONE = <time zone string>
Default: <NO TIME ZONE>

This parameter specifies the time zone where the server is located. The value is a time zone string indicating the abbreviated time zone name, the offset from UTC, and the alternate abbreviated name for daylight saving time. This parameter causes a UTC value to be recalculated from local time. To reduce confusion, we recommend that you set this parameter correctly for the actual physical server location.

The format for the time zone string is *xxx*N[*yyy*], where "*xxx*" is the time zone (MST = U.S. mountain standard time or EST = U.S. eastern standard time). The "N" is the number of hours offset from UTC (7 = U.S. mountain or 5 = U.S. east coast). The "*yyy*," which is optional, indicates that daylight saving time is in effect (MDT = U.S. mountain daylight saving time or EDT = U.S. eastern daylight saving time). Thus, the time zone string for the U.S. mountain time zone is:

```
MST7MDT
```

and that for the U.S. eastern time zone is:

```
EST5EDT
```

Daylight Saving Time Status = ON/OFF
Default: OFF

This parameter indicates whether daylight saving time is in effect. Possible values are ON and OFF. If this parameter is set to ON, the DST (daylight saving time) parameter should be used. The status of this parameter may be changed at any time. However, changing the status does not change the local time, but it does cause UTC to be recalculated.

Daylight Saving Time Offset = [+ | –]hour:minute:seconds
Default: +1:00:00

This parameter controls the offset applied to time calculations when daylight saving time is in effect. The offset, in seconds, is added to local time at the beginning of daylight saving time. A change causes UTC to be recalculated from local time.

Start of Daylight Saving Time = <Month [Day | Day of Week] [Condition] hour:minute:seconds>
Default: April Sunday First 2:00:00 AM

This parameter enables you to set up the local date and time or some simple rules for when the change from standard time to daylight saving time occurs. The following example sets the start of daylight saving time at 2:00 A.M. to the first Sunday of April (which is also the default):

```
SET START OF DAYLIGHT SAVING Time = (April Sunday First
2:00:00 AM)
```

End of Daylight Saving Time = <Month [Day | Day of Week] [Condition] hour:minute:seconds>
Default: October Sunday Last 2:00:00 AM

This parameter enables you to set up the local date and time or specify some simple rules for calculating when daylight saving time ends. The following example sets the end of daylight saving time at 2:00 A.M. on the last Sunday of October (which is also the default):

```
SET END OF DAYLIGHT SAVING Time = (October Sunday Last
2:00:00 AM)
```

The preferred method for setting the daylight saving time (DST) status is through the use of the SET Start of Daylight Saving Time and SET End of Daylight Saving Time commands placed in the AUTOEXEC.NCF file during system initialization.

Note that there are two ways to indicate when DST should start or end:

- Specify an exact date when the change to daylight saving time occurs.
- Specify a rule for calculating the dates. The operating system recalculates the next change and automatically schedules it for the next year.

Both the start and the end dates and times for daylight standard time (DST) must be set before either date is actually scheduled.

New Time with Daylight Saving Time Status = ON/OFF
Default: OFF

This parameter controls the adjustment of local time when DST is in effect. This command is similar to the TIMESYNC Daylight Saving Time Status parameter, but when this value is set to ON it adjusts the local time by adding or subtracting the DST time offset without changing the UTC for the server. This is accomplished by changing the daylight saving time status and adjusting the local time by the daylight saving time offset, effectively leaving the UTC unchanged. This is designed to correct a DST error. If a supervisor arrives and sees that DST did not change when it should have, this command will change it.

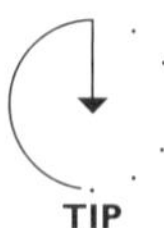
TIP

When changing daylight saving time information manually on a server, be aware that you may cause a UTC value to be recalculated from local time. The SET New Time with Daylight Saving Time Status command is expressly intended to avoid the recalculation of the UTC value and force local time to be recalculated instead. Use this command to change the daylight saving time status on a system that is otherwise correct and in time synchronization with the network.

Attempting to accomplish the same thing by changing local time and then changing the daylight saving time status will result in loss of time synchronization.

Additional TimeSync SET Commands

The following NetWare 5 SET commands for time synchronization are not documented in Novell manuals. These SET commands can assist you in fine-tuning your environment even further. However, these parameters may or may not work in future versions of NetWare 5. We have documented them here so that you can have all of the options when working with time synchronization. We recommend that you not adjust these parameters unless you are solving a specific problem and understand the use of each parameter.

TIMESYNC Immediate Synchronization = On/Off
Default: Off

This parameter triggers the time synchronization process, which simply means that it starts a polling process. After the value has been set to ON, it automatically resets to OFF, which is the default. This parameter is sometimes useful for creating screen output after the debug flag has been set, rather than waiting for the synchronization process to awaken normally.

Note that this SET parameter does not speed up synchronization in any way; it simply wakes up the synchronization process. Normally the synchronization process will respond within two seconds. Occasionally there may be a delay of several seconds (ten seconds or fewer) because of normal network overhead while attempting to reach the target server.

TIMESYNC Short Interval = <number (10 to 600 seconds)>
Default: 10

This parameter determines the shortest interval between polling processes. This parameter is used when the server falls out of time synchronization. In such a case, it immediately polls the network more frequently to establish time synchronization more quickly. The default interval is every ten seconds. You may want to increase this value for very expensive WAN links that should not monopolize all the bandwidth just to support time synchronization when it has been lost.

TIMESYNC Maximum Offset = <number (10 to 16,777,215 seconds)>
Default: 600

This parameter specifies the maximum amount of adjustment that the server will try to gain between polling processes. The default is 600 seconds, or 10 minutes. The greater the value, the faster the time server will adjust itself toward the network time.

TIMESYNC Correction Floor = <number (in milliseconds)>
Default: 1

This parameter sets the minimum value in milliseconds that any NDS server must differ from before the correction is applied. Any adjustment must be larger than this value, or the correction is ignored. This value must always be less than the synchronization radius. If it is not less than the synchronization radius, then time synchronization will not be possible.

This parameter is undocumented or hidden so that system administrators will not change it without knowing the consequences. We highly recommend that you leave the default setting of one millisecond to support NDS.

The only reason to change this parameter would be to eliminate the correction for the one-tick jitters that sometimes occur. This may be an issue if there are other applications that depend on time being synchronized and are extremely sensitive to larger amounts of error correction over a ten-minute period.

SET TIMESYNC Offset Ceiling = <number (0 to 315,532,800)>
Default: 10 years

A time provider whose clock is too far behind network time will not be able to participate in the voting process. This parameter sets the value that is used to determine if a server's clock is too far behind the network time. Again, if the time on a server is farther away from the network time than this value, it will be ignored and the time of the network will not be adjusted based on that server.

Timesync Debug Commands

NetWare 5 enables you to monitor the status of time synchronization on a server using the time synchronization debug commands. These commands are useful for debugging, testing, and fine-tuning the synchronization configuration. Note, however, that as undocumented commands they may or may not work in future versions of NetWare 5.

When executed, the debug commands start a separate time synchronization screen on the file server console. After the debug screen is started, information about the time synchronization function is written to the console. This information may be helpful when you are trying to determine if the servers are contacting each other in the manner you expect for time synchronization. It is also educational to read the debug messages to see the way the system changes the times on each server to converge on the network time. To turn on the time synchronization debug screen and its information, type the following:

```
SET TIMESYNC DEBUG = 7    (turns on the debug screen)

SET TIMESYNC DEBUG = 0    (turns off the debug screen)
```

Figure 7.31 illustrates the time synchronization debug screen.

FIGURE 7.31

The time synchronization debug screen

```
        offset.h = 00000000  offset.l = 0BF20F51

TIMESYNC: Polled server RIO-SRV1 (Primary/Chained Secondary)
        offset.h = 00000000  offset.l = 0DCB5F10

 *** TIMESYNC: Unable to communicate with server TOK-SRV1! ***

 *** TIMESYNC: Unable to communicate with server SYD-SRV1! ***

Uniform Adjustment Requested:  +0.0CDEB730
This server is configured as a REFERENCE
 *** Time is synchronized ***
TIMESYNC: Polled server NOR-SRV1 (Primary/Chained Secondary)
        offset.h = 00000000  offset.l = FD12AFC0

TIMESYNC: Polled server RIO-SRV1 (Primary/Chained Secondary)
        offset.h = 00000001  offset.l = 0CFB95E6

 *** TIMESYNC: Unable to communicate with server TOK-SRV1! ***

 *** TIMESYNC: Unable to communicate with server SYD-SRV1! ***

Uniform Adjustment Requested:  +1.050722D3
This server is configured as a REFERENCE
 *** Time is synchronized ***
```

TIP

You can set the debug flag to values other than 7, but the results are not very useful because each bit in the value controls a group of messages or disables output altogether. The debug information that appears on the screen is not particularly well formatted. Some portions are language enabled and may be translated.

The following messages are examples of the type of information provided by the debug screen:

```
TIMESYNC: Polled sever NOR-SRV1

Weight = 1, OFFSET.H = FFFFFFFF OFFSET.L = F1F06723
```

The most useful pieces of information are the name of the server (NOR-SRV1) and the weight (normally 0, 1, or 16). If time synchronization cannot actually exchange information with the other time server or if out-of-range data is detected, the weight will be zero. A weight of zero generally means that the server is not up or is not reachable across the network.

The values for OFFSET.H and OFFSET.L are the calculated deviation of the server's time from the target server's time. The values form a 64-bit signed number with an implied hexadecimal point separating the whole and fractional parts:

```
FFFFFFFF.F1F06723
```

This number means that this server is a fraction of a second ahead of NOR-SRV1. Another possibility that may occur is a weight of zero with nonzero offset values, indicating that the synchronization data is out of range (one server is more than ten years ahead of the other).

If this message does not appear at all, there are no time providers or sources in this server's list. Either the configured time source list is empty or no SAP time sources can be found, or both. Of course, if you have disabled the use of SAP, the only possible cause is that the configured time source list is empty. You can check the state of the list by typing

```
SET TIMESYNC TIME SOURCE =
```

at the system console screen. Notice that the equal sign with no parameter following is required to return the list of time sources.

The next message is

```
Uniform Adjustment Requested = -0.0E0F98DD
Server type = 2
```

This message shows the actual time adjustment that needs to be applied to the clock during the next polling interval. The message also shows the time server types, which are 2 = Secondary, 3 = Primary, 4 = Reference, and 5 = Single.

The adjustment value is hexadecimal, but the sign is displayed so that the magnitude of the adjustment is easier to understand. In this case, the value 0.0E0F98DD (one tick) is significant to time synchronization. This server is ahead of NOR-SRV1 by one tick. It is very common to see one-tick or one-half-tick errors that are caused by randomness between the two machines.

When the adjustment is +0.00000000, the servers are in exact synchronization, which really means that no error can be detected by the algorithm. It is also common to see this value stabilize at a very small negative value, such as –0.00000094, because of a small round-off error in the synchronization algorithm when slowing the clock. The error of 0.00000094 is 34 nanoseconds, much smaller than the resolution of the clock and nothing to worry about.

The next message,

```
Adjustment smaller than Correction Floor was ignored.
```

is mentioned because it is quite common. It means that the clock adjustment is so small that it is being ignored. Actually, the parameter that determines the cutoff point is called the TIMESYNC Correction Floor and is set to one millisecond by default.

Troubleshooting Time Synchronization

When time for a server fails to synchronize to the network, the most probable reason is that there are no reachable time providers. Check the configuration information to be sure it is correct. Make sure that the time providers are running and are synchronized themselves. Remember that a secondary server will not be synchronized until its time providers are synchronized. If necessary, turn on the debug option and verify that the server is actually contacting a time provider.

If the time on the file server has been set far ahead, time synchronization may take a long time. Remember that the server should not move time backward. So, for example, it takes at least two hours of real time to lose two hours.

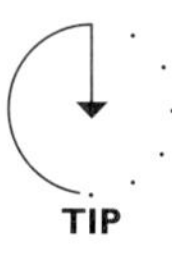

Setting time backward on a server is not a good thing to do for most applications that require synchronized timestamps. If you set the time backward on a server that is participating in NDS, the system will generate synthetic time to account for the local time being set backward. You should always set the DOS time before booting the server, just to make sure that the hardware clock has the correct time. (For more information on synthetic time see the "Synthetic Time" section later in this chapter.)

Remember that time synchronization requires routing information to make contact with the time provider. Sometimes it takes a while for routing information to get to a server, especially when the server has just been booted. Even though time synchronization normally happens quickly, wait a minute or two before jumping to conclusions. Also, try executing the DISPLAY SERVERS console command to see if the target server is known to the router.

Booting Time Servers

A rare condition exists when the only two time providers on a network are booted for the first time. Since the first action of any server is to find a time provider and set its own clock, determining which server will first set its clock from the other server (the first server polled sets the time) can be problematic. Once servers have synchronized, and as long as one time provider remains active, other time providers can be shut down and rebooted. The booting server will set its time to the network time. Since one server remains in operation, that server is not attempting to set its clock, and the rare condition does not exist.

Again, it is always a good idea to set the DOS time before booting a server to make sure that the hardware clock is correct and to minimize any possible time adjustment.

NDS Time Not Synchronized

NDS may report this error message:

```
Time_Not_Synchronized Error -659 (FD6D)
```

Yet when users check the server's status with the TIME command, it reports that time is synchronized. What this error message actually means is that NDS has received a timestamp that is older than information already in the Directory. The server time has probably been set backward because of a dead CMOS battery or because the time was incorrectly set when the server was booted.

This error message occurs mostly on small networks that use the default time synchronization configuration. Note that it is an NDS error, not a TIMESYNC.NLM error.

Correcting Local Time on a Server

Fortunately, once time information is correctly configured, there is little need to change it. When time synchronization is active, you need to be extremely cautious about changing local time information. If local time information is not configured correctly and time synchronization is active, the UTC will also be incorrect. Time synchronization will attempt to adjust local time to correspond to network time, which will, in turn, control the UTC. Time synchronization may, therefore, fight efforts to correct poorly configured local parameters.

To avoid this problem, you have to unload the TIMESYNC NLM, configure the local time information correctly, and then reload the NLM.

NOTE

The TIMESYNC NLM is automatically loaded when the NetWare server is booted.

As an alternative to unloading TIMESYNC, use the following command after correctly setting the server time and creating a TIMESYNC.CFG configuration file:

```
SET TIMESYNC RESTART/FLAG = On
```

Synthetic Time

When time synchronization is lost because the local time is set backward, NetWare 5 will continue to issue timestamps on the servers using synthetic time. When this situation occurs, the synthetic time message will appear on your server console screen as shown in Figure 7.32, indicating that synthetic time is being used to create timestamps for the partitions on the server. Synthetic time is also issued when DS.NLM loads and time synchronization has not yet been established.

FIGURE 7.32

Synthetic time is created when the time on the Reference or Single Reference servers is set backward. You will be notified with a server console message.

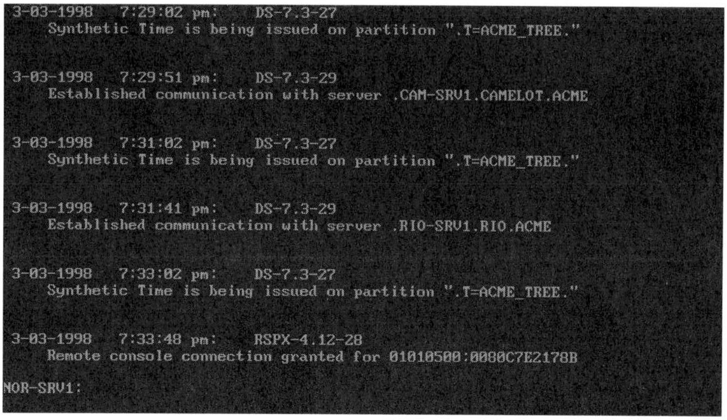

```
3-03-1998   7:29:02 pm:    DS-7.3-27
    Synthetic Time is being issued on partition ".T=ACME_TREE."

3-03-1998   7:29:51 pm:    DS-7.3-29
    Established communication with server .CAM-SRV1.CAMELOT.ACME

3-03-1998   7:31:02 pm:    DS-7.3-27
    Synthetic Time is being issued on partition ".T=ACME_TREE."

3-03-1998   7:31:41 pm:    DS-7.3-29
    Established communication with server .RIO-SRV1.RIO.ACME

3-03-1998   7:33:02 pm:    DS-7.3-27
    Synthetic Time is being issued on partition ".T=ACME_TREE."

3-03-1998   7:33:48 pm:    RSPX-4.12-28
    Remote console connection granted for 01010500:0080C7E2178B
NOR-SRV1:
```

Synthetic time is the process of creating timestamps from the most recent timestamp in NDS. Synthetic time will take the most recent timestamp and modify just the event counter to create a new timestamp. This means that the time is not incremented, just the event counter. The event counter is a two-byte value that will hold up to 65,535 events. Once the event counter rolls over, the number of seconds in the timestamp is incremented by one. Synthetic time will continue until the real time of day catches up with the synthetic timestamps being used.

Summary

Time synchronization is the method by which all the NetWare 5 servers maintain the same UTC value across the network. Although it is not directly part of NetWare Directory Services, time synchronization is used primarily by the

Directory to maintain the order of events that occur. Because the computer hardware does not inherently maintain consistent time, time synchronization continually attempts to correct time variations.

Time servers are either time providers or time consumers. The time consumer is the secondary time server type, whereas the time providers are primary, reference, and single reference time servers. The time providers determine the official network time. Secondary time servers only attempt to stay synchronized with one other server.

The default configuration of a single reference for time synchronization is easy to understand and requires no advanced planning. The single reference default is a great place to start your installation. Depending on your needs you can keep the defaults or configure a time provider group as your needs change. A custom configuration or time provider group offers you complete control of the time synchronization hierarchy and enables you to build fault tolerance into the system. There is very little maintenance with time synchronization once it has been configured.

You only need to determine which communication option works best in your environment. SAP is the default and adds very little additional traffic to your network as long as you keep the number of configured primary servers at no more than seven. You can also use a configured list in place of SAP.

You can set many time synchronization parameters on a NetWare 5 server. Altering these parameters can enhance system performance for time on the network.

Once configured, time synchronization is stable and dependable. It is one of those features that almost never needs changing unless your network changes in size or location.

PART III

NetWare 5 Operations and Maintenance

CHAPTER 8

NDS Internals Operations

"The first rule of intelligent tinkering is to save all the parts." — Paul R. Ehrlich

The main function of NDS (Novell Directory Services) is to provide a name service. The name service groups network resources together in a hierarchical structure called a *tree*. Each network resource can be represented in the NDS tree as a single NDS object. The information about all the objects or network resources can be distributed across the servers in the network. In NDS the object information and the rules to create and manage these objects are stored on the individual NetWare 5 servers in special data files. The data files associated with Directory Services are created during the server installation.

With NDS, information is not only distributed but also replicated to provide increased reliability and accessibility. These features provide Directory Services with the capacity to place the information close to the users for convenient access while enabling the job of the name service to be shared among the servers.

Since the information in the Directory can be distributed, the background processes that maintain the consistency of information are designed to support multiple servers. In order to support the operation between multiple servers, each server must be able to establish a connection and authenticate to the other NetWare 5 servers in the tree.

This chapter will focus on all NDS concepts and the internal operations that take place within the servers. This information will help you be able to better understand the "black box" called NDS.

First Server Installation

The best way to describe and examine the creation of NDS is to understand the installation procedure. We will discuss several basic concepts, including partitions, replicas, and bindery objects.

When you install the first NetWare 5 server and NDS, the installation program prompts you to enter the name of the NDS tree, the server context, and the password for the ADMIN user, which is created by default.

The name of the NDS tree is important because it names the hierarchy in which each of the objects or network resources will reside. The name you choose for the tree must be a unique value on the network. For example, the name that we have selected for our sample tree is ACME_TREE.

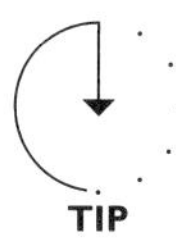

Each tree is identified by a name, containing up to 32 ASCII characters. The tree name may contain only the capital letters (A–Z), the digits (0–9), the hyphen (-), and the underscore (_) character. The tree name must not start or end with an underscore or a space. The tree name cannot have more than one underscore character in succession. This means that there cannot be back-to-back underscores in the NDS tree name. For example, "BAD__TREENAME" is illegal.

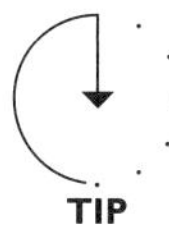

During the simple installation method for NetWare 5, the NDS tree name and the O=Organization container are named the same. In this case, the installation utility only prompts you for the password. This is the password for the ADMIN object.

The server context you choose is significant for several reasons. First, it forms the initial tree structure. Second, it becomes the parent or container object for the server object itself and all of its volumes. Third, it becomes the place in the tree where the bindery services context may be set for the server.

During the installation of the first server and of NDS several events take place. The following elements are created as part of this process:

1. NDS data files (partition, entry, value, and block files).

2. Internal NDS partitions, which consist of the following:

   - System partition
   - Bindery partition
   - External reference partition
   - Schema partition

3. Base schema.

4. System objects, which consist of the following:
   - Data storage for nonreplicating server data (a Pseudo Server object)
   - Data storage for the NetWare 5 server's dynamic SAP type 4 server object
5. The first user-created partition, called the [ROOT] partition.
6. The [ROOT] object for the tree.
7. An object for each container object in the server's name.
8. The server object in the appropriate container.
9. A volume object for each server volume, using the naming convention of "file server name_volume name."
10. The ADMIN user.
11. The bindery Supervisor account, which initially uses the ADMIN password. If the server is upgraded from the NetWare 3 bindery, it uses the password of the Supervisor from the bindery.

These remaining events also take place:

- The ADMIN user is granted Supervisor object rights to the [ROOT] object.
- [PUBLIC] is given object Browse rights to the [ROOT] object.
- Upgrade of existing bindery objects to NDS (if the server is being upgraded from NetWare 3).

The installation of the first server creates a single partition, named [ROOT], as the topmost object in the tree. The master replica of the [ROOT] partition is stored on the server. Each of the objects created by the installation of the first server is in the master replica of the [ROOT] partition. Figure 8.1 illustrates a logical view of the NDS tree for ACME after the first server CAM-SRV1 is installed.

FIGURE 8.1

A logical view of the NDS tree for ACME after the first server CAM-SRV1 is installed

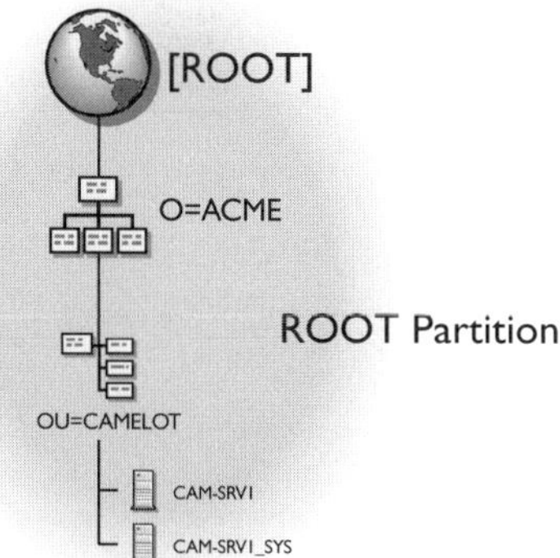

The NDS Program File (DS.NLM)

The NDS program code is found in the DS.NLM file, which is placed in the SYS:SYSTEM directory during installation. This NLM file is loaded by the operating system during server bootup. The DS.NLM provides the Directory name services on the server. The most important thing to remember is the build number for the NLM. For example, NetWare 5 ships with the build number DS 664.

The build number for DS.NLM can be found by running the NDIR.EXE program against the DS.NLM file. To find the build number for DS.NLM enter the following:

```
NDIR DS.NLM /ver
```

You can also find the build number for DS.NLM by using the MODULES console command and looking at the entry for the NLM. In order to use the MODULES command enter the following at the server console prompt and check the version of the DS.NLM that is loaded:

```
MODULES
```

One of the items shown by the MODULES command is the version of each module that is loaded at the server. See Figure 8.2.

FIGURE 8.2

You can check the build number for DS.NLM using the MODULES command at the server console prompt. The version shown here is DS.NLM 7.03.

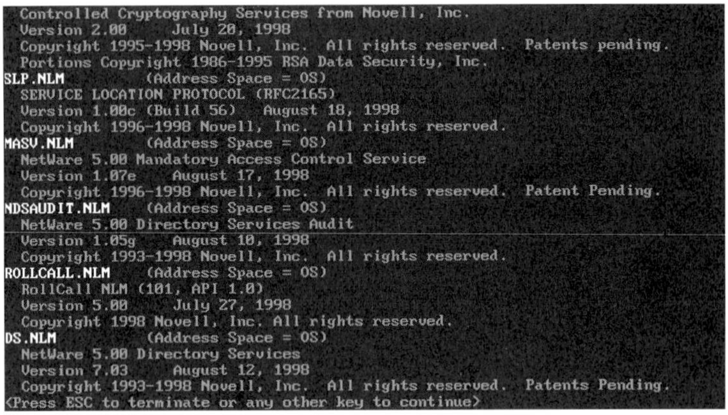

```
 Controlled Cryptography Services from Novell, Inc.
 Version 2.00      July 20, 1998
 Copyright 1995-1998 Novell, Inc.  All rights reserved.  Patents pending.
 Portions Copyright 1986-1995 RSA Data Security, Inc.
SLP.NLM          (Address Space = OS)
 SERVICE LOCATION PROTOCOL (RFC2165)
 Version 1.00c (Build 56)    August 18, 1998
 Copyright 1996-1998 Novell, Inc.  All rights reserved.
MASV.NLM         (Address Space = OS)
 NetWare 5.00 Mandatory Access Control Service
 Version 1.07e     August 17, 1998
 Copyright 1996-1998 Novell, Inc.  All rights reserved.  Patent Pending.
NDSAUDIT.NLM     (Address Space = OS)
 NetWare 5.00 Directory Services Audit
 Version 1.05g     August 10, 1998
 Copyright 1993-1998 Novell, Inc.  All rights reserved.
ROLLCALL.NLM     (Address Space = OS)
 RollCall NLM (101, API 1.0)
 Version 5.00      July 27, 1998
 Copyright 1998 Novell, Inc. All rights reserved.
DS.NLM           (Address Space = OS)
 NetWare 5.00 Directory Services
 Version 7.03      August 12, 1998
 Copyright 1993-1998 Novell, Inc.  All rights reserved.  Patents Pending.
<Press ESC to terminate or any other key to continue>
```

Newer versions of the DS.NLM can be copied to the SYS:SYSTEM directory on your server system. You may want to save the older DS.NLM by renaming it.

In order to unload and reload the new DS.NLM from the SYS:SYSTEM directory without taking the server down, enter the following DSTRACE command:

```
SET DSTRACE = *
```

You can perform the reload of DS.NLM using the more conventional method by simply entering the following server console commands:

```
UNLOAD DS
```

and

```
LOAD DS
```

A new workstation utility called DUPGRADE automatically copies the newer DS.NLM to each of your NetWare 5 servers and performs the reload of the software. This utility is available from the Novell corporate Web site at www.novell.com.

Locating a NetWare 5 Server

NDS is a distributed name service by which a client can locate the network resources anywhere in the network. Once the client or workstation is attached to any NetWare 5 server, then all the servers work together to locate the requested service.

The NetWare 5 servers that contain NDS replicas advertise the tree using the Service Advertising Protocol (SAP). Although the SLP protocol has replaced SAP in pure IP, SAP is still used for IPX communications. The SAP value contains two parts:

- **Service type** — 0x0278 hex (or 632 decimal). The SAP type is used to advertise the tree.
- **Service name** — The service name is 47 characters contained in two segments.

The first 32 characters of the Service Name are the NDS tree name. The tree is padded with the underscore characters to take up the entire 32 characters, if necessary.

The other 15 characters of the Service Name are made up from converting the server's network address. The server's network address contains the network address for the server, the internal IPX node number, and the NCP socket number in that order. The address is compressed to fit into the 15 bytes. The client connects to the server by reversing the compression and uses the address and socket numbers.

The workstation initially finds the first NetWare 5 server by broadcasting or making a service request indicating the Service Type 0x0278. Any server receiving this request that has NDS replicas of the NDS tree will respond to the request.

By looking at the Service Name field, the workstation or client determines the NDS tree name supported by the server and uses that information in choosing a server to contact. If the workstation has a setting for the Preferred Tree in the NET.CFG, it looks for the name equal to that of the Preferred Tree. The workstation can then connect to the server at the address and socket number extracted from the Service Name field.

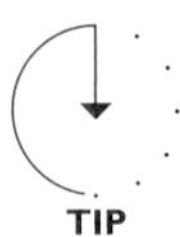
TIP

The other Service Advertising Protocols (SAPs) that you need to support NetWare 5 are type 0x0004 and type 0x026B. A normal NCP server or file server uses the SAP type 0x0004. This type is used for the SAP and RIP (Routing Information Protocol) broadcasts between servers. The SAP type 0x026B is used by Time Synchronization. Time servers use SAP type 0x026B to communicate with the time providers.

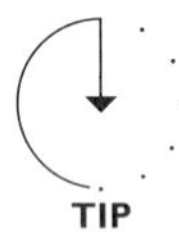
TIP

It is very important that you do not establish a Routing Information Protocol filter between NetWare 5 servers. Each NetWare 5 server needs to be able to see every other NetWare 5 server. This is especially true with NetWare 5 servers that do not have any NDS replicas. Some people think that, since a NetWare 5 server does not have replicas, it can be filtered out. The server needs to be able to do a service request for type 0x0278 to find the NDS tree. In addition, the clients or workstations need type 0x0278 to boot up.

NDS Data Files

The physical representation of the NDS tree and its objects relates to the actual NDS data files. The object and partition information are stored on the server in the data files under the SYS:_NETWARE directory, which is hidden by the operating system.

This directory is only visible through the RCONSOLE utility. After loading RCONSOLE and logging into the appropriate server, press ALT+F1 to bring up the main menu and then select the Scan Directory option. Figure 8.3 illustrates how to selectively scan SYS:_NETWARE using RCONSOLE. Figure 8.4 illustrates a view of the contents of the SYS:_NETWARE directory using RCONSOLE.

Five NDS files have the .DSD file extension, but a number of stream files may be used to support login script files, print job configurations, and so on. The stream files use the 8.3 DOS file-naming convention. However, they are distinguished from the others because their names consist of hexadecimal values only (0 to 9 and A to F). NDS uses the following files:

- Base File (0.DSB)

- Partition File (3.DSD)
- Entry File (0.DSD)
- Value File (1.DSD)
- Block File (2.DSD)
- Stream files (all have .DSD extensions)

FIGURE 8.3

Scanning the directory SYS:_NETWARE using RCONSOLE

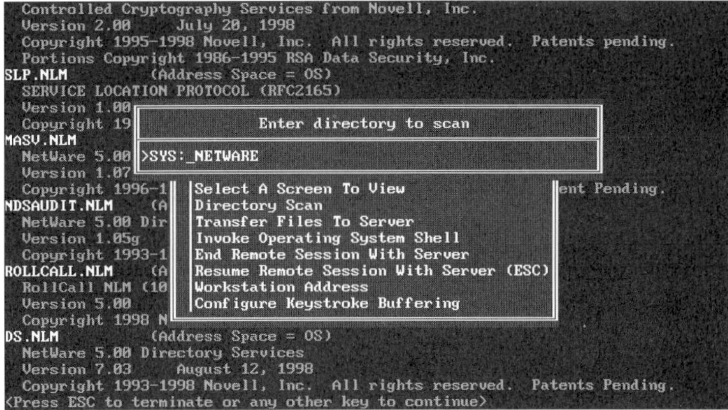

FIGURE 8.4

Viewing the contents of the directory SYS:_NETWARE using RCONSOLE

```
Controlled Cryptography Services from Novell, Inc.
Version 2.00      July 20, 1998
Copyright 1995-1998 Novell, Inc.  All rights reserved.  Patents pending.
Portions Copyright 1986-1995 RSA Data Security, Inc.
SLP.NLM
  Name              Type        Size    Date      Time
  0.DSB             <FILE>        28    8-20-98   9:15am
  0.DSD             <FILE>    206546    8-20-98   5:36pm
  1.DSD             <FILE>     80192    8-20-98   6:02pm
  2.DSD             <FILE>    427136    8-20-98   6:02pm
  3.DSD             <FILE>       200    8-20-98   9:15am
  CONNHAND.DAT      <FILE>     24000    8-20-98   4:41pm
  NLSLIST.DAT       <FILE>       494    8-20-98   5:04pm
  SERVCFG.000       <FILE>    327840    8-20-98   9:14am
  SERVHAND.DAT      <FILE>         4    8-20-98   9:30am
  XMGRCFG.DA0       <FILE>     20227    8-20-98   9:15am
<Press ESC to terminate or any other key to continue>
```

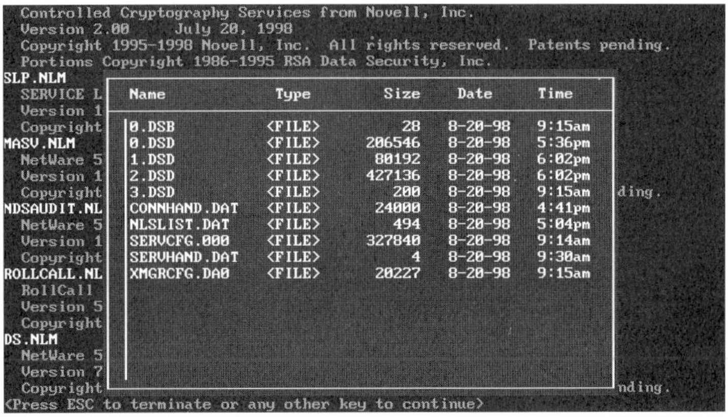

New in NetWare 5 is the base file (0.DSB), whose purpose is simply to hold the names of all the .DSD files. The other files hold the object, property, and partition information stored in NDS. These files work together to provide the complete NDS tree information for each server. The relationship between each of the NDS data files is illustrated in Figure 8.5. This figure shows how the partition record points to the first object in the partition, which, in turn, points to specific property values.

FIGURE 8.5

The NDS data files are related as shown here. Each partition record points to the first object in the partition, which, in turn, points to the specific property values.

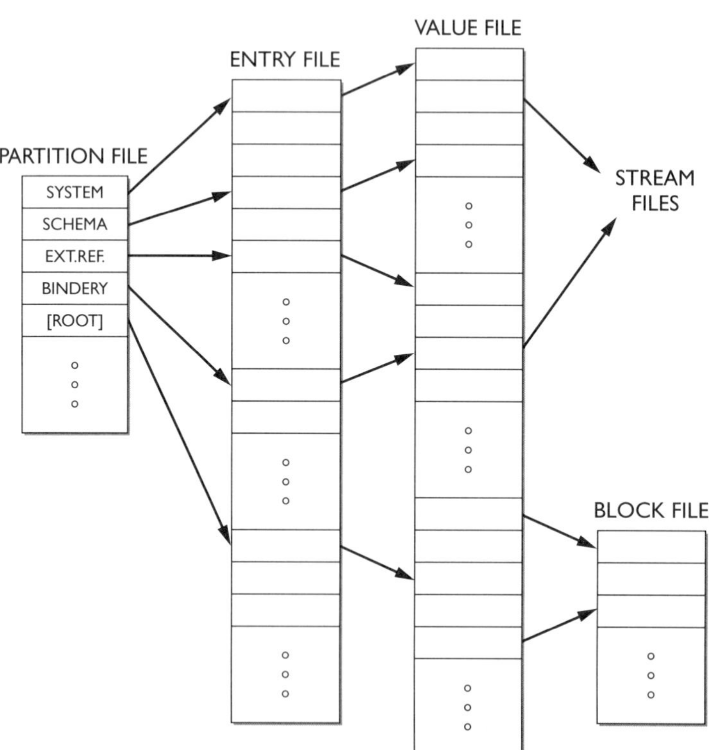

The filename and its description or purpose are presented in the following sections.

The Partition File (3.DSD)

The partition file named 3.DSD contains a list of each of the partitions defined on the local server and within the local NDS database. The partition file holds a record for each partition. Each partition record points to the starting record within the entry file for the specific objects.

There are always at least four NDS internal partitions on each NetWare 5 server. These partitions are stored in the partition file — the system, schema, external reference, and bindery partitions. They are discussed in the paragraphs that follow.

The System Partition

The first partition in the partition file is the system partition, which points or locates the Pseudo Server object as well as the NameBase version. Data available from this partition is server-specific information, such as the name of the tree as well as the version of the database. Because the information in this partition is server-centric, it is not synchronized with any other NetWare 5 server.

The Schema Partition

The second partition is the schema. The schema partition record is used to locate the top of the schema objects for NDS. The schema itself is the set of rules for the structure of the NDS tree and objects.

The initial installation of the server creates the base schema that ships with NetWare 5. The schema can be extended to include other custom objects and properties. In order to keep all copies of the schema on all servers throughout the tree the same, the information or objects in the schema partition are synchronized by NDS with the other NetWare 5 servers.

To be more exact, this file contains the information to locate the schema objects in the ENTRY.NDS file. There is nothing in this file specifically that is synchronized.

The External Reference Partition

The third partition in the partition file is the external reference partition. This partition record is used as the partition for the external reference objects stored on the server. An external reference is created for an NDS object that is not stored locally but needs an object ID on the local server. The external reference holds the object ID for the object that is external to this server.

The information in this partition is server-centric and is not synchronized with the other NetWare 5 servers. Again, to be more exact, this file contains just the information to locate the external reference objects in the entry file.

The external reference partition can be used to locate the top of the NDS tree, which refers to the [ROOT] object. Note that this partition is present even if the local database contains a copy of the [ROOT] partition.

The Bindery Partition

The fourth partition is the bindery partition. The bindery partition locates the bindery server SAP name and associated properties or attributes. The information in this partition is server-centric and is not synchronized by NDS to the other NetWare 5 servers.

The bindery partition also holds the dynamic bindery information, which contains the Service Advertising Protocol (SAP) and Routing Information Protocol (RIP) data received by the server during normal operation in the NDS tree.

The partition file contains a representation for every user-created partition on the server. These are the partitions that are created by the system administrators using the NetWare Administration utilities.

The Entry or Object File (0.DSD)

The entry file contains the individual records of the NDS objects that are created to form the NDS tree. In addition to the NDS objects, this file contains the information for each of the schema, bindery, and external reference objects. The term "entry" is often used to refer to an NDS object. The object's name and its partition and its parent within the NDS tree are among several pieces of data recorded in an individual entry.

One of the objects is the Pseudo Server object, which stores the information about the specific server. This object is not synchronized with the other NetWare 5 servers. The information held in the Pseudo Server object includes these items:

- The name of the NDS tree
- The server object's public key, which is used for authentication
- The server object's private key, which is used for authentication

- The synchronized up to vector for the schema partition
- The Remote ID list, which contains ID pairs consisting of a local ID and a remote ID (see the "Object IDs for Servers in NDS" section later in this chapter)
- The Monitored Connection, which cleans up connections that the client has terminated improperly

The Value, Block, and Stream Files

The property information can be stored in several different places within the internal structures of NDS. In order to store the property information in a variety of formats, NDS uses the value (1.DSD), block (2.DSD), and stream files. The majority of the structured property information is stored in the value file. If an overload area is needed for any properties, then the overload is written to the block file. If the property is free-form with no defined structure, then it is stored in a stream file.

VALUE.NDS (1.DSD)

The value file (1.DSD) contains the property or attribute records used by the objects contained within the entry file. There is an entry in this file for every attribute value whether the attribute is single-valued or multi-valued. For example, some of the attributes for the user object in NDS are multivalue fields. If there are multiple values defined for the user, each additional value will have an entry in this file. The access control list (ACL) attribute, for example, is multi-valued and may have many entries or values. Each of the values will have an entry in this file. The value file works in conjunction with both the block file and the stream files.

BLOCK.NDS (2.DSD)

The block file (2.DSD) contains records that are used by the record in the value file. If the data entered into a value field of a property or attribute is large, it overflows into this file. For example, if an attribute value is large, the remaining information for that attribute is stored in the block file. Any given value record may have multiple records assigned in this file.

Stream Files

The stream files are individual files that exist in the SYS:_NETWARE directory. These files contain the value information for attributes that are free form and of variable length. For example, the login scripts, printer control files, and print job definitions attributes are stored in stream files. The stream files use the 8.3 DOS file-naming convention. However, they are distinguished from the others because their names consist of hexadecimal values only (0 to 9 and A to F). In addition, each stream file has a .DSD extension.

The NDS .TMP Data Files

There is a complete set of temporary NDS data files that are created when the DSREPAIR utility is executed. There are no .TMP files created for any of the stream files. The temporary NDS data files are created by DSREPAIR when it is running and are used to perform all the changes against the partitions. At the end of the repair these temporary (.TMP) files become the permanent .NDS files, unless you choose not to accept the repairs that were made. The current NDS data files become .DOD files.

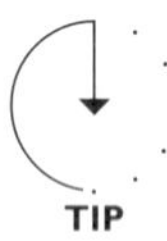

DSREPAIR creates the .DOD set of NDS data files. These .DOD files will be overwritten by DSREPAIR only after 72 hours. This feature helps the Novell Technical Support organization react to customer problems that may be recently caused.

The .DOD files are stored on the server in the same place where the regular NDS data files are stored under the SYS:_NETWARE directory. You can see these files by using the RCONSOLE utility and selecting the Scan Directory option from the main menu. Figure 8.6 shows the .DOD files created by DSREPAIR.

Timestamps

Since the NDS hierarchy can be distributed or replicated across the servers in the network, the information in each of the replicas can change without the other replicas immediately knowing about it. This form of synchronization is known as being loosely consistent.

FIGURE 8.6

RCONSOLE shows the .DOD files created by the DSREPAIR utility in the SYS:_NETWARE directory.

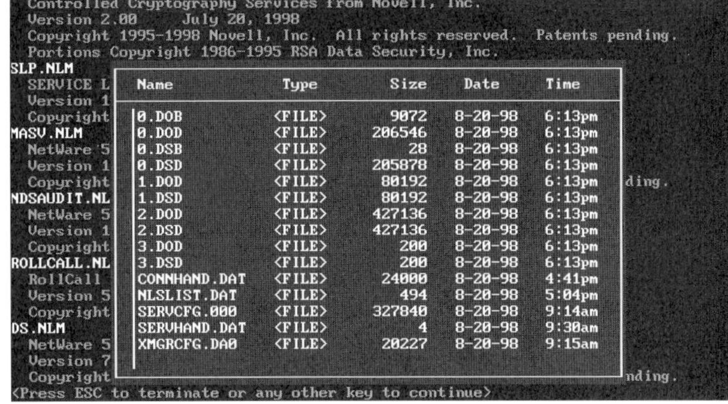

The sequence of events that occurs within NDS can become confused unless a mechanism is provided to ensure that the events are updated to each replica as they really happen. The term "event" is used to refer to a creation or modification to the NDS objects or properties.

The mechanism that ensures that the events are changed in sequence are the timestamps for each of the objects and properties. When an event occurs, NDS issues a new timestamp and associates the timestamp with the event. Synchronization between replicas of a partition uses the timestamps associated with every NDS object and property or attribute to indicate the time the modification was made. For example, if the same object (same property) is modified by two different administrators at approximately the same time, both updates may not take place, because the last timestamp wins the update.

The purpose of the timestamp in NDS is to ensure that the information stored in NDS will converge across all NetWare 5 servers over time.

There is a timestamp for each object when it is created, and one for when it is modified; the former is called the object creation timestamp and the latter, the last modification timestamp. There is also a timestamp issued for every change to a property value.

The timestamp value for objects and properties is unique within an NDS partition because the timestamps are assigned by the replica where the objects exist. This provides an ordering of the events that occur across all the servers holding replicas of a partition. Figure 8.7 illustrates the timestamp structure, which has three parts or fields.

FIGURE 8.7

The structure for a timestamp attribute

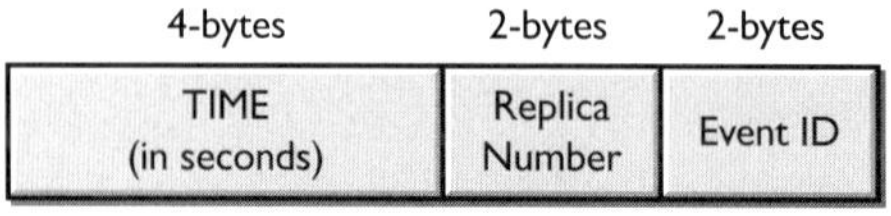

4-bytes	2-bytes	2-bytes
TIME (in seconds)	Replica Number	Event ID

- **Seconds** — This is a four-byte value that stores UTC time in whole seconds since midnight, January 1, 1970. The whole seconds represent the actual time that the event (creation or modification) took place.

- **Replica Number** — This is a two-byte field that stores the replica number where the event occurred and where the timestamp was issued. Every replica of a partition is assigned a unique number when it is created. The master replica is responsible for assigning a number to the new replica. The replica number ensures a unique timestamp within a partition.

- **Event ID** — This is a two-byte field that stores the number of events that occurred during a second. Because computers are so fast, many events can occur within any one second. The event ID permits a timestamp to be issued for events that occur in one second. The event ID is a sequence number that starts at 0 and can increment to 64K. The event ID is reset every second.

The timestamp is a critical component in the replica synchronization process. When NDS updates a replica, it requests the timestamps from that replica to identify the data. The timestamp provides a unique value for the object and properties that identify the time and place of the event's origin. If the same object or property is updated on different replicas (or servers) at exactly the same second and event ID, the replica number between the servers will be different. NDS will make the updates using the greater or latest timestamp. When compared, timestamps are treated as 32-bit, 16-bit, and 16-bit unsigned, with seconds as the most significant.

Whenever a client or workstation deletes an object or attribute from a replica on a server, the server does not immediately purge it from its local database. Instead, it issues a timestamp for the object or attribute and marks the object or attribute value as "not present" or deleted. After the replica synchronization process propagates the change to all other replicas, the janitor process purges the object or attribute (see the "Obituaries" section later in this chapter).

To support accurate timestamps, the servers must maintain accurate time and that time must be synchronized between the servers. Time synchronization provides the mechanism to ensure that each server is synchronized to the network time. You want accurate timestamps so that the order of modification is accurate, which means that the last modification timestamp is accepted.

NDS Structures for Objects and Properties

The NDS tree hierarchy is composed of NDS objects and properties. The objects and properties are stored as records in the NDS data files. The pieces of the data stored for each object are shown in Figure 8.8. Each record has seven fields.

FIGURE 8.8

The NDS object

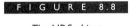

Object Class	Object Name	Creation Timestamp	Last Modification Timestamp	Object ID	Parent ID	Flags

- **Object class** — The object class is the base object class as defined in the schema for the object. An object is defined by a particular object type.
- **Object name** — The object name is the relative distinguished name of the object.
- **Creation timestamp** — The creation timestamp is issued to the object when it is created.
- **Last modification timestamp** — The last modification timestamp holds the timestamp of the last change received by this replica made to the object whether it was the object itself or its associated properties.
- **Object ID** — The object ID is a unique ID given to the object by the server where the replica is held.
- **Parent ID** — The parent ID is the object ID of the parent container object to this object.
- **Flags** — The flags are present, not present, alias, partition root, created by reference, and so on.

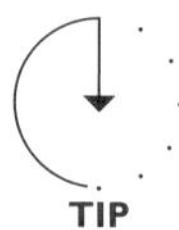

Sometimes the data contained in the object is called nonattribute object information because the information is stored with the object but not as attributes or properties.

The property or attribute shown in Figure 8.9 has four data items defined.

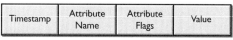

FIGURE 8.9

Timestamp	Attribute Name	Attribute Flags	Value

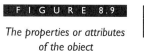

The properties or attributes of the object

- **Timestamp** — The timestamp holds the timestamp of the creation time for the attribute.
- **Attribute name** — The attribute name specifies the name of the attribute. The syntax or data type can be determined using the attribute name.
- **Attribute flags** — The attribute flags control the states of the attribute.
- **Value** — The value is the actual information or data stored.

An Object's Unique Name (Tuned Name)

An object's *tuned name* is the distinguished name of the object plus the creation timestamp for each of the parent container objects. The tuned name provides the NDS system with an absolutely unique ID structure for each of the objects in NDS. To illustrate the concept of a tuned name, we will use the following example. A system administrator decides to rename the user SIRGALAHAD to user GALAHAD. He or she then decides to create a new user called SIRGALAHAD. In order to guarantee that Directory Services knows that these two are separate objects, the concept of a tuned name is introduced. The tuned name is really a global unique name for the object.

A tuned name for an object is the distinguished name of the object with a little extra information. Each segment of the distinguished name is made up of a combination of the relative distinguished name bound with its creation timestamp. Remember that a distinguished name includes each parent object all the way back to and including [ROOT]. This means that the tuned name includes not only each relative distinguished name but also the creation timestamp for each to build the tuned name of the object.

As an example, the tuned name for the user SIRGALAHAD.CHARITY. CAMELOT.ACME would be as follows:

SIRGALAHAD (creation timestamp)
CHARITY (creation timestamp)
CAMELOT (creation timestamp)
ACME (creation timestamp)
[ROOT] (creation timestamp)

Including each creation timestamp for each object in the distinguished name removes any ambiguity about the object being identified. In the example, where SIRGALAHAD was created a second time under the same container, the first SIRGALAHAD differs from the second one created because of a difference in the creation timestamp.

The tuned name concept is used internally by NDS. You cannot see the tuned name for an object using the current NetWare Administration utilities.

Although objects have a unique object name or tuned name, you cannot have two objects with the same distinguished name. This would happen if two objects with the same relative distinguished name are in the same container. If two objects with the same name are synchronized into the same container but with different creation timestamps, NDS must rename one of the objects. The naming convention used by Directory Services to rename one of the objects is *number_number*. For example, a duplicate object is renamed to 1_2.

Object References

The values of some attributes in the Directory are other NDS objects. To truly understand objects in NDS, you need to understand how the objects are referenced. When an NDS object stores another object as an attribute value it is said to have an object reference.

For example, a group object has a membership attribute, and the values of this attribute are NDS objects. A printer object has an attribute whose values are other objects. The access control list is an example of an attribute for an object that stores other object IDs. The rights assignments for the NDS system are held in the access control list.

An object can also have its own object as one of its own attribute values. For example, a user object receives the read/write attribute for its own login script and print job configuration. The object becomes a trustee of itself.

To describe object references, we will use an example in the ACME tree. Consider Figure 8.10, where the user AEINSTEIN.LABS.NORAD.ACME is made security equivalent to the user KINGARTHUR.OPS.CAMELOT.ACME. The security equivalence attribute for AEINSTEIN has the value of the user to which he is security equivalent. In this case there is a value for KINGARTHUR. OPS.CAMELOT.ACME.

FIGURE 8.10

The user AEINSTEIN.LABS. NORAD.ACME is made security equivalent to the user KINGARTHUR.OPS. CAMELOT.ACME in the ACME tree.

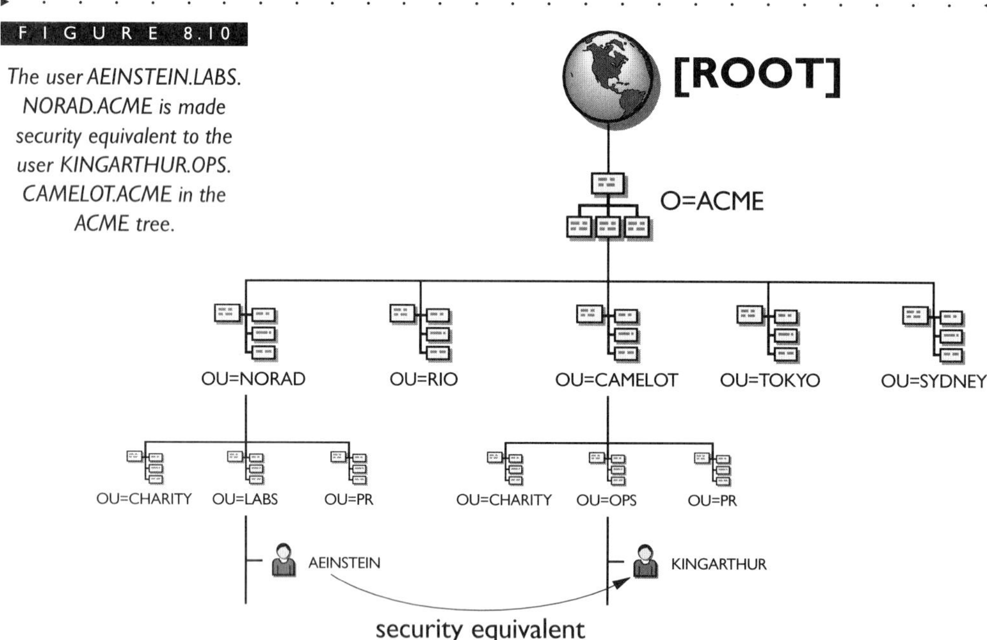

The object AEINSTEIN.LABS.NORAD.ACME is said to have an object reference to the object KINGARTHUR.OPS.CAMELOT.ACME. Internally, NDS stores the security equivalent attribute value as an object ID for the user KINGARTHUR. The client sees the value of the attribute as the distinguished name of the object.

A number of properties or attributes defined in the schema can contain object references. Some of these attributes are security equivalences, group membership, member, operator, and replica.

Consulting Experience

The rename problem has been noticed mostly in networks and servers that are migrating from NetWare 4.02 to NetWare 5.The reason is that NetWare 4.02 does not support tuned names and NetWare 5 requires them. In order to cure the problems experienced with renamed objects, you must run DSREPAIR, option number 8 on the NetWare 4.02 server before upgrading. Make sure that the DSREPAIR utility you are running is the updated version for NetWare 4.02. This updated DSREPAIR utility is available on the Novell corporate Web site.

The Object ID

One of the most important fields contained in the object structure is the object ID. Most of the operations that can be performed on the NDS objects require that the requesting client have or obtain the object ID. The object ID is a four-byte (32-bit) value that serves as a handle to the objects themselves.

Each object in a replica stored on a NetWare 5 server has a corresponding object ID on that server. The object ID is assigned on a per-server basis, which means that it is not a global ID and is valid only on the server that assigned it. Since the object ID is server-centric, it is not replicated, except for the backlinks and replica pointer table (both discussed later in this chapter).

Each server that stores a copy of the object will probably have a different object ID for the same NDS object. Figure 8.11 illustrates how each NetWare 5 server has a different object ID for the user object stored in different replicas. In this example, KINGARTHUR in the ACME tree has different object IDs on servers CAM-SRV1 and OPS-SRV1.

Obtaining the Object ID

The object ID is used in most of the internal operations performed by Directory Services. The client must first obtain the object ID for the object before it can execute the operation. There are several methods for the client to obtain the object ID.

The first method is known as *name resolution,* in which the client starts with the distinguished name of the object and makes the request to Directory Services to return the location and ID for the object. The name resolution method is used when logging into the network, capturing to printers, mapping network drives, and using NWADMIN to browse the tree. Each of the network resources is found using the name resolution process. The name resolution process is described in detail later in this chapter. The second method for obtaining the object ID is for the client to start with the current context and list the objects available in that container. Using the utilities provided, the client can then select any object and receive information that is of interest. This procedure is often called "yellow pages" or "white pages" in terms of the user interface and process.

FIGURE 8.11

Servers CAM-SRV1 and OPS-SRV1 have different object IDs for the user KINGARTHUR, which are stored in different replicas of the same partition.

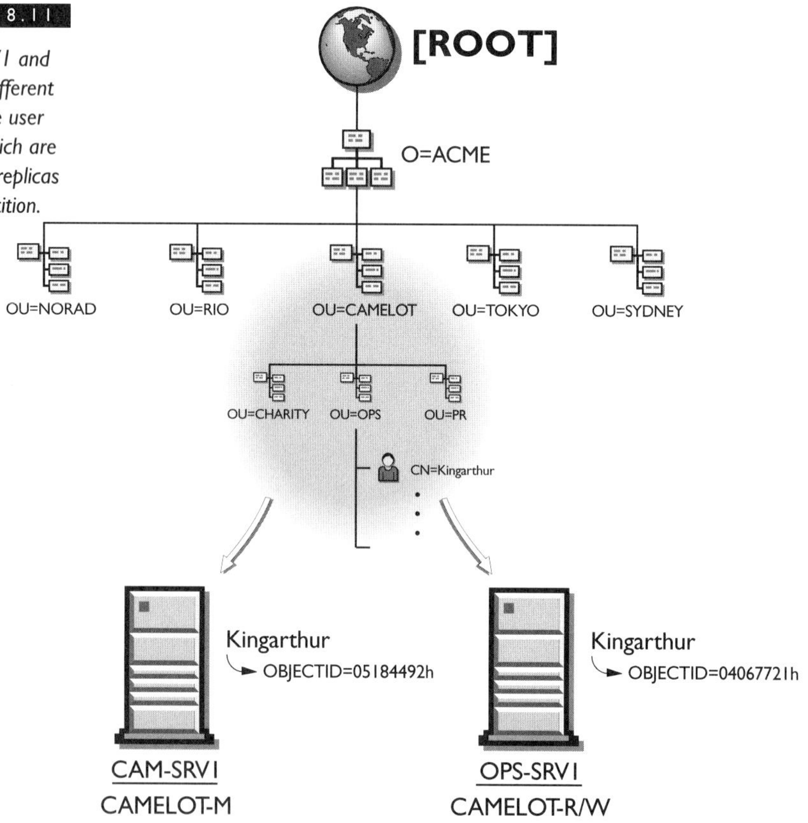

This method of obtaining the object ID is used mainly within the NWADMIN, NAL, or Z.E.N.works utilities. The user navigates through the tree listing all the objects. Depending on the utility, you can set a filter to weed out unwanted object types. Filters are available by name patterns, NDS object classes, or modification timestamps. An example of how to navigate through the NDS tree is shown in Chapter 2 in the section "Network Administration (NWADMIN.EXE)."

The third method for obtaining the object ID is for the client to execute a search. The search capabilities are the most powerful because you can select the objects by attribute values. The objects that match the value of the search criteria are returned. The search can be applied to the current container in the tree, or it can extend to the entire subtree. An example of how to perform a search against the NDS tree is shown in Chapter 2 in the section "Network Administration (NWADMIN.EXE)."

NDS Operations That Use the Object ID

Once the client has obtained a valid object ID, it operates on an object by sending requests to the NDS server where the object ID was obtained. Remember, the object ID is valid only on a per-server basis. The operating system also requires the object ID when performing operations. The file system, connection table, and other systems use this ID to identify the appropriate NDS object.

The most basic service provided is to read the detailed information about the object itself using the Read operation. The result of this operation is shown in NWADMIN when the Detail dialog box is opened for the object KINGARTHUR, as shown in Figure 8.12.

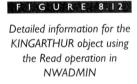

FIGURE 8.12

Detailed information for the KINGARTHUR object using the Read operation in NWADMIN

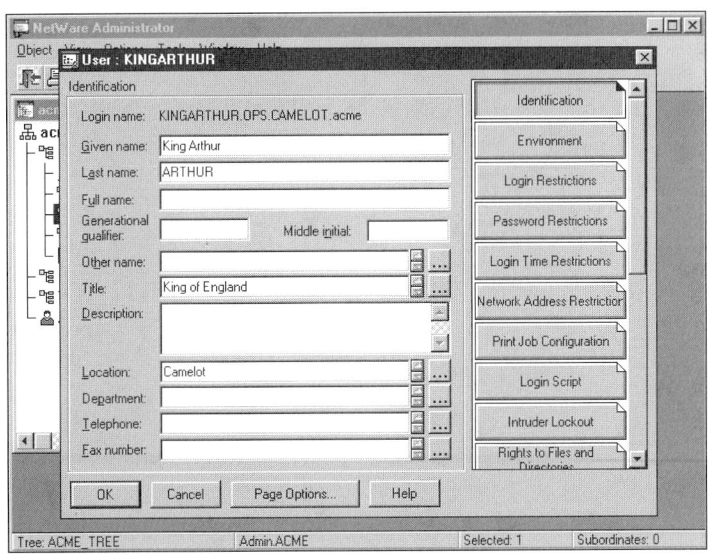

Other operations are Add, Delete, Modify, Get Effective Rights, Compare, and a lot more. Each operation that can be performed against an NDS object is self-explanatory.

Object IDs for Servers in NDS

The object ID for the NetWare server objects is stored in pairs consisting of a local server ID and a remote server ID. The server ID pairs are used as a shortcut for the server-to-server authentication that supports NDS operations such as replica synchronization. An authenticating object ID for the server object is required and is used in the connection table of the server. Thus, a server stores an object ID for all the other NetWare 5 servers that the local server has authenticated to. The following list illustrates how each server holds a server ID pair, which includes object IDs for the local server and the remote server.

- The local server ID is the local ID held for the remote server.
- The remote server ID is the local server's ID on the specific remote server.

For example, the server ID pairs that are held by each of the servers CAM-SRV1 and NOR-SRV1 are shown in Figure 8.13. The server ID pairs are also shown on a server basis in DSREPAIR under the Advanced menu option. Figure 8.14 illustrates the server ID pairs stored in NOR-SRV1.

FIGURE 8.13

The server ID pairs are held by each of the servers CAM-SRV1 and NOR-SRV1 in the ACME tree.

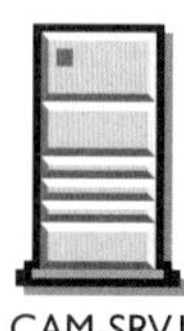

SERVER IDs

LOCAL ID	REMOTE ID
01023000	89007601

LOCAL ID	REMOTE ID
89007601	01023000

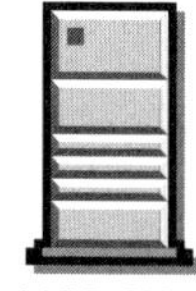

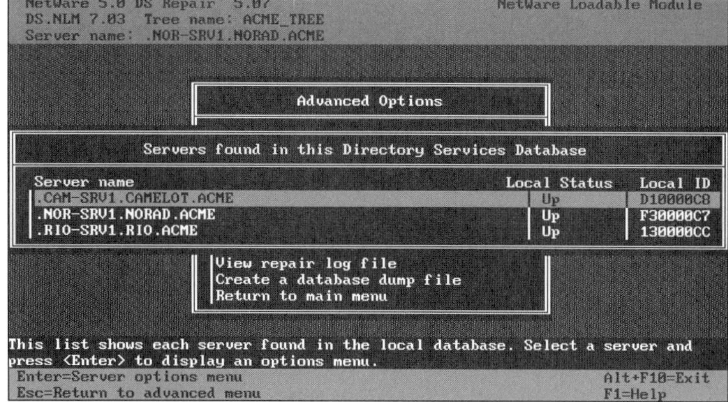

FIGURE 8.14

The server ID pairs are held by the server NOR-SRV1 as shown in the DSREPAIR utility.

Object IDs Used as File System Trustees

In order to maintain backward compatibility, the operating system uses the object ID rather than the object name to assign trustees for file system rights. The trustees of the file system are not stored in NDS; instead, they are stored in the same place as they are in NetWare 3, which is in the directory entry table (DET). The directory entry table is part of the file system. Figure 8.15 illustrates how assignments for the trustees of file system rights are made using the object ID. In this example, the user KINGARTHUR is assigned Read and File Scan rights to the SYS:APPS directory on the server CAM-SRV1.

External References and Backlinks

The object ID discussed in the previous section is valid on the server as long as the NDS object is stored in the replica on the server. Sometimes the server holds a temporary object ID for objects that are not stored locally. The temporary object ID is called an *external reference*. These external references work together with backlinks or distributive reference links to provide the distribution of the Directory Service.

FIGURE 8.15

The assignments for the trustees of file system rights are made using the object ID. KINGARTHUR is assigned Read and File Scan rights to the SYS:APPS directory on the server CAM-SRV1.

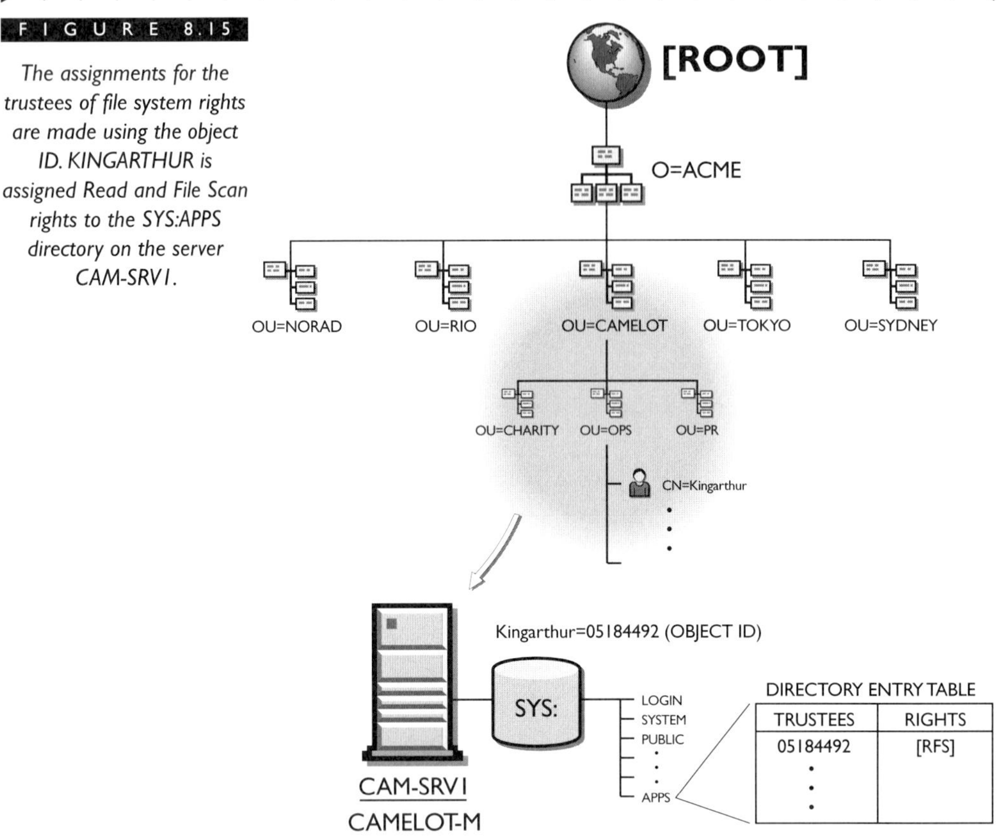

An external reference is created to reference an object that is not physically located on the local server. When a NetWare 5 server needs to reference information about an NDS object that is not held in any local replicas, that server creates an external reference, which provides a local object ID for the real NDS object on the other servers.

In order for NDS to keep track of all the external references created, each object can have a multivalued property called a *backlink*. The backlink points to the external reference with which it is associated. Each backlink value is periodically checked to verify that the associated external reference still exists. The backlink property of the object contains the name of the server that holds the external reference and the object ID that is assigned to the object on that server.

In order to understand how the external references and backlinks are used, you need to understand the object IDs on the server and when they are used. For example, the server needs the object IDs for use in the file system, connection table, and other systems.

In Figure 8.16, the object AEINSTEIN is contained in the NORAD partition, which is stored on server NOR-SRV1. The server CAM-SRV1 holds only a replica of the CAMELOT partition. Let's consider a situation in which AEINSTEIN maps a network drive to the server CAM-SRV1. The drive mapping forces the user to authenticate to CAM-SRV1, where a local object ID is needed by the connection table for assignment of file system rights.

The user object for AEINSTEIN, which mapped a drive to CAM-SRV1, is not physically stored on the server, and so it must create an external reference because a local object ID is needed to authenticate the real object. The real object is in the NORAD partition on the NOR-SRV1 server. The external reference created on the CAM-SRV1 server stores the object ID that is needed on the local server. In this case the object ID is 03 01 89 00 hex. Likewise, a backlink is created on the real object to track the external reference. Figure 8.17 illustrates the relationship of creating an external reference and backlink for the user object AEINSTEIN in the ACME tree.

The Purpose of External References

The purpose of the external reference is to be able to reference an object in Directory Services without requiring that object to be physically duplicated on the local server. The external reference architecture enables NDS to be distributed across the servers in the network while still being able to reference its objects. NDS can reference all the objects in Directory Services without having to store a complete replica of each partition on each NetWare 5 server.

FIGURE 8.16

The NORAD partition is stored on NOR-SRV1, and the CAMELOT partition is stored on CAM-SRV1.

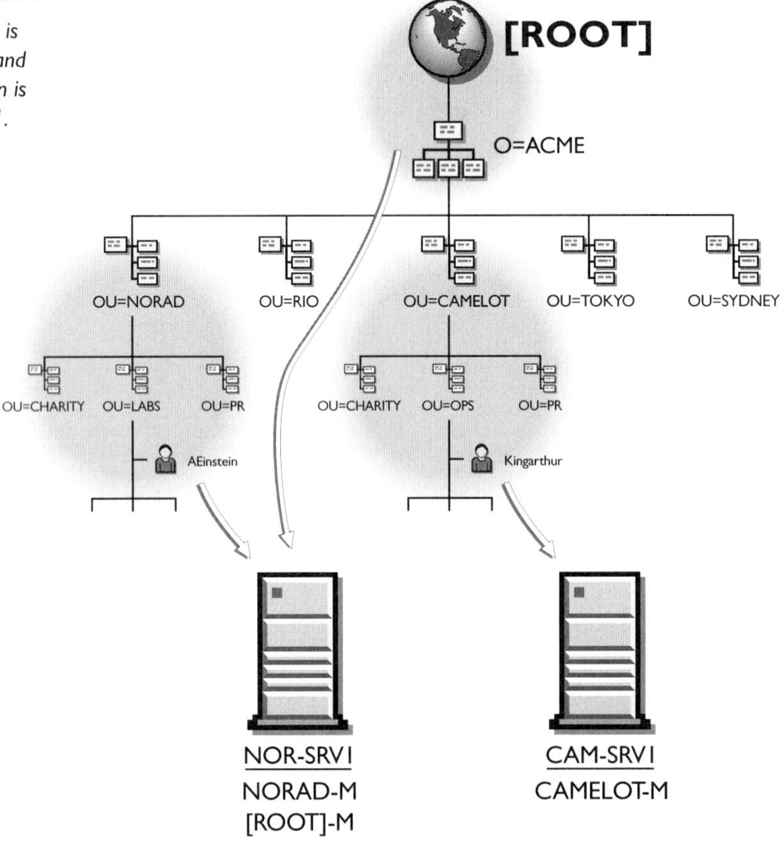

FIGURE 8.17

An example of an external reference and backlink for the user object AEINSTEIN

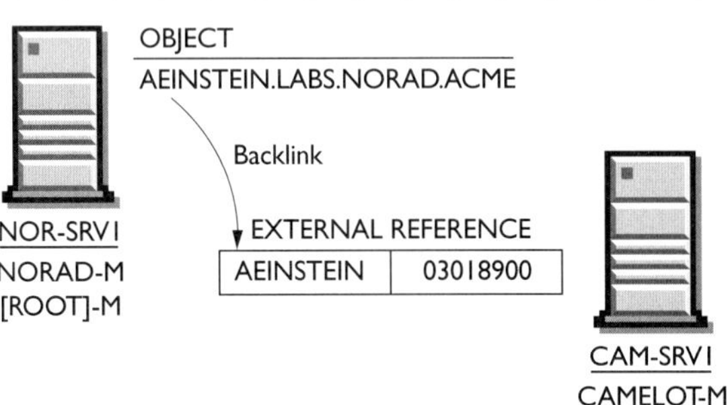

External references provide two major functions for NDS. First, they provide NDS with the capability to reference objects that are not local to the server. Second, they provide the complete NDS skeleton of the tree structure and maintain an object's lineage "up" the tree. The external references are stored on a per-server basis on each NetWare 5 server in the external reference partition. Since the data in this partition is server-centric, it is not synchronized to other NetWare 5 servers in the network.

External references improve system performance by caching frequently accessed information. Currently, NDS caches only an object's public key. Since authentication requires the client's public key, it is cached on the external reference so that it does not have to be read each time. The external references that are created for the server objects also store the server's status and DS revision or build number.

An external reference is an object stored in the ENTRY.NDS file as part of the external reference partition and has these components:

- **Object ID** — A unique object ID issued by the local server for the real object
- **Relative distinguished name** — The real object's relative distinguished name

Whenever a server creates an external reference for an object in the NDS tree, it also creates external references for each of the parent containers, if needed. These are the parent containers that are in the distinguished name of the object all the way back to and including [ROOT]. An external reference for the parent container is needed only when it has not been previously created.

The Purpose of Backlinks

The backlink property of an object is used by the NDS system to enable easy maintenance of the external references of that object. When an object is renamed, moved, or deleted from the system, the backlinks aid in modifying the external references to that object to reflect the changes. This process provides data integrity for Directory Services. For example, when an object is renamed, moved, or deleted, the backlinks make it possible to change all external references to the object.

The format for the backlink property or attribute includes these values:

- **Object ID** — The object ID value that is issued for the external reference on the remote server. This value enables NDS to find the associated external reference or object ID on the remote server.
- **Distinguished name** — The remote server object's distinguished name in the NDS tree. This value identifies the server holding the external reference.

Distributed Reference Links

New in NetWare 5 is a method for maintaining external references called *distributed reference links (DRL)*. These links are more efficient than backlinks when renaming, moving, and deleting the external references. The distributed reference links are more efficient because, unlike backlinks, they are not tied to a specific NetWare server; instead, they reference the partition that stores the external reference object. Alternatively, when a backlink (in NetWare 4.*x*) is created it stores the NetWare server name and object ID for each external reference object.

As mentioned, the major downside to using backlinks is that they are tied to a specific NetWare server and not tied to the external reference object's location in the NDS tree. The result of using backlinks is that each NetWare server tends to have a connection to every other server in the NDS tree. To alleviate this problem, distributed reference links have been added to NetWare 5 that store the partition name and object ID where each external reference object exists. By storing the partition name, the individual NetWare servers can resolve the DRLs by using the NDS tree structure.

Like backlinks, the DRLs have a periodic process that checks to verify that the associated external reference still exists. This process that periodically checks the DRLs provides data integrity for the NDS database. The distributed reference link is implemented using a new "Used By" property of the object. The "Used By" property contains the distinguished name of the partition that holds the external reference and the object ID that is assigned to the object.

Although distribution reference links are fully implemented in NetWare 5, backlinks will not go away. During certain situations, the backlinks will continue to be used to help maintain the external references. NetWare 5 uses both methods.

Creating External References and Backlinks

The external references are created for a number of reasons. For example, there are times when a server requires information about an object that is not stored locally. Having this information helps the local server maintain an object ID for an NDS object. NDS creates the object ID for each object. The external reference object supplies an object ID for the server where the real object is not stored. An example is a server that needs to grant file system rights to an object that is not local. The server requires the object ID to make the trustee assignment.

The corresponding property to the external reference is the backlink. A new value for the backlink property is written on the object each time an external reference is created. The backlink property value is used by Directory Services to keep track of where the external references of an object are located.

External references are required for five different situations on a NetWare 5 server. For these situations, it is assumed that the actual NDS object for which the external reference is created is not stored locally on the server. The five different methods or situations are as follows:

- Completing the distinguished names
- Authentication
- File system access control
- Dealing with attribute values that are NDS objects
- Replica removal

Complete the Distinguished Names

The name field for the object stores only the relative distinguished name of the object. Each object also requires the object ID for the parent objects. Therefore, external references are created on the server to complete the skeleton up the NDS tree for each of the objects that it holds in its partitions. One external reference is created for each relative distinguished name in the complete name. This means that external references are created for each of the parent container objects that are not physically stored on the server.

For example, the server CAM-SRV1 in the ACME tree holds only the CAMELOT partition, which defines each of the objects for that subtree. In order to complete the distinguished naming for the objects in the partition, the O=ACME and [ROOT] objects must have external references. The real objects for each external reference are stored in the [ROOT] partition on the server NOR-SRV1. Figure 8.18 illustrates this example.

FIGURE 8.18

External references are created on server CAM-SRV1 for the O=ACME and [ROOT] objects. The external references are needed to complete the distinguished names of the objects in the partition CAMELOT.

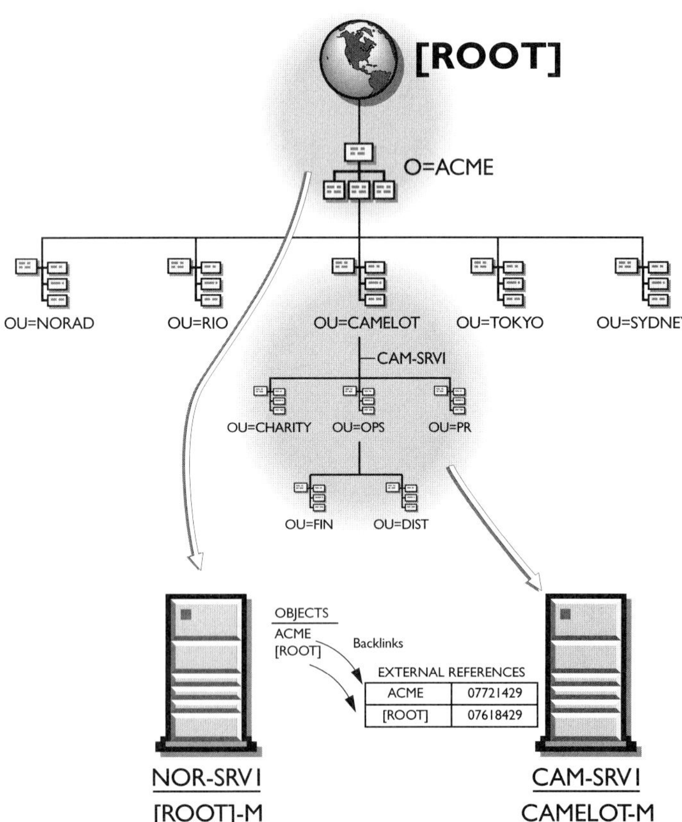

For each replica a server holds, it must know the distinguished name of the partition, which is defined by the partition [ROOT] object. This means that external references will be created to complete each relative distinguished name of the partition all the way back to the [ROOT] object.

Likewise, an external reference object cannot exist without the server knowing about every object in its distinguished name. The external reference objects themselves are stored as relative distinguished names, not simple distinguished names. This is true for every NDS object, not just the external references. When a server creates an external reference, it will most likely create external references to complete the distinguished name of the object contained in the external reference. If an external reference for the parent containers of the object has been previously created, another reference is not needed.

For example, in Figure 8.19, server RIO-SRV1 does not hold any NDS replicas in the ACME tree. The user object KINGARTHUR.OPS.CAMELOT.ACME is created as an external reference on the server RIO-SRV1. The server would need to create additional external references for each of the objects in the distinguished name of KINGARTHUR, including the [ROOT] object. [ROOT] is implied in every object name.

FIGURE 8.19

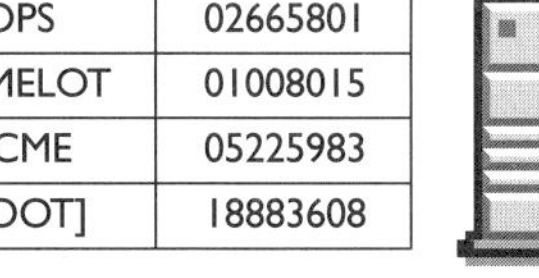

EXTERNAL REFERENCES

KINGARTHUR	0615360E
OPS	02665801
CAMELOT	01008015
ACME	05225983
[ROOT]	18883608

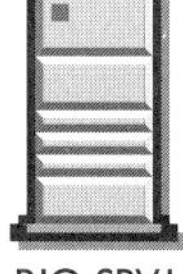

An example of an external reference created for the user KINGARTHUR on RIO-SRV1, as well as other external references created to complete the distinguished name for KINGARTHUR

Authentication

NDS objects (typically users and NDS servers) can authenticate themselves to a NetWare 5 server for access to specific network resources even though the objects are not stored locally on that server. The authentication mechanism needs an object ID defined for each NDS object that authenticates as well as an object ID for each security equivalence of the object.

The object ID is used in the server connection table to calculate the security privileges for the connection. One of the steps in the authentication process is the calculation of the object's security equivalences. The results of the calculation are stored in the object's entry of the connection table of the server. All security equivalences of the object that authenticate are included in the connection table. These security equivalences are stored in the server's connection table as object IDs and not names.

For those objects that are not stored locally, an external reference is created that supplies an object ID to the connection table. This is true even for the other NetWare 5 servers that attach and authenticate for purposes of synchronizing replicas.

An example of this situation is illustrated in Figure 8.20. (This is the same example that was illustrated in Figures 8.16 and 8.17.) The user object AEINSTEIN maps a network drive to the server CAM-SRV1. Since AEINSTEIN is not physically stored on the server, it must create an external reference for the real object. The real object is in the NORAD partition on the NOR-SRV1 server. The external reference created on the CAM-SRV1 server stores the object ID that is needed on the local server. Likewise, the real object stores a backlink property value to track the external reference.

FIGURE 8.20

An example of an external reference and backlink for the user object AEINSTEIN in the ACME tree

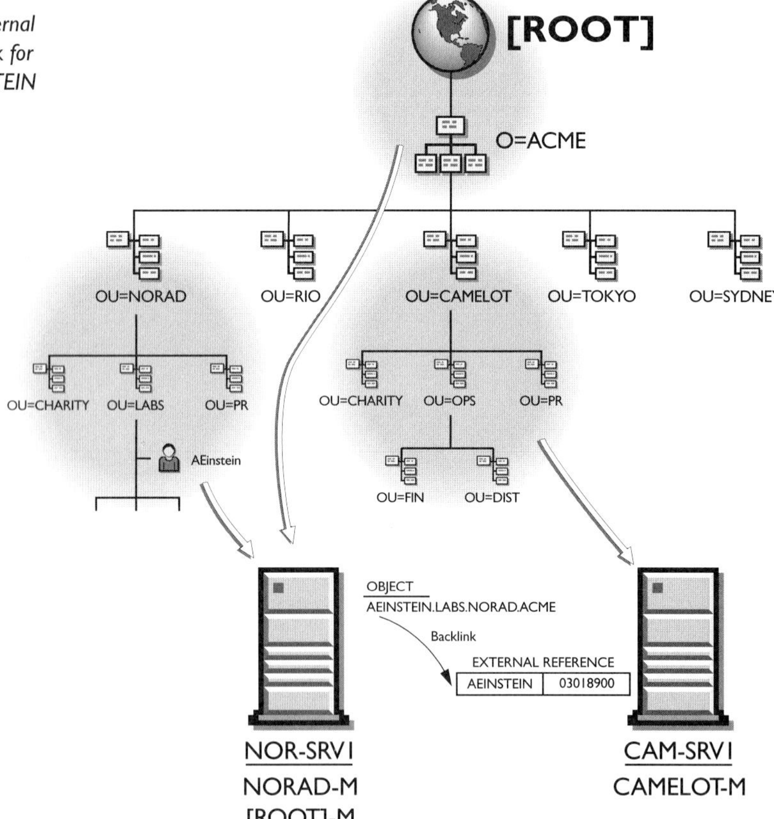

The server CAM-SRV1 will create an external reference for each of the other objects in the distinguished name of AEINSTEIN. These objects are OU=LABS, OU=NORAD, O=ACME, and [ROOT] as shown in Figure 8.21. The objects O=ACME and [ROOT] should already exist on the server CAM-SRV1 as external references because they are needed to complete the distinguished name of the objects in the CAMELOT partition.

FIGURE 8.21

An example of external references and backlinks for the objects OU=LABS, OU=NORAD, O=ACME, and [ROOT], which are part of the distinguished name for AEINSTEIN in the ACME tree

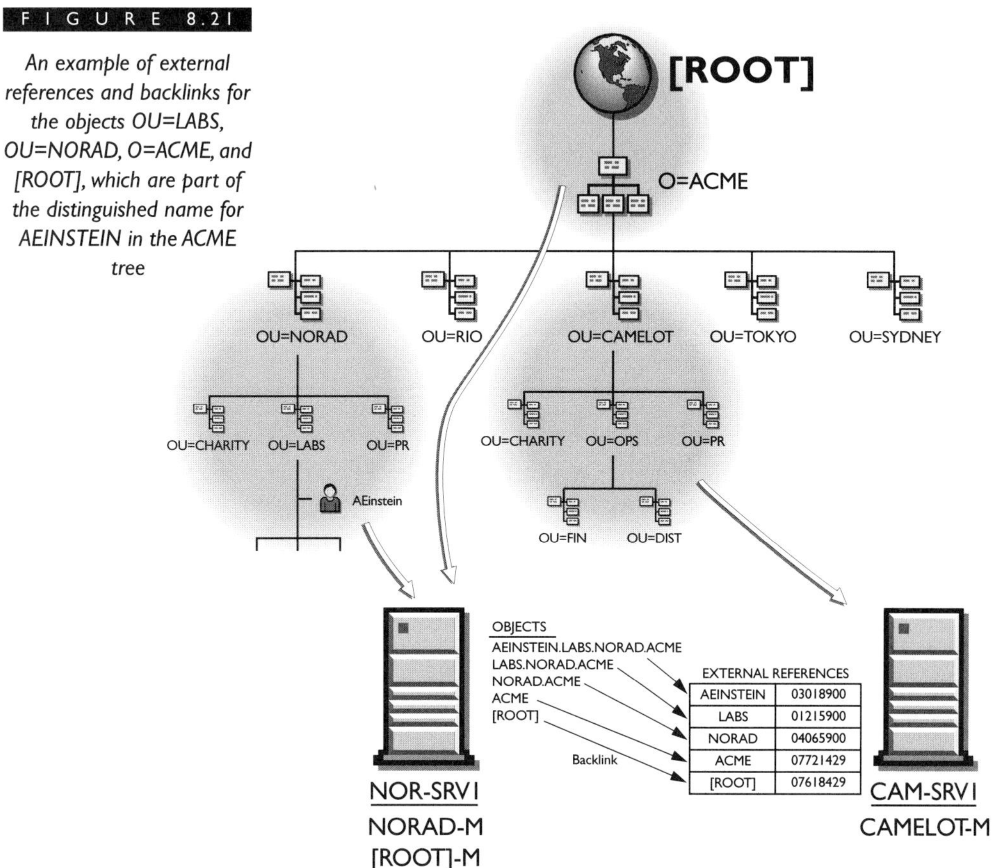

File System Access Control

An external reference object can be created to supply an object ID for the file system rights assignments. The assignment of file system rights is maintained by NetWare 5 using the object IDs. The object ID becomes the trustee for the files and directories rights assignments. The rights assignments for the file and directory system are stored in the directory entry table. This control list stores the object ID for the user that has the rights.

If the object does not exist on the server, an external reference is created, which supplies the file system's directory entry table with an object ID. For example, in Figure 8.22 a user KINGARTHUR can have file and directory rights to NOR-SRV1, even though the KINGARTHUR user object is not stored in a replica on the NOR-SRV1 server. In this example, KINGARTHUR is given Read and File Scan rights to the SYS:APPS directory on NOR-SRV1. The server requires an object ID for the user KINGARTHUR to place in the trustee list for the directory. An external reference is created for KINGARTHUR, but the real user object is stored on CAM-SRV1.

FIGURE 8.22

The user KINGARTHUR is granted Read and File Scan rights to the directory SYS:APPS on the server NOR-SRV1. An external reference is created for the user and its parents.

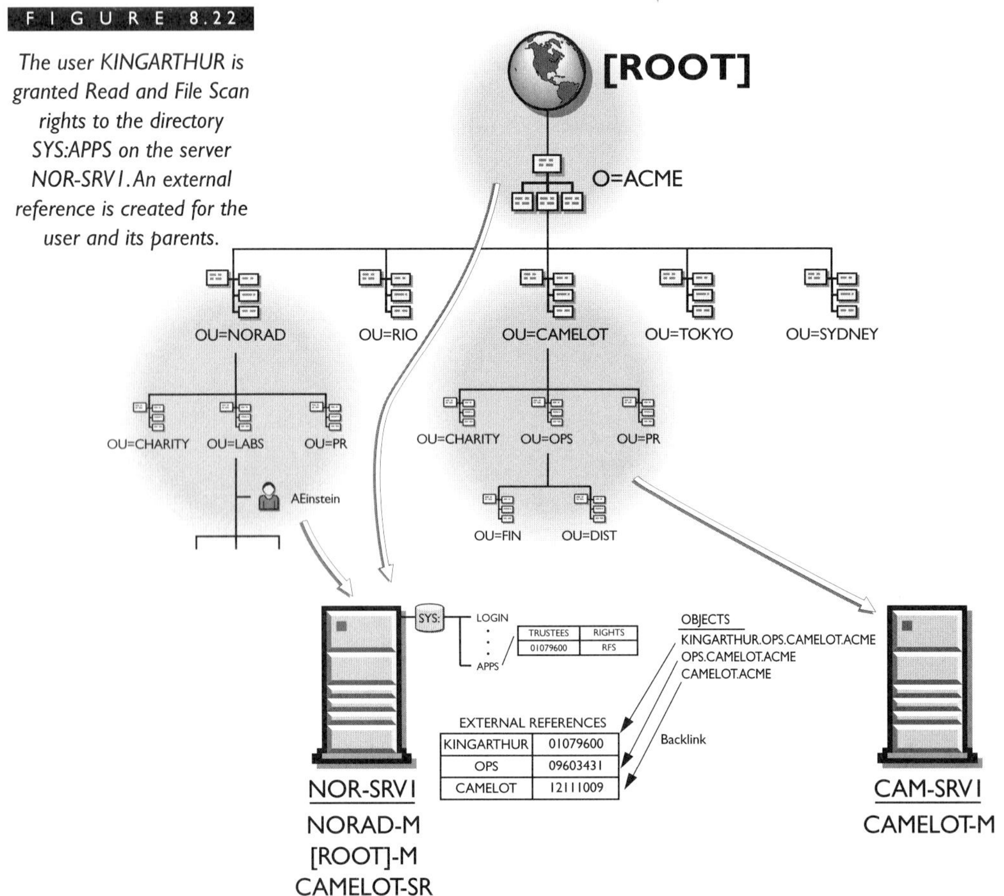

External references are also created for OU=OPS, which is the parent object in the distinguished name of the user. The OU=CAMELOT object already exists on the server NOR-SRV1 in a subordinate reference replica for the CAMELOT partition. The objects O=ACME and [ROOT] are not created as external references because they are real objects on the server NOR-SRV1 in the [ROOT] partition.

Attribute Values That Are NDS Objects

The values of some attributes are other NDS objects. These values are known as *object references*. For example, a group object has a membership attribute, and the value of this attribute is an NDS object. A printer object has an attribute whose values are objects. The access control list (ACL) is an example of an attribute for an object that stores other object IDs.

All object references are stored in the Directory as object IDs. Thus, if an attribute references an object that is not stored locally, the server creates an external reference for that object. This means that external references are created on a server if the object is placed as the value of an attribute or property of another object.

Replica Removal

When you remove a replica of a partition from a server, the NDS system will create an external reference for each object in the partition. Although each of the objects in the removed replica changes into an external reference, NDS marks each object with a zero modification timestamp. This means that the NDS system should check the external references at the next backlink interval to see if they are in use by the system. If the external references are not used, the system will clear them out as soon as possible.

Maintaining External References

External references require updating when the real object is deleted, moved, or renamed, or when the security equivalence has changed. After successfully synchronizing all the replicas of a partition, Directory Services checks any object that has been renamed, moved, or deleted. The operation that deletes, moves, and renames an object adds obituary attribute values to that object. To maintain consistency between the external references and backlinks, there are backlink obituaries for every backlink attribute of the object.

At the end of a successful replica synchronization of a partition, a portion of the janitor process (known as the *purger*) processes the obituaries on the object in the partition. If NDS finds any backlink obituaries, it notifies the server that contains the object's external reference to update that external reference appropriately. The janitor process is discussed in more detail in Chapter 9, "Troubleshooting Novell Directory Services."

Periodically, NDS checks the external references to see if the original object still exists. The NDS feature that checks the validity of the external references and backlinks is called the *backlink process*. The backlink process is discussed in more detail in Chapter 9, "Troubleshooting NDS."

Deleting External References

On each server Directory Services deletes external references if they have not been accessed for a period of time. The types of external references that will be deleted after a period of time are the ones created for temporary use. For example, the external references created to support authentication should be removed by the NDS system after a period of time.

External references that are used as attribute values of an NDS object or external references that are used by the server are not deleted even if they are not accessed for a period of time. The period of time is determined by a SET parameter called External Reference Life Span.

The system administrator can use this Directory Services SET parameter to set the number of hours after which NDS deletes external references that have not been used. The Directory Services SET parameter that controls the life span for external references is set as follows:

```
SET NDS External Reference Life Span = 192
```

The value of this SET parameter is set in hours. The default value of 192 (hours) or 8 days works well, and we recommend that you leave it. The range for this SET parameter is 1 to 384 (in hours). The default is set to 8 days so that this operation does not occur in exactly one-week intervals.

When an external reference is accessed, it updates the modification timestamp to the current time. The process that removes the external references builds a list of unused external references by checking the modification timestamp of each external reference compared with the life span interval. Using the default value for this SET parameter, the process will remove the external reference after the eight days. The process that checks each server to see if the external references are still in use is called the *backlink process* or *backlinker*.

Each time the backlink process runs, the server checks each object ID associated with an external reference to make sure it is still in use. This means that the directory entry tables for the file system need to be scanned, in a process that can be intensive. The janitor process then purges the deleted external references. For more information about the backlink and janitor processes, refer to Chapter 9, "Troubleshooting Novell Directory Services."

When Directory Services removes an external reference, the server holding the external reference requests that the server holding the original object or real object delete the backlink attribute value associated with the external reference.

Obituaries

Directory Services uses a special attribute of an NDS object called an *obituary* to track renames, moves, and deletions of both objects and external references. Since NDS is loosely consistent, each NetWare 5 server needs a mechanism to keep track or record the instances of the NDS objects. The purpose for the obituaries is to maintain consistency in the instances of objects across all the different replicas of a partition until synchronization is completed.

The obituaries help maintain consistency because each server cannot receive all updates simultaneously. This means that the servers may not hold the same information at a given time. For this reason, each server holds on to the latest set of information until all the other servers holding replicas for a partition receive the updates. Directory Services uses obituaries to coordinate or keep track of instances of objects.

Obituary Attribute Values

When an object is moved, renamed, or deleted in Directory Services, the system adds a new obituary attribute value to the object. There is one obituary for each move, rename, or delete operation. There is an obituary for each backlink attribute and one for each server in the replica pointer table (replica ring). See the "Obituary Types" section later in this chapter for more on the various obituaries.

Since obituaries are attribute values of the NDS object, they are synchronized to the other servers using the same mechanism that all replica synchronization uses. This means that obituaries for the objects are synchronized across replicas of a partition.

For example, when an object is deleted, Directory Services marks the object as not present, which means not visible to the clients. However, the object is retained in the name service until the removal is propagated to the other servers. The attribute values are removed, and the proper obituaries are established to indicate that the object is no longer logically present. In this case the obituary is of type "dead."

Obituary Data

The obituary attribute for an NDS object can be a multivalued attribute. The pieces of data for the obituary property or attribute are defined as a string. The obituary property or attribute is made up of the following pieces of data:

- **Obituary type** — Indicates the operation that has taken place on the object.
- **Obituary state** — An obituary goes through several different states as it is processed. The obituary state records the progress.
- **Old creation timestamp** — This is the creation time of the original object.

Obituary Types

The type of obituary determines the operation being performed. Directory Services classifies the obituary type internally into two categories: primary and secondary. Typically, when an object is changed, the primary obituary is the mechanism that conveys the change to servers holding replicas of the object. The primary obituaries are used for the types restored, dead, and moved.

Secondary obituaries convey the change to servers holding external references of the changed object. For any given primary obituary there can be several secondary obituaries.

The backlink obituary is the only secondary obituary currently in the system. It keeps external references synchronized with the real objects. All other obituaries are primary obituaries that keep track of changes made to the NDS objects themselves.

The specific obituary types are these:

- 0—Restored
- 1—Dead
- 2—Moved
- 3—Inhibit move
- 4—Old relative distinguished name
- 5—New relative distinguished name
- 6—Backlink
- 7—Tree old relative distinguished name
- 8—Tree new relative distinguished name
- 9—Purge all
- 10—Move subtree

Obituary States

An obituary goes through several states. The sequence of states progresses as the servers process the operation.

The specific obituary states are these:

- 0—Initial
- 1—Notified
- 2—OK to purge
- 4—Purgeable

Figure 8.23 shows how obituaries are used when an object is renamed. The servers CAM-SRV1 and OPS-SRV1 hold a replica of the CAMELOT partition. The user object SIRGALAHAD in the CAMELOT partition is renamed to GALAHAD.

FIGURE 8.23

The user object SIRGALAHAD in the CAMELOT partition is renamed to GALAHAD. The appropriate obituaries are established for each object.

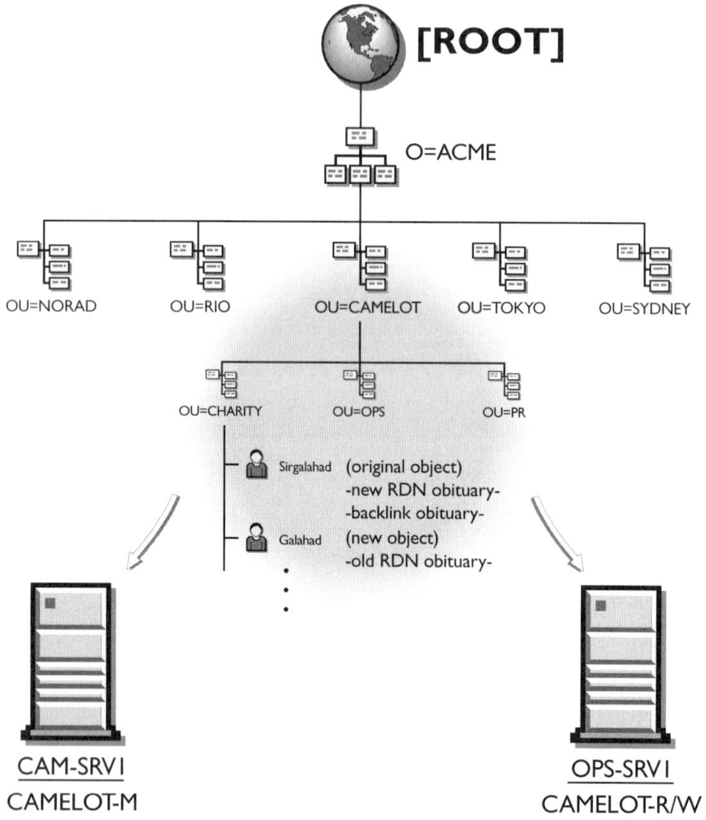

The rename operation for SIRGALAHAD to GALAHAD is started on the server CAM-SRV1, which establishes a New RDN obituary type for it. This obituary ensures that all servers can access the object using SIRGALAHAD, even if they have not been notified of the name change. The server then creates object GALAHAD and establishes an Old RDN obituary pointing back to the original object. Using this method, the object can be accessed either by the name SIRGALAHAD or GALAHAD while the rename is completed.

In order to complete the rename, each server holding a copy of the SIRGALAHAD object needs to be informed. In this case, the server OPS-SRV1 will receive the rename update via normal replica synchronization. After all replicas have been completely synchronized, the servers can delete the SIRGALAHAD object and remove the obituaries. The rename is completed, as shown in Figure 8.24.

FIGURE 8.24

The object SIRGALAHAD has completed the rename to GALAHAD, and the obituaries have been removed.

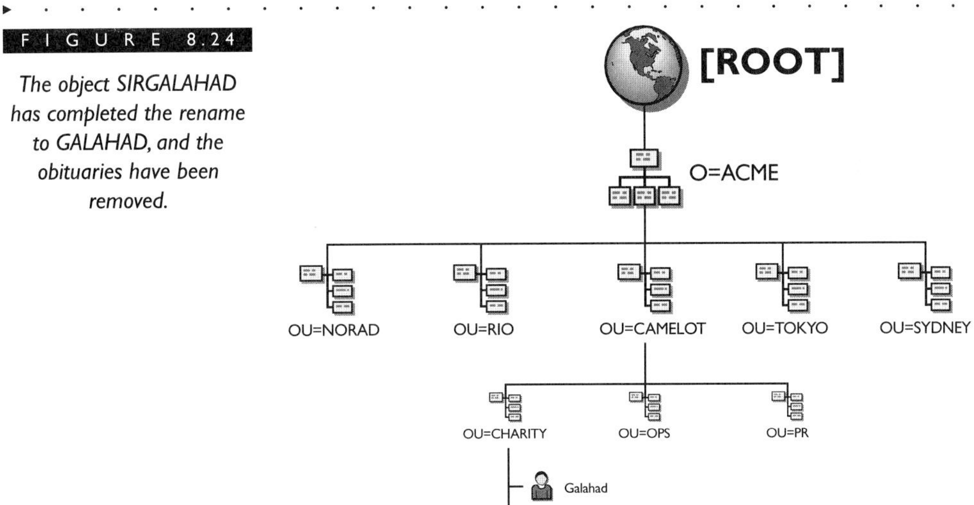

The process is a little more complicated than shown because the obituaries each go through all the state changes before the operation is completed. A more detailed discussion about the operation and how the obituaries function is included in Chapter 9, "Troubleshooting Novell Directory Services."

The Server Partition Table

Each NetWare 5 server maintains a list of the replicas that are physically stored in the server. This list is called the *server partition table*. You can think of the server partition table as the list of partitions that are stored on the server. The server partition table can be viewed using either NWADMIN under the NDS Manager or DSREPAIR under the Advanced Options menu and Replica and Partition

Operations. Figure 8.25 shows the server partition table on the server NOR-SRV1 as shown from the NDS Manager utility. The server NOR-SRV1 holds a replica of the partitions NORAD and [ROOT].

FIGURE 8.25

The server partition table on the server NOR-SRV1 as shown from the NDS Manager utility. The server NOR-SRV1 holds a replica of the partitions NORAD and [ROOT]. It also holds the subordinate reference for the CAMELOT, RIO, SYDNEY, and TOKYO partitions.

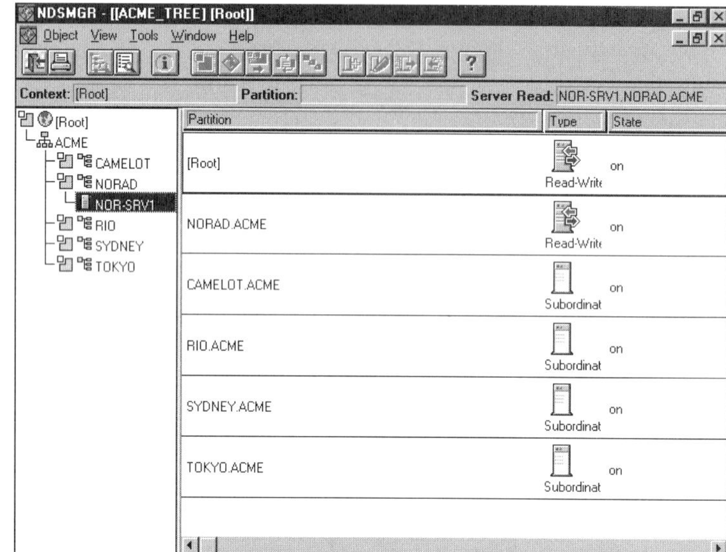

The records for the server partition table are stored in the NDS data file called PARTITIO.NDS. This information is stored for each replica of a partition located on the server:

- **Partition name** — The distinguished name of the topmost object in the partition, which is called the *partition root object*
- **Replica type** — Master, read/write, read-only, and subordinate reference
- **Replica state** — The current state of the replica
- **Replica timestamp** — The next timestamp issued for the replica, including the timestamps that are issued for any modification on the replica

The replica state field contains the current state of the replica. This field is used as an attribute that is stored by each replica as defined in Table 8.1.

TABLE 8.1

The Replica States Definitions

STATE	VALUE	DESCRIPTION
RS_ON	0	On
RS_NEW_REPLICA	1	New replica
RS_DYING_REPLICA	2	Replica in the process of being removed
RS_LOCKED	3	Locked
RS_CTR_0	4	Change Replica Type, State 0
RS_CTR_1	5	Change Replica Type, State 1
RS_TRANSITION_ON	6	Transition On State
RS_TRANSITION_MOVE	7	Transition Move State
RS_TRANSITION_SPLIT	8	Transition Split State
RS_SS_0	48	Split, State 0
RS_SS_1	49	Split, State 1
RS_JS_0	64	Join, State 0
RS_JS_1	65	Join, State 1
RS_JS_2	66	Join, State 2
RS_MS_0	80	Move Subtree, State 0
RS_MS_1	81	Move Subtree, State 1
RS_MS_2	82	Move Subtree, State 2

NDS Partition Structure

An NDS partition is created by selecting one NDS container object (usually an organizational unit) as the top of the partition boundary or root of the partition. The distinguished name of the topmost object becomes the name of the partition. This object is also referred to as the *partition root object*.

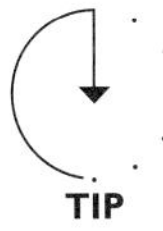
TIP

Do not confuse the partition root object with the [ROOT] object at the top of the NDS tree. The [ROOT] object is a special container object that defines the top of the NDS tree. The partition root object is just the topmost object in a particular partition.

When a partition is created, the NDS container object that is selected as the top of the partition has several new attributes added to support replica synchronization. The partition root object is the container object with additional properties or attributes defined that reveal the details of the partition's status and replica placement. These attributes are also used by NDS to synchronize the information between replicas of the partition.

The attributes of the partition root object that define the partition and support the NDS functions are defined here:

- **Replica pointer table** — This multivalued attribute stores the list of replicas for the partition.
- **Synchronized up to** — This multivalued attribute contains a timestamp for each replica in the replica pointer table. There should be a timestamp for every replica on which modifications have occurred. Each timestamp indicates the value received from other replicas of the partition. It represents the time that the data is modified up to for that replica. This attribute is often referred to as the *synchronized up to vector*.
- **Partition creation timestamp** — This attribute is known as the *epoch*. Although this attribute is in the timestamp syntax, it does not hold a time value. Instead, it holds a counter that begins at 1 and increments for each new epoch. An epoch indicates when the repair timestamp is executed.
- **Inherited access control list** — This attribute contains access control information inherited from a parent partition. It is the summary of the access control lists to that point in the NDS tree.
- **Partition control** — This attribute tracks the progress of partition operations such as splitting, joining, adding, and deleting replicas.
- **Replica up to** — This attribute contains a timestamp for each replica that is used to represent the purge time for replica. This is often called the *replica up to vector* because there is a timestamp for each replica. This attribute is a forerunner to the next release of NetWare 5. This attribute is localized to a particular server, which means that it is not synchronized to the other servers.

- **Partition status** — The status of the last synchronization effort. This value could show errors, if any. The partition status attribute is localized to the server and is not synchronized.

Each of these attributes is discussed in more detail in the following sections.

The Replica Pointer Table

The replica pointer table stores or references all the servers having a replica of a given partition. The replica pointer table is often referred to as the *replica ring* or *replica list*. Each of these names is equivalent. In this book we will refer to the attribute as the replica pointer table. The replica pointer table is an attribute of the partition root object. Each server with a replica of a particular partition will have the replica pointer table.

The replica pointer table attribute is extremely important to the internal function of NDS. The values in this attribute are used to perform replica synchronization between NetWare 5 servers. For example, when the local replica receives an update from the client, the replica can find the physical location of the other replicas by using the information in the replica pointer table attribute.

The replica pointer tables for each server should be identical. If the replica pointer tables are not identical, your NDS will not be able to complete replica synchronization for the partition.

You can view the replica pointer table using either NWADMIN under the NDS Manager option or DSREPAIR. Figure 8.26 displays the replica pointer table for the [ROOT] partition as seen on NOR-SRV1 using the DSREPAIR utility under the Replica Ring option from the Replica and Partition Operations menu.

As mentioned earlier, the replica pointer table should be consistent across all servers that hold a copy of the partition. This means you should get the same results when viewing the replica ring using DSREPAIR, regardless of which server you execute it on.

The replica pointer table attribute contains a list of the replicas for a partition. For each replica on the server, the replica pointer table has an attribute, which contains the server name, replica type, replica state, replica number, and internal IPX address for each server holding replicas of that partition.

FIGURE 8.26

The replica pointer table for the [ROOT] partition as seen on NOR-SRV1 using the DSREPAIR utility

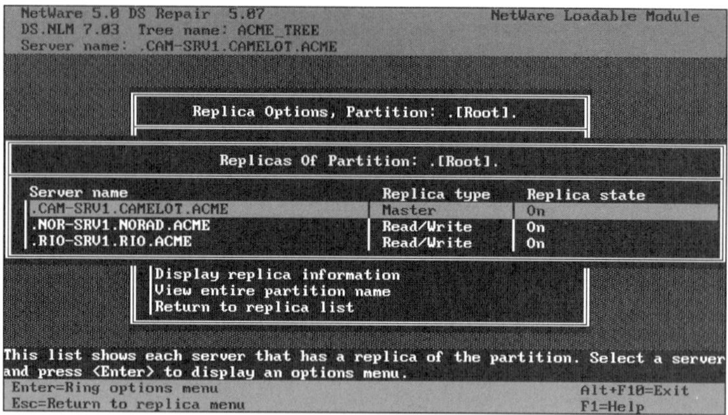

The replica pointer table attributes are as follows:

- **Server name** — The server name is the distinguished name of the server where the replica is physically located.
- **Replica type** — The replica type indicates the capabilities of the replica. The replica type will have one of the following values: 0=Master; 1=Read/Write (Secondary); 2=Read-Only; and 3=Subordinate Reference.
- **Replica state** — This value will typically be set to ON. During partition operations, a partition can go through several states. The states include On, New, Dying, Split, Join, and others. The complete list of replica states is provided in Table 8.1.
- **Replica number** — The replica number is assigned when the replica is created, by the master replica for the partition. Each replica for a partition has a unique number.
- **Partition root object ID** — This is the object ID of the partition root object on the server. The partition root object ID identifies the root-most NDS object of the partition. This value is valid only on the server that stores the local replica of the partition.

- **Number of addresses** — The network addresses for the server are held in this value. A server can be accessible over different protocols and will have different network addresses for each protocol. The number of addresses held in this value will depend on the number of protocols supported by the server. The IPX internal network number is always held in this value, which indicates the server's last known address. The address has three parts, including the address type (IPX, IP, and so on), address length, and address data.

The example of a replica pointer table in Figure 8.27 might help you understand how it looks. For this example, we will assume that the servers CAM-SRV1, NOR-SRV1, and TOK-SRV1 all hold replicas of the [ROOT] partition. It is also assumed that the servers NOR-SRV1, LABS-SRV1, and RD-SRV1 hold replicas of the NORAD partition. A logical representation for the replica pointer table for the [ROOT] partition on server CAM-SRV1 in the ACME tree is shown in the figure.

FIGURE 8.27

The replica pointer table for the [ROOT] partition on server CAM-SRV1 in the ACME tree

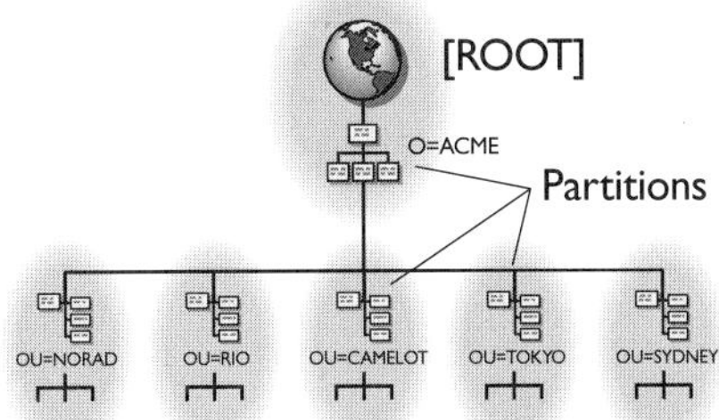

SERVER NAME	REPLICA TYPE	REPLICA STATE	REPLICA NUMBER	PARTITION ROOT OBJECT ID	ADDRESS
CAM-SRV1	READ/WRITE	ON	2	06001823	NET ADDRESS/ NODE/SOCKET
NOR-SRV1	MASTER	ON	1	50112030	NET/NODE/SOCKET
TOK-SRV1	READ/WRITE	ON	3	14830000	NET/NODE/SOCKET

A logical representation for the replica pointer table for the NORAD partition on server NOR-SRV1 in the ACME tree is shown in Figure 8.28.

FIGURE 8.28

The replica pointer table for the NORAD partition on server NOR-SRV1 in the ACME tree

SERVER NAME	REPLICA TYPE	REPLICA STATE	REPLICA NUMBER	PARTITION ROOT OBJECT ID	ADDRESS
NOR-SRV1	MASTER	ON	1	50112030	NET/NODE/SOCKET
LABS-SRV1	READ/WRITE	ON	3	81233010	NET/NODE/SOCKET
RD-SRV1	READ/WRITE	ON	2	61230010	NET/NODE/SOCKET
CAM-SRV1	SUBORDINATE REFERENCE	ON	5	06182300	NET/NODE/SOCKET
TOK-SRV1	SUBORDINATE REFERENCE	ON	4	14830000	NET/NODE/SOCKET

Synchronized Up To

The synchronized up to attribute is a multivalued attribute that contains a timestamp for each replica in the replica pointer table plus one for each replica on which modifications have been made. The timestamp indicates the last update and point in time that the local replica has received from other replicas of the partition. This attribute is often referred to as the *synchronized up to vector*.

The synchronized up to attribute is very important to the normal operation of NDS because using this list of timestamps, the replicas of the partition know what information to synchronize between servers. Since the synchronized up to attribute contains the timestamp for updates received for this replica up to a given time, other servers send updates only to this replica after that time. The synchronization process tests against it to determine if the other replicas on the other servers need updating. As mentioned earlier, this attribute is often referred to as the *vector* of timestamps for the server.

The Partition Creation Timestamp

The partition creation timestamp is the attribute that determines the epoch for the partition. The epoch indicates what instance of the partition this is and which replica number is the master. The epoch value starts with one and increments each time the repair timestamp operation is executed. The repair timestamp operation essentially changes the instance of the partition.

During the replica synchronization process, epoch values are compared to ensure that obsolete information is not passed.

Normal partition and replica operations preserve this partition creation timestamp, although an administrator can change it indirectly by using DSREPAIR and executing the repair timestamp function. Refer to Chapter 10, "NetWare 5

Features," before using the function to repair timestamps and declaring a new epoch.

The definitions of the partition creation timestamp attributes are given in the list that follows. The individual fields that make up the partition creation timestamp are the same as a regular timestamp. Although the data type or syntax of a timestamp is used, the parts of the timestamp are interpreted differently than those of a regular timestamp. The seconds, replica number, and event ID that make up the timestamp are defined as the following:

- **Seconds** — Holds the epoch counter, starting at 1 and incrementing sequentially.
- **Replica number** — Holds the replica number for the local replica that assigns the epoch for the partition. This is the replica number that holds the master replica.
- **Event ID** — Not used.

The Inherited Access Control List

The inherited access control list attribute contains the access control information inherited from all the previous parent partitions. The attribute is a summary or cumulative effect of all the access control lists inherited from parent containers down to the object's context in the tree.

The access control list attribute helps the server calculate the rights of the objects more quickly because the security information is local. This means that when calculating rights, the server does not have to go to other servers to find the security or rights information. A server should be able to make access control decisions using only local information.

NDS would be poorly designed if it forced the server to walk the tree and gather all the security or rights information for the users each time they accessed data. The inherited rights access control list attribute of the partition provides the capability of the server to look only at the local partition information to determine security rights all the way back to the [ROOT] object.

Partition Control

The partition control attribute tracks the progress of partition operations. However, its primary job is to lock out further partition operations until the current one is completed. The partition operations are split or create partition, join or merge partition, change replica type, move subtree, and repair timestamps. The add replica and delete replica operations are not tracked by the partition control attribute.

Typically, the partition will sequence through several states as the partition operation progresses. These states are the same used for the replica states. (See the "Server Partition Table" section earlier in this chapter.)

Because each replica of a partition can have only one state, there can be only one partition operation in progress at a time. The master replica of the partition controls the partition operations and acts as a traffic cop.

The partition operation in progress will use the partition control functions defined in Table 8.2.

TABLE 8.2

The Partition Control Function Definitions

FUNCTION	VALUE	DESCRIPTION
PC_IDLE	0	No operation in progress
PC_SPLITTING	1	Splitting
PC_SPLITTING_CHILD	2	Splitting child partition
PC_JOINING_UP	3	Child of two joining partitions
PC_JOINING_DOWN	4	Parent of two joining partitions
PC_MOVE_SUBTREE_SRC	5	Source of the move subtree
PC_MOVE_SUBTREE_DEST	6	Destination of the move subtree
PC_LOCKED	7	Partition locked
PC_REPAIRING_TIMESTAMPS	8	Timestamps being repaired
PC_CHANGING_REPLICATYPE	9	Replicas changing types

Replica Up To

New in NetWare 5 is a structure called the replica up to vector. The replica up to vector has been added to the partition root object of each partition. This attribute contains a timestamp for each replica that is used to represent the purge time for a replica. It is called the *replica up to vector* because there is a timestamp for each replica. This attribute is localized to a particular server, which means that it is not synchronized to the other servers.

Since replica up to is kept as a vector with an entry for each replica, the replica convergence can be achieved without having each replica talk to every other replica. The structure of the replica up to vector consists of received up to time stamps for all replicas in a given replica ring. The structure of the replica up to vector includes this information:

- **Flags** — Replica-specific information
- **Server** — The ID of the server that holds the replica
- **Received up to vector** — Time vector for the replica

One entry exists for each replica in the ring. However, subordinate reference replicas do not have an entry in the replica up to vector structure, which means that the subordinate reference replicas will no longer participate with the normal replica synchronization.

The replica synchronization process uses the replica up to time vector to determine which replicas it needs to synchronize with. Each server has a replica up to vector that keeps track of how up to date each replica is. After successful synchronization, the receiver merges the replica up to vector with that of the sender.

Partition Status

The partition status attribute provides information about the success or failure of the last replica synchronization cycle. The attribute could contain Directory Services error codes, if necessary. For more information about the Directory Services error codes, refer to Appendix B.

Bindery Services

In previous versions of NetWare, information was not available from a distributed Directory. Instead, each server in the network stored a database that contained information such as the name, object ID, and password of every user or object that had access to the services provided by that server. The bindery also included information about all the services provided by the server and network.

Because the servers in the network did not share or communicate this information, the user's or object's information was stored separately on every server to which it had rights. For example, if user BTHOMAS had rights to NetWare 3 servers called NCS, ENG1, and MKTG1, his information was stored on each of the three NetWare 3 servers. Each time BTHOMAS wanted to access services on a different server, he would have to establish a connection and log into that server.

Starting with NetWare 4 and continuing with NetWare 5, Directory Services provides the network user with a single login to the entire network with access to additional network resources as needed. The user does not have to log into each server to gain the resources on that server. Instead, Directory Services automatically authenticates the user to the server. The authentication process is completed seamlessly for the user.

However, in order for Directory Services to support backward compatibility for the bindery application and users, it provides the object information to these users through bindery services. These services are on a server-by-server basis. Bindery services enables the objects in a container to be accessed by both NDS clients and bindery-based servers and clients.

Unlike the NDS tree, which is hierarchical, objects in the bindery have no hierarchical relationship (a flat structure), and these objects are specific to one server. To provide access for bindery users and clients, NDS imitates a flat structure for leaf objects within one or more container objects.

The Server Bindery Context

The server bindery context is the name of the container object(s) where bindery services is set for the server. The server bindery context is also referred to as the *bindery path*. You can set the bindery context using a SET command at the console.

In order to set the bindery context for the server NOR-SRV1 in the ACME tree, enter the following command at the server console prompt:

```
SET BINDERY CONTEXT = "OU=NORAD.O=ACME"
```

Bindery-based clients and servers can access the objects subordinate to the containers where the bindery context is set. Because NetWare 5 enables you to set multiple bindery contexts for the server, the handling of the invalid context error has changed. NetWare 5 cannot fail the entire SET command, because one of the containers specified may be valid.

In order to see or verify the effective bindery path for a server, you should enter the following command at the server console prompt:

```
CONFIG
```

When you check the effective bindery path by using the CONFIG command, you will see the distinguished names of each NDS container object listed on separate lines. Each container listed here is a valid bindery path. Objects created through bindery services are created as subordinate to the first effective (or valid) bindery path.

In previous versions of NetWare 4, you were limited to setting the bindery context at only one container object. With NetWare 4.11 and NetWare 5, you can set up to sixteen container objects as the bindery context.

Multiple Bindery Contexts

When multiple bindery contexts have been defined, a client searches for a bindery object by looking through the containers in the order they appear in the list.

Setting multiple bindery contexts can create one potential problem, which is known as *eclipsing*. In NDS, two objects can have the same relative distinguished name, but the objects must be in different containers. For example, in Figure 8.29, there are two user objects created in the ACME tree, each with the relative distinguished name of JOHN. These objects exist in the OU=OPS and OU=PR containers. This example assumes that the server bindery context is set to both the OU=OPS and OU=PR containers in that order.

FIGURE 8.29

There are two user objects created in the ACME tree with the relative distinguished name of JOHN. These objects exist in the OU=OPS and OU=PR containers.

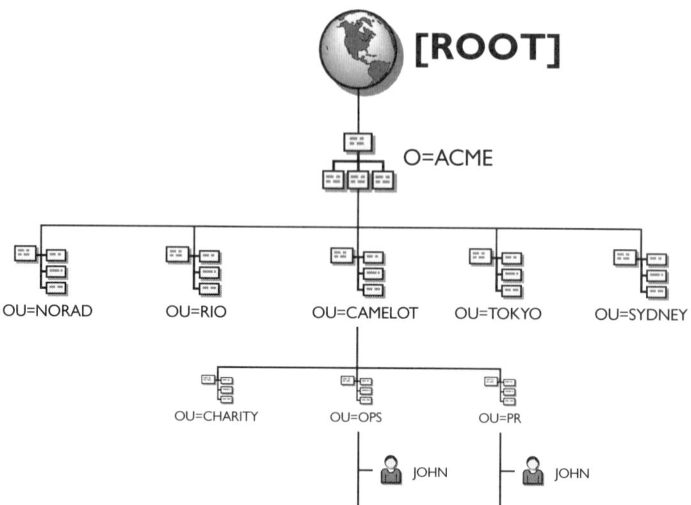

NDS distinguishes between the two objects because their distinguished names are different. However, the bindery client sees only the object's relative distinguished name. If a bindery client searches for the object JOHN, it finds an object in OU=OPS first and stops searching, whether or not that is the object the client is looking for. In this situation, the client is unable to access the object JOHN in the OU=PR container. This effect is called *eclipsing* and occurs only in bindery services, not in NDS.

You can solve this problem by making sure that no two objects in the NDS tree have the same relative distinguished name. A good naming standard is important and should be enforced.

Eclipsing also occurs when a dynamic bindery object has the same name as a static bindery object, although this situation is rare. In such cases, the dynamic object always eclipses the static object.

Objects in the Bindery

The bindery used in previous versions of NetWare enabled two categories of objects. These objects classes are as follows:

- Static bindery objects
- Dynamic bindery objects

These object categories are specified by a flag on the object itself. The difference between the two categories (static and dynamic) refers to the longevity expected for each of the objects rather than a specific type of object.

Static Bindery Objects

The static bindery objects consist of the normal user, group, print queue, print server, and profile objects defined in the bindery of NetWare 3. These objects are created permanently in the bindery until someone manually deletes them.

When migrated, the static bindery objects are stored in NDS container objects specified in the bindery context of the NetWare 5 server. If multiple containers are specified in the bindery context, the objects are migrated or placed in the first valid container in the bindery path.

The NDS schema defines what attributes each object class has, thus regulating the makeup or creation of each object class. The NetWare 3 bindery is not hierarchical and does not need to distinguish objects by classes. Therefore, the bindery does not have formal schema definitions. However, the bindery does enable specific object types. These object types are used to identify the object within the bindery. For example, objects of type 1 are user objects and group objects are type 2.

Some of the well-known object types have direct counterparts in the NDS schema and can be converted or mutated during installation, migration, or creation. The mutation occurs for object types from the bindery to the appropriate NDS object class. For each bindery object type to be mutated, it must have all the mandatory attributes of the targeted NDS object class and cannot have the same name as another object in the container.

The bindery object types that are mutated by NDS are as follows:

- User
- Group
- Print queue

- Print server
- Profile

For example, a client using a bindery-based application wants to create a user object called JOE on a NetWare 5 server in the NDS tree. The application makes a bindery API to create a user object. The request is made as follows:

```
CN=JOE+BinderyType = 1
```

The base object class is a bindery object type. The data are immediately converted to an NDS user object class, and the name then becomes:

```
CN=JOE
```

TIP

Not all the NDS objects in the tree are available or visible to the bindery APIs. Bindery services applies only to leaf objects that are in the NetWare 3 bindery definitions, including the objects for user, group, print queue, print server, and profile. Also included is the bindery object base class CN=XXXX+BinderyType=643.

Dynamic Bindery Objects

The dynamic bindery objects are used for Service Advertising Protocol object names and information. This allows the advertising servers or services to have their objects added to the bindery as dynamic objects. For example, these objects are the file server and print server names that use SAP to become known on the network. In NetWare 5 additional services use SAP to become known, such as the NDS tree and time synchronization.

If the bindery is closed and reopened, these objects and their properties are automatically deleted. Figure 8.30 illustrates how the information from the network would be directed logically to the appropriate section of the bindery according to the type of information.

Figure 8.30 is a logical representation of the bindery services. In reality, the bindery does not have separate sections for dynamic and static information. All bindery information is stored in the bindery files. The properties of the dynamic objects are mostly network addresses.

FIGURE 8.30

NetWare 3 bindery information from the network is directed to the appropriate section of the bindery according to the type of information.

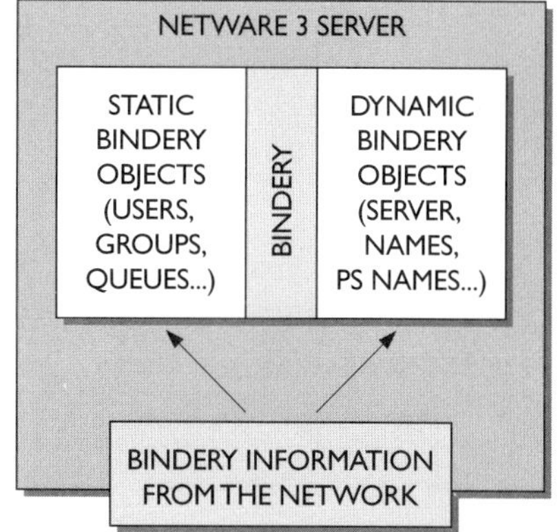

In order for NetWare 5 to be completely compatible with previous versions of NetWare, the dynamic bindery objects need to be supported. Since the bindery no longer stores objects in NetWare 5, NDS must provide this functionality.

The parent objects of dynamic bindery objects are not in the NDS hierarchy. They are not associated with a specific parent container in the tree. Instead, the dynamic bindery objects are stored in the NDS internal partition called the Bindery partition. These objects can be accessed by a bindery client or server and are not dependent on whether the bindery context is set for the server.

Figure 8.31 illustrates logically how the information from the network would be directed to the appropriate section of NDS to provide the same function as the bindery.

FIGURE 8.31

Information from the network is directed to the appropriate section of NDS to provide the same function as the bindery.

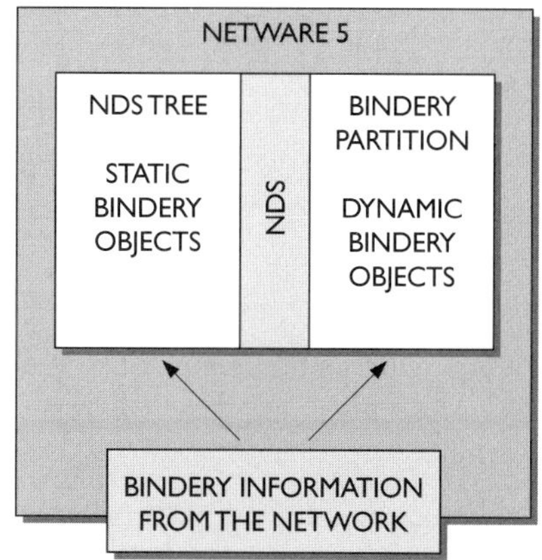

Figure 8.31, like Figure 8.30, is a logical representation of NDS. In reality, the Directory does not have separate sections for the dynamic bindery object information. All the dynamic bindery objects are located physically adjacent to the other NDS objects in the NDS data files. See Figure 8.32 for an illustration of the object data file in NDS. The properties of the dynamic objects are mostly network addresses.

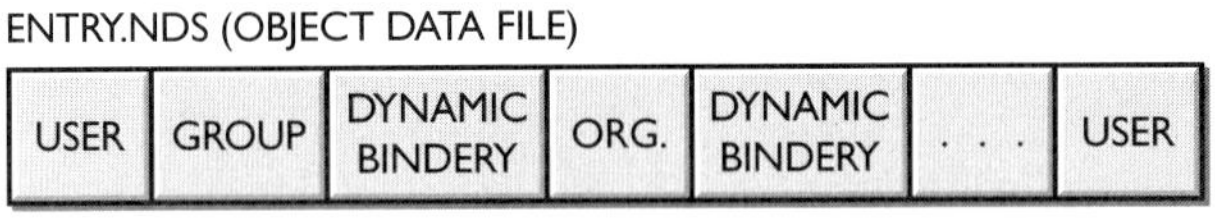

FIGURE 8.32

An example of the object data file in NDS. Notice that the dynamic bindery objects are stored adjacent to all the other NDS objects.

ENTRY.NDS (OBJECT DATA FILE)

USER	GROUP	DYNAMIC BINDERY	ORG.	DYNAMIC BINDERY	. . .	USER

The Bindery Supervisor Account

The bindery Supervisor account is created during the installation of the server. The Supervisor is a server-centric account created on every NetWare 5 server. This account is created even when NDS replicas are installed on that server or when a bindery services context is set on the server. However, the Supervisor user is only accessible if a valid bindery context is set for the server. This is true with the exception of the Server Console Lock and Unlock operation, which can be performed using the Supervisor password.

The Supervisor account is not seen as an object of the NDS tree because it is server-centric. The Supervisor user is stored in the bindery partition, which is one of the four partitions that exists even if an NDS replica is not installed on the server.

The Supervisor account has all rights to the individual server, which includes the objects and file system. This is the same as NetWare 3. If there is a bindery services context(s) set on the server, the Supervisor user will automatically have all rights to the bindery objects in the context(s). The Supervisor account has rights only to the NDS objects that are also bindery objects. For example, these objects are users, groups, queues, print servers, and profiles. The profile object was first made available in the bindery by the NetWare Name Service (NNS) product.

Since the Supervisor user does not show up in the NDS tree, you cannot log in as Supervisor using an NDS connection. This means that the NWADMIN utility cannot be used by someone logged in as Supervisor. The Supervisor account can only access the objects using the SYSCON utility in NetWare 3.

Consulting Experience

Although it is possible to use the administrative utilities such as NWADMIN to create an object in the Novell Directory Services tree called SUPERVISOR, the new user is not the same Supervisor user seen in the bindery. Any modifications made to the bindery Supervisor account are limited to bindery-based modifications. The individual logging in as the Supervisor user has to have a bindery connection to the server and use the bindery-based utilities.

The Supervisor account will always be assigned a password during creation. This was not the case in previous versions of NetWare 4 (specifically NetWare 4.01) because the individual installing the server was not required to have a password. The Supervisor user receives its password during creation under the following conditions:

- The server is a new NetWare 5 server that is not migrated from NetWare 3. The Supervisor is assigned the password of the user, typically the ADMIN user, that logs into the tree to perform the installation of the server.
- The server is being migrated from NetWare 3 to NetWare 5 using the INSTALL.NLM program. The Supervisor account information remains the same as before the upgrade. If the Supervisor account in NetWare 3 does not have a password, the password of the user (usually ADMIN) that logged in to the tree to do the installation is assigned to the bindery Supervisor in NetWare 5.
- The server is being migrated from NetWare 3 to NetWare 5 using the Novell Upgrade Wizard utility. When you migrate using the Upgrade Wizard utility, the NetWare 5 server is already installed and running. This means that the Supervisor account on the new NetWare 5 server is already created and has a password. The password is created according to the first condition in this list. Although the Upgrade Wizard utility does move passwords from NetWare 3 to NDS, it does not change the password for the Supervisor account using the password from the NetWare 3 server, since the Supervisor account on the NetWare 5 server is not stored in NDS.

It is very important that you safeguard the password for the Supervisor. The password that the Supervisor is assigned is not completely synchronized with the user that installs the new NetWare 5 server into the tree. If the ADMIN user ever changes its password, the password for the Supervisor account is not changed. The two accounts are completely separate after the initial installation.

The DS Client

We typically think of clients as the workstation software that logs the user into the network and accesses the network services. However, each NetWare 5 server uses the built-in NDS client software to attach and authenticate the server to the other NetWare 5 servers. Thus, the servers become clients of the other servers in the NDS tree. The client software used to support server-to-server connections is called the Directory Services client or DS client.

Since NDS is distributed and replicated among any of the NetWare 5 servers in the network, one server may need the NDS information stored by another server. This mechanism provides the interconnectivity needed to support all the NDS multiple server operations and processes. The DS client is sometimes referred to as the *virtual client*. (This term is used mainly in DSTRACE.)

The NetWare 5 servers use the same protocol as the workstation software to establish and authenticate to the other servers. The authentication process is initiated as a background authentication procedure.

Consulting Experience

If your servers are communicating using IPX, then it is very important that you do not filter the Routing Information Protocol (RIP) from your NetWare 5 network. If RIP is being filtered, the NetWare 5 servers will not be able to find each other to synchronize. Directory Services stores the addresses for the other NetWare 5 servers in its replica pointer table; however, it needs to find the route using RIP.

The connection made by the DS client between NetWare 5 servers is viewed in the MONITOR utility on the server. The connections made from server to server will authenticate using the distinguished name of the NetWare 5 server object. These connections are marked with an asterisk (*) character to indicate that the connection is not a licensed connection but rather an authenticated Directory Services connection.

Figure 8.33 shows the DS client connections made between servers on the MONITOR screen for the servers CAM-SRV1 and NOR-SRV1 in the ACME tree.

FIGURE 8.33

These DS client connections are made between servers on the MONITOR screen for the servers CAM-SRV1 and NOR-SRV1 in the ACME tree.

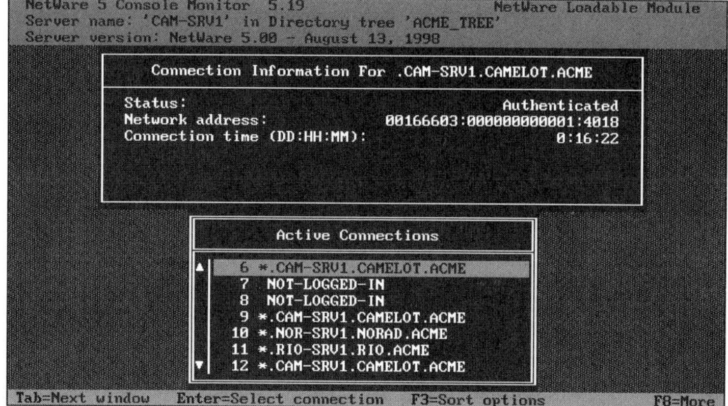

The messages related to the DS client can be viewed on the Directory Services screen at the server console using the SET DSTRACE command VCLIENT (VC or virtual client). The command is entered as follows:

```
SET DSTRACE = +VCLIENT
```

The other NetWare 5 servers occupy not only many of the Directory Services connections but also the NOT LOGGED IN connections that may be shown on the MONITOR screen. Other NetWare 5 servers perform the name resolution operation using the NOT LOGGED IN connection type and do not need to authenticate.

Name Resolution (Tree Walking) Operation

NDS's primary responsibility is to retrieve requested object or network resource information from the servers distributed across the network. NDS locates the object information using the operation or mechanism called *name resolution*. This operation walks the partitions of the NDS tree to locate objects or specific information requested by the user or client. Name resolution occurs when the client requests NDS object information from Directory Services and the NetWare 5 servers. If the object information is not on the server to which the client is connected, the process will walk or navigate through the partitions on the other NetWare 5 servers to find the correct information. The name resolution process is often called *tree walking*.

The name resolution operation starts with a distinguished name for an NDS object in the tree and attempts to obtain the object ID for the searched object on a specific server. The name resolution returns a list of addresses for servers that store the requested object information. Before we discuss the specific details associated with the name resolution operation, we need to quickly review the concepts of NDS partitions and replicas.

NDS Partition Review

As mentioned previously, the NDS tree can be divided into pieces or subtrees called partitions and stored on the NetWare 5 servers as NDS replicas. Partitioning provides distribution of the Directory Services information across the NetWare 5 servers.

Each partition is named by the container object at the root of the subtree called the partition root object. The partition root objects have additional properties or attributes that are used to find the NDS information on other servers and keep it synchronized. These additional attributes are as follows:

- **Replica pointer table** — Stores the list of replicas for the partition.
- **Synchronized up to** — Contains a timestamp for each replica in the replica pointer table.

- **Partition creation timestamp** — Determines the epoch for the partition.
- **Inherited access control list** — Contains access control information inherited from the parent partitions.
- **Partition control** — Tracks the progress of partition operations like splitting, joining, change replica type, and move subtree operations.
- **Partition status** — Contains information regarding the last synchronization attempt.

For more information about the partition root object, refer to the section about the partition root object earlier in this chapter.

Subordinate Reference Replica Review

Different types of replicas can be stored on the NetWare 5 servers. These replicas are the physical representation of the NDS tree. The replica type that helps the NDS tree stay physically connected is the subordinate reference replica. A subordinate reference replica is created by Directory Services on a server that holds a replica of the parent partition but not the child partitions.

The subordinate reference replica for a partition does not contain all of the objects in that partition. Instead, the subordinate reference contains only a copy of the partition root object (or the topmost object of the partition), including all its properties and attributes.

Since the subordinate reference replica holds a copy of the partition root object, it contains information such as the location of all the other replicas for the partition. An example of the contents of a subordinate reference replica for the partition CAMELOT, which is stored on server NOR-SRV1, is shown in Figure 8.34.

The replica pointer table property contains a list of the replicas for a partition. The list holds the server name, replica type, replica state, replica number, object ID for the partition root object, and addresses for each of the servers in the replica pointer table. Using this information, the subordinate reference replicas not only keep the NDS tree connected but also can aid in the procedure to resolve a name.

FIGURE 8.34

A subordinate reference replica for the partition CAMELOT, which is stored on server NOR-SRV1, contains the replica pointer table for the partition.

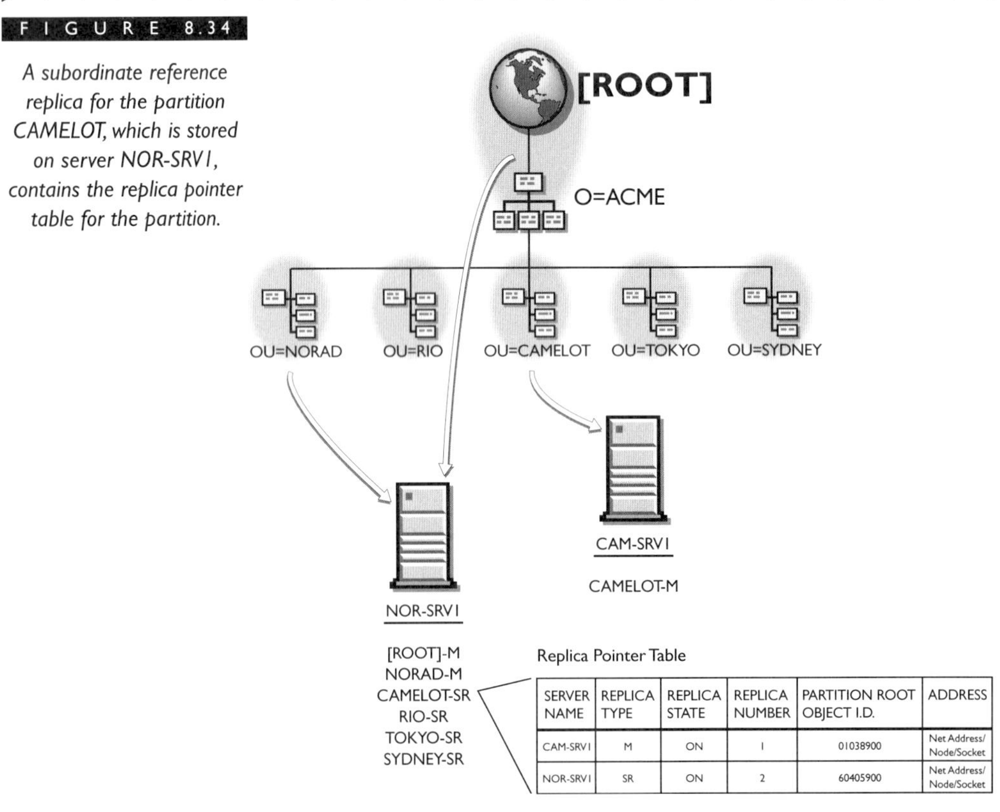

SERVER NAME	REPLICA TYPE	REPLICA STATE	REPLICA NUMBER	PARTITION ROOT OBJECT I.D.	ADDRESS
CAM-SRV1	M	ON	1	01038900	Net Address/ Node/Socket
NOR-SRV1	SR	ON	2	60405900	Net Address/ Node/Socket

Name Resolution Methods

The purpose of the name resolution or tree walking mechanism is to eliminate the necessity of the user's or client's awareness of the physical location of network resources. The term *name resolution* literally means resolving a name to an address; in this case, the address of the server where the requested object is stored.

In Figure 8.35 the client or workstation requests information about an NDS object. Because the client is currently authenticated to the server CAM-SRV1, that server will try to fulfill the request. Unable to fulfill the request, CAM-SRV1 walks the tree on behalf of the client. In this case, CAM-SRV1 contacts the server NOR-SRV1. The server NOR-SRV1 returns its lack of success. CAM-SRV1 contacts RIO-SRV1, which responds negatively. This process continues until the requested object information is located on SYD-SRV1. The physical location information is returned to the client. The client, in turn, connects directly to SYD-SRV1 to read the object information.

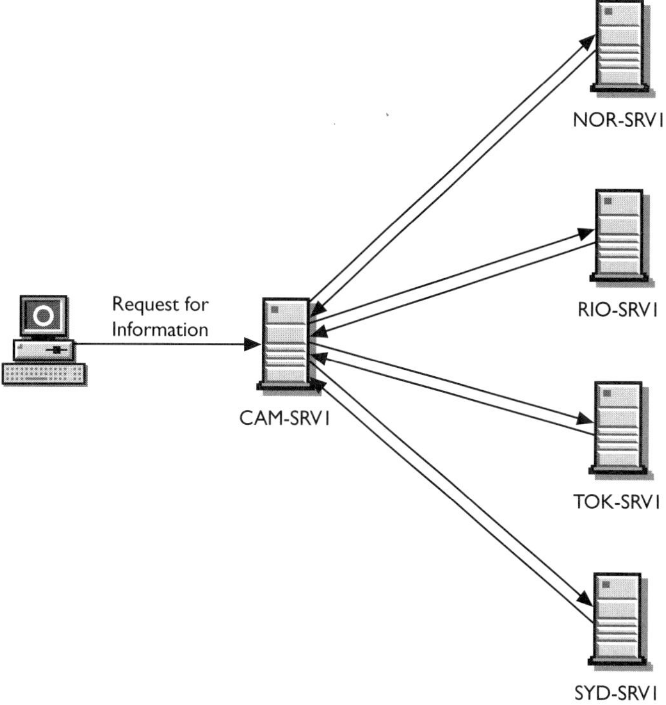

FIGURE 8.35

The workstation makes a request for information about an NDS object to the server CAM-SRV1. Then the server CAM-SRV1 will contact the other servers to find the object.

The name resolution requests are made for only specific replica types. Even though the server may have the object information requested, it may not have the right type of replica to support the request made by the client. For example, the client wants to modify a certain object. If a read-only replica responds, it will not help. The replica type is an important part of the request for name resolution.

The name resolution operation is used to access resources and find object information during login and authentication. In other words, a client requesting information about an object is serviced by the server using the name resolution or tree walking process in the following ways:

- Object found on the local server

- Walk down the tree to locate the object
- Walk up the tree to locate the object
- Walk up and down the tree to locate the object
- Server without a replica

When the client makes the request for object information, the distinguished name of the object is always used. NDS uses the individual relative distinguished name (RDN) to compare against the values at each server. Using this method, Directory Services will determine if the information is on the local servers or whether it needs to go to other servers holding information up or down the tree.

If the current NetWare 5 server contains a replica with the requested object information or target object, NDS completes the request by returning the physical location of the object information. In this case, the physical location of the object information is returned to the client. The physical location is the network address for the local server. If Directory Services determines that the name resolution operation will have to walk the tree (up or down), the local server acts as a proxy on behalf of the client to contact the other NetWare 5 servers.

Assuming that the object information exists down the tree from the information stored on the local server, the server will read the replica pointer table (replica ring) for the partitions that are down the tree. The server can use subordinate references replicas to locate the server(s) holding the child partition. In a very interesting twist, the name resolution operation will use the attributes of the subordinate reference replicas to navigate up the tree to locate the servers that store replicas for the parent partition. We will discuss the details of each case in the following sections.

Object Found on the Local Server

When the client makes the request for object information, it passes the distinguished name to the server it is connected to. If the NetWare 5 server contains a replica with the requested object information or target object, NDS completes the request by passing the physical location of the object information back to the client. In this case, the physical location of the object information is the network address of the local server. The client then makes the read request for the specific object or property information.

For example, a workstation is connected to the server NOR-SRV1 in the ACME tree. The server NOR-SRV1 holds the master replicas of the NORAD and [ROOT] partitions as illustrated in Figure 8.36.

FIGURE 8.36

The workstation is connected to the server NOR-SRV1 in the ACME tree. The server holds replicas of the NORAD and [ROOT] partitions.

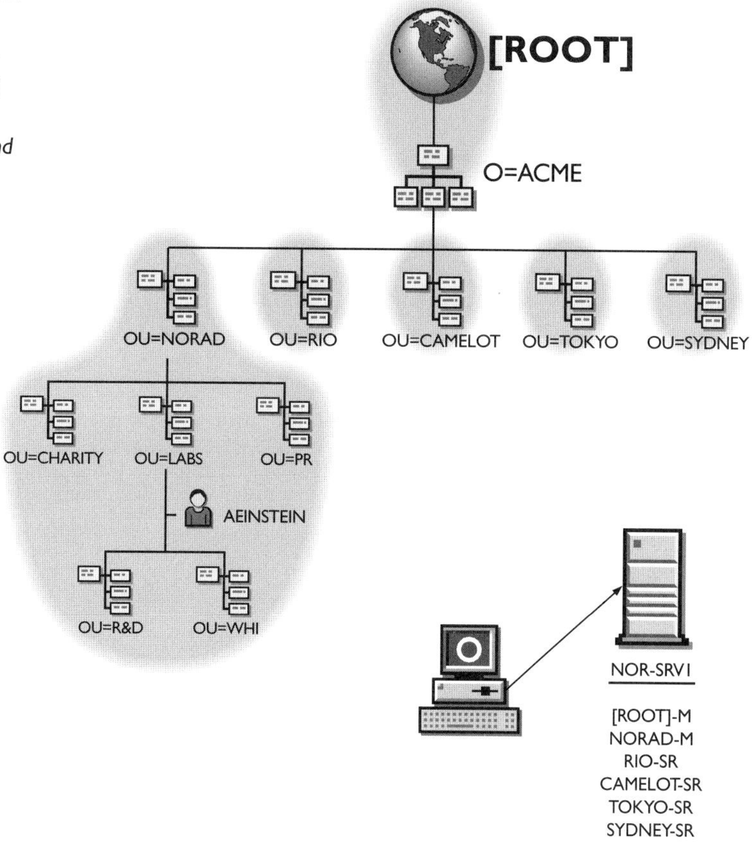

The workstation requests the location information about the user object AEINSTEIN.LABS.NORAD.ACME. The server NOR-SRV1 will check first to see if it has a copy of the requested object. Because NOR-SRV1 holds a replica (master replica) of the partition that contains the object information, it returns the physical location of the object information and the object ID back to the workstation. In this case, the physical location of the object information is the network address of NOR-SRV1. The workstation can then continue or complete the request (read, modify, and so on).

Walk down the Tree to Locate the Object

If the object information is not found on the local server, Directory Services will determine that it needs to either walk down or up the tree based on the distinguished name of the object being requested. The direction that the Directory will search, either up or down, is determined using a partial match on the distinguished name.

The matching that occurs for the names is processed from the root-to-leaf (top-down). Any given name is matched object by object or parent by parent, checking each of the subordinate objects. The name is processed in this fashion until the object is found, or the names do not match and there is not a subordinate object for the parent. The subordinate reference replicas are then read (if going down), and the process continues on the next server.

If Directory Services has determined that it must walk down the tree, the server that the workstation originally connected to uses the subordinate reference replicas of the name being located. Remember, the subordinate reference replicas are created on servers that have a copy of the parent partition but not the child partition. Therefore, each server that has a replica of a parent partition will know the location of each child partition using the subordinate reference replicas.

In this case, the subordinate reference replica of the partition is used to provide the best partial match to the distinguished name of the object requested. Using the DS client, the server will connect to the nearest server holding a correct replica type of the child partition based on a least-cost route.

For example, the workstation is connected to the server NOR-SRV1 in the ACME tree. The ACME tree is partitioned at each of the major cities. The NORAD partition is further partitioned at OU=R&D and OU=WHI as shown in Figure 8.37. The partitions [ROOT] and NORAD are held by the server NOR-SRV1. The servers R&D-SRV1 and WHI-SRV1 hold the master replicas of their respective partitions as illustrated.

A workstation sends a request to NOR-SRV1 for the information about the user object LDAVINCI.R&D.LABS.NORAD.ACME. NDS will check it first to see if it has a copy of the requested object. Since NOR-SRV1 does not hold the object information, DS must look on another server.

DS compares each segment of the distinguished name of the object with the information stored on the server. By comparing and matching the names available on the server, the name resolution operation determines whether the object information is subordinate (down) the tree or up the tree.

FIGURE 8.37

The workstation is connected to the server NOR-SRV1 in the ACME tree. The server NOR-SRV1 holds replicas of the NORAD and [ROOT] partitions. The servers R&D-SRV1 and WHI-SRV1 hold the master replicas of their respective partitions.

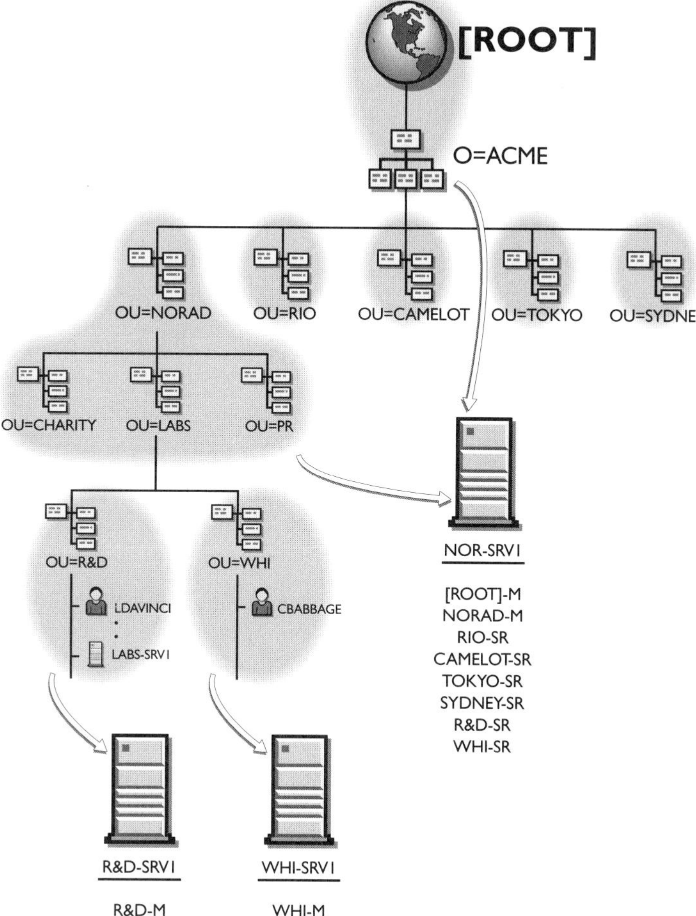

Determining that the object information is down the tree, the server that the workstation originally connected to will walk the NDS tree as a proxy agent on behalf of the workstation. In this case, the NOR-SRV1 will perform the proxy for the workstation. In order to locate the servers that contain the lower-level partitions, the server NOR-SRV1 uses the subordinate reference replicas that will go down according to the name matched. In this case, the R&D subordinate reference replica is used. The server NOR-SRV1 will read the replica pointer table for the R&D subordinate reference replica as shown in Figure 8.38.

FIGURE 8.38

The replica pointer table for the R&D partition. The replica pointer table is an attribute of a replica. In this case, the replica is the subordinate reference replica stored on the server NOR-SRV1.

SERVER NAME	REPLICA TYPE	REPLICA STATE	REPLICA NUMBER	PARTITION ROOT OBJECT I.D.	ADDRESS
R&D-SRV1	M	ON	1	06040000	Net Address/ Node/Socket
NOR-SRV1	SR	ON	2	14015016	Net Address/ Node/Socket

Using this information, the NOR-SRV1 will connect to the R&D-SRV1 using the DS client software (server-to-server connection). Because the server R&D-SRV1 holds the requested object information for LDAVINCI.R&D.LABS. NORAD.ACME, the tree walking phase is completed. The server R&D-SRV1 verifies to NOR-SRV1 that it has a copy of the object information. In turn, the server NOR-SRV1 returns the physical location of the object information back to the workstation. In this case, the physical location of the object information is the network address of R&D-SRV1. DS automatically authenticates the workstation to the server R&D-SRV1 to access or read the object information associated with the request.

Figure 8.39 logically illustrates the following name resolution steps that were performed for the preceding example:

1. The workstation makes a request to access specific object information. The server NOR-SRV1 receives the request.

2. The object information is not stored on the NOR-SRV1 server. The server checks the R&D subordinate reference replica and reads the replica pointer table for the R&D partition.

3. The server NOR-SRV1 makes a request for the object information to the server R&D-SRV1.

4. The server R&D-SRV1 sends a list of the physical locations of the object plus the object IDs. In this case, it is the server address of R&D-SRV1.

5. The list is returned to the workstation of the servers that contain the object location. In this case, the server R&D-SRV1 is the only server.

6. Directory Services automatically connects the workstation to server R&D-SRV1 to provide access to the object information.

FIGURE 8.39

Name resolution steps

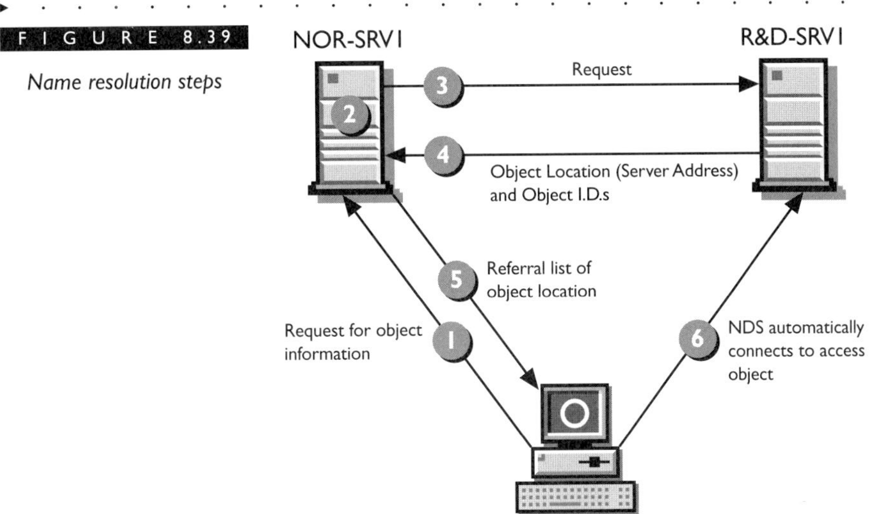

Requested Object Information on Multiple Servers

Consider the preceding example in which the workstation is requesting object information for the user object LDAVINCI.R&D.LABS.NORAD.ACME. Let's discuss what would happen if the server WHI-SRV1 also holds a read/write replica for the R&D partition. In this case, the replica pointer table for the partition R&D would appear as shown in Figure 8.40.

If more than one server holds a replica or copy of the partition that contains the information, DS will take that into account. Once the object information is located and the list of servers that can satisfy the request is found, a referral list (list of server addresses) is built from the replica pointer table of the object's partition. The server builds the referral list and passes it back to the client. This client may be the DS client of the current NetWare 5 server performing the proxy for the workstation. Again, the referral list is the list of all the server addresses that have the requested replica type for the partition.

FIGURE 8.40

SERVER NAME	REPLICA TYPE	REPLICA STATE	REPLICA NUMBER	PARTITION ROOT OBJECT I.D.	ADDRESS
R&D-SRV1	M	ON	1	06040000	Net Address/ Node/Socket
NOR-SRV1	SR	ON	2	14015016	Net Address/ Node/Socket
WHI-SRV1	R/W	ON	3	83621020	Net Address/ Node/Socket

The replica pointer table for the partition R&D with the WHI-SRV1 added. The WHI-SRV1 server has a read/write replica of the partition.

When the current server has found the referral list of servers by proxy for the workstation, it passes the list to the workstation. Once this referral list is received by the workstation, it makes a Routing Information Protocol (RIP) request for each server in the referral list. The purpose of the RIP requests is to determine which server is the closest according to the least-cost route. It is the responsibility of the workstation to determine the costing for each server based on a least-cost algorithm (number of ticks).

Walk up the Tree to Locate the Object

If Directory Services determines that it needs to walk up the tree, the servers use the replica pointer tables from the root-most partition stored on the server to find other NetWare 5 servers in the tree. In the previous example (walking down the tree), the subordinate references were used to locate object information lower in the tree. Well, the subordinate reference replicas stored in the replica pointer table of a server can also be used to walk up the tree to find an object.

Remember, the replica pointer table for a replica contains all the server names, server addresses, replica types, and so on for a particular partition. Using the information contained in a replica pointer table of a partition, DS can determine not only where the child partitions are but also the names and addresses for the server that holds copies of the parent partition.

DS creates a subordinate reference replica on a server that holds a replica of the parent partition but not the child partitions. Thus, it can be reasoned that a server holding a replica of the child partition will have knowledge of the parent servers storing the subordinate references. To illustrate how the information in the replica pointer table can be used to walk up the tree, see Figure 8.41.

For this example, assume that a workstation is connected to the server R&D-SRV1. The workstation requests information about the user object ADMIN.ACME. NDS will check the server R&D-SRV1 first to see if it has a copy of the requested object. Because R&D-SRV1 does not hold the object information, DS must look on another server.

FIGURE 8.41

The server NOR-SRV1 in the ACME tree holds replicas of the NORAD and [ROOT] partitions with subordinate reference replicas as needed. The servers R&D-SRV1 and WHI-SRV1 hold the master replicas of their respective partitions. The server WHI-SRV1 holds a read/write replica for the R&D partition.

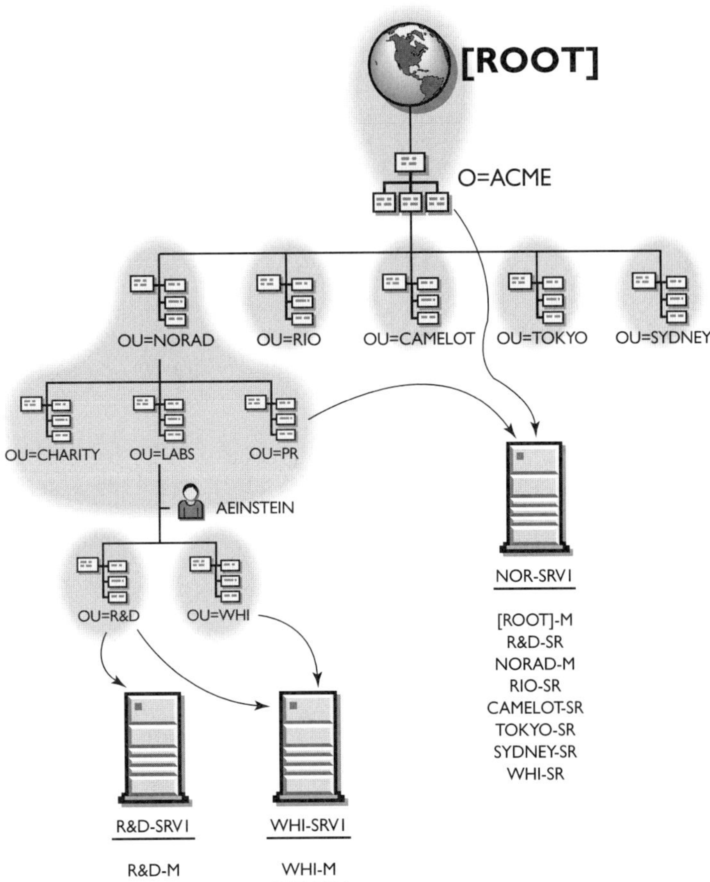

DS compares names and determines that the object information is up the tree. The server R&D-SRV1 will begin walking the NDS tree as a proxy agent on behalf of the workstation. In order to locate the servers that contain the upper-level information, the server will read the replica pointer table for the R&D partition as shown in Figure 8.42.

FIGURE 8.42

The replica pointer table for the partition R&D. The replica pointer table is the same on every server that stored a replica of the R&D partition. In this case, there are replicas on the servers R&D-SRV1 (master replica), WHI-SRV1 (read/write replica), and NOR-SRV1 (subordinate reference replica).

SERVER NAME	REPLICA TYPE	REPLICA STATE	REPLICA NUMBER	PARTITION ROOT OBJECT I.D.	ADDRESS
R&D-SRV1	M	ON	1	06040000	Net Address/ Node/Socket
NOR-SRV1	SR	ON	2	14015016	Net Address/ Node/Socket
WHI-SRV1	R/W	ON	3	83261020	Net Address/ Node/Socket

The replica pointer is an attribute of the partition root object of a replica, which means that this information is available on every server that stores a replica of the partition. In this case, there are replicas on the servers R&D-SRV1 (master replica), WHI-SRV1 (read/write replica), and NOR-SRV1 (subordinate reference replica).

By reading the replica pointer table, the server R&D-SRV1 sorts the server addresses according to least cost and contacts one. Either one of these addresses could have the object information. If the server WHI-SRV1 is contacted, then it reads its root-most partition and returns the referral list. In this case, WHI-SRV1 is no closer than R&D-SRV1. Next, the server NOR-SRV1 is contacted. NOR-SRV1 is able to match the name and find the object. The location and object ID are returned in the referral list to R&D-SRV1. In turn, R&D-SRV1 sends the referral list to the client.

You may think that because the server NOR-SRV1 holds the subordinate reference replica, it would be given preference as the first server to contact. However, servers with subordinate reference replicas are not given preference over other servers in the replica pointer table of the server R&D.

No Subordinate Reference Replicas for a Partition

It is possible for a NetWare 5 server to have replicas for a partition, and the partition not to have any subordinate reference replica types. This would be the case if all servers that held parent partitions also held the child partitions.

In this situation the server information in the replica pointer table will guarantee a server with a parent partition. Remember, if the server with a parent partition does not hold the child partition, then a subordinate reference replica is created.

To illustrate this issue, we will use the previous example but with a slight modification. We will change the replica type on the server NOR-SRV1 from a subordinate reference replica to a read/write replica for the R&D partition as shown in Figure 8.43.

FIGURE 8.43

The server NOR-SRV1 in the ACME tree holds replicas of the [ROOT], NORAD, and R&D partitions with subordinate reference replicas as needed. The servers R&D-SRV1 and WHI-SRV1 hold the master replicas of their respective partitions. In addition, the server WHI-SRV1 holds a read/write replica for the R&D partition.

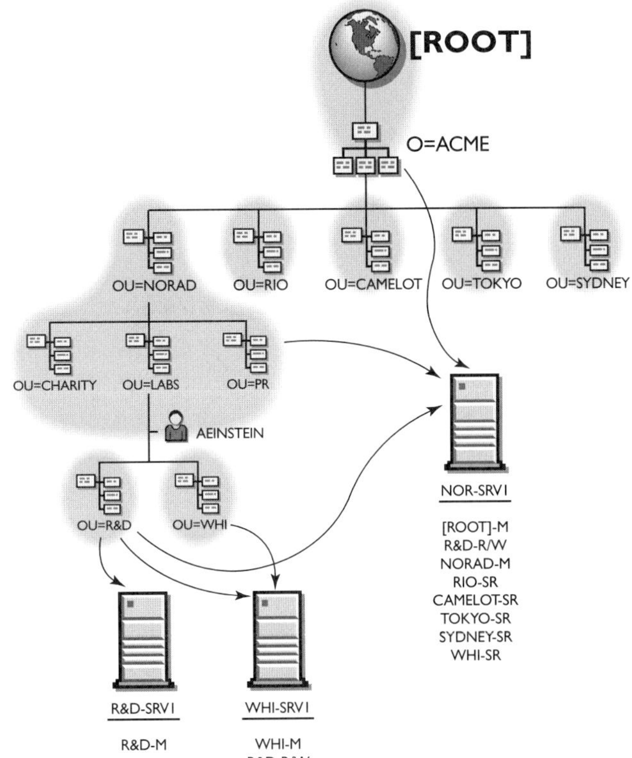

The station that is connected to the server R&D-SRV1 requests information about the user object AEINSTEIN.LABS.NORAD.ACME. NDS will check the R&D-SRV1 server to see if it has a copy of the requested object. R&D-SRV1 does not hold the object information, so NDS must find another server.

By comparing the names, Directory Services determines that the object information is up the tree. The server R&D-SRV1 will perform the tree walking as the proxy on behalf of the workstation. In order to locate the servers that contain the upper-level information, the server will read the replica pointer table for the R&D partition as shown in Figure 8.44.

FIGURE 8.44

SERVER NAME	REPLICA TYPE	REPLICA STATE	REPLICA NUMBER	PARTITION ROOT OBJECT I.D.	ADDRESS
R&D-SRV1	M	ON	1	06040000	Net Address/ Node/Socket
WHI-SRV1	R/W	ON	2	83261020	Net Address/ Node/Socket
NOR-SRV1	R/W	ON	3	47819010	Net Address/ Node/Socket

The replica pointer table for the partition R&D. The replica pointer table is the same on every server that stored a replica of the R&D partition. In this case, there are replicas on the servers R&D-SRV1 (master replica), WHI-SRV1 (read/write replica), and NOR-SRV1 (read/write replica). Notice that there are no subordinate references for this partition.

NDS reads the replica pointer table on the current server, which is R&D-SRV1. The closest server (least cost) in the replica pointer table is used.

R&D-SRV1 would connect to either server WHI-SRV1 or server NOR-SRV1 in the hope that they could offer more information about moving up the tree. If the server WHI-SRV1 is contacted, it would not be able to offer more information about walking up the tree because of the replicas it stores. The WHI-SRV1 does not have a replica closer to the [ROOT] than R&D, so the referral list returned is discarded by R&D-SRV1.

If the server NOR-SRV1 is contacted, then we have found the server that holds the parent partition. The object information is found in the NORAD partition, and the name resolution sends back a referral list. In this fashion, Directory Services can walk up the tree using the replica pointer table whether a subordinate reference replica exists or not.

Walk up and down the Tree to Locate the Object

When DS needs to find information about an object that is located in the NDS tree in peer partitions, the name resolution operation will walk up the tree to the nearest common parent and then back down.

For example, a workstation is connected to the server R&D-SRV1 in the ACME tree. The ACME tree is partitioned at each of the major cities. The NORAD partition is further partitioned at OU=R&D and OU=WHI as shown in Figure

8.45. The partitions [ROOT] and NORAD are held by the server NOR-SRV1. The server CAM-SRV1 holds the master replica of the CAMELOT partition, while the servers R&D-SRV1 and WHI-SRV1 hold their respective partitions as illustrated.

FIGURE 8.45

The workstation is connected to the server R&D-SRV1 in the ACME tree. The server NOR-SRV1 holds replicas of the NORAD and [ROOT] partitions. The server CAM-SRV1 holds the CAMELOT partition, while the servers R&D-SRV1 and WHI-SRV1 hold their respective partitions.

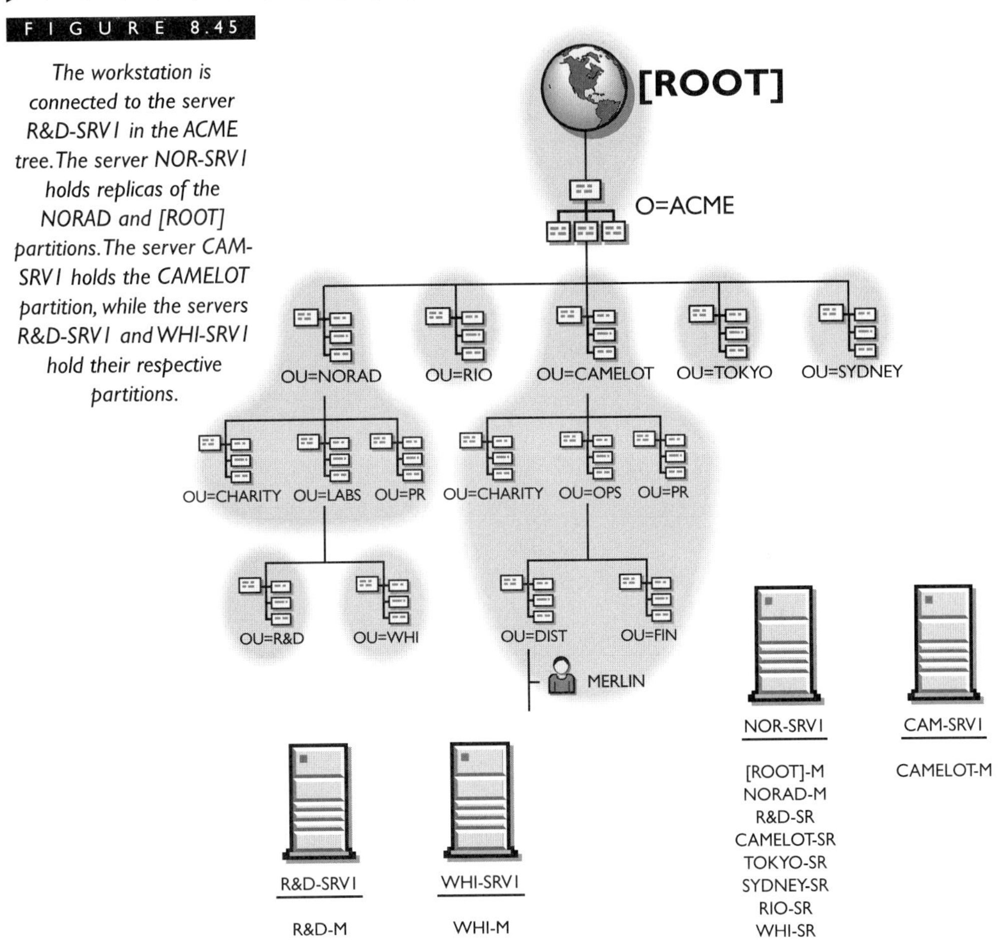

Figure 8.46 logically illustrates the name resolution steps that are performed to resolve the name MERLIN.DIST.OPS.CAMELOT.ACME starting from the server R&D-SRV1:

FIGURE 8.46

These name resolution steps are performed to resolve the name MERLIN.DIST.OPS.CAMELOT.ACME starting from the server R&D-SRV1.

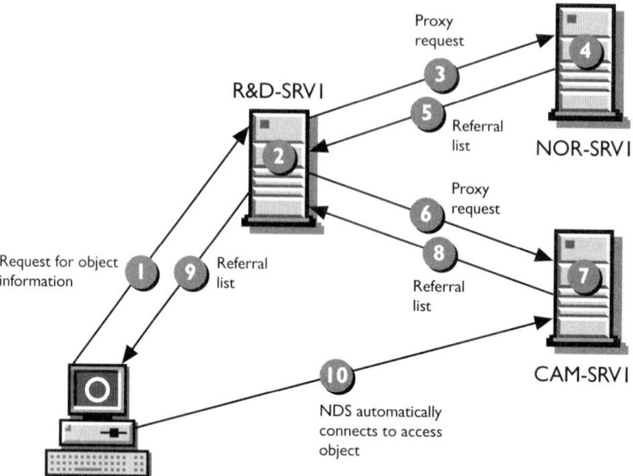

1. A workstation makes a request for information about the user object MERLIN.DIST.OPS.CAMELOT.ACME. The server R&D-SRV1 receives the request. The server R&D-SRV1 will perform the proxy on behalf of the workstation.

2. NDS checks R&D-SRV1 first to see if it has a copy of the requested object by comparing names. Because R&D-SRV1 does not hold the object information, Directory Services must look on another server. In order to locate the servers that possibly contain the proper partitions, the server R&D-SRV1 uses the replica pointer table of the root-most partition on the server — in this case, the R&D partition.

3. R&D-SRV1 makes a proxy request for the object information to the server NOR-SRV1 because it is the only other server in the replica pointer table (replica ring).

4. The server NOR-SRV1 then determines (by comparing names) if the object information is found locally or if Directory Services needs to continue walking up or down the tree. The object information is not found locally on NOR-SRV1. And because the server NOR-SRV1 has a subordinate reference replica of the CAMELOT partition, it continues walking down the tree to find MERLIN.DIST.OPS.CAMELOT.ACME in the CAMELOT partition.

5. NOR-SRV1 sends a referral list (replica pointer table of the partition CAMELOT) back to R&D-SRV1 of the servers that could possibly hold the object information. In this case, the referral list is the server address for CAM-SRV1.

6. R&D-SRV1 makes a proxy request for the object information to the server CAM-SRV1 because it contains the partition CAMELOT.

7. The server CAM-SRV1 determines (by comparing names) if the object information is found locally or if Directory Services needs to continue walking up or down the tree. The object information for MERLIN.DIST.OPS.CAMELOT.ACME is found locally on CAM-SRV1 in the CAMELOT partition.

8. CAM-SRV1 sends a referral list back to R&D-SRV1 of the servers that contain the object information. In this case, the list is the server address for CAM-SRV1.

9. The referral list is returned to the workstation for the servers that contain the object information, which includes the object ID. In this case, the server CAM-SRV1 is the only server.

10. The workstation contacts server CAM-SRV1 to provide access to the object information.

The DS client software provides the server-to-server connections for walking the trees. Because the server R&D-SRV1 did not hold the requested object information for MERLIN.DIST.OPS.CAMELOT.ACME, the tree walking was performed by Directory Services transparent to the user of the workstation.

Server without an NDS Replica

If the workstation attaches to a server that has no NDS replicas, DS must locate another NetWare 5 server. When a server without NDS replicas receives a request for object information, the server sends a service request for SAP type 0x0278 to the network. The SAP type 0x0278 is the NDS tree SAP. Another NetWare 5 server that is part of the NDS tree will respond.

NetWare 5 servers without NDS replicas connect to the tree using SAP type 0x0278. The servers without NDS replicas will run the limber process (described later in this chapter), check external references, and provide authentication services just like a server with NDS replicas.

Caching to Support Authentication

The total time required to authenticate between NetWare 5 servers is reduced through caching important information. The reduction is a result of the NetWare 5 servers remembering the object IDs of each of the servers they connected to during previous authentications. Storing the object ID for the other servers allows the time required to authenticate to those servers in the future to be reduced.

The specific information cached is the object ID of the server object on the other (remote) server. For example, if NOR-SRV1 authenticates to R&D-SRV1, then NOR-SRV1 stores the object ID for the R&D-SRV1 and vice versa.

NDS Background Processes

The information for NDS is loosely consistent, meaning that after a modification is made on a replica and before synchronization, the data will be different from one replica to another. Several NDS background processes are implemented to ensure synchronization of Directory data over a period of time. Most notable among these NDS background processes is the replica synchronization process, which synchronizes the information between replicas of the NDS partitions.

The other NDS background processes run periodically and are responsible for a number of internal operations that keep the information on all servers in the Directory tree consistent. All of these background processes will execute automatically without user or administrator intervention. Many of these processes can be forced to execute immediately using the SET parameters for DSTRACE. There are other SET parameters for NDS that control the interval between execution for a few of the NDS background processes.

The Replica Synchronization Process

NDS is a loosely consistent database, meaning that changes or updates can occur at various replicas and that not all the replicas may have the exact information at the same time. However, since NDS is loosely synchronized, an update made at one replica propagates to other replicas of the partition over time. The replicas work together to exchange the information to perform all updates. These changes are automatically sent to the other replicas of that partition by a background process called *replica synchronization*. The purpose of replica synchronization is to guarantee consistency of the information across all the replicas of a partition over a period of time.

The updates or modifications that affect the NDS data include adding, deleting, moving, or renaming an object, as well as changing the properties or attributes of the object. The replica synchronization process passes only the data that has changed for each object or property between the replicas of the partition. Passing only the information that is updated ensures that the total amount of information sent is reduced and network traffic for synchronization is kept to a minimum.

Replica synchronization is a background process that is event driven. Any modification to the NDS database activates the replica synchronization process. This means that replica synchronization is scheduled to run on a server after an object or property on that server has been updated. The process is scheduled according to the property or attribute being changed. Each property has a flag that determines if it is high convergence or not. The flag has the following settings:

- Fast synchronization (high convergence)
- Slow synchronization (not high convergence)

Fast Synchronization

Fast synchronization is the normal synchronization, which is scheduled to occur ten seconds after a client update event occurs on the server. The changes or updates to NDS objects that are made by the client are scheduled using fast synchronization. Synchronization scheduled for ten seconds after the first update is received enables several subsequent modifications, if any, to be processed at the same time.

Slow Synchronization

When a user logs into the NDS tree, four properties or attributes of the user object are changed. These properties are:

- Network address
- Last login time
- Current login time
- Revision count

Slow synchronization is login-related synchronization scheduled to occur thirty minutes after the login event. The properties or attributes that are used when a user logs in to the network are scheduled for slow synchronization.

The network address property added to the user objects when they log in indicates the physical workstation address from which the user is logging in. The last login time and current login time properties are modified to reflect the current status.

How Replica Synchronization Works

The replica synchronization process involves updating all the replicas for a specific partition with all the changes made to the partition since the last synchronization cycle. The process takes the replica pointer table (replica ring) and synchronizes each of these one at a time with the most recent changes. The process must contact the servers in the replica ring one at a time to complete a synchronization cycle for the partition.

Every time replica synchronization starts, it processes each of the replicas in the replica ring in a sequential order. Therefore, the first replica is synchronized first, followed by the second one, and so on. Since the replica ring is identical on all the servers holding copies of this partition, the synchronization process affects all the replicas for each partition in the same order. This may have an undesirable effect of multiple servers trying to synchronize with the same replica on the same server simultaneously. Since only one inbound synchronization is supported per partition (not per server), one of the synchronization processes will have to back off and attempt again at a later time. This situation only arises if the synchronization process tends to execute at approximately the same time on multiple servers.

To help alleviate this situation, NetWare 5 changes the sequence in which replicas are processed by randomizing the replica ring list before attempting to contact the first server. This reduces the possibility that one of the servers will have to back off and attempt to resynchronize with a replica.

The subordinate reference replicas are included in the synchronization process for a partition because they are found in the replica pointer table for a partition. This means that each of the replicas, including the subordinate reference replicas, is contacted during the synchronization cycle. The subordinate reference replica contains only the partition root object, and changes to that object are synchronized. The synchronized up to attribute of the partition root object changes frequently and is typically the only value synchronized for a subordinate reference replica.

After a server successfully sends all pending updates to a replica on another server, it proceeds to the next replica until all replicas have been updated. If the operation fails for any reason and is unable to update one or more replicas during the cycle, it reschedules the synchronization process to run at a later time.

Changes to Synchronization in NetWare 5

Several new changes to replica synchronization are available in NetWare 5. These changes make the synchronization process more efficient and manageable. The new features that help make NDS more scalable across your network servers include transitive synchronization, transitive vector, caching the replica changes, multiple objects per packet, and randomized replica lists. These new features will reduce traffic across your WAN infrastructure and enable you to more easily manage both the NDS tree contents and your network's overall system.

Transitive Synchronization and Transitive Vector The replica synchronization process in NetWare 5 uses transitive synchronization. Transitive synchronization is the method of using the transitive vectors during synchronizing between two NetWare 5 servers. Transitive synchronization uses the transitive vector instead of the Synchronized Up To property that was used in NetWare 4.

The transitive vector is a new structure that has been added to the Partition Root object for each partition. It is essentially a group of modification timestamps representing the values held by each replica. One transitive vector exists for each replica. The transitive vector differs from the Synchronized Up To property because it holds a group of timestamps for each replica, whereas the Synchronized Up To property holds only one value for each replica in the partition. Another major difference between the transitive vector and the Synchronization Up To property is that the transitive vector is synchronized between servers, whereas the Synchronization Up To property is not synchronized.

As mentioned, the transitive vector structure is kept as a vector with an attribute for each replica. Using the transitive vector, the synchronization process can achieve convergence among the replicas of a partition without having all replicas talk to every other replica. The structure of the transitive vector consists of modification timestamps for all replicas in a given replica ring. The transitive vector has been added to the Partition Root object of each partition in NetWare 5, as described here:

Server ID	Server ID that holds the replica
Timestamp Vectors	Timestamp vector for each replica in replica ring

Each time that the replica synchronization process is scheduled to run on the NetWare 5 server, transitive synchronization reads the transitive vector to determine which replicas it needs to synchronize with. Because each NetWare 5 server has a transitive vector, the process can immediately determine how up-to-date each of the other replicas are. Using transitive synchronization, a specific server does not have to contact each of the other servers in the partition to complete the replica synchronization process. After a successful synchronization, the target or destination server merges the transitive vector with that of the source server. In addition, the changes are guaranteed to converge across all replicas of a partition over time.

When a change occurs in an NDS object or property, the replica synchronization is scheduled to run. When the synchronization starts to execute, it determines which servers need to communicate by comparing the timestamps of the source and target servers in the transitive vector. The source server is the local server that received the update and the target server is the destination server of replica synchronization. If the time is greater for the local server, then the replica updates are sent. The local or source server does not request the target server's timestamps. The timestamps for the target server are already local in the transitive vector. After all updates are sent, then the source server sends its transitive vector values, which are merged into those of the target server.

As previously mentioned, this method of using the transitive vector during synchronizing between two NetWare 5 servers is called transitive synchronization. You may be wondering how the transitive vector works if the synchronization occurs on a replica ring with NetWare 5 servers and NetWare 4 servers. If a replica ring includes a mixed server environment, the two servers will synchronize using the NetWare 4 method of passing the Synchronized Up To vectors. After the synchronization has completed, either the transitive vector from the NetWare 5 server or the Synchronization Up To vector from the NetWare 4 server is merged.

Replica Ring is Randomized In NetWare 4, when the replica synchronization starts, it contacts and updates each of the replicas in the replica ring in a sequential order. The first replica in the replica ring is thus updated first, followed by the second one and so on. Because the replica ring is identical on all the servers holding copies of this partition, the synchronization processes all the replicas for each partition in the same order. This may have an undesirable effect if multiple servers are trying to synchronize with the same replica on the same server simultaneously. Because only one inbound synchronization is supported per partition (not per server) one of the synchronization processes will have to back off and try again at a later time. This situation only arises if the synchronization process tends to execute at approximately the same time on multiple servers. To help alleviate this situation, NetWare 5 changes the sequence in which replicas are processed by randomizing the replica ring list before attempting to contact the first server. Randomization greatly reduces the possibility that one of the servers will have to back off and attempt to resynchronize with a replica. By randomizing which replica receives the first update, transitive synchronization more quickly converges the data for each partition. As previously mentioned, the transitive synchronization process can converge the NDS data among all the replicas of a partition without having all replicas talk to every other replica.

Cache Changes Using a new feature—caching the changes to the NDS objects—enhances the performance of the replica synchronization process. Remember that the changes or updates that affect the NDS objects include adding, deleting, moving, or renaming an object, as well as changing the properties or attributes of the object.

Using NetWare 4, NDS sequentially searches the entire object file comparing timestamps to find the objects that have been updated since the last successful synchronization. The sequential searching effectively limited that size of the NDS partitions. When implementing the NDS tree in NetWare 4, we gave you a practical recommendation of 1,000–1,500 objects. To overcome this limitation, NetWare 5 eliminates the sequential search time by caching all changes to the objects. The ability to cache the objects in the NDS database greatly increases the speed of searching for and updating each replica and partition.

The object cache maintains a set of object IDs that have been modified since the last synchronization. The cache is populated by placing object IDs in the cache that have been modified as a result of client requests as well as inbound synchronization. Each cache entry has the modification time relative to the last synchronization. The cache that NDS maintains is for each partition stored on a server. The cache has a start time associated with it that identifies when the cache was built. Changes only need to be sent out if the transitive vector for the remote server is less than or equal to the transitive vector for the local server. The janitor process cleans up the cache periodically by removing the object IDS that have already been sent to all the replicas.

Multiple Objects per Synchronization Packet To help synchronize individual replicas faster, NetWare 5 supports more than one object in each communication packet. Formerly, NetWare 4 only allowed changes for one object in a single communication packet. By allowing multiple changes to different objects in a single packet, NetWare 5 reduces the total number of packets needed to synchronize with other replicas. If the number of changes between two replicas is small, it is feasible that all the updates between the two replicas can be accomplished in a single packet. Basically, this means that a partition can be synchronized in a minimum of one packet.

Scheduling the Replica Synchronization Process

As mentioned in previous chapters, every object and property that exists in Directory Services has an associated timestamp. Objects have a creation timestamp and a last modification timestamp. Properties have a timestamp that indicates when they were last changed. The modification to a property or attribute value consists of deleting the old value and creating the new one. Thus, the timestamp associated with the property could be called a creation timestamp.

By way of review, each replica of a partition on a server maintains a property or attribute called the synchronized up to vector. The synchronized up to vector is a list of timestamps, one for each replica in the partition plus one for every modification. The synchronization process will examine the timestamp held in the synchronized up to attribute for each replica and determine if the information needs to be updated. The synchronized up to values for each replica of a partition can be viewed using either the NDS Manager or DSREPAIR utilities. Figure 8.47

shows the replica information for the CAMELOT partition as shown in the NDS Manager utility.

Before starting the replica synchronization process and the first replica update, the server takes a snapshot of its own synchronized up to vector. The server saves the snapshot of these values in memory until all replicas have been contacted and successfully updated.

FIGURE 8.47

The replica information for the CAMELOT partition as shown in the NDS Manager utility

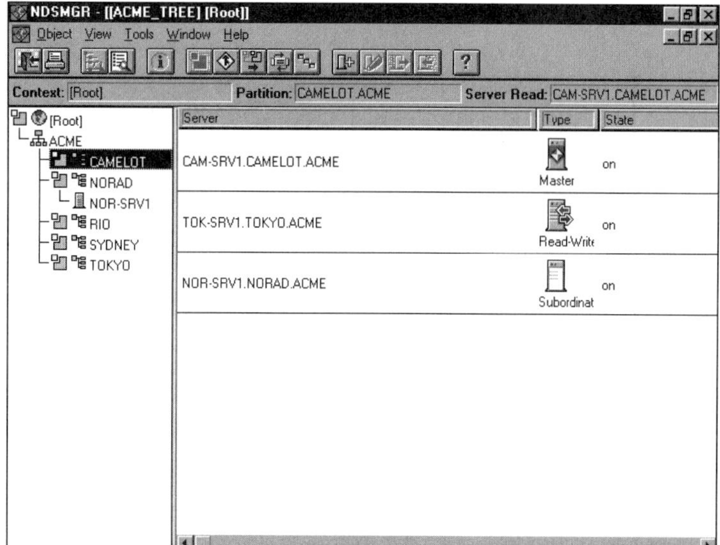

Performing the Replica Synchronization

The purpose of the replica synchronization process is to send any changes to the other servers that have a replica for a given partition. DSTRACE refers to this process as the *skulker*. Factors that determine whether synchronization is necessary are modifications or changes occurring with an associated timestamp. The synchronized up to vector from the other servers in the replica pointer table of a partition is compared with the local synchronized up to vector. If there are differences, the appropriate updates are made.

DS examines the replica pointer table (replica ring) for the local partition to locate the replicas of the partition. The timestamps in the synchronized up to vector are compared to determine the need to synchronize changes. Figure 8.48 gives you a logical representation of the dialog that occurs each time the local server contacts one of the other servers in the replica pointer table.

FIGURE 8.48

The dialog that occurs between servers during the replica synchronization process

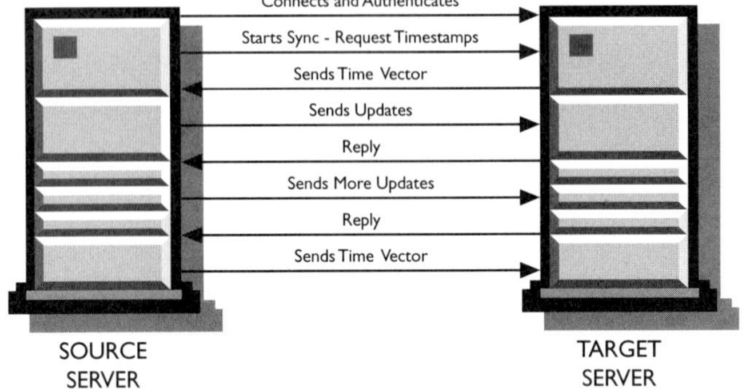

The specific operations and steps that are performed during a replica synchronization process are listed here:

1. The source (or local) server schedules its synchronization process after it receives a modification or event. If the process is flagged as fast synchronization, the source server schedules synchronization at the current time plus 10 seconds. Otherwise, the source server schedules synchronization at the current time plus 30 minutes.

2. The source server reads its synchronized up to vector.

3. The source server reads the replica pointer table to determine which servers hold replicas of the partition being synchronized.

4. The source server sets a flag that this partition is currently performing an outbound synchronization. This prevents the DSREPAIR utility from running multiple instances of synchronization for the same partition simultaneously.

5. The source server connects and authenticates to a target server holding a replica to be synchronized. If the server cannot establish a connection, it displays a DS error –625 for the server and proceeds to the next replica.

6. The source server requests the timestamp synchronized up to vector from the target server.

7. The target server reads its own replica pointer table to determine whether the source server is in its replica ring. If not, the server returns a DS error –672 denying access.

8. The target server checks if the specified replica is already processing incoming synchronization requests from another server. If so, the server returns a DS error –692. If not, the server returns a start reply to the source server.

9. The target server sends the requested synchronized up to vector of timestamps to the source server.

10. The source server determines whether it needs to send updates by comparing its own synchronized up to values to that of the target server. If the timestamps for the source server are more recent than the target's, the synchronization will proceed. If the timestamps are not more recent, the source server completes the synchronization request with that server and begins synchronizing with the next replica in the ring. The source server then skips to Step 14.

11. The source server sends the updates with the values to be changed for each object.

12. The target server verifies that the objects sent from the source server should be updated. The target server compares the local timestamps for each of its objects with the one received from the source server.

13. The target server updates the appropriate object and property information. The source and target servers repeat the update procedure until all updates are sent and received. The servers then send a reply indicating success or failure.

14. The source server sends the target server an end synchronization message and includes the source server's own synchronized up to vector.

15. The target server merges the timestamp values into its own synchronized up to vector using the higher values of the two vectors.

16. The target server replies to the end synchronization request with a completion code indicating success or failure.

17. The source server checks if all the replicas have been processed (All Processed=Yes).

   a. If all the replicas have not been processed, then the source server either retries the synchronization for the replicas that were previously busy or reschedules the process for the partition if retries are exceeded.

   b. The source server creates the partition status attribute to indicate synchronization results.

   c. If all the replicas have been processed, the source server writes the synchronized up to vector that it began the process with to its replica up to vector for the partition.

18. The replica synchronization process is completed.

By default the replica synchronization process is scheduled to execute only when changes are received to the object or properties in the NDS tree. However, using a DSTRACE command you can force the process to start (even if there are no changes to be propagated). To manually start the replica synchronization process, enter the following DSTRACE command at the server console:

```
SET DSTRACE = *S
```

This setting checks to see if the partition has been marked as changed; if not, it won't do anything. The DSTRACE command or setting to force the replica synchronization process to exchange the timestamp (synchronization up to) is entered at the server console as follows:

```
SET DSTRACE = *H
```

See "The Replica Synchronization Heartbeat" section that follows.

The Replica Synchronization Heartbeat

NDS provides a trigger, or heartbeat, every thirty minutes to schedule replica synchronization. The heartbeat enables each NetWare 5 server to contact all of the other NetWare 5 servers that it has in its replica pointer tables. This is checked in case the server has become disconnected from the network. The heartbeat starts the replica synchronization process for each partition that it holds.

The network administrator can adjust the heartbeat time interval using the SET command called the NDS inactivity synchronization interval. The default value for this parameter is 30 minutes, but you can set this parameter by entering the following command at the server console:

```
SET NDS INACTIVITY SYNCHRONIZATION INTERVAL = 60
```

A SET DSTRACE command may be used to initiate the heartbeat synchronization immediately. This command is entered as follows:

```
SET DSTRACE = *H
```

The SET DSTRACE command, SET DSTRACE = !H [time in minutes] may be used to change the default time interval parameter. Although you can change the default time interval using this SET parameter, we do not recommend it.

The Inspector Process

DS uses the inspector process to verify that the object and property information in the NDS data files is valid. The inspector process specifically checks and verifies that the Directory Services information stored on the server is formed correctly. If there are anomalies in the information, the inspector does not attempt to perform corrective action.

This process validates the object and property information, including the object name, class, timestamps, and references. It also checks to make sure that other objects reference the object correctly.

This process runs as needed with the flatcleaner process (described later in this chapter). The network administrator can manually activate the inspector using a DSTRACE SET command. To start the inspector process, enter the following:

```
SET DSTRACE = +INSP
```

This process can be very expensive in terms of CPU utilization and should not be executed manually on a server during normal working hours.

The Limber Process

The limber process maintains tree and server connectivity. At specific times, each NetWare 5 server in the NDS tree checks its distinguished name and addresses. The limber process will update or modify these values if necessary. The limber process checks the local server's entry to make sure that its distinguished name and address have not changed.

The limber process also ensures that if the relative distinguished name or internal IPX address is modified, the changes are replicated. The server name or IPX internal address can be changed in AUTOEXEC.NCF and then take effect when the server is restarted. The server name and IPX address are stored in the NDS server object created for the server.

If a server changes its name or address, the limber process is responsible for ensuring that the modifications are made to each replica pointer table in the partition. If the changes occur on the server with the master replica, the limber process changes its local address in the replica pointer table. If the changes occur on a server holding a nonmaster replica, the limber process tells the master replica. The limber process can initiate the backlink process, which does part of the checking for the limber process.

The limber process is initiated when each NetWare 5 server boots up or Novell Directory Services is restarted. The process is also initiated every three hours by default. The limber process can be event-driven, meaning it is started when a server address is added, changed, or deleted. An address can be added for another protocol while the system is running.

The limber process verifies that the server has the correct tree name. If the tree name is changed, the limber process affects the change on the server. The tree name modification is performed by the server holding the master replica of the root partition. This server then sends the request to all the other servers in the tree. If the update request fails to reach a server, the limber process will eventually make sure that the change is received by the server after it becomes available.

The limber process can be started on a server manually by executing a SET DSTRACE command at the server console prompt. The command to schedule the limber process to start is as follows:

```
SET DSTRACE = *L
```

The Backlink Process

When creating an external reference, NDS also schedules the creation of a backlink attribute for the object. Thus, the corresponding attribute to an external reference object is the backlink. The purpose of the backlink is to keep track of external reference objects on other servers.

The backlink process checks the local external reference objects that are on the server. It also verifies the backlink attribute values that have been created for the objects contained on the server.

DS periodically checks the external references to see if there is a reason for them to continue to exist. If an external reference is not needed, NDS will mark it to be removed.

The backlink process also enables maintenance of the external references by periodically verifying the information stored in the backlink attribute of the object. Each backlink attribute holds the remote server name and object ID of the associated external reference. By default, the backlink process checks consistency automatically every 780 minutes (13 hours). The default value can be changed for the backlink process by setting the SET parameter called the NDS backlink interval, which is entered in minutes. In order to change the SET parameter at the server console enter the following:

```
SET NDS BACKLINK INTERVAL = 900
```

The range for this parameter is 2 to 10080 minutes. The backlink interval can also be changed using DSTRACE by entering the following console command:

```
SET DSTRACE = !B [2-10080 minutes]
```

Using DSTRACE, the backlink process can be forced to execute immediately by setting the process flag. Enter the following DSTRACE server console command:

```
SET DSTRACE = *B
```

The backlink process will initiate sooner than the next regularly scheduled interval.

When an object is renamed, moved, or deleted, the backlinks make it possible for all the external references to that object to be changed. The backlink process has the responsibility to make the corresponding changes to the external references. Thus, the backlink process helps to maintain the integrity of external references by allowing them to be updated to reflect the changes made to the original objects.

Again, new in NetWare 5 is *distributed reference links,* which are a more efficient way to handle the renaming, moving, and deleting of external references. Although distribution reference links are fully implemented in NetWare 5, backlinks will not go away. Backlinks will also continue to be used to help maintain the external references. NetWare 5 will use both methods.

The Janitor Process

The primary responsibility of the janitor process is to keep everything in the DS clean. This process enables the DS to efficiently reuse the storage or disk resources of the server. It accomplishes this task by performing several functions associated with the objects and properties in the NDS data files. The janitor process performs the following tasks:

- Purges the deleted objects and values from the NDS data files
- Schedules the flatcleaner
- Updates the Inherited Rights ACLs for the partitions
- Alerts for synthetic time

Purging Deleted Objects and Properties

Before the object or property value is purged, the replica synchronization process makes sure that the object or value to be deleted is completely synchronized with all the other replicas of the partition. This ensures that each replica knows the object is going to be deleted before removing or purging it.

NDS reads the replica up to attribute of the partition and compares it against each object timestamp to determine which objects and property values need to be purged. A property value can be purged from an object if both of the following conditions are met:

- The property value is marked as deleted or not present.
- The timestamp for the property is less recent than the purge time (the purge time is the same as the synchronized up to timestamp).

Once the janitor process has inspected all the property values for an object, it determines whether the entire object itself can be purged. The janitor process will purge any object that meets the following criteria:

- Object is marked as deleted or not present
- Object has no property values

NDS also checks if the partition root object (the topmost object in the partition) has been renamed. If the container object has been renamed, the janitor notifies all external references of the partition root object of the new name.

While scanning the partition, the janitor builds two lists:

- **The release object ID list** — This is a list of objects that have been marked as moved. For each object in the list, the master replica processes the obituaries for the move, which releases the move inhibit destination object.
- **The notify external reference list** — The server with the master replica builds a list of objects that have backlink obituaries to be processed. For each object in the list, the janitor uses this list to send synchronization messages to the associated external references. The messages specify the operation that must be performed on the external reference.

Updating Inherited Rights ACLs

The janitor process determines the rights that should flow out through the inherited rights ACLs and updates the partitions. The inherited rights ACLs allows rights that are given at the higher levels in the tree to flow down from parent to child partitions. This enables all users to calculate all their rights in the entire tree from simply reading their local partition. The user does not need to walk the tree during login to calculate the rights.

By default, the janitor process is scheduled every hour (60 minutes). The default value can be changed by setting the SET parameter called NDS janitor interval, which is entered in minutes. In order to change the SET parameter at the server console, enter the following:

```
SET NDS JANITOR INTERVAL = 120
```

The range for this parameter is 1 to 10080 minutes. The janitor interval can also be changed using DSTRACE by entering the following console command:

```
SET DSTRACE = !J [1-10080 minutes]
```

The Flatcleaner Process

The flatcleaner process purges or removes the objects in DS that are marked as deleted. The flatcleaner purges the expired dynamic bindery objects and external reference objects from the NDS data files. This process purges only the objects that have been marked as deleted or not present.

The flatcleaner process is scheduled by the janitor process. It is started after the flatcleaner interval has expired. By default the flatcleaner interval is one hour (60 minutes). The default value can be changed by setting the DSTRACE SET parameter at the server console as follows:

```
SET DSTRACE = !F (in minutes)
```

The flatcleaner can be forced to execute using a DSTRACE command at the server console as follows:

```
SET DSTRACE = *F
```

The Schema Synchronization Process

The NDS schema can be modified or changed by creating new object classes or property definitions. The schema can be modified by client software. Typically, this would happen when new software applications are installed that require specific new kinds of objects or attributes. The user installing the software must have sufficient access rights before it can make the modifications.

For example, Novell's GroupWise software product has an optional feature that extends the NDS schema. The feature is a snap-in option to the NWADMIN utility, which enables the administrator to create GroupWise accounts at the same time a user object is created in the NDS tree.

Schema changes are replicated or propagated among all the servers containing NDS replicas. The schema is replicated using a similar synchronization process known as the replica synchronization process. Without this synchronization, the schema information on one server could become different from that on the other NetWare 5 servers in the tree.

Using the schema synchronization process, which is event driven, schema modifications are scheduled ten seconds after the change. The updates to the schema are propagated automatically from one server to another in much the same way as other NDS updates. However, the schema synchronization differs in that partitions replicate according to the replica pointer table (replica ring), but schema synchronization occurs according to a trickle-down method. In this trickle-down method the schema synchronization or updates propagate in two directions:

- Across servers holding a replica of a given partition
- Downward in the partition tree

Propagation across Replicas of a Partition

Like NDS objects, each schema object has a timestamp that indicates its last modification. The procedures for comparing and updating timestamps for the schema information between servers are the same as for any other NDS objects.

To propagate the latest schema updated information among the replicas of a partition, a server uses the schema synchronization process with a few slight changes. NetWare 5 servers without replicas can add themselves to the list of servers contacted. The specific operations and steps that are performed during a schema synchronization process for the replicas of a partition are listed here:

1. The source server takes a snapshot of its own local synchronized up to attribute.
2. The source server reads all the replica pointer tables (replica rings) in order to make a list of target servers to be sent the schema updates. The distribution list can include NetWare 5 servers that do not have NDS replicas. The reference replica to the source server is stripped from the list, as well as all subordinate reference replicas.

3. The source server pings each target server in the distribution list to determine the tree depth of the root-most replica on the target server. If the replica depth is less than the source server's depth, the target server is skipped.

4. A start synchronization request is then sent to the target server. The target server replies to the request by sending its synchronized up to vector.

5. The source server compares the synchronized up to vectors to determine if the schema updates should be sent.

6. The source server sends the updates to the schema.

7. The source server sends the target server an end synchronization request containing its own synchronized up to vector.

8. The target server merges the timestamp values into its own synchronized up to vector using the higher value of the two vectors.

9. The schema synchronization is terminated for a partition after the source server has contacted and updated all the target servers.

Propagation Down to the Lower Partitions

In order to propagate the schema modifications down to lower partitions, the server where the modification is received starts the schema synchronization process with its partitions. Each time a target server receives a modification, it will send the modification to lower partitions, if any. It will never send the modification to partitions that are higher. The procedures for the schema synchronization process are described earlier in this chapter in the section "Propagation across Replicas of a Partition."

The trickle-down method of synchronizing the schema occurs when a target server receives the updated schema and builds its own list of servers to distribute the schema it just received. The target first checks to see if the partition(s) is lower than the original partition (the partition where the modification is made). The procedures for updating the schema are performed across all replicas of a partition. In this way the schema updates are propagated downward to other partitions in the Directory tree and across all replicas of the partition.

Controlling Schema Synchronization

By default the schema synchronization process is scheduled to execute only when changes are made to the schema or after the expiration of the schema synchronization heartbeat. The default interval for the schema synchronization heartbeat is 4 hours (240 minutes). However, using a DSTRACE command you can force the process to start (even if there are no changes to be propagated). To manually start the schema synchronization process, enter the following DSTRACE command at the server console:

```
SET DSTRACE = *SS
```

This flag starts the process, which will check to see if the schema on that server needs to be synchronized. This is the schema synchronization heartbeat.

You can disable schema synchronization altogether by entering the following DSTRACE command at the server console:

```
SET DSTRACE = !S   [0 = ON, Nonzero = OFF]
```

This flag both enables and disables the schema synchronization. The flag value of 0 will enable the schema synchronization. A nonzero value will disable the schema synchronization.

NDS Partition and Replica Operations

An administrator using the NDS Manager utility can make structural changes to the NDS tree. For example, the administrator can add and remove replicas, change replica types, create or merge partitions, or move subtrees.

The NDS is a multithreaded system that enables the server to participate or perform multiple partition operations on different partitions on the server. A server can hold replicas of different partitions, and these replicas can be involved in their individual partition operations simultaneously on the server.

Partition and Replica Operation Control and Status

All partition and replica operations are initiated by contacting the master replica for the partition. Since each partition can have only one operation in progress at a time, the master replica of the partition controls the operation. The master replica ensures that other partition operations are not started until the first operation is completed. The master replica is the traffic cop for partition operations.

The partition has certain attributes that are used to manage the partition operations. For example, some of the attributes used to help with the partition operation are replica pointer table, replica status, partition control, and partition status. As the operation proceeds through several states, each server involved records the activity of these states in the partition control and status attributes.

Most partition operations are processed in several major passes. In the first pass, all affected servers are contacted with the details of the change. They report errors, if any. If any errors are detected in the first pass, this means the operation did not start and the message is returned to the utility. If there are no errors, the second pass contacts all the servers with replicas of the partition to finalize the modification.

The following sections summarize the operations that create and manage the NDS partitions and their replicas. The partition operations we will discuss include the following:

- Add replica
- Remove replica
- Change replica type
- Create (split) partition
- Merge (join) partition
- Move subtree or partition

Add Replica Operation

The add replica operation causes a new replica for a partition to be added to the partition's replica point table. The major events that occur during the add new replica operation are listed here:

1. An administrator with the proper rights issues a request using the NDS Manager utility to add a new replica for the partition. DS client

automatically authenticates the workstation to the server holding the master replica of the partition.

2. The administrator determines the replica type (read/write or read-only) and selects the target server that will store the new replica.

3. The server holding the master replica verifies the access rights of the user or administrator to the partition and destination server and checks that

    a. The target server object exists in the NDS tree

    b. The replica type requested is read/write or read-only

    c. The partition is not involved in another partition operation

4. The master replica server obtains the object ID for the partition root object on the target server.

5. The master replica assigns the first unused replica number to the new replica.

6. The master replica adds replica pointer table attribute values to the target server and sets the state for the new replica to RS_NEW_REPLICA. The master replica server adds the new replica created on the target server to its replica pointer table. This change to the replica pointer table will be synchronized out to the other replicas in the partition during the replica synchronization process already scheduled.

7. The master replica schedules an immediate replica synchronization process to begin downloading the contents of the partition to the target server.

8. The master replica server informs the client or workstation that the add new replica request was successful.

9. The replica state begins with the replica in the RS_NEW_REPLICA state. During this replica state,

    a. The target server accepts update requests from only the master replica

    b. Clients cannot access the new replica; it is treated as not available

10. After all the information is sent to the new replica, the master replica server changes its replica state attribute from RS_NEW_REPLICA to RS_TRANSITION_ON. The replica state attribute will be propagated to the other replicas of the partition by the normal replica synchronization process.

11. When the target server receives the replica state value of RS_TRANSITION_ON, it sends a request to the other replicas to obtain any updates more recent than those of the master replica.

12. The target server synchronizes with all other replicas of the partition as needed.

13. The target server then sends a request to the master replica server to change the replica state value to RS_ON.

14. The master replica server receives the request and sets the replica state for the new replica to RS_ON. The replica state attribute will be propagated to the other replicas of the partition by the normal replica synchronization process.

15. If needed, the master replica server sends a request to create the necessary reference replicas that are subordinate to the new replica. If the subordinate references replicas are created, the target server sends a request to the master of each child partition to update the replica pointer table to reflect the change.

16. Each change will be propagated to the other replicas of each partition by the normal replica synchronization process.

17. The add new replica operation is complete.

Remove Replica Operation

The remove replica operation deletes a replica from a specific server, and it also removes it from the replica pointer table of the partition. The master replica cannot be removed. To remove a replica, a user must have managed rights at the partition root object and the server from which the replica is being removed. The major events that occur during the remove replica operation are listed here:

1. An administrator with the proper rights issues a request using the NDS Manager utility to remove a replica from a server. DS automatically authenticates the workstation to the server holding the master replica of the partition.

2. The administrator selects the target server from which the replica is being removed.

3. The master replica server verifies the access rights of the user or administrator to the partition and server and checks that

   a. The master replica exists on that server

   b. The replica state is RS_ON

   c. The partition is not involved in another partition operation

4. The master replica server changes the replica state to RS_DYING_REPLICA.

5. The change to the replica state is propagated to the other replicas of the partition through the normal replica synchronization process.

6. The target server knows that it has a replica whose state is RS_DYING_REPLICA. It checks to see if it holds the parent of the partition being removed.

7. If the target server holds a parent,

   a. It sends a request to the server holding the master replica to update the replica pointer table to reflect the change. This request indicates that the replica being removed from the target server is changed to a subordinate reference replica.

   b. The target server sends the pending changes to at least one other replica not being removed and whose replica state is RS_ON.

   c. The master replica server changes the replica type in the replica pointer table to subordinate reference for the target server replica.
   d. The master replica server changes the replica state to RS_ON.

8. If the target server does not hold the parent partition,
   a. The target server sends the pending changes to at least one other replica not being removed and whose replica state is RS_ON.
   b. The target server sends a request to the master replica server to remove the replica from the replica pointer table of the partition.
   c. The change to the replica pointer table will be propagated to the other replicas of the partition by the normal replica synchronization process.

9. The target server converts its objects in the removed replica to external reference objects. It sends a request to create a backlink to a server holding the real object for each external reference created.

10. All changes are propagated to the other replicas for the partition through the replica synchronization process.

11. The remove replica operation is complete.

Change Replica Type Operation

The change replica type operation changes the type of any replica. The operation is started when an administrator decides to change the type of a replica on a specific server. The types of replicas that can be chosen are master, read/write, and read-only. You cannot change a replica to a subordinate reference. The subordinate reference replicas are maintained by NDS.

The change replica type operation differs when the operation assigns a new master replica. This section discusses changing both nonmaster replica types (read/write and read-only) and changing to a master replica. In order to change a replica to a master replica, the target server must hold a read/write or read-only replica of the partition.

The major events that occur during the change replica type operation of a nonmaster replica are listed here:

1. An administrator with the proper rights issues a request using the NDS Manager utility to change the replica type to either read/write or read-only. DS automatically authenticates the workstation to the server holding the master replica of the partition.

2. The master replica server checks the access rights of the user or administrator to the partition.

3. The master replica server changes the replica type in its copy of the replica pointer table.

4. The change to the replica pointer table will be propagated to the other replicas of the partition by the normal replica synchronization process.

5. The change replica type operation is complete.

The steps to change the Replica Type to a Master Replica are listed here:

1. An administrator with the proper rights issues a request using the NDS Manager utility to change the replica type to the master replica. DS automatically authenticates the workstation to the server holding the master replica of the partition. This server will be called the source server.

2. The source server checks the access rights of the user or administrator to the partition.

3. The source server identifies the target server in using the partition control attribute's distinguished name field.

4. The source server sets the partition control attribute to PC_CHANGING_REPLICATYPE.

5. The source sets the replica state of each replica in the replica pointer table to RS_CRT_0.

6. The change to the partition control and replica pointer table attributes will be propagated to the other replicas of the partition using the normal replica synchronization process. This enables all the replicas in the partition to change the partition state to RS_CRT_0.

7. The source server sends a request to the target server to set the replica to the new master. This routine tells the target server that it is now the master replica of the partition.

8. The target server waits until its clock is ahead of the timestamps issued by the source (old master replica) server. It then issues new timestamps on the replica pointer table of this partition.

9. The target server removes its name from the partition control attribute's distinguished name field.

10. The target server is now the master replica and sets the partition state in the replica pointer table to RS_CRT_1.

11. The target server changes its replica type in the replica pointer table to read/write (secondary) for the source server.

12. The target server replies to the source indicating that the replica type has been changed to master successfully.

13. The change to the replica pointer table on the target server will be propagated to the other replicas of the partition using the normal replica synchronization process.

14. The source server changes its own replica type to read/write in the replica pointer table.

15. The source server changes its replica state to RS_CRT_1.

16. The changes made to the source server will be propagated to the other replicas of the partition using the normal replica synchronization process.

17. The source server changes its replica state to RS_ON.

18. The change will be propagated to the other replicas of the partition.

19. The change replica type operation is complete.

Create (Split) Partition Operation

The create partition operation causes a partition (parent) to split and form a new child partition in the NDS tree. You can create any partition as long as it has a single container object as its partition root object. The major events that occur during the create partition operation are listed here:

1. An administrator with the proper rights issues a request using the NDS Manager utility to create a new partition in the NDS tree. DS automatically authenticates the workstation to the server holding the master replica of the partition.

2. The master replica server identifies the NDS container object that will become the new partition root object where the partition is created.

3. When the master replica server changes the master replica of the partition where the split will occur, the following events take place:

   a. The access rights of the user or administrator to the partitions and servers involved are checked.

   b. The replica state in each of the replica pointer tables is set to RS_SS_0.

   c. The partition control attribute is set with the distinguished name of the new partition root object and sets the current operation, which is a split partition.

4. The changes made to the master replica will be propagated to the other replicas of the partition using the normal replica synchronization process.

5. The master replica server sends a request to each server holding a replica of the partition to perform a split procedure. The subordinate references replicas are not included.

6. The servers holding replicas of the partition process the split request by taking the partition attributes and values from the parent to the partition root object of the child partition.

7. Each server returns a reply indicating success or failure to the split request.

8. The master replica server performs the split procedure on its own replica list.

9. The master replica server sets the replica state to RS_SS_1 (split state 1).

10. The replica state (RS_SS_1) is propagated from the master replica to each of the other replicas of the partition.

11. The master replica server advances the partition state and replica state to RS_ON for both the parent partition and new child partition.

12. The changes made to the master replica will be propagated to the other replicas of the partition.

13. The create or split partition operation is complete.

Merge (Join) Partition Operation

The merge partition operation causes a child partition to be joined back together with its parent partition. This operation requires that there is both a parent and child partition already existing in the NDS tree structure.

At the beginning of the merge operation, the replicas for each of the two partitions do not have to be stored on the same servers. However, the operation first proceeds by copying a replica of either the parent or child partition to all the servers involved. This ensures that each server will have the replicas for both the parent and child partition.

Consulting Experience

It is highly recommended that before you execute a merge operation of a parent and child partition, you manually place replicas of each partition on the servers that will be involved. If the replicas do not exist, the merge operation will place them for you. However, the merge operation will complete faster if you manually place the replicas in advance.

The merge operation will make the replica pointer table the same for both the parent and child partitions, excluding the subordinate references from the parent's replica list. When NDS creates all the replicas of the new partition, it simply erases the partition boundary between the parent partition and the child partition.

The major events that occur during the merge partition operation are listed here:

1. An administrator with the proper rights issues a request using the NDS Manager utility to merge a child partition with its parent. DS automatically authenticates the workstation to the server holding the master replica of the child partition.

2. The workstation sends the request to the server holding the child partition.

3. The master replica of the child partition locates the parent partition's master replica.

4. The master replica of the child partition verifies the access rights of the user or administrator to the partitions and servers involved and checks that

   a. The request is valid.

   b. The child partition is not involved in another partition operation.

   c. The software versions on the servers involved support the merge operation. This means that all servers involved must be running the DS.NLM v 4.63 or later.

5. The master replica of child partition sends a request to the server holding the master replica of the parent partition to start the merge procedure.

6. The master replica of the parent partition receives a request to start the merge operation and changes the master replica as follows:

   a. The replica state in the replica pointer tables and partition control attribute is set to RS_ JS_0.

   b. The partition control attribute also receives the distinguished name of the child partition root object.

   c. The current operation is set to PC_ JOINING_DOWN.

7. The changes made to the master replica will be propagated to the other replicas of the parent partition using the normal replica synchronization process.

8. The master replica of the parent partition replies to the server holding the master replica of the child partition the success or failure of the request to start the merge.

9. The master replica of the child partition receives the reply and changes the master replica as follows:

   a. The replica state in the replica pointer tables and partition control attribute is set to RS_ JS_0.

   b. The partition control attribute also receives the distinguished name of the parent partition root object.

   c. The current operation is set to PC_ JOINING_UP.

10. The master replica of the child partition replies to the client or workstation that the merge operation client is successful or not.

11. The changes made to the master replica will be propagated to the other replicas of the parent partition using the normal replica synchronization process.

12. The master replica servers for both the parent and child partitions check the replica pointer table (replica ring) to determine which servers must add replicas. Both a replica of the parent and child partitions are required before the merge can take place.

13. The master replica server sends a request to other servers as follows:

    a. Servers containing replicas of the child partition, but not the parent, receive new replicas of the parent with new replica numbers.

    b. Servers containing replicas of the parent partition, but not the child, receive new replicas of the child partition with new replica numbers. These do not include the servers containing subordinate reference replicas.

14. The master replica of the child partition advances the replica state to RS_JS_1.

15. The master replica of the parent partition checks that the child partition state is PC_JOINING_UP.

    a. If the state is not PC_JOINING_UP, it sets the partition and replica states to RS_ON. This stops the partition merge procedure.

    b. If the state is PC_JOINING_UP, it sends a request to all servers holding replicas of the two partitions to perform a merge procedure.

16. The nonmaster server receives the request and erases the boundary between the partitions by placing all objects from both partitions into one partition.

17. The master replica of the parent partition then performs the merge procedure on itself.

18. The master replica of the parent partition sets the replica state of the new merged partition to RS_JS_2.

19. The changes made to the master replica will be propagated to the other replicas of the parent partition.

20. The master replica of the child partition then performs the merge procedure on itself.

21. The master replica of the child partition sets the replica state of the new merged partition to RS_JS_2.

22. The changes made to the master replica will be propagated to the other replicas of the parent partition.

23. The master replica of the child partition sets the replica state to RS_ON.

24. The master replica of the parent partition sets the replica types as follows:

    a. The master replica of the parent becomes the master replica of the merged partition.

    b. The master replica of the child partition becomes a read/write replica.

    c. All other replicas of the child partition become replicas of the new partition.

25. The changes made to the master replicas will be propagated to the other replicas of the partition using the normal replica synchronization process.

26. The merge or split partition operation is complete.

Move Subtree or Partition Operation

NetWare DS allows you to move any subtree of the NDS tree as long as it is a partition. The subtree or partition being moved cannot have child partitions.

The move subtree operation moves a container with all its subordinate objects to another logical location in the NDS tree. The objects in the partition moved changed their distinguished name but the relative distinguished name remains the same. The servers that hold replicas for the partition being moved remain the same during the operation. This means that the move is logical (in the NDS tree) and not physical.

In the following example, the NDS tree has three partitions (NORAD, CAMELOT, and OPS), which are involved in moving the subtree. Figure 8.49 illustrates the OPS partition being moved from CAMELOT.ACME (source) to NORAD.ACME (destination).

FIGURE 8.49

The OPS partition will be moved from CAMELOT.ACME (source) to NORAD.ACME (destination).

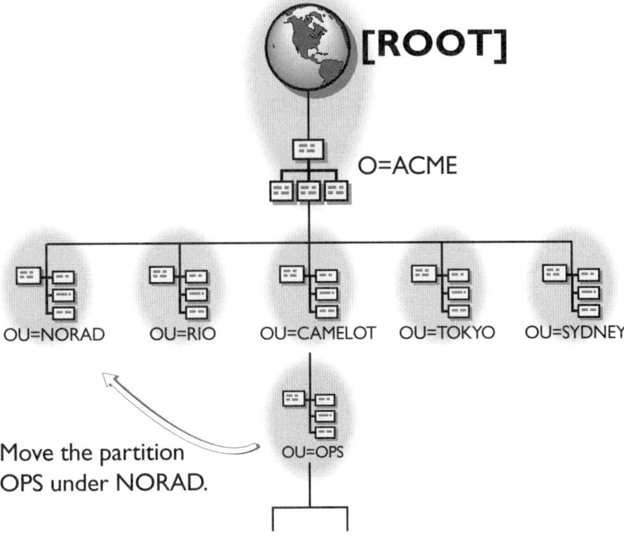

The major events that occur during the move subtree operation are listed here:

1. An administrator with the proper rights issues a request using the NDS Manager utility to move the subtree or partition OPS from CAMELOT.ACME (source) to NORAD.ACME (destination). DS automatically authenticates the workstation to the server holding the master replica of the OPS partition.

2. The workstation sends the request to server holding the master of the NORAD partition. This is the destination partition.

3. The master replica server of NORAD creates the following control list of information:

   a. The access rights of the user or administrator to the partitions and servers involved

   b. The operation's expiration time, which is set to one hour

   c. The partition root object ID for NORAD (the destination)

   d. The distinguished name of the server holding the master replica of OPS

   e. The new relative distinguished name of the moved object

4. If the expiration time passes before a moved object is received from the source server, the destination server purges its record of the move details and does not continue moving the partition.

5. The master replica of NORAD checks its ACL attribute to see that the administrator or client has create rights and that the partition is idle.

6. The client sends a message to finish the move to the master replica server of OPS.

7. The master replica server of OPS checks that its software version and all the other servers holding replicas of the OPS partition are at least DS v 4.63.

8. If the source and destination partitions are the same partition, then a PartitionOverlap flag is set.

9. At the request of the source server, the master replica of OPS sets the following:

   a. The replica state in the replica pointer table is set to RS_MS_0.

   b. The partition control function is set to PC_MOVE_SUBTREE_DEST.

   c. The partition control attribute also receives the distinguished name of the destination partition.

   d. An OBT_TREE_OLD_RDN is added to the source object if its relative distinguished name is being changed. This obituary records the old name of the partition being moved.

10. The master replica server of OPS sends the client a reply indicating success or failure.

11. The changes made to the master replica will be propagated to the other replicas of the CAMELOT partition using the normal replica synchronization process.

12. The master replica of NORAD sets the following:

   a. The replica states in the replica pointer table is set to RS_MS_0.

   b. Partition operation is set to PC_MOVE_SUBTREE_SRC.
   c. The partition control attribute also receives the distinguished name of the source partition.
   d. An OBT_TREE_OLD_RDN is added to the source object if its relative distinguished name is being changed. This obituary records the old name of the partition being moved.

13. The changes made to the master replica will be propagated to the other replicas of the NORAD partition.
14. The master replica of OPS builds a server notification list of servers that will participate in moving the subtree:
   a. Servers holding replicas of the CAMELOT partition
   b. Servers holding replicas of the NORAD partition
   c. Servers holding replicas of the OPS partition
   d. Servers holding external references to objects in the CAMELOT partition (as identified by backlinks)
15. The master replica server for OPS records the server notification list as an OBT_MOVE_TREE obituary for each server in the list.
16. If the PartitionOverlap flag was set in Step 8, then the master replica server for OPS sends a partition lock request to the server holding the master replica of the NORAD partition. This prevents other partition operations on the partitions while the subtree is being moved.
17. The master replica server for OPS sends a reply indicating success or failure. The client no longer participates in moving the subtree.
18. The master replica server for OPS will drive the completion of the move subtree operation.
19. The master replica server sends a request to every server in the server notification list to start the move subtree. This request is driven by the obituaries.

20. Each server on the notification list changes its replicas according to the new NDS tree structure. The change to each server depends on the replicas it holds.

21. The master replica server sends a request to each of the servers on the notification list to end the move operation.

22. Servers on the list set their obituary flags to OBF_PURGEABLE and return a reply.

23. The master replica sends a partition unlock request to the master replica of CAMELOT and also sends a partition unlock request to the server holding the master replica of NORAD if the PartitionOverlap flag was set.

24. The master replica server receiving the unlock request sets the partition state to RS_ON.

25. The master replica of OPS sets the replica states to RS_ON.

26. The changes made to the master replicas will be propagated to the other replicas of the appropriate partition.

27. The move subtree partition operation is complete.

Summary

NDS is a distributed and replicated system that has been designed to run on multiple servers across your network. In order to more effectively maintain and troubleshoot NDS, you need to understand the background processes, internal components, and overall architecture of NDS. This chapter has been focused on these components and processes.

CHAPTER 9

Troubleshooting Novell Directory Services

"What we anticipate seldom occurs; what we least expected generally happens." — Henrietta Temple

Chapter 8, "NDS Internals Operations," has given you a much better understanding of how the internal operations of NetWare 5 work together to provide an enterprise network system. In fact, you should make sure to read Chapter 8 before reading this chapter because the material covered here uses terms explained in that chapter. This chapter also deals with partition and replica operations. For the details on these concepts, you can refer back to Chapter 6, "Designing and Using NDS Partitions and Replicas," as well as Chapter 8.

Troubleshooting has been described as a combination of art, science, and luck. One reason troubleshooting tends not to be much fun is that administrators often do not know enough about the underlying technology to properly define network problems when they occur. Unfortunately, as networks grow larger and larger, they also become more complex. Under NetWare 3, troubleshooting was usually confined to tracking down a server or two that was experiencing a problem. Typically, you could focus on a single server and identify problems quickly.

Troubleshooting NetWare 5 has been made more easy. However, you are now dealing with a more complex multiserver environment in which servers communicate with one another. In addition, the technology may be new to many companies and may be unfamiliar to users and administrators. Novell continues to introduce improved repair utilities and procedures for maintaining your NetWare 5 network. Make sure to keep informed about patches and announcements by checking Novell's Web site regularly. Novell is dedicated to providing the best operating system available in the industry.

This chapter describes NDS primarily from the point of view of supportability. Based on information gathered, in part, by the staff on Novell's technical support teams, this chapter explains how to maintain and troubleshoot NDS. Experience has shown that, if NDS operations are properly verified before and after being initiated, NDS management can be virtually error free. This chapter covers three key topics:

- Understanding and using the NetWare 5 repair tools
- Performing and verifying partition operations
- Troubleshooting dos and don'ts

Understanding and Using the Repair Tools

The following sections describe the NetWare 5 repair tools: the DSREPAIR and the DSTRACE SET commands. These utilities are very important tools you will use during normal NDS maintenance and troubleshooting. By using a combination of DSREPAIR and DSTRACE, you will be able to perform three basic NDS troubleshooting steps.

- Identify the partition that is experiencing errors by using and understanding the DSTRACE set parameters and using the DSREPAIR utility.
- Identify the replica(s) in the partition that have errors. Identify these errors by using the DSTRACE SET commands and the DSREPAIR utility.
- Identify the error and take the appropriate action. Appendix B, "NDS Error Codes and Definitions," lists the errors and recommended remedies.

The DSREPAIR Utility

The DSREPAIR utility enables you to monitor NDS, check for errors, and correct problems in the name service on an individual server basis. The utility runs as a NetWare Loadable Module (NLM) at the server console. The utility is menu driven and is written with the well-known C-worthy user interface. These are the main functions of DSREPAIR:

- Correct or repair inconsistencies in the NDS database
- Check NDS partition and replica information and make changes where necessary
- Initiate replica synchronization

You can run the DSREPAIR utility on any NetWare 5 server in the Directory tree. Additionally, the utility can either be loaded from the server console or through access to a server via the RCONSOLE utility. The DSREPAIR utility can be run remotely in this manner. Figure 9.1 illustrates the DSREPAIR utility main menu.

FIGURE 9.1

The DSREPAIR utility main menu

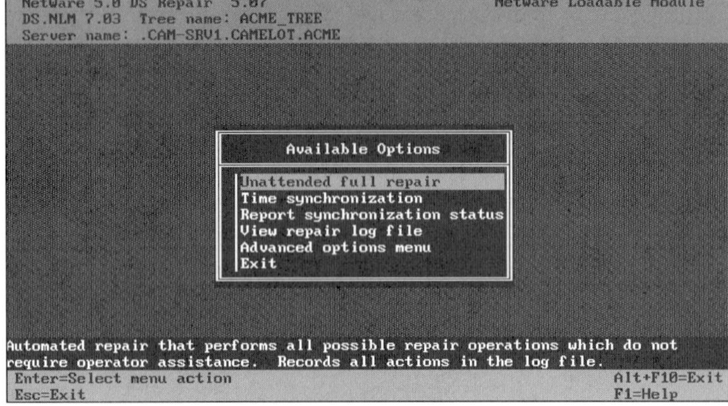

The DSREPAIR utility provides the following options:

- **Unattended Full Repair** — This feature automatically performs repair operations on the local NDS name service without operator assistance.
- **Time Synchronization** — This option checks the time synchronization for all servers that are known to the local server. You must monitor and correct time synchronization problems before performing any repair operation. A replica of the [ROOT] partition must be on the local server running DSREPAIR for this feature to contact all servers in the tree.
- **Report Synchronization Status** — This option lets you check the synchronization status of any partition on the server and the servers holding the association replicas.
- **View Repair Log File** — This option lets you view all the operations of the DSREPAIR utility by consulting a log file stored on your server. The default log file is SYS:SYSTEM\DSREPAIR.LOG. You should always view the log file after running the utility.

- **Advanced Options Menu** — The advanced options on this menu give you greater flexibility to manually control the repair of your NDS tree.

These options are discussed in the following sections.

Unattended Full Repair

The Unattended Full Repair option automatically performs all possible repair operations that do not require operator assistance. This option goes through five major repair procedures:

- It repairs the local NDS database, which locks the database during the repair operation so that no new database updates can occur until completed.
- It repairs any NCP server object's network address; the database is not locked during this operation.
- It verifies all remote NCP server object IDs; the database is not locked during this operation.
- It checks replica rings; the database is not locked during this operation.
- It authenticates every server in the ring and verifies information on the ring.

You can control which of the preceding items are checked or repaired by using the Repair Local DS Database option, which is described later in this chapter under the "Advanced Options Menu" section. Refer to the Repair Local DS Database selection screen for more information shown later in this chapter.

The log file records all the actions during the unattended full repair operation. When the repair operations are completed, the log file is opened so that you can see what repairs were made and check the current state of the database.

Time Synchronization

The Time Synchronization option contacts every server known to the local server and requests information about time synchronization, Directory Services, and server status. The information is written to the log file. When the operation has completed, the log file is opened so that you can check the status of time synchronization plus other Directory Services information. Figure 9.2 shows the log file after the time synchronization operation has been run on the ACME tree.

FIGURE 9.2

The log file after the time synchronization operation has been run on the ACME tree

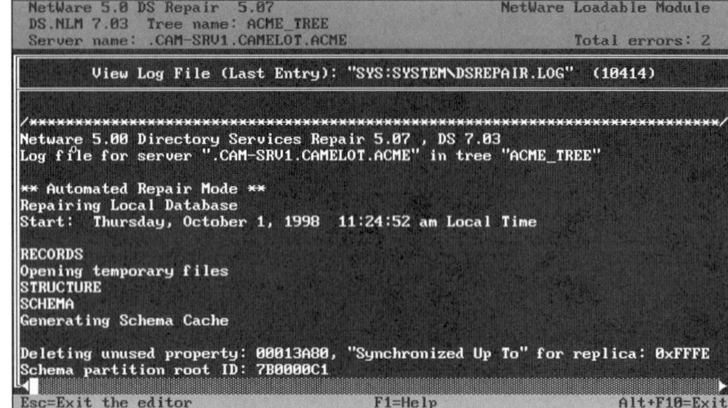

An explanation of each field in the log file is provided in Table 9.1.

TABLE 9.1

Fields in the Log File

FIELD	CONTENT
Server Name	This is the distinguished name of the server responding to the request.
DS.NLM Version	This is the version of the DS.NLM running on the responding server. This information is valuable as a quick reference to see the versions of NDS running on the servers of your network.
Replica Depth	The replica depth indicates how deep in the NDS tree moving away from [ROOT] the first replica is on the responding server. Each server knows which replica is highest in the NDS tree. This value is the number being reported. A positive number indicates how many objects there are from the [ROOT] to the highest replica. A value of –1 indicates that no replicas are stored on the server.
Time Source	The time source is the type of time server the responding server is configured to be.

FIELD	CONTENT
Time is in Sync	This field indicates the time synchronization status of the responding time server. The possible values are Yes and No. The value displayed is the status of the synchronization flag for each server. This means that the server's time is within the time synchronization radius. Refer to Chapter 7 for more information on time synchronization.
Time Delta	This field reports the time difference, if any, from the time synchronization radius for each server. The time synchronization radius is two seconds by default, so you will probably not see a server with more than a two-second difference. If the value is larger, the Time is in Sync field is probably set to No. The maximum the field can report is up to 999 minutes and 59 seconds.

Reporting Synchronization Status

The Report Synchronization Status option starts a replica synchronization process for all the partitions that have replicas on this server. This operation starts the synchronization process for all partitions and replicas. If you want to perform the same operation for individual partitions, you need to select the Replica and Partition Operations option from the Advanced Options menu.

The report synchronization status operation contacts each server in each of the replica lists stored on the server. A server does not attempt to synchronize to itself, so the status returned for a server's own replica is the value of "host."

The operation uses the log file to track the actions of the requests and displays any errors that occur. This operation is a quick and easy way to determine that the partitions and servers are communicating and synchronizing properly.

Viewing the Repair Log File

The View Repair Log File option lets you view the DSREPAIR log file, which contains the results of the previously performed operations. The default log file is stored in SYS:SYSTEM\DSREPAIR.LOG. When DSREPAIR performs an operation, the results are written to this log file. A record of each succeeding operation is appended to the log file, which increases in size with each repair operation. The size of the log file is displayed on the title line in parentheses after the name of the file.

Using the Advanced Options menu in DSREPAIR (discussed next), you can set current file size, reset the log file, log output to a new file name, and append to an existing file.

The Advanced Options Menu

The Advanced Options menu enables you to control the individual repair operations manually. You can also use it to monitor status and access diagnostic information about your NDS tree. These options provide advanced repair operations that you should execute only if you understand the procedures and how they function. The Advanced Options menu provides the options shown in Figure 9.3, several of which are identical to the main menu options.

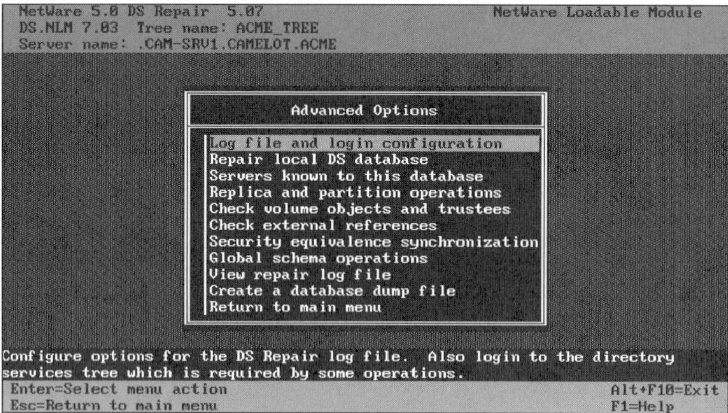

FIGURE 9.3

The Advanced Options menu in DSREPAIR

Log File and Login Configuration. This option lets you configure the log file and log into the Directory tree. Configuring the log file enables you to manage where DSREPAIR writes the information it gathers. You can turn the log file off, delete it, and change the name of the file itself. The file can be stored on any volume or DOS drive.

The login function presents a login screen that lets you enter an administrator user name and password. Once you have logged in, the authentication information is maintained in server memory for all other repair operations that require an administrator to log in.

Repair Local DS Database. This option repairs the local NDS name service and performs the same function as the Unattended Full Repair option in the main menu. Figure 9.4 shows the Repair Local DS Database selection screen. You can select or deselect each item to turn it on or off for the unattended full repair.

FIGURE 9.4

The Repair Local DS Database selection screen

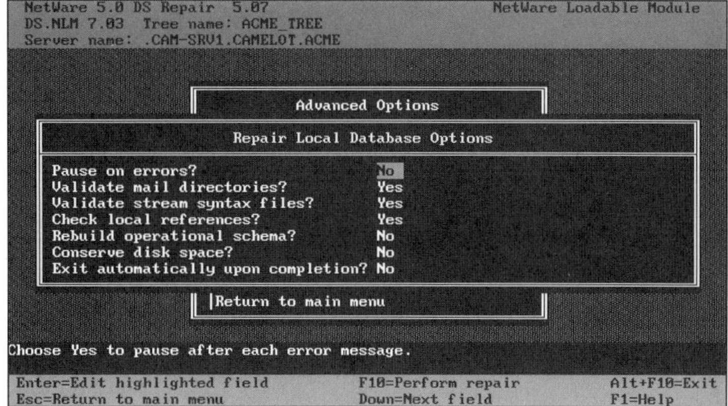

During the repair operations, NDS is temporarily locked, preventing clients from logging in. Several items are checked during the repair operation. For example, the Directory tree structure is checked to ensure that all records are linked to the [ROOT] object and that the object and property records are linked. The partition records are checked for validity, and any errors are fixed. A check is made for invalid checksums and links between records, and any errors are fixed.

The repair operation creates a set of temporary NDS files that are used to perform all the changes. The temporary files have the .TMP extension. At the end of the repair operation these temporary files become the permanent NDS files, unless you choose not to accept the repairs that were made.

Descriptions of the Repair Local DS Database options are listed in Table 9.2.

TABLE 9.2

The Repair Local DS Database Options

OPTION NAME	DEFAULT	DESCRIPTION
Pause on Errors	No	Turn on this option if you want DSREPAIR to stop on errors. After the repair is complete, you can view all actions it performed in the log file.
Validate Mail Directories	Yes	This option checks the mail directories on volume SYS for users who no longer exist after the repairs have been made. Novell Directory Services does not require the user to have a mail directory. The mail directories are migrated from NetWare 3 to support bindery users in NetWare 5.
Validate Stream Syntax Files	Yes	This option checks for valid stream files syntax files after the repair operation. Stream files contain data for a property whose data type syntax is stream, such as a login script. The files are associated with a specific user object or other object. If the user (or other object) no longer exists in NDS, the stream files associated with the user (or other object) are removed.
Rebuild Operational Schema	No	The operational schema is the set of rules that NDS uses to create objects and properties. The schema is required for base operations. If the schema becomes damaged or corrupted, you should rebuild it using this option. However, it is extremely unlikely that this situation will arise.

OPTION NAME	DEFAULT	DESCRIPTION
Conserve Disk Space	No	DSREPAIR creates temporary copies of the NDS files and operates on these files. You can choose to save or discard the changes after a repair has completed. If you save the changes by leaving this option set to No, the temporary files become the real NDS files and the current NDS files are assigned the .OLD extension. This ensures that DSREPAIR has an old set of files that Novell technical support can review in case of emergency. The drawback to saving at least one old copy of the NDS files is that it takes up a little more disk space. In most cases this will not be an issue because the NDS files don't take up a large amount of disk space.
Exit Automatically upon Completion	No	This option lets you look at the log file upon completion before saving the changes to the repaired NDS files. If you choose Yes, the utility automatically saves the changes and exits DSREPAIR.

Servers Known to this Database. This option displays all the servers that the local NDS knows about. Each server must contact all servers in the replica list during replica synchronization. The local server will only know about the servers it needs to contact. If the local server has a copy of the [ROOT] partition, the list of known servers most likely contains all the servers in the tree because of remote and local IDs.

Figure 9.5 shows the servers found in this Directory Services Database screen. This information shows servers from replica lists, servers from remote/local IDs, and NCP server objects in any partition.

FIGURE 9.5

The servers found in this Directory Services Database screen in DSREPAIR

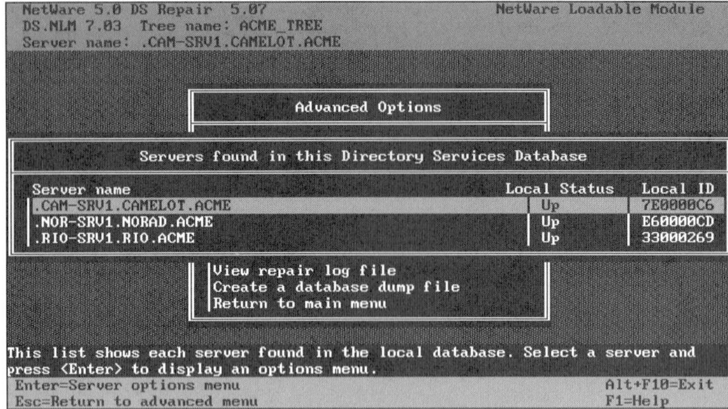

The Local Status field displays the state of the server as seen from the local server. If the value for a server is Up, the remote server is active. However, if the value is Down, the local server cannot communicate with the other server.

If you can select a server from the list, the Server Options menu shown in Figure 9.6 becomes available. This menu applies to the selected server.

FIGURE 9.6

The DSREPAIR Server Options menu

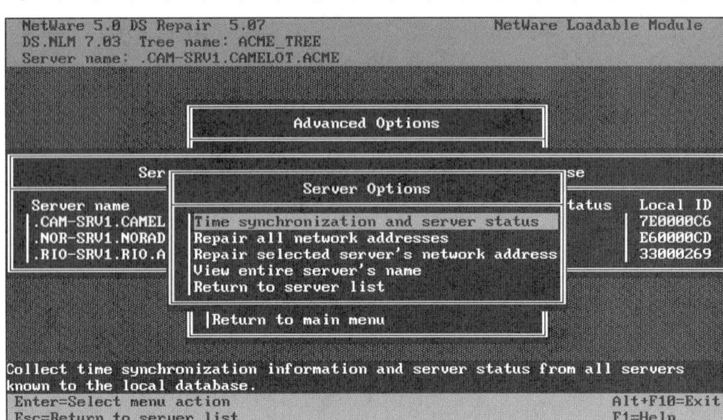

The Server Options menu provides the following options:

- **Time Synchronization and Server Status** — This option contacts every server known to the local server and requests information about time synchronization, Directory Services, and server status. This option is the same as the Time Synchronization option on the main menu.

- **Repair All Network Addresses** — This option checks every server object known to this server and searches for the server's name in the local SAP table. If the address is found in the SAP table, this address is compared with the value stored by the local server. If the two addresses do not match, the address in the SAP table is assumed to be correct and the other addresses are changed to match it. This operation is performed if you select the Unattended Full Repair option from the DSREPAIR main menu.
- **Repair Selected Server's Network Address** — This option repairs the highlighted server's network address in replica rings and server objects in the local database. As shown in Figure 9.7 you will see a log file displaying the results of this activity and any errors that may have been generated.
- **View Entire Server's Name** — This option allows you to view the server's distinguished name. Figure 9.8 shows a view of the server's full name from DSREPAIR.

FIGURE 9.7

The screen that is displayed when you select the Repair Selected Server's Network Address option in DSREPAIR

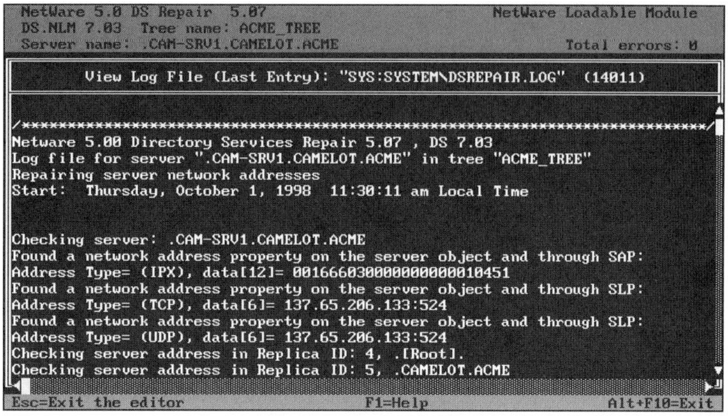

```
NetWare 5.0 DS Repair  5.07                              NetWare Loadable Module
DS.NLM 7.03  Tree name: ACME_TREE
Server name: .CAM-SRV1.CAMELOT.ACME                             Total errors: 0

     View Log File (Last Entry): "SYS:SYSTEM\DSREPAIR.LOG"  (14011)

/***************************************************************************/
Netware 5.00 Directory Services Repair 5.07 , DS 7.03
Log file for server ".CAM-SRV1.CAMELOT.ACME" in tree "ACME_TREE"
Repairing server network addresses
Start:  Thursday, October 1, 1998  11:30:11 am Local Time


Checking server: .CAM-SRV1.CAMELOT.ACME
Found a network address property on the server object and through SAP:
Address Type= (IPX), data[12]= 001666030000000000010451
Found a network address property on the server object and through SLP:
Address Type= (TCP), data[6]= 137.65.206.133:524
Found a network address property on the server object and through SLP:
Address Type= (UDP), data[6]= 137.65.206.133:524
Checking server address in Replica ID: 4, .[Root].
Checking server address in Replica ID: 5, .CAMELOT.ACME

Esc=Exit the editor                     F1=Help                    Alt+F10=Exit
```

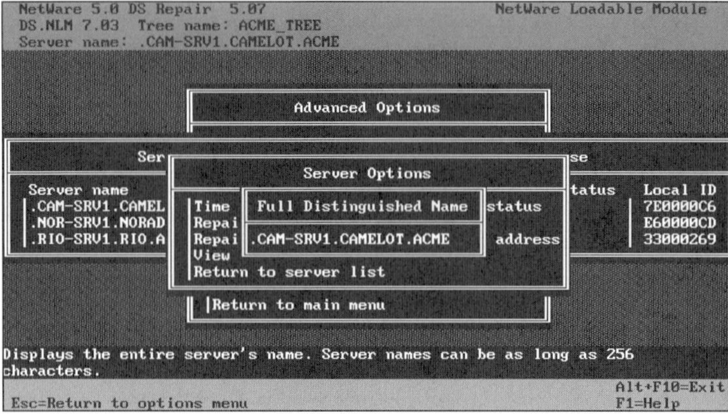

FIGURE 9.8

The DSREPAIR View Entire Server's Name Options menu

Replica and Partition Operations. You should become very familiar with the Replica and Partition Operations option on the Advanced Options menu. You will use this menu more than any other menu during the maintenance of NDS. When this option is selected, DSREPAIR displays a list of all the replicas stored on the server. This list applies only to the server on which you are running DSREPAIR. The menu option to view replicas is called Replicas Stored on This Server and is shown in Figure 9.9. Each replica is shown in list format, with the replica type (master, read/write, read-only, and subordinate reference) and replica state (ON, OFF, and so on).

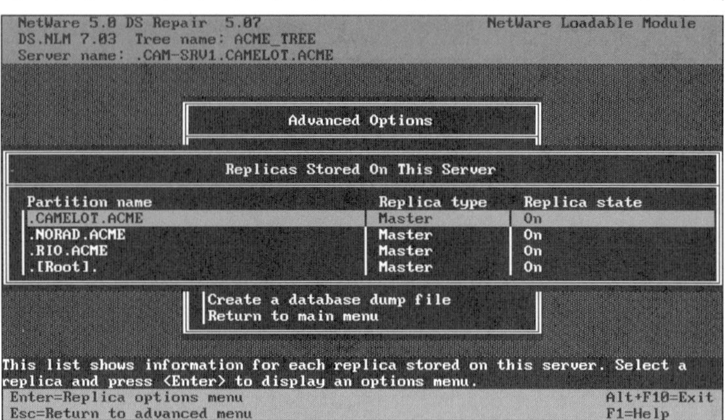

FIGURE 9.9

The Replicas Stored on This Server menu in DSREPAIR

From the Replicas Stored on This Server menu, you can select an individual replica or partition, which enables you to obtain more specific information and perform maintenance functions. After you select an individual replica or partition from the list, you'll see a larger Replica Options menu called Replica Options, Partition: *partition name*. Figure 9.10 shows this Replica Options menu. In the figure the name of the partition is CAMELOT.ACME. This menu includes an extensive list of specific options and operations that enable you to perform specific diagnostic and repair functions. These operations apply only to the partition selected.

FIGURE 9.10

The Replica Options menu in DSREPAIR for the CAMELOT.ACME partition

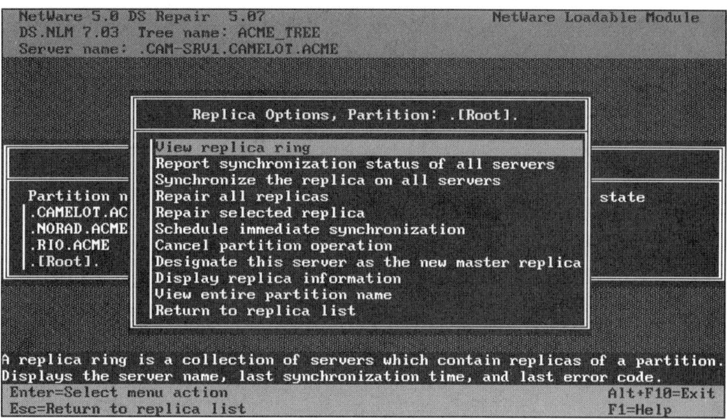

The Replica Options menu is the most heavily used menu in DSREPAIR because it enables you to monitor, diagnose, and repair specific problems with the replicas stored on a particular server. Several repair options in this menu require you to log in as a user who has rights to perform the operation. The utility makes you log in before running all of the important repair options as a final check that you are authorized to perform the operation.

The operations in this menu affect the entire partition and all of its replicas. This is one place that the DSREPAIR utility can start operations on the other servers through the use of a replica list.

If you want to affect only the replica that is stored on a specific server, select the View Replica Ring option, select a specific replica on any server, and then perform partition and replica operations on only that server.

The Replica Options menu supplies several additional options that you can execute for the partition and all of its replicas, as described next:

- **View Replica Ring** — This option provides another menu or list of all the servers that contain replicas for the selected partition. The menu that appears is called Replicas of Partition: *partition name*. A replica ring is equivalent to a replica list, which is a list of all the servers that hold replicas for a specific partition. The replica ring shows the replica type and replica state information for each server. You can choose a server or replica in this list and display the Replicas of Partition: *partition name* menu, as shown in Figure 9.11, which provides more functionality on the selected server. This figure illustrates information for the CAMELOT.ACME partition.

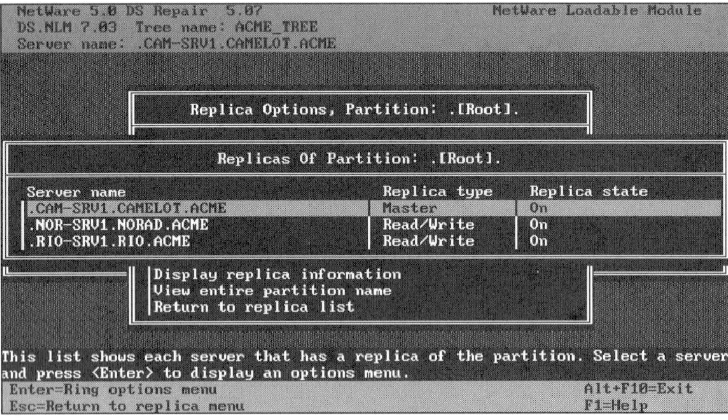

FIGURE 9.11

The Replicas of Partition menu in DSREPAIR

Selecting the View Replica Ring option will display the Replicas for Partition: *partition name* menu, which supplies the following options. These options affect only the selected partition:

- **Report Synchronization Status on the Selected Server** — This option checks the synchronization status of every server that has a replica of the selected partition. If all the servers with a replica response are synchronizing, the partition is functioning properly.

- **Synchronize the Replica on All Servers** — This option performs a synchronization of the selected partition on all servers that contain a replica and reports the status.

- **Repair All Replicas** — This option performs a repair of all replicas on this server. This option also checks and validates the information on each server that contains a replica, as well as the IDs of both the remote and local servers. This is the same information that is checked when you select the Unattended Full Repair option from the main menu. In other words, you can run an Unattended Full Repair or a Repair Local Database instead of choosing the Repair All Replicas option.

- **Repair Selected Replica** — This option performs a repair on only the highlighted replica. This option is the same as the Repair All Replicas option, except that it repairs only the selected replica. Before choosing this option, you can run an Unattended Full Repair or Repair Local Database, both of which are equivalent to this operation.

- **Schedule Immediate Synchronization** — This option causes the replica selected to begin the synchronization process immediately.

- **Schedule Immediate Synchronization** — This option starts an immediate synchronization of all the replicas stored on this server. You can use this option to initiate synchronization activity if you want to view the Directory Services trace screen started by DSTRACE.

- **Repair Timestamps and Declare a New Epoch** — This option always affects the master replica, even though the master replica may not be the local replica or the replica in the server where DSREPAIR is being run. This operation checks all the time value stamps in the master replica to see whether any of them are ahead of the current time. If they are, they are replaced with the current timestamp. After all the timestamps are consistent, a new epoch is declared.

  An *epoch* is a number (the first one is 1, next one, 2, and so on) selected as a point of reference for Directory Services. The epoch is also known as the *partition creation time*. An epoch is used to create a new timestamp, which controls the replica synchronization. When a new epoch is declared, it starts at the master replica, and the other replicas will not receive updates from a different epoch. The master replica sends out all objects until all replicas are fully synchronized with the new epoch. All objects on other replicas are tagged as unknown. The master then marks all replicas as new and resends all information.

Be careful with the Repair Timestamps and Declare a New Epoch option because it will lose changes made in a previous epoch. For example, changes to a read/write replica will be lost if they have not yet synchronized to all other copies, including the master. If a modification has not been synchronized to the master replica before a new epoch is declared, the change is lost.

Before using this option, make sure that all servers in the replica ring are communicating. You also should not perform this function during times of high server utilization.

- **Cancel Partition Operation** — This option attempts to cancel a partition operation that was started for the selected partition. This operation talks to the master replica, which is responsible for the partition operations. Some partition operations may not be canceled if they have progressed too far. Other partition operations — such as the add replica partition operation — cannot be canceled.

- **Destroy the Selected Replica on this Server** — This option removes the selected replica from this server. Therefore, it will be deleted or changed to a subordinate reference. Only use this option when other options such as using NDS Manager fail to remove the replica.

- **Designate this Server as the New Master Replica** — This option designates the local replica of the selected partition as the new master. Each partition can have only one master replica, so the previous master replica is changed to a read/write replica.

  This option is useful for designating a new master replica if the original one is lost. This situation may arise, for example, if the server holding the master replica has a hardware failure and will be down for a while or indefinitely.

- **Display Replica Information** — This option displays the distinguished name for the selected replica.
- **Delete Unknown Leaf Objects** — Delete the UNKNOWN class of leaf objects. This option should only be used when directed by Novell Technical Support.
- **View Entire Partition Name** — This option will display the full distinguished name of the selected partition.
- **Check Volume Objects and Trustees** — This option will check all mounted volumes on this server for valid volume objects and valid trustees on the volumes. This option does require you to log in as the ADMIN user before performing this operation.
- **Check External References** — This option will check each external reference object to determine if a replica containing the object can be located. If all servers that contain a replica of the partition where the object resides are inaccessible, the object will not be found during the check and a warning message will be issued.
- **Security Equivalence Synchronization** — The Security Equivalence Synchronization option allows synchronization of security equivalence properties throughout the global tree. This operation walks the Directory tree, checks each object for the Equivalent To Me property, and checks it with the corresponding Security Equals property on the referenced object.

  You should never have to run this option if you are using the standard NetWare security and rights administration. The Equivalent to Me property is not used by default. Enabling this option can cause performance degradation on your server.
- **Global Schema Update** — The Global Schema Update option checks that all servers in the NDS tree contain the correct schema up to the NetWare 5 base schema. If a NetWare 5 server does not contain the correct schema, it will be updated.

After you select the Global Schema Update option, you are provided with the following methods for updating the schema:

- **Update All Servers' Schema** — This option updates the schema on all servers in the tree and is useful for updating previous versions of NetWare 5 or NetWare 4 (4.0, 4.01, 4.02, 4.1, 4.11) to the current NetWare 5 schema.
- **Update the [ROOT] Server Only** — This option updates the schema on the server that contains the master replica of the [ROOT] partition.
- **Import Remote Schema** — This option is used for equalizing the schema before merging two trees.
- **View Repair Log File** — The View Repair Log File option allows you to manage the log file created when you run the other DSREPAIR options. The default log file is SYS:SYSTEM\DSREPAIR.LOG. When DSREPAIR is loaded, the log file is opened. When repair operations are performed, the activity is appended to the log file. The size of the file is displayed within parentheses on the far right side of the title line. You can use this option to control the log file. For example, you can turn the log file off, turn it on again, change the filename, and change its location. You can place the log file on a NetWare volume or on a DOS drive.
- **Create a Database Dump File** — The Create a Database Dump File option lets you copy the NDS files to disk in a compressed format to be used by Novell technical support. Creating a dump file can be useful for diagnostic and troubleshooting efforts. However, note that the dump file is not a backup that you can restore later.

  When you select this option, you are asked to enter the path name for a dump file. The default is SYS:SYSTEM\DSREPAIR.DIB. The dump file can be written only to a NetWare volume and not to a DOS drive.

DSTRACE SET Commands

In NetWare 4 DSTRACE referred to a group of SET commands available at the server console. DSTRACE was often referred to as a utility; however, it was really just a group of server SET commands. These SET commands were useful for monitoring how NDS was functioning. Now, in NetWare 5, DSTRACE is a utility (a NetWare Loadable Module) that provides expanded monitoring capabilities relative to its predecessor. Once it is loaded, you can use DSTRACE (also called the Novell Directory Services Trace Event Monitor) monitor synchronization status and errors. DSTRACE is primarily used to determine and track the health of NDS as it communicates with the other NetWare 5 servers in the network.

You can use DSTRACE commands to:

- Monitor the status of NDS synchronization processes.
- View errors that occur during NDS synchronization.

After you enable DSTRACE by typing **DSTRACE**, you can type **HELP DSTRACE** to see the list of options shown in Figure 9.12.

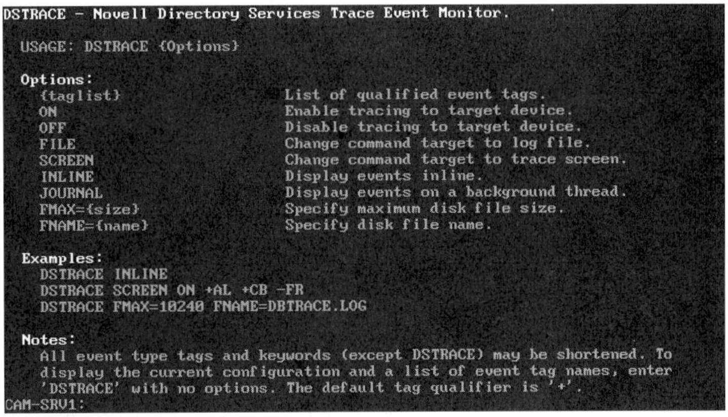

FIGURE 9.12

To start the Directory Services screen, type DSTRACE at the server console. After DSTRACE is enabled, you can type HELP DSTRACE to view the Help screen.

```
DSTRACE - Novell Directory Services Trace Event Monitor.

 USAGE: DSTRACE {Options}

 Options:
   {taglist}                  List of qualified event tags.
   ON                         Enable tracing to target device.
   OFF                        Disable tracing to target device.
   FILE                       Change command target to log file.
   SCREEN                     Change command target to trace screen.
   INLINE                     Display events inline.
   JOURNAL                    Display events on a background thread.
   FMAX={size}                Specify maximum disk file size.
   FNAME={name}               Specify disk file name.

 Examples:
   DSTRACE INLINE
   DSTRACE SCREEN ON +AL +CB -FR
   DSTRACE FMAX=10240 FNAME=DBTRACE.LOG

 Notes:
   All event type tags and keywords (except DSTRACE) may be shortened. To
   display the current configuration and a list of event tag names, enter
   'DSTRACE' with no options. The default tag qualifier is '+'.
CAM-SRV1:
```

To enable DSTRACE for viewing and event logging, you need to type the following commands while at the Help screen. Table 9.3 lists the commands that you can enter using the DSTRACE syntax.

TABLE 9.3

Basic DSTRACE Commands

COMMAND OPTION	DESCRIPTION
DSTRACE ON	Enable tracing the a target device.
DSTRACE OFF	Disable tracing to target device.
DSTRACE FILE	Change command target to log file.
DSTRACE SCREEN	Change command target to trace screen.
DSTRACE INLINE	Display events inline.
DSTRACE JOURNAL	Display events on a background thread.
DSTRACE FMAX={size}	Specify maximum disk file size.
DSTRACE FNAME={name}	Specify disk filename.

Once you have enabled DSTRACE, you can specify what you would like to view. You can select a whole array of information to view by specifying the DSTRACE command followed by a tag list. Note that when you select a view, that item is highlighted on your server screen in blue. Those items that you have not selected are displayed in gray.

The tag list is shown in Figure 9.13.

FIGURE 9.13

The tag list is a list of items you can select for viewing/logging with DSTRACE.

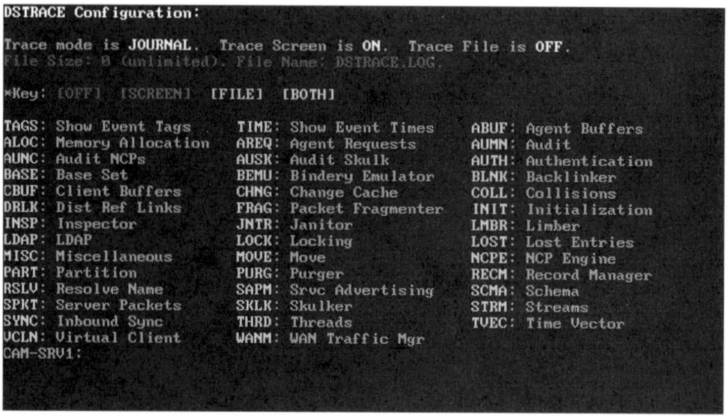

```
DSTRACE Configuration:

Trace mode is JOURNAL.  Trace Screen is ON.  Trace File is OFF.
File Size: 0 (unlimited). File Name: DSTRACE.LOG.

*Key: [OFF]  [SCREEN]  [FILE]  [BOTH]

TAGS: Show Event Tags      TIME: Show Event Times     ABUF: Agent Buffers
ALOC: Memory Allocation    AREQ: Agent Requests       AUMN: Audit
AUNC: Audit NCPs           AUSK: Audit Skulk          AUTH: Authentication
BASE: Base Set             BEMU: Bindery Emulator     BLNK: Backlinker
CBUF: Client Buffers       CHNG: Change Cache         COLL: Collisions
DRLK: Dist Ref Links       FRAG: Packet Fragmenter    INIT: Initialization
INSP: Inspector            JNTR: Janitor              LMBR: Limber
LDAP: LDAP                 LOCK: Locking              LOST: Lost Entries
MISC: Miscellaneous        MOVE: Move                 NCPE: NCP Engine
PART: Partition            PURG: Purger               RECM: Record Manager
RSLV: Resolve Name         SAPM: Srvc Advertising     SCMA: Schema
SPKT: Server Packets       SKLK: Skulker              STRM: Streams
SYNC: Inbound Sync         THRD: Threads              TVEC: Time Vector
VCLN: Virtual Client       WANM: WAN Traffic Mgr
CAM-SRV1:
```

To enable a tag, you simply type **DSTRACE** followed by the item you wish to view. Keep in mind that you have the options of viewing the file on the console only, logging the item to a file, or doing both. A legend at the top of the screen tells you whether you are viewing, logging to a file, or both. For example, you can type **DSTRACE TIME** to show event times. To disable this view you would type **DSTRACE –TIME** or to abbreviate, you can type **DSTRACE –TI**. The first two letters of each tag will work for disabling. You must always type **DSTRACE** in full.

NOTE

DSTRACE was originally developed and used by the Novell NDS engineers to help develop NDS. Novell technical support uses it to diagnose NDS errors and determine the health of the NetWare 5 system. The DSTRACE utility is also provided for the benefit of all administrators.

In NetWare 5, the DSTRACE screen displays the important information in color. Different colors highlight key events that occur during the synchronization process for the server. The trace screen displays synchronization information for every replica stored on that server.

Using DSTRACE

The quickest way to become familiar with the DSTRACE screen is to use it and learn what all the messages mean. Here is a standard set of DSTRACE commands that you can try:

```
DSTRACE  (load DSTRACE on the server)

DSTRACE+  <your preferred set tags or flags separated by
spaces>

DSTRACE SCREEN ON (Enables viewing on the screen)

DSTRACE FILE ON (Enables the events to be logged to a file)
```

DSTRACE has three main parts:

- Basic functions
- Debug messages
- Background process

Consulting Experience

Always check the DSTRACE screen to see that NDS is communicating before performing any partition operation. Never start a new partition operation if there is an error communicating to the other servers or replicas of the same partition.

Look for the message "ALL PROCESSED = YES" for each partition on the server, especially the partition you are going to modify. This message indicates that all replicas in the partition are synchronized without error.

Basic Functions

The basic functions of DSTRACE are to view the status of the Directory Services trace screen in NetWare 5 and initiate limited synchronization processes. If you are familiar with NetWare 4.*x*, you will notice that the DSTRACE screen has changed. However, you can still use the other DSTRACE options from NetWare 4.11.

Debugging Messages

When the DSTRACE screen is enabled, the information displayed is based on a default set of filters. If you want to view more or less information than the default, you can manipulate the filters using the debugging message flags. The debugging messages help you determine the status of NDS and verify that everything is working well.

Each NDS process has a set of debugging messages. To view the debugging messages on a particular process, use a plus sign (+) and the process name or option. To disable the display of a process, use a minus sign (–) and the process name or option. Here are some examples:

```
SET DSTRACE = +SYNC (Enables the synchronization messages)

SET DSTRACE = -SYNC (Disables the synchronization messages)

SET DSTRACE = +SCMA (Enables the schema messages)
```

You can also combine the debugging message flags by using the Boolean operators & (which means AND) and | (which means OR). The syntax for controlling the debugging messages at the server console is as follows:

```
SET DSTRACE = +<trace flag> [<trace flag>]
```

or

```
SET DSTRACE = -<trace flag> [& <trace flag>]
```

Table 9.4 describes the trace flags for the debugging messages. You can enter abbreviations for each of the trace flags. These abbreviations or alternatives are listed within parentheses in the table.

TABLE 9.4

Trace Flags for the Debugging Messages

TRACE FLAG	DESCRIPTION
ABUF	Display agent buffers.
ALOC	Display the memory allocation Information.
AREQ	Display messages relating to inbound client requests and what action is requested.
AUMN	Display messages and information related to auditing. In many cases, this will cause the server to pop into the debugger if auditing encounters an error.
AUNC	Audit NCP requests on this server.
AUSK	Audit skulker information.
AUTH	Display messages that are displayed while authenticating connections to the server.
BASE	Display a base set schema.
BLNK	Display messages related to verification of backlinks and external references. The backlink process resolves external references to make sure there is a real object in NDS. For real NDS objects the backlink process makes sure that an external reference exists for each backlink attribute.
BEMU	Display messages relating to Bindery Services (emulation).
CBUF	Display client buffer information.

Continued

TABLE 9.4

Continued

TRACE FLAG	DESCRIPTION
CHNG	Change cache.
COLL	Display collisions.
DRLK	Display distributed reference links.
ERRET	Display errors. Used only by the NDS engineers.
ERRORS (ERR, E)	Display error messages to show what the error was and where it came from.
FRAG	Display fragger debug messages. The fragger breaks up and rebuilds DS NCP packets — which can be up to 64K — into packets that can be transmitted on the network.
INIT	Display messages that occur during the process of initializing or opening the local name service.
INSP	Display messages related to the inspector process, which verifies the DS name service and object integrity on the local server. The inspector is part of the janitor process. If errors are detected, it could mean that you need to run DSREPAIR. Be aware that messages reported by this process may not all be actual errors. For this reason, you need to understand what the messages mean.
JNTR	Display messages related to the janitor process. The janitor controls the removal of deleted objects. It also finds the status and version of NCP servers and other miscellaneous record management.
LDAP	Display LDAP information.
LMBR	Display messages related to the limber process, which verifies tree connectivity by maintaining the server name, address, and replicas. This involves verifying and fixing the server name and server address if it changes.
LOCK	Display messages related to name service locking information.
LOST	Display lost entries.
MERGE	Not currently used.
MIN	Not currently used.

TRACE FLAG	DESCRIPTION
MISC	Miscellaneous information.
MOVE	Move.
NCPE	Display NCP Engine.
PART	Display messages related to partitioning operations. This trace flag may be useful for tracking partition operations as they proceed.
PURG	Purger.
RECM	Display messages related to the name base transactions, such as rebuilding and verifying the internal hash table and iteration state handling.
REPAIR	Not currently used.
RSLV	Display messages related to resolving name requests (tree walking). Resolve name resolves the name maps and object names to an ID on a particular server.
SAPM	Display Service Advertising packets.
SCMA	Display messages related to the schema being modified or synchronized across the network to the other servers.
SKLK	Display messages related to the synchronization process, which is responsible for synchronizing replicas on the servers with the other replicas on other servers. This is one of the most useful trace flags available.
STRM	Display messages related to stream attributes information.
SYNC	Display inbound synchronization information.
TAGS	Show entire list of event tags.
THRD	Display threads.
TIME	Display messages related to the synchronization or exchange of the timestamps between replicas. These messages display local and remote Synchronized Up To vectors, which contain the timestamps for the replica.

Continued

TABLE 9.4
Continued

TRACE FLAG	DESCRIPTION
TVEC	Display time vector information.
VCLN	Display messages related to the virtual client, which handles the outbound server connections needed to pass NDS information.
WANM	Display WAN Traffic Manager information.

The Background Process

In addition to the debugging messages, which help you check the status of NDS, there is a set of commands that force the NDS background processes to run. To force the background process to run, you precede the command with an asterisk (*). An example would be:

```
SET DSTRACE = *H
```

You can also change the status, timing, and control for a few of the background processes. To change these values, you must precede the command with an exclamation point (!) and enter a new parameter or value. An example would be:

```
SET DSTRACE = !H 15 (parameter value in minutes)
```

Here is the syntax for each statement controlling the background processes of NDS:

```
SET DSTRACE = *<trace flag> [parameter]
```

or

```
SET DSTRACE = !<trace flag> [parameter]
```

Table 9.5 lists the trace flags for the background processes, any required parameters, and the process the trace flags will display.

Consulting Experience

As you use the debugging messages in DSTRACE, you will find that some of the trace flags are more useful than others. One of the favorite DSTRACE settings of Novell technical support is actually a shortcut:

```
SET DSTRACE = A81164B91
```

This setting turns on (by setting the appropriate bits) a group of debugging messages.

TABLE 9.5

Trace Flags for Background Processes

FLAG	PARAMETERS	DESCRIPTION
*.	None	Unload and reload DS.NLM from the SYS:SYSTEM directory. For a short period of time, both DS.NLM and DSOLD.NLM will be loaded. This command is extremely useful when you are updating a version of DS.NLM. You can perform this operation during normal business hours without disrupting the users on that server.
*B	None	Force the backlink process to begin running. The backlink process can be traffic intensive, and you should probably wait until a slow time on the network before setting this command.
!B	Time (in minutes)	Set the backlink process interval used by NDS to check the backlink consistency. This command is the same as the NDS SET parameter NDS Backlink Interval, which is seen in the SERVMAN utility. The default is 1,500 minutes (25 hours). The range for this parameter is 2 to 10,080 minutes (168 hours).

Continued

TABLE 9.5

Continued

FLAG	PARAMETERS	DESCRIPTION
*D	Replica rootEntryID	Abort the Send All Updates or *I. This command is used only when a Send All Updates or *I cannot complete (and is therefore endlessly trying to send the objects to all replicas). This situation usually occurs when one of the servers is inaccessible.
*F	None	Force the flatcleaner process, which is part of the janitor process. The flatcleaner purges or removes the objects marked for deletion in the name service.
!F	Time (in minutes)	Set the flatcleaner process interval, changing when the flatcleaner process automatically begins. The flatcleaner process purges or removes the deleted objects and attributes from the name service. The default interval for this process is 240 minutes (4 hours). The value entered must be greater than 2 minutes.
*G	None	Give up on a server when there are too many requests being processed. The process gives up on the server and sets the server status to down.
*H	None	Force the heartbeat process to start. This flag starts immediate communication to exchange timestamps with all servers in replica lists. This command is useful for starting the synchronization between servers so that you can observe the status.
!H	Time (in minutes)	Set the heartbeat process interval. This parameter changes when the heartbeat process begins. The default interval for this process is 30 minutes.

FLAG	PARAMETERS	DESCRIPTION
*I	Replica rootEntryID	Force the replica on the server the command is issued to send a copy of all its objects to all other servers in the replica list. This command is the same as Send All Objects in DSREPAIR.
!I	Time (in minutes)	Set the heartbeat base schema interval. This parameter changes the schema heartbeat interval. The default interval for this process is 30 minutes.
!J	Time (in minutes)	Set the janitor process interval. This parameter changes when the janitor process executes. This command has the same function as SET command NDS Janitor Interval in the SERVMAN utility. The default interval is 2 minutes, with the limits of 1 to 10,080 minutes (168 hours).
*L	None	Start the limber process. The limber process checks the server name, server address, and tree connectivity of each replica.
*M	Bytes	Set the maximum size of the trace file in bytes, with a range of 10,000 to 10,000,000 bytes.
*P	None	Display the tunable parameters and their default settings.
*R	None	Reset the TTF file, which is the SYS:SYSTEM\ DSTRACE.DBG file by default. This command is the same as the SET parameter NDS Trace File Length Set to Zero.
*S	None	Schedule the skulker process, which checks whether any of the replicas on the server need to be synchronized.
*SS	None	Force immediate schema synchronization.

Continued

TABLE 9.5

Continued

FLAG	PARAMETERS	DESCRIPTION
!T	Time (in minutes)	Set the server UP threshold. This flag changes the server state threshold, which is the interval at which the server state is checked. The default interval is 30 minutes.
*U	Optional ID of server object	Force the server state to UP. If no server ID is specified, all servers in replica lists are set to UP. This command performs the same function as the SET parameter NDS Server Status.
!V	A list	List any restricted versions of the DS. If there are no versions listed in the return, there are no restrictions.
!W	Time (in ticks)	Change the IPX Request in Process (RIP) delay. This is the length of time to wait after getting an IPX timeout before resending the packet. The default value is 15 ticks. The range is 1 through 2,000 ticks.
!X	Number of retries	Change the number of IPX retries for the DS (server-to-server) client. After the retry count has been exceeded, an NDS error –625 is displayed. The default value is 3. The range is 1 through 50.
!Y	Number	Factor the estimated trip delay. It is used in the equation: IPX Timeout = (T *Y) + Z. This is where T is equal to the ticks required to get to the destination server. The default is value 2. The range is 0 through 530.
!Z	Number	Add additional delay for the IPX timeout. To increase the timeout, change this parameter first. It is used in the equation: IPX Timeout = (T *Y) + Z. This is where T is equal to the ticks required to get to the destination server. The default value is 4. The range is 0 through 500.

Performing and Verifying Partition Operations

Due to the loosely connected nature of NDS, any kind of partition operation change needs to be synchronized to other replicas of the partition. Because partition operations are performed by the master replica of that partition, master replicas should be used to verify any partition operation. The example of the NDS partition operations in this chapter uses the tree and partition information in Figure 9.14. The partitions are shown as circles. Figure 9.15 shows a view of the servers and their respective replicas. Some people prefer to view the different replicas of partitions stored on a particular server, whereas others prefer to view each partition and the servers on which they are stored.

FIGURE 9.14

A partitioned view of the ACME tree

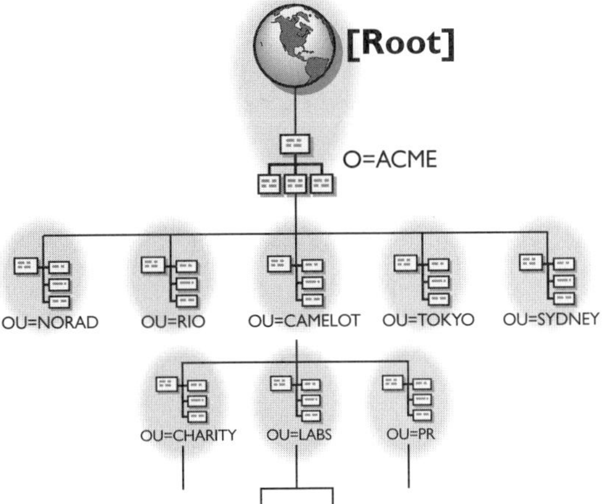

FIGURE 9.15

A grouping of ACME servers and their partitions

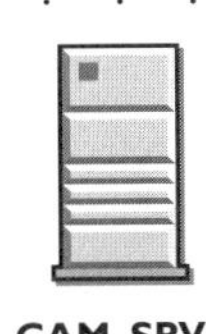
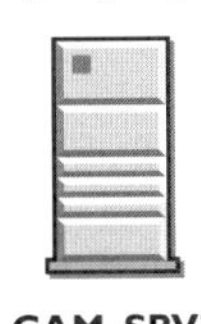
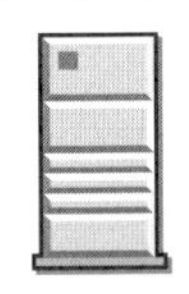
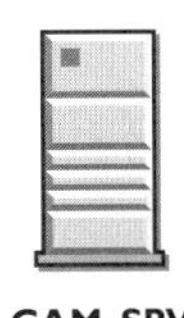

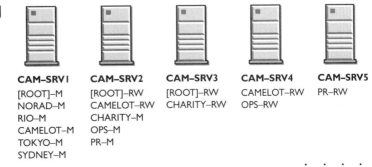

CAM-SRV1	CAM-SRV2	CAM-SRV3	CAM-SRV4	CAM-SRV5
[ROOT]-M	[ROOT]-RW	[ROOT]-RW	CAMELOT-RW	PR-RW
NORAD-M	CAMELOT-RW	CHARITY-RW	OPS-RW	
RIO-M	CHARITY-M			
CAMELOT-M	OPS-M			
TOKYO-M	PR-M			
SYDNEY-M				

Before starting any NDS partition operation, remember that there is a parent-child relationship between partitions. This entire section refers to the information in Figure 9.15. Notice in Figure 9.14 that the [ROOT] partition is a parent with five children—NORAD, RIO, CAMELOT, TOKYO, and SYDNEY. Notice that CAMELOT's parent partition is [ROOT]. The CAMELOT partition is also a parent partition with three child partitions: CHARITY, OPS, and PR. As shown in Figure 9.15, the tree includes the five servers CAM-SRV1, CAM-SRV2, CAM-SRV3, CAM-SRV4, CAM-SRV5. Most of the examples in this chapter will concentrate on the CAMELOT partition and its subordinate child partitions. Table 9.6 shows the replica assignments for [ROOT], NORAD, RIO, CAMELOT, TOKYO, SYDNEY, CHARITY, OPS, and PR.

NOTE

For discussion purposes only, we may place the replicas on the servers in a fashion that does not strictly follow our design recommendations. The examples used in this chapter do not imply a design recommendation for your replica placement; instead, these examples are simply used to explain the partition operations.

TABLE 9.6

Replica Assignments for [ROOT], NORAD, RIO, CAMELOT, TOKYO, SYDNEY, CHARITY, OPS, and PR (M indicates a master replica, and RW indicates a read/write replica)

[ROOT]	NORAD	RIO	CAMELOT	TOKYO	SYDNEY	CHARITY	OPS	PR
CAM-SRV1-M	CAM-SRV1-M	CAM-SRV1-M	CAM-SRV1-M	CAM-SRV1-M	CAM-SRV1-M	CAM-SRV1-M	CAM-SRV1-M	CAM-SRV2-M M
CAM-SRV2-RW			CAM-SRV2-RW			CAM-SRV3-RW	CAM-SRV4-RW	CAM-SRV5-RW
CAM-			CAM-	SRV3-RW			SRV4-RW	

As mentioned previously, some people prefer to view the partitions and replica assignments by server. Using the same set of information that is shown in Table 9.6 and displaying or representing this information by server is illustrated in Table 9.7. Notice that each server is shown and then the partitions.

TABLE 9.7

Partition and Replica Assignments for Each of the Servers CAM-SRV1, CAM-SRV2, CAM-SRV3, CAM-SRV4, and CAM-SRV5 (M indicates a master replica, and RW indicates a read/write replica)

CAM-SRV1	CAM-SRV2	CAM-SRV3	CAM-SRV4	CAM-SRV5
[ROOT]-M	[ROOT]-RW	[ROOT]-RW	CAMELOT-RW	PR-RW
NORAD-M	CAMELOT-RW	CHARITY-RW	OPS-RW	
RIO-M	CHARITY-M			
CAMELOT-M	OPS-M			
TOKYO-M	PR-M			
SYDNEY-M				

For each NDS partition, there is a replica list. In order to have a complete replica list for each partition, you have to consider the subordinate reference replicas (also known as subrefs) that are created automatically by NDS. When a server holds a copy of a partition such as a read/write (RW), read-only (RO), or master (M) of a parent partition, but does not hold the copy of the child partition, NDS automatically creates a subordinate reference, facilitating a link from the parent partition to the child partition. The link is necessary so that if the server holding the parent partition is queried about an object that exists on one of its child partitions, it knows which server to talk to. In other words, subordinate reference replicas are critical to the tree walking process, which is performed by the NetWare 5 servers. Therefore, including the subordinate reference replicas, the replica list just described will actually appear as shown in Table 9.8.

TABLE 9.8

Replica List for Each Server (M indicates a master replica, RW indicates a read/write replica, and SR indicates a subordinate reference replica)

CAM-SRV1	CAM-SRV2	CAM-SRV3	CAM-SRV4	CAM-SRV5
[ROOT]-M	[ROOT]-RW	[ROOT]-RW	CAMELOT-RW	PR-RW
NORAD-M	NORAD-SR	NORAD-SR	CHARITY-SR	
RIO-M	RIO-SR	RIO-SR	OPS-RW	
CAMELOT-M	CAMELOT-RW	CAMELOT-RW	PR-SR	

Continued

TABLE 9.8 Continued

CAM-SRV1	CAM-SRV2	CAM-SRV3	CAM-SRV4	CAM-SRV5
TOKYO-M	TOKYO-SR	TOKYO-SR		
SYDNEY-M	SYDNEY-SR	SYDNEY-SR		
CHARITY-SR	CHARITY-M	CHARITY-RW		
OPS-SR	OPS-M			
PR-SR	PR-M			

The following sections discuss the various partition operations that you can perform and explain how to properly verify their status and completion.

Consulting Experience

We are often asked "Is there something that we can do on a daily basis as a proactive measure to tell whether NDS is performing smoothly?" As a network administrator, you can follow the steps below to ensure that your NetWare 5 network is running smoothly. Take some time to learn and practice these steps. You should also follow these steps before you initiate any partition operations.

- Check the time synchronization status of the servers using DSREPAIR.
- Check to make sure that the servers are communicating properly. Use the replica synchronization option in DSREPAIR.
- Check to make sure the replica synchronization process has completed for the partitions. You can use DSTRACE to do the checking.
- Check the replica state for each partition. Use DSREPAIR to check the replica states. If the state of the partitions is okay, then you can initiate the partition operation that you choose. Make sure to check the state of all the partitions involved in the operation.
- Always check the log file in DSREPAIR for errors that may show up in the replica synchronization status.

Adding Replicas

The add replica operation adds a new replica to a partition's replica list and may be used fairly often by your administrators. Here are the steps involved in this operation:

1. The master replica of the partition adds the server name as New Replica to the replica list.
2. The master replica sends all the objects in the partition to the new replica. You have a NEW state until the master has successfully sent all changes to the new replica.
3. The master replica sets the state in the replica ring to TRANSITION ON.
4. All the other replicas begin synchronizing with the new replica.
5. The master replica sets the replica state to ON.

At this point, let's add a read/write replica of the CAMELOT partition to the CAM-SRV3 server. You should follow these steps to successfully carry out the add replica operation.

Phase One

1. Run DSREPAIR and choose the Report Synchronization Status option. The CAMELOT partition has both parent and child partitions. Therefore, the placement of a read/write replica of CAMELOT on CAM-SRV3 will cause the new replica to get involved in replica synchronization with servers that hold a replica of [ROOT] (the parent replica) and CHARITY, OPS, and PR (the child replicas). For this reason, you should check the synchronization status of the partition itself and of the child partitions. Use DSREPAIR to check the replica synchronization status.
2. Load DSREPAIR.NLM on the servers holding the master of CAMELOT and CHARITY, OPS, and PR partitions. In this case, CAM-SRV1 and CAM-SRV2 would need to be checked. In order to check the status of the replica synchronization, you need to choose the Report Synchronization Status option. An example of this report is shown in Figure 9.16.

FIGURE 9.16

A view of the Report Synchronization Status option

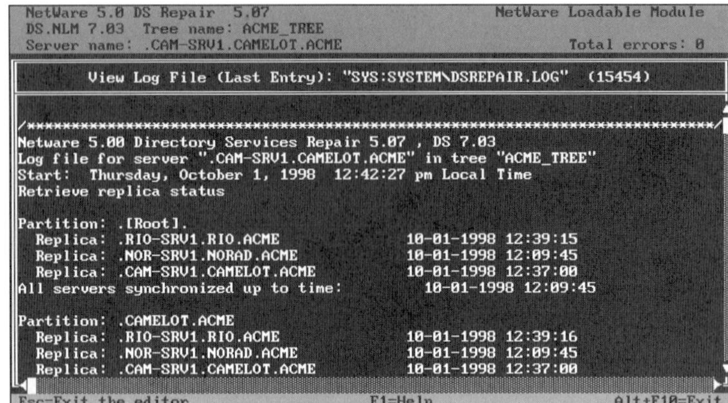

This first phase verifies that there are no synchronization errors on the partition itself, its parent, and its children. Only after you know that there are no errors should you initiate the add replica operation.

If any errors are reported by DSREPAIR's Report Synchronization Status option, you need to find out what they are before continuing with the add replica operation. For more information, refer to Appendix B, "NDS Error Codes and Definitions," for a listing of error codes and recommended actions.

TIP

You can also use the Partition Status option in DSREPAIR to search for any errors. For example, you may see a –698 error indicating that the partition is busy synchronizing. This is normal unless the error continues indefinitely.

Phase Two

1. Set the DSTRACE screen on the master replica to monitor the operation. In this case, the server holding the master replica is CAM-SRV1.

2. Follow this step if the partition status shows an error or the status does not change. If no errors are shown in the report from Phase One, it is time to SET DSTRACE on the server holding the master replica of the partition as follows:

```
SET DSTRACE = ON(Turn on debug trace screen. Press Alt+Esc
to see the trace debug screen.)

SET TTF = ON     (Open DSTRACE.DBG file)

SET DSTRACE = *R(Reset DSTRACE.DBG to zero length)

SET DSTRACE = 1 (Turn off all the switches)

SET DSTRACE = +S(Show detailed synchronization)
```

These steps capture the operations the master replica must take to finish the add replica operation. The text file that holds the trace information is in SYS: SYSTEM\DSTRACE.DBG file on the master.

Phase Three

1. Issue the add replica operation using NDS Manager.

Figure 9.17 shows an example of adding a replica.

FIGURE 9.17

An example of the Add Replica function using NDS Manager

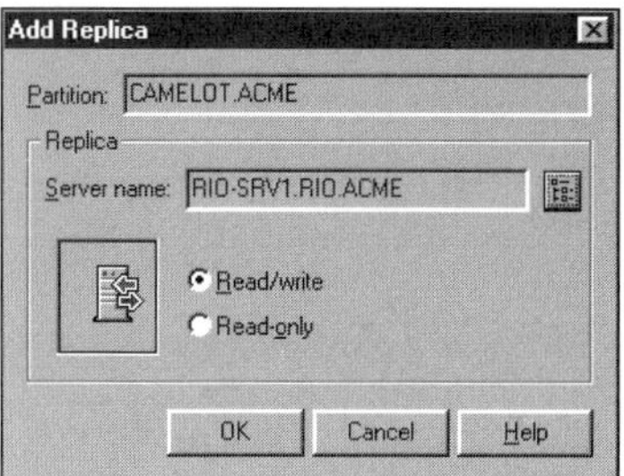

Phase Four

1. Verify the partition operation from the back end.

2. After issuing the call from the NDS Manager utility, you need to check the master server that controls the back-end process. You have two ways to verify that the add replica operation has completed: You can use DSTRACE, or you can use DSREPAIR and the Report Synchronization Status option. It is a good idea to use both methods to gather all possible information about the operation.

Checking Add Replica with DSTRACE

DSTRACE is a window to a NetWare 5 server's NDS activity. It shows what the background processes are doing. We set DSTRACE to ON in Step 2 of Phase Four to monitor the replica synchronization activity from the master while it is sending all the objects in the CAMELOT partition to CAM-SRV3. Now it is time to execute the following commands at the console prompt to stop the accumulation of trace information:

```
SET TTF = OFF (Closes the DSTRACE.DBG file)

LOAD EDIT SYS:SYSTEM\DSTRACE.DBG (Edit or view the trace
file)
```

You can also use your preferred editor to review the trace file and look for any errors that may have resulted from the Add Replica process.

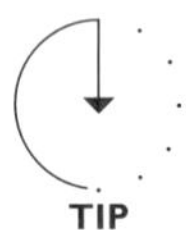

If the state of the partition goes from new to transition, you needn't run DSTRACE because you will see the error in Partition Status of DSREPAIR.

Checking Add Replica with DSREPAIR

Using DSREPAIR or Partition Manager, first check the master partition of CAMELOT, which is stored on CAM-SRV1, by doing these things:

1. Choose the replica partition operation.
2. Choose the CAMELOT partition.
3. View the replica ring.

DSREPAIR should confirm that CAM-SRV3 holds a read/write replica, and the state of the replica should say ON. If the state says New Replica, the add replica operation has not finished. The states of partitions range from New Replica to Transition ON to ON. The Transition ON state means the master replica has finished sending all the objects and CAM-SRV3 is waiting for other read/write replicas to send any other updates that the master didn't have when the operation was performed.

After confirming that the master replica has sent the updates to CAM-SRV3 as a read/write and confirming a state of ON in the replica list, you can use the DSREPAIR Report Synchronization Status option on the servers holding the master of [ROOT], CAMELOT, CHARITY, OPS, and PR to make sure that all the servers are successfully talking to CAM-SRV3.

Table 9.9 shows the replica list for the partitions in our scenario. Notice that the new replica added for the CAMELOT partition is stored on CAM-SRV3.

TABLE 9.9

A Replica List (M indicates a master replica, RW indicates a read/write replica, and SR indicates a subordinate reference replica)

CAM-SRV1	CAM-SRV2	CAM-SRV3	CAM-SRV4	CAM-SRV5
[ROOT]-M	[ROOT]-RW	[ROOT]-RW	CAMELOT-RW	PR-RW
NORAD-M	NORAD-SR	NORAD-SR	CHARITY-SR	
RIO-M	RIO-SR	RIO-SR	OPS-RW	
CAMELOT-M	CAMELOT-RW	CAMELOT-RW	PR-SR	
TOKYO-M	TOKYO-SR	TOKYO-SR		
SYDNEY-M	SYDNEY-SR	SYDNEY-SR		
CHARITY-SR	CHARITY-M	CHARITY-RW		
OPS-SR	OPS-M	OPS-SR		
PR-SR	PR-M	PR-SR		

Deleting Replicas

For a replica to be deleted successfully:

- Master(s) must remove the server from the replica list(s).
- The server holding the deleted replica must destroy the replica.

After the replica has been destroyed, the NetWare 5 server will turn all the objects on the deleted replica into external references.

NOTE

The external references will be removed from that server if they haven't been used by the next time the backlinker process runs. For more information on the backlinker process, refer to Chapter 8, "NDS Internals Operations."

For the delete replica operation, we will remove a read/write replica of CAMELOT from the server CAM-SRV4. Follow these steps to delete the replica from the server CAM-SRV4.

Phase One

1. Run the DSREPAIR Report Synchronization Status option. The CAMELOT partition has both parent and child partitions. Therefore, removing the replica of CAMELOT from CAM-SRV4 will also remove the subordinate reference replicas of CHARITY and PR from CAM-SRV4. Although the OPS partition is a child partition to CAMELOT, it is unaffected because it is a full read/write replica. The CHARITY and PR replicas are removed from the server because they are subordinate reference replicas. Subordinate reference replicas are removed once the parent replica is removed from CAM-SRV4. Therefore, we should also check the synchronization status on the parent and children using DSREPAIR.

2. Load DSREPAIR.NLM on the servers holding the CAMELOT, CHARITY, OPS, and PR partitions. You need to choose the Report Synchronization Status option.

The first phase verifies that there are no synchronization errors on the partition itself and its children. You must make this determination before running the delete replica operation.

If the DSREPAIR's Report Synchronization Status option discovers any errors, you need to find out what the error is before continuing with the operation. For more information, refer to Appendix B for a listing of error codes and recommended actions.

Phase Two

1. Set the DSTRACE screen on the master replica to monitor the operation.

2. If no errors are reported in Step 1, set DSTRACE on the server holding the master replica of the partition you intend to delete as follows:

```
SET DSTRACE = ON(Turn on trace screen)

SET TTF = ON     (Open DSTRACE.DBG file)

SET DSTRACE = *R(Reset DSTRACE.DBG)

SET DSTRACE = 1 (Turn off all the switches)

SET DSTRACE = +S(Show detailed synchronization)
```

With Phase Two, you can capture the operation the master replica must take to finish the operation. The information is in the SYS:SYSTEM\DSTRACE.DBG file on the master.

Phase Three

1. Issue the delete replica operation using NDS Manager.

Phase Four

1. Verify the delete replica operation from the back end.

2. After issuing the call from the front end, you must check the master server that controls the back end before the operation is considered complete. There are two ways to verify the delete replica operation. You can use DSTRACE, or you can use the DSREPAIR Report Synchronization Status option. It is a good idea to use both methods.

Checking Delete Replica with DSTRACE

DSTRACE is a window to a server's NDS activity. It shows what the background processes are doing. DSTRACE on the master shows us the process of removing CAM-SRV4 from the CAMELOT replica list. We can also capture DSTRACE on CAM-SRV2, which holds the master of CHARITY, OPS, and PR. Now you can issue the following commands at the console prompt:

```
SET TTF = OFF (Close DSTRACE.DBG file)

LOAD EDIT SYS:SYSTEM\DSTRACE.DBG
```

You can also use your preferred editor to review the trace file and look for any errors that may have resulted from the process.

Checking Delete Replica with DSREPAIR

In this scenario, we first check the master of CAMELOT, which is stored on server CAM-SRV1, and then choose the Replica and Partition Operations option. We next choose the CAMELOT partition and then choose View Replica Ring. This approach should confirm that CAM-SRV4 has been removed from the replica list of the master. If the state says Dying Replica, the delete replica operation has not yet finished.

After you confirm that the master replica of CAMELOT has CAM-SRV4 removed from the replica list, you can use DSREPAIR on CAM-SRV2 (the master of CHARITY, OPS, and PR) to make sure that CAM-SRV4 has been successfully removed from their replica lists. It is a good idea to check the Synchronization Report Status using DSREPAIR on CAMELOT, CHARITY, OPS, and PR.

The final phase is to run DSREPAIR on CAM-SRV4 to verify that delete operation has finished. Run the DSREPAIR.NLM Advanced Options menu and then select Replica and Partition Operations option to verify that CAMELOT, CHARITY, and PR have been removed.

The replica list for the partition in our scenario is shown in Table 9.10.

TABLE 9.10

A Replica List (M indicates a master replica, RW indicates a read/write replica, and SR indicates a subordinate reference replica)

CAM-SRV1	CAM-SRV2	CAM-SRV3	CAM-SRV4	CAM-SRV5
[ROOT]-M	[ROOT]-RW	[ROOT]-RW	OPS-RW	PR-RW
NORAD-M	NORAD-SR	NORAD-SR		
RIO-M	RIO-SR	RIO-SR		
CAMELOT-M	CAMELOT-RW	CAMELOT-RW		
TOKYO-M	TOKYO-SR	TOKYO-SR		

CAM-SRV1	CAM-SRV2	CAM-SRV3	CAM-SRV4	CAM-SRV5
SYDNEY-M	SYDNEY-SR	SYDNEY-SR		
CHARITY-SR	CHARITY-M	CHARITY-RW		
OPS-SR	OPS-M	OPS-SR		
PR-SR	PR-M	PR-SR		

Changing Replica Types

Change replica type is another very important partition operation. The master replica is in charge of all the partition operations. Any synchronization errors at the time of the change replica type operation can cause confusion between replicas and prevent the operation from completing. Therefore, no more partition operations are possible on that partition while it is in the change replica state.

To successfully change the read/write replica to a master, the old master changes the replica type in two stages and synchronizes the changes to the other replicas, including the new master.

This example changes the master of CAMELOT from CAM-SRV1 to CAM-SRV2.

Phase One

1. Run the DSREPAIR's Report Synchronization Status option. Change Replica Type is the only partition operation that requires a replica synchronization check of the partition itself. This operation affects only the CAMELOT partition in this example.

2. Load DSREPAIR.NLM on the master of CAMELOT partition. Choose the Report Synchronization Status option.

The first phase verifies that there are no synchronization errors on the CAMELOT partition before you issue a change replica type operation.

If there are any errors on DSREPAIR's Report Synchronization Status, you need to find out what the error is before continuing with the operation. For more information, refer to Appendix B for a listing of error codes and recommended actions.

Phase Two

1. Set the DSTRACE screen on the master replica to monitor the operation.

2. Once you have resolved any errors discovered in Phase One, you can set DSTRACE on the master of the partition as follows:

```
SET DSTRACE = ON(Turn on trace screen)
SET TTF = ON      (Open DSTRACE.DBG file)
SET DSTRACE = *R(Reset DSTRACE.DBG)
SET DSTRACE = 1 (Turn off all the switches)
SET DSTRACE = +S(Show detailed synchronization)
```

Phase Three captures the operation the master replica must take to finish the operation. The information is in the SYS:SYSTEM\DSTRACE.DBG file on the master.

Phase Three

1. Issue the change replica type operation using NDS Manager.

Phase Four

1. Verify the change replica type operation from the back end.

2. There are two ways to verify the change replica operation: DSTRACE and the DSREPAIR Report Synchronization Status option. It is a good idea to use both methods.

Checking the Change Replica Type with DSTRACE

DSTRACE is a window to a server's NDS activity. It shows what the background processes are doing. DSTRACE on the master shows us the process of changing the master replica type from CAM-SRV1 to CAM-SRV2. Now it is time to execute the following commands at the console prompt:

```
SET TTF = OFF (Close DSTRACE.DBG file)
LOAD EDIT SYS:SYSTEM\DSTRACE.DBG
```

You can also use your preferred editor to review the trace file and look for any errors that may have turned up as a result of the change replica type operation.

Checking the Change Replica Type with DSREPAIR

First check the old master of CAMELOT, which is CAM-SRV1, and choose the Replica and Partition Operation options, choose the CAMELOT partition, and then select the View Replica Ring option. It should confirm that CAM-SRV2 has been assigned as the new master replica. If the state says Changed Replica Type, the operation is not yet finished.

Next, check the new master CAM-SRV2, and then use DSREPAIR's View Replica Ring option to verify the change.

After confirming that the master replica of CAMELOT has been changed to CHR-SRV1, use DSREPAIR on CAM-SRV2 to check the Synchronization Report Status option for CAMELOT and make sure the change was successful.

The replica list for the partition in our scenario will now look like this:

<u>CAMELOT</u>
CAM-SRV1-RW
CAM-SRV2-M
CAM-SRV3-RW

Creating (Splitting) Partitions

Partitions are created when any container in the NDS Manager utility is marked as a new partition. In other words, the container is already part of another partition but gets split off as a new partition. This process establishes the new partition boundary. A new child partition gets created with respect to the parent. The servers that hold the copy of the parent partition will receive the copy of the new child partition with the same replica ring as the parent. It makes sense because the only servers that have the real copy of all the objects in the child partition will get a copy.

In a create partition operation:

- The master of the partition directs all the replicas in the list that a new partition is being created.
- The master of the parent becomes the master of the new child partition.

- Read/write copies of the parent will establish a new boundary for the read/write replica of the new child partition.
- Subordinate reference replicas of the parent are not involved in the operation.

The following example creates a new partition called OPS, which is a container below the CAMELOT partition.

Phase One

1. Run the DSREPAIR Report Synchronization Status option. As usual, you should check synchronization status before starting the operation. The CAMELOT partition needs to be checked. You don't need to check synchronization status on the sibling partitions to the new partition because the replicas of the sibling partitions won't get involved in the create operation.

2. Load DSREPAIR.NLM on the server holding the master of CAMELOT partition. Choose the Report Synchronization Status option.

The first phase verifies that there are no synchronization errors on the CAMELOT partition before you carry out the create partition operation.

If DSREPAIR's Report Synchronization Status should turn up any errors, you need to find out what they are before continuing with the operation. For more information, refer to Appendix B for a listing of error codes and recommended actions.

Phase Two

1. Set the DSTRACE screen on the master replica to monitor the operation.

2. Once you've determined that there are no errors as discussed in Phase One, it is time to set DSTRACE on the master of the partition as follows:

```
SET DSTRACE = ON(Turn on trace screen)

SET TTF = ON     (Open DSTRACE.DBG file)

SET DSTRACE = *R(Reset DSTRACE.DBG)
```

```
SET DSTRACE = 1 (Turn off all the switches)

SET DSTRACE = +S (Show detailed synchronization)
```

Phase Three captures the operation the master replica must take in order to finish the operation. The information is in the SYS:SYSTEM\DSTRACE.DBG file on the master.

Phase Three

1. Issue the create partition operation using NDS Manager.

Phase Four

1. Verify the create partition operation from the back end.

2. There are two ways to verify the create partition operation: DSTRACE and the DSREPAIR Report Synchronization Status option. It is a good idea to use both methods.

Checking the Create Partition with DSTRACE

DSTRACE shows what the background processes are doing. DSTRACE on the master shows us the process of creating the partition. Enter the following commands at the console prompt:

```
SET TTF = OFF (Close DSTRACE.DBG file)

LOAD EDIT SYS:SYSTEM\DSTRACE.DBG
```

You can also use your preferred editor to review the trace file and look for any errors that may have resulted from the Create Partition process.

Checking the Create Partition with DSREPAIR

DSTRACE shows what happened during the process. In contrast, DSREPAIR shows the state of the replicas and how they are synchronizing. First, check the master of CAMELOT, which is stored on CAM-SRV1, and choose Replica Partition Operation to make sure that the OPS partition is listed. Then choose the CAMELOT partition and View Replica Ring option; it should confirm that all the replicas are ON. Carry out the same procedure on the OPS partition. If the state says Split State, the operation has not yet finished.

After you confirm that the OPS partition has been successfully created, you can run DSREPAIR on CAM-SRV1, which contains the master of both CAMELOT and OPS, and run the Report Synchronization Status on the two partitions to make sure synchronization is successful after the operation.

Merging (Joining) Partitions

In the merge partition operation, the existing child partition will be merged with the parent partition. Because it is not possible to delete the partition, you must merge it with the parent. This process destroys the partition boundary and then removes all the partition properties. Thus, the container is simply an object in the tree that can hold other objects. Now you can delete the container object if it doesn't hold any objects.

By default, the Merge Operation option makes the replica ring the same for both the parent and child partitions, excluding the subrefs from the parent's replica ring. In other words, any server that holds the readable copy of the child or parent will get a read-only copy of either one. This is probably the most time-consuming part of the process and will possibly create network traffic if the partitions are large. The add replica operation is the first part of the process. A read-only replica of the child partition is added everywhere the parent is, and a read-only replica of the parent is added everywhere the child is.

In the merge partition operation:

- The master of the child partition finds the master of the parent partition to start the process.
- The master of the parent partition starts the first phase of the merge and the master of the child partition sets the states accordingly.
- The masters of parent and child compare replica rings to determine which servers they must add replicas to.
- The partition boundary is deleted.
- The parent's master replica becomes the master of the new partition. The child's master and read/write replicas become read/write copies of the new partition.

The following example merges the CHARITY partition into the CAMELOT partition.

Phase One

1. Run the DSREPAIR Report Synchronization Status option. As usual, you should check synchronization status before starting the operation. The CAMELOT and CHARITY partitions need to be checked.

2. Load DSREPAIR.NLM on the master of the CHARITY and CAMELOT partitions. Choose the Report Synchronization Status option.

The first phase verifies that there are no synchronization errors on the CAMELOT and CHARITY partitions before you perform the merge partition operation. If there are any errors on DSREPAIR's Report Synchronization Status option, you need to find out what the errors are before continuing with the operation. For more information, refer to Appendix B, "NDS Error Codes and Definitions," for a listing of error codes and recommended actions.

Phase Two

1. Set the DSTRACE screen on the master replica to monitor the operation.

2. Once you have eliminated any errors found in Phase One, set DSTRACE on the master of both the CHARITY and CAMELOT partitions as follows:

```
SET DSTRACE = ON (Turn on trace screen)

SET TTF = ON     (Open DSTRACE.DBG file)

SET DSTRACE = *R (Reset DSTRACE.DBG)

SET DSTRACE = 1  (Turn off all the switches)

SET DSTRACE = +S (Show detailed synchronization)
```

These steps shown in Phase Two capture all the operations the master replicas must take to finish the operation. The information is in the SYS:SYSTEM \DSTRACE.DBG file on the master.

Phase Three

1. Issue the merge partition operation using NDS Manager.

Phase Four

1. Verify the merge partition operation from the back end.

2. The replica list for the partition in our scenario is shown in Table 9.11.

TABLE 9.11

A Replica List (M indicates a master replica, RW indicates a read/write replica, and SR indicates a subordinate reference replica)

CAM-SRV1	CAM-SRV2	CAM-SRV3	CAM-SRV4	CAM-SRV5
[ROOT]-M	[ROOT]-RW	[ROOT]-RW	CAMELOT-RW	PR-RW
NORAD-M	NORAD-SR	NORAD-SR	OPS-RW	
RIO-M	RIO-SR	RIO-SR	PR-SR	
CAMELOT-M	CAMELOT-RW	CAMELOT-SW		
TOKYO-M	TOKYO-SR	TOKYO-SR		
SYDNEY-M	SYDNEY-SR	SYDNEY-SR		
OPS-M	OPS-M			
PR-SR	PR-M			

There are two ways of verifying the merge partition operation: DSTRACE and DSREPAIR's Report Synchronization Status option. It is a good idea to use both methods.

Checking the Merge Partition with DSTRACE

DSTRACE shows what the background processes are doing. DSTRACE on both master replicas shows us the process of merging the partitions. Enter the following commands at the console prompt:

```
SET TTF = OFF (Close DSTRACE.DBG file)

LOAD EDIT SYS:SYSTEM\DSTRACE.DBG
```

You can also use your preferred editor to review the trace file and look for any errors that may have resulted from the Merge Partition process.

Checking the Merge Partition with DSREPAIR

DSTRACE shows what happened during the process. In contrast, DSREPAIR shows the state of the replicas and how they are synchronizing. First, check the master of CAMELOT, which is held on CAM-SRV1, and choose the Replica and Partition Operations option to make sure that the CHARITY partition is not listed. Then choose the CAMELOT partition and the View Replica Ring option; it should confirm that all the replicas are ON. If the state says Join State, the operation has not yet finished.

After confirming that the CHARITY partition has been successfully merged, run DSREPAIR on CAM-SRV1, which holds the master of CAMELOT, and the Synchronization Report Status option to make sure synchronization is successful after the operation.

CHARITY should now be only an organizational unit inside the CAMELOT partition.

Moving Subtrees or Partitions

The move subtree operation moves a partition and all its child entries as a unit to another logical location in the tree. The replicas of the partition being moved are held on the same servers they were held on previously. In other words, NDS moves the subtree logically, not physically. However, the objects' full names in the partition will change.

A move subtree operation involves a destination server and a source server:

- The destination server is the server holding the master replica of the parent partition under which the child partition is moving. This server prepares for the operation and signals the source server.
- The source server is the server holding the master replica of the partition that is moving. This server forms a list of servers that will participate in moving the subtree.
- Large numbers of packets are exchanged between the source server and the destination server during a move subtree operation.

The following example moves the subtree CHARITY under the PR partition.

Phase One

1. Run the DSREPAIR Report Synchronization Status option. As usual, you should check synchronization status before starting the operation. The PR, CAMELOT, and CHARITY partitions need to be checked.

2. Load DSREPAIR.NLM on the servers holding the master of the CHARITY, CAMELOT, and PR partitions. In this case, the servers are CAM-SRV1 and CAM-SRV2. Choose the Report Synchronization Status option.

Phase One verifies that there are no synchronization errors on the CAMELOT, CHARITY, and PR partitions before the move subtree operation.

If there are any errors on DSREPAIR report synchronization status, you need to find out what they are before continuing with the operation. For more information, refer to Appendix B for a listing of error codes and recommended actions.

Phase Two

1. Set the DSTRACE screen on the master replica to monitor the operation.

2. Once you have resolved any errors that turned up in Phase One, set DSTRACE on the master of both the CHARITY and PR partitions as follows:

```
SET DSTRACE = ON (Turn on trace screen)

SET TTF = ON     (Open DSTRACE.DBG file)

SET DSTRACE = *R (Reset DSTRACE.DBG)

SET DSTRACE = 1  (Turn off all the switches)

SET DSTRACE = +S (Show detailed synchronization)
```

Phase Three captures all the operations the master replicas must take to finish the operation. The information is in the SYS:SYSTEM\DSTRACE.DBG file on the master.

Phase Three

1. Issue the move subtree operation using NDS Manager.

Phase Four

1. Verify the move subtree operation from the back end.

2. There are two ways of verifying the move subtree operation: DSTRACE and the DSREPAIR Report Synchronization Status option. It is a good idea to use both methods.

Checking the Move Subtree with DSTRACE

DSTRACE shows what the background processes are doing. DSTRACE on both master replicas shows how the process of merging the partitions finished. Enter the following commands at the console prompt:

```
SET TTF = OFF (Close DSTRACE.DBG file)

LOAD EDIT SYS:SYSTEM\DSTRACE.DBG
```

You can also use your preferred editor to review the trace file and look for any errors that may have resulted from the Move Subtree process.

Checking the Move Subtree with DSREPAIR

DSTRACE shows what happened during the process. In contrast, DSREPAIR shows the state of the replicas and how they are synchronizing. First, check the Master of PR, which is stored on CAM-SRV2, and choose Replica and Partition Operations. Make sure that the CHARITY partition's full name is under PR. Then choose CHARITY partition and the View Replica Ring option; it should confirm that all the replicas are ON. If the state says Move Subtree State, the operation has not finished. You should check the PR partition in the same way.

After confirming that CHARITY has been successfully moved, run DSREPAIR on CAM-SRV1, which holds the master of CAMELOT, and the Synchronization Report Status option to make sure synchronization is successful after the operation. Follow the same procedure for CHARITY and PR. Remember that the replica ring for CHARITY will remain the same.

Troubleshooting Do's and Don'ts

This section describes some of the most common mistakes people make when installing and managing NetWare 5 and Novell Directory Services.

Do Not Temporarily Change the Internal IPX or File Server Name

If a server is brought up without running AUTOEXEC.NCF for any reason, the NetWare OS requires that you enter a server name and internal IPX number. In NetWare 5, the server name and internal IPX number must be the same as what is stored in the AUTOEXEC.NCF. Otherwise the NetWare 5 server treats the change as permanent and synchronizes the change to all the other servers in your tree. Even if the server is not connected to the network, the change happens on its database, and as soon as the server is connected to the network it sends the change. If this happens, let the system resolve the change first, and then change the name or internal IPX back to what it should be. Do not change the server name and internal IPX number back immediately because this can cause problems with NDS.

Check Replica Ring Synchronization Before Doing a Partition Operation

Always run the DSREPAIR Check Report Synchronization option before starting any partition operation. This action will ensure that there are no synchronization errors and that any change you make will be synchronized to other replicas.

Do Not Change Read/Write to Master under Partition Error Conditions

If you change the master replica of a partition under error conditions, the operation can get stuck. This means that NDS has not properly or fully completed the process and NDS is in an inactive state. In this situation, no other partition operation is possible since the master replica controls all the partition operations. If you check the DSREPAIR option View Replica Ring, it should confirm that the replica states are Change Replica Type. If Change Replica Type doesn't resolve itself, you may have to call Novell technical support to resolve the issue.

Centralize the Partition Operation Administration

Novell technical support has found that centralized management of all the partitions in the tree is critical to maintaining a healthy NDS tree. Managing NDS should be divided into:

- Partition management
- User and server management

Partition management is the only area that needs to be centralized. User and server management can be decentralized, as in a NetWare 3 environment. NDS is loosely connected, and it takes a while for changes to synchronize to other replicas. If the change happens to be partition information and there are multiple administrators performing multiple partition operations, the replicas may not synchronize properly. Centralizing partition operations eliminates many of the related problems.

Do Not Design a Flat Tree

Flat tree design is inefficient and causes unnecessary overhead to the system. The reason is that a very wide and flat tree (meaning many peer organizational units) creates a large number of subordinate references if each container is partitioned. An inefficient tree design can compound NDS problems and actually decrease the performance of your network. For more information on designing an NDS tree, refer to Chapter 5, "Novell Directory Services Tree," and Chapter 6, "Designing and Using NDS Partitions and Replicas."

Use Install to Remove or Delete a Server

Always use the INSTALL.NLM option Remove Directory Services when deleting a server object. This option removes a server from the tree properly. Even if the server has a copy of any replica, INSTALL removes the copy from the server for you. Never delete a server object unless the server has been removed from the tree with the Remove Directory Services option.

If You Suspect Errors, Verify the Partition Operation on the Back End from the Master Replica

After issuing the call from the front end to perform a partition operation, check the master partition on the server that is controlling the back-end process before considering the operation completed. There are two ways to verify that the operation is completed: DSTRACE and the DSREPAIR Report Synchronization option. Verifying partition operations from the servers holding the master replicas will tell you whether the operation has finished or whether any errors have been generated as a result of the operation.

Be Careful with Declare New Epoch and Rebuild Replica Operations

This option can be issued from the DSREPAIR utility. Use this option only if instructed to do so by Novell technical support. It destroys all replicas of that partition except the master replica. In other words, the master will be the only copy left. Unsynchronized changes from other replicas will be lost. The master replica will resend every object in the partition to all the other replicas. Always run the DSREPAIR option Repair Local Database to determine how many unknown objects the partition has. Also make sure there are no synchronization errors on that partition before issuing the call.

Do Not Copy .NDS Files from One Server to Another

The .NDS files are located in the SYS:_NetWare directory and are specific to the server. Copying these files to another server will generate unexpected results and can cause serious problems for the tree.

Use NDS Replication before a Tape Restoration

Always rely on the replicas of a partition before using tape backup. This is why you should have at least three copies of any partition.

Consider How the Partition Operation Will Affect the Tree

Network administrators need to adjust to the new network-centric environment of NetWare 5, instead of thinking in terms of the server-centric world of NetWare 3. When you made a change in NetWare 3, it happened only on that server. However, when you make a change to a NetWare 5 server, the change affects both the tree and the network. In the NetWare 5 environment, you have to continually ask "How will the change affect the partitions of the tree?"

Avoid Duplicate Server Names, Internal IPX Numbers, or Tree Names

Duplicate server names, internal IPX numbers, and tree names can result in some irrational behaviors on the network, confusing all the clients and servers in the network.

Do Not Install the Same Server in More Than One Tree

Installing the same server name in multiple trees can create problems in replica synchronization. Normally, INSTALL.NLM will not let you do this, but if there are synchronization errors this situation is possible.

Basic NDS Troubleshooting Guidelines

- Identify the partition that is experiencing errors by using and understanding the DSTRACE set parameters and the DSREPAIR utility.
- Identify the replica(s) in the partition that have errors. Identify these errors by using the DSTRACE SET commands and the DSREPAIR utility.
- Identify the error and take the appropriate action. Appendix B of this book, "NDS Error Codes and Definitions," lists the errors and recommended remedies.

Using the DSDIAG Utility

The DSDIAG utility is a new utility found in NetWare 5 that provides an administrator with diagnostic information about NDS, background processes, and replica status and produces them in report files.

To initiate DSDIAG, simply type **DSDIAG** at a NetWare 5 server console. You will see the main screen appear as shown in Figure 9.18. You will see two options, which are covered in the next section.

FIGURE 9.18

The main screen for the DSDIAG utility

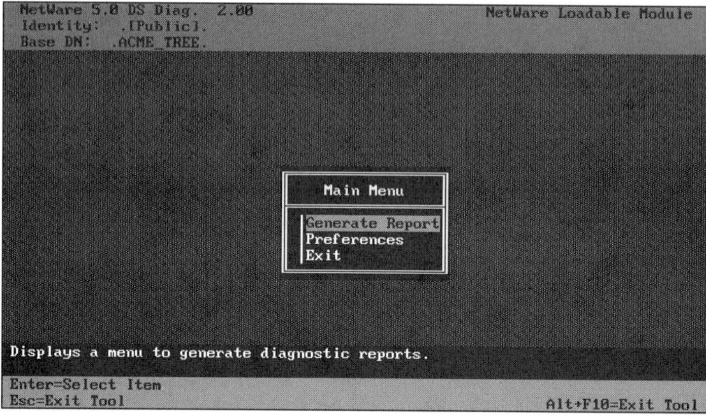

Generate Report and Preferences

You first select Generate Report, and you will be given the following list of report generation options. Be sure to select each option to define how you want the report to be created. Keep in mind that each of these options generates a separate report file and thus a separate report.

The second option is for preferences that you can set as defaults in DSDIAG. Both are explained in the text that follows.

Generate Report

Check NDS Versions — Returns the NDS version for each server in your NDS tree. Selecting this option allows you to do these things:

- Specify how you want the information gathered (that is, NDS, SAP, or by address).

- Specify a starting context for the search.
- Select the replica type you want to search on.
- Specify how far you want to search down the tree.
- Specify the report file format and options such as size and filename.

Check NDS Background Process Status—List the status of the NDS background processes for each server found. Selecting this option allows you to do these things:

- Specify how you want the information gathered (that is, NDS, SAP, or by address).
- Specify a starting context for the search.
- Select the replica type you want to search on.
- Specify how far you want to search down the tree.
- Indicate the type of status to be retrieved. The options are: All, Schema, Obituary, Xref Sync, and Limber.
- Specify the report file format and options such as size and filename.

List Server's Partition Table—List the partition table for each server found in the NDS tree. Selecting this option allows you to do these things:

- Specify how you want the information gathered (that is, NDS, SAP, or by address).
- Specify a starting context for the search.
- Select the replica type you want to search on.
- Specify how far you want to search down the tree.

- Specify a partition type match. The categories are All, Siblings, and Subtree.
- Specify a replica type. The categories are: All, Readable, Writable, Master, Read/Write, Read Only, and Sub Ref.
- Specify the report file format and options such as size and filename.

List Replica Rings — Search for all partitions in the tree and report each partition's replica ring. Selecting this option allows you to do these things:

- Specify how you want the information gathered (that is, NDS, SAP, or by address).
- Specify a starting context for the search.
- Select the replica type you want to search on.
- Specify how far you want to search down the tree.
- Retrieve the replica ring from a single replica, every server in the first ring found, or all servers from all rings.
- Specify the report file format and options such as size and filename.

Check Partition Status — Check the synchronization status of each partition root found in the tree. Selecting this option allows you to do these things:

- Specify how you want the information gathered (that is, NDS, SAP, or by address).
- Specify a starting context for the search.
- Select the replica type you want to search on.
- Specify how far you want to search down the tree.

- Retrieve the replica ring from a single replica, every server in the first ring found, or all servers from all rings.
- Specify the report file format and options such as size and file name.

Compare Replica Rings — For each partition root found in the NDS tree, compare the replica ring with other replicas in the ring. Selecting this option allows you to do these things:

- Specify how you want the information gathered (that is, NDS, SAP, or by address).
- Specify a starting context for the search.
- Select the replica type you want to search on.
- Specify how far you want to search down the tree.
- Retrieve the replica ring from a single replica, every server in the first ring found, or all servers from all rings.
- Specify the report file format and options such as size and filename.

Preferences

Selecting Preferences allows you to set up default configurations for all reports that you generate. You have the following options:

Manage Naming Conventions — Used to set the format of input and display of NDS names in DSDIAG and the report files. The options are:

- **File Output Context** — Set the naming conventions for file output to be the same or different from the naming conventions used for input.
- **Base DN** — Fully qualify relative names and reduce the size of displayed names.

- **Display Typed Relative Distinguished Name Values** — The default is ON.

- **Escape Non-local Characters** — The default is ON. Nonlocal code page characters will be accepted in escape format. Nonmappable characters are displayed using the escape character.

- **Delimiter Set** — Specify the delimiter to be used to display NDS names. DOT is the most common between names.

Manage Identities — Log in and out of identities and change the default identity. The only option here is to:

- List available identities found for this server.

Preferences — Configure the display or report preferences to be used.

Numeric Values — You can choose hexadecimal or decimal.

String Values — Select string translation or ON to show actual strings.

Flags Format — Select string translation or hexadecimal.

Time Format — Select local, UTC, or hexadecimal.

Primary Address Types — Select address types that are considered primary addresses during comparisons of servers, objects, and property values.

Generating a Report

As an example, let's say you want to generate a report that checks the NDS background process status. You would follow these steps:

1. Load DSDIAG on the NetWare 5 server where you want to generate the report. You can either run this straight from the console or use RCONSOLE.

2. Select "Generate Report."

3. Select the option "Check NDS Background Process Status." You will be presented with the screen shown in Figure 9.19.

FIGURE 9.19

The General Options screen

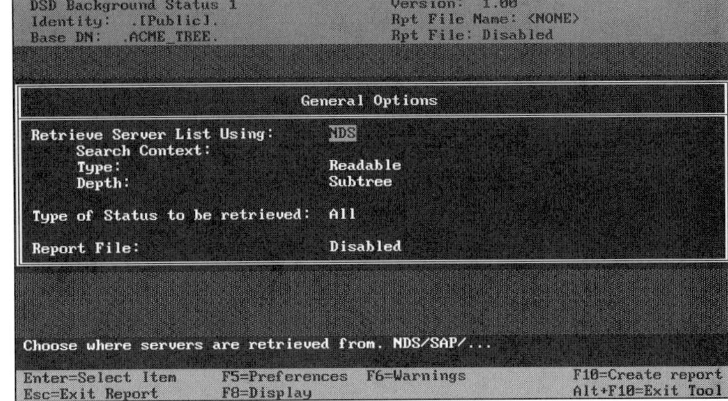

4. Keep the defaults for the first five options, arrow down to Report File, and press Enter twice.

5. Accept the defaults unless you want to change the filename.

6. Press F10 to return to the General Options screen.

7. Press F10 again to start report generation. You will see a status bar appear at the top of the server screen and the output shown on the screen. An example of this output is shown in Figure 9.20.

FIGURE 9.20

Output generated by running a DSDIAG report

```
DSD Background Status 1                          Version:  1.00
Method: NDS Server                               Identity: .[Public].
NDS Context:                                     Rpt File Name: <NONE>
                                    Complete
                                                             100% Complete
Server : CN=NOR-SRV1.OU=NORAD.O=ACME
     Status    Status         Network
               Type           Length
Server's Address: 0f2ac1ae
Unknown Status:
       -672

Server Name: CN=NOR-SRV1.OU=NORAD.O=ACME
Server's Address: 86177213
Unknown Status:
       -672

Contacted 3 server(s) out of 3 attempted.

Count    Error   Numbers     Message
   3     -672    FFFFFD60    no access

Report is complete. Press a key to continue.
```

Summary

As a system administrator responsible for the maintenance and troubleshooting of NDS, you need to know how to monitor NDS operations and check the health of the NDS tree. This chapter helps you understand first how to check the health of the tree before you start any new NDS partition operations and then how to monitor the operations to completion. As discussed, the first step to properly monitor any NDS partition operation is to check the current health or status of the partition involved in the operation. It is extremely important that you perform the health check before starting the operation. If a previous partition operation has not yet completed, you never want to start a new one. You learned how to use the DSREPAIR utility and DSTRACE to monitor the status of the replicas and synchronization. In addition, new to NetWare 5 is the DSDIAG utility that helps you determine the status of each replica list and each partition. The benefit is that you can effectively track NDS operations as they proceed through several states on several different servers and know if the operation is complete or needs more time.

CHAPTER 10

NetWare 5 Features

This chapter examines the many new and enhanced features of NetWare 5. While many of the changes are subtle and won't be noticed by many of your users, other changes are significant and require some additional understanding to implement in your network environment. In some cases you will find a topic that may also be covered in another chapter. We refer you to appropriate chapters for additional reading on that topic. In other cases the topic will be covered in the following sections. The NetWare 5 functions and features are categorized into the following sections:

- NetWare operating system
- File system
- Novell Directory Services (NDS)
- Network services
- Installation and upgrade
- Developer support
- Third-party add-ons

The NetWare Operating System

NetWare 5 offers many new changes to the core NetWare operating system that offer increased speed and reliability. This section describes the operating system changes, which include a new multiprocessor kernel, virtual memory, memory protection, the GUI console, Year 2000 readiness, and support for Hot Plug or I_2O hardware.

The NetWare 5 Multiprocessor Kernel

The core of the NetWare 5 operating system is a new kernel that supports multiple processors out of the box. The new NetWare 5 kernel is called the *NetWare multiprocessor kernel (MPK)*. The obvious benefit of having a multiprocessor kernel is that it automatically supports machines that have more than one processor. In fact, it supports single and multiple processors from the same kernel. This means that you can utilize existing processors in your servers more efficiently, or add processors as needed to help speed up specific services. An example of this concept is shown in Figure 10.1.

FIGURE 10.1

NetWare 5 provides a new kernel that supports multiple processors out of the box.

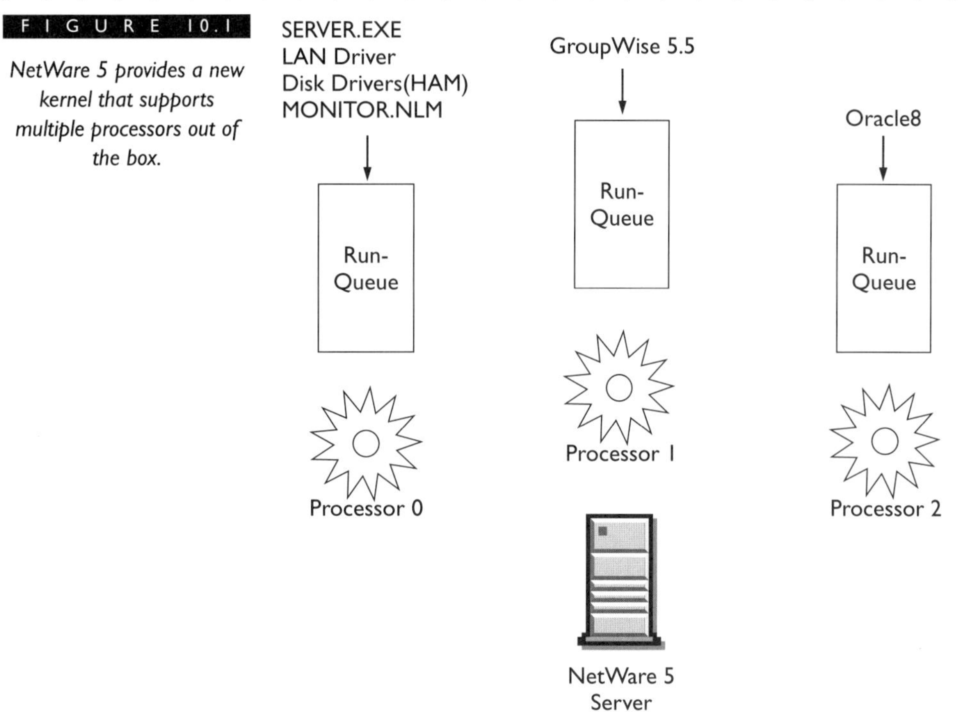

The NetWare MPK can support a machine with as many as 32 processors. During installation, NetWare 5 automatically detects the number of processors by reading the multiple processor table in the machine's BIOS. It then determines which of the NetWare 5 Platform Support Modules (PSM) matches the hardware platform. The PSM is a hardware abstraction layer or interface that NetWare 5 uses to support different hardware dependencies.

The new multiprocessor kernel provides many new services, including support for Java applications discussed later. The NetWare 5 operating system kernel adds the following additional functions: memory protection, virtual memory, preemption, and application prioritization.

Memory Protection

The memory protection feature in NetWare 5 allows you to load server applications in their own protected address space. The applications are then shielded from other applications and the operating system itself. The result is that if one application fails it does not affect any other applications or processing of the operating system. You can use protected address spaces to run untried or troublesome applications. Any program or module loaded into a protected address space cannot corrupt the operating system or cause server abends. The protected address space provides a safe place to run applications. All protected address spaces use virtual memory. An example of this concept is shown in Figure 10.2.

FIGURE 10.2

NetWare 5 allows applications to be loaded in their own memory space.

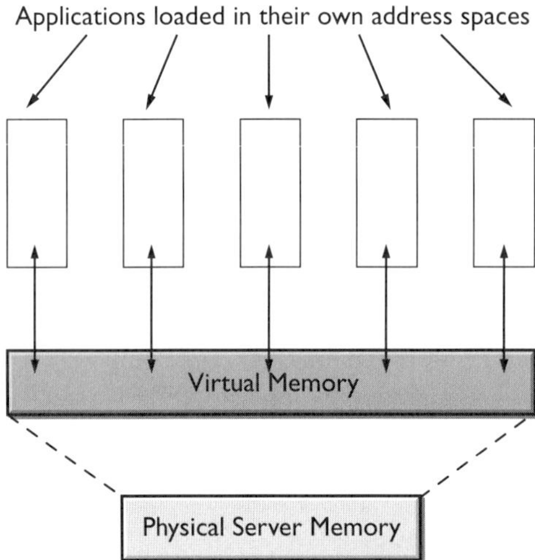

A protected address space is a portion of cache server memory that has controlled communication with the server's operating system. The protected address space is only a portion of cache memory that can be set aside. This is sometimes called user address spaces or ring 3. In contrast, the NetWare operating system does not run in a protected address space. The operating system address space is sometimes called ring 0 or the kernel address space. The kernel cannot run in virtual address space.

In the first release of NetWare 5, only a few NLMs or applications can be loaded into the protected memory space. NetWare 5 loads Java-based applications in protected mode by default. In addition, you can optionally load GroupWise 5.2, Lotus Notes 4.6 (except for the debugging module), Oracle 7.3, and Oracle8 into protected memory spaces. However, certain types of modules and programs cannot run in protected addresses. The protected address spaces run in ring 3, and others must be loaded at ring 0 instead. Here is a list of common NLM programs and executables that cannot be loaded into a protected address space:

- SERVER.EXE
- LAN drivers
- Disk drivers
- MONITOR.NLM
- Novell Storage Services (NSS)

Virtual Memory

Virtual memory is a memory management scheme that provides the NetWare 5 operating system with the capability to allocate more than the actual physical memory of the server machine. It does this by using the disk as an extension of memory and by swapping code and data between physical memory and disk as it is needed. When the data on disk is needed again, it is moved back into physical memory. Because data is swapped in and out of disk, available memory can be used for a larger amount of data than its actual physical capacity would allow. Virtual memory provides NetWare 5 with a more efficient use of memory and lessens the likelihood that low memory conditions could cause an abend condition.

NetWare 5 moves data out of physical memory to swap files on the hard drive if the data has not frequently been used. More specifically, available memory is assessed to see which data has been used less recently than the rest. How recently data has been used is determined by a bit in each field of the translation table that indicates whether the address space has been used since the last time it was checked. Data that has not been used for some time can be moved from memory to disk, thus freeing memory for other uses.

As mentioned earlier, protected memory uses virtual memory. The reason is to allow the memory management subsystem to allocate to each process a unique protected virtual address available to run the threads of the process. Thus, each process has a separate address space, so a thread in one process cannot view or modify the memory of another process. This architecture provides the protected memory for NetWare 5. An example of this concept is shown in Figure 10.3.

FIGURE 10.3

Virtual memory uses the disk as an extension of physical memory.

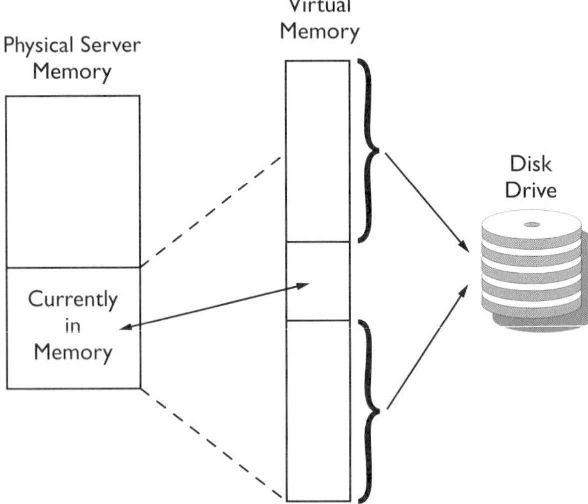

As an example, the server operating system (SERVER.EXE) cannot run in a virtual memory because it must always be resident in memory and cannot be swapped to disk.

Preemption

The NetWare 5 kernel has also been developed to support *preemption*. Preemption eliminates the problems associated with applications running on the server as NLMs that have been poorly written and monopolize too much of the processor time. In order to take advantage of preemption in NetWare 5, an application must be explicitly written or enabled by the developers to support the kernel's preemption.

Application Prioritization

The multiprocessor kernel also allows you to support what is known as *application prioritization* or *load balancing,* which ensures optimal application distribution among the processors. Application prioritization is implemented as part of the new NetWare 5 kernel, and the system administrator decides how to prioritize the applications running on the network's servers. You can specify the processor usage that you want to dedicate to each application.

The capability to adjust the usage dedicated to each application enables you to tune the quality of service provided. In addition, both single-processor and multiple-processor machines can benefit from the flexibility of application prioritization. Thus, if a single processor machine has multiple applications, you can allow one application to have more CPU cycles than the other applications.

The NetWare 5 GUI Console (ConsoleOne)

NetWare 5 allows the server console to appear in a graphical user interface (GUI) environment. Its appearance and operation are similar to the X Windows environment found on UNIX platforms. A GUI server environment permits the use of a graphical interface for programs such as the Novell Installation program and Java applications at the server console. To use ConsoleOne, the server must have a VGA or higher video adapter board and a VGA or higher display monitor, along with a mouse.

NOTE

The GUI environment requires additional server RAM. It is not recommended that you try to run the GUI environment on servers with less than 64MB of RAM.

ConsoleOne is very similar to the NWADMIN utility and allows you to use NDS to:

- Browse and organize network resources.
- Set up accounts for network users.

- Control access to network resources.
- Access remote server consoles.

Year 2000 Readiness

Like previous versions of NetWare 4 and NetWare 3.2, NetWare 5 is Year 2000 ready. For more information regarding Year 2000 compliance, visit Novell's Project 2000 Web site at `www.novell.com/p2000`.

PCI Hot Plug Hardware Management

NetWare 5 now provides the capability to upgrade or replace network interface cards while the server is up and running, easing server expansion and providing longer server uptime.

PCI Hot Plug technology allows industry-standard PCI adapters to be added or removed without disrupting operation of the NetWare 5 server. This reduces unplanned downtime for maintaining or adding disk or LAN adapters. Features of PCI Hot Plug technology include these:

- **Uninterrupted service** — You can add or replace network or other I/O controller boards while a system is operating. This can be done through "hot removal" or "hot insertion."
- **Compatibility** — Multiple system providers, operating system suppliers, and adapter vendors can implement Hot Plug, which is compatible with existing PCI standards.
- **Backward compatibility** — You can use a mix of Hot Plug and non–Hot Plug components in the same system. (But non–Hot Plug components cannot be added or removed without shutting down the server.)

Introduction to NCMCON

The Novell Configuration Manager console (NCMCON) allows you to view status information on PCI slots and to remove and add PCI Hot Plug adapters. The

NCMCON interface constantly monitors and displays the status of all slots. If there are any errors, the appropriate error message is displayed at the server.

Three menus are used in the NCMCON interface:

- The main menu
- Slot Options
- Slot Detailed Information

NCMCON Interface Menus

The main menu displays a list of all PCI slots in the system, as shown in Figure 10.4.

FIGURE 10.4

The main menu of NCMCON

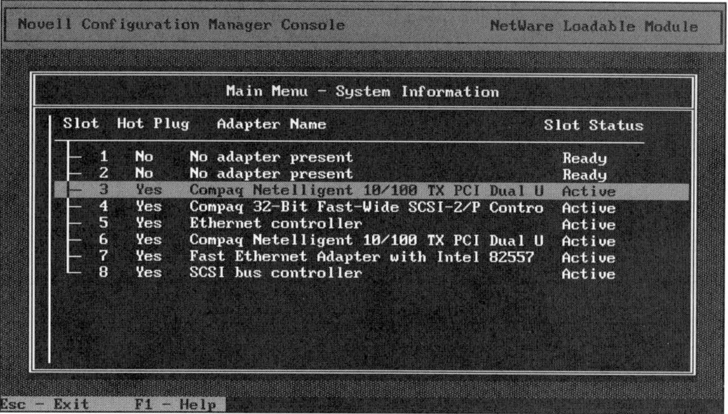

For each slot, the main menu displays the following information:

- The system board slot number
- Whether or not the slot is hot pluggable
- An adapter description field or name
- The status of the slot/adapter, which may have any of these states:

- **Powered Off** — The lever is open on the slot, and power to the slot is turned off.
- **Powered On** — The lever has been closed, power is on to the slot, and the slot is empty (this is different from Ready in that there is no card in the slot).
- **Ready** — An adapter is in the slot and ready to be used, but currently no driver is loaded for it.
- **Active** — A loaded driver is using this adapter, and the adapter is believed to be in good working order.
- **Failed** — This adapter's driver or Hot Plug driver indicated some type of device failure. The adapter can be removed, and a new one added, at this time.
- **Degraded** — A device on the multidevice adapter has failed, but other devices on the adapter continue to function.
- **Processing . . .** — An action is being performed on a slot/adapter.

Pressing Enter on a selected slot of the main menu displays the Slot Options screen as shown in Figure 10.5. Online, context-sensitive help is available to guide you through PCI Hot Plug actions.

FIGURE 10.5

The Slot Options screen

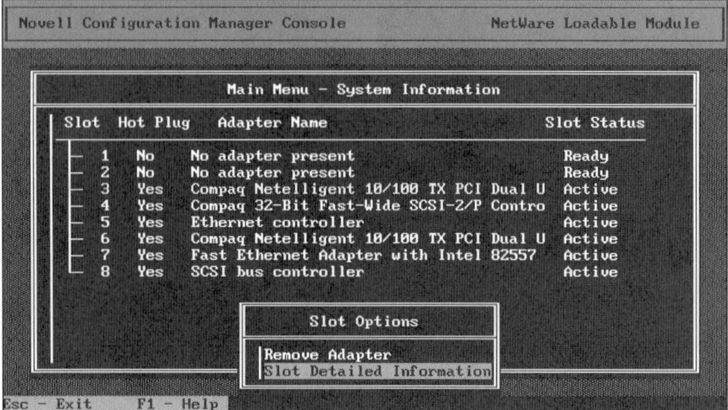

This menu lists the options available for the highlighted Hot Plug slot (selection of a non–Hot Plug slot automatically displays the Slot Detailed Information screen). An example of the detailed information is shown in Figure 10.6.

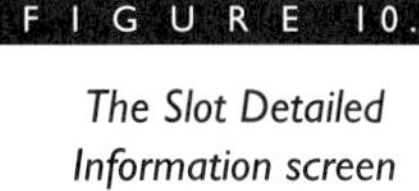
FIGURE 10.6

The Slot Detailed Information screen

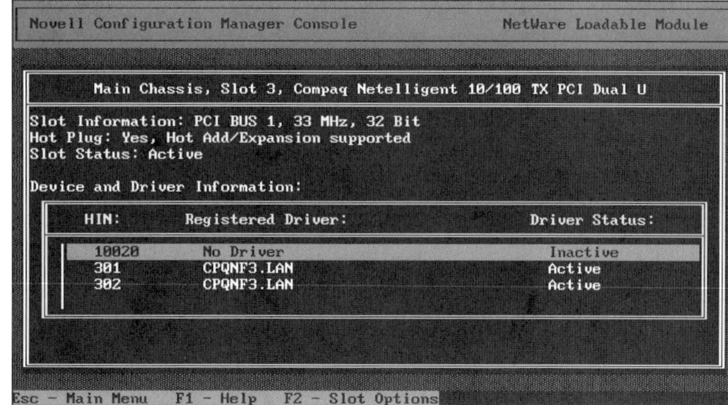

Items shown on the screen include these:

Main Chassis

- Slot number
- Description of the adapter in the slot

Slot Information

- The bus type (PCI, EISA, or EMBEDDED)
- The bus number of the slot

Hot Plug

- Hot pluggable, Yes or No

Slot Status

- The status of the slot/adapter, Active or Inactive

Device and Driver Information

- The NetWare hardware instance number (HIN) of each device

This last item includes the registered device driver name and status for each HIN. Status possibilities include these:

- **Active** — A driver is loaded for the device.
- **Inactive** — No driver is loaded for the device.
- **Failed** — The device has failed.
- **Suspended** — The driver is loaded, but activity is suspended while the adapter is being added.

Pressing F2 activates the Slot Options menu again, which allows you to take actions such as removing the card from a particular slot. Depending on the driver, the state of the slot or adapter, and the capabilities of the system, different options will appear on the menu.

For example, if you want to remove a card while the system is running, you can select the Remove Adapter option after hitting F2. This option is shown in Figure 10.7.

FIGURE 10.7

Removing a hot plug adapter from your NetWare 5 system

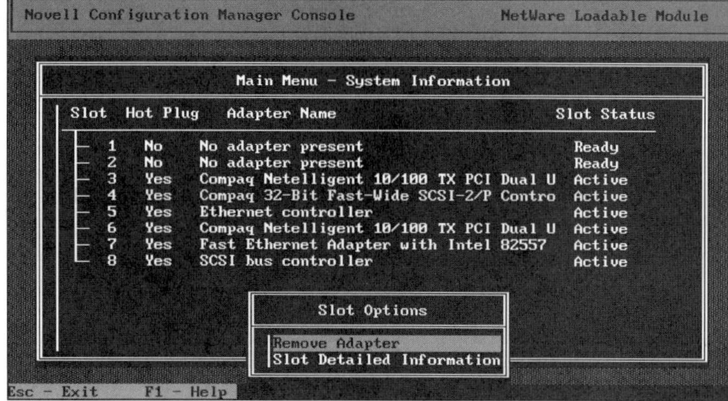

After selecting this option, you will be presented with a warning screen before you deactivate this card. An example is shown in Figure 10.8.

FIGURE 10.8

The warning screen shown before removing a card

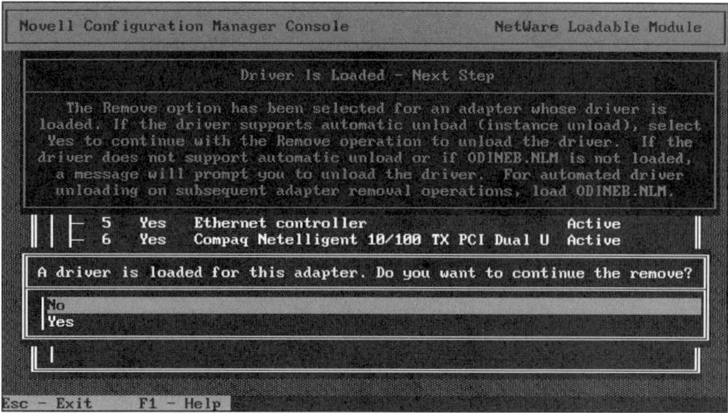

IMPORTANT

Before powering down your adapter cards with the manual switch on the hardware, follow the previous process to remove the software driver that is bound to the card. Failure to remove the driver before powering off the card can cause your server to abend. For example, if a disk controller in slot 4 is powered off, the process abends the server to protect your data.

Once you press Enter, the driver will be removed from the card and you will receive a message stating that the slot has been powered off, as shown in Figure 10.9.

FIGURE 10.9

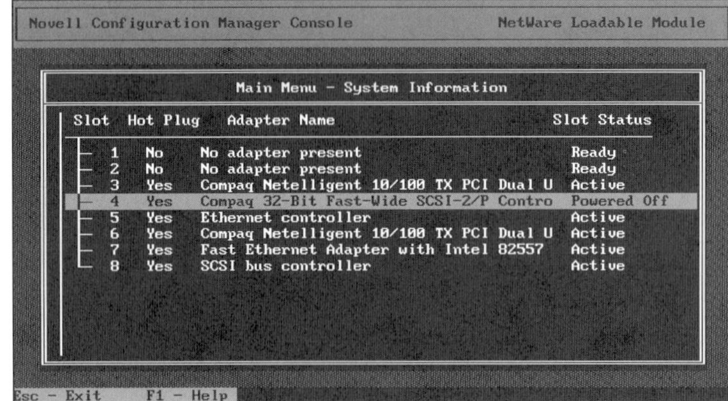

A status message indicating that the slot has been powered off

The interlock mechanism is one feature that can influence what appears on the Slot Options menu. The interlock is a safety mechanism that shuts off power to a slot if the slot is opened while the power is still on. Not all hardware manufacturers provide an interlock mechanism, and not all interlock mechanisms work the same way. You'll need to refer to your hardware documentation for more information.

When there is no power to the slot, the interlock mechanism is closed, and the driver supports what is known as *add functionality.* (Add functionality means that an adapter can be added to an empty slot or an existing adapter can be replaced with a different adapter.) When you remove a card from the slot, you will see the status appear on the NCMCON screen as shown in Figure 10.10.

When there is no power to the slot, the driver supports only replace functionality, and the interlock mechanism is either closed or not supported.

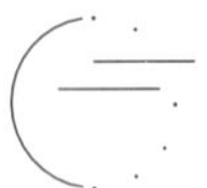

NOTE

Replace functionality **means that an existing adapter can be replaced only with an identical adapter.**

FIGURE 10.10

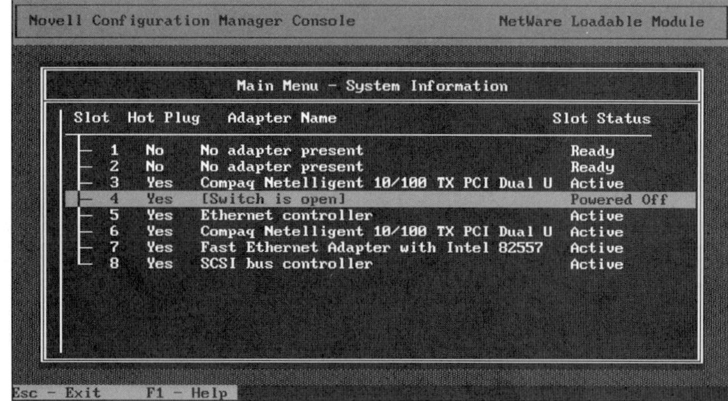

The Status screen indicates that the adapter card has been powered off.

When you replace an adapter, the Hot Plug PCI automatically detects the card, and the NCMCON utility will then ask if you want to have power turned on for this slot. This message is shown in Figure 10.11.

FIGURE 10.11

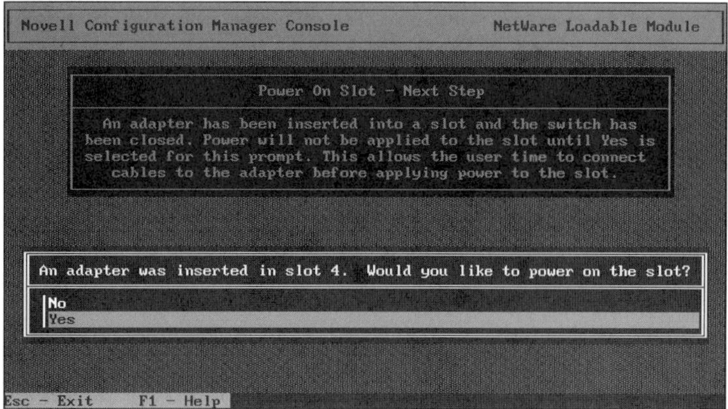

The NCMCON utility displays a message that a card has been detected in the slot.

Once power has been applied to the card, the utility will attempt to find the driver for this card and then load the driver. As you can see in Figure 10.12, the NCMCON utility initiates the NWCONFIG utility to perform this portion of the operation.

FIGURE 10.12

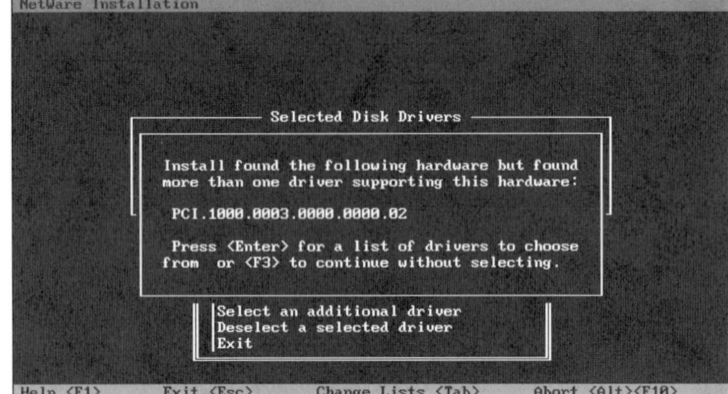

NCMCON uses the NWCONFIG utility to attempt to locate a driver for this card.

NOTE

This utility does configure IPX automatically but does not reinstate any IP addresses you may have had bound to this card. This step you must take manually.

Once you have completed this step to load the driver for the card, you will see the status screen indicate that the card is active for that slot. This is shown in Figure 10.13.

I_2O Support

I_2O (Intelligent I/O) is a relatively new technology that improves I/O throughput and server performance by relieving the CPU of interrupt-intensive tasks such as memory calls and system interrupts. I_2O is an industry-driven software specification designed to provide a standards-based solution to offload input/output traffic from the central processing unit and allow hardware vendors to develop a single driver to work with all networking platforms. NetWare 5 provides I_2O support for Ethernet- and SCSI-class devices and block storage, making server management easier while increasing application processing efficiency.

FIGURE 10.13

Status indicates that the highlighted card is active.

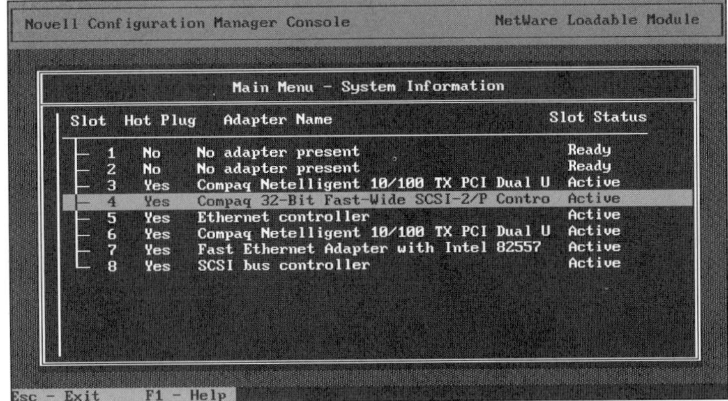

The NetWare 5 File System

In addition to the changes that have been made to the operating system in NetWare 5, the file system has seen some significant changes and improvements. This section describes the changes made to the file system, which include the Novell Storage Services (NSS) and Storage Management Services (SMS).

The Novell Storage Services

Novell Storage Services (NSS) is the new NetWare 5 file system designed to mount large server volumes in seconds, virtually eliminating the limits on the number or size of files that can be stored in volumes and directories. You can use NSS to quickly open and update large files, such as those found in databases.

NOTE

NSS cannot be used with the SYS volume. In addition, NSS cannot be used on servers running older versions of NetWare; however, use of NSS is optional. Also, NSS maintains compatibility with NetWare's traditional file system.

Novell Storage Services eliminates several limitations that currently exist in the NetWare file system. NSS provides an object-oriented storage with 64-bit internal and external interfaces. Without NSS, the NetWare file system supports a 32-bit interface that limits files to 2GB, directory entries to 16 million per volume, and volumes per server to 64. With NSS, the NetWare file system can host a single 8TB (terabyte) file. This capability may prove extremely useful for database applications. In addition, the NSS file system can support virtually unlimited directory entries (or number of files) per volume. During testing at Novell, a volume with a billion files was successfully created with three name spaces loaded. This demonstrates that the file system can support three billion directory entries on a single NetWare volume. Thousands of volumes can be created per server; however, the current NCP interface only supports 127 volumes per server.

In addition to larger volumes and greater numbers of files, NSS supports extremely fast volume mount times. A normal NSS volume will mount in less than one second regardless of size or number of files stored. If the NetWare 5 server crashes and the volume is not dismounted cleanly, when the server is brought back up it is restored and mounted in approximately 15 seconds to one minute. This is the case for all NSS volumes on the server. The older FAT-based file system is organized so that the greater the number and size of files, the greater the volume mount time. For more information about the configuration and use of NSS, refer to Chapter 2.

Consulting Experience

Here's a formula that can help you calculate your memory requirements using NSS:

1. Rate your users on a scale from 1 to 10, where 1 equals "light user" and 10 equals "power user."
2. Calculate the amount of memory required for NSS with the following formula, where R is the rating for users from step 1 and N is the number of users:

   ```
   (R X 7.5 X square root(N)) / Log10(N)
   ```

   This works for 10 to 10,000 users.

Storage Management Services

Storage Management Services (SMS) is a collection of software programs loaded on a NetWare 5 server that provide backup and restore services. SMS lets you back up, restore, and verify data stored on the network and on network clients. NetWare 5 SMS includes the Enhanced SBACKUP utility, which ensures regular and complete backups of all the data on your network, including the NDS database, bindery data, GroupWise data, and client and server file systems. The SMS services are performed by a collection of components that are independent of operating systems and hardware.

Enhanced SBACKUP for Backup and Restore

The Enhanced SBACKUP utility allows backups of SMS targets such as NDS, binderies, the file system, or an individual workstation's hard disk onto media that can be stored off-site. If you have a hardware failure, catastrophe, corrupted data, or incorrectly deleted or changed data, you can recover a previous version of the data.

Enhanced SBACKUP retrieves and reinstates backed up data. The restore session produces the requested data, which is retrieved from the storage media and restored to the location you specify. During a restore session, Enhanced SBACKUP reads the backup storage media, and the Target Service Agent compares the media data set to the existing hard disk data set.

For more information on backup and restore of the NetWare 5 file system and Novell Directory Services, see Chapter 18.

Novell Directory Services

Along with all the other exciting features of NetWare 5 comes increased functionality for Novell Directory Services (NDS). Several new enhancements make NDS more scalable, manageable, flexible, and secure in managing and administering the network. NetWare 5 ships with a new version of Novell Directory Services that will reduce traffic across your WAN infrastructure and enable you to more easily manage both the NDS tree contents and your network overall system. Several new features that help make NDS more scalable across your network servers include transitive synchronization, the transitive vector, caching the replica changes, multiple objects per packet, randomized replica lists, distributive reference links, and the WAN Traffic Manager. In addition, NetWare 5's NDS reduces network traffic by restricting all outbound synchronization from all read-only replicas, and it eliminates subordinate reference replicas from the normal replica synchronization process.

The new NDS features that enable you to more easily manage the NDS tree content include the role-based administration provided by the Inheritable ACLs, the Password Administrator property, and the Partition Administrator property. Using inheritable ACLs, you can provide role-based assignments by assigning supervisor rights to operators or help desk staff to manage specific types of objects or resources. For example, you can assign rights to a group to manage only the printers, servers, or users. Using the new Password Administrator property, you can specify a help desk group to reset only the user's password. With the Partition Administrator property, you can selectively assign rights to a specific group to perform partitioning and replication of the NDS tree without giving rights to the Supervisor for the entire tree. In addition, rights to perform partition operations can be assigned to any administrators that are lower in the tree structure without their acquiring all rights to the top.

Inheritable ACLs

Several new NDS features allow you to more easily manage the objects and properties of the NDS tree. One of the features is the capability to inherit specific property rights down the entire tree. This feature is possible because of the new inheritable ACLs. The inheritable ACLs allow you to assign Supervisor rights to operators or help desk staff for specific types of objects or resources without giving Supervisor rights to the entire tree. For example, you can assign rights to a group to manage just the printers, servers, or users. More important, you can create a group to manage only user passwords. For example, a help desk group can be given only enough rights to change a user's password or reset it. See the next section for the steps to do this.

In order to give inheritable rights to a specific property and have it flow down the NDS tree, you use NWADMIN. Inside the NWADMIN Property Rights dialog box is a new flag at the bottom of the rights list called "Inherit." You can give specific property rights to any object that will inherit by selecting the rights and then selecting the Inherit flag.

Another new feature in NetWare 5 is the capability to display all the schema-defined properties in a single list in NWADMIN anywhere in the NDS tree. The properties that are shown are for all the objects in the schema. This gives you the ability to select any property at any level in the NDS tree to be managed. For example, you can give a group the rights to manage all users' telephone numbers from the O=Organization level on down.

Enabling the Password Management Property

Follow these steps to enable the Password Management property and to create a Password Administration group that could be used by a help desk.

1. Using NWADMIN, create a Help Desk group for Password Administration, as shown in Figure 10.14.

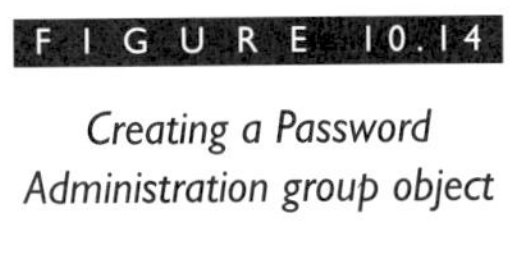

FIGURE 10.14

Creating a Password Administration group object

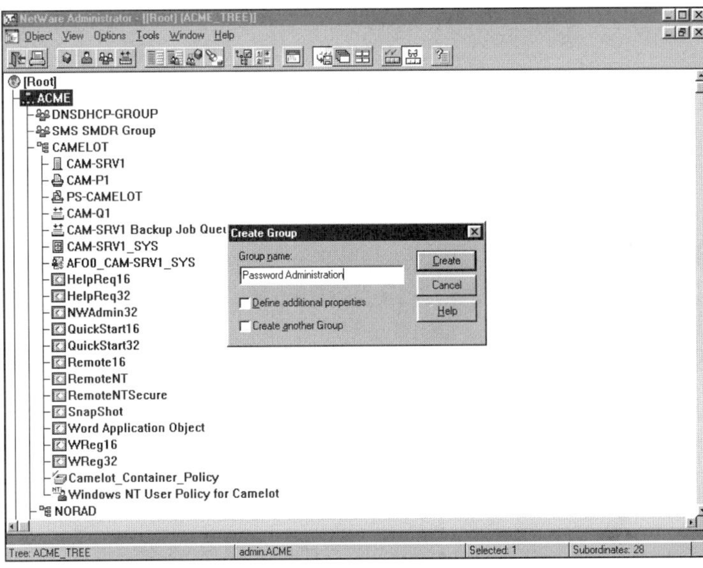

2. Next, select the container object where you want to activate the Password Administration group and select Trustees of This Object. Click Add Trustees and select the password group object you just created. It will appear in the trustee list. You will be presented with the dialog box shown in Figure 10.15.

FIGURE 10.15

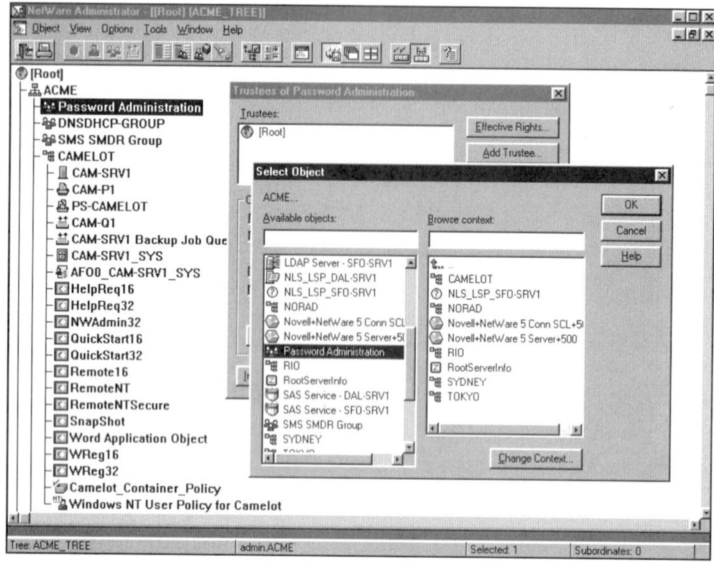

Adding trustees to the Password Group object

3. Under the Property Rights category on the same page scroll down to find the Password Management property. Select this property, mark it with the Supervisor property right, and as inheritable as shown in Figure 10.16.

FIGURE 10.16

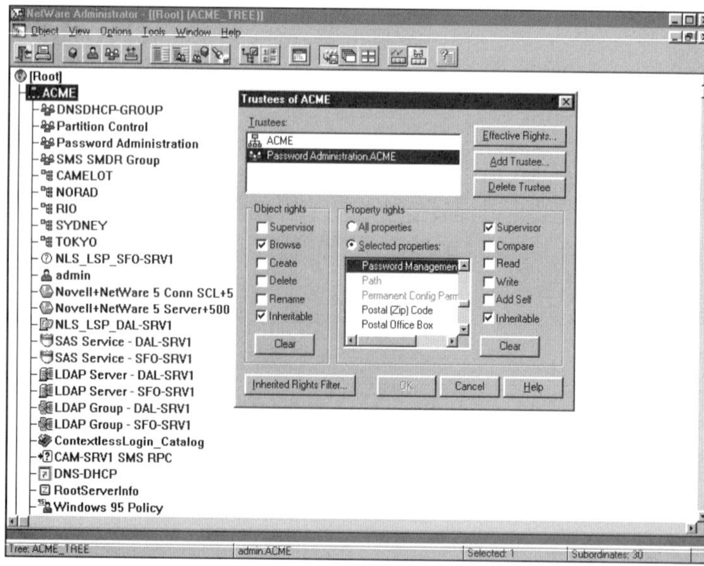

Selecting the Password Management property in the Password group and marking it with the Supervisor right and as inheritable

4. Click OK, and you have completed the steps necessary to create a password administration group.

Other new NDS utilities that allow you to more easily manage the overall NDS system are the DSDIAG utility and the Schema Manager utility. Using DSDIAG, you can quickly and easily determine how the partitions and replicas are synchronizing and detect errors, if any, between NetWare servers. An example of the main screen for this utility is shown in Figure 10.17. For more information on using DSDIAG, see Chapter 9.

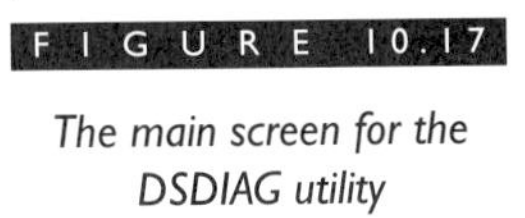
FIGURE 10.17

The main screen for the DSDIAG utility

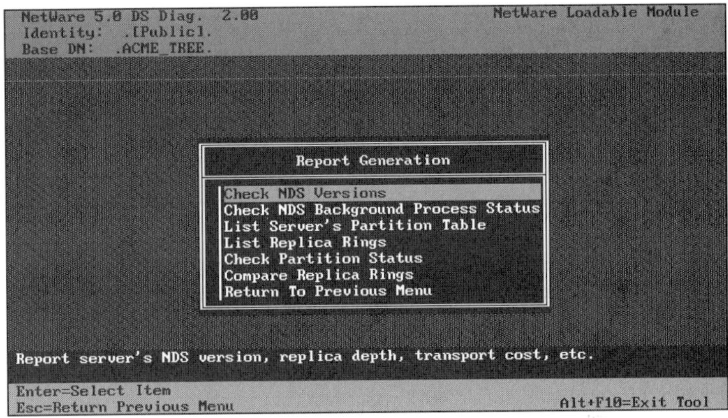

Another very useful utility is the Schema Manager, which enables you to view, update, and manage the NDS schema. The NDS schema is the internal set of rules for how NDS objects and properties are created and used. An example of the Schema Manager utility is shown in Figure 10.18. For more information on using the Schema Manager utility, see Chapter 3.

New Features Added to the Replica Synchronization Process

As you may know, NDS is a loosely consistent database, which means that changes or updates can occur at various replicas, and not all the replicas may have the exact same information at the same time. However, since NDS is loosely synchronized, an update made at one replica propagates to other replicas of the partition over time. These changes are automatically sent to the other replicas of that partition by a background process called *replica synchronization*.

FIGURE 10.18

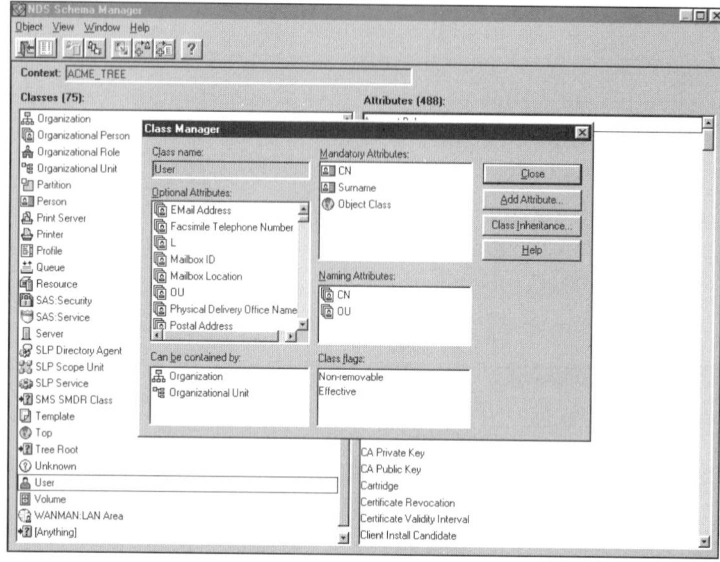

The Schema Manager utility allows you to view and modify the NDS schema.

The purpose of replica synchronization is to guarantee consistency of the information across all the replicas of a partition over a period of time.

The updates or modifications that affect the NDS data include adding, deleting, moving, or renaming an object, as well as changing the properties or attributes of the object. The replica synchronization process passes only the data that has changed for each object or property between the replicas of the partition. Passing only the information that is updated ensures that the total amount of information sent is reduced and network traffic for synchronization is kept to a minimum.

NetWare 5 has made significant changes to the replica synchronization process to make it even more streamlined and scalable. Remember that in NetWare 4, the replica synchronization process involved updating all the replicas for a specific partition with all the changes made to the partition since the last synchronization cycle. The process took the replica pointer table (replica ring) and synchronized each of the replicas one at a time with the most recent changes. The process had to contact each server in the replica ring one at a time to complete a synchronization cycle for the partition. This method of forcing the synchronization process to contact every server consumed valuable time and network resources. NetWare 5, on the other hand, makes the synchronization process more efficient and manageable by providing *transitive synchronization* and the *transitive vector.*

Transitive Synchronization and Transitive Vectors

The replica synchronization process in NetWare 5 uses *transitive synchronization* as a method of using the *transitive vector* during synchronization between two NetWare 5 servers. Transitive synchronization uses the transitive vector instead of the Synchronized Up To property that was used in NetWare 4.

With NetWare 5, server replication no longer happens within a replica ring or list as previously to determine who it must contact for synchronization. Transitive synchronization works through the transitive vector. If the source server's transitive vector is more recent than a target server's vector, the source server does not need to synchronize with that target server. This procedure reduces synchronization traffic and frees up bandwidth. It also employs either the IPX or IP protocol.

The transitive vector is a new structure that has been added to the Partition Root object for each partition. It is essentially a group of modification timestamps representing the values held by each replica. There is one transitive vector for each replica. The transitive vector differs from the Synchronized Up To property in that it holds a group of timestamps for each replica, whereas the Synchronized Up To property holds only one value for each replica in the partition. Another major difference between the transitive vector and the Synchronized Up To property is that the transitive vector is synchronized between servers, whereas Synchronized Up To is not synchronized. To view the status of transitive synchronization on your servers, use the NDS Manager utility, highlight a partition, right-click, and select the Partition Continuity option. At the top of the window select the Transitive Synchronization option. You will then be shown a dialog box like the one in Figure 10.19. This dialog box indicates the status of each transitive vector for each server and reports discrepancies between servers.

You can then highlight a replica and right-click to select information. The information dialog box shows detailed information on the replica stored on a particular server. An example of this information dialog box is shown in Figure 10.20.

FIGURE 10.19

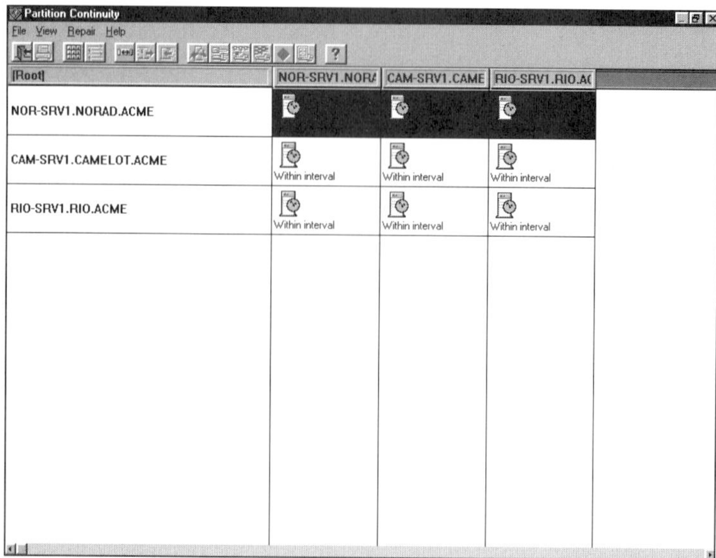

The results of selecting the Partition Continuity option in NDS Manager

FIGURE 10.20

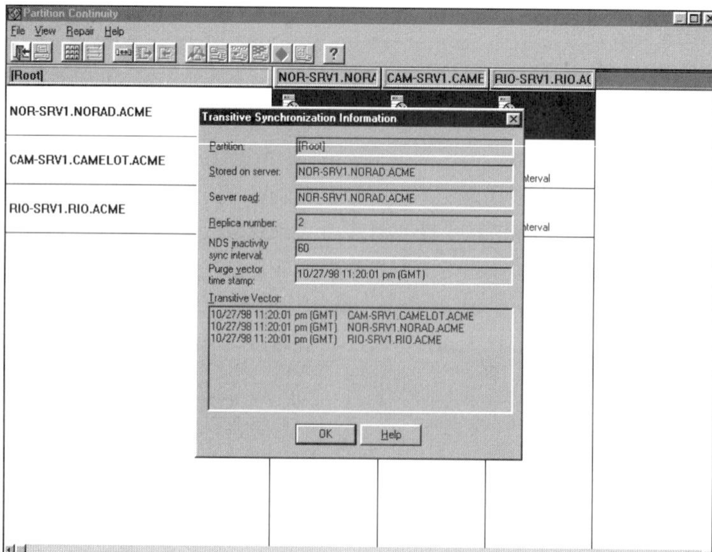

The Information dialog box for the transitive vector

As mentioned, the transitive vector structure is kept as a vector with an attribute for each replica. Using the transitive vector, the synchronization process can achieve convergence among the replicas of a partition without having each replica talk to every other replica. The structure of the transitive vector consists of modification timestamps for all replicas in a given replica ring. The transitive vector has been added to the partition root object of each partition in NetWare 5, as follows:

Server ID	The ID of the server that holds the replica
Timestamp vectors	A timestamp vector for each replica in the replica ring

Each time that the replica synchronization process is scheduled to run on the NetWare 5 server, transitive synchronization reads the transitive vector to determine which replicas it needs to synchronize with. Since each NetWare 5 server has a transitive vector, the process can immediately determine how up to date each of the other replicas is. Using transitive synchronization, a specific server does not have to contact each of the other servers in the partition to complete the replica synchronization process. After a successful synchronization, the target or destination server merges the transitive vector with that of the source server. In addition, the changes are guaranteed to converge across all replicas of a partition over time.

When a change occurs in an NDS object or property, replica synchronization is scheduled to run. When the synchronization starts to execute, it determines which servers need to communicate by comparing the timestamps of the source and target servers in the transitive vector. The source server is the local server that received the update, and the target server is the destination server for replica synchronization. If the time is greater for the local server, then the replica updates are sent. The local or source server does not request the target server's timestamps. The timestamps for the target server are already local in the transitive vector. After all updates are sent, then the source server sends its transitive vector values, which are merged into those of the target server.

You may be wondering how the transitive vector works if the synchronization occurs on a replica ring with NetWare 5 servers and NetWare 4 servers. If a replica ring includes a mixed server environment, the two servers will synchronize using the NetWare 4 method of passing the synchronized up to vectors. After synchronization has completed, either the transitive vector from the NetWare 5 server or the synchronized up to vector from the NetWare 4 server is merged.

The Replica Ring Is Randomized

In NetWare 4, when the replica synchronization started, it contacted and updated each of the replicas in the replica ring in a sequential order. Therefore, the first replica in the replica ring was updated, followed by the second one, and so on. Since the replica ring was identical on all the servers holding copies of this partition, the synchronization process affected all the replicas for each partition in the same order. This could have an undesirable effect if multiple servers were trying to synchronize with the same replica on the same server simultaneously. Since only one inbound synchronization was supported per partition (not per server), one of the synchronization processes would have to back off and attempt again at a later time. This situation only arose if the synchronization process tended to execute at approximately the same time on multiple servers.

To help alleviate this situation, NetWare 5 changes the sequence in which replicas are processed by randomizing the replica ring list before attempting to contact the first server. This greatly reduces the possibility that one of the servers will have to back off and attempt to resynchronize with a replica. By randomizing which replica receives the first update, transitive synchronization will more quickly converge the data for each partition. As previously mentioned, the transitive synchronization process can converge the NDS data among all the replicas of a partition without having each replica talk to every other replica.

Cache Object Changes

Novell Directory Services caches NDS changes to enhance the performance of the replica synchronization process. Remember that the changes or updates that affect the NDS objects include adding, deleting, moving, or renaming an object, as well as changing the properties or attributes of the object.

Using NetWare 4, NDS sequentially searched the entire object file, comparing timestamps to find the objects that had been updated since the last successful synchronization. Sequential searching effectively limited the size of the NDS partitions. When discussing implementation of the NDS tree in NetWare 4, we gave you a practical recommendation of 1000–1500 objects. In order to overcome this limitation, NetWare 5 eliminates the sequential search time by caching all changes to the objects. The capability to cache the objects in the NDS database greatly increases the speed of searching for and updating each replica and partition.

The object cache maintains a set of object IDs that have been modified since the last synchronization. The cache is populated by placing object IDs in the cache that have been modified as a result of client requests as well as inbound synchronization. Each cache entry has the modification time relative to the last synchronization. The cache that NDS maintains is for each partition that is stored on a server. The cache has a start time associated with it that identifies when the cache was built. Changes only need to be sent out if the transitive vector for the remote server is less than or equal to the transitive vector for the local server. The janitor process cleans up the cache periodically by removing the object IDs that have already been sent to all the replicas.

Multiple Objects per Synchronization Packet

In order to help synchronize individual replicas faster, NetWare 5 supports more than one object in each communication packet. Formerly, NetWare 4 only allowed changes for one object in a single communication packet. By allowing multiple changes to different objects in a single packet, NetWare 5 reduces the total number of packets needed to synchronize them with other replicas. If the number of changes between two replicas is small, all the updates between two replicas may be accomplished in a single packet. Basically, this means that a partition can be synchronized in a minimum of one packet.

Distributed Reference Links

New in NetWare 5 is a method for maintaining external references called *distributed reference links (DRLs)*. These links are more efficient than backlinks when renaming, moving, and deleting external references. The distributed reference links are more efficient because unlike backlinks they are not tied to a specific NetWare server but instead reference the partition that stores the external reference object. Alternatively, when a backlink is created, it stores the NetWare server name and object ID for each external reference object.

As mentioned, the major downside to using backlinks is that they are tied to specific NetWare servers and not tied to the external reference object's location in the NDS tree. The result of using backlinks is that each NetWare server tends to have a connection to every another server in the NDS tree. In order to alleviate this problem, distributed reference links have been added to NetWare 5 that store the partition name and object ID where each external reference object exists. By storing the partition name, they permit the individual NetWare servers to resolve the DRLs by using the NDS tree structure. An example of a distributed reference link is shown in Figure 10.21.

FIGURE 10.21

Distributed reference links maintain external references in NetWare 5.

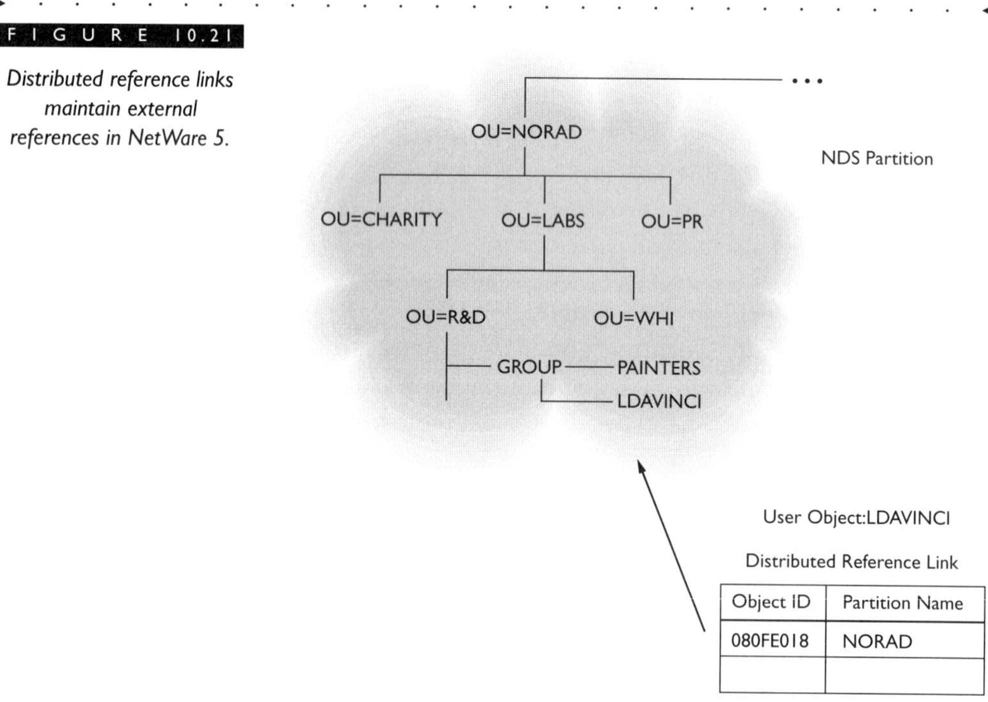

Like backlinks, the DRLs have a periodic process that checks to verify that the associated external reference still exists. This process that periodically checks the DRLs provides data integrity for the NDS database. Distributed reference links are implemented using a new "Used By" property of the object. The "Used By" property contains the distinguished name of the partition that holds the external reference and the object ID that is assigned to the object.

Although distribution reference links are fully implemented in NetWare 5, backlinks will not go away. During certain situations, backlinks will continue to be used to help maintain the external references. NetWare 5 uses both methods.

The WAN Traffic Manager

The *WAN Traffic Manager* (WTM) allows you to manage NDS traffic across WAN links, reducing network costs and increasing performance benefits. This product would generally be used where you have slow WAN links or are using ISDN lines. Many European sites use ISDN and will benefit from this product. This product ships with Novell Directory Services.

The WAN Traffic Manager is a policy-based tool for managing the cost and congestion of WAN traffic. Its clients (such as NDS traffic) request a policy decision before initiating WAN traffic. WTM, as a policy evaluator, checks administrator-supplied policies and attempts to match input criteria to one of them. If it succeeds, it runs the rest of the policy to see whether to allow the WAN traffic to proceed or be delayed. WTM is a valuable tool for networks that have significant congestion on their WAN links (for example, with ISDN or slow dial-up links), allowing administrators to control and manage bandwidth use and congestion.

How WAN Traffic Manager Works

The WAN Traffic Manager consists of three elements:

- **WTM.NLM** — WTM.NLM will reside on each NetWare 5 server in the tree. Before NDS sends server-to-server traffic, WTM.NLM will read a WAN traffic policy to determine whether that traffic will be sent.
- **WAN traffic policies** — Policies are rules that control the generation of NDS traffic. WAN traffic policies are text stored as NDS property values on the NetWare Server object, the LAN Area object, or both.
- **NWAdmin Snap-In** — This snap-in is the interface to WAN Traffic Manager. It allows you to create or modify policies, to create LAN Area objects, and to apply policies to LAN areas or to individual servers. When the WAN Traffic Manager is installed, your NDS schema will be extended to include a LAN Area object and three new detail pages for the NetWare Server object. These pages are the LAN Area Membership page, the WAN Policies page, and the Cost page.

Keep in mind that WTM allows you to control server-to-server traffic, which is defined as traffic generated from replica synchronization, schema synchronization, heartbeat, limber, backlink, connection management, and server status checking.

NOTE

The WAN Traffic Manager is not the older Novell product known as PingFilt/DSFilter. PingFilt used a dirty hook into NDS and inspected every packet that NDS attempted to send. On ping packets, it recorded the values returned and used them to spoof ping packets when filtering was active. Otherwise, PingFilt either allowed packets to proceed or returned the error –625 ERR_TRANSPORT_FAILURE to NDS.

The WAN Traffic Manager provides a policy service using WAN policy and cost attributes that are stored in NDS. When it receives a request from a client application (via the GetWanPolicy API), it selects the most appropriate policy and evaluates it. It then returns the results (SEND_NOW or DONT_SEND) to the client application.

The client application must supply WanMan with a traffic type and with optional source and destination network addresses, along with optional application-specific information in the form of named variable and value pairs. The executed policy can modify these variables, which are returned to the client application as part of the results. This enables a policy to tell the application more than just SEND_NOW or DONT_SEND. For example the policy might indicate to send the data at a particular later time or when certain conditions (such as queue sizes) are met.

WanMan provides its services in two ways: directly and indirectly via the RollCall NLM. In the direct approach, the client application calls WanMan's exported APIs. This introduces a load order dependence—WanMan must be loaded before and while the client application is loaded. Because this is most often undesirable, WanMan also makes its APIs available via RollCall. Both WanMan and the client application will have a load order dependence on roll call, but not on each other. They can be loaded and unloaded independently. Novell anticipates that most applications will use the indirect approach via roll call.

The WAN Traffic Manager controls server-to-server traffic generated by NDS. It can restrict traffic according to cost of traffic, time of day, type of traffic, or any combination of these. Although the WAN Traffic Manager was designed to control traffic across WAN links, it can control NDS traffic between any servers in an NDS tree. The WAN Traffic Manager controls only periodic events initiated by NDS, such as replica synchronization, the janitor process, and the limber process. It does not control events initiated by administrators or users, nor does it control non-NDS server-to-server traffic such as time synchronization.

Installing and Configuring WTM

Follow these steps to install and configure WTM:

1. Move the snap-in DLL WANMAN.DLL to your SYS:\Public\win32\snapins directory.

2. After moving the DLL to this directory, restart NWADMIN. Once in NWADMIN select Tools → Add Wanman Schema, as shown in Figure 10.22. This will extend your NDS schema and add the new policy pages to the server object.

FIGURE 10.22

Extending the NDS schema to include the Wanman policy pages

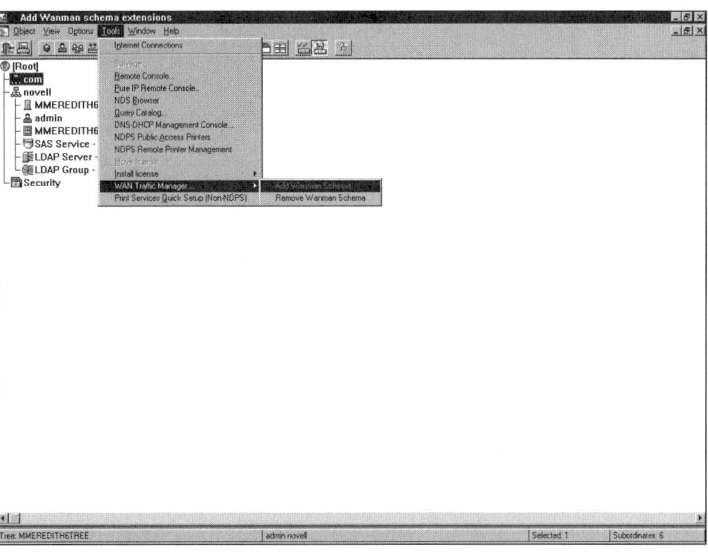

After this operation is complete, you will have a LAN area object available in the Create Objects menu of NWADMIN. The next step is create a LAN area object if you want to have multiple servers assigned to the same WAN policy. Using this object saves time because the policy is shared by multiple servers and you avoid configuring multiple servers. An example of creating a LAN area object is shown in Figure 10.23.

FIGURE 10.23

Creating a LAN area object for the WAN Traffic Manager

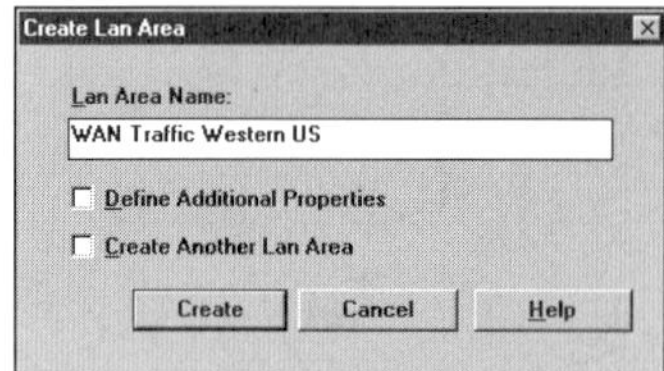

3. Once you have created the new LAN area object, you can click Details and then select Servers Belonging to LAN Area and Add. This allows you to indicate the servers that you want to participate in this LAN area group. Adding a new server to the group is shown in Figure 10.24.

FIGURE 10.24

Adding a server to the LAN area group

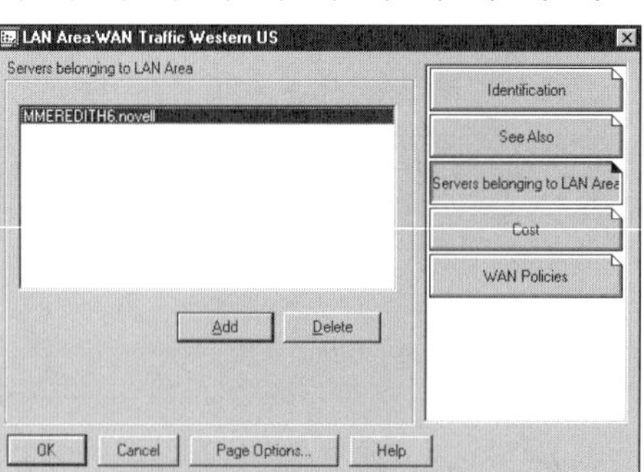

4. The next step is to define a WAN policy page. We highly recommend that you use the predefined policies that are provided. Be very careful if you make modifications to these policies. The WAN Traffic Manager selects and runs administrator-supplied policies to manage WAN costs and congestion. NDS uses policies to control synchronization and other background tasks based on time of day, network addresses, network costs, and so on. The WAN Traffic Manager is extensible so that clients can supply extra information to the policies. WAN Policies are stored in NDS to enable

global administration, and you can use constraints such as time of day, connection cost, source and destination addresses, other connection and address specifics, and information supplied by the WTM client.

5. To create or enable a policy, select the WAN Policy page in the Details of the LAN area object you previously created. An example of this is shown in Figure 10.25. Notice the drop-down menu that includes many predefined policies for your use. Using a predefined policy is the easiest and fastest method for using policies.

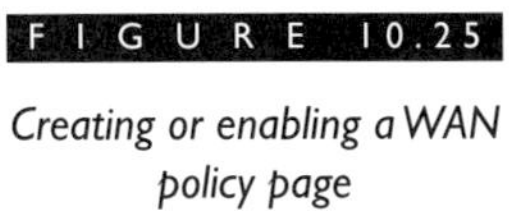
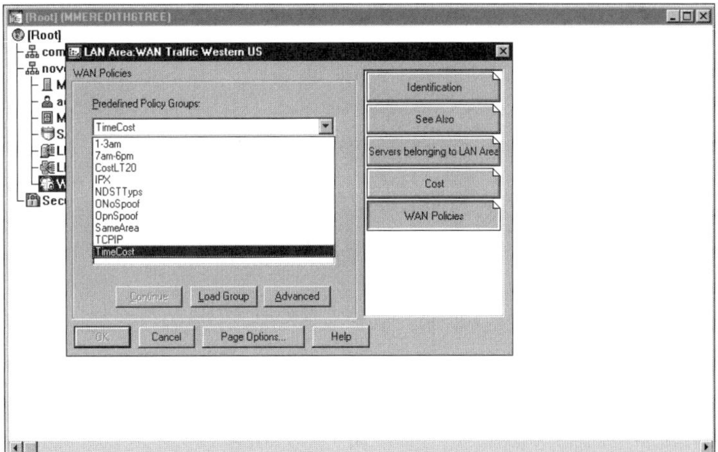

FIGURE 10.25

Creating or enabling a WAN policy page

6. You then need to select the Load Group option to load the policy. You will see a status message, and any errors will be displayed if discovered. An example of this output is shown in Figure 10.26. If you have created your own policy, any errors in the policy will be displayed here.

7. The next step is to define a destination range and a cost for this range. This range can be a range of either IPX addresses or IP addresses, and the cost can be any value that you wish to measure, such as dollars or hours.

An example of selecting an IPX or IP range and a cost is shown in Figure 10.27.

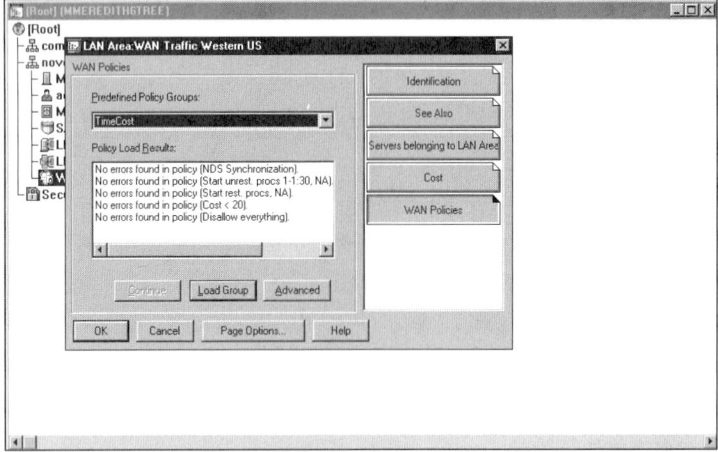

FIGURE 10.26

Loading a policy will reveal any errors present in the policy.

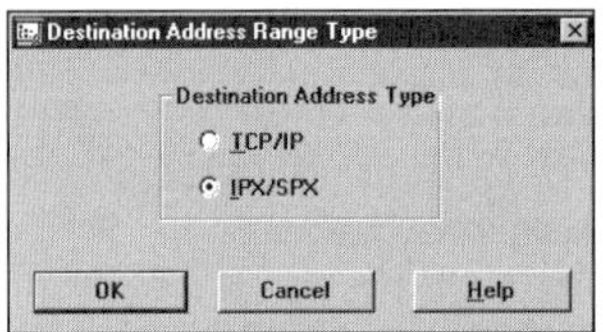

FIGURE 10.27

Selecting an IPX or IP range and a cost for this policy

If you choose not to use the LAN area object or select an individual server to create a policy, simply highlight the server and select Details. You will notice the tabs for WAN Policies and costs on the right side of the dialog box. You also have the option of adding this server to a LAN area group by selecting the LAN Area Membership tab.

Catalog Services

NDS Catalog Services provides a method to store directory data in a non-partitioned, indexed format on your NetWare 5 server for rapid access. Directory information stored in catalog or index format can be easily customized for searching, sorting, and reporting purposes. Distribution and replication of a catalog allows administrators to quickly access a "snap shot" of the complete network directory as opposed to performing a query across the entire network and walking the NDS tree.

Catalog Services enables the development of applications, which need rapid access to directory data in a centralized repository. These applications can include contextless login, NDS white pages, and fast lookup for LDAP gateways, along with many others. NetWare 5 provides one of these new Catalog Services applications, called *contextless login*. The contextless login leverages the NDS catalog by allowing users to authenticate from any point on the network by typing their login name and password, removing the need to know the location of their user object in the NDS tree.

Catalog databases can be scoped to include data from the entire directory tree or from one or more subtrees. The attributes stored in the catalog can be filtered according to user or administrator requirements. Catalog Services includes a dredger that reads the directory to build catalogs; an NWADMIN snap-in that controls the scope, filtering, time interval, and other aspects of catalog creation; and a set of query APIs that support development of applications that can find catalogs and read data from them.

The catalog services dredger is a server-based program that creates catalogs by periodically scanning the NDS tree for the data that was previously requested by the administrator of the catalog. The dredger runs on the following platforms:

- NetWare 4.10 (NDS build 5.01 and above)
- NetWare 4.11 (NDS build 5.73 and above)
- NetWare 5 (all builds)

You can completely control scheduling of the dredger operations. You select how and when the dredger refreshes the catalogs at periodic intervals, or you can start a refresh manually at any time. Although the catalog is updated during the refresh operation, it remains available to users. In addition, dredging for multiple catalogs can occur simultaneously.

It is extremely important that after you define the Catalog Services object in the NDS object you grant it the proper access rights. The access rights used by the dredger while creating a catalog are the rights assigned to the catalog object in NDS. The access rights are controllable through access control lists (ACLs) in the same manner that all other access rights are controlled.

In addition to controlling the rights, you can control the scope of the directory data included in a catalog by specifying a base object where dredging will begin and a tree depth of single object, subordinate objects, or full subtree. Multiple base objects can be specified, each with a corresponding tree depth. You can also create filters to control the object classes, attribute classes, and values to be included in the catalog.

Included with the Catalog Services product is a management utility that runs as a snap-in to the NWADMIN console on Windows NT and Windows 95/98. The management utility provides the capability to create and edit filter expressions that determine what data is included in the catalog according to object classes, attribute classes, and attribute values. The management utility includes a simple browser for viewing catalog contents that is part of the Tools option.

The management utility provides a dredger server page, which allows the administrator to control certain aspects of the operation of the server on which the dredger is running. These include the number of threads allocated for dredger operation and the sync interval length at which the dredger checks its catalog list against the list on the server object in NDS. The page also displays a list of the catalogs dredged by the server. The management utility provides a summary page, which lists summary information about the dredger, including time of last dredge and log file statistics.

Catalog Services is easily installed during regular installation of a NetWare 5 server. When Catalog Services is installed, it extends the NDS schema. It also places the dredger and the management utilities on the appropriate servers. The Install Wizard provides the capability to remove SDK components and registry entries installed by Catalog Services on the local machine. It does not remove components that are installed on a file server. Components not removed include NDS schema extensions, the dredger, and the management utility.

Catalog Services consists of these components:

- **DSCAT.NLM** — This NetWare Loadable Module (NLM) is installed and loaded during NetWare server installation. It contains the dredger that searches the NDS database for the objects and properties that you have defined in the catalog.

- **DSCQRY16.DLL or DSCQRY32.DLL** — These DLLs are the query engines (16-bit or 32-bit) that the NetWare Administrator snap-in (or other applications) uses to query the directory.

- **NetWare Administrator snap-in (DSCATMGR.DLL)** — This provides an interface to Catalog Services through NetWare Administrator. It lets you create, modify, query, index, and delete catalog objects.

Creating a Master Catalog

Creating a master catalog allows you to create a place to store information extracted from the Directory database. The catalog stores only the objects and attributes you specify and lets your users find information about those objects without a time-consuming search of the entire Directory. The master catalog will periodically receive updates from the catalog dredger (search engine) and distribute this information to any existing slave catalogs.

These steps will walk you through creation of a catalog:

1. Load the NetWare Administrator and choose the container in which you want to create the catalog object.

2. Choose the NDSCat:Master Catalog object icon and click OK as shown in Figure 10.28.

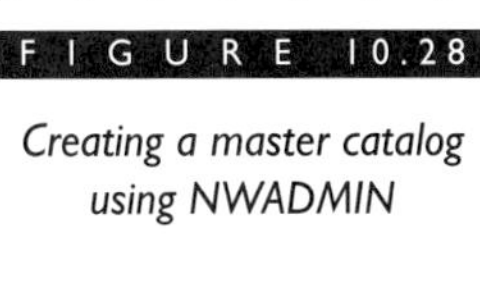

Creating a master catalog using NWADMIN

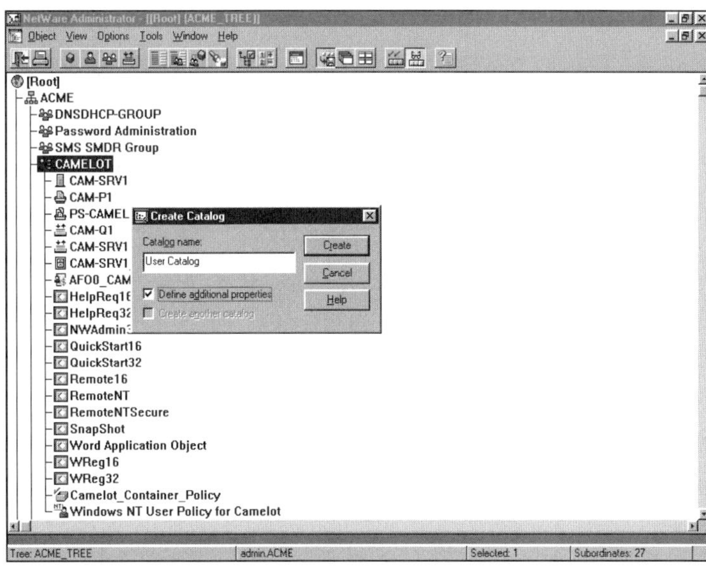

3. In the Create Catalog dialog box, specify the catalog name, check Define Additional Attributes, and then click Create.

4. In the Details dialog box select a host server. The host server hosts the catalog dredger that populates and updates this master catalog. Type in the server's Complete Name (for example, CAM-SRV1.CAMELOT.ACME).

5. Make the catalog object security equivalent to another object so that the catalog has rights to read and browse the tree. An example of the Details dialog box is shown in Figure 10.29.

FIGURE 10.29

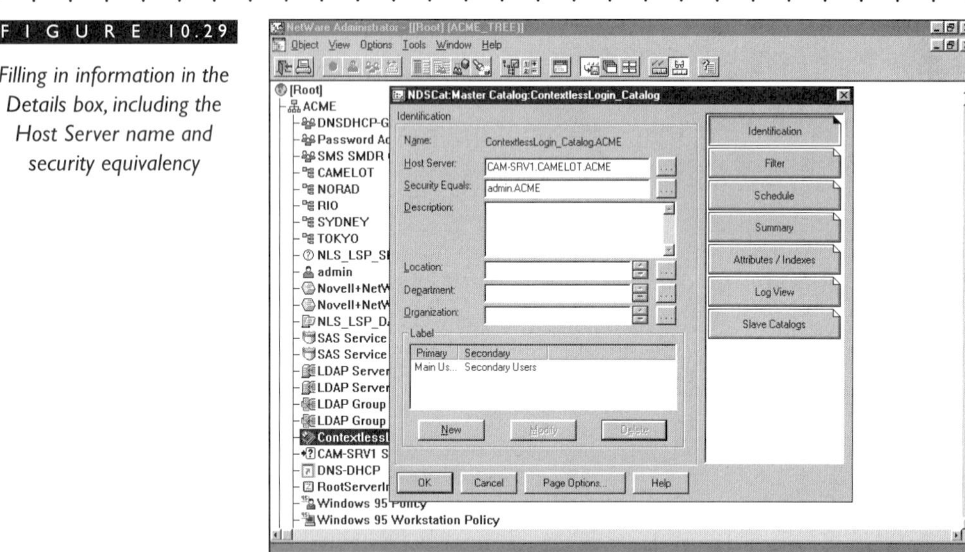

Filling in information in the Details box, including the Host Server name and security equivalency

IMPORTANT

Be sure to make the catalog security equivalent to a leaf object (typically a user) with read and browse rights *only* where you want the catalog to browse the tree. For example, making the catalog security equivalent to the Admin object would allow the catalog object all rights allowed to the Admin object. You are better off assigning read and browse rights to the catalog object at the container level where you want the catalog to start a search. You could also create a dummy user with read and browse rights to the container.

6. (Optional) Enter a description, location, department, and organization for the master catalog.

7. Label the catalog. You need to enter both primary and secondary labels. A label is a name that is used by an application. Multiple applications can reference the same label. A primary label can be a global name such as your company's name. A secondary label can be more specific such as a department name. An example of creating the labels is shown in Figure 10.30.

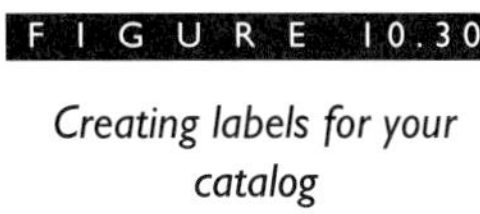

FIGURE 10.30

Creating labels for your catalog

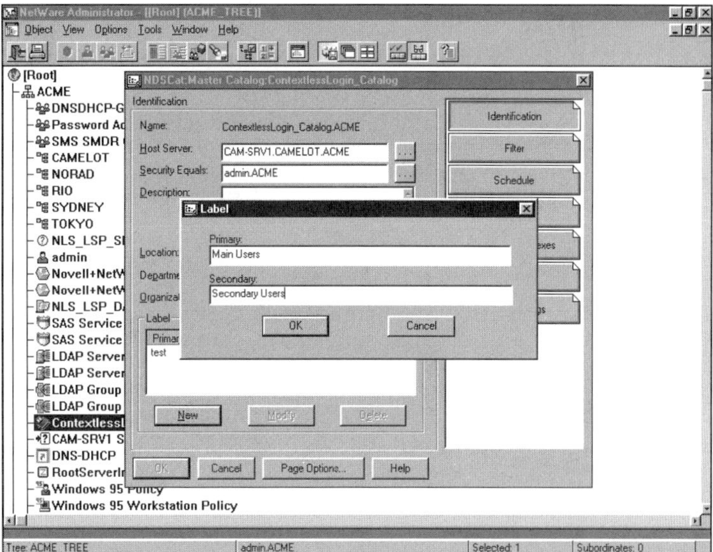

8. Click Filter, and then enter a statement in the Filter box. The filter is an attribute name and attribute value such as "object class" = "user" and so on. An example of this box is shown in Figure 10.31.

9. Define the scope of the catalog. You can search the subtree, search immediate subordinates, or search aliases as shown in the dialog box. You can also enter the context limits for the search.

FIGURE 10.31

Specifying a filter to search NDS and build the catalog

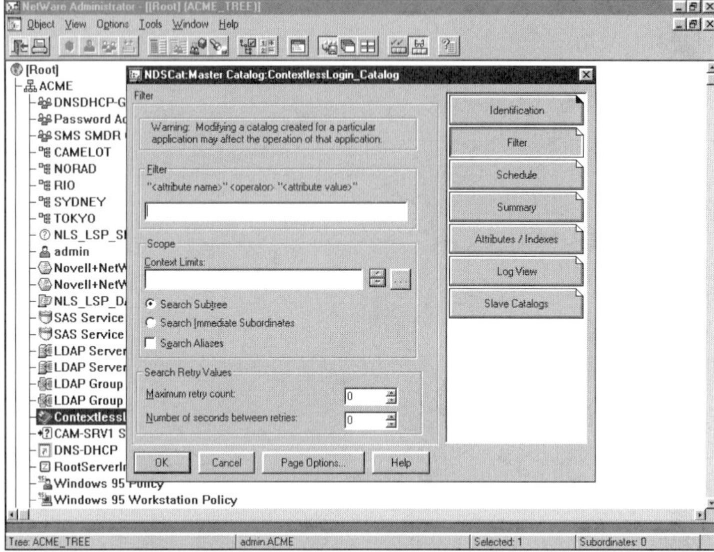

10. Click Schedule to specify when the catalog should be updated. If you select Update Now, the dredger component on your NetWare 5 server initiates creation of the catalog. Click the Summary tab to see a summary of the catalog findings, as shown in Figure 10.32. You will see a message on your NetWare 5 server indicating the times the dredge began and was completed. You can also choose to schedule a time for building the catalog by specifying an automatic time with a frequency, start time, and start date.

11. Click Attributes/Indexes and then choose All Attributes or Selected Attributes. If you choose Selected Attributes, you can choose individual attributes to include in your catalog. You can select any available attributes by highlighting them and clicking Add. An example of this is shown in Figure 10.33.

12. Click Select Indexes on the same page to specify the attribute by which the catalog is to be indexed. You can index on any attribute that you have previously selected.

FIGURE 10.32

The Summary Information tab shows the results of catalog creation.

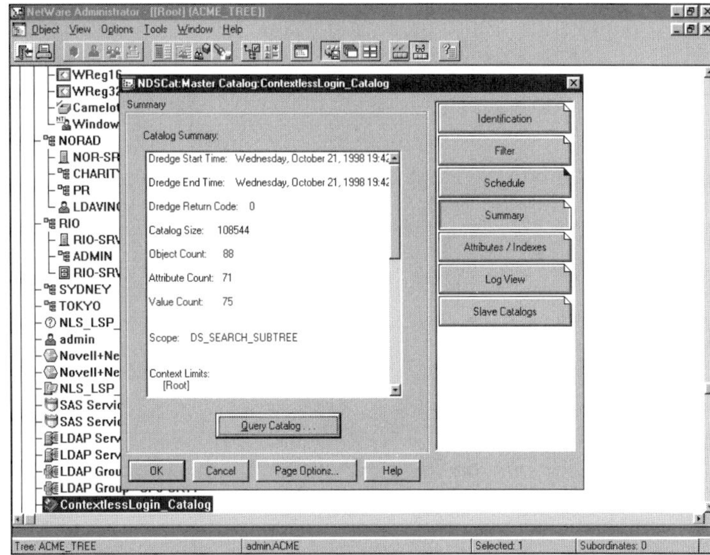

FIGURE 10.33

Selecting attributes to add to your catalog

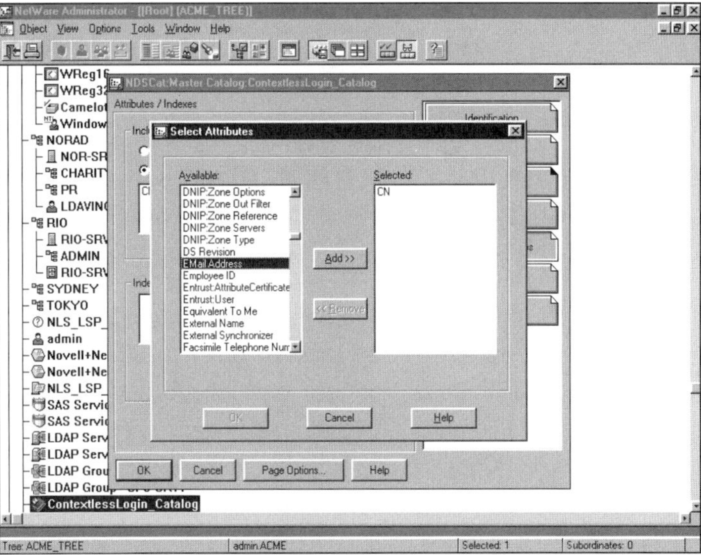

Installation of Contextless Login

Perhaps one of the most important features of Catalog Services is its capability to create a contextless login for your users. This feature allows users to log into the NDS tree without knowing their full context. They can simply enter their user name without knowing their location in the tree. This is a big benefit for mobile users. Follow these steps to implement contextless login:

1. LGNCON32.DLL is the contextless login extension that is installed as part of the NetWare Client for Windows NT install program. Verify that this file exists on your machine by examining the Windows system directory.

For Windows 95/98 this is C:\WINDOWS\SYSTEM; for NT it is C:\WINNT\SYSTEM32. For Windows 3.1, the file is LGNCON16.DLL and is in the WINDOWS\SYSTEM directory.

2. Log in as a user with Administrative rights to the target tree.

3. If you have not already done so, install NDS Catalog Services using the NetWare 5 installation program. Select to install all except the NDS Catalog Services SDK. During the Catalog Services setup, select a tree and server to copy the dredger (DSCAT.NLM) to.

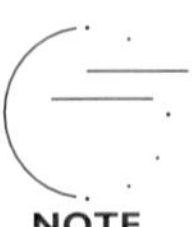

The install program modifies the server AUTOEXEC.NCF to automatically load DSCAT.NLM. You may wish to edit this file after installation completes so that you can load it manually in the future, if you desire.

4. Check the local WINDOWS\SYSTEM directory for a DSCQRY32.DLL. If this file does not exist, look for DSCATQRY.DLL and rename it to DSCQRY32.DLL (Note: for Windows 3.1 this file should be renamed to DSCQRY16.DLL). This file may also exist on the server in SYS:PUBLIC. If it does, copy it to the appropriate local Windows directory as described previously. This file is needed for contextless login to use NDS Catalog Services.

5. From the Start menu, run a NetWare Administration Utility program such as Z:\public\win95\NWADMN32.EXE.

6. Create the catalog object: Type **NDSCat:Master Catalog**, name it "usrcat" in any organizational unit or container in your tree, and save it.

7. Select the catalog object just created and define these additional attributes:

   Identification page:

   - Select the Browse button to the right of the Host Server: field. Browse to and select the HOST server (this is the one that runs the dredger as in Step 3).
   - Click the New button in the Label section. Enter **LGNCON** for the primary label and **Users** for the secondary label. *Please note that case is important.*

   Filter page:

   - Input this text in the Filter field: **"Object Class" = "User".** *Note that case is important and be sure to include the double quote marks.*
   - Select the Search Subtree radio button and leave the Context Limits field blank, or designate the context limiting container. This will be the starting point for the dredger to fill the catalog with users; in other words, only users in this container and below will be added to the usrcat database. (When this field is blank, the entire tree will be cataloged from the [root] container down.)

   Attributes/Indexes page:

   - Select the Selected Attributes radio button.
   - Select Full Name from the Available list and click the Add button. Click OK.
   - Click the Select Indexes button. Select Full Name from the Available list and click Add. Click OK. *Please note: This will allow the use of Full Name searching by contextless login if the administrator has included Full Name attributes for User objects in the tree.*

Schedule page:

- Select the Manual radio button. *Note: If you add more users to your tree, you'll need to update the catalog (redredge the tree) as well.*

8. Click OK to save all changes.

9. Right-click on Root or the container used in Step 7 for the filter page, and select Trustees of This Object.

10. Click Add Trustee. Locate the catalog "usrcat" created and add it as a trustee. It should now appear in the Trustees list for this container. Verify that Browse is enabled under Object rights, and that Compare and Read are enabled under Property rights. This gives the catalog object rights to the container in order to read objects and populate the catalog.

11. Click OK to save changes.

12. Locate the catalog and right-click it to select Trustees of This Object.

13. Click Add Trustee. Select [Public] under the Available objects listing, and select OK. [Public] should now appear in the Trustees list for the catalog usrcat. Verify that Browse is enabled under Object rights, and that Compare and Read are enabled under Property rights. This gives contextless login the capability to open and read a catalog using [public] rights. This is necessary, as the user is not currently "Authenticated" to the tree; [public] rights are used.

14. Click OK to save changes.

15. Go to the server and load DSCAT.NLM or verify that it is loaded.

16. Return to the workstation and run the Administration tool again. Select the catalog object. Open the Schedule page and select the Update Now button (unless you are using automatic updating).

17. Return to the server and wait for a successful dredge of the catalog. After the line appears that says "USRCAT dredge is complete," you may unload DSCAT.NLM if you wish.

18. Return to Administration tool and verify that the catalog has data by reselecting the USRCAT object. Select the summary page. Verify the dates and times listed on this page. Click the Query button and query this catalog. You should only see a listing of distinguished names for all users currently defined in the database (tree).

19. Exit the Administration tool.

20. Verify that the settings for contextless login are set. You may use the Registry editor or go through the Client Configuration property page for contextless login.

21. To use the Client Configuration property page, simply enable contextless login.

22. Using a Registry editor, locate the following key:

For Win95:

```
\\HKEY_LOCAL_MACHINE\Network\Novell\System Config\
Network Provider\Graphical Login\NWLGE\Z Xcontext
```

For Winnt:

```
\\HKEY_LOCAL_MACHINE\Software\Novell\Graphical Login\
NWLGE\Z XContext
```

23. Under Z XContext, verify or create the following key value pairs:

KEY NAME	KEY TYPE	KEY VALUE
LoginExtDesc	String	"Login Extension Contextless Login"
LoginExtName	String	"LGNCON32.DLL"
LoginExtType	Binary	01 80 00 00

24. Save these settings and exit.

NOTE

After any new users are created in the future, rerun the dredge by loading DSCAT.NLM on the server, waiting for a successful dredge, and then unloading (see Steps 14 through 16).

Testing the Functionality of Contextless Login

Test if contextless login is running correctly by following these steps:

1. Run Loginw32.exe.
2. In the Tree field, enter the tree that has the catalog "usrcat" as created previously.
3. Input any existing user name into the Username field.
4. Hit the Tab key.
5. If the user name only exists once on the server, the user's corresponding context should now appear in the Context field.

   If the user name exists in multiple contexts in NDS, a Users dialog box should appear that states "Select your user and context from the list shown on the screen below." Click OK.
6. A list of all matching users and contexts should appear below the prompt.
7. Partial names will also work but only if contextless login is configured for wild card searches.

LDAP Services for NDS

NetWare 5 supports Lightweight Directory Access Protocol (LDAP) version 3, an industry-standard protocol that allows a user to easily access X.500-based directories including but not limited to NDS. LDAP Services for NDS is a server-based interface between NDS and any LDAP-compliant applications running optionally under Secure Sockets Layer (SSL). In NetWare 5, the performance of

LDAP access to NDS has also been significantly enhanced from previous versions, allowing unlimited scalability through NDS's advanced replication and management of directory functions.

The Lightweight Directory Access Protocol (LDAP) in NetWare 5 is configured and managed using LDAP Services for NDS, a snap-in to the NetWare Administrator utility (NWADMN32.EXE). LDAP Services for NDS 3.0 is a server application that allows LDAP clients to access read and write information stored in NDS. With LDAP Services for NDS, all your NDS data is available and you define the directory information that is accessible to LDAP clients and the clients that can access the directory. You can also give different clients different levels of directory access or access the directory over a secure connection. These security mechanisms allow you to make some types of directory information available to the public, other types available to your organization, and certain types available only to specified groups or individuals.

Installing LDAP Services for NDS

LDAP Services for NDS is installed when you install NetWare 5 and choose product options. The NetWare 5 server loads NLDAP.NLM, and a snap-in is added to NWADMIN to provide new object functionality.

Understanding LDAP Services for NDS

LDAP Services for NDS is a NetWare server application (NLDAP.NLM) that allows LDAP clients to access information stored in NDS. With LDAP Services for NDS, you define the directory information you want to make accessible to your LDAP users and grant the rights to the LDAP clients that you want to have access to the directory. Using the NetWare Administrator utility, you can specify all the attributes of the LDAP clients and set all security information in one place.

The directory features available to LDAP clients depend on the features built into the manufacturer's LDAP server and the LDAP client. For example, LDAP Services for NDS allows LDAP clients to read and write data in the NDS database if the client has the necessary permissions. Some clients have the capability to read and write data; others can only read directory data.

LDAP Clients

LDAP Services for NDS allows LDAP clients to access data in NDS directories. All LDAP clients bind, or connect, to NDS as one of the following types of users:

- [Public] user
- Proxy user
- NDS user

Login restrictions and password restrictions will still apply; however, any restrictions will be relative to where LDAP is running.

Time and address restrictions are also used, but address restrictions are relative to where the NDS login occurred — in this case, the LDAP server. Also, as LDAP does not support grace logins, it is possible to log into NetWare and yet not be able to bind to LDAP.

[Public] User (Anonymous Bind) An anonymous bind is a bind that does not contain a username or password. If an LDAP client binds to LDAP Services for NDS and the service is not configured to use a proxy user, the user is authenticated to NDS as user [Public]. User [Public] is an authenticated NDS user. By default, user [Public] is assigned the Browse right to the objects and attributes in the NDS tree.

The default Browse right for user [Public] allows users to browse NDS objects but blocks user access to object attributes. The default [Public] rights are typically too limited for most LDAP clients. Although you can change the [Public] rights, this will give these rights to all users. Because of this, use of the proxy user anonymous bind is suggested.

NOTE

To enable user [Public] access to object attributes, you must make user [Public] a trustee of the appropriate container or containers and assign the appropriate object and attribute rights.

Proxy User (Proxy User Anonymous Bind) A proxy user anonymous bind is an anonymous bind that is linked to a normal NDS username. If an LDAP client binds to LDAP Services for NDS anonymously and the service is configured to use a proxy user, the user is authenticated to NDS as the proxy user, whose name is configured in LDAP Services for NDS and in NDS.

To implement proxy user anonymous binds, you must create the proxy user object in NDS and assign the appropriate rights to that user. Assign the Proxy User Read and Search rights to all objects and attributes in each subtree where access is needed. Use LDAP access control lists (ACLs) to restrict access as necessary. You also need to enable the proxy user in LDAP Services for NDS by specifying the same proxy username.

The key concepts of proxy user anonymous binds are as follows:

- All LDAP client access through anonymous binds is assigned through the proxy user object.
- The proxy user cannot have a password or any password restrictions (such as password change intervals), because LDAP clients do not supply passwords during anonymous binds. You should not force the password to expire or allow the proxy user to change passwords. You may want to limit the locations from which the user can log in by setting address restrictions for the proxy user object through the Network Address Restrictions page of NetWare Administrator.
- The proxy user object must be created in NDS and assigned rights to the NDS objects you want to publish. The default user rights provide Read access to a limited set of objects and attributes. Assign the Proxy User Read and Search rights to all objects and attributes in each subtree where access is needed. Use LDAP ACLs to restrict access as necessary.
- The proxy user object must be enabled on the General page of the LDAP Group object that configures LDAP Services for NDS. Because of this, there is only one proxy user object for all servers in an LDAP group.

NOTE

You can configure access control lists (ACLs) in the LDAP Group object to add access controls for the proxy user. For example, you can create an access control list that allows the proxy user access through one IP address or a group of IP addresses.

NDS User (NDS User Bind) An NDS user bind is a bind that an LDAP client makes using a complete NDS username and password. The NDS user bind is authenticated in NDS, and the LDAP client is allowed access to any information the NDS user is allowed to access.

When LDAP Services for NDS is installed, NDS user bind requests using clear-text (unencrypted) passwords are refused by default. Clear-text passwords and NDS usernames entered by LDAP clients on non–Secure Sockets Layer (SSL) connections are vulnerable to capture by network monitoring equipment. Anyone who captures an NDS username and password has immediate access through an LDAP or NDS client to all the NDS objects to which the captured username has access. NDS user binds should only be used on LDAP servers that are configured to use SSL.

NOTE

Even though clear-text passwords are not accepted by default, this does not prevent users from trying to bind with their usernames and passwords. On an unsecured connection, all attempted binds expose the username and password to eavesdropping, whether or not the bind is successful. However, not allowing clear-text passwords for NDS user binds discourages users from using their names and passwords, because this method of binding will be unsuccessful.

To support NDS user binds on non-SSL connections, you must allow clear-text passwords within the LDAP Group object.

The key concepts of NDS user binds are as follows:

- NDS user binds are authenticated to NDS using the username and password entered at the LDAP client.
- On non-SSL connections, the NDS password is transmitted in clear text on the path between the LDAP client and LDAP Services for NDS.
- Any NDS username and password used for LDAP client access can also be used for NetWare client access to NDS.

To support NDS user binds on non-SSL connections, you must allow clear-text passwords. To enable this feature, check the Allow Cleartext Passwords check box on the LDAP Group object using NetWare Administrator for Windows 95/98 or NetWare Administrator for Windows NT. If clear-text passwords are not enabled, all NDS bind requests that include a username or password on non-SSL connections are rejected.

If an NDS user password has expired, NDS bind requests for that user are rejected. The type of bind with which the user authenticates has a direct effect on the content the LDAP client can access. LDAP clients access a directory by building a request and sending it to the directory. When an LDAP client sends a request through LDAP Services for NDS, NDS completes the request for only those attributes to which the LDAP client has the appropriate access rights. For example, if the LDAP client requests an attribute value (which requires the Read right) and the username is granted only the Compare right to that attribute, the request is rejected.

LDAP Services for NDS supports the Secure Sockets Layer (SSL) protocol to ensure that the connection over which data is transmitted is secure and private. SSL is a protocol that establishes and maintains secure communication between SSL-enabled servers and clients across the Internet. To ensure message integrity, SSL uses a hashing algorithm. To ensure message privacy, SSL provides for the creation and use of encrypted communications channels. To prevent message forgery, SSL allows the server and, optionally, the client to authenticate each other during the establishment of the secure connection. This release of LDAP does not ask the LDAP client to authenticate itself.

Key Material Object To implement the authentication and encryption processes, SSL uses a cryptographic mechanism called *public keys.* To establish a secure connection, the server and the client exchange their public keys to establish a session key. The session key will be used to encrypt the data for the life of the connection. A subsequent LDAP connection over SSL will result in the generation of a new session key that is different from the previous one.

Digital certificates, digital IDs, digital passports, or public key certificates are critical for verifying the identity of the contacted server. They are similar to an employee badge that identifies the wearer as an employee of a company. Each LDAP server requires a digital certificate to implement SSL. Digital certificates are issued by a certificate authority (CA).

Certificates are stored in a new NDS object, the key material object. Use Novell PKI Services, a snap-in of the NetWare Administrator utility (NWADMN32.EXE), to request, manage, and store certificates in NDS. Refer to the section on PKI Services later in this chapter for details on setting up a certificate on a server. You can access Novell PKI Services help by selecting the Help button from any key material object page.

In order for the LDAP server to use a specific certificate for LDAP SSL connectivity once it is stored in NDS, you must indicate the key material object containing the certificate on the LDAP Server General page in NetWare Administrator.

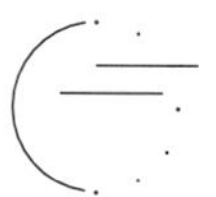
NOTE

The key material object must be in the same container as the NetWare server object that will use it.

SSL Configuration

Although SSL can be configured on both the client and the server to ensure the identity of both parties, clients do not require digital certificates to communicate securely. As the LDAP server listens for SSL connections on a special port, all the client needs to do is initiate the connection over that port.

Note that when you make changes to your LDAP Services for NDS configuration using NetWare Administrator, many of the changes take effect dynamically without your having to restart the LDAP server. However, most SSL configuration changes require a restart. Also note these points:

- If SSL is disabled, you can enable it without restarting the LDAP server, and the enabling will occur dynamically. If SSL is enabled and you disable it, you must restart the LDAP server in order for the disabling to take effect.
- If you make any configuration changes to the SSL port or the SSL certificate, you must restart the LDAP server for the changes to take effect.

To restart the LDAP server, type these commands at the NetWare server console prompt:

```
UNLOAD NLDAP

LOAD NLDAP
```

Understanding Class and Attribute Mappings

A *class* is a type of object in a Directory, such as a user, a server, or a group. An *attribute* is a Directory element that defines additional information about a specific object. For example, a User object attribute might be a user's surname or phone number. In NetWare Administrator, classes are called *object types* or *classes*, and attributes are called *properties*.

A *schema* is a set of rules that defines the classes and attributes allowed in a Directory and the structure of a Directory (where the classes can be in relationship to one another). Because the schemas of the LDAP Directory and the NDS Directory are different, mapping of LDAP classes and attributes to the appropriate NDS objects and attributes is necessary. These mappings define the name conversion from the LDAP schema to the NDS schema.

LDAP Services for NDS provides default mappings. In many cases, the correspondence between the LDAP classes and attributes and the NDS object types and properties is logical and intuitive. Depending on your implementation needs, however, you may want to reconfigure the class and attribute mapping.

In most instances, the LDAP class to NDS object type mapping is a one-to-one relationship. However, the LDAP schema supports a feature called *auxiliary class support* that allows an object to be associated with more than one class. To view the mappings, select the LDAP group object you have created and select Details. You then select the Attribute Map tab to view the default settings and make changes to the mapping if necessary. This will depend on the type of LDAP client you are using. An example of this view is shown in Figure 10.34.

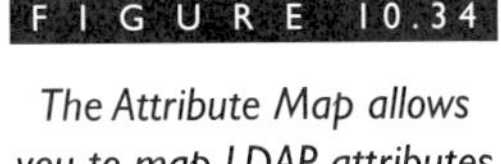

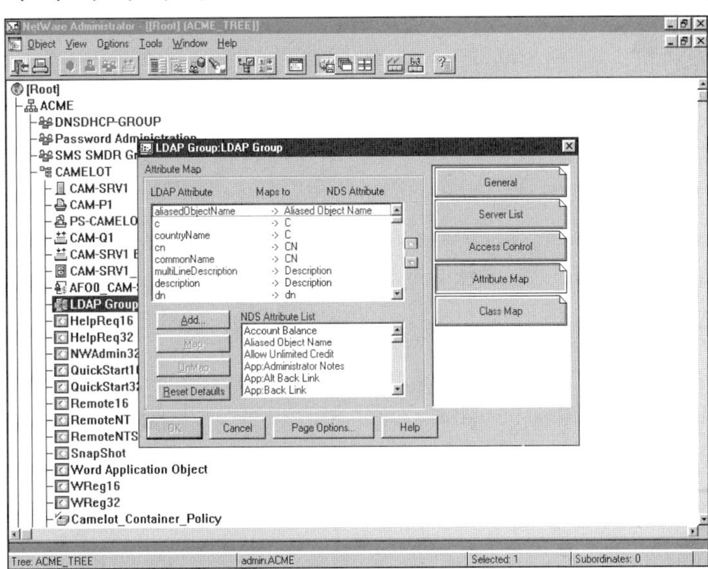

FIGURE 10.34

The Attribute Map allows you to map LDAP attributes to NDS attributes.

LDAP and NDS Syntax

LDAP and NDS use different syntaxes. Some important differences are:

- Commas
- Typeful names only
- Escape character
- Multiple naming attributes

Commas LDAP uses commas rather than periods as delimiters. For example, a distinguished, or complete, name in NDS looks like this:

CN=ALINCOLN.OU=ADMIN.OU=RIO.O=ACME.

Using LDAP syntax, the same distinguished name would be:

CN=ALINCOLN,OU=ADMIN,OU=RIO,O=ACME.

Typeful Names Only NDS uses both typeless (.LDAVINCI.NORAD.ACME) and typeful (CN=LDAVINCI.OU=NORAD.O=ACME) names. LDAP uses only typeful names with commas as the delimiters (CN=LDAVINCI,OU=NORAD, O=ACME).

Escape Character The backslash (\) is used in LDAP distinguished names as an escape character. If you use the plus (+) character or the comma (,) character, you can escape them with a single backslash character. Some examples include:

CN=A\+EINSTEIN,OU=LABS,OU=NORAD,O=ACME (CN is A+EINSTEIN)

Multiple Naming Attributes Objects can be defined with multiple naming attributes in the schema. In both LDAP and NDS, the user object has two: CN and OU. The plus symbol (+) separates the naming attributes in the distinguished name. If the attributes are not explicitly labeled, the schema determines which string goes with which attribute (the first would be CN, the second is OU for NDS and LDAP). You may reorder them in a distinguished name if you manually label each portion.

For example, here are two relative distinguished names:

SIRKAY (CN is Sirkay)

Sirkay+Charity (CN is Sirkay, the OU is Charity)

Both relative distinguished names (Sirkay and Sirkay+Charity) can exist in the same context because they must be referenced by two completely different relative distinguished names.

Configuring the LDAP Server Object

The LDAP server object stores configuration data for one LDAP Services for NDS server. During installation, an LDAP server object named LDAP Server *servername* (where *servername* is the name of the server on which LDAP Services for NDS is installed) is created. The object is created in the same container as the NetWare server object on which the product is installed. An example of the Details dialog box is shown in Figure 10.35.

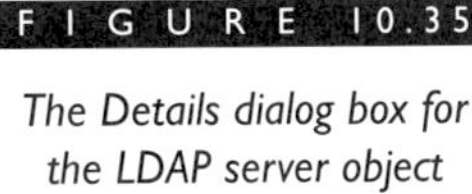

FIGURE 10.35

The Details dialog box for the LDAP server object

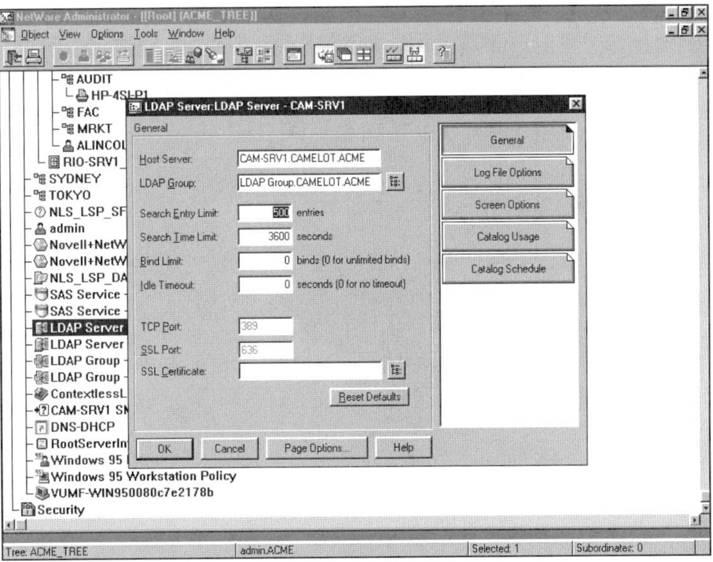

Each LDAP server object configures one LDAP Services for NDS server. Do not assign the same LDAP server object to more than one LDAP Services for NDS server. If you assign the LDAP server object to another server, it is no longer assigned to the previous server. The LDAP server object contains five property pages from which you set configuration options. These are the General (Details) page, log file options, screen options, catalog usage, and catalog schedule.

Using LDAP in a Wide Area Network Environment

In order to reduce network traffic when using a wide area network (WAN), you can specify exact times when you want to refresh LDAP objects in NDS.

Type one of the following three commands at the NetWare 5 server console.

LDAP REFRESH This command refreshes LDAP at a specified interval. You can use the following syntax:

```
LDAP REFRESH = 'date' 'time' 'interval'
```

Use the following formats for the arguments:

Date format: mm:dd:yyyy (If zeros are entered for all date fields, then the current date will be used.)

Time format: hh:mm:ss (If zeros are entered for all time fields, then the current time will be used.)

Interval format in minutes: a value greater than or equal to 1. The default is 30 seconds. If zero is entered, 30 seconds is used.

LDAP REFRESH IMMEDIATE This command refreshes the LDAP objects immediately. If you have already set the LDAP REFRESH command, the set interval will be saved.

```
LDAP REFRESH
```

This command displays the time and interval of the next scheduled refresh.

LDAP HELP To display help information at the server console, type the command:

```
LDAP HELP
```

The NetWare Time Protocol

Time synchronization in NetWare 5 always uses TIMESYNC, whether servers are using IP only, IPX only, or IPX and IP protocols. TIMESYNC.NLM is automatically installed on the NetWare 5 server installation program, but NTP.NLM must be manually loaded on your NetWare 5 server whenever the network has an IP stack in use.

When NetWare Time Protocol (NTP) is loaded on an IP server, TIMESYNC will operate as an NCP request responder only, and NTP will manage and set the clock. This means that when NTP is loaded on any IP server, NTP will become the main source of time for both the IP and IPX networks. The IPX/TIMESYNC servers have to become secondary time sources and will point to IP/NTP through the Migration Agent for the primary source of time. For more information on time synchronization in NetWare 5, see Chapter 7.

Configuring NTP

The Network TP is configured with NTP.CFG, located in the SYS:ETC directory. When NTP is installed, a default NTP.CFG is created. This file should be edited to define the user's time synchronization subnetwork. The default NTP.CFG file specifies the local clock (147.86.1.0) as the time source.

These two commands specify the mode in which to operate and the time server hostname or address to be used:

- Peer address
- Server address

Address The address can be either a DNS name or an IP address in dotted-quad notation, such as 147.85.1.0. See the default NTP.CFG file on your server's SYS:ETC directory.

Peer The peer command specifies that the local server is to operate in symmetric active mode with the remote server. In this mode, the local server can be synchronized to the remote server, and in addition, the remote server can be synchronized by the local server. This is useful in a network of servers where, depending on various reliability scenarios, either the local or a remote server might be a better source of time.

Server The server command specifies that the local server will operate in client mode with the specified remote server. In this mode, the local server can be synchronized to the remote server, but the remote server can never be synchronized to the local server. On a local network without Internet access, the server can use its own clock as the reference clock by using IP address 147.85.1.0 with the server option. The local reference clock is useful if you want to use NTP in an isolated environment where no other time sources are available. When there are no synchronization sources, the local reference clock can use the local hardware clock as a last resort.

Loading NTP.NLM At NetWare 5 server console, type **NTP.NLM**; the following message will display:

```
"NTP is synchronizing local clock to remote time source
145.87.3.1""NTP is synchronizing local clock to remote time
source 147.86.16.63""NTP is synchronizing local clock to
remote time source 129.7.1.66"Time synchronization has been
established with remote time source 129.7.1.66Date and Time
is Thursday, October 22, 1998 05:00:30 PM MDT
```

If you modify the NTP.CFG file and specify more than one time source, the time servers will be loaded in reverse order, much like a DNS file entry.

Figure 10.36 shows an example NTP.CFG file created on your NetWare 5 server. To use any of the other time providers listed, remove the comment from the time server of your choice. Time servers can also be added to the configuration file. Use either the hostname or IP address to denote the server.

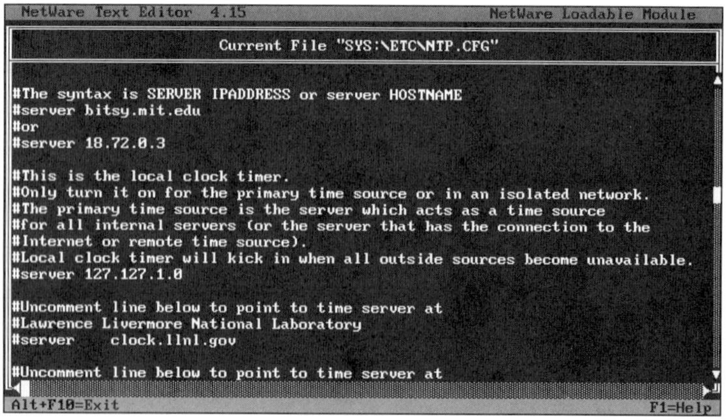

FIGURE 10.36

The NTP.CFG file is created on your NetWare 5 server when you type NTP at the console prompt.

```
NetWare Text Editor  4.15                          NetWare Loadable Module
                 Current File "SYS:\ETC\NTP.CFG"

#The syntax is SERVER IPADDRESS or server HOSTNAME
#server bitsy.mit.edu
#or
#server 18.72.0.3

#This is the local clock timer.
#Only turn it on for the primary time source or in an isolated network.
#The primary time source is the server which acts as a time source
#for all internal servers (or the server that has the connection to the
#Internet or remote time source).
#Local clock timer will kick in when all outside sources become unavailable.
#server 127.127.1.0

#Uncomment line below to point to time server at
#Lawrence Livermore National Laboratory
#server    clock.llnl.gov

#Uncomment line below to point to time server at
Alt+F10=Exit                                                       F1=Help
```

Network Services

Several new enhancements make the basic network services in NetWare 5 more flexible, manageable, and secure. The new network services included in NetWare 5 are pure IP, Service Location Protocol (SLP), DNS/DNCP integration, Z.E.N.works Starter Pack, Cryptographic Services, Secure Authentication Services (SAS), Public Key Infrastructure Services (PKIS), Auditing Services, NetWare Licensing Services, and Internet Connectivity.

Pure IP

New in NetWare 5 is pure IP, which enables NetWare to support TCP/IP in a pure sense. It does not encapsulate or tunnel IPX/SPX communications. Pure IP enables servers and clients to make NetWare Core Protocol (NCP) calls directly over the TCP/IP stack; such calls can then be routed by any IP router on the network. Although NetWare 5 maintains support for IPX/SPX protocols, you now have the option of implementing a pure TCP/IP environment or using IPX/SPX alone or as part of a mixed TCP/IP and IPX/SPX environment. This is advantageous for customers who require a pure IP environment because it eliminates multiple protocols and frees up valuable network bandwidth, while allowing them to control IP implementation at their own pace.

Novell has severed the operating system's dependence on IPX/SPX and has rewritten IPX-only applications and utilities to support TCP/IP. As a result, NetWare 5 servers and workstations can use TCP/IP, IPX/SPX, or both. The major advantages of supporting pure IP in NetWare are:

- Consolidation to one protocol in your network
- More efficient use of your LAN and WAN bandwidth
- A wider range of opportunities for remote user connectivity

Although there are major advantages to pure IP, Novell is committed to remain backward compatible to IPX/SPX. NetWare 5 is shipping with features that provide seamless compatibility between IPX- and IP-based technologies. NetWare 5's Compatibility Mode enables customers to move to an IP-only environment without having to replace valuable IPX-based applications and without having to introduce disruptions to their network operations. In addition, NetWare 5 ships an IP Compatibility Mode Migration Gateway that allows you to move to an IP-only network, incrementally if desired.

In essence, it is your choice whether to use IPX/SPX or TCP/IP as your network protocols. In order to install pure IP, you use the standard NetWare 5 installation program. During the installation process, you select the protocols that you want your server to support. If you enable IPX/SPX, you must select an internal IPX address for the server, as you normally would. If you enable TCP/IP, you must select an IP address for the server. For more information, see Chapter 23.

Service Location Protocol

Service Location Protocol (SLP) provides automatic resource discovery and registration over TCP/IP connections. Network resources such as servers and printers use SLP. SLP is more efficient than Service Advertisement Protocol (SAP) because it creates less ongoing network traffic than SAP. In addition, SLP allows network resources to carry extended description attributes. For example, a printer could be categorized as a "PostScript printer loaded with legal-sized paper used by Consulting." For more information on installing and configuring SLP in NetWare 5, see Chapter 23.

DNS/DHCP

Domain Name Service (DNS) converts domain names (such as `www.novell.com`) to numerical IP addresses (*xxx.xxx.xxx.xxx*). NetWare 5 integrates DNS with NDS. With NDS integration, each user can automatically be assigned an appropriate DNS server upon login. For example, a mobile user in a distant location might be assigned a DNS server with a faster response time than a desktop user in a local office.

Dynamic Host Configuration Protocol (DHCP) provides unique IP addresses upon request to users and network devices. NetWare 5 uses NDS to help automate DHCP services, and this means you can store IP address in NDS. When the user logs into the network, DHCP consults NDS and provides an appropriate IP address to that user. DHCP eliminates the older methods of manually tracking and assigning IP addresses, and NDS ensures that DHCP provides managed IP addresses throughout the enterprise. For more information about DNS/DHCP, see Chapter 23.

The Z.E.N.works Starter Pack

NetWare 5 ships with the Z.E.N.works Starter Pack, which includes Novell Application Launcher (NAL) and Workstation Manager as part of the NetWare 5 installation. Z.E.N.works, which stands for Zero Effort Networking, is a bundle of management utilities that assist you in managing individual workstations in an enterprise.

The components of Z.E.N.works allow administrators to solve a user's workstation problems without visiting the user's workstation. By adding workstation objects and workstation group objects to the NDS tree, administrators can manage the desktop configuration, distribute applications, and perform maintenance on the workstation through NDS.

With Z.E.N.works installed, workstations are registered with NDS each time a user logs into the network. Registration enables administrators to look at a workstation object's details and centrally manage workstations through NDS.

Features Available in the Full Z.E.N.works Product

Additional Z.E.N.works functionality can be obtained by purchasing the full-featured product. Once you install Z.E.N.works and the Novell Client provided on the Z.E.N.works CD, you can take advantage of the additional features described under the next few headings.

The Help Requester

This application lets users send messages about a workstation problem to the administrator or Help Desk. A message automatically includes the workstation object's details stored in NDS. You can use the message and the workstation object in NWAdmin to solve the problem. This saves time and effort, especially when problem workstations are located on a WAN.

Workstation Inventory

Z.E.N.works allows you to easily inventory and track all the configuration data for Windows workstations on the network.

Remote Control of Workstations

By enabling remote control access on the network's workstations, you can connect to a workstation remotely and navigate the desktop to troubleshoot workstation problems without having to visit the workstation.

For more information on installation and use of Z.E.N.works, see Chapter 19.

New Security Features in NetWare 5

Several new security features build upon NetWare 4's existing security features. For a complete description of NDS and file system security, see Chapter 13. The new security features found in NetWare 5 have been integrated with Novell Directory Services (NDS) and help simplify administration of each new feature. They also provide security for improved Internet data integrity and privacy across public networks. Novell's PKI infrastructure enables the use of public key cryptography and public key certificates on your network.

Before diving into this relatively new technology, it's important to understand the basics. Over the past couple of years we've witnessed the explosion of the Internet and its capabilities. With Internet commerce and other transactions, security has moved to the forefront of importance. Internet communications such as Web browsing or public forums lend themselves to be monitored easily by anyone with the right equipment and knowledge. However, credit card information and other sensitive data must be made secure across the Internet. Public key cryptography is the most widely used method for securing sensitive data and credit card transactions.

Public key cryptography secures data transmissions through authentication and encryption. *Authentication* is the method by which the data receiver knows that the data sender is exactly who or what it claims to be. *Encryption* is the scrambling of data such that it can only be read by the intended receiver.

Both authentication and encryption utilize the technology known as *key pairs*. Key pairs are mathematically related codes or "keys" that provide a secure method of communication. One key in each pair is publicly distributed, while the other key in the pair remains strictly private.

Therefore, during authentication, the data receiver knows that the data sender is exactly who or what it claims to be. An example of this concept is shown in Figure 10.37, in which a user authenticates to a NetWare server.

FIGURE 10.37

The authentication process using public/private key cryptography

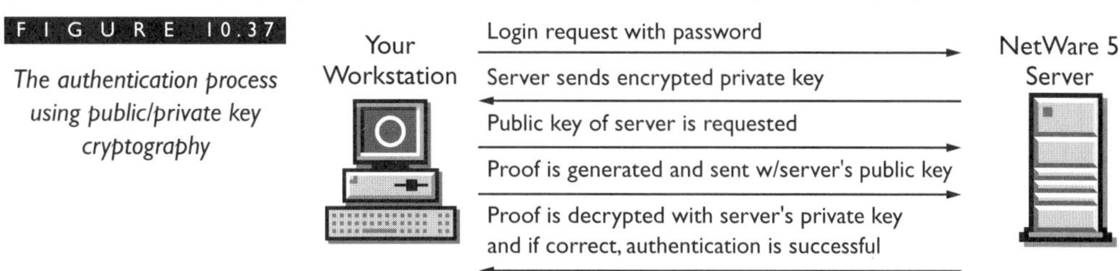
Your Workstation
Login request with password
Server sends encrypted private key
Public key of server is requested
Proof is generated and sent w/server's public key
Proof is decrypted with server's private key and if correct, authentication is successful
NetWare 5 Server

These are the basic steps of the authentication process:

1. You initiate a login request from your NetWare client.
2. Your client receives an encrypted private key from the server. This is used to generate a signature.
3. The public key of the NetWare server is requested by the client.
4. A proof is generated and encrypted with the server's public key and sent to the server.
5. The server decrypts the proof with the server's private key.
6. The server validates your signature against the request using your public key. If the results compute correctly, the signature is authenticated. Otherwise, a message is displayed that the login attempt has failed.

The encryption process scrambles the data before it is transmitted across the Internet to ensure that the data can be read only by the intended receiver. For example, you order a product over the Internet and must enter your credit card number. An example of this process is shown in Figure 10.38.

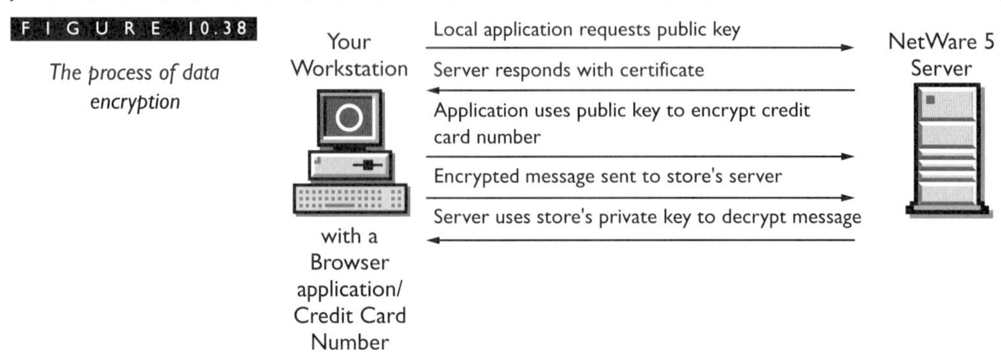

FIGURE 10.38

The process of data encryption

These are the basic steps of the encryption process:

1. You are viewing a Web browser with the vendor's Web site and enter your credit card number in the store's application.

2. The store's application gets the store's public key directly from the store or a public directory.

3. The store's application uses this key to encrypt the message containing your credit card number.

4. The application sends the encrypted credit card information to the store's server.

5. The store's server uses the store's private key to decrypt the message.

Another important aspect of PKI is the concept of establishing a trust. If a sender and receiver know and trust each other, they can exchange public keys and establish a secure data transmission, including authentication and encryption. This is accomplished through the use of each other's public keys and their own private keys. But neither party can typically trust each other, and so a third party is introduced whom they both trust, to provide proof of their identity.

A party needing to prove its identity in a public key cryptography environment enlists the services of a trusted third party known as a *certificate authority* or CA. There are commercial CAs such as VeriSign that provide this type of service. A CA service can also be operated by an internal organization such as a corporate MIS department that can issue public key certificates internally. The NDS tree CA can easily serve this purpose and allows you to save money by not using a commercial CA. A CA can also offer services such as key pair generation, key pair archival, public key certificate revocation, and public key certificate publishing services.

The CA's purpose is to verify that a party is who or what it claims to be; it will then issue a public key certificate for that party to use. The public key certificate verifies that the public key contained in the certificate belongs to the party named in the certificate. When the identity of the requesting party has been established to the satisfaction of the CA, the CA will issue an electronic certificate and apply to it what is called a digital signature. The digital signature verifies the authenticity of the certificate.

Digital Signatures

A digital signature is similar to a personal signature that you would place on a document such as a check or other legal paper. Digital signatures can also be referred to as public key certificates, digital Ids, digital passports, or just certificates. A digital signature provides proof that electronic data is authentic. In order to create a digital signature, software must link the data being signed with the private key of the signer. For example, a company can request from a CA that they certify the company's public key. In this process, the company sends their public key information to the certificate authority for verification. Once the information is verified by the CA through the CA's own rules of verification, the certificate authority takes a series of actions:

1. The CA creates a public key certificate containing the necessary information.

2. The CA runs a computation on the information in the public key to produce a small data string of 16 to 20 bytes.

3. The CA encrypts the small data string using the CA's private key. The encrypted string is the CA's signature for the certificate information.

4. The CA sends the public key certificate containing the requester's public key and the CA's signature to the requesting party.

Therefore, a digital signature is linked to the entity that signs it and the data. No other entity can duplicate the signature because each entity has its own private key. Even the entity that creates a signature cannot deny having signed the data. This is often referred to as nonrepudiation. So when a CA signs a public key certificate, it guarantees that it has verified the identity of the public key owner according to the CA's guidelines and policies.

The certificates generated by most commercial certificate authorities and also Novell's NDS Tree CA are encoded using the X.509 v3 format. A public key contains the information shown in Table 10.1.

TABLE 10.1

Contents of the Public Key Certificate

The public key of the user or organization
The length of time the public key certificate is valid (typically this is one year)
The serial number of the public key certificate
The name of the CA that digitally signs the public key certificate
The digital signature created by the CA
Additional Encoded Attributes
Alternate names
Phone numbers
E-mail addresses
Key usage constraints
Certification practice statements
Other critical or noncritical attributes

Now let's apply these concepts to the NetWare 5 environment. The security provided by the public key cryptography components in NetWare 5 include:

- Novell International Cryptographic Infrastructure
- Public Key Infrastructure Services

- Secure Authentication Services
- The Audit system

The next four sections discuss these new features and explain why they are important and how they provide NetWare 5 with advanced security services. The following section describes how you can configure Novell's PKI services in your NetWare environment.

The Novell International Cryptographic Infrastructure

NetWare 5 includes cryptographic services known as the *Novell International Cryptographic Infrastructure (NICI)*. NICI allows developers to use the Controlled Cryptography Service (CCS) API to integrate cryptographic schemes with their applications. Therefore, an application must be written to take advantage of this service provided on NetWare 5. The big benefit is that NICI allows developers to write a single application using cryptography that can be used in different countries, regardless of the differences in countries' cryptographic laws. For example, a developer could write a single application that uses 128-bit cryptographic keys for use within the United States and 40-bit cryptographic keys when used within countries that allow only keys of that length.

NICI provides the infrastructure for network cryptographic services on a worldwide basis because it supports strong cryptography and multiple cryptographic technologies. This infrastructure has been developed in accordance with customer and internal Novell needs and at the same time abiding by the national policies and laws regarding the shipment and use of cryptography. NICI services were designed to be modular in nature, which allows for new cryptographic engines, libraries, and policy managers to be added at any time. The infrastructure is also tightly controlled, enforced through an integral OS loader that verifies modules before loading and controls access to modules only via standardized interfaces. For developers the cryptographic services are provided via a Novell SDK.

Some important features that NICI offers NetWare 5 include these:

- Developers do not have to include cryptographic code in their products. This is handled by the Controlled Cryptography Service API.

- A cryptographic library can be dynamically bound. This library delivers controlled cryptographic services to applications regardless of the country where they are used.
- U.S. export approval is expedited for international applications.
- Integrity of key management is ensured.
- An infrastructure supports key escrow in future releases.
- A uniform cryptographic services API is included.
- Network security services are built on NICI.

NICI is the foundation for future network cryptographic services from any vendor. It ensures that your product complies with international cryptography import and export laws through enforced region-specific cryptographic laws and regulations. NICI also provides for single, worldwide commodity vendor products and supports extensible, application-specific cryptographic libraries and interchangeable cryptographic technologies.

In the past, applications had to provide their own services if they needed to employ cryptography. Because of the way the Novell cryptographic services are designed, application vendors can take full advantage of the services without having to incorporate complex and expensive cryptography inside their applications. The vendor can ship just one version of its product worldwide, instead of having multiple versions to accommodate the many and varied national cryptography regulations. Novell will ensure compliance with international laws and export requirements—leaving application developers free from these concerns. Novell's PKI services for application developers are provided through Novell's SDK.

Public Key Infrastructure Services

NetWare 5 includes *Public Key Infrastructure Services (PKIS)*, which supports public-key cryptography and digital certificates in a NetWare 5 environment. Digital certificates provide a method for verifying the authenticity of keys used in a public-key process. In NetWare 5, PKIS allows you to act as your own certificate authority or to use the services of third-party certificate authorities. Through PKIS, you can generate and sign digital certificates and store and manage these certificates within NDS.

PKIS allows any NetWare 5 administrators with Supervisor rights to the NDS tree CA to establish a certificate authority (CA) management domain within NDS. Additionally, PKIS allows administrators to manage certificates and keys for Secure Sockets Layer (SSL) security for LDAP servers.

Some important features that PKIS offers NetWare 5 include:

- Integrity of Certificate and Private Key Storage through NDS's trusted directory capabilities
- The capability to manage such tasks as automated artificial certificate creation, using the local CA through the NetWare Administrator as a single point of administration
- Standards Support for the PKIS-generated certificates. This is according to the X.509 v3 standard. PKIS is compatible with X.509 v1 and v2 certificates. The X.509 standard defines an internationally recognized format for providing identity and public key ownership.
- Standards Support for PKIS-generated PKCS #10 certificate signing requests. A PKCS #10 certificate signing request is a public key and identity bound for certification by a signing authority. The PKCS #10 certificate request is sent to the certificate authority for a signature.
- The capability to securely manage the private keys for server applications.
- Worldwide exportable public key management capabilities with Novell's international cryptographic infrastructure

PKIS helps you to build a working public key infrastructure on your network. You can create a CA specific to your organization and use the services of an external CA. You can also use a combination of both as your certificate authority needs dictate.

Using PKIS, you can control the costs associated with obtaining key pairs and managing public key certificates. PKIS helps you create a local CA based on NDS that signs certificates for other services on the network. With PKIS you can also generate unlimited key pairs and issue unlimited public key certificates through the local CA at no charge.

Secure Authentication Services

Secure Authentication Services (SAS) is an infrastructure for supporting both existing and emerging authentication mechanisms, such as biometric and token-authentication systems. Through SAS, NetWare 5 supports SSL version 3. Developers can use the SAS API to write applications that can establish encrypted SSL connections. Additionally, developers can then use NICI to ensure that these SSL connections conform to the laws of each country in which the applications are used.

Authentication recognizes and protects the end user. It is how people and things identify themselves. So without authentication, you cannot secure your network. SAS security properties are attributed to applications running on the network inside of the NetWare 5 security boundary. Because SAS is a service, not a library, applications do not have access to protected authentication materials or users' secrets. It also provides worldwide exportable cryptographic services for authentication.

SAS is built entirely on NICI. SAS has the following capabilities:

- The SAS service is based on a single executable file. Because no cryptography is included in the SAS NLM, you can ship a single NLM worldwide. This provides easy administrator management and tracking. Also, any applications written to the SAS API can be based on a single executable file.

- Applications written to the SAS application can go through a one-time and usually expedited export approval process. Novell has already received export approval for SAS and NICI. This means that application developers benefit from expedited export procedures.

- PKIS provides key management for the SSL services. Any application written to the SAS interface inherits the capability to have PKIS manage its certificates. NDS access control lists (ACLs) manage access to the private key that enables SSL. Because SAS is a network service, it has its own network identity. ACLs are set up on the SSL key object in a way that allows only the SAS identity to read the private key. This guarantees that nonauthorized entities such as users, other server applications, and even the application built on top of SAS cannot gain access to and expose or subvert the private key.

The Audit System

NetWare 5 includes auditing services, which allow administrators to monitor users' access to an organization's network and to record this monitoring information in audit log files. You can create NDS objects to represent audit log files, and you can then manage these objects just as you manage other objects in the NDS tree. You can also grant rights to the NDS objects representing audit log files, just as you grant rights to other objects in the NDS tree. As a result, you can assign administrators to view and manage audit log files.

The audit system now takes advantage of exposed NDS audit services in the following ways:

- Audit log files are represented and managed as NDS objects.
- Access to audit and configuration information is controlled by standard NDS rights.
- Auditing is configured at the container and volume levels.
- The audit policy for a container or volume specifies what is audited within the volume or container and which users are audited.

Auditing services are an essential element of the total NetWare security environment. You must have network audit integrity to ensure that the network is secure. As previously mentioned, the NetWare 5 auditing system can monitor and record every relevant network transaction. It detects which user performed the transaction, and when the transaction occurred. This is important because businesses and other organizations such as government agencies often contract with independent parties to audit network transactions. These auditors review various events as requested. Generally, auditors are granted rights only to track events and activities, but they cannot open or modify network files (other than audit files).

NetWare 5 provides the highest level of audit data granularity. This includes which events are audited, control of audit configuration, and access to audit data. In order to enable auditing, you can use the AUDITCON utility. After auditing is enabled, audit data and history files are automatically created for the volumes and containers you specify. Audit files continue to accept records until auditing is disabled or the file becomes full.

Some important features that Audit offers NetWare 5 include:

- The capability to assign independent auditors that are separate and distinct from administrator privileges
- Distributed and replicated audit information
- A multiple-auditors capability
- A high granularity of auditable events, to the user level
- An auditing system that the auditor can configure to meet company policies
- New audit events added for NetWare 5 (for example, SSL connections)
- Exportable audit data for use by reporting programs

Installing and Using Novell's PKI Services

In this section we'll walk you through the steps required to set up a NetWare 5 server as a certificate authority to generate certificates and key pairs. Novell's PKI services are installed when you install your NetWare 5 server. When you install NetWare 5, your server installs the Novell Secure Authentication Services (SAS), the Novell PKI Services, and the NICI cryptographic modules. If these components were not installed during the installation of NetWare 5, you can use the NWCONFIG utility and select Other Installation Items/Products to complete this step.

IMPORTANT

The server to which a key material object is associated must be able to communicate with at least one other server holding a writable replica of the key material object. You must also ensure that the servers are running the same protocol (IP/IPX).

Server and Workstation Requirements

Novell's PKI services require that your server and the workstation administering PKI services have certain basic requirement as outlined here.

Server Requirements

- NetWare 5 or NetWare 4.11 (with BorderManager installed in an NDS tree)
- Novell Secure Authentication Services (SAS) installed on the server that will be associated with the NDS tree CA
- Novell PKI services installed on the server
- NICI cryptographic modules installed

Workstation Requirements

- A Novell client with the capability to run NWADMN32.EXE

The following objects are available in the NDS schema when you install this service:

- **Certificate authority object** — This object contains the public key, the private key, the public key certificate, the certificate chain, and other information that is used by this object. This object resides in the security container. The certificate authority service runs on only one NetWare 5 server in your NDS tree. Be sure to choose a NetWare 5 server that is physically secure so that you don't compromise the integrity of your system.

- **Key material objects** — These objects contain the public key, the private key, the public key certificate, and the certificate chain. The private key is stored in the key material object in encrypted form. Any applications taking advantage of these security services will access a key material object.
- **Security container** — This container holds all the security-related objects for the entire NDS tree. This container, which resides at the top of your NDS tree, holds the key material objects and the certificate authority object. This container is installed automatically when SAS is installed on your NetWare 5 server.

The first step to enabling these security features is to create a certificate authority object.

Creating a Certificate Authority Object

The certificate authority object should be placed on a server that is dependable and stored in a secure location. Because this server will be the centerpiece of your public key infrastructure system, you don't want to compromise the integrity of your network.

You have the option of using the NDS tree CA or an external CA as your certificate authority, but you must still create the NDS tree CA for rights management for PKI. Your choice of whether to use the NDS tree CA versus an external CA depends on a number of factors including compatibility with Novell products, cost savings, and simplified management through NDS. However, an external CA can provide liability protection and availability to outside applications.

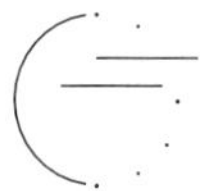
NOTE

Both types of CAs can be used simultaneously. Using one type of CA does not preclude the use of the other.

If you have already installed the security services during the NetWare 5 installation, you will see that a security container is already created in your tree below the [Root] object. Then follow these steps to create your certificate authority object:

1. Launch the NetWare Administrator.

2. Set your context to [Root].

3. You will see a security container in NWADMIN. Right-click this object and select Create; a certificate authority object will be created as shown in Figure 10.39.

FIGURE 10.39

Using NWADMIN to create an NDS tree CA object

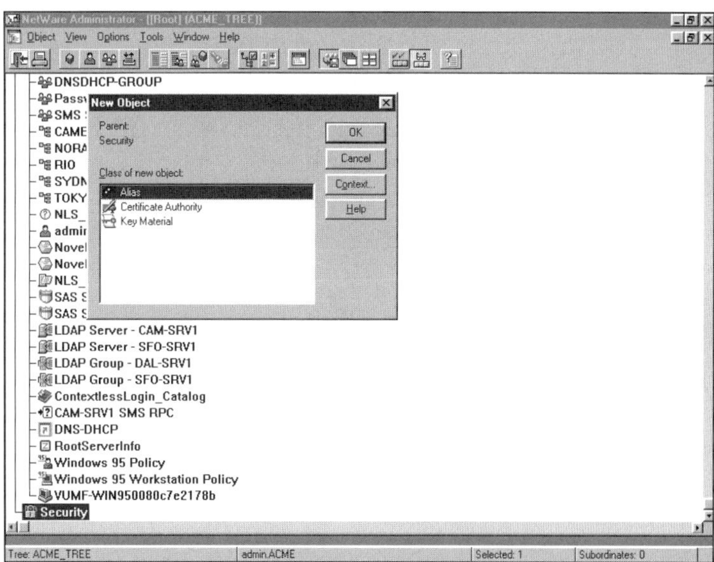

4. From the dialog box, choose the certificate authority object and click OK. Follow the instructions shown in the Certificate Authority Object Wizard. An example is shown in Figure 10.40.

Once this process is completed, you'll notice that the CA object will be placed in the security container. By double-clicking this object, you can view the details of this certificate authority object. An example is shown in Figure 10.41.

FIGURE 10.40

Using the wizard to create a standard or custom certificate authority object

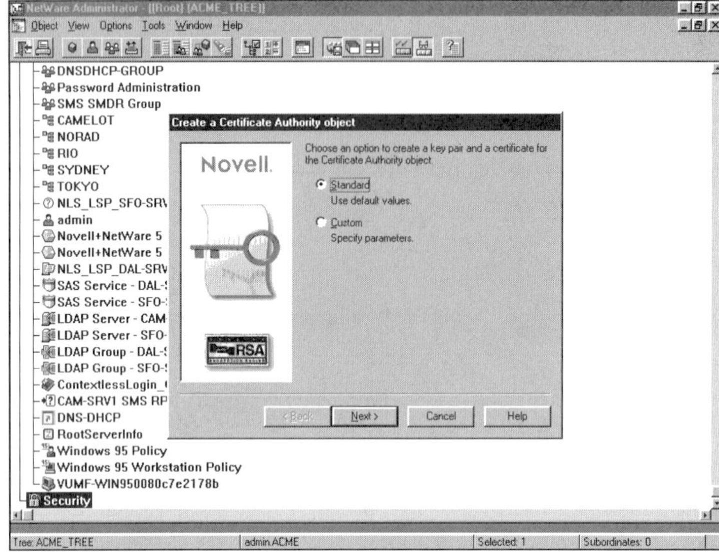

FIGURE 10.41

Viewing details of a certificate

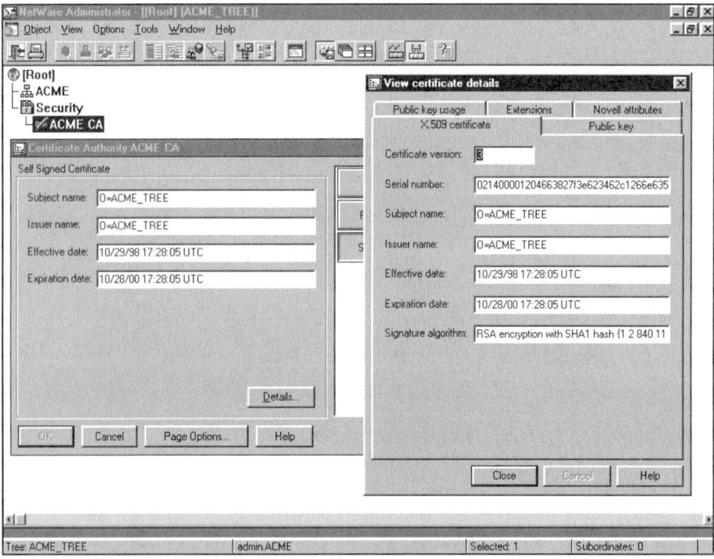

Creating Key Material Objects

A key material object must be created in the container where the NetWare server object resides. Follow these steps to create a key material object:

1. Identify the server that is going to run your security-based applications.

2. Launch the NetWare Administrator.

3. Right-click the container object containing the server identified in Step 1 and choose Create. An example of the resulting dialog box is shown in Figure 10.42. If you select a container where no server is present, you will get an error message.

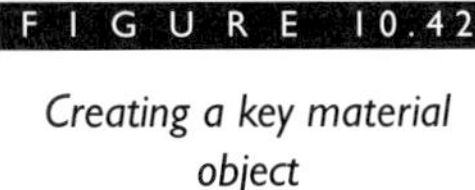

FIGURE 10.42

Creating a key material object

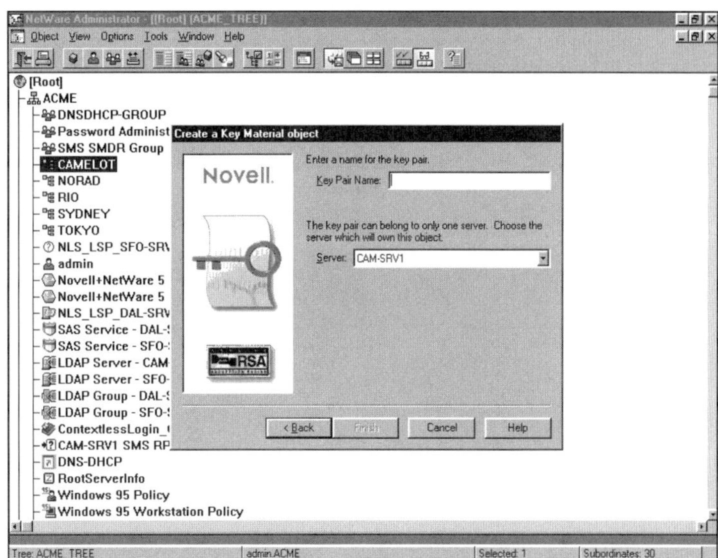

4. Enter an key pair name and click OK. Follow the instructions shown on the Key Material Object Wizard page. You will then see a new key material object placed in that container.

Once you have configured PKI services for your network, you must configure your individual security applications so that they can use the key material objects that you established. Since the configuration procedures are unique to the individual applications, they are not discussed here. You must refer to your application's documentation for specific security information. To view the configuration information, select the key material object and select Details.

Installing a Public Key Certificate

The process of installing a public key certificate involves creating a new key material object using the Standard installation option. If you have not done so, see the previous section on how to create a key material object. You can also choose to use the NDS tree through the Custom installation option, which will automatically sign the public key certificate by the NDS tree CA.

To install a public key certificate signed by an external CA, follow these steps:

1. Launch the NetWare Administrator.
2. Double-click the key material object you have just created.
3. Select the public key certificate page. You will see a message that there is no public key certificate.
4. Select Import.
5. Choose a location of the public key certificate to install.
6. Either you can copy and paste the certificate using any text editor or the Clipboard utility, or you can select a file option and specify the file's location.
7. Click Add. This will store the public key in the key material object. If you now click the Public Key Certificate page, you will see the distinguished name of the subject, the distinguished name of the issuer, and the validity period of the public key certificate as shown in Figure 10.43.

Using the NWADMIN utility, you can also renew a public key certificate, revoke a public key certificate, or export a trusted root certificate.

NetWare Management Agents

NetWare 5 includes NetWare management agents (NMAs) that are used to manage the operating system via the Simple Network Management Protocol (SNMP). These agents are SERVINSTR.NLM, HOSTMIB.NLM, and NWTRAP. NLM. With these agents you can use any SNMP-based console such as

ManageWise, CA UniCenter, HP Openview, IBM Tivoli, SunNet Manager, and others to view and manage over 400 objects and 400 traps that are exposed by the NetWare Management Agents. Alerts can be set up to notify administrators of problems before end users start calling and escalating a network problem.

FIGURE 10.43

The Public Key Certificate information page in NWADMIN

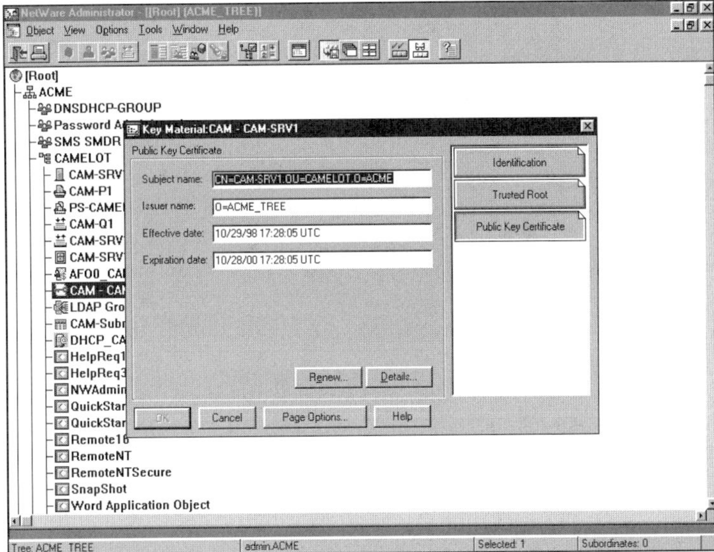

These agents can be installed automatically during the installation of NetWare 5. For more information on using ManageWise with NetWare 5, see your Novell documentation.

NetWare Licensing Services

This service simplifies installation and licensing of new Novell products. It works on your NetWare 5 server to reduce the time and effort you must spend on installing and licensing. Common utilities and interfaces now standardize each of these tasks. NLS provides a single utility (NLSMANAGER.EXE) that you can use to license all future NetWare products. This new capability ensures consistent, efficient, and rapid licensing for NetWare products, and it permits licensing for any non-Novell products conforming to NLS requirements.

Implementing NLS

When a certificate for an NLS-aware application is installed, NLS adds a license container object to the NDS tree and a license certificate object to that container object. You select the context or location in the NDS tree for that license container object. An example of a license container object is shown in Figure 10.44.

FIGURE 10.44

A license container object and a license object are created when you create a license certificate.

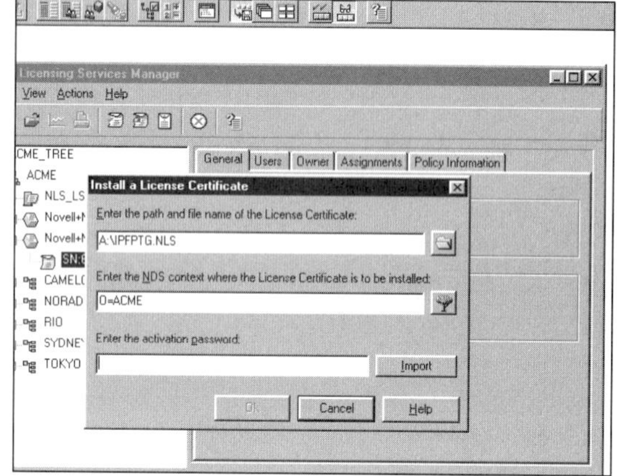

In the next section we walk you through how to create a license certificate, a metered certificate, and an install envelope.

Installing a License Certificate

If you purchase and install additional licenses, they will also be added to the NDS tree as objects in the appropriate license container object. When adding license certificates to the NDS tree, you should be aware of where in the tree you want to install the license. This location or context will determine who can use the license units associated with that license certificate. You install license certificates by accessing .NLS files from the application you are installing. Installation of the license certificate can be done through either the NWADMIN utility or the NLSManager utility.

To install license certificates using the NetWare Administrator utility, follow this step: After loading NWADMIN, select Tools → Install License → Install License Certificate. An example of this selection is shown in Figure 10.45. You can then follow the instructions on the screen. These instructions are similar to the instructions that follow for creating a license using NLS Manager.

FIGURE 10.45

Installing a license certificate using NWADMIN

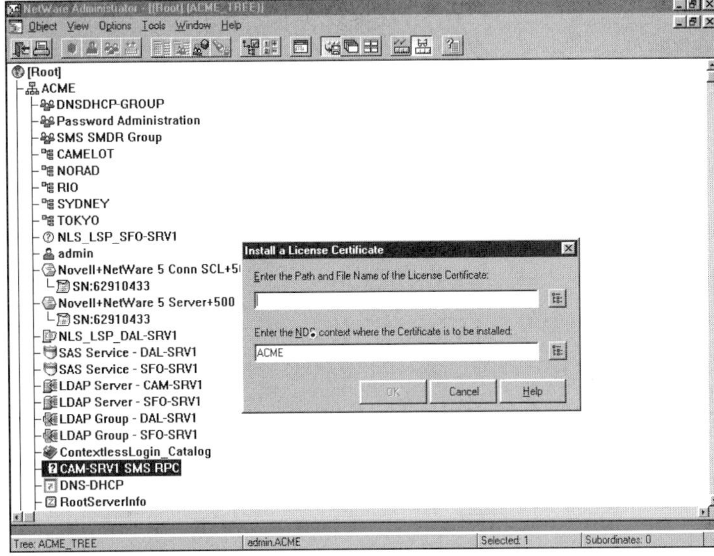

The NLS Manager utility provides greater functionality for managing licenses. You can also use the NLS Manager utility by completing the following steps.

1. Select View → Tree View to see the dialog box shown in Figure 10.46.

FIGURE 10.46

The first screen of the NLS Manager utility

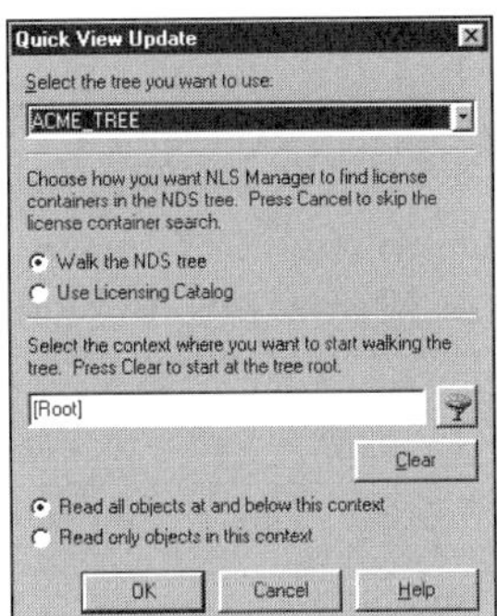

2. Select Actions → Install License Certificate. You can also click the first license certificate icon on the toolbar. Be sure to select the tree icon before selecting Actions. If not, the option to Install License Certificate will be grayed out.

3. Enter the path and filename of the certificate. To locate the filename, click the folder icon next to the filename field. Then navigate the directory structure. The file may be on a disk in drive A: or on a CD-ROM. The .NLS file is linked to an activation password file (key) and automatically retrieves the password.

4. Select the NDS context where the certificate object will be installed. To locate the context, click the tree icon next to the NDS Context field, browse the tree, and select a context. If you are installing an additional certificate in an existing license container object, select the container's parent, not the license container object.

5. With both fields filled, click OK to install the license certificate, OK to acknowledge the "need to update" message, and then OK to acknowledge the successful installation.

6. (Optional) In the Activation Key window, enter the key that you received for this license.

NOTE

If the file containing the activation key is in the same directory as the license file you select, the key will be read automatically. You only see the Activation Key window when the file containing the activation key is not detected in the same directory or on the floppy disk or CD-ROM containing the file.

A license certificate requires an activation key. If the NLS Manager utility can't find an activation key while you are installing a certificate, an Activation Key window allows you to enter a key.

An activation key is like a password. It's a sequence of numbers and letters that allows you to complete the installation of a license for a product you purchased.

Software vendors provide this key at the time of purchase. During installation, you enter the activation key, which allows you to complete an installation.

With electronic purchases and distribution, activation keys allow you to install additional licenses for a product you already have. You may have purchased a product that came in a suite, or you can subsequently purchase the additional products in that suite and then use them by activating their keys. If you know the activation key, you can enter it without browsing for the file. To browse for the file containing the activation key, however, click Import.

Creating a Metered Certificate

Metered certificates allow you to track usage of applications, even those not written to the Licensing Service Application Programming Interface (LSAPI) specifications. Most likely, you have already invested in legacy applications that are not NLS-aware. By using metered certificates, you can allow users to continue using these applications while you track and manage the licenses for those applications.

You can configure Z.E.N.works to function as the NLS client for non-license-enabled applications. Z.E.N.works will then request licenses on behalf of the applications.

To create metered certificates using the NetWare Administrator utility, follow these steps:

1. Select Tools → Install License → Create Metered Certificate.
2. Next, use the instructions in the online help. (The steps are similar to those for the NLS Manager utility.)

You can also use the NLS Manager utility by completing the following steps:

1. Select View → Tree View.
2. Select Actions → Create Metered Certificate. You can also click the second certificate icon on the toolbar. The dialog box that appears is shown in Figure 10.47.

FIGURE 10.47

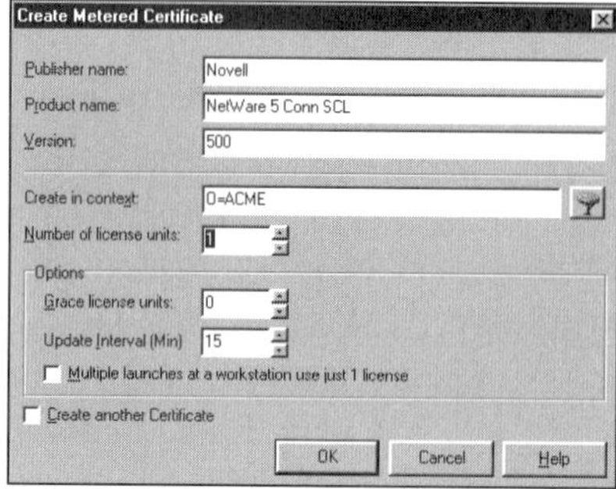

Creating a metered certificate using the NLS Manager utility

3. Enter the publisher's name. This is the name of the software company, such as Novell.

4. Enter the product name. This is the name of the software package, such as GroupWise.

5. Enter the version. This is the version number, for example, 500 for NetWare version 5.00. If a period (.) is used as part of the version number, the License container object will add a backslash to its NDS name. For example, 5.00 will display in an NDS tree as "5\.00."

6. Choose the NDS context for the certificate. To locate the desired context, click the Browse button next to the NDS Location field. Browse by clicking the + or – symbols in the Select window. Double-click the desired context or select it and click OK.

7. Enter or select the number of licenses for the certificate. This is the number of licenses you have purchased. For example, if you own a 500-user version of NetWare 5, enter 500.

8. Enter or select the number of grace licenses you will allow. This option enables additional users to run applications until you have time to purchase additional licenses. That is, this option helps you comply with your software license agreement without interrupting users' work flow or productivity. If you don't enter a number here, users will not be allowed to

open additional applications beyond the number specified in Number of Licenses. To ensure that no one is denied access to an application, enter a number that protects the users while also protecting the software vendor.

9. Select an update interval. This setting determines how often an application is to check whether a license is still being used and to inform the LSP of the status.

10. Select whether or not users use a single license when launching an application multiple times from one workstation.

11. Click OK twice. The first OK acknowledges that Quick View must be updated. (A new product license container for the certificate may not appear until you refresh the screen.) The second OK acknowledges that the certificate installed successfully.

You can see the license container object (for example, Novell+NetWare 5 Conn+500) and the license certificate object in the Tree view. An example is shown in Figure 10.48.

FIGURE 10.48

The NLS Manager view of the license container object and its contents

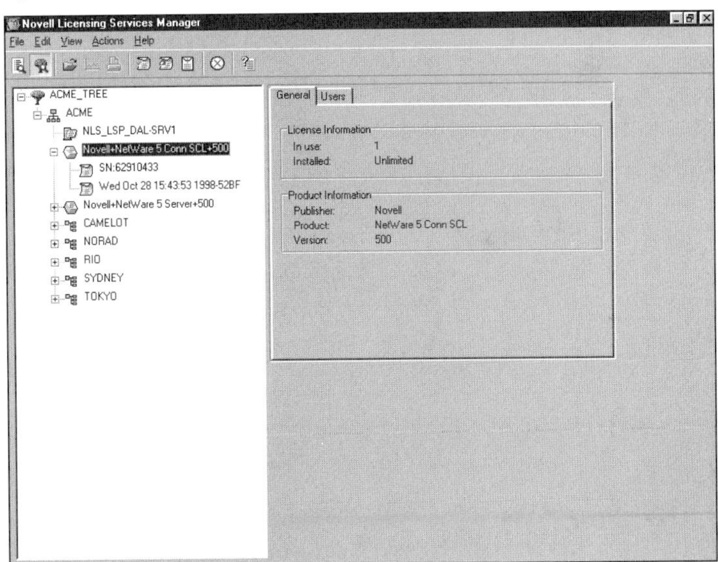

Installing an Envelope

An envelope is a file containing one or more license certificates. (It may have just one certificate because the envelope also contains other information — for example, for NIS-enabled installations — associated with the product.)

Envelopes allow you to install more than one license certificate at a time into license container objects. For example, you may have purchased three products in a suite. An envelope allows you to simultaneously install license certificates for all three products.

To install envelopes using the NetWare Administrator utility, select Tools → Install License → Install Envelope. Then use the instructions in the online help. (The steps are similar to those for the NLS Manager utility.)

You can also use the NLS Manager utility by completing the following steps:

1. Select View → Tree View.

2. Select Actions → Install Envelope. You can also click the envelope icon on the toolbar. The Envelope Installation Wizard appears, as shown in Figure 10.49.

FIGURE 10.49

Creating a license envelope using the Installation Wizard in NLS Manager

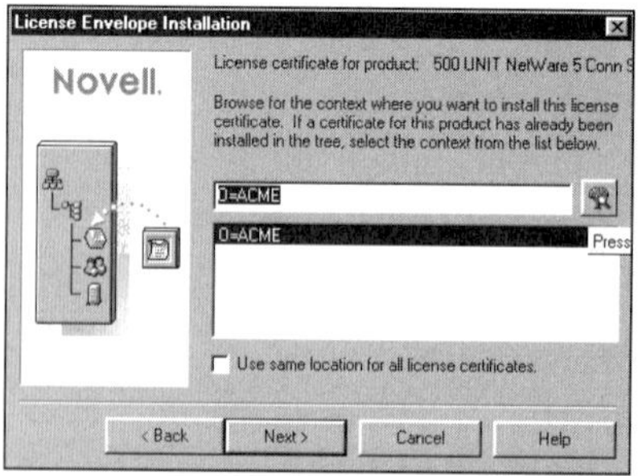

3. Follow on-screen prompts in the Envelope Installation Wizard:

   a. Select an envelope. Click Next, click the folder icon, navigate to the folder containing the envelope, and select the envelope (.NLF file).

   b. Choose certificates within the envelope. Click Next, select the certificates to install, and click Next.

c. Specify where in the NDS tree to install the certificates. Browse by clicking the tree icon and the + and – symbols as shown in Figure 10.50. Click the desired context and then click OK.

FIGURE 10.50

Selecting a context to install the License Certificate

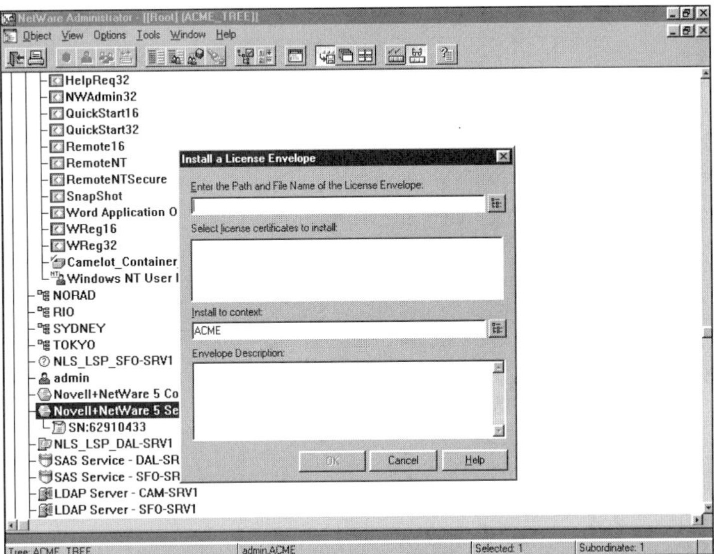

d. Select whether or not to install all certificates in the same location or context and then click Next. Click Next for each certificate you selected.

e. Verify that you selected the correct certificates and then click Finish.

f. Acknowledge that the certificates installed successfully by clicking Close.

Assigning Licenses to Users

Access to a license certificate is determined by the location of the license certificate and whether any assignments have been made to the license certificate. The owner of a license certificate is the NDS object (typically a user) that installed the license certificate. As an owner, you can assign the following objects access to the licenses:

- Users
- Groups
- Organizations
- Organizational Units
- Servers

If you assign a container object to use a certificate, all users in and below that container will be able to use the certificate through the mechanism of security equivalence. If you do not want to restrict access to licenses in this way, do not make any assignments to the license certificates.

Once you make assignments, only those objects that have been assigned to the license certificates can use the license. You can add and delete assignments to licenses through the Assignments property page.

You can assign licenses by using the NetWare Administrator utility. After you select a certificate in the Browse window, right-click → Details → Assignments → Add. Then browse, select an object, and click OK twice. (Steps in the online help are similar to those for the NLS Manager utility.)

You can also use the NLS Manager utility by completing the following steps:

1. Select View → Tree View.
2. Select the license certificate that you want users to access.
3. Select the Assignments property page as shown in Figure 10.51.
4. Click Add.
5. Locate and select the object that allows appropriate users to access the certificate's licenses, and then click OK. Browse the NDS tree by clicking the + or – symbols in the Select Object(s) window.

FIGURE 10.51

An example of assigning the container ACME to this license

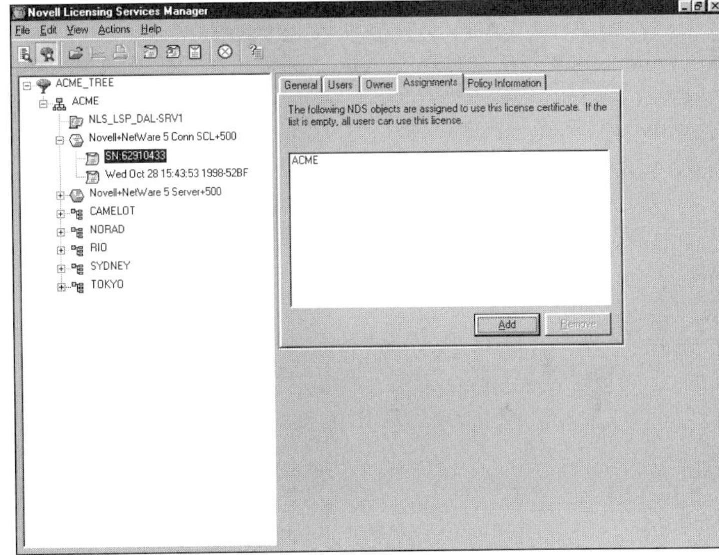

Delete assignments to a license certificate by completing the following steps:

1. Navigate to the Assignments property page of the license certificate object as explained previously.

2. Select the object you would like to remove from the list of assigned users and click Remove and then Yes.

Internet Connectivity

NetWare 5 ships with the Novell Internet Access Server (NIAS) 4.1. NIAS provides routing between local and remote LANs, remote access to all company network resources (including e-mail and Internet access) through a modem or other connection, and remote service management of all connectivity services and servers from your workstation. For more information on installing and using NIAS, see Chapter 22.

Installation and Upgrade

Several new installation or upgrade utilities are available in NetWare 5, including new upgrade utilities that easily move your NetWare 3 or NetWare 4 server to NetWare 5. In addition, there are utilities to help you upgrade your clients. These new installation and upgrade tools allow you to choose the options that best reflect your organization's network structure or design.

The NetWare 5 Installation Program (INSTALL.EXE and -.NLM)

The NetWare 5 installation program is used either to install a new NetWare 5 server or to upgrade an existing NetWare 4 server to NetWare 5. Upgrading an existing NetWare 4 server to NetWare 5 is often called an in-place upgrade. For complete information on installing NetWare 5, see Chapter 2.

The Novell Upgrade Wizard

New in NetWare 5 is the Novell Upgrade Wizard, which moves the NetWare 3 source server's bindery (including print information) and file system to the destination NetWare 5 server. The utility is a wizard-based interface, which ensures ease of use for across-the-wire upgrades. The wizard can also detect potential conflicts and provide options to resolve them before the upgrade begins.

The Rexxware Migration Toolkit

The Rexxware Migration Toolkit (RMT) is a batch-oriented, server-based tool with an unlimited capacity for migration and consolidation of servers, users, and data. This utility moves files and network bindery information from NetWare 3 source servers to NetWare 5 destination servers. RMT includes capabilities designed specifically for enhanced performance and customization during the upgrade.

The Rexxware Migration Toolkit is provided free of charge to existing NetWare 3 customers who wish to upgrade to either NetWare 5 or NetWare 4. The utility is created by Simware, Inc., and can be downloaded from the company's Web site at `www.simware.com`.

The Automatic Client Update

The Automated Client Update (ACU) ships with NetWare 5. This utility is used to upgrade all kinds of NetWare clients. For example, you can upgrade NetWare 3 clients to NetWare 5 clients automatically from a central location. For more information on using ACU, see Chapter 17.

Developer Support

NetWare 5 caters to network developers by providing the world's fastest Java Virtual Machine (JVM) for running server-based Java applications and services. Listed here are several additional enhancements made to the NetWare 5 system.

Java Support in NetWare 5

NetWare 5 supports Java applications running on the server. This allows a wide range of Java-developed applications to serve your network and users. Java support on NetWare 5 allows you to run Java applets on the server console, display Java applications in X Windows–style formats with full mouse and graphic support, and run multiple Java applications on the server while the server performs other tasks.

Java support in NetWare 5 is provided by JAVA.NLM. This NLM starts the Java engine, which enables Java applications to run. You can load Java support by calling JAVA.NLM at the server console prompt, and you can run Java applications using the APPLET console command.

The Java run-time environment consists of the following components:

- JVM
- Java Services Framework

- Support for GUI installation
- ORB

For more information, see your Novell documentation.

Scripting

NetWare 5 scripting and component services offer you choice, compatibility, and speed. NetWare 5 supports the major scripting languages available, including Perl 5, NetBasic 6.0, NetBasic 7.0, and JavaScript. For more information, refer to Novell's documentation.

Third-Party Add-Ons

Several third-party products are included at no cost in NetWare 5. Novell is including these third-party products as part of the NetWare 5 package software in order to integrate them with NDS and takes advantage of the security and services of NetWare 5. The third-party products are listed in the sections that follow.

Oracle8 for NetWare

NetWare 5 includes a five-user license for Oracle8 for NetWare. This version of Oracle (specifically Oracle8) has been integrated with NDS. As a result, you can use NDS to control access to your company's Oracle database.

The five-user version of Oracle8 for NetWare in NetWare 5 includes:

- An intuitive installation for getting a pretuned and preconfigured Oracle8 database up and running
- Wizards to help you create databases and migrate Oracle7 server databases to Oracle8
- HTML Web page creation based on data retrieved from Oracle8 (no knowledge of SQL or HTML syntax is required)

- The Oracle Migration Assistant for Microsoft Access for complete and easy migration from your Microsoft Access database to Oracle8 for NetWare.

Oracle8 for NetWare requires a NetWare 4.1*x* or NetWare 5 server with the following resources:

- 48MB free RAM (minimum)
- 16MB additional free RAM for the Advanced Replication option
- 200MB free disk space (minimum)

Oracle8 client software requires:

- A 486 or higher processor
- Windows 95/98, Windows NT Workstation version 4, or Windows NT Server version 4
- 16MB free RAM
- 25MB free disk space (minimum)

The Oracle Enterprise Manager running on an Oracle8 client requires:

- 32MB free RAM
- 25MB free disk space for the manager

The Netscape FastTrack Server

NetWare 5 provides a fully integrated version of the Netscape FastTrack server. This Web server uses Netscape Web server code specifically adapted for maximum performance on NetWare 5 and integration with NDS. This integration with NDS makes the Web server easier to administer and more secure by restricting who can administer the Web server and what content users can publish. The Netscape FastTrack server supports the following Web enhancing technologies: NDS, LDAP,

Common Gateway Interface (CGI), PERL, and NetBasic. For more information regarding installation of the FastTrack server, see Chapter 21.

Btrieve

The Btrieve key-indexed record management system is designed for high-performance data handling and improved programming productivity. Btrieve allows an application to retrieve, insert, update, or delete records either by key value or by sequential or random access methods.

Starting NetWare Btrieve 6.*x*

After installing Btrieve 6.1*x* using the NetWare installation utility, you can start it by entering this command at the server console or at a workstation running RCONSOLE:

```
bstart
```

If you have created a Btrieve server object, the BSTART.NCF command file for Btrieve 6.*x* automatically loads the NDS Support utility (BDIRECT.NLM). This utility checks to see whether a Btrieve server object exists, in which case the utility activates it.

NOTE

The Btrieve server object is installed at the level of the current directory context, as defined by the server's start-up script.

Stopping NetWare Btrieve 6.1*x*

To stop Btrieve 6.1*x*, enter this command at the server console or at a workstation running RCONSOLE:

```
bstop
```

The BSTOP command runs a NetWare command file (BSTOP.NCF) that unloads the following modules in the order shown:

1. BROUTER.NLM
2. BSPXCOM.NLM
3. BTRIEVE.NLM

NOTE

BSTOP.NCF does not unload BSPXSTUB, RSPXSTUB, or BDROUTER. To unload these modules, enter the UNLOAD command followed by the module name.

If you have created a Btrieve server object, the BSTOP.NCF command file for Btrieve 6.*x* automatically loads the NDS Support utility (BDIRECT.NLM). If an active Btrieve server object exists, it is deactivated and the NDS Support utility unloads.

NOTE

Before issuing the NetWare DOWN command on a server that has an active Btrieve server object, you must first issue the BSTOP command.

Summary

The new features and enhancements to NetWare 5 offer superior network management and control for system administrators and a more friendly and flexible interface for your users. NetWare 5 is also one of the most secure and cost-effective network operating systems available, offering comprehensive security features including cryptography, public key infrastructure, and Secure Authentication Services.

CHAPTER 11

Tuning and Optimizing the NetWare 5 Operating System

"Good is not good, where better is expected." — Thomas Fuller

Tuning and optimizing the NetWare 5 operating system is one of the responsibilities of the network administrator. These tasks can seem difficult because modifications are not always immediately perceived by the users. However, the question most people ask is, "What do I change in order to tune the operating system?"

One of the first steps in the tuning and optimizing process requires you to understand the basic characteristics of your network, servers, and user community. You should measure the baseline performance of your system during periods of both peak and off-peak production. Having a baseline beforehand allows you to gauge the changes in performance and reliability during the tuning effort.

For most implementations of the NetWare 5 operating system, the default settings for each of the internal parameters work very well. There are some server implementations that may make it necessary to modify some of the system settings to increase the capacity and performance of your system. These implementations may include heavy use of imaging or document retrieval types of software.

This chapter will provide you with a better understanding of the vital configurable NetWare 5 system parameters. Becoming familiar with the internal system parameters will help you to make changes to increase capacity and performance without compromising the reliability of your server. This information will also help you prioritize the tuning options and reduce the trade-off between system performance and reliability.

Performance versus Reliability

As most network administrators know, tuning and optimizing the operating system for performance and providing maximum reliability involve a kind of balancing act. For example, a setting in NetWare 5 allows disk writes to the NetWare volumes to be verified. This parameter is called "read after write verification" and should always be enabled on NetWare 5 volumes, which utilize disk hardware devices that do not perform write verification inherently. Turning the parameter to ON will increase reliability of the data being written to disk but will decrease the overall performance of the system. In this case, the reliability gained through verifying all writes to disk usually outweighs any side effects of slightly slower performance. NetWare 5 turns the read after write verification parameter ON by default.

Consulting Experience

For most systems with high-end (RAID 5) hardware and advanced disk drive technology, the parameter "read after write verification" is automatically enabled in the hardware. Most high-end disk drive manufacturers provide read after write verification within the hardware drive itself. The setting in NetWare is redundant and can be turned off to increase the performance.

Before you turn the "read after write verification" setting off for NetWare 5, make sure that the disk drive device is doing this process for you.

Surprisingly, for many users and administrators performance is not the single most important issue for their NetWare 5 servers. When forced to prioritize the different functions of a network server, many users will rank reliability and security as the two most important, with performance coming in a close third. Of course, each of these areas is important and each needs attention when you are the network administrator. But it's important to understand that tuning for performance's sake should not be allowed to compromise reliability and security.

Since most of the server resources or subsystems are closely tied together, changing the parameters on one subsystem can affect the performance of other subsystems. The best place to start the process of tuning the NetWare 5 operating system is with the defaults after installation. For the most part the system will tune itself and simplify your efforts.

NetWare 5 Is Self-Tuning

One of the key traits of Novell's NetWare operating system is its capacity to self-tune to provide your users with the best possible performance. Autotuning is NetWare's capacity to automatically increase necessary resources for the NetWare operating system. It determines workload requirements and makes enough resources, such as memory, available to provide maximum efficiencies. The procedure used to self-tune offers the capability to dynamically alter the internal system parameters and configuration in order to accommodate changing or increasing user demands.

Autotuning occurs when there are not enough service requests to handle all the incoming requests. Therefore, autotuning will request greater bandwidth by increasing some of the operating system parameters. Keep in mind that once the parameters are increased, they are never decreased automatically. For this reason maximums are applied to all parameters, so that bandwidth allocation is very carefully controlled on the server and is not allowed to dominate all available resources. To restore these parameters to their original state, you must restart the operating system or change them manually with the SET command.

Using the SET Parameters

For most resources on the server, the SET parameters are available to adjust the values to help fine-tune a particular resource. These parameters cover a wide variety of internal systems all the way from communications to the file system. The SET parameters enable you to set minimum and maximum limits.

NetWare 5 uses SET commands to manage the minimum and maximum values and wait times for its adjustable features. The minimum values define the number of resources that the operating system will allocate immediately upon startup. The maximum values set the upper limits for resource allocations. A wait time is a specified length of time that the operating system must wait before allocating a new resource.

There are also wait times or conditions that prevent the operating system from reacting to peak loads by performing only one specific operation well. The wait time limits parameters help smooth out the peak load demands for server resources.

The SET parameters can be controlled, adjusted, or viewed using either the server console SET commands or through MONITOR.NLM, which is a server utility introduced in NetWare 5. One important note is that the SERVMAN.NLM utility is no longer available in NetWare 5. All the features and functionality that SERVMAN provided have been placed in the MONITOR utility.

The server console SET command is issued at the server prompt as follows:

```
SET
```

The SET command responds with a listing of all the server resource categories or subsystems that can be controlled or configured with the individual SET parameters. Figure 11.1 illustrates the category list that can be configured using the SET commands at the server console.

FIGURE 11.1

The server resource category list can be configured using the SET commands at the server console.

```
CAM-SRV1:set
Settable configuration parameter categories
   1. Communications
   2. Memory
   3. File caching
   4. Directory caching
   5. File system
   6. Locks
   7. Transaction tracking
   8. Disk
   9. Time
   10. NCP
   11. Miscellaneous
   12. Error Handling
   13. Directory Services
   14. Multiprocessor
   15. Service Location Protocol
   16. Licensing Services
```

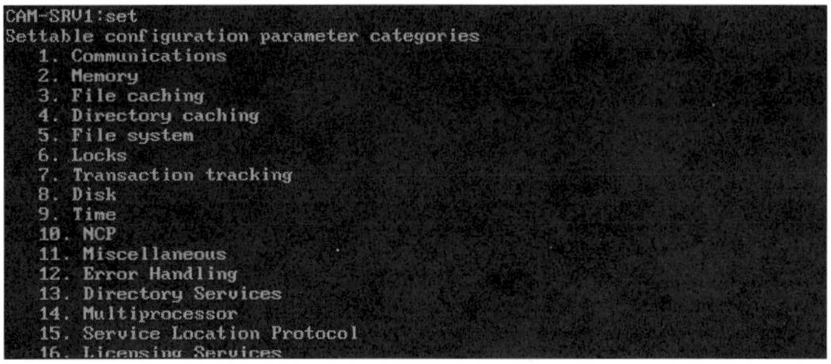

In order to view the current settings for each of the server resources categories or subsystems listed, simply select the corresponding number and scroll through the listings. Figure 11.2 shows the screen that is displayed for the Communications category or subsystem.

FIGURE 11.2

Viewing the settings for the Communications category using the SET commands at the server console

```
SPX Maximum Window Size:  0
   Limits: 0 to 16

Load Balance Local LAN:  OFF
   Description: Whether load balancing is ON or OFF.

TCP Defend Land Attacks:  ON
   Can be set in the startup ncf file.
   Description: Defend against Land Attacks. default: ON

TCP Defend SYN Attacks:  OFF
   Can be set in the startup ncf file.
   Description: Defend against SYN Attacks. default: OFF

IP Wan Client Validation:  OFF
   Can be set in the startup ncf file.
   Description: Start or Stop IP WAN Client Validation for remote client
                dialing through NetWare Connect. By default IP WAN Client
                Validation is OFF

<Press ESC to terminate or any other key to continue>
```

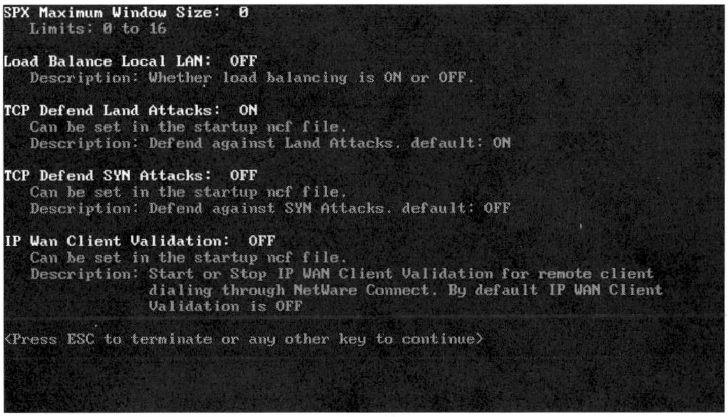

The syntax for viewing the setting for an individual SET parameter is to use this command at the server console:

```
SET parameter_description
```

The syntax for changing the individual SET parameter is to use this command at the server console:

```
SET parameter_description = new_value
```

Use the MONITOR Utility to Change Server Parameters

MONITOR.NLM is a server-based utility that helps you easily manage and configure each of the system SET parameters through a menu interface. The MONITOR utility enables you to view and set each parameter, as well as observe network performance statistics at a glance.

For example, the General Information screen, visible at the top when the utility is loaded, enables you to view processor utilization, server up time, processor speed, server processes, and connections used (which typically represents the number of users logged in). Figure 11.3 shows the main screen, which includes general information about server performance.

The main menu in MONITOR provides you with a menu-driven interface to the system SET parameters available on the server. From the main menu, select the menu item called Server Parameters. Other options from the main menu cover connection information, LAN configuration, storage information, volume information, and network information. Once you have selected the Server Parameters, a list of categories (similar to the one displayed if you type SET at the server console) is displayed. At this point you can select a specific category or area to view and edit.

Throughout the rest of this chapter, we will use both the SET command and the MONITOR utility to show how you can change the individual parameters.

FIGURE 11.3

The MONITOR main screen includes general information about server performance.

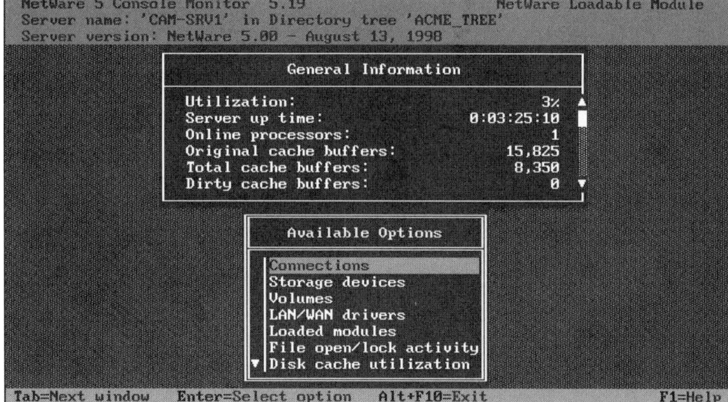

Subsystems of the Operating System

From a performance standpoint, many of the system parameters are closely related and can be separated into specific subsystems of NetWare 5. Because of the association, we have categorized many of the most important SET parameters into the subsystems categories as follows:

- LAN communications subsystem
- Disk and file system
- Server processes and CPU utilization
- Memory

The LAN Communications Subsystem

The LAN communications SET parameters control the characteristics of the memory buffers used to send and receive data packets to and from the LAN. In order to tune and optimize the server for communications, you will need to address several issues:

- Physical packet size
- Packet receive buffers
- Media statistics
- Large Internet Packets (LIP)
- Packet burst
- NCP requests
- NetWare Link State Protocol (NLSP)

Physical Packet Size

The physical size of the packet that is transmitted on the network is determined by the network topology or media access attached to the server. NetWare 5 enables you to use the SET command to set or define the maximum physical packet size that the server will support:

```
SET MAXIMUM PHYSICAL RECEIVE PACKET SIZE = n
```

The default physical packet size for Ethernet is 1,514 bytes, and the default for Token Ring is 4,202 bytes. NetWare 5 defaults the physical receive packet size to 4,224 bytes to accommodate the larger size. This is true even if the network uses only Ethernet. When a workstation makes a connection to the server, the packet size for the session is negotiated. The value set for the session with the workstation is typically established as the largest packet the workstation can support.

Figure 11.4 shows the screen used in MONITOR, called the Communications Parameters screen, that lets you set the maximum size of the buffers for incoming and outgoing packets. You should set this size to the largest packet size on your network.

You should always make sure the MAXIMUM PHYSICAL RECEIVE PACKET SIZE parameter is set large enough to support the protocols for the server. If the setting for the SET parameter MAXIMUM PHYSICAL RECEIVE PACKET SIZE is 1514 bytes, you should change it if you need to support Token Ring workstations as well.

FIGURE 11.4

The Communications Parameters screen used in MONITOR lets you set the maximum size of the buffers for incoming and outgoing packets.

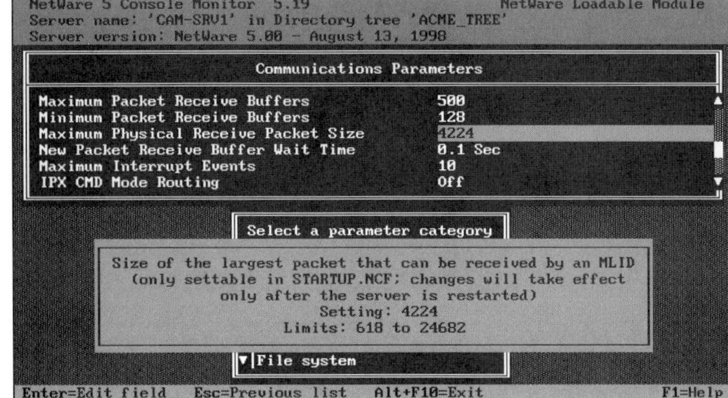

To set the value for Token Ring, you need to enter this command at the server console or in MONITOR:

```
SET MAXIMUM PHYSICAL RECEIVE PACKET SIZE = 4224
```

The parameter value ranges from 618 to 24682 (in bytes). If you want to have this value established each time the server is started, you will need to place it in STARTUP.NCF. You cannot add this parameter to AUTOEXEC.NCF. The reason is that the server needs to know how large each packet receive buffer should be as the server is booting. The packet receive buffers are taken from memory, and the size is not adjustable after the server is running.

Packet Receive Buffers

The server needs to keep a certain number of packet receive buffers free to service incoming requests from clients. Having additional packet receive buffers available will reduce the chance that the server will be overrun by incoming or outgoing requests that share these buffers. Each packet receive buffer is equal in size to the maximum physical receive packet size. In most cases, this is 1,514 bytes for Ethernet segments and 4,202 bytes for Token Ring.

A lack of packet receive buffers results in a "No ECB Available Count" error message, as shown in the Media Statistics section in this chapter. ECB stands for Event Control Block in NetWare. When a client sends a packet to a server that has no available packet receive buffers, the server is forced to discard the packet. The client waits for the specified time-out period and will receive no reply from the server. It is then the client's responsibility to retry and resend the packet. If a buffer has become available in the meantime, the incoming packet is received and the client notices no network errors — just a slightly slower response time.

Meanwhile, at the server, NetWare 5 starts a timer after the server discards the packet due to no available buffers. If no buffer is freed up after 0.1 seconds (default setting) have elapsed, the operating system will allocate a new packet receive buffer for incoming and outgoing packets. You can view the current number of packet receive buffers that the operating system has allocated by using the main screen of MONITOR.NLM. Figure 11.5 illustrates an example of current packet receive buffers.

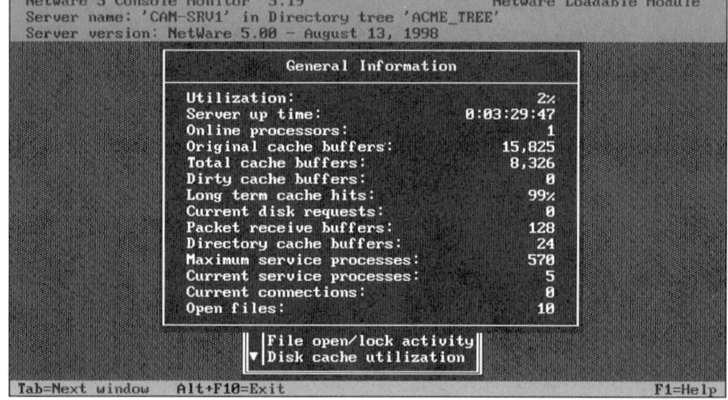

FIGURE 11.5

View the current number of packet receive buffers that the operating system has allocated using the main screen of MONITOR.NLM.

As an administrator, you will want to pay special attention to the number of current packet receive buffers on your system, especially if your users are complaining of slow response time from the server. An occasional problem is that the server receives so many packets that it runs up to the maximum packet receive buffer count. If all buffers are full, the incoming packets will be dropped. This usually means that the workstations will have to resend any packets to the server multiple times, slowing response time for each user.

Setting the Packet Receive Buffer Values: Normally, NetWare dynamically allocates the packet receive buffers based on its needs. However, the operating system allows you to set both a minimum number of buffers that can be preallocated when the server boots and a maximum number or upper limit that prevents them from allocating too many resources during very high utilization.

Consulting Experience

We recommend that you have at least one packet receive buffer for each client that will be attached to your server. For example, a server supporting 500 users needs the capability to allocate 500 packet receive buffers if necessary. In addition, you should allow 10 packet receive buffers for each LAN adapter installed in the file server.

Thus, we recommend that you use the following formula to calculate the proper value for the MAXIMUM PACKET RECEIVE BUFFERS:

Maximum = (1 × (# of connections)) + (10 × (# of LAN cards))

The proper setting for the MINIMUM PACKET RECEIVE BUFFERS parameter is the value currently in use at the file server. Using the MONITOR utility, you can compare the number configured versus the number currently in use. For example, the total number of packet receive buffers may peak at 350 after several days or weeks of continuous server operation. You can take advantage of the SET MINIMUM PACKET RECEIVE BUFFERS parameter to preallocate more than the default of 50 buffers the next time the server is rebooted. This will help overcome any sluggishness of the server after it is rebooted. Thus, we recommend that you use the following formula to calculate the proper value for the MINIMUM PACKET RECEIVE BUFFERS:

Minimum = Number of packet receive buffers in use currently

You can adjust the settings for packet receive buffers by using the communications parameters SET commands described here:

```
SET MINIMUM PACKET RECEIVE BUFFERS = n
```

In this parameter *n* can be 10 to 4294967295, with the default being 128. This setting specifies the minimum number of buffers that will be immediately allocated by the operating system when it is booted. This parameter can only be permanently set in the STARTUP.NCF file:

```
SET MAXIMUM PACKET RECEIVE BUFFERS = n
```

In this parameter *n* can be 50 to 294967295, with the default being 500. This parameter specifies the maximum number of packet receive buffers to be used by the NetWare 5 operating system. Once the maximum is reached, no more packet receive buffers will be allocated even if more are needed. If all the allocated buffers are in use, the operating system will have no choice but to discard incoming packets. This parameter should be changed to meet the needs of your network environment. The parameter is set in the AUTOEXEC.NCF file.

It is extremely important to monitor the value of the current packet receive buffers to see if the value is close to the maximum value. If this is the case, you should increase the maximum to account for the increased workload performed by the server.

One of the most common errors people encounter when using these parameters is that the current packet receive buffers become equal to the maximum and the system can no longer dynamically tune itself.

```
SET NEW PACKET RECEIVE BUFFER WAIT TIME = n
```

In this parameter *n* can be 0.1 to 20, with the default being 0.1 seconds. This setting specifies the wait time necessary before allocating any new packet receive buffers. It is recommended that you not change this setting.

Media Statistics

The communications media statistics are reported by each LAN adapter installed in the server through the LAN driver. The statistics can be viewed using the MONITOR.NLM program at the server. These statistics can help you diagnose specific problems with the physical network media and supporting software.

For example, a lack of packet receive buffers results in a "No ECB Available Count" error message, which is reported and viewed on the media statistics screen in MONITOR. An example of the statistics screen for a LAN driver is seen in Figure 11.6.

As mentioned in the previous section, when a client sends a packet to a server that has no available packet receive buffers, the server is forced to discard the packet. Each time the server or LAN driver discards a packet, the "No ECB Available Count" is incremented.

FIGURE 11.6

These statistics are reported by the individual LAN driver in the server, using the MONITOR.NLM program.

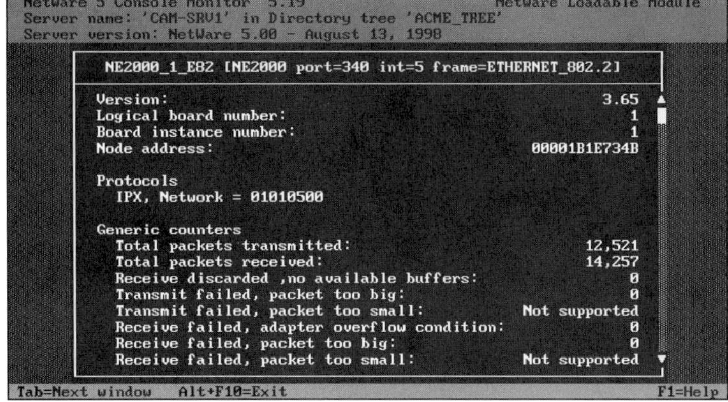

Large Internet Packets (LIP)

One feature in NetWare 5 that has greatly improved the performance of the communications between workstations and servers is the support for Large Internet Packets (LIP). The capability of the server to inherently support LIP solves a problem in previous versions that the maximum physical packet size was not always used during the negotiation from a server to a workstation.

During the process that connects the workstation to the server, a physical packet size is negotiated that is used for the duration of the session. The packet size selected is the largest physical packet size that both the workstation and the server can support. For this reason, it is a good idea to set the MAXIMUM PHYSICAL PACKET SIZE parameter on the server according to the protocols of the workstations.

Prior to NetWare 4, when the workstation and server negotiated the physical packet size and the packet passed through a router device (such as a file server or hardware router), the packet size was always set to 512 bytes. At the time of the client login, the server looked at the transport control field in the IPX header of the packet. If it was incremented (meaning the packet had crossed at least one router), the server responded with a 512-byte packet size.

The reason for the reduced packet size is that a server cannot anticipate what packet size might be supported on the other side of a router. NetWare supports a mixture of Ethernet, Token Ring, and seldom used Arcnet, with their respective packet sizes. To accommodate the different topologies, the NetWare router decides to use the least common denominator, which—at the time the NetWare router software was developed—happened to be Arcnet at 512 bytes.

The Large Internet Packet support gives you a way to get around this 512-byte router packet size limitation. The LIP software allows the largest common physical packet size to be used when a workstation and server communicate through an intermediate router. With LIP, the packet size proposed by the client is accepted regardless of the information in the IPX header.

In order to enable Large Internet Packets type:

```
SET ALLOW LIP = ON
```

The default for this SET parameter in NetWare 5 is already set to ON.

In order to enable the LIP features for the workstation or client, the user must have the VLMs (Virtual Loadable Modules) or NetWare 32-bit client. The older NETX code does not inherently support LIP without the addition of special client software called *packet burst.*

Packet Burst

NetWare 5 automatically supports packet burst, which improves data delivery over latent links. Packet burst technology eliminates the ping-pong effect of sent/returned packets during communication. For example, using packet burst, the client sends a request to the server. The server responds to the client with multiple packets without requiring a "return receipt" for every packet. The server is content to have just one return receipt for the whole transmission. This means that the total transmission time is reduced and the "chattiness" of the NCP protocol is eliminated. This is particularly beneficial for communication across WANs where line speeds are often a bottleneck.

A SET command is available that enables a separate packet burst statistics screen to be used to see if specific workstations or clients are connected using packet burst. In order to start the packet burst statistics screen, enter this command at the server console:

```
SET ENABLE PACKET BURST STATISTICS SCREEN = ON
```

NCP Requests

This section discusses the adjustments you can make to the NetWare Core Protocol (NCP) requests.

```
Set NCP packet signature option = n
```

where *n* is 0, 1, 2, or 3. The default setting is 1. The purpose of this setting is to enable Novell's packet signature security. Packet signature attaches a unique signature to each NCP packet that is transmitted between a NetWare client and a NetWare server. You use these parameters to enable or disable packet signature and to designate varying levels of security. This feature is only used where extremely high levels of security are required. Packet signature does impact performance because of the translation that must take place between receiving and sending entities on your network. What follows are the settings for packet signature at the server. The packet signature for the client is set in the user's NET.CFG file.

Server settings:

- 0—Do not do packet signature.
- 1—Do packet signatures only if the client requires them.
- 2—Do packet signatures if the client can, but don't require them if the client doesn't support them.
- 3—Require packet signatures.

For most companies packet signature is not used. If you do have a client using packet signature, the default setting of 1 is sufficient to have that client use this feature.

```
SET ENABLE IPX CHECKSUMS = n
```

where *n* is 0, 1, or 2. The default setting is 1. The purpose of this setting is to require a checksum calculation on packets. A checksum is calculated and placed in the packet being sent across the network. Once received, the checksum can be recalculated to ensure that the same number of bits are received as were sent. This parameter allows you to enable or disable IPX checksums. The values for the checksum have the following meanings:

- 0—No checksums
- 1—Checksums if enabled at the client
- 2—Require checksumming

Most sites will not need to enable checksumming because this type of checking is done at the data link level of your network. However, some older bridges have been known to cause IPX packet corruption. So in some unique circumstances you may want to enable this parameter. Keep in mind that you will experience performance degradation with this feature enabled. Additionally, this feature is only supported by Ethernet 802.2 frame type, not 802.3.

The NetWare Link Services Protocol (NLSP)

Novell's NetWare Link Services Protocol (NLSP) provides a solution for routing RIP and SAP protocols across a wide area network. For network administrators who have a concern about routing such protocols in a WAN environment, NLSP offers a more efficient approach to routing these protocols across your WAN.

The basic concern with SAP and RIP is that it will broadcast its information every 60 seconds using a distance vector routing protocol. A distance vector protocol will try to rebuild all the information in the routing tables every time the servers communicate routing information. NLSP is architected using a link-state routing protocol to eliminate all the RIP and SAP broadcasts. NLSP, for instance, only sends out changes to the routing information when a change occurs. Thus, link-state routing protocols are smarter, cause less network chatter, and are more efficient than distance vector protocols.

Network users find network resources such as file and print services using both RIP and SAP. The servers on the network automatically discover all the services and route those services through SAP and RIP. This feature makes the network dynamic, flexible, and easy to access. The other network protocols such as IP, XNS, and AppleTalk also use SAP and RIP to propagate information. Therefore, it is difficult to entirely eliminate SAP and RIP because other protocols use it as well.

NLSP does not replace the SAP information and RIP information but only handles its propagation in a manner that is complete and efficient. With NLSP, the SAP and RIP information will no longer be broadcast every minute. Once the NLSP routers and servers have learned about all the routes and services available on the network, they will communicate with each other only when changes occur. When a server or link is added to a network, NLSP servers and routers communicate that change throughout the network. When a server or link disappears, that change is also communicated.

For backward compatibility, NLSP automatically detects the presence of routers and servers that require SAP and RIP broadcasts and will generate these periodic advertisements.

Pure IP

New in NetWare 5 is the pure IP product, which enables NetWare to support TCP/IP in a pure sense. It does not encapsulate or tunnel IPX/SPX communications. Pure IP enables the servers and clients to make NetWare Core Protocol (NCP) calls directly over the TCP/IP stack so that they can be routed by any IP router on the network. Novell has severed the operating system's dependence on IPX/SPX and has rewritten the IPX-only applications and utilities to support TCP/IP. As a result, the NetWare 5 servers and workstations can use TCP/IP, IPX/SPX, or both. The major advantages of supporting pure IP in NetWare are:

- Consolidation to one protocol in your network
- More efficient use of your LAN and WAN bandwidth
- A wider range of opportunities for remote user connectivity

Although there are major advantages to pure IP, Novell is committed to remain backward compatible to IPX/SPX. NetWare 5 will ship with features that provide a seamless compatibility between IPX and IP-based technologies. NetWare 5's Compatibility Mode enables customers to move to an IP-only environment without having to replace valuable IPX-based applications and without having to introduce disruptions to their network operations. In addition, NetWare 5 ships an IP Compatibility Mode Migration Gateway that allows you to move to an IP-only network incrementally, and if desired.

In essence, it is your choice whether to use IPX/SPX or TCP/IP as your network protocols. In order to install pure IP, you use the standard NetWare 5 installation program. During the installation process, you select the protocols that you want your server to support. If you enable IPX/SPX, you must select an internal IPX address for the server, as you normally would. If you enable TCP/IP, you must select an IP address for the server.

NCP takes advantage of both TCP and UDP as transport protocols. Like IPX, UDP provides connectionless datagram services, which do not require a "handshake" to set up communications. TCP, on the other hand, is similar to SPX, which provides connection-oriented services. Connection-oriented services require communication partners to perform a "handshake" before exchanging data and enable these partners to acknowledge the receipt of transmitted data. Although both SPX and TCP provide connection-oriented services, TCP's windowing and streaming capabilities provide greater throughput than SPX.

Some NCP calls use UDP for its communication, whereas others use strictly TCP. For example, the "control" NCP call (which requests information for a server) uses UDP communication. TCP is used typically for large transactions, such as NCP file reads, writes, and NDS synchronization. Large transactions use TCP because TCP's streaming capability is similar to IPX's burst-mode technology. This capability provides quicker and more efficient file transfers. With IPX/SPX the developers use sockets to define the sending or receiving process during communications. In the TCP/IP world the Internet Registration Group assigns port numbers to vendors, thereby differentiating between the various processes on the network. For example, NetWare 5's port number is 524.

To ensure that NCP UDP packets do not become corrupted, you can control the checksumming required during the client-to-server communication. Use the following SET parameter:

```
SET ENABLE UDP CHECKSUMS ON NCP PACKETS = n
```

where *n* is 0, 1, or 2. The default setting is 1. The purpose of this setting is to enable the use of checksumming of NCP UDP packets. A checksum is calculated and placed in the packet being sent across the network. Once the packet is received, the checksum can be recalculated to ensure that the same number of bits are received as were sent. This parameter allows you to enable or disable UDP checksums. The values for the checksum have the following meanings:

- 0 — No checksums
- 1 — Checksums if enabled at the client
- 2 — Require checksumming

Most sites will not need to enable checksumming, because this type of checking is done at the data link level of your network. However, some older bridges have been known to cause packet corruption.

A workstation on an IPX/SPX network sends a SAP Get Nearest Server request to locate a NetWare server. A workstation on a TCP/IP network, on the other hand, uses the Dynamic Host Configuration Protocol (DHCP) to locate a NetWare server. After the workstation locates a server using DHCP, this workstation transmits an Address Resolution Protocol (ARP) request to find the server's hardware address. After the server's address is obtained, the workstation uses NCP calls to retrieve the server information, authenticate to NDS, and log into the server.

As mentioned, you can configure a workstation to automatically obtain an IP address from a DHCP host. Using a DHCP host can dramatically reduce the amount of time required to configure and maintain IP addressing on your network. NetWare 5 offers DHCP support through a DHCP configuration NLM (DHCPCFG.NLM). You use this NLM to configure DHCP addressing, and it performs the DHCP functions for your NetWare 5 network.

On the other hand, you can manually assign an IP address to your workstation. For example, if you wanted to manually assign an IP address to a Windows 95 workstation, you would define the IP address and subnetwork mask in the TCP/IP Properties window. To access the IP Address Configuration window, select Run, and then select Settings. Next, select Control Panel, select Network, and finally, select the TCP/IP entry listed. (For DOS and Windows 3.1 workstations, you can define individual IP addresses in the NET.CFG file.)

The Disk and File System

NetWare 5 optimizes the use of the server file system with several new improvements over previous versions of NetWare. These improvements enable NetWare 5 to take full advantage of the available disk space and offer speed improvements as well as savings in server memory. The specific improvements that are addressed in this chapter are:

- Novell Storage Services (NSS)
- Volume block size
- Suballocation

- File compression
- Read ahead
- Prioritization of disk requests

Novell Storage Services

Novell Storage Services (NSS) eliminates several limitations that currently exist in the NetWare file system. NSS provides object-oriented storage with 64-bit internal and external interfaces. Without NSS, the NetWare file system only supports a 32-bit interface that allows files of up to 2GB, up to 16 million directory entries per volume, and up to 64 volumes per server. With NSS, the NetWare file system can host a single 8 TB (terabyte) file. This would be extremely useful for database applications. In addition, the NSS file system can support virtually unlimited directory entries (or number of files) per volume. During testing, a volume with a billion files was successfully created with three name spaces loaded. This demonstrates that the file system can support three billion directory entries on a single NetWare volume. Thousands of volumes can be created per server; however, the current NCP interface only supports 127 volumes per server.

In addition to larger volumes and more files, NSS supports very much faster volume mount times. A normal NSS volume will mount in less than one second regardless of size or number of files stored. If the NetWare 5 server crashes and the volume is not dismounted cleanly, then when the server is brought back up the volume is restored and mounted in 15 seconds to one minute. This is the case for all NSS volumes on the server. The older FAT-based file system is organized so that volume mount time increases with the number of files and their size.

The amount of server memory required to support NSS is 8MB, as a minimum. Although this is the minimum memory requirement, NSS is capable of mounting any size volume or any number of volumes in this amount of memory. This fact basically eliminates the need for any complicated server memory calculations.

Even though NSS has many new features, it is also completely compatible with the standard FAT-based file system. The server volumes running NSS will look the same as the standard FAT-based volumes to the workstations and users. In addition, NSS is architected to support both NetWare 4.11 and NetWare 5. NSS automatically detects which of these two operating systems it is running on and loads the appropriate NLMs for that server.

In order to fine-tune NSS on each of your servers, you can adjust many parameters. To view the current parameters settings and other NSS commands, enter this command at the server console:

```
NSS HELP
```

or just

```
NSS /?
```

Figure 11.7 shows an example of the NSS help screen. Before you attempt to use the NSS commands available from the help screen, you must first load NSS.NLM.

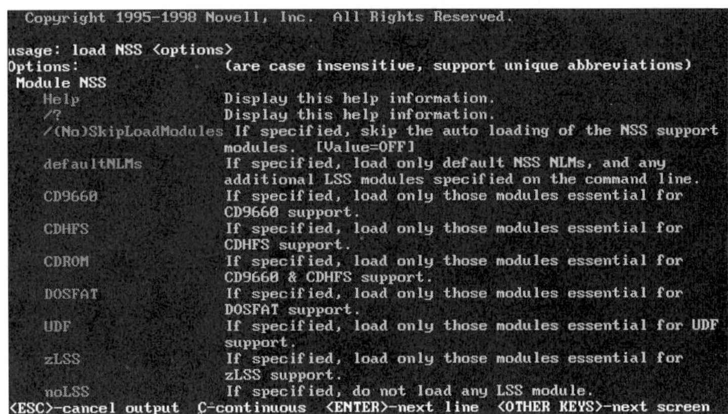

FIGURE 11.7

The NSS help screen is available on the server.

You can view the current settings for each of the NSS parameters by simply entering the command: NSS STATUS. Figure 11.8 illustrates the screen on the server that enables you to see the current settings for the NSS parameters.

In addition to the NSS commands available at the server console, you can use the NSS Configuration Menu or utility. This utility enables you to manage and configure the NSS volumes. You can rebuild or verify specific NSS volumes or simply view the volume's information. You can load the NSS Configuration Menu by entering the following command at the server console:

```
NSS MENU
```

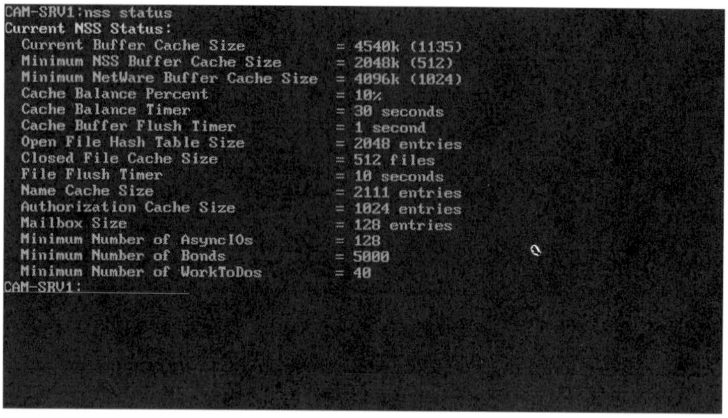

FIGURE 11.8

The current NSS parameters can be viewed using the NSS status command at the server console.

```
CAM-SRV1:nss status
Current NSS Status:
  Current Buffer Cache Size             = 4540k (1135)
  Minimum NSS Buffer Cache Size         = 2048k (512)
  Minimum NetWare Buffer Cache Size     = 4096k (1024)
  Cache Balance Percent                 = 10%
  Cache Balance Timer                   = 30 seconds
  Cache Buffer Flush Timer              = 1 second
  Open File Hash Table Size             = 2048 entries
  Closed File Cache Size                = 512 files
  File Flush Timer                      = 10 seconds
  Name Cache Size                       = 2111 entries
  Authorization Cache Size              = 1024 entries
  Mailbox Size                          = 128 entries
  Minimum Number of AsyncIOs            = 128
  Minimum Number of Bonds               = 5000
  Minimum Number of WorkToDos           = 40
CAM-SRV1:
```

One of the major drawbacks to NSS is that it does not currently support the transaction tracking system (TTS). This means that the SYS volume of the server cannot be an NSS volume because NDS requires TTS for its operation and NDS is physically stored on SYS. This drawback is only temporary and will be fixed in later releases of NSS.

Volume Block Size

One of the features in the NetWare 5 operating system is the capability to support large volume block sizes. The large volume block size increases the performance of almost every associated subsystem, such as disk channel, file cache, directory cache, directory entry table, and file allocation table (FAT). This large volume block size does not waste disk capacity when storing lots of small files because of how the files are suballocated.

In the previous versions of NetWare (including the initial releases of NetWare 3), the volume block size or allocation unit was typically set at 4K. In NetWare 3 larger volume block sizes were possible, but they resulted in a lot of unused disk space at the end of files. For example, if the last part of a file took up 1K of a 16K block, the remaining 15K was wasted.

With the release of NetWare 5, the default volume block size is no longer 4K. The default volume block sizes calculated during volume creation are not based on performance criteria but on volume size to conserve server cache memory. The new defaults are listed in Table 11.1.

TABLE 11.1

Default Volume Block Sizes Are Based on Volume Size

VOLUME SIZE	DEFAULT BLOCK SIZE
Less than 32MB	4K
32 to 150MB	8K
150 to 500MB	16K
500 to 2,000MB	32K
2,000MB and up	64K

Consulting Experience

We recommend a 64K volume block size for all volumes regardless of size. The larger 64K volume block size allows NetWare 5 to use the disk channel more efficiently by reading and writing more data at once. This results in faster access to mass storage devices and improved response times for network users.

Suballocation

One of the greatest cost benefits to upgrading to NetWare 5 is the use of volume block suballocation. Suballocation in NetWare 5 subdivides the volume blocks, regardless of size, into smaller suballocation units of 512 bytes. This process ensures that you will never waste more than 511 bytes when saving any file. You now have the flexibility to set your NetWare 5 volume block size to the recommended maximum of 64K without sacrificing valuable hard disk space. This ensures the disk space is more efficiently used.

As mentioned previously, earlier versions of NetWare worked with a 4K volume block size determined at the time of installation. The block size became the smallest unit of storage on the NetWare volume and server's hard drive. Generally, the larger the block size, the better the throughput between file server hard drive and file server's RAM or cache. But the large block sizes also had the most potential of wasting disk space or creating disk slack.

For example, if your volume block size is 16K (without suballocation) and you save a small file of 1K, the remaining 15K in the disk block is not used. The used space is referred to as "slack." Figure 11.9 shows that there is a problem with large block sizes without suballocation because it creates slack.

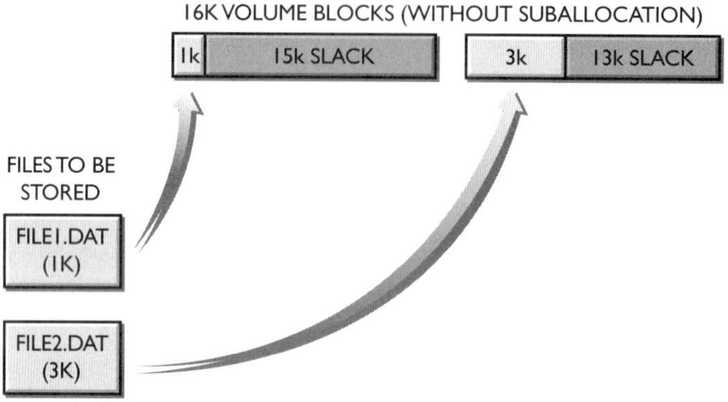

FIGURE 11.9

The problem with large block sizes without suballocation is that it creates slack.

Figure 11.10 shows the same example as the preceding one but with suballocation of the volume block to reduce the slack. You will notice that the volume block size is still 16K, but the volume block has been suballocated by the NetWare 5 operating system into 512 byte blocks. FILE1.DAT (a 1K file) would ordinarily be allocated a full 16K but only takes the required 1K using two suballocated blocks. The other 15K is not wasted but can be used by other files. Another file, FILE2.DAT (3K file), is written to disk and starts in the middle of the volume block using six more suballocated blocks. There is no slack in this example.

Notice that new files can start in the middle of a volume block that has been suballocated. They do not have to start on the volume block boundary. This means that if you select the recommended 64K volume block size, then several files can be started and stored in the middle of the 64K block.

From a performance standpoint, suballocation enhances the performance of write operations within NetWare 5 by allowing the ends of multiple files to be consolidated within a single write operation. Of course, this minor improvement will often be counterbalanced by the increased overhead of managing the suballocation process. The major advantage is the optimization of the disk channel and cache around the 64K disk allocation unit.

FIGURE 11.10

Large block size with suballocation of the volume block reduces the slack.

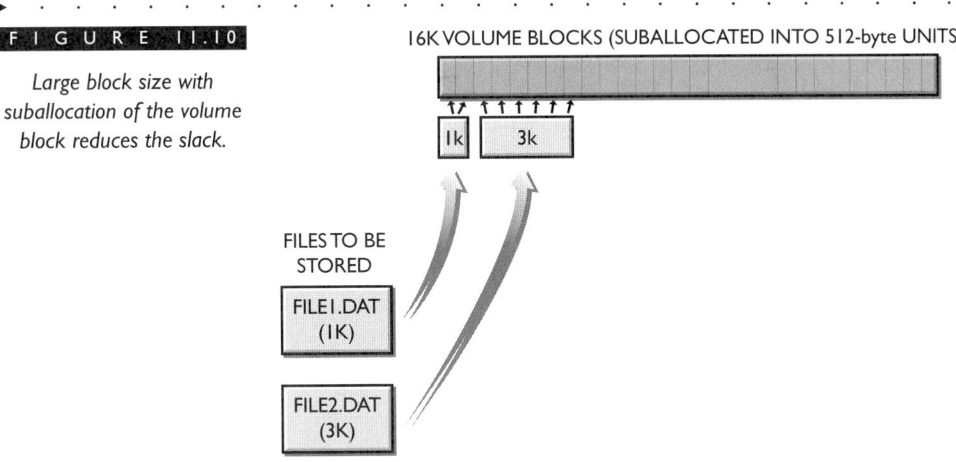

As imaging, multimedia, and other workloads involving streaming data become more prevalent, the 64K block size will become invaluable. We recommend that everyone use the 64K disk block size to realize greater efficiency, eliminate wasted space, and take advantage of read-ahead.

File Compression

NetWare 5 provides the capability to automatically compress any files on the server that have not been used for a period of time. This compression can result in space savings of up to 50 to 60 percent in some cases for a particular file. The file listing in the directory structure (FAT table) shows the file as if no change has occurred. When the user wants to retrieve the file, the operating system automatically decompresses the file. This file compression and decompression process is completely transparent to the user.

The file compression feature in NetWare 5 is completely optional, and you can determine which servers can benefit from its use. You can choose which files, directories, or volumes to compress. The compression process runs as a background task, which means that it will usually not affect the performance of the file server. In order to enable file compression, use the following SET parameter at the server console:

```
SET ENABLE FILE COMPRESSION = ON
```

Consulting Experience

The NetWare 3 customers that we have visited have experienced significant benefits from upgrading to NetWare 5 and suballocation. A typical customer has seen a return of about 25 to 30 percent of hard disk space after upgrading to NetWare 5. The savings do not include file compression.

This implies that their NetWare 3 servers had more than 25 to 30 percent slack, and that this slack was reduced by moving to NetWare 5. It is obvious that the suballocation feature alone is reason to upgrade.

The slack can be estimated to equal the total number of files ×_(volume block size / 2). The total savings in disk space from upgrading from NetWare 3 to NetWare 5 can be estimated using the following formula:

Savings = total number of files × ((old block size / 2) – (new block size / 2))

Some example numbers follow:

1. Slack in NetWare 3: 50,000 files (4096 bytes / 2) = 102.4MB
2. Slack in NetWare 5: 50,000 files (512 bytes / 2) = 12.8MB
3. Savings for upgrading to NetWare 5 from NetWare 3 is:

   50,000 ((4096 / 2) – (512 / 2)) = 89.6MB

You can decide the hours during the day when you want the file compression process to start and stop scanning for files that meet the compression criteria. The default start time is 0, which represents 12:00 P.M. The possible range is 0 through 23, which represents each hour of the day. To set the hour in the day to start scanning type:

```
SET COMPRESSION DAILY CHECK STARTING HOUR = 0
```

To stop scanning, type (default is 6, or 6:00 A.M.):

```
SET COMPRESSION DAILY CHECK STOP HOUR = 6
```

If the COMPRESSION DAILY CHECK STARTING HOUR parameter is the same as the COMPRESSION DAILY CHECK STOP HOUR, then it starts each day at that time and runs as long as necessary to finish all files that meet the criteria.

You can also set a parameter at the server that specifies the period of time the file has not been accessed before the system compresses it. The default setting is 14 days. The parameter to specify the period of time can be set at the server console by entering:

```
SET DAYS UNTOUCHED BEFORE COMPRESSION = 14
```

You can control the minimum space savings that must be accomplished before the compressed file is saved. If the operating system cannot gain a given amount of space from compressing a file, it does not compress the file. The default for this parameter is 20, or 2 percent. The parameter to set the minimum space saving is entered at the server console as follows:

```
SET MINIMUM COMPRESSION PERCENTAGE GAIN = 20
```

Decompression is automatic when the user requests a compressed file. The algorithms provided are extremely fast and do not affect either the client's or the server's performance. You can also control the decompression options when the compressed file is accessed by users. The default setting is 1, but the range is 0 to 2. Enter the compression/decompression options as follows:

```
SET CONVERT COMPRESSION TO UNCOMPRESSED OPTION = 0
```

(0 — means that the operating system will always leave compressed)

```
SET CONVERT COMPRESSION TO UNCOMPRESSED OPTION = 1
```

(1 — means leave compressed if it has only been read once in the last seven days or DAYS UNTOUCHED parameter; see the previous discussion)

```
SET CONVERT COMPRESSION TO UNCOMPRESSED OPTION = 2
```

(2 — means always decompress)

NetWare 5 also enables you to control the percentage of disk space that must be present before the system attempts to decompress a file. The default is 10 percent. The parameter is entered at the server console as follows:

```
SET DECOMPRESS PERCENT DISK SPACE FREE TO ALLOW COMMIT = 10
```

Read Ahead

The read ahead feature in NetWare 5 provides the requesting workstation faster response when reading files from the server. The operating system anticipates the read requests from the workstation and caches the next volume or disk block of a file.

For example, when the workstation makes a request for a file open, the operating system opens the file and assumes that the next request from the workstation is going be a read request. In anticipation of the read request, the read ahead feature caches (places into file cache) the first block of the file.

The result is that when the request from the workstation comes in for the first block, the server already has the block available in cache. The workstation request is serviced immediately instead of waiting for a hard disk access. As the workstation reads the information out of the block in cache, the operating system will fetch the next block of the file and place it in cache anticipating more read requests. When the workstation has read one-half of the current block in memory (or cache), the operating system determines that the next block is needed. Using this algorithm, the operating system can calculate when the next blocks are needed and reads them from disk before the request is made.

This read ahead feature is a low-priority task that will not be executed when the server is busy handling other processes. The greatest impact of read ahead is when accessing optical media. A CD-ROM drive, for example, is not as fast as a hard drive. Read ahead pulls the next block into cache so that it is ready when the workstation needs it.

Prioritization of Disk Requests

In previous versions of NetWare, there were situations when a server would start servicing heavy write requests and would seem to ignore other transactions involving read requests. For example, if a user would perform a large COPY to the file server, the other users would see poor performance for the duration of the COPY.

This condition resulted when a large number of cached writes (dirty cache buffers) hit a threshold where the server needed to switch writes from background to foreground in order to service all the requests. However, when the server switched priorities, it switched completely to foreground writes, leaving less consideration for the higher-priority read requests.

NetWare 5 includes a tiered prioritization of the disk elevator that reduces the possibility of ignored reads. It also supports lower priorities for read ahead requests. There are four bins, prioritized as follows:

- Critical events (such as file commits and TTS log file writes)
- Read requests
- Write requests
- Read ahead requests

Critical events are typically guaranteed events and are always processed with greater priority. Reads are almost always generated by client foreground tasks and make up the majority of work processed by any server. Most writes can occur in the background as a write-behind process. Read ahead requests are prioritized so as not to preclude the processing of any higher priority events.

Instead of using the normal first-in, first-out (FIFO) build sequence for the disk elevators, NetWare 5 takes a percentage of requests from each priority bin. The higher the priority, the more requests are placed on the current elevator. In this way, none of the levels gets locked out due to an overabundance of requests in one of the levels.

New Client 32 NetWare Core Protocols (NCPs)

New NetWare Core Protocols (NCPs) have been added to the NetWare 5 server to enable the new Client 32 software to operate more efficiently and deliver a higher level of performance. The result is that the file system responds more efficiently to the new 32-bit NetWare client architecture by delivering a higher level of performance to the workstations.

Support for Long Filenames

LONG.NAM provides the extended name spaces available with the Windows 95/98, Windows NT, and OS/2 workstation platforms on a NetWare volume. LONG.NAM is a special type of NLM that enables non-DOS filenames on a NetWare volume. Because extended name spaces are used more often now,

LONG.NAM is loaded as part of the default server configuration. In previous versions of NetWare 3 and NetWare 4, the OS/2 name space was provided by OS2.NAM. LONG.NAM replaces OS2.NAM.

The Kernel, Server Processes, and CPU Utilization

The core of the NetWare 5 operating system is a new kernel that supports multiple processors out of the box. In fact, it supports single and multiple processors from the same kernel. This means that you can utilize existing processors in your servers better, or add processors as needed to help speed up specific services. In addition, the new kernel offers memory protection, virtual memory, and application prioritization.

NetWare 5 supports up to 32 processors with the new kernel, which is called the multiprocessor kernel (MPK). During installation, NetWare 5 automatically detects the number of multiple processors by reading the multiple processor table in the machine's BIOS. It then determines which of the NetWare 5 Platform Support Modules (PSM) matches the hardware platform. The PSM is a hardware abstraction layer or interface that NetWare 5 uses to support different hardware dependencies.

Symmetric Multiprocessing

As mentioned, the core of NetWare 5 is the kernel. The kernel executes individual threads that have been placed in a queue waiting to be serviced. A *thread* is a stream of control or a unit of execution. In NetWare 5, the new kernel maintains the structure called a *run queue,* which contains all the threads that are ready to be processed. Since NetWare 5 supports multiprocessor machines, it can execute individual threads on different processors. In comparison, a uniprocessor machine or system can only execute the threads one at a time. NetWare 5 creates only one run queue for a uniprocessor machine. A machine with multiple processors creates a run queue for each processor and distributes the threads appropriately.

Threads are scheduled on the processor's run queue that they arrive on. However, an internal algorithm determines how many threads are on the queue and how long the time is from the time that the thread has been scheduled to run until it has run. If the number of threads exceed a set threshold called the *load balance threshold,* then it is determined that it will be more advantageous to move the thread to another processor. Using this method, NetWare 5 can balance between processors.

NetWare 5 periodically monitors each of the processors' run queues to make sure that none of the processors become overloaded. The load balance threshold that is set in the system parameters is used to determine how much the run queues can handle before becoming overloaded. The scheduler in the kernel calculates the system-wide load and the mean load or average length of each processor's run queue against the predetermined threshold. If one processor's run queue is determined to be overloaded, any new threads targeted for that processor are moved to another processor for execution.

Figure 11.11 illustrates how you can configure the system threshold by using the MONITOR utility. In MONITOR, select the Server Parameters, and then Multiprocessor. Next, see the setting for System Threshold. The System Threshold parameter is used in calculating load balances between server threads. Although this threshold is configurable, we strongly recommend that you keep the value at the preset or factory setting. The factory setting is optimal for every machine. If after careful consideration you decide to modify the threshold, experiment with a new value only in a lab environment.

FIGURE 11.11

The processors in a multiprocessor machine can be automatically load-balanced using the SET parameter shown in MONITOR. The SET parameter is the System Threshold. We strongly recommend that you leave the value at the factory setting.

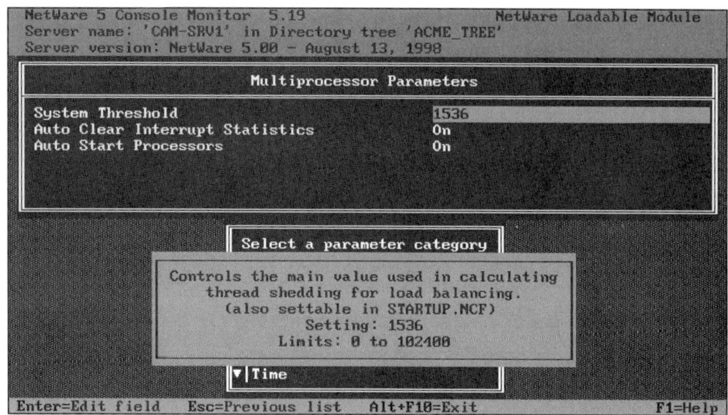

To take advantage of multiple processors in a server, the server application code must be written to be multithreaded. For example, the NetWare 5 core components or processes that are enabled for multiple processors are NWPA, Media Manager, LSL, memory, Open Data-link Interface (ODI), C-library (CLIB), RSA encryption, routing functions, and the direct file system.

Application Priorities

The new NetWare 5 kernel enables you to prioritize the applications running on your servers. You can specify the processor use that you want to dedicate to each application. More specifically, the NetWare 5 kernel applies the processor use to a collection of threads called a *share group*. Each collection of threads, or share group, tracks its use of the processor resources. The amount of processor time reserved for each share group is only used when multiple applications want the processing power simultaneously. If only one application is using the CPU at any one time, then naturally it will get 100 percent of the processing power regardless of its priority. Therefore, a NetWare 5 server must have at least two share groups to benefit from the prioritization of the applications.

By adjusting the share value for each application, you can tune the quality of service provided. In addition, both single-processor and multiprocessor machines can benefit from the flexibility of the application prioritization. Thus, if a single processor machine has multiple applications or share groups, then you can allow one application to have more CPU cycles than the others.

In order to set or establish the share value for each application, you use the MONITOR utility at the server console. At the main menu select the Kernel option and then Applications. Next, select one of the specific applications running on that NetWare 5 server. Figure 11.12 illustrates how you use the MONITOR utility to set the share value for an application. In this example, the application is the default NetWare application. This share group represents all the NLMs loaded by the basic NetWare 5 server, which include the storage drivers, communication drivers, NDS, and others.

The default share value in NetWare 5 is 100, but share values can range from 1 to 10,000. The most important thing to remember is not the actual value of the share, but the ratio between multiple share groups. For example, for two share groups, an assignment of 200 and 100 respectively entitles the first share group to twice the amount of processing resources. The same is true if the two share groups are assigned 400 and 200, or 100 and 50. The ratio between the share groups is the key.

FIGURE 11.12

Using the MONITOR utility, you can set the percentage of CPU time that the operating system will guarantee to one application if multiple applications request the CPU simultaneously.

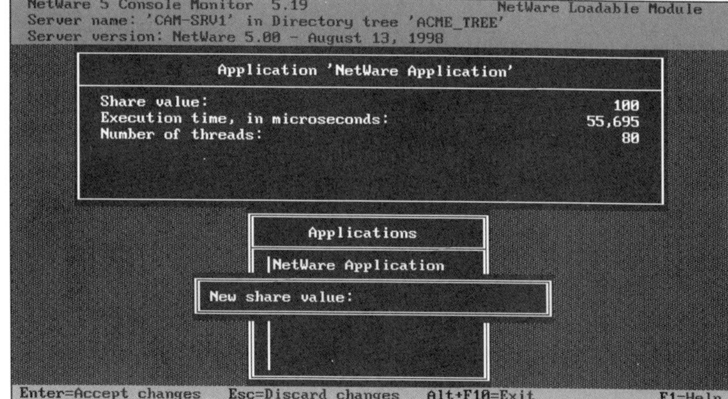

Share groups with equal values assigned to each will be given the same amount of processor resources regardless of how many threads each share group has. This feature prevents applications with large numbers of threads from swamping applications with fewer threads. The share value, not the number of threads, determines the amount of processing power for each application.

When using NetWare 5 as an application server, you will find that this feature gives you more detailed control over each individual service or application. For example, if you run a Web site using the FastTrack Web Server and Oracle8 database on the same server, you can specifically establish parameters for each in sharing the CPU. You will want to give the application that is more critical a higher share value percentage.

Preemption

The NetWare 5 kernel has also been developed to support preemption. *Preemption* eliminates the problems associated with poorly written applications running on the server as NLM and monopolizing the processor. In order to take advantage of preemption in NetWare 5, the application must be explicitly written or enabled by the developers to support the kernel's preemption.

Service Processes

A service process is an execution thread that handles incoming service requests to the server. NetWare 5 has the capability to allocate up to 100 service processes. Typically, your NetWare 5 server will not use more than 40 service processes. In fact, most installations may never see this number rise above 10 because of how well NetWare handles multiple user connections. However, you can use the server set parameters to manage this function by typing:

```
Set maximum service processes = n
```

where *n* can be a value from 5 to 100. The default is 40. This setting controls the maximum number of service processes available for the server.

To control the wait time for new service processes, type:

```
Set new service process wait time = n
```

where *n* can be 0.3 to 20 seconds. The default is 2.2 seconds. This setting specifies the wait time before the operating system can allocate any new service processes.

You can view the number of service processes in use by using the MONITOR.NLM utility and viewing the first screen as shown in Figure 11.13.

FIGURE 11.13

Using MONITOR.NLM to view the number of service processes in use on an NetWare 5 server

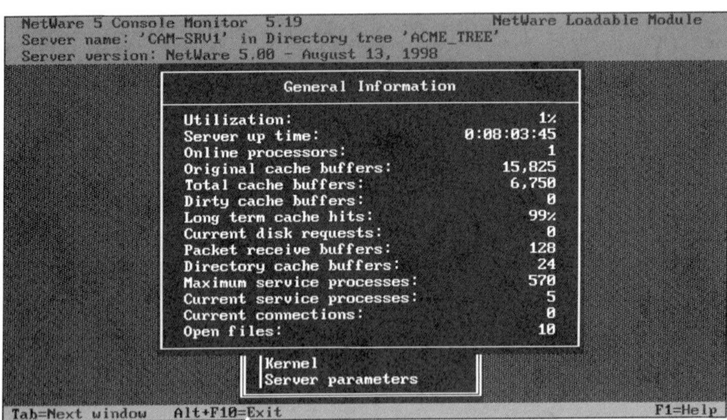

Changing these parameters is only necessary in a few circumstances. For example, if you are running 500 to 1,000 users on a single server, you will want to increase the maximum service processes parameter. You might also consider increasing this value if you are using this service to store imaging or other graphics-intensive data. Do not increase this value to the maximum in one single adjustment. Instead, keep raising the number of service processes in small increments until your performance improves.

CPU Utilization

The CPU is usually the last place to look for a bottleneck on your server. Naturally, if you are trying to run 500 users on a 486/33 with NetWare 5, you are going to have some performance issues. But most of your tuning should be with the server's subsystems and not the CPU itself.

For example, if you were to use a bus mastering NIC in your server, you would have very little CPU activity in terms of disk read and writes. Almost all activity is handled on the NIC card itself without the intervention of the CPU. You can easily check the performance of your server's CPU through MONITOR.NLM's main screen. If you select Kernel and then select Applications, you will see groups of applications. For example, all the NetWare processes are grouped in a single application called the NetWare Application. To view the individual processes or threads, select the application. If you want to see the busiest threads, press the F4 key. You will see a screen similar to the one shown in Figure 11.14.

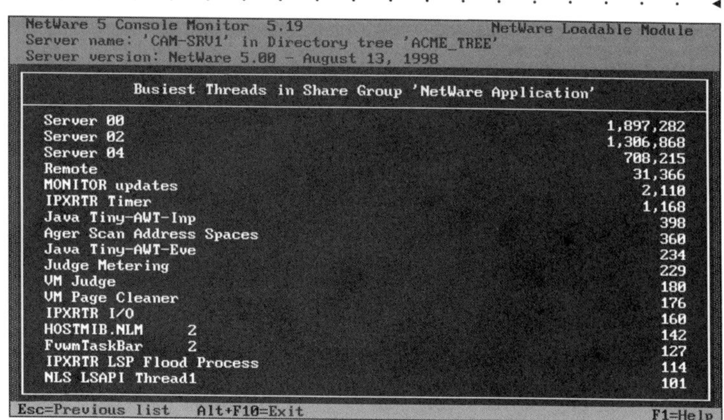

FIGURE 11.14

The Busiest Threads in a Share Group screen found in MONITOR.NLM

Paging down the Processor Utilization screen displays the percentage of CPU utilization that each process on your server is using. The Idle Loop category shows the percentage of time that the CPU is sitting idle. Look carefully at this statistic to see how busy your CPU actually is. If you are using only 20 to 30 percent of the CPU time, that means 70 to 80 percent is going unused and is sitting idle. The idle loop value is the inverse of the most accurate CPU percent utilization figure available from NetWare.

Not all processes are calculated when this screen is active. Novell Directory Services, for example, uses a process known as the work-to-do process. These types of processes are not monitored by the Process Utilization screen. They are not too significant in terms of CPU power and therefore are not registered on the MONITOR screens.

TIP

Novell provides a custom utility called STAT.NLM that can record your server's long-running CPU percent utilization. STAT is available from the Novell Web site at `www.novell.com` in a self-extracting file called STAT.EXE. Use this utility to gain a better perspective on what your average utilization is for a server.

Keep in mind that when you make a determination to purchase new hardware, you want to spend money where it will have the greatest impact for performance on your systems. Sometimes your money may be better spent on the subsystems of the server rather than the CPU itself.

If your CPU appears to still have capacity, you should look at the following suggestions for other ways of improving performance on your current system:

- Avoid the use of ISA systems and upgrade to the EISA or MCA bus architectures to increase I/O channel capacity. Consider upgrading EISA or MCA systems to PCI to further increase I/O channel capacity.
- Increase the server RAM for additional file caching.
- Upgrade the LAN channel to 32-bit intelligent bus master adapters.
- Segment the LAN across multiple LAN adapters.
- Upgrade the disk channel to SCSI-2.

In some cases you may have a server experiencing high utilization and actually see the CPU reach 100 percent utilization. In some cases this activity is normal and generally does not pose a problem for your server or users. If you notice high utilization occurring for long periods of time there are some areas that you will want to look at to understand why this may be occurring.

NDS Design

Having an efficient tree design is essential to avoiding utilization problems. The size and number of partition replicas can cause utilization problems if they are not managed properly. NDS needs to keep synchronization among all servers in its replica ring. The more replicas there are of any partition, the more traffic there will be on the wire. Novell recommends having three replicas of each partition in the tree. This provides Directory Services fault tolerance and allows for a recovery if a replica were to become corrupt.

For more information on designing your NDS tree refer to Chapters 5, 6, and 7.

Abend Recovery Options

NetWare 5 provides recovery options for handling abends (abnormal ends) in the operating system. In addition, the NetWare 5 operating system source code has been modified to reduce the total number of abend conditions. For example, software errors in previous versions of the operating system caused the system to abend. Some of these errors could have been corrected or ignored with no adverse effect. Other errors could have been changed to be conditional based upon whether the developer option in the operating system is set to OFF. This reduces the number of events that can potentially disrupt the NetWare 5 operating system but allows them to be turned back on when the software engineers or developers are debugging a new NLM product.

You may now be wondering if abends are good or bad. The answer depends on your perspective. An abend stops the server processes before data is damaged or harmed. While this is a positive feature, an abend will disrupt or halt the entire service. This disruption in service is definitely an inconvenience. However, the abend information about the software or hardware problems helps the administrators troubleshoot the server. Thus, the abend information can decrease the troubleshooting time. One of the primary goals of the new abend recovery options is to improve the information or messages displayed on the server console. The abend recovery enhancements that are new to NetWare 5 include the following features and capabilities:

- Additional abend information is displayed on the server console.

- When an abend occurs, the header "Additional Information:" is displayed on the server console followed by the probable cause of the abend. The information displayed will identify the specific NLM or hardware problem that caused the abend so that the administrator can take immediate corrective action to prevent the problem from occurring again.

The new abend recovery options are:

- The ABEND.LOG file
- The SET AUTO RESTART AFTER ABEND parameter
- The SET AUTO RESTART AFTER ABEND DELAY TIME parameter

The ABEND.LOG File

When an abend occurs, information about the abend is automatically written to a text file called ABEND.LOG. The abend information is formatted and written to appear like a mini–core dump. The ABEND.LOG file is initially created on the DOS partition of the server. However, the next time the SYS: volume is mounted, the information is appended to the ABEND.LOG file stored in the SYS:SYSTEM directory, and the ABEND.LOG file on the DOS partition is removed. This method will provide a running history of all the abends that occur on a specific server and also provide detailed information about abends. This will help the administrators and support engineers identify and resolve server problems.

The SET AUTO RESTART AFTER ABEND Parameter

There is a SET parameter called AUTO RESTART AFTER ABEND that enables the NetWare 5 server to automatically recover from an abend. According to the value selected, the server will recover in a variety of ways. The three values you can set are 0, 1, or 2. The default value for this parameter is 1.

If the parameter is set to 0, the server will not try to recover from the abend. However, the server will display the standard abend information to the system console screen and write it to the ABEND.LOG file. The server will also provide the option to the user to attempt to take the server down gracefully (as if the option had been turned ON). The administrator has the option to do a core dump or simply exit to DOS at that point.

If you set the parameter to 1 (which is the default), the server will attempt to recover from the abend. In order for the server to recover from the abend, it must first check the state of the SET DEVELOPER OPTION parameter. If the DEVELOPER OPTION parameter is set to OFF (which is the default), then when the abend occurs the standard abend information will be displayed on the system console screen and logged to the ABEND.LOG file. Next, if the running process is a Page Fault, Protection Fault, Invalid Opcode, or Divide Overflow Exception, or if the process can be restored to a stable state, the server will continue to run and service all requests. If the SET DEVELOPER OPTION parameter is set to ON, then the server is scheduled to be restarted after two minutes. When the server is scheduled to be restarted, a broadcast message is automatically sent to the system error log file and to all the users notifying them that the server will be going down in two minutes. The server is then automatically downed and automatically restarted. The server will then come up in a clean state, reloading all the drivers and NLMs previously loaded. The clients running the new client requesters with auto-reconnect will automatically reconnect to the server and continue accessing the same network files they had open before the abend occurred.

If you set the parameter to 2, the server attempts to recover from the abend while suspending the faulting process. If the SET DEVELOPER OPTION parameter is off when the abend occurs, the standard abend information will be displayed on the system console screen and logged to the ABEND.LOG. The running process, which is the faulting process, will be suspended (if possible). Next, the server is scheduled to go down after two minutes. A broadcast message is sent to the system error log file and to all the users notifying them that the server will be going down in two minutes. The server is then automatically downed and restarted and all the drivers and NLMs are reloaded. The clients running the new client requesters with auto-reconnect will automatically reconnect to the server and continue accessing the same network files they had open before the abend occurred. The faulting process continues to be suspended.

A value of 1 or 2 allows the NetWare 5 servers to automatically recover from abends and come back online rather than sitting in a halted state waiting for administrator intervention. All the error messages, conditions, and necessary information are written to a file to help the system administrator debug the problem after it occurs. These settings also allow the server to go down in a graceful fashion, which prevents both client and server file system data from being lost. This greatly reduces the need to run VREPAIR after an abend.

The SET AUTO RESTART AFTER ABEND DELAY TIME Parameter

This SET parameter allows the user to configure the amount of time (in minutes) the server will wait before going down and restarting automatically if the SET AUTO RESTART AFTER ABEND parameter is turned on (set to 1 or 2). Although the default for this parameter is 2 minutes, it can be set anywhere between 2 and 60 minutes, in one-minute intervals. It can be changed at any time after the abend has occurred but before the server actually goes down.

When you enter the SECURE CONSOLE command at the server prompt, DOS is not removed from memory automatically. To remove DOS from memory, you have to explicitly use the REMOVE DOS command. This enables abend logging and the SET AUTO RESTART AFTER ABEND functionality when the console is secured.

The Memory Subsystem

The total amount of server memory has a larger impact on the overall performance of the operating system than any other subsystem. The memory supports the file server cache, which provides both file and directory caching. The cache memory allocates space for the hash table, the File Allocation Table (FAT), the Turbo FAT, directory caching, and finally file caching. The minimum amount of memory for NetWare 5 is 64MB, but we recommend that you have at least 128MB.

Calculating server memory requirements for NetWare 3 and NetWare 4 was a common pastime; however, NetWare 5 eliminates the need to do a lengthy memory calculation. For the most part NetWare 5 requires far less memory because of NSS. In the past, the server memory calculations were highly dependent on the file system size, number of volumes, number of files, and name spaces wanted. For example, in NetWare 4 a server with 10GB volume would need roughly 160MB of RAM and would grow with every gigabyte installed afterward. In NetWare 5, the memory requirements are more constant because NSS only requires 8MB. The 8MB requirement is minimum, but NSS guarantees that it will mount and support all volumes on the server regardless of the size. Thus, a server with 10MB, 10GB, or 100GB requires the same amount of server memory.

Memory Protection

NetWare 5 has been enhanced to include several new memory features. These features include memory protection and virtual memory. Although NetWare 4 had some features for memory protection, NetWare 5 has complete memory protection. The memory protection in NetWare 5 allows you to load any server applications in their own protected address space. The applications are then shielded from the other applications and the operating system itself. The result is that if one application fails it does not affect any of the other applications or processing of the operating system. You can use protected address spaces to run untried or troublesome applications. Any program or module loaded into a protected address space can't corrupt the operating system or cause server abends. The protected address space provides a safe place to run applications. All protected address spaces use virtual memory. For more information about virtual memory, see the section "Virtual Memory" later in this chapter.

Protected Address Spaces

As mentioned, each application can be loaded into its own protected address space. A *protected address space* is a portion of cache server memory that has controlled communication with the server operating system. The protected address space is only a portion of cache memory that can be set aside. This is sometimes called user address spaces or ring 3. In contrast, the NetWare operating system does not run in a protected address space. The operating system address space is sometimes called ring 0 or the kernel address space.

Although running applications in ring 0 offers greater performance benefits, doing so can be risky. Modules or applications that are executed in ring 0 do not have protected memory. Thus, if an application has problems, it could start overwriting memory outside its own address space. As a result, the operating system could crash or abend. We recommend that you only load trusted modules in ring 0 and new or suspect modules in ring 3. This provides a layer of protection between the new module and the NetWare operating system.

Since the protected address space runs in ring 3 and the operating system runs at ring 0, there must be an interface between the two areas. This interface, in conjunction with the memory protection subsystem, prevents modules in a protected address space from having direct access to anything outside the address space, especially the server operating system. The interface prevents NLM programs in protected spaces from passing calls to the operating system address space that would corrupt or abend the core operating system.

Each protected address space has its own page translation table to provide logical memory addressing. The memory management subsystem ensures that the page translation table of each protected address space points to a different set of physical memory addresses. Only one translation table can be loaded into the memory management subsystem at a time. When there is more than one protected address space, the memory management subsystem loads one translation table for a specified time and then replaces it with another. Figure 11.15 illustrates how the memory management subsystem only loads one translation table for the protected address space at a time.

FIGURE 11.15

The memory management subsystem loads the translation tables one at a time.

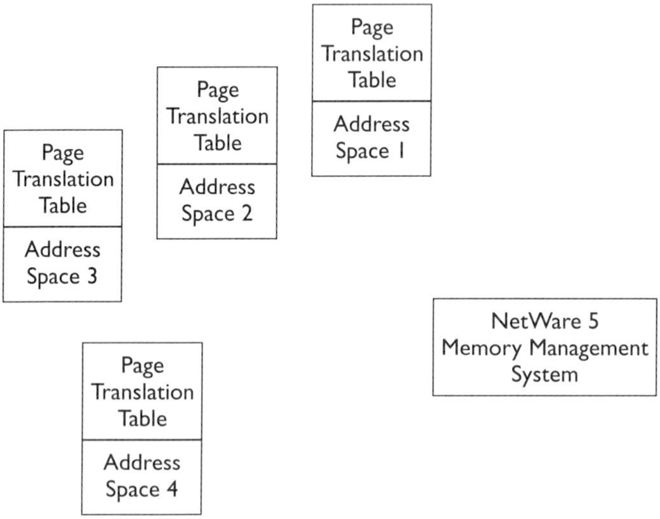

Loading and unloading translation tables is called a *context switch.* As you may know, context switches can be somewhat time consuming for the CPU. Thus, we recommend that you do not create more protected address spaces than you need.

In the first release of NetWare 5, there will only be a few NLMs or applications that can be loaded into the protected memory space. NetWare 5 loads Java-based applications in protected mode by default. In addition, you can optionally load GroupWise 5.2, Lotus Notes 4.6 (except for the debugging module), Oracle 7.3, and Oracle8. However, there are certain types of modules and programs that cannot run in protected addresses. The protected address spaces run in ring 3, and others must be loaded at ring 0 instead. What follows is a list of common NLM programs and executables that cannot be loaded into a protected address space:

- SERVER.EXE
- LAN drivers
- Disk drivers
- MONITOR.NLM
- Novell Storage System (NSS)

The server operating system (SERVER.EXE) cannot run in a protected address space because software running in a protected space is subject to being temporarily stopped and swapped to disk (see the section "Virtual Memory"). LAN and disk drivers must run in ring 0 or the operating system address space because they use physical memory addresses. Protected address spaces use logical memory addressing.

Any software modules or server applications that need to access physical memory directly or engage in direct hardware I/O (such as LAN drivers, HAM or disk drivers, and I/O services) cannot be loaded in the protected address spaces. The same is true for applications such as MONITOR that make calls directly to the operating system that are not allowed from protected address spaces. Additionally, some modules and applications aren't designed to run in protected address spaces.

Loading Protected Address Spaces

In order to manage an application's performance and reliability, you can move it into and out of protected address space. In order to create a protected address space, you load the individual module with specific commands. Table 11.2 shows the list of commands that control creation of protected address spaces.

TABLE 11.2

Server Console Commands for Creating a Protected Address Space

COMMAND	DESCRIPTION
[LOAD] PROTECTED module_name	Loads the module and automatically creates a new protected address space called ADDRESS_SPACE *n*, where *n* is a number.
[LOAD] RESTART module_name	Loads the module and automatically creates a new protected address space with restart functionality. The restart functionality means that if the protected address space abends, the operating system closes the space, cleans up its resources, restarts the space again, and reloads the modules. To prevent the server from restarting a memory space that continues to abend, the operating system uses the SET parameter called Memory Protection No Restart Interval. This parameter is found in the Miscellaneous section of the Server Parameters in MONITOR.
[LOAD] ADDRESS SPACE = space_name module_name	Loads modules into a new protected address space with a user-defined name. You can use this command when you want to create your own name for the space. You can also use this command when you want to load more than one module into an address space. In order to do this, repeat the command multiple times.
PROTECT filename. NCF	Use this command to use an NCF file to load multiple modules at once. This command creates a protected address space with the same name as the NCF file.
PROTECTION RESTART space_name	Adds restart functionality to an existing address space. Restart functionality means that if the protected address space abends, the operating system closes the space, cleans up its resources, restarts the space again, and reloads the modules.

COMMAND	DESCRIPTION
	To prevent the server from restarting a memory space that continues to abend, the operating system uses the SET parameter called Memory Protection No Restart Interval. This parameter is found in the Miscellaneous section of the Server Parameters in MONITOR.
PROTECTION NO RESTART space_name	Removes restart capability from an existing address space.

You may be wondering is there a limit to the number of modules that can be run in protected mode simultaneously. The answer is that there is no built-in limit to the number of protected address spaces that can be used, or the number of modules that can be loaded into a given address space. The only limit is dictated by the amount of physical memory and disk space available.

Unloading Protected Address Spaces

In order to unload a module or application from a protected address space, you can use the commands shown in Table 11.3. This table not only shows you each command to unload a module or application from a protected space but also shows you how to unload the space itself. The commands are only valid at the server console.

TABLE 11.3

Server Console Commands for Unloading Applications or Unloading the Protected Address Space

COMMAND	DESCRIPTION
UNLOAD ADDRESS SPACE = space_name module_name	Unloads the specified module or application for the specified address space, but does not remove the address space. If the module is loaded into more than one address space, this command removes only the module from the designated address space.
UNLOAD ADDRESS SPACE = space_name	Unloads all modules from the specified protected address space plus removes the address space itself from memory.

Continued

TABLE 11.3 *Continued*

COMMAND	DESCRIPTION
UNLOAD KILL ADDRESS SPACE = space_name	Unconditionally removes the address space without having to unload each module first. This returns all the resources used by the protected address space to the system. You will only want to use this command if you have tried and failed to unload it using the normal method.

Under certain circumstances, a module that is being unloaded with the UNLOAD ADDRESS SPACE command will hang. The system waits a predetermined time before it displays an error message. The error message that is shown on the server console is as follows:

```
<module name> in <address space> did not unload yet. Killing
the address space is the only way to remove the NLM. Should
the address space be killed? Yes/No.
```

If you answer Yes, the system kills the address space without unloading modules from it. If you answer No, the system waits a specified time and displays the message again. You can use a SET parameter to designate the amount of time the system waits under these conditions. The SET parameter is called Hung Unload Wait Delay and is found in the error handling section of the SET parameters. The default is 30 seconds, but you can change it to wait less time.

If you find that during an UNLOAD of an address space the server does not completely clean up all the assigned resources, a message is sent to the server console. The message may include the words "clean up failure," and you will not be able to unload the address space. In order to recover from the error and recover the resources assigned to the address space, you will need to schedule a shutdown and restart of the server.

Virtual Memory

Virtual memory provides the NetWare 5 operating system the ability to allocate more than the actual physical memory of the server machine. It does this by using the disk as an extension of memory and by swapping code and data between physical memory and disk as it is needed. When the data on disk is needed again, it is moved back into the physical memory. Because data is swapped in and out of disk, the available memory can be used for a larger amount of data than its actual physical capacity would allow. Virtual memory provides NetWare 5 with a more efficient use of memory and lessens the likelihood that low memory conditions will cause an abend condition.

NetWare 5 moves the data out of physical memory to swap files on the hard drive if the data has not frequently been used. More specifically, the available memory is assessed to see which data has been used less recently than the rest. How recently data has been used is determined by a bit in each field of the translation table that indicates whether the address space has been used since the last time it was checked. Data that has not been used for some time can be moved from memory to disk, thus freeing memory for other uses.

As mentioned earlier, protected memory uses virtual memory. The reason is that the memory management subsystem can allocate to each process a unique protected virtual address available to run the threads of the process. Thus, each process has a separate address space, so a thread in one process cannot view or modify the memory of another process. This architecture provides the protected memory for NetWare 5.

NetWare 5 will load a few applications or modules into virtual memory by default. One of those is the Java Virtual Machine (JVM). Any other modules that are loaded by the JVM will run in virtual memory. As in the case of protected memory, however, certain types of modules and programs cannot run in virtual memory. Not surprisingly these types of programs are the same as those that cannot use protected memory. The reason is that protected memory uses virtual memory. What follows is a list of common NLM programs and executables that cannot be loaded into virtual memory:

- SERVER.EXE
- LAN drivers
- Disk drivers
- MONITOR.NLM
- Novell Storage System (NSS)

As an example, the server operating system (SERVER.EXE) cannot run in virtual memory because it must always be resident in memory and cannot be swapped to disk. The same condition exists for all the other modules.

Managing Virtual Memory

The memory management subsystem assesses the memory needs of all server and NLM processes and determines where the freed memory should be used. The subsystem stores freed memory in disk cache. When data is moved from memory to disk, it is stored in a swap file. Swapping the data between memory and disk requires additional system resources, but it increases the memory available for use. The availability of the additional memory can improve overall server performance.

You can manage the swapping of data by controlling the swap files where the data is stored on disk. You can use the SWAP command to create a swap file, delete a swap file, change swap file parameters, and view information about the swap file. You can also view information about the swap file in MONITOR. You can create one swap file for each NetWare 5 volume. A swap file is created for the SYS volume by default.

Table 11.4 describes each of the commands you can use to create, delete, and manage swap files that are used by virtual memory. The commands described are all executed from the server console.

TABLE 11.4

Server Console Commands for Creating, Deleting, and Managing the Swap Files Needed for Virtual Memory

COMMAND	DESCRIPTION
HELP SWAP	Learn about the SWAP command.
SWAP	Display a Virtual Memory Information Screen containing information about swap files. Alternatively, you can use MONITOR to view information about the swap files under the Available Options, select Virtual Memory, and then Swap Files.

COMMAND	DESCRIPTION
SWAP ADD volume_name [parameter= value...]	Create a swap file on a designated volume. The optional parameters are MIN=, MAX=, and MIN FREE=. These parameters specify the minimum and maximum sizes of the swap file and the minimum free space that must be left on the volume. The values are in MB (millions of bytes). If no parameters are included, then the command uses the default values of MIN=2, MAX=Free volume space, and MIN FREE=5. You will generally want to place swap files on the fastest volume or the volume with the most available space.
SWAP DEL volume_name	Delete a swap file from a designated volume. If you are using protected address spaces, the Java Virtual Machine, or any other application that uses virtual memory, make sure that you have at least one swap file for your system. Remember, by default a swap file for volume SYS is created automatically. If you do not want a swap file for SYS, place the SWAP DEL command in the STATUP.NCF file before the command to mount volumes. If the swap file is being used when it is deleted, the swapped data is then moved to another swap file. If there is no other swap file, an error message is displayed and the file is not deleted.
SWAP PARAMETER volume_name parameter =value...	Change the parameter values for a swap file on a designated volume. Again, the parameters are MIN=, MAX=, and MIN FREE=. These parameters specify the minimum and maximum sizes of the swap file and the minimum free space that must be left on the volume. Values are in millions of bytes.

When using swap files in a production NetWare 5 environment, you should be aware of several important facts. The facts about swap files are as follows:

- You can create one swap file per volume.
- The swap file for the SYS volume is created by default; you can delete it if necessary.
- Data moved to disk by virtual memory will be stored in any available swap file. It does not matter which volume the swap file is on.
- You can add a swap file to a volume even if the volume is not mounted. Once the volume is mounted, the swap file will be created.
- When you dismount a volume, the swap file is deleted. To keep a swap file on that volume, you must create the swap file again. Again, the only exception is volume SYS, which is created by default.
- You will typically want to place the commands to create swap files into the AUTOEXEC.NCF file so that the files will be created each time the server is started.
- Swap files are dynamic; they change size as data is swapped in and out of memory.

If the overall supply of memory in the server is running low, then swapping within virtual memory will occur more often. If memory is extremely low, the system may spend all its time swapping memory in and out of disk and have no time to accomplish useful work. This is called disk "thrashing."

In extremely low memory conditions, NetWare will move all the data from a protected address space into the disk swap file, temporarily stopping the modules within the space. After a period of time, NetWare will move the data back into the memory space and shut down another space, moving its data to disk. Without virtual memory, these extremely low memory conditions would cause processes to fail. With virtual memory, the server keeps running, although very slowly.

When disk thrashing occurs, the solution is to add more RAM. Virtual memory cannot compensate for an overall lack of server memory, although it can prevent processes from failing and allow a server to continue to function. The real value of virtual memory is in using a sufficient supply of memory more efficiently, thus improving server performance.

File Caching

NetWare 5 uses cache memory on the server to speed up file access for clients. The file cache provides a temporary data storage area (in RAM) for files that are being read or written to the server.

The most dramatic file server performance increase can be seen when the appropriate number of file cache buffers are allocated. The file cache buffers should be sufficient to keep the cache hit ratio high. The greatest performance increase is achieved when the hit ratio is between 90 and 100 percent. As a rule of thumb, the 90 percent hit ratio is achievable (in a read-intensive environment) when the cache buffers are 75 to 80 percent of total server work memory. File cache buffers are assigned from the memory that is left after the operating system is booted and the core functions and NLMs are loaded.

The most important parameter to measure cache efficiency is the LRU sitting time statistic that is updated and displayed once per second in MONITOR.NLM. LRU stands for least recently used. This statistic is found under the Cache Statistics menu as shown in Figure 11.16 and is calculated by taking the difference between the current time and the time stamp of the LRU cache block at the end of the cache list. The result is then updated every second and is displayed. The LRU sitting time measures the length of time for a most recently used (MRU) cache buffer at the beginning of the list to work its way down to the end of the list, where it becomes the LRU cache buffer. This measurement is also known as the cache churn rate.

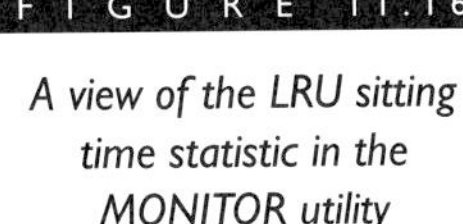

A view of the LRU sitting time statistic in the MONITOR utility

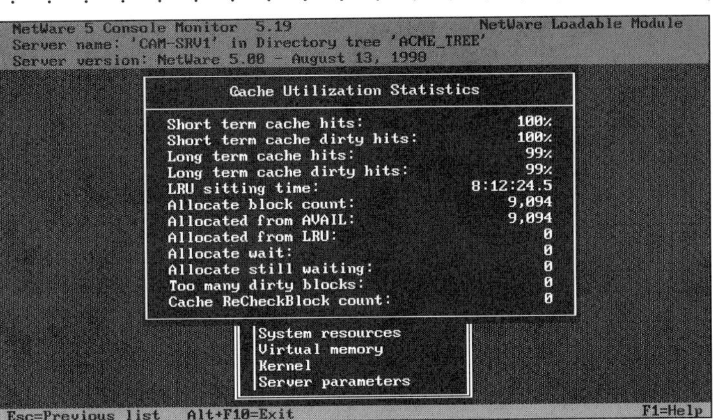

In environments with very large amounts of cache, the LRU sitting time will be up in the hours of time. A good rule of thumb is that your LRU sitting time should not go below 15 minutes. If your LRU value falls below 15 minutes, it usually means that you do not have enough memory to create a large enough cache for your directories. Therefore, the sitting time is very short because of the churn rate of MRUs versus LRUs. It's time to take a look at adding more memory to your server if this value remains consistently below 15 minutes. Here are some other helpful ideas to tuning your cache:

1. **Estimate your server memory requirements.** You can use the previous memory calculation worksheet to estimate your server memory requirements. You must first determine if your server has adequate memory overall.

2. **Observe the Cache Statistics parameter.** You should monitor the LRU sitting time during peak workload periods and record that information. You should then monitor the LRU sitting time at other, slower, times of the day. Obtain an average for your LRU sitting time. Record your observations for at least one week or longer to obtain a pattern of activity on your server. Estimate a low watermark based on the information you have gained from your observations. This low watermark will help you to adjust cache if necessary.

3. **Tune the Cache parameter by increasing its size.** A simple rule of thumb is if your LRU sitting time falls below 15 minutes, you should probably increase the cache size by adding more memory to your server. You'll need to add memory to increase the LRU Sitting Time during your peak workloads. The added memory increases the likelihood that repeatedly used data will still be cached when the next user request is received from a client.

On the other hand, if your LRU sitting time is several hours, you have more than adequate cache resources. In this case, it is not necessary to increase your memory, and you can leave the memory in the server to support additional growth.

The point is not whether you actually add or remove memory from your server. We hope to improve your ability to interpret the LRU sitting time statistic and thereby provide you with a meaningful way to understand the efficiency and performance of NetWare 5's file cache.

Directory Caching

Directory caching is the ability of NetWare to read directories and cache directory entries for faster lookup. Rather than search the disk for directory entries, the server can hold the entries in memory. Disk access performance is greatly increased with this feature. Because some directories can be extremely large, the directory cache uses what is called the least recently used (LRU) algorithm to store only the most recent directory cache blocks. By doing this, the operating system can more efficiently make use of memory. Each cache buffer is 4K and holds up to 32 directory entries. This parameter can be set as follows:

```
SET MAXIMUM DIRECTORY CACHE BUFFERS = n
```

where *n* is a number between 20 and 4000. The default is 500. This setting allows you to define what the maximum number of directory cache buffers are that NetWare 5 can allocate. NetWare 5 will only allocate extra buffers if necessary.

```
SET MINIMUM DIRECTORY CACHE BUFFERS = n
```

where *n* is a number between 10 and 2000. The default is 20. This setting defines the minimum number of directory cache buffers that can be allocated by the NetWare 5 operating system without waiting for the directory cache allocation wait time.

```
SET DIRECTORY CACHE ALLOCATION WAIT TIME = n
```

where *n* is a value between 0.5 and 120. The default is 2.2 seconds. This parameter specifies how long the NetWare 5 operating system must wait before allocating one more directory cache buffer.

In very few circumstances do you need to adjust this parameter upward. Keep in mind that the minimum number of buffers is the number of directory cache buffers that can be set by the operating system using the wait time. If your server is functioning as a document server where many searches are being performed, you may want to increase this parameter.

Additional directory set parameters allow you to control cache functions listed here. They are also set parameters that are manipulated at your server console.

```
SET MAXIMUM CONCURRENT DIRECTORY CACHE WRITES = n
```

where *n* is from 5 to 10. The default setting is 10. This parameter allows you to control the number of cache writes through the disk channel. When you create a new directory addition, deletion, or other modification, a directory cache write is created. You can limit the number of cache writes through your disk channel if your disk subsystem is not extremely fast.

```
SET DIRECTORY CACHE BUFFER NONREFERENCED DELAY = n
```

where *n* can be 1 to 300 seconds. The default setting is 5.5 seconds. The purpose of this SET parameter is to specify the amount of time a cache buffer can remain unreferenced before it is removed. Novell does not recommend that you make any changes to this parameter, as you can better control performance by setting the number of cache buffers.

```
SET DIRTY DIRECTORY CACHE DELAY TIME = n
```

where *n* can be 0 to 10 seconds. The default is 0.5 seconds. The purpose of this parameter is to reduce the likelihood of redundant cache writes. This setting causes NetWare 5 to wait for the delay time specified before performing a directory request (write) to the directory cache. The reason for the wait is to see if there are any more requests to change the same block. If there are duplicate requests, then the operating system only processes those requests once with a single write. This makes writing more efficient. Only very large directory caches (hundreds of thousands of entries) will realize any benefit by changing this parameter.

Obtaining the Latest Patches

Make sure that you have the latest patches loaded for the NetWare 5 operating system and Novell Directory Services. Each Novell patch contains a readme file that explains the problems being resolved and any special loading instructions. To download the latest patches, you need to go to the Novell corporate Web site: `www.novell.com/download`.

Summary

Before you can adequately tune or optimize the NetWare 5 operating system, you must first understand the basic characteristics of your network, servers, and workstations. In addition, you need to become familiar with the internal server components and processes.

A variety of SET parameters help you accomplish the task of tuning and optimizing the NetWare 5 server. These SET parameters can be adjusted either up or down to help fine-tune your system. Although the SET parameters can be manually adjusted, the default settings for each of the internal parameters work very well for most implementations. Some server implementations may make it necessary to modify some of the system settings to increase the capacity and performance of your system. These implementations may include heavy use of imaging or document retrieval types of software.

You should measure the baseline performance of your system during periods of both peak and off-peak production. Having a baseline beforehand allows you to gauge changes in performance and reliability during the tuning effort.

PART IV

NetWare 5 Administration

CHAPTER 12

Understanding and Managing Client Access

"Good counselors lack no clients." — Shakespeare

The network client provides an extension to each network user to access the corporate resources on the network servers. The network client is tasked to communicate with the desktop operating system and the network operating system and serves as a liaison between the two. If a desktop application requires the use of network services, the client redirects the output to a server. If a server application needs to communicate with a client, it directs that communication to the network client in response to the client request.

Because of the variety of clients that may exist in your network, your responsibility as a LAN administrator will be to determine what type of client access is needed for a workstation to connect to NetWare 5 and to create the appropriate accessibility to meet those needs. Providing access to NDS will be accomplished through the different client software components available in conjunction with NetWare login scripts. The client software provides access to NetWare 5, and the login script creates the environment for the user. Client software is discussed in detail in the sections that follow.

NetWare 5 Network Client Software

The NetWare 5 client software is designed to support connectivity to workstations including the DOS/Windows, Windows 95/98, OS/2, Macintosh, NT, and UNIX operating systems. Through various connections discussed in this chapter, you can connect to a NetWare 5 server and access files, applications, and Novell Directory Services.

As a network designer, you will hopefully have most of your users running on the same desktop operating system, with a few exceptions that use other systems across your departments. As you design for user access to the NDS tree and NetWare 5 servers, you should first begin by designing access (login scripts and so on) for the majority of your user community that uses the same operating system. You can then create your access designs for the less commonly used workstations on your network. You may also have some mobile users that require special login scripts.

This chapter reviews the user login scripts for setting up user environments. We will review container, profile, and user login scripts and how they can be used to meet any user need. At the end of the chapter we provide sample login scripts for Windows 95 and Windows NT clients. Figure 12.1 illustrates the different client access mechanisms and will serve as the basis of our discussion. As shown in the diagram, client access can be broken down into multiple categories. Each of these categories is discussed in this chapter.

FIGURE 12.1

The components of client accessibility for NetWare 5 Networks are based on a variety of connections, workstation software, services, login scripts, and users.

Access			
Type of Connection	Authenticated and Licensed	Not Authenticated Not Licensed	Authenticated
Workstation Software	NETX		VLM and 32-bit Client
Type of Service	Bindery		NDS
Login Scripts	User Script in Mail Directory	System Script NET$LOG.DAT	Container L.S. Profile L.S. User L.S.
Type of User	Network / Remote / Mobile		

Desktop support is key to NetWare 5. A server cannot serve the user community unless access is provided for the clients to communicate with NetWare servers across the entire network. This access requires speed and reliability for all users and must make good use of limited memory at each workstation. Once a connection is made, the login script can set up the user's environment. Chapter 17, "Installing and Configuring NetWare Clients," provides a description of currently supported clients with their latest version of software.

Workstation Software

The newest client software is Novell's 32-bit Client architecture, which provides network connections for both DOS/Windows 3.1 and Windows 95/98. Novell also provides a 32-bit client for Windows NT users that also uses the 32-bit architecture, although it is slightly different than the Novell DOS/Windows client.

The older DOS Requester technology is discussed first, and then the new 32-bit client technology.

The DOS Requester

The DOS Requester is the older technology (first introduced in NetWare 4.0) and is a group of Virtual Loadable Modules (VLMs) that work together to provide client connectivity to a NetWare 5, NetWare 4, or NetWare 3 server. Using the VLM software, you can install only the VLM modules that are required for your user environment. You can create a standard configuration for the majority of your users.

An important difference between the older NetWare 3 NETX.EXE shell and the NetWare DOS Requester is how each client handles network requests. Because NETX.EXE is a shell, all calls from an application to the workstation operating system are intercepted by the shell and then directed to either the network or to DOS.

The NetWare DOS Requester, on the other hand, receives all calls from DOS through the DOS Redirector interface known as Int2Fh. Therefore, any calls sent to this interrupt are always intended for the network. Each of these approaches has its advantages and disadvantages in terms of memory usage and performance.

A visual example of how the NETX.EXE shell works is found in Figure 12.2.

FIGURE 12.2

A view of NETX.EXE routing operating system requests from an application

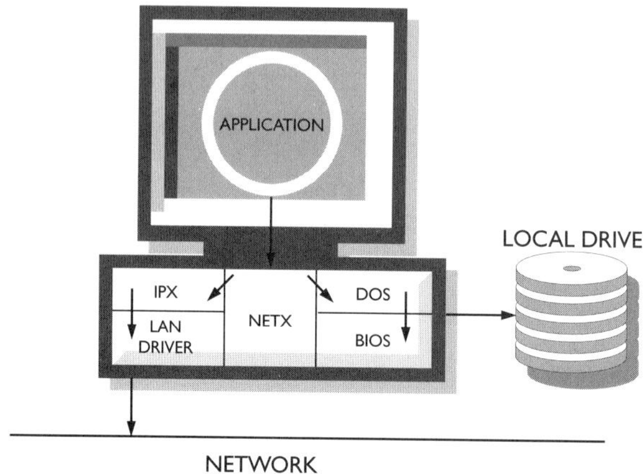

A visual example of how the NetWare DOS Requester receives the network requests from DOS is shown in Figure 12.3.

FIGURE 12.3

A view of the NetWare DOS Requester routing operating system requests from an application

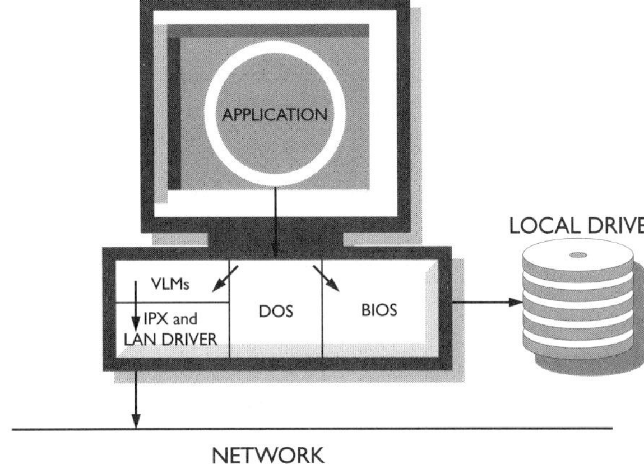

Novell Client 32 Technology

The NetWare clients for DOS/Windows, Windows 95, and Windows NT are based on a 32-bit architecture and combine the best of both technologies, the NetWare Shell (NETX) and the NetWare DOS Requester (VLMs). Both of these technologies operate in 16-bit real mode that requires conventional memory, which is typically scarce on many PC systems. Installations get especially complicated in multiprotocol configurations with network connectivity using a large amount of memory. The NetWare Client 32 architecture provides a 32-bit protected-mode environment for its clients. The CPU gets switched to protected mode when the client software loads. Therefore, memory beyond 1MB is addressable as a continuous range. Figure 12.4 shows a view of the NetWare Client 32 process.

FIGURE 12.4

A view of the requester process of Client 32

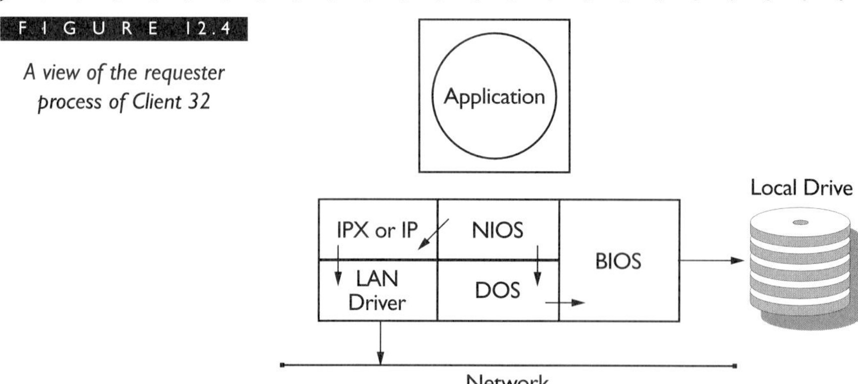

Types of Service

Two types of connections exist for NetWare 5—the NDS connection and a bindery services connection. The basic difference between these two connections is that a bindery services connection is server-centric. Server-centric means that connections to multiple servers require a username and password at each server, and the login process is repeated at every server.

With the NDS connection, on the other hand, you can have a single login to multiple NetWare 5 servers. A single login enables the user to enter a name and password once. Any additional drive mappings to other NetWare 5 servers will be handled in the background by NDS. The great benefit of the NDS connection is that administrators need to manage only a single user account if they are operating completely on NetWare 5 servers. Novell also provides NDS for NT, which, among many things, provides authentication for users on NT as well. For more information regarding NDS for NT, refer to IDG Books' *NDS for NT* by Jeffrey F. Hughes and Blair W. Thomas.

NDS Connections

An NDS connection requires the use of the NetWare 32-bit client software for authentication to a NetWare 5 server. An NDS connection provides a security mechanism known as RSA encryption between the client and server to provide background authentication for a single sign-on to multiple NetWare 5 servers.

An NDS connection is said to be in one of three states:

- Connected but not logged in
- Authenticated
- Licensed/authenticated

Each of these states are discussed as follows.

Connected but Not Logged In This state occurs when a user has attached to a NetWare 5 server through NETX l, the VLM client, or a NetWare 32 Client. An NDS connection that is not logged in can exist for NetWare 3, NetWare 4, or NetWare 5 users to the first attached server. If a connection is made after walking the tree, the state can exist after the first attached server.

For example, when a connection is neither authenticated nor licensed, users can navigate the NDS tree through the CX (**c**hange conte**x**t) command. At this point they have attached to a server but have not yet authenticated.

Authenticated *Authentication* is a process of proving identity to a server. In NetWare 3, this meant logging in with a user id and password. In NetWare 4 and NetWare 5, the authentication process happens as a "behind the scenes task" at the client.

This type of connection indicates that a NetWare 5 server has established a user's identity after the user has entered a correct name and password. Once authenticated, NDS can provide connections (background authentication) to other servers on the network. Authentication occurs for NetWare 3, NetWare 4, and NetWare 5 users alike, but NetWare 4 and NetWare 5 add more security to this process.

Authentication is invisible to the user. During the login sequence, the user will enter a password when prompted, and the remainder of the process occurs behind the scenes. No sensitive data are transmitted across the wire for security purposes. Authentication relies on encryption algorithms that are based on a public/private key system.

After successful authentication has taken place, a process known as *background authentication* may occur if the user's login script specifies connections to other servers. A connection to another NetWare 5 server, for example, does not require the user to reenter his or her password. However, all connections are authenticated the same way; the process makes no distinction between the first and subsequent server logins.

Licensed/Authenticated A connection is said to be *licensed* when a user has made a request of the server, such as mapping a drive or capturing to a printer. Each user will cause the user license to decrement by one after a connection has been licensed. Only an authenticated connection can be licensed.

A combination of these states determines what level a user currently has in a NetWare 5 environment.

If users are licensed and authenticated, they can access NDS and file system information to the extent allowed by their rights.

Additive licensing increases the total number of licenses on any given NetWare 5 server. This feature enables administrators to more closely match the number of licensed users to their company's needs. A company that currently has a 100-user license can add a 25-user license to the NetWare 5 server to accommodate increased growth. NetWare 5 supports 5-, 10-, 25-, 50-, 100-, 250-, 500-, and 1,000-user versions in any combination.

Bindery Services Connections

The NetWare client software provides compatibility with previous versions of NetWare through bindery services connections. This connection does not provide the capability of a single login to the network. For example, a client using the NETX.EXE shell or the LOGIN/B option with VLMs to log into a NetWare 5 server must enter a username and password for that server. Additional connections to other NetWare 5 servers would require the user to enter another username and password.

Bindery services can be enabled on any NetWare 5 server through the SET BINDERY CONTEXT command. The server can select one container or multiple containers in the NDS tree to set as the bindery context. All the leaf objects in the NDS container(s) that are also objects in the NetWare 3 bindery (for example, users, groups, queues, print servers, and profiles) are seen as the bindery.

Bindery services in NetWare 5 allows you to select up to 16 containers as the server bindery context. Bindery services requires that the server store at least a read/write replica of the partitions where the bindery context is set.

Login Scripts

Network users will execute login scripts to access NetWare 5 servers and other network resources. Traditionally, login scripts were used to establish the user's network environment. Login scripts for NetWare 5, however, are used to map network drives, map to applications, capture to printers and print queues, and set other important environment variables. Login scripts are the standard mechanism for user access and may require careful consideration.

When a user logs into the NetWare 5 network or server, login scripts associated with the user are executed. Two categories of login scripts are available to the user of the NetWare 5 network—NDS login scripts and bindery-based login scripts. NDS login scripts support the Directory connections, and bindery-based login scripts support the bindery services connections.

Our focus on login scripts in this chapter is to provide information on designing access to NetWare 5, not to encompass every login script variable and command. (Definitions and functions of all variables and commands are included at the end of this chapter.) Well-designed login scripts will help you create effective working environments for your users.

TIP

It is recommended that you execute the login scripts before launching Windows 3.1. If there are users who access Windows immediately after they boot their workstations, you need to have them log into the network, which runs the login scripts before launching Windows 3.1. The exception to this tip is if you are running the newer NetWare Client for DOS/Windows that provides a Windows login utility. See Chapter 17, "Installing and Configuring NetWare Clients" for more information on NetWare Client for DOS/Windows.

Login scripts execute in a specific order as shown in the following sequence of login script execution for NetWare 5:

1. The user logs into a server.

2. The user executes a container script if it is available.

3. The user executes a profile if that user's Profile property is set.

4. The user executes a user script if one is available.

5. If a user login script is not available, then the user executes the default script.

Bindery-based login scripts and NDS login scripts are both discussed in the next two sections.

Bindery-Based Login Scripts

The bindery-based login scripts that you may place in NetWare 5 are the same bindery login scripts found in NetWare 2 and NetWare 3. These login scripts can be copied onto the NetWare 5 servers to provide bindery services scripts to your NETX.EXE clients. For example, a user attaching to a NetWare 5 server with the NETX.EXE workstation software will have a bindery connection and look for the system and user login scripts on the server. The user script is in the SYS:MAIL directory, and the system login script would be placed in the SYS:PUBLIC directory as NET$LOG.DAT. Even if the user is using the VLM workstation software and selects the LOGIN/B option, that user will be attached to the server as a bindery connection.

The system login script is used for commands that affect all the bindery-based users on that server. Commands that might be placed in the system login script include the commands for displaying messages, mapping network drives and search drives, and setting environment variables. The system login script is the best place to manage the mapping and capture statements for all the bindery users that may still exist on your NetWare 5 network.

After a user successfully attaches to the server with a bindery connection, the system login script will execute from SYS:PUBLIC\NET$LOG.DAT if it exists. If the user login script is present, it will execute from the SYS:MAIL\USERID subdirectory. If the user login script does not exist, then the default login script is executed. The default login script is hard-coded into the LOGIN.EXE program.

Figure 12.5 shows the order of execution for bindery-based login scripts. If you are familiar with NetWare 3, notice that the bindery-based login scripts for NetWare 5 are executed in the same order.

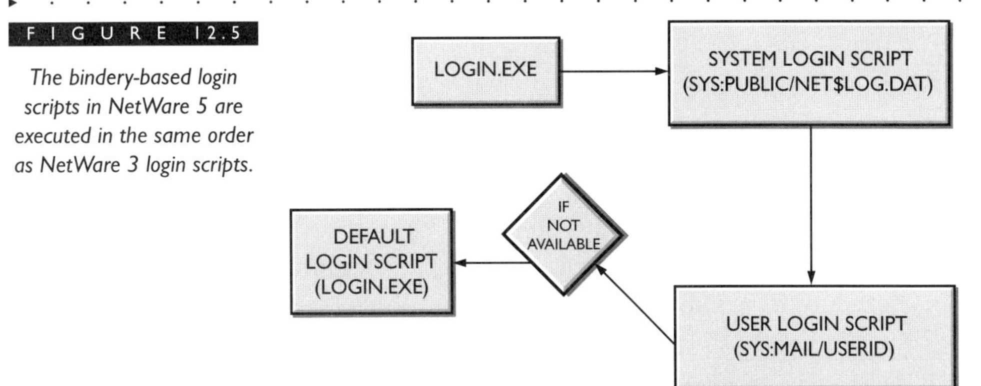

FIGURE 12.5

The bindery-based login scripts in NetWare 5 are executed in the same order as NetWare 3 login scripts.

The individual user login scripts are stored in each user's mail subdirectory on the SYS volume of any server where a bindery account exists. For example, user GWASHINGTON (with object ID of 19000023) stores the bindery-based user login scripts in the SYS:MAIL\19000023 subdirectory.

The individual user login script customizes the user environment to the specific needs of the user. The same commands placed in the system login scripts can also be placed in the individual user login scripts. It is recommended that the user login scripts be used only in situations in which the system login script will not suffice.

The bindery-based login scripts are server-centric, meaning that they are used only if a bindery user logs into the server that is holding them. Because the login scripts are server-centric, there are not a lot of design issues to consider. However, you should try to move all the users to the NDS login scripts as soon as possible so that you have fewer scripts to support.

You can make changes to both the system and user login scripts using the NetWare 3 SYSCON.EXE utility. You can also edit the NET$LOG.DAT file (or any script) directly with any text editing program. Although the bindery-based login scripts can be edited, any changes you make to the scripts are not automatically synchronized to the corresponding NDS login scripts. You can use Novell's NETSYNC utility to synchronize login scripts if you need to maintain consistency between NetWare 3 and NetWare 5. Refer to Chapter 2, "Installation and Management Utilities for NetWare," for more information on NETSYNC.

NDS Login Scripts

The login scripts used in NDS are different from those used by bindery services. The NDS login scripts are a property of an object and are accessible only through an NDS connection. The only NDS objects that have the login script property are the container objects (O=Organization and OU=Organizational Unit), profile objects, and user objects.

Users who obtain an NDS connection to the network and run LOGIN.EXE will execute the NDS container login script in the container in which they reside. The container script is roughly equivalent to the NetWare 3 system login script. After the container login script is executed, a profile login script can be executed if the user is associated with one. The user may also have a user script, which is executed after the container and profile scripts. If no user login script exists, the user will execute a default script. Again, the default login script is hard-coded into the LOGIN.EXE program.

Figure 12.6 shows the order of execution for the NDS login scripts. Notice the profile login script, which falls between the container and user login scripts. Each type of login script is discussed later in this section.

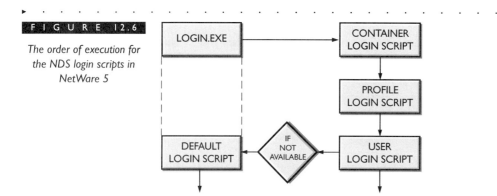

FIGURE 12.6

The order of execution for the NDS login scripts in NetWare 5

LOGIN.EXE

CONTAINER LOGIN SCRIPT

PROFILE LOGIN SCRIPT

USER LOGIN SCRIPT

IF NOT AVAILABLE

DEFAULT LOGIN SCRIPT

In order to manage the NDS login scripts, you can use either the NWADMIN or NETADMIN utility that ships with NetWare 5. With these utilities, you can create and edit all the login scripts, except for the default login script. You can also add a profile login script for execution by selected users. An example of editing a login script is shown in Figure 12.7. In this example, the administrator is editing a container login script for the FAC container.

FIGURE 12.7

You can use the NWADMIN utility to add or modify an NDS login script.

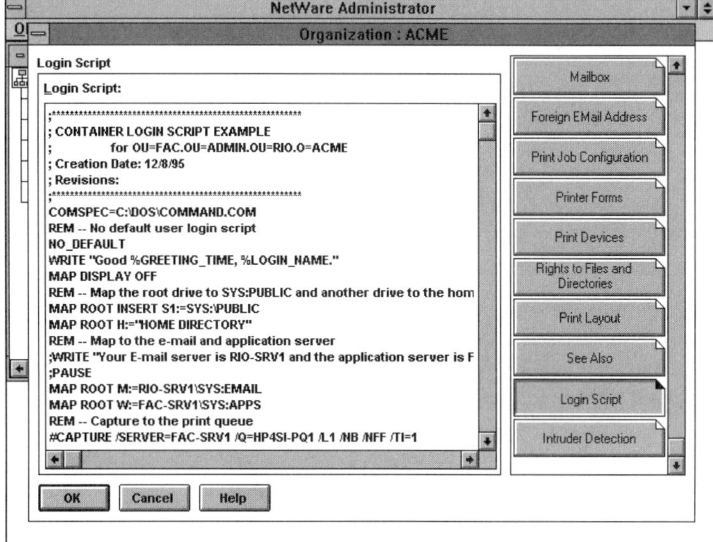

NDS Container Login Scripts Typically, the NDS users needing the same network resources will be grouped together in the same NDS container. These users will probably need similar drive mappings and capture statements to establish access to the network resources with which the users are grouped. You can then use the container login script to provide users access to the NDS tree in this fashion.

After the LOGIN utility has authenticated a user to the NetWare 5 network, the program checks the container login script in which the user resides. If the container login script exists, it will then be executed. NDS will search only the immediate container (O or OU) in which the user is a member. If the container login script is not defined, the system will not automatically search higher in the tree for another container login script.

For example, Figure 12.8 shows the user JMadison in the ACME tree named under the container OU=FAC.OU=ADMIN.OU=RIO.O=ACME. The container OU=FAC does not have a login script. There is, however, a container login script defined higher in the tree at OU=ADMIN. The user JMadison is an occupant of OU=FAC and will not execute a container login script because there is not one currently in FAC. The user JMadison will not search up the tree for a container login script. In other words, no other container login scripts above the user JMadison will be executed.

Consulting Experience

It is highly recommended that you use the NDS container login script to replace the functionality of the NetWare 3 system login script. The container login script is stored as a property of the O=Organization object, the OU=Organizational Unit object, and other container objects. Maintaining one set of login scripts allows for easier administration.

FIGURE 12.8

Container login scripts are executed only for the immediate occupants of a container. In this example, the user JMadison does not have a container login script in FAC.

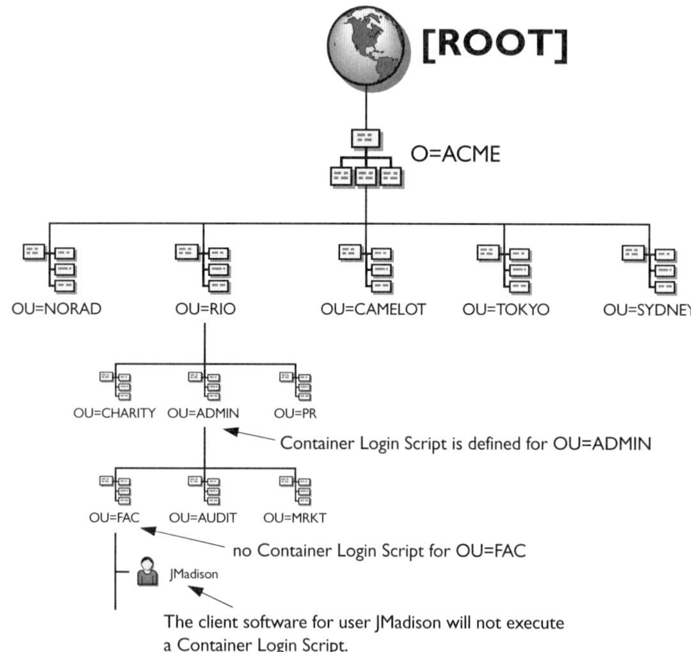

The NDS container login script commands should establish the network environment of the users. These commands include the network drive mappings, printer and print queue captures, and other environment settings. The users in the container are best managed by using the NDS container login script.

Here is an example of a container login script that we have just added for the OU=FAC container in the RIO location of ACME tree.

```
;*****************************************************
; CONTAINER LOGIN SCRIPT EXAMPLE
; for OU=FAC.OU=ADMIN.OU=RIO.O=ACME
; Creation Date: 03/18/9
; Revisions:
;*****************************************************
COMSPEC=C:\DOS\COMMAND.COM
REM — No default user login script
NO_DEFAULT
WRITE "Good %GREETING_TIME, %LOGIN_NAME."
MAP DISPLAY OFF
REM — Map the root drive to SYS:PUBLIC and another drive to
the home directory
MAP ROOT INSERT S1:=SYS:\PUBLIC
MAP ROOT H:="HOME DIRECTORY"
REM — Map to the e-mail and application server
;WRITE "Your E-mail server is RIO-SRV1 and the application
server is FAC-SRV1"
;PAUSE
MAP ROOT M:=RIO-SRV1\SYS:EMAIL
MAP ROOT W:=FAC-SRV1\SYS:APPS
REM — Capture to the print queue
#CAPTURE /SERVER=FAC-SRV1 /Q=HP4SI-PQ1 /L1 /NB /NFF /TI=1
```

The previous script can be created in either the NWADMIN utility or the NETADMIN utility as shown in Figure 12.9.

FIGURE 12.9

Using the NWADMIN utility to create a script for the FAC container

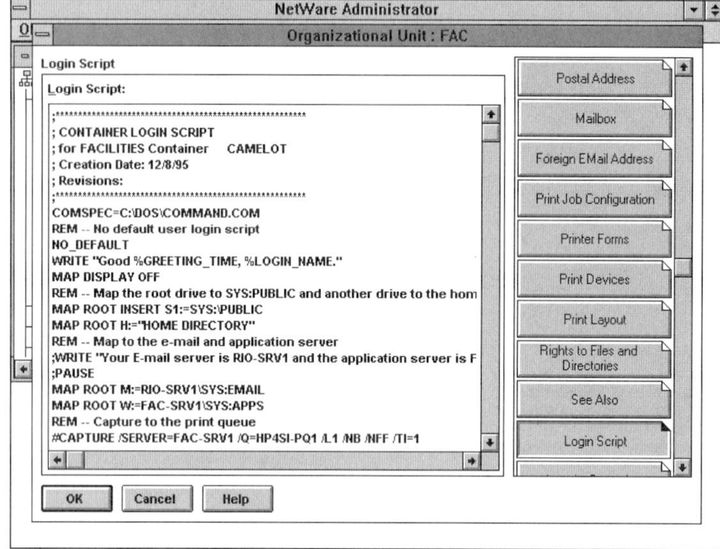

Profile Login Scripts If a user has a profile script assigned, it will be executed immediately after the container login script. The profile login script is optional and is used in special cases or for groups with special needs. The profile has the capability to include users that are in different containers in the tree. Its purpose is to assign additional environment settings that you may not want to assign to everyone in the profile. The scripts and the commands used in the profile login script are identical to the NDS container login scripts.

Because the profile login script is a special-purpose login script, it can provide you with greater flexibility during the login process. Multiple users can be associated with the profile login script, and they can reside in different containers in your tree. Figure 12.10 shows the creation of a profile login script through the NWADMIN utility. You can enable individual users to execute the profile script by assigning them to it; make the assignments to the user objects at creation. This method can be accomplished through the NWADMIN utility as shown in Figure 12.11.

FIGURE 12.10

Assigning an individual user to execute a profile login script

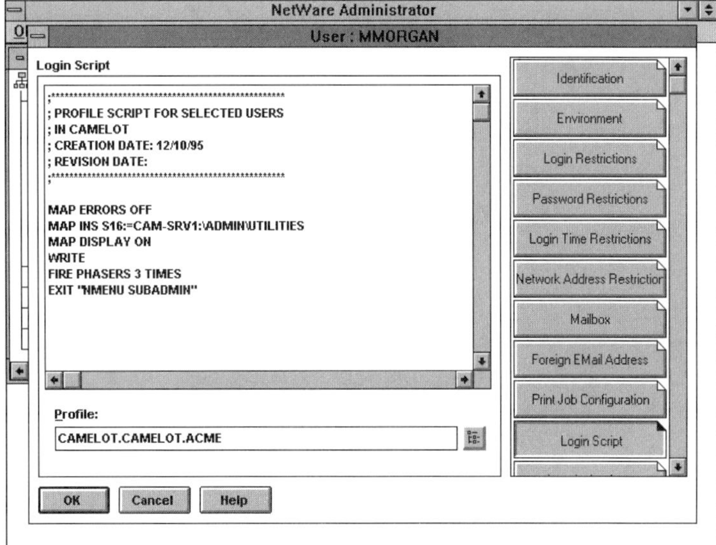

FIGURE 12.11

Creation of a profile login script through NWADMIN

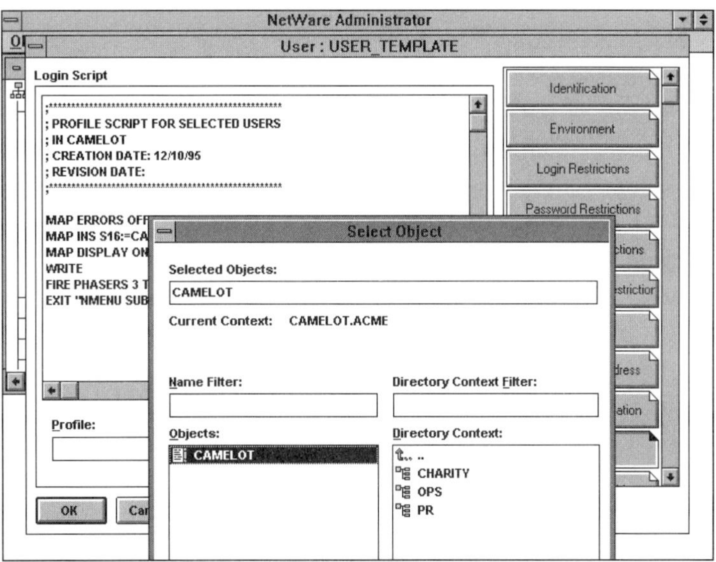

Typically, the profile login script is used as follows:

- For an entire company (if the company and tree are small)
- To create a user environment based on location
- For a special group of users

The profile script is represented by the profile object, which can be placed anywhere in the Directory tree. Using the profile login script to span all the users in the entire company is recommended only for small networks. A small network consists of fewer than ten servers and is not widely distributed over wide area links. In general, we recommend using the profile login script only across small networks. Our basis for this recommendation is that using a profile script across a very large tree is expensive in terms of the amount of NDS traffic that will be generated to locate and manage this object.

The profile login script is also used to create a user environment for a location. This method is similar to simply using a container script, except that you may want to create an environment for specific users within the container. Users that are organized around a particular site, building, or floor can have specific environment settings based on their particular needs. With the profile login script it is not necessary to create floor or building containers in your tree just to have a common login script.

For example, you have a specific set of users in a building and you want them to always map to the same e-mail and applications servers. You may also have users on one floor who want to capture to the same printers. You can accomplish these tasks using the profile login script. Using the profile login script in this fashion is considered to be a *locational* use of the script.

Figure 12.12 illustrates a profile login script being used as a locational login script that includes the containers in the ACME tree below the OU=ADMIN container in the RIO location. Specifically, OU=FAC and OU=AUDIT are in the same building and need similar environment settings.

FIGURE 12.12

The users in both the OU=FAC and OU=AUDIT containers are using the same profile login script.

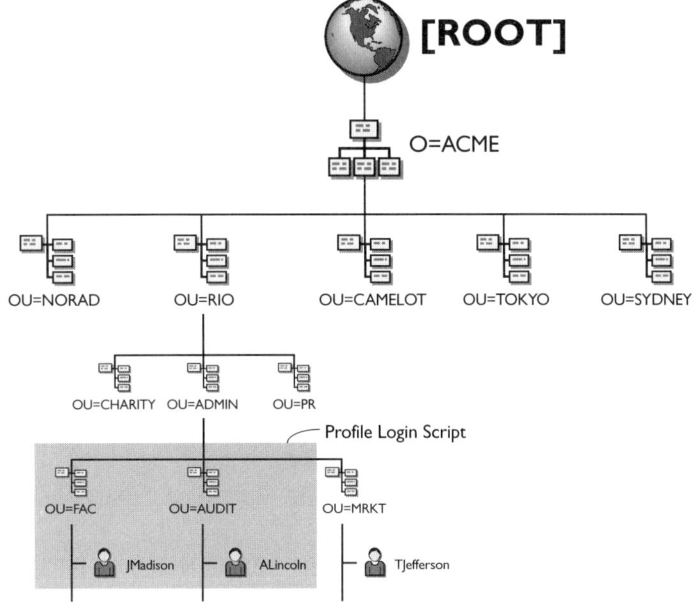

The profile login script can also serve as a special-purpose login script for a group of users. The group members can all be in the same NDS container, or they can span across a number of OUs. If the profile login script makes assignments for users within a single OU, then the profile login script is similar to a group object with its sole purpose being to execute a script.

A more powerful use of the profile login script is to span more than one NDS container. In Figure 12.13, you see three users in a different NDS container. These users are members of a special group of administrators who need specialized access to resources in the NDS tree. When each user logs in to the network, he receives the additional drive mapping to perform various job functions. Users JMadison, ALincoln, and TJefferson are each associated with the same profile login script that gives them the extra drive mappings.

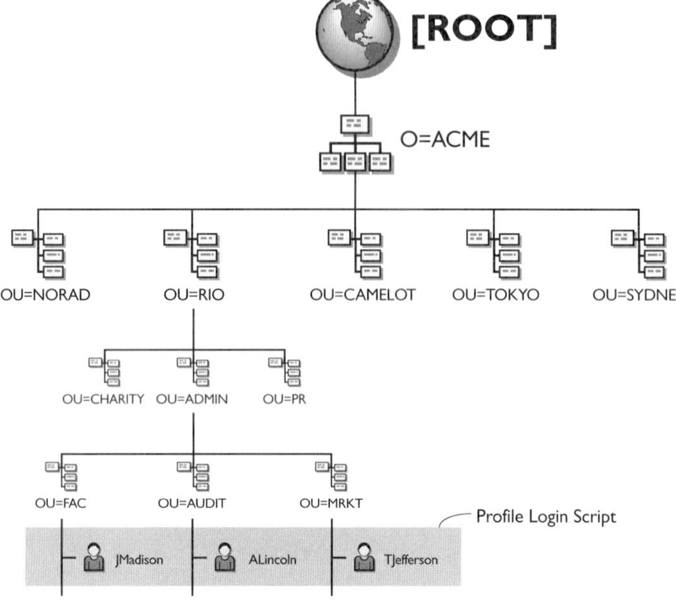

FIGURE 12.13

The users JMadison, ALincoln, and TJefferson are each associated with the same profile login script.

NDS User Login Scripts The NDS user login scripts are stored as a property in each of the user objects. Like the bindery-based user login script, the NDS user login script customizes the user environment to the specific needs of that user. All the login script commands and variables can be used in the individual user login scripts. However, we strongly recommend that user login scripts be used only when the commands in the container system login script are not adequate.

Most, if not all, scripting can be accomplished through container login scripts. For most large NetWare environments it is generally unfeasible to implement user scripts, because of the difficulty in maintaining them. As a network administrator you don't need the extra work.

If you decide to let your users have personal login scripts, keep in mind that maintaining all the users' login scripts will be a difficult task.

Here is an example of a user login script for JMadison in the OU=FAC container in the RIO location of the ACME tree. These users support their own user login scripts and do not request the assistance of a network administrator.

```
MAP DISPLAY OFF
MAP ERROR OFF
MAP F:=FAC-SRV1\SYS:USERS\JMADISON
;***** EMAIL *****
SET EMAILUSER = "JMADISON"
MAP M:=RIO-SRV1\SYS:POSTOFF
;***** PRINTERS *****
#capture L=1 Q=HP4SI-PQ1 NB NFF TI=1
;***** WINDOWS *****
MAP ROOT W:=FAC-SRV1\SYS:APPS\WINDOWS
;***** BRIEF EDITOR FLAGS *****
MAP S16:=FAC-SRV1\SYS:APPS\BRIEF
SET BPACKAGES = "c:t;h:t,r"
SET BPATH ="z:\\apps\\brief\\macros"
SET BHELP = "z:\\apps\\brief\\help"
SET BBACKUP = "c:\\backup"
SET BFLAGS = "—i70 —u300 —l200 —Dega —kl M"
SET BFILE = ""
SET BTMP = "c:\\tmp"
SET BCC = "\"cl /c %s.c\""
SET BCH = "\"cl —c —Tc %s.h\""
;***** WP *****
MAP S16:=FAC-SRV1\SYS:APPS\WP\6.1
SET WP = "/U=JM"
;***** Misc. *****
```

```
MAP S16:=FAC-SRV1\SYS:APPS\PROGRAMS\BIN

MAP
```

Default Login Scripts The default login script is executed only when the user login script does not exist. The default login script is hard-coded into the LOGIN.EXE program and tries to create enough drive mappings to the server that the user can function properly. The purpose of the default login script is to serve as backup in the absence of a user login script. The default login script will execute even if you have a container or profile login script.

If you do not want to run the default script, then you need to place the NO_DEFAULT command in the container login script or in a profile script. The container login script can also have an EXIT command at the bottom of the script. The EXIT command prevents any other login script from running, including the default login script.

The following commands are executed as the default login script:

```
WRITE "Good %GREETING_TIME, %LOGIN_NAME."

MAP DISPLAY OFF

MAP ERRORS OFF

MAP *1:=%FILE_SERVER\SYS:

MAP *1:=%FILE_SERVER\SYS:%LOGIN_NAME

IF "%1" = "SUPERVISOR" || "%1" = "ADMIN" THEN MAP
*1:=%FILE_SERVER\SYS:SYSTEM

MAP INS S1:=%FILE_SERVER\SYS:PUBLIC

MAP INS

S2:=%FILE_SERVER\SYS:PUBLIC\%MACHINE\%OS\%OS_VERSION

MAP DISPLAY ON

MAP
```

Mobile or Traveling Users

NetWare 5 lets the user log in and access resources from anywhere in the network. This feature helps you to manage the mobile or traveling user more easily. In order to completely support traveling users and their specific computing requirements, you will need to consider the following questions:

- Does the user carry a laptop computer?
- Where is the user geographically located?
- Where is the user's home office?

As users move from one location to another, they access the network and its resources differently. Knowing how each user wants to access the network will help you set up the user environments. For example, some users just want dial-in access to the network from remote locations. These locations can range from their homes, hotel rooms, and even airplanes. Typically, this type of user dials into the network from a laptop or home computer.

Some users may travel from one office to another and need full access to all the local network resources of the office they are visiting. Although the users need full access to the local resources, they still want the data from their home directory and server. Essentially, the definition of a traveling user is broken into two types: remote users and mobile users. Both types are discussed in the sections that follow.

Consulting Experience

Your approach to designing access for NetWare 5 should be to first design for the majority of the users and then design for the traveling users. In order to design the access properly, you need to know how many users in the network are traveling users. Then determine from the total number of traveling users how many are remote users and how many are true mobile users.

Remote Users

The *remote users* are the individuals who travel or carry a laptop computer and simply access the network resources through dial-in. The remote user who takes a laptop on the road is usually self-contained, meaning that the laptop computer is configured with all the necessary applications software. The user can continue to work when on the road and merely dials into the network to transfer e-mail messages, download files, or briefly access other resources.

Remote users require less design considerations for access because they will access the NDS tree only as needed for a connection to the network. Supporting remote users will not impact the design of the Directory tree or require you to create any special NDS objects. Users simply dial into specific predetermined access points in the network and use their normal NDS context or location. After the normal login to the network, the users can download files and access other necessary resources.

Some remote users dial in just to transfer their e-mail messages. Typically, a company may dedicate special phone lines for just the remote e-mail users. These lines may have their own security and access method and would not affect the Directory tree access.

If a remote user travels to another office and plugs his or her laptop computer into the network and wants access to all the local resources, that user has really become a mobile user. The design considerations for the mobile users are addressed in the following section.

Mobile Users

The *mobile users* are individuals who travel from one office to another or from one computer to another. They expect full access to all the local network resources of the office they are visiting while maintaining the ability to access data from their home server. The mobile user may not carry around a computer (laptop) but expects to have a computer available at the other site. Some mobile users decide to carry laptop computers and plug them into the network when they arrive. Thus, the best definition of a mobile user is an individual who uses a computer on the network from a location that is away from his or her home office.

Whether the user travels thousands of miles or across the building, the issues are the same for mobile users. The user wants access to the network applications, such as word processing, spreadsheets, e-mail, and printing from the local servers, but also wants to retrieve the data from his or her home server. The user wants these capabilities to be as seamless as possible.

In order to support the needs of the mobile user, you need to answer the following questions:

- Where is the user geographically located?
- Where is the user's home office?

There are several mechanisms in NetWare 5 to help you answer each of these questions. These mechanisms include the NDS name context, alias objects, configuration files, login scripts, login script variables, and environment variables.

NDS Name Context The *name context* in NDS helps you determine where in the NDS tree the user belongs. The name context is important because NDS requires it for every user logging into the network. The context can be set in the user's NET.CFG file or by typing the user's full name during login as well. While a mobile user's physical location may change, his or her context will remain constant.

If the mobile user has traveled without a laptop computer, that user expects to use any available computer in the office he or she is visiting and log into the network. The main issue with this scenario is how to determine the user's name context for login purposes. There are several ways to work around this problem:

Consulting Experience

Users who carry laptop computers to a new location are not considered mobile users if they do not need access to the local network resources. If the users are content to access their home resources across the network, then they are simply remote users. There are no special design considerations for remote users. Remember, NetWare 5 enables the users to log in from anywhere on the network. A user simply looks for a network connection and logs into the server at his or her home office.

- Manually enter the context at the computer console before login.
- Create alias objects that point to the user in his or her normal context.
- Set the name context of the alias in the workstation configuration file.

Manually Changing the NDS Name Context The first option involves the mobile user manually entering his or her name context into the computer he or she is using. This option assumes that the user understands how to use the proper utilities and is familiar with their complete context in the NDS tree. The CX utility is used to set the user's context before login.

For example, the user JMadison in the ACME tree as shown in Figure 12.14 would need to set his or her name context by typing the following:

```
CX .FAC.ADMIN.RIO.ACME
```

FIGURE 12.14

The name context for the user JMadison in the ACME tree

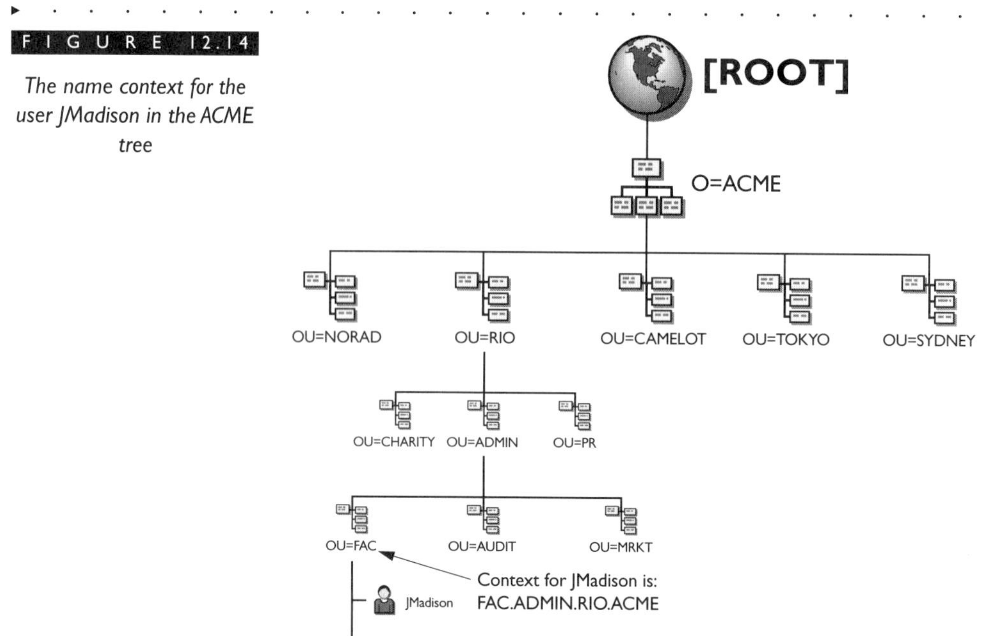

Notice the leading period in the CX command line. The leading period tells the utility that this is a distinguished name and to start at the [ROOT] object when setting the name context. This is a little easier than trying to figure out where your current context is set in the tree.

The CX utility is stored in the LOGIN subdirectory on the server. The user must have a connection to a server and be in the directory (typically the F: drive) or type the path before running this utility.

Using an Alias Object to Help Set the Name Context The second option that could help set the name context is the use of alias objects. If you have a small number of mobile users, you can create an alias object below the O=Organization for each mobile user. The alias would point to the user's primary object in the appropriate container.

The value of this strategy is that it creates a simple context for each of the mobile users. The users do not need to know where the context is or even how to set it. The users would simply enter the name of the alias object during the login process.

For example, an alias object has been created for the user JMadison in the ACME tree. Figure 12.15 shows that the alias object called JMADISON was created directly in the O=ACME container. The alias object points to the real object in the OU=FAC in the RIO location. When the user JMadison wants to log into the network from any site, he or she uses the name of the alias object as follows:

```
LOGIN .JMADISON.ACME
```

Notice the leading period in the LOGIN command line before the name of the alias object. The leading period instructs the utility to start at the [ROOT] object when looking for the alias object.

This method of using the alias object to support the mobile users works well if you have a small number of mobile users at your site. Setting up an alias object for each individual mobile user is feasible if the total number is small. This method may not work if your mobile user population is high. You will need to determine how many alias objects you can manage.

FIGURE 12.15

An alias object called JMADISON has been created under the O=ACME container.

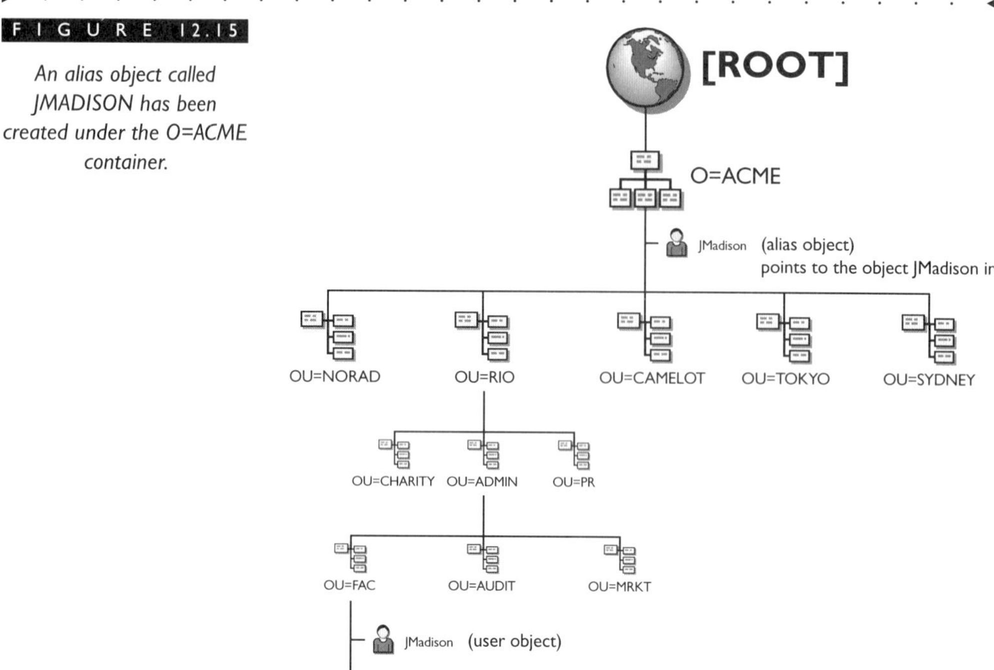

TIP

You can also use third-party utilities that search the tree for a user object and set the appropriate context for your mobile user. You should consider these types of utilities when you have many mobile users.

Using the Configuration Files to Set the Name Context The name context for the user can be set using the standard workstation configuration file called NET.CFG. The NET.CFG file is read during the loading of the workstation client. What follows is an example of setting the name context for the user JMadison in the ACME tree. Within the NET.CFG file a section called the NetWare DOS Requester holds the NAME CONTEXT = "OU.FAC.OU=ADMIN.OU=RIO.O= ACME." Users traveling to different locations with their own notebooks or laptops will typically have the NET.CFG file set already. When they arrive on site and connect to the network, their name context is resolved from the setting in the NET.CFG file on the laptop.

```
Link Support
   MemPool 6192
   Buffers 10 1580
   MAX STACKS 8
Link Driver NE2000
   INT 5
   PORT 300
   MEM D0000
   FRAME Ethernet_802.2
NetWare DOS Requester
   NAME CONTEXT = "OU=FAC.OU=ADMIN.OU=RIO.O=ACME"
   PREFERRED SERVER = FAC-SRV1
   FIRST NETWORK DRIVE = F
   NETWARE PROTOCOL = NDS,BIND
   SHOW DOTS = ON
   USE DEFAULTS = ON
   PB BUFFERS = 10
```

You can use the PREFERRED SERVER variable in the NET.CFG file (in the NetWare DOS Requester section) or PREFERRED SERVER setting in the Windows Registry to connect the mobile user to the server that has this user's bindery context. If you force the user to connect to the proper server using the PREFERRED SERVER variable, the user can log in using bindery services. This enables users running the older NETX.EXE workstation client to participate in mobile computing if needed. For example, in the previous NET.CFG file, the variable is set as PREFERRED SERVER = FAC-SRV1. This enables the user JMadison to log in and access the server using bindery services if he is still running NETX.EXE.

Login Scripts for Mobile Users

The two mechanisms for creating a mobile user login script are the login script variables and an environment variable that can be called NW_SITE.

What follows is an example of a container login script for mobile users. In this example, we have defined a mobile script that will allow the user to easily log into the network from any of the five major sites shown in the ACME tree. The script demonstrates how a user is mapped to the local e-mail server and the local application server. This login script is used as a container login script and also requires the NW_SITE DOS environment variable to be set on the user's workstation in the CONFIG.SYS file.

```
;*********************************************************
; MOBILE CONTAINER LOGIN SCRIPT
; for OU=FAC.OU=ADMIN.OU=RIO.O=ACME
; Creation Date: 03/18/98
; Revisions:
;*********************************************************
REM Do not execute default script
NO_DEFAULT
Write "Good %GREETING_TIME, %LOGIN_NAME"
REM Map public drive to local server
MAP S16:=SYS:\PUBLIC
REM Map F drive to the user's home server
MAP F:="HOME_DIRECTORY"
REM Map NetWare Drives according to the NW_SITE variable

IF <NW_SITE> == "NORAD" THEN BEGIN
     MAP ROOT M:= NOR-SRV1\SYS:MAIL
     MAP ROOT W:= NOR-SRV1\SYS:APPS\WP
```

```
    MAP ROOT Q:= NOR-SRV1\SYS:APPS\QPRO
    END
IF <NW_SITE> == "RIO" THEN BEGIN
    MAP ROOT M:= RIO-SRV1\SYS:MAIL
    MAP ROOT W:= RIO-SRV1\SYS:APPS\WP
    MAP ROOT Q:= RIO-SRV1\SYS:APPS\QPRO
    END
IF <NW_SITE> == "CAMELOT" THEN BEGIN
    MAP ROOT M:= CAM-SRV1\SYS:MAIL
    MAP ROOT W:= CAM-SRV1\SYS:APPS\WP
    MAP ROOT Q:= CAM-SRV1\SYS:APPS\QPRO
    END
IF <NW_SITE> == "TOKYO" THEN BEGIN
    MAP ROOT M:= TOK-SRV1\SYS:MAIL
    MAP ROOT W:= TOK-SRV1\SYS:APPS\WP
    MAP ROOT Q:= TOK-SRV1\SYS:APPS\QPRO
    END
IF <NW_SITE> == "SYDNEY" THEN BEGIN
    MAP ROOT M:= SYD-SRV1\SYS:MAIL
    MAP ROOT W:= SYD-SRV1\SYS:APPS\WP
    MAP ROOT Q:= SYD-SRV1\SYS:APPS\QPRO
    END
EXIT
```

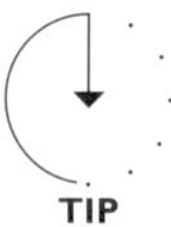

TIP

In the previous script you can specify the actual NDS volume object names instead of the server names for mapping drives. The drives M and W in our example default to searching in the bindery, which relies on SAP because we do not specify the NDS volume object names in the login script.

A Container Script Using Additional SET Parameters

For even greater flexibility you can use the %NETWORK and %NETWORK_ADDRESS variables to point the user to the nearest application server or printer in your company. This variable is used in the script because all resources that reside on the network have a network address. This basic script makes use of the user's context and the network context. Therefore, you can assign a resource such as an application server to every network. When users execute their container login scripts, you can use the %NETWORK_ADDRESS variable to determine their location and "map" them to the closest application server. What follows is a sample container login script emphasizing this method.

```
;*****************************************************

; MOBILE CONTAINER LOGIN SCRIPT

; for OU=FAC.OU=ADMIN.OU=RIO.O=ACME

; Creation Date: 03/18/98

; Sample login script for nearest Application Server

; Revisions:


;*****************************************************

; Login script for users physically located in the office

IF NETWORK_ADDRESS ="0101C9DA"

      SET LOCATION= "ATLANTA OFFICE"

      SET APPSRV =  "ATL-APP-1"

      SET DEFPRNT = \\ATL-PS-1\HP4SI-Q
```

```
        GOTO COMMON
END
; Start script for users from same office on the road
IF NETWORK_ADDRESS<>"0101C9DA" THEN BEGIN
        INCLUDE .TRAVEL.NOVELL
        GOTO COMMON
END
; Start Common info for all users
COMMON:
        WRITE "SUBNET: %NETWORK_ADDRESS"
        WRITE "LOCATION: %<LOCATION>"
        WRITE "APP SERVER: %<APPSRV>"
        WRITE "DEFAULT PRINTER: %<DEFPRNT>"
        MAP INS S1:="%FILE_SERVER\SYS:PUBLIC"
        MAP H:="%HOME_DIRECTORY"
        WRITE ""
END
EXIT
EXIT
```

As you can tell in the previous example, if a user is away from his or her home office the network number will be different. This implies that you must maintain a network number for each office or segment in the login script. These numbers (hopefully) remain static, so this shouldn't present much of an administrative problem for you. You would duplicate the preceding script for each location by changing the network address for each location.

Next, you need to create the Profile script that we have called TRAVEL.PROFILE. An example of this script is shown here:

```
;TRAVEL PROFILE

; NOTE: The administrator must configure this file. For best
performance configure this script so that the most frequently
accessed network addresses are at the top of this list where
they will be found first. This form is parsed from top to
bottom until the correct network number is found. For
example, if you have many users going to the same office on
business, then you should have the network address for that
office at the top of the list of network addresses.


START:

;************************************************************
****

IIF NETWORK_ADDRESS ="0101D9CB" THEN BEGIN

      SET LOCATION = "NEW YORK OFFICE"

      SET APPSRV = "NYC-APP-1"

      SET DEFPRNT = \\NYC-PS-1\HP4SI-Q

      GOTO EXIT

END

;************************************************************
****

IF NETWORK ADDRESS = "0101D9CD" THEN BEGIN

      SET LOCATION = "LOS ANGELES"

      SET APPSRV = "LAX-APP-2"

      SET DEFPRNT = \\LAX-PS-2\HP5S1-Q

      GOTO EXIT

END
```

```
: NOTE: CONTINUE THIS SEQUENCE FOR EACH NETWORK ADDRESS
REMEMBERING TO PLACE THE MOST WIDELY USED LOCATIONS FIRST IN
YOUR LIST.

; ERROR GENERATION

Write "Contact your network administrator to add the
following network address to the Travel Profile Script."

Write "Network = %NETWORK_ADDRESS"

PAUSE

GOTO ERROR1

END

:**********************************************************

ERROR1

      Write "Has the administrator updated the script?"

      GOTO START

END

EXIT:

EXIT
```

NetWare Login Command Switches

Table 12.1 lists the NetWare general login command switches and their syntaxes. Keep in mind that these command switches are for the DOS-based LOGIN.EXE only and do not apply to the Windows-based graphical login.

TABLE 12.1

NetWare Login Command Switches

COMMAND	COMMAND SYNTAX	PURPOSE
General Login Commands	LOGIN [File Server\] username [options]	Logs clients into a NetWare server with a bindery or NDS connection.
/NS (No Script option)	LOGIN /NS	Executes a login without a login script.
/CLS (Clear Screen option)	LOGIN /CLS	Clears screen before execution of the login script.
/S (Script option)	LOGIN /S filename or LOGIN /S object name	Executes a login script contained in the text filename or NDS object name.
/B (Bindery option)	LOGIN /B	Logs into a server using bindery services.
/TR (Tree option)	LOGIN /TR treename	Specifies a certain NDS tree by its tree name for logging in.
/SWAP	LOGIN /SWAP	Swaps LOGIN.EXE into extended RAM if you use external commands from inside the login script.
/? (help option)	LOGIN /?	Provides a help screen.

Login Script Commands

Many login script commands can be used in any of the login scripts. Table 12.2 lists each login script command and its function.

TABLE 12.2 *Login Script Commands*

COMMAND	FUNCTION
ATTACH	The ATTACH command allows you to attach workstations to other NetWare servers. The ATTACH command only provides a bindery services connection to the selected server. This command enables you to have login scripts that are compatible and coexist with previous versions of NetWare (specifically NetWare 2 and NetWare 3). This command no longer works on the command line for NetWare 5 but is still provided in login scripts as a means of backward compatibility with NetWare 3 scripts that may be migrated into NetWare 5.
BREAK	The BREAK command has two settings, either ON or OFF. The ON setting enables you to execute your login scripts by pressing Ctrl+C or Ctrl+Break. The default setting is always OFF.
# CHARACTER	The # character provides external program execution. For example, to execute the capture program from within a login script, type: #CAPTURE L=1 Q=HP4SI NB NFF TI=1 You can enter a complete pathname/ filename for the external program or make sure that the proper drive mapping and search drives have been set. The # character must be the first character on the line.
CLS	The CLS command clears the workstation screen or display. It is functionally similar to the CLS command that you can execute from DOS.
COMSPEC	The COMSPEC command specifies the subdirectory where DOS should load the command line processor called COMMAND.COM.

Continued

TABLE 12.2

Continued

COMMAND	FUNCTION
CONTEXT	The CONTEXT command is a smaller version of the CX.EXE command line utility that enables you to set the workstation context in the NDS tree. An example of using the CONTEXT command is as follows: CONTEXT .R&D.NORAD.ACME
DISPLAY	The DISPLAY command enables you to show the contents of any file on the screen. The following syntax is used: DISPLAY [pathname]\filename The difference between this command and the DISPLAY command discussed later in this section is that this command shows all the characters in the file including control codes and ESC sequences.
DOS BREAK	The DOS BREAK command has two settings, either ON or OFF. The ON setting enables you to terminate any DOS program that has been executed from the login script by pressing Ctrl+C or Ctrl+Break. The difference between this command and the BREAK command is that this command enables Ctrl+Breakchecking for DOS. The BREAK command checks only Ctrl+Break within the login script itself.
DOS SET, TEMP SET, or SET	These commands can be used to establish the DOS environment variables for the workstation and user. The syntax is as follows: [OPTION] [DOS] SET name = "value" The [OPTION] parameter can be used or replaced with an optional keyword. The keywords are TEMP, TEMPORARY, and LOCAL, which means that the variable is set only during the processing of the login script. The variable is not set in DOS.
DOS VERIFY	The DOS VERIFY command has two settings, either ON or OFF. The ON setting means that the data copied to the local drive is written without errors.

COMMAND	FUNCTION
DRIVE	The DRIVE command specifies which network drive will be used as the default drive.
EXIT	The EXIT command tells the login script to terminate the processing of the login script and exit immediately. You can use the EXIT command in conjunction with the following program name: EXIT [filename] The login script passes control to the program specified. You should place the EXIT command statement as the last line in the individual login script. The EXIT command can be placed in system or container login scripts to guarantee that no individual user login scripts are executed.
FDISPLAY	The FDISPLAY command shows the contents of the specified text file on the screen. The following syntax is used: FDISPLAY [pathname]\filename Only the text or characters in the file are displayed. The control characters in the file are not shown.
FIRE PHASERS	The FIRE PHASERS command produces blasts that sound like you are firing a toy weapon. You can fire 1 to 9 phasers as dictated in the following syntax: FIRE PHASERS *n* TIMES (where *n* is the number of times) You typically use this command for special effects during the login process.
GOTO	The GOTO command enables you to program the login script and jump or repeat specific locations in the login script. You can place labels in the login script to control the GOTO statements.

Continued

TABLE 12.2 *Continued*

COMMAND	FUNCTION
IF . . . THEN . . . ELSE	The IF . . . THEN . . . ELSE command enables you to build conditional logic into the login scripts. This command lets you execute certain portions of the login scripts conditionally.
INCLUDE	The INCLUDE command enables you to direct the login script to specific files that you have predefined. The following syntax is used: INCLUDE [pathname]\filename The contents of the file specified in the INCLUDE statement are the next lines processed in the script. After the file has been processed, control is returned to the stat ement immediately following the INCLUDE statement in your login script.
LASTLOGINTIME	The LASTLOGINTIME command checks or displays the last date and time of login.
MACHINE	The MACHINE command sets the hardware machine type. This variable receives its value from the LONG MACHINE TYPE variable in the NET.CFG. The default value is IBM_PC.
MAP and MAP DISPLAY	The MAP command is equivalent to the MAP.EXE program. The command enables you to establish network drive mapping. The MAP DISPLAY command can be set to either ON or OFF. The ON setting shows all the drive mapping during the login process. The default is ON. The OFF setting will not show the drive mapping during the login procedure.
NO_DEFAULT	The NO_DEFAULT command disables the execution of the default login script, which is part of the LOGIN.EXE program. Disabling the default login script can be useful when you want to control all the drive mapping for the user. This includes the drive mapping to the SYS:PUBLIC subdirectory.

COMMAND	FUNCTION
PAUSE or WAIT	The PAUSE or WAIT commands cause the login script to stop execution until a key is pressed. This command permits long messages to be read without scrolling off the screen. This command can also be helpful when debugging the login script.
PCCOMPATIBLE	The PCCOMPATIBLE command indicates that the workstation hardware is compatible with an IBM PC. For some workstations, if you do not use this command, then some NetWare utilities such as NETADMIN and FILER will not work.
REMARK or REM	The REMARK command documents the lines or place comments in the login script file. The use of comments will always improve the readability and maintenance of the scripts. To place comments in the login scripts the following syntax is used: REM [text] or * text or ; text
WRITE	The WRITE command displays text messages to the workstation screen during the login process. The following syntax is used: WRITE [text] You can use the semicolon (;) to join together text messages.

Login Variables

NetWare 5 has always had the capability to use login variables in login scripts to help you manage the login scripts and make them more efficient and flexible. Table 12.3 lists the login script variables and their definitions that can be used to enhance your login scripts. These variables can be used in the login script to help you do the following:

- Build conditional statements
- Provide date and time functions
- Establish DOS environment and workstation settings
- Provide NDS properties to the user

TABLE 12.3

Conditional Statement Login Script Variables

VARIABLE	FUNCTION
%ACCESS_SERVER	Displays or checks if the access server is functional (TRUE=functional, FALSE=not functional).
%ERROR_LEVEL	Displays or checks the DOS error level. A value of 0 indicates that no DOS errors have occurred. For example, this variable can be used to see if a drive mapping was successful.
%MEMBER OF "group"	Tests to see whether user is a member of the "group." Returns TRUE or FALSE.
%NOT MEMBER OF "group"	Returns TRUE if the user is *not* a member of the "group."

Most of the variables can be displayed using the WRITE login script command preceding the variable. There are also some examples provided in the use of these variables. In Table 12.3, note that some of the variables have underscores in them and some do not. This is perhaps due to inconsistencies in coding these parameters.

Table 12.4 lists the date and time login variables.

TABLE 12.4

Date and Time Login Script Variables

VARIABLE	FUNCTION
%AM_PM	Displays time as day or night, using A.M. or P.M.
%DAY	Displays the current day value ranging from 01 to 31.
%DAY_OF_WEEK	Displays the written day of the week.

VARIABLE	FUNCTION
%GREETING_TIME	Displays the time of day as morning, afternoon, or evening.
%HOUR	Displays the time of day in hours ranging from 1 to 12.
%HOUR24	Displays the hour in 24-hour time ranging from 00 to 23.
%MINUTE	Displays the minutes ranging from 00 to 59.
%MONTH	Displays the month (from 01 to 12).
%MONTH_NAME	Displays the name of the month.
%NDAY_OF_WEEK	Displays the number of the week day.
%SECOND	Displays the seconds ranging from 00 to 59.
%SHORT_YEAR	Displays the year in short format (92, 93, 94, 95, 96, 97, and so on).
%YEAR	Displays the year in full format (1992, 1993, and so on).

Any DOS environment variable can be used in a login script if you place angle brackets (< and >) around the variable. A common example of a DOS variable used in login scripts is as follows:

```
<COMSPEC>
```

In order to use a DOS environment variable with login script commands, you need to add a percent sign (%) in front of the variable. For example, to map a drive to the COMSPEC DOS environment variable type this:

```
MAP S16:=%<COMSPEC>
```

The list of DOS environment and workstation variables in Table 12.5 will help to set up the workstation for the specific network users. Some variables have more than one keyword, which is shown in parentheses.

TABLE 12.5

DOS Environment and Workstation Variables

VARIABLE	FUNCTION
%LAST_NAME	Displays the user's last name (surname) in Novell Directory Services, or full login name in bindery-based NetWare. This value returns the same result as the SURNAME variable in the user properties.
%LOGIN_ALIAS_CONTEXT	Displays the context of the alias object the user logged in with. This variable is valid only with NDS.
%LOGIN_CONTEXT	Displays the context for the user. Returns the context where the user exists in the NDS tree. This variable works only with NetWare 5.
%LOGIN_NAME	Displays the user's login name. This returns the same result as the CN variable in the user property list, although CN is multivalued.
%MACHINE	Displays the machine type of a workstation (IBM_PC, and so on).
%NEW_MAIL	Displays the status of the variable.
%OS	Displays the type of operating system on the workstation (MSDOS, OS2, and so on).
%OS_VERSION	Displays the operating system version on the workstation (3.30, and so on).
%P_STATION (PHYSICAL_STATION)	The workstation's node number is shown as a 12-digit hexadecimal.
%PASSWORD_EXPIRES	Displays the number of days before the user password will expire.
%REQUESTER_VERSION	(optional names: NETWARE_REQUESTER, REQUESTER) Displays the version of the VLM requester.
%REQUESTER_CONTEXT	Displays the context that is found in the workstation's NET.CFG file at the time of login.

VARIABLE	FUNCTION
%SHELL_TYPE (SHELL_VERSION)	Displays the version of the workstation's DOS shell (1.02, and so on); supports NetWare 2 and 3 shells and NetWare 4 Requester for DOS.
%STATION (CONNECTION)	Displays the workstation address for that user.

NetWare 5 extends the list of login variables, as shown in Table 12.6, through the use of the user properties found in NDS. If the property includes a space, enclose the name in quotation marks or replace the spaces with an underscore.

TABLE 12.6

NDS User Properties Variables

VARIABLE	FUNCTION
%ACCOUNT_BALANCE	Displays account balance information if being used.
%ALLOW UNLIMITED CREDIT	Displays whether unlimited credit has been assigned for that user. The value returned is "Y" or "N."
%BACKLINK	Established for any user object in which there is an associated external reference on a different server.
%BINDERY PROPERTY	Used to emulate the bindery properties that are not represented by the other user properties.
%CN	Displays the login name of the user who logs in to the network.
%DESCRIPTION	Displays any value contained in the description property for the user.
%EMAIL ADDRESS	Displays the first value in the e-mail address property for the user.
%EQUIVALENT TO ME	Displays only the first value in the list.
%FACSIMILE TELEPHONE NUMBER	Displays the first number in the fax number property for the user.

Continued

TABLE 12.6

Continued

VARIABLE	FUNCTION
%FULL NAME	Displays the user's full name value. This value is the property stored in NDS and the bindery if the server is bindery-based NetWare. Spaces are replaced with underscores.
%GROUP MEMBERSHIP	Displays the values of the membership attributes.
%HOME DIRECTORY	Displays the complete path for the home directory property set for the user who has logged in.
%INITIALS	Displays the value of the user's middle initial property.
%L	Displays the first value of the location property for the user.
%LANGUAGE	Displays the current language being used by the user.
%LOCKED BY INTRUDER	Displays the status of the locked by intruder property. The value returned is "Y" for yes or "N" for no.
%LOGIN DISABLED	Displays the account disable status. The value returned is "Y" for yes or "N" for no.
%LOGIN GRACE LIMIT	Displays the value of the login grace limit property.
%LOGIN GRACE REMAINING	Displays the number of remaining grace logins for the user.
%LOGIN INTRUDER ATTEMPTS	Displays the number of incorrect login attempts for the user.
%LOGIN MAXIMUM SIMULTANEOUS	Displays the value of the maximum simultaneous connections for the user.
%LOGIN TIME	Displays both the date and time of the login time for the user.
%MAILBOX ID	Displays the mailbox ID for the user.

VARIABLE	FUNCTION
%MAILBOX LOCATION	Displays the mailbox location for the user. MHS can, but does not have to, be installed in order to have a value for the mailbox location.
%MESSAGE SERVER	Displays the default server or message server name.
%MINIMUM ACCOUNT BALANCE	Displays the value of the minimum account balance or low balance limit.
%NETWORK ADDRESS	Displays the physical network address, node, and socket number for the workstation.
%OBJECT CLASS	Displays the base class for the user object.
%OU	Shows the first value defined in the Department list for the user.
%PASSWORD ALLOW CHANGE	Shows the value of this user property "Y" or "N."
%PASSWORD EXPIRATION INTERVAL	Displays the time in total seconds before the user password will expire.
%PASSWORD MINIMUM LENGTH	Displays the minimum password length setting for the user.
%PASSWORD REQUIRED	Displays the value of the password required. Displays or returns "Y" or "N."
%PASSWORD UNIQUE REQUIRED	Displays the property value of unique password required. Displays or returns "Y" or "N."
%PHYSICAL DELIVERY OFFICE NAME	Displays the value of the city property for the user.
%POSTAL ADDRESS	Displays the value of the user's postal address property, if any.
%POSTAL CODE	Displays the value of the user's postal zip code, if any.
%POSTAL OFFICE BOX	Displays the user's postal office box value, if any.

Continued

TABLE 12.6

Continued

VARIABLE	FUNCTION
%PROFILE	Displays the name of the profile object if the user is associated with a profile.
%REVISION	Displays the value of the revision property for the user. The revision increments each time the user is accessed.
%S	Displays the value of the state or province property for the user.
%SA	Displays the value of the street address for the user.
%SECURITY EQUALS	Displays security equivalence assignments made for that user. Only displays the first value in the list.
%SEE ALSO	Displays the first value in the see also property for the user.
%SERVER HOLDS	Displays the number of accounting charges pending while the server performs a chargeable action.
%SURNAME (LAST_NAME)	Displays the user's surname property value, if any — the user's last name (surname) in NetWare Directory Services, or full login name in bindery-based NetWare.
%TELEPHONE NUMBER	Shows the user's phone entered in his phone number property. Only displays the first value in the list.
%TITLE	Displays the title for the user if one has been entered as a user property. Only shows the first value in the list.
%UID	Displays a unique user ID assigned to the user for use by UNIX clients.

Additional Login Scripts for Your Desktops

The following scripts provide a sample script for Windows 95, Windows NT, and mixed environments.

LOGIN Script Information for Windows 95

The file locations are as follows:

NET$LOG.DAT	SYS:PUBLIC
***.BAT files**	SYS:PUBLIC\CLIENT\WIN95\IBM_ENU
***.REG files**	SYS:PUBLIC\CLIENT\WIN95\IBM_ENU

The *.BAT and *.REG files will reflect the user location in the NDS tree to set up the proper context on the workstation. If you place the client update information at the end of the login script, you will not affect any other clients using that script provided you have not made any typing errors. For this reason you may want to create a TESTC32 user ID and use the "%LOGIN_NAME" variable. Once the script is tested, you may then use "IF MEMBER OF GROUP" to automate multiple client upgrades without having to touch the workstations.

NET$LOG.DAT

```
Write "Good %GREETING_TIME, %FULL_NAME"

IF "%LOGIN_NAME" = "TESTC32" THEN GOTO UPDATE

IF MEMBER OF GROUP "TESTC32" THEN GOTO UPDATE

Write "This is the Bindery Login Script"

END

EXIT

UPDATE:

Write "This will update the MS Client to Client 32"

IF "%LOGIN_NAME" = "TESTC32" BEGIN

IF MEMBER OF "GROUP1" THEN BEGIN
```

```
MAP Y:=DEMOSRVR\SYS:PUBLIC\CLIENT\WIN95\IBM_ENU
DRIVE Y:
EXIT "GROUP1.BAT"
END
IF MEMBER OF "GROUP2" THEN BEGIN
MAP Y:=DEMOSRVR\SYS:PUBLIC\CLIENT\WIN95\IBM_ENU
DRIVE Y:
EXIT "GROUP2.BAT"
END
```

GROUP1.BAT

```
SETUP.EXE /ACU /N
/U:Y:DEMOSRVR\SYS:PUBLIC\CLIENT\WIN95\IBM_ENU\GROUP1.TXT
REGEDIT /S GROUP1.REG
```

GROUP1.REG

```
REGEDIT4
[HKEY_LOCAL_MACHINE\Network\Novell\System Config\Network
Provider\Graphical Login]
"Tree Login"=dword:00000001
"Server Login"=dword:00000000
"Connection Tab"=dword:00000001
"Bindery Connections"=dword:00000000
"Clear Connections"=dword:00000001
"Script Tab"=dword:00000000
"Display Results"=dword:00000001
"Close Results"=dword:00000001
```

```
"Login Script"=dword:00000001

"Script Variable Tab"=dword:00000000

"Save On Exit"=dword:00000000

[HKEY_LOCAL_MACHINE\Network\Novell\System Config\Network
Provider\Graphical Login\Scripts]

[HKEY_LOCAL_MACHINE\Network\Novell\System Config\Network
Provider\Graphical Login\Scripts\1]

@=""

[HKEY_LOCAL_MACHINE\Network\Novell\System Config\Network
Provider\Graphical Login\Profiles]

[HKEY_LOCAL_MACHINE\Network\Novell\System Config\Network
Provider\Graphical Login\Profiles\1]

@=""

[HKEY_LOCAL_MACHINE\Network\Novell\System Config\Network
Provider\Graphical Login\Variables]

[HKEY_LOCAL_MACHINE\Network\Novell\System Config\Network
Provider\Graphical Login\Variables\2]

@=""

[HKEY_LOCAL_MACHINE\Network\Novell\System Config\Network
Provider\Graphical Login\Variables\3]

@=""

[HKEY_LOCAL_MACHINE\Network\Novell\System Config\Network
Provider\Graphical Login\Variables\4]

@=""

[HKEY_LOCAL_MACHINE\Network\Novell\System Config\Network
Provider\Graphical Login\Variables\5]

@=""
```

```
[HKEY_LOCAL_MACHINE\Network\Novell\System Config\Network
Provider\Graphical Login\NWLGE]

[HKEY_LOCAL_MACHINE\Network\Novell\System Config\Network
Provider\Graphical Login\NWLGE\Z XContext]

"LoginExtType"=hex:01,80,00,00

"LoginExtName"="LGNCON32.DLL"

"LoginExtDesc"="Login Extension Contextless Login"

"AllowWild"=hex:00,00,00,00

"RunContext"=hex:00,00,00,00

[HKEY_LOCAL_MACHINE\Network\Novell\System Config\Network
Provider\Graphical Login\Results Pos]

"Left"=dword:0000014f

"Top"=dword:0000011d

"Right"=dword:000002b0

"Bottom"=dword:000001e1

"XRes"=dword:00000400

"YRes"=dword:00000300

"State"=dword:00000000

[HKEY_LOCAL_MACHINE\Network\Novell\System Config\Network
Provider\Graphical Login\Trees]

[HKEY_LOCAL_MACHINE\Network\Novell\System Config\Network
Provider\Graphical Login\Trees\2]

@="TREE_NAME"

[HKEY_LOCAL_MACHINE\Network\Novell\System Config\Network
Provider\Graphical Login\Context]

[HKEY_LOCAL_MACHINE\Network\Novell\System Config\Network
Provider\Graphical Login\Context\2]
```

```
@="GROUP1.DALLAS.NOVELL"

[HKEY_LOCAL_MACHINE\Network\Novell\System Config\NetWare DOS
Requester]

[HKEY_LOCAL_MACHINE\Network\Novell\System Config\NetWare DOS
Requester\Preferred Server]

"0"=""

[HKEY_LOCAL_MACHINE\Network\Novell\System Config\NetWare DOS
Requester\First Network Drive]

"0"="F"

[HKEY_LOCAL_MACHINE\Network\Novell\System Config\NetWare DOS
Requester\module]

@="C:\\NOVELL\\CLIENT32\\CLIENT32.NLM"

[HKEY_LOCAL_MACHINE\Network\Novell\System Config\NetWare DOS
Requester\init order]

@="A0010100"

[HKEY_LOCAL_MACHINE\Network\Novell\System Config\NetWare DOS
Requester\Preferred Tree]

"0"="TREE_NAME"

[HKEY_LOCAL_MACHINE\Network\Novell\System Config\NetWare DOS
Requester\Preferred Tree\Trees]

"TREE_NAME"="GROUP1.DALLAS.NOVELL"

[HKEY_LOCAL_MACHINE\Network\Novell\System Config\NetWare DOS
Requester\Name Context]

"0"="GROUP1.DALLAS.NOVELL"

[HKEY_CURRENT_USER\InstallLocationsMRU]

"a"="\\\\DEMOSRVR\\SYS\\DESKTOPS\\WIN95\\"

"MRUList"="a"

[HKEY_USERS\.Default\InstallLocationsMRU]
```

```
"a"="\\\\DEMOSRVR\\SYS\\DESKTOPS\\WIN95\\"
"MRUList"="a"
```

These last six lines on this page were added simply to assist in pointing the desktop machines to a location where the Windows 95 install files (*.CAB) are located.

An NDS Container Login Script for Windows 95 Clients

After Client 32 is installed, the container login scripts will need to be updated to reflect the information these clients were getting in the NET$LOG.DAT file. Also, any necessary changes to a Windows 95 Client 32 configuration can be made via the container login script or a profile login script. To do this, simply add these lines to the end of the login script:

```
REM The Novell Login Interpreter will read the %OS variable
and the Microsoft interpreter will not
REM and continue to the next line
IF "%OS" = "WIN95" THEN
   IF ERRORLEVEL = "0"
      WRITE "You are currently using Novell Client 32 for
Windows 95"
      ELSE
         GOTO NOC32
      END
      GOTO WIN95C32
END

NOC32:
IF <OS> ="WIN95" THEN
   IF ERRORLEVEL = "0"
```

```
         WRITE "You are currently using Microsoft Client for
Novell Networks"
         ELSE
            GOTO NOT95
         END
      GOTO MAPLE
END

WIN95C32:
   REM This Win95 client is currently using Client 32 and
will automatically update if needed
   REM If the client is up to date no changes are made. To
make a change edit the
   REM  NWSETUP.INI and change the version number. This file
is located in the
   REM SYS:PUBLIC\CLIENT\WIN95\IBM_ENU directory.
   @\\DEMOSRVR\sys\public\client\win95\ibm_enu\setup.exe /acu
/n
   MAP K:=DEMOSRVR\SYS:
   END
EXIT

   REM You may also use NCIMAN.EXE to create an update file
and use the following line:
   @\\DEMOSRVR\sys\public\client\win95\ibm_enu\setup.exe /acu
/n /U:\\DEMOSRVR\sys\public\client\win95\ibm_enu\update.txt
   END
```

```
EXIT
NOT95:
   REM Clients that are NOT Win95 will now EXIT
   Write "You are seeing this because you are not using a
recognizable Desktop OS"
   Write "Please call your network administrator or the help
desk"
   PAUSE
   END
EXIT
```

An NDS Container Login Script for Windows NT Clients

Windows NT clients are handled a bit different than in the Windows 95 script. The Microsoft Client for NetWare on NT will read the container login script. To update the NT workstations, change the login script by adding these lines to the end:

```
IF "%OS" = "WINNT" THEN
   GOTO WINNTC32
END
IF <OS> = "Windows_NT" THEN
   GOTO WINNTMS
END
WINNTC32:
   REM This WINNT client is currently using Client 32 and
will automatically update if needed
   REM If the client is up to date no changes are made. To
make a change edit the
```

```
   REM UNATTEND.TXT and change the version number. This file
is located in the

   REM SYS:PUBLIC\CLIENT\WINNT\I386\NLS\ENGLISH directory.

@\\DEMOSRVR\sys\public\client\winnt\i386\setup.exe /acu
/u:\\DEMOSRVR\sys\public\client\winnt\i386\nls\english\unatte
nd.txt

   END

EXIT

WINNTMS:

   WRITE "This is an NT Client and the current seen is %OS"

   Write "This is MS Client  section for Windows NT"

   IF <COMSPEC> = "C:\WINNT\COMMAND.COM"  OR  <COMSPEC> =
"C:\WINNT\SYSTEM32\CMD.EXE" THEN BEGIN

   Write "The IF COMSPEC Worked and the next 2 lines will
execute"

REM If the next 2 lines are NOT read than check the COMSPEC
on the NT Workstation and edit

REM the login script to reflect additional COMSPEC.

MAP M:=DEMOSRVR\SYS:PUBLIC\WINNT

#\\DEMOSRVR\sys\public\client\winnt\i386\setupnw.exe /acu
/u:\\DEMOSRVR\sys\public\client\winnt\i386\nls\english\
unattend.txt

END

EXIT
```

A Login Script for Mixed Environment of Windows Clients

NCIMAN.EXE is a new 32-bit GUI tool that provides an easy way to automatically update the clients using Novell Client 32.

Using NCIMAN.EXE

The Win95.TXT file looks like this:

```
[Novell_Client_Install_Manager]
Novell_Client=95


[Novell_Client_Parameters]
Preferred_Server=DEMOSRVR
Preferred_Tree=NOVELL_INC
Name_Context=OU=NORAD.O=ACME
Clear_Current_Connections=NO
Close_Script_Results_Automatically=NO
Save_Settings_When_Exiting_Login=NO
Show_Location_List=YES
Show_Clear_Connections=NO
Log_File=C:\Novell\Client32\LOG.TXT
Preferred_Server_Distribute=Always
Preferred_Tree_Distribute=Always
Name_Context_Distribute=Always
Clear_Current_Connections_Distribute=Always
Close_Script_Results_Automatically_Distribute=Always
Save_Settings_When_Exiting_Login_Distribute=Always
Show_Location_List_Distribute=Always
Show_Clear_Connections_Distribute=Always
Log_File_Distribute=Always
```

```
Windows NT file

[Novell_Client_Install_Manager]
Novell_Client=NT

[SetupNWInstallOptions]
!DisplayInitialScreen=NO
!AskReboot=NO

[NovellNetWareClientParameters]
!AcceptLicenseAgreement=YES
!Preferred_Server=DEMOSRVR
!Preferred_Server_Distribute=Always
!Preferred_Tree=KP_DEMO_TREE
!Preferred_Tree_Distribute=Always
!Tree_List1=KP_DEMO_TREE
!Tree_List_Distribute=Replace
!Default_Context_List1=Norad.Acme
!Default_Context_List_Distribute=Replace
!Welcome_Screen_Caption=Novell Consulting
!Welcome_Screen_Caption_Distribute=Always

[RemoteControlParameters]
!DoInstall=YES
```

```
[WorkstationManagerParameters]
!Workstation_Manager_Tree=KP_DEMO_TREE
!Workstation_Manager_Tree_Distribute=Always

[Unattended]
OemPreinstall=YES

[Network]
InstallServices=ServicesList

[ServicesList]
NWFS=NovellNetwareClientParameters, \$OEM$\NET\NTCLIENT\I386
WM=WorkstationManagerParameters, \$OEM$\NET\NTCLIENT\I386
WUA=RemoteControlParameters, \$OEM$\NET\NTCLIENT\I386
```

Summary

In this chapter we have reviewed the Novell Client 32 architecture and the basic methods for client access, including types of NDS scripts and sample login scripts. Designing for network access is an important step in your NDS design, and this chapter has highlighted the different types of access available with the Novell clients and the benefits of using an NDS connection. We also have presented sample login scripts for Windows 95 and Windows NT users.

CHAPTER 13

Managing NetWare Security

"Even in the common affairs of life, in love, friendship, and marriage, how little security have we when we trust our happiness in the hands of others!" —William Hazlitt

As networks become increasingly more distributed, the exposure of information has also increased. Therefore, it makes sense that in large networked environments, you'll have to pay more attention to security and take measures to ensure that your data is protected.

Securing your network actually encompasses many areas of security including physical access, login, NDS, and file system restrictions. Other areas that can be classified within the physical access category include natural disasters and hardware failures. Another area of security violations is caused unintentionally by users who have authorized access and simply make mistakes. Computer viruses also pose a threat to security and can be caused intentionally or unintentionally.

While each of these areas is important, the goal is to secure your important data from theft, eavesdropping, or destruction. Every organization may place greater emphasis on a particular aspect of security depending on the sensitivity of the data. Some organizations may attempt to enforce all available aspects of security, while other companies may only concentrate on a few areas. As a network administrator you must decide along with your other managers what is an acceptable level of security versus risk for your department or company's data. Any level of security you implement is more than what your users will want because of additional burdens placed on their ability to freely work on the network.

Some companies may be especially prone to disasters because of their geographical location and natural weather conditions. Other companies may be at a greater hardware risk because they are running their network in a factory or plant where the possibility of fire or other damage is greater.

This chapter discusses these topics including securing physical access to hardware, understanding the authentication and login process, and applying NDS restrictions. NDS restrictions include security for objects and properties as well as for the file system. These various levels of security are represented in Figure 13.1.

FIGURE 13.1

Security can be broken down into the categories of physical security, login security, and NDS security.

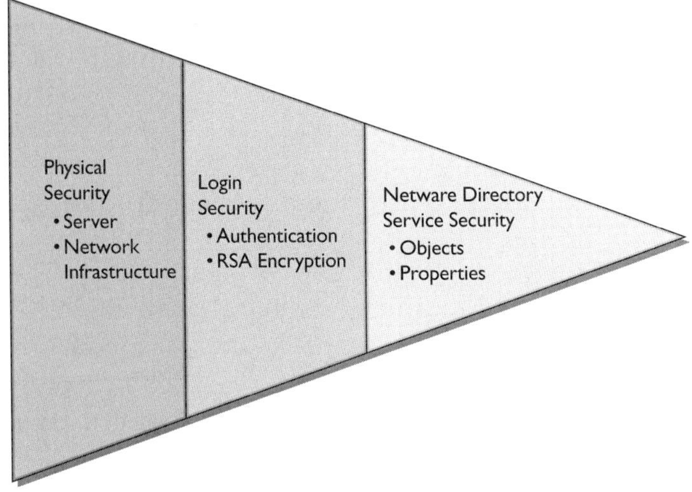

Designing a Security Policy

One of the first steps to implementing security for your environment is to design what is commonly referred to as a security policy. A *security policy* is basically your own company's road map for implementing security. Consider the following questions when implementing your security plan:

- What security threats do you have at your company?
- You must evaluate all aspects of threats including your building's age and entrance policies, the geographic location, the experience level of your users, the number of users, the age of your server hardware, and access points to your network from locations outside your company. *Access points* refer to gateways or other routing devices connected to the Internet or other wide-area links.
- What security do you currently have in place and what improvements can be made?

- Most companies usually have some form of network security in place. If your network is growing or if you have recently connected to the Internet, you should consider increasing your security. If your company is in the process of relocating to a new building, you should reevaluate your security measures.

- What costs are associated with increasing your security?

- You have to take into account what the costs will be when increasing your security. Will your added security measures require more staff to assist with this aspect? Will the changes require the purchase of newer, more expensive hardware such as tape backups and virus protection software? How much more administration time is needed to service each user? What is the cost of your downtime if your network should have a failure?

- Are you reviewing your security processes on a continual basis?

- Each network administrator should perform a regular security check on the network to determine if new workstations or any other new devices have been added to the network. A review will also determine if any security policies need to be modified based on any other changes that may have occurred on the network.

Controlling Physical Access to Your Hardware

One of the most basic aspects of providing a secure network is to physically secure your servers and workstations. If possible, your servers should be protected in a locked room such as a data center or wiring closet. Many large companies already place servers in their data centers. Smaller companies may not have this option, but other steps can be taken to help safeguard your servers, as explained in the next section.

Network Hardware Security

Network administrators can secure their physical networks by encasing their network wiring in conduit to prohibit intrusion. Again, your company and administrators must determine if such an enormous expense is needed to secure your particular data.

You also should consider taking the following steps to secure your servers:

- Keep all servers in a data center or an air-conditioned locked room and limit access to these areas.
- Provide a tape backup for all servers on your network to back up files as well as NDS. Restore data to a test directory to periodically check that the restore procedure is working properly.
- Remove DOS from the file server by typing REMOVE DOS at the server console.
- Use an auditing tool such as Novell's AUDITCON or another third-party utility to track server events on highly sensitive servers.
- Lock the file server console using MONITOR.NLM and do not store the password in the AUTOEXEC.NCF file.
- Require passwords for print servers that need to log into the NetWare 5 servers.
- Periodically check containers that are under your responsibility for new objects. Investigate all new objects added to your containers.
- Carefully control the use of RCONSOLE and its password. You can encrypt the RCONSOLE password for your AUTOEXEC.NCF by following these steps:

  1. At a NetWare 5 console type **REMOTE ENCRYPT**.
  2. You will then be prompted for an RCONSOLE password to be encrypted.

3. After you enter the password, the file LDREMOTE.NCF will be created.
4. You can call this file in your AUTOEXEC.NCF or copy the contents out of the file into your AUTOEXEC.NCF.

Controlling Physical Access to Workstations

Workstations are more problematic to secure because some of your employees may use notebook computers that are transported away from the office each day. Also, very few companies ever go to the bother of physically securing workstations to desks or tables. Even if your users have stationary computers, there is always the possibility that unauthorized individuals will have access to your data.

You may also want to consider using a protocol analyzer such as Novell's LANalyzer, which provides a feature known as "new station" alarm to notify network administrators when a new node address has been discovered on your network. This application could be run on a nightly basis to search for any new hardware that may have been added to your network. It is usually quite easy for anyone to attach a notebook computer to your network infrastructure.

You can also limit access to your servers through Novell's station restriction and time restrictions procedures, which can be accomplished with the NWADMIN utility. These procedures limit a user to a particular workstation for logging in and also limit access to specific times of the day.

You should consider taking the following steps to secure your workstations:

- Encourage users not to leave their workstations unattended while logged into the network unless they are using password-protected screen saver software.
- Always log out of the network before leaving your work location for the day.
- Keep office doors locked when not in use and workstations powered off if possible.
- Administrators especially should not leave their workstations unattended while logged in with Supervisor rights to the tree, its containers, or servers.

- At a minimum you should have an asset tag for each piece of hardware on your network in case of theft or other damage.
- Use an antivirus product for your network that is loaded from the container login script.
- Carefully monitor the use of the ADMIN or any tree administrator user object. Change the password frequently.
- Require periodic changes in users' passwords. Do not allow them to use the same password twice.
- Have a company policy that no floppy disks are to be brought into the workplace unless they are scanned for viruses first.
- Closely monitor dial-in access and employ automatic callback features built into remote dial software.

Understanding the Login and Authentication Process

After you have physically secured your servers, the NetWare 5 login security is the next line of defense in network security. The authentication procedure verifies that any requests the server receives are from legitimate clients. The authentication process consists of the login and the authentication. NetWare 5 uses its own authentication process that is compatible with NetWare 3 as well. The mechanism used to make the authentication process extremely secure is known as encryption and is discussed later in this section.

Password Security and Verification

The purpose in having a password is to prevent unauthorized access to your network resources. NetWare 5 security must be reinforced by all network users and administrators practicing good password security. Any disclosure of passwords will allow a user to access that account to the extent of that user's rights. Therefore, you can take numerous precautions to secure your network, but the human factor is always the biggest threat to your security. You can take some steps to help minimize the threat of a password breach in your security:

- Without exception, require user passwords for all users.
- Always require periodic changes of passwords for mobile users dialing into your network or users who work from home.
- Users should never post their passwords anywhere.
- Users should be encouraged to avoid easy passwords such as family member names, and so on.

Through the NetWare 5 utilities you can:

- Require a minimum password length of five to eight characters.
- Enforce periodic changes of passwords.
- Enforce unique passwords.
- Frequently change the password for your ADMIN or tree administrator user objects.

RSA Encryption/Decryption

NDS uses encryption to secure authentication information that is being sent across the network from one server to other servers or from a workstation to a server for authentication purposes. NetWare 5 uses the RSA encryption technology to provide public and private key encryption. The encryption process produces transmissions across the network that are unreadable except to the receiving entity.

Public and private key encryption is also known as *asymmetrical cryptography* because there is a mathematical relationship between the two keys. If data is encrypted with the object's public key, the receiving object will use its private key to decrypt the information. The public key can be read by any requesting object. The receiving object holds the private key but never discloses it. Figure 13.2 shows the relationship between the public and private keys during transmission of authentication data. Keep in mind that only server objects keep their own private keys. Users obtain their encrypted private keys during the login process. These keys are then decrypted, used to generate a signature, and discarded.

FIGURE 13.2

The use of public and private key encryption of authentication data

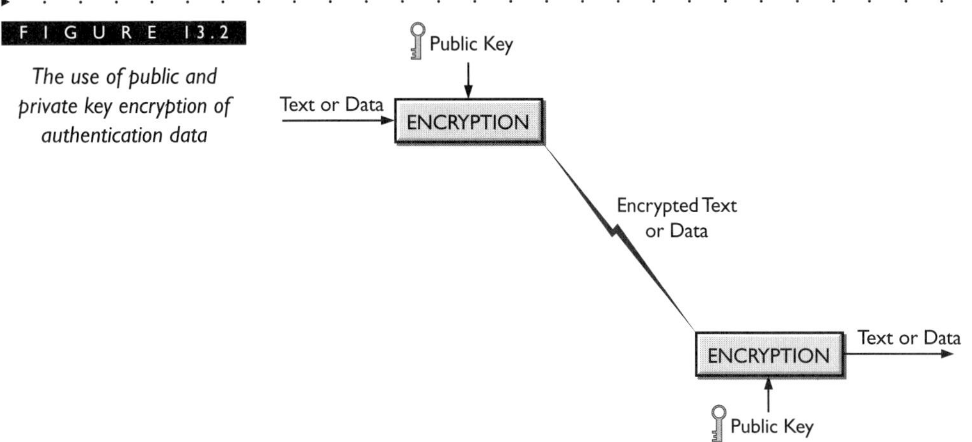

Directory Services uses encryption to ensure that authentication information is secure while it is being transmitted on the wire. There will always be a public key/private key pair for each encrypted transaction. To prevent intrusion during a transmission by capturing and replaying encrypted messages, the NetWare authentication process uses what is known as a nonce value. A *nonce value* is a random value that is generated for each encrypted transaction. The nonce value is associated only once with each encrypted message. Because the nonce is used only once, it will not do an intruder any good to capture an encrypted message and attempt to impersonate the sender.

Each transaction uses the network layer infrastructure to send and receive packets. This means that for authentication IPX and NCP requests are made between a client and a server, but for NDS authentication the data is encrypted before transmission on the wire. Keep in mind that the term "client" can mean a

Directory Services server communicating with another server. As discussed previously in Chapter 12, "Understanding and Managing Client Access," there are varying degrees of authentication access. We list them here again briefly.

Connected But Not Logged In

This state applies to a client who has attached to a NetWare 5 server either through the NETX shell or the VLM client. It could also be a DS server that does not use NETX or VLMs. A connected but not logged in state can exist for NetWare 3 or NetWare 5 users either to the first attached server or, if a connection is made for tree walking, after the first attached server. This state is seen in the MONITOR utility as NOT LOGGED IN and does not take a licensed connection.

Authenticated

Authentication is a process of proving identity to a server. In NetWare 3, this meant logging in. In NetWare 5, it happens as a "behind the scenes task" at the client.

This type of connection indicates that a NetWare 5 server has established a user's identity after the client has entered a correct name and password to obtain the encrypted private key. Authentication occurs for both NetWare 3 and NetWare 5 users, with NetWare 5 adding more security to this process. The authentication process includes creating a proof and a server's verifying that proof. Proof is constructed with the client's public key, signature, and credential and is built at the time of login.

Licensed

A connection is said to be *licensed* when a client has made a request of the server such as mapping a drive or capturing to a printer. At that time the client requests the server to license the connection. This will cause the license count on the server to be decremented by one. Only an authenticated connection can be licensed.

A combination of these states determines what level a user currently has in a NetWare 5 environment. For example, when a connection is neither authenticated nor licensed, users can navigate the NDS tree through the use of the CX (Change conteXt) program (presuming [PUBLIC] has the Browse right at the [ROOT] object of the tree) and the execution of the LOGIN.EXE utility as well. They have attached to a server but have not yet authenticated.

If a user is licensed and authenticated, he or she can access NDS and file system information to the extent allowed by his or her rights.

NOTE

The Change Connection State NCP call switches the connection between Not Licensed and Licensed.

The User Login

The first step to authenticating in a NetWare 5 environment is the identification phase, also known as the login phase. When the user first logs into a NetWare 5 server, the user must establish his identity with the server and then proceed through the authentication phase. This is accomplished by the client broadcasting a service request, with the broadcast type 0x0278 if the preferred tree is set on, or the broadcast type 0x0004 if the preferred server is set. A server or router that receives this request will reply with a response. The client will examine the response and accept the first response with the correct tree/server being sought. This gets the client a connection to begin the tree walking (resolve name operation). NDS will then search the tree to find a writable replica of the user's object. At that point the login and authentication phases that are discussed next will occur.

Login Phase

The following steps occur during the login phase:

1. Once a writable replica is found with the user object, the user is prompted for a name and password.

2. After successfully proving knowledge of the password, the client receives the encrypted private key from the server.

3. The private key of the client is used to generate a signature.

4. The public key of the client is used to generate a credential.

5. The signature and credential are used to build a proof that is used later in this sequence.

Authentication Phase

The following steps occur during the authentication phase:

1. The public key attribute of the server is read by the requesting client.

2. The proof previously generated is encrypted with the server's public key and sent to the server.

3. The server decrypts the proof with the server's private key.

4. The proof is verified by the server through a mathematical computation of the client's public key and the client key stored on the server.

5. If the proof is correct, then authentication is successful.

6. The finished authentication request will then call Directory Services for the user's security equivalence vector.

7. The login process is then passed back to Directory Services to execute the applicable login script and apply NDS access controls.

NOTE

For more information on user login and authentication, you can refer to Novell's October 1994 Application Notes, "Identification and Authentication in NetWare 4." To order AppNotes, call 1-800-377-4136 or 303-297-2725. Orders can also be faxed to 303-294-0930. The AppNotes and other Novell Research publications (such as Research Reports and Novell Developer Notes) are also available on the Web at `www.novell.com/research`**.**

Keep in mind that the client's password is never transmitted across the wire. Therefore, it is not possible for anyone to capture a password packet on the wire. In addition, the authentication data is valid only during the current login session. If a user terminates the session and then reconnects, the authentication process is repeated.

NOTE

Another feature, known as *packet signing*, requires each packet to have a valid signature in order to be executed by the server. Packet signing makes it far more difficult for someone to forge NCP packets and send them on to the server for processing.

Background Authentication

During the initial login process a NetWare client will identify a hosting server. Although the login process in NetWare 5 is performed only once, the authentication process may occur throughout the entire session in order to enable services from other servers.

Background authentication is the ongoing identification process that occurs after the initial login. If a connection needs to be made to other network services, authentication is done through the process of background authentication. Background authentication can occur because the NetWare 5 servers can verify the proof provided by the client from the client's public key without additional user intervention. A server making a request of another server is also considered a client. Keep in mind that the proof is constructed at the client using the signature, credential, and public key.

When a user logs out of the network, the NetWare 5 license manager is notified and makes the license available to any other validated user needing a license. The logout includes destroying the service connection to all but one server along with all bindings that were part of the user connection. The authentication data is also destroyed on the workstation at logout.

Changes in NetWare 5 to Security

Several new security features come with NetWare 5, which builds upon NetWare 4's existing security features. The new features have been integrated with Novell Directory Services (NDS) and help simplify administration of each new feature. They also provide security for improved Internet data integrity and privacy across public networks. The new security features include Public Key Infrastructure Services (PKIS), Novell International Cryptographic Infrastructure (NICI), Secure Authentication Services (SAS), and the audit system. This section discusses these new features and explains why they are important and how they provide NetWare 5 with advanced security services.

The information presented in this chapter is only a brief description for each new feature. For a more complete reference refer to the section "Security" in Chapter 10, which discusses all the newest NetWare 5 features.

Public Key Infrastructure Services (PKIS)

NetWare 5 includes PKIS, which supports public-key cryptography and digital certificates in a NetWare 5 environment. Digital certificates provide a method for checking the authenticity of keys used in a public-key cryptographic session. In NetWare 5, PKIS allows you either to act as your own certificate authority or to use the services of third-party certificate authorities. Through PKIS, you can generate and sign various types of digital certificates and store and manage these certificates within NDS.

PKIS allows any designated NetWare 5 administrators to establish a Certificate Authority (CA) management domain within NDS. PKIS allows administrators to manage certificates and keys for Secure Sockets Layer (SSL) security for LDAP servers.

Certificate management includes services such as establishment of a CA local to your organization, certificate renewal, simplified certificate revocation with certificate suspension (without complex certificate revocation lists), creation of certificate signing requests (for use with external CAs), unlimited certificate minting services for applications, and using SSL in the NetWare environment (such as Novell LDAP Services for NDS).

Using PKIS, you can control the costs associated with obtaining key pairs and managing public key certificates. PKIS helps you create a local CA based on NDS that signs certificates for other services on the network. With PKIS you can also generate unlimited key pairs and issue unlimited public key certificates through the local CA at no charge.

NDS stores all keys and certificates that are generated by PKIS or obtained from external CAs. NDS's trusted directory features means that public keys can be openly published while private keys are securely protected. For more information about PKIS, refer to Chapter 10.

Novell International Cryptographic Infrastructure (NICI)

NetWare 5 includes cryptographic services named Novell International Cryptographic Infrastructure (NICI). NICI allows developers to use the Controlled Cryptography Service (CCS) API to integrate cryptographic schemes with their applications. NICI also allows developers to write a single application that can be used in several countries, regardless of the differences in countries' cryptographic laws. For example, a developer could write a single application that uses 128-bit cryptographic keys when used within the United States and 40-bit cryptographic keys when used within countries that allow only keys of that length.

NICI is an infrastructure of network cryptographic services for worldwide consumption that will support strong cryptography and multiple cryptographic technologies. The NICI infrastructure has been developed in response to customer and internal Novell needs while complying with various national policies on the shipment and use of cryptography. Cryptography services on the NetWare platform provide fundamental security features such as confidentiality, integrity, authentication, and nonrepudiation.

The services are modular in nature, which will allow new cryptographic engines, libraries, and policy managers to be dynamically added. The infrastructure is also tightly controlled, enforced through an integral OS loader that verifies modules before loading, and controls access to modules only via standardized interfaces. Available cryptographic services will be provided via a Novell SDK.

NICI is the foundation for future network cryptographic services. It ensures that your product complies with international cryptography import and export laws through enforced region-specific cryptographic policies. NICI also provides for single, worldwide commodity vendor products and supports extensible, application-specific cryptographic libraries and interchangeable cryptographic technologies. For more information about NICI, refer to Chapter 10.

Secure Authentication Services

NetWare 5 includes Secure Authentication Services (SAS), an infrastructure for supporting both existing and emerging authentication mechanisms, such as biometric and token-authentication systems. Through SAS, NetWare 5 also supports SSL version 3. Developers can use the SAS API to write applications that can establish encrypted SSL connections. (Developers can then use NICI to ensure that these SSL connections conform to the laws of each country in which the applications are used.)

Authentication is a fundamental component of a robust network service — it is how you identify yourself. Without authentication, you cannot secure a network. Novell's Secure Authentication Services (SAS) provides next generation authentication services, as well as serving as an evolving industry authentication mechanism for the future. In NetWare 5, SAS provides Secure Sockets Layer (SSL) support. Server applications use the SAS API set to establish encrypted SSL connections.

SAS is built entirely on NICI. This means that the SAS service itself is based on a single executable file. Because no cryptography is included in the SAS NLM, you can ship a single NLM worldwide. This provides easy administrator management and tracking. Also, any applications written to the SAS API can also be based on a single executable file.

In addition, applications written to the SAS application can go through a one-time and usually expedited export approval process. Novell has already received export approval for SAS and NICI. This means that application developers benefit with expedited export procedures.

PKIS also provides key management for the SSL services. Any application written to the SAS interface inherits the ability to have PKIS manage its certificates. NDS access control lists (ACLs) manage access to the private key that enables SSL. Because SAS is a network service, it has its own network identity. ACLs are set up on the SSL key object in such a way that allows only the SAS identity to read the private key. This guarantees that nonauthorized entities such as users, other server applications, and even the application built on top of SAS cannot gain access to and expose or subvert the private key. For more information about SAS, refer to Chapter 10.

Auditing Services

NetWare 5 includes auditing services, which allow administrators to monitor users' access to an organization's network and to record this monitoring information in audit log files. You can create NDS objects to represent audit log files, and you can then manage these objects just as you manage other objects in the NDS tree. You can also grant rights to the NDS objects representing audit log files, just as you grant rights to other objects in the NDS tree. As a result, you can assign administrators to view and manage audit log files.

The audit system now takes advantage of exposed NDS audit services in the following ways:

- Audit log files are represented and managed as NDS objects.

- The access to the audit information and configuration is controlled by the standard NDS rights.
- Auditing is configured at the container and volume levels.
- The audit policy for a container or volume specifies what is audited within the volume or container and which users are audited.

The audit system is an essential element of the total NetWare security environment. You must have network audit integrity to ensure that the network is secure. Additionally, some industries such as banking require auditing to be done as part of business operations. The NetWare auditing system can monitor and record every relevant network transaction, which user performed the transaction, and when the transaction occurred.

NetWare provides the highest level of audit data granularity. This includes which events are audited, control of audit configuration, and access to audit data. For more information about audit services, refer to Chapter 10.

NDS Access Control

NDS security actually consists of two parts known as file system security and object security. Both aspects of NetWare 5 security work together to provide a flexible and effective method for controlling access to your network. *File system security* provides access control to files and directories. *Object security* provides access control to NDS objects and associated operations. You must determine to what extent you want to enable the many file system and NDS security features at your disposal. NetWare is well regarded for providing a high degree of network security, and much of the security administration happens by default as explained later in this chapter.

The first step to understanding NetWare security is to begin with file system security. File system security consists of the security that was introduced in previous versions of NetWare. Your familiarity with the security concepts in NetWare 3 will be a great help to you in understanding security in NetWare 5.

Understanding File System Security

Very little has changed in file system security since NetWare 3. All the rules governing rights administration are the same in NetWare 5. As an administrator you don't have to learn any new concepts to manage your NetWare 5 files. However, if you are new to NetWare you will want to read this section and refer to Novell's documentation on managing the file system. NetWare 5 does introduce some additional file system attributes that can be useful for particular situations.

File system security basically consists of assigning trustee rights and file/directory attributes. The trustee rights assignments can be applied to any NDS object including containers, user objects, group objects, and organizational roles. Table 13.1 shows the file system rights available in NetWare 5. The rights are in order as typically seen in most of the NetWare applications.

TABLE 13.1

File System Rights

RIGHT	DEFINITION
Access Control	Adds/modifies rights to files and directories.
Supervisor	Enables all file and directory assignments to be made and grants all rights listed in this table.
Read	Enables the trustee to open, read, and execute application files.
Write	Enables the trustee user to open, write to, and modify a file.
Create	Enables the trustee to create subdirectories and files.
Erase	Enables the trustee to delete directories and files.
Modify	Enables the trustee to modify and rename directories and files, and to change file attributes.
File Scan	Enables the trustee to view file and directory names in the file system.

NetWare 5 file system security includes the capability to manage access at file and directory levels just as it did in previous versions of NetWare. Attributes control what actions can or cannot be taken on a file or directory. For certain files, such as application files on the network, you may want to make sure they are flagged as Read Only and Sharable so that no unintentional or intentional deletions occur.

Additional file and directory attributes have been added to the NetWare 4 and NetWare 5 file system to provide more functionality to NetWare 5. These new file system attributes are listed in Table 13.2. For a complete list of all attributes associated with NetWare 5 files and directories, refer to Novell's documentation. The attributes are in order as normally seen in the NetWare utilities.

TABLE 13.2

New File System Attributes That Have Been Added to NetWare 5

ATTRIBUTE	ABBREVIATION	DEFINITION
Compress	Co	Status attribute that indicates the file is compressed
Can't Compress	Cc	Status attribute that indicates the file cannot be compressed because of limited space savings
Don't Compress	Dc	Added to a directory, this attribute keeps all files within the directory from being compressed. This attribute can also be added to a specific file.
Immediate	Ic	Added to directories or files, this Compress attribute alerts the file system to compress a file as soon as the operating system can handle the action.
Migrated	M	This status attribute indicates that the file has been migrated.
Don't Migrate	Dm	Added to a directory, this attribute will not allow files within the directory to be migrated to secondary storage. This attribute can also be added to a specific file.

For more information on administering file system security, refer to Novell's NetWare 5 manual, *Supervising the Network.*

Understanding Object Security

Your understanding of NetWare 3 file system security will assist you in mastering NetWare 5 security because both use the same terminology and the same rules. The rules for file system security in both versions of NetWare are identical. NetWare 5 extends security to the NDS environment by adding access controls to all objects and properties found in your tree.

As shown in Figure 13.3, security features in the NetWare 5 environment are similar to those in NetWare 3.

FIGURE 13.3

Security features between the two versions of NetWare are similar.

NETWARE 3	NetWare 5
BINDERY	NOVELL DIRECTORY SERVICES
FILE & DIRECTORY RIGHTS FILE ATTRIBUTES	FILE & DIRECTORY RIGHTS FILE ATTRIBUTES
SUPERVISOR OPERATOR OBJECT RIGHTS ONLY	OBJECT & PROPERTY RIGHTS
SUPERVISOR USER	ADMIN USER AND BINDERY SUPERVISOR
EVERYONE GROUP	O=ORGANIZATION
GUEST USER	[PUBLIC] TRUSTEE (NOT THE SAME AS GUEST)
INHERIT RIGHTS MASK (IRM)	INHERITED RIGHTS FILTER (IRF)
DIRECTORY ENTERY TABLE (DET)	DET, ACL (ACCESS CONTROL LIST)

The exceptions between NetWare 3 and NetWare 5 are as follows:

- Inherited rights filter (IRF) terminology is used instead of inherited rights mask (IRM) language. In NetWare 5, the term IRF describes the operation of filtering out rights for a particular object. IRFs are explained in detail later in this chapter.

- NetWare Object classes have been expanded from 4 in NetWare 3 to 32 in NetWare 5.
- The SUPERVISOR user is used only for bindery requests in NetWare 5. Another NDS user object (typically called ADMIN) is granted Supervisor object rights at the [ROOT] of the tree. This user object is the functional equivalent of the Supervisor found in NetWare 3 and has default Supervisor rights over all NDS objects in the tree as well as the file system for any NetWare 5 server installed. One other major difference to note is that you cannot filter Supervisor rights in the NetWare 5 file system, which is just like NetWare 3. You can, however, filter Supervisor rights in the NetWare Directory Services tree.
- Guest is not automatically created in NetWare 5. The [PUBLIC] Trustee is similar to Guest in enabling users to see the NDS tree before logging into a server. However, Guest is a real object and [PUBLIC] is not, so the similarities are few.
- Group Everyone is not automatically created in NetWare 5. However, an equivalent feature is available by using either the [ROOT] object or O=Organization object. For example, O=ACME includes every object in the NDS tree, and rights can be assigned to O=ACME, which all users receive automatically.
- Operators for print queues found in NetWare 3 are now an attribute of the Queue object found in NetWare 5 Directory Services.
- Directory entry tables are still used to store file system trustees in NetWare 5. In addition, NetWare 5 uses the access control list (ACL) to store NDS trustee information.

Object Rights Defined

Object rights are simply rights granted to a particular object to access or manage another object. In NetWare 3 servers the Supervisor object has rights to manage all other bindery objects on the server. NetWare 5 has expanded on this concept by allowing all NDS objects rights to other objects. As shown in Table 13.3, NDS objects can receive many different rights. The NDS objects rights are in order as seen in the NWADMIN utility.

TABLE 13.3

An Object Can Receive Many Different Object Level Rights to Manage Other Objects in the Directory

NDS OBJECT	OBJECT LEVEL RIGHTS
Supervisor (S)	Grants full privileges to the trustee over an object and has complete access to all the object's property rights.
Browse (B)	Enables a trustee to see an NDS object in the tree during a browse of the tree.
Create (C)	Enables a trustee to create objects below this object (applies to container objects only).
Delete (D)	Enables a trustee to delete an object. Subordinate objects must be deleted first if you are deleting a container.
Rename (R)	Enables a trustee to rename an object.

An example of how object rights appear in the NWADMIN utility is shown in Figure 13.4.

FIGURE 13.4

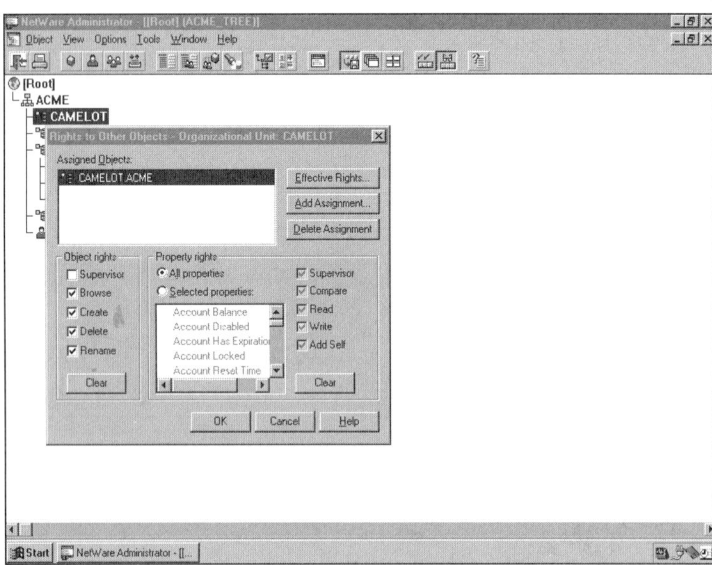

An example of object rights as they are displayed in the NWADMIN utility

Property Rights Defined

Property rights enable a trustee to view or change the values of a particular object's properties. You can have rights to certain properties (selected property rights) or to all properties (all property rights) for a particular object. For example, the Supervisor right over an NDS object also grants Supervisor privileges for all properties in that object. All other rights assignments made at the object level do not affect the properties. In fact, Supervisor rights at the property level do not grant Supervisor rights at the object level. Only the reverse is true. Table 13.4 shows a list of the available property rights in NetWare 5. The NDS property rights are in order as seen in the NWADMIN utility.

TABLE 13.4

NetWare 5 Property Rights

PROPERTY RIGHT	FUNCTION
Supervisor (S)	Grants all rights to the object's properties.
Compare (C)	Enables a test for a value match and returns a true or false. Compare is a subset of read. If you have Read/Write rights, you automatically have Compare rights at the property level.
Read (R)	Returns a value (contents) of a property. Read contains the Compare right.
Write (W)	Enables you to modify, add, change, and delete a property value.
Add/Remove Self (A)	Enables you to add or remove yourself as a value of a property. It is a subset of the Write right. If you have Write rights to a property, you automatically have the Add/Remove Self right.

An example of how property rights are displayed in NWADMIN is shown in Figure 13.5.

FIGURE 13.5

Property rights in the NWADMIN utility

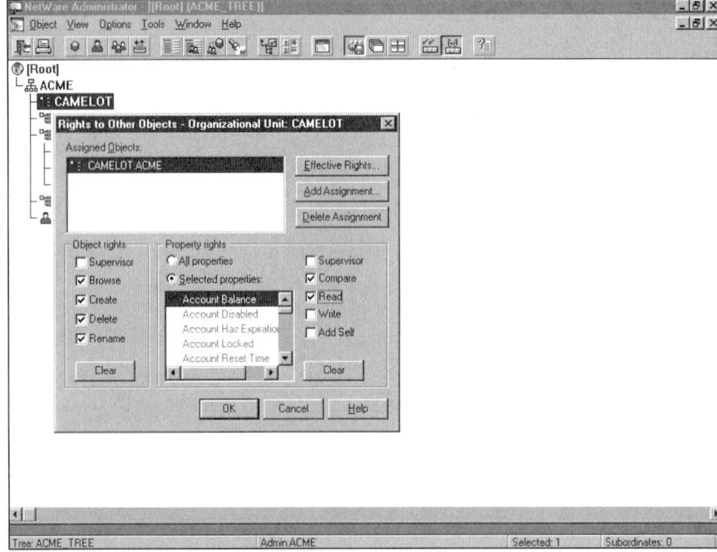

The Access Control List

The access control list (ACL) is a special property of every object. It can actually be considered the most important mechanism for determining NDS access. The access control list contains trustee assignments for an object and its properties. A user object, for example, with the Write right to the ACL of another user object has what is known as *managed rights* over that user object. This means that an object with the Write right to any object's ACL can make any rights assignments to that object.

Each object can have an ACL. The ACL is a property value and contains three entries: the trustee ID, the type of access (object or property), and the actual rights assignment. This concept is shown in Figure 13.6.

FIGURE 13.6

Every object may have an access control list as one of its properties.

ACCESS CONTROL LIST (ACL)

TRANSFER OBJECT ID	TYPE OF ACCESS (OBJECT OR PROPERTY)	RIGHTS ASSIGNMENT
07721429	OBJECT	[S]
07618424	OBJECT	[CR]
01099600	PROPERTY	{S }

NOTE

The ACL is extremely powerful, and its access should be closely controlled for every object on your network. Because the ACL is a property of an object, it can be modified by anyone who has Write rights to the ACL property for the object. This means that someone with the Write rights to the ACL can make rights assignments for that object.

The ACL has three categories:

- Object rights
- [All Properties]
- Selected properties

The [All Properties] category is a property under the ACL, and if given the Write right to the ACL, you can modify the object's trustee assignments. As a security rule, be careful how you grant the Write right to ordinary users under the ACL. Selected property rights overwrite those rights assigned by [All Property Rights] — they are not cumulative.

By default, users do not receive Write rights to their own ACL. In the NDS schema, some of the object classes specify a default ACL template. The default ACL template grants basic access control to newly created objects. If the object (for example, the organizational unit object) contains a default ACL template when created, it would have information in its ACL as shown in Table 13.5.

TABLE 13.5

The Container Object Default ACL

OBJECT NAME	DEFAULT RIGHTS	AFFECTED
[ROOT]	Read	Login script and print job configuration

When a container object is created, the [ROOT] object automatically obtains the Read property right to the container's login script and print job configuration.

The user class is another example of an object that receives a default ACL during initial creation. Its default ACL would appear as shown in Table 13.6.

TABLE 13.6

The User Object Default ACL

OBJECT NAME	DEFAULT RIGHTS	AFFECTED ATTRIBUTES
[PUBLIC]	Read	Message server
[ROOT]	Browse	Object rights
[ROOT]	Read	Group membership
[ROOT]	Read	Network address
[self]	Read	All attributes
[self]	Read/Write	Login script
[self]	Read/Write	Print job configuration

Therefore, as was mentioned earlier, access control is limited, and your default security is a closed-door approach. As a NetWare administrator, you must open up security doors (granting additional rights) only when necessary. Otherwise, the majority of your users receive by default sufficient access rights when they are created.

NOTE

As we have stated earlier, an object may or may not have an ACL. If an object already has the effective right, the ACL is not created. For example, all objects have the default ACL that specifies that the ADMIN (or appropriate object) has object Supervisor rights to the user object. If the ADMIN already has the Supervisor object right (and it does if it creates a user object), the default ACL is not created when the NDS user object is created.

New Inheritable ACLs

Inheritable ACLs are a new feature in NetWare 5 that allows you to more easily manage the objects and properties of the NDS tree. This feature gives you the ability to inherit specific property rights down the entire tree. The NDS inheritable ACLs allow you to assign Supervisor rights to operators or help desk staff for specific types of objects or resources without giving Supervisor rights to the entire tree. For example, you can assign rights to a group to manage just the printers, servers, or users.

You need to use NWADMIN in order to give inheritable rights to a specific property and have it flow down the NDS tree. In the NWADMIN object and property rights screen are two new buttons at the bottom of the rights list called Inherit. By selecting the Inherit button, when giving specific object or property rights to any other object, you are making then inherit down the NDS tree. Figure 13.7 shows an example of using the Inherit button to grant rights to a specific property and have those rights flow down to the NDS tree.

FIGURE 13.7

The NDS inheritable ACLs have been implemented in NWADMIN as the Inherit button for either object of property rights. You can have specific property rights flow down the NDS tree by selecting the Inherit button when assigning the rights.

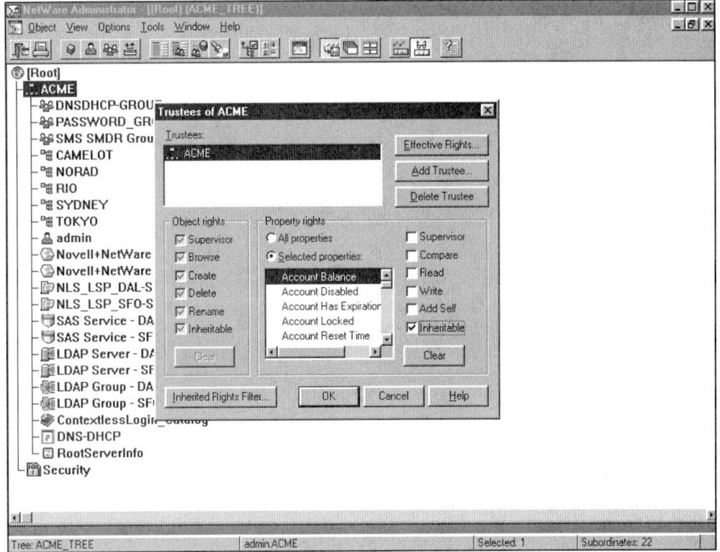

You may be wondering how specific property rights can be assigned using the new inheritable ACLs if NWADMIN only displays the property for the object in use. For example, in NetWare 4, if you wanted to grant a group (TELE-GROUP) rights to manage all users' telephone numbers at the O=ACME level, then you would select the O=ACME object. However, using NetWare 4 you would see only the properties that are associated with the O=ACME object, and thus the users' telephone number could not be selected.

Enhancements to NWADMIN

To overcome this limitation, NetWare 5 offers a new feature that allows NWADMIN to list all the schema-defined properties in a single list in NWADMIN. This means that regardless of the location in the NDS tree, the properties listed for the object are all properties defined in the schema.

The NWADMIN feature that lists all schema-defined properties gives you the ability to select any property at any level in the NDS tree. As mentioned, if you wanted to grant a group (Telephone_Group) rights to manage all users' telephone numbers at the O=ACME level, then you would select the O=ACME object. The new feature lists the users' telephone numbers as a property, and you can grant specific property rights that will inherit. Figure 13.8 illustrates how you can use NWADMIN to grant the group, Telephone_Group, the rights to manage all users' telephone numbers at the O=Organization level.

FIGURE 13.8

In order to grant a group, Telephone_Group, rights to manage all users' telephone numbers at the O=ACME level, you use NWADMIN. Select the O=ACME container object and grant the group the Supervisor rights to manage all users' telephone numbers.

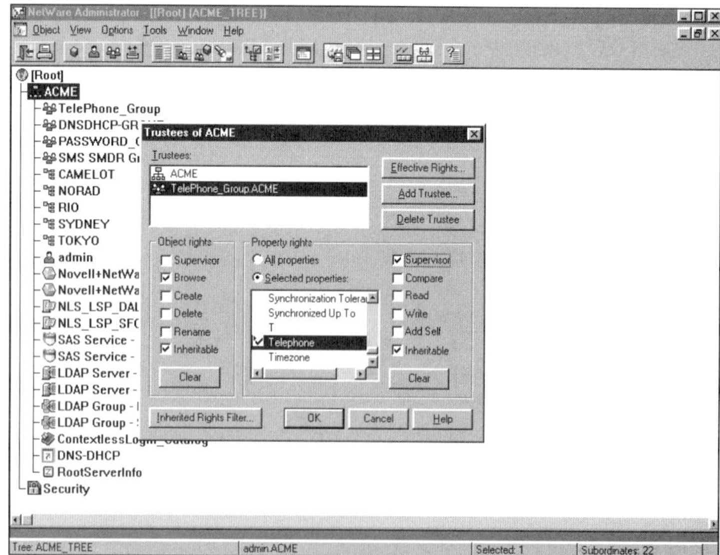

The Password Management Property

In addition to the NDS Inheritable ACLs feature, NetWare 5 has added a new user property called Password Management. The Password Management property allows you the ability to assign rights to manage just the users' passwords.

Using the new Password Management property, you can grant a specific group, PASSWORD-GROUP, the ability to reset just the users' passwords and accounts. To accomplish the same thing using NetWare 4, you had to give all rights or Supervisor rights to the individual user objects or to the entire container or tree. Using the Password Management property, in combination with the new Inherit button, you can grant rights that will flow down the entire tree. Figure 13.9 illustrates the example of granting the group, PASSWORD-GROUP, the rights to manage all users' passwords and accounts for the entire ACME tree.

FIGURE 13.9

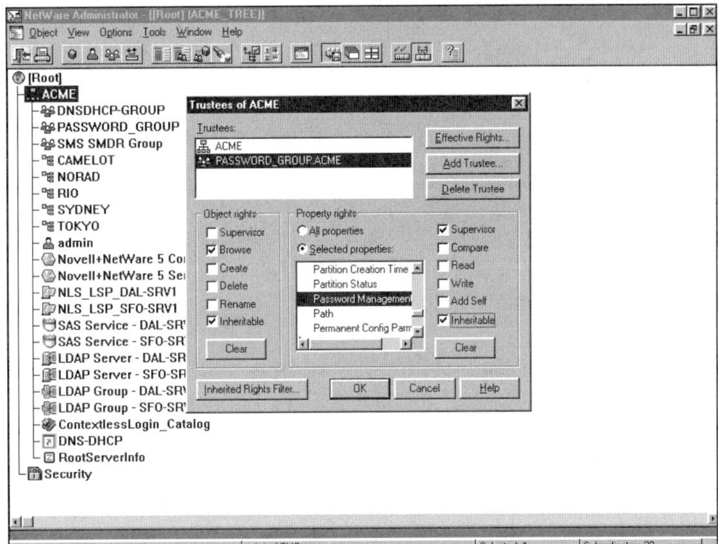

Using the new Password Management property in NWADMIN, you can grant a specific group, PASSWORD_GROUP, the Supervisor rights to manage the users' passwords and accounts at O=ACME. Select the Inherit button so that these rights flow down the entire NDS tree.

Learning the Rules of NDS Security

There are a number of security rules that every network manager should be aware of when setting up a secured NetWare 5 system. These rules affect both the file system security and NetWare Directory Service (NDS) security.

NetWare does a very good job with security (out of the box) just using the defaults that are implemented during installation. NetWare security is not an open door system. The NetWare 5 installation process closes all the necessary doors and gives you default security settings for servers, for users, and for NetWare Directory Service access. Then if users need additional access, the administrator can grant those additions to them.

For example, the installation process creates the Admin user object. Install creates the [Public] trustee, and each user receives rights to the [Public] trustee through security equivalence. The [Public] trustee is granted Browse rights to the [Root] object during initial installation. The install process also gives user objects the appropriate rights that they need for themselves, such as to read and modify their login scripts, to log in, and so forth. System administrators can give additional file and object rights when they are needed.

The first step in understanding NDS security is to understand the rules that govern it. This section will outline the concepts and rules for each area of security. With the groundwork in place we will then focus on some specific examples and explain how security is implemented for each.

NDS security uses the same terminology as file system security. In fact, your familiarity with NetWare 3 file system security will provide you with a great foundation for understanding NetWare 5 security. The following concepts will be discussed and are shown in Figure 13.10:

- Trustee assignments
- Security equivalence
- Inheritance
- The inherited rights filter (IRF)
- Effective rights

Trustee Assignments

A *trustee assignment* indicates the rights granted to an object for a specific file, directory, object, or property. An object that has been granted rights to manage another object is said to be a *trustee* of that object. Trustee assignments for the file system are stored in the directory entry table, whereas trustee assignments for NDS objects and properties are stored in the ACL (access control list).

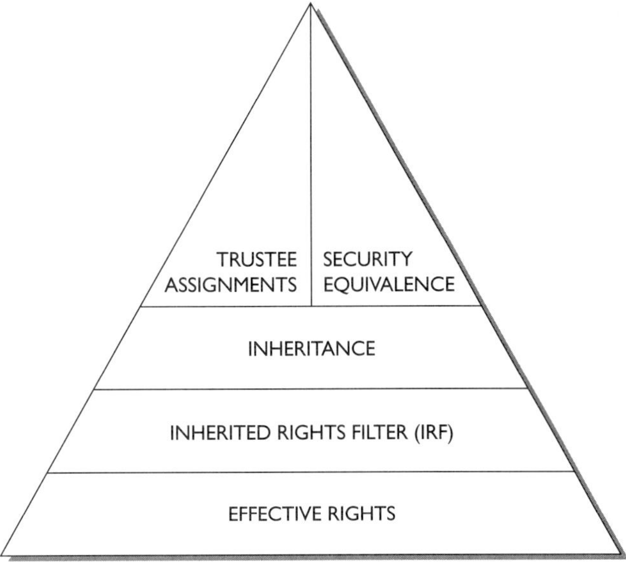

FIGURE 13.10

The NDS security pyramid serves as a visual basis for understanding the order and concepts of NDS security.

A trustee assignment is a direct, explicit assignment of rights to a particular object. Sometimes you will hear the term *explicit trustee assignment*, which means the same thing. Trustee assignments are listed first in our pyramid diagram because it is the first point at which rights assignments are made. It is the basis for all subsequent security assignments, such as security equivalence and inheritance. In fact, a trustee assignment is the lowest level where you can make assignments. Security always begins with a trustee assignment. For example, the use of a group object requires you to grant the group a trustee assignment that the members of the group receive through security equivalence.

The installation of NetWare 5, as another example, causes some default trustee assignments (templates) to be made for user and server objects. As an administrator you will most likely make additional trustee assignments for groups, containers, and other administrators as explained in the following section.

Default Trustee Assignments for Users

During the installation of your first NetWare 5 server the ADMIN user object (if you've named it that) receives an explicit assignment of object Supervisor at object [ROOT] as shown in Figure 13.11.

NOTE

The ADMIN object is just a user object like any other object, but it has been granted object Supervisor rights at [ROOT]. It can be renamed, deleted, and moved like any other user object. Be careful.

This assignment is the first trustee assignment made by the NetWare 5 installation software and initially is the only object in the tree with object Supervisor rights at [ROOT].

FIGURE 13.11

This diagram shows the default trustee assignments made at the installation of NetWare 5.

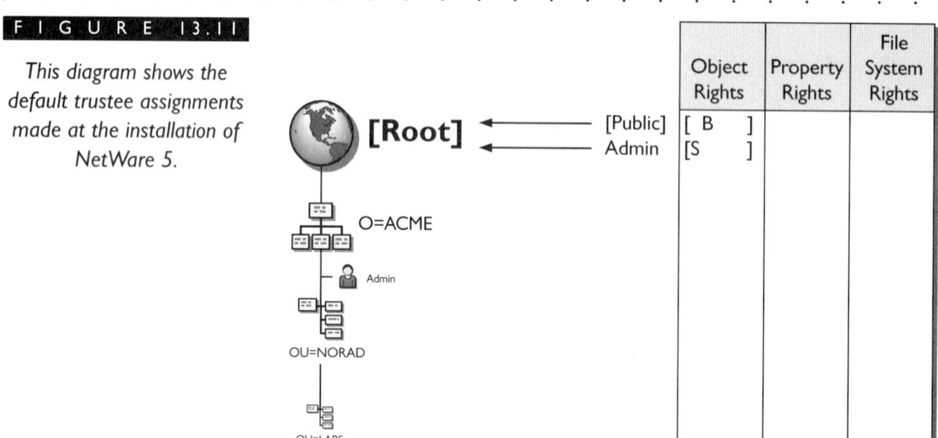

Also during installation of NetWare 5, [PUBLIC] receives an object trustee assignment of object Browse at object [ROOT]. With this right all users can browse the tree after attaching to a server before logging in. This enables users to use the CX command to browse the tree and discover object names once they have loaded the NetWare client software and have attached to a NetWare 5 server. Figure 13.11 shows a graphic representation of the PUBLIC rights received at the time of installation of NetWare 5.

NetWare 5 Server Default Trustee Assignments

The NetWare 5 installation utility also makes trustee assignments at the file system level. The ADMIN object has object Supervisor rights to the tree. The server object is in the tree and therefore has rights to your servers. Because the ADMIN object has object Supervisor rights to the server object, the ADMIN object also receives Supervisor rights to the NetWare file system of that server. This is the only instance in NetWare 5 security where object rights have an impact on file system rights. In fact, any object with Write rights on a server's ACL has Supervisor rights on the file system of that server.

[PUBLIC] receives the Read property right to the server object's Messaging Server property right so that if the server is being used as the default login server, its property can be located. This assignment is in the template for the server object.

The container object that the new server is installed into receives Read and File Scan rights to the server's \PUBLIC directory. This default access enables all users in the container to execute any files stored on the server's \PUBLIC directory.

The container also receives Create rights to the server's \MAIL directory.

Figure 13.12 shows how these trustee assignments are made when a server object is first created.

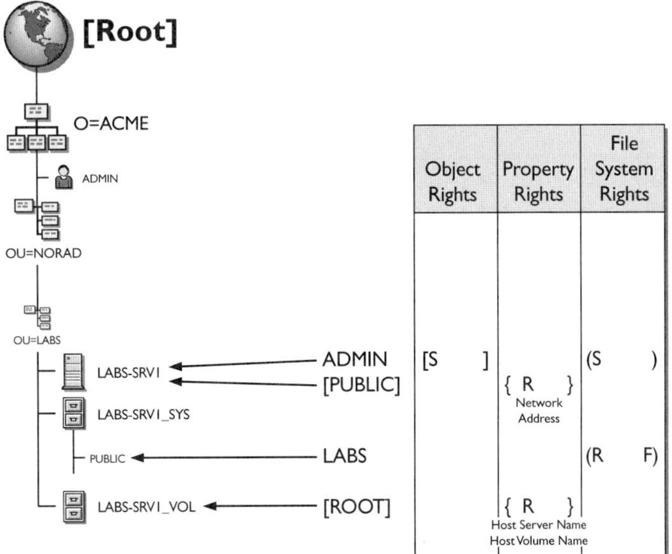

FIGURE 13.12

This example shows how trustee assignments are made for a server object during installation of NetWare 5.

Default Trustee Assignments for Users

When user objects are created, they also receive some default trustee assignments (refer to the section "The Access Control List" earlier in this chapter, which discusses ACLs and default ACLs). These assignments greatly reduce the amount of work required by a NetWare administrator to set up user accounts and provide for their access. The following access is automatically granted during creation of a user object.

For our purposes let's assume that a new user object has been created in the TOKYO container. The newly created user object receives the Read and Compare rights to All Properties by default. All Properties is a category that is visible using NWADMIN by selecting Rights to Other Objects as shown in Figure 13.13. Having the Read right to All Properties allows the user to read the values of his or her own user properties. The Compare right is a subset of Read and enables the value of the property to be compared with another value.

FIGURE 13.13

The user object SIRKAY.TOKYO.ACME receives by default the Read and Compare rights to All Properties for its own object.

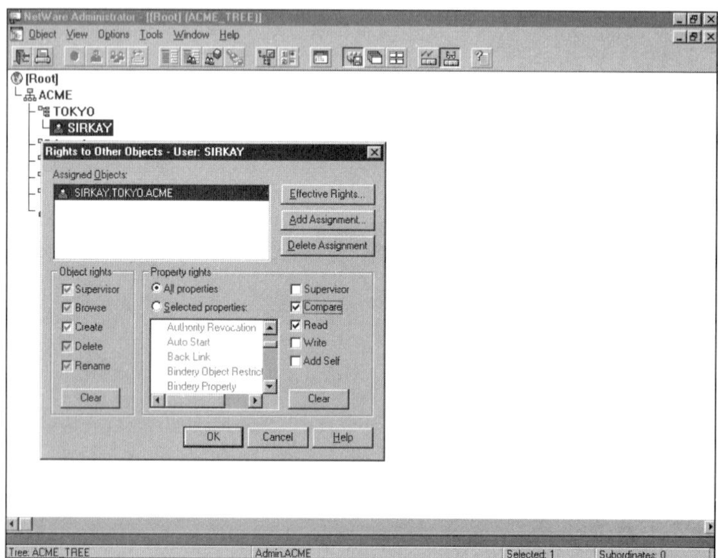

The user object is granted Read and Write rights to its own login script and print job configuration. These rights permit the users to change their own login scripts and print job configurations if they want. Figure 13.14 shows these rights assigned along with the others when a user object is created.

FIGURE 13.14

Rights assignments are made when a user object is created.

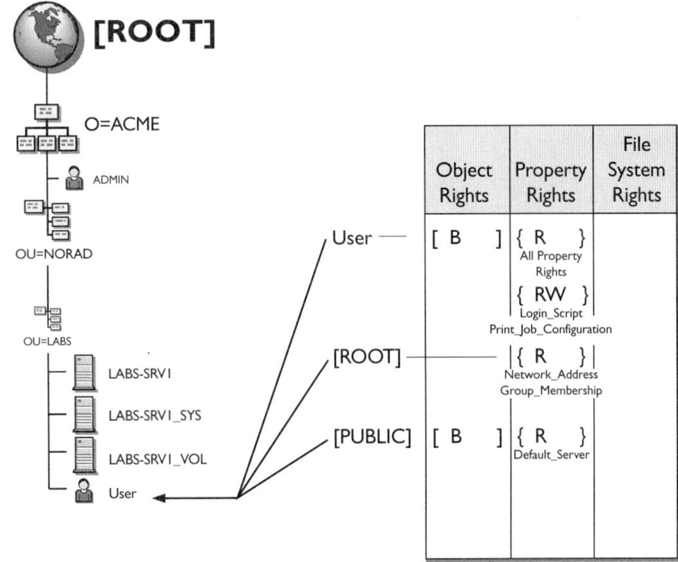

Understanding the Rules of Trustee Assignments

As was mentioned earlier, there are rules that govern the functionality of trustee assignments. Learning these rules can make it much easier for you to understand and use NetWare security.

- **Trustee assignments flow down the tree** — A trustee assignment for objects and [All Property Rights] flows down the tree unless it is blocked by an inherited rights filter (IRF). (The IRF is explained later in this chapter.) For example, if user SIRKAY were granted Supervisor rights to the TOKYO container, these rights would flow down to any subsequent containers and objects below TOKYO unless an object has an inherited rights filter.

- **An explicit trustee assignment at a lower level in the tree replaces all previous trustee assignments** — As shown in Figure 13.15, user SIRKAY has been granted explicit Create and Rename rights beginning at object TOKYO. This trustee assignment flows down until it is blocked by an IRF or reassigned by another explicit assignment. In this example, we reassign the object the Browse right at the OU=CRIME. This explicit assignment will replace all other higher assignments at the OU=CRIME level in the tree.

FIGURE 13.15

An explicit rights assignment made at a lower level in the tree will replace any previous explicit assignment made to that object.

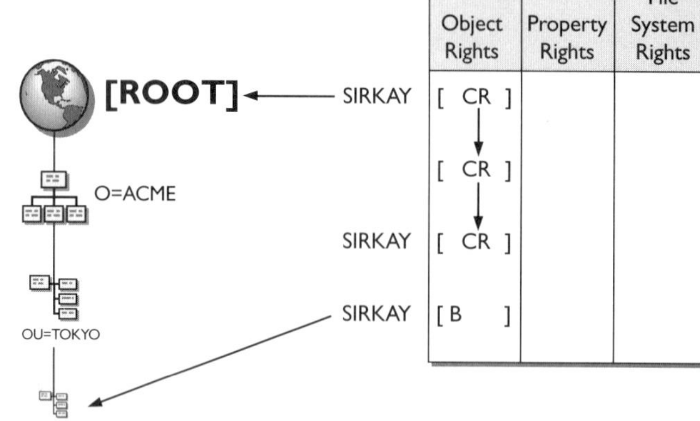

- **Selected property rights override any assignment made in the All Properties category** — At the time of user creation, a user object receives the Read property right to all of its own properties. Any selective assignment of a property right using the Selected Properties category will override anything assigned through the All Properties category. For example, by default all users have the Read property right to all of their own user object properties. Notice also that a user also receives by default the Read and Write rights to his or her login script and print job configuration. The fact that the read write is given again in the selected properties assignment indicates that it has overridden the previous assignment made in the All Properties category.

- **The access control list (ACL) property of every object stores trustee assignments to that object** — Each object can contain a property known as the ACL. A user by default does not have Write rights to the user's own ACL or to that of any other object. Keep in mind that some objects may not have ACLs if they already have received the explicit right.

IMPORTANT

Do not grant users Write rights to any ACL, including their own user objects, because the Write right to the ACL controls all access to those particular objects.

For example, a user possessing the Write right to a container ACL has the ability to make any changes to that object's ACL. The user could assign anyone Supervisor object rights to that container and could modify the object as well.

Understanding Security Equivalence

Security equivalence simply means that one object can be equivalent in rights to another object. The majority of rights assignments should be made by administrators through the use of security equivalence. It is quick and easy to use security equivalence because you can deal with a large number of users rather than a single user at a time. Time is always a factor for network administrators, and we recommend that you assign security equivalence to groups or containers as the best way to make rights assignments to large numbers of people.

To meet the needs of many users requiring the same rights to a directory or file, you can create a group, assign rights to the newly created group, and add members to the group. The members of the group are security equivalent in rights to the group object. Therefore, any assignment made to a group will be received by its members through security equivalence. An example of this process is shown in Figure 13.16.

FIGURE 13.16

An example of creating a group and granting rights to the group. The users receive rights through security equivalence.

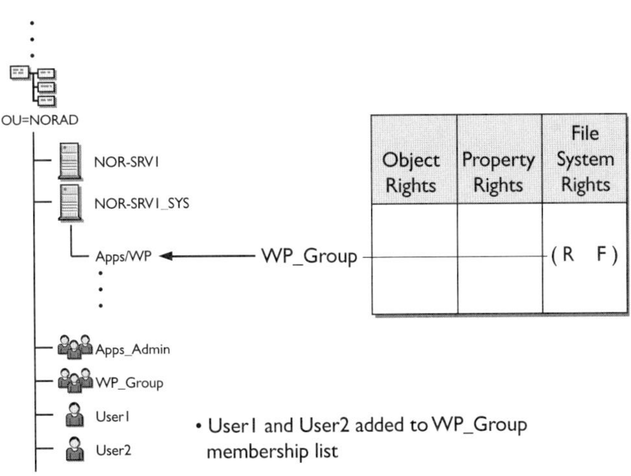

In addition, a container functions much the same way as a group except that the group is used in your login scripts and a group can span multiple containers. If all users in a container access the same resources, it may not be necessary to use groups. However, if you want to further differentiate your environment setting within a container, the group object is an effective way to go.

Because the use of security equivalence will be so common on your network, it is very important to understand how NetWare 5 security functions. You will save time as a network administrator if you understand the rules that govern security equivalence.

- **Security equivalent rights cannot be masked** — If you receive a security equivalence, this assignment cannot be masked by an IRF.
- **Every object is security equivalent to all container objects that are part of its distinguished name** — This security is known as *implied security* equivalence. For example, the user GUINEVERE.FIN.OPS.CAMELOT in the ACME tree is security equivalent to every object in its name. Therefore, if you were to grant the container FIN rights to a particular e-mail server, user GUINEVERE would receive those rights through security equivalence.

NOTE

You cannot use an IRF to single out users to be denied rights granted to a container. If you grant rights to a container, *all* users in or subordinate to that container will always receive those rights.

- **Every object is security equivalent to [ROOT]** — Once a user has successfully logged into a server, that user is security equivalent to [ROOT].
- **Every object is security equivalent to [PUBLIC]** — [PUBLIC] with the default rights of Browse enables users to browse the tree before logging into a server. Each user is security equivalent to [PUBLIC], and [PUBLIC] has been granted Browse rights at object [ROOT]. This assignment can be changed if you like.

- **An object is security equivalent to all objects listed in its Security Equals property** — An NDS object will keep a list (known as the Security Equals property) of all objects that it equals in rights.
- **Security equivalence is not transitive** — This means that Object A can be security equivalent to Object B, but if Object B is security equivalent to Object C, then Object A won't be security equivalent to Object C through Object B.

As mentioned in the rules, security equivalence allows an object to be equivalent in rights to another object. Every object is security equivalent to [Root]. Every object is security equivalent to all container objects that are a part of its name. This is known as implied security equivalence; you don't see this equivalence listed in NWADMIN utilities.

This means that the users are security equivalent to every object above them that is a part of their context name. If you grant rights to an OU that contains the user's name, you have given that individual rights to that context. Conversely, if you are at an Organizational level (O = Novell) and you grant rights to that Organization, then any user located in that Organizational level is going to receive whatever rights were granted to O = Novell by virtue of security equivalence. Those rights cannot be revoked because users are security equivalent to every object that is contained in their context name.

Consulting Experience

Be very careful with assigning rights to the [PUBLIC] trustee because of the security equivalence with all users, since they do not need to be authenticated to receive those rights. The assignment of file system rights is nonfunctional when using the [PUBLIC] trustee. This means that you cannot grant access to files before the user has successfully logged into the server. Generally, the use of the [PUBLIC] trustee for granting rights should be avoided.

Keep in mind that when a user logs into a NetWare 5 server and authenticates to the Directory, Directory Services creates what is known as a *security equivalence vector* that is stored in the connection table on the server. The security equivalence vector contains a list of that object's security equivalencies and is created on every server that the client authenticates to.

Inheritance

Inheritance is the method by which rights to objects and files flow down to subordinate levels of the tree. Only two types of rights are inherited: trustee assignments and security equivalence. Rights given through these two methods can flow downward. This is called inheritance.

As previously stated, explicit trustee assignments at a higher level in your tree will flow down. The rights you receive at lower levels without assignment are known as *inherited rights*. Inherited rights include only the object rights and the All Properties rights. Selected property rights are not inherited.

An important rule to note here is that trustee assignments and security equivalence rights flow down independently. Many think that a trustee rights reassignment affects security equivalence, but that is not the case. For example, suppose you have security equivalence rights flowing down, as well as trustee assignments flowing down at Level A. If you reassign trustee rights at Level B, that affects the trustee rights on that level and below (unless you explicitly reassign trustee assignments again).

But the security equivalence rights continue to flow down and are not affected by the change. If you have an explicit Browse trustee assignment but you still have Read and Write rights through security equivalency, those rights will continue to flow down unless they are affected by an inherited rights filter (IRF) at that level.

Sometimes there is the tendency to confuse security equivalence and inheritance. Keep in mind that inheritance is simply the way that previously granted rights flow down the tree to subordinate levels.

The following rights can be inherited: Object rights, File and Directory rights, and [All Property Rights]. Individual or selected property rights are not inherited.

Through trustee assignments and inheritance, you can make a user as powerful as Admin by assigning the user the Supervisor object right to the [ROOT] object.

By virtue of inheritance, the user is supervisor at all subordinate levels unless filtered by an IRF.

Earlier in our discussion we mentioned that explicit rights, such as the ADMIN user object possessing the Supervisor right at the [ROOT] object, flow down the tree. As shown in Figure 13.17, the Supervisor assignment continues to flow down the tree unless it is otherwise blocked or reassigned. Therefore, at each subsequent level in the tree the ADMIN object's rights are being received through inheritance.

FIGURE 13.17

Inheritance of the Supervisor right at the second and third levels of the tree

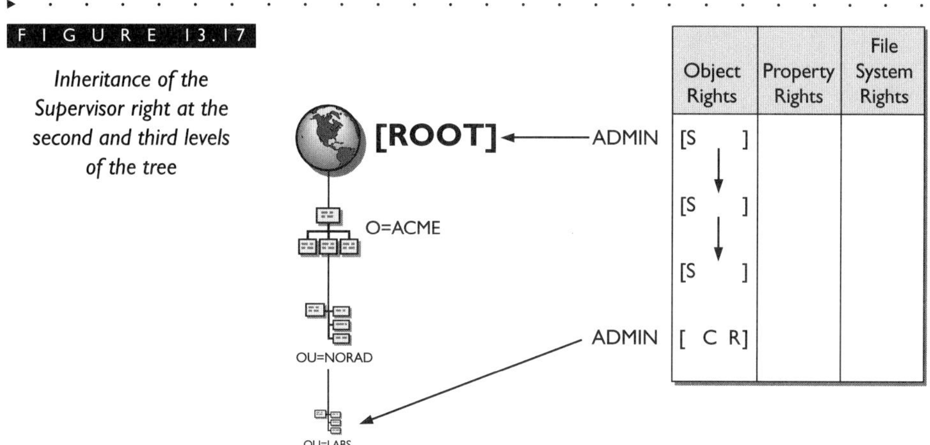

Inherited rights also flow down independently of other rights assignments, such as those obtained through security equivalence. This means that the rights received through inheritance are not affected by actions you may take on other explicit rights assignments. The two operate under separate rules. Do not mix up your security rules. Figure 13.18 shows how explicit rights assignments flow down independently of security equivalence rights.

Understanding Inherited Rights Filters (IRFs)

The filter known as the inherited rights filter (IRF) is used to block inheritance. In reality, the inherited rights filter can only revoke inherited rights and is an inclusive filter. The IRF can be applied to object rights, the All Properties category, and the Selected Properties category.

There is an IRF for every file, directory, object, and property.

FIGURE 13.18

The explicit assignment of the Supervisor right flows down the tree independently of the Browse right, which was received because user ALincoln is security equivalent to the [PUBLIC] trustee.

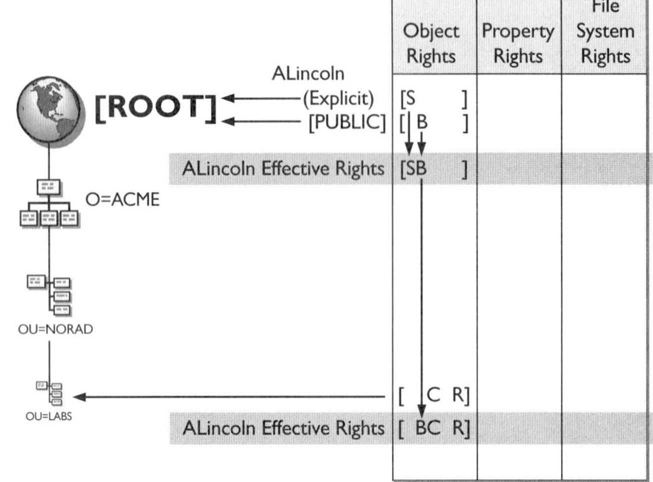

NOTE

As mentioned earlier, you cannot place an IRF on rights received through security equivalence. You can apply the IRF only to object rights, the All Properties category, and the Selected Properties category.

The IRF enables the NetWare administrator to specify which rights can be inherited from an object. It is easier to understand the concept of the IRF if you compare it to a shell around an object. When you place an IRF on an object, you are placing an imaginary shell around the object. The rights that are enabled in the IRF are the only rights that users will have to an object. For example, you could place an IRF of Browse on a server object in a container. One user must maintain Supervisor rights over the object, however. All other users can inherit only the Browse right because of the IRF that is placed around the server object.

Many are confused between security equivalence and inheritance. You can block inheritance through the IRF, but you cannot block security equivalence or trustee assignments through the IRF.

The main difference between Directory Services security and file system security is that the Supervisor right granted in the file system can never be blocked at the file and directory level. This works the same in NetWare 4 and 5 as it does in NetWare 3.*x*. In NDS, however, the Supervisor object and the property Supervisor right can be blocked with an IRF.

Another rule is that you don't inherit the container's rights — you are security equivalent to the OU container object to which you belong. For example, if you are a member of an OU (OU = ABC) and there are rights explicitly assigned to ABC, you receive those rights through security equivalency. Many think they can place an IRF on the container and block all rights, but this is not so.

Also, if you assign explicit trustee assignments directly to users (underneath the IRF), the users will still have rights to the objects through the trustee assignments. Again, the IRF only blocks inherited rights.

NOTE

The ACL is both the trustee assignments made and the filters applied. The same attribute (property) name is used for both.

Rules that Govern the IRF

The following rules govern the inherited rights filter:

- **The IRF cannot grant rights** — It only revokes previously assigned rights. Keep in mind that the IRF is an imaginary shell wrapped around an object.
- **You can enable an IRF for every object, property, file, and directory** — In most cases you will not need to use that many IRFs, because the user's default rights are limited to begin with. As shown in the scenarios at the end of the chapter, most IRFs are used to protect servers and to separate file system and NDS administration.
- **The Supervisor object/property rights can be revoked by an IRF** — An IRF can be applied to all objects, including the server object. Therefore, you can limit a person's Supervisor access to a NetWare 5 file server by applying an IRF to the server object. Remember that a user possessing the managed right (Write right to the ACL) to a server object also has rights to the file system volumes for that server as well.
- **The Supervisor file/directory rights cannot be revoked by an IRF** — This feature is identical to NetWare 3 Supervisor rights in that any user that has Supervisor rights to a file system directly cannot have file system rights masked on that file server.

Inherited ACLs

Each partition [ROOT] object contains a property known as the inherited access control list. For more information on the partition [ROOT] object, refer to Chapter 6, "Designing and Using NDS Partitions and Replicas." The inherited ACL property contains the summation of ACLs from parent containers. Unless an IRF is in effect, all objects in the partition will receive the rights contained in the inherited ACL. NDS can then calculate rights for objects in its partition without having to walk the Directory tree. As changes to ACLs are made to the Directory tree, NDS will update the multivalued inherited ACL property.

The NDS janitor process has the responsibility to maintain the inherited ACLs by recalculating inheritance if any changes are made to the inherited ACLs. For more information on the janitor process, refer to Chapters 8, "NDS Internals Operations," and 9, "Novell Directory Services Objects and Properties."

Understanding Effective Rights

The last step in the security pyramid is the calculation of effective rights. *Effective rights* are what an object can actually do after all other security factors are calculated against the object. The following sources are used in the calculation of effective rights of one object to another:

- The object's ACL
- The object's explicit assignments
- All security equivalent access privileges

For example, we will discuss an object A with access to object B using security equivalence calculated at the time of authentication. The rights would be calculated as follows:

1. Calculate the sum of explicit assignments back to the partition root. Object B would be calculated back to object B's partition root. Of course, an IRF would negate some assignments.

2. Add in the inherited ACLs from the partition root.

3. Object A receives all explicit and inherited ACLs to which A is security equivalent.

As mentioned, effective rights are what an object can actually do at a particular level in the tree. You may have explicit trustee assignments at the Organizational level, but once you get down to a lower OU, an IRF may be placed there and you will end up with different effective rights.

For example, at the OU=ABC level, you may have Admin rights, but at O=TOPGUN level, you may only have Browse rights. What your effective rights are depends on where you are in the directory tree. If you look at your effective rights through some of the utilities, know that those rights are calculated for the context in the tree where you currently are.

The effective rights for specific NDS objects can be viewed using the NWADMIN utility in the "Trustee of this object" screen. The effective rights are the summation of all rights, and objects can receive them through explicit assignments, inheritance, and security equivalences.

Understanding Managed Rights

Managed rights (or management rights) is a term used to describe an object (ADMIN, for example) that has the Write right to an object's ACL. Managed rights means that the trustee has all power over an object and can modify anything pertaining to that object. For some operations in NDS you must have managed rights to perform that operation. Here is a list of NDS operations and the managed rights that are required to perform them:

- All partition operations including Create, Merge, Add Replica, and Move Subtree require the trustee to have Write rights to the target partition server object. The Merge operation requires managed rights to the [ROOT] objects of both trees.

- A schema modification requires the trustee to have Write rights to the ACL of the Directory's [ROOT] object.

- Any modifications to the following properties require Write rights to that object's ACL:
  - Security Equals
  - Group Membership
  - Profile Membership
- Backup requires managed rights on the object(s) being backed up.
- The Add/Remove replica operation requires:
  - Managed rights on the partition root
  - Managed rights on the target server

Managed rights is a term that is used to signify all rights to a specific NDS object. Managed rights are not viewed using any utility; rather, this is a concept, not an actual assignment of rights.

Implementing NDS Security

With an understanding of the basic concepts of security, we can now begin a discussion of how to use and implement NDS security for your network. Refer back to Figure 13.10 as the basis for our security discussion. As stated earlier, the pyramid shown in this figure shows a very logical approach to understanding NetWare 5 security. Each section of the pyramid will now be explained with examples on how you can implement security in your environment for the greatest benefit. First let's consider some general security guidelines or tips.

1. When implementing security, you want to give rights to objects at the highest level possible in your environment, such as at the O or OU levels. If you have a small shop and you want to assign rights to the Mail directory, it may make sense to do this at [Root], or O=TOPGUN. But in large-scale networks, an OU level is probably a better place to assign the more global rights, because not all users need the same kind of rights. For

example, if you want everyone to have file system rights to an APPS directory on a specific file server, you can grant those rights at the O or OU container level through a trustee assignment. Then everybody will get those rights to that file system by virtue of security equivalence, and it won't be blocked by an IRF.

2. Understand how to use the [Public] trustee. You don't want to give the [Public] trustee broad rights because users get those rights before they log in.

3. If you have the Supervisor object right to a file server object, you get all file system rights. This is the only place where NDS rights cross over to the file system rights. If you have the Supervisor object right to the volume object, you do not get all file system rights.

For the specific examples that follow, we will refer to the ACME tree for the model to implement security. The following scenarios will be discussed in terms of NetWare security. All scenarios make the assumption that you are an administrator, and object Supervisor rights at the [ROOT] of your tree are assigned.

Server-Level Security

First consider the security required to install a NetWare 5 server under the OU=NORAD center in our example system.

It is important to understand the following security concepts:

- Trustee assignments
- Security equivalence

As a temporary administrator you are asked to install a NetWare 5 server in the NORAD container into the ACME tree. There are currently no administrators in your location, and this server must be brought up immediately. You would begin by contacting your main administrator to obtain Create rights for the NORAD container. Supervisor rights at your container are needed to install a NetWare 5 server into your own container or to add a partition replica to partition root. This can be accomplished in several ways as described in the following steps.

1. The first way is to simply have the administrator explicitly grant you Supervisor rights to the NORAD container. This method is difficult to track if many similar requests are made to the main NDS administrator. The administrator soon forgets who has been granted rights.

2. The second and recommended way is to use NWADMIN to create an organizational role in the NORAD location and grant the role Supervisor rights to the NORAD container known as NORAD_ADMIN.

3. The main administrator can then move you into the role temporarily as an administrator so that you can install the NetWare 5 server. A NetWare 5 installation with an add replica will *not* complete unless you have Supervisor rights to the container in which the server is being installed.

An example of this entire scenario is shown in Figure 13.19.

FIGURE 13.19

Rights necessary to install a server in the NORAD container

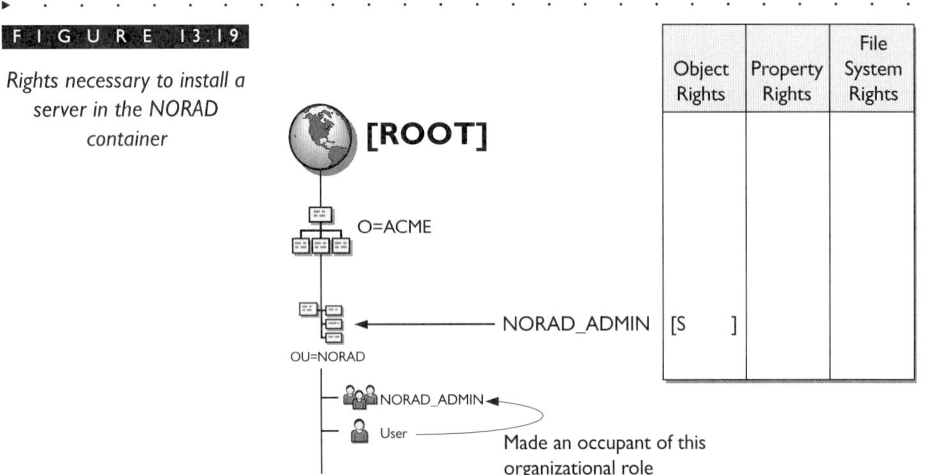

An example of an organizational role being created with NWADMIN is shown in Figures 13.20, 13.21, and 13.22.

FIGURE 13.20

Creating an organizational role

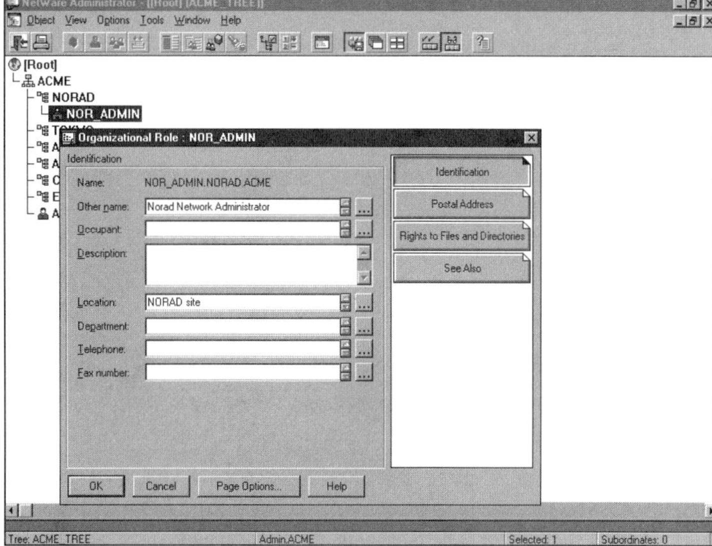

FIGURE 13.21

Assigning the necessary rights

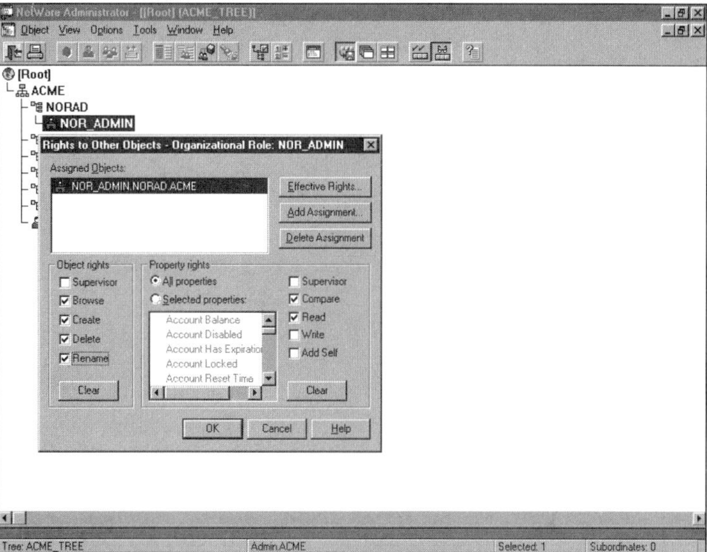

FIGURE 13.22

Moving a user into the role as an occupant

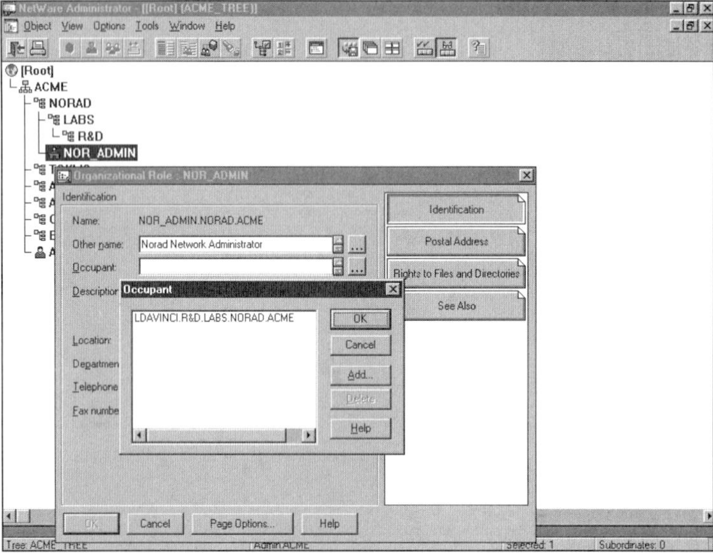

The necessary rights for installing servers into the NDS tree are essentially the Supervisor rights at an NDS-specific container that is also the top object in an NDS partition. The rights needed can be assigned using the NWADMIN utility.

Application-Level Security

The next step in our example scenario is to consider the security required to install an application on your NetWare 5 server in the CAMELOT container and grant application access to your users.

It is important to understand the following security concepts:

- File system trustee assignments
- Supervisor rights to a server object

You are a file system administrator in the LABS location responsible for installing all new applications on the location's file servers.

1. You must have at a minimum the Create right to the APPS subdirectory on your NetWare 5, for example. In most cases you will use Supervisor trustee rights to perform these operations.

2. If you have Supervisor object rights over the file server object, you will also have Supervisor rights over the file system.

3. Install your application according to the directions.

4. Make sure that all executable files related to this application are flagged as sharable read-only. Most application installations automatically do this for you, but it doesn't hurt to check.

5. Create any supporting objects that may be needed such as groups or directory maps. This requires Create rights at the container. You may also need file system rights as well.

6. Consider using Novell's NetWare Application Manager to launch applications as NDS objects from a user's desktop. For more information on the NetWare Application Manager, refer to Chapter 2, "Installation and Management Utilities for NetWare."

An example of this entire scenario is shown in Figure 13.23.

The rights for creating and assigning application into the NDS tree have been detailed. In addition, the assigned user will want to use the NWADMIN utility to grant the appropriate access rights to the network users.

Security on the Level of Individual Rights

Consider security procedures for granting an individual rights to manage a help desk center at the CAMELOT location.

It is important to understand the following security concepts:

- Trustee assignments
- Security equivalence

FIGURE 13.23

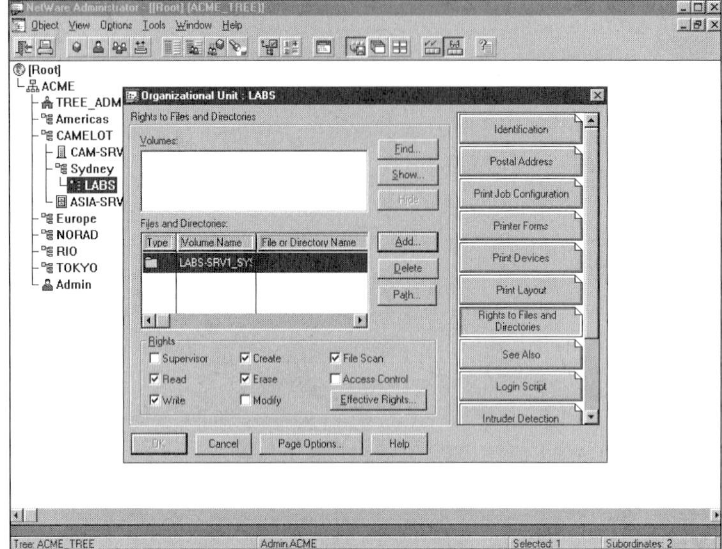

Using NWADMIN to assign rights necessary to install an application on a NetWare 5 server in the LABS container

Your responsibility is to assist in managing a help desk at the CAMELOT location.

1. Using NWADMIN, create a series of specialized organizational roles for your help desk administration such as user administrators, server administrators, and tree administrators. Although currently Directory Services does not enforce rights to a specific object class, you can create organizational roles that designate these type of administrators.

2. Assign Create, Delete, and Rename rights to the user administrator's role.

3. Assign Supervisor file system rights to the server administrator's role for each server in the container to be managed.

4. Create an organizational role at the top of your tree with explicit Supervisor rights at [ROOT]. Move the top help desk administrators into the organizational role as occupants.

5. Make IRF assignments where appropriate to limit administrator access to certain areas of your system.

Examples of this entire scenario are shown in Figures 13.24, 13.25, and 13.26.

FIGURE 13.24

Creating an organizational role for the user administrator

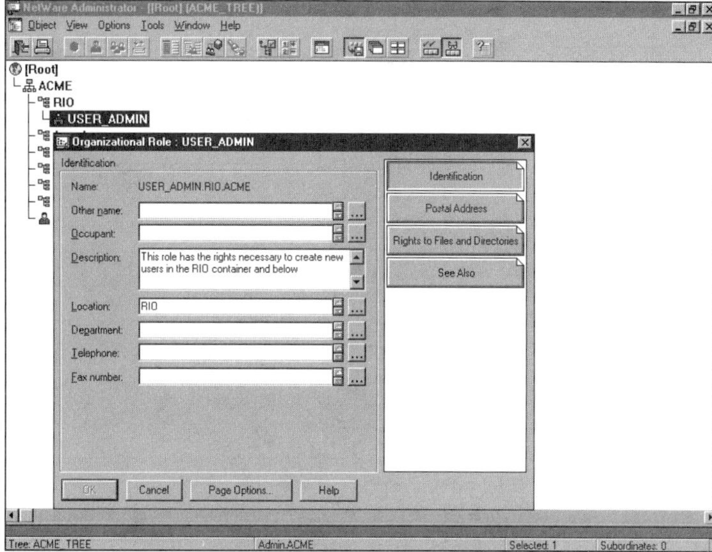

FIGURE 13.25

Creating an organizational role for the server administrator

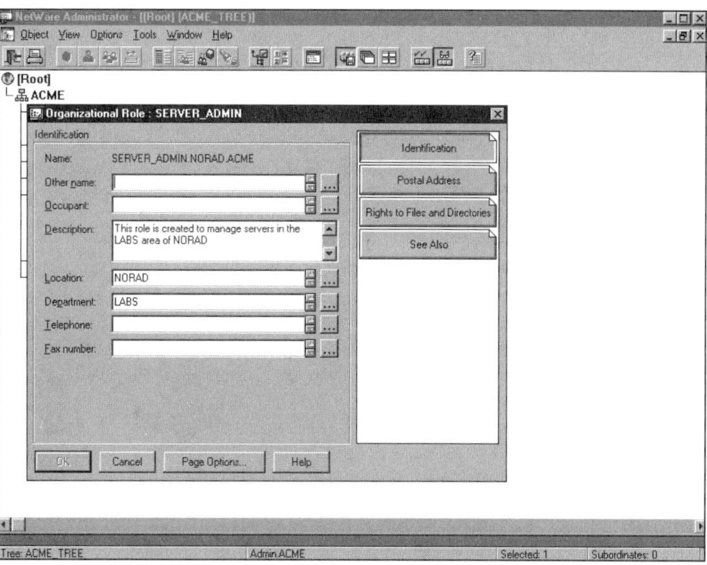

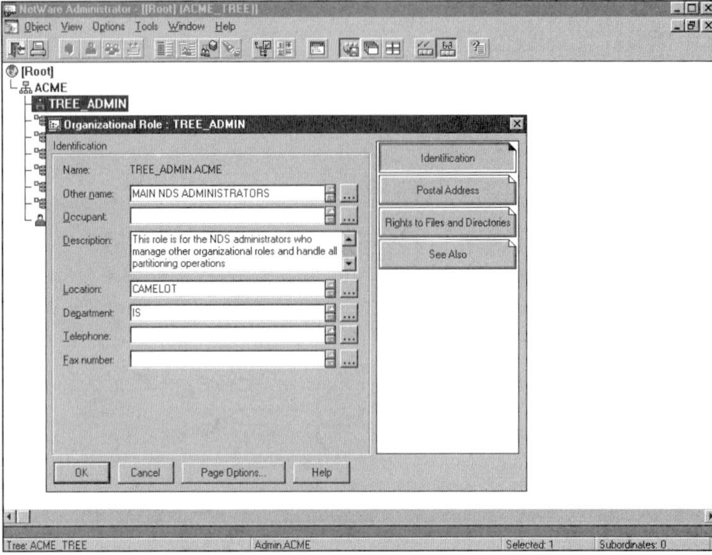

FIGURE 13.26

Creating an organizational role for the tree administrators

The necessary rights for creating a help desk for your organization have been detailed. You will want to use the NWADMIN utility to make the rights assignments.

Security on the Level of Subadministrators

Next, we turn to the creation of subadministrators for each major location in the ACME tree.

It is important to understand the following security concepts:

- Trustee assignments
- Security equivalence
- Inheritance

You have been given the assignment to create subadministrators for each major location in the ACME network and assign individuals to manage the network from that level down. You currently manage the network with only the ADMIN user object.

1. Using NWADMIN, create organizational role objects in the containers NORAD, RIO, TOKYO, CAMELOT, SYDNEY, and TOKYO.

2. Using NWADMIN, grant the newly created organizational role objects Supervisor rights to their respective containers.

3. Choose an administrator or administrators to participate in the organizational role and add them as role occupants using NWADMIN.

4. Assign the ADMIN user explicit Supervisor rights to each of the organizational role objects.

5. Using NWADMIN, place an inherited rights filter of Browse (and possibly Read) on each of the organizational roles to prohibit management of the role by the occupants.

6. These new administrators will have the power to create additional objects, including subordinate containers, in their respective locations. The administrators have Supervisor rights at these lower levels in the tree through inheritance.

An example of this entire scenario is shown in Figure 13.27.

If you need to decentralize the administration of NDS for your company, the rights for doing so have been detailed. In order to assign the appropriate rights to the specific users or groups of users that will become the subadministrators, you want to use the NWADMIN utility.

Administrator-Level Security

Next, create a file system administrator and an NDS administrator in the OU=TOKYO location.

FIGURE 13.27

Creating organizational roles for each location in the ACME tree

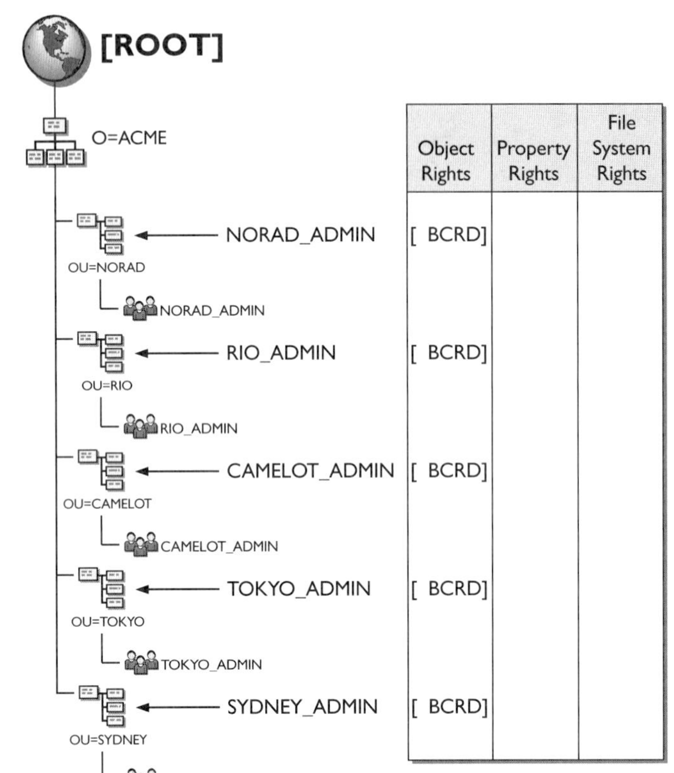

It is important to understand the following security concepts:

- Trustee assignments
- Security equivalence
- Inherited rights filter

Administration in the TOKYO container is being broken out into two responsibilities. One individual will handle only the file system administration, while the other administrator will handle NDS administration. Each must have separate rights.

1. Using NWADMIN, create two organizational roles. Name the first role NDS_ADMIN and the second role FILE_ADMIN.

2. Using NWADMIN, assign the NDS_ADMIN role Supervisor rights to the TOKYO container.

3. Using NWADMIN, assign the FILE_ADMIN role Supervisor rights to the server objects TOK-SRV1 and TOK-SRV2.

4. Using NWADMIN, place an inherited rights filter of Browse (and possibly Read) on the server objects TOK-SRV1 and TOK-SRV2.

An example of this entire scenario is shown in Figure 13.28.

FIGURE 13.28

Separating NDS and file system administration

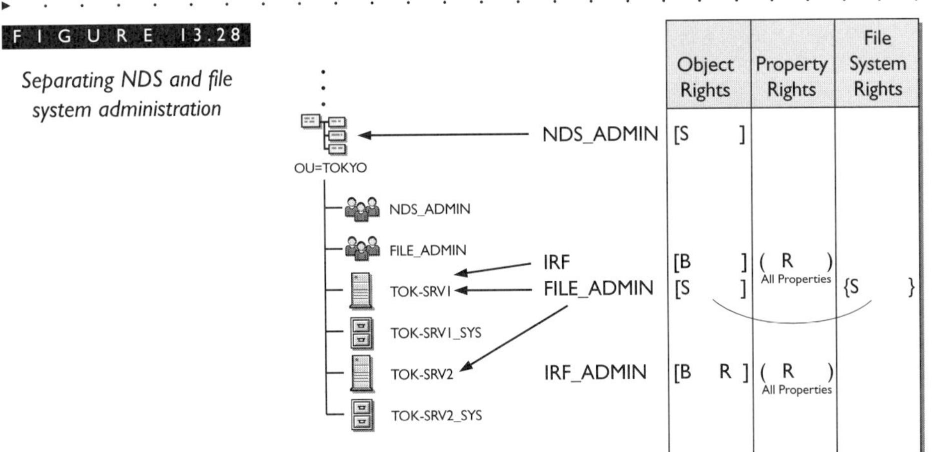

Using NDS rights, you can separate the administration of the NDS tree from the NetWare file system. This method is helpful if you need to decentralize the administration of either the NDS tree or your file system, and then make those assignments to other administrators in your company. In order to assign the appropriate rights to the specific users or groups of users that will become the subadministrators, you want to use the NWADMIN utility.

Security in Partitioning Operations

As a final step in our scenario, consider the rights necessary to perform partitioning operations at different levels in the NDS tree.

You have been made responsible for partitioning operations on the ACME network. You want to prohibit all partitioning operations except those performed by you and another administrator.

1. Using NWADMIN, grant the other administrators in their organizational roles all rights to their respective containers except the Supervisor object right. Grant Read and Create rights on the container ACL also. (Keep in mind that other administrators will not be able to install NetWare 5 servers into the tree without the Supervisor right to the container if they are adding a replica. You can grant them the right temporarily to handle this situation or add the replica for them.)

2. Create an organizational role for yourself and other tree administrators for partitioning operations called OR_PARTITIONS.

3. If you have not already done so, grant the organizational role explicit object Supervisor rights to each container immediately subordinate to [ROOT].

An example of this entire scenario is shown in Figure 13.29.

By using NDS rights, you can separate the administration of the partitioning and replicas for the NDS tree from the administration of the objects and properties in NDS. This method is helpful if you need to decentralize the administration of the NDS tree. In order to assign the appropriate rights to the specific users or groups of users that will become the subadministrators, you want to use the NWADMIN utility.

FIGURE 13.29

Rights needed to perform partitioning operations on the ACME tree

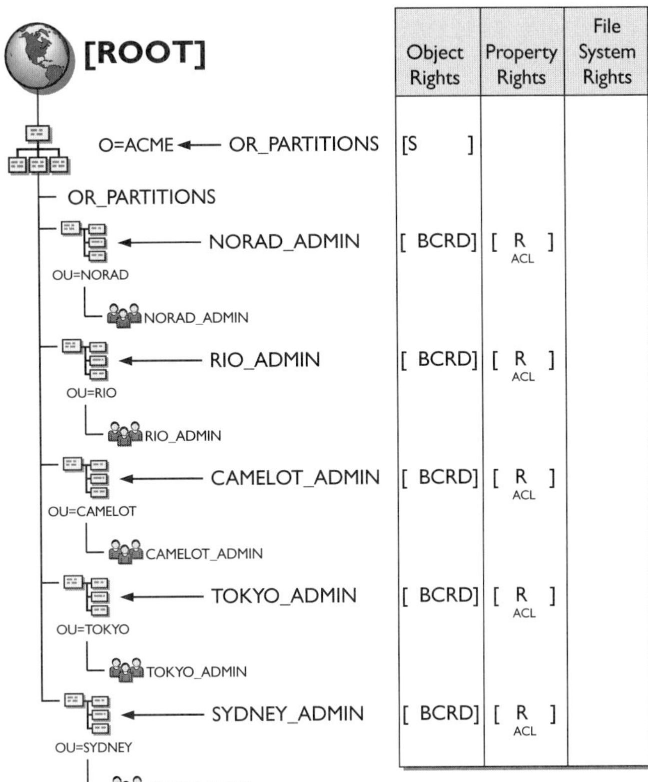

Summary

This chapter has presented you with an understanding of NDS object and file system rights. As an administrator, you can assign rights to other administrators to perform specific tasks such as managing the users in their part of the tree or performing certain operations such as doing server backups or creating new NDS users. NetWare 5 provides expanded security functions including Public Key Infrastructure (PKI) and Secure Authentication Services (SAS).

CHAPTER 14

NetWare 5 Print Services

"Learning hath gained most by those books by which the printers have lost."
—Thomas Fuller

NetWare 5 enables a printer to be shared by any or all network users. In order to print, an entire print job must be created and placed in a print queue on the server and then wait until a print server can process the job and send it to the network printer.

NetWare 5 print services uses the same basic concepts and architecture available in earlier versions of NetWare, which are based on print queues. In addition, NetWare 5 includes the next generation in network printing, called Novell Distributed Print Services (NDPS). NDPS has been created by Novell joining forces with the leaders of printer hardware technologies, including Hewlett-Packard, Xerox, Lexmark, Ricoh, and many others.

In this chapter we will discuss these concepts and demonstrate how to design and implement NetWare 5 print services in either a queue-based printing environment or the newer NDPS print environment. We also discuss setting up a pure NetWare 5 printing environment and mixed NetWare 3 and NetWare 5 print environments. Because there is little difference between setting up a pure NetWare 5 printing environment and a mixed NetWare 4 and NetWare 5 environment, we will not discuss the latter problem in this chapter. The queue-based services and NDPS are available on both NetWare 4 and NetWare 5. The major difference between the two versions lies in the pure IP protocol support in NetWare 5, which enables easier setup for some printers.

In the first several sections of this chapter, we will exclusively address setting up the more familiar queue-based print services for NetWare 5. Next, we will discuss how you can integrate the NetWare 3 printing environment, which uses the bindery instead of NDS to store its print objects. Finally, we will discuss the newest printing environment called NDPS, which makes network printing completely bidirectional, giving users and administrators complete control.

The NDS Print Objects for Queue-Based Printing

The print objects are the building blocks for the NetWare 5 print services architecture. These print objects define the network's printing infrastructure. In

NetWare 5, these objects are stored in NDS as these three separate objects:

- Print queue
- Print server
- Printer

The NetWare 5 print services infrastructure is created by the association or relationship you set up between these three objects. The print queue should be assigned to represent a specific network printer or group of printers. The printer, in turn, is assigned to a print server, and the print server is assigned to service specific print queues. With these structures, a user creates a print job that is stored in a print queue until a print server can service the print job and send it directly to a printer. The print server waits until the printer is ready to accept the print job before sending it. This relationship is shown in Figure 14.1.

FIGURE 14.1

The relationship between the print objects in the NetWare 5 print services infrastructure

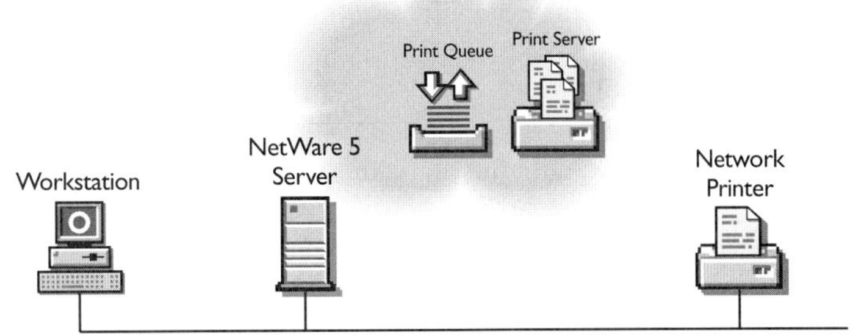

Users using NetWare 5 print services redirect their print jobs to network printers or to printers attached to the network workstations. The user's data (or print job) is not sent directly from the workstation to the printer. Instead, the data is captured and redirected to a file in a print queue, where it is stored waiting to be sent to the printer. The data is first sent to a print queue to avoid multiple print jobs contending for the same shared printer. Multiple print jobs from different network users may stack up in the print queue until the print server is able to send them to the printer. The print server will service the print jobs in the order they are received unless otherwise stipulated by the network administrator or print server operator.

The Print Queue

The *print queue* is a key object or component in NetWare 5 printing. When a network user sends a print job to a network printer, NetWare temporarily stores the print job as a file in a directory on the server called a print queue. The print jobs wait in the print queue until the print server is able to process them and then send them to the waiting printer. The print queue objects represent the directories where the print jobs are sent to be serviced.

The print queues store print jobs in subdirectories on server volumes that you specify when you create them. In NetWare 3, the print queue subdirectory was located in SYS:SYSTEM by default and could not be moved. In NetWare 5, the print queue subdirectory can be created on any server volume. The print queue will then be found in a default root subdirectory called QUEUES of that selected server volume. This subdirectory name can also be changed if you like.

Consulting Experience

Print queues and printers in the NDS tree should be placed with the users who will use their print services. For example, place print queues and printers in the same OUs as their users. If you have users in different OUs in the tree who want to use these print objects, you can either alias the print objects or place them at upper levels in the tree to support the greatest number of users.

Consulting Experience

It is a good idea to take advantage the NetWare 5 feature that enables you to create the print queues on server volumes other than SYS:SYSTEM. We recommend that you leave extra space on the SYS volume because NDS files are stored on the SYS:SYSTEM in a hidden directory. NDS will stop accepting changes if the SYS volume fills up.

You can create print queues using the NWADMIN utility. When you define a print queue using this utility, you give it a descriptive name. This name should follow your naming convention and identify the kind of printer the print queue is associated with, where the printer is located, or the type of print jobs that can be sent. For example, the print queue associated with a Hewlett-Packard Laser Jet 4si could be called HP4SI-PQ1.

The print queue name is used by the users and should be as clear and convenient as possible. Internally, NetWare 5 assigns a print queue a server-centric ID number, which is an eight-digit hexadecimal number. For example, the print queue named HP4SI-PQ1 might have an ID with the value of 8034D4CF. You can view this ID number in the utilities. This number is important because it is used as the corresponding subdirectory name under the QUEUES directory.

The use of print queues provides an orderly method for multiple users to send print jobs to a single printer device. Queuing print jobs at the NetWare 5 server ensures that the printer deals with only one print job at a time.

Consulting Experience

Although you can set up a print queue associated with multiple printers, we recommend that for simplicity and manageability you set up only one print queue for each printer on your network.

The print jobs are stored as files in the print queue subdirectory. Their filenames always start with a "Q$" and include the last four digits of the print queue ID, plus a three-digit job number as the file extension. For example, the seventh print job in the print queue with the ID of 8034D4CF would have a file name of Q$D4CF.007.

When a user creates a print job and forwards it to the print queue, the print job passes through several states before being printed. These states are outlined in Table 14.1.

TABLE 14.1

Print Job States in the Print Queue

STATE	DESCRIPTION
Adding	The print job is being added to the print queue by the workstation.
Ready	The print job is waiting to be serviced by the associated print server.
Active	The print job is being sent to the appropriate printer.
Removed	The print job is finished and is removed from the print queue.

Print Servers

Another key software component of NetWare 5 printing is the print server, which binds the print queues to the network printers. A print server takes print jobs from the print queue and sends them to the assigned network printer. The print server software program can either be loaded as a NetWare Loadable Module on a NetWare 5 server or run as firmware in a network-attached printer.

In NetWare 5 PSERVER.NLM supports up to 256 printers, a fact that can help you consolidate or reduce the total number of print servers you have in the network. In order to start the print server on the server, type this at the server console prompt:

```
LOAD PSERVER PrintServerName
```

Substitute the name of the specific print server for PrintServerName. You can place this command in the AUTOEXEC.NCF file if you want the print server to load automatically during server bootup. Figure 14.2 displays the main screen for the print server software.

FIGURE 14.2

The main screen for the print server software running on the NetWare 5 server

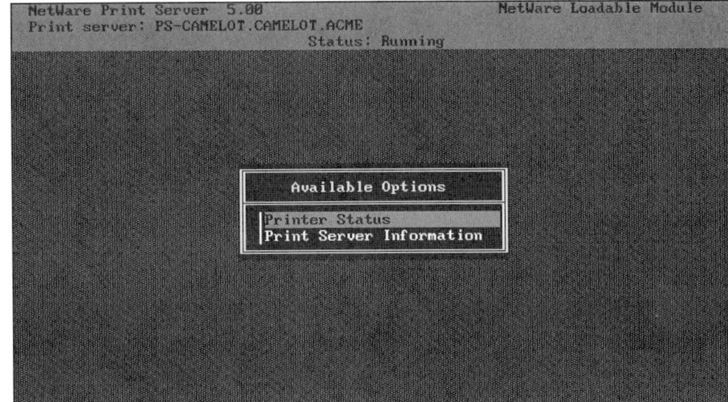

The print server software running at the network attached printer is often referred to as a *queue server* because the printer is set up to service the print queue directly. The queue server software logs into the server where the print queue is stored and polls the print queue to see if it has any print jobs ready for the printer. In this configuration the printer device performs both functions of the print server and printer.

Consulting Experience

For ease of administration and use, we recommend that you configure the network printers as queue servers. This configuration requires that you connect the printers directly to the network cable system.

Printers

If you use the NLM-based print server, you need to use the new NPRINTER printer program that enables the print server to send jobs to a network printer. This printer can either be physically attached to the back of the NetWare 5 server, a DOS or OS/2 workstation, or directly to the network itself. Each printer requires the NPRINTER program to attach to the printer server and service print jobs.

Several different versions of the NPRINTER printer program can be loaded in several different situations. For instance, NPRINTER can be loaded as a terminate-and-stay resident (TSR) program, as a NetWare Loadable Module, or in the memory of the printer device itself. NPRINTER can be loaded in the following three ways according to the printer configuration:

- Workstations with printer devices connected should run NPRINTER.EXE to support the network printer. The printer is cabled to the parallel or serial port of the workstation. There is now a 32-bit version of NPRINTER called NPRINTER Manager for use on Windows 95/98/NT machines.

- Printer devices that are connected to a NetWare 5 server use the NPRINTER.NLM. The printer is cabled to the parallel or serial port of the NetWare 5 server.

- Printer devices connected directly to the network run the NPRINTER program from firmware or flash memory.

With NPRINTER loaded on a workstation, the user of that workstation can run applications and function normally. The user can even access the printer device as a local printer in stand-alone fashion, as well as a network printer. However, users are not encouraged to use the printer as a local printer because it might conflict with network printing activities. Naturally, the type of workstation and CPU speed will affect printing performance. For most large network sites this type of configuration is not used.

NetWare 5 enables users to specify the printer object instead of a print queue when sending their print jobs. Users no longer have to know anything about print queues; they can simply send their print jobs to a printer by specifying the printer name. The network takes care of all print queue and print server activities. Sending a print job to a printer instead of a print queue is more intuitive to the user.

NetWare 5 Print Utilities

In order for you to create and manage NetWare 5 print services, you should become familiar with several utilities that help you set up, control, and monitor network printing. One major change that you may notice immediately is that NetWare 5 no longer supports the DOS-based print utilities, such as PCONSOLE, PRINTCON, PRINTDEF, PSERVER, PSC, PUPGRADE, MIGPRINT, and ENDCAP. Instead of using the DOS-based utilities, you can use NWADMIN to create the printing objects and establish their relationship. The DOS-based utilities still available are CAPTURE, NPRINT, and NPRINTER. In addition, the server-based print utilities, PSERVER.NLM and NPRINTER.NLM, are also still supported.

The NetWare 5 print utilities and their functionality are described in the sections that follow.

NWADMIN (NetWare Administrator)

The NetWare Administrator is a windows-based program that enables you to manage NDS objects, including the printing objects. You can browse, create, modify, and grant rights to the printing objects. This utility offers the graphical interface for managing objects.

Capture

The Capture utility runs as a TSR to intercept the output to a local printer port and redirect it to the appropriate network print queue. This program is used mainly with applications and situations that are not network aware.

NPRINT (Network Print)

The Network Print utility is used from the command line to submit text files or previously formatted printer-ready files to the network print queues. This program is similar to the DOS PRINT command line utility.

NPRINTER.EXE (NetWare Printer)

The free-standing form of the NetWare printer program runs at a DOS workstation and connects the printer to the print server. With NPRINTER.EXE, the workstation printers wait to receive the print jobs passed to it. The workstation can run any application while printing takes place in the background. This program must be used in conjunction with the PSERVER program running at the server.

NPRINTER.NLM (NetWare Printer)

The NetWare 5 printer program can also be loaded at the server as NPRINTER.NLM. This utility supports printers attached directly to the server and must be used in conjunction with the PSERVER program running at the server.

PSERVER.NLM (Print Server)

The Print Server utility loads and runs on a NetWare 5 server that can act as a print server. The print server supports the remote and local printers running NPRINTER. The print server runs as an NLM called PSERVER.NLM. The print server can support up to 256 printers.

Queue-Based Print Services Configurations

You should plan your printing needs in advance to determine which users need what kind of printers. For example, some users need strictly laser printers, whereas others may need dot matrix printers, plotters, and color printers. The type of printer has a significant effect on overall printing speeds. Where performance is a necessity, choose printers with a high page-per-minute (PPM) rating.

You need to consider five printer configurations or relationships when planning the printing infrastructure for your network. These five configurations are:

- Non-network workstation printers
- Network workstation printers

- Network server printers
- Network-direct printers (remote printer mode)
- Network-direct printers (queue server mode)

Non-Network Workstation Printers

A non-network workstation printer is connected to a workstation but is not set up as a network printer. This means that the workstation is not running the NPRINTER program, which shares the printer among all network users. Without the network software NPRINTER, the users of this workstation are the only ones that can print to the local printer. The users simply send the print jobs from the workstation to the stand-alone printer. Figure 14.3 illustrates this configuration.

FIGURE 14.3

The printer is set up as a non-network workstation printer. This is a stand-alone printer configuration.

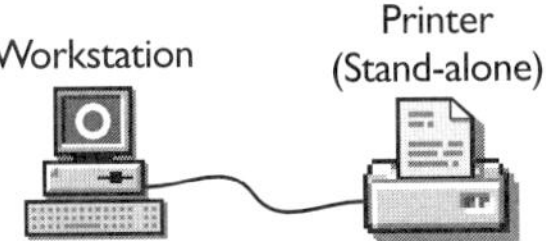

This configuration is simple for the user to set up and understand but is limited in a network environment. Because the printer is not shared by the other network users, the only person who can use the printer is the user sitting at the workstation.

You may want to consider setting up the printer in this fashion when the user requires a special-purpose workstation/printer combination. For example, the user who is responsible for printing invoices or checks may have a dedicated printer with all the forms preloaded and therefore may need a separate printer that should not be used by everyone on the network.

Network Workstation Printers (Remote Printers)

A printer that is connected to a workstation can be a network printer if the proper network software is loaded. The NetWare 5 printer software NPRINTER.EXE needs to be loaded at the workstation, and the PSERVER.NLM software needs to be running at the server to communicate with the printer. The PSERVER is configured with the setup for the printer at the workstation.

The workstation that has the printer attached always needs be powered on (but not necessarily logged in) and running the NPRINTER.EXE program. The NPRINTER.EXE program connects the workstation printer to the print server and waits to receive the print jobs passed to it. Figure 14.4 illustrates the network workstation printer or remote printer configuration.

FIGURE 14.4

A network workstation printer, also called a remote printer

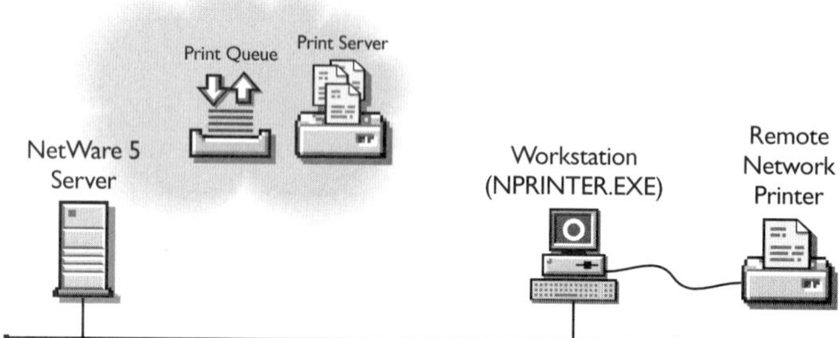

This configuration is also called a *remote printer configuration* because the printers are not physically attached to the server running the print server. Instead the printers are connected to the workstations in the network so that all the network users can print to them. You must start NPRINTER.EXE for each remote printer you defined for the print server. Run NPRINTER.EXE on the workstation to which the remote printer is physically attached. If you have more than one remote printer attached to the same workstation, you need to run NPRINTER once for each printer.

The easiest way to execute NPRINTER is by using the AUTOEXEC.BAT file for the PC. In this way, the NPRINTER software is running once the workstation is booted and even before a user logs in. Here is an example of loading the NPRINTER software using an AUTOEXEC.BAT file:

```
ECHO Off
PATH C:\DOS;C:\WINDOWS
PROMPT $P$G
LOADHIGH C:\NWCLIENT\LSL
```

```
LOADHIGH C:\NWCLIENT\NE2000
LOADHIGH C:\NWCLIENT\IPXODI
LOADHIGH C:\NWCLIENT\VLM
F:
NPRINTER PrintServer N
PAUSE
LOGIN...
```

Remember, NPRINTER doesn't have to be logged in to run, but it does need to be attached to the network, meaning that the NetWare shell or VLMs need to be loaded at the workstation. In order to execute the NPRINTER program before the user has logged in, you should copy it to the SYS:LOGIN directory of each server.

The remote printer configuration is a good option because the printing resources can be easily distributed around the network and placed close to the users that need them. One downside to this setup is that if the workstation is ever turned off or fails, the network printer becomes unavailable.

Network Server Printers

A printer that is connected directly to the server can be a network printer if you load the NPRINTER.NLM software on the server. The PSERVER.NLM software also needs to be loaded to communicate with the NPRINTER software and printer.

Using this configuration, network users have the option to print to printers that are connected directly to the server. As with the network workstation printer, the users' print jobs are redirected to print queues that are serviced by the print server or PSERVER. Figure 14.5 illustrates the network server printer configuration.

Because the printer is connected directly to the server, this configuration becomes less flexible in most large network environments. Typically, in large networks the servers are placed in the computer room and may not be close to the network users. The printer cable can only extend a limited distance, thus making access for the users difficult, if not impossible.

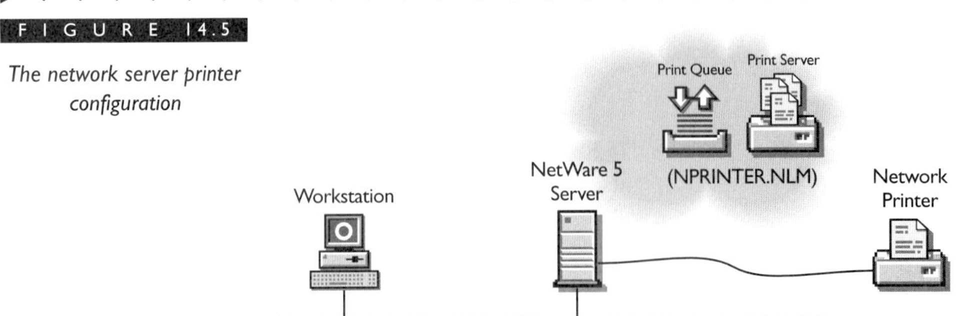

FIGURE 14.5

The network server printer configuration

This configuration is very popular in networks or remote office configurations in which the number of users is small. The server in this case can be situated close to the network users, and access to the printers is not limited. An important issue to remember when placing printers is that the users should not have to walk too far to pick up their print jobs. Printers should be placed in convenient locations.

Another issue with connecting printers directly to the server is that the printing load could slow the performance of the server. A printer connected to a server will demand CPU interrupts to process the print jobs. In a high-traffic environment, it is not wise to connect printers directly to the server.

Network-Direct Printers (Remote Printer Mode)

A network-direct printer in remote printer mode is connected directly to the network using a special hardware device. These special hardware printing devices provide the connectivity to the network and are supplied by vendors such as Castelle, Compaq, Eagle Technologies, Hewlett-Packard, Intel, and Lexmark. Depending on the hardware, this device is either connected to the port of the printer and then to the network or is installed in a slot in the printer.

In the remote printer mode, the printer functions much like a network workstation running NPRINTER.EXE. The NPRINTER program resides in the firmware or flash memory of the printer device. This configuration requires that the PSERVER.NLM be loaded on a NetWare server. The printer device then logs into the NetWare 5 server. It connects to the NetWare print server and polls print jobs. Figure 14.6 illustrates a network-direct printer running in remote printer mode.

FIGURE 14.6

A network-direct printer running in remote printer mode

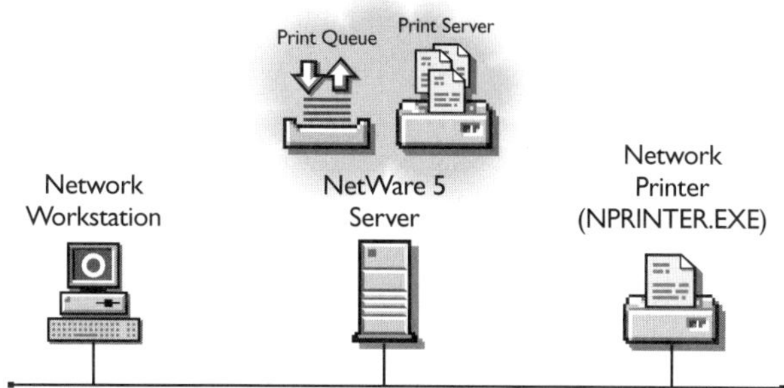

Using this configuration, you can distribute the printers around the network and place them close to the network users who use them. The printers running in remote printer mode under NetWare 5 run considerably faster than they did under NetWare 3. The increased speed and flexibility of NetWare 5 makes remote printer mode a very effective way of providing network print services with these devices.

NetWare 5 and NetWare 3 use the same NetWare SPX communication protocol between the print server and network-direct devices running in remote printer mode. This means that your existing NetWare 3 network-direct devices can attach and receive print jobs from a NetWare 5 print server. Supporting a mixed NetWare 3 and NetWare 5 printing environment will be discussed in more detail later in this chapter.

In general, setting up a network-direct print device in remote printer mode involves the following steps:

1. Use the printer configuration utility supplied by the vendor to set up specific assignments.

2. Start NWADMIN to create your print service objects.

3. Create one or more print queues to be associated with the printer.

4. Select Other/Unknown and assign it to the print queue(s) previously created.

5. Create the print server object to service the printer and assign the printer to the print server object. If you already have an existing print server, you can use it for this purpose. Simply assign to it the printer to be serviced.

6. Run the network-attached printer configuration software supplied by the vendor.

7. Select the printer to be configured.

8. Configure the printer as a remote printer.

9. Select the print server and printer number to represent this printer.

One possible inconvenience in this process is that some printer devices require the print server to be running in order to be configured. Typically, this is not a problem, because the print server is running and servicing other printers. The new assignments made to the print server will take effect immediately, and there is no need to recycle (take down and bring back up) the print server.

Another possible inconvenience comes with some of the older varieties of network-direct devices. These devices need to be configured on the print server with a 16-printer limitation. (This 16-printer limitation was introduced in the NetWare 3 print servers.) You should reserve printer connections 0 to 15 for these printer devices. The remaining slots (16 to 255) can then be used for your other, newer network printers.

Consulting Experience

Some of the printer configuration utilities supplied by the vendors of the hardware can be operated only with explicit SUPERVISOR rights to the server; these utilities do not recognize a Supervisor equivalent. As a result, you will need to log in using the SUPERVISOR account in bindery mode rather than logging in as ADMIN or other administrative user under NDS.

Network-Direct Printers (Queue Server Mode)

A network-direct printer is set up in queue server mode much as in the preceding case, in which the printer is connected directly to the network using a special hardware device. The difference with this configuration is that the printer in queue server mode acts like a special-purpose print server.

The queue server logs into the NetWare 5 server and services the associated print queue directly. The network-direct printers set up as queue servers are created and displayed in the NDS tree as print server objects.

In general, setting up a network-direct print device in queue server mode involves the following steps:

1. Use the printer configuration utility supplied by the vendor to set up specific assignments.
2. Start NWADMIN to create your print service objects.
3. Create one or more print queues to be associated with the printer.
4. Create a printer object for the network-direct printer. Configure the printer object as Other/Unknown and assign it to the print queue(s) previously created.
5. Create the print server object to service the printer, and assign the printer to the print server object. This name must be unique on the network. A new print server object is created for each network-direct printer set up in queue server mode.
6. Run the network-attached printer configuration software supplied by the vendor.
7. Select the printer to be configured.
8. Configure the printer as a queue server.
9. Type in the name of the print server.
10. Select the file server where the print queues are located.

The network-direct printer setup in queue server mode is the most popular printing solution in the industry. In many cases, it offers a fast, effective, and low-cost method for printing. This configuration also offers a good distribution of the printers across the network because the printers are placed next to the network users. This configuration is also not dependent on any external software or hardware systems such as PSERVER.NLM or a workstation. Figure 14.7 illustrates the network-direct printer running in queue server mode.

FIGURE 14.7

A network-direct printer running in queue server mode

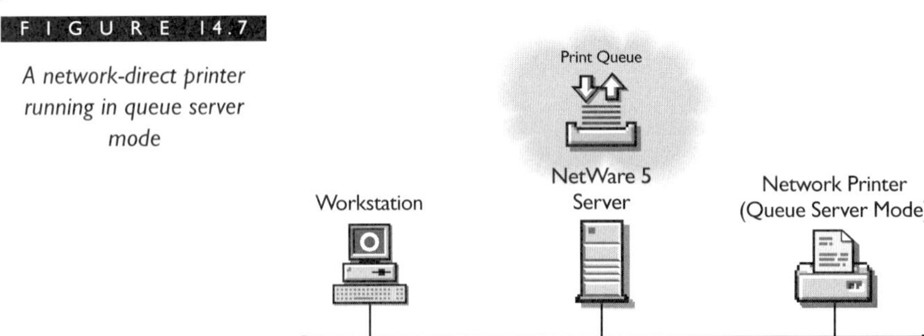

Several issues need to be considered when you implement this configuration:

- One common drawback of this configuration is that the queue servers are required to log into the network or server where the print queue resides. The queue server logs in using the normal user connection slots and will take one of the server's license connections, leaving you fewer connections for the network users. You should plan the distribution of the print queues accordingly. Of course, the PSERVER does the same thing as well.
- Some older print hardware devices are not yet NDS aware. This means the queue servers will log into the NetWare 5 servers using bindery services mode and cannot read the print server configuration files from NDS.
- In order for the queue server to log in using bindery services, the NDS object definitions for the print queues must be in the server's bindery context. Any additional print queues serviced by the network-direct printers should also exist in the server's bindery context.

- NetWare 3 creates the group EVERYONE by default. Many network-direct print devices assume that this group exists and will not function properly in its absence. For these devices running in NetWare 5, you may need to manually create a group called EVERYONE in the context where the print server is defined. This way the print server or queue server will be able to communicate with the network. Users do not have to be in the Group EVERYONE to print.

NetWare 5 Queue-Based Printing Setup

In order to set up NetWare 5 print services, you should start by defining the print queues, print server, and printers using the NWADMIN utility. The following list outlines the steps necessary to install NetWare 5 print services:

1. Create network print queues on the file server by using NWADMIN.
2. Assign queue operators and queue users to the printer queue through NWADMIN.
3. Create a print server definition.
4. Specify the file servers that have the print queues the print server will service.
5. Create printers to be associated with the print server.
6. Assign the print queues to the appropriate printers.
7. Optionally, set up printing for additional file servers.
8. Load PSERVER.NLM on the server.
9. If a remote printer was assigned to the print server, run NPRINTER.EXE at the appropriate workstation or run NPRINTER.NLM at the server.
10. Network printing should now be ready.

The Quick Setup Option

The Quick Setup option is a quick way to create and set up each of the three print objects (print queue, printer, and print server) and automatically establish the appropriate relationships. This option is the simplest way to set up NetWare 5 print services, especially if you are starting without existing printing objects. Quick Setup is available in NWADMIN.

In order to run the Quick Setup option, perform the following steps:

1. Log into the network as an ADMIN user with the Create object right to the specific NDS container.

2. Load NWADMIN and change to the appropriate context.

3. Select the Quick Setup menu under the Tools menu.

4. Enter the information required on the screen by selecting names for each of the printing objects.

5. After saving the configuration, load the PSERVER.NLM software at a server console with the new print server object's name.

6. Load NPRINTER.EXE at the workstation with the printer or NPRINTER.NLM if the printer is attached directly to the server.

7. Network printing should now be ready.

We recommend that you use the Quick Setup option in NWADMIN if you are setting up NetWare 5 print services for the first time. Figure 14.8 shows the Quick Setup option screen in NWADMIN.

After a print queue is created, the user who created the queue is automatically assigned as a queue operator, and the users that exist in the same container in the NDS tree are assigned as print queue users. This is the default setup, and it works well for most networks.

If you want to delegate the responsibility for managing the print queues to other users, you can assign the other users to be queue operators through the NWADMIN utility.

FIGURE 14.8

The Quick Setup option screen in the NWADMIN utility

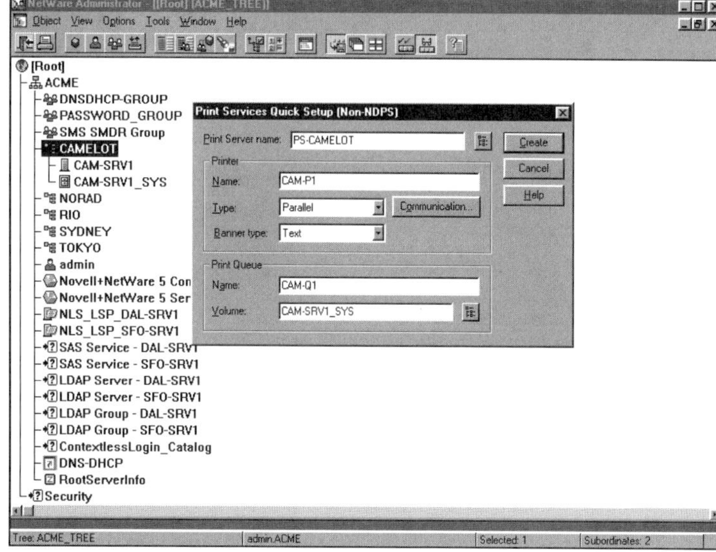

Only users designated as queue users can submit print jobs to the print queue. In larger networks, delegate responsibility to queue operators for a location or department and make only the members of the location or department queue users. The queue operators can then manage the print jobs for their areas.

Setting Print Services Environments

You are now able to set up a mixed NetWare 5 and NetWare 3 printing infrastructure. The compatibility of the print services between the two NetWare versions is bidirectional. This means that NetWare 5 can share printing services with NetWare 3. NetWare 3, in turn, can share print services with NetWare 5. The benefit of this compatibility is that the users may capture to print queues whether they are on NetWare 5 servers or NetWare 3 servers.

The best way to illustrate the capabilities of mixed print services is through the following examples:

- **Pure NetWare 5 print services** — In this configuration network users send their print jobs to NetWare 5 print queues.

- **Pure NetWare 3 print services** — In this configuration network users send their print jobs to print queues stored on NetWare 3 servers.
- **Mixed NetWare 5 and NetWare 3 print services** — In this configuration network users can send their print jobs to either NetWare 5 or NetWare 3 print queues.

A Pure NetWare 5 Print Services Implementation

You can choose to create all the print queues, printers, and print servers in NDS and store them on only NetWare 5 server volumes. This configuration is known as a pure NetWare 5 print services implementation. NetWare 5 users or users running the Novell Client 32 or Virtual Loadable Modules (VLMs) will access the print queue and read the configuration information from NDS.

Because NetWare 3 users or users running the older NETX workstation software will access the print queue and the configuration information from NDS through bindery services, you will be required to support bindery services at each NetWare 5 server that has print queues. The NetWare 3 users will be able to use only the print queues in the server's bindery context. The NetWare 3 users must also be able to log into the server using bindery services, which means that each user will have an account in the server's bindery context. You could implement a group or collective account that many users use just for printing services.

NOTE

If the printers are using the NPRINTER program, the NetWare 5 servers will need to load the appropriate PSERVER.NLM to support them.

If the printers are running the queue server mode, then the printer device is truly a print server and printer combination. Using the queue server mode, the printer device logs into the server in order to service the assigned print queue. Only some of the newest versions of the queue server software support an NDS authentication. The older versions require bindery services–supported logins at each NetWare 5 server that has print queues. The bindery services requirement forces you to place the print queue, print server, and printer NDS objects in the same container so that each can be resolved.

Figure 14.9 illustrates a pure NetWare 5 printing infrastructure.

FIGURE 14.9

A pure NetWare 5 print services implementation

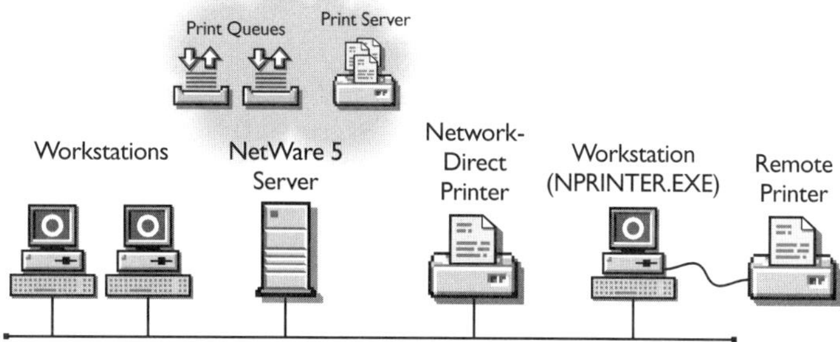

A Pure NetWare 3 Print Services Implementation

If you are upgrading from a NetWare 3 network environment, you may have a temporary need to keep all the print services back on NetWare 3. This configuration means that all the print queues and print server definitions are retained on the NetWare 3 servers for the duration of the upgrade project. Figure 14.10 illustrates a pure NetWare 3 print services implementation running with NetWare 5 servers and users.

FIGURE 14.10

A pure NetWare 3 print services implementation running with NetWare 5 users

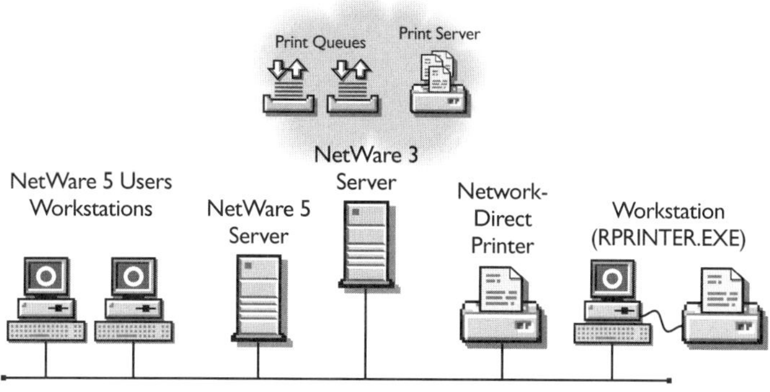

Even with a pure NetWare 3 printing implementation, the NetWare 5 users are able to send print jobs to any of the print queues on a NetWare 3 server. The user must first log into every server with a print queue that the user wants to access. You should also create an NDS print queue in the tree that points to the NetWare 3 volume. The user can then select the print queue using either the NetWare 3 utilities or NetWare 5 utilities. The NDS print queue object is a logical representation for the print queue that is physically located on the NetWare 3 server volume.

TIP

This approach implies that your NetWare 5 users also need to have accounts on NetWare 3 servers if they plan to log into servers and access print queues. You may want to consider Novell's NETSYNC utility to at least synchronize the same passwords between server types. Refer to Chapter 2, "Installation and Management Utilities for NetWare," for more information on NETSYNC.

In order to create an NDS print queue object to represent a NetWare 3 queue, you can use the NWADMIN utility. On the Create Print Queue screen select the Print Queue Volume item, which will prompt you for the file server and volume where the print queue will be placed. You should enter the NetWare 3 server and volume name. Figure 14.11 illustrates the process of setting up an NDS print queue that is stored on the NetWare 3 server but that both NetWare 3 and NetWare 5 users can share.

FIGURE 14.11

Creating an NDS print queue in NWADMIN, which is physically stored on a NetWare 3 server

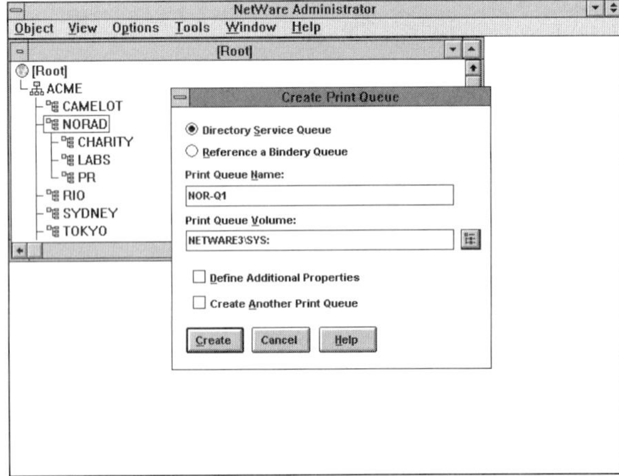

NOTE

The print queue stored in the NetWare 3 server can be serviced by a print server running on either the NetWare 5 or NetWare 3 operating systems. For more information on setting up a mixed print service environment, refer to the section "A Mixed NetWare 5 and NetWare 3 Print Services Implementation" that follows.

A Mixed NetWare 5 and NetWare 3 Print Services Implementation

If you are upgrading from a NetWare 3 network environment, then the most common configuration is to have the print services defined on both the NetWare 5 and the NetWare 3 servers. This configuration means that the print queues, print servers, and printer definitions are separated according to the version of the NetWare server. For example, the print services upgraded to NetWare 5 are those print services that the users need on that server. Likewise, the print services left on NetWare 3 are those needed by the users of that server. Figure 14.12 illustrates a mixed NetWare 5 and NetWare 3 print services implementation.

FIGURE 14.12

A mixed NetWare 5 and NetWare 3 print services implementation

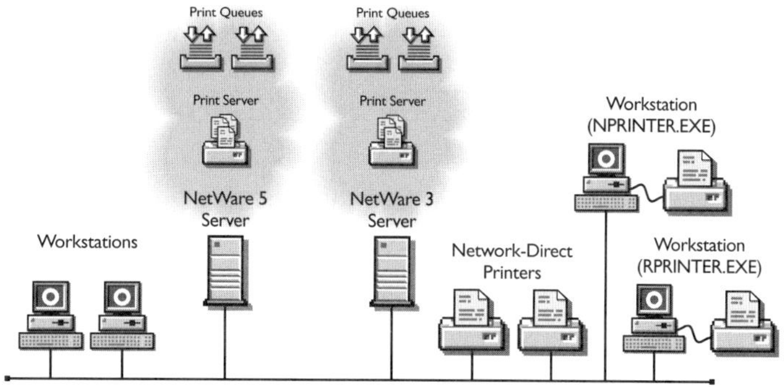

The print queues on either class of servers can be serviced by a print server running on the NetWare 5 servers or the NetWare 3 servers.

A printer device operating in queue server mode could also service any print queue on any servers in the network. Because all of the older network-direct print devices are not NDS aware, you must create the print server information in PCONSOLE (available with NetWare 3). The reason you need to use the older PCONSOLE is that in NetWare 3 the print server configuration files are stored in SYS:SYSTEM. In NetWare 5, by contrast, the print server configuration files are stored in NDS as properties of the printer server object. You should also use the PCONSOLE utility that comes with NetWare 3 when setting up a NetWare 3 print server to service NetWare 5 print queues. In order for the NetWare 5 print queues to be serviced from a print server running on the NetWare 3 servers, the print server software must log into the target server. The NetWare 3 print server logs into the NetWare 5 server using a print server object by the same name, which is defined on the NetWare 5 server. The NetWare 5 print server definition is used only for login purposes.

Upgrading the Print Services

The Novell Upgrade Wizard will upgrade the printing objects from NetWare 3 to NetWare 5. The printing objects are converted into NDS and become true NDS objects.

When you are upgrading from NetWare 3 to NetWare 5, you should consider the effect the upgrade will have on the print services. This is important if you are upgrading a NetWare 3 server to NetWare 5 and using the Novell Upgrade Wizard utility. If you want the print queues on the upgraded NetWare 5 server to be serviced by the original NetWare 3 print server, you must recreate each print server and print queue object. Because the printing objects have been converted to NetWare 5 and NDS, NetWare 3 will not be able to read them. Thus, you may be required to recreate each printing object in bindery mode to support the mixed NetWare 3 and NetWare 5 environments.

Upgrade Printing Using the Novell Upgrade Wizard Utility

If you are upgrading a NetWare 3 server using the Novell Upgrade Wizard utility, all the print services objects, including print queues, print servers, and printers, are moved to NDS. The PRINTCON and PRINTDEF databases (these files are named after the DOS utility that administers them) are upgraded directly into NDS. Although the database files are physically copied during the upgrade process of the volume data to their respective areas, they may not be useful. For example, the PRINTCON files are copied from the SYS:MAIL\USERID# directory from the source NetWare 3 server to SYS:MAIL\USERID# on the destination NetWare 5 server. Instead, the PRINTCON information should be an NDS property of either the user or a container object (such as an Organizational Unit).

The PRINTDEF files are copied from the SYS:PUBLIC directory on the source server to the SYS:PUBLIC directory on the NetWare 5 server. This information should be stored as an NDS property of a container object, such as an Organizational Unit.

Novell Distributed Print Services

Novell Distributed Print Services (NDPS) is the next generation of print services. NDPS is designed to simplify access and administration of the network print services. Novell Distributed Print Services (NDPS) is a distributed service that consists of client, server, and the connectivity software components to seamlessly connect the applications to the network printers.

In the past, the Novell Distributed Print Services product has been offered as an add-on product that could be integrated into your existing NetWare 4 networks. In NetWare 5, NDPS is included as the regular print services for the operating system. If you are currently satisfied with your current NetWare printing infrastructure, however, NetWare 5 will continue to support it. Then you can incrementally deploy NDPS at your own pace to gain the features and benefits.

NDPS gives users and administrators greater control over their printing. Features such as bidirectional feedback, print job status, automatic driver downloading, and event notification for printer status help simplify and streamline the usability and administration of the network printing. NDPS provides the following major benefits, features, and printing capabilities:

- NDPS allows the network administrator to centrally manage printing services from a single location.
- Users submit print jobs directly to the printers; no print queues need to be created.
- NDPS supports bidirectional communications with the printers.
- Administrators can move, copy, delete, prioritize, and pause print jobs.
- Network administrators are able to monitor and control print jobs, and they can receive print alerts or event notifications through e-mail, pop-up windows, event logs, and other methods, such as beepers and faxes.
- Users can determine whether a printer is available or busy and can copy or move print jobs between network printers as necessary.

- Plug-and-print option allows you to quickly install printers that can be immediately used by everyone with set-up rights.
- NDPS reduces the network traffic associated with SAP broadcast because direct-connect printer devices no longer require SAP.
- Any NDPS printer can be managed through a standard SNMP console using the standard printer Management Information Base (MIB).
- NDPS completely supports the current NetWare queue-based printing environment and thus will allow you to upgrade to NDPS as quickly or slowly as necessary.

NDPS uses a snap-in to NWADMIN to provide a single comprehensive management utility that enables and controls network printing for all major brands and models of printers. In the queue-based print services, the initial setup currently requires creating print queues, printer objects, and print servers, and then establishing a relationship between them. NDPS eliminates the need to create and configure print queues, printers, and print server objects. In fact, NDPS doesn't require you to manage print queues at all. Instead, using an NDPS-aware printer, you simply connect the printer to the network; users can begin sending print jobs to it at once. The printer will indicate which driver it needs, and the driver will be automatically downloaded to the users. This eliminates the administrator's having to configure the users' workstations with drivers for specific printers and other devices.

Simple Printer Access

When the client software is installed, a list of available printers (called a "short list") is immediately available. The printers are created and configured as NDS printers, which allows users to browse the NDS tree for new printers based on a printer's properties, such as location, type, and supported languages. Because NDPS allows bidirectional information to be passed between the client and printers, users can match print jobs with the printer's capabilities. Users can also query and receive the status of the individual printers. This enables the users to know whether a printer is available, to get information about the status of the print jobs, and to receive notification that the paper tray is empty. One of the favorite features for many users is notification when the print job has been completed.

Users also have the flexibility to indicate that a print job or document needs to be printed on a special paper type. The printer will then notify the user when the paper needs to be loaded or inserted and then print only that document on the special paper. For example, if the user specifies that a letter needs to be printed on single sheets of letterhead, the printer will prompt the user to insert the letterhead, and then only that letter or document will be printed on the letterhead.

Easier Setup and Administration

New printers that are added to the system automatically register with NDPS, a feature that reduces the initial administrative setup and installation costs. For example, using the queue-based print services, when a new printer (set up as a queue server) is added to the network, the printer immediately starts advertising its availability, which results in increased network traffic. This advertising continues as long as the printer is turned on. Using NDPS, when a new printer is added to the network, it registers with a single registration agent. The agent will then notify all the appropriate clients of the printer's availability and will advertise all the printers. This greatly reduces the overall network traffic caused by network printers.

Using NWADMIN, administrators have a centralized, simplified, and common interface to manage print services. Because NPDS is completely integrated with Novell Directory Services, administrators can create a printer object in the NDS tree and manage printers even if they come from different vendors. Because printer objects appear as NDS objects, they can easily monitor and control the printer. Figure 14.13 illustrates how the printer object in NDS can be used to monitor and control the features of the network printer directly from NWADMIN.

FIGURE 14.13

Using NWADMIN and the printer object in NDS, you can easily monitor and control the features of the network printer.

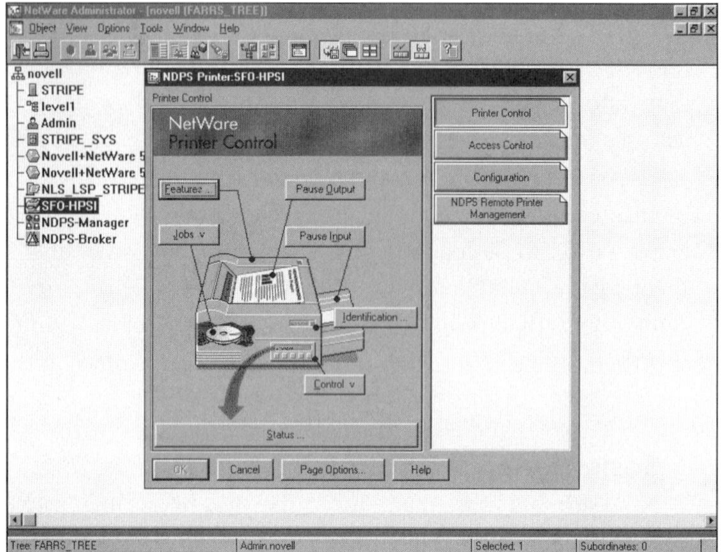

NDPS Architecture

The components that make up the Novell Distributed Print Services architecture are independent of any single operating system. Thus, the architecture is designed to be portable to different environments. The major components of NDPS are as follows:

- **Broker** — The Broker provides several network support services to NDPS. These services are the Service Registry Service, the Event Notification Service, and the Resource Management Service. When you first install NDPS, a Broker is automatically created and added to the NDS tree.
- **Client software** — All printing starts when the user sends print jobs to the network printers. Thus, in order to take full advantage of NDPS, you must upgrade the NetWare client software to the NetWare 5 client. The print client's responsibility is to send network print jobs from the workstation to the appropriate network printer on the network. The print clients communicate with a printer agent using the Novell Distributed Print Service Protocol (DPSP).

- **Gateway** — The gateways allow NDPS clients to send jobs to network printers that are not NDPS aware. They also allow non-NDPS clients in a pure NDPS environment to continue to access printers and send jobs to print queues just as they always have in the past. There are two types of gateways: third-party gateways developed by the printer manufacturer and the Novell standard gateway, which is used to support any non-NDPS-aware printers.
- **NDPS Manager** — The NDPS Manager is an NLM loaded on the NetWare server that enables you to create and manage the printer agents in the system.
- **Physical printer** — The physical printer is the actual printer device that is attached to the network to service the print jobs sent by the users. In order for the physical printer to be involved with the Novell Distributed Print Services, it must either have the Printer Agent component embedded or be able to communicate to such a component running on a NetWare 5 server.
- **Print device subsystem** — The print device subsystem (PDS) is part of the Novell standard gateway. It is a driver that is implemented and customized to control feedback and send it to the physical print device.
- **Printer agent** — A printer with an embedded printer agent is called an NDPS-enabled printer. It performs all the tasks of the current print server, spooler, and print queue. These tasks are combined into a logical print management agent that maintains information about the specific physical printer, such as printer availability, status, and other factors.
- **Port handler** — The port handler is part of the Novell standard gateway, which ensures that the print device subsystem (PDS) can communicate with the printer no matter what type of physical port is being used (such as a parallel port, serial port, or network port).

Physical printer devices that are attached as network printers can become NDPS printers in two different ways. The printer can have an embedded printer agent, which enables the printer to become an NDPS-aware printer. The other method, used for printer hardware that does not have an embedded printer agent, must have the printer agent running on the NetWare 5 server to represent it to NDPS. However, the printer agent running at the server must communicate to a printer gateway, which in turn talks directly to the printers. The printer agents running on the NetWare 5 server are controlled and managed by the NDPS Manager. Figure 14.14 illustrates how all of these components work together to provide the printing solution.

FIGURE 14.14

The NDPS components work together to provide the network printing solution.

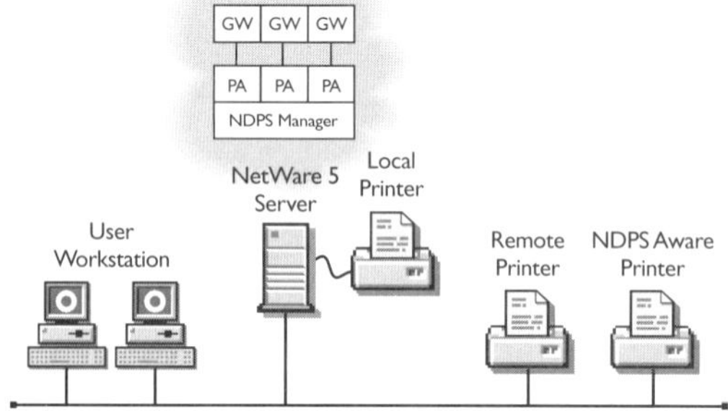

In addition to all the components for NDPS, several utilities help you manage the printing environment. These software utilities are the snap-in to NWADMIN, Novell Printer Manager, and NDPS Remote Workstation Printer Management. Next we will discuss each of these components and software utilities in more depth.

Printer Agents

Administrators create printer objects in the NDS tree, which represents a physical printer and allows users to submit print jobs to the printers. The printer agent represents the printer object to NDPS, and thus, the printer agent becomes the heart of NDPS. The printer agent acts as the major liaison between the network users and the physical printer devices. The printer agent receives information about the printer devices and resources that it is managing. It validates security information and provides direct notification and feedback to the appropriate client. The information received by the printer agent can be viewed using

NWADMIN by selecting the individual printer object in NDS. Figure 14.15 shows the NWADMIN printer control screen for the printer object SFO-HPSI in the NDS tree. This screen allows you to manage and control the physical printer through the printer agent.

FIGURE 14.15

Using NWADMIN, you can manage the physical printer through logical representation of the NDS printer object and print agent.

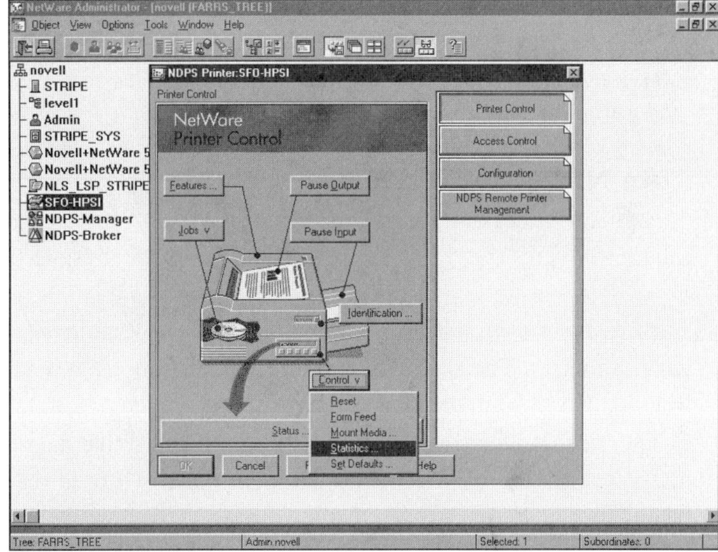

Before you can add a specific printer device into NDPS, you are required to represent the printer using a printer agent. The printer manufacturer typically develops these print agents. In addition, only one instance of the printer agent can represent a single physical printer, and no physical printer can be represented by more than one printer agent.

The printer agent may reside in several places on the system. The printer agent may be embedded within the physical printer device that is connected directly to the network. Or the printer agent may be run on the NetWare server as an NLM, which represents a printer that is either connected directly to the network or attached to a server or workstation. Figure 14.16 illustrates how the printer agent can be loaded and running on the NetWare 5 server and still represent the physical printer device or be embedded in the physical printer itself.

FIGURE 14.16

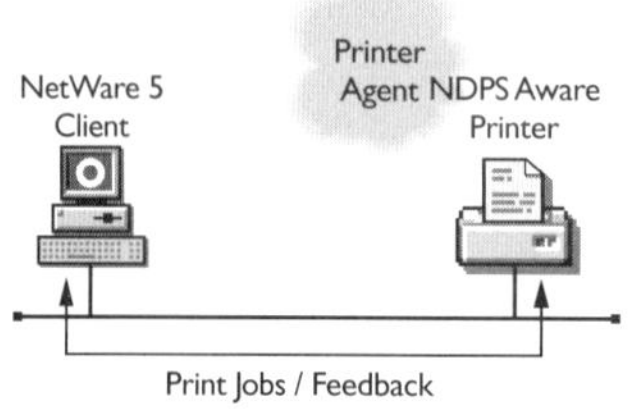

The printer agent may be embedded in the physical printer or loaded on the NetWare 5 server, and it may represent either a printer connected directly to the network or one attached to a server or workstation.

An NDPS-Aware Printer

As mentioned, a physical printer device with an embedded printer agent is called an NDPS-aware printer. This is typically a physical printer that is attached directly to the network. The printer agent is the NDPS component that receives and processes the print job requests, providing a standard NDPS communication with the users. The physical printer device communicates with the printer agent in its native printer language.

The strength of this type of configuration is that it allows users to directly interact with the printer. They can send prints jobs directly to the printer and receive notifications and feedback from it. In this setup the client and printer will have full bidirectional communication and feedback capabilities. Other major benefits of this configuration are that you get true plug and print, peer-to-peer printing, simple management, automatic driver download, and exceptional feedback and control. These benefits are gained because of the embedded printer agent, which maintains information about the specific physical printer. The printer agent also performs all the tasks of the current print server, spooler, and print queue. If a user queries the printer for status information or other attributes, the printer agent responds to the user on behalf of the physical device. In addition, the printer agent manages processing of all print jobs and other operations typically performed by the printer device itself. The printer agent also generates event or error notification for job completion, printing problems, or changes in printer status. Finally, the printer agent ensures scalability of the printing environment by supporting a wide range of devices, such as dot matrix, laser, and large-scale printers.

As of this writing (fall 1998), a number of printer manufacturers are developing NDPS-aware printers with the embedded printer agent. Once these new printers become available, they can be used in the configuration just described.

The NDPS Manager

If the printer agent is loaded on the NetWare 5 server, it is created and managed by the NDPS Manager. The NDPS Manager is an NLM, called NDPSM.NLM, which enables you to load the printer agent entities on the system. The NDPS Manager is an object that is created in the NDS tree. In fact, you must create the NDPS Manager object before you can create or manage the printer agents. Figure 14.17 shows the main screen for the NDPS Manager in NWADMIN. You can load this screen by selecting or double-clicking the NDPS Manager object in the NDS tree.

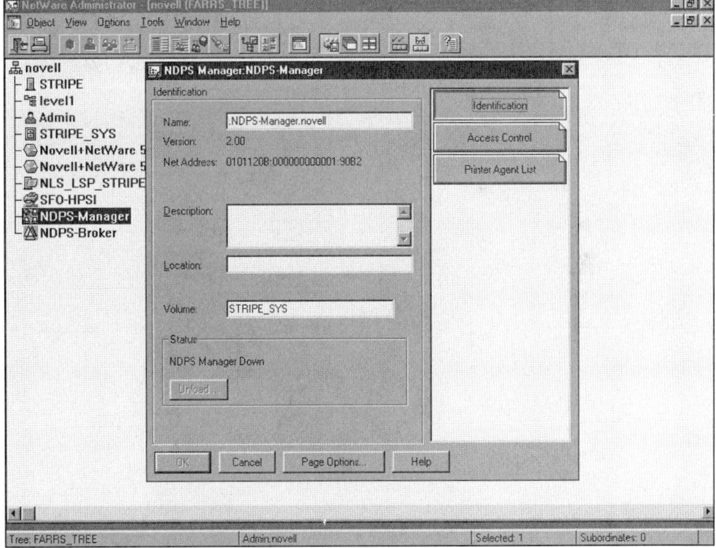

FIGURE 14.17

The NDPS Manager screen can be viewed through the NWADMIN utility. To activate the screen, double-click the NDPS Manager stored in the NDS tree.

A user wanting to create an NDPS Manager object in the NDS tree must have at least Create rights for the container in which it will be created. In addition, the user must have at least file system rights of Read, Write, Modify, Create, and File Scan at the root of the volume. Although you can perform some configuration and maintenance tasks directly through the NDPS Manager software running on the server, you will want to mainly use the NWADMIN utility to manage the different printer agents.

Because the NDPS Manager is an object in the NDS tree, you must create the NDPS Manager object before you can create or manage the printer agents. This NDPS Manager object stores information used by NDPS.NLM. A printer agent that has been created by the NDPS Manager but not been officially registered as an NDS object in the tree can advertise its presence and availability as a *public access printer,* which is a network printer that is available to anyone attached to the network (even if they are not NDS users). On the other hand, printer agents that have been represented in the tree as NDS objects are called *controlled access printers* because this configuration does take advantage of the security.

As mentioned, the NDPS Manager enables you to create and manage the printer agents. Figure 14.18 illustrates how the NDPS Manager controls and manages the printer agents in the system.

FIGURE 14.18

The NDPS Manager allows you to create and manage the printer agents stored on the NetWare 5 server.

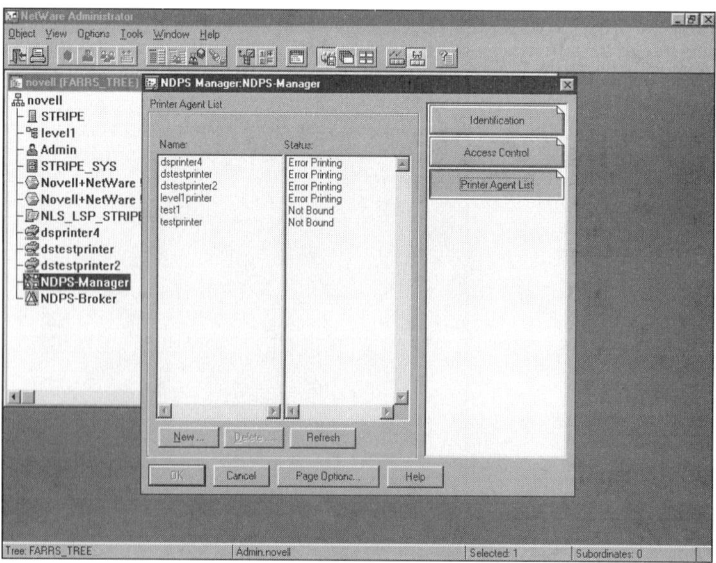

Once the printer agents have been created to represent the physical printer device, the users need to install the printer on their workstations and be given access to the printer. Both these tasks can be easily accomplished by the administrators, using NWADMIN. The administrators can select the specific printer in the NDS tree and grant users access to use it. Figure 14.19 illustrates how the administrators can grant rights to the print object in NDS using NWADMIN through the printer Access Control page.

FIGURE 14.19

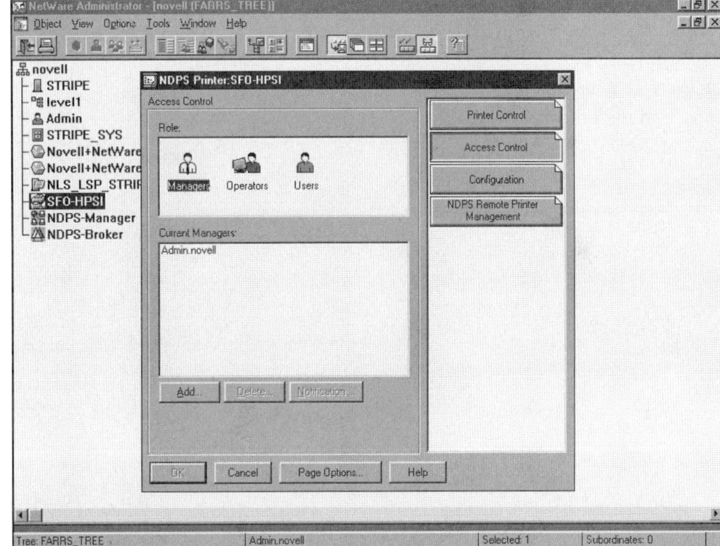

The administrators can use NWADMIN and the Access Control page to grant rights to users, managers, and operators.

NDPS Remote Workstation Printer Management

Although users may have rights to a printer, in order for them to access it using NDPS, the printer needs to be installed on the users' workstations. With NDPS, you can remotely change the configuration of the workstation to add, delete, or change printer configurations. These tasks are performed remotely using the remote workstation management software that comes with NDPS. The software is called the NDPS Remote Workstation Printer Management. Figure 14.20 illustrates how you can add a specific printer to the user's workstation configuration remotely using the NDPS Remote Printer Management page in NWADMIN. This example is for the specific printer SFO-HPSI.

FIGURE 14.20

An NDPS printer can be added to the user's workstation configuration remotely using the NDPS Remote Printer Management page in NWADMIN. This example is specific to the printer SFO-HPSI.

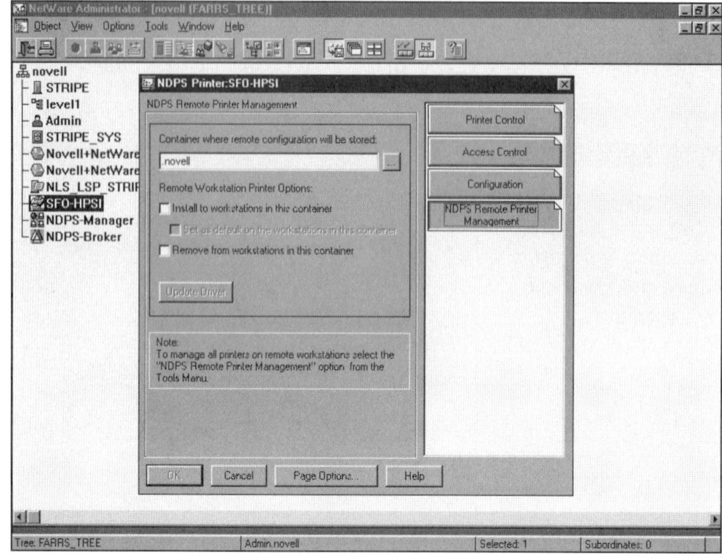

The NDPS Remote Workstation Printer Management software can be executed as a stand-alone utility from the Tools menu in NWADMIN. Running it from the Tools menu enables you to make changes for multiple printers at the same time. Figure 14.21 illustrates the interface for the utility after it has been executed from the Tools menu.

In order to support the NDPS Remote Workstation Printer Management from the workstation or client side, you must be running the NetWare 5 client. The NetWare 5 client is also required to print directly to the printer agents either embedded in the printer device itself or on the server. Some of the major advantages of the NetWare 5 client with NDPS are as follows:

- Automatic driver download
- Remote workstation management
- Public access printing
- Print queues no longer needed
- Event notification

FIGURE 14.21

The NDPS Remote Workstation Printer Management software can be executed from the Tools menu in NWADMIN, which enables you to make changes for multiple printers at the same time.

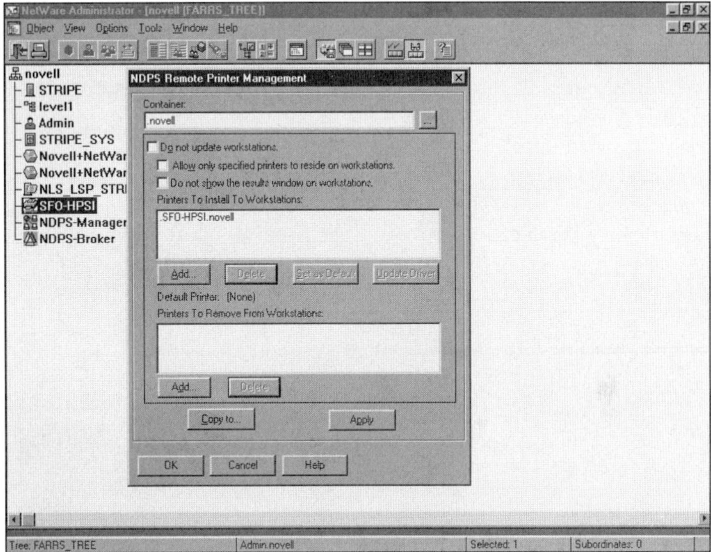

Novell Printer Manager

Once users have an NDPS printer defined on their workstations, they can use the Novell Printer Manager to view the printer status, print jobs, and other information. In addition, they can move print jobs between printers. Figure 14.22 shows the main screen of the Novell Printer Manager, which shows the list of printers available to users. In this case, the printer shown is SFO-HPSI with its print jobs.

Figures 14.23 and 14.24 illustrate how the Novell Printer Manager can be used by users to receive status information from the printer. In Figure 14.23, the printer is reporting a caution status symbolized by the yellow icon with an exclamation mark in it. In Figure 14.24, the printer is reporting a critical error, which has halted or stopped the printer from functioning.

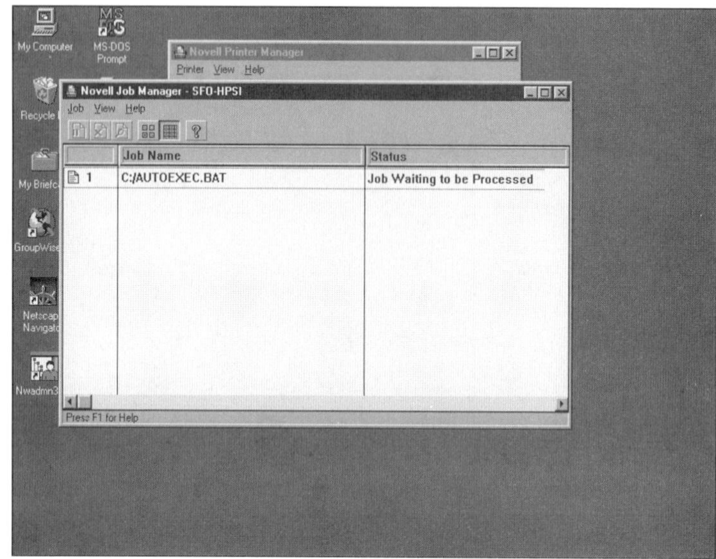

FIGURE 14.22

The Novell Printer Manager can be used by the users to view the list of printers available. In this case, the printer shown is SFO-HPSI. In addition, the print jobs that are currently placed at the printer are shown.

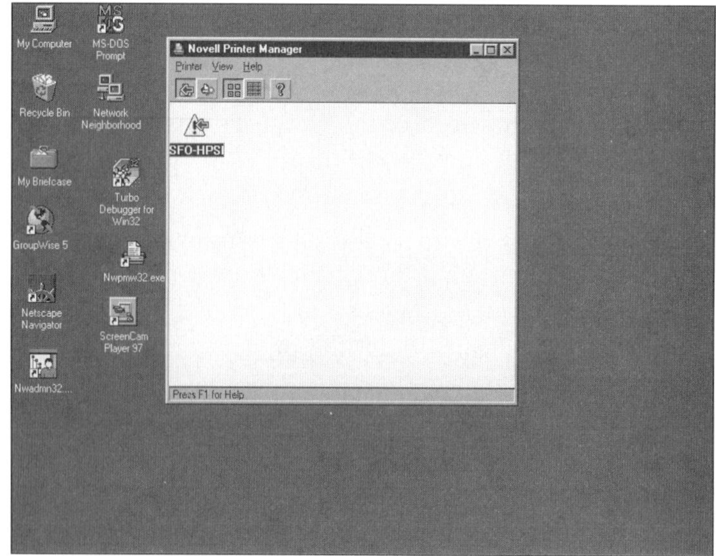

FIGURE 14.23

Using the Novell Printer Manager, the user has received a caution status report from the printer. The caution status is symbolized by the yellow icon with an exclamation mark in it.

FIGURE 14.24

Using the Novell Printer Manager, the user has received a critical error from the printer. The critical error has halted or stopped the printer.

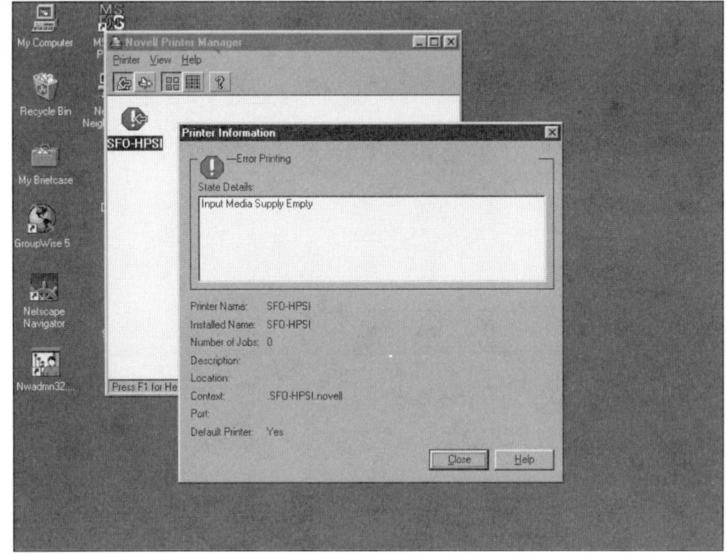

NDPS Printer Gateways

As mentioned previously, a physical printer device that does not have an embedded printer agent must have the printer agent running on the NetWare 5 server to represent it to NDPS. However, the printer agent running at the server must communicate to a printer gateway, which in turn talks directly to the printers. The printer gateway communicates to the printer device in its native language to provide complete bidirectional feedback to the users. Thus, in order to support network printers that are not NDPS aware, you need to use NDPS printer gateways.

The NDPS printer gateway allows NDPS clients to send jobs to network printers that are not NDPS aware. They also allow non-NDPS clients in a pure NDPS environment to continue to access printers and send jobs to print queues just as they always have in the past. In the absence of true NDPS-aware printers, it is important that you know and understand how to support non-NDPS-aware printers in your network. To accomplish this, you need to set up the appropriate gateway and printer agent running on the server. Figure 14.25 illustrates how the printer gateway communicates directly to the printer device and then passes the information on to the printer agent. Print jobs are handled by the printer agent, which passes them to the gateway and then on to the printer itself.

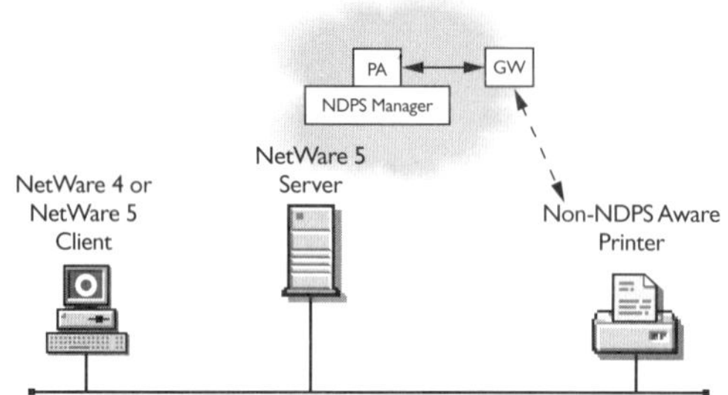

FIGURE 14.25

The printer gateway enables the users to print to printers that are not NPDS aware, meaning that the printer agent is not embedded in the printer device itself.

NDPS supports two different categories of printer gateways, third-party gateways and the Novell gateway.

Third-Party Printer Gateways

The third-party gateways are developed by printer manufacturers to support printers directly attached to the network. Printer manufacturers may provide utilities that can be configured to automatically create printer agents using their gateways to support one of their non-NDPS printers. Currently, the Hewlett-Packard and Xerox gateways are included with the NDPS software. For example, the Hewlett-Packard gateway is called HPGATE.NLM.

You can also download the latest copies of a third-party gateway from the appropriate web site. For example, the Xerox gateway is available for download at `www.xerox.networkprinters.com`. Gateways from other printer vendors will be available soon.

The Novell Printer Gateway

The Novell gateway supports printers connected as remote printers, such as those using NPRINTER to support queue-based print services. This gateway provides the functionality to be backward-compatible with the queue-based services. The Novell gateway enables you to support not only remote printers in the network but also local printers (printers connected directly to the server ports) and printers connected to a PSERVER. Figure 14.26 illustrates how the Novell gateway supports network printers connected as remote printers and local printers.

FIGURE 14.26

The Novell gateway supports network printers connected as remote printers and local printers. The gateway provides backward compatibility with the queue-based services.

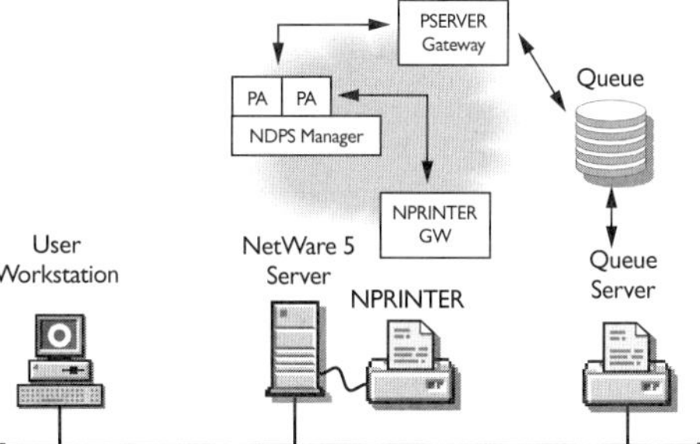

The Novell gateway is implemented through the print device subsystem and the port handler. These two components of NDPS are unique to the Novell gateway and are not used for the third-party gateways.

The Print Device Subsystem The print device subsystem (PDS) is a driver that can be implemented and customized to control feedback and send it to the physical print device. The PDS retrieves printer-specific information and stores it in a database. A port handler can then use the information that is stored in the database to communicate with the physical printer. Normally, the print device subsystem is developed by original equipment manufacturers (OEMs) and independent software vendors (ISVs) to take advantage of the functionality of each of the physical printer devices.

The PDS is implemented as a NetWare Loadable Module (NLM) and is automatically loaded when a printer agent is created using the PDS configuration utility. You should use the Novell PDS when you are creating a printer agent for either of the following situations:

- A network printer that is not connected directly to the network, which includes local printers and remote printers
- A printer that is directly connected to the network but whose manufacturer has not provided a proprietary NDPS gateway

The Port Handler The port handler ensures that the print device subsystem (PDS) can communicate with the printer no matter what type of physical port is being used (such as a parallel port, serial port, or network port).

The Broker

When you first install the NDPS software on your network, a Broker is automatically created and added into your NDS tree. For performance purposes, an additional Broker is created if NDPS is installed on a server that is more than three hops away from the existing Broker. The Broker provides three services that are distinct from one another. These services are called the Service Registry Service (SRS), the Event Notification Service (ENS), and the Resource Management Service (RMS).

The Service Registry Service

The Service Registry Service (SRS) allows public access printers to advertise themselves so that users can find them. This service maintains information about the printer type, printer name, and printer address, as well as printer-specific information (such as manufacturer and model number). Figure 14.27 shows the SRS screen found in NWADMIN under the Broker object in NDS.

FIGURE 14.27

You can use the NWADMIN utility to manage the Service Registry Service (SRS) in the Broker object in NDS.

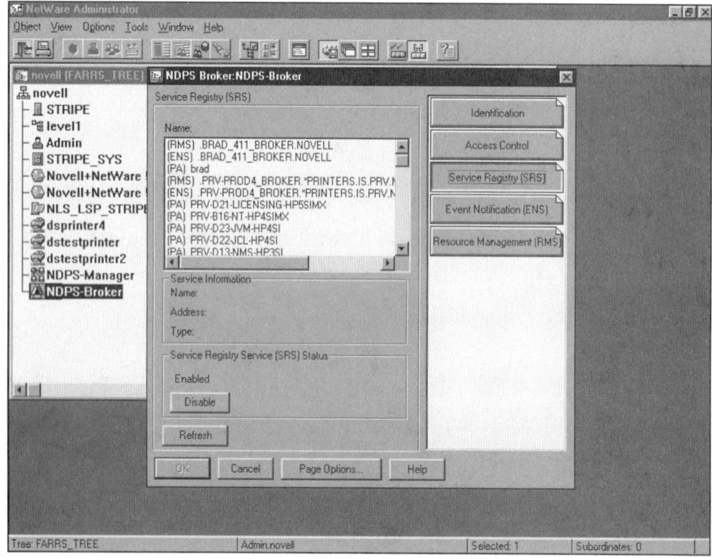

SRS helps reduce the network traffic and overhead problem created when printers connected directly to the network advertise using SAP. Before NDPS, all printers set up in queue server mode periodically advertised their availability through the Novell Service Advertising Protocol (SAP). This method caused an inefficient use of the network. Now, when an NDPS printer is set up on the network, it registers with SRS. In turn, when users request the use of a printer, they contact SRS and retrieve a list of registered printers on the network.

The Event Notification Service

The Event Notification Service (ENS) allows printers to send customizable notifications to users and operators about printer events and print job status. This service supports a variety of notification delivery methods including log files, pop-up windows, e-mail, and other third-party interfaces (such as pagers). Figure 14.28 shows the screen in NWADMIN for the Event Notification Service, which is included in the Broker.

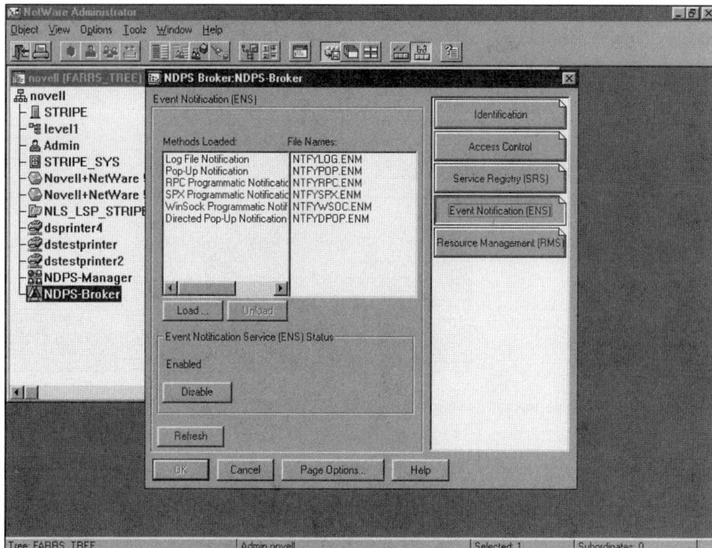

FIGURE 14.28

The Event Notification Service (ENS) is managed by the Broker and can be seen in the NWADMIN utility.

ENS not only allows the administrators to configure event notification but also allows non–job owners who wish to be notified of the existence of a defined printer event that occurs during the processing of the job. For example, the boss requests a print job but wants the secretary to pick it up for him. At the workstation, individual users can use the Novell Printer Manager to configure event notification pertaining to their own print jobs.

The Resource Management Service

The Resource Management Service (RMS) allows resources to be installed in a central location and then have those resources downloaded to the individual workstations, or printers. The RMS supports adding, listing, replacing, and deleting resources including printer drivers, printer definition files (PDFs), banners, and fonts. Figure 14.29 shows the Resource Management Service screen found in NWADMIN under the Broker NDS object.

FIGURE 14.29

You can use the NWADMIN utility to manage the Resource Management Service (RMS) in the Broker NDS object.

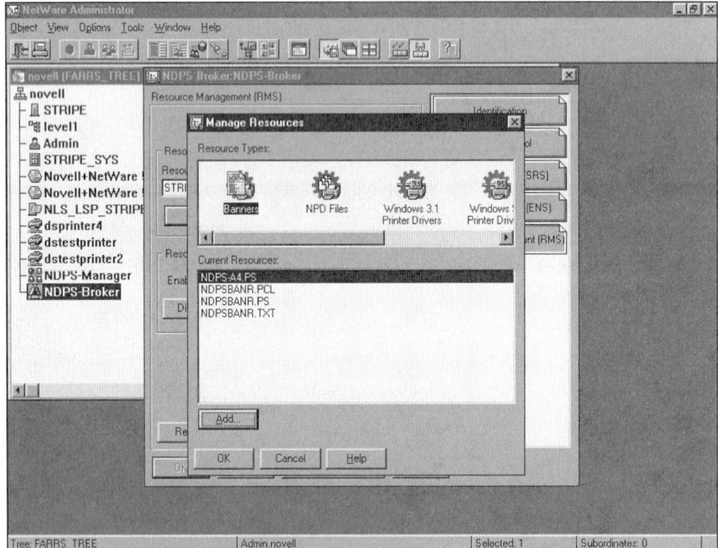

The Future Direction of NDPS

NDPS is making printing easier for the users and management easier for the administrators. This means that NDPS is reducing printing costs by making the printing environment consolidated and more simplified. But what is the future?

A draft of the Internet Printing Protocol (IPP) definition, currently in the IETF standards committee, includes many of the NDPS principles. Novell is actively participating in the definition development and plans to provide support for this standard and NDPS as IPP becomes generally available. Novell is also working to further its longstanding commitment to printer manufacturers. These companies depend on the NEST product line to provide embedded software, which will enable connectivity between hardware devices and Novell software on the network. This will eliminate the need for server involvement in the printing process and provides improved plug-and-print capabilities. Novell plans to extend the NDPS technology into the NEST space, enabling printer companies to ship NDPS–ready systems. One quick note about the NEST technology, to help clear up any confusion, is that although Novell spun off NEST, it is still being developed. The company that purchased NEST from Novell is currently developing the product.

Summary

The printing solution for NetWare 5 includes both traditional queue-based and new NDPS print architectures. Queue-based printing is well known; it requires users to know which physical printers are associated with each print queue. On the other hand, NDPS is easy to set up and use because users can send their print jobs directly to the physical printers. In addition, printers can send status information or error messages back to the users.

CHAPTER 15

Preparing to Upgrade to NetWare 5

*"If you want things to stay as they are,
things will have to change."* — Giuseppe di Lampedusa

This chapter will help you prepare for and begin the process of upgrading your current system, which is either NetWare 3 or NetWare 4, to NetWare 5. You will want to do several things to prepare to upgrade your servers and workstations to NetWare 5. You will want to organize and educate the NetWare 5 project team, create an implementation schedule, set up a testing lab, and do the pilot system.

In order to create a good implementation schedule and prepare for the design, implementation, and upgrade to NetWare 5, you need to organize and educate your NetWare 5 project team.

Organize and Educate the NetWare 5 Project Team

Your first objective is to organize the NetWare 5 project team with one individual assigned as the project manager. The project manager should choose the members of the team, matching the network responsibilities needed with the individual's skills.

The project team will create the master schedule to manage all of the implementation tasks. In order to accomplish the individual tasks, the team members can be assembled into functional areas, with each individual presiding over a functional area and responsible for seeing that task to completion. Here is a list of some suggested functional areas:

- Training
- Novell Directory Services
- Servers
- Clients

- Protocols
- Printing
- Administration

Project Team Assignments

The size of the NetWare 5 project team will vary depending on the size of the corporation or the overall project. A team may consist of only one person performing all the tasks and functional assignments or of dozens of persons helping the project to succeed. Again, each team or functional area can include one individual or many people depending on the size or scope of the project. You must determine the scope of your project and how many people are needed to complete and maintain the installation of NetWare 5.

The primary responsibility of the entire project team is to determine the overall scope of the project, which includes a list of deliverables that the project team will create and accomplish for the company or steering committee. Depending on the demands of the project, the deliverables might also include a list of milestones, critical paths, success factors, risk analyses, and tracking mechanisms.

After assignments are made for the entire project team, you should consider the responsibilities and areas of focus for each of the individual teams and its members. We will discuss each individually.

Training

One person or team is responsible for providing the other members of the project team, the network administrator, and the users with the proper NetWare 5 training. This includes a lab environment for hands-on training, which is discussed later in this chapter.

Several methods and sources of training are available for your network personnel. The training includes formal Novell education, Novell-sponsored workshops or conferences, lab experience, white papers, Novell AppNotes, user groups, related books, and other available media.

Formal Education

Instructor-led courses are available through Novell Authorized Education Centers (NAECs) and Novell Education Academic Partners (NEAPs) worldwide. CBT (computer-based training) products, videos, and self-study workbooks are available through NAECs and Novell resellers. For more information on Novell's education programs, or to find the NAEC or NEAP nearest you, in the United States and Canada call 1-800-233-EDUC. Outside the United States and Canada, call 1-801-429-5508, or contact your nearest Novell office.

Another quick 24-hour-per-day tool for information is the Novell Education FaxBack. Call 1-801-429-5363 for access to FaxBack. Ask for document 1448 for current courses.

Novell-Sponsored Workshops and Conferences

Novell develops and delivers various workshops throughout the year at the local sales offices. You should contact the local office account teams for the scheduled workshops in your area. Novell presents several BrainShare Conferences throughout the world. BrainShare is a conference for developers, consultants, and system integrators. Currently, there are BrainShare conferences held in the United States (March in Salt Lake City, Utah), Europe, Australia, Japan, China, South Africa, Russia, and China.

Lab Experience

There is no substitute for hands-on experience. You will provide skills that transfer to your system administrators in the lab environment. A test upgrade of the servers from a copy of a production server in the lab, for example, will give your personnel valuable experience as well as an understanding of the upgrade issues before an actual upgrade is attempted in a production environment.

Application Notes

Novell AppNotes (formerly Novell Application Notes) is published monthly by Novell. The material in the AppNotes is based on actual field experience and technical research performed by Novell personnel, covering topics in the following main areas:

- Network design and optimization strategies
- Network management tactics

- NetWare internals and theory of operations
- Novell product implementation guidelines
- Integration solutions for third-party products
- NetWare programming techniques

Current AppNotes is a good source of information for NetWare 5. The AppNotes subscription rate for a one-year subscription (12 issues) is $95 in the United States and $135 outside the United States. To order AppNotes, call 1-800-377-4136 or 303-297-2725. Orders can also be faxed to 303-294-0930. The AppNotes and other Novell Research publications (such as Research Reports and Novell Developer Notes) are also available on the Web at `www.novell.com/research`.

AppNotes and other Novell Research publications (such as Research Reports and Novell Developer Notes) are also available on the Web at `www.novell.com/research`.

NetWare User International (NUI) Group

We also recommend that you join a NetWare User Group in order to share information and experiences with other NetWare 5 users. They also periodically invite speakers from Novell to speak on topics of interest.

Online Support Services

Novell provides online support through Novell's corporate Web site at `www.novell.com` on the Internet. The Web page provides customers with the latest Novell information, which includes fixes and patches, questions and answers, technical documentation, and support knowledge.

Novell Directory Services

One person or team is responsible for designing Novell Directory Services. The design includes design of the NDS tree, NDS partitions and replicas, and time synchronization. This team will work closely with other company personnel to establish the NDS naming standards as well. This team should have a good understanding of NDS objects and properties as well as an understanding of administration of the network. This team will also help manage and monitor the NDS system once it is moved into production.

If the new NetWare 5 servers are going to be installed into an existing NetWare 4.10 or NetWare 4.11 environment, then this team must install the proper versions of NDS (DS.NLM) on all the NetWare 4.10 and NetWare 4.11 servers. NetWare 5 will not synchronize with older versions of the NetWare 4 DS.NLM. You must install or upgrade the DS.NLM version before installing the first NetWare 5 server into the production tree.

The versions DS.NLM that will work correctly with NetWare 5 are found in Table 15.1.

TABLE 15.1

Necessary DS.NLM Upgrades for NetWare 4 Versions

NETWARE 4 VERSION	DS.NLM VERSION REQUIRED
NetWare 4.10	5.13 or later
NetWare 4.11	5.99a or later

The DS.NLM versions 5.13 and 5.99a (or later) are now available from `support.novell.com`. For example, the upgrade for version 4.11 can be found as filename DS411L.EXE or in the operating support packs. DS.NLM version 5.99a will be incorporated in the NetWare 4.11 support as IWSP6.EXE. As of this writing, the only files that are available are DS411L.EXE and IWSP5b.EXE.

WARNING

Do not attempt to install a NetWare 5 server into an existing NDS tree unless the proper DS.NLM version requirements for NetWare 4.10 and NetWare 4.11 have been met.

Four main problem areas have been addressed in NDS 4.11 update v5.99a in order for it to correctly function in a mixed environment:

- Schema synchronization (both classes and attributes)
- Synchronization of new NetWare 5 schema additions
- NDS object and property ACL inheritance
- Restoration of object references on NetWare 5 servers

Deleting Schema (Classes and Attributes)

Schema synchronization will not work correctly with the older NetWare 4 DS.NLM versions. For example, NetWare 5 schema deletes will not correctly synchronize to NetWare 4.11 servers without replicas. This is not particularly bad in most instances, because it just means that some items are defined in the schema that are not being used, but the schema in that tree is technically out of sync. The fact that the schema is not synchronized across all servers causes a couple of problems.

One problem is that NetWare 5 has some NLM-based applications that read the schema and can possibly obtain misleading results from a server with no replicas. For example, Novell License Services (NLS) reads the schema to verify that previous NLS attributes and classes have been removed. If the previous attributes and classes have not been removed, you will be prompted (frequently) to remove the old schema from the tree.

The second problem is that if the administrator adds a replica where none existed before, the incorrect schema information may be synchronized to other servers in the tree. This could require support intervention to clean up the schema so that the replica will synchronize.

Synchronizing NetWare 5 Schema Additions

The DS.NLM version 5.99a addresses a problem with schema synchronization when synchronizing the new NetWare 5 schema additions from one NetWare 4.11 server to another NetWare 4.11 server. In NetWare 5 a new Tree Root dependence was added to the schema. This new schema is synchronized correctly from a NetWare 5 server to a NetWare 4.11 server, but the NetWare 4.11 server does not pass the same new schema on to other NetWare 4.11 servers correctly. DS.NLM version 5.99a fixes this problem.

Consulting Experience

Running the new version of DS.NLM and the new version of DSREPAIR (v4.56) can fix these problems. Use the Reset Local Schema option in DSREPAIR.

ACL Inheritance

A new feature of NetWare 5 allows specific attribute ACLs to be inherited. This feature will be masked if the inheritance path includes a server running any DS.NLM version prior to 5.99a. Note that 5.99a will not act upon these inheritable ACLs, but it will allow them to properly flow through to a NetWare 5 server holding replicas subordinate to the replicas on the NetWare 4.11 server. Without 5.99a, you might get inconsistent results when evaluating rights on NetWare 5 servers that rely on this new feature.

Restoring an Object Reference on a NetWare 5 Server

DS.NLM version 5.99a restores required referenced objects on NetWare 5 servers when you restore an object reference. If the referenced object resides on a NetWare 4.11 server that is not running 5.99a, NDS will not create the referenced object properly, and this may cause collisions.

For example, suppose we have a mixed NetWare 5 and 4.11 tree:

- The administrator restores object Group1.Dept1.Company (an object with many member attributes) to the tree.
- Group1 has a member attribute Member1.Dept2.Company.
- Member1 does not currently exist in the tree, and all replicas of Dept2.Company exist only on NetWare 4.11 servers, none of which are running 5.99a.

The result could be one of these:

- The restore will fail.
- NDS will not correctly create the object Member1.Dept2.Company.
- The restore will not fail but NDS will not create the group member Member1.Dept2.Company.

If it isn't possible to upgrade all of the NetWare 4.11 servers to DS v5.99a, then at least install the new DS on any server that is without a replica, or one that is reporting an NLS error of "An older NLS schema extension has been detected," or one that is in the same replica ring as a NetWare 5 server, to keep inherited ACLs in synchronization.

Also, make the installation on at least one server in every replica ring that is more than one partition level removed from a NetWare 5 server. This enables the NetWare 5 Tree Root schema extension to properly synchronize between NetWare 4.11 servers.

Servers

One person or team is responsible for upgrading the file servers from your current network operating system to NetWare 5. This group will work closely with or be a part of the NDS design group and will also assist in setting up the lab for testing and staging upgrades. This includes the first pilot servers and all the additional servers added into the NDS tree. This group will also be responsible for operational issues such as protocol support, backup and restore, and performance tuning of the NetWare 5 servers.

If you are upgrading from NetWare 2 or 3, the server team should spend some time cleaning up and preparing the NetWare 3 servers. This team can create guidelines for cleaning up the files in the file system as well as the NetWare 3 binderies. Cleaning up the files ensures that only files and objects you need are transferred during the upgrade process.

The server team may also want to consider upgrading the server hardware to newer and faster machines because NetWare 5 requires more resources to load and operate than previous NetWare operating systems. The server team should work with your company's hardware vendor to procure the optimal hardware for NetWare 5.

Minimum Server Hardware Requirements

The hardware requirements for NetWare 5 have increased over those for earlier versions of NetWare. As a minimum, a NetWare 5 server must have:

- A Pentium-class processor
- 64MB of RAM
- A 50MB minimum DOS partition

- A 500MB SYS volume
- Network cards with HAM drivers

The NetWare 5 documentation calls for a minimum processor speed of 1500, which would qualify a 486-100 processor as adequate. However, the performance issues for the products installed mandate at least a Pentium 90 or better for NetWare 5.

NetWare 5 specifies a minimum of 50MB of space in a DOS partition. An install will work with as little as 35MB of space, but this is not recommended. In addition, we recommend that the DOS partition include enough additional space to cover core dumps from server RAM. For example, a 128MB RAM system should have 128MB + 50MB = 178MB for the DOS partition.

Note that this DOS partition must be created using a non–Windows 95/98 format program (DOS 3.3 or higher). NetWare 5 will not install on a partition created by or with a Win95/98 or WinNT COMMAND.COM on it. To help you get around this, the NetWare 5 CD-ROM is bootable using the El Torito specification (which will work with most IDE and SCSI CD-ROM equipped servers that support El Torito, except for Compaq SCSI systems). You may have to configure the CMOS to boot from the CD-ROM drive letter to get this to work.

Novell also includes the DR DOS 7.02 OS on the License Diskette. This includes such basic DOS utilities as FORMAT, FDISK, and COMMAND.COM in versions that will work with NetWare 5. You can then use this diskette to boot from and recreate the DOS partition if needed.

One of the major changes in the server hardware for NetWare 5 is the replacement of the .DSK drivers with the .HAM drivers. NetWare 5 includes .HAM drivers for most adapters on the installation CD-ROM. If the adapter in your system is not available on the CD-ROM, please check developer.novell.com/infosys/mastr_02.htm for a list of all NetWare-certified adapters and drivers.

Upgrading ROLLCALL.NLM

In a mixed NetWare 4.11 and 5 tree, the server team must upgrade existing 4.11 servers to ROLLCALL.NLM version 4.10. The 4.10 version of ROLLCALL.NLM became available with the intraNetWare Support Pack 5, called IWSP5b.EXE. NDS Manager can perform this function, or you can manually copy the file from one server to another.

NetWare 3 to NetWare 5 Server Preparations

If you have NetWare 3 servers that need to be upgraded to NetWare 5, the server team should also consider performing the following functions in preparation for the upgrade of each server:

- Apply the corporate NDS naming standard while the objects are still in the bindery.

  NDS does not support different object types having the same name. By contrast, the binderies in previous versions of NetWare do support different object types with the same name. For example, in NetWare 3, a group object called HP4SI and a print queue called HP4SI can have the same name because they are different object types. In NetWare 5 you cannot have any leaf object with the same name in the same container. This conflict needs to be resolved before the upgrade of the server to NetWare 5. If there are duplicate object names, the upgrade utilities need to know how to handle the duplication. Should the objects be merged or brought over as a second occurrence of the same object name? There are several utilities that can help you find duplicate object names in the NetWare 3 bindery, for example, the Rexxware Migration Toolkit (RMT) or the DUPBIND (found on `www.novell.com`), among others. These utilities display the duplicate object names in the binderies so that they can be changed before an upgrade begins. You can easily download the Rexxware Migration Toolkit for free directly from `www.simware.com`.

- Clean up the binderies and delete users and other objects that are no longer in use.

  Take this opportunity to remove security and access privileges that are no longer required. The SECURITY.EXE program in NetWare 3 will help you find and expose the detailed security information for each object in the bindery. Users who have left the company or who are no longer using that server should be removed.

- Make a complete backup of your servers before beginning an upgrade.

  Some companies have individuals in an operations group that are responsible for backups. The server team should work with this group to ensure that a recent backup has been performed on any server that is about to be updated.

- Run the BINDFIX utility in NetWare 3 to remove any objects that are corrupted in the bindery.

  If you are upgrading multiple NetWare 2 or NetWare 3 servers into a single NetWare 5 server, the server team should check for users with accounts on the multiple servers.

- Decide on a strategy for upgrading multiple servers and duplicate users, a process that will present you with several challenges during the upgrade process to NetWare 5. First, you need to determine how you want to handle the duplicate users. You can merge the users into the same NDS user object, or you can create separate objects. By default the upgrade utility will merge the user objects that have the same name into a single NDS object with cumulative rights. This may or may not be what you had intended.

  If each one of the multiple NetWare 2 or NetWare 3 servers is moved into different containers in the NDS tree (OUs), the duplicate usernames will be moved to each individual container that has the same relative distinguished name but a different context. In most cases you do not want to manage the same user twice in the tree.

- Delete old files and applications from the file system. This will free up disk space for other purposes. You will discover many old, unused, and duplicated applications that are wasting disk space.

- Determine which protocols you want loaded on your servers. There are a variety of protocol configurations, namely IP, IPX, or IPX Compatibility. In addition, ensure that your network uses the NetWare 5 default Ethernet frame type of 802.2.

Although NetWare 5 will support both the 802.3 raw and IEEE 802.2 frame types, 802.2 is the preferred standard and provides automatic checksumming of packets to ensure greater communications reliability.

The server team should understand how to install a new NetWare 5 server from scratch and should have experience in the upgrade of your current servers to NetWare 5.

In order to perform a new installation of NetWare 5, run the INSTALL.BAT program from the NetWare 5 CD-ROM. The NetWare 5 CD-ROM can be mounted as a DOS device on the server machine, or it can be mounted as a NetWare volume where the server is logged in as a client. The CD-ROM can also be completely copied to a server volume; this method is referred to as server-to-server installation.

Installing a new NetWare 5 server on new hardware is simple and can be accomplished by referring to Chapter 16, "Upgrading to NetWare 5."

The server team needs to become familiar with the upgrade options available to them. In upgrading an existing network server to NetWare 5, you have several utilities available to you. These include the normal In-Place (using the installation program), Across-the-Wire (using the Novell Upgrade Wizard), and Rexxware Migration Toolkit (RMT) utilities. The installation program offers support for upgrading from NetWare 3 and previous versions of NetWare 4. The Novell Upgrade Wizard and RMT utilities upgrade NetWare 2 and NetWare 3. The DS Migrate program that was shipped in previous versions of NetWare 4 is no longer available in NetWare 5. However, the Novell Upgrade Wizard and Rexxware Migration Toolkit are both graphical upgrade utilities that enable you to upgrade a NetWare 2 or NetWare 3 server bindery by upgrading modeled bindery information to an existing NetWare 5 tree. For more detailed information on the Novell Upgrade Wizard and RMT, refer to Chapter 16, "Upgrading to NetWare 5." The In-Place upgrade method is the fastest way to upgrade because it does not move any data or files. This method is also recommended when you are upgrading an existing NetWare 3 server to NetWare 5 on the existing hardware device.

The other upgrade methods are slower because the workstation has to move all the data across the network. It is recommended that you use the Novell Upgrade Wizard or Rexxware Migration Toolkit method when you want to upgrade an existing network server from one machine to another. These methods enable you to replace or upgrade the server hardware.

Consulting Experience

Always try to use the 802.2 frame type and begin phasing out the 802.3 raw frame type if it is in use at your site. Choosing just one frame type will eliminate additional network traffic.

Clients

One person or team is responsible for upgrading the workstations or clients to the latest client software for the preferred desktop operating system. If there are several different types of operating systems, then the team can be divided to support each desktop operating system. For example, DOS/Windows, Windows 95, OS/2, Macintosh, NT, and UNIX desktops can be supported by different people with the client team. This team would be responsible for optimizing, configuring, and updating or migrating the workstations.

Upgrade at least one workstation to the latest version of Client 32 for use by the system administrator. You should do this for either new installations of NetWare 5 or installations of NetWare 5 into an existing NetWare 4 tree. NetWare 5 includes version 2.7 of the Client 32 software. Earlier clients either did not fully support NDPS or lacked the extended capabilities of the newer NWAdmin, NDS Manager, or other GUI utilities. Attempting to use an older Client 32 v2.2 or earlier workstation to administer NetWare 5 with its Win32 utilities on the new server will either cause one or more of these utilities to fail or result in one or more features of the utility failing to perform as expected.

For example, an NDPS configuration in NWADMIN cannot function with the older workstation software. Also, attempting to launch the NDS Manager from such a workstation will cause a failure to load error message.

The new client software for NetWare 5 is found on the Client CD-ROM included with the operating system. It ships on the same CD-ROM as the Z.E.N.works Starter Pack included with the package.

Consulting Experience

Consider moving the client team and other IS staff to the NetWare 32-bit Client first. This will enable your administrators to become familiar with the technology before they upgrade the user community.

It is recommended that the client team upgrade the workstations to the latest client software before upgrading any servers to NetWare 5. For example, the NetWare Client 32 can provide your workstation with more conventional memory. Once the server is upgraded to NetWare 5, the user will have immediate support for single login and other services unique to the NetWare 5 operating system.

The OS/2 Requester for NDS also provides many of the same benefits as the NetWare Client 32, such as full backward compatibility.

The Macintosh client for NetWare 5 also provides single login to any NetWare 5 servers.

The client team should plan for about 10 minutes per workstation to complete the installation of the latest client software for the desktop operating system. The team should also combine all necessary changes into a single visit to each workstation. Here are some things to consider:

- Determine and define the contents for each of the configuration files on the workstation. These configuration files include CONFIG.SYS, AUTOEXEC.BAT, NET.CFG, and STARTNET.BAT. You should define a standardized set of files across all workstations in the network.
- During the upgrade or installation of the new client software, the fastest installation method is to download from a server rather than using floppy disks. This method is possible if you are upgrading from NETX workstations. If you have VLMs or NetWare Client 32, then there are automated methods for updating the client software.
- Consider upgrading other system software for the workstations. For example, you could take this opportunity to upgrade the workstations to the latest revision of Windows or to perform other upgrades.

- Schedule the upgrade of your workstations during a period that is long enough to upgrade your selected set of users. You may need to schedule this process during a weekend. Obviously, the more people involved in the upgrade of workstations, the faster this process will go.
- The client team could also consider an automated strategy for upgrades from the server. For instance, when the user logs into a NetWare 5 server, the automated program will download the required programs to the workstations. This implies that the workstations are standardized in their file structure.

Protocols

The responsibilities of the protocol team include determining which protocols will be used in the network. Large companies, however, typically have an entire organization called Router Engineering or Telecommunication, which manages and controls the network infrastructure. This group usually mandates the specific protocols and frame types for the networking teams.

NetWare 5 defaults to a pure IP installation. This means that if it is installed into an existing tree with only IPX, it would essentially be invisible to the servers and clients in that tree. However, you can load and bind both IP and IPX on the same NetWare 5 server to make the servers visible in an IPX environment. NetWare 5 also includes a middle-of-the-road solution called IPX Compatibility Mode.

When you select to install IP, passive support for IPX is also automatically provided. If an IPX request arrives at the server, NetWare 5 will process the IPX request. This passive support for IPX is called Compatibility Mode and is automatically enabled to provide service for applications that require IPX.

In Compatibility Mode, the server will respond to IPX-based applications without having IPX bound to one of its LAN boards. The server will listen for IPX requests on a specific network number and respond. Compatibility Mode provides a way to migrate easily to IP without having to reconfigure every client and server to support IP immediately.

The protocol team is responsible for determining how to implement or migrate from the current IPX segments to IP. There are several options or configurations that each use various degrees of Pure IP. For example, there is IP-only, IP and IPX both, or IP/CMD (which is the IPX compatibility). In order to implement the protocol solution, this team must be familiar with the following technologies:

- Migration Gateway (links the logical IPX and IP worlds)
- Compatibility Mode (CMD)
- IPX to NetWare 5
- NWIP to IP Migration
- SLP Agents (UA, SA, DA)
- SLP Design

DNS/DHCP Printing

One person or team is responsible for designing the printing strategies for NetWare 5. The strategies may include installation and configuration of the new NPDS printing product. All the print software and hardware should be tested for compatibility, which includes connections greater than 255 users. The printing strategies could encompass printing in a mixed environment from both bindery-based and NDS-based configurations. This team should address the following issues for both methods of printing. In addition, this team should address how and when to implement the Novell Distributed Print Services (NDPS) strategy:

- Setup for an NDS-based printing strategy
- Quick Setup
  - Default Print Queue for printers
  - Workstations running VLMs
  - Workstations running NETX
  - Workstations running Client 32 for Windows and Windows 95

- Support for a mixed bindery-based and NDS-based printing strategy
  - Queues on NetWare 5, with the Print Servers on NetWare 3
  - Queues on NetWare 3, with the Print Servers on NetWare 5
  - Queues and Print Servers on NetWare 3, with Client on NetWare 5, VLMs, and Client 32 for Windows and Windows 95
- New support for Novell Distributed Print Services (NDPS):
  - Install NDPS-aware printers. This could be as simple as upgrading the flash memory of the printer hardware.
  - Install and manage Printer Agents with printer-specific gateways using the NDPS Manager to support non-NDPS-aware printers.
  - Install and manage the NDPS Broker.
  - Set up the Novell printer gateway to support NDS- and bindery-based print jobs to non-NDPS-aware printers.
  - Set up IP printing (LPR/LPD) using the Novell printer gateway, as needed.
  - Load compatibility support for RPRINTER and NPRINTER printers using the Novell printer gateway.

The print team should test all the possible printing configurations and help with the upgrade of the printing infrastructure to NetWare 5 and NDPS.

Applications

One person or team is responsible for performing compatibility testing for applications running on the servers and clients. There are several issues to consider during the compatibility testing. These issues include, but are not restricted to:

- Bindery-based software programs
- DS-aware applications

- Connections greater than 255 users
- VLM and NetWare Client 32 compatibility

This group is also responsible for upgrading and implementing the applications into the NetWare 5 production environment, as well as for testing the server and workstation applications to make sure that they will run properly. Certain types of applications may not work properly when more than 255 users are connected to one NetWare 5 server. However, if the applications were already used in a production NetWare 4 (which is the predecessor to NetWare 5) environment with more than 255 users, they will work in NetWare 5. If your company has applications that were written by an internal staff, they should be tested for compatibility with NetWare 5.

Administration

One person or group is responsible for assigning system administrators and users access to both the network and NDS. This includes login scripts, bindery services, mobile users, security, and the administration of NDS. This team will determine and establish the auditing requirements for the corporation.

These team members with their assignments perform your NetWare 5 design and installation. Some or all of these tasks may be performed by one person or by a team of people with specific assignments. After you have selected your project team, you are now ready to define the implementation tasks and schedule.

Implementing Tasks and Schedules

This section of the chapter focuses on the key objectives and tasks in order to implement NetWare 5. These are the major objectives that need to be accomplished to implement NetWare 5:

1. Set project scope.
2. Determine training needs.

3. Understand NetWare 5 core OS enhancements.
4. Conduct NDS design or review.
5. Make server upgrades.
6. Change over protocols from IPX to IP.
7. Upgrade clients.
8. Upgrade the printing environment.
9. Convert applications and other services.

From these objectives you can create specific tasks and associated schedules that will provide you the time line for accomplishing the various upgrade and installation tasks. Having such a document helps you to keep the process moving and gives focus to the remaining tasks. The implementation schedule should provide detailed tasks that you will accomplish or perform during the installation or upgrade of your network servers. The implementation schedule should also include the time line and the individuals or team members assigned to complete the tasks. The schedule can also provide specific guidelines and recommendations necessary to properly perform the assigned tasks.

The objective for the NetWare 5 implementation schedule is to establish and perform the implementation tasks in the proper order. The individual tasks also need to provide a continual process for the upgrade to NetWare 5. This objective can be met only if all the network administrators work together using the same goals, schedules, and task lists.

The schedule helps you track the status of the project and can provide immediate feedback or reports to your staff and management. A well-planned implementation schedule will not only help you manage and track the status of the NetWare 5 design and implementation project but can be used to set the deadlines for each task. You should lay out a chart or schedule for each task that includes a description, guidelines, duration, start and end date, team or person assigned, and the percentage of the task completed. If possible, the schedule can also show the interdependencies of the tasks, measure team members' progress in completing tasks, review the work, and produce reports for management.

The main responsibility of the project team as a whole is to create and lay out the implementation schedule to determine the overall scope of the project. This schedule should define what the end result of your upgrade will be.

The purpose for the implementation schedule is to provide the project team with a consistent set of tasks and objectives for the NetWare 5 upgrade and roll out. The final goal of the project team is to establish a NetWare 5 network that provides a single point of login for the users and simplifies network administration. You are also trying to enhance your network services by increasing the capacity of existing systems.

For example, in the ACME tree, we need to define an implementation schedule to accomplish the upgrade of 40 NetWare 4 servers. The schedule should outline each task, which includes the description, guidelines, duration, start and end dates, team or person assigned, and the percentage of the task completed. The implementation schedule presented in this section may be changed or customized to more closely meet the needs of your company. Table 15.2 outlines the ACME implementation schedule.

Setting Up a Testing Lab

You can gain valuable experience with a product such as NetWare 5 by creating a lab environment. The lab experience provides the opportunity to understand how NetWare 5 operates at your particular site with your particular network characteristics. We recommend a lab for any company or organization that can afford the additional resources or may already have a lab in place. At a smaller site without the resources of a lab you can obtain hands-on experience with NetWare 5 through educational training or perhaps through your integrator.

The lab is a safe environment where you can make changes and view the impact of those changes on the NDS tree. You can test many of the features and functions of NetWare 5 and become acquainted with the product. This section will first discuss the components of a lab. Next, it will cover the areas that you should test in your lab. Keep in mind that the lab experience can be short yet productive. After reading this section you should be able to define the areas of lab testing that fit your needs. You can create a checklist of these items to help you focus on a completion date for the lab process.

TABLE 15.2

A Proposed ACME Implementation Schedule

TASK DESCRIPTION	DURATION	START DATE	END DATE	TEAM ASSIGNED	PERCENT COMPLETE
1. Set Project Scope	12w	1/1/99	2/1/99	Project Team	
1.1 Determine Roles and Responsibilities					
1.2 Determine Milestones					
1.3 Determine Critical Path					
1.4 Determine Success Factors					
1.5 Conduct Risk Analysis					
1.6 Establish Reporting and Tracking					
1.7 Establish Documentation Procedures					
1.8 Design Test Strategies and Acceptance Testing					
2. Set Up Training	20w	1/1/99	6/1/99	Training	
2.1 Determine Training Needs					
2.2 Design Training Strategies					
2.2.1 Administrative					
2.2.2 NDS Design					
2.2.3 Server Installation and Upgrades					
2.2.4 Etc.					
2.3 Set Up Formal Training Courses or Classes					
2.4 Obtain Training					
2.5 Set Up the Lab					
3. Understand NetWare 5 Core OS Enhancements	4w	1/1/99	2/1/99		
3.1 Multiprocessor Kernel					
3.1.1 Virtual Memory					
3.1.2 Memory Protection					
3.2 NetWare Peripheral Architecture					
3.2.1 Hot Plug PCI					
3.3 New RCONSOLEJ					
3.3.1 RCONSOLEJ					

TASK DESCRIPTION	DURATION	START DATE	END DATE	TEAM ASSIGNED	PERCENT COMPLETE
3.4 New Security Features					
3.4.1 PKI					
3.4.2 X.509					
3.4.3 SSL					
3.5 JAVA					
3.5.1 Virtual Machine					
3.5.2 Console One					
3.6 SMS					
3.7 Licensing					
3.8 Clustering Support					
3.9 New Debuggers					
3.9.1 Assembly Level					
3.9.2 Source Level					
3.9.3 Virtual Level					
4. Conduct NDS Design or Review	6w	3/1/99	4/15/99	NDS Team	Training
4.1 Understand New NDS Features					
4.1.1 Transitive Synchronization					
4.1.2 Multiple Objects per Packet					
4.1.3 Distributive Reference Links					
4.1.4 WAN Manager					
4.1.5 Inheritable ACLs					
4.1.6 Password Administrator					
4.1.7 Partition Administrator					
4.1.8 Schema Manager					
4.1.9 Catalog Services					
4.1.10 WAN Traffic Management					
4.1.11 LDAP					
4.1.12 DSDIAF					

Continued

TABLE 15.2
Continued

TASK DESCRIPTION	DURATION	START DATE	END DATE	TEAM ASSIGNED	PERCENT COMPLETE
4.2 If Upgrading from NetWare 4 to NetWare 5, Review NDS Design					
4.2.1 NDS Health Check					
4.2.2 NDS Tree Design Review					
4.2.3 Coexistence Issues					
4.2.4 NDS Versions					
4.2.5 Synchronization Issues					
4.2.6 Upgrade Issues					
4.3 If Upgrading from NetWare 3 to NetWare 5, Design New NDS					
4.3.1 Understand Basic NDS Concepts					
4.3.2 Understand New NDS Features					
4.4 Incorporate NDS Naming Standard	2w	3/1/99	3/15/99	NDS Team	
4.4.1 Identify Existing Standards					
4.4.2 Create NDS Naming Documents					
4.4.3 Create File System Standard Structure					
4.4.4 Deliver Standards Documents					
4.5 Design NDS Tree	5d	3/15/99	3/20/99	NDS Team	
4.5.1 Review WAN Maps					
4.5.2 Review Campus Maps					
4.5.3 Design Top of the Tree					
4.5.4 Review Organization					
4.5.5 Review Resource List					
4.5.6 Design Bottom of the Tree					
4.5.7 Place Network Resources in Containers					
4.5.8 Apply Design Considerations					
4.5.8.1 Administration					
4.5.8.2 Partitioning					

TASK DESCRIPTION	DURATION	START DATE	END DATE	TEAM ASSIGNED	PERCENT COMPLETE
4.5.8.3 Login Scripts					
4.5.8.4 Bindery Services					
4.5.9 Test NDS Tree Design					
4.6 Design Partitions and Replicas	5d	3/21/99	3/26/99	NDS Team	
4.6.1 Review WAN Map					
4.6.2 Partition Top of the Tree					
4.6.3 Devise Replica Strategy					
4.6.3.1 Replicate Locality					
4.6.3.2 Replicate for Fault Tolerance					
4.6.4 Partition Bottom as Needed					
4.6.5 Develop Partition and Replica Guidelines					
4.6.6 Test Partitions and Replica Strategy					
4.7 Design Time Synchronization	1d	3/27/99	3/28/99	NDS Team	
4.7.1 Evaluate TimeSync Options					
4.7.1.1 Single Reference (Default)					
4.7.1.2 Time Provider Group					
4.7.2 Choose Option Based on WAN					
4.7.3 Evaluate TimeSync Communications					
4.7.3.1 Service Advertising Protocol (SAP)					
4.7.3.2 Configured List					
4.7.4 Develop Time Synchronization Strategy					
4.7.5 Test Time Synchronization Strategy					
4.8 Design NDS Accessibility Plan	4d	3/30/99	4/4/99	NDS Team	
4.8.1 Analyze Existing Login Scripts					
4.8.2 Move System Login Script to Container Login Script					
4.8.3 Test Login Scripts					
4.8.3.1 Container Login Scripts					
4.8.3.2 Profile Login Scripts					
4.9 Establish Access with Z.E.N.works					

Continued

TABLE 15.2

Continued

TASK DESCRIPTION	DURATION	START DATE	END DATE	TEAM ASSIGNED	PERCENT COMPLETE
4.10 Establish Access with NDS for NT					
4.11 Develop Mobile User Strategy					
4.11.1 Test Mobile User Access					
4.12 Deliver Accessibility Plan					
5. Design Security and Audit Strategy	10d	4/5/99	4/15/99	Administration	
5.1 Server Security					
5.1.1 Server Settings					
5.2 NDS Security					
5.2.1 Object Security					
5.2.2 Property Security					
5.2.3 Develop NDS Security Strategy					
5.3 Test Security Strategy					
5.4 File System Security					
5.4.1 Develop File System Strategy					
5.4.2 Test File System Strategy					
5.5 Audit					
5.5.1 Define Audit Procedures					
5.5.2 Understand Audit Utilities					
5.5.3 Develop Audit Strategy					
5.5.4 Test Audit Strategy					
6. Make Server Upgrades	20w	5/1/99	10/1/99	Server Team	
6.1 Server Installation					
6.1.1 Preparatory Steps					
6.1.2 Impact Study					
6.1.3 Planning the Upgrade Process					
6.1.4 Develop Schedule					
6.1.5 Determine Minimum Hardware Requirements					
6.1.6 Set Recommendations for Hardware Requirements					

TASK DESCRIPTION	DURATION	START DATE	END DATE	TEAM ASSIGNED	PERCENT COMPLETE
6.2 Perform Server Upgrade from NetWare 4 to NetWare 5					
6.2.1 Evaluate In-Place Utility (INSTALL)					
6.2.2 Conduct Mass Upgrades and Run Automated Scripts					
6.2.3 Evaluate Enterprise Upgrade Utility					
6.3 Perform Server Upgrade from NetWare 3 to NetWare 5					
6.3.1 Evaluate Across-the-Wire Utility					
6.3.2 Evaluate Upgrade Utilities					
6.3.3 Evaluate Upgrade Wizard					
6.3.4 Evaluate Simware's Rexxware Migration Toolkit (RMT)					
6.4 Perform Mock Upgrade in the Lab					
6.5 Test Server Upgrade Strategy					
6.6 Develop and Establish File System Standards					
6.7 Determine Cleanup Procedures					
6.8 Develop Backup and Restore Strategy					
6.9 Upgrade Volumes to NSS					
6.9.1 Volume Conversions to NSS issues					
6.9.2 NSS Conversion Utilities					
6.10 Incorporate New Backup Utilities					
6.10.1 New GUI Backup Utility					
6.10.2 NDS Backup Utility					
6.11 Prepare Server Pilot and Rollout					
6.11.1 Server Preparation					
6.11.2 Perform Cleanup (Objects and Files)					
6.11.3 Back up the Server					
6.11.4 Install or Upgrade Server to NetWare 5					
6.11.5 Test Server (Production-Like)					
6.11.6 Document Any Problems					
6.11.7 Modify Procedures Based on Results					
6.11.8 Perform Acceptance Testing					
6.11.9 Provide Daily Support to User					
6.11.10 Validate Functionality of the Servers					

Continued

TABLE 15.2

Continued

TASK DESCRIPTION	DURATION	START DATE	END DATE	TEAM ASSIGNED	PERCENT COMPLETE
7. Make Protocol Change Over (IPX to IP)	4w	3/1/99	4/1/99	Protocol Team	
7.1 Determine Migrate Method					
7.1.1 IP only					
7.1.2 IP and IPX					
7.1.3 IP/CMD (IPX Compatibility)					
7.2 Migration Gateway /g (IP to IPX)					
7.3 Migration Gateway /bs (IPX to IP to IPX)					
7.4 Compatibility Mode (CMD)					
7.5 NWIP to IP Migration					
7.6 SLP Agents (UA, SA, DA)					
7.7 SLP Design					
7.8 DNS/DHCP					
8. Perform Client Upgrade	10w	3/1/99	5/15/99	Client Team	
8.1 Undertake Preparatory Steps					
8.1.1 Develop Schedule					
8.1.2 Impact Study					
8.1.3 Determine Hardware Requirements					
8.1.4 Set Hardware Recommendations					
8.2 Evaluate Client Upgrade Options					
8.3 Determine Client Upgrade Strategy					
8.4 Test Client Upgrade Strategy					
8.4.1 Functional Testing for Each Desktop					
8.5 Plan the Upgrade Process					
8.6 Conduct Client Implementation					
8.6.1 IP-enabled Windows 95					
8.6.2 IP-enabled Windows NT					
8.6.3 IP-enabled DOS/Windows					

TASK DESCRIPTION	DURATION	START DATE	END DATE	TEAM ASSIGNED	PERCENT COMPLETE
9. Make Printing Environment Upgrade	5w	3/1/99	4/15/99	Print Team	
9.1 Identify Existing Printing Environment					
9.1.1 Bindery-Based					
9.1.2 NDS Queue-Based					
9.2 Design NDPS Printing Environment					
9.2.1 Printer Agent					
9.2.2 Management Console					
9.2.3 Queue-Based Printing Upgrade					
9.3 Determine NDPS Gateway Placement					
9.4 Evaluate Direct Print Cards and Printers					
9.5 Design Printing Upgrade Strategy					
9.5.1 Bindery-Based to NDPS-Based					
9.5.2 NDS Queue-Based to NDPS-Based					
9.6 Test Printing Upgrade Strategy					
10. Upgrade Applications	5w	3/1/99	4/15/99	Applications	
10.1 Identify All Server-Based and Client-Based Applications					
10.1.1 Identify and Create Application Objects in NDS					
10.2 Upgrade from NetWare 4 to NetWare 5					
10.2.1 Differences in Utilities					
10.2.2 DOS Utilities Not Supported					
10.3 Identify and Create Application Objects in NDS					
10.4 For Internally Written Applications					
10.5 Install					
10.6 Test on a Desktop					
10.7 Test on Server					
10.8 Test Printing					
10.9 Test Document Compatibility					
10.10 Deliver Applications in Production Using NAL					
10.11 Upgrade Other Services					
10.11.1 Oracle 8					
10.11.2 Netscape FastTrack Server					
10.11.3 BTRIEVE					

Evaluating the Need for a Lab

The decision to have a lab is entirely dependent upon your circumstances. Although most small sites do not have the resources to install a lab, they can benefit by gaining some hands-on experience through their integrator or education center. For a small site where you plan to use the default configurations, the lab is not as crucial but can provide you with valuable administrative experience. If your site is small and you do have a lab, we recommend a brief testing period in the lab to familiarize yourself with NetWare 5, especially from an administrative standpoint. Setting up a lab and installing NetWare 5 will also instill confidence in your project team as they learn about the features and capabilities of NetWare 5. It will also give you time to work with the operating system, perform diagnostics, and test utilities and applications.

Implementation of a NetWare 5 lab is recommended for any site that will install or upgrade more than 30 NetWare 5 servers. Many customers will move from the default settings of NetWare 5 to configurable parameters at approximately this number of servers. Therefore, the lab gives you the opportunity to adjust and test various configuration parameters.

If you have a larger site with a Wide Area Network (WAN) in place, we recommend that you follow, where applicable, the lab procedures presented in this section. Network administrators of large sites should fully familiarize themselves with the functions and features of NetWare 5 before beginning a full-scale upgrade to NetWare 5.

For the ACME site, lab testing is being handled at the NORAD facility in the LABS department. All new software and hardware is evaluated at this facility before being deployed onto the production network. Therefore, the new operating system being deployed in the ACME tree has gone through the lab process.

The Lab Setup

Many large organizations have a permanent lab for testing all new software and hardware that may be placed into production at their site. Others may be considering the creation of a temporary lab for this project. In either case, you will need to dedicate some hardware for use as NetWare 5 servers and workstations for the duration of your lab project.

Your lab should consist of a minimum of four nodes — two NetWare 5 servers and two workstations. The servers and adapter cards should be similar to the hardware that will be used in your network environment. If you are planning to upgrade your hardware, then use the new hardware in your lab environment. Each NetWare 5 server should exceed the minimum recommendations provided by Novell. You want to duplicate your actual environment as closely as possible. In addition, you will want to duplicate your LAN topology where possible.

Figure 15.1 shows the ACME lab for testing NetWare 5 for the entire ACME tree installation. This lab has four dedicated NetWare 5 servers and three workstations to run the Novell and third-party utilities. In addition, because the ACME network is primarily a token ring, we have a token ring concentrator in the lab to connect the servers and workstations together. All file servers have a CD-ROM drive as well as sufficient disk and memory capacity. The lab ring also has a connection to the corporate backbone located in the labs division of NORAD.

FIGURE 15.1

The ACME lab consists of four NetWare 5 servers and three workstations.

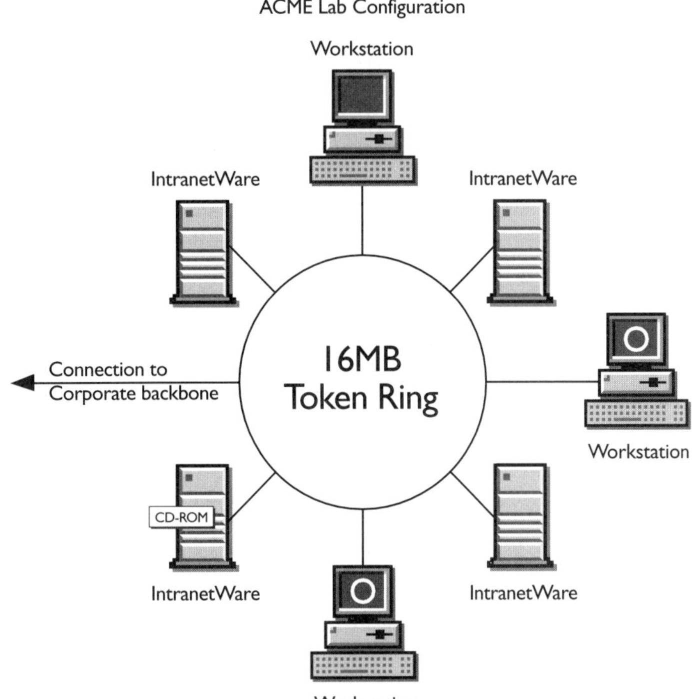

Your lab can be smaller; it can even consist of only three nodes. A three-node network would consist of two NetWare 5 file servers and a single workstation.

One of the servers must have a CD-ROM device for installing NetWare 5. Also, if possible, have a network connection to your backbone so that you can access any servers currently in operation on your network. A minimal configuration is shown in Figure 15.2.

FIGURE 15.2

A minimal lab configuration would have two NetWare 5 servers and a single workstation.

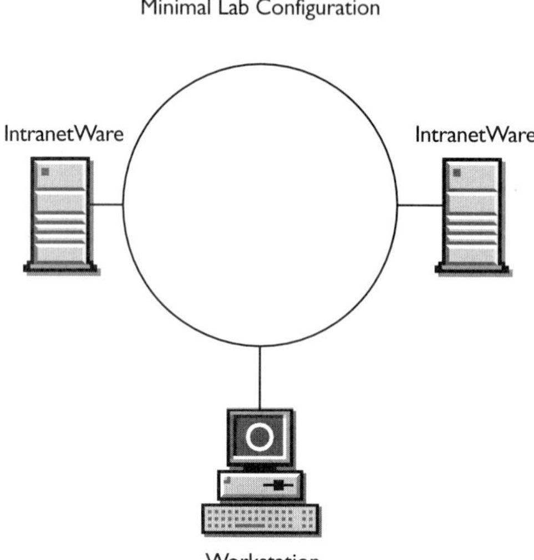

The Lab Process

The lab process simply provides order and direction to help you accomplish your objectives in the lab. Without such direction, a lab simply becomes a bunch of PCs that are not utilized, and the lab experience wears on until people lose interest in what they are trying to accomplish. With some specific objectives, you will be able to provide a thorough test of NetWare 5 and obtain experience before beginning a large-scale upgrade.

Your network administrators can put into practice the information presented in this book such as NDS tree design, partitioning and replication strategies, and security procedures. You can evaluate the following areas in your lab (which will be discussed here):

- Lab installation
- Hardware setup and required components

- Mounting a CD-ROM as a NetWare volume
- Installation of NetWare 5
- NDS tree review and implementation
- NDS partitions and replicas review
- Time synchronization configuration review
- Design and test container login scripts
- Design and test administration/security procedures
- Software testing
- Application testing
- Novell utility testing
- Third-party utilities
- Backup and restore procedures
- Implementation of the NetWare 5 pilot system

Lab Installation

If your site already has a lab in place, you can simply designate a group of servers for your test along with a few workstations. You will want to follow the NetWare 5 installation procedures discussed in Chapter 16, "Upgrading to NetWare 5," as well as the procedures discussed in the "Install NetWare 5" section later in this chapter.

Companies creating a lab from scratch can follow the procedures outlined in the text to follow.

Hardware and Required Components

Perhaps the most time-consuming aspect of installing NetWare 5 is installing and connecting a CD-ROM drive. Your job will be made much simpler if you obtain the latest CD-ROM drivers from Novell and/or your third-party manufacturers. You'll save hours of frustration when mounting your CD-ROMs if you have the latest drivers running on your hardware.

For most hardware products, you can obtain their latest drivers by connecting to their bulletin boards. All drivers that are contained on the Novell NetWare 5 CD-ROM have been tested with NetWare 5.

Mounting a CD-ROM as a NetWare Volume

Mounting a CD-ROM as a NetWare volume has become extremely easy compare to the method that was needed in NetWare 4. The following steps illustrate how to install your CD-ROM as a NetWare volume:

1. From the server console type:

   ```
   LOAD CDROM.NLM
   ```

2. The LOAD command is optional and no longer required in NetWare 5. The effect of the command is that the CD that is placed in your server machine will automatically be mounted as a NetWare volume.

3. After loading the CDROM.NLM, type this command at the console to verify that the CD-ROM was mounted:

   ```
   VOLUMES
   ```

4. The CD should be mounted as a NetWare 5 volume and available.

With a NetWare volume mounted you can then map a drive to this volume and access the CD-ROM device.

Installing NetWare 5

You can refer to Chapter 16, "Upgrading to NetWare 5," for detailed information on installation procedures. For the lab exercise you can install the NetWare 5 operating system on each of your lab servers. Loading the software is not difficult, but you should familiarize yourself with the different installation options. For example, new to NetWare 5 is a GUI installation utility with an intuitive, graphical interface.

You should also practice removing NDS from the server. On occasion you may have to remove a server from the tree because of hardware repairs or shipment to another location, and you should follow the appropriate steps to remove a server from the tree.

Familiarize yourself with the new NWCONFIG utility, which replaces the INSTALL utility from NetWare 4. You may have to add new NLMs or additional licenses, and the NWCONFIG utility handles these procedures.

If you are upgrading from NetWare 3 to NetWare 5 and you have the hardware, you can perform an upgrade of a current NetWare 3 server to a lab NetWare 5 server. This approach allows you to upgrade your hardware to a new platform for NetWare 5 and does not endanger your current NetWare 3 server.

Creating the NDS tree

The creation of your NDS tree in your lab should be based on the information discussed in the other chapters in this book. For modeling your lab tree, you can use the Rexxware Migration Toolkit to simplify this process. In addition, refer back to Chapter 5, "Novell Directory Services Tree," for information and design strategies.

The lab tree that you install will eventually become your production tree, so take the necessary time to define the appropriate levels and placement of resources. If you have a successful and functional lab tree, you do not need to recreate another tree unless you want to maintain separate trees for testing purposes.

Creating Partitions and Replicas

The first partition created is the default [ROOT] partition. After your lab servers are up and running, you can use the NDS Manager utility to further partition each of your sites into separate partitions subordinate to [ROOT]. Use your lab to learn how to create replicas as well. Because the size of your lab may be somewhat limited, you still should learn how the partition utilities place replicas on servers. You can also learn how to identify the locations of the replicas by viewing them with the utilities.

Configuring Time Synchronization

Your lab servers will initially have time synchronization set up with the defaults. Your first NetWare 5 server is installed as a Single Reference server. All other servers are Secondary.

Familiarize yourself with the TimeSync parameters through the various SET commands as well as the MONITOR utility. You can change the default settings through the MONITOR utility. For example, you can create a small-time provider group by changing your Single Reference server to a Reference server. Then change the other two or three lab servers to Primary servers. With a LANalyzer or other equipment you can view the packets sent and received for each time synchronization interval.

Use other commands such as SET TIMESYNC DEBUG=7 to enable the time synchronization screen on your NetWare 5 server. This screen will show you the status of time synchronization and the adjustments being made if this server's time is not synchronized.

Designing and Testing Container Login Scripts

The lab is a great place to design and test your container login scripts. Populate one of your containers with actual user objects from your company. Test the container login script for errors and to verify that all necessary environment variables have been defined.

If you are planning to use Profile scripts as well, the lab is the perfect place to test the functionality of these scripts.

Designing and Testing Administration/Security Procedures

The lab testing facility is an excellent place to test your security and administrative policies and procedures. NetWare 5 includes several new security and administrative features that you may want to test, for example, the ability to inherit specific property rights down the entire tree. This feature is possible because of the new inheritable ACLs. The inheritable ACLs allow you to assign supervisor rights to operators or help desk staff for specific types of objects or resources without giving supervisor rights to the entire tree. For example, you can assign rights to a group to manage just the printers, servers, or users.

Before making these types of rights assignments, you will want test and determine which specific property you want to have flow down the NDS tree. In order to establish the rights, you use the NWADMIN property rights screen. On this screen, there is a new button at the bottom of the rights list called Inherit. You can give specific property rights to any object that will inherit by selecting the rights and then selecting the Inherit button.

In addition to the inherited ACL feature, NetWare 5 now provides you the ability to assign rights to manage just the users' passwords or NDS partitions. NetWare 5 provides you with two new properties called Password Administrator property and Partition Administrator property. Again, you will want to test implementation of these rights before rolling it directly into you production tree.

Application Testing in Your Lab

Not all applications need to be tested for NetWare 5 compatibility. Some applications, however, especially those written inside your corporation, may require some testing. The following points should be considered when you are testing applications:

- Is the application bindery-based? Bindery-based applications require bindery services to be enabled on that server as well as a read/write replica of the defined context.

- Were these applications written specifically for the NETX or VLM client? Were the applications written specifically for the NetWare 3 or NetWare 4 operating system? If so, they should be tested with the software. Some basic and easy tests you can perform are listed here:

  - Run the application to completion or proper termination.
  - Print a document with the application.
  - Using the application, do a file save of your work onto the NetWare 5 server.
  - Run the application on the new IP client software, if applicable. Test your tape backup application support for NetWare 5 and NDS.
  - Keep your application testing procedure short and simple. You will never be able to test every feature and function of every product. Concentrate your efforts on the specialty applications that are not in the mainstream.

Administer network applications using Z.E.N.works, which stands for Zero Effort Networking. Z.E.N.works enables you to represent applications and workstations as objects in the Novell Directory. You can manage the application and workstation objects as Directory objects the same way you manage other objects, using the NWADMIN utility. Using application objects you can:

- Define an application's directory, icon, command line parameters, and other properties in one place.
- Use trustee assignments to manage access to an application.
- Define startup scripts that establish the appropriate network environment for the application (drive mappings, print captures, and so on) and cleanup scripts that restore the workstation's environment.

Gaining Experience with Your Utilities

The fact that you have installed a lab will automatically give you experience with Novell and NetWare and, most likely, third-party utilities. You will be exposed to the following utilities with a lab in place:

- NDS Manager
- NWADMIN
- MONITOR.NLM
- INWCONFIG.NLM (formerly INSTALL.NLM)
- DSREPAIR.NLM
- DSTRACE (not really a utility, but a group of set commands)
- NWUSER
- Novell Upgrade Wizard
- Rexxware Migration Toolkit

Review and work through each utility to gain experience and confidence with the operation of these tools.

Backup and Restore Procedures

Perform a full backup and restore of a NetWare 5 server. This backup includes files as well as NDS tree information. Always have a clear understanding of backup procedures related to your specific backup product. The lab is the best place to gain experience in backup and recovery procedures. For more information on backup and restoration of NDS, refer to Chapter 18.

The NetWare 5 Pilot System

A *pilot system* is the first NetWare 5 server placed into production on your network. A pilot system will be the baseline system you will use to test all the operational procedures that you have developed for the upgrade to NetWare 5. You can use either the In-Place or Across-the-Wire upgrade to perform the upgrade of users and data, depending on the previous network operating system from which you are upgrading.

If you can use separate hardware for an upgrade, you can safely move a server without affecting the production server. Once you have successfully performed the upgrade, you can redirect the actual users or group of users to the new NetWare 5 server. The server you choose to upgrade as the pilot system should probably be a server that is used by the technical staff at your facility. This way the staff members will become familiar with the operation of the NetWare 5 server in production.

Use the pilot system to optimize your workstation configurations including AUTOEXEC.BAT, CONFIG.SYS, NET.CFG, and any other files required for your installation.

The pilot system process for NetWare 5 does not require an enormous amount of time. The purpose of the pilot system is to provide adequate experience for you and your staff with the NetWare 5 server in your production environment. If you feel you have reached that point after only a couple of weeks, then the pilot system has most likely served its purpose.

Summary

This chapter covers the major features and options that are available to you to prepare for upgrading your current NetWare servers and environment to NetWare 5. Depending on the size of your organization, you may need to create an in-depth implementation schedule or just have a couple of basic tasks. The individual tasks, which include NDS design, training, understanding the new features, upgrading servers and clients, and upgrading the printing infrastructure, may be accomplished by different teams or all by the same person. Again, the number of people involved in the process depends on the overall size of the company and number of servers.

CHAPTER 16

Basics of NetWare 5 Server Upgrades

"A permanent state of transition is man's most noble condition."—Juan Ramon Jimenez

This chapter explores the many methods for upgrading your NetWare 3 and NetWare 4 servers to NetWare 5. Each method has its merits, and you can choose the method that most closely meets your needs and circumstances. You face many considerations when determining which upgrade method to use. These considerations are discussed here in each upgrade section. Some network upgrades may require multiple methods depending on the circumstances of the upgrade. For example, some sites may decide to purchase new hardware to support NetWare 5 and use one upgrade utility for the entire process. Other companies may have multiple departments, each responsible for its own upgrade and each with its own budgetary constraints. They may choose to keep their existing hardware, and hence a different upgrade process may be used. This chapter focuses on upgrades from previous versions of NetWare only. NetWare 5 provides you with the following upgrade methods:

- In-place upgrades for NetWare 3 to NetWare 5
- In-place upgrades for NetWare 4 to NetWare 5
- In-place NetWare 4 to NetWare 5 mass upgrades
- The Novell Upgrade Wizard
- The Rexxware Migration Toolkit (RMT)

There is an important new feature in NetWare 5: for new installations, the CD-ROM is bootable; booting from the CD automatically creates a DOS partition and installs NetWare 5 from the CD. This includes automatic install and loading of the DOS CD-ROM drivers. The previous versions of NetWare forced you to manually create the DOS partition and to locate and configure the DOS drivers and server installation. For more information on actual installation steps and procedures for NetWare 5, see Chapter 2.

Consulting Experience

Take some time to review and practice the upgrade options in your lab if you can. If you do not have the additional hardware to create a new server, make sure that you take all the necessary precautions to back up your current servers before beginning a upgrade. Our experience has shown that those who can practice upgrades in a lab will have fewer problems during an actual upgrade to NetWare 5.

In addition to new installations, you need to understand each of the upgrades so that you can choose the method that best suits your needs. The advantages and disadvantages of each upgrade method are discussed in this chapter. Figure 16.1 illustrates graphically the strengths and weaknesses of each of the upgrade options. In this figure all of the in-place options appear together under the heading of In-Place.

FIGURE 16.1

The strengths and weaknesses of each upgrade method

Upgrade Needs	In-Place Upgrade	Novell Upgrades Wizard	RMT
Same Hardware	X		
Bindery (converts to NDS)		X	X
Data (moves file system)		X	X
Name Spaces		X	X
Passwords		X	X
Printing		X	X
Easiest upgrade method		X	
Fastest upgrade method			X
Customization			X
Modeling			X
Strongest reports			X
Checkpoint restart and undo capability			X

Basic Hardware Requirements

Novell's success over the years has been the capability of its products to operate on a large variety of hardware at either the server or workstation levels. As with the earlier versions of NetWare, NetWare 5 and its associated client products operate well on a variety of hardware platforms. The speed of your server hardware, however, has become much more important when you are using NetWare 5 servers to interoperate on the network. Obviously, the faster your hardware, the better performance you will have with NetWare 5. Enhanced performance will not only increase the speed of access for your clients, it will improve the speed of NDS synchronization operations and the associated NDS background processes. So look closely at your current hardware and understand that your most heavily utilized servers should be your fastest and most powerful. What follows is a list of the minimum server hardware needed to operate NetWare 5. We also include a recommended list of hardware for NetWare 5.

A Minimum Configuration

The following minimum configuration is for 10 users:

- A PC with a 486 processor
- 48MB RAM
- 1GB hard disk space (SYS volume requires 500MB)
- 16-bit NIC card
- CD-ROM device installed on the server to be upgraded
- 3.5-inch floppy drive
- Any low-cost monitor with VGA card

A Recommended Configuration for Your Busiest Servers

The following configuration is recommended for 250 users:

- Intel Pentium II class or better
- 128MB RAM (even more is better)
- 4GB hard disk minimum
- EISA or PCI bus-mastering NIC card
- 24X speed CD-ROM drive
- 3.5-inch floppy drive
- Any low-cost monitor with VGA card

Preparing for Your Upgrade

Regardless of the upgrade method you choose you must accomplish some basic preparations before you start your upgrade. These steps are listed and explained here.

Prepare Your NetWare Server for Upgrade

Refer to Chapters 15 and 18 for more information regarding the following preparations:

1. Back up your NetWare server before beginning an upgrade. Always make sure that you have tested the restoration of a tape backup as well.
2. Delete unneeded files and directories before beginning an upgrade. Your upgrade will be shortened if you have fewer files to move. Besides, this is a good time to perform that long-overdue cleanup of your volumes.

3. Run the FILER utility to salvage or purge deleted files. Once an upgrade is performed, you cannot salvage previously deleted files. So if any deleted files need to be restored, you must do it before the upgrade.

4. Prepare your bindery by deleting unnecessary objects. Keep in mind that duplicate user names upgraded into the same container will have their trustee assignments combined into one user with the same name. For other duplicate objects, the first object upgraded is accepted, whereas the second duplicate is discarded. Therefore, if you have a group and a print queue with the same name, the first is upgraded and the second is discarded.

5. Run the BINDFIX utility to clean up your bindery and discard entries for users that no longer exist on that server.

Design Your Novell Directory Services Tree

Refer to Chapters 4–7 for more information regarding the preparations that follow:

1. Implement your NDS naming standards.

2. Make an NDS tree design before starting your upgrade to NetWare 5. The design consists of three steps:

   a. Designing a Novell Directory Services tree

   b. Designing NDS partitions and replicas

   c. Designing time synchronization

3. Before starting an upgrade, determine where you will install the new server in the Directory tree. Also, determine where you want to move the users, groups, and printing objects. For example, using the INSTALL program, these objects will be moved to the container specified as the destination NetWare 5 server's bindery context.

Perform the Upgrade and Post Upgrade Activities

Refer to Chapters 2, 12, and 14 for more information regarding the following preparations:

1. You can use the information explained later to help you make a decision on which upgrade option to use.

2. Update your login scripts for your users and containers. For small sites you may have user login scripts that are being upgraded from NetWare 3 to NetWare 5. Verify that the scripts were upgraded properly after the upgrade. The upgrade method you used will create a container login script from the NetWare 3 system login script. Make sure that the commands in the container login script will work for NetWare 5 and NDS.

3. Distribute the upgraded objects to their appropriate containers. The bindery objects are upgraded into the same context as the server object. After an upgrade you may have to move some objects to other containers in your tree.

4. Check any user restrictions that you may have set in NetWare 3 to make sure they are in effect in NetWare 5. There is no need to check all users; a few randomly chosen users will suffice to verify that things are okay.

5. Verify that your print services are functioning properly. Verify that your users can print to the appropriate print queues and that all print services have upgraded properly.

6. Verify that your users' applications work properly on NetWare 5. This should be a very simple test to see if the application can perform basic functions such as PRINT and SAVE. Further testing is not necessary for most commercially available applications.

The In-Place Upgrade Method

The in-place method is used primarily for upgrading servers from either NetWare 3 or NetWare 4 to NetWare 5 using the same hardware. You can also use this method for upgrading from NetWare 2 to NetWare 5, as explained in the second half of this section.

For example, Figure 16.2 illustrates the process of upgrading a NetWare 3 or NetWare 4 server to NetWare 5 on the same server hardware device.

FIGURE 16.2

Upgrading a NetWare 3 or NetWare 4 server to NetWare 5 using the same server hardware device

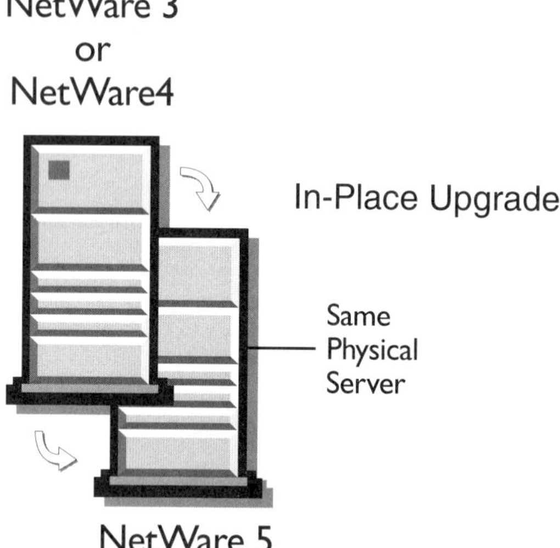

Since the file server hardware stays the same, the data volumes remain the same. Only new files are added to the SYS: volume in the system subdirectories and the DOS partition during the in-place upgrade process. The data files on the other volumes on the NetWare 3 server will not be moved or changed. The files that do get upgraded include LOGIN, SERVER.EXE, LAN drivers (*.LAN), disk drivers, and other NetWare Loadable Modules (*.NLM).

The NetWare 5 INSTALL utility will install NDS onto a NetWare 3 server and then upgrade the bindery to NDS. This utility will attempt to upgrade all objects found in the bindery to NDS.

The in-place method is the fastest upgrade method because it does not move the data files to another server. The other upgrade methods, such as across-the-wire and file copy, are slower because all the user data must be upgraded across the LAN or WAN networks.

The upgrade to NetWare 5 is accomplished by running the NetWare 5 INSTALL.EXE program. The NetWare 5 installation program can be started in DOS on the device being used as the server hardware by accessing the NetWare 5 CD-ROM. The main menu for the installation program appears as shown in Figure 16.3. From the main menu, select the NetWare Server Installation option.

FIGURE 16.3

The main menu for the NetWare 5 installation program INSTALL.EXE

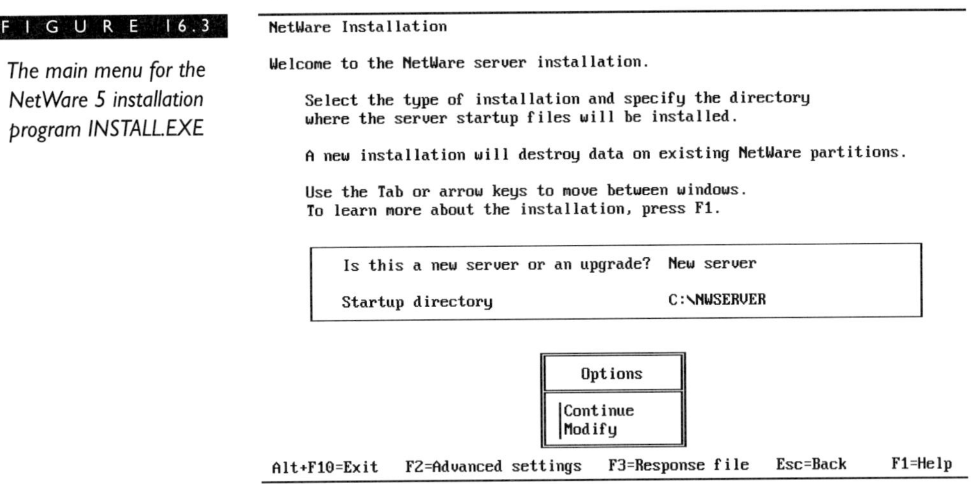
NetWare Installation
Welcome to the NetWare server installation.
Select the type of installation and specify the directory
where the server startup files will be installed.
A new installation will destroy data on existing NetWare partitions.
Use the Tab or arrow keys to move between windows.
To learn more about the installation, press F1.
Is this a new server or an upgrade? New server
Startup directory C:\NWSERVER
Options
Continue
Modify
Alt+F10=Exit F2=Advanced settings F3=Response file Esc=Back F1=Help

When making your decision on the type of upgrade method to use, keep in mind the following advantages and disadvantages of the in-place upgrade process.

Advantages of the In-Place Upgrade

This list gives the advantages of the in-place upgrade method:

- It uses the same physical server hardware, thus eliminating the cost of a new server hardware system just to perform the upgrade. Look carefully at your hardware at this point, however. That old 386 NetWare 3 server buried in your wiring closet somewhere may not pass muster with NetWare 5. You may still have to upgrade your hardware.

- It preserves passwords. Once on NetWare 5, your users will not need to enter a new password when they initially log in.

- It upgrades the existing bindery information with full NDS compatibility, meaning that all the users, groups, and trustee assignments are upgraded and preserved on NetWare 5. Users' login scripts will be placed directly into the corresponding NDS property for each user if they are present in the bindery.

- It preserves all the user print configuration databases. The PRINTCON. DAT and PRINTDEF.DAT databases are written directly into the NDS property for each user.

- It upgrades the server faster than any other method available. The data in the file system or volumes remain unmodified. Only the bindery files need to be converted. The bindery files are moved to NDS.

- It maintains name spaces. Because the data files are not changing the name spaces (MAC, NFS, and so on), they are fully supported.

Disadvantages of the In-Place Upgrade

Disadvantages of using the in-place upgrade method are as follows:

- It does not allow the volume block size of the server to be changed. Whenever possible, we recommend that each NetWare 5 server have 64K volume blocks, which provide for the greatest performance of disk reads and writes. But since the file system remains intact during the in-place upgrade, you will have the original volume block size set for your NetWare 3 servers (possibly 4K blocks).

- It does not allow suballocation for the file system to be turned on before the upgrade begins. Suballocation can easily be turned on after the upgrade, but the suballocation will affect only the subsequent writing of files to the disk. Therefore, any file that is rewritten to the disk will be suballocated.

- It may require a restoration from a tape backup if a failure occurs during the upgrade process.

Consulting Experience

If you use the In-Place Upgrade utility, you can still change your volume block size after upgrade but only with some effort. In order to change the volume block size, follow these steps:

1. Back up the data to tape.
2. Delete the NetWare volume.
3. Create the volume and specify the 64K block size.
4. Restore data from the tape.
5. Bring the NetWare 5 server back up.

NOTE

The in-place upgrade process is restartable if a failure should occur. There are, however, windows of vulnerability that may cause a failure and still require you to restore from tape.

The In-Place NetWare 4 to NetWare 5 Mass Upgrade

You can use any of several different methods to upgrade your NetWare 4 server to NetWare 5. The method discussed in this section is used for automatically upgrading your NetWare 4 server to NetWare 5 and can be used in a mass rollout.

Although the INSTALL.NLM program does a great job upgrading a server, it is a manual process designed to upgrade one server at a time. For example, in order to do the upgrade, you first connect to a NetWare 4 server, start the install process, select a few options, answer a few questions, and then finish by bringing the server down and back up. This same sequence needs to happen for each server that you wish to upgrade. This works well if you only have a few servers and they are all local. If you have hundreds of servers and some of them are remote, however, then you may need a better option.

In this section, we explore an option to automate large-scale or mass server upgrades both for local and remote servers across your network. This upgrade option uses Novell's CDWARE scripting language and other commonly available utilities. The greatest advantage of this solution is the ability to automate the upgrade process so that it can be accomplished quickly. This solution shows you how to automatically upgrade hundreds of remote servers in just a few hours.

Although the example mentions of this upgrade was used for NetWare 4.1 to NetWare 4.11, it can also be used to upgrade NetWare 4.11 to NetWare 5. In fact, we have included an upgrade script (based on CDWARE) that will enable you to move your servers from NetWare 4.11 to NetWare 5. In addition, this same solution can be used to apply service packs, patches, drivers, and application updates to the NetWare operating system as needed.

In the simplest terms, you can think of an in-place upgrade from NetWare 4 to NetWare 5 as a bunch of newer files that replace older files on your server. The NDS tree structure and location of files for NetWare 4 is typically the same as NetWare 5. For example, CLIB.NLM resides in the SYS:\SYSTEM subdirectory on NetWare 4, and it is in exactly the same place for NetWare 5. Thus if the upgrade process updates or replaces the CLIB.NLM, the new version of CLIB copies over the old version of CLIB in the SYS:\SYSTEM directory. Although the files in NetWare 4 and NetWare 5 are in the same location and can be easily updated, a few files need to have their content changed. These files are the configuration files that require different information. These configuration files include STARTUP. NCF, AUTOEXEC.NCF, NETINFO.CFG, TIMESYNC.CFG, and a few others.

The upgrade process involves these six steps:

1. Create an image for the upgrade.
2. Store the upgrade image on a file server's directory structure.
3. Compress the upgrade image into one single file.
4. Create an upgrade script using CDWARE.
5. Move the upgrade image and script to the destination servers to be updated.
6. Schedule and launch upgrade process.

In order to create the upgrade script, you should use the CDWARE scripting language, which is native to the NetWare operating system. CDWARE is the name of the product that Novell uses to script their installation processes. As mentioned, CDWARE is built into the operating system and is not a product that you need to buy. CDWARE scripting is a very powerful scripting tool, but it is cryptic. The CDWARE scripting interpreter is provided by INSTALL.NLM for NetWare 4.11 and NWCONFIG.NLM in NetWare 5. Since CDWARE is built into the operating system, to use it you simply need to obtain the documentation from Novell. The CDWARE documentation can be found on the Novell corporate Web site at `www.novell.com`.

Creating an Upgrade Image

In order to create an upgrade image, start by creating or building a blank directory structure on a server or workstation that looks like the NetWare 5 directory structure. This is where you will construct the upgrade image. In other words create subdirectories that match the subdirectories structure on the NetWare 5 server. The best way to create the upgrade image for NetWare 5 is to simply install the NetWare 5 operating system on a new server using the standard installation process. Then just copy the entire image to the blank directory that you have created.

The upgrade image should include such directories as SYSTEM, PUBLIC, LOGIN, and others. The content of these directories and subdirectories will then replace the files on the existing NetWare 4.11 server. For example, the files under the subdirectory NetWare5\SYS\PUBLIC that you create will replace the files in SYS:\PUBLIC on your destination server. Remember to include the files found in the COMMON and SYS directories as needed.

Next, select the products that need to be upgraded and copy the files and subdirectories to the upgrade image. If you have specific products that need to be installed on the NetWare 5 server, then create a specific product subdirectory with the product installed in it. For example, if you want to have DHCP installed on your destination servers, you want to create the subdirectory in your local area under NETWARE5\PRODUCTS\DHCP\SYSTEM. These files will then be moved or replace the appropriate files in SYS:\SYSTEM.

Next, create a SYS:\NWSERVER directory on the upgrade image. This directory corresponds to the DOS boot directory where SERVER.EXE resides, usually

C:\NWSERVER. Place any files that need to be updated on the DOS boot directory in this directory. This directory should include disk and LAN drivers and other NLMs. To get an idea of what type of files are placed in this directory, look at any server's C :\NWSERVER directory. As part of the upgrade script the files from SYS:\NWSERVER will get copied to the C:\NWSERVER directory.

The nice thing about having and keeping an upgrade image of your servers is that you can now add any patches, utilities, and applications that you want to download to your servers. For example, now that you have built an upgrade image for NetWare 5, as patches become available for different products or the operating system itself, you can add them to your upgrade image. This enables you to run only one additional upgrade process on each server, instead of one upgrade for one product and then one for another. You can also customize your upgrade image to include any needed NCF files, any custom NLMs or drivers, and even application files. In addition, you can also remove unneeded files from the upgrade image. For example, if you don't need Unix Print Services, don't include the UXP files.

Compressing the Upgrade Image

After you have built the upgrade image for NetWare 5 that can be used to upgrade a NetWare 4.11 server, the next step is to compress the entire image into one single file. In order to accomplish this, you can use any type of compression program. For example, you can use the PKZIP.EXE program in either DOS or Windows. If you use the DOS PKZIP program to compress your upgrade image, use this command:

```
PKZIP -~ -r -p UPGRADE.ZIP driveletter:\*.*
```

This command will store all the files and directories from the upgrade image into one file UPGRADE.ZIP. Using PKZIP.EXE, you can expect about 50 percent compression of the original file image.

In order to uncompress the UPGRADE.ZIP file once it has been downloaded to the destination server, you can use the UNZIP.NLM file found on the Novell Consulting Web page at `www.novell.com/toolkit`. This NLM is used to uncompress UPGRADE.ZIP on the destination server. UNZIP.NLM can uncompress the files in UPGRADE.ZIP and keep the correct directory structure. It will even overwrite read-only files. You will want to copy UPGRADE.ZIP and

UNZIP.NLM to the SYS: volume on the destination server. Then in order to uncompress the upgrade file image manually, enter the command:

```
LOAD SYS:\UNZIP.NLM -o -$ SYS:\UPGRADE.ZIP
```

After the image is uncompressed, the files from the SYS:\NWSERVER need to be copied to DOS boot directory at C:\NWSERVER. This can be accomplished using a NETBASIC script or the COPY.NLM utility. The COPY.NLM utility can be found on the Novell Consulting Web site at `www.novell.com/toolkit`.

Creating the Upgrade Script

After you have created an upgrade image and compressed it, you need to develop an upgrade script. The upgrade script should end in an .ILS extension. An example script for upgrading a NetWare 4.11 server to NetWare 5 called UPGRADE.ILS follows. Notice that the CDWARE code for the upgrade process includes support for making backup copies of SYS:\SYSTEM and C:\NWSERVER on the destination server. This enables you to back out of the procedure more gracefully, if need be. In addition, you will notice that the display command pauses execution of the script for debugging purposes. This upgrade script is called UPGRADE.ILS and is only an example; the upgrade script you develop for your production servers may be different.

The following listing, UPGRADE.ILS, is the CDWARE script that you can use to migrate your NetWare 4.11 servers to NetWare 5:

```
; This is a sample CDWARE Script to upgrade a NetWare 4.11
Server to NetWare 5.

; Server 4.11 upgrade to IWSP4B.

; Script Version 1.00 10-15-98


Command ICMD.NLM


; The steps for upgrading a server are:

;

; 1. Minimize the processes that are running on the server
```

```
; 2. Make any backup copies of files if needed
; 3. Copy files to backup directories
; 4. Erase system files to avoid conflict with new operating
system
; 5. Uncompress the upgrade image on the destination server
; 6. Restore files for backup directory
; 7. Move new drivers and SERVER.EXE to C: or boot drive
; 8. Reboot the server
;
; 1) Unload Running Programs on Server
  Display 1,"Unload Running Programs."
  console 'UNLOAD MONITOR',5
  console 'UNLOAD SERVMAN',5
; 2) Make Backup Copy of Important Directories
Display 1,"Make Backup Directories for SYS:SYSTEM and
C:NWSERVER"
; Make the BACKUP Directories on SYS: and C:
GetPath Source, 1,'SYS:\\',""
SetDir Source,BACKUP,'','',10,0,0
GetPath Source, 1,'C:\\',""
SetDir Source,BACKUP,'','',10,0,0
; 3) Copy files to the Backup Directories on SYS: and C:
Display 1,"Backup Directories of SYS:SYSTEM and C:NWSERVER"
GetPath Source, 1,'SYS:\\SYSTEM\\',""
GetPath Target, 1, 'SYS:\\BACKUP',''
CopyFile 1,1,1,1,0,Source,'','','',Target,'','',''
```

```
GetPath Source, 1,'C:\\NWSERVER\\',""
GetPath Target, 1, 'C:\\BACKUP',''
CopyFile 1,1,1,1,0,Source,'','','',Target,'','',''
console 'SEARCH ADD SYS:\\BACKUP',1
; 4) Erase files on SYS:\SYSTEM and C:\NWSERVER
Display 1,"Erase File on SYS:SYSTEM and C:NWSERVER"
GetPath Source, 1,'SYS:\\SYSTEM',""
EraseFile 2,Source,'','',''
GetPath Source, 1,'C:\\NWSERVER',""
EraseFile 2,Source,'','',''
GetPath Source, 1,'SYS:\\NWSERVER',""
EraseFile 2,Source,'','',''
; 5) UNZIP the compressed file to sys: volume.
Display 1,"UNZIP File UPGRADE.ZIP Image"
NLMexec 1,'sys:\\unzip.nlm -o -$ sys:\\upgrade.zip'
; 6) Restore Files from the backup subdirectory
Display 1,"Restore NCF files from backup directories."
GetPath Source, 1,'SYS:\\BACKUP\\',""
GetPath Target, 1, 'SYS:\\SYSTEM',''
CopyFile 0,0,0,1,0,Source,'*.NCF','','',Target,'','',''
GetPath Source, 1,'C:\\BACKUP\\',""
GetPath Target, 1, 'SYS:\\NWSERVER',''
CopyFile 0,0,0,1,0,Source,'*.NCF','','',Target,'','',''
; 7) Move the files to the C: drive
Display 1,"Move Server Files to C: Drive."
GetPath Source, 1,'SYS:\\NWSERVER\\',""
```

```
GetPath Target, 1, 'C:\\NWSERVER',''
CopyFile 1,1,1,1,0,Source,'','','',Target,'','',''
; 8) Reboot the file server and exit
Display 1,"Reboot Server Now."
console 'REMOVE DOS',5
console 'DOWN',2
console 'Y',5
console 'EXIT',5
END;
```

Launching the Upgrade Script

In addition to developing the upgrade script, you also need to create an NCF (NetWare control file) that enables you to launch the upgrade script. The NCF is for your convenience and is not required. To launch the upgrade CDWARE script, load INSTALL.NLM and point it to the script file. To launch this upgrade script, you can use this example for an UPGRADE.NCF:

```
LOAD INSTALL
B=SYS:\UPGRADE.ILS,S=C:\DOS,E=SYS:\ERR.FIL,NOSTATUS
```

As mentioned previously, the INSTALL.NLM program provides the interpreter for the CDWARE scripting for NetWare 4.11. The NWCONFIG.NLM program provides the interpreter for the CDWARE in NetWare 5. Since we are running the upgrade script on the NetWare 4.11 server (soon to be upgraded to NetWare 5), however, the command to launch the script should LOAD the INSTALL program.

Distributing the Upgrade Image

After you have created the upgrade image, compressed the upgrade image, and developed the upgrade script, you need to distribute the files to the destination servers. You should now have at least four files that you will want to distribute to the server that are used to upgrade to NetWare 5. Table 16.1 shows the files that you need to download or distribute to each NetWare 4.11 server that you want to upgrade.

TABLE 16.1

Files to Distribute to Each NetWare 4.11 Server to Be Upgraded to NetWare 5

FILE NAME	DESCRIPTION
UPGRADE.ZIP	Compressed upgrade image
UNZIP.NLM	NLM that uncompresses the upgrade image
UPGRADE.ILS	CDWARE script to move files and reboot server
UPGRADE.NCF	File to launch the UPGRADE.ILS script (optional)

As mentioned, each of the files needs to be downloaded to the destination NetWare 4.11 server that you will be upgrading to NetWare 5. According to the upgrade script example, these files need to be copied to the root directory of the SYS: volume on the destination server. There is a variety of methods for copying these files. You can use NCOPY, COPY, or FTP. If you are copying the files across the WAN to remote servers and your network WAN is running TCP/IP, then we recommend that you use FTP, because it will be the fastest.

Performing the Upgrade

Once you have successfully completed your upgrade image and script file and your files have been moved to the appropriate destination servers, you are ready to perform the upgrade process. You can manually launch the upgrade process by simply running UPGRADE.NCF. The process just described to upgrade a NetWare 4.11 server to NetWare 5 takes approximately 15 minutes to complete. In addition to running the process manually, you can launch the upgrade process automatically using a scheduling program for the NetWare servers.

One scheduling program available is CRON.NLM, which is available for no cost from the Novell Consulting Web site at `www.novell.com/toolkit`. With the CROM NLM loaded or running on your servers, you can launch any NLM, NCF, or script file at a specified time or a specified interval. This enables you to perform the upgrade process automatically from any number of servers. For example you can set all your servers to upgrade themselves at 2:00 A.M. on Friday night, or have all your servers in a specific location be upgraded at 1:00 A.M. Then the next day or week, you can upgrade another location or site automatically. The CRON.NLM program comes with documentation.

Make sure you test your upgrade process and image thoroughly before applying it to a production network. It is also important that you check compatibility issues with NDS and other applications running on the server. Once your servers are upgraded to NetWare 5, you may want to revisit each server and clean up the server by deleting the zip file and the SYS:\NWSERVER directory.

At stated earlier, this upgrade process works well on a large enterprise network and has many advantages, including standardizing the operating system on all the servers while minimizing network impact during upgrade of the servers.

Applying Patches

You can also use this process to automatically apply patches to the operating system, as they become available. Using this process, you will find that applying patches can almost be a nonevent. An example of a CDWARE script for applying patches can be seen in the listing that follows; it is called PATCHES.ILS.

This is a sample CDWARE script to apply patches to your NetWare server:

```
; Server 4.11 upgrade to IWSP4B.
; Script Version 1.01 3-12-98

Command ICMD.NLM

; 1.) Unload Running Programs on Server.
console 'UNLOAD MONITOR',5
console 'UNLOAD SERVMAN',5
; 2.) Unzip the Upgrade File image to server.
NLMexec 1,'SYS:\UNZIP.NLM -o -$ SYS:\\UNGRADE.ZIP'
; 3.) Move the files to the C: drive.
GetPath Source, 1,'SYS:\\NWSERVER\\',""
GetPath Target, 1, 'C:\\NWSERVER',''
CopyFile 0,1,1,1,0,Source,'','','',Target,'','',''
; 4.) Now reboot the file server and exit.
console 'REMOVE DOS',5
```

```
console 'DOWN',2

console 'EXIT',5

; END
```

Again, to launch the CDWARE script, load INSTALL.NLM and point it to the script file. To launch or apply this patch, enter this command at the server prompt:

```
LOAD INSTALL
B=SYS:\UPGRADE.ILS,S=C:\DOS,E=SYS:\ERR.FIL,NOSTATUS
```

The In-Place Upgrade for NetWare 2 to NetWare 3

For servers running NetWare 2, you can use the in-place upgrade utility called 2XUPGRDE.NLM to upgrade from NetWare 2 to NetWare 3.12. Then use the NetWare 5 installation program to finish upgrading to NetWare 5. The in-place upgrade NetWare Loadable Module (2XUPGRDE.NLM) reformats a server's NetWare 2.1*x* or NetWare 2.2 partition, without losing any data, and transforms it into a NetWare 3.12 file system partition.

The in-place upgrade method upgrades only NetWare 2.1*x* or NetWare 2.2 servers to NetWare 5. For previous versions of NetWare, you will have to first upgrade to these versions before proceeding.

The upgrade process actually occurs in several stages in which the NetWare 2 file system and bindery are upgraded to NetWare 3.12. The second stage is to install the new operating system.

Many servers running any version of NetWare 2 will not have the horsepower to support NetWare 5. Carefully evaluate this situation, as you may want to use the in-place upgrade option only to move to NetWare 3.12 so that you can upgrade your data to a newer, more powerful server platform using the Across-the-Wire Upgrade utility.

Keep in mind that user passwords are not retained when you upgrade to NetWare 3.12. As with the across-the-wire upgrade, you can have the utility generate random passwords. These random passwords are stored in a file called NEW.PWD in your SYS:SYSTEM directory. In addition, no Value Added Processes (VAPs) or core printing services are upgraded with this process. Refer to the Novell documentation for step-by-step instructions for upgrading from NetWare 2 to NetWare 3.

The Across-the-Wire Upgrade Using the Novell Upgrade Wizard

The across-the-wire upgrade method will move your data and bindery files from NetWare 3 to NetWare 5. The Novell Upgrade Wizard utility that comes with NetWare is run on a Windows 95/98 or Windows NT workstation and facilitates the transfer of the files and bindery information. The workstation running the Novell Upgrade Wizard utility will read the bindery information and data files from the source server and write them to the NetWare 5 server. The connected workstation running the Upgrade Wizard utility must be logged into the NetWare 3 and NetWare 5 servers with Supervisor access on both servers. Figure 16.4 illustrates conceptually how the Novell Upgrade Wizard runs as an across-the-wire upgrade process. It runs on a Windows 95/98 or Windows NT workstation between the servers being upgraded.

Because the utility runs on the workstation and has the responsibility to move all the data, the faster the workstation's CPU, the faster the upgrade. The workstation needs at least a 16-bit LAN card, although a 32-bit card will increase performance.

Although a slower workstation with an 8-bit LAN card will perform an across-the-wire upgrade, it will increase the time needed to complete. We recommend that you find the fastest PC possible and place it on the same network segment as the server being upgraded.

FIGURE 16.4

The Novell Upgrade Wizard utility is run on a Windows 95/98 or Windows NT workstation between the NetWare 3 and NetWare 5 servers being upgraded.

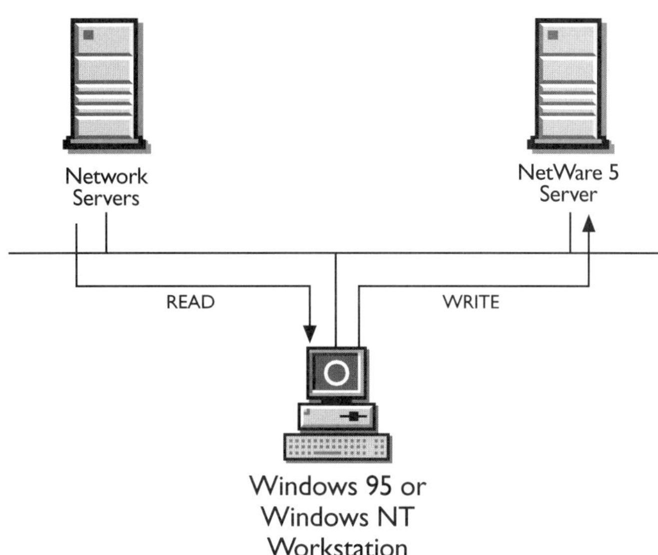

To start the upgrade process at the Windows workstation, you will be asked to first connect to both the source (NetWare 3) and destination (NetWare 5) servers with Supervisor or equivalent access rights. The Novell Upgrade Wizard utility screen that is displayed enables you to select each server, as shown in Figure 16.5.

FIGURE 16.5

The Novell Upgrade Wizard utility requires that you select the source and destination server during the upgrade. You must have Supervisor access to both the NetWare 3 and NetWare 5 servers.

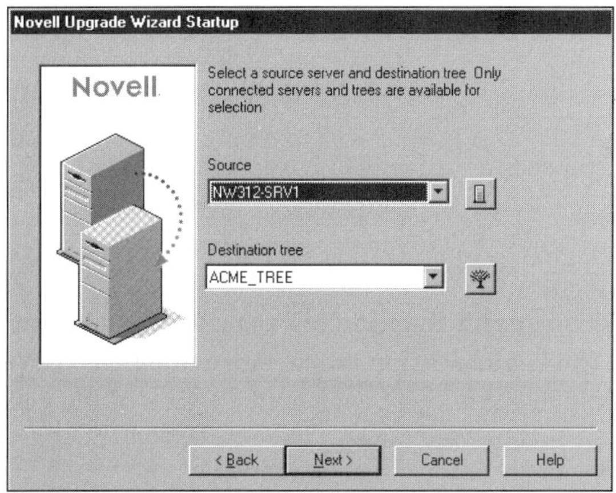

Advantages of the Across-the-Wire Upgrade

Here are advantages of the across-the-wire upgrade method:

- It upgrades all the bindery information into NDS (bindery services mode). The users, groups, and trustee assignments are maintained.
- The NetWare 3 server being upgraded is read-only, and the data files and bindery remain intact, thus preserving your original server if the upgrade cannot be completed because of any problems.
- It consolidates multiple source servers into a single NetWare 5 server. The source servers can be upgraded into a single, larger NetWare 5 server.
- It gives you the opportunity to replace or upgrade the server to newer, more powerful hardware.
- Passwords are preserved or moved from the NetWare 3 server to NetWare 5.
- Multiple Windows workstations can upgrade the same server with different volumes at the same time, meaning that you can have more than one workstation processing the information and upgrading it.
- You can change the volume block size on the new server volumes. You can select the volume block size during the installation of the NetWare 5 server to the recommended 64K.
- It enables file suballocation before the upgrade of the data files.
- All name spaces are supported. Specifically, the DOS, MAC, NFS, and LONG (or OS2.NAM) name spaces are supported.

TIP

We recommend that you always select a volume block size of 64K. With the suballocation feature provided in NetWare 5, a block size of 64K will give you the best performance of file reads and writes without losing disk space.

Disadvantages of the Across-the-Wire Upgrade

However, there are a couple of disadvantages to the across-the-wire upgrade method:

- The procedure is slower than the in-place upgrade method. Because all data files are transferred across the network, the selected data being copied could disrupt other network traffic. For this reason, the across-the-wire upgrade process may need to be executed during off-peak hours.
- Two separate servers are required. If you have limited hardware or budget, then buying a new machine just for the upgrade may not be possible.

The Novell Upgrade Wizard

The Novell Upgrade Wizard (NUW) is a new upgrade utility that enables you to upgrade your NetWare 3 servers to NetWare 5. The utility lets you move the NetWare 3 bindery and file system across the wire and place them in a desired location in an existing NDS tree. This utility does not currently support NetWare 4 to NetWare 5 upgrades across the wire.

You need to consider a couple of prerequisites before running the Novell Upgrade Wizard. For example, since the Novell Upgrade Wizard can be run from either a Windows 95/98 or Windows NT workstation, verify that you are running the latest NetWare Client 32 for each. As of this writing the latest NetWare Client 32 for Windows 95 is version 2.2, and the latest Windows NT Client is 4.11a (revision a). Thus, any version of the client software that is equal to or greater than these values will be valid. The NetWare client software for both Windows 95/98 and Windows NT can be downloaded from the Novell main Web site at the URL location `novell.com/download`.

In addition, you should make accommodations for SAP filtering. You should ensure that SAP filtering is disabled on each server involved in the upgrade. If SAP filtering cannot be disabled, you should ensure that the default server (preferred server) for the client is on the same LAN segment as the other servers you are upgrading to and from.

Consulting Experience

If you need to know the current version of the client software and have Windows 95/98, you can select the Start button, the Settings menu, and the Control Panel, and then double-click the Network icon. Next, choose Novell NetWare or IntranetWare Client and then click the Properties button. The client page appears with the client version at the bottom. If the client version number does not appear, then you have an older client that must definitely be updated. The version number of the NetWare Client for Windows NT can be found on the title bar of the Novell login dialog box.

You also need to make sure that you have the latest or updated NLMs on your NetWare 3 server that will be involved in the upgrade process. In order for the Novell Upgrade Wizard to work properly, a number of NLMs need to be updated with the latest versions. These NLMs are found in PRODUCTS\NW3X subdirectory in the location where you installed the Novell Upgrade Wizard. For example, if you installed using the default path, the NLMs are at:

```
C:\PROGRAM FILES\UPGRADE\PRODUCTS\NW3X
```

Several NLMs must be upgraded and loaded on the NetWare 3 server before the Novell Upgrade Wizard can function properly:

- TSA311.NLM or TSA312.NLM
- SMDR.NLM
- SMDR31X.NLM
- SPXS.NLM
- TLI.NLM
- AFTER311.NLM

- CLIB.NLM
- A3112.NLM
- STREAMS.NLM

In order to upgrade and change the NLMs on the NetWare 3 server, unload the NLMs in the sequence indicated in the list. Next, copy the latest NLMs to the server.

TSA311.NLM or TSA312.NLM (depending on the version of NetWare 3) must be loaded on the NetWare 3 server prior to doing the upgrade. If you did not reboot after updating the NLMs, you will need to load TSA311.NLM or TSA312.NLM manually. Since the TSA31X.NLM is dependent upon all of the other NLMs listed, loading it will automatically load all of the other updated NLMs that you copied earlier. If the server's AUTOEXEC.NCF file includes a LOAD command for TSA311.NLM or TSA312.NLM, TSA31X.NLM will automatically load during the boot cycle and you do not need to load it manually.

Another prerequisite to the upgrade process is loading and adding the proper name space support. If any of the volumes you are going to migrate contain files with non-DOS naming conventions, you must load the appropriate name spaces on the destination NetWare 5 volumes and then add the name spaces to the volume prior to the upgrade process. Windows 95/98, Windows NT, OS/2, FTAM, and NFS name spaces are loaded through LONG.NAM, which stands for long names (formally called OS2.NAM). The Macintosh name space is loaded through MAC.NAM.

Consulting Experience

Some NLMs may require you to unload additional interdependent NLMs. If doing so becomes too cumbersome or impossible, you can reboot your server. When the server is rebooted, the recently copied NLMs will be loaded.

Running the Novell Upgrade Wizard Utility

After you have determined the objects and volumes that you want to upgrade to NetWare 5, you can launch the Novell Upgrade Wizard utility by simply clicking the Windows 95/98 or Windows NT Start menu and then selecting the location of the program. By default, the utility will be located under the Programs and Novell menu items.

Once the utility is launched, a dialog box appears, ready for you to create a new project. A *project* is a model the utility uses to save the settings and options that will be used during the upgrade process. The project is created and completed before the actual upgrade takes place. In this dialog box, you are asked to select or create a project filename. If this is the first time you have executed the Novell Upgrade Wizard, you need to choose the Create New Upgrade Project option and click OK. Next the wizard is launched; the first page of the wizard asks you to indicate the name and location of the new project. In this startup menu, you are asked to select a project filename. Figure 16.6 shows the startup screen, which enables you to select the project filename. In this example, the project name is NW3 Upgrade.

FIGURE 16.6

The Novell Upgrade Wizard requires you to select a project name to be used to save the settings and options used by the upgrade process. In this example, "NW3 Upgrade" is the name of the project.

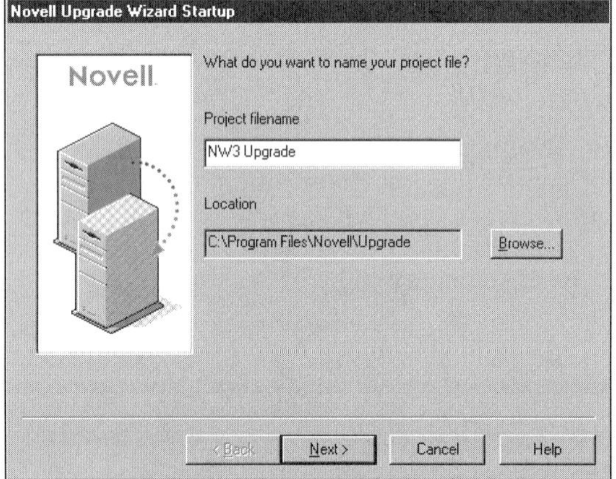

After selecting a project name or using the Browse button to indicate the location where you want the project saved, you simply click the Next button at the bottom of the screen. A new page appears asking you to select or indicate the NetWare 3 server you will be upgrading. This is referred to as the source. Next, select the name of the NDS tree where you will be placing the information. The selected NDS tree is referred to as the destination tree. Figure 16.7 shows an example for this screen.

FIGURE 16.7

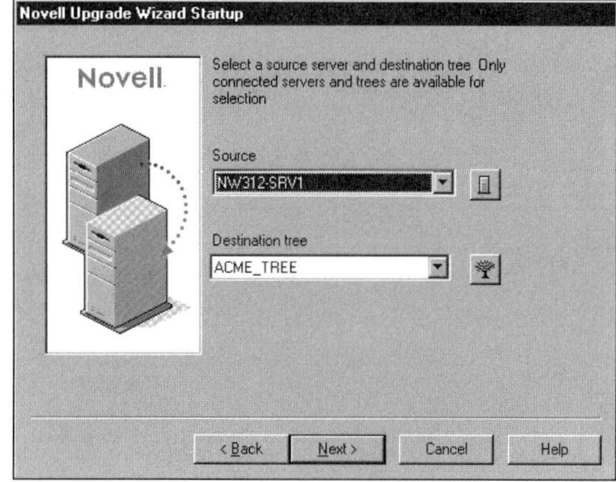

The Novell Upgrade Wizard asks you to define the source NetWare 3 server and the destination NDS tree before starting the upgrade process.

You can use the two drop-down list boxes to indicate the source server and destination NDS tree. If the desired server and/or NDS tree is not displayed, use the Server button or Tree button to log into a server or NDS tree. Once you have indicated the server and NDS tree, click the Next button.

The next screen that appears is an animated information screen that graphically shows you how to drag and drop the NetWare 3 bindery and volumes into the NDS tree. After the bindery and volumes have been placed, you simply start the upgrade process. Figure 16.8 shows the information screen with its hints or tips on running the utility.

Drag and Drop Objects in the Project Window

In the main project window for the Novell Upgrade Wizard, the indicated source NetWare 3 server and destination NDS tree are displayed. Using this project window, you can drag and drop the NetWare 3 bindery and volume from the source side to desired locations in the NDS tree. Figure 16.9 illustrates the main project window in the Novell Upgrade Wizard.

FIGURE 16.8

The information screen graphically shows you how to drag and drop the NetWare 3 bindery and volumes into the NDS tree.

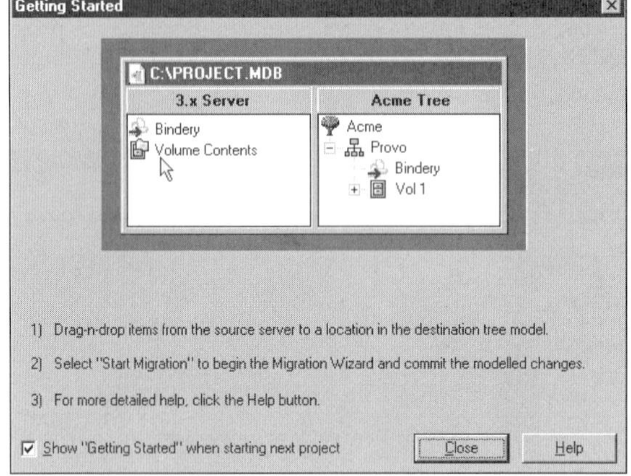

FIGURE 16.9

The Novell Upgrade Wizard main project window displays the NetWare 3 bindery and volumes, which will be upgraded to the NDS tree, which is also shown.

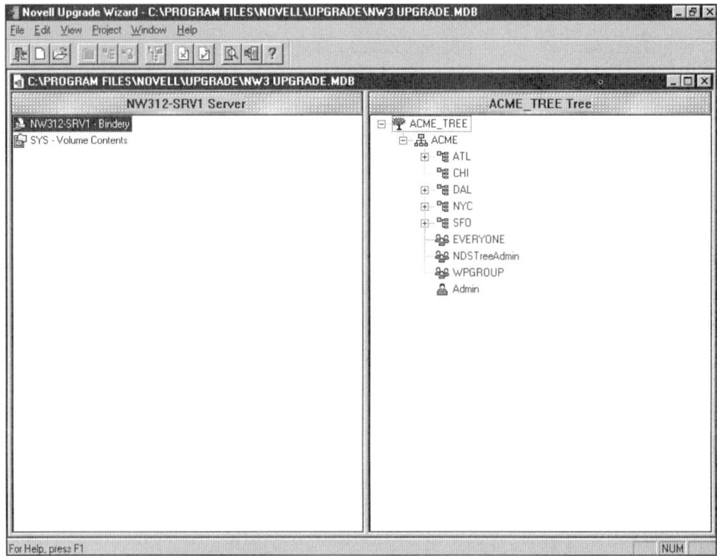

Before dragging and dropping the bindery or volume data, first determine where in the destination NDS tree you want the bindery and volumes placed. If the desired container for the bindery or volume folder (for the volume data) does not already exist in the NDS tree, right-click the parent and create and name the new container or folder. The Create New Container option is available if the selected object is an NDS container. The Create New Folder option is available if the selected parent is a volume folder.

Figures 16.10 and 16.11 illustrate how the project window might appear if the NetWare 3 bindery and volume have been dragged and dropped into the NDS tree. Figure 16.10 shows the bindery being placed directly under O=ACME in the tree. Figure 16.11 shows how the volumes can be placed anywhere in the tree and do not have to be located with the bindery.

FIGURE 16.10

The project window in the Upgrade Wizard shows the NetWare 3 bindery placed in the NDS tree directly under O=ACME in the tree.

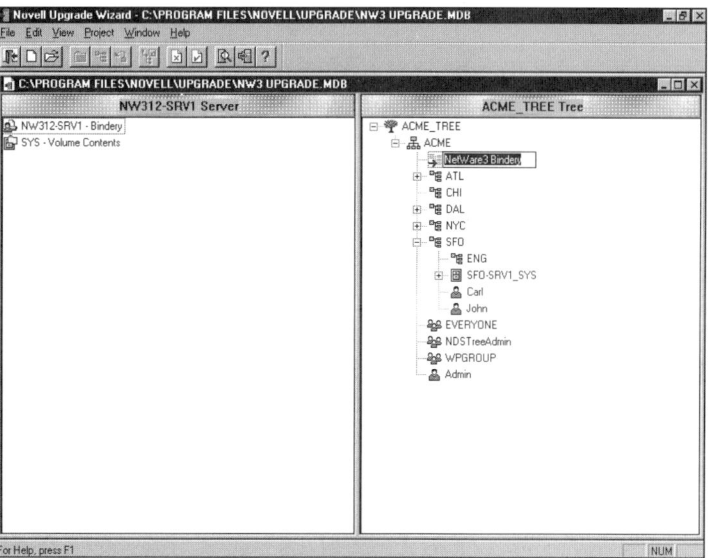

Once the bindery and volumes have been moved to the destination NDS tree, you should verify that the upgrade can proceed. The verification process checks for object conflicts, sufficient NDS and file system rights, disk space limitations, and a variety of other criteria that could impede the upgrade process. In order to start the verification, select the Start Migration button from the toolbar on the project window. You can also choose it from the main menu under the Project option. Once you start the upgrade process, a verification phase is handled by a wizard that is launched. The first page of the wizard gives an overview of how the verification works. Figure 16.12 illustrates the first page of the Verification Wizard after you have started the upgrade process within the Upgrade Wizard project.

FIGURE 16.11

The NetWare 3 volume has been dragged and dropped in the NDS tree.

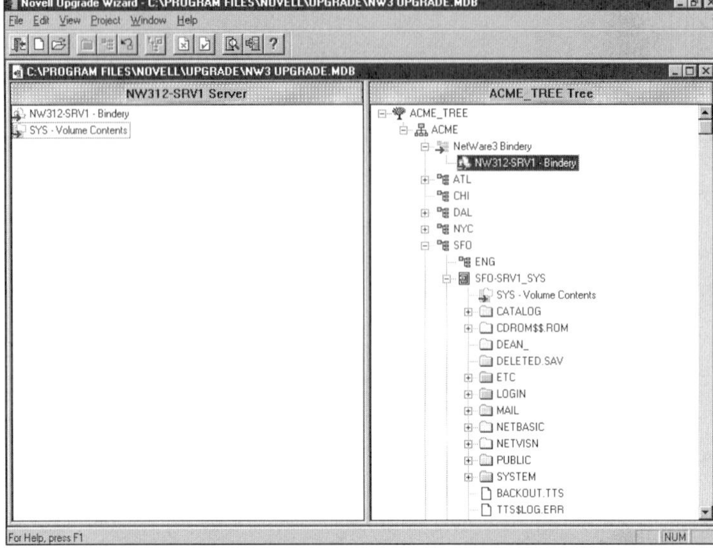

FIGURE 16.12

The verification process checks and displays for several different options that are covered in this screen.

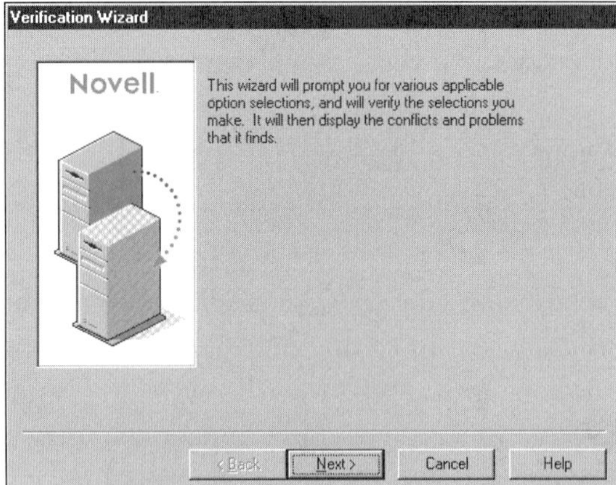

The next page that appears enables you to indicate whether you would like to upgrade your NetWare 3 print information, and if so, to which volume. If you do not want to upgrade the print information, uncheck the check box at the top of the page (it is checked by default). If you do want to upgrade the print information, choose the desired volume in the tree browser and click the Next button.

A new page appears enabling you to apply an existing NDS Template object to all users being upgraded. The template is a user template that can be used to apply the same user characteristics during the upgrade process. If you do not want to apply a template object, uncheck the check box at the top of the page. If you do want to apply a template object, choose the desired Template object and click the Next button.

The next page is the password verification, which makes sure that you have sufficient rights to run the upgrade. You need Supervisor rights to the NetWare 3 server and Supervisor rights to the container in NDS where the users and groups will be upgraded. In addition, you need Supervisor rights to the volume where the NetWare 3 volume will be written.

Next is a screen with check boxes on which items to perform verification. The type of verification is either Check for Duplicate Objects or Check for Disk Space. The check boxes let you indicate what categories you want to verify. It is important that you check to see if there is sufficient disk space to complete the upgrade process.

After running the verification, a wizard page appears showing any object naming conflicts that the process has found. The only object conflicts that the process checks are those between objects of the same type. The Novell Upgrade Wizard can handle the object naming conflicts in several different ways. The following options are available to handle conflicts:

- Let the wizard rename the object automatically.
- Choose not to upgrade the object.
- Merge the objects and maintain the bindery properties.
- Merge the objects and maintain the NDS properties.

Figure 16.13 shows an example of the results of the verification process.

If conflicts are shown in the list box, select the object and choose an appropriate conflict resolution option. Repeat this section for each conflict listed.

FIGURE 16.13

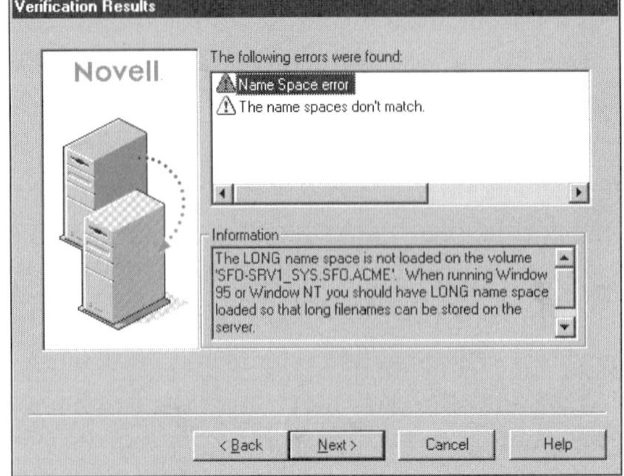

The results of the verification for object conflicts are shown. If no naming conflicts are found, the list box in the wizard page is blank.

Once you have resolved all the conflicts or errors, you can begin the upgrade of the bindery objects and file system volumes. The Novell Upgrade Wizard first copies the contents of the bindery and then the file system, according to where you dragged and dropped objects in the Project window. A progress bar indicates the relative percentage of objects that have been upgraded and those yet to be upgraded.

You can stop the upgrade at any time by simply clicking the Stop button shown during the upgrade process. A dialog box appears asking you to confirm your choice. If you still want to stop the upgrade, click the Yes button. The upgrade is immediately terminated; however, all NetWare 3 bindery objects and files copied up to that point remain and are not backed out. If you want to remove the upgraded objects from the NDS tree, you must delete them manually. The same is true for files that have been moved to the NetWare 5 server from the NetWare 3 server.

Consulting Experience

When conflicts are shown in the list box of the verification process, you should choose a method for the utility to perform for each object. If you do not choose a conflict resolution option, however, the object in the list box will be renamed by default.

The Rexxware Migration Toolkit

The Rexxware Migration Toolkit (RMT) is another resource available to you to help you upgrade your NetWare 3 servers to NetWare 5. This product has been developed by Simware, Inc. This upgrade product does not ship directly on the NetWare 5 CD-ROM but is available for no cost from the Simware Web site at `www.simware.com`.

This product is the most robust and full-featured product available for NetWare 3 to NetWare 5 upgrades. The strength of RMT is the product's ability to handle both simple upgrades and very large and complex ones. RMT should be your choice for upgrading from a NetWare 3 server when you want the fastest and most robust upgrade utility. This utility is the fastest at moving your data files because the file transfer is strictly between servers. No data passes through the server or workstation running the program. This utility offers full password support, name space support, check-point restart, and complete roll back of the upgrade.

The latest release of the RMT utility is a GUI interface that enables you to run it either on the NetWare 5 server in Java or at a Windows NT workstation running Java.

How RMT Works

When running the RMT utility, seven major tasks will be completed, as follows:

1. Extracting Objects from Your NetWare 3 Server

The RMT utility will first extract the standard bindery objects and their properties (such as user objects and the groups to which they belong) from NetWare 3 server binderies and store the resulting records and properties in a NetWare 3 database. Before this process occurs, you can perform these options:

- Choose filter options to display all servers or only NetWare 3 servers in the network.
- Select which object types to extract (ALL, USERS, GROUPS, PRINT_QUEUES, PRINT_SERVERS).

2. Generating a Report on Your NetWare 3 Database

Find out exactly which user, group, and print server and print queue objects are on each of your NetWare 3 servers. The options for this process are:

- Report on any object classes or objects that have common attributes (that is, all user objects with supervisor equivalence).
- Select the detail level you want for your 3.*x* version reports.

3. Preparing the NetWare 5 Database

Create a NetWare 5 database and make it ready to receive the NetWare 3 database information. These options are available:

- Create your NetWare 5 database (extract an existing NDS tree or emulate an NDS installation).
- Create the container structure from your NDS plan.
- Associate NetWare 3 servers to NDS server objects.
- Associate NetWare 3 volumes to NDS volume objects.
- Set the time zone for each NDS server object.

4. Applying the NetWare 3 Database to a NetWare 4 Database

Bring the information or objects from the NetWare 3 database to the corresponding NetWare 5 database objects. Several actions and options are available to you for this step:

- Select a NetWare 5 database to receive the NetWare 3 information.
- Configure the user identification template to parse first names and last names correctly.
- Apply the NetWare 3 database object information to the NetWare 5 database.

At this point, the NetWare 5 database becomes a virtual NDS tree, which you will edit.

5. Generating a Report on Your NetWare 5 Database

Run a report to check whether your NetWare 5 database model matches your actual NDS or planned NDS tree. The actions and options available for this step are these:

- Report on any object class or objects that have common attributes (for example, all users with Admin equivalence).
- Select the detail level you want for reports on the virtual NDS tree.

6. Editing Your NetWare 5 Database

Model your NetWare 5 database into the exact NDS tree structure you have in existence or are planning. The actions and options are:

- Move all your NetWare 5 database objects to the NDS contexts that are in your existing tree or planned tree.
- Edit objects to give them new NDS attributes (for example, Email Address).
- Combine duplicate objects of the same class originating from different NetWare 3 servers (for example, consolidate the contents of several servers in the same container).
- Resolve duplicate objects of different classes originating from the same NetWare 3 server.

7. Committing the Upgrade to the Destination NetWare 5 Server

Bring the NetWare 5 database or model of your NDS tree into your "live" NDS environment. The actions and options that you may perform for this step are as follows:

- Choose the type of initial passwords you want to give users on the NetWare 5 servers (null, random, or passwords from an external file you create).

- Upgrade users, groups, and print-system objects to the live NDS tree.
- Update references within objects in the live NDS tree.
- Choose the type of file migration (test or real).
- Migrate files and directories from the DOS name space.
- Migrate from name spaces, such as Mac, OS/2, NT, and NFS.

More detailed information on how to use the RMT utility to provide complete general and line-of-business upgrade solutions is available on the Novell corporate Web site. The information available is extremely detailed and is beyond the scope of this book.

An Across-the-Wire Upgrade Using File Copy

Another across-the-wire method that you can use, although it may not be the easiest, is copying the files and data from your current operating system to the NetWare 5 file system. This is a very dynamic upgrade method because you can choose which files and subdirectories you want to move. You can move an entire volume, a group of subdirectories, or a single file.

In order to perform a file copy, you must have your new NetWare 5 server installed and running on the network along with the server you intend to upgrade. You will need to choose a workstation and establish a concurrent connection to both servers using accounts with sufficient rights to read and write the data to and from the appropriate source and destination servers. Your workstation must have enough memory to support the concurrent login to both servers.

In a mixed operating system environment the workstation performing the upgrade will have to be loaded with two protocols to support both operating systems.

Both the source and destination servers must be visible to the workstation performing the copy. In Figure 16.14, a user logs into a NetWare 3.12 server called NetWare_312 and a NetWare 5 server called NetWare_5. After connecting to both servers from a DOS workstation, the user maps a drive to the source server and the destination server. Then the user issues an XCOPY command with appropriate parameters and copies the data for volume VOL1 to the DATA volume on the destination server.

FIGURE 16.14

File copy for the volume VOL1 data from a NetWare 3.12 server to the NetWare 5 server using a DOS XCOPY command

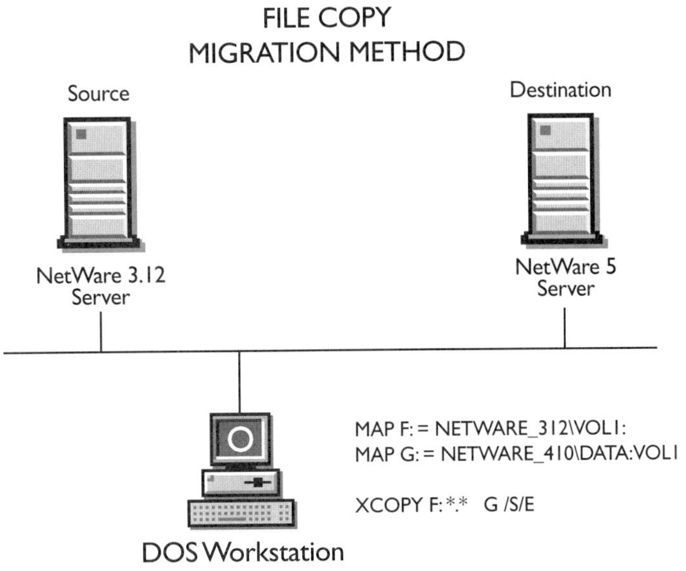

The drive mappings for the workstations are as follows:

```
MAP F:=SERVER_312\VOL1:
MAP G:=SERVER_5\DATA:VOL1
```

The Copy command will appear as:

```
XCOPY F:*.* G: /S/E
```

to specify a copy of all files from the F drive to the G drive, including all subdirectories (/S) even if empty (/E).

Although the file copy upgrade method seems to be straightforward and easy, it may not be practical for those who require other information besides just the data. Other information could include the bindery information and the trustee assignments, for example.

The file copy method is valuable for those who only need to move the data from the old server to the new one. In addition, for some upgrades, the file copy method is currently the only option. For example, to upgrade a network from DEC Pathworks to NetWare 5 requires the use of the COPY command. There is currently no other mechanism. For accounts that do not wish to migrate trustee assignments but only data, this option is certainly viable. The advantages and disadvantages of the file copy upgrade method are listed in the next section.

File Copy Advantages

This list summarizes the advantages of the file copy method:

- It restricts the copy of the source server to Read Only on the data files. The copy procedure provides fault tolerance because the source server is only being read, not altered in any way.
- It selects volumes, directories, or files that you want to move. For example, the entire drive does not need to be immediately copied to the other server; you can do upgrades in stages.
- It moves different kinds of name spaces. The file copy method supports MAC, NFS, and other name spaces if the native desktops connect to perform the copy of the data files.
- It supports file transfers between all popular network operating systems. For example, Windows NT Server, LAN Manager, DEC Pathworks, or LANtastic files can be copied.
- It moves data files anytime because the procedure is nondisruptive to the user. However, the increased network traffic may impact performance.
- Many different utilities can be used to perform the file copy — COPY, XCOPY, NCOPY, Windows Explorer in Windows 95/98 or Windows NT, Norton Utilities, XTREE, or other third-party products.

File Copy Disadvantages

The file copy method also has a number of disadvantages:

- It does not move the bindery in NetWare 2 and NetWare 3. Thus, users, groups, and print services are not upgraded to the new server.
- It does not maintain the existing file trustee assignments contained on the source server.
- It requires additional server hardware. Both the source and destination servers need to be installed and running on the network. This method also requires availability of a workstation.
- It requires a concurrent connection to both the source and destination servers. Both servers need to be visible to the workstation unless you attach to only the source server to move the data files to a temporary storage device such as a tape unit or the hard drive of the workstation. You can then move the files to the destination server in stages.
- Operation is slow because the file copy moves the data files across the network from one server to another.

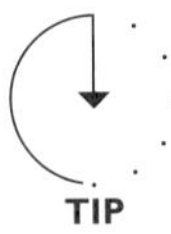

TIP

If the servers are not visible or if you have problems communicating with the network, you should check to see if your workstation is set up with the same frame types as the NetWare servers. With recent releases of NetWare (including NetWare 4 and NetWare 5), Novell has changed the default frame type from 802.3 to 802.2.

Before performing a file copy, take time to review the data structure on the source server. In particular, you should remove or clean outdated or unused files and programs from the system before starting the upgrade. This saves time and space when copying to the new server and prevents carrying around the old baggage. If the workstation cannot set up a concurrent connection to both the source and destination servers, you may want to move the file temporarily to the workstation. Then you can move the file to the destination server in stages. This method implies that there is a very large storage device at the workstation, such as a tape unit or additional hard drives. The workstation can move the data files in sets or stages according to the limitations of the workstation hardware. Follow these steps to perform the workstation copy:

1. Guarantee that the workstation has enough capacity to hold the selected data files. Add a tape unit or extra drive to increase the capacity.
2. Copy the selected data files from the source server to the appropriate workstation device.
3. Change connections to the new server or the destination server.
4. Copy the data files over to the destination server.
5. Continue this process in stages until all the data files are upgraded.

Figure 16.15 illustrates how you can use a workstation to temporarily hold the data files from the source server.

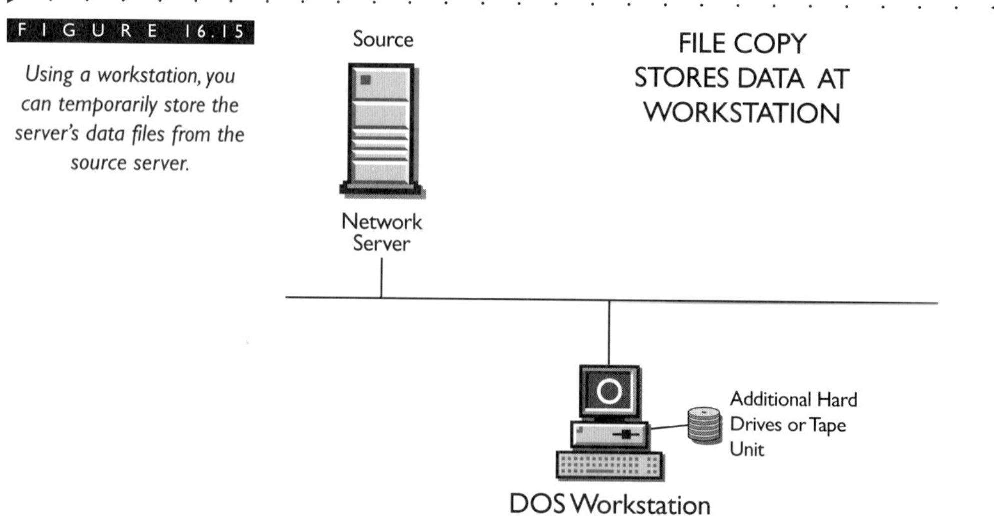

FIGURE 16.15

Using a workstation, you can temporarily store the server's data files from the source server.

If you are using the same hardware device as the source and destination servers, you will need to move the entire contents of the server to the workstation. Once the workstation holds all the information, you can down the source server and install NetWare 5 at the destination server. You can then copy the data file to the NetWare 5 server.

The file copy upgrade method is valuable to companies that are performing file server data restructuring. If you need to change the layout of the server significantly or apply large changes in the naming of subdirectories, you may choose just to copy the files from server to server.

Summary

When upgrading your current NetWare servers to NetWare 5 you can use any of several different methods. Each method has its strengths or weakness depending on the type of upgrade that you want to perform. This chapter focused on upgrades from previous versions of NetWare only and provided details about several different options. For example, when upgrading from NetWare 3 to NetWare 5 you need either to perform the in-place upgrade using the INSTALL program or to use the across-the-wire program. The best across-the-wire methods are the Novell Upgrade Wizard and the Rexxware Migration Toolkit (RMT). The Novell Upgrade Wizard is the simplest method, whereas the Rexxware Migration Toolkit (RMT) is the fastest and most robust.

If you are upgrading your NetWare 4 servers to NetWare 5, then you need to use the in-place upgrade method using the INSTALL utility that can be executed directly from the NetWare 5 CD-ROM. If you have a great number of NetWare servers that you want to upgrade rapidly, then you may want to develop or use the CDWARE scripts as outlined in the previous sections.

Once you have decided on an upgrade method for your servers, you will want to immediately start thinking about upgrading the workstation or client software to the latest NetWare 5 client. The next chapter addresses how to best upgrade your workstation clients to the latest software.

CHAPTER 17

Installing and Configuring the Novell Clients

"Change must be measured from a known base line." — Evan Shute

The Novell Client 32 allows workstations to take advantage of all features in NetWare, and Novell provides a set of utilities to upgrade from both NETX and VLMs to Novell Client 32. Once these utilities are in place, there is no need to visit workstations for future updates, as this can all be managed centrally and updates can take place in an unattended mode.

Novell Client 32 works with DOS, Windows 3.*x*, Windows 95/98, and Windows NT, providing a common network client base for all workstation types in many organizations today. Microsoft Client for Novell Networks workstations can attach to servers running NetWare but cannot take full advantage of NetWare 5, as this client operates in "bindery emulation" mode. Therefore, in order to take advantage of utilities such as Z.E.N.works, your Microsoft Client for Novell Networks workstations need to be upgraded to Novell Client 32 software.

For simplicity many companies are standardizing the majority of their workstations on a common desktop OS to provide for easier administration, updates, and support of their end users. Many larger organizations have selected Windows NT. Others are standardizing on Windows 95 (or eventually Windows 98) as their desktop. In this chapter you will find the necessary information for installing, configuring, or migrating to the Novell Client that corresponds to the desktop or desktops you are deploying at your site.

Installation and Configuration of the Novell Clients

This chapter discusses the features, installation options, and configuration options for the following clients:

- Windows 95/98
- Windows NT
- DOS/Windows 3.*x*

- Mac OS
- OS/2

Novell Client for Windows 95/98

The Novell Client for Windows 95/98 provides complete NDS functionality and provides you with the following NetWare functions:

- Utilize pure Internet Protocol (IP) (NetWare 5 only) as well as IPX applications and services
- Display a list of NetWare servers and trees
- Connect to and browse multiple Directory trees
- Log into and out of NetWare servers and Directory trees
- Map drives
- Capture ports
- Change passwords and synchronize with other servers when a password expires
- Synchronize a workstation password with an NDS password for a single-password login
- Use any of the NetWare DOS-based utilities with Windows 95/98

Novell Client for Windows 95/98 Installation

The following tools can be used to install the Novell Client for Windows 95/98 software:

- Z.E.N.works

- MSBATCH
- Automatic Client Upgrade (ACU)
- WINSETUP.EXE

Z.E.N.works

Z.E.N.works, or Zero Effort Networks, is an integrated set of tools that allows you to deliver and manage applications, configure Windows desktops, and remotely repair workstation software problems using a single management utility — NetWare Administrator 32.

For extensive information on using this product, refer to Chapter 19.

MSBATCH

MSBATCH is used to install and configure Novell Client for Windows 95 and Windows 98 without actually visiting the workstation. This process saves a great deal of time, especially if you need to install the software on multiple workstations. MSBATCH requires some preparation but can simplify installation on each workstation. This process also uses some Windows 95 utility programs. They are found on the Windows 95 Upgrade CD-ROM, but not on the Windows 95 floppy disks. These programs prepare the Windows 95 and Novell Client for Windows 95 files on a file server, so you can install both Windows 95 and the Client at the same time. The installation process then copies the files from the server to the workstation.

Prerequisites:

- A workstation running Windows 95 and Novell Client for Windows 95/98
- The Windows 95/98 Upgrade CD-ROM
- Enough available disk space (approximately 115MB on your NetWare 5 server)

IMPORTANT

The CD-ROM must have the ADMIN\APPTOOLS folder and .cab files. Your CD's path to these files may differ from the paths documented here.

Install Windows 95 Files onto the NetWare 5 Server Use these steps to load the workstation software on your NetWare 5 server. The server will serve as the distribution point for the client installations:

1. While logged into the NetWare 5 server, map a network drive to a volume from which you want users to copy Windows 95 and the Novell Client for Windows 95/98 files. For example, map drive g: to volume sys:.

2. Create two folders. One folder is for the Windows 95 files, for example, G:\WIN95. The second folder is for the Novell Client files. Although you won't copy client files right now, you can go ahead and create the folder. For example, create G:\CLIENT95.

3. Run NETSETUP.EXE under Windows 95/98. NETSETUP.EXE is in the ADMIN\NETTOOLS\NETSETUP folder on the Windows 95/98 Upgrade CD. It opens the Server Based Setup dialog box. An example of this dialog box is shown in Figure 17.1.

FIGURE 17.1

The Netsetup dialog box

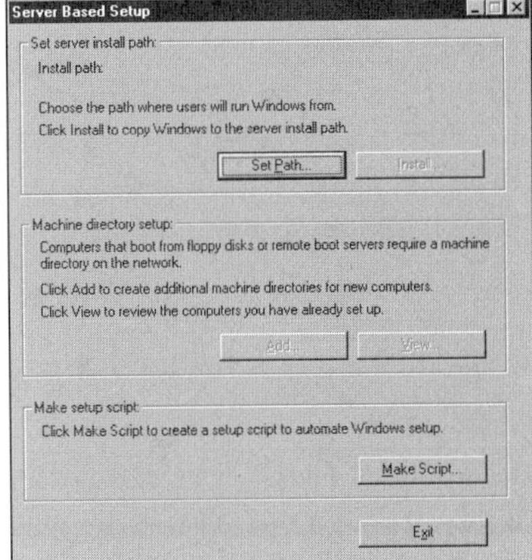

4. Specify where NETSETUP places files.
   a. Click Set Path.
   b. Enter the path (**G:\WIN95**). If this folder isn't already on the server, NETSETUP.EXE creates it for you. This folder eventually will contain the Windows 95 files and directories, including SETUP.EXE and the setup script (MSBATCH.INF). These files simultaneously install Windows 95 and the Client software.
   c. Click OK.
5. Install the Windows 95/98 source files.
   a. Click Install → Local Hard Drive. Please note that the Novell Client for Windows 95 does not support running Windows 95/98 from shared files on a server.
   b. Enter the path that has the Windows 95/98 .cab files as the Path to Install From. The files are on the Microsoft Windows 95/98 Upgrade CD. For example, **D:\WIN95**.
   c. Click OK → Don't Create Default.
   d. Click OK to bypass the Product Identification Number box. NETSETUP copies files to G:\WIN95. This might take 15 to 45 minutes.
6. Exit Server Based Setup by clicking OK and then Exit.
7. Change the MSBATCH.INF and NETDET.INI files to Read/Write.
   a. From a command prompt, go to G:\WIN95.
   b. Using the FLAG command, change the two files' attributes to Read/Write. For example: flag msbatch.inf +rw -ri -di

Be sure to change both files. They are overwritten later.

Copy and Prepare the Novell Client Files Use these steps to copy the Novell Client software from the Z.E.N.works CD-ROM to your NetWare 5 server:

1. Copy the Novell Client files to the server (G:\CLIENT95). The Client files are on the Clients and Z.E.N.works CD-ROM in the PRODUCTS\WIN95\IBM_ LANGUAGE folder.

IMPORTANT

Do not copy the files from the PRODUCTS\ADM32\IBM_ LANGUAGE \BATCH95\NLS\ LANGUAGE folder of the Clients and Z.E.N.works CD-ROM.

2. Remove or rename the .inf files from the client95 folder.
3. Copy the .inf files from the Clients and Z.E.N.works CD-ROM to G:\CLIENT95. The files are in the PRODUCTS\ADM32\IBM_ LANGUAGE \BATCH95\NLS\ LANGUAGE folder. Always copy these three files: NWCLIENT.INF, NWTRANS.INF, and NWLAYOUT.INF. For additional product support, copy these files as well:
   a. For IPX/IP Gateway support, also copy NWIPXIP.INF.
   b. For NDPS support, also copy NWNDPS.INF.
   c. For NetWare/IP support, also copy NWIP.INF.
   d. For Remote Access Dialer support, also copy NWDIAL.INF, located in the PRODUCTS\WIN95\IBM_ LANGUAGE folder.
   e. For SNMP support, also copy NWSERV.INF.
4. (Optional.) Edit NWCLIENT.INF if you want to integrate the Novell Client help with Windows 95 System help. Remove the semicolon (;) at the beginning of the line that contains OEM.CNT.

Create a New MSBATCH.INF File Next, you follow these steps to create a new MSBATCH.INF file:

1. Run BATCH.EXE. This file is on the Microsoft Windows 95 Upgrade CD, in the ADMIN\NETTOOLS\NETSETUP folder. You can run BATCH.EXE under Windows 3.*x* or Windows 95. An example of this utility is shown in Figure 17.2.

FIGURE 17.2

The BATCH.EXE utility will assist you in setting up a client install.

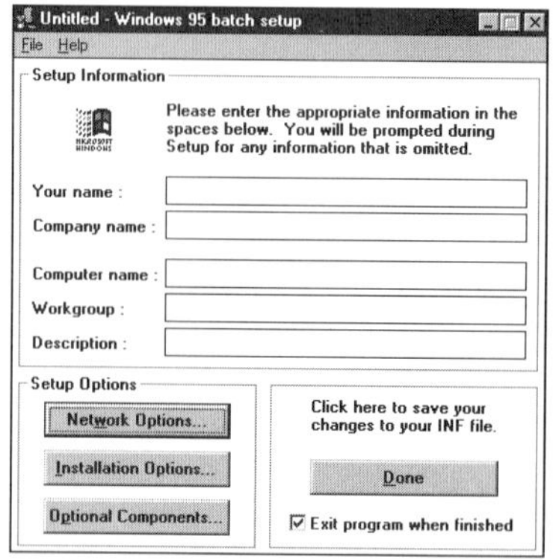

2. (Optional) Fill in Setup Information. For an unattended install, enter general information in all fields.

3. Remove options.

   a. Click Network Options. An example of this dialog box is shown on Figure 17.3.

   b. Uncheck any protocols, services, clients, or other options that are checked.

FIGURE 17.3

The Network Options dialog box

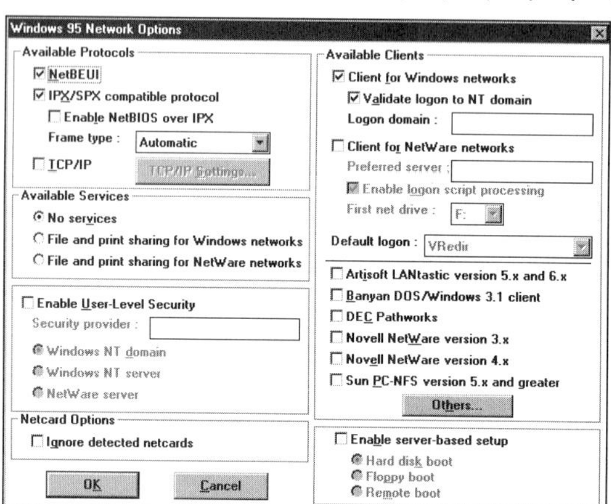

c. Check IPX/SPX Compatible Protocol. If you are setting up TCP/IP, check that box, click TCP/IP Settings, and enter required data, including DNS, DHCP, and gateway options. Once you are done, exit this dialog box.

4. Click Installation Options. An example of this dialog box is shown in Figure 17.4. Completing this step allows users to have minimal interaction while MSBATCH updates workstations.

FIGURE 17.4

An example of the Installation Options dialog box

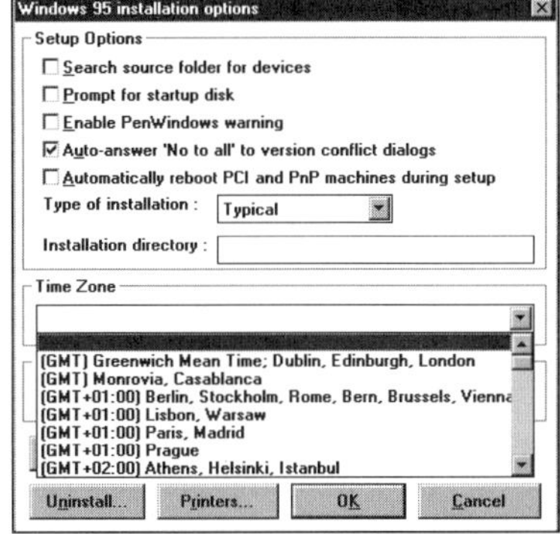

a. Select all options *except* Search Source Folder for Devices and Prompt for Startup Disk.

b. Set Type of Installation to Typical. Typical is the recommended option.

c. Enter Installation Directory as **C:\WINDOWS**.

d. Set the time zone for your appropriate time zone.

e. Click Printers shown at the bottom of the Installation options dialog box. Don't Prompt to Install Printers during Setup. Click OK.

f. Return to the Untitled dialog box by again clicking OK.

Skip Optional Components. Choosing this will negate the Typical settings you selected earlier.

5. Click Done.

6. You will now be prompted for a location to save the file. Save the MSBATCH.INF file to the G:\WIN95 folder.

   Enter **MSBATCH.INF** in the FileName box. Using the Drives box and the Folders box, choose the path to G:\WIN95 on your NetWare 5 server. This file overwrites the one that NETSETUP copied previously.

7. Click OK.

Add the Client to MSBATCH.INF The next step is to add the Novell client to the MSBATCH.INF file:

1. Run the INF Installer (INFINST.EXE). INFINST.EXE can be found in the ADMIN\NETTOOLS\NETSETUP folder of the Windows 95 Upgrade CD. An example of this dialog box is shown in Figure 17.5.

FIGURE 17.5

An example of the INF Installer utility

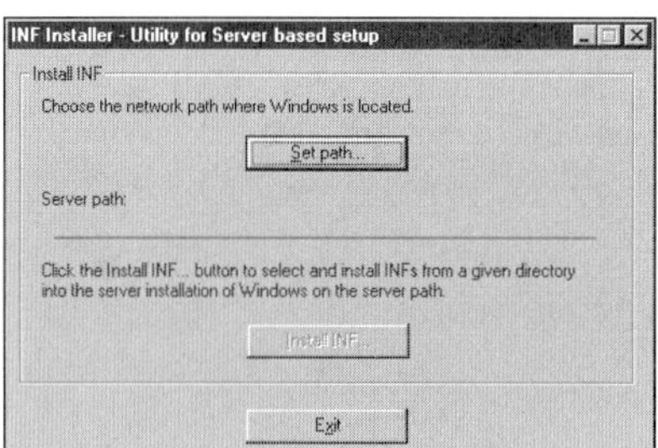

2. Specify where Installer places files.
   a. Click Set Path.
   b. Enter the server path. Specify the drive and folder, for example, **G:\WIN95**.
   c. Click OK.

3. Install .inf files.
   a. Click Install INF.

b. Click NWCLIENT.INF.

Use the Drives and Folders boxes to select G:\CLIENT95. Then you can click NWCLIENT.INF. You must use the NWCLIENT.INF file in this folder, which contains the Client files to be installed. Once you select NWCLIENT.INF, the Installer integrates the Client files into the MSBATCH.INF file.

4. Click OK.

During this process, the Installer copies a number of files in a process that may take a few minutes to complete. Don't click the Exit button until after you select OK from the small inf Installer dialog box.

Do not keep the existing NETWARE.DRV file even if it is newer than the NETWARE.DRV file that shipped with this Novell Client for Windows 95/98 software. Click No in response to the Version Conflict message that will be shown. Do not skip files. If the INF Installer cannot find a file, specify the path where you think the file may exist. You must locate all files before proceeding.

5. Click OK at the small INF Installer dialog box and then click Exit at the main INF Installer dialog box.

Check the MSBATCH.INF file Review the sample MSBATCH.INF file in the PRODUCTS\ADM32\IBM_ LANGUAGE\BATCH95\NLS\ LANGUAGE folder of the Clients and Z.E.N.works CD-ROM.

This sample file illustrates three items:

- The settings necessary to install the Client
- Which client settings you can directly configure
- Valid values for the settings

1. (Optional) Compare the registry keys shown in the sample MSBATCH.INF file with the ones generated by the inf Installer.

2. (Optional) Adjust as necessary.

You can set the values of the Client properties automatically during installation by placing values in the ADMIN.CFG file. This file is found on your Z.E.N.works CD-ROM.

Simultaneously Install Windows 95/98 and Novell Client for Windows 95/98 By following these steps, you can simultaneously install both Windows 95/98 and the Novell Client for Windows 95/98:

1. Log into your NetWare 5 server from a workstation to be upgraded.

   Map a network drive to the folder containing MSBATCH.INF. For example, map G:=SYS:\WIN95.

2. Run SETUP.EXE with MSBATCH.INF as the first parameter.

   To avoid having Windows 95 query for accepting the license agreement, use the /IW (in capital letters) command line option, for example, setup /IW G:\WIN95\MSBATCH.INF.

Automatic Client Upgrade (ACU)

Novell's Automatic Client Upgrade (ACU) is used to automatically upgrade multiple workstations from the Microsoft Client for NetWare Networks to the Novell Client for Windows 95/98. It also provides a way for you to upgrade from earlier Novell Client software to the latest Novell Client for Windows 95/98 software. This upgrade happens when users log into your NetWare 5 server.

ACU is the name of a process rather than a specific utility. The process requires that you complete the following tasks:

1. Create a folder on the NetWare 5 server.

2. Copy Novell Client files and Windows 95/98 installation .cab files into the folder. Workstations can then read the files during logins.

3. Grant rights to the new folder using NWADMIN.

4. Update the NWSETUP.INI file.

5. Modify the appropriate login script.

Create a Folder Follow these steps to create a folder:

1. Log into a NetWare 5 server with Supervisor rights. You will need sufficient rights to copy files to the folder that all users can access. You will also need rights to modify login scripts on that server.

2. Create a folder, for example, SYS:\PUBLIC\CLIENTS\W95.

Copy Files Use the following steps to copy files:

1. Copy the Client files to the new folder. The files are on the Clients and Z.E.N.works CD-ROM in the PRODUCTS\WIN95\IBM_ LANGUAGE folder.

2. Copy Windows 95 .cab files to the new folder. These files are found on the Microsoft Windows 95 CD (and Upgrade CD) in the win95 folder.

Grant Rights Follow these steps to grant rights to the ACU group:

1. Create an NDS group called ACU.

2. Place into the ACU group the users whose workstations need to be upgraded.

3. Grant the group ACU Read and File Scan rights to the new folder.

Updating NWSETUP.INI To get information such as where to copy drivers during installation, SETUP.EXE reads a configuration file named NWSETUP.INI. This file is in the same folder (iwc95) as SETUP.EXE. To determine whether a workstation should be upgraded, ACU uses the Client Version section of NWSETUP.INI. For example:

```
[Client Version]

Version=3.0.0.0
```

The Version= line contains four fields: 3.0.0.0. These fields refer to the version of client software. The first field (3) is the MajorVersion field. The second field (0) is the MinorVersion field. The third and fourth fields (0.0) are the Revision and Level fields.

You can view the version number on the Novell Client property page of the Network Control Panel. Each new version of Novell Client has updated fields. You can define the Revision and Level fields. Although Novell initially sets these to 0, you can set them to any number from 0 to 65000. You can change the fields to cause updates for other changes you want, even if the Client software has not changed.

The upgrade takes place if any part of the version number is greater than the number stored in the registry. For example, 2.2.1.1 is greater than 2.2.1.0, and 2.2.2.0 is greater than 2.2.1.999.

To have ACU show the user a dialog box stating that there are more recent files, you can set options in [AcuOptions]. Doing this allows users to continue with the upgrade or cancel the upgrade.

To allow the user to choose whether to upgrade, set DisplayFirstScreen=Yes. Otherwise, the upgrade starts automatically. With this setting in place, the user sees a dialog box before the upgrade begins and can then choose to upgrade or cancel the upgrade. Until the user upgrades, that user encounters the dialog box at every subsequent login.

To allow the user to choose whether to restart the workstation, set DisplayLastScreen=Yes. Otherwise, the workstation restarts automatically. With this setting in place, the user sees a dialog box after the upgrade completes and can choose whether to restart the workstation. The workstation must be restarted to activate the upgraded Client files.

Modifying the Login Script You will need to modify login scripts for users whose workstations will be upgraded. To upgrade specific users' workstations, modify those users' separate login scripts. You can do this with FILER, NetWare Administrator, or any text editor. To upgrade workstations for users in a container, modify that container's login script. You can do this with the NetWare Administrator utility. To upgrade workstations for users in a profile, modify that profile login script through the NetWare Administrator.

To upgrade a workstation running bindery-based client software (such as the version of Microsoft Client for NetWare Networks that ships with Windows 95), edit the system login script (SYS:PUBLIC\NET$LOG.DAT).

You can use a Universal Naming Convention (UNC) path as shown here. Add this line to the login script (where, after the volume name, all directories are separated by a backslash [\]):

```
#\\ servername\ volume\...\setup.exe /acu
```

For example:

```
#\\atl-srv1\sys\...\setup.exe /acu
```

Both the Login Processor from Microsoft and Novell's GUI Login utility allow Windows programs to run using the # (external command) notation.

You can also map a drive to the folder (G:\W95) and call SETUP.EXE from there.

When using SETUP.EXE, you can use any of six command line parameters: /ACU, /N, /O, /NCF, /RB, and /U.

Using /ACU To perform an Automatic Client Upgrade (ACU), use /ACU. When you use this parameter, by default no screens will show during the installation.

Using /N and /O The Custom option for the Client has an Upgrade NDIS Driver to ODI Automatically if Available check box. Using command line parameters, you can change the default state of the check box:

- To install without upgrading NDIS to ODI, use /N.
- To install and upgrade NDIS to ODI, use /O.

Users can still check the check box during installation. Doing so overrides the command line parameters.

Using /NCF To allow Windows 95 to copy some .cab files, use /NCF, the Network Configuration File. Novell's SETUP.EXE performs a CAB FIX, checking to see if .cab files exist on the workstation. If the files exist, CAB FIX disables this file copy. Not using CAB FIX means that the user has to insert the Win95 CD-ROM to complete the installation.

Using /RB Before the client is installed, Rollback (RB) backs up the current client configuration to the NOVELL\CLIENT32\NWBACKUP directory. After the client is installed and the workstation is rebooted, Rollback checks to see if the client was able to connect to the network. If installation and connection are successful, Rollback deletes the backup. If installation and connection are not successful, Rollback reverts to the previous client using the backup.

Using /U The /U parameter specifies the default parameters by using a configuration file created by Novell Client Install Manager. Novell Client Install Manager is located on the Clients and Z.E.N.works CD-ROM in the Products → Win95 → Ibm_ language → Admin directory.

For example:

```
SETUP /U:F:\PUBLIC\95CLIENT\NOVELL.TXT
```

specifies the default parameters set in the text file NOVELL.TXT.

Using Novell Client Install Manager to Create a Configuration File If you are using the /U command line parameter with SETUP.EXE, you must create a configuration file using the Novell Client Install Manager. Follow these steps:

1. Start the Novell Client Install Manager.

   The Novell Client Install Manager is located on the Clients and Z.E.N.works CD-ROM in the Products → Win95 → Ibm_ language → Admin directory.

2. Click File → New File, and then select Windows 95 to create a new file.

3. Modify the installation options as needed by following these steps:

   a. Double-click the configuration option you want to modify in the Installation options for Windows 95 list box.

   b. In the property pages, set the parameters, and then click OK. The values you set appear in the right list box.

NOTE

You can set up one workstation the way you want all of the workstations set up and then use Novell Client Install Manager to import the settings from that workstation's registry and save them to the configuration file you use during the ACU install. Once you set up the workstation, click File → Open Registry to import the settings into Novell Client Install Manager.

4. Click File → Save.

You can save the file with any filename you want to use. For example, you could rename the file NOVELL.TXT. You can use this file in conjunction with other command line parameters to customize the Client install.

If workstations have older software, ACU upgrades the client software when users log in and then restarts the workstation. Users see system messages as ACU upgrades their workstations. If workstations already have current software, the client login runs as usual.

WINSETUP.EXE

WINSETUP.EXE is used if you are installing the Novell Client for Windows 95/98 for the first time on one or more workstations, or if you want to upgrade a workstation. WINSETUP.EXE provides a graphical interface for an easy installation.

To further simplify installation, especially if you are installing the Novell Client for Windows 95/98 on multiple workstations, you can set configuration options by using the NWSETUP.INI file.

To run winsetup, simply insert your Novell Clients and Z.E.N.works CD-ROM. The CD will autorun and load winsetup as shown in the example in Figure 17.6. Select the language option you desire.

You will then be presented with a screen with the clients for Windows 95/98, Windows NT, and Windows 3.*x*. Additionally, you can install Z.E.N.works as well. An example of this screen is shown in Figure 17.7.

FIGURE 17.6

The winsetup screen from the Novell Clients and Z.E.N.works CD-ROM

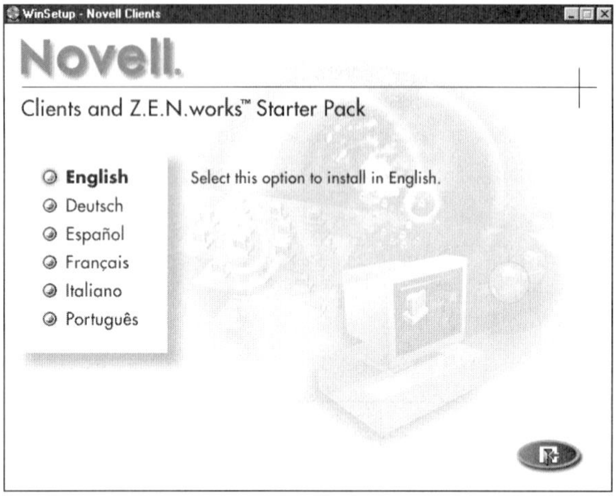

FIGURE 17.7

The winsetup screen presenting client install choices

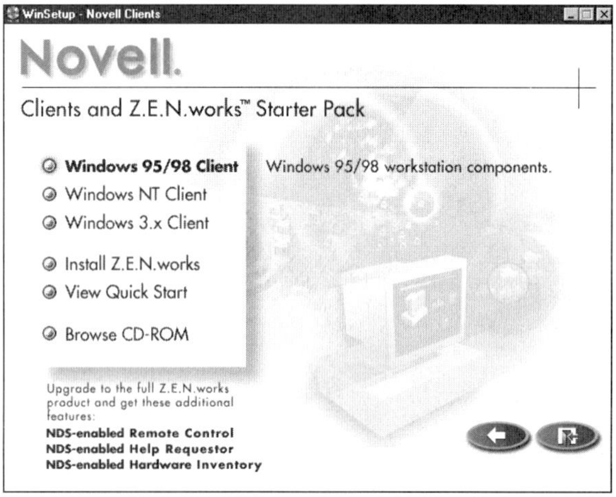

Novell Client for Windows 95/98 Configuration

If NetWare 5 is running on your network, the Novell Client for Windows 95 can be installed with one of the following three protocol options:

- IP Only allows the client to run in IP-only networks. This includes IP Compatibility Mode, which allows IPX applications to function in IP-only networks. IPX Compatibility Mode also allows the client to communicate with services in IPX-only networks if the Migration Agent is installed on any NetWare 5 server. IPX Compatibility Mode is dependent on the Service Location Protocol (SLP) for its operation.

- IP + IPX allows the client to run in both IP and IPX networks.

- IPX Only allows the client to run in IPX-only networks.

NOTE

Pure IP is available only in NetWare 5. If your network is running a version of NetWare earlier than NetWare 5, install the Novell Client for Windows 95/98 with the IPX Only option.

NetWare 4 included NetWare/IP. This feature provided an IP solution over IPX networks but was not a native IP solution. NetWare/IP allows a Novell Client for Windows 95/98 workstation to access NetWare services over a TCP/IP network.

NetWare 5, on the other hand, supports pure IP connectivity. In order for NetWare 5 to communicate with an existing NetWare/IP network, a NetWare 5 server with the Migration Agent installed must exist in the NetWare/IP environment. More information on this can be found in Chapter 23.

NetWare/IP provided the Domain SAP/RIP Service (DSS), which maintained two types of information required by NetWare servers and clients:

- Service Advertising Protocol (SAP) information about the available NetWare services

- Routing Information Protocol (RIP) information about routes between NetWare servers

Once configured, the DSS automatically maintained this information and made it available to all NetWare/IP nodes. NetWare/IP servers and clients also used DSS servers to obtain service and routing information. The Domain Name System (DNS) is a distributed database system used to locate computers in TCP/IP internetworks. NetWare/IP servers and clients would use DNS to locate the DSS server.

The Novell Client for Windows 95/98 uses NWSIPX for 32-bit API support of IPX/SPX and for full 32-bit Packet Burst support.

To select a protocol, load the Client and Z.E.N.works CD-ROM and select English (or other language) and then select the Windows95/98 Client.

You will then be presented with a dialog box to select the typical installation (the default is whatever you have running when you install this client). If IPX is the default on this client, then IPX will be the default if you select the default installation. The typical install does not prompt you further but simply installs the client software on your workstation.

To customize your desktop or to select another protocol, you need to select the Custom option rather than the typical install. An example of this dialog box is shown in Figure 17.8.

FIGURE 17.8

Select the Custom option to configure your client to a protocol other than the default your client is currently running.

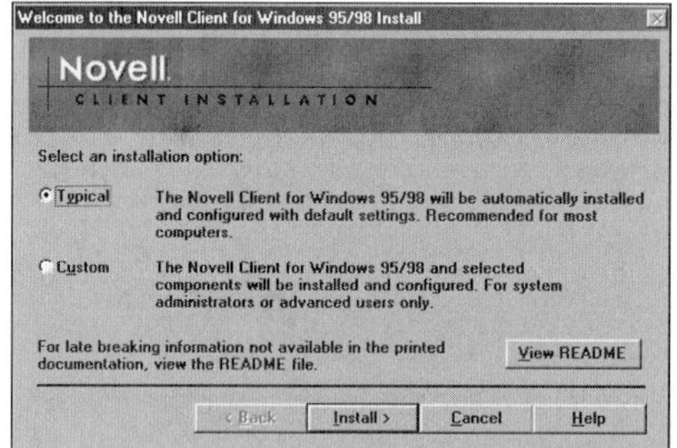

You will then be presented with the dialog box shown in Figure 17.9, which allows you to select the protocol or protocols you wish to run.

FIGURE 17.9

The Protocol Preference dialog box

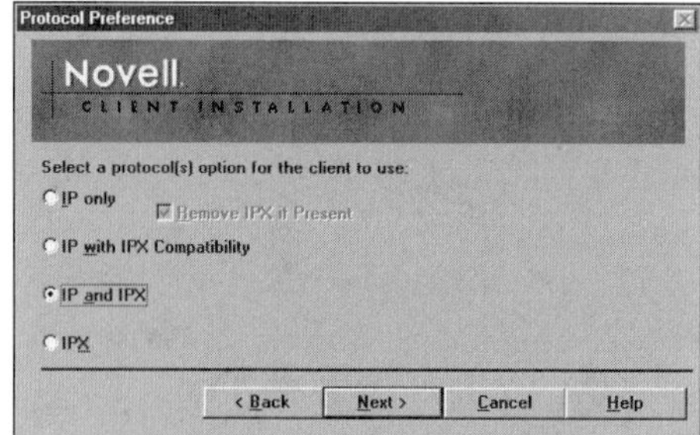

The next step is to choose your client connection type, either NDS or Bindery. As shown in Figure 17.10, you select what type of connection you desire.

FIGURE 17.10

The Login Authenticator dialog box allows you to choose the type of connection for this client, either NDS or Bindery.

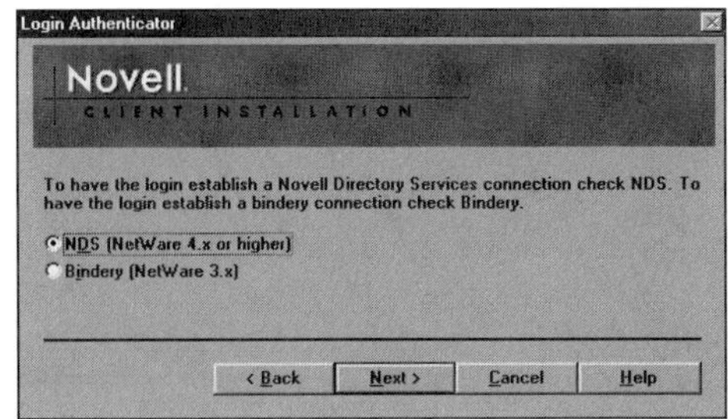

Continuing the custom installation, you will be presented with the Novell Client for Windows 95/98 Custom Options dialog box. It is here that you can select to install optional components of the client such as the Novell Workstation Manager and Novell Distributed Print Services. This dialog box is shown in Figure 17.11.

FIGURE 17.11

The Custom Options dialog box allows you to install optional components of the client.

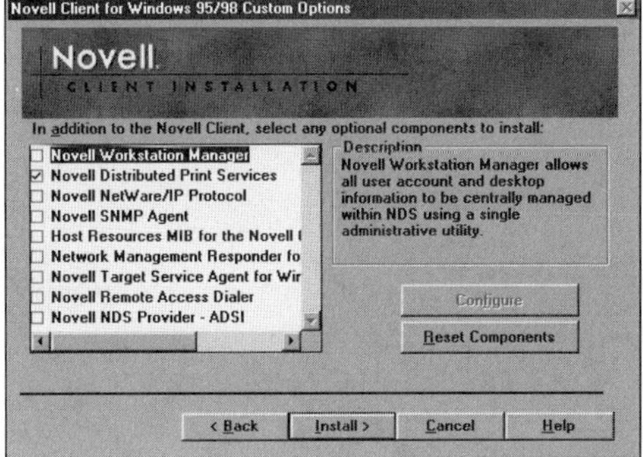

The client install will now begin the copy process and run to completion. You will then be presented with the installation completion dialog box, where you have the option to reboot or close without rebooting the workstation. You must reboot to activate the new client software. This dialog box is shown in Figure 17.12.

FIGURE 17.12

The Installation Completion dialog box for the Windows 95/98 installation

API Support for Novell Client for Windows 95/98

The Novell Client for Windows 95/98 supports the following applications and APIs:

- 32-bit applications that are supported by Windows 95/98
- 16-bit Microsoft Windows applications that use the 16-bit NWCALLS library set
- NWSIPX.API (32-bit)
- NWIPXSPX.API (16-bit)

The NWCALLS Library

The following 16-bit NetWare Windows libraries are supported in Windows 95/98:

- NWCALLS.DLL
- NWIPXSPX.DLL
- NWCLIENT.DLL
- NWNET.DLL
- NWNETAPI.DLL

These libraries have the same names as the traditional NetWare 16-bit Windows libraries but provide functionality unique to Windows 95. If you have 16-bit Windows applications that are not running correctly in Windows 95, verify that the preceding 16-bit Windows libraries are being used.

Some applications install to the network with one or more of the traditional 16-bit Windows libraries (DLLs) being installed with the application. In this case, we recommend that you delete the traditional DLLs that have the same name as the preceding DLLs from the application directory and have the DLLs accessible only from the client. This option lets you run the same 16-bit Windows applications from the NetWare server for both Windows 3.*x* and Windows 95 workstations.

If your installation has the traditional 16-bit windows DLLs only in the application directory on the server and they are not accessible at the client, you can duplicate your application structure under a directory on the server. Then remove all the NetWare traditional 16-bit Windows DLLs and replace them with the preceding 16-bit Windows 95–specific DLLs.

If a 16-bit Windows application still does not function after completing these tasks, it is possible that the application requires a NetWare 16-bit DLL that is not supported by Windows 95.

Configuring the Novell Client for Windows 95/98 Before Installing

The Novell Client for Windows 95/98 software minimizes the need for configuration, adjusting many settings dynamically. Most settings have default values that work well in most environments. The Novell Client uses some settings as a guide or as an initial value and then dynamically adjusts their run-time equivalents for maximum performance. Before installing the Client, you can use two files that assist with the install-configured workstations:

- ADMIN.CFG
- NWSETUP.INI

Editing ADMIN.CFG

ADMIN.CFG is an Administrator Defaults file. By specifying default values for configuration settings in an ADMIN.CFG file, you can simplify installation of the client software. This configuration method is useful for network supervisors who are familiar with the NET.CFG syntax, want to install and configure the Novell Client at the same time, and need to configure settings that can't be configured using the System Policy Editor.

By installing from a NetWare server, you can configure multiple workstations using the same ADMIN.CFG file. You should set critical defaults in ADMIN.CFG, as described in the following list, before running any of the network installations. The ADMIN.CFG file uses the same syntax as a NET.CFG file. However, you should be familiar with the settings that the Novell Client supports. Follow these steps:

1. Open ADMIN.CFG using a text editor.

   ADMIN.CFG can be found in the PRODUCTS\WIN95\IBM_ENU folder of the Clients and Z.E.N.works CD-ROM. You need to copy this file to a network install directory and edit it from there.

   The first line of the file must have the words "Admin Defaults." The valid parameters for this option are Overwrite and Version.

2. On the Overwrite= line, enter **True** or **False**.

   True specifies that all configuration settings in the ADMIN.CFG file are written to the registry. False means that the configuration settings in the ADMIN.CFG file are written to the registry only if they aren't already there.

3. On the Version= line, enter the parameters and values you want to set as defaults.

   The following lines illustrate the Overwrite and Version parameters:

   ```
   Admin Defaults
   Overwrite = false
   Version = 0
   ```

   An example of this is shown in Figure 17.13.

FIGURE 17.13

An example of the ADMIN.CFG file

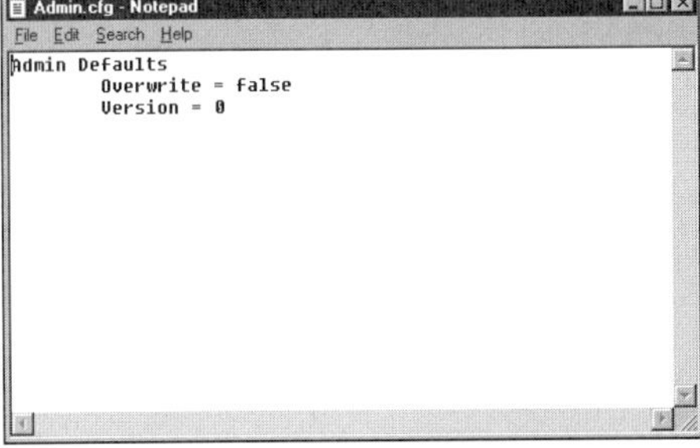

The Version parameter can be set to any number from 0 through 4,294,967,295. If this number is greater than the version number stored in the registry, the configuration settings in the ADMIN.CFG file are written to the registry, and this number is stored as the new version number. For example, if the previously installed Client version was set to 3, then the number in the version field must be greater than 3 for the new settings to take effect.

The first time the Novell Client software is installed, no version number is in the registry. In this case, the Administrator Defaults are written to the registry, including the version number.

4. Below the Version= line, enter any parameters and values you want to set as defaults.

   Use the syntax for a NET.CFG file. Make sure you include the group name for the parameters you set. For example, if you want to include settings for a preferred tree, you can add the following lines to ADMIN.CFG after the "Version=" line:

   ```
   NetWare dos requester
   preferred tree=tree_name
   ```

   For details about the configuration settings that you can specify in the ADMIN.CFG file, see Administrator Defaults Parameters in the PROP.HLP file located in the PRODUCTS\WIN95\IBM_LANGUAGE directory.

5. Save your changes and exit the editor.

Editing NWSETUP.INI

The Novell Client supports NDIS and ODI LAN drivers. The Novell Client supports 16-bit drivers. But for increased performance and stability, you should use a 32-bit driver when one is available for your LAN adapter.

In addition, you can change the default installation settings for protocols and custom installation options by editing the NWSETUP.INI file.

Installing ODI LAN Drivers Novell and many third-party ODI LAN drivers (.lan files) are on the Clients and Z.E.N.works CD-ROM in the PRODUCTS\WIN95\IBM_ENU folder. Setup will detect them and configure the workstation during installation. If you want to use an additional ODI LAN driver, you need to copy the driver to the network install folder and specify the driver in the NWSETUP.INI file. Follow these steps:

1. Create a network install folder on the server and copy to it the Client install files from the CD-ROM. For example, copy all the files from PRODUCTS\WIN95\IBM_ENU on the Clients and Z.E.N.works CD-ROM to SYS:\PUBLIC\CLIENTS\W95.

2. Copy the driver to the network install folder. For example, copy the driver to SYS:\PUBLIC\CLIENTS\W95.

3. Open NWSETUP.INI in a text editor. NWSETUP.INI is located in the network install folder (for example, SYS:\PUBLIC\CLIENTS\W95).

4. Search for the .inf file that corresponds to the LAN driver you want to use. The .inf files for third-party LAN drivers are named odi*.inf, where the asterisk represents the manufacturer of the network adapter. For example, ODI3COM.INF specifies a 3Com driver.

5. Delete the semicolon at the front of the line or, if the .inf file is not listed, add the .inf filename to the [INF Files] section.

6. Save your changes and exit the editor.

7. Run Setup.

An example of the NWSETUP.INI file is shown in Figure 17.14.

FIGURE 17.14

The NWSETUP.INI file

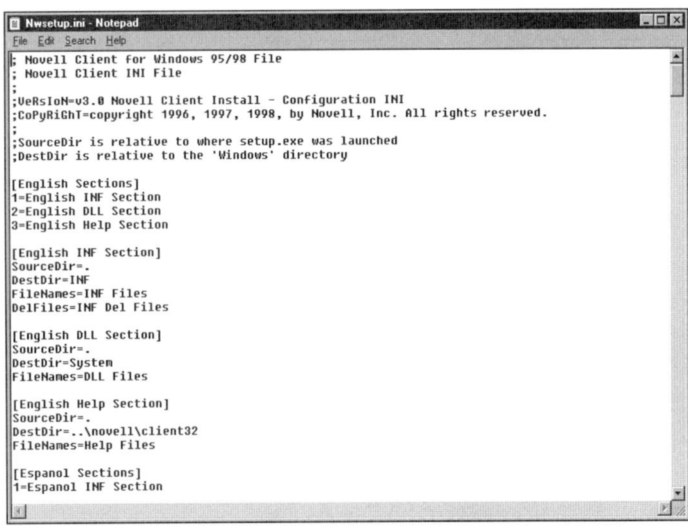

```
; Novell Client for Windows 95/98 File
; Novell Client INI File
;
;VeRsIoN=v3.0 Novell Client Install - Configuration INI
;CoPyRiGhT=copyright 1996, 1997, 1998, by Novell, Inc. All rights reserved.
;
;SourceDir is relative to where setup.exe was launched
;DestDir is relative to the 'Windows' directory

[English Sections]
1=English INF Section
2=English DLL Section
3=English Help Section

[English INF Section]
SourceDir=.
DestDir=INF
FileNames=INF Files
DelFiles=INF Del Files

[English DLL Section]
SourceDir=.
DestDir=System
FileNames=DLL Files

[English Help Section]
SourceDir=.
DestDir=..\novell\client32
FileNames=Help Files

[Espanol Sections]
1=Espanol INF Section
```

Installing NDIS LAN Drivers If you want to switch from an ODI LAN driver to an NDIS LAN driver, you need to remove the ODI information in the NWSETUP. INI file before installing the Novell Client. Follow these steps:

1. Change to the network install folder and open NWSETUP.INI in a text editor. For example, change to SYS:\PUBLIC\CLIENTS\W95. If the file isn't already in the folder, copy it from the Clients and Z.E.N.works CD-ROM (PRODUCTS\WIN95\IBM_LANGUAGE).

2. In the [INF Files] section, add a semicolon (;) to the front of each line containing an ODI setup information file (odi*.inf). Record each filename. You will need this information for Step 6.

3. Add a semicolon to the front of each line that lists a Novell ODI setup information file (NE.INF). Record each filename. You will need this information for Step 6.

4. Add a semicolon to the front of the line containing ntr2000.inf.

5. Save your changes and exit the editor.

6. Rename or delete the .inf files you commented out of NWSETUP.INI in Steps 2, 3, and 4 from the client workstation's WINDOWS\INF folder.

7. Reinstall the Novell Client software.

Changing the Default Protocol You can change the default protocol of the Novell Client at installation by commenting out with a semicolon the protocols you don't want to use and removing the semicolon from the protocol you do want to use. Only one protocol should be uncommented. For example, to use only IPX, uncomment (remove the semicolon from) DefaultProtocol=IPX under [ProtocolOptions].

Novell Client for Windows NT

The Novell Client for Windows NT allows you to log into NDS and Windows NT, and to use the following NetWare 5 functions:

- Install pure Internet Protocol (IP) support (NetWare 5 only) as well as support for IPX applications and services.
- List NetWare servers and trees.
- Connect to and browse multiple Directory trees.
- Log into and out of NetWare servers and trees.
- Map drives to NetWare servers.
- Capture ports.
- Change passwords and synchronize with other servers when a password expires.
- Synchronize workstation passwords with NDS passwords for single-password logins.

The Novell Client for Windows NT supports the Internet Protocol (IP) running natively on a NetWare 5 server. If you use the client with a version of NetWare other than NetWare 5, you can use NetWare/IP for IP connectivity. The Novell Client for Windows NT also supports IPX/SPX protocols. This client can also coexist with other protocol stacks, such as NetBEUI protocols.

Additionally, the Novell Client for Windows NT also supports a 32-bit interface, NWSIPX to IPX/SPX, and can coexist with the WinSock API, Named Pipes, and NetBIOS APIs.

With NetWare 5 running on your Novell network, the Novell Client for Windows NT can be installed with one of the following three protocol options:

- IP Only
- IP and IPX
- IPX Only

Novell Client for Windows NT Installation

The Novell Client for Windows NT allows a Windows NT workstation to connect to a NetWare 5 server via NDS. One of the following methods can be used to install the Novell Client for Windows NT software:

- Winsetup
- Unattended install
- The SETUPNW.EXE utility
- Automatic Client Upgrade (ACU)
- The Windows NT Network Control Panel
- Winsetup install of Novell Client for Windows NT

WINSETUP.EXE is used if you are installing the Novell Client for Windows NT for the first time on one or more workstations, or if you want to upgrade a workstation. WINSETUP.EXE provides a graphical interface for an easy installation.

To further simplify installation, especially if you are installing the Novell Client for Windows NT on multiple workstations, you can set configuration options by using the NWSETUP.INI file.

To run winsetup, simply insert your Novell Clients and Z.E.N.works CD-ROM. The CD-ROM will autorun and load winsetup as shown in the example in Figure 17.15. Select the language option you desire and the Windows NT client.

FIGURE 17.15

The winsetup screen with the Novell Client for Windows NT selection

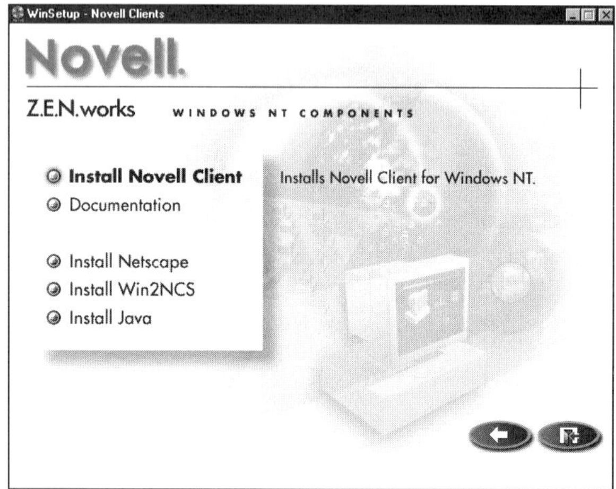

You will then be presented with a screen to select the typical installation (the default is whatever you have running when installing this client). If IPX is the default on this client, then IPX will be the default if you select the default installation. The typical install does not prompt you further but simply installs the client software on your workstation.

To customize your desktop or to select another protocol, you need to select the Custom option rather than the typical install. An example of this screen is shown in Figure 17.16.

FIGURE 17.16

Select the Custom option to configure your client to a protocol other than the default your client is currently running.

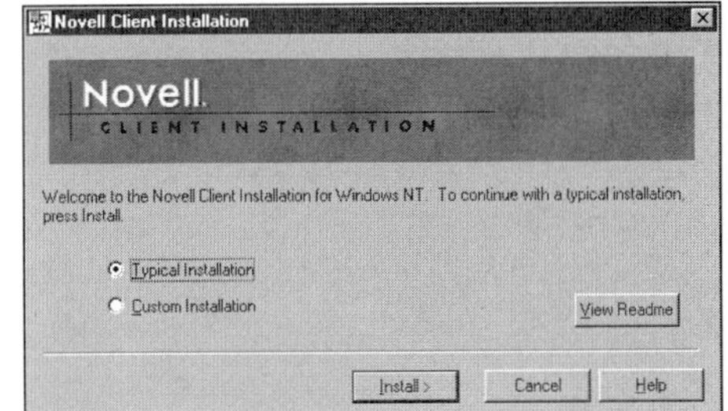

You will then be presented with the dialog box shown in Figure 17.17 that allows you to select optional components for this workstation such as the Workstation Manager and Novell Distributed Print Services.

FIGURE 17.17

The Client Installation Preference dialog box

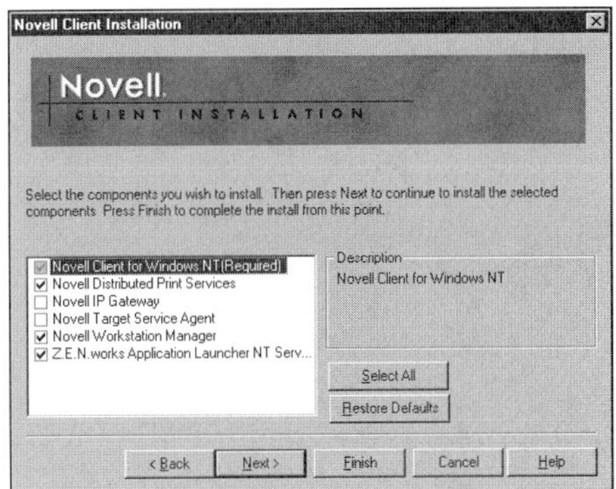

You will then be presented with the dialog box shown in Figure 17.18, which allows you to select the protocol or protocols you wish to run.

The next step is to choose your client connection type, either NDS or Bindery. As shown in Figure 17.19 you select what type of connection you desire.

The client install will now begin the copy process and finish to completion. You will now be presented with the installation completion dialog box where you have the option to reboot or close without rebooting the workstation. You must reboot to activate the new client software. This dialog box is shown in Figure 17.20.

FIGURE 17.18

The Protocol Preference dialog box

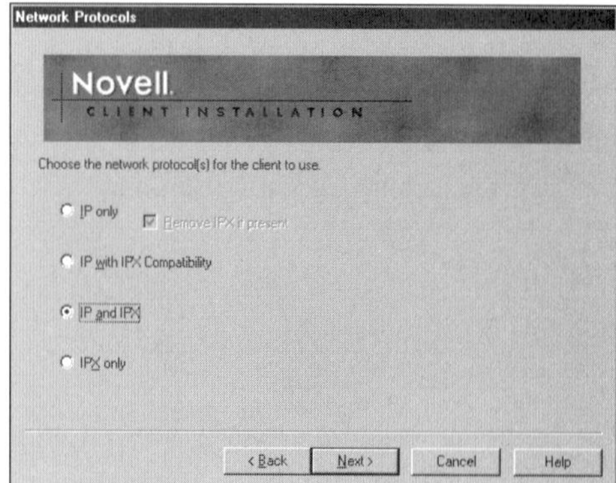

FIGURE 17.19

The Login Authenticator dialog box allows you to choose the type of connection for this client, either NDS or Bindery.

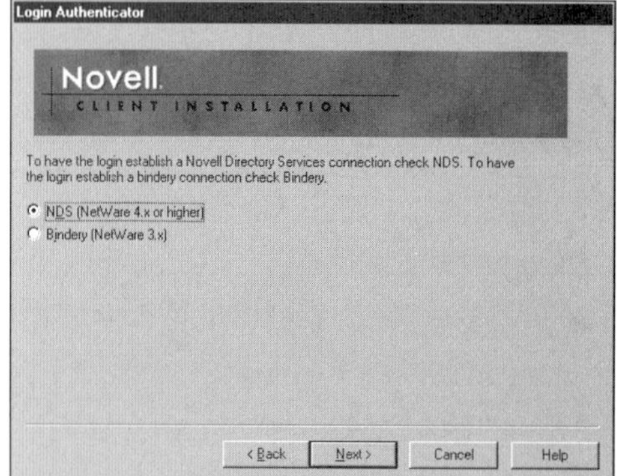

FIGURE 17.20

The Installation Completion dialog box for the Windows NT installation

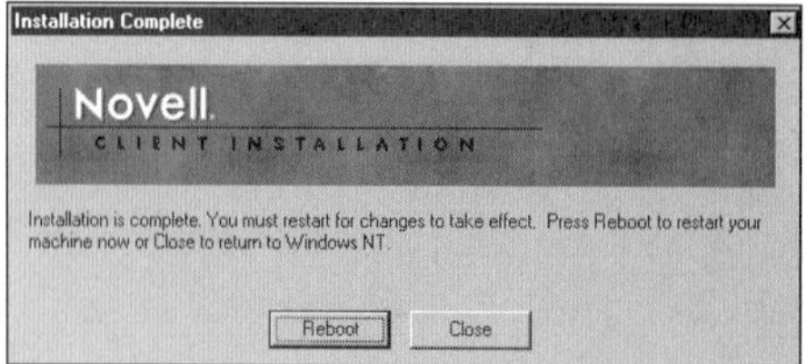

Unattended Installation of Novell Client and Windows NT

Windows NT and Novell Client for Windows NT can be installed at the same time through an unattended install option. This method can save time if you are installing the software on many workstations. Follow these steps to create an unattended install:

1. Enable the long name space on the NetWare 5 volume you will use to store the Windows NT installation files.

2. Copy the Windows NT CD to the existing NetWare 5 network.

   a. Create a directory at the root of a NetWare volume that has the long name space enabled.

   b. Open the Windows NT CD by double-clicking the CD icon in My Computer as shown in Figure 17.21.

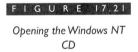

FIGURE 17.21

Opening the Windows NT CD

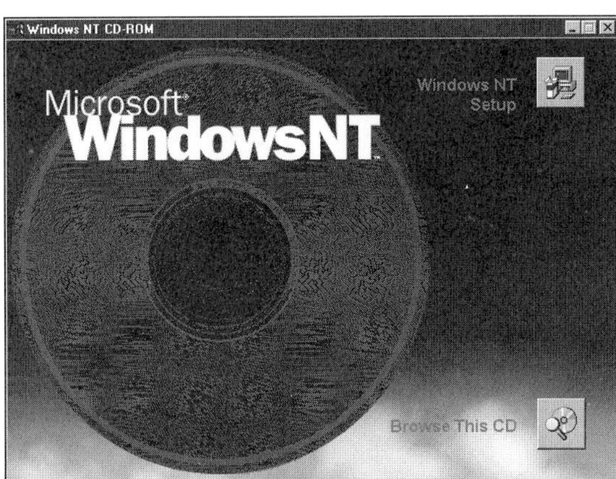

   c. Choose Select All from the Edit menu.

   d. Drag the highlighted folders and files to the directory you created at the root of your NetWare 5 volume.

3. Inside the I386 directory, make a directory called oem. The I386 directory is one of the directories you copied from the Windows NT CD.

4. Inside the oem directory, make a directory called Net.

5. Inside the Net directory, make another directory with any name of your choice. Many administrators name the directory based on the date of the version being installed, or based on the name of the group you're installing for. In this example the directory is called Ntclient.

6. Use the Microsoft Setup Manager to configure the Microsoft portion of the UNATTEND.TXT file. The Microsoft UNATTEND.TXT file includes several options that prompt the installer for information during setup. If you do not provide answers to these prompts in the UNATTEND.TXT file, a user must be present to answer the prompts as they appear on the screen. To install Windows NT without user intervention, preconfigure the answers.

7. Use the Novell Client Install Manager to create a configuration file. The Novell Client Install Manager can be found on the Z.E.N.works CD:

   ```
   D:\PRODUCTS\WINNT\I386\ADMIN\NCIMAN.EXE
   ```

   An example of this is shown in Figure 17.22.

FIGURE 17.22

The Novell Client Install Manager

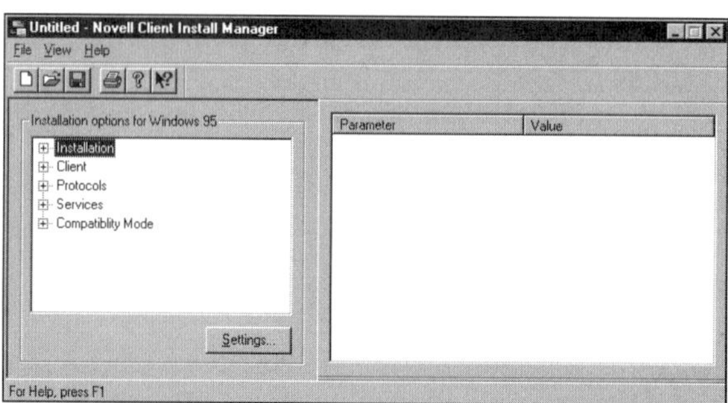

8. Save the configuration file.

9. Copy the contents of the D:\PRODUCTS\WINNT directory of the Z.E.N.works CD-ROM to the network directory that you created in Step 4.

10. To install Windows NT, log each workstation into the network.

11. To start the installation, change to the directory on the Windows NT installation CD to the WINNT.EXE file found in the I386 directory.

12. Enter this command at the prompt from the NT installation directory:

    `winnt /s:`*`source path`*`/b /u:`*`path to configuration file`*

    For example:

    ```
    winnt /s:f:\i386
    /b/u:f:\public\winnt40\i386\$oem$\net\ntclient\novell.txt
    ```

13. The unattended install process automatically installs Windows NT and the Novell Client for Windows NT on each workstation.

Unattended Install of Novell Client Only

You can install the Novell Client for Windows NT (without installing Windows NT) on several workstations at the same time by using the unattended install process. Follow these steps to accomplish this task:

1. Use Novell Client Install Manager to set up a configuration file. See the information in the next section to set up this configuration file.

2. Log each of the new machines into the network.

3. To start the installation, enter the following command:

    `setupnw /u:`*`path to configuration file`*

    For example:

    ```
    setupnw /u:f:\public\ntclient\novell.txt
    ```

Using SETUPNW.EXE for Installation

SETUPNW.EXE provides an alternative for installing the Novell Client for Windows NT software. It lets you install the client software without using the Windows control panel. SETUPNW.EXE also has options for specifying which Unattended file to use and deciding whether to prompt for default information.

SETUPNW.EXE Actions SETUPNW.EXE will perform the following actions during installation:

- Remove any existing client software, such as the Microsoft Client Services for NetWare.
- Install the Novell Client for Windows NT software.
- Update the system registry with information needed to start the Novell Client for Windows NT automatically each time Windows NT starts.

SETUPNW.EXE also provides a mechanism for you to automatically configure the client parameters when you install the client software. You can find SETUPNW.EXE on the Z.E.N.works CD at D:\PRODUCTS\WINNT\I386.

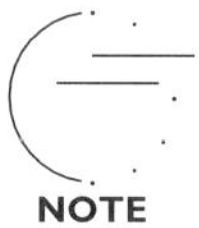
NOTE

SETUPNW.EXE is automatically run from WINSETUP.EXE, the install program that automatically runs when you insert the Novell Clients CD. If you want to use command line switches such as /ACU, however, you must run SETUPNW.EXE from the command line.

Syntax and Command Line Switches When you run SETUPNW.EXE directly from a command line, you can use switches that enable advanced installation options, such as Automatic Client Upgrade and unattended install. Keep in mind that the switches are not available if setupnw is launched from the winsetup utility.

The syntax for SETUPNW.EXE is as follows:

```
setupnw.exe [/u[: configuration file path]] [/acu] [/?]
```

/U uses a configuration file to specify the default functionality. The default text file, UNATTEND.TXT, is used if no alternative is presented with the /U:*configuration file path* option. The UNATTEND.TXT file can be found on the Z.E.N.works CD at:

```
d:\products\winnt\i386\nls\english\unattend.txt
```

You can modify the UNATTEND.TXT file with the Novell Client Install Manager as described previously in this section.

The /ACU option specifies that the install is to check the version stamp and proceed without interaction to use the defaults. If all the values are not found by default, the program will prompt you. If used in conjunction with the /U option, the defaults will be taken from the configuration file.

/W installs the Workstation Manager utility. See Chapter 19 for more information on the Workstation Manager utility.

/? displays information about using SETUPNW.EXE.

Automatic Client Upgrade

The Automatic Client Upgrade is a process by which you can update your workstations to the latest Novell Client for Windows NT software. When SETUPNW.EXE (in the D:\PRODUCTS\WINNT\I386 directory) is run with the /ACU option, ACU examines the workstation and determines whether the Novell Client software is an older version and needs to be updated. If the workstation is running an older version, the latest version is automatically installed on that workstation.

As discussed in the Windows 95/98 section of this chapter, the ACU uses version numbers to determine whether the client needs to be upgraded. The ACU compares the version number of the currently installed client with the number of the new client in the new install directory. If the new client software version number is greater than the current client version number, SETUPNW.EXE continues with the installation. The user will then see a dialog box indicating that a newer version of the client is available. If the user clicks Continue, the upgrade continues uninterrupted. The user will see an installation progress indicator as the newer files are copied. If the user should click Cancel instead, the existing client continues to function without the upgrade. However, each time the user logs in with the older version of the client, the files are compared and the option to upgrade is presented. If the version number is not greater, then SETUPNW.EXE exits without installing a new version of the software.

You can run setupnw /ACU from any login script or profile, provided that the proper drives are mapped and paths and filenames are specified using the UNC style (DRIVE:\PATH\FILENAME).

After the client has been updated, the user sees a dialog box presenting the option to reboot the workstation, unless ACU was run with the /U option (for an unattended install) and the parameter was configured so that it would not show this dialog box. To prevent the welcome and reboot dialog boxes from appearing, use the Novell Client Install Manager to set the following parameters in the UNATTEND.TXT configuration file:

```
DisplayInitialScreen = no
AskReboot = no
```

The client workstation must be rebooted in order for the newer version of the client to take effect.

Using the ACU Option To use the Automatic Client Upgrade option, complete the following steps:

1. Create an ACU folder on a NetWare server. In order for the Automatic Client Upgrade to work, the client needs access to a folder where all the installation files are stored.
   - **a.** Create a folder for the Automatic Client Upgrade. A good place to create this folder is in the public directory on volume sys: on a server that users have access to when they log in.
   - **b.** Copy all Novell Client for Windows NT installation files into the ACU install folder. You'll need at least 12MB of free disk space for this step.
   - **c.** Make sure that all users scheduled for automatic upgrade have Read and File Scan rights to the ACU install folder.

2. Modify the appropriate login script or profile script and the UNATTEND.TXT file. Depending on which login script is modified, different clients can be allowed to upgrade. If the user login script is modified, only that user will automatically be upgraded. If the container login script is modified, all clients in that container automatically upgrade. If the profile login script is modified, all clients using that login script automatically upgrade.
   - **a.** Add this line to the login script:

     #\\ *servername*\ *volume*\...\setupnw.exe /acu /u

     For example:

     ```
     #\\nor-srv1\sys\public\client\acu\setupnw.exe /acu /u
     ```

   - **b.** In addition to modifying the login script, you can use the Novell Client Install Manager to modify the UNATTEND.TXT configuration file. An UNATTEND.TXT configuration file allows the setupnw utility to set the client's configuration options automatically. The following command installs the Novell Client for Windows NT using both the ACU and Unattended options:

```
setupnw.exe /acu /u:path to unattend.txt file
```

3. Log into the NetWare 5 server. If you are using the bindery-based Microsoft Client for NetWare Networks, SETUPNW.EXE must be run from the user's bindery login script (located in the sys:mail directory) in order for the Automatic Client Upgrade to work. When using ACU with the Microsoft Client for NetWare Networks Service for NDS, SETUPNW.EXE must be placed in the login script that corresponds with the type of login (bindery or NDS).

4. Upgrade the Novell Client for Windows NT software.

Forcing an Upgrade In some cases, you might want to update one or more files without upgrading the entire client. For example, if Novell releases a new version of a file with additional functionality, you might decide that all clients need to use this file. Because this isn't a new version of the Novell Client for Windows NT software, ACU has no client revision number to check and the client will not be automatically upgraded. In this case, you can force the clients to upgrade, using ACU, so that all clients use the newer file.

In the configuration file used for unattended install (created with Novell Client Install Manager), there are two version parameter numbers:

- Major Internal Version
- Minor Internal Version

The version parameters can be any number from 0 through 4,294,967,295. These version numbers are used to decide when the client upgrades. To force the upgrade, you must make at least one version number higher than it was when the client was first installed (for example, if the number is 0, make it a 1). With this done, ACU compares the version numbers upon client login, finds the discrepancy, and upgrades the client to the system's newer files.

Installing from the Network Control Panel

Follow these steps to install the client from the Control Panel:

1. Log into the Windows NT workstation as an NT user with administrator rights.
2. Click Start → Settings → Control Panel → Network → Add → Have Disk as shown in Figure 17.23.

FIGURE 17.23

Using the Network Control Panel to install

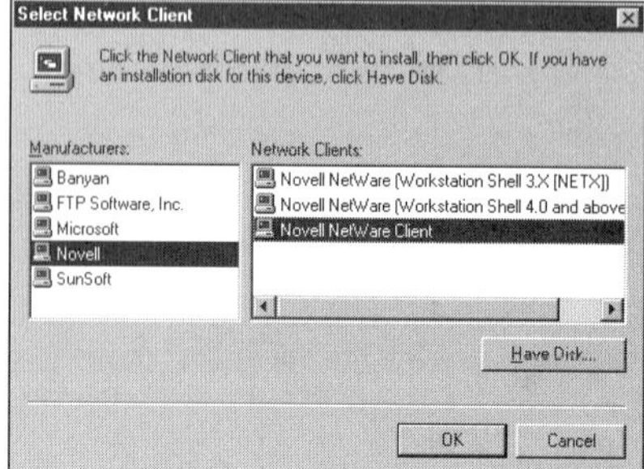

3. Enter the path to the Novell Client for Windows NT files on the CD or network. For example, enter **D:\I386**.

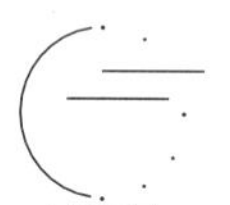

NOTE

If you are installing from the network, map root to the drive you are installing from.

4. From the Select OEM Option dialog box, select the Novell Client for Windows NT and then click OK. The client software and driver are installed on the workstation.

Novell Client for Windows NT Configuration

In this section we discuss how to configure your workstation to use the various protocol options that are available.

Before you can use the NetWare/IP Support, you must have Microsoft's TCP/IP Services installed on your Windows NT workstation. See your Windows NT documentation for instructions on installing TCP/IP.

If you are running NetWare 5, the client install presents you with a set of IP installation options. To install IP, select one of the IP installation options when you install the Novell Client for Windows NT software. To change IP setup after installing with one of the options, you must run the client install again.

Here are the available options:

- IP Only
- IP and IPX

Installing Novell IP Gateway

Follow these steps to install the Novell IP Gateway feature:

1. Right-click Network Neighborhood.
2. Click Properties → Protocols → Add. An example of this is shown in Figure 17.24.

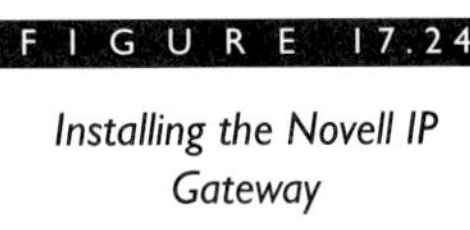

Installing the Novell IP Gateway

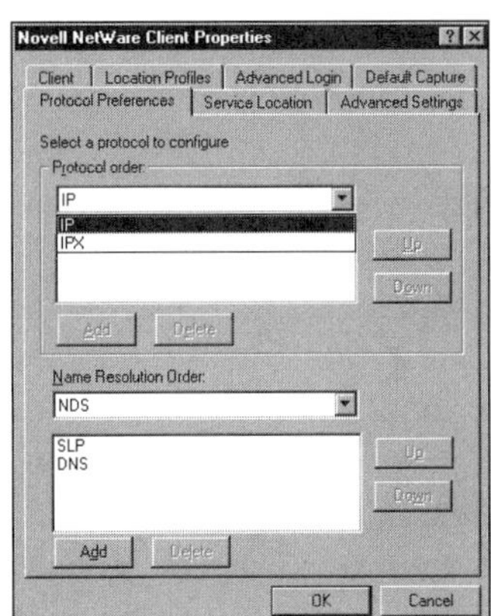

3. Select Novell IP Gateway and then click OK.

4. Select the gateway in the Network Protocols list and then click Properties.

5. Enter a preferred server and tree name as appropriate.

Enter your gateway server's NDS name or SAP name, or leave this field blank to let the gateway autodetect a server. If you entered an NDS name in the Preferred Server field, enter its tree name here.

Installing NetWare/IP

There are two ways to install NetWare/IP: at the same time as the Novell Client for Windows NT software during an unattended install or from the Network Control Panel after the client has been installed.

Installing NetWare/IP during an Unattended Install

The configuration file includes two options that allow you to install NetWare/IP during an unattended install:

- Ask NetWareIP

- Install NetWareIP

These two options work together. The following scenarios are possible:

1. AskNetWareIP=No, InstallNetWareIP=No

   With this option nothing happens. You are not asked whether you want to install NetWare/IP, and NetWare/IP is not installed.

2. AskNetWareIP=No, InstallNetWareIP=Yes

   With this setting NetWare/IP is installed automatically without asking whether you want to install it.

3. AskNetWareIP=Yes

   This option will ask whether you want to install NetWare/IP. You can choose Yes to install or No not to install. If you set AskNetWareIP to Yes, it is not necessary to set the InstallNetWareIP parameter. You can, however, set the InstallNetWareIP parameter anyway to determine whether the Yes or No button is the default button on the prompt that appears.

4. AskNetWareIP=Yes, InstallNetWareIP=Yes

   With this option the prompt asks whether you want to install NetWare/IP and displays with the Yes button as the default.

5. AskNetWareIP=Yes, InstallNetWareIP=No

   With this option the prompt asks whether you want to install NetWare/IP and displays with the No button as the default.

Installing NetWare/IP with the Network Control Panel

Install NetWare/IP from the Network Control Panel if you need to install NetWare/IP on only one workstation and do not want to reinstall the entire Novell Client for Windows NT. Use the following steps to perform this install:

1. Click Start → Settings → Control Panel.
2. Double-click Network.
3. Click Services → Add → Novell NetWare/IP Support (NWIP) → OK.
4. Configure NetWare/IP.
5. (Conditional) If TCP/IP isn't already configured, configure it.

Installing Remote Access Service

You can follow these steps to install the remote access portion of the client:

1. Click Start → Settings → Control Panel.
2. Double-click Network.
3. Click Services → Add → Remote Access Service.

4. Answer the questions for the components that are needed.

   This sets up a group for the Remote Access Services.

5. On the Novell Client Configuration property page, specify the preferred server and tree you want to log into.

   To open the property page:

   a. Right-click Network Neighborhood.

   b. Click Services → Novell Client for Windows NT → Properties → Client.

6. Start Remote Access Service.

   a. Log into the workstation.

   b. From the Remote Access Service group, click the Remote Access icon.

   c. Enter the phone number for the RAS server and then click Dial.

   d. After a connection has been established, log in and run the login script.

Do this by going to the NetWare (Common) group and clicking NetWare Login → Login to run the login script and log into the tree or server.

Uninstalling the Client

If you ever need to uninstall the Novell Client for Windows NT software, follow these procedures:

1. Click Start → Settings → Control Panel.

2. Double-click Network.

3. Click Services → Novell Client for Windows NT → Remove.

4. Restart your workstation after the client is removed.

It is not necessary to uninstall the client before installing a new version. The install utility automatically removes the existing client if it is an older version than the one being installed and can also be configured to remove a newer client if you want to install an older client.

IMPORTANT

If you remove Novell Client for Windows NT software, you will not be able to connect to NetWare 5 or any version of NetWare. To connect to NetWare, you must first install a Novell Client.

Novell Client for DOS/Windows 3.*x*

The Novell Client for DOS/Windows 3.*x* improves network performance by providing you full 32-bit access to any of NetWare's network services and resources, including Novell Directory Services, integrated messaging, and multiprotocol support. Replacing the Virtual Loadable Module software used in the 16-bit client, Novell Client for DOS/Windows is implemented as a set of NetWare Loadable Modules, making it dynamic and portable.

The following features are available with this client:

- Extended memory and improved client-side caching
- Novell Application Launcher (NAL) support, which provides simplified network management
- Expanded autoreconnect capabilities
- Simple Installation — from either Windows or DOS — including an Automatic Client Update (ACU) capability, Packet Burst technology, and Large Internet Packets (LIPs)
- Simple Network Management Protocol (SNMP)

Novell Client for DOS/Windows Installation

If you are upgrading several existing clients, installing from the network is easiest. You can edit the Windows 3.*x* SETUP.INI or the DOS INSTALL.CFG file to limit or eliminate user input during installation and automatically configure the client settings.

If you previously installed the Novell Client software using the Windows 3.1*x* installation (SETUP.EXE) and you are using multiple locations profiles, you should update the client using the Windows installation. The DOS installation does not support Novell Dial-up Services or locations and disables previously installed versions of the Locations Manager.

You must first set up a network directory and choose the appropriate method for installing the client software over the network. There are three network installation methods:

- **Winsetup.** If you are installing the client software on a small number of workstations, or if the workstations are not yet connected to a network, you can install the client from a local drive or from a network drive.
- **Automatic Client Upgrade (ACU).** This process allows network supervisors to set up and standardize the installation process. During installation, the ACU automatically configures each workstation's client settings.
- **Z.E.N.works** is an integrated set of products for managing workstations and user desktops while reducing the total cost of ownership.

Installing from CD-ROM is the quickest and easiest installation method on local or remote workstations that have a CD-ROM drive.

Installing from floppy disks is the method for workstations that do not have a CD-ROM drive. This is a much slower process and should be avoided if possible.

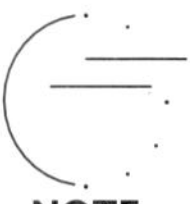

In order to use Z.E.N.works, you must manage your network from a 32-bit workstation. Many of the Z.E.N.works application and desktop management features can be administered from a 32-bit workstation to a Windows 3.*x* workstation.

Novell Client for DOS/Windows Configuration

Make sure your workstations have the following configuration before installing the Novell Client software.

Hardware Requirements

Your workstations must have the following minimum hardware to run the Novell Client software:

- 386 processor or later
- Minimum 15MB of free disk space
- Minimum 8MB of RAM
- Memory manager (such as HIMEM.SYS, EMM386.EXE, qemm, or 386max)
- Network board with the appropriate LAN driver
- Physical connection to a NetWare network
- (Optional) Additional disk space for optional Windows 3.*x* software components such as Novell Directory Print Services (NDPS).

The Windows installation program informs you of the amount of additional disk space needed to accommodate the additional components.

Software Requirements

Your network must have one of the following operating systems to run the Novell Client for DOS and Windows 3.*x*:

- Novell DOS 7
- MS-DOS 5.*x* or 6.*x*
- PC-DOS 5.*x*, 6.*x*, or 7.0
- Windows 3.1*x* or Windows for Workgroups 3.11

Minimum Components for Users of Windows for Workgroups 3.11 At least the following components of Novell Client for DOS and Windows 3.*x* client must be installed to allow users of Windows for Workgroups 3.11 to access Microsoft Network's peer clients and Novell's network directories with the same LAN card:

- NIOS.EXE
- NBIC32.NLM
- LSLC32.NLM
- CMSM.NLM
- A TSM such as ETHERTSM.NLM
- A LAN driver with each supported frame type

The Novell Client for DOS and Windows 3.*x* can connect to IPX-only, IP-only, or mixed networks. NetWare 5 IP-only servers must be running Compatibility Mode (SCMD.NLM), and the network must have a Migration Agent on a NetWare 5 server in order for the client to successfully connect to them. Compatibility Mode allows IPX applications to function in IP-only networks. Compatibility Mode also allows your workstations to communicate with services in IP-only networks if the Migration Agent is installed on any NetWare 5 servers. Compatibility Mode is dependent on the Service Location Protocol (SLP) for its operation. If you are running a NetWare 3 or 4 server, you should load all server patches provided on the Novell Web site at `www.novell.com`.

Setup for Network Installation If you are upgrading several existing clients, installing over the network is easiest. You can even edit the Windows 3.*x* SETUP.INI or the DOS INSTALL.CFG file to limit or eliminate user input during installation and automatically configure the client settings.

NOTE

If you previously installed the Novell Client software using the Windows 3.*x* installation (SETUP.EXE) and you are using multiple locations profiles, you should update the client using the Windows installation. The DOS installation does not support Novell Dial-up Services or locations and disables previously installed versions of the Locations Manager.

You must first set up a network directory and choose the appropriate method for installing the client software over the network. There are three network installation methods:

- **Automatic Client Upgrade (ACU)** allows network supervisors to set up and standardize the installation process. During installation, the ACU automatically configures each workstation's client settings.
- **User-initiated installation** allows network supervisors to set up an installation procedure that will run with little or no user intervention. Once users are notified of the installation procedure, they can install the client whenever it is convenient.
- **Z.E.N.works**, or Zero Effort Networking, is an integrated set of products for managing workstations and user desktops while reducing the total cost of ownership. Z.E.N.works includes application management and distribution features and desktop configuration, management, and maintenance features. Application Launcher, a component of Z.E.N.works, lets you distribute applications to workstations and manage those applications as objects in the NDS tree. Users do not need to worry about workstation configurations, drives, ports, command line parameters, application source directories, or whether they have the latest upgrade.

Installing with ACU

The Automatic Client Upgrade (ACU) is a process designed to upgrade all of your systems currently using a VLM, NETX, or 32-bit client. To run Automatic Client Upgrade, you need to add commands to the system, container, or personal login script for the users you want to upgrade. The ACU process varies depending on the way users log into the network and which installation program is used (DOS INSTALL.EXE or Windows SETUP.EXE).

To upgrade specific users' workstations, modify those users' login scripts using the NetWare Administrator. To upgrade workstations for users in a container, modify that container's login script. To upgrade workstations for users in a profile, modify that profile login script. To upgrade a workstation running bindery-based client software, edit the system login script (PUBLIC\NET$LOG.DAT).

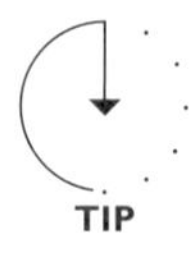
TIP

Once users have upgraded the client, you can remove the ACU information from the login scripts.

Installing from the Network

After you create a network install directory, you can instruct your network users to run either the DOS (INSTALL.EXE) or Windows (SETUP.EXE) installation program from the network to update the client software on their workstations. Follow these steps:

1. Create a network install directory and then copy the doswin32 directory to it.
2. (Optional) Modify SETUP.INI or INSTALL.CFG to supply default values for the installation and to reduce or eliminate the need for user intervention.
3. Copy the modified SETUP.INI or INSTALL.CFG file to the network install directory.

Once you have modified the default values, instruct the users to complete the following steps:

1. Log in to the network.
2. Map root a drive to the network installation directory.

   For example:

   ```
   MAP ROOT I:SYS:PUBLIC\CLIENT\DOSWIN32
   ```

3. If you are installing from Windows, make sure you are running Windows 3.1*x*, and then run WINSETUP.EXE from the installation directory. If you are installing from DOS, make sure you are in the directory, and then enter **install**.
4. If you are asked to provide information during the installation, follow the on-screen instructions.
5. Reboot your computer.

Installing from CD-ROM

If you are installing the client software only, on a small number of workstations, or if the workstations are not yet connected to a network, you can install the Novell Client for DOS and Windows 3.*x* software from the CD-ROM using either the Windows installation utility or the DOS installation utility.

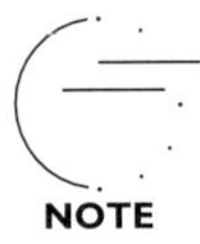

NOTE

If you are installing the software on several workstations that have network connections, using one of the network installation options is generally better.

Keep in mind that if you are running DOS only you must run install as explained here. Otherwise you can run WINSETUP.EXE if you are installing the Novell Client for Windows 3.*x* for the first time on one or more workstations, or if you want to upgrade a workstation. WINSETUP.EXE provides a graphical interface for an easy installation.

To run winsetup, simply insert your Novell Clients and Z.E.N.works CD-ROM. The CD-ROM will autorun and load winsetup and select the language option you desire as shown in the example in Figure 17.25.

FIGURE 17.25

The winsetup screen from the Novell Clients and Z.E.N.works CD-ROM

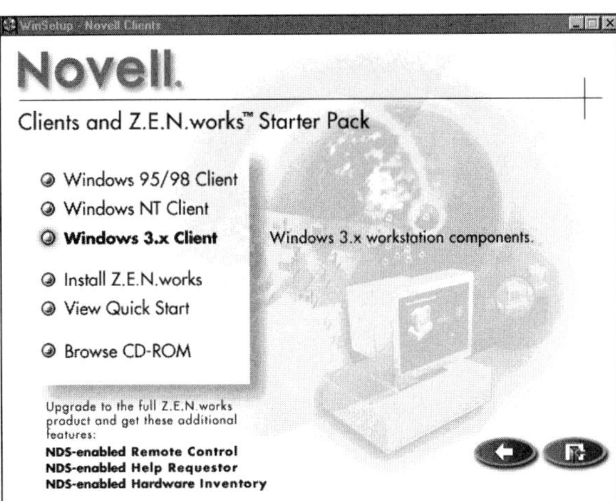

Follow the installation instructions on the screen to complete the client install for Windows 3.*x*.

If you are installing the client on a DOS machine, then you can use the following procedure:

1. Insert the Z.E.N.works CD-ROM and go to the following subdirectory:

   ```
   D:\products\doswin32
   ```

2. Run install in this subdirectory.

3. You will be presented with an installation screen. You can select options such as the Novell Client for DOS only or the Novell Client with Windows support. An example of this screen is shown in Figure 17.26.

FIGURE 17.26

The Novell Client for DOS installation screen

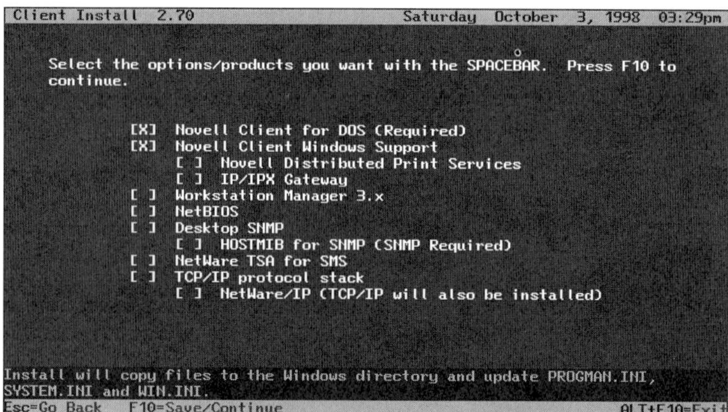

4. You will then be presented with the custom support screen. You can bypass the custom support screen.

5. Then you will be prompted to choose between a 32-bit or 16-bit LAN driver as shown in Figure 17.27. A LAN driver list is presented. Select your appropriate LAN driver.

FIGURE 17.27

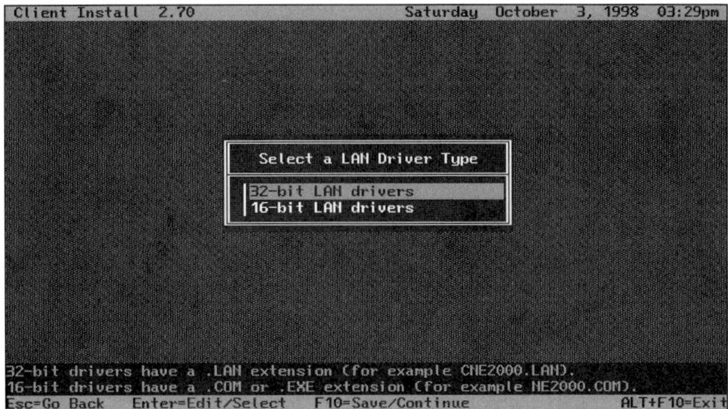

Selection between 32-bit and 16-bit LAN drivers

6. After all your selections have been made you will see a summary screen. If you are finished, then the copy will begin on this workstation.

7. You will then see an installation complete screen indicating that the install has finished successfully.

Peer-to-Peer Networking

The Novell clients also support peer-to-peer networking. If your workstation uses Windows for Workgroups 3.11 and you want access to Microsoft Networking's peer clients as well as Novell's network directories, you should load odinsup.386. This allows Windows for Workgroups 3.11 users to access peer clients and network directories with the same LAN card.

In addition to loading odinsup.386, at least the following minimum components of Novell Client for DOS and Windows 3.1*x* must be loaded in the STARTNET.BAT file:

- NIOS.EXE
- NBIC32.NLM
- LSLC32.NLM

- CMSM.NLM
- A TSM such as ETHERTSM.NLM
- A LAN driver with each supported frame type

If the client is also desired, the modules that support the correct protocols, the client (client32.nlm), and other network management features must be loaded:

1. From Windows 3.*x*, close all other programs running on the workstation.
2. From Program Manager, double-click the Network program group.
3. Double-click Network Setup.
4. (Conditional) If Microsoft Networking is not already installed, click Networks and install it as directed.
5. Click Drivers.
6. (Conditional) If you have an NDIS driver loaded, click it in the Network Drivers list and then click Remove.
7. Click Yes.

   ODINSUP replaces the NDIS driver.
8. Click Add Adapter.
9. In the Select a Network Adapter to Install list, click Unlisted or Updated Network Adapter, and then click OK.
10. When asked for the location of the driver, enter the location of odinsup.386 and its corresponding OEMSETUP.INF file.

    These files are located on the Novell CD-ROM in the DOSWIN32\WINDRV directory.

11. Verify that the ODINSUP driver type is NDIS3.

    If the driver type is something other than NDIS3, complete the following steps:

    a. Click Setup.

    b. From the Driver Type list, click Enhanced Mode NDIS Driver.

    c. Click OK.

12. Verify that the protocol stacks available on your network appear in the Network Drivers list.

    If the protocol stacks available on your network do not appear, complete the following steps:

    a. Click Add Protocol.

    b. Click the missing protocol in the list.

    c. Click OK.

13. Finish the installation by clicking OK until the Network Setup is closed.

14. Check the STARTNET.BAT file to make sure that the modules you want are loaded.

When Windows is restarted, ODINSUP is loaded and binds to the first ODI driver registered with the Link Support Layer (LSL). The Microsoft client and NDIS protocols are channeled through ODINSUP and the ODI driver.

Uninstalling the Novell Client for DOS/Windows

Novell Client for DOS and Windows 3.*x* software does not have an uninstall program, so you must edit system files and delete directories if you want to remove the software.

NOTE

If you plan to use the client again on the workstation, you can disable the client by commenting out the line in AUTOEXEC.BAT that calls STARTNET.BAT in the client32 directory.

Novell Client does not replace the VLM or NETX client, so you can revert to these clients simply by specifying the STARTNET.BAT file in the nwclient directory. However, you might not be able to link to an IP-only NetWare 5 server with the older clients. This procedure is generalized for Windows 3.1 and Windows for Workgroups 3.11. Some tasks might not be applicable to removing Novell Client support for Windows from your particular workstation.

Remove the Novell Client by following these steps:

1. Delete the client32 directory.
2. In Program Manager, switch to the Novell Client window.
3. Select each icon in the group and click Delete.
4. With the Novell Client window still highlighted, click Delete.
5. In Program Manager, click File → Run.
6. Enter **SYSEDIT** on the command line.
7. Click the AUTOEXEC.BAT window and do these things:
   - **a.** Delete path C:\NOVELL\CLIENT32; %path%.
   - **b.** Delete the line that calls the STARTNET.BAT file.
8. Click the CONFIG.SYS window and do these things:
   - **a.** Delete device=C:\NOVELL\CLIENT32\LOCATION.EXE.
   - **b.** Delete device=C:\NOVELL\CLIENT32\DIDB.SYS.
9. Click the SYSTEM.INI window and do these things:
   - **a.** Delete vnetware.386 from the network = line in the [386 Enh] section.
   - **b.** Delete the device = vlanint.386 line from the [386 Enh] section.
   - **c.** Delete netware.drv from the secondnet.drv = or the network.drv = line in the [boot] section.

   d. Delete the Novell Client for DOS/Windows from the secondnet.drv = or the network.drv = line in the [boot.description] section.

10. Click the WIN.INI window and do these things:
   a. Delete run = C:\NOVELL\CLIENT32\NWMSTART.EXE.
   b. Delete the load = nwpop.exe line from the [Windows] section.

11. Save your changes to the files and close SYSEDIT.

12. Delete the client files from the Windows root and Windows System directories.

13. If you installed support for TCP/IP, rename WINSOCK.OLD and WLIBSOCK.OLD in the Windows root and Windows System directories to WINSOCK.DLL and WLIBSOCK.DLL, respectively.

Disabling the Client

You can temporarily remove the client functionality from a workstation. If you want to remove it completely, see the previous section. Follow these steps to disable the client:

1. Open AUTOEXEC.BAT in a text editor.

2. Comment out the line that calls STARTNET.BAT. For example:

   ```
   rem @call startnet
   ```

3. Save the change and close the AUTOEXEC.BAT file.

4. Open CONFIG.SYS in the text editor.

5. Comment out LOCATION.EXE in the [common] section. For example:

   ```
   rem c:\novell\client32\location.exe
   ```

6. Save the change and exit the editor.

You can also disable support for protocols by commenting out references to the drivers associated with the protocols in the STARTNET.BAT file. If you also want to disable the protocol settings, you can comment them out in the STARTNET.BAT file.

If you have multiple location profiles, there are both STARTNET.BAT and NET.CFG files for each location profile you create. Edit these files for the location profile you are using. If you did not create a location profile during installation, then these are the files in the default location profile subdirectory, PROFILE\LOC_. The old file is located in loc_0.

Disabling Protocol Support You can use the following steps if you want to disable support for a particular protocol. This may occur if you are in the process of changing protocols on your network:

1. Open STARTNET.BAT in a text editor.

   The simplest way to ensure that you are opening the STARTNET.BAT file for the correct location profile is to run the Locations program. Select the profile and then click Advanced → Edit STARTNET.BAT. The file is opened in an editor.

2. Comment out the driver load line for the protocol you do not want.

   For example, if you want to disable protocol support for TCP/IP, place a REM statement before the line that loads the TCP/IP protocol (Ethernet II):

   ```
   rem load cne2000.lan frame=ethernet_II
   ```

3. Save your changes and exit the editor.

4. Reboot the workstation.

Disabling Protocol Settings You can also disable the protocol settings in your NET.CFG file by using the following steps:

1. Disable protocol support.

2. Open NET.CFG in a text editor.

   The simplest way to ensure that you are opening the NET.CFG file for the correct location profile is to run the Locations program. Select the profile and then click Advanced → Edit NET.CFG. The file is opened in an editor.

3. Comment out the section that maintains the settings for the protocol you want to disable.

4. Save your changes and exit the editor.

5. Reboot the workstation.

Reverting to a Previously Installed VLM or NETX Client In some rare occasions you may need to revert to a previously installed set of VLMs or a NETX client. This usually occurs in situations where the workstation has insufficient memory to run to the newer Novell clients:

1. Open AUTOEXEC.BAT in a text editor.

2. Change the path to STARTNET.BAT to the file you used in the previous installation. For example:

   ```
   @call c:\nwclient\startnet.bat
   ```

3. Save the change and close the AUTOEXEC.BAT file.

4. Open CONFIG.SYS in the text editor.

5. Comment out the LOCATION.EXE in the [common] section. For example:

   ```
   rem c:\novell\client32\location.exe
   ```

6. Save your changes and exit the editor.

7. Reboot the workstation.

NOTE

To restore full VLM functionality for Windows, you will need to run the VLM install. Make sure you answer Yes when asked to replace the existing files with the VLM files.

Novell Client for Mac OS

The Novell Client for Mac OS is workstation software that enables Mac OS users to take advantage of all NetWare services and resources, including Novell Directory Services. This is the first Mac OS client that can use either the native IPX protocol or TCP/IP.

In addition, the Novell Client for Mac OS lets network supervisors manage Mac OS clients in the same way they administer Windows, DOS, and other clients, greatly reducing administrative tasks. The Novell Client for Mac OS also eliminates the need for running NetWare for Macintosh on the server (although it is compatible with NetWare for Macintosh).

The Novell Client for MAC OS provides the following features:

- Access network servers or printers from an intranet or the Internet
- Realize improved network performance through Packet Burst and Large Internet Packet (LIP) technologies
- Navigate a network easily with the NetWare Directory Browser
- Log into or browse multiple NDS trees simultaneously
- Drag NDS server and printer objects to your Macintosh desktop
- Use a single protocol (IPX or TCP/IP) for the entire network
- Access all authorized resources with a single password
- Use AppleTalk, IPX, and TCP/IP simultaneously
- Accomplish remote management of servers

The Novell Client for Mac OS enables Mac OS users to access NetWare servers and printers from their organization's intranet or the Internet using NetWare/IP version 2.2. With Novell Client for Mac OS, remote and mobile Mac OS users can access servers and printers on their NetWare network from any location on the Internet (if no firewalls exist to prevent server access).

The Novell Client for Mac OS uses Packet Burst and LIP technologies for faster network performance. Packet Burst technology greatly reduces network traffic by transferring multiple packets before requiring a response, enabling users to send large amounts of data more quickly across both local and wide area networks. LIP technology significantly increases the maximum packet size that can be sent over bridges or routers, thereby greatly increasing the rate of internetwork data transfer.

Network supervisors can also improve server performance by removing NetWare for Macintosh NetWare Loadable Modules (NLMs). Rather than using NLMs to give Mac OS users access to network services, Novell Client for Mac OS uses native NetWare Core Protocols to communicate directly with the server.

You can use the NetWare Directory Browser application for Mac OS, an application that lets you navigate the network easily and view information in the NDS tree. Using a point-and-click interface, you can browse through information and select objects, such as server volumes and printers.

The NetWare Directory Browser also has a context-sensitive Help dialog box that provides a definition of objects in the browser when you point to them. The Help dialog box makes the browser easier to use by explaining how to select and access resources. In addition, for Mac OS workstations running Mac OS System 7.5 or above, Apple Guide Help is also available when the NetWare Directory Browser is open.

With Novell Client for Mac OS, users can simultaneously log into their local NDS tree as well as additional trees to access other servers on the network. For instance, if each department in your company uses its own NDS tree, Mac OS users in the marketing department can print expense reports to the printer in the accounting department simply by logging into the accounting department's tree and selecting the desired printer.

The Novell Client for Mac OS gives network supervisors and Mac OS users the ability to drag and drop objects from the NetWare Directory Browser to their Macintosh desktops or to a folder. Users can then double-click the icon to change printers, for example, or access server volumes.

Novell Client for Mac OS is the first Mac OS client to offer the choice of either the native IPX protocol or TCP/IP. This gives users and network supervisors the freedom to choose the right protocol for their networks. Because Novell Client for Mac OS uses IPX or TCP/IP for network communications, network supervisors can manage Mac OS clients as they would any other client, rather than managing the Mac OS users separately. And network supervisors can use familiar tools, such as the NetWare Administrator utility, to manage all clients, rather than having to use separate tools for different platforms.

Novell Client for Mac OS is the first client software that enables Mac OS users to access all the resources and services of a NetWare network through NDS. With NDS, users enter a single password only once to log into the network, regardless of how many servers are on the network, and to gain access to any network resource to which they have been given rights.

Because Novell Client for Mac OS is compatible with the simultaneous, transparent use of AppleTalk, IPX, and TCP/IP, users can easily access the services they need. For example, users can log into the network server through IPX, browse the Internet using TCP/IP, and print using AppleTalk.

In the past, Mac OS users were unable to take full advantage of the network. Mac OS workstations could access only printers that were configured for AppleTalk, servers that ran NetWare for Macintosh, and parts of the network with routers configured for AppleTalk.

The Novell Client for Mac OS communicates on the network using IPX or TCP/IP, enabling Mac OS users to access printers, servers, and other resources that were previously unavailable to them.

Because Novell Client for Mac OS is compatible with NetWare for Macintosh, which is compliant with AppleTalk Filing Protocol, network supervisors can upgrade their networks over time. If NetWare for Macintosh NLMs remain on the servers, users can access network resources through the Chooser or the NetWare Directory Browser.

The Novell Client for Mac OS includes a remote console application, which allows remote management of servers from a Mac OS workstation. After installing the remote console, you can back up servers or workstations, load and unload NLMs, install and remove products, and change server configuration parameters from the Mac OS workstation. In addition, you can simultaneously open windows to multiple servers—a capability not available in the DOS version of the remote console.

The Novell Client for Mac OS takes advantage of the sophisticated security features of NDS, such as packet signing, RSA public/private key encryption, and passwords with as many as 128 characters. With NDS security features, the user's password never crosses the wire. In addition, NetWare security has been incorporated with Apple's alias technology to provide secure access to files, folders, and resources.

Novell Client for Mac OS Installation

You have several options when installing Novell Client for Mac OS. With the CD-ROM, you can install the software directly on a Mac OS workstation or run Install on the server. You can also install Novell Client for Mac OS from a PC or from another Mac OS computer with File Sharing.

The Novell Client for Mac OS features autodetection, which means that it automatically uses the correct frame type. In addition, it supports Ethernet, token-ring, and LocalTalk cabling.

To run the Novell Client for Mac OS on Mac OS 8, download the patch that is available, free of charge, from the Novell Support ConnectionWeb site at `support.novell.com` under filename MCLUPD3.BIN.

Novell Client for OS/2

The Novell Client for OS/2 provides seamless integration of OS/2 workstations into NetWare and NetWare networks. The OS/2 Client supports OS/2 1.3 and above, including Warp 3.0. An OS/2 workstation running Novell Client for OS/2 gives users transparent access to NetWare and NetWare resources such as file, print, database, and communication services.

The Novell Client for OS/2 can be used to connect an OS/2 workstation to NetWare networks and OS/2 servers running applications such as Lotus Notes or Microsoft/Sybase SQL Server.

The Novell Client for OS/2 enables an OS/2 workstation to concurrently access multiple servers. For example, you can access information from a NetWare or NetWare file server and simultaneously query a database on an application server.

This client has the following features:

- Connects with any NetWare 2.15c or above network, including NetWare 5.
- Supports OS/2 application servers (SPX, NetBIOS, and Named Pipes).
- Coexists with IBM's Communication Manager and LAN Services.
- Supports connection to a NetWare network from Virtual DOS and WINOS2 sessions.
- Supports Novell Directory Services (NDS).
- Supports Packet Burst and Large Internet Packet (LIP) services.
- Provides built-in diagnostic capabilities.
- Includes a graphical tool for using NetWare resources.

You can use Novell Client for OS/2 with any NetWare network using NetWare 2.15c and above, including NetWare 5, NetWare 4, NetWare 3, NetWare for UNIX, and NetWare 4.11 for OS/2. It supports all NetWare application programming interfaces (APIs) and provides connectivity to NetWare servers through the IPX protocols and to OS/2 application servers through SPX, NetBIOS, and Named Pipes.

Accessing the network is easy using the Presentation Manager workstation tools and the LAN WorkPlace Shell in OS/2 2.*x*. OS/2 workstations can act as nondedicated print servers (through the NetWare remote printer capability) and can support as many as 1,000 simultaneous Named Pipes connections.

Support for OS/2 Application Servers

With Novell Client for OS/2, you can access an OS/2 application server. Novell Client for OS/2 supports SPX, NetBIOS, and Named Pipes for application servers. For example, you can run SQL Server as an application on an OS/2 server to service Named Pipes clients running Windows, OS/2, or DOS.

Novell Client for OS/2 coexists with all OS/2 programs, including the following products:

- IBM's Communication Manager (connects to IBM mainframes)
- Remote Data Services
- PC Support — AS/400
- IBM LAN Services (connects to IBM's LAN servers)

Novell Client for OS/2 supports both LANSUP and ODINSUP for sharing a network adapter with non-IPX applications. You can use LANSUP with a Network Device Interface Specification (NDIS) driver or ODINSUP with an Open Data-Link Interface (ODI) driver.

Support for Virtual DOS and WINOS2 Connections to NetWare Networks

OS/2 is capable of emulating different operating systems and running concurrent OS/2 sessions on one machine. Thus, Novell Client for OS/2 enables you to have multiple, simultaneous, private connections to NetWare. For example, you can simultaneously have a DOS connection, a Windows connection, and an OS/2 connection, all from the same OS/2 machine. Multiple, concurrent connections can be combined or virtualized to create one global connection. A global connection enables you to use one NetWare connection while maintaining full NetWare API support in all sessions. The Novell Client for OS/2 fully supports NetWare NDS. While you are in an OS/2 session, you can log into a NetWare server and use NDS functionality to seamlessly access the entire network. You can view and access any authorized network service or resource, regardless of its physical location. Novell Client for OS/2 includes a graphical user tool for viewing and accessing your directory tree and other network resources.

The Novell Client for OS/2 includes built-in support for Packet Burst and LIP services. On servers that support Packet Burst and LIPs, Novell Client for OS/2 will automatically take advantage of this technology, transmitting data faster and more efficiently than by conventional methods.

Novell Client for OS/2 automatically captures diagnostic information. When Novell Client for OS/2 is used in conjunction with Novell's ManageWise 2.1 or 2.5, ManageWise can graphically display the client as a part of the network. This information can aid network supervisors in troubleshooting and fine-tuning their networks.

Installation of the Novell Client for OS/2

The Novell Client for OS/2's Presentation Manager installation program provides an easy-to-use graphical interface for installing and configuring OS/2 workstations to run the client, Presentation Manager workstation tools, Remote Initial Program Load (RIPL), and printing services.

The Novell Client for OS/2 is required if you want to run OS/2 workstations on NetWare networks. It also supplies the network connection protocols and interprocess communications mechanisms (Named Pipes, NetBIOS, and Novell's IPX/SPX) needed to run OS/2 distributed applications.

Summary

This chapter has outlined the steps necessary to install, configure, or upgrade to the Novell Clients. These clients provide you with a secure and reliable desktop that can take advantage of Novell's Z.E.N.works product to manage your desktop environment.

CHAPTER 18

Backing Up and Restoring Novell Directory Services

"Put all thine eggs in one basket and—watch that basket."—Mark Twain

Because Novell Directory Services (NDS) is a global and distributed name service, it requires a specialized approach to backup and restore processes. Not only must you back up your files and directories, but you should have a backup of your NDS tree for all situations that may occur, including catastrophes. In most cases you may simply need to restore a few objects or a subtree. Because NetWare 5 is not server-centric, as were previous versions such as NetWare 3, NDS information may be stored on multiple servers. Therefore, you must have a backup solution that can read this specialized NDS information across multiple servers and store it properly. The backup solutions for NetWare 5 must be able to "see" the entire NDS tree by communicating with the other servers. A restore solution must also have the same capability.

This chapter refers frequently to NDS objects and partitions. Proper partitioning and replication can provide you with a greater degree of fault tolerance. For more information on these topics, see Chapters 3 and 6 of this book.

This chapter describes how to back up and restore NDS using the Novell Enhanced SBACKUP system and explains what steps you should take to institute a comprehensive backup plan in your company. The text will also cover how to devise a backup procedure through the use of replication, your first (and easiest) line of defense against NDS data loss. First, you'll learn about the components of the NetWare 5 backup architecture.

NOTE

This chapter will not try to discuss specific implementation of NetWare 5 backup/restore products. There are a variety of products available from third-party companies that you may also consider using.

Understanding the Basics

Before backing up and restoring NDS information, you should understand the basic components and architecture of NDS backup solutions. The process of backing up and, especially, restoring NDS information is complex, and you can always first rely on your replicas for NDS fault tolerance. For more information on providing fault tolerance with replica placement, refer to Chapter 6.

NOTE

Replication, however, is not sufficient protection for a single-server network or when all copies of the replicas are destroyed or corrupted. In these instances, if the NDS data has been backed up regularly, the NDS tree structure can be restored using backup and restore procedures.

The NDS name service (Directory) actually exists as a set of files stored on one or many NetWare 5 servers. These NDS files are stored on the SYS volume as hidden files for your network's protection. These are files that you definitely don't want deleted, accidentally or otherwise. When you do a Storage Management Services (SMS) backup of NDS, you are backing up this NDS file information. You do not back up information regarding the partition boundaries of the NDS tree. Instead, you back up every server that contains a portion of the NDS database. You basically have an image of your entire NDS tree that appears as a single partition on a tape backup.

Consequently, during a restore of NDS, the image partition is split into its appropriate partitions as they exist on your actual tree. Some backup solutions also let you restore subtrees or individual objects. Novell's TSANDS.NLM, which ships with NetWare 5, supports this capability, as discussed later in this chapter. If there is no partition information on your tree because of a total loss of NDS, the entire image is restored to a single ([ROOT]) partition.

During a restore you will often see unknown objects, or objects that are lacking a mandatory attribute. When you use the NWADMIN utility, unknown objects appear with a "?" icon. During a restore, any number of your objects will have pointers to attributes of other objects that do not yet appear in your tree. For example, one user object may have been granted rights to another user object. Because the process restores only one object at a time, you may see a whole series of unknown objects until the restore is completed and these discrepancies are resolved.

Storage Management Services

Novell's Storage Management Services (SMS) is an open architecture for interfacing storage management engines with Novell Directory Services. Third-party developers can develop backup solutions with their own functions and features written to the SMS standard interface. This platform provides a consistent architecture for storing, accessing, and managing data on many different client platforms, including NetWare servers, Windows 95/98, and Windows NT clients. Although the file systems may be different, SMS provides a consistent view of this data.

The SMS architecture was developed with the assistance of third-party developers, and many backup products now comply with the SMS standard. In fact, you should not purchase any NetWare 5 backup product that is not SMS compliant.

The SMS architecture actually consists of these three components:

- The Storage Management Engine (SME)
- Target Service Agent (TSA)
- The Storage Management Data Requester (SMDR)

These components are discussed in the following sections.

The Storage Management Engine

One of the key components of the SMS architecture is the Storage Management Engine (SME). The SME is software that communicates with network clients through a common interface. The software provides cross-platform support and is easily modified to add new features or support. Novell's Enhanced SBACKUP utility is an SME. Most third-party developers provide functions and features to support NetWare 5 backups by including an SME with their product. The most common use of the SME is a backup and restore application.

The SME operates on a NetWare 5 server as a NetWare Loadable Module (NLM). The SME manages all user requests and interaction between the Target Service Agents, discussed next, and the device driver for your tape backup system.

The Target Service Agent

The Target Service Agent (TSA) is software that can scan, read, and write data found on a target file system. A target can be any item on the network that needs backing up; in most cases this means a file server or group of file servers and NDS. Targets can also be SQL database engines or print servers or even workstations.

A TSA must understand the file structure for the particular platform that it is accessing. Therefore, the TSA is specifically written for each type of platform that you need to back up. The TSA understands all the unique features of the platform you are backing up, such as name spaces, file and directory attributes, and security rights. The TSA can also present the data to the SME in a common format. For this reason, the SME can interact with many different types of TSAs, as shown in Figure 18.1.

FIGURE 18.1

Each TSA can talk to its operating system platform. The TSA then presents this information to the SME in a common format.

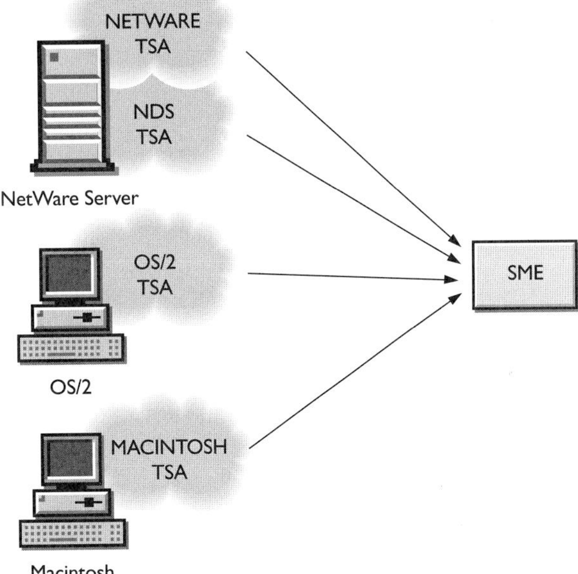

Because the SMS components are very modular in nature, they make it easy to support many operating systems. A vendor releasing a new version of an operating system only needs to provide a TSA to support that operating system. That way all vendors selling an SMS-compliant backup solution can support the new operating system. Novell, for example, currently provides TSAs for the following operating systems:

- NetWare 3.11 and 3.12
- NetWare 4.01, 4.02, 4.1, 4.11, and NetWare 5

- Novell Directory Services
- NetWare SQL
- DOS/MS Windows 95/98 clients
- OS/2 clients
- Macintosh clients
- UnixWare clients

SMS TSAs are loaded as NLMs on the host or target server. You can also load them as memory-resident modules on your client workstations. For backing up your file systems, Novell provides the TSA400, TSA410, and TSA500 modules.

The latest version of the TSA500.NLM supports NetWare 5 and is backward-compatible with NetWare 4.1. A new feature that became available with the TSA410.NLM is the capability to back up server specific information. Server Specific Info is a new resource that the NetWare 4 and NetWare 5 system Target Service Agents provide. This resource is provided in the Storage Management Engine's (SME's) Resource list. The SYS volume and other volumes are major resources that can be selected from most backup utilities and backed up.

Select Server Specific Info packages contain critical data for recovery purposes. SERVDATA.NDS, DSMISC.LOG, STARTUP.NCF, AUTOEXEC.NCF, and VOLSINFO.TXT are all backed up by selecting Server Specific Info. There are two ways to back up server specific information. The first way is to select a full file system backup on your NetWare Server. The second way is to select the Server Specific Information option from the resource list for a file system backup. Table 18.1 lists each TSA version that you need to load for a particular operating system.

TABLE 18.1

TSA Version Requirements by Operating System

BACKUP/RESTORE	AT THIS CONSOLE	ENTER THIS COMMAND
5.00 host server	5.00 host server	LOAD TSA500
5.00 target server	Target server	LOAD TSA500
3.12 target server	Target server	LOAD TSA312
3.11 target server	Target server	LOAD TSA311

BACKUP/RESTORE	AT THIS CONSOLE	ENTER THIS COMMAND
NDS database	Any 4.*x* or 5 server (preferably a server with a copy of the largest partition)	LOAD TSANDS
DOS partition on NetWare	Host server	LOAD TSADOSP
OS/2, Unix, and Macintosh	Host server, target workstation	LOAD TSAPROXY
Windows 95/98	Target workstation	W95TSA.EXE (installed with the Novell Client). See Help in your Windows 95/98 client.
Windows NT	Target workstation	TSAPrefs.exe, TSAMain.exe, NT TSA (installed with the Novell Client). See Help in your Windows NT client.

When the server specific information is restored, it places the files in the SYS:\SYSTEM*SOURCE_SERVER_NAME* directory on the target server (by default). The *SOURCE_ SERVER_NAME* directory is created using the 8.3 naming convention. If your backed-up server name is SMS500_S1 and you restore the Server Specific Info to server S2, the source server name in the path just given will be SMS500_S1. The new directory on S2 will be SYS:SYSTEM\SMS500_S1. All the Server Specific Info files will be put into this directory (SERVDATA.NDS, DSMISC.LOG, AUTOEXEC.NCF, STARTUP.NCF, and VOLSINFO.TXT). The following is a description of the server-specific files that are backed up.

SERVDATA.NDS contains server-specific NDS information. This file is used by INSTALL to recover from an unplanned SYS volume failure. The restore procedures show how to use this file to recover from a SYS volume failure in a multiserver environment with existing replicas on other servers that will be used to provide a complete recovery.

DSMISC.LOG is a text file that contains the replica list and replica types that the backed-up server held at the time of backup. This file is used in the restore procedures to provide helpful information needed to prepare NDS for recovery of the failed server. It also provides a list of the other servers that were in the failed server's replica ring. Here is a sample DSMISC.LOG:

```
Wednesday, August 28, 1998   2:30:21 pm
Backing up server-specific NDS data
Successfully read addresses of the local server object.
Current partition/replica list
Partition OU=NORAD.O=ACME, current replica list:
    CN=SMS50_S5.O=ACME, type read/write
    CN=SMS50_S4.O=ACME, type read/write
    CN=SMS50_S3.O=ACME, type master
Partition OU=LABS.OU=RIO.O=ACME, current replica list:
    CN=SMS50_S5.O=ACME, type read/write
    CN=SMS50_S4.O=ACME, type read/write
    CN=SMS50_S3.O=ACME, type master
Partition OU=CHARITY.OU=NORAD.O=ACME, current replica list:
    CN=SMS50_S5.O=ACME, type read/write
    CN=SMS50_S4.O=ACME, type read/write
    CN=SMS50_S3.O=ACME, type master
Partition OU=PR.O=ACME, current replica list:
    CN=SMS50_S5.O=ACME, type subordinate reference
    CN=SMS50_S4.O=ACME, type read/write
    CN=SMS50_S3.O=ACME, type master
Partition [Root], current replica list:
```

```
CN=SMS50_S5.O=ACME, type read/write
CN=SMS50_S4.O=ACME, type read/write
CN=SMS50_S3.O=ACME, type master
```

AUTOEXEC.NCF is the NetWare server executable batch file located in the NetWare partition of the server's disk. This file is used to load modules and set the NetWare operating system configuration.

STARTUP.NCF is the NetWare server boot file that loads the NetWare server's disk driver and name spaces and various SET parameters.

VOL$INFO.TXT is a text file that contains needed information about the volumes on the server at the time of backup, including name spaces, compression, and migration information. This file can be used during restore procedures to provide helpful information in preparing volumes correctly for a restore. A sample VOL$INFO.TXT is given here:

```
SMS500_s123456789
Current File System Information by Volume
Wednesday, August 28, 1998 2:15:25 pm
SYS:
Supported Name Spaces:
    DOS
    MACINTOSH
    NFS
    LONG
Extended File Formats:
    Compression is enabled.
VOL1:
Supported Name Spaces:
    DOS
    MACINTOSH
```

```
Extended File Formats:
    Compression is enabled.
VOL2:
Supported Name Spaces:
    DOS
```

A special TSA known as TSANDS.NLM supports the backup and restoration of Novell Directory Services, including objects and trustee assignments. The backup includes NDS partitions and other crucial information. TSANDS can walk the entire NDS tree to access the appropriate NDS files for backup. Novell's Enhanced SBACKUP utility and the other third-party SMS-based backup solutions use this TSA.

The TSANDS.NLM has a number of features covered in the following sections.

Extended Schema Backup

Extensions to the NDS base schema are included in the backup and restore function set of TSANDS.NLM. Backup and restore of the NDS schema will be handled by TSANDS.NLM as a complete data set. A new target service resource schema is now exported by TSANDS.NLM. The backup of the schema resource consists of the packaging of all attributes followed by all class definitions from the working NDS schema. A restore of the schema data set will consist of the addition of all attributes from the backup that are not part of the current working schema. After the additions of the backup attribute set have been restored, the class definitions will be restored by updating the current classes with missing attributes from the backup or by the addition of a complete class when none is present.

Selecting the Full Directory Backup option includes the schema resource in its backup by default. If the backup application enables selection of resources, the schema resource can be selected and backed up separately. The schema resource can be handled the same way for restores.

Error Handling

TSANDS.NLM now has the capability to log objects to an error log when an object cannot be backed up for whatever reason. For example, you are backing up a big tree with thousands of objects and by chance one or more of the replicas are off line so that no referrals can be found, or an object is corrupt and cannot be read properly. The object name or container name will be logged to the backup error log file. The TSANDS.NLM will then continue to get the next object and continue the backup if possible. This enables TSANDS.NLM to discover and back up all the objects that are resolvable in the tree. After the backup is complete, you can view the error log file and see what objects or container objects have not been backed up.

The Resource Configuration Option

The following options ("How to scan what you are backing up:" and the TSANDS.CFG configuration file) are included to improve the scaling of the TSANDS.NLM. These options enable administrators to back up subsections of NDS trees by assigning rights to backup users. Supervisor rights are required to back up NDS objects. It is the tree administrator's responsibility to assign Supervisor rights to any additional backup administrators. Backup administrators should be assigned supervisory rights to the subsection of the NDS tree that they will be responsible for backing up. For example, suppose you have five containers, NORAD, RIO, CAMELOT, TOKYO, and SYDNEY, that need to be backed up. You can create five backup administrators — BAdmin1, BAdmin2, BAdmin3, BAdmin4, BAdmin5 — and give each backup administrator Supervisor rights to his respective container.

This enables the backup administrator to back up only the objects for which he has been given Supervisor rights. If BAdmin1 has been given Supervisor rights to container NORAD, then he can only back up objects in the container NORAD and below as long as his Supervisor rights are not filtered at a subordinate level to NORAD.

Since BAdmin1 has not been given Supervisor rights to organization ACME, he cannot start the backup from ACME context. The TSANDS.CFG file can be created to help identify the starting context for each backup administrator. The TSANDS.CFG resides in SYS:SYSTEM\TSA\ directory. The content is shown here:

```
.OU=NORAD.O=ACME

.OU=RIO.O=ACME

.OU=CAMELOT.ACME
```

```
.OU=TOKYO.ACME
.OU=SYDNEY.ACME
```

You will need to create this .CFG file and enter the starting context for each backup administrator that you have in your tree. The starting context will show up in your backup utility as a selection item that each backup administrator can select as his or her starting context and initiate the backup from that point. This eliminates walking down a deep tree to select the correct starting context each time a backup needs to be performed. This also provides a starting context if browse rights are removed from each backup administrator and he cannot see below the [ROOT] object to start walking the tree down to the assigned container starting context. The backup administrator that possesses the Supervisor right to ACME does not need an entry in the TSANDS.CFG because that starting context is visible from the selection resource list.

In addition, the Supervisor rights are assigned by a tree administrator and can be assigned or filtered either at partition boundaries or at a container level. Depending on how you design and administer your tree backup procedure, these new options can help in effectively and efficiently improving your backup and restore of your NDS tree. More about using the Enhanced SBACKUP utility is discussed in the section "Using the Enhanced SBACKUP Utility" later in this chapter.

The Storage Management Data Requester

The Storage Management Data Requester (SMDR) is the link between a vendor's backup application engine (SME) and the SMS TSAs. Its job is to locate and provide instructions to the TSAs on your network. The SMDR also provides the link to the storage device interface. For example, during a backup sequence, the SME receives from the TSAs data processed into the correct format. This information is communicated through the storage device interface to the backup device.

Figure 18.2 shows all of the components of the SMS architecture.

For data restoration, the SME talks to the device driver to tell it which data to restore from tape. After receiving the data, the SME passes it back to the TSA, which writes the data to the target. Again, the target could be a NetWare server, a SQL database, a print server, and so on.

FIGURE 18.2

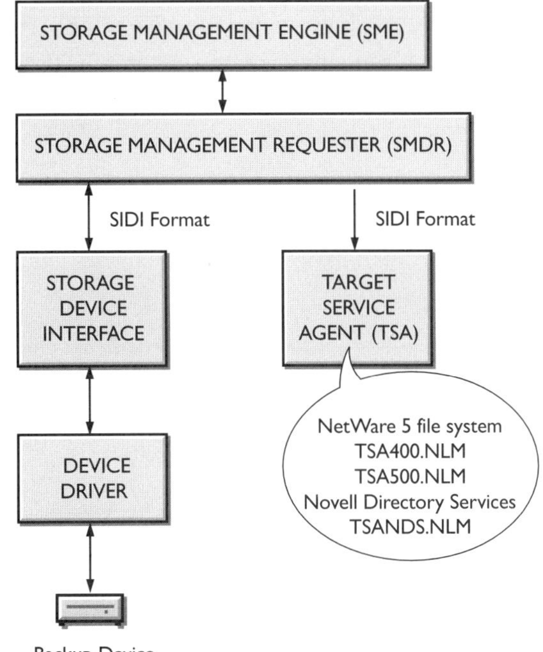

The SMS architecture consists of multiple components, including the Storage Management Engine (SME), the Target Service Agent (TSA), and the Storage Management Data Requester (SMDR).

Backing Up Novell Directory Services

An NDS replica is generally your first mechanism for fault tolerance in NDS because of the time-sensitive nature of NDS. The replica can maintain the most recent event information about its objects and properties. You can use replicas to restore or rebuild information from a replica of the same partition that has been damaged. In contrast, a tape backup is like a snapshot in time and will become out of date, unlike the actual replica.

Nonetheless, you should have a tape backup of NDS for increased fault tolerance of your NetWare 5 network. In some cases, such as single-server environments, tape backup provides fault tolerance for NDS. In addition, a tape backup protects data and NDS information in the event of a catastrophe such as a fire or flood. Novell highly recommends that you always have a tape backup of NDS and maintain this copy by performing regular backups.

A replica is a copy of a partition. Having multiple copies of replicas increases fault tolerance for your system. As discussed in Chapter 6, there is a point at which too many replicas can result in a performance decrease. Typically, three replicas are sufficient for fault tolerance. This would include a Master Replica and two Read/Write replicas. Figure 18.3 shows an example of the replication process.

FIGURE 18.3

Using replication as a means of avoiding NDS data loss

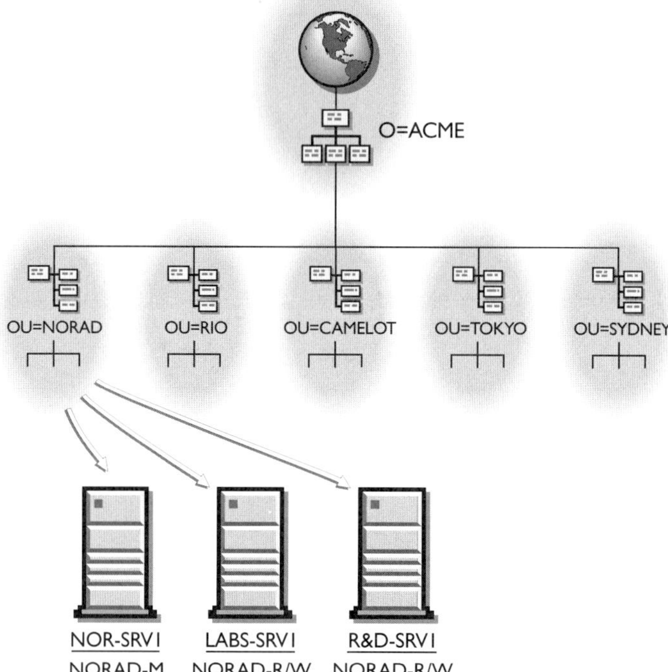

Object IDs and the Backup Process

An object ID is generated for each NetWare 5 object created in your tree. In NetWare 3 the same process occurs and the object IDs plus all the file system data are placed on tape during the backup process. Instead of storing object IDs on tape, SMS-compatible backup products store an object's distinguished name in typeful format. Each object has a distinguished name that serves as the object's unique identifier. For example, the user object LDAVINCI.R&D.LABS.NORAD. ACME is backed up in its typeful format:

```
CN=.LDAVINCI.OU=R&D.OU=LABS.OU=NORAD.O=ACME
```

For more information on distinguished names, refer to Chapter 4.

NetWare 5 objects only have one distinguished name that is unique across the entire tree. However, when a replica of a partition is placed on a server, NDS generates a unique object ID for the same object. Therefore, each NDS object has one distinguished name with possibly many object IDs, depending on the number of replicas created for that partition. Each server uses the object IDs to coordinate activity on the local server between the local object and, for example, file services. During a tape restore, if an object ID already exists for that object, the server receiving the restore does not create a new object ID. If the object on the tree were deleted and you subsequently did a restore, a new object ID would be created on the server receiving the restore. Figure 18.4 shows an example of this process.

FIGURE 18.4

A restore of an object creates a new object ID if the object does not currently exist on the tree.

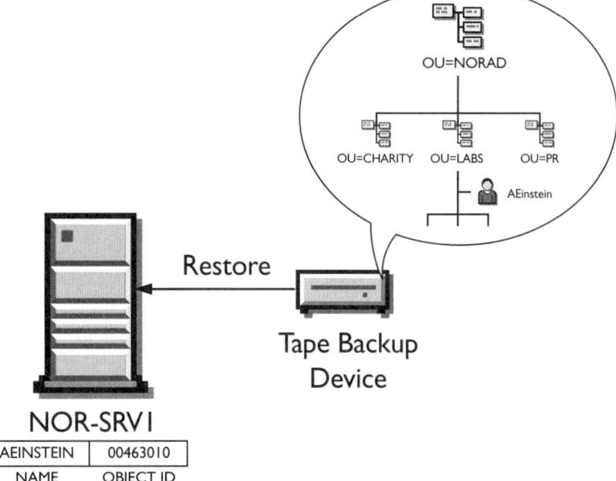

As in NetWare 3, trustee assignments for the file system are backed up along with the file system. The SMA TSA uses the object's distinguished name to back up the trustee rights from the file system in order to preserve an object's trustee assignments during restoration. For example, suppose a user object is deleted from the tree and subsequently recreated. If you then restored the user's files from tape, the TSA could match the file system assignments to the user because of the distinguished name. This also assumes that when you recreated the user you used the same name that was in use before.

NOTE

The preceding paragraph explains why you *must* restore your objects to NDS *before* you can restore file system information. The file system restore attempts to match the file assignments to the user object's distinguished names. If they are not on the server first, the files will not be assigned back to the users.

Choose a backup approach that fits your needs. Whenever possible, you should have a centralized approach to the backup of your NDS tree. Ideally, a single administrator will have rights to all servers in the tree in order to perform backup functions. However, this may not always be possible because of the size of some corporate networks and the geographic nature of the network. In large environments you may want to designate a site administrator who is responsible for backups in his or her portion of the tree. Keep in mind that each administrator must have Supervisor rights to the servers for which he or she needs to perform backups. If several people are responsible for backups, it takes more coordination and organization to ensure that each location backs up their portion of the NDS tree consistently. Figure 18.5 illustrates an example of centralized backup approach.

FIGURE 18.5

You should use a centralized backup approach for NDS whenever possible.

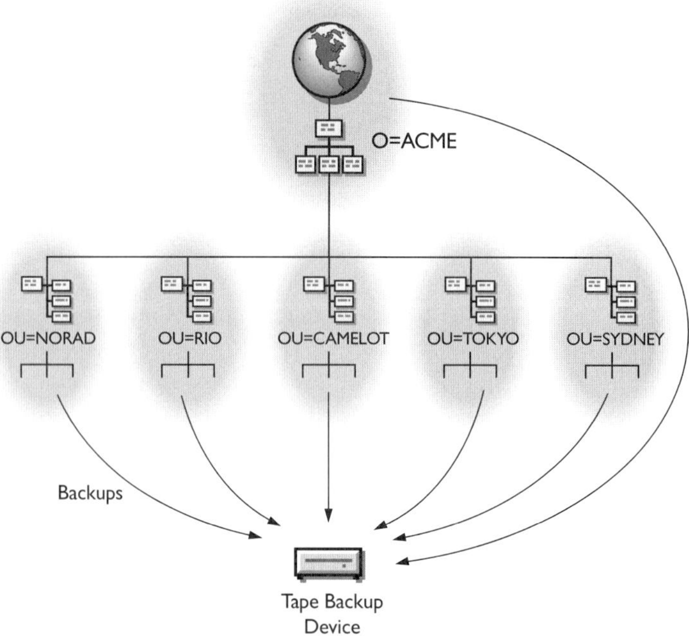

You can follow these guidelines when backing up your tree:

- Perform backups regularly — once a week, for example. The number of backups you perform depends on how many changes are made to your tree. (Examples of changes are adding new users, moving subtrees, and so on.) If your tree does not change much, backups can be performed weekly. If it changes a great deal, backups should be more frequent.
- Create a company policy stating how often NDS backups should be performed. You may simply want to have your administrators perform the NDS backup each time they do a full server backup.
- Load TSANDS.NLM on one NetWare 5 server in your tree. Choose the server containing a replica of the largest partition in your tree. For more complex networks, TSANDS.NLM can be loaded on more than one server.
- Keep a written record of your partitions and replicas. If you need to do a total restoration of NDS, you may need to know where to create your partitions and replicas. You can also use DSREPAIR to log partition and replica information to a file.
- Create an alternate administrative type user if you decide to reduce your ADMIN user rights. Typically, when you install the first NetWare 5 server, you call the first user ADMIN, and this user has Supervisor rights at the [ROOT] of your tree. If you subsequently reduce the rights of the ADMIN (or equivalent) user and perform a tape backup on that object, the object will be backed up with the reduced rights. Subsequently, when you restore the ADMIN (or equivalent) object, it will be restored with the reduced rights, which will not allow you to complete your restore.

Using the Enhanced SBACKUP Utility

In this section we discuss the steps to launching and using the Enhanced SBACKUP utility. This utility can be launched from a NetWare 5 server or from a Windows 95/98 or Windows NT workstation. This utility is run from a server through the command line prompt. It is run from a workstation through a graphical interface. Both methods are discussed here.

The first step is to load the necessary modules at the NetWare 5 server. To load the Storage Management Engine (SME), follow these steps:

1. At the NetWare 5 server, type **SMDR**. If this module has never been loaded before, you will be prompted to create a new SMDR group. Enter the name of the new group in the SMDR Group Context field.

2. Enter the full context of your user name. This is the name of the person who will be performing the backups and restore. The name must begin with a period (.), for example: .Aeinstein.Labs.Norad.Acme.

3. Enter your administrator password.

4. Type **TSA500**.

5. Type **SMSDI**.

6. Type **QMAN**. If this is the first time you have loaded the module, the queue is created automatically once you enter the following information:

   - Queue Context is the context that will be used for the job queue. You need this when you create backup or restore jobs. You can select the default if it is correct.
   - Queue Name is the name of the job queue. You need this when you create backup or restore jobs. You can select the default if it is correct.
   - User Name is the name of the person who will be submitting the jobs.
   - Password is the password of the person who will be submitting the jobs. For example: .ADMIN.ACME.

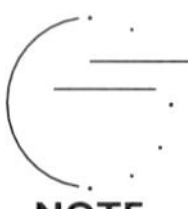
NOTE

If you enter an incorrect password or user name, you must rerun QMAN. First type UNLOAD QMAN and then type QMAN NEW at the server console.

7. Type SBSC.

8. Type SBCON.

NOTE

If you use backup and restore on the server, load SBCON. If you use NWBACK32 on a client, you do not need to load this module.

When this module is loaded, you will see a startup screen as shown in Figure 18.6.

FIGURE 18.6

The Enhanced SBACKUP utility running from a NetWare 5 server console

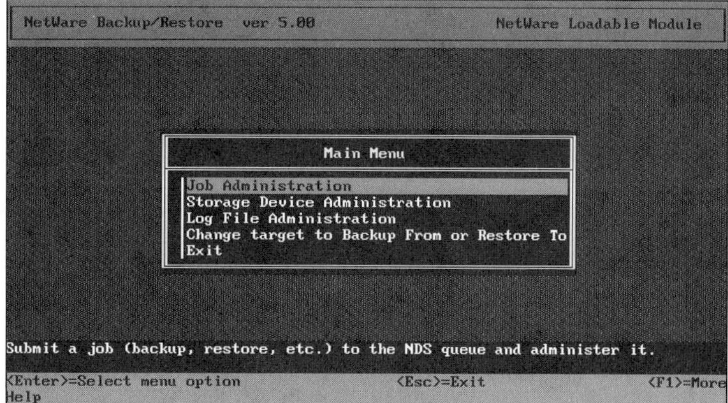

Backup Options at the Server

From the main menu, the following options are available:

- Job Administration
- Log/Error File Administration, which contains the session and error files
- Storage Device Administration, which contains the options to monitor the properties of a device
- Change Target to Back Up From or Restore To, which contains the options to change your target

From the main menu at the prompt Job Administration, the following options are available:

- Backup
- Restore
- Verify

When you select Backup Options, you are prompted to fill in the information screen as shown in Figure 18.7. You will need to log in with Supervisor rights to the server you have selected as the target.

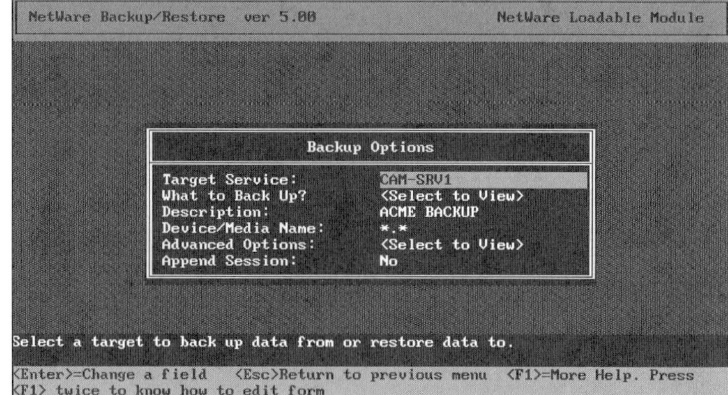

FIGURE 18.7

The Job Administration Backup screen

The Target Service is the server that you wish to back up or restore to. The "What to Back Up?" screen enables you to select the entire server, sys volume, individual files, and so on to be backed up. An example of selecting individual files for backup is shown in Figure 18.8.

Other options on this screen include selecting the media type that you are using. Press Insert to be shown a list of the installed backup media on your server. You must have at least one option appearing in the list in order to run a successful backup. You can also give the backup job a name such as NDS Weekly Backup.

FIGURE 18.8

Selecting individual files for back up

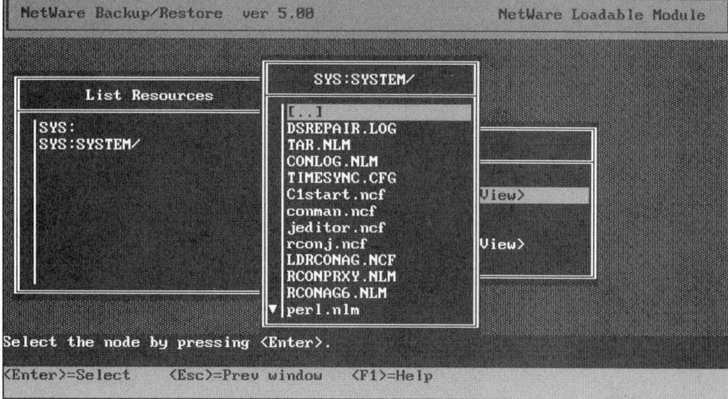

The Advanced Backup Options screen is shown in Figure 18.9. This screen enables you to specify with greater detail how and when you want a backup to occur. For example, you can specify a Full, Incremental, or Differential backup. You can also specify the time and date you want to the backup to begin.

FIGURE 18.9

The Advanced Backup Options screen of the SBCON utility

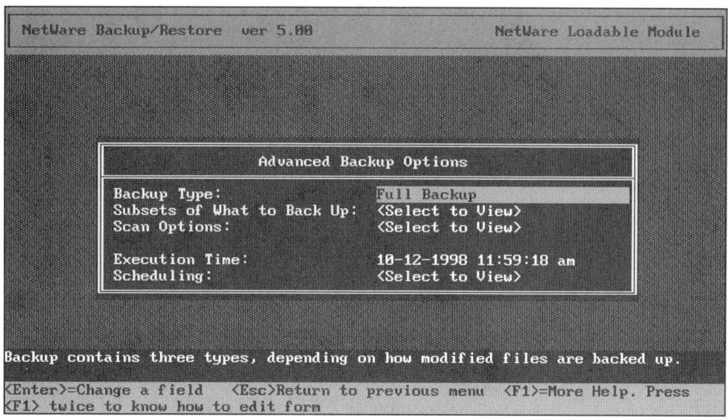

Once you have completed these screens, you can exit by hitting Esc. You will then be prompted if you want to submit the backup job for processing. If you say Yes, the job will then be scheduled for processing based on the criteria you have previously defined for that job.

An example of the job submission screen is shown in Figure 18.10.

FIGURE 18.10

The job submission screen for SBCON

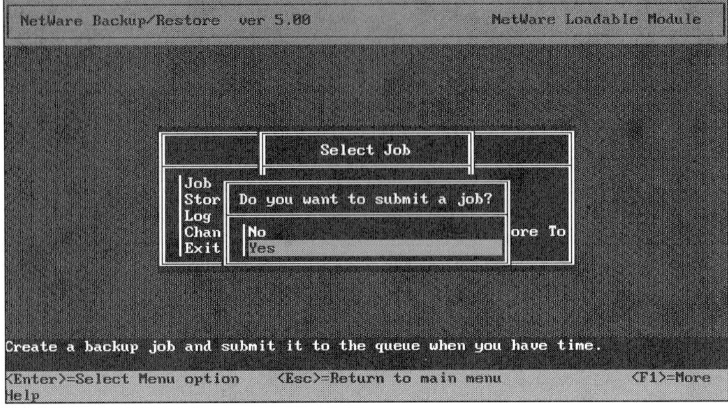

Enhanced SBACKUP from a Workstation

You can also load the Enhanced SBACKUP utility at a Windows 95/98 or Windows NT workstation by doing the following steps. The workstation backup utility is stored on the SYS:Public directory and is known as NWBACK32.EXE. It accomplishes the same tasks as the SBCON utility on your NetWare 5 server but uses a graphical interface:

1. Log into your NDS tree structure. Be sure to log into the desired tree if you have more than one tree on your network.

2. Click Network Neighborhood → Novell → sys:public.

3. If this is the first time you have used NWBACK32, you will be prompted to configure the SMDR information including tree name, SMDR context, and the SMDR group context. Enter the name of the NDS tree you will be using to back up and restore data. Enter the context you created during the server configuration. Check the SAP (IPX) box if you want to use IPX. Uncheck the box for IP. An example of this dialog box is shown in Figure 18.11.

The application will then launch, and you will see a dialog box as shown in Figure 18.12. You can then select an option. Keep in mind the same options exist in both the SBCON (server-based utility) and NWBACK32.EXE (workstation-based utility).

FIGURE 18.11

The SMDR configuration dialog box is initialized the first time you run NWBACK32 from a workstation.

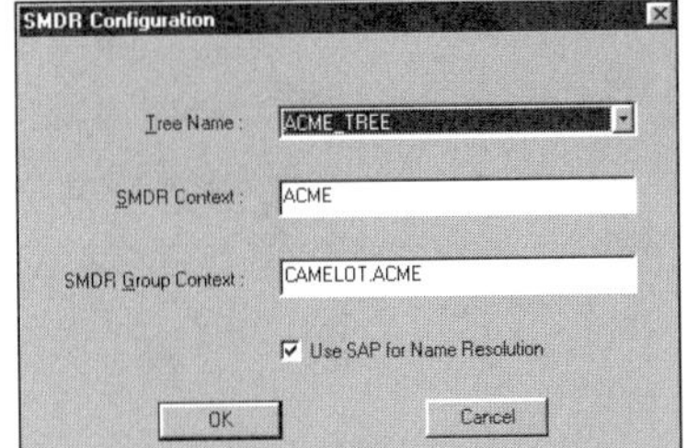

FIGURE 18.12

The main dialog box for NWBACK.EXE

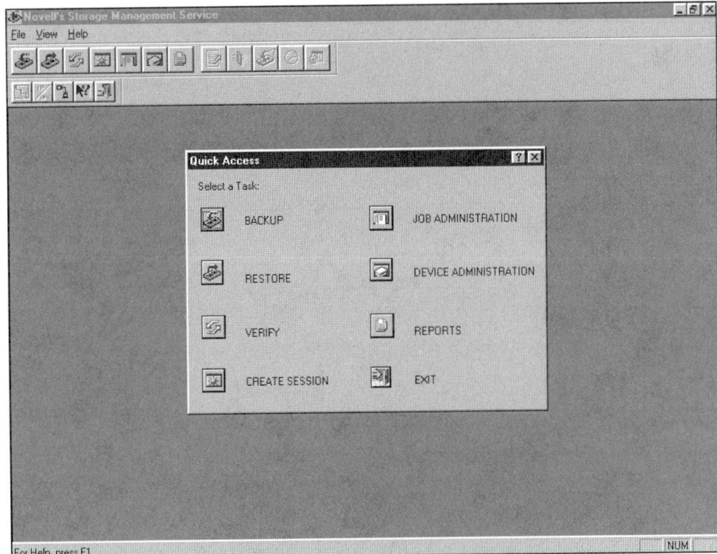

If you select the Backup task, you will be presented with the What to Backup dialog box.

Double-click What to Backup. Click to back up NDS, NetWare Servers, or Workstations. A list of servers will appear. Double-click to select the server you want to back up. An example of this window is shown in Figure 18.13.

FIGURE 18.13

Selecting what you want to back up through the NWBack32 Utility

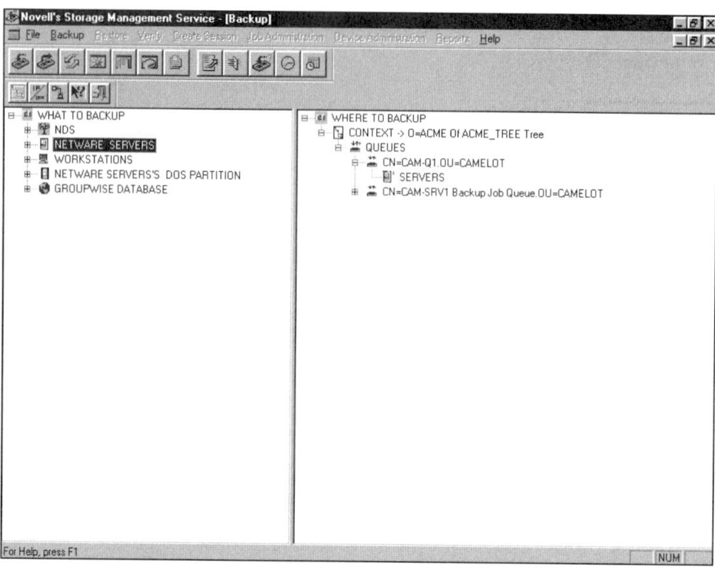

You will then be prompted to enter the username and password to authenticate to the server. A list of resources to back up appears, such as volumes and files. You can then click the resources to back up.

Next, select where you want your backup data to go. Double-click Where to Backup.

Change to the correct NDS tree structure and context by clicking the Change to Context button on the toolbar. Double-click Queues; a list of Queue objects appears. Click to highlight a Queue object. Right-click to open the drop-down box.

You are now ready to submit the backup job as shown in Figure 18.14.

FIGURE 18.14

Submitting a backup job for processing

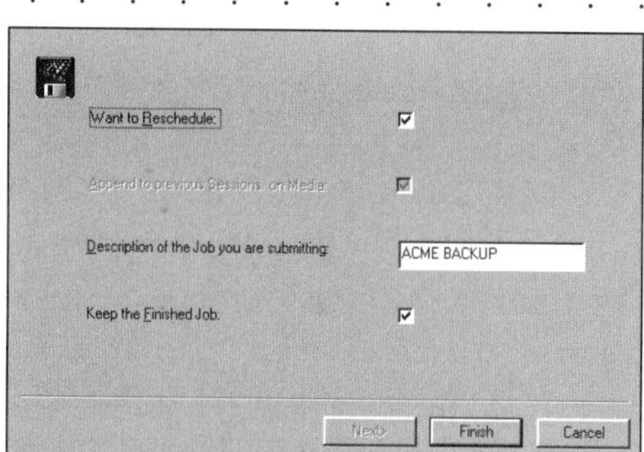

This step enables you to submit the job to a queue, on the chosen server, or on the chosen media type.

Backing Up Your Workstations

To back up the workstation (the target), a Target Service Agent (TSA) must be loaded on the workstation. You can select the individual directories to back up or back up the entire workstation.

Backing Up a Windows 95/98 Workstation Make sure that the W95TSA is installed and configured. It is a part of the Novell Client modules (check box for Target Service Agent for Windows 95).

NOTE

To configure W95TSA, refer to Help that comes with the Novell Client modules. If it is installed and registered, a shield-like icon appears in the shell tray and indicates "Novell TSA (Listening)" when the mouse pointer reaches the icon. You will also see an SMS window pop up when you log in to NetWare.

To prepare for a backup on a Windows 95/98 workstation, follow these steps:

1. At the target workstation, register with W95TSA by double-clicking the shield-like icon that appears in the shell tray. The Novell Target Service Agent for Windows 95 Properties box appears. You then must follow these steps:
    - a. Enter your user name and password for the TSA.
    - b. Enter the server name that will be servicing this Windows 95/98 client.
    - c. Choose the disk drive you want to register.
    - d. (Recommended) Check Auto Register. This automatically registers your workstation with the server.
    - e. Click OK.
    - f. Restart your workstation.
2. The TSA must be installed and registered with the host server, along with the TSA username and password. At the host server, type **TSAPROXY**. You can then select or click the NetWare server running the target service agent.

3. Next, select or click the target workstation you want to back up and enter the username and password when prompted. Follow the steps in the procedures to back up data to complete your backup.

Backing Up a Windows NT Workstation Make sure that the NT TSA is installed and configured. It is a part of the Novell Client modules (check box for Novell Target Service Agent). The Windows NT TSA has two parts:

- The TSA Service (TSAmain.exe) is a service that waits for and acts when there is a request from the backup engine.
- The TSAPrefs (TSAPrefs.exe) enables an NT administrator to set preferences and monitor the activities of the TSA Service.

The first step is to configure the NT TSA on your Windows NT client. To configure, follow these steps:

1. In Windows NT, click the Properties page. The TSAPrefs page appears with tabs for Preferences, Registration, Connections, and Event Logs.
2. Click Preferences.
3. Fill in the following fields:
   a. Workstation: Enter the name of the workstation.
   b. Preferred Server: Enter the name of the server on which you want to connect. This server must have TSAProxy installed.
   c. Protocol: Select SPX/IPX or TCP/IP.
   d. Events to Log: Check the items you want to log: Connection, Registration, Security, or Service.
   e. Allow Backup User: This grants the backup user rights depending on the group.
   f. Auto Register: This automatically registers the Windows NT workstation with the server.

4. Click Registration.

5. Check the fields in the Registration page and click Register if the fields are correct. If information in any of the fields is incorrect, click Withdraw and return to the Preferences page to change the information, then repeat Steps 4 and 5.

6. Click Connections.

7. Check the fields in the Connections page and click OK. If you need to add or change information, click Apply. You can delete connections in this page under Current Connections if preferred. Click Apply.

Restoring Novell Directory Services

As mentioned, before doing a tape backup restore of Novell Directory Services you should attempt to restore NDS information through replicas and repair operations. For more information on these processes, refer to Chapter 9. If you have to restore NDS information, an active replica is faster and more up to date than a tape backup. Remember, two or three replicas are adequate for fault tolerance. Your particular circumstances may require more or fewer replicas.

Take the following precautionary measures before you begin your restoration:

1. Make sure that your current tree is functioning properly in terms of replica synchronization. Use NDS Manager or DSTRACE to verify that all partitions are error free. Doing a restore when you still have replica synchronization errors will only compound your problems.

2. Always restore NDS information first, and then restore file system data and trustees. Failure to do so may result in the loss of trustee assignments for your user objects.

Performing a Partial NDS Restore

NetWare 5 provides SMS TSAs that enable you to selectively restore objects and groups of objects from your tape backup. This is known as a partial restore.

You need to determine whether a partial restore is the fastest solution to your particular problem. For example, if you are trying to restore a single object, it might be quicker to simply recreate the object using NWADMIN than to perform a partial restore. Remember, you must understand how the restore process works in terms of object IDs and dependent objects to successfully carry out a partial restore. A full or partial restore can be done with either the SBCON or NWBACK32 utilities by selecting Job Administration/Restore and entering the same information as was entered for the backup. Keep in mind that you must have created a previous backup session to restore from.

Object IDs

If you are restoring an object that no longer exists in your NDS tree, a new object ID is created when you restore the object. Any (old) object ID associated with the file system trustees, such as directories for user mail, is affected in this situation. The new object ID will not match the old file system ID assignments. If an object already exists in the tree and you do a restore, you will copy the object's properties from tape backup over the existing object's properties. This may or may not be what you intended to do.

Dependent Objects

Dependent objects are dependent upon other objects to exist in your tree. A print queue object, for example, maintains directory and host server properties to determine where the queue is stored and on what server. Without this information, the print queue object cannot function. Therefore, if you restore any dependent objects, they will not be functional in your tree without the other supporting objects.

You may restore some dependent objects, including Directory Map objects, print queue objects, and any schema extension objects you have created. Once restored, these types of objects are nonfunctional. The best way to resolve this problem is to restore the supporting objects for the dependent object, delete the previously restored dependent object, and recreate it with NWADMIN. Once you recreate the object, it will make use of the supporting objects.

Unknown Objects

Restoring the NDS may create unknown objects. If a restored object is dependent on other objects in the tree that do not currently exist, the object will be designated as unknown. NDS creates an unknown object until the real object is restored. If the actual object is restored during the restore, the unknown category is replaced by the actual object name.

You will always see unknown objects during a restore until all the resources—servers, volumes, users, and so on—are in place in your tree. Most objects should be cleaned up once the restore is completed. If not, you can delete the unknown objects and recreate the actual objects, or you can attempt to selectively restore the actual objects and overwrite the unknown objects. Again, you have to determine whether it's easier to restore the objects or to recreate them with NWADMIN.

Bindery Objects and Applications

As mentioned, new object IDs are created for restored objects that do not exist in the tree. Bindery-based applications such as printing, e-mail, and others will probably not function because they use object IDs to communicate. If the bindery application has one list of object IDs and you restore the objects with new IDs, these applications will not function properly. In most cases, you will need to reinstall and reconfigure these applications after you restore the tree.

The login scripts of bindery-based user objects are stored in their mail subdirectories if the scripts were created with a utility such as SYSCON. These subdirectories are based on an object ID. Therefore, when you restore the user objects with a new object ID, the mail subdirectories are not automatically renamed.

A Novell utility called RENMDIRS.NLM changes the mail directory name (old object ID) to that of the new object ID created after a restore. This utility is available from the NSD section of Novell's corporate Web site.

Print Services

After restoring NDS, you have to restore print services objects from your tape backup if you are using queue server mode printing. You also have to run any setup software from your third-party print package to reconfigure your printing environment. Because your queue ID has changed during the restore, you have to recreate the queue to allow for a reassignment of the queue ID to the new print server object ID. You will most likely need to reset your printers after reconfiguration as well.

For remote printing mode, your printing should be fully functional after a tape restore of NDS.

Performing a Full NDS Restore

You would need to perform a full NDS tree restore if all servers in the tree suffered a catastrophic failure. In large, geographically dispersed networks this situation is all but impossible. Some smaller companies in a single building or a few buildings in the same location are more likely to experience this situation.

Follow these steps to carry out a full NDS restore:

1. Reinstall NetWare 5 on your file servers to regain a [ROOT] partition of your network on the first server. Be sure to specify the exact tree structure organization (Organization and Organizational Unit objects) that was present in your first tree. Now is not the time to make changes to your tree.

2. Reinstall additional NetWare 5 servers as you had them before the failure. Any servers that you cannot install before the restore may cause some errors due to dependent objects that do not restore properly. This may require you to go back with NWADMIN and recreate objects.

IMPORTANT

Be sure to recreate the ADMIN or equivalent user with the same name, same container, and same password that was used to create the original backup. If you made and backed up extensions to the schema, you need to make those extensions again. Extensions to the default schema are not backed up, but the objects created with these extensions are. Therefore, you must extend the schema on your tree before restoring your objects. Failure to do so will result in an incomplete restoration.

3. If you have reinstalled more than one NetWare 5 server, you should remove the default replicas of [ROOT] before beginning the restoration. Having a single copy of the [ROOT] partition will simplify the restore process. This process assumes that you have a server holding [ROOT] with enough disk space to restore the entire NDS tree.

4. Install your tape backup drivers and bring up your backup software. Restore the entire NDS backup to your server. The NDS tree will be placed in your [ROOT] partition.

5. Restore the file information to each NetWare 5 server in your tree. When performing a restore, be sure to set your backup software to delete any existing trustees before restoring the data. This purges any existing trustees before the tape backup; its trustee assignments are restored to the server.

6. Recreate your partition boundaries using your written record of the partition boundaries. Alternatively, you can designate and place replicas of your partitions where they are needed.

7. Run DSREPAIR on each server to verify the accuracy of your database.

Server/SYS Volume Failure

It's common to have a single server fail in your NDS tree. Often this occurs because of a SYS volume failure. Such a failure is serious because your SYS volume contains all or portions of the NetWare Directory and can affect other servers in your tree that participate in the same partition as the failed server.

If your SYS volume fails on a single-server network, the situation is similar to a total tree failure of many servers. The restore procedure is basically the same as a full NDS restoration, with the addition of a few steps:

1. Replace or resolve the problem that caused your SYS volume to fail. This usually means replacing the hard drive unit itself.

2. Reinstall NetWare 5 on your file servers to regain a [ROOT] partition of your network on the first server. Be sure to specify the exact tree structure organization (Organization and Organizational Unit objects) that was present in your first tree. Now is not the time to make changes to your tree. Specify 64K for your volume block size. Have INSTALL mount all volumes during the installation process. Make sure that you install all the patches and updates to the operating system and utilities as well.

Again, be sure to recreate the ADMIN or equivalent user with the same name, same container, and same password that was used to create the original backup. If you made and backed up extensions to the schema, you need to make those extensions again. Failure to do so will result in an incomplete restoration.

3. Run DSREPAIR on any volumes other than SYS on the server to purge invalid trustees contained on those volumes. Run the option UNATTENDED FULL REPAIR to purge any invalid trustee information.

4. Install your tape backup drivers and bring up your backup software. Load TSANDS and TSA500 NLMs.

5. Restore the entire NDS backup to your server. The NDS tree will be placed in your [ROOT] partition.

6. Restore the file system information to your NetWare 5 SYS volume from your tape backup. You need to choose an option for restoring without session files.

7. Restore any trustee assignments (without data streams) for any other volumes that existed before the failure.

If you restore data on volume SYS, you will no longer have trustee assignments for the other volumes because you ran DSREPAIR in Step 3. You can restore only the directory without data streams on these volumes. Because the data files already exist, you only need the directory structure to obtain the trustee assignments. Consult the instructions for your third-party backup program for details on how to accomplish this task.

8. Run DSREPAIR on each server to verify the accuracy of your NDS database.

When there is a multiserver environment in a partition, it's also extremely common to have a single server fail for whatever reason, including the failure of the SYS volume. This does not mean, however, that you have lost all your replicas of that partition. This situation requires a slightly different approach:

1. Remove this server from the NDS by using the NDS Manager utility. Start by deleting the failed server's Server object and volume objects from the tree. If your failed server holds a master replica, you must run DSREPAIR or NDS Manager to designate another active replica in the partition as the master. Verify through NDS Manager or DSREPAIR that the server has been removed from the replica list and that your tree is functioning properly. If the server is not returning for use in your tree, this is all you need to do. If your server is returning to the tree, continue reading the following steps.

IMPORTANT

Only follow these procedures if your server has failed and is completely inoperable. If you have a functioning NetWare 5 server that you want to remove from the tree, instead load INSTALL and use the option Remove Directory Services from that server.

2. Once you have repaired the failed server hardware, you can reinstall NetWare 5 on that server. Make sure that your install includes all the latest patches and versions of the operating system and utilities that you were using before the failure.

3. Restore the replica(s) that were present on the server before the failure. Allow the synchronization process to place the objects on the server. You do not need to use your SMS tape backup to restore NDS information. Verify through DSREPAIR and Partition Manager that the replicas are synchronizing properly on the restored server hardware.

4. Use your SMS backup to restore the data and trustee assignments for the SYS volume that was lost during the server failure.

5. Restore any other volumes besides SYS that were not affected by the failure. Again, you can only restore the trustee assignments without the data streams for those volumes.

Be sure to delete existing trustees before restoring. This option will purge existing trustees before restoring the backed up trustee assignments from the backup. You can simply restore the directory structure without data streams on these volumes. Because the data files already exist, you only need the directory structure to get the trustee assignments back. Follow your backup vendor's guidelines to accomplish this task.

Devising a Disaster Recovery Plan

You should have a disaster recovery plan to protect your system and your data in case of an emergency. Your disaster recovery plan can include redundant hardware along with proper replication and tape backup.

For some sites requiring a high degree of redundancy, you can consider using disk mirroring or disk duplexing, which provide you with varying degrees of safety.

Always maintain at least two to three replicas of your partitions as one of your strongest backup defenses for NDS. Some sites create one or two NDS servers that contain all replicas of all partitions for backup purposes. If you use an NDS server for replica storage, consider these recommendations:

- Have a centralized NDS server across the fastest WAN link possible.
- Use only fast hardware (Pentium-class machines) for your NDS replica server.
- If you have more than 100 replicas, distribute the replicas on two servers for greater synchronization performance.
- The synchronization process on these servers should complete in 30 minutes or less. If the server cannot complete a synchronization cycle (synchronizing all replicas on the server) in this amount of time, place some of the replicas on a second replica server. This recommendation is based on the fact that the background NDS synchronization interval occurs each 30 minutes.
- Make sure that you have a regular tape backup of your entire NDS tree, as discussed in this chapter.

Summary

This chapter has provided you with the basics of the backup and restore mechanism for NetWare 5 and NDS. We have covered the architecture of the Storage Management Services including the Storage Management Engine, the Target Service Agent, and the Storage Management Data Requester. Additionally, we have covered the Enhanced SBACKUP utility for NetWare 5. This utility enables you to perform file system and NDS backups with greater flexibility and reliability.

PART V

Integrating Additional Services with NetWare 5

CHAPTER 19

Integrating Novell Z.E.N.works with NetWare 5

This chapter provides you with guidelines and recommendations for designing and implementing Novell's Zero Effort Networks (Z.E.N.works) product on your NetWare 5 network. Z.E.N.works is a combination of Novell products that provide you with application management, workstation management, and desktop maintenance of your Windows 3.1, Windows 95/98, and Windows NT desktops.

These features enable the network administrator to reduce the overall cost and complexity of configuring and maintaining workstation desktops on the network. For example, desktop management features create a workstation inventory and store this inventory as workstation objects in NDS. Inventory information can include hard disk space, workstation memory, and versions of software.

Desktop management features also enable an administrator to store and configure Windows 95/98 and Windows NT desktop policies in NDS. These policies can then follow a user from desktop to desktop. Because the policies are stored in NDS, the users can easily move from one desktop to another and have their associated policies follow them. Printer drivers can also be delivered to the desktop via Z.E.N.works so that users can easily print from any desktop to any printer.

Novell's Desktop Management software (previously known as Workstation Manager) enables all user account and desktop information for Windows 3.*x*, Windows NT, and Windows 95/98 to be centrally managed within NDS using a single administrative utility. For NT environments, it also eliminates the need for NT domains or for a large number of NT user accounts to reside in the local SAM of each workstation.

Configuration information is stored in policy package objects that are particular to the platform. For example, for Windows NT and Windows 95/98 there are NT package objects and Windows 95 package objects. Each package contains policies that can be enabled, configured, and scheduled for downloading to the workstations. Note that most of the examples in this chapter use the NT desktop. The same concepts can be applied to the other previously mentioned desktops as well.

Z.E.N.works provides you with these features:

- **NDS policy support** — Enables you to customize import of workstation object information into NDS and to set rules on how the remote control feature and the end-user help request system can be used.
- **Hardware inventory** — Automatically stores the hardware inventory into NDS for tracking and troubleshooting.

- **Dynamic print configuration** — Provides dynamic distribution and updating of print drivers.
- **Profile management** — Provides centralized location and administration of user profiles.
- **Client configurations stored in NDS** — Enables you to view and update client configurations without visiting the workstation.
- **Update clients on workstations** — Enables you to update during off hours or when users are not logged in.
- **NDS-authenticated remote control of a workstation or NT server** — Enables you to solve user problems without visiting the workstation or NT server.
- **Administrative control of an end-user help request system** — The Help Requester is an end-user program that helps users provide pertinent information on themselves and their workstation to the help desk through e-mail or phone. This can mean faster problem resolution.
- **Applications Delivered via NDS** — Using the Novell Application Launcher within Z.E.N.works, you can create and configure application objects that can be delivered to the user's desktop via NDS.

Z.E.N.works defines several new object types in NDS:

- Workstation object
- Workstation group object
- Policy package object including:
  - Container search policy object
  - Platform-specific user policy package objects
  - Platform-specific workstation policy package objects

Figure 19.1 shows a diagram of the available policy packages within Z.E.N.works.

FIGURE 19.1

The policy packages that are available with Z.E.N.works

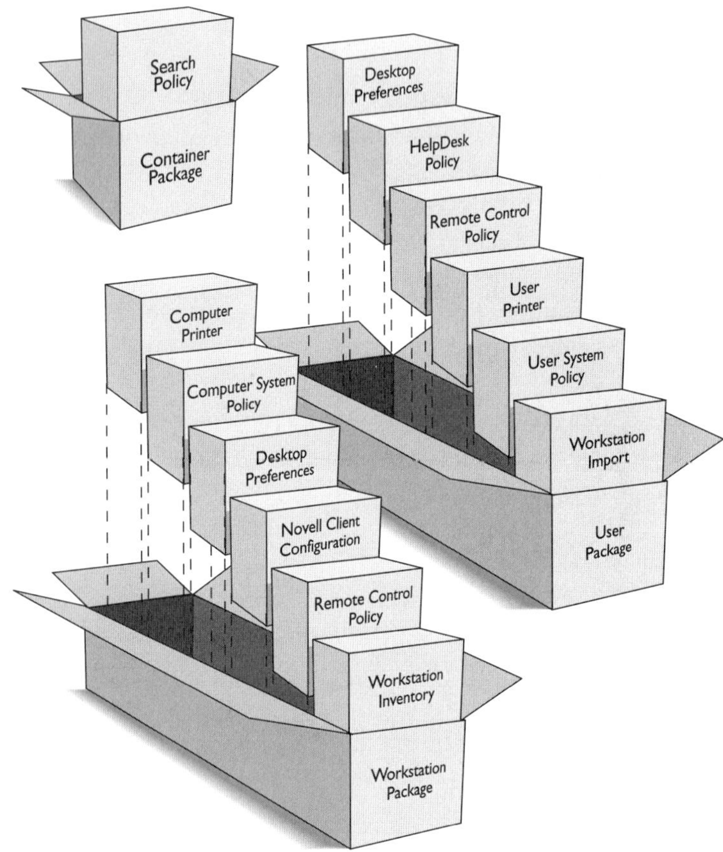

Table 19.1 lists and explains the function of each new policy object.

TABLE 19.1

New Objects Created with Z.E.N.works

NEW OBJECTS	FUNCTION
Windows 3.*x* Workstation	Represents a Windows 3.*x* workstation.
Windows 3.*x* User	Represents a Windows 3.*x* user.
Windows 95/98 Workstations	Represents a Windows 95/98 workstation.

NEW OBJECTS	FUNCTION
Windows 95/98 User	Represents a Windows 95/98 user.
Windows NT Workstation	Represents a Windows NT workstation.
Windows NT User	Represents a Windows NT user.
Workstation Group	Represents a group of workstations, either Windows 95/98 or Windows NT.
Policy Packages	Groups specific policies together.

NOTE

Workstation objects can be associated with users, workstation groups, containers, and certain policy packages.

Installing Z.E.N.works

The first step to using Z.E.N.works is to install the software on your server and clients. This section will take you through these steps. The installation of Z.E.N.works consists of two parts:

- Server installation
- Novell Client installation

Z.E.N.works Server Installation

The Z.E.N.works installation CD provides an autorun feature that automatically loads the installation window shown in Figure 19.2. You can install the server software first and then the NT workstation client software, or you can browse the CD before installation. We use NT as an example, although you can install the Novell clients for Windows 3.*x*, 95, and 98 as well.

FIGURE 19.2

The initial installation window for Z.E.N.works is automatically run when you insert the Z.E.N.works CD-ROM.

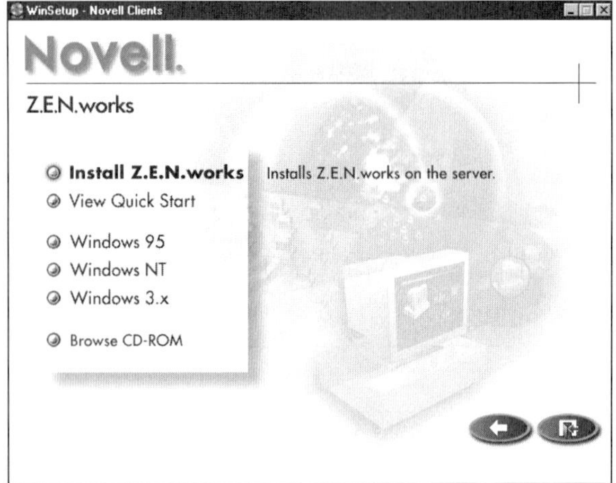

Figure 19.3 shows the Typical installation dialog box. By selecting a Typical install, you will receive all the necessary server components of this product. Your only option under Typical Install is the tree/servers that you want to install to. If you select the Custom installation option, you are able to select individual components that are specified in Figure 19.4. These components include the software components of Z.E.N.works such as the application software, workstation maintenance software, desktop management software, and NWADMIN utility. You can also copy the Novell Client software to the server for easy distribution to the desktops.

FIGURE 19.3

The Server Installation dialog box for Z.E.N.works, typical install

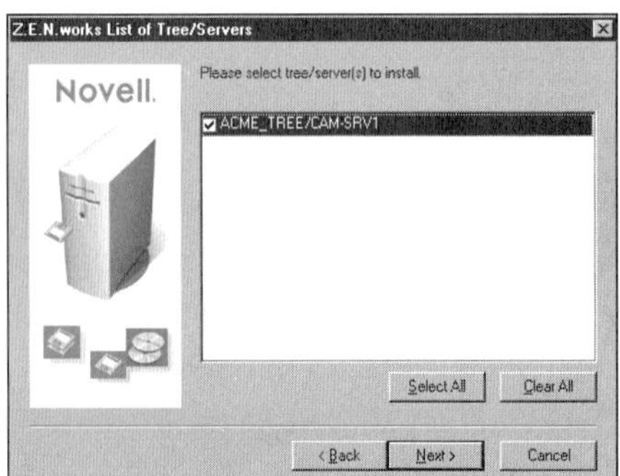

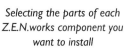

FIGURE 19.4

The Custom Installation dialog box for Z.E.N.works

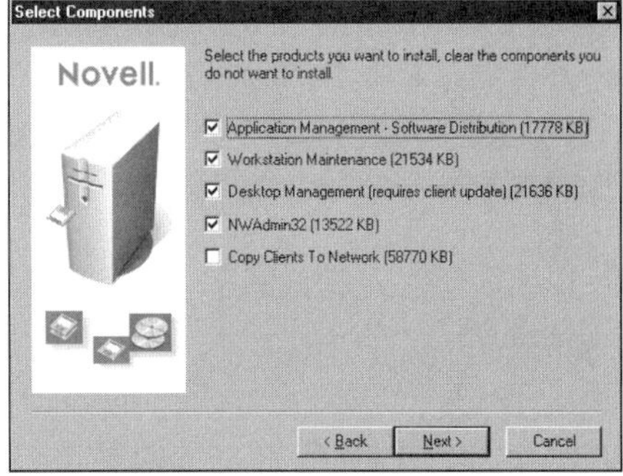

You will then be presented with additional options to select the parts you want to install for each component shown in the previous figure including files, schema extensions, application objects, and workstation registry entries. An example of this is shown in Figure 19.5.

FIGURE 19.5

Selecting the parts of each Z.E.N.works component you want to install

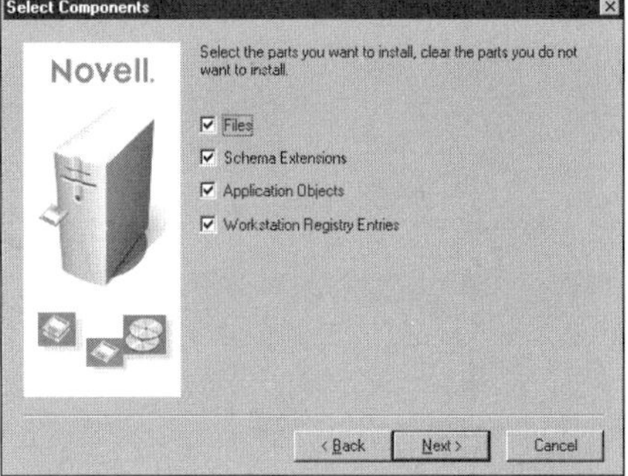

Once you specify the type of installation and go through the install options, you will be prompted to select the NDS tree and server(s) to install the product. Keep in mind that you must have Supervisor rights at [Root] for the servers you wish to install onto and you must have previously logged into the tree on which you want to install the product. An example of this dialog box is shown in Figure 19.6.

Select the language option you desire and press Next. You will then be presented with an information summary dialog box. You can then press Enter to begin the install process.

The appropriate files will then be installed to the server.

FIGURE 19.6

Selecting the NDS tree and server(s) to install Z.E.N.works

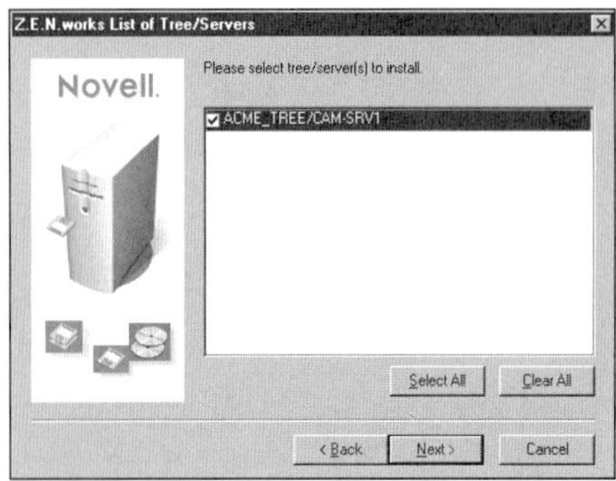

Once you have completed the server install, you can move to the Novell Client install. You can use Novell's Automatic Client Upgrade (ACU) feature or other install options to assist you with your client upgrades. For more information about client installations see Chapter 17.

Once the install is completed, you will be prompted to specify a context where you want rights granted to all users. In order for Z.E.N.works to create workstation objects in NDS, users of those workstation must be granted appropriate rights to write a workstation registration entry to their container. An example of specifying a context is shown in Figure 19.7.

FIGURE 19.7

Specify a context where you want rights granted to users to write their workstation registration to their container.

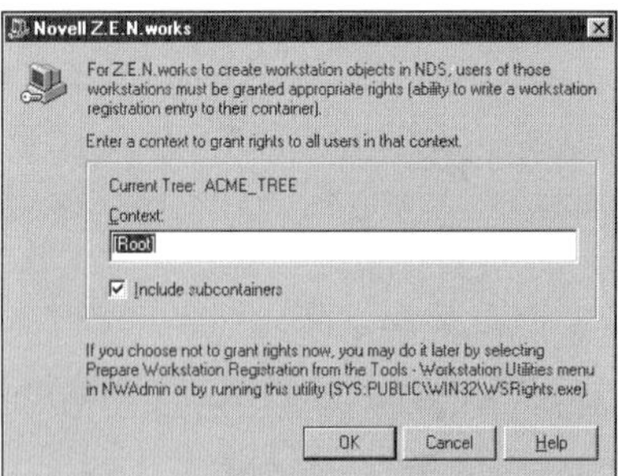

If you choose not to grant rights at this time, you can do it later by selecting the option Prepare Workstation Registration from the Tools → Workstation Utilities menu in NWADMIN.

Z.E.N.works NT Client Installation

You can also install Novell's NT client (or other clients) from this CD as well. Simply select this option to perform a client installation. For more information on NT client installation options refer to Chapter 17.

Automating Remote Control Installations with Windows NT

There are two different methods of installing the remote control components on Windows NT workstations. You can use the installation program, NTSTACFG.EXE. Starting this installation program will automatically install the System Service on the NT workstation. As installation of services requires Administrator rights on the local machine, this method is only usable when the user has Administrator rights to the local machine or if the NTSTACFG.EXE program is used during unattended installation of Windows NT with the RunOnce option.

The second method involves using the predefined NAL application, which is created by the setup program of Z.E.N.works to distribute the Remote Control Service to NT Workstations. The installation of services with NAL is accomplished by the NAL NT Service, which installs applications with System rights.

Creating Workstation Objects

Once you have completed installation of Z.E.N.works, you are now ready to begin using the workstation objects that you will need to manage the workstations on your network. Unlike most NDS objects, workstation objects in Z.E.N.works are created automatically in NDS when these two things occur:

- A workstation registers with NDS
- The registered workstation is imported into a container object

A Workstation Registers with NDS

Z.E.N.works invokes a workstation registration process to notify NDS of the existence of a workstation. The registration program can be run in three ways:

- An executable file (WSREG32.EXE or WSREG16.EXE) is placed in a workstation's login script. When the login script is executed, the executable is launched and the workstation registers with NDS.
- An application object can be created in the Novell Application Launcher to run the executable file (WSREG32.EXE or WSREG16.EXE). An example of this is shown in Figure 19.8.

FIGURE 19.8

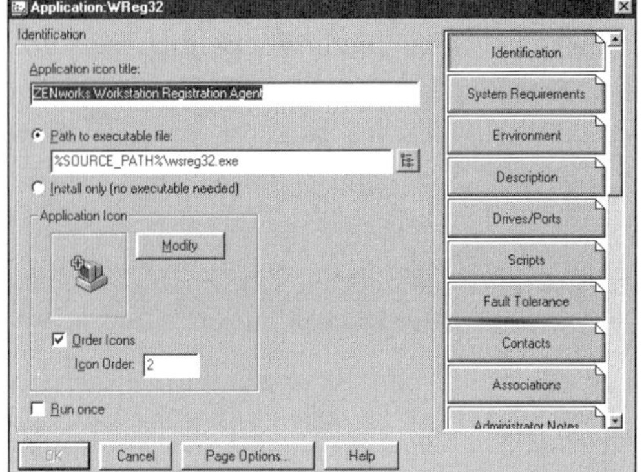

The application object to launch WSREG32.EXE is created automatically during the installation of Z.E.N.works.

- Desktop Management features can be used. The Desktop Manager will, if scheduled, automatically run WSREG32.DLL, which accomplishes the same thing as the executable files. You can simply double-click the executable under Windows Explorer.

As an administrator you must determine which method makes the most sense for your size of network. If you are deploying Z.E.N.works to a large number of workstations, you should consider placing the executable file in the container script so that all users will register their workstation when they log in.

The Registered Workstation Is Imported into a Container

The second step in this process is to import the workstation object into a container. To do this, you must first create an import policy package. This object determines how and when you want the workstation object imported into the container.

Consulting Experience

Sometimes a workstation fails to register properly because it has been connecting to multiple trees. You can enforce the tree name and server at login by going into your Network Neighborhood. This will ensure that the next time the workstation logs in, it will go to the right tree. You can go through these steps to check what tree has been registered in the registry:

1. Run the Regedit utility.
2. Drill down in the workstation's registry to HKEY_LOCAL_MACHINE/SOFTWARE/Novell/Workstation Manager/Identification.
3. Open the Registered In tab; you should see the location in your tree. Check to see if the correct tree is shown.
4. If not, delete the Identification folder and rerun DSREG.EXE.

To create a policy package, go to NWADMIN and highlight the container where you want to create the policy package. Go to Object → Create and select the policy package for the type of desktop you want to manage. Be sure to select User Package. In Figure 19.9 we show a Windows 95 user package being created.

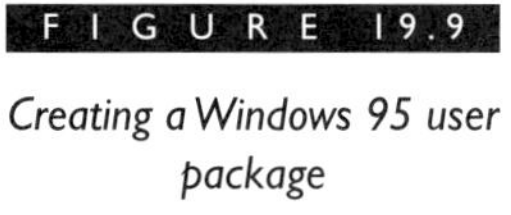

FIGURE 19.9

Creating a Windows 95 user package

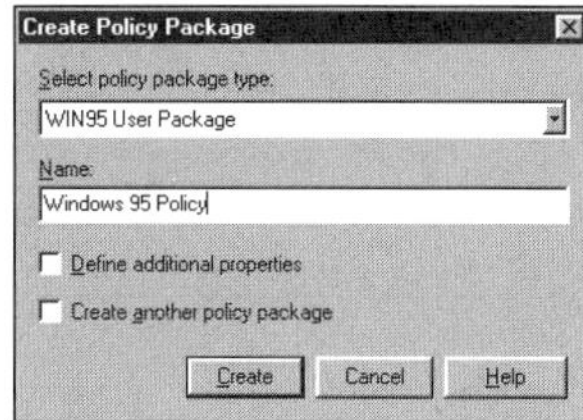

Once you have created the user package for your desktop, double-click this object in NWADMIN. You now must enable the package for the action you want to take on these desktops. As shown in Figure 19.10 we are enabling the workstation import policy. This will enable us to import all workstations of this type into our NDS container.

FIGURE 19.10

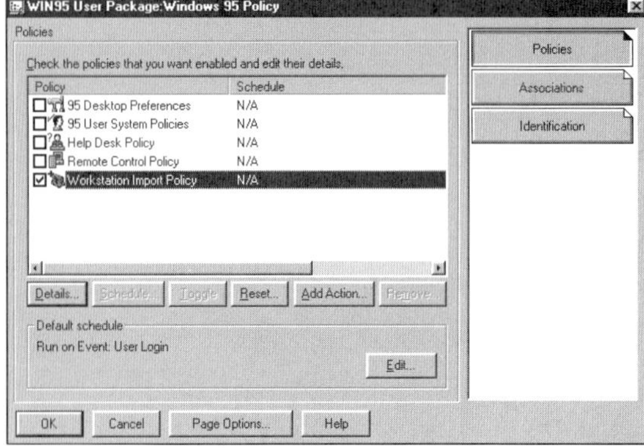

Selecting the workstation import policy on the newly created user package

You now need to select the container location where you want the workstations imported. Where you create the workstation objects is important from the standpoint of NDS design. (See organizing Z.E.N.works objects later in this chapter and also Chapter 5 for more information on NDS design concepts and object placement.) You have the option to create the workstation object in the same container as the corresponding user object or to create a separate container. Most small installations can simply create the workstation object in the same container as the user object. Large installations as specified later in this chapter and in Chapter 5 should create a separate container called OU=Workstations. An example of selecting the user container to create the workstation objects is shown in Figure 19.11. This dialog box is found by selecting the Details tab while inside the dialog box to select the import workstation policy.

FIGURE 19.11

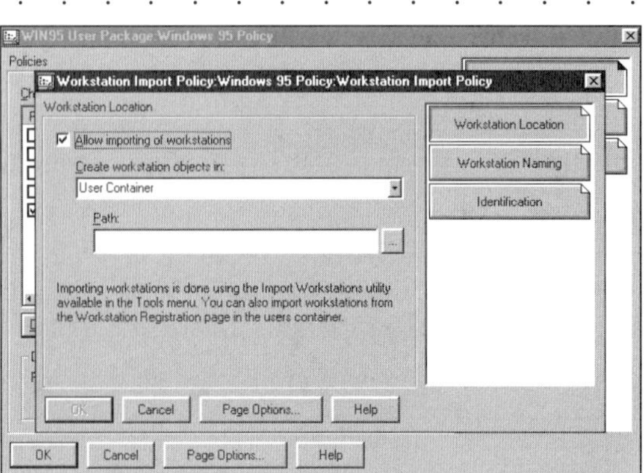

Selecting where you want the workstation objects created. In this example the user container is selected.

The last thing you need to do before importing a workstation is to associate the user package with the container you have selected. This is accomplished by selecting the Associations tab and adding the container to the associations list as shown in Figure 19.12.

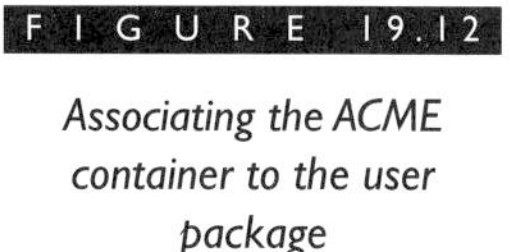

FIGURE 19.12

Associating the ACME container to the user package

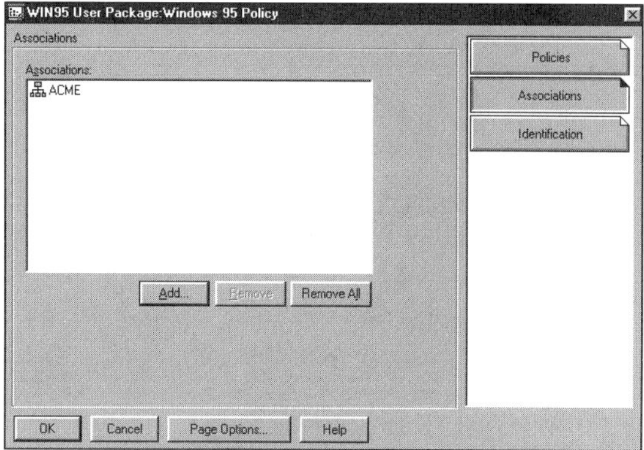

NOTE

The association step is crucial to successfully import workstations into a container. If you run the import utility and discover that no workstations have been imported, it is likely you failed to associate the package with a container.

The workstation objects can then be imported into NDS in any of these three ways:

- Select a container in NetWare Administrator, and choose Tools → Import Workstation. This action will create a workstation object for the registered workstation.
- Select a container in NetWare Administrator, and choose the Import button from the container object. This action will import all registered workstations in the selected container (see Figure 19.13).
- If desktop management features are used, the Import process can be scheduled by creating a scheduled action for WSIMPORT.EXE.

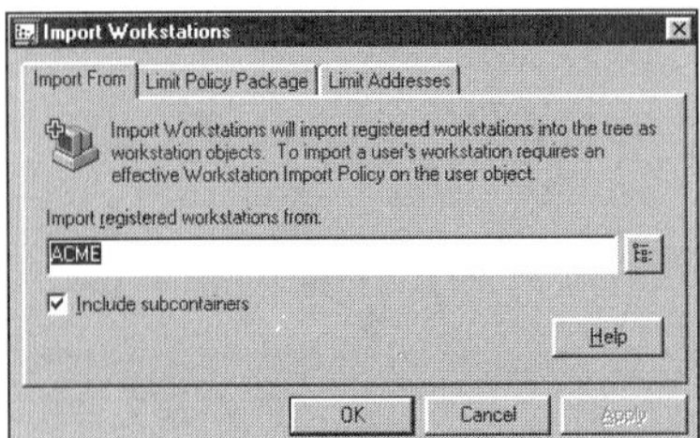

FIGURE 19.13

Importing a workstation into an NDS container by selecting the ACME container

Registered workstations are automatically named in NDS. The name format is specified in the Workstation Name field in the workstation import policy that is associated with the applicable container. The container is associated with the user logging in. When a workstation has been successfully registered you will see the dialog box shown in Figure 19.14.

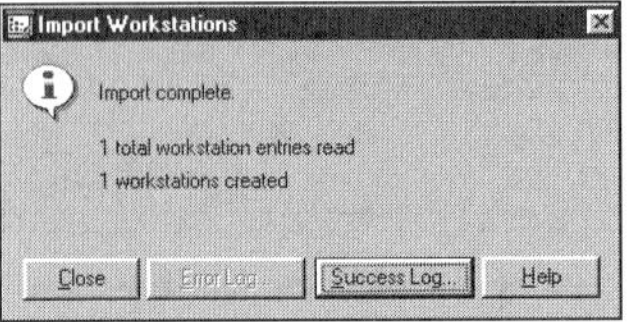

FIGURE 19.14

A Status dialog box is displayed when a successful NDS Import of workstations has occurred.

Consulting Experience

Network supervisors must periodically (as often as network addresses can change) choose to import workstations in order for workstation objects to be maintained in NDS. The workstation object is created when a registered workstation is initially imported. On the second and subsequent import sessions, the following items are updated in the workstation object: registration time, network address, last server, and last user. Imports are done on a container-by-container basis, although it can be chosen to import a container and all of its subcontainers.

Understanding Z.E.N.works Policy Package Objects

Network administrators can now create and store policy packages within NDS. Policy packages are a collection of policies that relate to the configuration of a workstation. The policy packages are broken down by desktop OS, user, and workstation in the desktop OS. The seven policy packages are listed and discussed here:

- Container package
- WIN31 user package
- WIN31 workstation package
- WIN95 user package (includes Windows 98)
- WIN95 workstation package (includes Windows 98)
- WINNT user package
- WINNT workstation package

Z.E.N.works defines seven policy packages. Each policy package and the policies it contains are outlined in the following section. The types of objects the policy package can be associated with are also noted.

Consulting Experience

Some policies exist in more than one policy package. In general, Z.E.N.works defines policy packages that are either associated to a user or a group of users or associated to a workstation or a group of workstations. Different packages are defined for every operating system type (Windows 3.*x*, Windows 95/98, and Windows NT).

Container Package/Search Policy

The container policy is only associated to containers and defines how the Z.E.N.works client components search in NDS for associated policy packages. The search policy is included in the container package. Use the search policy to set a limit on how the system will search for associated policy packages and effective policies. Search policies can be associated to a container only (by associating the container package to a specific container). You may want to limit searches to the parent container only to reduce LAN traffic. An example of the search level policy is shown in Figure 19.15.

FIGURE 19.15

Search levels can be set using the container package search policy.

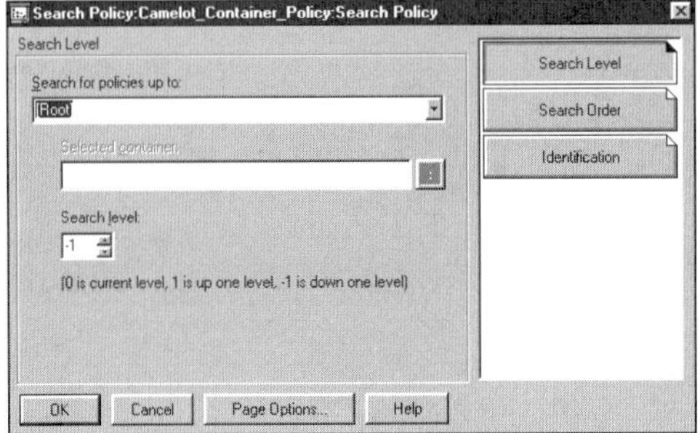

Windows 3.*x* User Package

The Windows 3.*x* user package is used to represent a Windows 3.*x* user and can be associated with users, groups, or containers. The Windows 3.*x* user package can define these types of policies:

- **Help desk policy** — You can use this primarily to establish communication rules between users and your help desk. You must set a help desk policy in order for your users to be able to use the Help Requester program. If you choose to, you can enable users to send requests for help to an e-mail address; the program will automatically supply the e-mail with the pertinent information you require.

- **Remote control policy** — Use this policy to manage remote control functions for this workstation (or the workstations associated with this policy) or to begin a remote control session and access the remote control console.

- **Workstation import policy**—Use this policy to manage remote control functions for this workstation (or the workstations associated with this policy) or to begin a remote control session and access the remote control console.

Windows 3.*x* Workstation Package

The Windows 3.*x* workstation package is used to represent Windows 3.*x* workstations and can be associated with workstations, workstation groups, or containers. The policies included are:

- **3x Computer system policy**—Use this to manage one or more files and make them part of a workstation policy package. The types of files that can be managed are ASCII text (such as .BAT, .INI, or .CTG) or binary files (such as .EXE, .COM, or .DLL).

- **Remote control policy**—Use this policy to manage remote control functions for this workstation (or the workstations associated with this policy) or to begin a remote control session and access the remote control console.

Windows 95/98 User Package

The Windows 95 user packages are used to represent a Windows 95/98 user and can be associated with users, groups, or containers. The policies included are:

- **95/98 desktop preferences**—This policy contains Control Panel contents with nothing enabled. Use it to set default display preferences and mouse buttons for the desktops.

- **95/98 user system policy**—Use this to create settings for a default Windows 95/98 user.

- **Help desk policy**—You can use this primarily to establish communication rules between users and your help desk. You must set a help desk policy in order for your users to be able to use the Help Requester program. If you choose to, you can enable users to send requests for help to an e-mail address; the program will automatically supply the e-mail with the pertinent information you require.

- **Remote control policy** — Use this policy to manage remote control functions for this workstation (or the workstations associated with this policy) or to begin a remote control session and access the remote control console.
- **Workstation import policy** — Use this policy to manage remote control functions for this workstation (or the workstations associated with this policy) or to begin a remote control session and access the remote control console.

Windows 95/98 Workstation Package

The Windows 95 workstation packages are used to represent Windows 95/98 users and can be associated with workstations, workstation groups, or containers. The policies included are:

- **95 computer printer policy** — Use this to list printers and drivers available to the Windows 95/98 workstations associated to this policy.
- **95 computer system policy** — Use this to set a collection of settings for a default Windows 95/98 computer.
- **95 RAS configuration** — Use this option to create a policy for a remote access server and dial-up networking.
- **Novell Client configuration** — Use this policy to configure workstation clients for large-scale updates. You can set numerous parameters for a workstation, including preferred server, preferred tree, and so on. You can also change protocol preferences, printer preferences, and much more.
- **Remote control policy** — Use this policy to manage remote control functions for this workstation (or the workstations associated with this policy) or to begin a remote control session and access the remote control console.
- **Restrict login policy** — This policy enables you to control from which workstations access to the network can be made. To restrict login, simply add NDS objects to either the Allow Login From or Deny Login From area on the Restrict Login page. To remove a login restriction previously added to either side, click the object and press the Remove tab.

- **Workstation inventory** — Enabling the workstation inventory policy causes the workstation to create a workstation object in the NDS tree and provide information about itself to be put into that workstation object. The information about that workstation can then be periodically updated.

Windows NT User Package

The Windows NT user packages are used to represent NT users and can be associated with users, groups, or containers. The policies included are:

- **Dynamic local user policy** — You can use this policy to configure the user created on an NT workstation after successfully authenticating to NDS. A dynamic local user is a user object that the Workstation Manager (rather than the administrator) creates temporarily or permanently in the workstation's SAM database. A temporary user or account is known as a volatile user, the duration of which is determined by the administrator. This type of account prevents the workstation SAM from becoming too large.

- **Help desk policy** — You can use this primarily to establish communication rules between users and your help desk. You must set a help desk policy in order for your users to be able to use the Help Requester program. If you choose to, you can enable users to send requests for help to an e-mail address, and the program will automatically supply the e-mail with the pertinent information you require.

- **NT desktop preferences** — This policy contains Control Panel contents with nothing enabled. Use it to set default display preferences and mouse buttons.

- **NT user printer policy** — Use this to list printers and drivers available to the Windows NT users associated to this policy.

- **NT user system policy** — This policy page lets the administrator set a variety of attributes related to the computer system the user is running. Unlike the computer system policy, which applies to the individual workstation, the user system policy follows users regardless of which workstation they use to access the network.

- **Remote control policy** — Use this policy to manage remote control functions for this workstation (or the workstations associated with this policy) or to begin a remote control session and access the remote control console.

- **Workstation import policy** — Use this page to specify where workstation objects are created and how they are named when they are associated with the policy package containing this policy.

Windows NT Workstation Package

The Windows NT workstation packages are used to represent a Windows NT workstation and can be associated with workstations, workstation groups, or containers. The policies that are included are:

- **Novell Client configuration** — Use this policy to configure workstation clients for large-scale updates. You can set numerous parameters for a workstation, including preferred server, preferred tree, and so on. You can also change protocol preferences, printer preferences, and much more.

- **NT computer printer policy** — Use this to list printers and drivers available to the Windows NT workstations associated to this policy.

- **NT computer system policy** — Use this to set a collection of settings for a default Windows NT computer.

- **Remote control policy** — This policy is the first step in enabling a workstation to be controlled remotely, which can help you resolve workstation problems from the comfort of your own office. Here you specify whether or not remote control is enabled for workstations associated to the policy package containing this policy.

- **Restrict login policy** — This policy enables you to control from which workstations access to the network can be made. To restrict login, simply add NDS objects to either the Allow Login From or Deny Login From area on the Restrict Login page. To remove a login restriction previously added to either side, click the object and press the Remove tab.

- **Workstation inventory** — Enabling the workstation inventory policy causes the workstation to create a workstation object in the NDS tree for that user and provide information about itself to be put into NDS for that object. This information can be periodically updated to give administrators an accurate picture of their workstation hardware.

Organizing Z.E.N.works NDS Objects in NDS

This section covers guidelines for organizing Z.E.N.works objects in NDS. As we mentioned earlier, the workstation import policy defines where the workstation objects are created in NDS.

There are three different approaches for creating these objects:

- Create the workstation object in the same Organizational Unit as the user object. Use this option if you have less than 1,000–1,500 objects in the same partition.
- Create the workstation in a separately defined organizational unit. Use this option if you have a container with users that approaches or exceeds 1,500 objects. Be sure to partition this workstation container separately.
- Create the workstation in an organizational unit relative to the organizational unit where the user policy package is associated. This depends on how many objects are in the same container.

We'll walk you through an example of creating a policy package. You can follow these steps to create any of the available policy packages after you have installed Z.E.N.works:

1. Load NWADMIN at your workstation.
2. Select a container where you want to create the policy package as shown in Figure 19.16. Select Policy Packages from the list.

FIGURE 19.16

Creating a new policy in the selected container

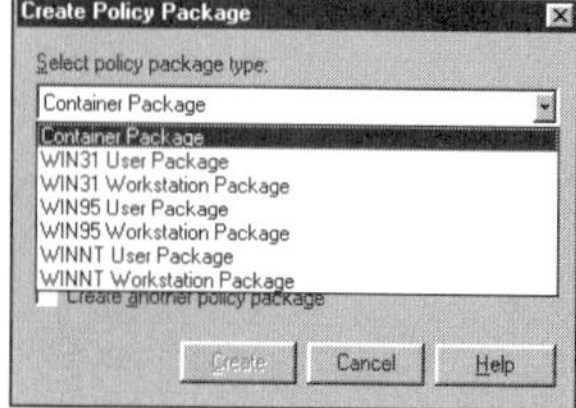

3. A dialog box will be displayed showing the packages available. In Figure 19.17, we select the WINNT user package.

FIGURE 19.17

Creating a WINNT user package

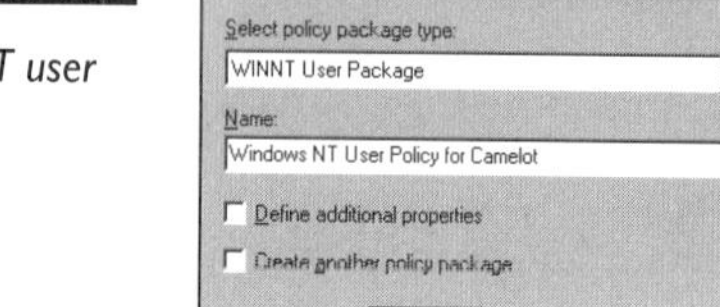

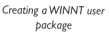

4. The next step is to select the newly created object and right-click Details as shown in Figure 19.18.

FIGURE 19.18

Selecting Details of the newly created object

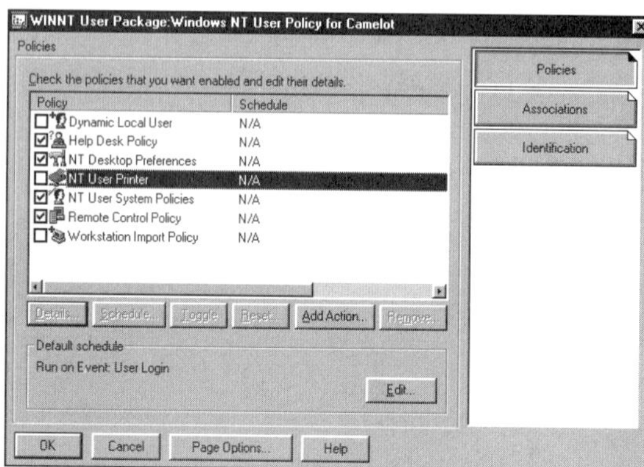

5. Once you are in the Details dialog box with the Policy tab selected, you will see that you have the capability to check boxes for the types of policies you want to create. We previously discussed creating the workstation import policy, and many other policies can be created, as shown on the previous dialog box. For example you can select the help desk policy for your workstation as shown in Figure 19.19.

FIGURE 19.19

Creating a help desk policy for your workstations

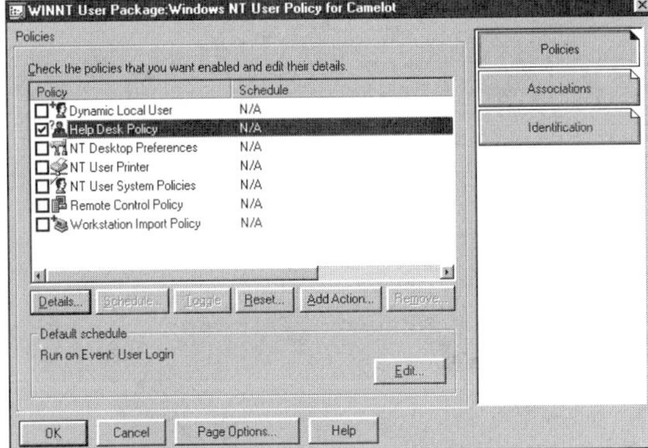

6. Now select Details for the help desk policy and fill in the contact information as shown in Figure 19.20.

FIGURE 19.20

Providing the details for the help desk policy

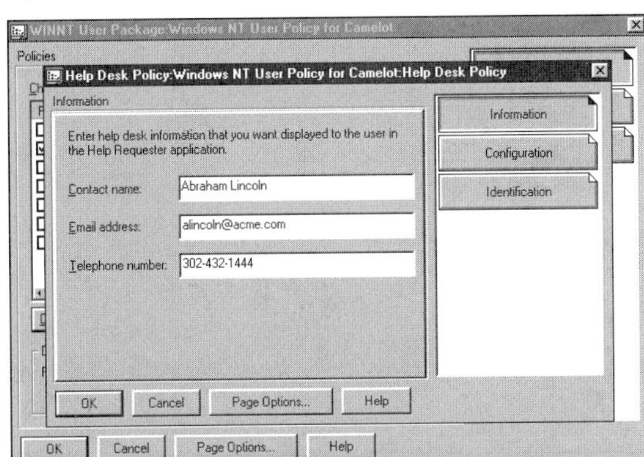

7. After you have defined the policies you wish to use, you need to associate the policy with a user, group, or container. As previously discussed, select the Associations button to view the available associations in your NDS tree. Associate the help desk policy to a container. A user logging into a workstation sees the help desk icon appear on the workstation as shown in Figure 19.21. The user can click the icon to provide the Help Disk with critical information regarding the workstation.

FIGURE 19.21

The Help Desk icon as it appears on the user's desktop

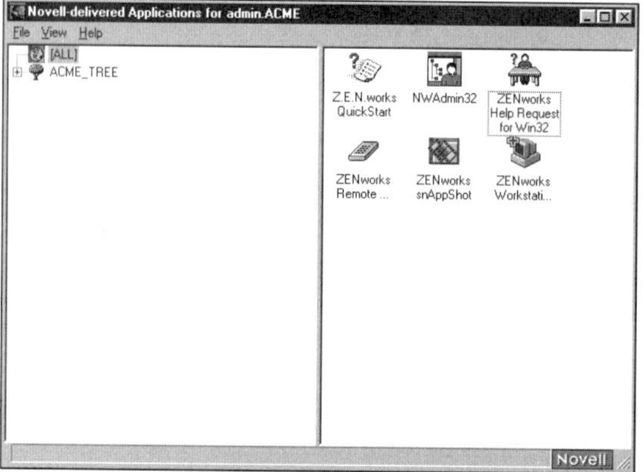

Using Z.E.N.works to Copy Printer Drivers to Workstations

Z.E.N.works printer policies can be used to create printers in Windows 95/98 or Windows NT and to copy the appropriate printer drivers to the local workstations. Z.E.N.works uses what is known as the Z.E.N.works Scheduler to install the printers. Therefore, a logged-in user does not need to have Administrator privileges.

You can define these printer policies:

- NT user printer policy
- NT workstation printer policy
- 95 user printer policy
- 95 workstation printer policy

Consulting Experience

For every group of workstations using the same standard printer create a workstation printer policy for the entire group. You can define a workstation printer policy for every room or every floor, depending on your environment. Standard printers should be grouped together. For example, 10 workstations in one room accessing three different printers located in the same room should be grouped together with one workstation printer policy.

A specific workstation or a specific user can only use one policy of the same type. Therefore, a printing environment for a user working on a workstation will be defined by one NT user printer policy and one NT workstation printer policy. Future versions of Z.E.N.works will allow the association of multiple printer policies.

An example of creating a workstation printer policy for a Windows NT workstation is discussed here:

1. Using NWADMIN, create a WINNT user package if one has not already been created.

2. Select the Details of the new object and click NT User Printer to see the dialog box shown in Figure 19.22. Select the printer and print queue that you want for this policy.

When you create an association, the printers are created as NDS objects and the appropriate drivers are installed on any workstation that the user uses. Therefore, a printer setup can follow the user to any workstation.

Printers and printer drivers can also be associated with workstations through the Windows workstation packages. So when you make an association to a workstation, the printers are available to any user that uses that workstation.

FIGURE 19.22

Creating an NT user printer object in NWADMIN

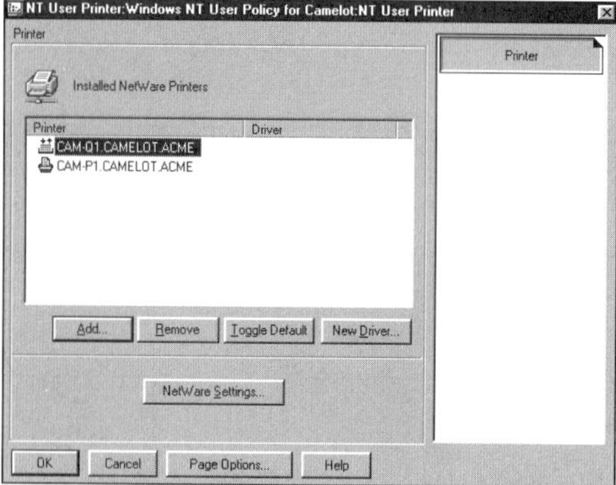

Using Profiles with Z.E.N.works

A Windows NT 4.0 user profile describes the Windows NT configuration for a specific user, including the user's environment and preference settings. For example, those settings and configuration options specific to the user, such as installed applications, desktop icons, and color options, are contained in a user profile. This profile is built in part from system policy information (for example, those things that a user has access to and those things that the user can and cannot change) and in part from permitted, saved changes that a user makes to customize his or her desktop.

A system policy for Windows 95/98 or a Windows NT workstation is a set of registry settings that together define the computer resources available to a group of users or an individual. Policies define the various facets of the desktop environment that a system administrator needs to control, such as the applications available, the applications that appear on the user's desktop, the applications and options that appear in the Start menu, and who can change attributes of their desktops and who cannot.

With the addition of system policies and the new user profile structure to Windows NT 4.0, network administrators have a greater ability to control the user environment than ever before. Z.E.N.works enables you to define this policy for Windows 95/98 and Windows NT workstations.

Creating and Administering User Profiles

In this section we discuss in more detail the components of user profiles and how to use them. User profiles can be created and administered in several different ways as we will describe here. As a system administrator, you determine whether users can modify their profiles. You can create a user profile that is not modifiable for a particular user or group. This is known as a *mandatory profile*.

You can also establish a network default user profile that applies to all new users on Windows NT 4.0 (or Windows 95/98) computers. After downloading this default profile and logging in, a user can customize the profile if he or she has been given access to do so.

You can also copy a template user profile and assign the copy to a user. The user can then customize the profile. Profiles can be stored on a network server or cached on the local machine. Cached profiles are located in the \%SystemRoot%\Profiles directory. Caching a profile reduces the total time to log in and load the profile; however, in a roaming user environment, this approach may not be optimal. This option is controllable by the administrator.

User Profile Structure

A user profile comprises a Windows NT registry hive and a set of profile directories. The registry is a database used to store machine- and user-specific settings, and portions of the registry can be saved as separate files, called *hives*. These hives can then be reloaded for use as necessary. User profiles take advantage of the hive feature to provide roaming profile functionality.

The user profile registry hive is the NTuser.dat in file form and is mapped to the HKEY_CURRENT_USER portion of the registry when the user logs in. The NTuser.dat hive maintains the user's environment preferences when the user is logged in. It stores those settings that maintain network connections, Control Panel configurations unique to the user (such as the desktop color and mouse), and application-specific settings. The series of profile directories store shortcut links, desktop icons, startup applications, and so forth. Together, these two components record all user-configurable settings that can migrate from computer to computer.

Setting Permissions for User Profiles

As an administrator you will decide how user profiles can be used and by which users. When preparing for a rollout of user profiles, you should pay careful attention to file trustees at the file server. If the user profile is mandatory, the user account should have at least Read rights on the network directory where that user's user profile is stored. If the user's profile is roaming, the user must have Write rights (or better) because the client will need to write the changes back to the central profile on the shared network drive when the user logs out.

Permissions are also important on a client machine where the user is logging on interactively. If Windows NT is installed in an NTFS partition on the client computer and the user does not have at least the default permissions, errors can occur. For example, if permissions are incorrect on the root of the system directory, this message appears: "Can't access this folder, the path is too long." A blank desktop is displayed, and the user's only option is to log out.

If permissions are set incorrectly in the %SystemRoot%, %SystemRoot%\System, %SystemRoot%\System32, or %SystemRoot%\System32\ Config directories, this message appears: "Unable to log you on because your profile could not be loaded."

Selecting a Location to Save User Profiles

As with Windows NT 3.5*x*, you can place a roaming profile on any network directory and then configure the user account profile path with Z.E.N.works to point to the profile. The Profiles directory in the system root stores local user profiles, "All Users" profile settings (which apply to any user who uses the computer), the "Default User" profile, and cached user profiles of Z.E.N.works users.

Consulting Experience

Directories containing roaming user profiles need at least Create and Read rights for profiles to be read correctly. If you use Create permissions only, when Windows NT checks for the existence of the profile it will fail because it looks for the path first, and if Read rights are not given, the check will fail.

Consulting Experience

In situations where the same user account logs into multiple machines, the last user to log out dictates the profile settings because that user was the last one to write data to the profile. Similarly, if a group of users all point to the same profile, the final logout settings are saved and will overwrite previous settings.

If the user profile is flagged as a local profile and is not mandatory, any changes the user makes while logged in are written to the locally cached version of the profile, but not to the server-based copy.

Windows NT 4.0 profiles can be saved on every NetWare server because the client computer uses the path where the profile is stored only as a location to download the profile and to write the modified user profile at logout. This enables profiles to be stored on any shared network drive. The process of downloading the profile is controlled by the client computer. The only thing a client needs is the correct path.

Except in the case of mandatory profiles or when a slow network is detected, any changes to the user's profile are saved to the central profile when the user logs out. (Because users cannot modify mandatory profiles, changes do not need to be written to the server.)

Creating a New Roaming User Profile for Windows NT 4.0

To create a new roaming user profile, you must first determine where the user's profile will be stored. You then must create an NDS user account (if one doesn't already exist), and specify a user profile path with Z.E.N.works. Finally, you must specify whether a given user will use a specific profile or can use a default profile. These procedures are described in the following sections.

Creating a New Roaming User Profile Follow these steps to create a new roaming user profile:

1. If a location has not already been prepared, create a directory on the server. Give the user a minimum of Read/Write permissions to the shared directory. If your implementation stores user profiles within users' home directories, Z.E.N.works uses a subdirectory of the user's home directory called "Windows NT 4.0 Workstation Profile."

2. Define where in the NT User Package/NT Desktop Preferences the roaming profile is stored as shown in Figure 19.23.

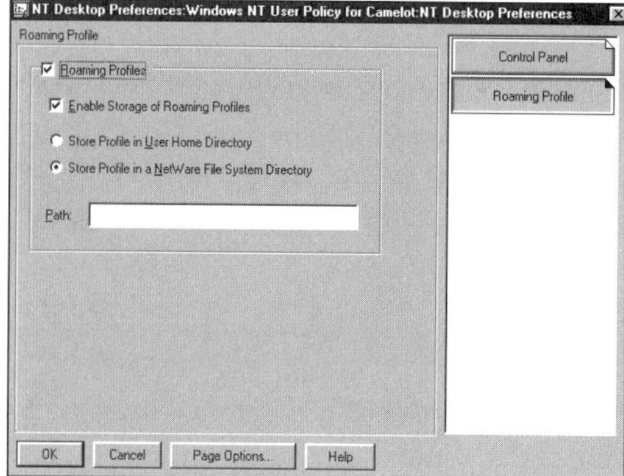

FIGURE 19.23

Defining a roaming profile in the NT user package

3. Enter the user profile path. This is the location where the user profile will be stored. It could be either the user's NDS home directory or a fixed path like \\SERVER\VOL\PROFILES\%LOGIN_NAME.

4. If the user is to receive the default user profile from the workstation where he or she will interactively log in, no further administration is required. Otherwise, use User Manager to create an account for establishing a template profile. So that you can easily identify this account, we recommend that it be called TemplateUser.

5. Using the template account (TemplateUser), log in to the local machine. A new directory with the same name as the user name created in Step 4 will be created in the %SystemRoot%\Profiles directory when you first log in. For example, if the user name is TemplateUser, the resulting directory name will be %SystemRoot%\Profiles\TemplateUser.

6. Modify any items that need to differ from the current default (for example, you may choose to modify the background color or bitmap, shortcuts on the desktop, and View options in My Computer).

7. Log out, and then log back into the same computer using an account with administrative privileges.

8. Place the template profile in the appropriate location for the type of profile distribution that will be used. (The template profile, including customization, is stored initially in %SystemRoot%\Profiles\TemplateUser.)

Copying an Existing User's Profile to Another User If you want to copy an existing user's profile to another user, then follow these steps:

1. From the Windows NT — based machine hosting the profile to be used, log in as an administrator.

2. From the Control Panel, click System. On the User Profiles page, select the profile to be copied and use the Copy To option to enter the path of the directory.

3. Modify the permissions to reflect the proper account. To do this, click the Change button, select the account, and click OK. Click OK again to copy the profile.

To copy the template profile to the Default User folder on validating domain controllers:

1. From the Windows NT–based machine hosting the profile to be used, log in as an administrator.

2. From the Control Panel, click System. On the User Profiles page, select the profile to be copied and use the Copy To option to enter the path of the Default User directory on the validating domain controller.

3. Modify the permissions to reflect the Everyone group. To do this, click the Change button, select the account, and click OK. Click OK again to copy the profile.

To copy a template profile manually to a number of users:

1. Copy the entire contents (files and subdirectories) from the directory containing the template user profile created in Step 8 under the section "Creating a New Roaming Profile" to the directory previously created.

2. Repeat this for each of the user profile directories that will receive the template user profile. The profile does not need to be stored one directory below the server\volume. The profile can be nested several directories below, or the profile path can be local. When building a path, you can use a combination like \\Server\Vol\Dir\Dir\%LOGIN_NAME\Dir\NTUser.MAN. We recommend that the Everyone group be given permission to use template profiles.

Creating a New Mandatory User Profile for Windows NT 4.0 To create a new mandatory user profile:

1. If a location has not already been prepared, create a directory on the server. Users who will have mandatory profiles need only Read permissions to the shared directory. If your implementation stores user profiles within users' home directories, make the profile directory a subdirectory of the user's home directory.

2. Make sure that the NDS user account is created and associated to an NT desktop preferences policy in Z.E.N.works.

3. Enter the user profile path in the NT desktop preferences policy. This is the location where the user profile will be stored, for example: \\server\volumes\Profiles\All. You can also use a UNC pathname pointing to an NDS Directory map object.

   If the profile is to be stored within the user's home directory, just click Store Profile in User's Home Directory in the policy.

4. Determine if an extension needs to be appended to the user profile path. If it will be mandatory that the user read the profile from the server, and if login will be denied unless this is the case, add the extension .MAN to the user profile path; for example: \\server\volumes\Profiles\All\NTUSER.MAN

5. Use User Manager to create an account for establishing the template profile. So that you can easily identify this account, we recommend that it be called TemplateUser.

6. Using the template account (TemplateUser), log into the local machine. A new directory with the same name as the user name created in Step 5 will be created in the %SystemRoot%\Profiles directory when you first log in. For example, if the user name is TemplateUser, the resulting directory name will be %SystemRoot%\Profiles\TemplateUser.

7. Modify any items that need to differ from the current default (for example, you may choose to modify the background color or bitmap, shortcuts on the desktop, and View options in My Computer).

8. Log out, and then log back into the same computer using an account with administrative privileges.

9. In \\server\volumes\Profiles\All, create the directory structure you specified as the path in Step 5. For example, you would need to create the directory user name under \\server\volumes\Profiles\. Or if the profile is stored in the user's home directory, the directory has been automatically created by NetWare Administrator.

   If you appended the .MAN extension to the user profile path in Step 4, append the .MAN suffix to the directory name for the folder where the profile will be stored. The .MAN extension identifies a Windows NT 4.0 mandatory profile that must be accessible for the user to log in. For example, if the user name is "username," the path to the mandatory profile would be \\server\volumes\Profiles\username.man.

   If you also have a mandatory Windows NT 3.5*x* profile for the user, use the .pdm extension in place of the .man extension (for example, \\server\volumes\Profiles\username.man). The .pdm extension is required because the profile folder cannot have the same name as the Windows NT 3.5*x* user profile located in the same parent folder.

Consulting Experience

The profile does not need to be stored one directory below server\volume. The profile can be nested several directories below, or the profile path can be local. When building a path, a combination like \\Server\vol\Dir\Dir\%LOGIN_NAME\Dir\NTUser.MAN can be used.

10. From the Windows NT–based machine hosting the template profile to be used, log in as an administrator.

11. From the Control Panel, click System. From the User Profiles page, select the profile to be copied and use the Copy To option to enter the path of the directory you created in Step 6.

12. Modify the permissions to allow the group Everyone to use the profile. To do this, click the Change button, select the account Everyone, and click OK.

    The profile including the folder trees and the NTuser.*xxx* file originally included with the profile is written to the location you designated. The permissions are also encoded into the binary NTuser.*xxx* file.

13. In the directory that the profile was copied to in Step 11, check the NTUSER.*xxx* file for the .man extension. If the extension is .dat, the profile will still be modifiable. Change the extension to .man if necessary.

Making a Roaming Profile Mandatory in Windows NT 4.0 You have two options when configuring a mandatory roaming profile: You can change the user's ability to modify the user profile, or you can change the user's ability to modify the user profile and enforce the use of the server-based profile at login. With the second option, the user is not able to log into the system if the network profile is unavailable. Each of these procedures will be explained more fully in the sections that follow.

Consulting Experience

If you make this change while the user is logged in, the user's copy of the profile will overwrite your changes, because at the time the user logged in, he or she had permission to overwrite the profile.

Changing the User's Ability to Modify a Profile When creating a user profile or at any time thereafter, you have the option of enforcing whether or not the user can modify the profile by changing the extension on the NTuser.dat file. The NTuser.dat file is located in the root of the user's profile directory. If you change the name of this file to NTuser.man, when Windows NT reads the profile, it marks the profile as read-only, and any changes that the user makes while logged in are not written back to the server-based profile when he or she logs out.

To change the user's ability to make modifications to their user profile, you can use these steps:

1. Locate the user's profile in the account's user profile path.

2. While the user is logged out, rename the NTuser.dat file to NTuser.man.

Be cautious if you use the Explorer interface to make these changes. If you have the "Hide file extensions for known file types" option enabled (this is the default), be sure to check the properties to be sure that there are not two extensions. For example, say you want to make a profile mandatory and you use Explorer to rename the NTuser.dat filename to NTuser.man. Because of the Hide extensions default, Explorer saves the file as type .man but does not display the .man extension. Later, you decide to allow the user to make changes again, and through Explorer, you rename the file back to NTuser.dat. However, because Explorer was hiding that part of the filename that determines its type, the only thing you rename is the prefix. The filename is now NTuser.dat.man. To avoid this situation, you can either rename files from the command line or change the behavior of Explorer.

Enforcing the Use of the Server-Based Profile In addition to enforcing the read-only property of a profile, the administrator can duplicate the functionality that was available in Windows NT 3.5*x* of not allowing the user to log in unless the server profile is available.

To enforce the use of the server-based profile for a given user:

1. Append the .man extension to the user profile path in User Manager as explained in the previous section. (Skip this step for users who have existing Windows NT 3.5*x* profiles and who already have the .man extension appended to their profile paths.)

2. If the user already has a Windows NT 3.5*x* mandatory profile on the server, change the name of the folder where the Windows NT 4.0 roaming profile currently exists to foldername.pdm. If the user logs into a Windows NT 4.0–based workstation and the user profile path contains the .man extension, Windows NT will determine that a mandatory Windows NT 3.5*x* profile exists and will automatically replace the .man extension with .pdm and will look for the directory path configured in the user profile path. For example, at login if the user profile path is configured to use \\server\volume\profiles\username.man, Windows NT will look for \\server\volume\profiles\username.pdm for the correct profile to load.

   If only the Windows NT 4.0 user profile exists, change the name of the folder where the Windows NT 4.0 roaming profile exists to foldername.man. If the user logs into a Windows NT 4.0–based workstation and the user profile path contains the extension .man, Windows NT will look for the directory path configured in the user profile path. If Windows NT does not find the directory, it will replace the .man extension with .pdm and will check again.

3. If you haven't already done so, change the name of the NTuser.*xxx* file to NTuser.dat. (Refer to the section "Changing the User's Ability to Modify a Profile," earlier in this chapter.)

Distributing Applications with the Z.E.N.works Application Launcher

The Novell Application Launcher component of Z.E.N.works lets you distribute applications to users' workstations and manage those applications as objects in your NDS tree. Users can then access the applications that you assign to them using the Application Launcher window.

The Application Launcher Components

In this section we discuss the components of the application launcher, which include the application launcher snap-in and the Application Launcher window. The Application Launcher consists of two administrator components and two user components. The administrator components are as follows:

- Application Launcher snap-in
- Application Launcher
- Application Launcher window
- Application Launcher Explorer

The Application Launcher Snap-In

The Application Launcher snap-in component is a Windows DLL that "snaps in" to the NetWare Administrator utility. The Application Launcher snap-in makes it possible to create application objects in your NDS tree. Like other objects in the NDS tree, application objects contain their own set of properties. These properties give you a high level of control over the application object after it has been distributed to workstations.

In addition to adding the application object type, the Application Launcher snap-in also adds new property pages to the user, group, organization, and organizational unit objects. These property pages enable your administrators to associate applications with one specific user object, or with a group, organization, or organizational unit objects. Using the added property pages, it is also possible to specify how the application will run a users' workstation.

The Application Launcher snAppShot

When you install a complex application on a workstation, changes will need to be made to the workstation, including the Windows Registry, .INI files, file system files, CONFIG.SYS and AUTOEXEC.BAT files, and any other configurations that support the application. The Application Launcher snAppShot component takes two "snapshot" pictures: the workstation's preinstallation configuration state (before an application is installed) and the workstation's postinstallation state (after an application is installed). Application Launcher snAppShot then compares the two snapshots and records any differences in an Application Object Template (.AOT) file or in an Application Object Text Template (.AXT) file. The Application Launcher snAppShot also keeps track of all the files that an application Setup program installs to the workstation. These files are copied and stored in a series of .FIL files.

NOTE

An .AOT file is written in binary format and cannot be modified by an administrator. The .AXT file is in text format and can be modified using a text editor. Editing these text files can introduce problems into the application object, so be careful when editing an .AXT file.

The user components for the Application Launcher are as follows:

The Application Launcher Window

The Application Launcher window is the workstation component that displays the icons of the application objects that you set up using Application Launcher snap-in. The Application Launcher window lets users create personal folders, refresh applications, change views, and get information about folders and applications. Because the applications are centrally managed, users cannot disturb the drive paths of the application.

The Application Launcher Explorer

The Application Launcher Explorer adds another level of Windows 95/98 and Windows NT desktop integration. In addition to using the Application Launcher Explorer window, users also have access to the applications you assign to them in the Windows Explorer, Start menu, System Tray, or Desktop.

Both the Application Launcher window and Application Launcher Explorer rely on the configurations that are set up in the Launcher Configuration property page on the user, organization, or organizational unit object to which the application objects are associated. For example, if a user object is set to use parent container settings, then the Application Launcher window and Application Launcher Explorer look to the immediate parent organizational unit object. If the parent organizational unit is set to use a default configuration, then the default configuration is used.

Defining Application Objects with snAppShot

When a complex application is installed to a workstation, it is possible that the application's Setup program makes changes to the workstation including the Windows registry, .INI files, system files, CONFIG.SYS and AUTOEXEC.BAT files, and any other configurations that support the application.

The information gathered by NAL snAppShot is to be used when creating and setting up application objects using the NetWare Administrator and the NAL snap-in component.

Using snAppShot

The following steps explain how to use the Novell Application Launcher snAppShot ("NAL" snAppShot) component, including how to compare the pre- and postinstallation states of a workstation, how to create Application Object Template (.AOT) and .FIL files, and how to make those files available to the NetWare Administrator using the NAL snap-in.

Use NAL snAppShot to make the .AOT and .FIL files available to the NAL snap-in. The steps listed here will walk you through an example of using snAppShot to make this happen:

1. Find a workstation that is representative of the ones on your network to which you will distribute applications. This workstation should be configured the same as the workstations you use on your network.

NOTE

Although no two workstations are exactly the same, find a workstation that is configured similarly to the other target workstations. The more representative the workstation is, the fewer manual setup procedures you need to do during and after distribution.

2. For best results, close all other applications on the workstation you have chosen to use.

3. Run NAL snAppShot by executing the SNAPSHOT32.EXE file from the directory where you installed it (most likely SYS:\Public\Snapshot\); then read the introductory window, and choose the appropriate option. An example is shown in Figure 19.24.

FIGURE 19.24

Using the snAppShot utility

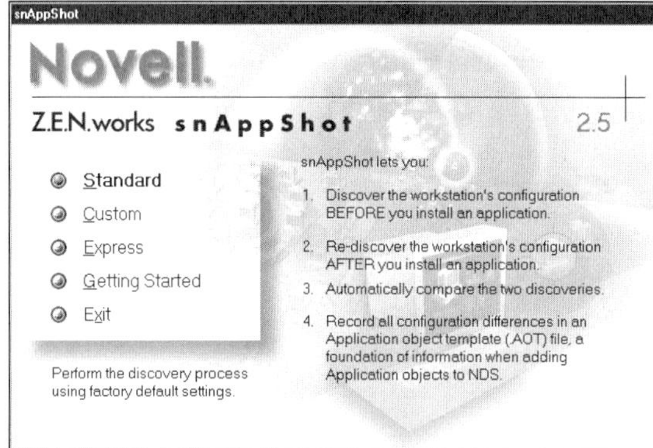

4. You can choose among these discovery options:

   - **Standard** — Performs the discovery process using the factory default settings.
   - **Custom** — Enables you to specify the drives, files, folders, registry hive, and shortcuts you want to include or exclude in the discovery process.
   - **Express** — Quickly scans for changes on the desktop using a snAppShot Preferences file created during a previous discovery process.

Be sure to read the Getting Started option before choosing a discovery option. This will give you a good overview of snAppShot.

For example purposes we will describe the Standard installation here. Select the Standard option to be presented with an information dialog box. Fill in a name for the NDS application object and an application icon title, and then click Next. An example of this is shown in Figure 19.25.

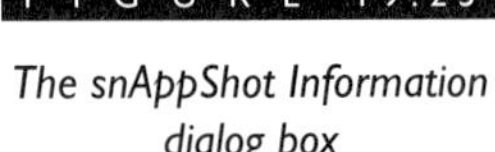
FIGURE 19.25

The snAppShot Information dialog box

5. Specify the application file location for the .FIL files that will be created as a result of running NAL snAppShot. Also specify the Windows Drive and Boot Drive. Click Next. An example of this procedure is shown in Figure 19.26.

FIGURE 19.26

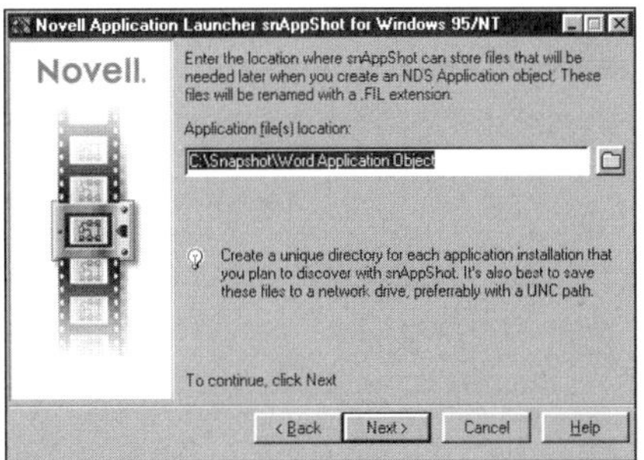

Specifying the network or workstation directory of the .AOT

The next dialog box will ask you to enter the filename and location you want to use for the Application Object Template (.AOT) file. In our example, the name will default to WordApplicationObject.AOT. You can change this if you desire another name.

IMPORTANT

If you are going to use NAL snAppShot again to discover the changes of additional application installations, we recommend creating unique directories on the network for each application. If you don't use unique source directories, .AOT and .FIL files could be overwritten and cause you problems.

6. Specify the drives you want snAppShot to scan. If you select the custom option, specify which files, directories, .INI Files, .TXT files, and Registry keys you want to include or exclude during the NAL snAppShot discovery process and then click Next. For example, because you might not want to record the changes to the Windows 95/98 Recycle Bin as a result of installing an application, you can exclude this directory from the discovery process.

7. After reviewing the snAppShot settings summary, you are ready to take the preinstallation snapshot of the workstation. Click Next or click Back to check or change a previous setting.

   The preinstallation discovery process records all current files and configurations on the workstation and stores the information in a hidden file. When NAL snAppShot finishes the preinstallation discovery, it is ready for you to run the application's Setup program. An example of this information gathering is shown in Figure 19.27.

   When the process is completed, the utility will display a dialog box stating that it's time to install the application. Click the button that says Run Application Install. An example of this is shown in Figure 19.28.

8. Complete the installation of the application. Your application installation files can reside anywhere and can be located by browsing.

FIGURE 19.27

The snAppShot utility first does a scan of the workstation.

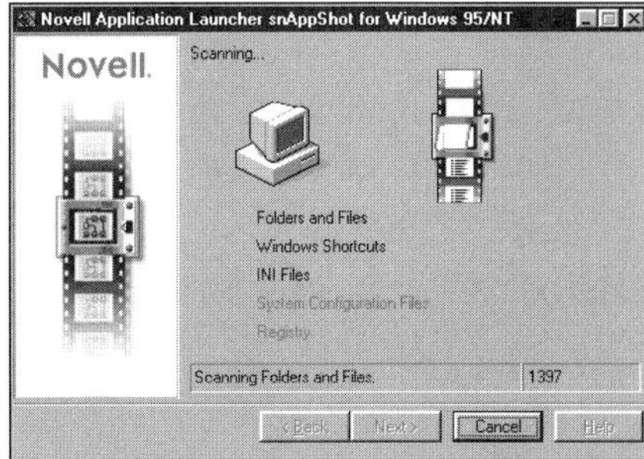

FIGURE 19.28

After scanning the workstation, snAppShot will display this dialog box to install your application.

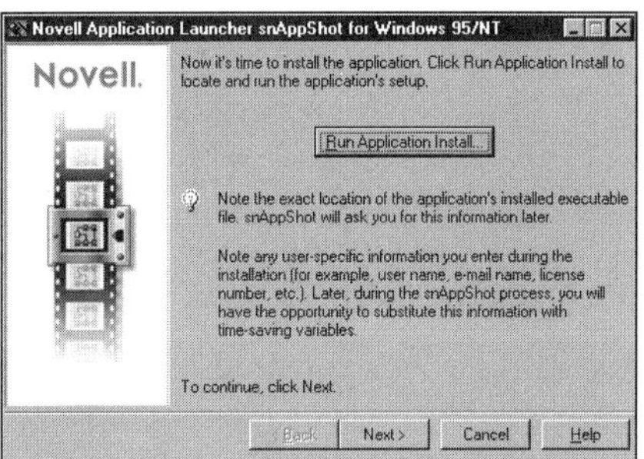

9. When the application is installed, the snAppShot utility will automatically go to the postinstallation discovery. This step will note any changes made to the files and configurations on the workstation as a result of the application's Setup program. An example of the postapplication install scan is shown in Figure 19.29.

FIGURE 19.29

A postapplication install scan of the workstation

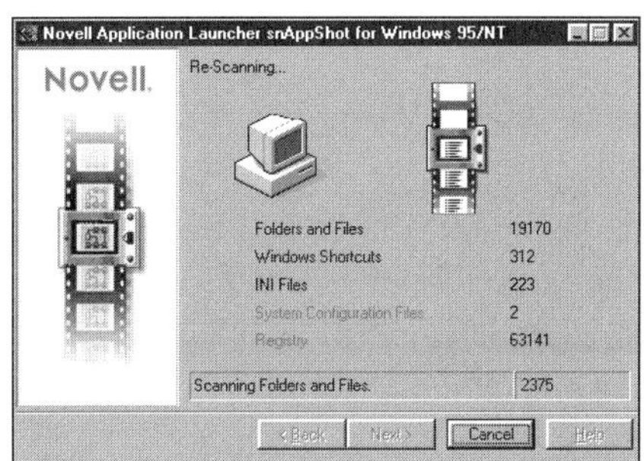

You will then be shown a dialog box that notifies you that an AOT template is being generated. This will take a few minutes depending on how many files you have on your workstation (see Figure 19.30).

FIGURE 19.30

The final stage in the snAppShot process is to generate the template file.

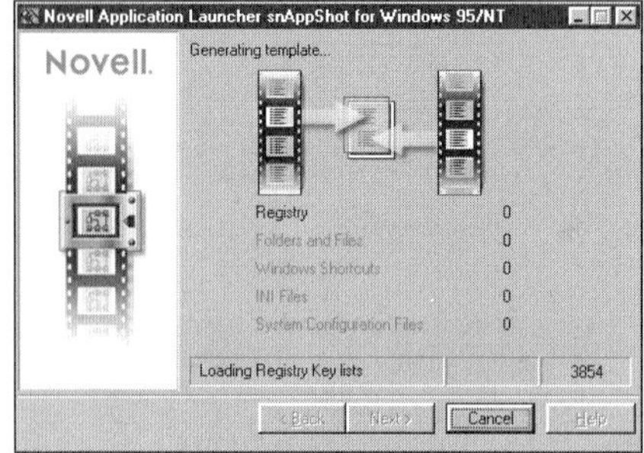

Once complete, a dialog box (shown in Figure 19.31) will be displayed showing that the process is finished. The template is stored as both an .AOT file and an .AXT (text) file in the locations that you've previously specified.

FIGURE 19.31

The SnAppShot Completion dialog box

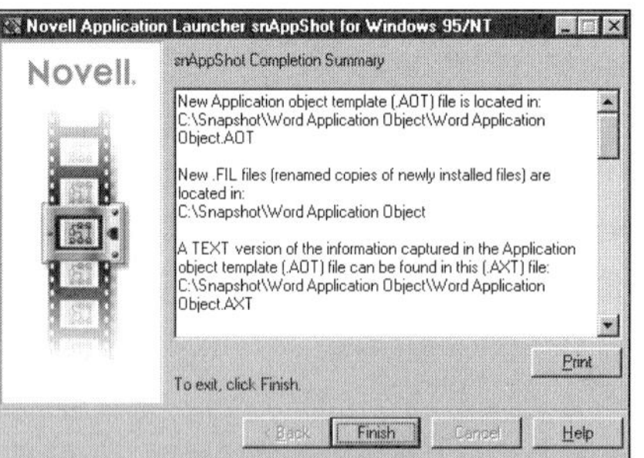

Creating an Application Object Using the .AOT and .FIL Files That You Generated

Now that you have successfully completed the creation of the .AOT files for an application, you are ready to create an application object that will represent the application to your NDS users. Follow these steps:

1. Start the NetWare Administrator.

2. Right-click the organization or organizational unit object under which you want to create an application object and click Create. Select Application and then click OK.

3. The resulting dialog box is shown in Figure 19.32.

FIGURE 19.32

Creating an application object

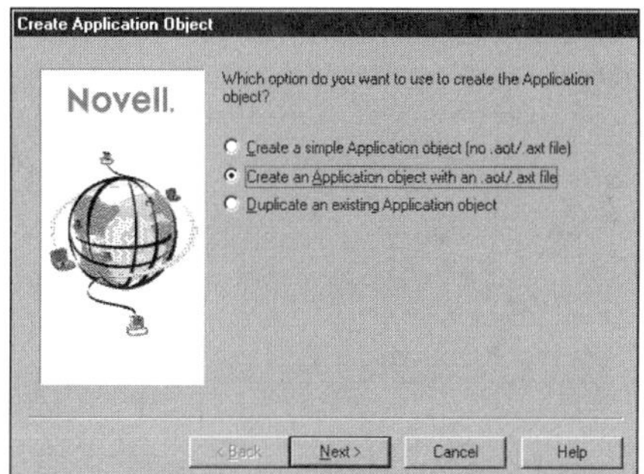

4. You can create an application object with or without an associated .AOT/.AXT file.

5. Browse for the .AOT files, if necessary, and then click Next to see the dialog box shown in Figure 19.33.

FIGURE 19.33

Selecting a predefined .AOT file to associate with an application object

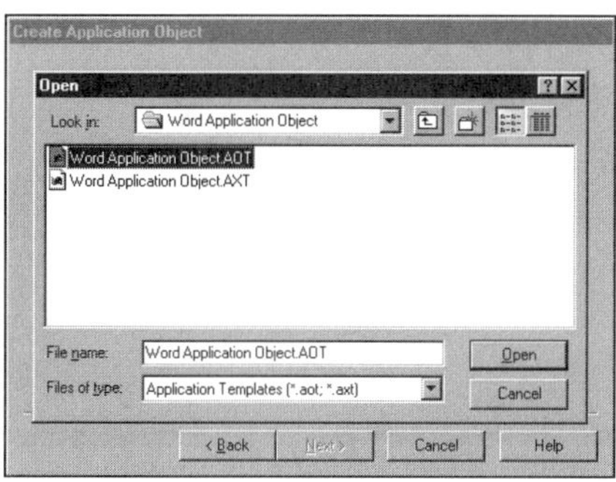

6. Check (and change if necessary) the target and source directories of the application object, and then click Next.

7. Review the information about the application object, and then click Create to see the dialog box shown in Figure 19.34.

FIGURE 19.34

You can review the settings for the application object before its creation.

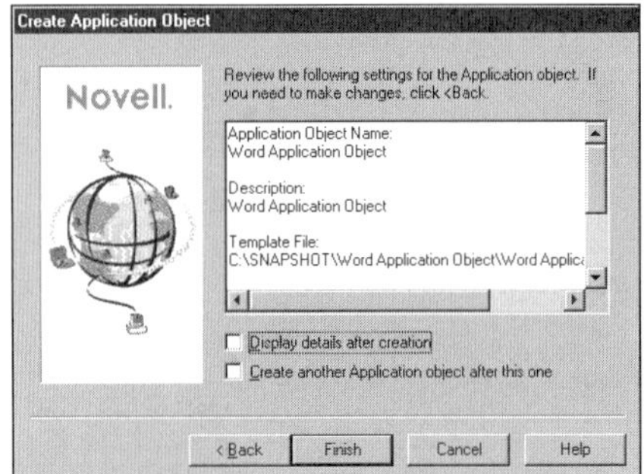

8. Associate the application object with a user, group, organization, or organizational unit object. To associate an application, right-click the application object, click Details, and then click the Associations button found on the right side of the dialog box. Use this property page to assign other objects to the application object. An example of creating associations is shown in Figure 19.35.

FIGURE 19.35

Associating the application object with users in NDS

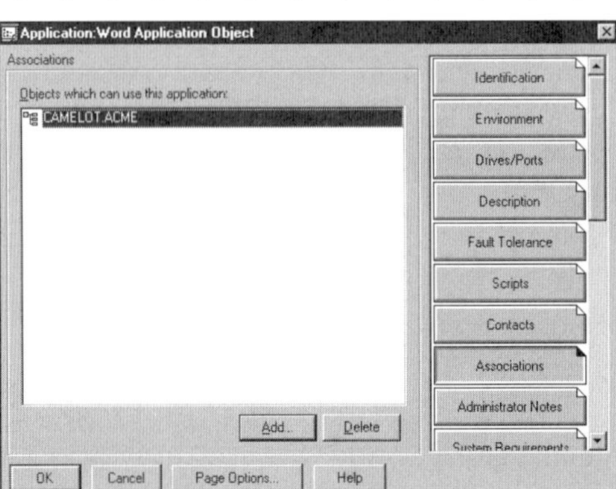

Customizing Application Objects

For your reference, all configuration options for an application object are listed in the next section. You can view these options by selecting the application object and double-clicking it or by right-clicking Details. An example of the Details dialog box is shown in Figure 19.36.

FIGURE 19.36

Customizing the application object through the Details dialog box

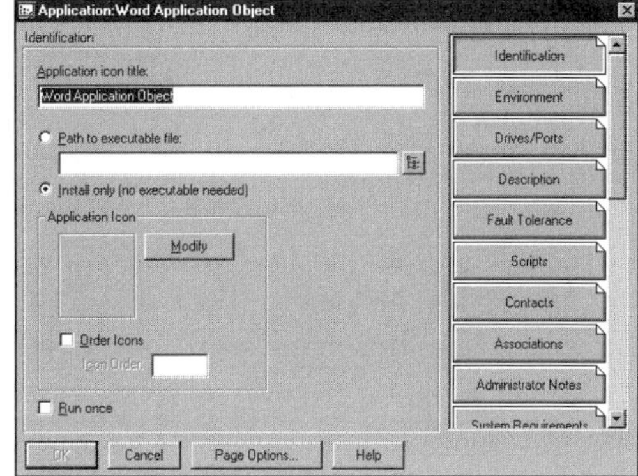

The next section lists each section of the Details dialog box.

The Identification Page

Use the Identification property page to control the application icon that the user sees at the workstation. For example, you can select a different icon picture, write the icon's title, and give the icon a display and run priority. You can also specify the path to the application's executable file and set up the application to run just one time.

Application Icon Title The text you type here appears as the caption beneath the application icon in the Application Launcher window or Application Launcher Explorer software. The application icon title, which is mandatory, can be different from the application object name (that is, the name that NDS uses to identify the application) and can contain periods and other special characters. Use the Description property page for longer descriptions of the application.

Path to Executable File The path you specify here is to the executable that is run when an Application Object icon is double-clicked in the Application Launcher window or Application Launcher Explorer. You can type in the path as a UNC path or a file directory path. Use the Browse button to browse the file directory structure and to find the executable you want. Refer to the following example syntax when mapping a drive:

```
SERVER\VOLUME:PATH

\\SERVER\VOLUME\PATH

\\TREE\.DIRECTORY_MAP_OBJECT_NAME\PATH

VOLUME_OBJECT_NAME:PATH

DIRECTORY_MAP_OBJECT_NAME:PATH

DRIVELETTER:\PATH
```

Install Only (No Executable Needed) Use this option if there isn't an application to run. For example, this application object's purpose might be to just update some files on the workstation. When you select the Install Only option, the software is installed but not run.

Application Icon This option lets you assign an icon to an application object. The icon you choose appears in the Application Launcher window or Application Launcher Explorer, depending on what you have specified on the Applications property page. If you do not specify an icon, a default Application Launcher icon is used.

Consulting Experience

You should use the variable %TARGET_PATH% wherever possible. Example: Start Netscape Communication with %TARGET_PATH%\Program\Netscape.EXE where %TARGET_PATH% is equal to C:\Program Files\Netscape\Communicator. If you don't want to run an application (for example, this application object's purpose might be to just update some files on the workstation), use the Install Only option and do not specify a path.

Order Icons This option performs two useful functions. First, it organizes the icons in the Application Launcher window and Application Launcher Explorer. Second, it dictates the order in which application objects set as Force Run will run.

Ordering is left to right or top to bottom, depending upon the way the user views icons in the Application Launcher window and Application Launcher Explorer. You achieve ordering by entering a numeric value into the Icon Order text box. All application objects you wish to order must have a numeric value. The value of zero gives the icon the highest priority and thus the highest prominence in the list. The maximum value is 999. If you do not order application objects, they will be ordered alphabetically (the default).

Example: Suppose that you have ten icons that you want to organize in the Application Launcher window. In each of those ten application objects, select Order Icons on the Identification property page and type the icon's order number. If you want the icon to be the sixth icon in the list, type the number 5. If you want it to be the first one, type 0.

If two application objects have the same Icon number, then they will be arranged alphabetically. This works well if you want to order sets of Application Object icons.

Example: Suppose you are distributing, in order of highest priority, a productivity suite with five icons, a set of utilities with seven icons, and a set of tools with four icons. You want the group of highest priority (the suite) to display most prominently.

To achieve this, give all icons in the first group a value of zero. Give the next set a value of one, and the third set a value of two. When users (who have been associated with the application objects of the three groups) run the Application Launcher window or Application Launcher Explorer, they will see three sets of icons, arranged alphabetically within each set. The very top set will be the suite applications.

Run Once When an application object's purpose is to install software to a workstation, it can be confusing to users if the icon remains on their workstations after the software has been installed. Use the Run Once option if you want the application to run just once and then have its icon disappear so as to not cause confusion.

There are a variety of ways to use Run Once in combination with other object properties. For example, if the application is specified as a Force Run on the Applications property page (meaning that the user is not involved, the application runs when Windows starts), the application is forced to run one time.

If you selected Run Once and also specified a version stamp for this application, the application runs once until the next time you change the version stamp, whereupon the application runs one more time. This latter method is useful for upgrading applications.

The Environment Property Page

Use the Environment property page (shown in Figure 19.37) to identify the environment that might be required for an application object. Some applications require custom configuration parameters to function properly. Before launching the application, the Application Launcher window or Application Launcher Explorer software configures the workstation to properly run the application. The parameters, directories, mappings, and printer ports associated with the application automatically execute (mappings and captures don't actually happen until the user launches the application). After exiting the application, the application's posttermination script removes any drive mappings or port captures it created during execution.

FIGURE 19.37

The NAL Environment page

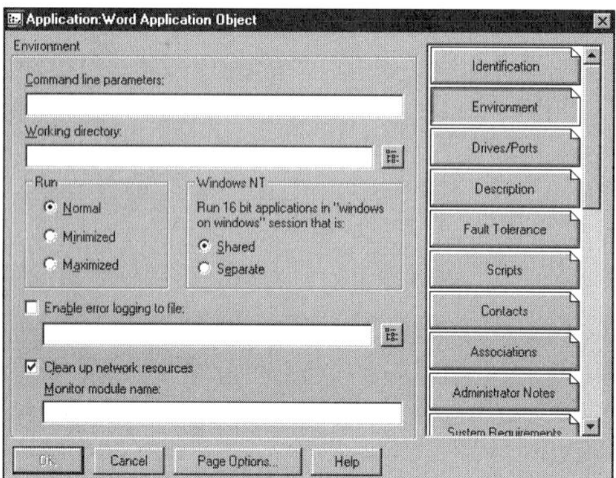

To set up the application's environment:

1. Right-click the application object and click Details.

2. Click the Environment button.

3. Change the following Environment properties as needed, and then click OK.

Command Line Parameters Some applications require application-specific parameters to run in a desired mode or view. You can place one or more parameters here. See your application's documentation for more information about the types of parameters that you can use.

Working Directory This option can be designated for any application object and might be required by some applications (your application's documentation describes the working directories it needs). You can look for the working directory by using the Browse button to the right of the Working Directory field.

Run This group box sets the application's initial window size. Choose whether you want to run the application in Normal, Minimized, or Maximized mode.

If you are setting up a 16-bit application to run on Windows NT, you need to specify either a shared or separate "Windows on Windows" (WOW) session.

To run on Windows NT (a 32-bit operating system), 16-bit applications must run in a Virtual DOS Machine (VDM) that emulates Windows 3.1 functionality. The 16-bit Windows emulator called WOW (for Win16-on-Win32) isolates 16-bit application errors from the rest of the 32-bit operating system.

Sixteen-bit Windows applications can run in their own separate WOW sessions, or they can share a WOW session with other 16-bit applications. Sharing a WOW session saves memory and enables applications to use DDE or OLE to communicate with other applications in the same WOW session. Running an application in its own separate WOW session allows for more robust operation because the application is isolated from other 16-bit applications. Because some applications do not run properly in a separate WOW session, the default option is to run the 16-bit Windows application in a shared WOW session.

Enable Error Logging to File Specify the path to a file where any errors are logged if the application fails to install or launch. No status is tracked here except for errors.

Consulting Experience

Users running this application object must be given rights to write to this file for this option to work correctly.

Clean Up Network Resources The process of "cleaning up" means that the license for a particular network connection is removed. This prevents users from using a network connection when they don't need it.

If the Clean Up Network Resources option is selected, drive mappings and printer ports associated with the applications launched by the Application Launcher window or Application Launcher Explorer are cleaned up. If this check box is not selected, drive mappings and printer ports established earlier remain in effect.

Consulting Experience

If the resource (a connection, map, or capture) is already in use when the Application Launcher window or Application Launcher Explorer is started, the Application Launcher window or Application Launcher Explorer uses it and does not clean it up. Otherwise, the resource is created and cleaned up when all other Application Launcher window or Application Launcher Explorer applications are finished using it. The connection to the server containing the resource is removed as well. If the applications that the Application Launcher window or Application Launcher Explorer launched are still running when the Application Launcher window or Application Launcher Explorer is terminated, the allocated resources remain intact.

Monitor Module Name When an application is launched, the Application Launcher window or Application Launcher Explorer monitors the executable of the application. When the executable terminates, the process of cleaning up network resources begins. However, the executable filename may actually be a "wrapper" that sets up environments, runs other executables, and then terminates. If the Application Launcher window or Application Launcher Explorer monitors the wrapper executable, it might prematurely start cleaning up network resources before the application has terminated.

Consult your application documentation about whether the application uses a wrapper executable. If it does, find out the name of the module that remains running. Type this name (without the extension) in the text box provided.

The Drives/Ports Page

Because the applications that users see in the Application Launcher window or Application Launcher Explorer are linked directly to application objects, users do not need drive mappings established through their login scripts.

However, each application object can map additional drives and capture printers as needed. Use the settings on the Drives/Ports property page to set up drive mappings and port captures for printers for an application. Such drive mappings and port captures are set up before the Application Launcher window or Application Launcher Explorer software executes the application.

If the Clean Up Network Resources option is selected on the Environment property page, the drive mappings and port captures that the Application Launcher window or Application Launcher Explorer creates are released when the user exits all applications that use the resources.

For example, suppose you are configuring a word processing application that requires a specific mapped drive. This application is installed and runs from the same drive letter. You choose to map drive w: for this application and specify w:\apps\word1\word1.exe in the Path to Executable File text box on the Identification property page. Then, in the Drives/Ports property page, you map drive W: to the server where the application exists. When the Application Launcher window or Application Launcher Explorer runs the application, it checks for a mapping of drive w:. If w: is mapped to the correct volume and server, the drive is used. If w: is mapped to some other server or volume, it is not used, and the application does not run. If w: is not mapped at all, the Application Launcher window or Application Launcher Explorer maps it. Only in the case where the Application Launcher window or Application Launcher Explorer actually maps the drive, it cleans up the mapping after the application terminates. If several applications use the same drive mapping, then drive mappings aren't cleaned up until the last application terminates.

Consulting Experience

The paths to executable files, drive mappings, and port captures are stored as strings and not as NDS object names. Therefore, if a subtree is moved, some application objects might still point to the previous, but possibly invalid, objects.

The Description Property Page

Use the Description property page to give your users more complete information than the application icon caption allows. Users can right-click an application object in the Application Launcher window or Application Launcher Explorer to see details containing both the descriptive name of the application and the more lengthy description that you provide using the Description property page.

For example, suppose you are creating an application object that installs a word processor to the users workstation. The description you type, which is longer than the icon's title can contain, might include a description and any special instructions you'd like your users to see. The description is also used with the function "Prompt before distribution."

The Fault Tolerance Property Page

Use the Fault Tolerance property page to make sure your users can access the applications they need even if the server containing those applications becomes inaccessible.

An application object pulls application source files from a specific server. If that server is inaccessible, you can set up alternative servers from which the application files can be accessed. By doing this, you keep the applications running with no disruptions in availability to your users. You can use two methods for setting up alternative servers: load balancing and fault tolerance. Both of these are discussed in the sections that follow.

Load Balancing Load balancing lets the Application Launcher window or Application Launcher Explorer software spread the user load across multiple application objects. Ordinarily, you use load balancing when all the servers the application objects use are located in a single site on a local area network. If a particular server goes down, rendering that application object inoperable, the application object is removed from the list of available applications, the list is randomized again, and a server is selected.

Fault Tolerance Fault tolerance lets the Application Launcher window or Application Launcher Explorer search the specified servers in the order in which you have set them up. If the first server specified is too busy or is not available, the Application Launcher window or Application Launcher Explorer tries each server in the order listed until it comes to a server that is available; it accesses the application from that server. Ordinarily, you use fault tolerance when the servers are located at various sites throughout a wide area network. However, the servers that you are using for fault tolerance must reside in the same NDS tree.

Combining Both Methods You can set up your applications to take advantage of both load balancing and fault tolerance. If you do so, the Application Launcher window or Application Launcher Explorer first attempts to locate an available server among those designated for load balancing. If none of those is available, the Application Launcher window or Application Launcher Explorer then goes in order through the servers listed for fault tolerance.

To set up load balancing:

1. Right-click the application object and click Details.

2. Click the Fault Tolerance button.

3. Choose the Enable Load Balance check box.

4. Click the Add button (below the Load Balancing text box).

After the Select Object window is displayed, find the next application to launch by using the browser in the panel on the right. The applications are contained in the object you created for them. Your current context is shown above the Browser text box. To change your current context, click the Change Context button below the Browser text box.

The application now appears in the Load Balancing text box.

To set up fault tolerance:

1. Right-click the application object and click Details.
2. Click the Fault Tolerance button.
3. Choose the Enable Fault Tolerance check box.
4. Click the Add button.

After the Select Object window is displayed, find the next application to launch by using the browser in the panel on the right. The applications are contained in the object you created for them. Your current context is shown above the browser panel. To change your current context, click the Change Context button located below the browser text box.

The application now appears in the Fault Tolerance text box.

To delete an application object from the load balancing or fault tolerance lists:

1. Right-click the application object and click Details.
2. Click the Fault Tolerance button.
3. Choose the load balanced — or fault tolerant — enabled application that you want to remove from the list, and then click the Delete button.
4. Click OK to save changes.

The System Requirements Page

Use the System Requirements property page as a filter to display application icons only on workstations that meet certain criteria that you specify, such as the specific version of an operating system, the amount of RAM, or free disk space. If workstations do not meet the criteria you specify, the icons do not appear on that workstation.

Consulting Experience

The Windows 3.*x* Application Programming Interface does not return values higher than 486. Therefore, if Application Launcher queries the processor type of a Windows 3.*x* workstation using a Pentium processor, Windows 3.*x* returns "486." In other words, even if you select the Pentium processor type for the Processor option, the application is displayed on 486 workstations running Windows 3.*x*.

For example, suppose you want a word processing application icon to appear only on Windows 95/98 workstations that have at least 32MB of RAM, a Pentium processor, and 500MB of free disk space on the C: drive. Using the options on the System Requirements property page, you can tailor the requirements in this way.

Display Applications on a Particular Operating System As there might be a mixture of platforms on your network, you can select one or more platforms, such as Windows 3.*x*, Windows 95/98, and Windows NT.

For example, suppose you want the application to run only Windows NT 4.0 or later workstations. To specify this configuration, select Windows NT, and then type **4** in the Major text box and **0** in the Minor text box. If you leave the Major and Minor text boxes empty, only the operating system is verified.

Display Applications on Machines That Have at Least Use the options in this group box if you need further filtering. For example, if the application object sets up a suite of applications, minimum disk space and memory requirements may need to be met.

MB of RAM This field is valid only for Windows 95/98 and Windows NT workstations (Windows 3.x is ignored). Use it by entering the minimum amount of total installed RAM that the workstation must have to see and run this application.

For example, if the application requires 8MB of RAM (8 × 1,024 × 1,024 bytes), you enter **8** in this text box. If you leave this text box blank, no memory checking is done.

Consulting Experience

If the drives selected for any of the three fields happen to be the same drive, Application Launcher adds those minimum requirements together to determine available space. For example, if you specify 20MB free on the Windows directory drive (which happens to be the C: drive), 10MB free on the TEMP drive (which is also the C: drive), and 50MB free on the D: drive, Application Launcher only shows the application object as if there were 30MB available on the C: drive and 50MB free on the D: drive.

Processor This field shows the minimum processor needed to run this application. The choices are 386, 486, or Pentium. For example, if you select 486 and the user has a 386 workstation, the application object is not displayed on the workstation.

Free Disk Space Use this group box to check three different drives for available disk space. For example, you can check the workstation for 20MB free (20 × 1024 × 1024 bytes) on the Windows directory drive, 10MB free on the TEMP drive, and 80MB free on the D: drive. As with the other settings, if you leave these text boxes blank, no checking is done for available disk space.

The Scripts Property Page

Use the Scripts property page to set up scripts that are executed automatically each time the application is launched and closed. Unlike environment parameters, scripts can overwrite existing drive mappings and printer ports. You can use these options when running these scripts:

- Run Before Launching (or Startup) scripts are executed after the environment is set and before the application is launched.
- Run After Termination (or posttermination) scripts are executed after the application is closed and before the network resources are cleaned up. The Scripts property page uses the same syntax as a NetWare login script. Refer to your NetWare documentation for more syntax descriptions and examples.

Examples of What You Can Do with Application Scripts An application script can provide extra mappings beyond those defined on the Drives/Ports property page. For example, you can take any of these actions with an application script:

- Provide a mapping to override another mapping.
- Run other applications.
- Log into other servers or NDS trees.
- Terminate applications under certain circumstances.

Create Application Object Scripts To enable an application object script, type the appropriate commands in either the Run before Launching or Run after Termination text box.

Commands for cleaning up the changes made by the prelaunch script should be placed in the posttermination script. The posttermination script is run after Application Launcher detects that the application has terminated. Both scripts follow the login script language syntax, and all login script variables are allowed (that is, %FULL_NAME, %LOGIN_NAME, <PATH>, and so forth).

The Application Launcher supports these scripting commands:

- DAY
- FILESERVER or FILE_SERVER
- FULL_NAME
- HOUR24 (24HOUR)
- HOUR (HOURS)
- LAST_NAME
- LOGIN_NAME
- MINUTE (MINUTES)

- MONTH
- NDAY_OF_WEEK
- NETWORK (NETWORK_ADDRESS)
- OS_VERSION
- OS
- PLATFORM
- PHYSICAL_STATION (P_STATION)
- REQUESTER_CONTEXT
- SECOND (SECONDS)
- SHORT_YEAR
- TERM
- WINVER
- YEAR

The Application Launcher currently does not support these scripting commands:

- ACCESS_SERVER
- AM_PM
- CLS
- DAY_OF_WEEK
- DIALUP

- DISPLAY
- ERROR_LEVEL
- EXIT
- FDISPLAY
- GREETING_TIME
- INCLUDE
- LASTLOGINTIME
- LOCATION
- LOGIN_ALIAS_CONTEXT
- LOGIN_CONTEXT
- MACHINE
- MONTH_NAME
- NEW_MAIL
- NO_DEFAULT
- NOSWAP
- OFFLINE
- PASSWORD_EXPIRES
- PAUSE
- PCCOMPATIBLE

- REQUESTER_VERSION
- SCRIPT_SERVER
- SET_TIME
- SHELL_VERSION
- SMACHINE
- STATION
- SWAP
- USERID
- WRITE

The Application Launcher scripting does not pause or output display errors to the screen.

The Contacts Property Page

Use the Contacts property page to add, delete, and list the users who are resources or support contacts for specific application objects. This information is displayed in the properties of each application icon on a user's workstation through the Application Launcher window or Application Launcher Explorer.

The Help information can be tailored so that users are directed to the support group at their locations. Designating a user support contact helps channel problems to knowledgeable people and alleviate your workload.

A user can find out who is assigned to what application by choosing File → Properties and clicking the Contacts tab from the Application Launcher window or Application Launcher Explorer. The user can contact the assigned contact in person, by phone, or by using the Application Launcher window or Application Launcher Explorer to send an e-mail.

Consulting Experience

Using the Applications property page, you can assign user, group, organizational unit, organization, or country objects to multiple application objects. For example, if you create several application objects, you can use the Applications property page for a given user object to assign those applications to the user. Furthermore, you can specify how applications are displayed on the workstation (that is, through the Application Launcher window, Application Launcher Explorer, Windows Explorer, Start menu, Desktop, and System Tray).

The Associations Property Page

Use the Associations property page to grant multiple users, groups, organizations, or organizational units the right to see and use the application object. If you do not associate applications with these objects, they are not available to users in the Application Launcher window or Application Launcher Explorer.

When the association is complete, the object and application contain information about each other. The user, group, organizational unit, organization, or country object shows which applications it can use, and the application shows what other objects can access it. Only direct associations appear. For example, if a user is a member of a group and the group is associated with an application, viewing the user object does not show the application association and viewing the application does not show the user association. However, the group object shows both the user and the application associations.

The Administrator Notes Property Page

Use the Administrator Notes property page to create a section of notes that only you, as the administrator, can view and edit.

For example, you might want to remind yourself about some special settings for a particular application. Or if your system is managed by several administrators, you could use the Administrator Notes property page to provide a history of application upgrades and file changes.

The System Requirements Page

Use the System Requirements property page as a filter to display application icons only on workstations that meet certain criteria that you specify, such as the specific version of an operating system, the amount of RAM, or free disk space. If workstations do not meet the criteria you specify, the icons do not appear on that workstation.

For example, suppose you want a word processing application icon to appear only on Windows 95/98 workstations that have at least 32MB of RAM, a Pentium processor, and 500MB of free disk space on the C: drive. Using the options on the System Requirements property page, you can tailor the requirements in this way.

The Macros Property Page

Use the Macros property page to manage the macros that are used on other property pages of the application object. You can use macros in these application object locations:

- Full path
- Command line
- Working directory
- Mapping path
- Capture port path
- Registry property page: key, name, value (string only)
- .INI Files property page: group, name, value
- Application Files property page: source/target, directory
- Text Files property page: find and add string
- Icons/Shortcuts property page: all locations

Consulting Experience

Before any change on this property page goes into effect, you must change the version stamp value on the Distribution property page. Changing this value signals Application Launcher to re-distribute the application.

For example, suppose that you have a complex application object that uses the %SOURCE_PATH% macro throughout numerous property pages. What if the path that %SOURCE_PATH% points to changes? Rather than change each case, you can change the value of %SOURCE_PATH% one time on the Macros property page; the change will be reflected on all other property pages where the macro is used.

The Registry Settings Property Page

Use the Registry Settings property page to add, change, delete, and import Registry keys, names, and values as if you were working with the actual Windows Registry. You specify whether these settings are created or removed in the Windows Registry when the application runs or distributes.

The Application Files Property Page

Use the Application Files property page to make changes to application-related files on the target workstation when the application is distributed.

The easiest way to use the Application Files property page is to run the snAppShot first. Application Launcher snAppShot compares the configuration settings on a representative workstation before and after you install an application on it. These differences are recorded in an Application Object Template (.AOT) file. If files are copied during the installation, the changes are imported to the Application Files property page when you create the application object. Giving you a point of reference, the .AOT file method takes the guesswork out of knowing which files and settings are required to run an application. If you need to upgrade an application and there are new files to copy, you import a new .AOT file into the Application Files property page. These application files can be conditionally installed:

- Always Copy
- Copy If Does Not Exist
- Copy If Exists
- Copy If Newer
- Copy If Newer and Exists
- Request Confirmation or deleted.

The Text Files Property Page

Use the Text Files property page to add, change, or delete workstation text files (such as CONFIG.SYS and AUTOEXEC.BAT). Text file changes go into effect after you change the application object's version stamp.

For example, suppose that users are experiencing problems due to an incorrect text string found in their workstation's CONFIG.SYS file. Rather than visit and change each workstation or run the risk of users incorrectly and inconsistently implementing a change, you can set up a Text File template that finds, deletes, modifies, or adds text strings to the text file of your choice. The Text File template implements the changes the next time the application runs.

The easiest way to use the Text Files property page is to use snAppShot first that compares the configuration settings on a representative workstation before and after you install an application on it. These differences are recorded in an Application Object Template (.AOT) file. If changes are made to text files during the installation, the changes are imported to the Text Files property page when you create the application object. Giving you a point of reference, the .AOT file method takes the guesswork out of knowing which files and settings are required to run an application. If you need to upgrade an application and there are new text file changes, you import a new .AOT file into the Text Files property page.

Use the Text File Edit dialog box to find, delete, and add text strings to the text file template that is used to change text files when related applications are run.

The Schedule Property Page

Use the Schedule property page to define when you want a particular application to run or how long you want an application's icon to appear in the Application Launcher window or Application Launcher Explorer.

For example, suppose you want users to have access to a particular application for only five days. After that, you want to remove the application from their view. Using the settings on the Schedule property page, you can automatically remove the icon from users' workstations.

Or suppose that you want to run a virus detection application on users' workstations at a certain time, and only one time. The Schedule property page contains settings that make this possible as well.

The Icons/Shortcuts Page

Use the Icons/Shortcuts property page to control the icons of application objects that appear in Program Manager (Windows 3.*x*) and Shortcuts in Windows Explorer (Windows 95/98 and Windows NT 4.*x*). The items that appear in the Icons/Shortcuts list control the Program Group, Program Group Item, and Shortcuts.

Example: Suppose that your company uses special icons for the applications that users run on their Windows 95/98, Windows NT, and Windows 3.*x* workstations. Using the Icons/Shortcuts property page for this application object, you can change the icons for the other applications.

The Distribution Property Page

Use the Distribution property page to configure general distribution behavior when an application object distributes.

To access the Distribution Property Page:

1. Right-click the application object and click Details.
2. Click the Distribute button.
3. Use the options to change settings, and then click OK.

Show Distribution Progress to User

The Show Distribution Progress option displays an easy-to-read progress bar to users the first time they distribute an application to their workstations. Turn off this option if you are distributing only a small change to the application, such as a Registry modification. Turn it on if you are distributing a large application and want to give the user a general idea of how long to expect the distribution will take.

The Folders Property Page

Use the Folders property page to create Custom or Linked folders in which to organize application objects. A Custom folder is tied to one application object. A Linked folder might contain many application objects. All folders appear in the Application Launcher window or Explorer browser view and also in the Start Menu. Using folders, you can achieve "subfoldering" or the placing of folders within folders.

Use the Folders property page on the application object to create both Custom and Linked folders. Use the folder object to create one Linked folder to which you link other application objects.

The Create a Folder for an Application Object

Follow these steps if you want to create a folder for an application object.

1. Right-click the application object.

2. Click the Folders button.

3. Click Add and select Custom to create a folder exclusively for this application object or choose Linked to create a separate folder object that can be shared by this and other application objects.

4. If you want to change or delete the name of a folder, highlight it and use the Modify or Delete buttons.

5. Select Launcher Window and/or Start Menu depending on whether you want to display the folders in the Application Launcher window or Application Launcher Explorer browser view or on the Start menu.

The .INI Settings Property Page

Use the .INI Settings property page to create or change the .INI files on the target workstation when the application runs. The easiest way to use the .INI Files property page is to run the Novell Application Launcher snAppShot component ("Application Launcher" snAppShot) first. Application Launcher snAppShot compares the configuration settings on a representative workstation before and after you install an application on it. These differences are recorded in an Application Object Template (.AOT) file. If changes are made to .INI files during the installation, the changes are imported to the .INI Files property page when you create the application object. Giving you a point of reference, the .AOT file method takes the guesswork out of knowing which files and settings are required to run an application. If you need to upgrade an application and there are new .INI file changes, you import a new .AOT file into the Text Files property page.

The File Rights Property Page

Use the File Rights property page to grant rights to files, directories, and volumes when this application object is associated to a user object or a group, organizational unit, organization, or country to which the user is already associated. Such rights are removed when the application object is unassociated.

The file rights are stored in the NetWare file system. The file page eases the administration of the file rights and synchronizes these to the associated users, groups, organizational units, organizations, or countries.

If two separate application objects give file rights to the same file, directory, or volume and just one of them is unassociated with the user, then the user loses all rights even though the user might still be associated with the other application object.

File rights are not dynamic. For example, the file rights you set up are not dependent on whether or not the user is actually using the application.

The Termination Property Page

Use the Termination property page to terminate an Application Launcher–delivered application. There are several methods to terminate the application, ranging from simple requests for users to exit an application on their own, all the way to revoking the application without warning.

To terminate an application object follow these steps:

1. Right-click the application object and click Details.

2. Click the Termination button.

3. Choose one of the termination behaviors from the drop-down list.

The Application Site List Property Page

Use the Application Site List property page to set up a site "ring" or "chain" of applications to ensure that users who travel from site to site always access applications from the server that is geographically closest to them. An application site list gives users faster access to their applications and reduces WAN traffic and associated costs. A site list must include application objects located within the same NDS Tree.

To set up an application site list:

1. Right-click the application object.

2. Click the Application Site List button.

3. Click Link To and specify the application objects that would be geographically close to the user should that user travel to a different site.

4. To unlink a site, highlight its name and click Unlink This Site.

Summary

This chapter has presented the basics of using Z.E.N.works with NetWare 5. We have discussed installation of the Z.E.N.works components including the creation of workstation objects to manage desktops and application objects to manage your NDS applications. NDS provides a powerful system for delivering applications to your users and managing their desktops.

CHAPTER 20

NDS for NT

NDS for NT is a simple solution for making it easier to manage the resources in your network, whether they are NetWare or Windows NT resources. If you use Novell Directory Services (NDS) to store and manage information about your network in one place or tree, then you should also use NDS for NT to manage the NT domains.

You may have discovered that as Windows NT servers are installed on your company's network, managing these servers in your existing NetWare 5 environment becomes a nightmare. By default, there is no cohesive method for managing both systems. For example, when making any change to NetWare 5 and NDS, you must turn around and make the same change in the Windows NT domains. For example, when a system administrator adds a new user, he or she would first check to see if the user name is unique within the NT domain. This is due to the "flat file" nature of Windows NT. The user is then created in NDS and then added again in Windows NT via User Manager for Domains. The result is that a user must enter multiple passwords to log in to this environment. The user first enters the NetWare 5 name and password and then the NT server name and password. This causes confusion to users and will increase the volume of support calls to the IS or support staff. If several hundred users need accounts in a domain and on NDS, the amount of work required to maintain those accounts can be prohibitive.

This problem gets worse if Microsoft Exchange is installed on your system. Your network administration is then spread over three platforms. The result is that you will use NWADMIN for the NetWare 5 and NDS environment, User Manager for Domains for the NT Server environment, and Exchange ADMIN for e-mail users. Fortunately Windows NT has a link to Exchange, which creates the user there automatically. However, ongoing management of the Exchange user is done from the Exchange ADMIN utility. This whole process obviously creates extra work and can be prone to errors.

To alleviate these problems, you should install and configure NDS for NT, which integrates Windows NT domains directly into your NDS tree. This allows you to manage all aspects of the NT server domain through NDS. The result is the inherent ability to provide a single login, which will reduce user confusion, and a single point of administration for the entire network. Thus, if changes are made using the User Manager for Domains, they will be automatically replicated in the NDS tree. If the changes are made first in NDS using NWADMIN, they are represented in the NT server domain. Therefore, you can use either User Manager or NWADMIN to manage your network and NDS will remain consistent. This is significant if some system administrators primarily apply the User Manager to administered objects.

Advantages of NDS for NT

NDS for NT extends the normal advantages and benefits of Novell Directory Services. These benefits are extended to the Windows NT platform through the integration of NDS for NT. Among other advantages, NDS for NT:

- Gives you a single login to both NetWare and Windows NT servers.
- Provides a single point of administration for your entire network.
- Reduces the complexity and cost of managing domains.
- Simplifies the deployment of NT applications.
- Manages the Windows NT desktops.
- Dramatically cuts your total cost of owning a network.

Because NDS for NT gives you the ability to integrate Windows NT domains directly into your NDS tree, it allows you to administer all aspects of the NT domain through NDS. For example, NDS for NT has been designed so that any application requiring Windows NT domain information will receive that information directly from NDS. This is accomplished with no change to the application. NDS for NT is installed entirely on the Windows NT servers. No workstation components or workstation configuration is required. From the perspective of the Microsoft clients or applications using that domain, nothing has changed. All workstations and applications will continue to function as they always did before NDS for NT was installed.

Single login is one of the major benefits of having the NT domain integrated into NDS. In this situation, single login means that when a user needs to access network resources from NetWare 5 or Windows NT, the user only enters one username and password. When an NT domain is migrated to NDS, the hashed user passwords are also migrated. This allows a user to log into a recently migrated domain using the same password that was defined before the migration took place. NDS holds both hashed passwords for the user, one encrypted using the MD4 algorithm (Microsoft) and one encrypted using RSA (NDS).

Because there is no modification to the workstation, the login process used to authenticate to NDS and the NT server does not change. The login process hashes the user password with RSA and sends that directly to the NetWare 5 server for authentication to NDS. The login process also hashes the password using MD4 and sends that to the Windows NT domain controller. The redirected domain controller retrieves the hashed user password from NDS and compares it to that sent from the workstation. If they match, the user is authenticated to the Windows NT domain. Please note that NDS for NT does not compromise NT security in any way. In fact, you have increased security because NT passwords are stored in NDS.

You are now ready for the increased penetration of Windows NT Workstation into your NetWare 5 network. NDS is the key to central management of all aspects of the Windows NT domains. By installing and configuring the NDS for NT, you are upgrading the Windows NT domain system to a true directory service that gives you a single login, a single point of administration, and full NT application support for mixed NetWare 5 and NT networks.

How NDS for NT Works

The Windows NT Security Accounts Manager (SAM) is the database where the NT domain namebase is stored. NDS for NT works by integrating the SAM database for Windows NT domains into NDS. This is accomplished by replacing SAMSRV.DLL on each Windows NT server that is designated as a primary domain controller (PDC) or a backup domain controller (BDC). Next, you need to install the Novell NetWare 5 Client for Windows NT on all the Windows NT servers. This enables the NT servers to connect to the NetWare 5 servers. The SAMSRV.DLL being replaced redirects all domain access calls to NDS. Figure 20.1 illustrates how SAMSRV.DLL is replaced to redirect the domain access calls to NDS instead of to the SAM database on NT.

FIGURE 20.1

SAMSRV.DLL is replaced to redirect the domain access calls to NDS instead of to the SAM database on NT.

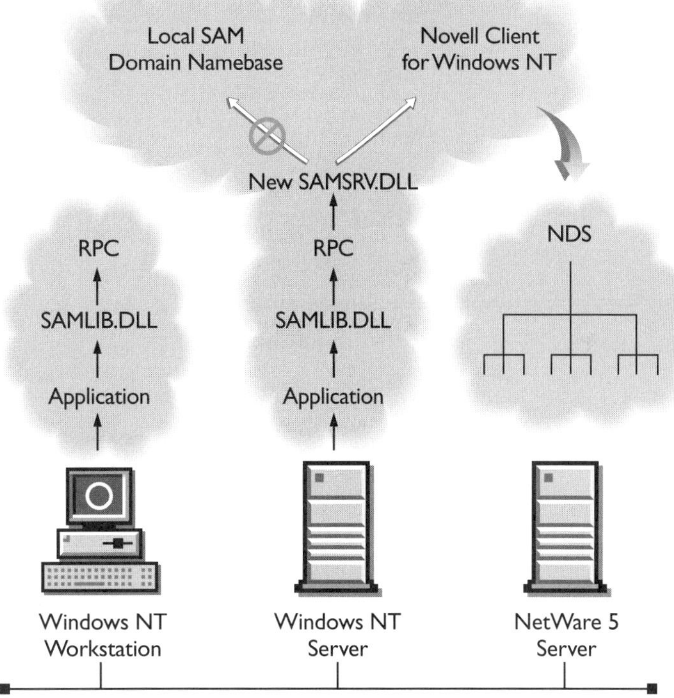

When you configure the NDS for NT software, you select a specific context in the tree where the current NT domain objects will be migrated. The migration is performed using the Domain Object Wizard. During the execution of the wizard, you are asked to provide a name for the NT domain object that is created in the selected context. This domain object in NDS represents the NT domain. This object behaves similarly to a Group object in that it not only holds information about the domain and users who are members of the domain, but it also contains member objects such as computers and groups just as an actual domain. This is illustrated in Figure 20.2.

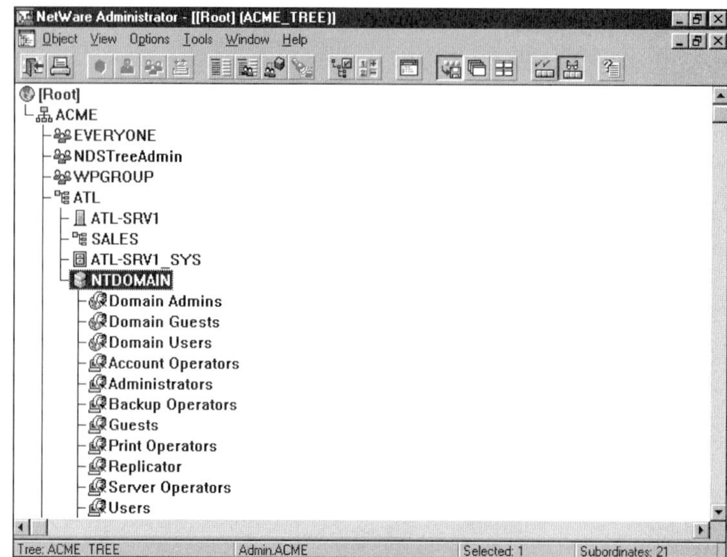

FIGURE 20.2

A domain object (in this case, NTDOMAIN) is created in the NDS tree, which represents the NT domain. Users added to the domain object in NDS are immediately visible to the NT server domain.

The domain object acts as a group with a list of domain members. The computers and groups associated with the domain are represented as objects contained within the NDS domain object. By making user objects "members" of the domain rather than actually residing within the domain, administrators can place the NDS user objects anywhere in the tree and still give them access to specific domains.

As previously mentioned, the Windows NT Security Accounts Manager (SAM) is the database where the NT domain namebase is stored. A unique number identifies the NT domain. This number, called the *Security Identifier* or *SID*, uniquely identifies an NT domain across a network. A SID that is created by combining the domain SID with a Relative Identifier or RID also identifies objects within the domain. This object SID is used throughout the Microsoft network to identify the object and its access to various system resources. Because NDS stores each domain user's Relative Identifier (RID) in the NT domain object and not as a property of the user object, one NDS user object can be a member of more than one NT Domain object. This provides a simple way for a single NDS user to access resources in multiple domains without having to set up complicated trust relationships.

NDS for NT is installed completely on the NT server. No workstation components or configurations are needed. To the workstation running normal Microsoft clients or applications using the domain, nothing has changed. All workstations and applications will continue to function as they did before the installation. All clients and applications communicate to the servers using Remote Procedure Calls (RPCs). Any request passed from the workstations using RPCs is extracted and passed to the SAMSRV.DLL layer. Normally SAMSRV.DLL accesses the Windows NT Security Accounts Manager (SAM), where the domain namebase is stored, and performs the requested operation. However, when SAMSRV.DLL is replaced, the request is not forwarded the local SAM namebase but instead passes directly to NDS. Using this method, NDS becomes the single directory where everything is stored. Replacing just SAMSRV.DLL ensures that the level of compatibility is 100 percent.

Once a Windows NT domain has been brought into the NDS tree, the NT domain controller must be able to authenticate to the NDS tree. The NT server that is a primary domain controller (PDC) or backup domain controller (BDC) now needs to store, modify, and retrieve domain information from the domain object placed in NDS. In order for the NT server to authenticate, an NDS object is created for its use. This NDS object is referred to as a *service account*, which must have the appropriate rights assigned. The service account object must have administrative rights to create and modify all containers holding the NDS user objects of the domain membership. This may require you to grant trustee rights to the service account where future domain members may exist. The service account may be an existing NDS user object or a new user object created automatically during domain migration into NDS.

NDS for NT Core Components

NDS for NT versions 1.0 and 1.2 include these core product components:

- **NDS for NT Domain Object Wizard** — The NDS for NT Domain Object Wizard is a network administrative tool that migrates or relocates an NT domain to the NDS tree. The users are migrated and created as NDS users.

The users that were migrated to NDS are not physically stored in the NDS Domain object; however, they are members of the objects. Once it is inside the NDS tree, you can manage an NT domain as you would an NDS group object.

- **Domain Object snap-in** — The Domain Object snap-in is an administrative snap-in to NWADMIN for NT that allows Domain objects to be viewed and managed within NDS. With this tool, you can perform network administrative tasks, such as create a local group, create a new global group, or create a new workstation for an NT user. You can also continue to use User Manager for your NT users as well. Any updates made to your NT users will be stored in the NDS domain object if they are part of that domain.
- **NetWare Client for Windows NT** — Network users want to be able to access their NetWare 5 network from an NT workstation. The NetWare Client for Windows NT allows users of NT workstations to access and use all of the services available on NetWare 3, NetWare 4, and NetWare 5 servers. The NetWare Client for Windows NT brings the full power, ease of use, manageability, and security of NetWare 5 to Windows NT workstations. The NetWare Client is installed with NDS for NT. It is a required component in using the Domain Object utilities.

Bundled Administration Utilities

In addition to the core NDS for NT components other NT integration products are also included with NDS for NT to assist you with administration and management of your network. These utilities are discussed here, and their installation is covered in subsequent sections:

- **Novell Application Launcher 2.01** — This utility helps customers reduce the cost of software management by automating application distribution and updates to NT Workstations and other desktops via NDS.

- **The NAL snap-in** — This is an administrative snap-in to NWADMIN that lets you manage the NAL software. Installing NAL installs this snap-in and provides NWADMIN with the additional capability to create and configure NAL objects.
- **NDS Manager v1.25** — This is an administrative tool that allows network administrators to manage partitions, replicas, servers, repair operations, printing, and preferences.
- **Workstation Manager** — This utility is included with the Novell NetWare Client and is a software component that enables administrators to manage both Windows NT workstation user accounts and NetWare 5 user accounts from within NDS.
- **NWADMIN for NT (32 bit version)** — This is included as a graphical network administrative tool that allows a single point of administration for your mixed NetWare 5 and Windows NT network. NWADMIN for NT helps network administrators manage network resources from a single interface. All peripheral products that work with NWADMIN for NT require snap-ins (new DLLs) to provide additional functionality.
- **Novell Administrator for Windows NT 2.0c** — This utility allows administrators to synchronize NT domains with NDS. Novell Administrator for Windows NT provides a solution to the problem of dual administration between NetWare 5 and NT servers. The Novell Administrator for Windows NT integrates the NetWare 5 and Windows NT networks so that they can be administered from a central point of administration using NWADMIN.
- **Mailbox Manager for Exchange snap-in** — This is a new product included as an administrative snap-in to NWADMIN for NT that lets you manage Microsoft Exchange Mail accounts in NDS. It enhances NDS for NT by offering single-point administration for Exchange mailboxes.

Novell Application Launcher 2.01 and NAL Snap-In

The Novell Application Launcher (NAL) provides simple, powerful software application management and deployment. NAL lets network administrators distribute network applications to users' workstations and manage those applications as objects in the NDS tree on their mixed NetWare and Windows NT network. With the Novell Application Launcher you can deliver applications to Windows 3.1, Windows 95/98, and Windows NT desktops. NAL also gives network administrators powerful, unparalleled control over applications after they have been distributed to workstations. Instead of visiting every desktop each time an application needs to be installed or updated, NAL allows all applications to be managed from a single utility called NWADMIN. Built on Novell Directory Services (NDS), NAL allows you to deliver new and updated applications and data to users across your network quickly and easily.

Using the Novell Application Launcher 2.01 makes it easy to distribute new applications and application updates to your desktops. You can deliver applications from NetWare 5 and NT servers to your Windows 3.1, Windows 95/98, and Windows NT workstations running Novell's Client 32 for DOS/Windows, Windows 95/98, or Windows NT; or Virtual Loadable Module (VLM) client software 1.2. This greatly reduces the cost of managing your network and its services. The user of NAL gets applications that work every time and are always available.

Network users will not need to worry about workstation configurations, drives, ports, command-line parameters, application source directories, or the latest software upgrades. NAL is installed separately from the NDS for NT product. The install utilities for NAL are located in the i386\GOODIES\NAL directory on the NDS for NT CD.

The Novell Application Launcher has several major components that work together to create and manage NDS application objects in the NDS tree. The components are:

- The Novell Application Launcher (NAL) Window program
- The NAL Explorer

- The NWADMIN snap-in module (APPSNAP.DLL)
- The NAL snAppShot
- The NAL Library (NWAPP)

The NAL program component is a user tool that allows users to run applications set up by a system administrator through NWADMIN. The APPSNAP.DLL is a snap-in to the NWADMIN utility, which expands the NDS schema to include a new class of objects called "Application," and to provide descriptions of the attributes for application objects. It also provides additional functionality to your NWADMIN utility so that you can create and define application objects in NDS. The NAL snAppShot is a subset utility that allows you to install complex applications on workstations that require updates to a Windows Registry, .INI files, file system files, and CONFIG.SYS and AUTOEXEC.BAT files.

The NAL Window is the workstation component that delivers icons of the NDS application objects that you have set up using the NAL snap-in feature in NWADMIN. The NAL Explorer adds greater functionality for Windows 95/98 and Windows NT by delivering application objects to the Windows Explorer, Start Menu, System Tray, and desktop.

In addition to the other components a special library called NWAPP enables the NAL Window, Explorer, snap-in, and snAppShot to access the application objects in the NDS tree. This library provides a simple interface the developer can use to create and access the NDS objects. Figure 20.3 illustrates how each of the NAL components uses the NWAPP library to access NetWare 5 and NDS.

NDS Manager v1.25

This utility is installed automatically with the NWADMIN utility. See Chapter 6, "Designing and Using NDS Partitions and Replicas," for examples on partitioning and replication using NDS Manager. The Schema Manager is a utility that is installed as part of NDS Manager. This utility allows you to view and make changes to your NDS schema.

FIGURE 20.3

The NAL components use the NWAPP library interface to access the application objects stored in NDS and NetWare 5.

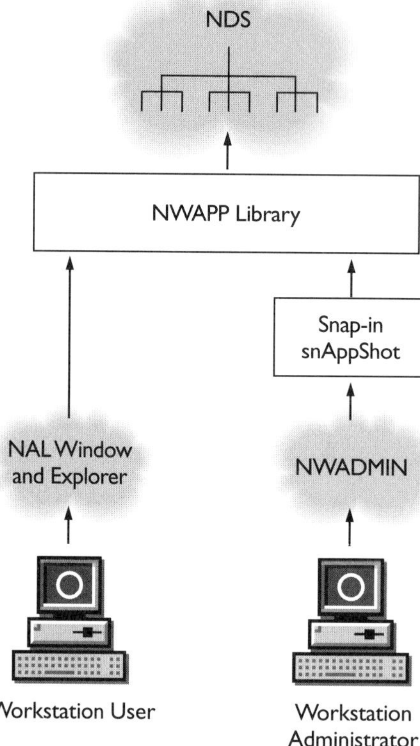

Workstation Manager

NetWare Client for Windows NT also includes Workstation Manager for NT, which makes managing NT workstations simple without the troubles of deploying domains. This solution is extremely useful if you have discovered that integrating Windows NT desktops into your current NetWare network can be a challenge. (For example, a typical Windows NT user is required to log into first the network and then the workstation — two accounts for just one user with one for the NT workstation and one for the network.) In addition, you choose to either manage all the Windows NT workstation configuration settings manually or centrally using NT domains.

If you are like most NetWare administrators, the idea of creating and managing Windows NT domains is painful. Instead, we suggest that you use your existing Novell Directory Services (NDS) structure to more easily and quickly integrate the Windows NT desktops into your current network without having to install Windows NT domains. This can be accomplished by installing your NT workstations into the NDS using a combination of Novell's NetWare Client for Windows NT and the Novell Workstation Manager utility. The client software supports NT workstations running both versions 3.5 or 4.0. It also supports all services over IPX or IP transport protocols. The Novell Workstation Manager works between the client software and NDS through a NWADMIN snap-in interface to store the NT workstation configuration files for both local and roaming workstations.

After the client software has been installed on the NT workstation, you can place the workstation in the NDS tree by creating a new workstation object. The workstation object is a new type of object in NDS called the NT Configuration object. This object holds the information necessary for the Novell client software to dynamically create a preconfigured user account on any NT workstation. The object grants security access to both the network and the desktop PC. It controls individual desktop preferences, such as colors, shortcuts, cursors, and backgrounds. Figure 20.4 shows the individual tabs for the NT Configuration objects that are used to set up and control the various configurations and forms of access.

FIGURE 20.4

The NT Configuration object main dialog box showing the specific tabs used as the key to tight NDS and Windows integration. Through NDS, the NT Configuration object allows you to centrally configure and control any number of Windows NT user desktops.

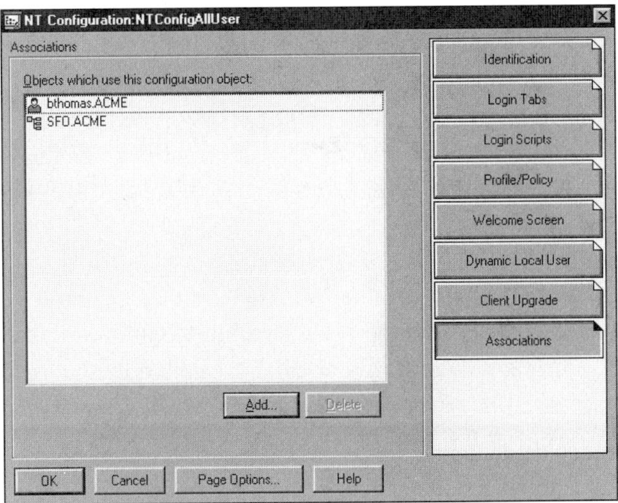

To associate an individual NT Configuration object with specific users, click on the Associations tab and choose country, organization, organizational units, groups, or users. When a user logs in from an NT workstation, the client software uses these associations to find the appropriate NT Configuration objects for each user. The influences of the NT Configuration object on the local desktop are applied after network login but before login to Windows NT.

The client software or NT requester is designed to expose the desktop to all of the available functionality in a NetWare environment, not just basic file and print. Some of the most significant features are NWIP support, autoreconnect, multitree support, customizable GINA (graphical pop-up login box), roaming profile support, policy support, and ODI or NDIS.

NetWare Administrator for Windows NT 2.0c

The NetWare Administrator for Windows NT product provides you with a different method for integrating your Windows NT server with NetWare 5. This solution synchronizes your NT domains with the NDS tree. The NetWare Administrator for Windows NT differs from the basic NDS for NT method in that it synchronizes domains and NDS while maintaining two separate databases. All the user and group information is stored in both the Windows NT and NDS databases. You can use this tool if you want to synchronize your NT domains with NDS instead of redirecting the information.

Like NDS for NT, this product is designed to alleviate the dual administration necessary in managing NT domains and an NDS tree. With NetWare Administrator for Windows NT, all administration is done with the NWADMIN tool. NWADMIN will store all information necessary in the NDS tree, and a back-end process will synchronize the tree to the appropriate NT domains. This solution ensures all changes in the tree are synchronized to the domain in a reliable, secure manner.

In addition, you will create NT user objects in the NDS tree to represent the NT domain users. Administrators can then manage all the NT domain users from NWADMIN. Optionally, the NT user objects can be linked to standard NDS user objects. Objects linked in this manner are called *hybrid user objects* and are used to grant access to both the NT domain and the NDS tree. This provides a single point of administration for both worlds.

Mailbox Manager for Exchange

The Mailbox Manager for Exchange is an extra goodie utility included for you to use to manage the Exchange user on your network. This tool enhances NDS for NT by offering single-point administration for Exchange mailboxes.

For a complete description on how to install, configure, and manage your network using the Mailbox Manager for Exchange refer to the installation section later in this chapter.

Installing NDS for NT

As mentioned previously, the NDS for NT product provides you with tools you need to manage your mixed NetWare 4, NetWare 5, and Windows NT networks. Installing NDS for NT relocates NT domains that you specify to the NDS tree. This relocation is transparent to your users but enables NT domains as NDS domain objects and makes them manageable through Novell's NWADMIN utility. You can also continue to use Microsoft utilities to manage Microsoft domains.

When using NDS for NT, a Domain object in NDS represents each Windows NT domain. This object behaves much like a Group object in that it not only holds information about the domain and users who are members of the domain but also contains member objects such as Computers and Groups just like an actual domain. One significant difference, however, is that NDS for NT stores each user's RID in the NT Domain object and not as part of the User object. This means that one NDS User object can be a member of more than one NT Domain object. This provides a way for a single NDS user to access resources in multiple domains without having to set up complicated trust relationships.

In this section we discuss how to install the core components of NDS for NT. In order to run the NDS for NT installation programs, you will need these things:

- The NDS for NT CD-ROM containing the NDS4NT.EXE file
- Windows NT 3.51 with Service Pack 5.0 or Windows NT 4.0 server with Service Pack 3.0
- Windows NT 4.0 workstation

- At least one NetWare 4.11 or NetWare 5 server
- Administrator (Supervisor) rights to the NetWare server and [Root] of the Directory tree
- Administrator rights to the Windows NT domain you want to move over to NDS

Installation Files

The installation of NDS for NT requires you to run the following two programs, which can be run from a singe install menu known as WINSETUP.EXE. When you run WINSETUP.EXE, you will select to either Install NDS for NT files on the NT Server or Install NDS for NT Administrative Utilities. The selection causes these executable files to be run:

- NDSSETUP.EXE
- ADMSETUP.EXE

Running the WINSETUP.EXE Utility

In this section we'll explain how to install NDS for NT using the WINSETUP utility.

Phase One

1. If you are using the NDS for NT CD-ROM, insert the CD into the NT server CD-ROM drive. When the autostart installation window appears (WINSETUP.EXE), select Install NDS for NT. If you downloaded NDS for NT from the Novell Web site, run the WINSETUP.EXE file located at the root of the NDS for NT directory you created. The installation window will appear. Select Install NDS for NT. The main menu for WINSETUP is shown in Figure 20.5.

Consulting Experience

Before beginning your installation of NDS for NT, be sure you know the NT server name, the NT domain name, and the NT domain administrator password. You will also need to know the NetWare 5 server name, the NDS tree name, and the administrator password for the NDS tree. You then will perform the steps described here to install NDS for NT.

FIGURE 20.5

The main installation window for WINSETUP

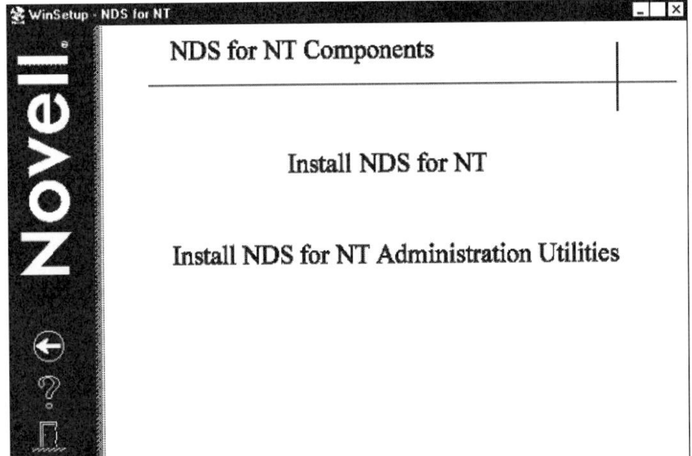

2. The setup program can be run by using the NDSSETUP.EXE file located in the I386 directory of the NDS for NT CD-ROM or by using the NDSSETUP.EXE file in the NDS for NT directory you created. In any case, selecting Install NDS for NT will do these things:
   - Copy the NDS for NT files to your NT server.
   - Install the latest version of NetWare (NetWare 5) Client for Windows NT on your NT server.
   - Launch the Domain Object Wizard, which will create the Domain object(s) for your NDS Directory tree.

An example of the dialog box that appears is shown in Figure 20.6.

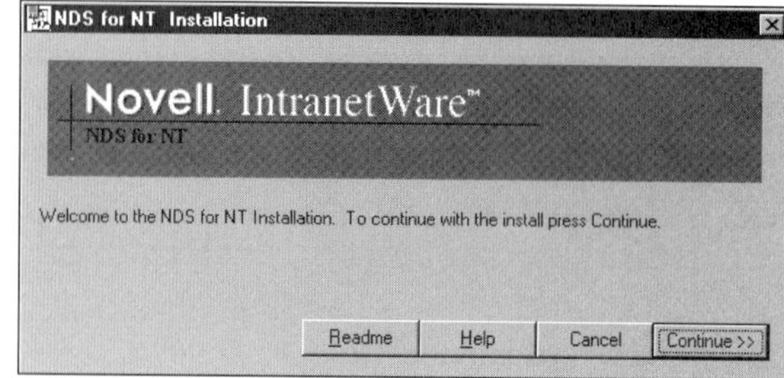

FIGURE 20.6

The main dialog box for NDS for NT installation

An example of the file copy process is shown in Figure 20.7.

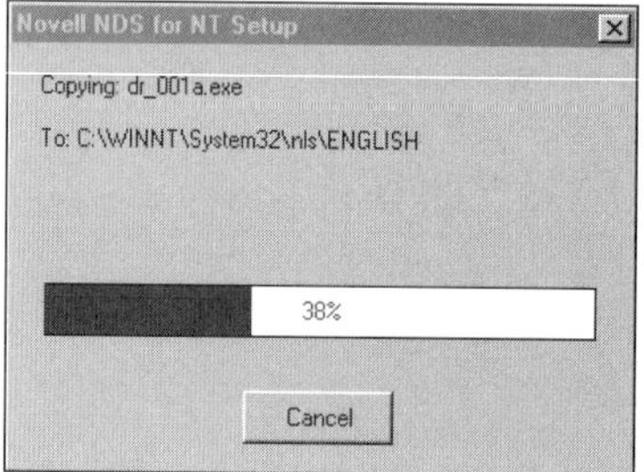

FIGURE 20.7

The file copy process of NDS for NT installation

Phase Two

- When the software installation is complete, you will be prompted to reboot your machine as shown in Figure 20.8. Log in as Admin or its equivalent to the NDS tree that will hold the NT Domain objects. An example of this login is shown in Figure 20.9. You may also need to log in to your NT workstation if prompted.

Phase Three

- After you log in, the Domain Object Wizard launches automatically. An example of the Domain Object Wizard main window is shown in Figure 20.10.

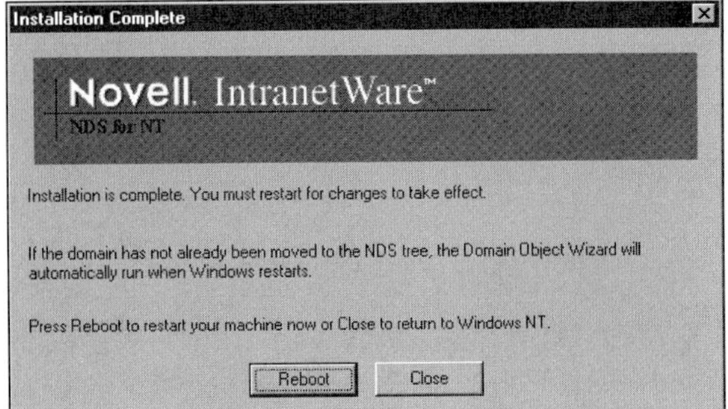

FIGURE 20.8

The NDS for NT installation is complete; you must reboot the machine.

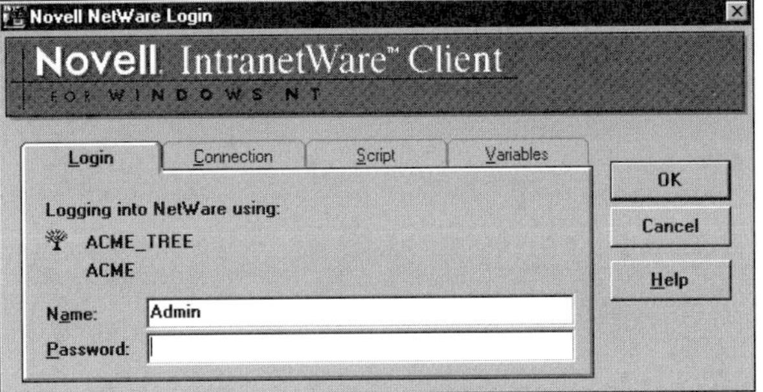

FIGURE 20.9

The login dialog box using the NetWare (NetWare 5) Client for Windows NT

Phase Four

- Follow the on-screen instructions. If you need additional information while using the Domain Object Wizard, click the Help button. Once you have completed the domain migration, reboot the Windows NT server. The installation of the core NDS for NT components is complete.

Installing the NDS for NT Administration Utilities

If you are using the NDS for NT CD-ROM, insert the CD into the NT server CD-ROM drive. When the autostart installation screen appears (WINSETUP.EXE), select Install NDS for NT Administration Utilities.

FIGURE 20.10

The Domain Object Wizard assists you in migrating your NT domains into NDS.

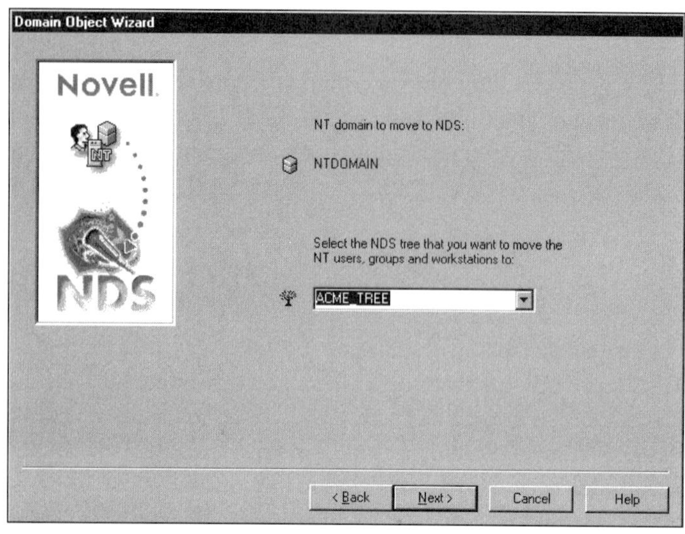

If you downloaded NDS for NT, run the WINSETUP.EXE file located at the root of the NDS for NT directory you created. If you downloaded the program from the Web, you can execute ADMSETUP.EXE from the directory you created to store the program. The installation screen will appear. Select Install NDS for NT Administration Utilities.

In either case, running WINSETUP.EXE and selecting the Install NDS for NT Administration Utilities will install the following Novell administration utilities:

- NetWare Administrator for NT (includes NDS Manager and Schema Manager)
- Novell Workstation Manager

The following conditions are necessary before you can install the NDS for NT Administration Utilities:

- You must have Administrator (Supervisor) rights on the NetWare 5 server and in the container or tree where you are installing the administration utilities.
- The Directory tree that contains the NetWare server where you want to install the utilities must be set as your current tree before you run ADMSETUP.EXE.

Use the following steps to install the NDS for NT Administration Utilities.

Phase One

- From a Windows NT workstation, run WINSETUP.EXE and select Install NDS for NT Administration Utilities.

Phase Two

- Choose Yes to accept the Novell Terms and Conditions. If you choose No, you will not be able to install the administration utilities and you will exit the utility.

Phase Three

- Choose Continue after reading the Administrator Utility title screen. If you choose Cancel, you will not be able to complete the installation and you will exit the utility.

Phase Four

- Choose the utilities you want to install by checking the check box next to each utility's name. There are two choices: The NetWare Administrator and the Novell Workstation Manager. If you select the NetWare Administrator, the install program will also install NDS Manager and Schema Manager.

Phase Five

- Choose a NetWare 5 server from the To Server list. You must have sufficient rights to write files to the server. You should choose a server for which you have Administrator rights. An example of this dialog box is shown in Figure 20.11.

Phase Six

- Choose OK. A progress screen with two progress bars appears. The top bar shows which application is being installed. The bottom bar shows the percentage of files that have been installed. When the files are installed, the Installation Complete dialog box appears.

FIGURE 20.11

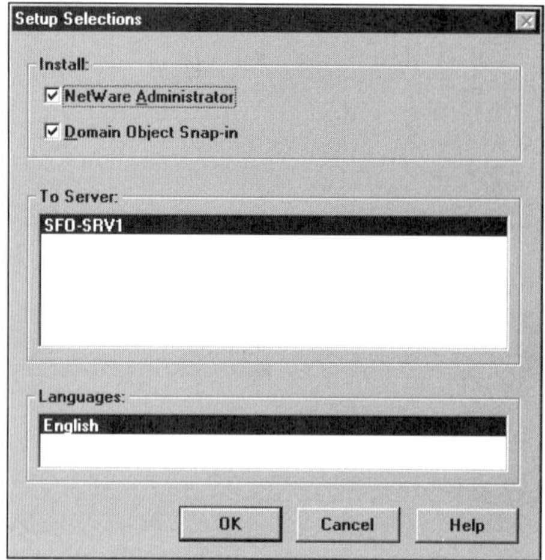

Choosing a server from the Administrator Setup dialog box

Phase Seven

- Choose Run NWADMIN to start NetWare Administrator or choose Close to exit the installer without starting NetWare Administrator.

Novell Workstation Manager Configuration

If you selected the Novell Workstation Manager under Install NDS for NT Administration Utilities you have a few more steps to enable the use of this product. This section covers those steps.

Workstation Manager Components

The Workstation Manager consists of two components. *The NT Workstation Component* is included as part of the NetWare (NetWare 5) Client for Windows NT and runs at the workstation. You can use this client to create and delete NT user accounts because the Novell Client runs with administrator privileges. Novell has created an implementation of the Graphical Identification and Authentication module for Windows NT (NWGINA). NWGINA gathers the username and password and then authenticates the user to NDS and the NT workstation.

Because NWGINA runs on the NT workstation with administrative privileges, you can dynamically create and delete NT user accounts, provided NWGINA can obtain the necessary user information from the NT Configuration object.

The NetWare Administrator Component is a snap-in DLL to Novell Administrator (NWADMIN). From this utility the administrator can enter workstation configuration information into NDS and associate it with users and groups. This snap-in stores the NT user information in an NT Configuration object that is placed into NDS. The snap-in consists of two DLLs that provide functionality for the NT version of the NWADMIN utility (NWADMNNT.EXE). A network supervisor can create NT Configuration objects within NDS containers. These NT Configuration objects store all the information necessary for NWGINA to dynamically create a user account on the NT workstation and grant a user access to NT.

Workstation Manager Installation

The installation of Workstation Manager is accomplished by loading the NetWare Client for NT at the workstation and enabling some parameters to use the utility at that desktop. You also need to install the NWADMIN for NT snap-in modules to extend the schema and manage your desktops from this utility. Therefore, we first discuss how to install the NetWare Client for NT software and enable the Workstation Manager at the desktop. The next section discusses the installation of the snap-in for NWADMIN for NT.

The installation program for the NetWare 5 Client for Windows NT is known as SETUPNW.EXE and installs the default client configuration. SETUPNW.EXE makes the following changes to a user's computer:

- Removes any existing NetWare client software such as the Microsoft Client for NetWare Networks and Microsoft Service for Novell Directory Services.
- Installs Novell's NetWare 5 Client for Windows NT.
- Copies the Novell NetWare 5 Client for Windows NT files to the local hard disk.
- Creates the folder for the Novell NetWare 5 Client for Windows NT under the WINNT\SYSTEM32\NETWARE directory on the workstation's Windows drive.

SETUPNW.EXE has the following switches to assist you in the installation:

- /U — Uses a text file to specify the default functionality. The default text file, UNATTEND.TXT, is used if no alternative is presented with the /U:<unattended file path> option.
- /ACU — Specifies that the program is to check the version stamp and proceed to install using the defaults if an older version of the client software is detected. If not all the values can be defaulted, the user will be prompted only if absolutely necessary. If used in conjunction with the /U option, the defaults will be taken from the Unattended file.
- /W — Installs the Workstation Manager utility.
- /? — Displays help information about using SETUPNW.EXE.

To install the Workstation Manager, run:

```
SETUPNW.EXE /W:NDSTree1
```

You can specify the names of the NDS trees to look for NT Configuration objects. If you only have one NDS tree, then select the tree name.

Enabling the NWADMIN Snap-In Settings

Included with the NetWare Client for Windows NT is a file called WORKMAN.REG, where the NT client configuration settings are stored. This file must be run for the client to view and manage an NT Configuration object. If this file is not run, you will not be able to administer NT Configuration objects and a "?" (denoting an unknown object) will appear in the NDS tree for this object.

Simply double-click on the WORKMAN.REG file to enable these settings. Failing to double-click on this file will prevent the updates from being made, and you will be unable to create or manage any NT Configuration objects.

Enabling the Workstation Manager Settings

If Workstation Manager has not been enabled on a workstation, the NetWare Client for Windows NT was not installed using the SETUPNW /W or SETUPNW /U option. You can enable the NT Workstation Manager without reinstalling the client by enabling Workstation Manager on the Novell Workstation Manager property page in the Novell NetWare Client Services Configuration dialog box, accessible from the Network Control Panel.

Once Workstation Manager is activated, you will need to add at least one tree to the Trusted Trees list on the property page. The Trusted Trees list contains the names of the NDS trees that Workstation Manager searches to find NT Configuration objects.

Therefore, you have four ways to enable the NT Workstation Manager:

- Run SETUPNW.EXE /W:NDSTree1, NDSTree2, NDSTree3.
- Update the information in the UNATTEND.TXT file to include Workstation Manager settings and run SETUPNW.EXE /U.
- Enable a Trusted Tree from START → Control Panel → Network → Services → Novell NetWare 5 Client for Windows NT → Novell Workstation Manager → Enable Workstation Manager on these Trusted Trees. Type in the tree name(s) and click on Add.
- Manually edit the registry (not recommended).

Novell Application Launcher Installation

In this section we describe how you can install the Novell Application Launcher (NAL). A NetWare 4.10 or later (NDS) server is required to support Application objects.

The applications you wish to distribute can reside on NetWare 4, NetWare 5, or Windows NT servers.

Consulting Experience

You can distribute applications off Windows NT servers if the workstation is running both the Novell and Microsoft network client software. Distribution of applications off NetWare 3 servers is not supported.

Client Requirements

Your workstation must meet the following requirements:

- Windows 3.1*x*, Windows 95/98, or Windows NT
- The latest version of Novell's Client 32 for DOS/Windows, Windows 95/98, or Windows NT; or Virtual Loadable Module (VLM) client software 1.2.1
- A Directory Services connection between the workstation and server; no bindery connection

Administrator Workstations

An administrator's workstation must be configured with the following elements in order to perform NAL administration:

- Windows 95/98 or Windows NT
- The latest version of Client 32 for Windows 95/98 or Windows NT; or Workstation Manager 1.0
- NetWare Administrator (NWADMIN) 4.11 or later

Product Components

The Novell Application Launcher 2.01 consists of four product components: two for administrator functions and two for user functions. They are as follows:

- snAppShot and NAL snap-in (administrator components)
- NAL Window and NAL Explorer (user components)

snAppShot

The snAppShot component (when used with the NAL snap-in) provides for advanced server-to-client software distribution capabilities.

NAL Snap-In

NAL snap-in is a Windows DLL that extends NWADMIN, making it possible to create and properly display Application objects. NAL Snap-In adds an Application object to the NDS Tree, which supports Windows 3.1*x*, Windows 95/98, and Windows NT. Earlier versions of NAL added three separate Application objects for each of these three operating systems. This version adds a three-in-one configurable object. Two new NWADMIN property pages are added for Container and User objects: Applications page and Launcher Configuration page.

One new NWADMIN property page is added for the Group object called Applications (the same property as for Container and User objects).

By applying various settings at the container or group level for these property pages, you arrange that they apply to all users in that container or group. By setting them at the user level, you make them apply only for that user.

A container's default Launcher Configuration property is "Use Default Settings," which means:

Exit the Launcher is	On
Log In is	On
Refresh Icons is	On
View Folders is	On
Create Personal Folders is	Off
Save Window Size and Position on Local Drive is	On
Enable Timed Refresh is	Off
Enabled Timed Refresh is	3600 Seconds (if preceding is on)
Inherit Container Applications	1 Level

To modify any of these, you simply select the button next to Use Current Settings and modify these properties, as appropriate. A user's default Launcher Configuration property is Use Parent Container Settings, which uses the preceding chart, then, by default.

The NAL snap-in also adds:

- An Export Application Object selection in the Tools menu
- A Show All Inherited Applications selection in the Tools menu
- A Migrate Application Objects selection in the Tools menu

NAL Window

NAL Window is the workstation component that displays the icons of NAL-delivered applications set up for the user. The NAL Window can be run on Windows 3.1*x*, Windows 95/98, or Windows NT workstations.

SYS:PUBLIC\NAL.EXE is the executable file for the NAL Window. It is a wrapper technology meaning that NAL.EXE takes care of several initialization functions and then runs the correct executable: either NALW31.EXE or NALWIN32.EXE. Once the correct executable is started, NAL.EXE terminates. One of the main functions of the wrapper (NAL.EXE) is to determine the proper launcher executable, based on the operating system of the client.

NAL Explorer

NAL Explorer is an alternative to using the NAL Window. It lets network administrators deliver applications not only into the NAL Explorer Window but also into Windows Explorer, the Start Menu, the System Tray, the Desktop, or any combination of these. NAL Explorer can only be run on Windows 95/98 or Windows NT 4.0 workstations. NAL Explorer requires a newer version of SHELL32.DLL for Windows 95/98, which is part of the Microsoft Windows 95/98 Service Pack 1 Update.

SYS:PUBLIC\NALEXPLD.EXE is the executable file for the NAL Explorer. When installed, it will add a NAL Explorer folder on the desktop. To uninstall the NAL Explorer (the only way to remove the NAL Explorer folder from the desktop), execute NALEXPLD /U. You may have to reboot your workstation for this process to finish. This removes NAL Explorer from the desktop, removes the DLLs installed, and cleans the registry settings from this program.

Rights Requirements for Using NAL

The installation of the Novell Application Launcher requires certain rights.

NDS Rights

Supervisor Object rights to the [ROOT] of the NDS Tree are needed when the network administrator installs NAL, as NAL extends the NDS base schema to support Application objects and adds new properties to existing objects (as discussed previously). As always, an NDS "Health Check" should be performed before installing any application that extends the schema to ensure that NDS is properly synchronized among all servers in the Tree.

Consulting Experience

We recommend that the workstation always start NAL.EXE rather than going directly to one of the launching executables. Additionally, if you run NAL.EXE from a login script (which is generally the way to do it), then you don't have to anticipate the operating system of the attaching client.

No manual assignment of NDS rights is necessary for users to access Application objects. Read and Compare "All Property Rights" will automatically be assigned to any container, group, or user a network administrator associates with an Application object.

Users need Read and Write property rights to their User object's NRD: Registry Data and NRD: Registry Index properties to create personal folders. This assignment is not automatically given. Personal folders allow users to create their own folders and move NAL-delivered applications into these folders. The "Create Personal Folders" must be turned on (remember the default from the preceding table is off) in either the container's or user's Launcher Configuration property to support this feature.

File System Rights

Users accessing NAL need file system rights to:

- The directory in which NAL is installed (default is SYS:PUBLIC)
- The directories where the applications to be distributed reside

A future release of NAL will support automatic assignment of file system rights when a user launches a NAL-delivered application and will remove these rights when the NAL-delivered application is exited.

NAL Installation

The NAL 2.01 installation software consists of two executable files:

- **SETUPNAL.EXE** — This installs three of the four NAL product components mentioned earlier (for example, NAL snap-in, NAL Window, and NAL Explorer) into a default directory of SYS:PUBLIC. The steps for installing NAL are discussed under "Running SETUPNAL.EXE."
- **SETUPSNP.EXE** — This installs the fourth NAL product component mentioned earlier (for example, snAppShot) into a default directory of C:\SNAPSHOT. Remember that snAppShot is an administrator utility and does not need to be installed on user workstations. The steps involved for installing snAppShot will not be discussed, as it is a very straightforward installation process.

Running SETUPNAL.EXE

In this section we describe how to install the Novell Application Launcher using SETUPNAL.EXE.

1. Log into a server in the NDS Tree where NAL is to be installed. Remember to log in as a user with Supervisor Object rights to the [ROOT] of the Tree.
2. Close all applications on the workstation you are using. If NAL 1.1 has previously been installed in this Tree, make sure no users are running it, as NAL 2.01 will automatically upgrade NAL 1.1 Application objects during the installation process.
3. Run SETUPNAL.EXE and respond to the prompts below (italicized). Notice that it says Novell Application Launcher 2.0 even though you are installing NAL 2.01. This was intentional because NAL 2.01 was primarily a maintenance release from NAL 2.0.

Choose Destination Location

We recommended you install to the default SYS:PUBLIC directory. Make sure that your mapping to SYS:PUBLIC is not a Root mapping. SETUPNAL.EXE installs product files in the following directory structure:

- SYS:PUBLIC
- SYS:PUBLIC\NLS\ENGLISH
- SYS:PUBLIC\WIN95
- SYS:PUBLIC\WIN95\NLS\ENGLISH
- SYS:PUBLIC\WINNT
- SYS:PUBLIC\WINNT\NLS\ENGLISH

Additionally, a NALLIB directory structure will be created under the directory in which you installed NAL:

- SYS:PUBLIC\NALLIB\WIN31\NLS\ENGLISH
- SYS:PUBLIC\NALLIB\WIN95\NLS\ENGLISH
- SYS:PUBLIC\NALLIB\WINNT\NLS\ENGLISH

Do You Want to Extend the NDS Schema?

Figure 20.12 shows an example of the NAL installation and making an extension to the schema.

Consulting Experience

NAL 1.0*x* Application objects are not automatically upgraded to 2.01. However, NAL 2.01 offers a migration utility that creates NAL 2.01 Application objects from existing NAL 1.0*x* Application objects. The migration utility is available from the Tools menu in NWADMIN, and this selection will only be active if you select a NAL 1.0*x* object in the Tree to migrate. Refer to the online Help (within NWADMIN) on "Migrating Application Objects from 1.0*x* to 2.0*x*" for more information.

FIGURE 20.12

NAL installation and schema extension

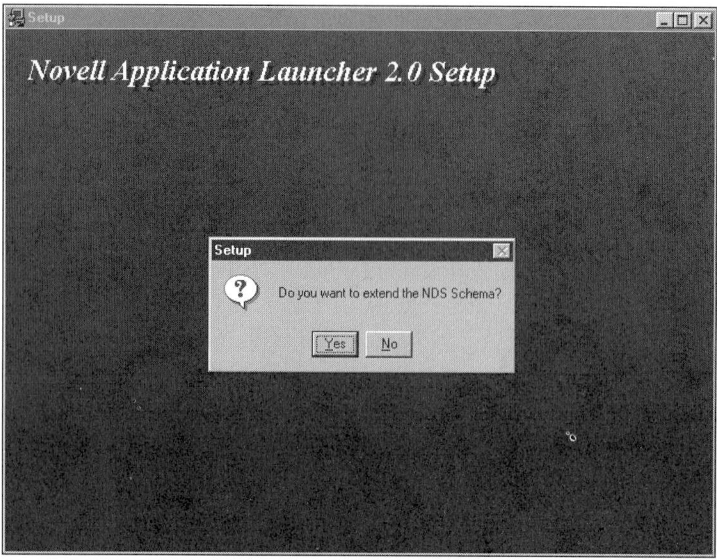

You must extend the schema to use NAL (it is a one-time process per NDS Tree). It can be done now or after NAL installation is complete. If you select Yes, Setup extends the schema in the NDS Tree that contains the directory in which you are installing the NAL software. If you select No, the first time you open NWADMIN after NAL is installed, a prompt will ask you on which NDS Tree you want to extend the schema. Select the appropriate NDS Tree and click Modify.

NOTE

If you have NAL 2.0 installed in your Tree, you will not be asked to extend the schema as the schema has not changed from NAL 2.0 to NAL 2.01.

Do You Want Setup to Create Sample Application Objects?

It is recommended you select "Yes" so that after installation you can explore Application object properties. The context-sensitive Help available on each of these properties is very helpful in learning about NAL's features. These sample Application objects (that is, NWADMIN95, NWADMINNT, and snAppShot) will be placed in the server context on which you are installing the NAL software and can safely be deleted at any time.

NOTE

If you have NAL 2.0 installed in your Tree, you will not be asked to create sample Application objects.

Do You Want to View the Readme?

It is recommended you select Yes to view READNAL.TXT. The Appendix contains caveats, limitations, and known problems network administrators should be aware of.

Mailbox Manager for Exchange Snap-In Installation

Mailbox Manager for Exchange synchronizes NDS and existing Exchange Sites, Mailboxes, and Distribution Lists to dramatically simplify management of Exchange user accounts. Mailbox Manager for Exchange lets the administrator create and maintain all Exchange mailbox information using the NWADMIN utility, eliminating the need to use Microsoft Exchange Administrator for creating, editing, and deleting mailbox information (including site information).

Components of the Mailbox Manager

In this section we describe the components of the Mailbox Manager for Exchange and how to install this utility.

NWADMIN Snap-In

During installation, a component of Mailbox Manager for Exchange snaps into NWADMIN, allowing administrators to use NWADMIN to centrally manage Exchange sites, mailboxes, recipient containers, distribution lists, and servers. These Exchange objects are represented in NWADMIN as native NDS objects. The NDS User object is also extended to include an attribute that identifies the user's Exchange mailbox attributes.

Because all Exchange mailbox information is synchronized to NDS, you don't need to use Microsoft Exchange Administrator for managing user mailbox accounts. In fact, changes made using Exchange Administrator will not get forwarded to NDS. Only changes made using NWADMIN will get synchronized with the Exchange system.

NDS Schema Extensions

The NDS schema defines the types of NDS objects that are allowed and the properties associated with each object type. Users with administrator or equivalent rights can define additional types of NDS objects and additional properties for existing objects. To manage Exchange objects from NDS, Mailbox Manager for Exchange extends the standard NDS schema to accommodate the new objects. New Exchange-related objects include:

- Site
- Recipient Container
- Distribution List
- Exchange Server

The schema extensions are performed during the installation of Mailbox Manager for Exchange. Once the schema extensions are in place, NWADMIN must be able to manage the new objects. The Mailbox Manager for Exchange snap-in extends the capabilities of the NWADMIN to include this feature.

The Import Utility Mailbox Manager for Exchange includes a utility (IMPORT.EXE) to import existing Exchange mailbox information into your NDS directory tree. NDS then becomes the master repository for all Exchange mailbox account information. The Import utility can be launched from the Tools menu of NWADMIN or run as a stand-alone utility.

This version of Mailbox Manager does not include automatic synchronization from Microsoft's Exchange Administrator to NDS. But it does include the ability to manually synchronize Exchange data with NDS at any time. To do this, an administrator simply chooses Upload Exchange Mailboxes from the Tools menu in NWADMIN. Mailbox Manager requires NDS for NT and uses the domain association NDS for NT creates to simplify and automate its installation.

BACKEND.DLL When you make a change to an Exchange-related object in NWADMIN, BACKEND.DLL makes the corresponding change on the Exchange server, keeping records in NDS and Exchange in sync. For example, if you use NWADMIN to add an NDS user to a recipient container, BACKEND.DLL makes the corresponding update in the Exchange database on the Exchange server.

Consulting Experience

If you're installing Mailbox Manager to a workstation that is not an Exchange Server, the Mailbox Manager Installation Wizard will prompt you to log into your nearest Exchange Server so that Mailbox Manager can copy five required DLLs to your local System32 directory.

Once Mailbox Manager is installed, to successfully run the Import utility, you must have Administrator or equivalent rights to the Exchange directory from which you want to upload Exchange mailbox information.

BACKEND.DLL also sends appropriate changes to an Exchange server that has been down. Once the system comes back online, it is brought up to date with the current Exchange mailbox information in the NDS database.

Prerequisites

To successfully install and use Mailbox Manager for Exchange, you must have the following things:

- Exchange Server 5.0 with Service Pack 1
- Administrator rights to the NT domain
- A NetWare server using DS.NLM version 594 or higher

You should have a NetWare 4.11 server with DS.NLM version 5.94 and Support Pack 4 or NetWare 5. You can download these files from Novell's Web site at `www.novell.com`.

The installation process is a very simple two-step process:

1. Run the Mailbox Manager for Exchange setup program (SETUP.EXE).
2. Run the Import Exchange Mailboxes utility.

The Mailbox Manager for Exchange installation program (SETUP.EXE) is located in the i386\GOODIES\MAILMGR directory on the NDS for NT CD. The setup program is a wizard that walks you through the installation step by step. An example of the installation window is shown in Figure 20.13. Simply follow the instructions as they appear in the dialog boxes.

The installation program modifies the schema and adds a snap-in interface to NWADMIN so that you can manage the Exchange mailbox information once it is imported, and it copies the Import utility (IMPORT.EXE) to SYS\PUBIC\WINNT on the NetWare server.

Once you have installed Mailbox Manager, you need to import your Exchange mailbox information. To do so, in NWADMIN choose Tools → Import Exchange Mailboxes, or run IMPORT.EXE from SYS\PUBLIC\WINNT on the NetWare server. The Import utility is a wizard that walks you through the process of importing your Exchange sites into NDS.

FIGURE 20.13

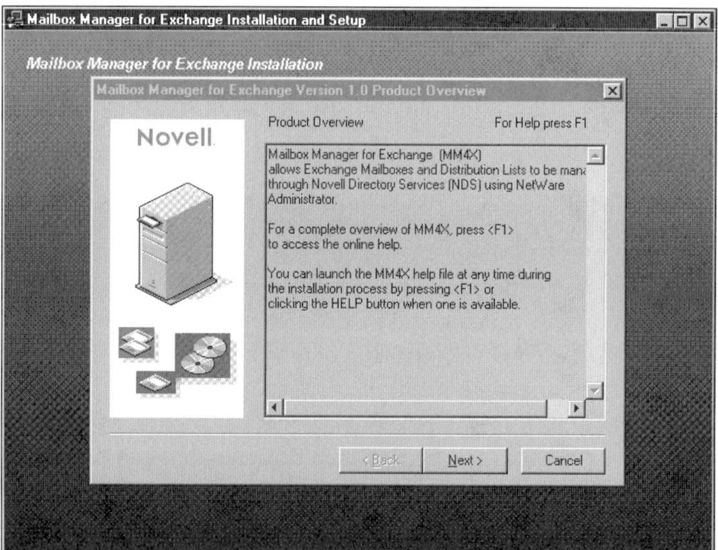

The Main installation window for Mailbox Manager for Exchange

The Import utility does the following things:

- Searches the NDS tree for NT domains.
- Recreates the Exchange hierarchy in the NDS container you specify.

- Using the Domains found in Step 1 and the NT information in each mailbox, matches mailboxes to NDS users.

- Imports mailbox attributes into NDS users.

Once your Exchange information is imported, you can manage the Exchange mailboxes with NWADMIN.

NetWare Administrator for Windows NT Installation

The NetWare Administrator for Windows NT gives network managers a single, centralized point of administration for users and groups in a mixed NetWare and Windows NT environment. It allows user information to be created and managed in NDS and synchronized to the NT domain.

Installation Prerequisites

Perform the following prerequisites before beginning the installation:

- Each NetWare 4.1*x* or NetWare 5 server must have the NetWare Administrator utility (NWADMIN for NT) installed.

- As an administrator you need Supervisor rights at the root of the NDS tree and you will need administrative rights to all NT domains or NT workgroups to be brought under NDS administration.

Each NetWare server must run SAP. To check for SAP, complete the following procedure:

1. From the server console, type **LOAD INETCFG**.

2. Select Bindings.

3. For SAP, select IPX External Net.

4. Select Expert Bind Options.

5. Select SAP Bind Options

6. Set SAP State to ON.

An example of the INETCFG screen is shown in Figure 20.14.

FIGURE 20.14

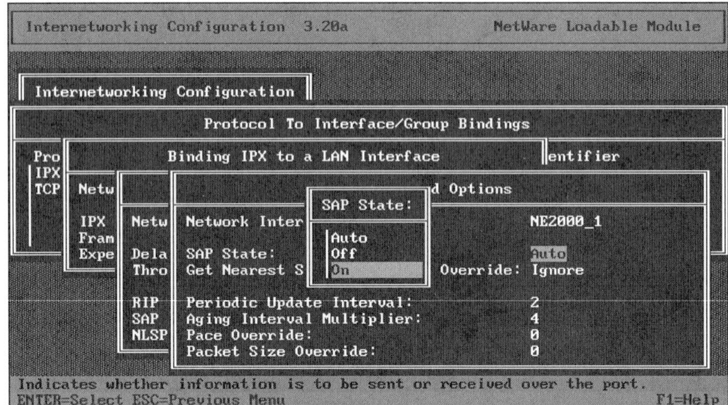

Checking the SAP configuration with the INETCFG Utility

Make sure each NetWare server has NetWare 4.1*x* CLIB Update Kit installed. You can download the update (LIBUPB.EXE) from Novell's Web site at:

`http://support.novell.com/cgi-bin/search/downloads/pub/updates/nwos/nw311/libupb.exe`

To install the CLIB Update Kit, download LIBUPB.EXE onto your workstation and execute LIBUPB.EXE (it is a self-extracting executable). See the LIBUPB.TXT file for the rest of the installation instructions.

Each NT System must have the Novell NT Client installed. You can download the NetWare 5 Client for Windows NT — NTENU41N.EXE (network version) or NTENU41D.EXE (floppy disk version) — from Novell's Web site at `www.novell.com`.

- Ensure you have the TCPIP.NLM loaded on the NetWare server.

- Ensure that the NT Event Log Viewer is not open on the systems where you're installing the NDS Object Replication Service.
- During the installation process — ensure that the system from which you are running the installation program has no NT connections or drive mappings to any NT systems upon which you are going to install the NT agent.

Installation of Novell Administrator for Windows NT

The NAdminNT installation program is a wizard that walks you through each step. If you have questions at any point of the installation process, press F1 or choose the Help button.

IMPORTANT

The first time you install NAdminNT, you should not receive any CRITICAL or WARNING messages in the Event Log. If you do, you should remove the program and reinstall, troubleshoot the error, or get technical support.

After installing NAdminNT, make sure the NDS Object Replication Service (ORS) is started on the NT machine. To do so, open the Control Panel and launch the Services applet. Then locate the ORS service. If it is not started, start it manually.

Integrating and Synchronizing Users with the Integration Utility

You can run the Integration Utility (IGRATE.EXE) either from the Tools menu of NWADMIN or as a stand-alone utility. This utility lets you integrate NDS users to NT, integrate NT users to NDS, or synchronize an existing NDS user with an existing NT user.

NOTE

Before performing any integration or synchronization operation, you must upload NT domain information into NDS using the Integration Utility's "Update" feature.

If you experience any kind of failure during an upload from NT to NDS with the Integration Utility, you should *not* delete the users that were uploaded to NDS before the failure and start over. Simply recover from the failure and then rerun the "Update" operation.

If you should want to delete the users and clean things up and start completely over, you should unload NDSDM.NLM before deleting the objects from NDS with NWADMIN. If the NLM is loaded when you delete the objects, it will keep track of the delete operations — and when the ORS comes back online, the objects will be deleted from the NT domain.

For procedures and overview information, choose Help once you are in the Integration utility.

Compatibility Issues

For an explanation of compatibility issues, see "Compatibility Issues" under the "Troubleshooting and Reference" section of the help file (MWA.HLP). The following issues are *not* documented in the help file:

- When large numbers of events are being placed in the application event log, the "Log Settings" for the "Application" log in the "Event Viewer" should be set to "Overwrite Events as Needed."

- Large multiserver trees take longer to propagate the schema extensions. Installation to such environments should run schema extensions during the first install of this product. Be sure to wait some time for the schema extension to propagate to all NetWare 4 and NetWare 5 servers and then install NetWare and NT systems. If the NDSDM event monitor NLM fails to load, complaining that the schema is not up to date, the most likely reason is that the schema extensions have not yet propagated to that NetWare server.

- If you have large domains and you are uploading the domain into a partition that already has a large number of objects, you should make sure that the server has sufficient memory and the tree is partitioned properly. The help file (MWA.HLP) gives recommendations on how many objects should be uploaded into a particular partition. See Chapters 4 and 5 for more information on partitioning.

- In order to run the NWADMIN snap-in on a Windows 95/98 workstation, you must have Microsoft's Internet Explorer version 3.01 or later.

Designing and Managing NDS for NT

Since NDS for NT is an add-on software product to NetWare 4 and NetWare 5, it makes it easier to manage the resources in both your NetWare and Windows NT networks. It alleviates the dual administration necessary in managing NT domains and an NDS tree. With NDS for NT, all administration is done from a single point using NWADMIN. NWADMIN will store all information necessary in the NDS tree, and all NT requests to the domain are redirected to NDS. This provides a single point of administration for both worlds. The result is that you can manage all aspects of the NT server domain through NDS. The result is the inherent ability to provide a single login, which would reduce user confusion, and a single point of administration for the entire network. Thus, if changes are made using the User Manager for Domains, they will be automatically changed in the NDS tree. If the changes are made first in NDS using NWADMIN, they are represented in the NT server domain. Therefore, you can use either User Manager or NWADMIN to manage your network and NDS will remain consistent. This is significant if some system administrators primarily use the User Manager to administer objects.

In this chapter, we will discuss how to manage all aspects of the NT domain as a part of your NDS tree. But first, we need to discuss how to design your NDS tree to include the domain and all of its users and groups.

Designing NDS for NT

Since NDS for NT gives you the ability to integrate Windows NT domains directly into your NDS tree, it requires you to design your NDS tree to accommodate the new objects. New topics that we need to cover include how to design NDS trees with NT domains in them to support the NDS for NT product and also what is the best way to design domains.

Before we introduce the addition requirements of NDS for NT, let's quickly summarize the Novell Directory Services (NDS) design guidelines that you should have learned from the previous chapters. We strongly recommend that you learn and follow these design principles before you attempt to integrate the NT domains.

Summary of NDS Design Guidelines

The basic NDS tree design can be done very quickly once the concepts are understood. An NDS design for companies large and small can be mapped out in literally hours. In addition, having a plan before beginning an installation will save you time in the long run. Your design can even serve as your installation guide. No two trees will be exactly alike, and yet all trees have common characteristics that can be summarized in the following guidelines.

NDS Tree

1. Design the top of the tree based on WAN infrastructure.

2. Design the bottom of the tree based on organization of network resources.

3. Allow no global groups or groups that have users from multiple partitions.

NDS Partitions

1. Partition the top of the tree based on the WAN infrastructure.

2. Do not create a partition that spans your WAN.

3. Partition around the local servers in each geographic area.

4. Partition the top of the tree based on size (1000–1500 objects).

NDS Replicas

1. Maintain three replicas for fault tolerance.

2. Replicate locally (if possible).

3. Replicate to provide bindery service access.

4. Place master replica on servers at hub sites, not remote sites.

A balance of replication for fault tolerance and performance can be achieved if the preceding rules for partitioning and replication are followed as closely as possible. NDS was built to be scalable to meet the growth needs of your network environment. Partitioning and replication constitute the method by which NDS can be logically segmented for greater efficiency across multiple NetWare 5 servers.

The specific design rules for partitioning and replication of Directory Services can be separated into two different categories depending on your specific implementation requirements, your hardware, and the knowledge level of your staff. The two categories defined for the partition and replica design rules are the Quick Design and the Advanced Design options. We *strongly* recommend that you always use the Quick Design numbers for the design of your NDS tree. You should only use the Advanced Design numbers in extreme situations. Your NDS design tree will work better and more efficiently if you always use the Quick Design rules.

Quick Design (Strongly Recommended)

Partition size:	1,000–1,500 objects
Number of child partitions per parent:	10–15 partitions
Number of replicas per partition:	2–5 replicas (typically 3)
Number of replicas per server:	7–10 replicas
Number of replicas per Replica Server:	30 replicas
Minimum server hardware:	Pentium 100+MHz (64MB RAM)

Advanced Design (Use Only in Extreme Situations)

Partition size:	3,500 objects
Number of child partitions per parent:	35–40 partitions
Number of replicas per partition:	10 replicas (typically 3)
Number of replicas per server:	20 replicas
Number of replicas per Replica Server:	70–80 replicas
Minimum server hardware:	Pentium 200+MHz (128MB RAM)

A *replica server* is a dedicated NetWare 4 or NetWare 5 server that just stores NDS replicas. This type of server is sometimes referred to as a "DSMASTER server." This configuration has become popular with some companies that have a lot of single server remote offices. The replica server provides a place for you to store additional replicas for the partition of a remote office location.

The ultimate limiting factor for the number of replicas on any server is that the replica synchronization process on the server must be able to complete in 30 minutes or less. The factors that affect the time it takes to complete the sync are:

1. CPU speed of the replica server hardware
2. Number of replicas
3. Number of objects in each replica
4. Number of servers in each replica ring
5. Location of replicas in the replica ring (local or remote)
6. Speed of the WAN links connecting remote replicas
7. Amount of RAM on the replica server hardware
8. Frequency of inbound replica synchronization

Designing the NDS Tree for NDS for NT

When you configure the NDS for NT software, you select a specific context in the tree where the current NT domain objects will be migrated. The migration is performed using the Domain Object Wizard. During the execution of the wizard, you are asked to provide a name for the NT domain object that is created in the selected context. This domain object in NDS represents the NT domain. This object behaves similarly to a Group object and a Container object in that it holds information about the domain and users who are members of the domain, but it also contains member objects such as computers and groups just as an actual domain does. Figure 20.15 illustrates how the domain object placed in the NDS tree represents the NT domain.

FIGURE 20.15

The domain object (in this case, NTDOMAIN) created in the NDS tree, which represents the NT domain. Users added to the domain object in NDS are immediately visible to the NT server domain.

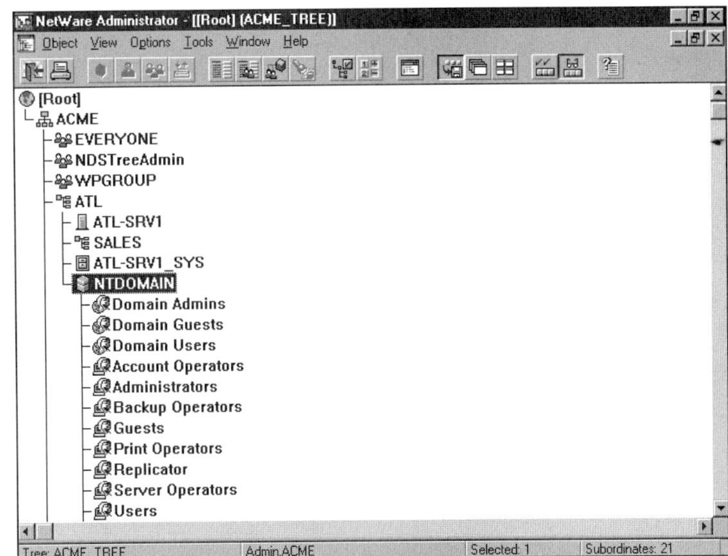

Since the NT domain object in NDS acts as a group with a list of domain members, it takes on the NDS design characteristics of an NDS Group object. However, it is also a special NDS container object that holds NDS for NT Local Group objects, NDS for NT Global Group objects, and NDS for NT Workstation objects that are migrated from the original NT domain. Figure 20.16 illustrates how the NTDOMAIN object contains the NDS for NT Local Group objects, NDS for NT Global Group objects, and NDS for NT Workstation objects that have been migrated.

Because this new NDS object called the NT Domain object acts as both a group and a container, it has unique design characteristics. One of the unique design characteristics is the fact that you can create an NDS partition at the domain object. In other words, the NT domain object in the tree can become its own partition. Figure 20.17 illustrates how a domain object can be partitioned using the NDS Manager utility. In this case, the NT domain object called NTDOMAIN in ATL.ACME is being created as an NDS partition.

FIGURE 20.16

The NTDOMAIN object in the NDS tree contains the NDS for NT Local Group objects, NDS for NT Global Group objects, and NDS for NT Workstation objects that have been migrated.

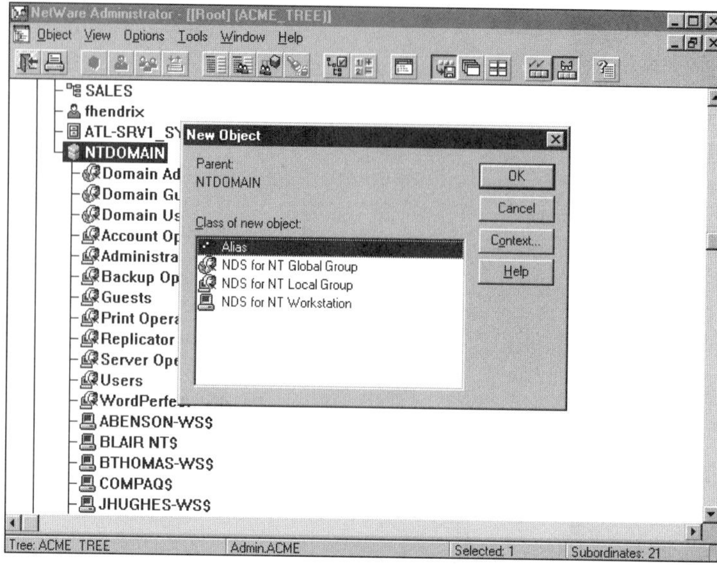

FIGURE 20.17

The NT domain object, NTDOMAIN.ATL.ACME, is being partitioned using the NDS Manager utility.

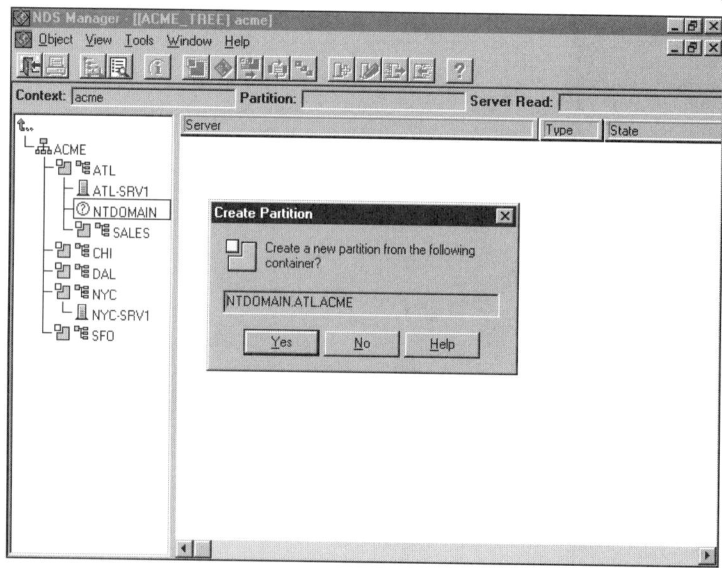

Consulting Experience

The domain object in NDS can only partition using NDS Manager. And NDS Manager version 1.25 is the only version that will let you make this change. Versions of NDS Manager shipped with NetWare 4 will not let you perform the operation. Version 1.25 of NDS Manager comes with the NDS for NT product and is installed automatically on the server that you select to install NDS for NT. Make sure that you are using the correct version of NDS Manager before trying to do the partition operation.

The NDS Manager version 1.25 is the latest version available from Novell. The version of NDS Manager that ships with Novell's latest NetWare 4 support pack (INWSP4.EXE) is only 1.24. To help reduce the confusion, you can copy the NDS Manager version 1.25 to all of your NetWare 4 servers.

The information that is stored in the partition created from the domain object includes just the objects found under the domain. These objects are NDS for NT Local Group objects, NDS for NT Global Group objects, NDS for NT Workstation objects, and Alias objects. The users that were migrated from the original NT domain cannot be part of a partition created from the NT domain object in NDS.

NDS for NT Design Guidelines

Since the domain object represents the original NT domain, one of the first design decisions is where to create or place the domain object in the NDS tree. We recommend that the object be placed in a container that is local to the domain users. For example, if there is a Windows NT domain at the Atlanta site or location, then the NT domain object in NDS (NTDOMAIN) should be created within the ATL.ACME container of the NDS tree as shown in Figure 20.18.

In addition, the user objects should be migrated to the appropriate department containers under ATL.ACME. In the example, the users for the original NT domain have been moved under the SALES.ATL.ACME container. Figure 20.19 illustrates how the users can be moved using the Domain Object Wizard. In this case, the users are being migrated into the SALES.ATL.ACME container, even though they are managed through the NTDOMAIN.ATL.ACME domain object in the tree. You want to place the users in the container with the network resources that they use.

FIGURE 20.18

The original NT domain users are located in the Atlanta site and have been migrated into the NDS tree under the SALES.ATL.ACME container. The object called NTDOMAIN represents the NT domain. Users added to the domain object in NDS are immediately visible to the NT server domain.

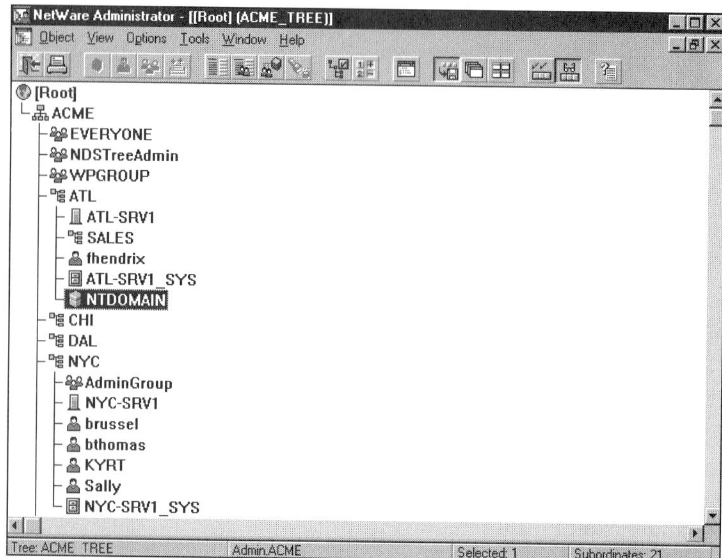

FIGURE 20.19

The original NT domain users are migrated into the NDS tree using the Domain Object Wizard. The SALES.ATL.ACME container has been chosen as the default destination.

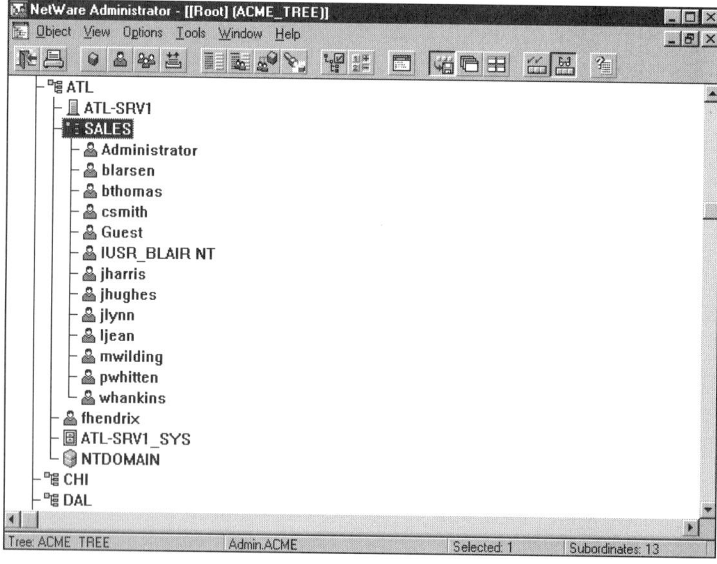

Figure 20.20 illustrates that after the users have been migrated into the tree they become true NDS user objects. It addition, they obtain all the rights and benefits of being a part of NDS. The users are located in the SALES.ATL.ACME container.

FIGURE 20.20

The NT users have been migrated into the SALES.ATL.ACME container.

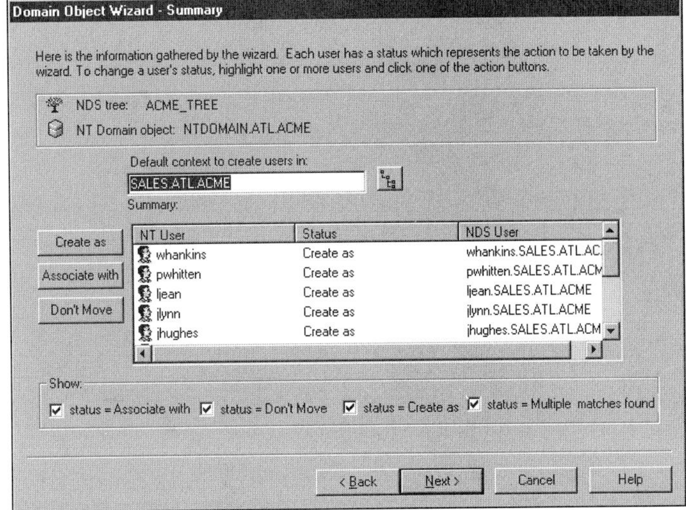

After you have decide where in the NDS tree that the domain object and users will be placed, consider the following design rules for NDS for NT:

- Limit the number of members in the membership list of the NT domain object to 3,000. This implies that you limit the number of users in the original NT domains to less than 3,000 users.
- If possible, keep the users associated with the NT domain in the same partition. The result is that you minimize external references and associated traffic.
- If you have multiple NT domains in your NDS tree, place each NT domain and its associated users in separate partitions.
- Create the NT domain object as its own partition when the number of objects contained is greater than 1,000.

- Always have NDS for NT running on the master replica of the partition holding the NT domain.
- The NT domain PDC or BDC must be in the same SAP domain as the NDS domains supporting the user objects.

Managing NDS for NT

The NT domain object you create in the NDS tree represents the original NT domain. With NDS for NT, all administration for both the NDS and NT systems can be done from a single point using NWADMIN. For example, you can manage all the NT domain users from NWADMIN. Figure 20.21 illustrates how NDS users can be associated with an NT domain by making them members of the NT domain object in NDS. These users are typically the original NT users that you have migrated into NDS.

FIGURE 20.21

The NDS users can be associated with an NT domain by making them members of the NT domain object in NDS.

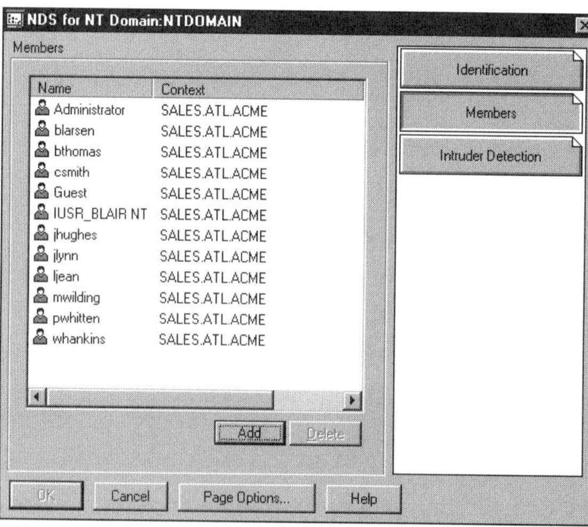

In order to associate the user with the NT domain, you add the user as a member (which is similar to a group). By making user objects members of the domain rather than actually having them reside within the domain, you can place the NDS user objects anywhere in the tree and give them access to one or many NT domain objects. Because NDS stores each domain user's Relative Identifier (RID) in the NT domain object and not as a property of the user object, one NDS user object can be a member of more than one NT Domain object. This provides a simple way for a single NDS user to access resources in multiple domains without having to set up complicated trust relationships in NT.

Creating NT Users in NDS

NWADMIN is used to create a new user and associate it with the NT domain object in the tree. Since NWADMIN is the primary utility used by administrators to manage the information in the NDS tree, and all NT requests are redirected to NDS, it provides a single point of administration for both worlds. As an example, if you need to add a new user with access to an NT server using NDS for NT, you first use NWADMIN to create the user and then associate it with the NT domain object. In addition, using the provided NWADMIN you can grant the user in NDS rights to the NT server. Figure 20.22 illustrates how you add a new user to the NT domain using NWADMIN.

FIGURE 20.22

In order to add a new user into the NT domain, the user must first be created in NDS.

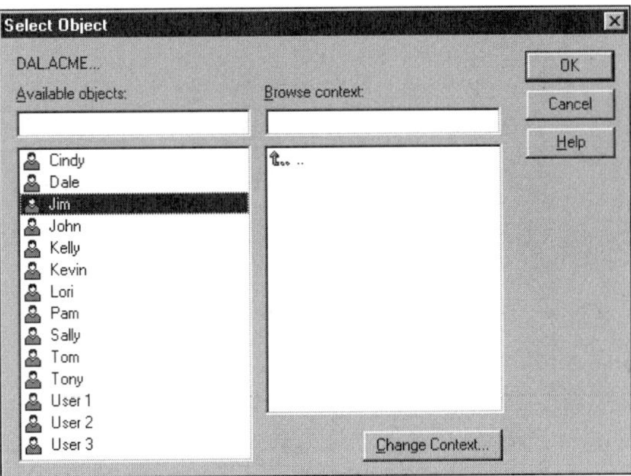

Alternatively, you could use Microsoft User Manager to create the user. User Manager sends requests to the NT server to create the user in the domain, and NDS for NT directs those requests to the NDS database. The user is created in NDS with the same properties and access restrictions that are available from the domain itself.

Any subsequent modifications made to that user with User Manager or any other domain administration utility is serviced in the same way. Figure 20.23 shows the main screen in Microsoft's User Manager utility, which can be used to create and modify users. With NDS for NT installed, the request is redirected to NDS.

Creating a user with the User Manager utility and having it automatically created in NDS is possible because NDS for NT is installed only on the NT server. No workstation components or configurations are needed. So for the workstation running the User Manager utility, nothing has changed, In fact, nothing has changed for any normal Microsoft clients or applications using the domain. The domain requests are simply redirected to NDS, which responds in turn. All workstations and applications will continue to function as they did before the installation. For this reason the User Manager utility can be used without modification.

FIGURE 20.23

With NDS for NT installed on the NT server, you can use Microsoft's User Manager utility to create and modify users because the request is redirected to NDS.

User Manager

User Policies Options Help

Username	Full Name	Description
Administrator		Built-in account for administering the computer/dom
blarsen	Brad Larsen	
bthomas	Blair Thomas	
csmith	Corey Smith	
Guest		Built-in account for guest access to the computer/d
jhughes	Jeff Hughes	
jlynn	Jessa Lynn	
knay	Kyrt Nay	
ljean	Laurin Jean	
mashley	McKenna Ashley	
pwhitten	Pam Whitten	
whankins	Wendy Hankins	

Groups	Description
Administrators	Members can fully administer the computer/domain
Backup Operators	Members can bypass file security to back up files
Guests	Users granted guest access to the computer/domain
HP4SI Printer	Shared Printer
Power Users	Members can share directories and printers
Replicator	Supports file replication in a domain
Users	Ordinary users
WordPrefect	WordPrefect Application

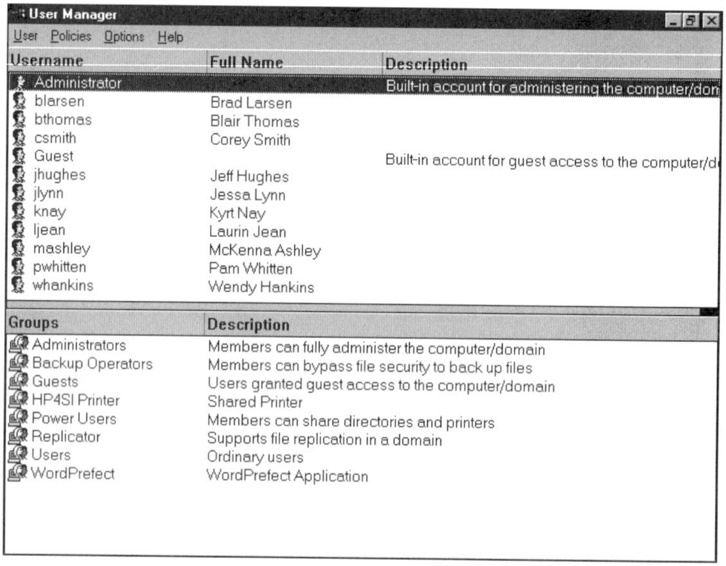

Consulting Experience

All NT clients and applications communicate to the NT servers using Remote Procedure Calls (RPCs). Any request passed from the workstations using RPCs is extracted and passed to the SAMSRV.DLL layer. Normally the SAMSRV.DLL accesses the Windows NT Security Accounts Manager (SAM), where the domain namebase is stored, and performs the requested operation. However, NDS for NT replaces SAMSRV.DLL, and the request is forwarded to NDS instead of the local SAM namebase. Using this method, NDS becomes the single directory where everything is stored. Replacing just the SAMSRV.DLL ensures that the level of compatibility is 100 percent.

Once a Windows NT domain has been brought into the NDS tree, the NT domain controller must be able to authenticate to the NDS tree. The NT server that is a PDC or BDC needs to store, modify, and retrieve domain information from the domain object placed in NDS. In order for the NT server to authenticate, the NDS domain object is used. The domain object is given the appropriate administrative rights of create and modify to all containers holding the NDS user objects of the domain membership. This may require you to grant trustee rights to the domain object where future domain members may exist. You can configure the NT domain object in NDS with a default location in NDS where all new objects are created with the User Manager utility. Figure 20.24 illustrates how you can select a default location for creation of all new NT users. You can set the Default User Creation Context for the NT domain object using NWADMIN and going to the Identification page. The result of setting this value is that all new users created with the User Manager utility are automatically created in the NDS tree at the selected location.

FIGURE 20.24

You can set the Default User Creation Context for the NT domain object in Identification. Setting this value allows you to create new users with the User Manager utility and have them automatically created in the NDS tree at the selected location.

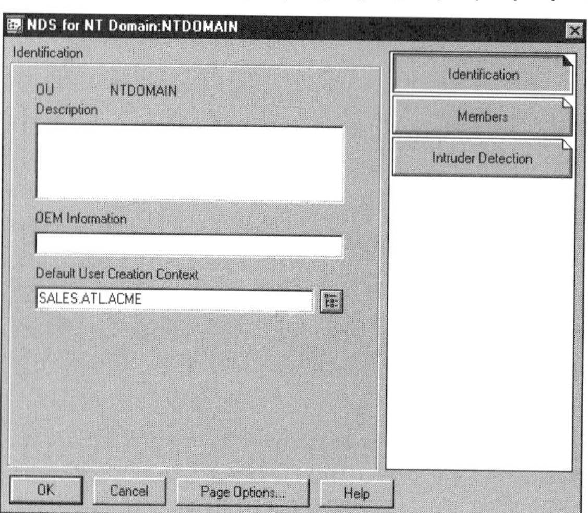

For NT servers that should be brought into the NDS tree but already have a large number of users and computers defined, NDS for NT provides a utility that allows the NT Server administrator to easily migrate Windows NT domains into NDS. This utility guides the administrator easily through the process of creating the Domain object in NDS and then proceeds to create all defined local groups, global groups, and Workstation objects. User objects from the domain can either have new NDS User objects created for them or they may be associated with existing NDS User objects. This greatly simplifies the task of moving an existing domain to NDS.

User Authentication and Single Login

Single login is one of the major benefits of having the NT domain integrated into NDS. In this situation, single login means that when a user needs to access network resources from NetWare 5 or Windows NT, the user only enters one username and password. When an NT domain is migrated to NDS, the hashed user passwords are also migrated. This allows a user to log into the domain using the same password that was defined before the migration took place. NDS holds both hashed passwords for the user, one encrypted using the MD4 algorithm (Microsoft) and one encrypted using RSA (NDS).

Windows NT uses an MD4 password encryption algorithm, whereas NDS uses the more robust RSA encryption. When user passwords are created, they are hashed (encrypted or scrambled) by the respective algorithms, and then these hashed values are stored on the respective servers. Because there is no modification to the workstation, the login process used to authenticate to NDS and the NT server does not change. The login process hashes the user password with RSA and sends that directly to the NetWare 4 or NetWare 5 server for authentication to NDS. When a user logs in, the password is passed through the RSA encryption algorithm at the workstation and the encrypted value is sent to NDS for verification. If the hashed value of the entered password matches that stored in NDS, the user is authenticated to NDS.

At the same time, the password is also hashed with the MD4 algorithm and sent to the Windows NT domain controller. This hashed value is compared to that stored in the domain User object; if they match, the user is authenticated to the NT server. This authentication process is secure because the encryption process that is performed on each password is nonreversible. This means that even though the hashed value is sent on the wire, there is no way to reverse the encryption process and determine the clear text password from the encrypted value.

Figure 20.25 illustrates how the workstation running the NetWare 5 Client is responsible for password and authentication to both the NetWare 4 or NetWare 5 and Windows NT servers.

FIGURE 20.25

The workstation running the NetWare 4 or NetWare 5 client is responsible to hash the password and use it to authenticate to both the NetWare 4 or NetWare 5 and Windows NT servers.

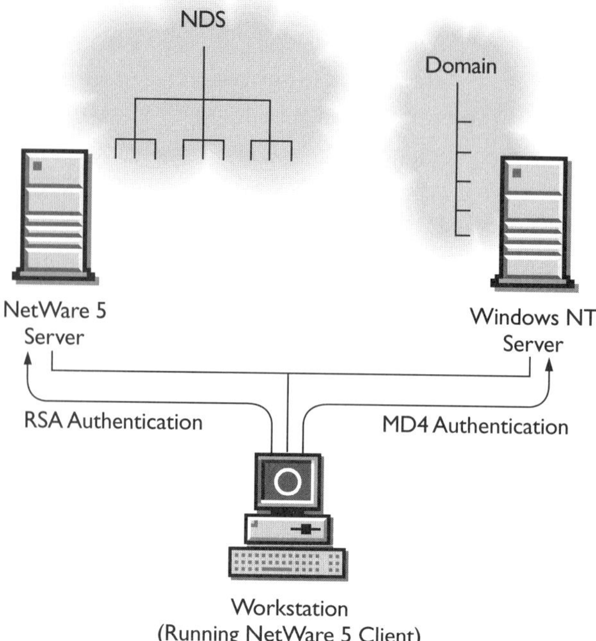

Maintaining Password Synchronization

Because Novell maintains Microsoft's security, it is necessary to keep the NDS and NT passwords synchronized. Most users will change their password when prompted or when they have forgotten and have to call their network administrator. In either case, the passwords are easily changed and synchronized. The methods used to maintain this synchronization are identical to those used when authenticating users to standard NT domains.

The best way to maintain synchronized passwords involves setting up the client workstation to authenticate to both NDS and Windows NT simultaneously. The following methods and utilities will help you maintain password synchronization:

- Use the NetWare 5 Client for Windows NT and check the Automatically Synchronize Passwords check box at login if the passwords are not currently synchronized. The NetWare 5 Client change password feature is made through the NWGINA module.

- Use the NWADMIN and the snap-in provided with NDS for NT to change user passwords. This snap-in provides a change password option that will change both the NDS and NT passwords. Using the snap-in for NWADMIN instead of User Manager, NETADMIN, or SETPASS will ensure password synchronization.
- Set the passwords to expire through NDS and not through NT. This ensures that an NT password is not changed without changing the corresponding NDS password.
- Make sure users who need both NDS and NT resources authenticate to both NDS and NT simultaneously. This method helps avoid any rare password synchronization issues.

NDS for NT and Windows NT Domain Controllers

Windows NT networks are installed with a primary domain controller (PDC) and one or more backup domain controllers (BDCs). The NT domain namebase is stored on each of these domain controllers in a single master configuration. This means that each domain controller can provide information requested by workstations but all changes to the domain must be made at the PDC. The PDC then replicates the changes down to each of the backup domain controllers.

NDS for NT moves the domain namebase into NDS where it is referenced by both primary and backup domain controllers. In order for all domain controllers to have access to the domain information stored in NDS, all primary and backup domain controllers must have NDS for NT installed. In addition, each of the domain controllers needs to be associated with the same NT domain object in NDS. Next, make sure that the NT server is installed with the Novell NetWare 5 Client for Windows NT. The client is installed by default. The client enables the NT servers to connect to the NetWare 4 servers and NDS that enable the domain redirection to NDS.

Summary

NDS for NT upgrades the Windows NT domain system to a true directory service and gives you single login, a single point of administration, and full NT application support for mixed NetWare 5 and NT networks. NDS for NT alleviates the need to manage users on both systems. Thus, NDS for NT greatly reduces the amount of time network administrators spend managing the mixed server networks. It allows administrators the flexibility of managing all Windows NT domains and their resources in NDS using either NWADMIN or the Windows NT utilities. NDS for NT also allows a single NDS User object to become a member of multiple domains, doing away with the complexity of trust relationships.

CHAPTER 21

Netscape FastTrack Server for NetWare

The Netscape FastTrack Server for NetWare is the Web server product designed for NetWare by Novonyx, a joint venture between Novell and Netscape. NetWare 5 includes this product as a replacement for the NetWare Web Server product that was shipped with previous versions of NetWare.

This chapter introduces you to Novell's FastTrack Server, which provides you with the capability of running the Netscape Web server software on the NetWare platform. We will discuss how to install the FastTrack software and then how to manage it on a NetWare platform. This chapter does not explain how to create a Web site or design a site with sound, graphics, and so on. We explain how to manage and deliver the Web content, but not how to create it.

The FastTrack Server offers the following capabilities:

- **Ease of Web Publishing** — Web publishing is made easier through one-button publishing to a Web site, using authoring tools such as Communicator or Composer. A Web designer can create graphics and add content and links quickly and easily.

- **Simple Administration** — The FastTrack Server is administered through a common, graphical, browser-based server console. You can use the same interface to manage FastTrack, Enterprise, or other Novonyx servers.

- **Reliability** — With the proven NetWare network operating system, you now have Netscape reliability on that platform with security provided through NDS.

- **Open Standards** — FastTrack supports all industry standards such as HTML, HTTP, TCP/IP, SSL, and so on, for complete Web application development.

- **Application Development** — FastTrack provides tools for Web application development including Perl, JavaScript, and NetBasic for development on NetWare.

- **Upgrade Path** — FastTrack servers can easily be migrated to the more powerful Enterprise Servers without impacting your users.

- **Security** — FastTrack provides SSL and NDS authentication for increased security. You can limit access to specific pages or directories on your servers.

The Netscape FastTrack Server for NetWare consists of two server installations: the administration server and the Web server. The administration server is a Web-based server containing forms that you use to configure your Netscape server on NetWare and manage other Netscape servers. You can manage multiple servers from a single location. The installation of the FastTrack server will prompt you for an IP address and port number for your administration server. The Web server is the server that is configured by the administration server to deliver Web pages to the Internet or intranet.

NOTE

A single computer can be used to run the administration server and the FastTrack server.

Requirements for the Netscape FastTrack Server

In this section we identify the client and server requirements for running the FastTrack software on your network. Additionally, you need to take a few other steps such as obtaining the appropriate administrative rights and having valid IP addresses for your FastTrack server.

Client Requirements

You will need to verify that the client you use to install this software meets the following requirements:

- Windows 95/98 or Windows NT 4.0. Be sure to have a good understanding of how these platforms work.
- Novell's 32-bit NetWare Client for either platform. Make sure the client is functioning properly before beginning your installation.
- Netscape 3.*x* or higher. A copy of Communicator 4.04 is included on the FastTrack Server CD for installation of this product only.

- A CD-ROM drive for CD installation.
- 100MB of free space on the workstation hard drive for installation files and workspace.

Server Requirements

Verify that the server you are installing this software on has met the following minimum requirements:

- Configured for IPX and running NetWare 4.11 or higher.
- CLIB 4.11J. This version of CLIB is included on the FastTrack Server CD and must be installed if not currently running on this server.
- Long filename support. The FastTrack installation will prompt to install long filename support if it's not currently on this server.
- NLDAP gateway. This product is used if you want to integrate users and groups with NDS via the administration server. You can download a copy of the gateway from `www.novell.com`.
- Minimum 32MB of RAM. 64MB is recommended.
- 100MB minimum free space on the SYS volume.

Other Requirements

In addition to the client and server requirements, you must also meet the following prerequisites or have the following information:

- Supervisor rights to the SYS volume of the NetWare 4.11 or higher server.
- The IP address for the server on which you intend to install FastTrack Server.

- The subnet mask of the IP network for which the server is attached.
- The IP gateway address that the server will use.
- The DNS host name for the server and at least one DNS server that the FastTrack server will use for IP address resolution. Make sure DNS is resolving properly before beginning your installation.
- Unique port numbers for administration and Web servers. You will need two port numbers: one for the administration server and one for the Web server.

Installation of the FastTrack Server

The following steps outline the installation of the FastTrack Server software:

1. Insert the Netscape FastTrack Server CD into the CD-ROM drive of your Windows 95 or Windows NT client.
2. Choose the FastTrack Setup program, which displays the screen shown in Figure 21.1.

FIGURE 21.1

The FastTrack Startup dialog box

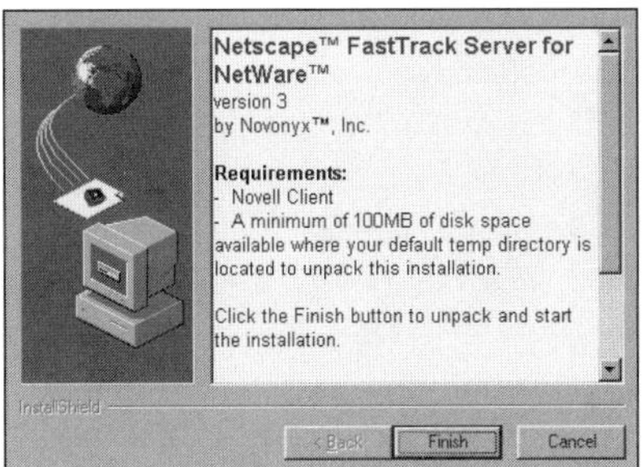

3. A series of files will load, and then you will be prompted with the main FastTrack Server for NetWare installation screen as shown in Figure 21.2. Accept the license terms and then continue.

FIGURE 21.2

FastTrack Server for NetWare installation

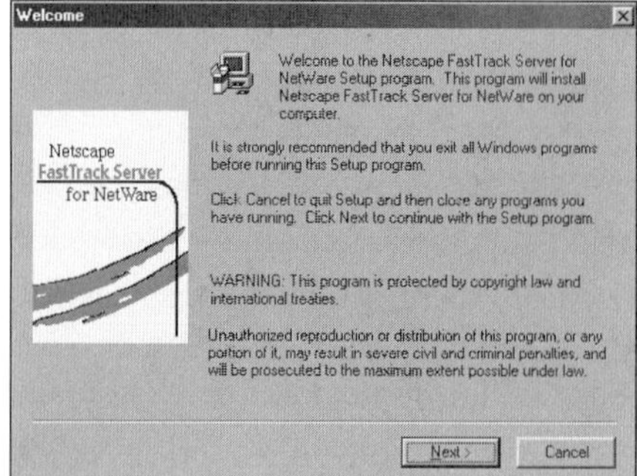

4. You will be prompted now to select a drive mapped to the SYS volume of a NetWare 4.11 or later server.

5. You must now enter the host name and IP address of the server you have selected. Confirm that these are the right settings as shown in Figure 21.3.

FIGURE 21.3

The Configure Server dialog box

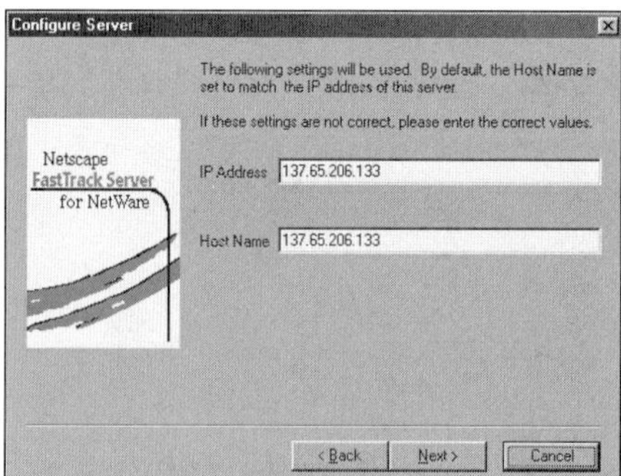

6. Follow the prompts on the screen, paying close attention to the information prompt. It is important that you remember the I/O address and port information, which is used to access the administration server.

7. You will now be prompted to enter a username and password to restrict access to the administration server as shown in Figure 21.4.

FIGURE 21.4

Enter a username and password to restrict access to the administration server.

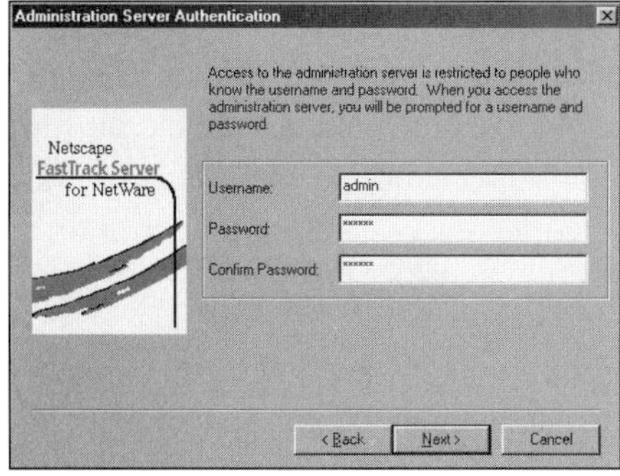

8. Respond to the rest of the prompts on the screen. You will then be presented with a summary page of all your current selections as shown in Figure 21.5.

FIGURE 21.5

A summary dialog box lists all settings before performing the installation.

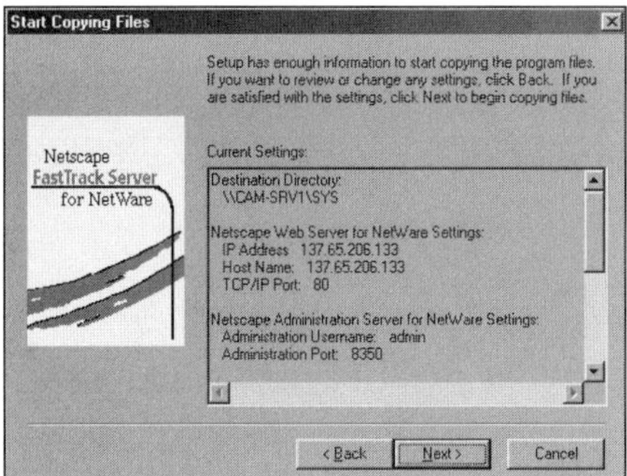

9. Click Finish. The file extraction process will then begin. Follow the instructions on screen to completion.

NOTE

If you are installing this product over a beta version, the installation program will match existing files that are currently on your system with a file of the same name from the installation CD and then determine if they are newer or older. The installation will prompt to overwrite files that are older than those on the CD. Be sure to back up any Web content before doing an upgrade.

Using the Administration Server

All Novonyx-based servers (Enterprise, FastTrack, and Netscape) are configured using the administration server and Server Manager forms. You can use any workstation on your network to access the administration server and the forms.

The administration server contains Java and JavaScript forms that you can use to configure your Novonyx servers. All forms have a consistent look and feel, so you can easily manage any type of Novonyx server. You use your browser to navigate the administration server and create/modify forms to configure a Web server. You use a URL you have defined in the setup to navigate the server.

Connecting the Administration Server

The following steps are used to connect to the administration server:

1. From your browser, enter the URL you selected during installation and configuration of FastTrack. This URL will depend on the host name and port number you selected. The format for the URL is http://*servername*:*portnumber*/. For example, your URL and port number may look something like this:

   ```
   http://cam-srv1.acme.com:8350
   ```

2. The browser will prompt you for a user id and password. You have three levels of users:

   - **Superuser** — The Superuser is a special user that you created during the installation of FastTrack. This user has full access to the administration server.
   - **Administrators** — The Administrators bypass the server administration page and go directly to the Server Manager forms. What forms they can access depend on the access granted to them by the Superuser.
   - **End Users** — End users will see a limited set of forms and can modify information specific to themselves such as passwords.

3. You will then be presented with the Server Administration window.

You can start and stop a Web server by clicking the On/Off icon located to the left of the server's name at the bottom of the Administration screen. You'll notice that a server that is running will show "On" with a green light to the left of the server's name. You can also start or stop the server from the Server Manager forms by clicking Server Preferences → On/Off and then clicking On or Off. If the server is currently on and you click On, it will restart. You will see the Preferences option once you are at a Server Manager form.

By default, the Web server will stop accepting new connections after three seconds. In most cases you won't need to change this value. If you do need to change the value, you must edit the magnus.conf file and modify the line that reads:

```
TerminateTimeout seconds
```

To restart a server at a NetWare console, use the following steps:

1. Type **unload nshttpd**.

2. Type **nsweb** to load the server again.

Using Server Manager Forms

Server Manager forms are the collection of forms that are used to manage a single Web server. Therefore, there is a Server Manager (set of forms) for each Novonyx server installed on the computer, including a Server Manager for the administration server itself.

The forms are accessed by clicking the Webserver button found below the heading "Servers Supporting General Administration." You will see a server's name there to click. After clicking a button, you will be shown the Server Manager for that server.

You then select a category button in the top frame and click a link in the left frame. The remaining portion of the screen displays a form where you can specify values to configure that Web server. You can return to server administration by clicking the Server Administration button, always displayed at the upper-right side of your browser.

NOTE

When changing any server information, be sure to always save and apply your changes so that they take effect.

Managing the Server Content

You also use the Server Manager to manage the server's content. The content includes the HTML files and graphics that make up your Web site. Clients may view files depending on the access that they have been granted. This section provides information on how you can manage the Web server's content.

The Primary Document Directory

A *primary document directory* is a central or root location for all your server's Web documents. You can more fully control who has access to files on your server if you have all Web-related documents stored in the primary document directory. You need to perform the following steps to set up a primary document directory:

1. Within Server Manager, choose Content Management → Primary Document Directory.

2. In the Primary Directory field, type the full pathname of the directory that you want to be the primary document directory.

3. Click OK.

4. Save and apply your changes.

You may also have additional document directories if all the files to be accessed are not stored in the Primary Document Directory. You can use this procedure if you want someone else to manage a subset of documents to the total set of Web files. To specify additional document directories, follow these steps:

1. Select Content Management → Additional Document Directories.

2. Type the URL prefix that you want to map. For example, you could have a mapped URL that reads

```
http://www.acme.com/marketing/index.html
```

where `marketing` is the prefix you specify.

3. Type the absolute path of the directory you want the URL prefix to map to. For example you could have

```
\acme\marketing\pubdocs\index.html
```

4. Select a configuration style to apply to this directory's configuration (optional).

5. Click OK.

6. Save and apply changes.

Document Preferences

Document preferences refer to how files are located and indexed when a client makes a request to the Web server, and how they are then presented to the client. This section describes the configuration options available for the Web server documents.

Index File

If a specific document is not specified in the URL, the default is to first look for a file called `index.html` and then for one called `home.html`. If it finds a file called "index" it assumes that it is the index file and displays that page. The index file is a file you create that maintains an overview of the directory's contents. You can specify any file as an index file for your directory by simply naming it one of the default names, "index" or "home."

If an index file is not found, the server will generate an index file that lists all the files in the document root. You can specify that the index displayed appear:

- **Fancy** — A detailed directory index. Includes a graphic that represents the type of file, last file modification date, file size.
- **Simple** — A less detailed directory index.

You can also specify that no directory index be displayed if the default index file is not available. Instead, an error message will be returned to the user.

The Server Home Page

By default, the server will display the index file as the server home page when a client first requests the Web site's URL. However, you can also specify a file to use as the server's home page by setting the radio button to Home Page and entering the filename for the home page in the field next to the radio button. You can access this page by using the Server Manager and choosing Content Management → Document Preferences.

Parsed HTML

When a client makes a request for an HTML document, it is sent exactly as it exists on the disk. However, you can have the server search HTML files for special commands that will insert request-specific information or files when the document is sent. To provide this capability, you must first enable HTML parsing. Use the following steps:

1. Within the Server Manager select Content Management → Parse HTML.
2. From the Resource Picker, choose the server resource you want to edit.
3. Select whether you want to activate parsed HTML. If you activate it, you must choose whether to activate it with or without the EXEC tag. This tag allows an HTML file to execute an arbitrary program on the server. The EXEC tag can by used for security reasons.
4. Choose the files to parse.

The most common choice is to select files to parse that only have the .shtml extension.

You can specify that the server parse all its HTML file. However, this option will slow your server's performance.

Document Footer

A document footer is information appended to a file that includes last modified time to the page's output and other defined text. The footer will work for all files except output of CGI scripts or parsed HTML files, as discussed previously. To specify a document footer, use the following steps:

1. From within the Server Manager, select Content Management → Document Footer.

2. From the Resource Picker, select the resource to which you want to apply the document footer.

3. Select the type of files you to want to include in the footer. The default is text/html.

4. Choose the time format for the drop-down list. You can also type a custom date format in the Custom Date Format field.

5. Enter the footer text. The maximum number of characters is 765. Type the string **:LASTMOD:** if you want to include the date the document was last modified.

6. Click OK.

7. Click Save and Apply to confirm changes.

Configuration Styles

Configuration styles can be considered templates that you create to specify a set of options for a set of files or directories. For example, you can create a configuration style for access logging. You then select a set of files or directories that you want to log; the style (template) is applied for all files. You create a configuration style by following these steps:

1. From within the Server Manager, select Configuration Styles → New Style.
2. Enter the name you want for the configuration style.
3. Click OK. The Edit Configuration Style form will appear.
4. From the drop-down list, choose a configuration style to edit and click Edit this Style.
5. From the list of links available, click the category you want to configure for your style. You will be able to configure the following information:
   - **CGI File Type** — Allows you to activate CGI as a file type.
   - **Character Set** — Change the character set for a resource.
   - **Default Query Handler** — Set a default query handler for a server resource.
   - **Document Footer** — Add a document footer to a server resource.
   - **Error Responses** — Customize error responses that a client will see when encountering an error from the Web server.
   - **Log Preferences** — Set preferences for access logs.
   - **Restrict Access** — Restrict access to the entire server or parts of it.
   - **Server Parsed HTML** — Specify whether the server parses files before they are sent to the client.
6. Fill out the form that appears, and then click OK.
7. Repeat Steps 5 and 6 to make additional changes to the configuration style.
8. Click OK.
9. Click Save and Apply.

Once you have created a configuration style, you can apply it to the files or directories on your Web server. You may specify either single files and directories or multiple files by using a wildcard pattern such as *.gif. Follow these steps to apply a configuration style:

1. Select Configuration Styles → Assign Configuration Style.

2. Enter the prefix of the URL to which you are applying this configuration style. If you choose a directory inside the document root, only enter the path after the document root. If you enter /* after the directory, you will apply the configuration style to all of the directory's contents.

3. Select the configuration style you want to apply. To remove any configuration style previously applied to the resource, select None.

4. Click OK.

Tuning for Performance

The FastTrack server provides a number of tuning options to improve performance and throughput. The following options are discussed in this section:

- Maximum Simultaneous Requests
- Domain Name System Lookups
- Listen-Queue Size
- HTTP Persistent Connection Timeout
- MIME Types

Maximum Simultaneous Requests

Simultaneous requests are the number of active page requests allowed for the server at one time. The default is 128 requests; you probably don't need to adjust this value, because a typical Web server can handle approximately 200 requests a second (considering a response time of 5 milliseconds per page). If you need to change the request value, use the following steps:

1. Select Server Preferences → Performance Tuning.
2. Indicate the new value for requests.
3. Click OK.
4. Click Save and Apply.

Domain Name System Lookups

The server can be configured to use DNS lookups for a host name based on IP address. By default, the server does not enable DNS lookups, because of the performance hit. The benefits to using DNS lookups are that you can use hostname restrictions (limit sites where a client can go) and view the hostname (rather than the IP address) in the log file. The DNS queries are cached for faster performance and can contain from 32 to 32,768 entries, with the default being 1,024 entries. You may also set an expiration on the cache from 1 second to 1 year, specified by seconds. The default value is 20 minutes (1,200 seconds). To enable a DNS system lookup, use the following steps:

1. Create a file named resolve.cfg.
2. Add the following text to the newly created file:

```
Domain <domain-name> (refers to a qualified domain name
such as www.novell.com)

Name server <dns-ip-address> (refers to the IP address of
your DNS server)
```

3. Save the new file at the root of sys:/etc.

4. Restart the server or reload TCP/IP.

Listen-Queue Size

The *listen-queue size* specifies the number of incoming connections that the system accepts for that socket. The default setting is 48 incoming connections. This setting is sufficient for most Web sites.

Setting the listen-queue size too high will degrade server performance. The larger the size, the more incoming connections the server tries to handle, which can cause it to fall further behind.

To make a change to the listen-queue size, do these things:

1. Select Server Preferences → Performance Tuning.

2. Enter a value for Persistent Connection Timeout.

3. Click OK.

4. Save and apply changes.

HTTP Persistent Connection Timeout

All connections have a timeout value so that they don't consume system resources. There is rarely a need to change the timeout value. If you should have to change this value, follow these steps:

1. Select Server Preferences → Performance Tuning.

2. Enter a value in seconds for the HTTP Persistent Connection Timeout entry.

3. Click OK.

4. Save and apply changes.

MIME Types

Multipurpose Internet Mail Extension (MIME) controls what types of multimedia files your mail system supports. You can also use the MIME types setting to specify what file extensions belong to certain server file type. To add a new MIME type, follow these steps:

1. Select Server Preferences → MIME types.
2. Enter the category, content type, and file suffix.
3. Click New Type.

To edit an existing MIME type, do these things:

1. Repeat Step 1 from the previous instructions.
2. Click Edit next to the MIME type you want to edit.
3. Change the category, content type, or file suffix where necessary.
4. Click Change MIME Type to update.

You can also remove a mime type by clicking Remove next to the type you want to remove.

The MIME type can include these file types:

Text/plain	Text/html
Text/richtext	Image/tiff
Image/jpeg	Image/gif
Application/x-tar	Application/postscript
Application/x-gzip	Audio/basic

Network Settings

The FastTrack server provides server settings that allow you to make changes to the configuration. The following parameters can be changed on the FastTrack server:

- The server name
- The server port number
- The server binding address
- The MTA host
- The NNTP host

Changing the Server Name

The format for your server name is:

```
machinename.yourdomain.domain
```

If you make a change to the server name (Web server) and are using DNS, be sure to specify the change using the Network Preferences form.

Changing the Server Port Number

You may change the server port number on the Network Preferences Form. If you choose a nonstandard port, your users will have to enter the server name and port in the URL. For example, if the port you select is 8150, the user would have to enter a URL such as:

```
http://www.acme.com:8150
```

Changing the Server Binding Address

On occasion you may want the server to respond to two URLs. If you want to use this feature, follow these steps:

1. Select the Network Preferences → Bind to Address.
2. Indicate which IP address(s) is/are associated with this hostname.

Be sure that you configure your system to listen to multiple IP addresses.

Changing the MTA Host

To change the Message Transfer Agent host, follow these steps:

1. Select Network Preferences → MTA Host.
2. Change the name of the SMTP mail server.
3. Click OK.
4. Save and apply changes.

Changing the NNTP Host

To change the Network News Transfer Protocol, do these steps:

1. Select Network Preferences → NNTP Host.
2. Change the name of the new server.
3. Click OK.
4. Save and apply changes.

Summary

In this chapter, we detailed the steps for installing and configuring the Netscape FastTrack Server for NetWare. This product allows you to install and manage a Web site on NetWare 5 by providing familiar Netscape server functionality in a high-performance NetWare environment.

CHAPTER 22

Installing the Novell Internet Access Server and FTP Services

In this chapter we take a look at the installation and configuration of the Novell Internet Access Server. We'll first discuss how you install the software and then how you manage the components.

Installing and Managing Novell Internet Access Server Components

In this section we discuss the components of the Novell Internet Access Server.

- To install the Novell Internet Access Server components on the server, use INSTALL.NLM, select Product Options, and choose Install a Product Not Listed. Then specify the path to the Novell Internet Access Server 5 CD-ROM.
- To configure the IPX/IP gateway on the server, use INETCFG.NLM.
- To install the client support for the IPX/IP gateway on workstations, install NetWare Client 32 and choose Additional Options (on Windows 3.1*x*) or Customize (on Windows 95 or Windows 98).
- To work with the IPX/IP gateway object in NDS and to configure access rights, add the IPX/IP gateway snap-in utility to the NetWare Administrator utility by editing the NWADMN3X.INI file.

Installing and Managing FTP Services for NetWare 5

In this section we review the steps to install FTP Services for NetWare 5.

- To install FTP Services for NetWare 5, use INSTALL.NLM, select Product Options, and choose Install a Product Not Listed. Then specify the path to the FTP Services for NetWare 5 CD-ROM.

- To configure FTP Services for NetWare 5 and to create an Anonymous FTP user account, use UNICON.NLM.

Just when we were beginning to get comfortable with the Internet technology, the intranet technology appeared. From a technical standpoint, an *intranet* is simply a Web server that is confined to a private internal network and publishes files to a private audience such as the employees of a corporation. A true Web server is connected to the Internet and publishes files to the world.

The reason that intranet technology is so popular is that people can use their Web browsers to view private information. The intranet server publishes shared information in HTML files that can be created with almost any word processor or text editor and can be viewed with Internet browsers on almost every operating system.

NetWare 5 is Novell's comprehensive operating system for a modern, full-service intranet. It starts with the NetWare 5 operating system then adds the following intranet and Internet features:

- **IPX/IP gateway** — This gateway enables administrators to allow IPX-based workstations to access TCP/IP-based resources, such as FTP and the World Wide Web, without having to install or configure TCP/IP on those workstations. The gateway also lets you implement access control — you can limit users by TCP port number, IP address or target host, and time of day.

- **MultiProtocol Router 3.1** — This feature provides WAN (Wide Area Network) connectivity, routing multiple protocols over leased lines, frame relay, or ISDN lines. This capability allows you to connect network users to an Internet service provider (ISP).

- **Netscape Navigator** — This is the Web browser that lets you locate and read information stored on the Internet or intranet.

- **FTP Services for NetWare 5** — FTP services let you configure FTP access for your intranet.

In your NetWare 5 package, you'll find the following CD-ROMs:

- The NetWare 5 Operating System CD-ROM, which contains the regular NetWare 5 product software and the NetWare Web server. The NetWare Web server also contains the Netscape Navigator Web browser (and a single-user license for the browser).
- The NetWare 5 Online Documentation CD-ROM, which contains HTML documentation for NetWare 5.
- The Novell Internet Access Server 5 CD-ROM, which contains most of the NetWare 5 features: the IPX/IP gateway, MultiProtocol Router 3.1 for WAN connectivity, and the Netscape Navigator Web browser (multiuser license). This CD-ROM also contains HTML-formatted documentation for the IPX/IP gateway.
- The FTP Services for NetWare 5 CD-ROM, which contains the FTP services and configuration utilities.

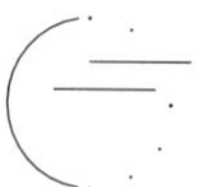
NOTE

To read the HTML-formatted documentation for the Novell Internet Access Server product, use a Web browser from a workstation.

For instructions on installing the Netscape Navigator browser that comes with the NetWare Web server on the NetWare 5 Operating System CD-ROM, see Chapter 14, "NetWare 5 Print Services." For instructions on installing the browser from the Novell Internet Access Server CD-ROM, see the Internet Access Server 4 Quick Reference Guide, which comes with your NetWare 5 kit. The two browsers are identical, and they are placed on both CD-ROMs primarily for convenience.

NOTE

If you have NetWare 5, you are allowed to use as many copies of the Web browser as your NetWare 5 user license permits. In other words, if you bought a 50-user version of NetWare 5, you can let 50 users use the browser. If you have NetWare 5 alone, you have only a single-user license to the browser.

Installing the Novell Internet Access Server Software

Before installing the Novell Internet Access Server software, which will provide the software necessary to run the routing, WAN connectivity, and IPX/IP gateway, you must first install a NetWare 5 server as usual. Then you can install the Novell Internet Access Server software. During the installation, the Netscape Navigator browser will be copied to SYS:NETSCAPE so that you can later install it on workstations.

To install Novell Internet Access Server components on the NetWare 5 server, complete the following steps.

1. Insert the Novell Internet Access Server 4 CD-ROM in a drive on the server and mount the CD-ROM as a NetWare volume.

2. At the server console, load INSTALL.NLM.

3. From the Installation Options menu, choose Product Options, and then choose Install a Product Not Listed.

4. To specify a path to the installation software, press F3 and type

   ```
   NIAS4:\NIAS\INSTALL
   ```

5. Choose Install Product. The Install To Servers list displays the local server name. The value in the title reflects the number of servers to be installed. If you want to install Novell Internet Access Server software on a remote server, press Insert to add the server to the list. If an expected server is not displayed, ensure that the latest version of RSPAWN.NLM is loaded on that server. To remove a server from the Install To Servers list, select the server, press Delete, and select Yes at the prompt.

6. From the Install To Servers menu, press Enter and select Yes to begin the installation. Servers are installed in alphabetical order. If you are installing to a remote server, you will be prompted to log in as an administrator. Enter the administrator's full login name and password.

7. When the prompt "Install previously created configuration files?" appears, select No.

8. When prompted for the Novell Internet Access Server license diskette, insert the NetWare 5 license diskette in the specified drive and press Enter. Once the login, license, and configuration file information for each server is provided, the installation begins copying files to the destinations.

9. When the installation is completed, you can read the installation log file if you desire. Choose Display Log File. When you're finished reviewing the log, press Esc to return to the Installation Options menu.

10. To verify that the Novell Internet Access Server software installed correctly, choose Product Options from the Installation Options menu, and then select Configure/View/Remove Installed Products. The Currently Installed Products list appears, showing entries for the NetWare MultiProtocol Router 3.1 software, WAN Extensions 3.1, and Novell Internet Access Server 4. Press Esc to return to the Installation Options menu.

11. From the Installation Options menu, select NCF Files Options, and then choose the Edit STARTUP.NCF file. Modify the STARTUP.NCF file for each installed server to include the following line at the end of the file if you are using the NetWare 5 server to make a WAN connection:

    ```
    SET MINIMUM PACKET RECEIVE BUFFERS=400
    SET MAXIMUM PACKET RECEIVE BUFFERS=1000
    ```

    The value of the second parameter can be increased as needed.

12. To exit the installation screen, press Esc and then select Yes to save the changes.

13. Bring down and restart the server to make sure all the correct NLMs are loaded. At the server's console, type:

    ```
    DOWN
    RESTART SERVER
    ```

In addition to updating server NLM files stored in SYS:\SYSTEM, the installation process installs the client files in the SYS:\PUBLIC\CLIENT\WIN95 and SYS:\PUBLIC\CLIENT\WIN31 directories. The Netscape Navigator files are installed in the SYS:\NETSCAPE\32 and SYS:\NETSCAPE\16 directories.

The IPX/IP Gateway

NetWare 5 includes an IP Compatibility Mode feature that provides much of the same functionality as the IPX/IP gateway. You can either install this gateway or use the new functionality provided by NetWare 5. For more information on IP Compatibility Mode see Chapter 10, "NetWare 5 Features."

The IPX/IP gateway is an important part of the Novell Internet Access Server components of NetWare 5. With this gateway, IPX-based clients can access the Internet and other IP-based resources without having to install TCP/IP on the workstations themselves. The IPX/IP gateway gets installed on the server as part of the Novell Internet Access Server installation. To take advantage of the gateway, you must install IPX/IP gateway support on each workstation. Client gateway support is included as an option in the NetWare Client 32 installation.

Not having to use TCP/IP on each workstation is a benefit in many cases because there are significant management tasks associated with maintaining TCP/IP workstations. With TCP/IP, you have to manually keep track of and configure many items for each individual workstation, such as the unique IP address, subnet mask, IP addresses of the default router and the domain name servers, and the domain name.

An IPX/IP gateway removes many of the individual management hassles that occur with maintaining TCP/IP workstations by letting you retain IPX on those workstations.

When the IPX/IP gateway is installed on the NetWare 5 server, the server runs IPX to communicate with the IPX workstations on the network and TCP/IP so that it can communicate with the Internet. From the viewpoint of a remote host on the Internet, all traffic through the gateway seems to originate from the IP address assigned to the gateway server. Because the IPX/IP gateway uses only a single IP address, regardless of the number of users it supports, the private network is safe from outside interference. Using the Novell IPX/IP gateway alleviates the difficulties of administering a TCP/IP environment by providing ease of management and centralized control over Internet access.

By using Novell's IPX/IP gateway, you can run only IPX on the network workstations. Compared to IP, IPX is simple to manage. It assigns user connections dynamically, eliminating the need for a registered address to be configured at each desktop. Since IPX addresses are assigned dynamically, workstation IPX address conflicts do not occur. Users can move transparently between IPX networks, and traveling IPX users can roam between multiple networks within an enterprise.

The Novell IPX/IP gateway allows you to limit access to Internet services by the type of traffic (for example, Web browsing or FTP) and by remote host. Either type of restriction can be limited to specific times during the day to reduce "rush hour" traffic on an Internet connection.

Configuring the IPX/IP Gateway

After you've installed Novell Internet Access Server on the server, you can configure the IPX/IP gateway. To do this, complete the following steps:

1. At the server console, load INETCFG.NLM. If you are asked if you want to transfer your LAN driver, protocol, and remote access commands, choose Yes. What this really means is that you will move the LOAD and BIND commands from the AUTOEXEC.NCF file to INETCFG's startup files.

2. From the main menu, select Protocols, then choose TCP/IP, and then choose IPX/IP Gateway Configuration.

3. Specify "enabled" in the Enabled for the IPX/IP Gateway field so that the gateway will become operational.

4. If you want to record when clients access a service over the gateway, enable the Client Logging field. The log is stored in a field called GW_AUDIT.LOG in the SYS volume.

5. In the Console Messages field, specify the type of messages you want to display on the gateway logging screen and the gateway status log file (GW_INFO.LOG in the SYS volume). You can choose "Informational, warning, and errors" (the default), "Warnings and errors only," or "Errors only."

6. To enforce access restrictions (which you set using the NetWare Administrator utility), enable the Access Control field.

7. In the Domain Name field, specify the name of the domain in which the gateway is installed. Your Internet service provider may provide you with this name.

8. In the Name Server fields, specify the IP addresses of any active domain name servers. Your Internet service provider may provide these addresses.

9. Press Esc twice, and then log in as user Admin when prompted.

10. If you want to configure the gateway to use leased lines, frame relay, or ISDN lines, complete the following steps (see the documentation that came with Novell Internet Access Server for more specific details about parameters):

    a. Choose Boards from the INETCFG.NLM main menu. Then specify the appropriate WAN driver and configure any necessary parameters.

    b. Choose Network Interfaces from the INETCFG.NLM main menu. Then configure the appropriate WAN interfaces.

    c. Choose WAN Call Directory from INETCFG's main menu and press Insert to configure a new WAN call destination. Then configure any necessary parameters.

    d. Choose Bindings from INETCFG's main menu, press Insert, and bind TCP/IP to the appropriate board or driver.

11. Exit INETCFG.NLM and save the changes you made.

12. Reboot the server to make the changes take effect.

After you've enabled and configured the gateway, a gateway server NDS object appears in the NDS tree in the same context as the server on which it is installed. The gateway object's name is the same as the server's name, with -GW added to the end of the name. This gateway object assists gateway clients in locating active IPX/IP gateway servers.

Adding IPX/IP Gateway Tools to the NetWare Administrator Utility

To work with the IPX/IP gateway object, you'll need to add the gateway's snap-in utility to the NetWare Administrator utility. This will allow NetWare Administrator to recognize the new gateway object and the new access control property that was added to certain objects. (This property is explained later in this chapter.)

The IPX/IP gateway snap-in utility works only with the 16-bit version of NetWare Administrator (which runs on Windows 3.1*x*).

To add the IPX/IP gateway support to the NetWare Administrator utility on a Windows 3.1 workstation, complete the following steps:

1. If you haven't yet opened the NetWare Administrator utility, open it and close it.

2. From the Windows File Manager on your workstation, double-click on the NWADMN3X.INI file (located in the WINDOWS directory) to open it for editing.

3. Under the heading [Snapin Object DLLs WIN3X], add the following line:

   ```
   IPXGW3X=IPXGW3X.DLL
   ```

4. Save and close the file. Now the NetWare Administrator utility will recognize the IPX/IP gateway object.

Controlling Access to the IPX/IP Gateway

After the IPX/IP gateway server is fully installed and configured, you can use the NetWare Administrator utility to give the IPX/IP gateway server access control information for the various objects in the NDS tree. Then you can use NetWare Administrator to set restrictions for users, groups, or containers.

To give the gateway server access control information, use the NetWare Administrator utility to make the following changes to the NDS tree:

- Make the Public object a trustee of the gateway object, with browse object rights and read and compare property rights (for all properties).
- Make the Public object a trustee of the File Server object that is running the IPX/IP gateway, with browse object rights and read and compare property rights for the Network Address property only (under selected properties).
- Make the gateway object a trustee in the Root object, with browse object rights and read and compare property rights (for all properties).

You control user access through the IPX/IP gateway by using the NetWare Administrator utility. As the point of connection between a NetWare network and a TCP/IP network, an IPX/IP gateway is in an ideal position to enforce restrictions on traffic between the two networks.

These access restrictions can be stored in two properties that are added to the User, Group, Organization, or Organizational Unit objects when the gateway is enabled:

- The first property, service restrictions, tells the gateway object which applications may be used by the object and which are restricted. These restrictions are based on the port number.
- The second property, host restrictions, tells the gateway which remote hosts are restricted from the object. These restrictions are based on the IP address.

Storing access restrictions in the NDS objects provides a single database of restrictions that all gateway servers share. You do not need to configure access control separately on each gateway. Restrictions are active on all gateways regardless of whether they are applied to an entire organization or created individually for each user.

To place access restrictions on a User, Group, Organization, or Organizational Unit object, use the NetWare Administrator utility and select the object in question. Then choose Details under the Object menu and open the IPX/IP Gateway Service Restrictions page. On this page, you can enter restrictions for this object.

To restrict access to a specific Internet site, place a host restriction on the IP address of that site. To prevent certain types of traffic from being forwarded by the server, create a service restriction for the appropriate port number. For example, you might restrict Web browser access to certain hours during the day but allow FTP or Telnet access during those same hours. You could also place the remote host "www.games.com" off-limits. To prevent news readers from operating across the gateway, you might place a restriction on traffic to port number 119 (News) at any site.

Installing the IPX/IP Gateway Client

The IPX/IP gateway support is installed as an option in the NetWare Client 32 workstation software. The following instructions explain how to install this support on Windows 3.1*x* workstations and Windows 95 and 98 workstations.

The Windows 3.1*x* Client

To configure the IPX/IP gateway support on a Windows 3.1*x* workstation, you install NetWare Client 32 as explained in Chapter 4, "Directory Services Naming Conventions." During the installation process when the Additional Options screen appears, complete the following steps:

1. Select the NetWare IPX/IP Gateway check box, and then select Next to continue.

2. When the Configuration menu for these options appears, enter the appropriate information and select Next to continue.

3. When you've finished, choose OK to restart your computer. When the workstation comes back up, the Novell IPX/IP Gateway Switcher icon appears in the NetWare Tools program group. The gateway switcher program switches the client from gateway operation to native TCP/IP operation (if TCP/IP is available on the client).

4. Double-click the Gateway Switcher icon, and then click Enable Gateway to enable the gateway. You can also enter the name of a preferred gateway server if you have more than one gateway installed in the network. If a preferred gateway server is configured, the gateway task will attempt to locate that gateway server through NDS and connect to it. If the preferred gateway server is not available, the gateway client will search for other gateway servers, first in the user's NDS context, then in the bindery of the attached server, and then finally by querying for a SAP broadcast of any gateway server.

NOTE

There is no linkage between the preferred file server and the preferred gateway server. A user may be attached to file server A while using a gateway server that resides on file server B.

The Windows 95 Client

To configure the IPX/IP gateway support on a Windows 95 or 98 workstation, you install NetWare Client 32 as explained in Chapter 4, "Directory Services Naming Conventions." When the installation is finished, complete the following steps:

1. Click on Customize to customize the client.

2. Choose Add.

3. In the Type of Network Component You Want to Install box, double-click on Protocol.

4. In the Manufacturers box, choose Novell, and then double-click on Novell NetWare IPX/IP Gateway.

5. Choose OK to exit the Network configuration screen.

6. If you receive a prompt to select a preferred gateway server, click Yes, enter the name of your preferred IPX/IP gateway server, and select OK. If a preferred gateway server is configured, the gateway task will attempt to locate that gateway server through NDS and connect to it. If the preferred gateway server is not available, the gateway client will search for other gateway servers, first in the user's NDS context, then in the bindery of the attached server, and then finally by querying for a SAP broadcast of any gateway server.

7. If you are asked for additional files, type the location of those files in the Copy Files From box. If you are asked for Client 32 files, type in the path to the directory from which you ran SETUP.EXE.

8. Click Yes to restart the computer. The IPX/IP Gateway Switcher program runs automatically during the first restart after installation. This switcher program switches the client from gateway operation to native TCP/IP operation (if TCP/IP is available on the client).

9. To enable the gateway, click the Enable IPX/IP Gateway button and then click OK.

Installing FTP Services for NetWare 5

In addition to the Novell Internet Access Server components, NetWare 5 also includes FTP Services. This feature, which is a subset of the NetWare UNIX Print Services 2.11 product, allows NetWare clients to use FTP to work with files on the Internet or intranet.

To install FTP Services for NetWare 5 on your server, complete the following steps:

1. Mount the FTP Services CD-ROM as a volume on the NetWare 5 server.

2. Load INSTALL.NLM on the server.

3. Choose Product Options, and then choose Install a Product Not Listed.

4. Press F3 and then type in the following path to the FTP Services files on the CD-ROM:

   ```
   NWUXPS:\NWUXPS
   ```

5. If you are asked to specify a host name, either press Enter to accept the default name displayed or enter the correct host name.

6. Accept the default boot drive (or specify the correct drive from which the server boots).

7. To install the online documentation for FTP Services, choose Yes. This documentation is separate from the regular NetWare online documentation and describes how to install and use FTP Services.

8. If you have already installed the NetWare 5 Online Documentation viewer, choose No when asked if you want to install a new one.

   Note: If you receive the message "hosts.db does not exist," ignore it.

9. When prompted for a user name, enter the ADMIN name and password.

10. Choose the name service option you want to use on this server and answer any prompts necessary for the name service you choose. If you choose to use a local name service, the database that holds the name service information will be stored on this server and will be the master database. You can use the UNICON.NLM utility to work with the master database on a local server. If you choose to use a remote name service, that database will reside on another server. You can use UNICON.NLM only to view the database information but not modify it. You can choose one of the following options:

    - **Local DNS and Local NIS** — This option stores both master databases on this server.
    - **Remote DNS and Remote NIS** — This option uses the master databases stored on another server.

- **Remote DNS and Local NIS** — This option stores the master NIS database on this server and the DNS database on another server.
- **No DNS and Remote NIS** — This option stores the master NIS database on another server and does not provide DNS service at all.

11. Follow any prompts necessary to initialize the name service and the product.

12. To start FTP Services, press Insert and choose FTP Server. FTP Services will start running and will appear in the Running Services menu.

13. To exit the installation program, press Esc as many times as necessary.

14. Restart the server to make the new settings take effect, by typing:

```
DOWN

RESTART SERVER
```

CONFIGURING FTP SERVICES

With FTP Services, users can use FTP to access and transfer files from the intranet or Internet. If you desire, you can create an Anonymous FTP account for users to use. With an Anonymous account, any user can access the FTP service by typing in any password. (Any password will work; the FTP service doesn't actually authenticate the password.)

To configure an Anonymous FTP account, complete the following steps:

1. At the server console, load UNICON.NLM.

2. When prompted, enter the ADMIN user name and password.

3. Choose Manage Services, then choose FTP Server, and then choose Set Parameters.

4. Choose Default Name Space and enter NFS. This will install the NFS name space on the server, which will allow the server to store UNIX files.

5. Change the Anonymous User Access field to Yes so that the Anonymous account will be enabled.

6. Choose Anonymous User's Home Directory and change the path from the volume SYS (displayed as /sys) to a directory you prefer to use as the login directory for Anonymous FTP users.

7. When finished, press Esc to exit the installation program and save the changes you've made.

8. Return to the main menu by pressing Esc twice, then choose Perform File Operations, and then choose View/Set File Permissions.

9. Enter the path to the Anonymous user's home directory (specified in Step 6) and press F9 to see the permissions (the UNIX equivalent of trustee rights) that have been set for this directory. If the permissions are not correct, modify them on this screen. The permissions should be:

   ```
   [U = rwx] [G = --] [o = --]
   ```

10. Press Esc multiple times to exit UNICON and save the changes you've made.

11. Even though you specified the NFS name space in Step 4, you still need to add it to the volume. (You only need to add the name space to the volume once. To see if you've already added NFS name space to a volume, type **VOLUMES** at the server console — the display will show which name spaces are supported on each volume.) If you need to add the name space, type the following command, replacing "volume" with the name of the volume:

    ```
    ADD NAME SPACE NFS TO volume
    ```

Summary

This chapter has discussed how to install the Internet Access Server component for NetWare 5 and FTP services.

CHAPTER 23

Pure IP in NetWare 5

One of the most anticipated features of NetWare 5 is pure IP, which provides the capability to access NetWare services through the use of the IP networking protocol instead of only IPX/SPX as in previous versions of NetWare. This means that the NetWare Core Protocol (NCP) services can run over the TCP/IP stack. The NetWare Core Protocol (NCP) services that will run over TCP/IP are file reads and writes, user login and authentication, and Novell Directory Services (NDS) synchronization.

The term "pure" implies that IPX encapsulation is not required. In NetWare 5, pure IP allows NCP to sit directly on top of User Datagram Protocol (UDP) or Transmission Control Protocol (TCP) headers and use IP services for discovery, addressing, and data-transfer operations. The IP port for the NetWare Core Protocol (NCP) was registered by IANA as port 524. The NetWare system implements the IP connection as a TCP connection.

Support for Pure IP in NetWare 5

The pure IP feature makes NetWare 5 protocol-independent. One of the advantages of a protocol-independent system is that the system can support TCP/IP, IPX/SPX, or both concurrently. Although traditional NetWare networks have primarily used IPX as the network protocol, a pure IP network is more easily integrated with other systems such as Windows NT and UNIX. Thus, there is significant opportunity for mixing and matching the multiple protocols to achieve migration goals.

NetWare 5 Client Support

The foundation of pure IP lies in the protocol-independent communication for both the server and the NetWare client. Like the NetWare 5 server, the NetWare client also can use either IP or IPX, or both. This is the case for NetWare clients running on Windows 95/98, Windows NT, and Windows 3.1. Thus, both the NetWare 5 client and NetWare 5 server allow the user to implement dual protocol stacks. As mentioned, the system is designed to prefer IP, if an IP connection can be made. IPX is available for communication with the remaining IPX network. Such an approach minimizes the risk of discontinuity; most network clients already use both IP and IPX stacks.

Novell Directory Services Support

Novell Directory Services (NDS) has been modified in NetWare 5 to support the IP protocol suite in addition to the IPX protocol suite. The Novell Directory Access Protocol (NDAP) is able to provide NDS communications via UDP or TCP. This support extends to the partition level, where an NDS tree can support some partitions that are located on IPX-based machines, other partitions that are located on IP-based machines, and yet other partitions that are based on machines that support both IP and IPX stacks concurrently.

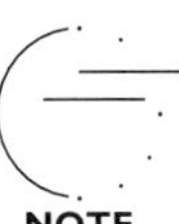
NOTE

It is important to remember that all servers in a tree must be able to talk to all the other servers in a tree to handle NDS backlink obituaries and external references.

Winsock Support

Within the NetWare 5 server, the WinSock 2 API was selected as the portal to the communications infrastructure. The developer is able to write to a single API and gain access to UDP, TCP, IPX, and SPX. Additionally, the WinSock API provides a single interface to naming services. Novell has implemented name service providers for NDS, DNS, DHCP, SLP, and SAP. NetWare 5 still supports the existing BSD and TLI interfaces to the protocol stacks.

In addition to those mentioned, NetWare 5 uses an array of IP-related protocols, services, and tools to make migrating to a pure IP network manageable. These services and tools allow migration of your network from IPX to IP without losing connectivity or IPX application support. Before we consider all the different options for upgrading or migrating your network protocols to pure IP, we must first introduce some of the migration components and IP-related services.

Migration Components in Pure IP

As previously mentioned, NetWare 5 provides the option to run the pure IP protocol on your network. However, if IPX applications are required, then you will need to bind the IPX protocol or the Compatibility Mode. In order to help you migrate to pure IP or to configure your network to support both IPX/SPX and TCP/IP, NetWare 5 offers several possible IP and IPX configurations. These configurations are dependent upon the IP-related services and are as follows:

- IPX Compatibility Mode (CMD)
- Client Compatibility Mode driver
- Server Compatibility Mode driver
- Migration agent with gateway support
- Migration agent with backbone support

To allow flexibility in migrating an IPX-based network to an IP-based network, these migration components have been integrated into NetWare 5 rather than placed in a separate migration tool. The migration components, and more specifically, the IPX Compatibility Mode drivers, are used by the server only when an IPX application requires them. And because an IPX stack is loaded on the server, some IPX symbols may persist. This does not mean, though, that the system is using IPX on the wire, only that the system is compatible with IPX if it is needed by an IPX application. If there are no requests for IPX services, then the IPX stack is not used.

The following description of each key component in pure IP is intended to give you just enough information to understand the migration options and strategies mentioned in this chapter. For more detailed information about each component refer to the associated information found later in this chapter.

The IPX Compatibility Mode Driver (CMD)

The IPX Compatibility Mode driver (CMD) has two parts, one for the server and one for the client. At the server, the Compatibility Mode driver is viewed as a network adapter. When it functions in this capacity, you can bind both IPX and IP protocols to the CMD adapter and it acts like a router. The CMD at the server is called the *Server Compatibility Mode driver.*

At the workstation, the CMD is invisible because it is an integral part of the new client. It provides the IP communications link required by an IP client. Because NetWare 5 is pure IP, there is no need for IPX at the client. The Compatibility Mode driver at the workstation or client is called the *Client Compatibility Mode driver.*

The Client Compatibility Mode Driver

The NetWare 5 client automatically supports the Compatibility Mode driver, which ensures that IPX-dependent applications running on the NetWare 5 clients transmit only IP communications. This means that any IPX application will be able to communicate to other IPX services across the IP-only network. For example, if a printer driver were IPX dependent and required a SAP broadcast to locate a print server (PSERVER.NLM), the Client Compatibility Mode driver would change this SAP query to an SLP query. Figure 23.1 illustrates how a SAP request or query is redirected to SLP.

FIGURE 23.1

When the client needs to discover services from SAP and you have an IP-only network, the client request for SAP services will be redirected to SLP.

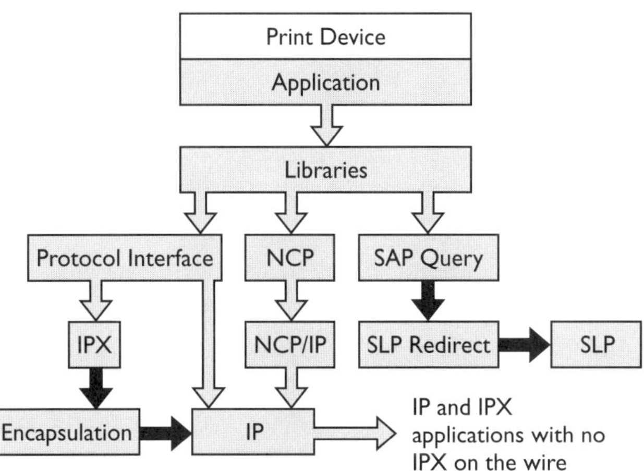

The Service Location Protocol (SLP) is introduced in this section. For more detailed information on SLP, please refer to the later sections.

The Server Compatibility Mode Driver

By default, the Server Compatibility Mode driver (SCMD.NLM) runs on every NetWare 5 server to support any server-based applications that are IPX dependent. SCMD is often referred to as the Compatibility Mode server process, which allows all IPX applications to communicate in a pure IP network. This server component supports IPX-based applications without having to bind IPX to the wire. A virtual IPX network is created to support the IPX applications.

Although the Server Compatibility Mode driver is loaded by default, you can manually load and unload the process using its name (SCMD.NLM). For example, to load the Server Compatibility Mode driver manually at the server console, type:

```
LOAD SCMD ( the LOAD keyword is optional)
```

To remove or unload the Compatibility Mode server, type:

```
UNLOAD SCMD (the UNLOAD keyword is mandatory)
```

The SCMD process translates IPX communications — such as Service Advertising Protocol (SAP) queries, SAP broadcasts, and IPX packets — into the pure IP format. For example, suppose that a NetWare Loadable Module (NLM) such as PSERVER.NLM needs to broadcast its presence on the network using SAP broadcasts. SCMD will redirect the SAP broadcasts to the Service Location Protocol (SLP) process running on the NetWare 5 server. The SLP process will register the IPX-dependent NLM, enabling workstations to discover this NLM just as they discover IP services. PSERVER.NLM will be unaware that its service announcement has been redirected. Figure 23.2 illustrates how SAP broadcasts from the PSERVER.NLM program are redirected to SLP.

The IPX compatibility driver treats the IP Network as a virtual IPX network segment (CMD network segment), by encapsulating IPX datagrams inside UDP datagrams, and by resolving RIP and SAP requests through the use of the Service Location Protocol (SLP). To run IPX applications in your IP network or to connect IP systems with IPX systems, Service Location Protocol (SLP) must be enabled across the network, since the IPX compatibility drivers are dependent upon the capabilities of SLP. Additionally, at least one migration agent must be used on the network if you interconnect IPX and IP systems.

FIGURE 23.2

PSERVER.NLM will send SAP broadcasts to announce its presence on the network. If you have an IP-only network, then the SAP broadcasts will be redirected to SLP, which enables discover of services through IP.

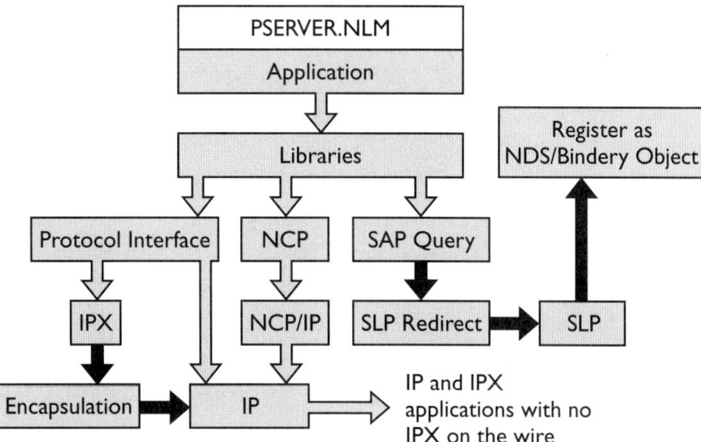

The default IPX network number (CMD network number) assigned to the virtual IPX network created by the IPX compatibility drivers is 0xFFFFFFFD. Migration agents that interconnect IP Systems with IPX systems must have a CMD network number that does not conflict with the internal IPX network number of a server or the IPX network number of a network segment. Be aware that IPX routers should not filter this address.

If a system or a segment conflicts with the CMD network number, you can either override the default CMD network number by modifying the configuration of the IP-only clients and servers, or change the network number of the conflicting system or segment.

The Migration Agent with Gateway Support

The migration agent (MA) is a migration component that enables communication between the IPX stack and the IP stack. It can only run on the NetWare 5 server because it is a special condition of the SCMD.NLM program, and it is enabled by loading the SCMD /G or /GATEWAY option. The migration agent is often referred to as the SCMD with gateway support. The terms "migration agent" and "SCMD /G" are equivalent.

The SCMD.NLM provides both the Server Compatibility Mode driver and the migration agent with gateway service. Although the Server Compatibility Mode driver is enabled by default, you must manually enable and configure the migration agent to get gateway support. To enable the migration agent, you load SCMD.NLM reentrantly by entering the following commands:

```
LOAD SCMD.NLM /G (the LOAD keyword is optional)
```

The migration agent allows access between IPX and IP networks and vice versa: It enables users on a pure IP network to access services located on an IPX network. Likewise, the migration agent enables users on an IPX network to access services located on a pure IP network. Figure 23.3 illustrates how the migration agent using the SCMD /G option is used as a router between the services on the IPX network and the virtual IPX network segment created by the IPX compatibility drivers. The migration agent with gateway support resides on the server that acts as a gateway between the existing IPX network and the newer pure IP network. The server running as the gateway should be accessible to all the nodes from both the IPX and IP networks so that the services provided by each are fully accessible.

FIGURE 23.3

The migration agent using the SCMD /G is set up as a router between the IPX network and nodes and the IP services. All pure IP servers and clients use the gateway to the IPX segments and vice versa.

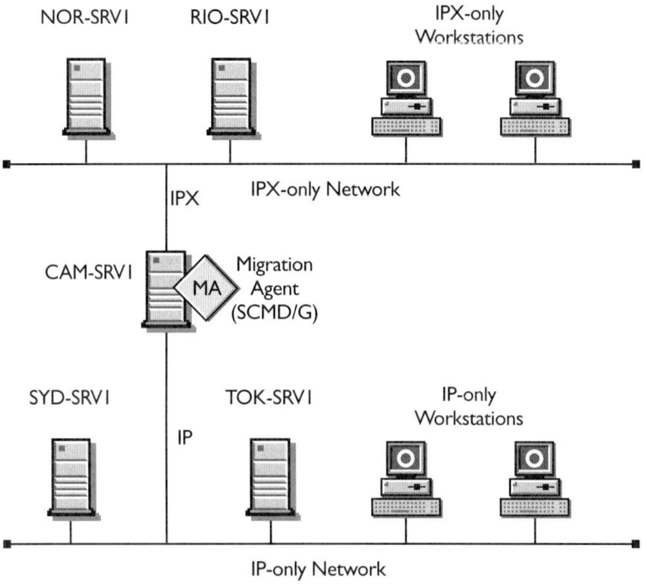

In this example, the servers named SYD-SRV1 and TOK-SRV1 are both configured to support only IP. The servers called NOR-SRV1 and RIO-SRV1 are configured with the IPX stack only. To enable these two networks to communicate with one another, you can load the migration agent on the NetWare 5 server, CAM-SRV1. To accomplish loading the gateway, load SCMD /G to allow the server on the pure IP network to communicate with the servers on the IPX network. The servers on the IPX network may be running NetWare 2, NetWare 3, NetWare 4, or NetWare 5 but are configured to support only IPX.

The migration agent provides protocol translation services, changing IPX-based queries into pure IP–based queries. As a result, any workstation or clients on the IPX network could access services that resided on the pure IP network.

You should use the /G option only if you want to configure a migration agent to connect one IPX network and one pure IP network. When configuring the migration agent, you can set it up to use either one network board or two. Figure 23.4 illustrates how you run the migration agent on a NetWare 5 server with only one network board. The pure IP and IPX stacks are bound to this single network card.

FIGURE 23.4

The migration agent supports the gateway service on a NetWare 5 server that only has one network board with both the pure IP and IPX stacks bound to it.

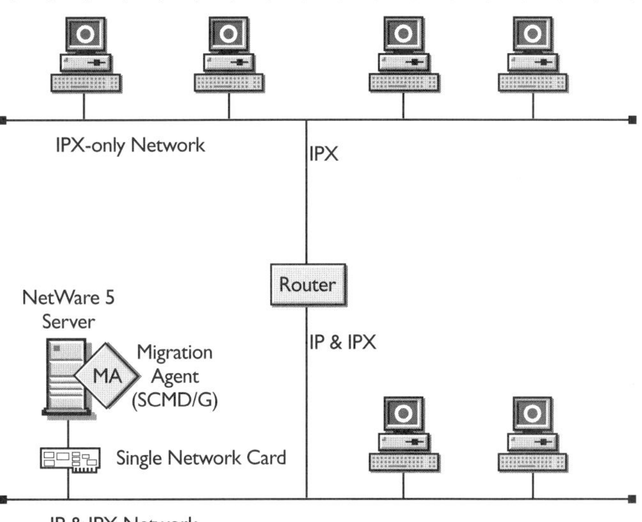

In addition to the single network board support, the migration agent can provide the gateway service on a NetWare 5 server with two network boards. In this configuration, both the pure IP and IPX stacks are bound to the separate network cards. Figure 23.5 illustrates how the migration agent can be run on a NetWare 5 server with two network boards with pure IP and IPX bound to each card.

FIGURE 23.5

The migration agent with gateway support can be run on a NetWare 5 server with two network boards. In this configuration, both the pure IP and IPX stacks are bound to the separate network cards.

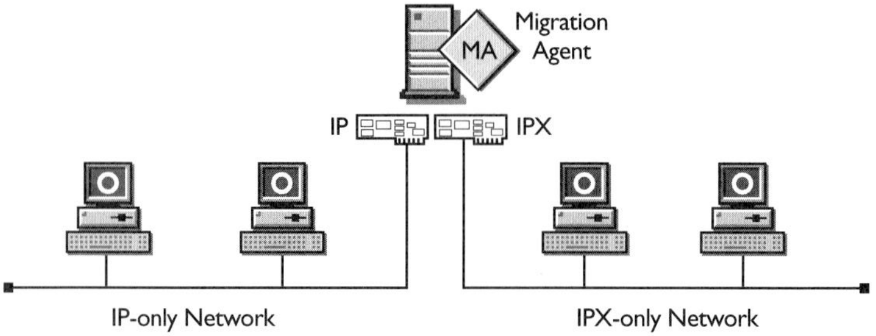

The Migration Agent with Backbone Support

As mentioned previously, SCMD.NLM provides both the Server Compatibility Mode driver and the migration agent with gateway service. In addition, SCMD.NLM provides the backbone support that allows the IPX services to connect to other IPX services across an IP-only communication link.

The migration agent with backbone support is a migration component that enables IPX services to communicate across an IP-only segment. The migration agent with backbone support can only run on the NetWare 5 server because it is a special condition of the SCMD.NLM program. The migration agent with backbone support is enabled by loading the SCMD /BS option.

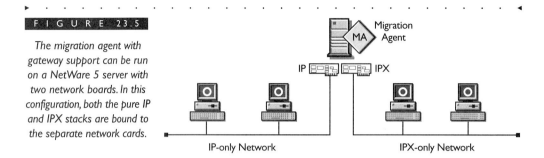

The backbone support allows access between IPX services connected with only an IP network. The backbone support is used if you want two disconnected IPX networks to communicate through a pure IP network. Figure 23.6 illustrates how you can use the migration agent with backbone support to allow two remote IPX networks to communicate over an IP-only network.

Although SCMD.NLM is typically loaded automatically when the server is booted, you must manually enable and configure the migration agent to get backbone support. To enable the migration agent, you load SCMD.NLM reentrantly by entering one of the following commands:

```
LOAD SCMD.NLM /BS (the LOAD keyword is optional)
```

By enabling the /BS option, you have configured the migration agent to forward IPX packets through the IP network bound to the server. This allows the migration agents to exchange SAP and Routing Information Protocol (RIP) information about the disconnected IPX networks.

FIGURE 23.6

Two disconnected IPX networks are communicating through an IP-only WAN link. If you load the SCMD.NLM with the /BS option, the migration agent will encapsulate IPX packets inside IP, thus enabling these disconnected IPX networks to communicate.

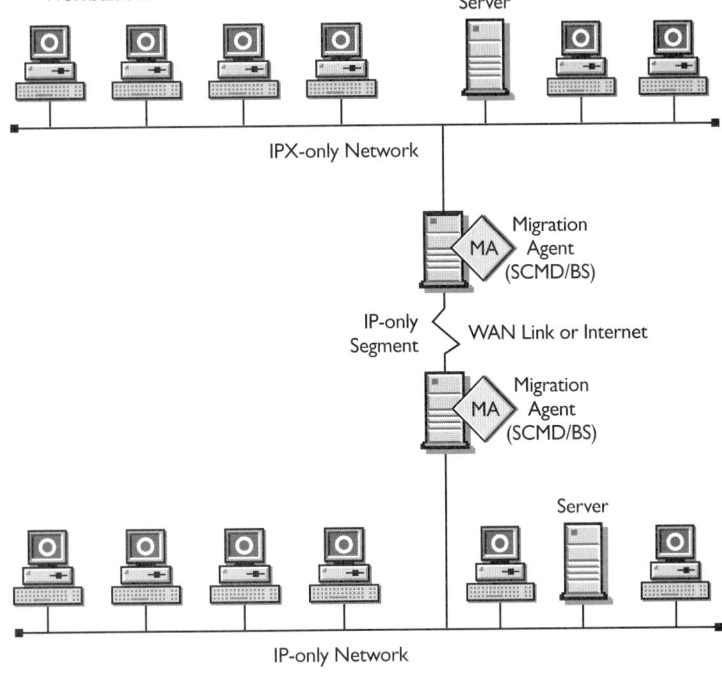

Comparison of the SCMD Options

You may be wondering what are the similarities and differences among the SCMD options? For example, how does the Server Compatibility Mode driver (SCMD) differ from the migration agent with gateway support (SCMD /G)? Or how does SCMD /G differ from SCMD /BS? For the most part the options are very similar. They can be viewed or considered as concentric circles, with each option adding functionality. This means that when you load SCMD /G, it loads all the features of SCMD (Compatibility Mode) plus the gateway function. When you load SCMD /BS, you will get the SCMD /G and SCMD features plus the backbone support. Figure 23.7 illustrates how each of the options available for SCMD.NLM adds functionality. The least functionality is SCMD, with SCMD /G adding the gateway support. The most functionality comes with the SCMD /BS option, which provides features for each of the other options.

FIGURE 23.7

The SCMD.NLM options are Compatibility Mode, gateway support, and backbone support. The options can be viewed or considered as concentric circles with each option adding functionality.

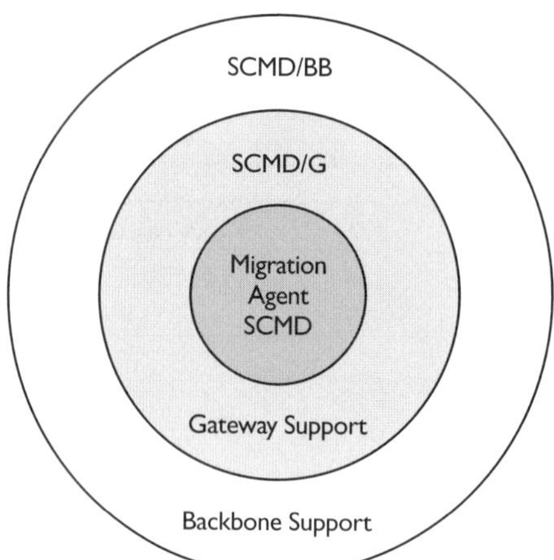

The two migration agent options have many similarities; for example, they each perform the following five functions:

- Registers migration agent services with an SLP service agent. (An SLP service agent works on behalf of a service to respond directly to queries for specific services. For more information about SLP service agents, see the section on Service Location Protocol later in this chapter.)
- Registers SAP services with an SLP service agent.
- Unencapsulates and forwards SAP queries to an IPX network.
- Unencapsulates and forwards RIP queries to an IPX network.
- Encapsulates and unencapsulates IPX traffic that is coming from or going to a pure IP network.

Registering Migration Agent Services with an SLP Service Agent

Migration agents register their services with a local SLP service agent, making the services available to devices on the pure IP network. Sometimes a NetWare 5 client running the Compatibility Mode client process might require the services of the migration agent. In this case, the NetWare 5 client would use SLP to discover the migration agent.

Registering SAP Services with an SLP Service Agent

As the translator between an IPX network and a pure IP network, a migration agent receives SAP broadcasts from the IPX network. For example, a server would send a SAP broadcast every 60 seconds on the IPX network, announcing the server's file, directory, and other services. After receiving this SAP broadcast, the migration agent would send an SLP packet to the SLP service agent, registering the server's services.

If a NetWare 5 client running the Compatibility Mode client process wants to use an IPX service, this client sends an SLP query to the SLP service agent. The SLP service agent then returns the network address of the device providing the requested IPX service.

Unencapsulating and Forwarding SAP Queries to an IPX Network

If a NetWare 5 client running the Compatibility Mode client process queries an SLP service agent for an IPX service and that service is not registered with the SLP service agent, this client can encapsulate a SAP query inside IP and send the query directly to the migration agent. The migration agent, in turn, unencapsulates the SAP query and forwards it to the IPX network. The migration agent then encapsulates the SAP reply inside IP and sends this reply to the requesting NetWare 5 client.

Unencapsulating and Forwarding RIP Queries to an IPX Network

After a NetWare 5 client running the Compatibility Mode client process locates an IPX service, this client encapsulates a RIP query inside IP and sends the query directly to the migration agent. Next, the migration agent unencapsulates the RIP query and forwards it to the IPX network. The migration agent then encapsulates the RIP reply inside IP and sends this reply to the requesting NetWare 5 client.

Encapsulating and Unencapsulating IPX Traffic

If a NetWare/IP client exists on a pure IP network, the migration agent can unencapsulate IPX packets and forward them in native IPX format to the IPX network. For example, if a NetWare/IP client resided on a pure IP network, this client would encapsulate IPX packets within a UDP/IP header.

When a NetWare/IP client needs to locate a service on an IPX network, the client sends a SAP request to the migration agent. The migration agent then unencapsulates the SAP request and sends it in its native IPX format onto the IPX network.

Pure IP Migration Options and Strategies

Migrating a NetWare network from IPX to IP reduces administrative costs, especially if you are already supporting both protocols, or if you are expending a significant portion of your Information Services (IS) budget managing IPX. Because of the flexibility of pure IP, there is no single migration utility or method. Anyone wanting to migrate from IPX to IP needs to implement the newer technology while providing continued access to all existing network services.

The client and server can be installed to support several different configurations. In some cases the customer may want to mix and match IP and IPX. Certainly the migration process will require compatibility of both protocols during the transition period. NetWare 5 provides tremendous flexibility in configuring the IPX and IP protocols. The following configuration options are supported within NetWare 5:

- Pure IP only (no legacy IPX application support)
- Pure IP and IPX dual stack (assumes both IP and IPX protocols routed everywhere)
- Pure IP with IPX application support (SCMD)
- Pure IP with IPX connected segment (SCMD /G, assumes IPX filtering)
- Pure IP backbone with IPX linked segments (SCMD /BS)

Although NetWare 5 fully supports the IPX/SPX stack as a protocol option, it will not be discussed in this section. For obvious reasons it is not a migration strategy to pure IP. However, IPX remains 100 percent supported in NetWare 5 with native support for all the current IPX applications and services.

Typically, the protocol installation screen determines the binding between protocol stacks and the network adapters. It does not determine which protocol stacks are loaded in the system. For example, if the IP-only installation option is selected, only the TCP/IP stack is attached to the network adapter. Figure 23.8 shows the Protocol Installation window that allows you to choose the protocols that you want the server to run.

FIGURE 23.8

This protocol installation window that appears during server installation allows you to select which protocols the server will have available to requesting services.

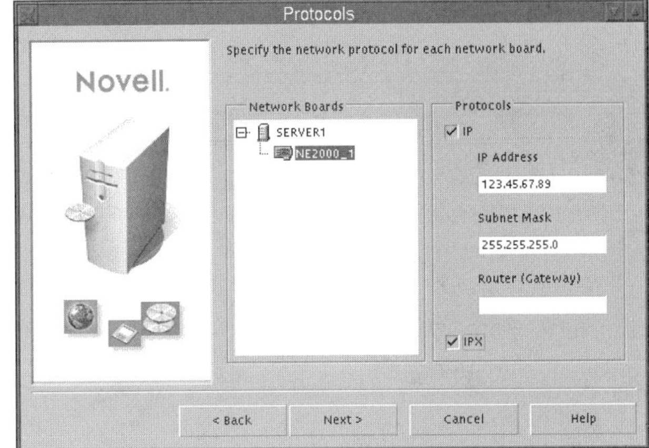

Pure IP Only

NetWare 5 can be configured to support a pure IP network. Systems installed using the IP-only installation option have both the TCP/IP and IPX stacks loaded by default, but only the TCP/IP stack is bound to the network adapter. If a pure IP network in the strictest sense is required, the IPX stack loaded as the CMD driver that helps support IPX application compatibility will need to be unloaded (as it is loaded by default). Figure 23.9 illustrates the layout for the IP-only protocol architecture.

NOTE

The pure IP–only migration strategy or option assumes that no legacy IPX applications will be supported on either the client or the server.

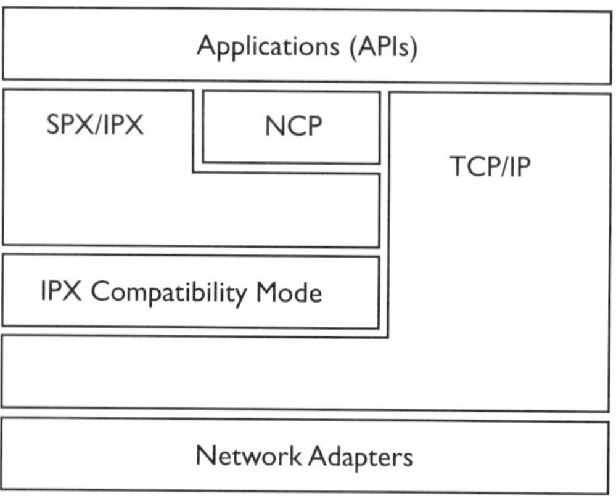

FIGURE 23.9

The IP-only protocol architecture layout

As mentioned, during installation of the NetWare 5 server the IPX stack is loaded on the system with the IP-only option to give those systems the capability to execute IPX applications and to connect with IPX services through a migration agent. Any NetWare 5 servers installed with the IP-only option have the following capabilities:

- Establish NCP connections with clients installed with one of the install options that include IP.
- Establish NCP connections through migration agent with pre–NetWare 5 clients whose clients only support NCP connections over IPX or with NetWare 5 clients installed with the IPX-only option.
- Execute IPX applications and communicate directly with NetWare 5 systems installed with the IP-only option.
- Execute IPX application and communicate through a migration agent with IPX nodes.

Pure IP and IPX Dual Stack

NetWare 5 allows both native IPX and IP protocols to be bound to the server. This configuration can be very useful where bandwidth and administration issues are not relevant. Systems installed with the IP and IPX option are configured to establish NCP connections over either the TCP/IP stack or over the IPX stack. The NetWare 5 server by default will seek to transmit on the IP network whenever possible. Figure 23.10 illustrates the relationship between the protocol stacks for the IP and IPX protocol stacks.

FIGURE 23.10

The IP and IPX protocol relationship and architecture layout

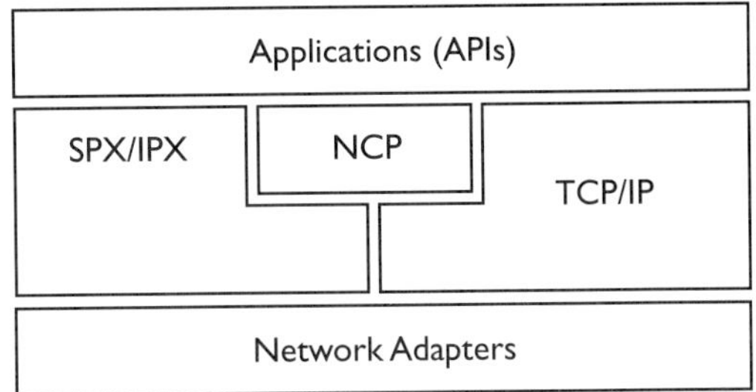

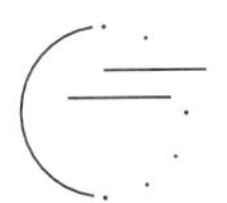
NOTE

The dual stack approach assumes that both protocols are freely routed—thus providing global access for either IPX or IP clients.

With both the IPX and pure IP stacks bound, Novell Directory Services will communicate to appropriate partitions depending on local protocol communications. In a dual-stack environment, the NCP engine will select an IP connection before an IPX connection, if available. If an IP connection is made, then all of the NCP packets will use the TCP transport for communication between the client and server. Any NetWare 5 servers installed with both the IP and IPX protocol stacks have the following capabilities:

- Establish NCP connections with NetWare clients that are previous to NetWare 5 or with NetWare 5 clients without regard for the option used to install them.
- Execute IPX applications and communicate directly with other IPX services or nodes.
- Execute IPX applications and communicate through a migration agent with NetWare 5 systems installed with the IP-only option.

Having a NetWare client installed with the IP and IPX option does not guarantee that the client will be able to establish an NCP connection with a server installed with the IP-only option without the use of a migration agent. The type of address obtained by the client when trying to connect to a server determines the protocol stack utilized to establish the connection.

Applications that obtain address information from the bindery will not be able to connect with servers installed with the IP-only option if there is no migration agent installed and if the client is installed with both the IP and IPX stacks. This is not the case if the client has been installed with the IP-only option.

Pure IP with IPX Application Support (SCMD)

If pure IP with the IPX Compatibility Mode (SCMD) is loaded, the NetWare 5 server can communicate with existing IPX services. The IPX Compatibility Mode driver's job is to provide IPX connectivity over the IP network. In other words, applications using the IPX stack for communications will still be able to function properly. The IPX Compatibility Mode driver also allows IP systems to communicate with IPX systems by utilizing the services of migration agents. The IPX Compatibility Mode driver achieves its job by treating the IP network as a virtual IPX network segment (CMD network segment), by encapsulating IPX datagrams inside of UDP datagrams, and by resolving RIP and SAP requests through the use of the Service Location Protocol (SLP).

The services of the IPX compatibility drivers are only utilized when the user wishes to execute an IPX application or wishes to establish connections between IP and IPX systems. If the IPX Compatibility Mode is not used, it does not affect network communications.

Figure 23.11 illustrates how you can install and configure the pure IP and IPX Compatibility Mode (SCMD). In the figure, the server called SERVER1 is upgraded from 4.11 to NetWare 5, whereas the server called SERVER 2 is a new NetWare 5 server, with one IP printer and two workstations. The clients have Compatibility Mode enabled, although they are sitting on a pure IP segment.

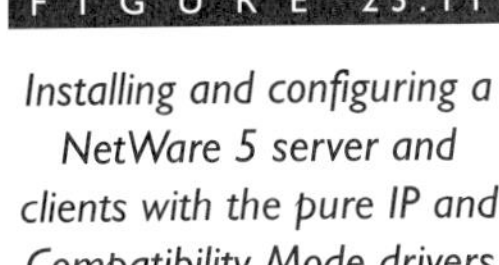

FIGURE 23.11

Installing and configuring a NetWare 5 server and clients with the pure IP and Compatibility Mode drivers

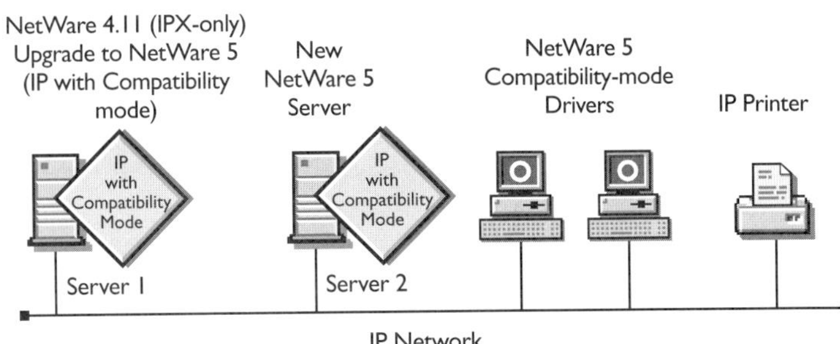

Installation to Support Pure IP with the IPX Compatibility Mode Option

In order to install and configure the servers and clients to support pure IP with the IPX Compatibility Mode option, follow these steps:

1. After your NetWare 4.11 server has been upgraded to NetWare 5, you need to unbind and remove IPX from the network board. To accomplish this task, you will want to load the Internetworking Configuration utility at the server console by typing **INETCFG**. From the Internetworking Configuration utility's startup screen, select Protocols. From the Protocol Configuration screen, select IPX and press Delete. Select Yes to disable IPX. Then exit INETCFG and down and reinitialize the server. Figure 23.12 illustrates an example of removing the IPX protocol using the Internetworking Configuration utility.

FIGURE 23.12

You can remove the IPX protocol from the upgraded server using the Internetworking Configuration utility.

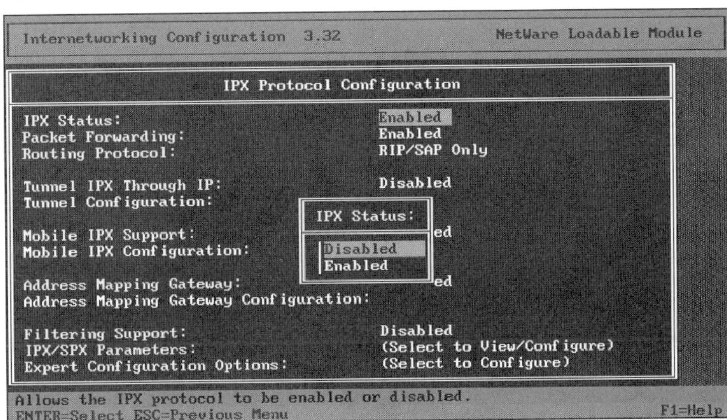

2. Now you need to bind the TCP/IP protocol stack to the appropriate board using the Internetworking Configuration utility. Type **INETCFG** to enter the utility and view the first screen. Select the Protocols option from the main menu. From the Protocol Configuration screen, enable TCP/IP and then press Esc to save the settings. Next, from the main menu, select Bindings. Press Insert. Select TCP/IP from the List of Protocols. Select the first interface board and press Enter. Enter the IP address and Subnet mask, as shown in Figure 23.13. Then exit INETCFG and restart the server.

FIGURE 23.13

You can install and bind the TCP/IP protocol stack on the upgraded server using the Internetworking Configuration utility.

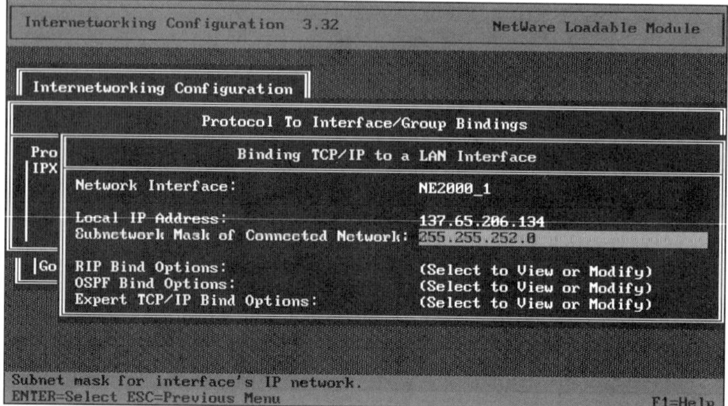

NOTE

If you need to have static routing enabled, you can select the Protocol option for the INETCFG menu. Select TCP/IP, enable static routing, and configure the static routing table.

3. Next, you need to load the Compatibility Mode driver (SCMD.NLM) on the upgraded NetWare 5 server. This can be accomplished by entering the following command at the NetWare 5 server console:

```
LOAD SCMD (the LOAD keyword is optional)
```

4. Finally, you will want to verify the installation and configuration settings that you have made by typing the **CONFIG** command at the server console. You need to make and verify that SCMD is loaded with the board name as CMD Server. If it was installed and configured correctly, you should see information similar to the screen shown in Figure 23.14.

FIGURE 23.14

After you have changed the settings from the previous steps, you will want to verify that the installation and configuration settings are correct. You can do this by typing CONFIG at the server console.

```
File server name: RIO-SRV1
IPX internal network number: 0F2AC1AE
Server Up Time: 18 Hours 46 Minutes 55 Seconds

Novell NE2000
   Version 3.65a December 27, 1997
   Hardware setting: I/O ports 30 Ch to 31FH, Interrupt 3h
   Node address: 008029E1D27F
   Frame type: ETHERNET_II
   Board name: NE2000_1_II
   LAN protocol: ARP
   LAN protocol: IP Address 147.87.206.134 Mask
                 FF.FF.FF.0(255.255.252.0) Interfaces 1

Compatibility Mode Driver
   Version 1.04c August 13, 1998
   Hardware setting: I/O ports A55h
   Node address: 7E00C04FBFFE73
   Frame type: CMD
   Board name: CMD Server
   LAN protocol: IPX network FFFFFFD

Tree Name: ACME_TREE
Bindery Context(s): .acme.rio.
```

Compare this list with the information in Figure 23.14:

- **Hardware setting** — CMD server uses a reserved UDP port 2645 (A55 H).
- **Node address** — 7E01< IP address of the first interface bound>; the node address starts with 7E01 to distinguish from NWIP nodes.
- **Frame type** — Signifies Compatibility Mode driver.
- **Board name** — Signifies SCMD is functioning as the CMD server.
- **LAN protocol** — This is the IPX CMD network number.

In order to have SCMD.NLM loaded as the CMD server, the IPX protocol stack should not be bound to any network card. If IPX is bound, it will come out with the following error message: "SCMD: Could not set the router in CMD Mode routing. Unbind IPX network(s) from IPX stack/router if bound."

When you install a new NetWare 5 server and configure it for IP-only support, it will automatically load the SCMD.NLM module as CMD server. To verify that the CMD server is functioning correctly, at the server console type **DISPLAY SERVERS**. This will show the SAP services of the IPX servers on the network. The DISPLAY SERVERS command is a good test because it is an IPX application on the server and will not run if SCMD is not set up correctly.

CMD Server Configuration Parameters

The current implementation of SCMD.NLM provides several different configuration parameters that allow you to control the features of the program. The configuration parameters are the following:

- Changing the CMD network number
- Configuring the preferred migration agent
- Setting the CMD preferred IP address

Changing the CMD Network Number By default the CMD network number is set to FFFFFFFD, but this can be changed either through the MONITOR utility or by using the SET parameter as follows:

```
SET CMD NETWORK NUMBER=XXXXXXXX
```

The SCMD module has to be loaded before you can change the SET parameter value. Subsequently, you can unload and reload the module in order to make the change take effect permanently. Optionally, the CMD network number can be changed dynamically as the module is loaded. To do this, at the console prompt type:

```
LOAD SCMD /NET=XXXXXXXX
```

Configuring Preferred Migration Agent The CMD server, when configured on the network, will register itself with the SLP, learn all the available registered SLP services, and build a link list in memory. It will query the SLP server agent or directory agent every five minutes to refresh its records. CMD clients attached to this server can access all the services learned by this server.

If a registered migration agent (MA) is available on the network, CMD Server will discover the migration agent from the SLP database and register it with the MA. The CMD server, once registered with MA, will subsequently get its updates from MA through an event-driven delta transfer. The CMD server algorithm will discover the best MA registered with SLP. However, we can statically set the list of MAs by typing:

```
SET PREFERRED MIGRATION AGENTS LIST = xxx.xxx.xxx.xxx/
```

The IP address for the preferred MAs needs to be entered in decimal notation separated by periods. You can create a list of preferred migration agents. This list has a maximum of five elements. Each element in the list needs to be separated by a semicolon. You can specify the end of the list with a backslash character (/) . For the changes to be effective, unload and reload SCMD.NLM.

Setting the Preferred IP Address If the server is configured with multiple-interface IP-bound boards, you can specify on which IP address CMD (all modes of operation) should advertise its services and availability. To do this, type the following at the console prompt:

```
SET CMD PREFERRED IP ADDRESS = xxx.xxx.xxx.xxx
```

The IP address for the preferred IP address needs to be entered in decimal notation. For the change to take effect, unload and reload SCMD.NLM.

Pure IP with an IPX Connected Segment (SCMD /G)

The SCMD /G option for pure IP provides a gateway to IPX services. The SCMD /G option is also called a migration agent. Having the migration agent with a gateway on the IPX network will build up the SAP/RIP list for the CMD servers on the IP network registered with the SLP and generate the SAP on the local IPX segments. On the other hand, all IPX services available on the IPX segments are provided to all the CMD servers registered with MA. The CMD server provides service and route visibility between IPX and Pure IP networks.

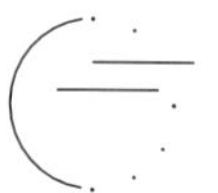
NOTE

This scenario assumes that IPX has been filtered (not allowed on the IP network).

In order to install and configure the NetWare 5 server to support pure IP with the SCMD /G option, follow these steps:

1. Install the NetWare 5 server as the CMD server.

2. Unload the SCMD.NLM module.

3. Bind IPX to the network adapter.

4. Load the SCMD module with the /G or /Gateway option by typing: **SCMD /G**.

5. Type **CONFIG** at the server console to ensure the settings are correct. Make sure that both IP and IPX are bound to the interface.

6. To verify that SCMD /G is advertising its services, type the command **DISPLAY SERVERS** at the server console prompt of the CMD server. You should see all of the IPX services of the IPX servers on the IPX segment. On the other hand when you type **DISPLAY SERVERS** on the IPX servers, you should see the SAPs of the CMD servers on the IP segment.

7. If there are multiple MAs on the network segment, to distribute the load you can configure CMD servers to register with the specific MA by setting the preferred migration agent list, as discussed previously in this chapter.

8. To view the list of migration agents on the network that have been registered with the SLP database, type the following at the console:

```
DISPLAY SLP SERVICES mgw.novell
```

If you wonder why the command DISPLAY SLP SERVICES mgw.novell uses the name of Novell on the end, the reason is that SLP is an open standard and each type of service needs to register. In this example, the Novell migration agents are a specific type of service provided in SLP.

Pure IP Backbone with IPX Linked Segments (SCMD /BS)

The SCMD /BS option for pure IP allows you to connect network IPX segments over an IP-only segment. This type of situation can occur during the migration from IPX networks to pure IP networks. In such scenarios, the IPX networks must be able to see and access each other's services. Since the service discovery mechanisms in IPX and IP are different, such access is not possible directly. The feature that facilitates visibility and accessibility between disconnected IPX segments connected via CMD is referred to as *IP backbone support*.

For instance consider a network that has two different IPX segments as shown in Figure 23.15. Further, say they are connected via an IP-only link. Since the link between the two segments is IP only, they cannot communicate with each other in IPX. The feature that facilitates communication between the two IPX segments is referred to as IP backbone support.

FIGURE 23.15

Two separate IPX network segments are connected via an IP-only WAN link. SCMD /BS provides the support to forward the IPX communication packets across the IP link.

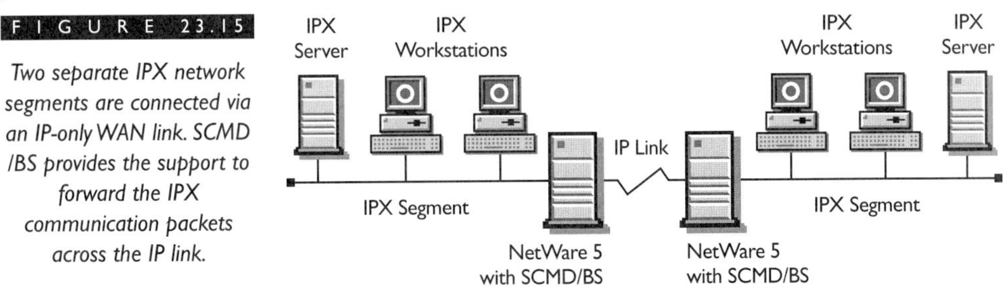

The IP Backbone Feature in CMD

The IP backbone component in CMD achieves the functionality of providing visibility and accessibility between disconnected IPX segments, as mentioned previously. The IP backbone component resides on the different migration agents at the IPX/IP network borders and helps them exchange information. The migration agents exchange information about the services and routes they are aware of and thus connect the different IPX segments. Figure 23.16 shows how the NetWare 5 servers with the module SCMD /BS loaded provide the IPX packet forwarding capabilities. In the figure are two IPX networks (IPX1 and IPX2), which are connected by a pure IP network. The two NetWare 5 servers each have the SCMD /BS or migration agent loaded. These migration agents provide service and route visibility between the IPX segments and the pure IP network.

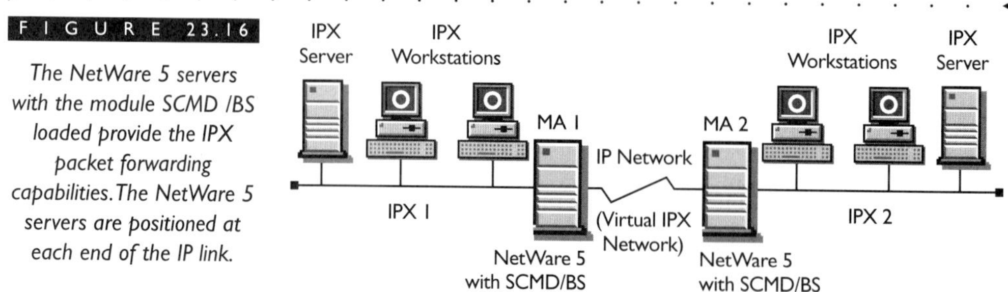

FIGURE 23.16 *The NetWare 5 servers with the module SCMD /BS loaded provide the IPX packet forwarding capabilities. The NetWare 5 servers are positioned at each end of the IP link.*

If a client in IPX1 wants to access a service in IPX2 (or vice versa), then the migration agent called MA1 should be aware of the services in IPX2. In turn, the migration agent called MA2 should be aware of services in IPX1. This is possible only if MA1 and MA2 exchange information about the respective IPX networks to which they are connected.

Such an information exchange has to be reliable and efficient, and it should not generate much traffic. To achieve all this and still keep the implementation simple enough, the IP backbone component uses the NetWare Link Services Protocol (NLSP) as a carrier for this information exchange. NLSP takes care of reliability, load balancing, efficient routing, and other such desirable features.

Usage of the IP Backbone Component

The IP backbone feature can be activated only on a migration agent. Since this component may not be required on all migration agents, it can be enabled or disabled according to the requirement with a command line load option. By default, when CMD is loaded in the MA mode, this component is switched off. To enable it, SCMD.NLM should be loaded with the /BS (backbone support) option as shown here:

```
LOAD SCMD /BS (the LOAD keyword is optional)
```

In order for this feature to work, the IPXRTR.NLM has to be loaded in the server with Routing = NLSP option. This is transparent to the user as IPXRTR is loaded automatically by SCMD if not already loaded. Apart from this option, the IPX Router should be configured to use NLSP as its routing protocol.

A migration agent that has been loaded with the /BS option (on which the IP backbone feature has been enabled) exchanges data about the IPX networks only with other migration agents on which this component is enabled.

How to Set Up the IP Backbone Feature

In order to set up or configure the IP backbone feature, follow these steps:

1. At the borders between the IPX networks and the IP-only link, place two NetWare 5 servers having two network interface cards each.
2. Bind IPX on the interfaces connecting the server(s) with the IPX network(s).
3. Bind IP on the interfaces connecting the server(s) with the IP-only link.
4. Check to make sure that the Service Location Protocol (SLP) is loaded on the servers.
5. Check whether SLP is able to communicate between the two servers. This can be done by issuing the command DISPLAY SLP SERVICES, which should display all the SLP services visible to that server.
6. Load SCMD.NLM with the /BS option on both the NetWare servers as shown later.

After you have set up the IP backbone feature, you need to check or verify that it is working. You can check whether the IPX server in one of the IPX networks is able to see the IPX server in the other IPX network and vice versa by using the command DISPLAY SERVERS, which displays all the services the server is aware of. If the DISPLAY SERVERS command does not work, then you can perform the following checks to determine the problem with the IP backbone feature:

1. Check to make sure that both migration agents have the same CMD network number.
2. Check to make sure the IP link between the migration agents is OK.
3. Check whether SLP is loaded on both migration agents.
4. Check whether SLP is communicating properly between the migration agents. You can use the DISPLAY SLP SERVICES command as described previously.

Filter Issues with the IP Backbone Component in CMD

The IP backbone feature uses the NLSP protocol to achieve its functionality. One of the issues with NLSP is that SAP/RIP filtering is not applicable to NLSP; that is, if any SAP/RIP filtering is applied on the migration agents, this filtering is overridden, as the filtering does not apply to NLSP. The filter issue is illustrated in Figure 23.17. In the figure, the two IPX networks are connected via an IP-only link. The migration agents MA1 and MA2 help the IPX networks to see and access services across the two networks. If there is a need to filter some of the services in IPX1 from IPX2, then any kind of SAP/RIP filtering on the migration agents will not work. This is because the two migration agents exchange service/route information using NLSP, and NLSP overrides SAP/RIP filtering. To achieve filtering in such a situation, do the following on all the migration agents' IPX interfaces:

1. Load the INETCFG utility.
2. Select Bindings.
3. Select IPX.
4. Select Expert Bind Options.
5. Select RIP Bind Options and change the RIP State to ON.
6. Select SAP Bind Options and change the SAP State to ON.
7. Select NLSP Bind Options and change the NLSP State to OFF.

FIGURE 23.17

The two separate IPX segments communicate through an IP-only link. Two migration agents with the backbone feature support the communication.

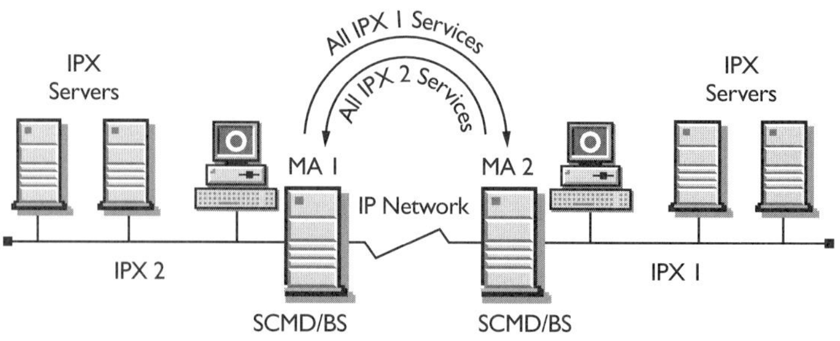

Configuration Issues with the IP Backbone Component in CMD

The IP backbone feature uses the NLSP protocol for its functionality. The IPX router (IPXRTR.NLM) is auto-loaded in this mode of operation of CMD if it is not already loaded. If IPXRTR is already loaded, CMD does not ensure that the routing protocol used is NLSP. In such a case, the user has to configure IPX to use NLSP as its routing protocol. This can be done using the INETCFG utility in the server as follows:

1. Load the INETCFG utility.
2. Select Protocols.
3. Select IPX.
4. Select Routing Protocol.
5. Select NLSP with RIP/SAP Compatibility.
6. Reinitialize the system.

If this configuration is not present, then the IP backbone feature will not work.

Dependence on the Service Location Protocol

For different migration agents to exchange information, they must discover each other in the first place. This discovery is achieved using the Service Location Protocol (SLP). Thus in a way, the IP backbone feature in CMD is dependent on SLP. The following issue with the usage of SLP affects functioning of this feature.

Multicasting over WAN

SLP uses multicasting as its mechanism for communication. Multicasting may not be supported over a WAN link. As a result SLP cannot communicate over the WAN link. This in turn affects the IP backbone feature, as it depends on SLP to discover the services across the WAN link. This issue can be overcome by using an SLP DA (directory agent) on the migration agents on either side of the IP-only link.

An Issue with the CMD Clients (Split Horizon)

When using the IP backbone feature, you can create a situation in which clients requesting the services will have a split horizon. The split-horizon issue will happen if you set up the migration agents as shown in Figure 23.18. The migration agents MA1 and MA2 are using the backbone support with MA1, MA2, and the CMD client in the same CMD network. The CMD client is configured to contact MA1 to get all IPX service/route information. If the CMD client wants to know the route to the IPX server in IPX2, it queries MA1 for it. But since MA1 has obtained the service/route information about IPX2 from the interface over which it is connected to the client, it will not respond to the client query, due to the split-horizon algorithm. Thus, the CMD client is unable to access services in IPX2 in such a scenario.

FIGURE 23.18

A situation can arise in which clients cannot access desired services because of the split horizon among migration agents.

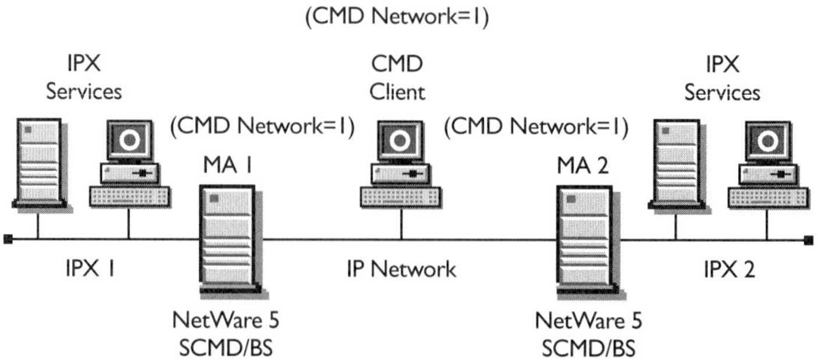

The split-horizon issue can be resolved by installing a new migration agent as shown in Figure 23.19. In this figure, MA1 and MA2 are still using the backbone support mode, but they now have a different CMD network number. MA3 is the new migration agent, which has a different CMD network number. The CMD client is also in the CMD network that the new migration agent is in. Thus, the client will contact MA3 to get the IPX service/route information.

In such a configuration, MA1 and MA2 achieve the MA-MA functionality. MA1 thus populates IPX1 with the service/route information of IPX2. MA3 will get all the service/route information about IPX1 and IPX2 through the IPX interface only. So when the client queries MA3 about IPX2, the split horizon does not apply, since it gets the information from a different interface.

FIGURE 23.19

The split-horizon issue can be resolved by installing a new migration agent with a different CMD network number.

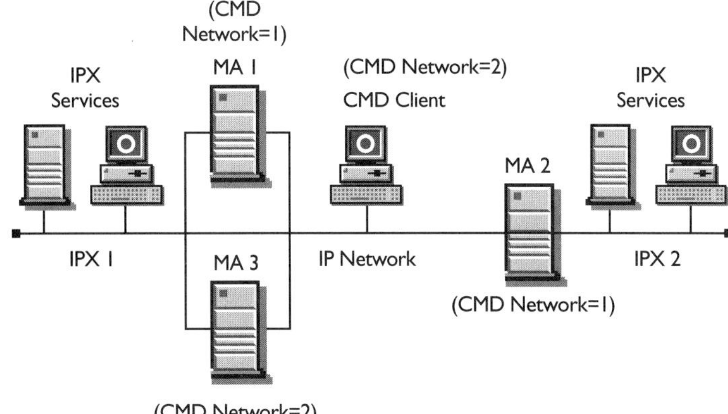

Your Migration Strategy Depends upon Your Goals

The migration options that we have discussed do not take into account your goals or needs in migrating your network protocols. The most common goals for changing your IPX networks to pure IP are the following:

- Migrate to obtain Internet connectivity.
- Migrate to cut administrative costs associated with IPX networking.
- Migrate to have an IP-only network.

Migrate to Obtain Internet Connectivity

In order to add Internet connectivity to NetWare systems, simply upgrade your network servers to NetWare 5 using the IP and IPX option, as described previously. Although this upgrade path requires administration of both the IP and IPX networking protocols, you do not have to worry about setting up any migration agents to maintain connectivity to IPX as you upgrade your systems.

Migrate to Cut IPX Administrative Costs

If you want to migrate your networks from IPX to IP to maximize your return on your investment, you will probably want to take advantage of the functionality provided by the IPX compatibility drivers and migration agents. The IPX compatibility feature is critical in this scenario because it allows migration without losing connectivity and without your having to upgrade existing applications. When utilizing the IPX compatibility feature to migrate, start the migration with the leaves of the network and finish with the backbone of the network or vice-versa.

Administrators wanting to migrate networks using the IPX compatibility feature must understand that the IPX compatibility drivers are dependent upon the functions of SLP and that there are costs associated with setting up an SLP infrastructure. On the other hand, setting up an SLP infrastructure is an investment in the future because SLP is an emerging Internet standard that will be leveraged by future applications and devices.

Migrate to Have an IP-Only Network

The choice to migrate your network to IP only on both servers and workstations depends completely on whether you have to support IPX applications anywhere in the network. If you do not have any applications that need IPX, then you can configure your servers and workstations to use IP. The definition of a pure IP segment is one that does not pass IPX through the router to the other network segments.

By using the Compatibility Mode drivers, you can configure your network segments to run only IP but still support IPX applications. The Compatibility Mode drivers can be loaded on both servers and workstations. Using the Compatibility Mode drivers, you ensure that IPX applications are 100 percent supported without having to bind IPX to the network.

Applications are considered IPX applications if they use the interfaces provided by the IPX stack or they specify IPX addresses when trying to establish NCP connections. The best way to screen out IPX applications is to run them on a test network on which IPX is absent (no IPX stacks loaded). Many applications let you specify the networking protocol to use when communicating.

In order to convert all services on a network segment from IPX to pure IP, you will typically need to configure the Compatibility Mode to support IPX applications and then turn IPX routing off at the router. These steps are as follows:

1. Place a migration agent in a central location within the network topology. Since the rest of the network will still have IPX, the migration agent must be placed outside of the segment being converted so that it can collect the SAP/RIP information for clients and servers in the pure IP area.

2. Before you start upgrading clients to IP/CMD, you should upgrade all the servers in the pure IP area to NetWare 5 with IP and IPX bound. IPX clients and IP clients will then be able to access these servers while you are converting the clients from IPX to IP/CMD.

3. Before you start upgrading clients in the pure IP area to IP/CMD, you may want to convert the printers in the area to NDPS and configure NDPS to print via IP.

4. To avoid upgrading the clients twice (IPX/IP and later to IPX/CMD), you must place migration agents in a central location within the network topology. During the client upgrade, you can configure the clients to use the migration agents to access IPX services.

5. Once the clients have been upgraded to IP/CMD, you can remove IPX from the NetWare 5 servers and load SCMD (which provides IPX application support).

6. Once the clients, servers, and printers in the pure IP area have been upgraded to IP/CMD, you can shut off IPX routing to the pure IP segment.

Sometimes pure IP only is the final goal but there is an immediate need to remove IPX from the network. The following migration path requires migration of all applications from IPX to IP before IPX is disabled on the network.

In order for this migration method to function properly, the NetWare clients must be configured twice during the course of this migration. Taking advantage of the Automatic Client Update (ACU) feature of NetWare 5 and the Workstation Manager feature can minimize the cost of modifying client configurations.

If it is later discovered that your applications require IPX, you must switch to one of the migration strategies outlined in this chapter.

The steps that follow describe how to migrate a network from IPX to IP without relying on the IPX Compatibility Mode feature:

1. Identify IPX applications and make sure that they can be configured/upgraded/replaced to run over the TCP/IP stack.

2. Start upgrading/installing your servers and clients using the IP and IPX option.

3. Start migrating applications from IPX to IP.

4. Turn off IPX networking at the routers when all the IPX applications have been migrated and all the NetWare clients and servers have been upgraded/installed using the IP and IPX option.

5. Modify the configuration of the NetWare servers and clients to be IP-only servers and clients.

Migrating a Section of the Network

In order to successfully convert your network protocols, you need to know how to migrate just a portion of the network. You have the option to first migrate your networks starting with the leaf nodes or with the backbone. In order to migrate only a section of your network at a time, follow the steps outlined here. In order to complete these steps successfully, you must ensure that the network section being migrated is not used to interconnect other sections of the network using IPX. Figure 23.20 illustrates the setup for migrating a segment of your network.

FIGURE 23.20

The IPX segment can be migrated to IP.

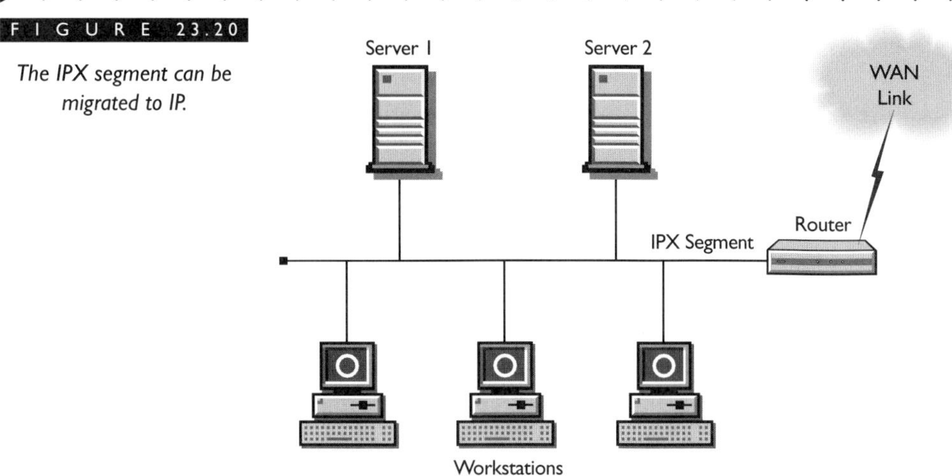

Using this example, you can follow these steps to convert the IPX segment in your network to pure IP. The steps are:

1. Upgrade Server 1 to NetWare 5 as a migration agent.

2. Upgrade Server 2 to NetWare 5 using the IP and IPX install option.

3. Upgrade clients to NetWare 5 using the IP-only install option.

4. Unbind IPX from the network adapters in Server 1 and load SCMD.NLM. Unbind IPX from the network adapters in Server 1 and reload SCMD.NLM without the migration agent option.

5. Turn off IPX routing at the router.

Migrating Leaf Networks First

Migrating leaf networks first reduces the impact of the migration on the IPX routing infrastructure of the network, and it allows the administrator to focus efforts on specific sites. Since the backbone is the last portion of the network migrated, however, administrative costs may not be offset as quickly.

These steps describe how to migrate a network from IPX to IP starting with the leaf networks first:

1. Identify the nodes and links that form the backbone of the network.

2. Select and Upgrade/Install some servers in the backbone to serve as migration agents.

3. Select the leaf portion of the network to be migrated. This may be a group of segments connected to the backbone via a WAN link. Migrate the selected portion of the network following the steps outlined previously in the section called "Migrating a Section of the Network."

4. Repeat Step 3 until all networks connected to the backbone are migrated.

5. Migrate the backbone section using the steps outlined in the section called "Migrating a Section of the Network."

Figure 23.21 shows an example of converting the leaf segments in your network before you convert the backbone segment.

The segment marked C is the backbone in the network. You will want to upgrade or install two servers on this segment to NetWare 5. These two servers should also be running as migration agents. After you have set up the migration agents, you will want to select the portion of the network consisting of leaf segments to perform the migration. In the example, the segments marked A and B are the ones that you will want to target. Next, follow the migration instructions as outlined in the section called "Migrating a Section of the Network." Make sure that you first upgrade or install servers in both segment A and segment B as NetWare 5 migration agents to minimize performance degradation while each segment is being migrated. After you have successfully installed the migration agents on the segments, turn off IPX routing in routers A and B when all the nodes in the section have been migrated to IP only. After all the leaf segments have been converted or migrated to segment C, use the steps outlined in the section called "Migrating a Section of the Network."

FIGURE 23.21

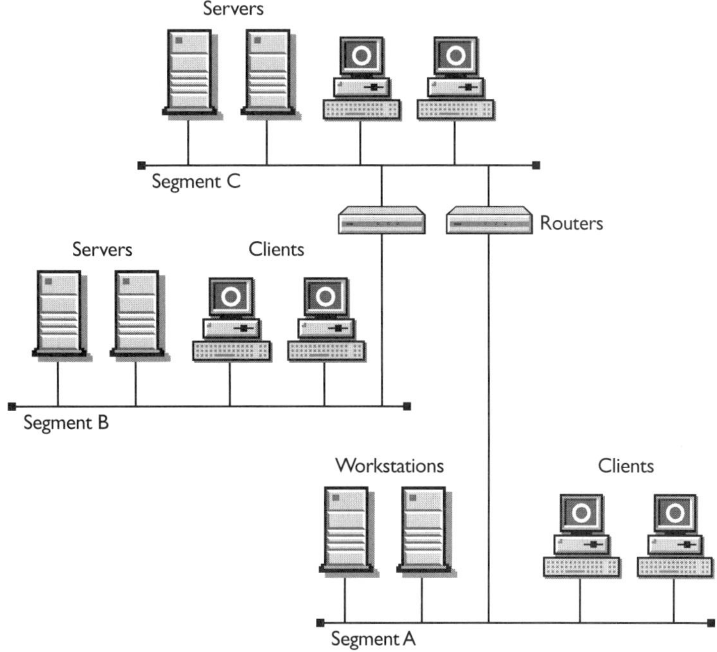

An example of migrating a leaf segment of the network before the backbone

Migrating the Backbone First

Migrating the backbone first alleviates administrative costs associated with maintaining IPX over the backbone. This migration path requires migration agents at each of the segments connected to the backbone and the backbone support feature of the migration agents before IPX routing is disabled on the backbone. The migration agents with the backbone support feature enabled are able to interconnect IPX segments by exchanging RIP and SAP information and by routing encapsulated IPX datagrams.

These steps describe how to migrate a network from IPX to IP starting with the backbone:

1. Identify the nodes and links that form the backbone of your network.

2. Select and upgrade or install some servers to NetWare 5 in each one of the segments connected to the backbone. These servers should serve as migration agents with the backbone support feature enabled.

3. Migrate the nodes on the backbone section using the steps outlined in the section called "Migrating a Section of the Network."

4. Select all leaf segments of the network to migrate. These may consist of a group of segments connected to the backbone via a WAN link. Migrate the selected portion of the network following the steps outlined in the section called "Migrating a Section of the Network." Repeat this step until all networks connected to the backbone are migrated.

Figure 23.22 shows an example of converting the backbone segment in your network before you convert the leaf segments.

FIGURE 23.22

An example of migrating the backbone segment before migrating the leaf networks

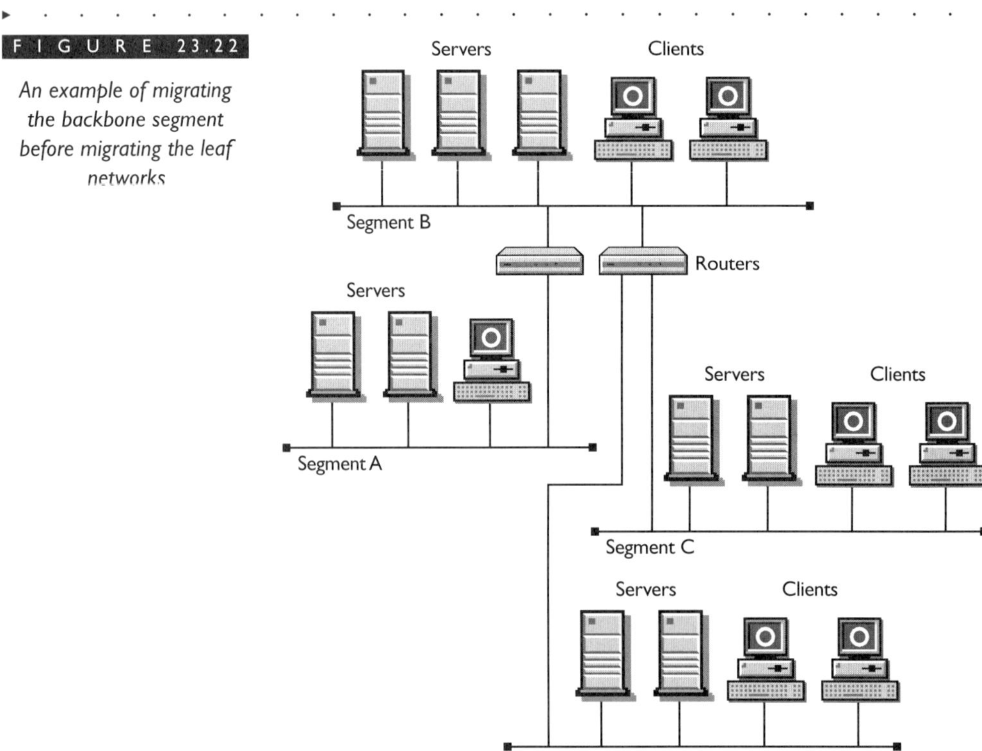

The segment marked B is the backbone in the network. You will want to upgrade or install servers on each leaf segment to NetWare 5. The leaf networks are marked as segment A, segment C, and segment D. You will need to run the migration agent with backbone support on each of the leaf segments. After you have set up the migration agents (SCMD /BS), you will want to convert or migrate the nodes on the backbone segment, which is marked as segment B. Follow the migration instructions outlined in the section called "Migrating a Section of the Network." After you have successfully migrated the backbone segment, you will then need to turn off IPX routing in routers A, C, and D. Finally, migrate segments A, C, and D.

NetWare/IP Networks Rely on Migrating Leaf Segments First

Migrating a NetWare/IP network to IP relies heavily on the IPX Compatibility Mode feature to maintain connectivity. This typically means that you will want to migrate the leaf segments or networks first. In addition, you will want to upgrade or install the NetWare 5 servers with the IP and IPX protocols.

NOTE

Migrating a NetWare/IP network to IP only using the migrate backbone (first) method is not recommended because it will seriously disrupt the NetWare/IP infrastructure.

The workstation and servers that utilize NetWare/IP to communicate are viewed as IPX nodes to clients running IP only, They are reached through the migration agents. Workstations and servers using the IP-only protocol are viewed as IPX nodes by NetWare/IP. This implies migration agents also need to function as NetWare/IP gateways. This allows the NetWare/IP clients to communicate with machines using IP only.

Migrating NetWare/IP to pure IP without using the migration agents (Compatibility Mode) is accomplished by simply installing the IPX or IP network protocol that you wish. However, be aware that you are removing the NetWare/IP component for the workstation or server and replacing it with either IPX or pure IP. Be aware that without using the migration agent at the server a disruption in service between NetWare/IP and IPX or pure IP may result.

Other Migration Considerations

In addition to the normal issues, you may need to understand several miscellaneous migration issues. These issues are not presented in any specific order.

SAP/RIP Filters and the Migration Agent Backbone Support Feature

If the backbone support feature of the migration agents is enabled, then the RIP/SAP information exchange between these agents may bypass the RIP/SAP filters that you may have set up in your routers. Refer to the migration agent documentation to learn how to set up RIP/SAP filters using the migration agents.

Turning Off Microsoft IPX Networking

Clients may be set up to do Microsoft Networking using IPX and/or IP. If clients are set up to do Microsoft Networking over IPX and you want to migrate them from IPX to IP, you may want to enable Microsoft Networking over TCP/IP and then disable Microsoft Networking over IPX. This may be necessary to reduce the demand on the services provided by the IPX Compatibility feature.

IPX-, Bindery-, and SAP-Based Applications and Utilities

Most networks have evolved slowly over the years and are generally a combination of old and new software and hardware. Legacy software and legacy network infrastructure remain necessary for many years after newer replacements have been made available. Sometimes these applications and infrastructure elements limit the ease of migration. The situations described here might present such limitations when migrating from an IPX to an IP network.

Many of the DOS utilities that were released in the intraNetWare (4.11) release were modified to work with both NDS and the older bindery. These utilities will make their first attempt at discovery by going to the bindery context of NDS. If the discovery attempt fails, then these utilities will attempt to use SAP and bindery calls to use the older technology.

Many of the scripts that IS&T staffs use to run their daily operations are based on both NCP and DOS batch processing files. In both cases, the NetWare-specific elements are generally command line versions of NetWare DOS utilities or NetWare NLMs. The reasons for continuing to use these commands should be reevaluated in light of the newer technology shipped with NetWare 5.

The Filtered Network

The first question that needs to be addressed with regard to filtering is whether it remains necessary in the IP environment. Filtering in the IPX environment sought to address congestion control and service access. With an IP-based system, the SAP that created congestion no longer exists. Service visibility is a different issue.

The real solution for this issue is the use of NDS rather than the SAP/bindery infrastructure. The filtering capability within the IP routers can still be used to replace the IPX routing. But in the IPX environment, SAP was just a special packet type that could be easily managed at the routing level. SLP, DHCP, DNS, NCP, NDS, and other protocols are just data within the IP packet and not so easily managed at the router.

The Service Location Protocol

The *Service Location Protocol* (SLP) is an Internet standard protocol as defined by the Request for Comments (RFC) 2165. SLP is defined as a discovery method for TCP/IP-based communications. It is not a name resolution service like NDS or DNS. The main purpose or function of SLP is discovery. SLP discovers infrastructure services such as NDS servers, DNS servers, DHCP servers, NDPS registration servers, and various protocol gateways. In addition, SLP encapsulates SAP broadcasts in IP packets if you have IPX Compatibility Mode running.

The Service Location Protocol basically provides the same type of information in IP networks as SAP provides in IPX networks. It registers information in a database and allows clients to query the database to find services. There are, however, two principal differences between SAP and SLP:

- SLP does not maintain a global database of services. It registers services only in the local area. It discovers services in the local area via multicast requests, which are forwarded using NDS replication from network to network within a site.
- SLP assumes that the client is able to locate either services themselves or a database server representing those services using these pan-network multicasts.

If a global database of services is required for your network, then you can configure SLP to store its information in the NDS tree. Using this method, local SLP information is compiled to provide a global representation of all available services on the network. This provides dynamic discovery of services locally and scalability in large networks.

NOTE

SLP and pure IP require that NetWare 5 be running on at least one NetWare server in the network.

The Service Location Protocol provides a method for registering and discovering network services dynamically in IP networks. The Novell Client for Windows 95/98 can use SLP to dynamically discover NDS trees and NetWare servers, providing plug-and-play capabilities similar to what Novell customers have enjoyed for many years with their IPX networks. Figure 23.23 illustrates how the Service Location Protocol provides a method to register and discover network services.

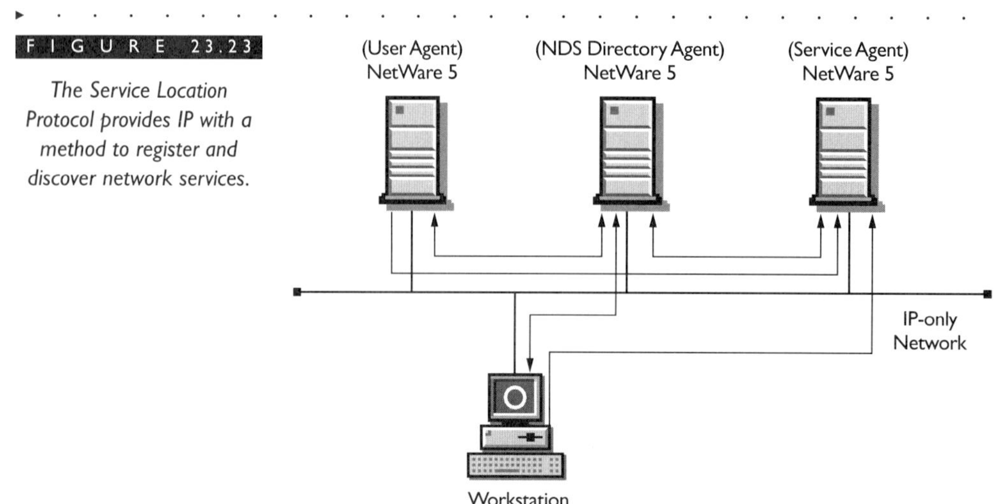

FIGURE 23.23

The Service Location Protocol provides IP with a method to register and discover network services.

SLP is not router-based. It uses standard UDP and TCP packets to register and discover network services. Network routers are not involved in maintaining SLP service information. This feature eliminates the need for constant router synchronization traffic (for example, once-a-minute SAP broadcasts in IPX networks).

If you do not use IPX Compatibility Mode (in other words, if your network does not include any IPX applications or services), or if you are not planning on using SLP for NDS tree or NetWare server discovery, then SLP does not need to be enabled for your IP network.

SLP Agents

The three types of agents that NetWare 5 SLP uses are the following:

- User agents, which acquire service handles for user applications
- Service agents, which advertise service handles
- Directory agents, which collect service handles in internetworked enterprises

Applications running on a computer are represented by a user agent that understands the service and resource needs of the application. Each network service is represented by a service agent, which makes it available to user agents. SLP dynamically maintains service attributes, so that a user agent can obtain current information.

NetWare 5 includes a Compatibility Mode feature, which enables SLP to register services that are SAP dependent. When a service that relies upon service discovery is loaded on a NetWare 5 server, the server reroutes the SAP broadcast to SLP. The service can then be registered by a service agent or by a directory agent, and a user agent can locate this service.

User Agents

A *user agent* initiates a discovery on behalf of an application. The NetWare 5 client software contains a user agent that is enabled by default and is launched during the bootup process. In a pure IP environment, SLP is the client software's preferred method to locate an NDS tree and server when this client software does not support DHCP.

Service Agents

A *service agent* works on behalf of a service to respond directly to a user agent's query for specific services. You can also configure a service agent to register the service with one or more directory agents. A user agent queries a service agent directly if no directory agent exists or if a directory agent does not respond to discovery queries.

Directory Agents

A *directory agent* collects and maintains information about service agents. A directory agent responds to a user agent's query only if the directory agent maintains information about the requested service.

If you use directory agents on a NetWare 5 network, the NetWare 5 client software queries the directory agent for service information during the bootup process. To configure a NetWare 5 server as a directory agent, you load an optional NetWare Loadable Module (NLM). However, you do not configure every server as a directory agent. You configure one local server as a directory agent, which provides service information for many other NetWare 5 servers.

The point of interface between SLP and NDS is the SLP directory agent. The directory agent provides common data storage of network service information collected through SLP. The directory agent uses NDS as its database for network service information that is distributed globally. NDS adds significant value to SLP by leveraging existing NDS standards for configuring NDS tree structures, for providing a central point of administration, and for enabling NDS to replicate service information. NDS replication services allow directory agent–to–directory agent communication. This is unique in SLP implementations, and it facilitates global distribution of SLP database information. NDS replica services give the directory agent the capability to access global services from a local replica.

Scopes

A *scope* can be thought of as a collection of services within a logical group. You might want to implement a scope for a very large installation to create a group of directory agents and services registered with these directory agents.

SLP NDS Objects

SLP in NetWare 5 has several new NDS objects. These objects are represented by SLP:

- Scope container object
- SLP service object
- SLP directory agent object

The SLP scope container object represents an SLP scope and is the container in which SLP service objects are stored. SLP service objects represent a network service discovered through the Service Location Protocol. They contain all of the SLP information about the network service, including its network address and attributes. The SLP Directory agent object represents the actual SLP directory agent.

The SLP Scope Container Object

The SLP scope container object is the storage container for SLP service information. Each object contains all the SLP service objects for the specific scope. The NDS administrator can replicate the container into other partitions within the tree or within federated trees. The object is a stand-alone entity within the NDS tree, and there is no relationship between its distinguished name, the tree name, and the scope name. When a Service agent forwards a service record to a directory agent within a specific scope, the scope name is mapped to the scope object by using the name attribute within the container object. The SLP scope object must contain rights to read, write, and browse the container because the access rights of the directory agent object access are equivalent to the access rights of the scope object. Because the scope object uses distinguished name syntax, the scope object can be moved to a different location in the tree and NDS will automatically change all values to reflect the new location.

The SLP Service Object

The SLP service object is a leaf object that represents a service registration. SLP service objects are subordinate to the SLP scope object and contain all information supplied by a service registration. SLP service objects are stored in the appropriate SLP scope object according to their scope.

The Directory Agent Object

The SLP directory agent object is a leaf object that represents a single instance of a directory agent. Multiple directory agents cannot share a single object. This object defines the directory agent's configuration, scope, and security. The directory agent uses this object to log into the server and operate under the access control requirements assigned to the NCP server object.

Major Features of SLP

As mentioned, pure IP uses Service Location Protocol, which is a service discovery mechanism that allows NetWare 5 clients to locate servers and services that are Service Advertising Protocol (SAP)–dependent during the bootup process.

NetWare 5 provides several methods to discover services, including the following:

- **Novell Directory Services (NDS) query** — The preferred method for an application to locate a service is through NDS, which provides authentication and security services for devices that can be registered as NDS objects.
- **Domain Naming System (DNS) lookup** — An application that is not NDS aware can use DNS to locate a service.
- **Dynamic Host Configuration Protocol (DHCP) query** — The NetWare 5 client software uses DHCP to locate an NDS tree and server when the client is configured to use DHCP services. DHCP offers three new options for obtaining NDS tree, server, and context information from a NetWare DHCP server daemon (a DHCP server process running on a NetWare 5 server).
- **Lightweight Directory Access Protocol (LDAP) lookup** — NetWare 5 provides LDAP support when an application specifically sends an LDAP query.
- **SLP query** — NetWare 5 clients in a pure IP environment use SLP to discover the preferred NDS tree and server when the clients are not configured to use DHCP services. Although SLP can be used as a more fully functional mechanism to discover services, the best implementation is to use SLP only during the bootup process.

The application itself determines which discovery method to use. For example, an NCP-based application queries NDS directly to locate a service. However, another application could use an LDAP query to locate a service.

The NetWare 5 client software has two options for locating an NDS tree and server in a pure IP environment: DHCP or SLP. The NetWare 5 client software uses DHCP if you have configured the client to use DHCP services. For example, you can configure the client to obtain an IP address from a DHCP server. The NetWare 5 client software uses SLP if you have not configured the client to use DHCP services.

NOTE

In NetWare's IPX/SPX-based communications architecture, the NetWare client software issues a SAP broadcast (also known as a Get Nearest Server request) during the bootup process to locate services. When a NetWare 5 network is configured to support only pure IP, however, the NetWare 5 client software cannot use SAP to locate services. (Of course, losing SAP is not really a bad thing because devices that use SAP continually broadcast their services on the network.)

Discovery of Infrastructure Service Providers

SLP works with NDS to help bring together the IP infrastructure services, which include NDS trees, DNS servers, NCP servers, NDPS service registries, and some of the protocol gateways. Doing so allows NetWare clients to discover services by querying one database rather than the whole network. The NetWare Client uses this information to gain access to infrastructure services. The SLP system does not create end user–accessible NDS objects from these infrastructure services. Instead, it uses NDS to collect and replicate knowledge of these services for the benefit of the client.

In previous IPX-based versions of NetWare, this kind of global distribution of infrastructure knowledge was accomplished through the SAP/bindery architecture. SAP was global, and each machine had a bindery. Consequently, any service that could place a SAP packet on the wire could be globally known. Unfortunately, there was a price to be paid for this global distribution. Bandwidth was consumed and network administrators had to engage in significant filtering to regulate line congestion and service visibility. With the advent of NDS, this began to change. Newer applications were able to forego SAP, register themselves directly with NDS, and take advantage of the NDS replication to attain global visibility.

Many administrators, however, wanted not one, but many, NDS trees to service their companies. So how was the network client to find these many trees? Each tree generated a SAP advertisement that was saved in the router tables of each NetWare server. The client had only to make it to an initial server to find this global infrastructure information.

SAP was created in the early days of networking with a worst-case scenario in mind. The system refreshed itself every 60 seconds whether anything had changed or not. This was advantageous for plug and play in the LAN but impractical across WAN links. Services are registered in SLP with a lifetime that defines the amount of time the service will be available. If the service goes away before the lifetime has elapsed, a request to that service fails.

NDPS makes significant use of SLP in the IP environment. The presence of SLP allows a degree of automated management in the IP environment that is equivalent to that found in the IPX environment. NDPS will function without SLP, but automated management is reduced.

Where to Place the Directory Agents

A small network may not need SLP configuration. The user and service agents on both client and server are automatically loaded and require no configuration. In a small network (up to 25–30 servers) there is probably no need to implement a directory agent. For larger networks, a directory agent will be needed to provide scaling and enterprise visibility of services. Placement and frequency of directory agents in the network will depend on several factors:

- Is the company centralized, or is it distributed, or does it support many small branch offices?
- Should IP multicast be routed outside the local segment?
- What does the existing NDS replication infrastructure look like?
- Will there be a need to use SLP scoping for congestion control?
- What degree of fault tolerance is desired in the system?
- Will every network segment need to work with every other network segment?

- How many services will be represented on the network?
- What is an acceptable response time for service discovery?

If you set up the SLP infrastructure using directory agents, and if you rely on the IPX Compatibility Mode feature to accomplish the migration, you must place directory agents so as to minimize the round-trip distance between the IP-only nodes and their closest directory agent. This is necessary to avoid having IPX applications timing out when they perform RIP or SAP requests.

Finally, within the corporate LAN, the administrator could easily use any of the technologies presented as well as IP multicast for SLP directory agent synchronization. A mixture of technologies could work concurrently in the LAN environment. The following issues should be considered.

IP Multicast The advent of IP multicast technology creates an additional factor that the system administrator must consider. On a local segment, multicast is manageable. But when routers are configured to enable multicast, the multicast packet enters the router, which checks to determine whether any other local segments have registered to listen to multicast. Upon finding a registered listener, the router moves the multicast packet into another segment. With the wrong configuration, multicast takes on characteristics of broadcast, consuming bandwidth. Properly configured, however, IP multicast can provide a global distribution of critical information.

In its default mode in a local network segment environment, the SLP user agent uses IP multicast to access the several SLP service agents. Or IP multicast can be configured and made available across the networks. Then SLP will utilize the available bandwidth to continue seeking service agents. If you decide to restrict multicast traffic, you can implement DHCP to help the user agents find service and directory agents that are not local and cannot be discovered through multicast.

NDS Replication NDS replication can be used to synchronize the data in numerous SLP directory agents across the enterprise. Synchronization traffic across a WAN link can be expensive though, and consume bandwidth. Within the LAN, however, this replication service is a viable alternative. System administrators should consult the existing literature on NDS deployment to understand the administrative requirements and network impacts of NDS replication.

Fault Tolerance While a single SLP directory agent could provide service for a fairly large company, that would create a single point of failure. The presence of multiple directory agents provides a degree of fault tolerance so that the failure of a single DA will not impact the network. Once again, there is the issue of synchronizing the multiple directory agents. Each of the alternatives previously presented carries both costs and benefits.

Service Visibility Services do not necessarily have to be provided to the whole network. For many years, NetWare administrators have been regulating network congestion and service visibility through IPX packet filtering at the routers. Not every user of the network saw every service that SAP advertised in the network. A similar situation can be achieved by disabling IP multicast. A network can be configured to use multiple SLP directory agents, each containing different data and servicing a different region of the network.

SLP Design

In a large network, the system administrator will have to use the SLP directory agent to achieve scalability across the network. The directory agent may be installed with system defaults that make it immediately usable. On installation, the directory agent will extend the NDS NCP object schema and create a SLP-DA record within the NCP server object. It will also create a default container in the NDS name base for SLP entries. This container may be replicated at the discretion of the system administrator.

In the largest networks, however, the use of a flat SLP implementation may prove inadequate for scalability and traffic management. SLP scopes subdivide services. For example, some services may be regularly registered on the machines in the engineering department and have no use to anyone outside of that department. Thus, the administrator could configure the system to attach a scope attribute of "ENG" to each service in that area. These services would then be seen only by requests that included the attribute of SCOPE=ENG. Such subdividing of services provides a kind of filtering that administrators are used to in both IP and IPX environments. SLP implementations that don't utilize scopes are said to be "unscoped."

You may not use every SLP option on your company's network. The set of processes you use depends on which SLP network design you choose. The SLP network design you choose, in turn, depends on the size and complexity of your company's network. Essentially, you determine the number of services running on the network, and you choose the best SLP network design to handle these services. You can choose one of the following SLP network designs:

- Small service radius
- Medium service radius
- Large service radius

Small Service Radius

You can use the small service radius design for an installation that supports 50 servers or less. In this design, user agents query service agents to locate services. If you use a small service radius design on a NetWare 5 network, you simply keep the default settings for NetWare 5 and the NetWare 5 client software. Figure 23.24 illustrates a small network with less than 25 servers. This size network gains no advantage from an SLP directory agent. All SLP communication can be handled by the SLP service and user agents with local segment IP multicast. With this simple system, the network client is able to have dynamic discovery of NDS trees, NCP servers, the NDPS Service Registry, and other infrastructure services such as gateways. NDS-aware services could register themselves with NDS.

FIGURE 23.24

You can implement the small service radius SLP design when there are less than 25 NetWare 5 servers.

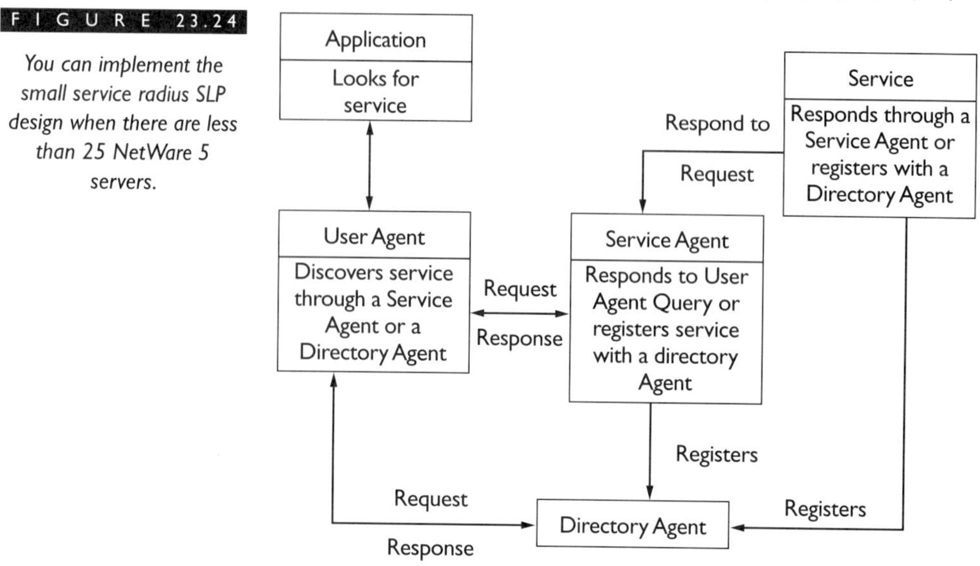

Medium Service Radius

In a large installation, however, you may not want hundreds of service agents replying to queries from user agents. In this case, you can load the directory agent on one NetWare server. When service agents for NetWare 5 servers discover that a directory agent is available, these service agents register with the directory agent. The directory agent then replies to queries from user agents. By default, the NetWare 5 client software can locate and use a directory agent if one exists on the NetWare 5 network. You do not have to reconfigure the NetWare 5 client software to use a directory agent.

As shown in Figure 23.25, a medium network using Service Location Protocol will require SLP directory agents to provide scaling and WAN support. If the network is architected to be a rather flat network, then a single directory agent might be sufficient. Unlike on the smaller systems, there may be no IP multicast in this network. In that case, the directory agent can be found by the user agents through the use of DHCP. Also, with the directory agent, information can be stored in an NDS container that can be replicated through the corporate network and have information that can be made available to other directory agents. Classification of service information would not normally be necessary in this environment.

FIGURE 23.25

When you implement the medium service radius SLP design, you will want to implement the SLP agents to provide scaling and WAN support.

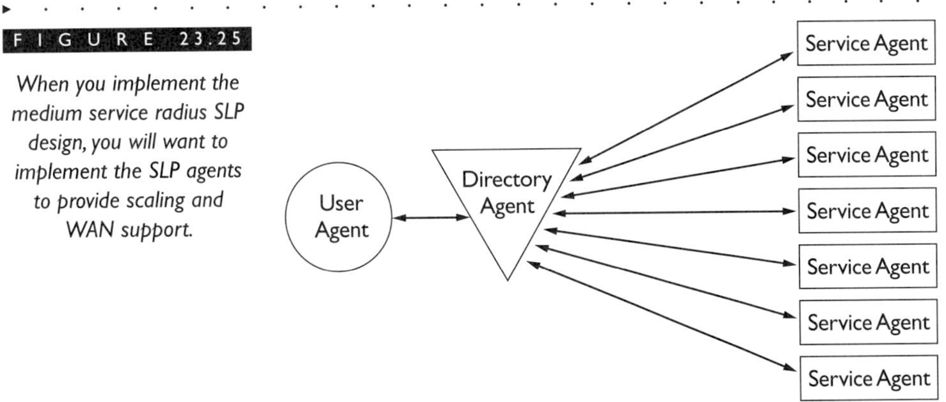

Large Service Radius

You can use the large service radius design for a very large installation that has services spanning WAN links. In this design, you group services in scopes. For example, if your company had two offices—one in London and one in Paris—you could configure two scopes: a London scope and a Paris scope. When a user in the London office requested a service, the request would indicate which scope contained the requested service. In this way, you would prevent SLP queries from being sent over a WAN link, which is typically a low-bandwidth, high-latency link that is not designed to handle excessive traffic.

You can also use the large service radius design to reduce the load on a particular directory agent: You separate services into scopes and set up a directory agent for each scope, ensuring that a single directory agent does not have to handle all SLP queries.

Large-scale implementation of Service Location Protocol will most likely require a combination of SLP directory agents, Novell Directory Services, DHCP, and local IP multicast. Figure 23.26 illustrates the role that NDS would play in such an environment. The SLP directory agent would collect service information from the local service agents. That information would then be loaded to a container in NDS. That container would then be replicated as necessary with other SLP directory agents feeding in information from different parts of the network and retrieving information collected from other directory agents. Thus, the local service can receive global distribution (at the system administrator's discretion).

FIGURE 23.26

In the large service radius design you can assign several scopes to a particular directory agent, and you can assign several directory agents to one scope.

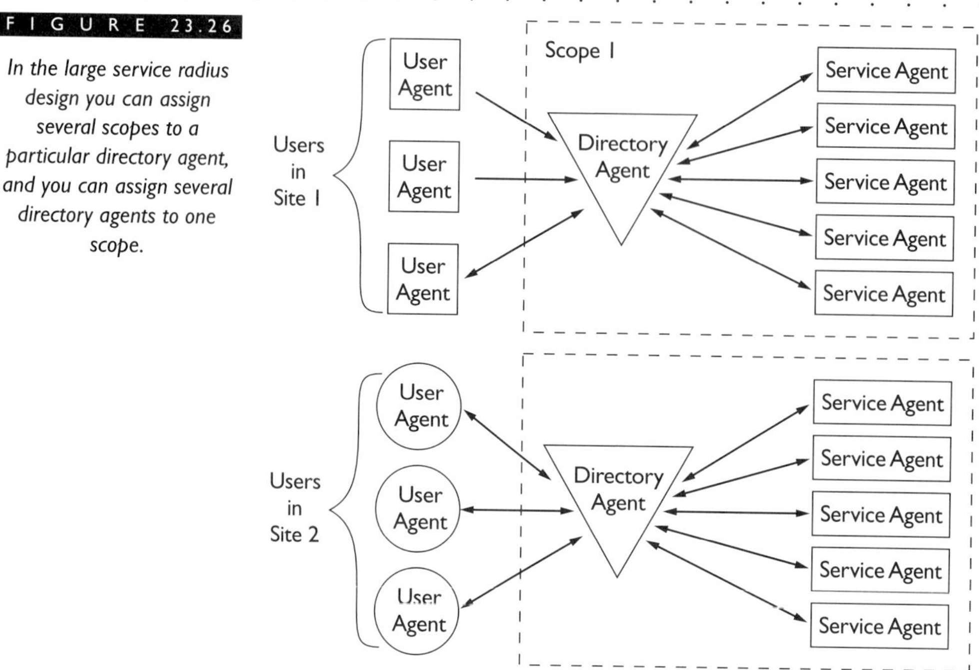

SLP Communications

SLP communications can use the User Datagram Protocol (UDP) or Transmission Control Protocol (TCP) with registered port 427. Although most SLP communications use UDP, TCP can be used for bulk information transfer—that is, traffic generated by a single request with multiple replies. (If you use an access filter or a security filter on routers or gateways, you must remove the filter on port 427 to enable SLP communications to work properly.)

SLP uses a combination of several types of communications:

- Directory agent discovery multicast packets (147.85.1.35)
- SLP general multicast packets (147.85.1.22)

- Internet Group Message Protocol (IGMP) multicast packets
- Unicast packets (station address)

Locating a Directory Agent

During the bootup process, an SLP device sends a directory agent discovery multicast packet, looking for a directory agent. If the service agent locates a directory agent, the service agent uses unicast packets to communicate with that directory agent.

If your company's network doesn't support multicast packets or DHCP services, broadcast communications or static configurations can be used to discover directory agents. For example, if your company has a large network, you might have disabled multicast forwarding on routers to control traffic. In addition, you might have manually assigned IP addresses, eliminating the need for DHCP services.

Broadcast communications are, however, an undesirable way to implement SLP because a broadcast is considered a local operation and typically isn't allowed to propagate throughout an entire internetwork. As a result, using a broadcast reduces the radius in which services can be discovered to the local network only. A device cannot discover services on the other side of a router, unless the router forwards broadcast packets.

If no directory agent exists, the user agent sends an SLP general multicast packet to locate the requested service (rather than the directory agent).

Joining a Multicast Group

SLP devices join a multicast group during the bootup process by sending an IGMP multicast packet on the network. Based on the IGMP multicast packets that IP routers receive from SLP devices, these routers decide whether or not to forward multicast packets to particular subnetworks. IP routers forward multicast packets only to subnetworks in which other devices have joined the multicast group. In this way, SLP uses multicast groups to reduce traffic.

To get a better idea of how SLP works, let's take a look at the NetWare 5 client software's bootup process. If the NetWare 5 client software is using SLP to discover services on a network that does not use directory agents or scopes, this client software completes the following bootup process:

- The client software's user agent sends an SLP directory agent discovery multicast packet.
- The client software's user agent sends an SLP general multicast packet for the migration gateway. (The migration gateway offers a gateway service between pure IP and pure IPX configurations on a NetWare 5 network.)
- The client software's user agent sends an SLP general multicast packet to discover the preferred NDS tree and server.
- The client software's DHCP stack sends DHCP attempts.
- The service agent replies.

SLP Service Types

The services that register in SLP have specific types associated with them. The service types are used as categories for the services and are used for query and display purposes. The service types in SLP appear with URLs to define the specific resource that registered. This method of defining resources creates more flexible communications and naming mechanisms that take advantage of existing technology. For example, when a user agent sends an SLP query to find the preferred NDS tree and server, either a service agent or a directory agent replies with the following information:

```
service:ndap.novell:///CAMELOT.ACME.ACME_TREE
```

The information displayed shows the CAMELOT.ACME.ACME_TREE information that has registered with SLP. An example of the CAM-SRV1 server registering with the SLP would appear as follows:

```
service:bindery.novell:///CAM-SRV1
```

The IP address of the service provider (the NDS server, in this example) is located in the attributes of the reply. Devices can also use SLP to discover other types of services. The following list shows some of the most common Novell SLP service types and what they are used for:

- The MGW.NOVELL service type is used for migration agents that register with SLP.
- The NDAP.NOVELL service type is used by the NDS partitions. A NetWare 5 server that has IP bound with a replica for a given partition in an NDS tree will register with SLP on behalf of that NDS partition.
- The BINDERY.NOVELL service type is used by NetWare 5 servers. Every NetWare 5 server with a Pure IP stack will register with SLP as a BINDERY.NOVELL server.
- The SAPSRV.NOVELL service type is used for NetWare5 servers with IPX Compatibility Mode, which redirects all the IPX SAP requests to SLP as SAPSRV.NOVELL objects.
- The RMS.NOVELL service type is used by the NDPS brokers. The Resource Management Service of NDPS registers with SLP.
- The RCONSOLE.NOVELL service type registers the new NetWare 5 rconsole registers with SLP.
- The DIRECTORY-AGENT service type is used to send an SLP multicast packet to rediscover the directory agents on the network.

SLP Console Commands

Many SLP commands have been made available to you at the server console. These commands allow you to display, query, monitor, debug, and set up the Service Location Protocol information.

DISPLAY SLP SERVICES <SERVICE TYPE> [<RESTRICTION CLAUSE>]

The console command to display SLP services allows you to display or view all the IP services that have been registered. You can restrict the display of services by providing the specific service type or using a restriction clause. An example of using the Display SLP Services console command is shown in Figure 23.27.

```
service:sapsrv.novell:/ipx/00166603:000000000001:0451/0004/8941ce85/8941cc00/C
AM-SRV1
service:sapsrv.novell:/ipx/00166603:000000000001:0840/0278/8941ce85/8941cc00/A
CME_TREE_____________________________@xXÇ@@@@@@DàPJ
service:sapsrv.novell:/ipx/00166603:000000000001:8104/0107/8941ce85/8941cc00/C
AM-SRV1
service:rconsole.novell:///137.65.206.133:2034;DAL-SRV1
service:ndap.novell:///ACME_TREE.
service:ndap.novell:///CAMELOT.ACME.ACME_TREE.
service:ndap.novell:///NORAD.ACME.ACME_TREE.
service:ndap.novell:///ACME.ACME_TREE.
service:bindery.novell:///CAM-SRV1
service:mgw.novell://137.65.206.134
service:sapsrv.novell:/ipx/0f2ac1ae:000000000001:0451/0004/8941ce86/8941cc00/R
IO-SRV1
service:sapsrv.novell:/ipx/0f2ac1ae:000000000001:0840/0278/8941ce86/8941cc00/A
CME_TREE_____________________________0±D±J@@@@@DàPJ
service:sapsrv.novell:/ipx/0f2ac1ae:000000000001:000a/026b/8941ce86/8941cc00/A
CME_TREE_____________________________0±D±J@@@@@DàPJ
service:rconsole.novell:///137.65.206.134:2034;SFO-SRV1

10-30-1998  10:57:12 am:    RSPX-4.12-28
     Remote console connection granted for 01010500:0080C7E2178B

<Press ESC to terminate or any other key to continue>
```

FIGURE 23.27

An example of using the Display SLP Services console command

In order to restrict the view using a service type, you can use some of the most common Novell SLP service types. They are:

- MGW.NOVELL
- NDAP.NOVELL
- BINDERY.NOVELL
- SAPSRV.NOVELL
- RMS.NOVELL
- RCONSOLE.NOVELL
- DIRECTORY-AGENT

DISPLAY SLP ATTRIBUTES [<RESTRICTION CLAUSE>]

The console command to display the SLP attributes for a specific service allows you to display or view all the SLP attributes for the services that have been registered. You can restrict the display of attributes for a specific service by providing a restriction clause. An example of using the Display SLP attributes console command is shown in Figure 23.28.

FIGURE 23.28

An example of using the Display SLP Attributes console command

```
CME_TREE_______________________________@ẋXÇ@@@@@@DàPJ
  service:sapsrv.novell:/ipx/00166603:000000000001:8104/0107/8941ce85/8941cc00/C
AM-SRV1
  service:rconsole.novell:///137.65.206.133:2034;DAL-SRV1
  service:ndap.novell:///ACME_TREE.
  service:ndap.novell:///CAMELOT.ACME.ACME_TREE.
  service:ndap.novell:///NORAD.ACME.ACME_TREE.
  service:ndap.novell:///ACME.ACME_TREE.
  service:bindery.novell:///CAM-SRV1
  service:mgw.novell://137.65.206.134
  service:sapsrv.novell:/ipx/0f2ac1ae:000000000001:0451/0004/8941ce86/8941cc00/R
IO-SRV1
  service:sapsrv.novell:/ipx/0f2ac1ae:000000000001:0840/0278/8941ce86/8941cc00/A
CME_TREE_______________________________0╧D±J@@@@@DàPJ
  service:sapsrv.novell:/ipx/0f2ac1ae:000000000001:000a/026b/8941ce86/8941cc00/A
CME_TREE_______________________________0╧D±J@@@@@DàPJ
  service:rconsole.novell:///137.65.206.134:2034;SFO-SRV1

  service:bindery.novell:///RIO-SRV1
Display complete.
CAM-SRV1:lp attributes service:rconsole.novell:///137.65.206.134:2034;SFO-SRV1

Searching Network . . .
    type=Agent
CAM-SRV1:
```

SLP query restrictions are in parentheses at the end of the SLP query string. The format for restriction clauses are as follows (<slp attribute>==<value>). Also, <=, >= can be used in place of ==. For example, if you want to list all the migration agents servicing the CMD network number 01010000, enter the following SLP query from the server console:

```
DISPLAY SLP SERVICES MGW.NOVELL (CMD NETWORK==01010000)
```

DISPLAY SLP DA

This console command displays the list of SLP directory agents and their current status. You can use the command SLP DEBUG LEVEL = 8 to display all the requests made to the DA including the type of SLP request and the IP address of the UA or SA sending the request. In order to log this information to a file for a period of time, you can use SLP OPEN and SLP CLOSE. The SLP trace file can then be GREPed to find any UAs or SAs that are requesting more from the DA than they should. In addition, you may also use the following command:

```
DISPLAY SLP SERVICES DIRECTORY-AGENT
```

This command enables you to discover and view the status of all the directory agents that exist in the network. You can also change the status of the directory agents from inactive to active using the following SET SLP DEBUG command:

```
SET SLP DEBUG = <numeric option>
```

The numeric options are defined as 0x01=COMM, 0x02=TRAN, 0x04=API, 0x08=DA, 0x010=ERR, 0x020=SA. These bits can be OR'd together for multiple values. For example, the COMM and API could be 5, or the COMM, API, and DA could be 13.

SLP OPEN <FILENAME.LOG>

You can enable a trace file to track the information for SLP. When you specify the filename for the trace file, it will be created in the root of SYS volume.

SLP CLOSE

You can close the SLP trace file that was active or open. The SLP trace file must be open before you can close it. You can use SLP DEBUG LEVEL = 8 to display all the requests made to the DA including the type of SLP request and the IP address of the UA or SA sending the request. Log this information to a file for a period of time using SLP OPEN and SLP CLOSE. The SLP trace file can then be GREPed to find any UAs or SAs that are requesting more from the DA than they should.

SLP Set Parameters

Several SLP SET parameters and commands enable you to monitor and control many of the features and activities of the Service Location Protocol. Table 23.1 outlines each of the SLP SET parameters and describes their purpose or use.

TABLE 23.1

SLP SET Parameters Used to Monitor and Control the Features and Activities of the Service Location Protocol.

SET PARAMETER	DESCRIPTION
SLP DA Discovery Options = *value*	The SLP DA discovery uses multicast DA advertisements. The settings for the options value are: 0x01 = Use multicast directory agent advertisements 0x02 = Use DHCP discovery 0x04 = Use static file SYS:ETC\\SLP.CFG 0x08 = Scopes required These bits can be ordered together for multiple values. The supported values are 0 to 8, with the default set at 3. This parameter can be set in the STARTUP.NCF file.
SLP TCP = *value*	Use TCP packets instead of UDP packets when possible. The supported values are ON or OFF, with the default set at OFF. This parameter can be set in STARTUP.NCF.
SLP Debug = *value*	You can use the SLP debug command to enable debugging or change the mode. The common settings are called: 0x01 = COMM 0x02 = TRAN 0x04 = API 0x08 = DA 0x10 = ERR 0x20 = SA The supported values are 0 to 4294967255, with the default of zero. This parameter can be set in STARTUP.NCF.
SLP Multicast Radius = *value*	This parameter is used to specify an integer describing the multicast radius. The supported values are 0 to 32, with the default of 32. This parameter can be set in STARTUP.NCF.
SLP Broadcast = *value*	This parameter allows you to use broadcast packets instead of multicast packets for SLP. The supported values are ON and OFF, with the default being OFF. This parameter can be set in STARTUP.NCF.

Continued

TABLE 23.1
Continued

SET PARAMETER	DESCRIPTION
SLP MTU Size = *value*	Use this parameter to specify an integer describing the maximum transfer unit size. The supported values are 0 to 4294967255, with the default set at 1472. This parameter can be set in STARTUP.NCF.
SLP Rediscover Inactive Directory Agents = *value*	This parameter allows you to specify the minimum time period in seconds that SLP will wait to issue service requests to rediscover inactive directory agents. The supported values are 0 to 4294967255, with the default of 60. This parameter can be set in STARTUP.NCF.
SLP Retry Count = *value*	Using this parameter, you can specify an integer value describing the maximum number of retries. The supported values for this parameter are 0 to 128. The default for this parameter is set to 3. This parameter can be set in STARTUP.NCF.
SLP Scope List = *value*	This parameter allows you to specify a comma-delimited scope policy list. The maximum length value for this parameter is 1023, with the default set at 1023. This parameter can be set in STARTUP.NCF.
SLP SA Default Lifetime = *value*	This parameter specifies an integer value describing the default lifetime in seconds of service registers. The supported values for this parameter are 0 to 4294967255. The default for this parameter is set to 900. This parameter can be set in STARTUP.NCF.
SLP Event Timeout = *value*	This parameter specifies an integer value describing the number of seconds to wait before timing out multicast packet requests. The supported values for this parameter are 0 to 4294967255. The default for this parameter is set to 53. This parameter can be set in STARTUP.NCF.

SET PARAMETER	DESCRIPTION
SLP DA Heart Beat Time = *value*	This parameter allows you to specify an integer value describing the number of seconds before sending the next directory agent heartbeat packet. The supported values for this parameter are 0 to 4294967255. The default for this parameter is set to 10800. This parameter can be set in STARTUP.NCF.
SLP Close Idle TCP Connections Time = *value*	Using this parameter, you can specify an integer value describing the number of seconds before idle TCP connections should be terminated. The supported values for this parameter are 0 to 4294967255. The default for this parameter is set to 300. This parameter can be set in STARTUP.NCF.
SLP DA Event Timeout = *value*	This parameter allows you to specify an integer value describing the number of seconds to wait before timing out directory agent packet requests. The supported values for this parameter are 0 to 429. The default for this parameter is set to 5. This parameter can be set in STARTUP.NCF.

SLP Client Configuration Settings

In addition to Server SLP SET parameters that allow you to fine-tune the configuration, the NetWare 5 Client and SLP interaction can be configured from the client property pages in NWADMIN. The client settings are as follows.

SLP Active Discovery

This parameter specifies that SLP is required to look up services from a directory agent and not use IP multicasting directly to SLP service agents for services. During normal operation of SLP, it first checks directory agents. If no directory agent is found, SLP multicasts to service agents.

Property Page: Novell Client Configuration

Tab: Advanced Settings

Parameter Group: SLP General

Default: On

SLP Cache Replies

When SLP receives a service request from a User Agent, the SLP reply is saved for the amount of time specified by the SLP Cache Replies parameter. If SLP receives a duplicate of this request, the cached reply is sent, so the same reply does not have to be generated again. The default value for this parameter is one minute. Setting this value higher will consume more memory to retain replies longer. We recommend that you not change the default setting, because any duplicate requests should occur within the first minute.

Property Page: Novell Client Configuration
Tab: Advanced Settings
Parameter Group: SLP Times
Range: 1 to 60 (minutes)
Default: 1

SLP Default Registration Lifetime

This parameter specifies the lifetime of a service registration that is registered by a service provider requesting the default lifetime value. If the service provider specifies a lifetime value when the service is registered, this value is not used.

The directory agent deletes the service when the lifetime expires, if it hasn't been specifically renewed or unregistered before then. This prevents the directory agent's information from becoming too stale if the server agent registering the service goes down. The server agent automatically renews the service so that the application doesn't need to.

The default value for this parameter is 10,800 seconds, which is three hours. Using a smaller value will make the directory agent's information less stale at the expense of more network traffic to renew services more frequently. This parameter does not affect how long the service is registered by the server agent.

Property Page: Novell Client Configuration
Tab: Advanced Settings
Parameter Group: SLP Times
Range: 60 to 60000 (seconds)
Default: 10800

SLP Maximum Transmission Unit

This parameter specifies the maximum transmission unit (UDP packet size) for the link layer used. Setting this parameter either too large or too small will adversely affect performance of SLP. For this reason, we recommend that you leave the parameter with the default setting of 1,400.

Property Page: Novell Client Configuration
Tab: Advanced Settings
Parameter Group: SLP General
Range: 576 to 4096
Default: 1400

SLP Multicast Radius

SLP uses IP multicasting to dynamically discover other SLP service agents and directory agents. This parameter specifies the maximum number of subnets (number of routers plus 1) that SLP's multicasting should traverse. A value of 1 confines multicasting to the local segment (no routers).

Property Page: Novell Client Configuration
Tab: Advanced Settings
Parameter Group: SLP General
Range: 1 to 32 (number of routers plus 1)
Default: 32

DNS/DHCP Services

Because NetWare 5 provides pure IP capabilities, your clients will most likely use IP at the desktop as well. Therefore, your users will take advantage of IP for their applications and their software and will need an IP address at their workstation. Because assigning an IP address to every user is cumbersome and time consuming, NetWare 5 provides Dynamic Host Configuration Protocol (DHCP) services and a Domain Name Service (DNS). These two features provide an administrator with the capability to supply IP addresses quickly and easily to the user community.

Domain Name Services (DNS)

A Domain Name Service is a database that matches computer names to their corresponding IP address. The DNS is broken into two categories; the hierarchy and the name service. The hierarchy specifies a host's domain in relation to other hosts on the domain. As in NDS, the domain is considered an upside-down tree with a root at the top followed by the top-level domains such as .com, .edu, and .org. Following these are the subdomains, which would include the name of your company, if registered (for example, novell.com).

The name service component of DNS maps the host name to an IP address. Clients known as *resolvers* can query the name server for host address information. If one name server does not contain the information in the query, the request is sent on to other servers up and down the domain hierarchy until a response to the query is received.

The Dynamic Host Configuration Protocol (DHCP)

In order for a computer or any other device to function on an IP network, the device must be configured with the appropriate IP information, including the client's own domain name and IP address, the DNS server's IP address, and the subnet mask. Dynamic Host Configuration Protocol (DHCP) servers provide the capability to automatically hand out IP addresses and other network information to your network's workstations.

A client that is using DHCP will initialize and contact a DHCP server on your network. The server will respond to the client with an IP address that it has selected from a pool. The server will also send the client any necessary DHCP information. The server also includes a lease time of how long the IP address is valid for this client. Clients will periodically ask for a renewal of the lease, and the DHCP server will grant it. If the client does not renew, the IP address goes back into the pool of IP addresses available to other users.

Dynamic DNS (DDNS)

The nature of DHCP is dynamic because users are constantly obtaining new and different IP addresses each time they log into the network. Because DNS has the responsibility of providing a current address for any host name sent to it by a resolver, DNS would constantly be out of sync with the devices on its network.

Dynamic DNS allows a DNS database to be notified immediately of address assignments made by DHCP servers. Through NDS, DNS can easily be updated when a change is sent over from DHCP, because all information is maintained in the Directory.

NDS-Enabled DHCP

In the previous version of NetWare 4 known as intraNetWare, DHCP was provided by using a flat text file to track distributed IP addresses. Because networks have grown considerably with IP, Novell has introduced NDS-enabled DHCP in NetWare 5. NDS is now used as the database to store all DHCP objects. Also new to NetWare 5's DHCP is its capability to "ping ahead." This process pings the network before allocating an IP address to the client. This ensures that a duplicate IP address will not be issued. As shown in Figure 23.29, you can enable the ping option using the DNS/DHCP Management Console utility when you create a DHCP server for your tree. The DNS/DHCP utility can be run in stand-alone mode or inside of the NWADMIN utility. Installation of this utility is discussed in a later section.

FIGURE 23.29

Check the box Ping Enabled at the bottom of this screen to have the server ping the network before allocating an IP address.

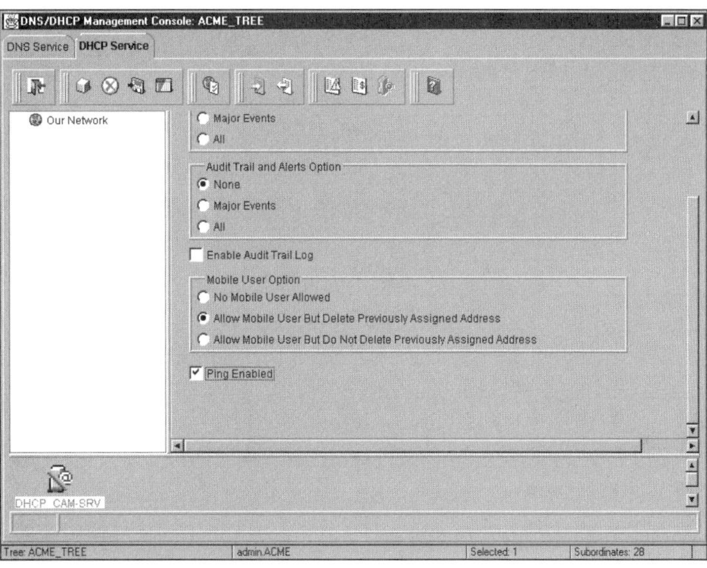

DNS/DHCP in a Mixed NetWare Environment

NetWare 5 works well in a mixed environment with NetWare 4.11 servers. If you are currently running in a NetWare 4.11 environment, you can utilize DNS/DHCP services by adding one NetWare 5 server as long as the NetWare 4.11 servers are running DS version 5.99 or later. You can use the NetWare 5 DHCP server to issue IP addresses to any client, such as Windows 95/98, UNIX, Macintosh, or NT, in a mixed NetWare 4 and NetWare 5 environment.

NDS Objects for DNS and DHCP

Five objects are created when you enable DHCP on your NetWare 5 server. The schema in your NDS tree is extended to support these new DNS/DHCP objects. The new objects for DHCP are:

- **DHCP server object** — This object contains the configuration information for a DHCP server with a multivalued attribute listing all subnet ranges that the DHCP server is servicing. This object is created for you when you install DNS/DHCP services on your NetWare 5 server for the first time.

- **Subnet object** — This object represents a subnet and can be contained in an O, OU, C, or L object. The subnet object is a container object for the IP address and address range objects.

- **Subnet pool object** — This object provides support for multiple subnets through a DHCP or BOOTP forwarder on a router and by identifying a pool of subnets for remote LAN address assignments. This object can be contained in O, OU, C, or L containers.

- **Address range object** — This object is used to denote a range of addresses to create a pool of addresses for dynamic address assignment. It's also used to identify a range of addresses to be excluded from address assignment.

- **IP address object** — This object represents a single IP address. This object must include an address number and an assignment type. This address can be assigned manually, automatically, or dynamically, and it can be excluded from DHCP address assignment.

Additionally, three new objects are also created for DNS. These object are:

- **DNS zone object** — This object is a container object to hold all data for a single DNS zone. A zone object is the first level of the DNS zone description. A zone object can be contained under an O, OU, C, or L object.
- **DNS resource record set object** — This object is an NDS leaf object that is contained in a DNS zone object. This object represents an individual domain name within a DNS zone.
- **DNS name server object** — This object is different from the regular server object in NDS. A DNS server has configuration information about DNS such as a list of forwarders and a list of zone servers. This object can be contained in an O, OU, C, or L container.

Design Guidelines for DNS and DHCP Objects

As we've mentioned at many points throughout this book, NDS is a distributed database and therefore updates are exchanged with other servers at periodic intervals. Unless you are only managing a few IP objects, we recommend that you create a separate container to maintain the DNS and DHCP objects in your tree.

Create an OU near the top of the tree. You can then locate the DNS/DHCP Group and Locator objects under the container object. You can also create an administrator group object in this container. The administrator group should have Read and Write rights to all DNS/DHCP locator object attributes except the global and data options fields. Members of this group can use the Management Console to modify and create DNS and DHCP objects.

Try to place your DNS and DHCP servers at locations where they are geographically close to the hosts that require their services. You can have one DHCP server in each partition of your network to minimize any WAN communications problems caused by normal load, configuration changes, or replication.

The location of group and locator objects is also very important. Each NDS tree has only one set of group and locator objects. Try to keep these objects no more than two or three levels deep in the tree. The NDS Group object is created automatically during installation and has DNS/DHCP servers as members of the group. Servers gain rights to DNS and DHCP data within the tree because of their security equivalence to the group object. An example of the group object as seen at the management console in NWADMIN is shown in Figure 23.30.

FIGURE 23.30

Create a group object for DNS/DHCP servers.

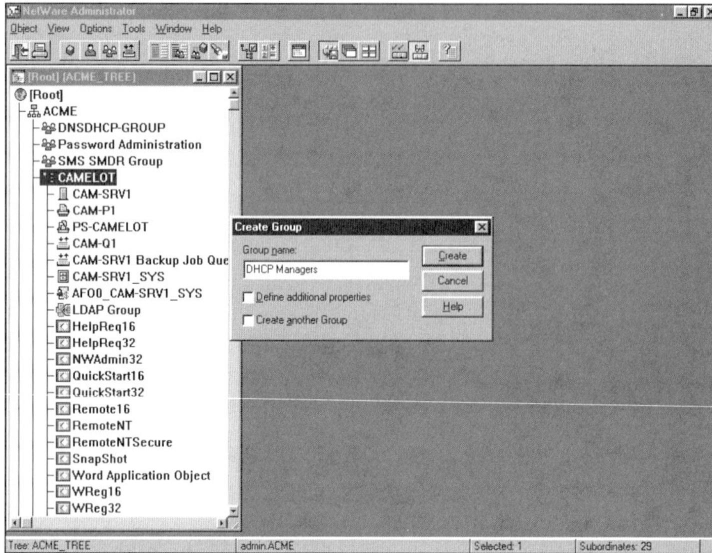

The locator object is used for DNS/DHCP operation. This object contains global defaults; DHCP options; and all DNS and DHCP servers, subnets, subnet pools, and zones in the tree. You create only one locator object per NDS tree. This object is created automatically during the installation of the DNS/DHCP software. An example of how this object is placed in your NDS tree is shown in Figure 23.31.

Using DHCP Over Routers

Novell's DHCP allows a NetWare client to traverse a router and obtain an IP address from the Novell DHCP server. Obtaining an IP address is done by using the subnet pool object to provide an address to a router that is running a BOOTP forwarder. The subnet pool identifies a pool of subnet address assignments and forwards an address to a DHCP or BOOTP forwarder. You must configure your BOOTP forwarder with your DHCP server's address so that the requests are relayed from the clients.

FIGURE 23.31

An example of using the DHCP objects in your NDS tree

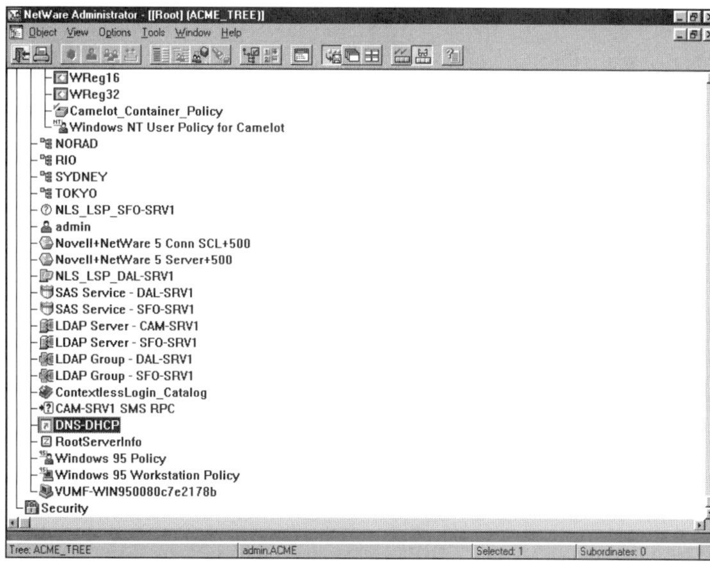

In many situations you may have more than one subnet. Using the subnet pool object in NDS, you can define multiple numbers of subnets.

Using the DNS/DHCP Management Console

The DNS/DHCP Management Console runs on Microsoft Windows 95/98 and Windows NT client workstations with the Novell Client software delivered with NetWare 5. The DNS/DHCP Management Console provides the following management functions from the client's desktop:

- Importing and exporting DNS/DHCP configuration to and from NDS
- Creating, updating, reading, or browsing configuration information
- Viewing DNS and DHCP server status, events, and alerts
- Viewing audit trail logs

After the software installation, existing DNS information is converted to master file format and can be imported to the server where NetWare 5 has been installed. You must use the DNS/DHCP Management Console to import any existing DHCP information. If you have no existing configuration information to import, you must use the DNS/DHCP Management Console to create the necessary objects to support your network. If you have imported configuration information, use the DNS/DHCP Management Console to create the DNS and DHCP server objects prior to operation.

Installing the DNS/DHCP Management Console

Installation of the DNS/DHCP Management Console software on a client workstation requires the following:

- 12.5MB of free disk space.
- 64MB of memory (recommended), 32MB minimum.
- Novell NetWare 5 Client (or higher) software installed.

The installation process uses Install Shield to install the DNS/DHCP Management Console on the client's hard disk. Exit all Windows programs before beginning the software installation.

To install the DNS/DHCP Management Console on a client workstation, complete the following steps:

1. Map a drive to the SYS: volume on a server on which you have installed NetWare 5.
2. Click Start and then select Run.
3. Use the Browse button to select the drive mapped to the SYS: volume on the selected server. Then select the Public and DNSDHCP folders.
4. Double-click Setup and then click OK in the Run dialog box.

You can also begin the installation from the DOS prompt by entering:

```
X:\PUBLIC\DNSDHCP\SETUP.EXE
```

where *x* is the drive mapped to volume SYS on the server on which NetWare 5 has been installed. A welcome window is displayed, and you are reminded to exit all Windows programs before running the Setup program. After the installation has completed, you must restart your computer before attempting to use the DNS/DHCP Management Console.

After the DNS/DHCP Management Console has been installed on a workstation, a DNSDHCP icon is added to the client's desktop and the DNSDHCP folder. Double-click the DNSDHCP icon to launch the DNS/DHCP Management Console. The DNS/DHCP Management Console can also be launched from NetWare Administrator by selecting DNS/DHCP Management Console from the Tools menu.

Using the DNS/DHCP Management Console

You must first log into the tree you want to administer before launching the DNS/DHCP Management Console. Additionally, you must have sufficient rights to use the DNS/DHCP Management Console. All network administrators must have Read and Write rights to the container where the DNS/DHCP Locator and Group objects are located.

Administrators also must have Read and Write rights to the specific containers they manage. For example, if your company has offices in Sydney, Tokyo, and Norad, all administrators would require Read and Write rights to the container storing the Locator and Group objects. However, the administrator in Sydney would require Read and Write rights only to the Sydney part of the tree for the following objects:

- DNS and DHCP server objects
- DNS zone object
- Subnet container object
- Subnet pool object

It is convenient to create an NDS group object for administrators and grant that object the necessary rights as explained in the previous section.

Managing DNS is managing primary and secondary zones. When beginning configuration, it might be better to import the data, especially if you have a large zone. Doing so reduces the chances of error.

If you are using Dynamic DNS (DDNS), when a client receives an address assignment from the DHCP server, a request is made to update NDS. The only way to override DDNS is by using the DNS/DHCP Management Console.

After you have installed and configured your zones, you must still use the DNS/DHCP Management Console to assign a DNS server to service the zones.

Managing DHCP

After configuring your DHCP servers and beginning to provide DHCP services, you can also perform auditing or generate SNMP traps. Deciding which DHCP options to use depends on your implementation. Managing DDNS is complicated because each Subnet Address Range type requires a different configuration.

It is important to understand the difference between static (or manual) and dynamic address assignment. If you use static address assignment, you must use the DNS/DHCP Management Console to assign permanent IP addresses to the clients in your tree. If you are using dynamic address assignment, the DHCP server assigns the address to a client when it starts. You can deny address assignment to clients based on hardware address-based exclusion.

Events and Alerts

You can configure the DNS and DHCP servers to maintain a history of server activity in the events log. Events are activities that are considered significant, such as loading or unloading the server or problems the server encounters. The events logged depend on parameters set on the server's Options tab page.

You can configure DNS and DHCP servers to log major events, all events, or none (the default). Event logs can be saved for future reference. When you are logging events, it is important to pay attention to the event log size. Event logs grow rapidly, especially if you are experiencing or researching problems. Event logs should be maintained or purged regularly to control the amount of disk space used. You can launch the CSAUDIT management utility by typing **CSAUDIT** at the server console.

Configuring DHCP

To manage an organization's IP address database, you must define the global address pool in the form of Class A, B, and C network addresses. The addresses available to a network are managed by the DNS/DHCP Management Console and logically organized into the following types of objects:

- Subnet
- Subnet address range
- IP address
- DHCP server
- Subnet pool

The Novell DHCP server views an organization's network as a collection of DHCP objects.

Importing DHCP Configuration Information

You can use the DNS/DHCP Management Console to import existing DHCP configuration information. The DHCP information should be in DHCP version 2.0 or 3.0 file format. To import existing DHCP configuration information, complete the following steps:

1. Launch the Management Console by double-clicking the icon.
2. Click the DHCP Service tab.
3. Click Import. The Import-File Input dialog box is displayed, requesting the location of the DHCP database file.
4. Enter the drive and path to the DHCP database file, or use the Browse button to navigate your way to the file. After you select the file to import, the path to that file is displayed in the DHCP File dialog box.

5. Click Next. The Import DHCP - Subnet List dialog box is displayed, listing each subnet found in the configuration file.

6. Select the desired subnet or subnets and click Add, or click Add All to import all the subnets on the list.

7. Select the Subnet Context and click Next.

8. The Import dialog box is displayed, indicating the subnet context and the subnets to import. (The subnet address and name are displayed on the list.)

9. Click Import.

10. The Server Input dialog box is displayed, prompting you to select a default NCP server to manage the newly imported subnet.

11. Use the Browse button to select the target server and click OK.

If an error occurs during the importing process, an error message will be displayed, and the Details button will be enabled, allowing you to display more information.

Setting Up DHCP

This section provides basic information about the steps required to set up DHCP. This section does not describe how to enable all the available features. The following steps must be completed prior to setting up DHCP:

1. Load NetWare 5 on the selected server or servers.

2. Load the Novell Client software delivered with NetWare 5 on client computers that will be used to administer DNS and DHCP.

3. Install the DNS/DHCP Management Console on client computers that will be used to administer DNS and DHCP.

Logging into the Tree

To complete the steps required to set up DHCP, you must first log into the tree where NetWare 5 has been installed. To log into the server, complete the following steps:

1. Right-click Network Neighborhood and select NetWare Login on a NetWare 5 client workstation on which you have installed the DNS/DHCP Management Console.

   The NetWare Client login dialog box is displayed.

2. Under the Login tab, enter your user name and password, and then click Connection.

3. Under the Connection tab, enter the Tree, Server, and Context of the server on which you have installed NetWare 5, and then click OK.

Launching the DNS/DHCP Management Console

Launch the DNS/DHCP Management Console by double-clicking its icon. The DNS/DHCP Management Console can be installed on a client workstation, or it can be accessed from the Tools menu of the NetWare Administrator utility. When the DNS/DHCP Management Console loads, you are prompted to enter the NDS Tree Name where you want to set up DHCP.

Setting Global DHCP Options You use the DNS/DHCP Management Console to set global DHCP options. Setting global DHCP options is not required to set up DHCP, however. To set global DHCP options, complete the following steps:

1. Click the DHCP Service tab of the DNS/DHCP Management Console.

2. Click Global Preferences on the toolbar. The Global DHCP Options tab of the Global Preferences dialog box is displayed, listing code, name, and value of any global DHCP options selected. Two other tab pages are available. One shows any global DHCP defaults set for the selected object; the other is the DHCP Options table. An example of this dialog box is shown in Figure 23.32.

FIGURE 23.32

Setting global preferences for DHCP

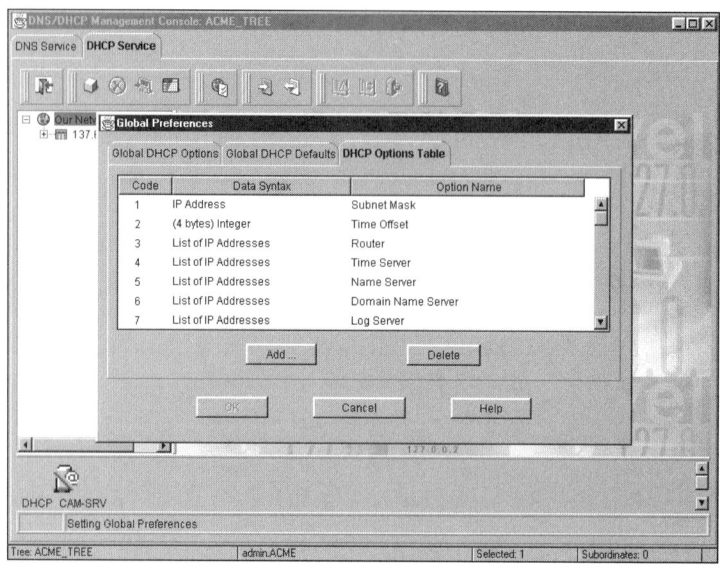

3. Click the Global DHCP Defaults tab and then click Add. The Add Exclude Hardware Address dialog box is displayed. Any devices or addresses you configure here will be excluded from any global defaults or global options. An asterisk (*) can be used as a wildcard character to select a range of addresses to exclude. The asterisk can be used only as a trailing character, however. It cannot be used as a prefix or in the middle of a hardware address. The default delimiter for hardware addresses is a colon (:), but a dash (–) or a period (.) can also be used. Only one type of delimiter can be used within an address.

4. Click in the Hardware Type field to select a type of hardware to exclude, and enter an address in the Exclude Hardware Address field. An example of this is shown in Figure 23.33. You can use the wildcard character (*) and a different delimiter if you choose.

FIGURE 23.33

Excluding hardware in the Global Preferences section

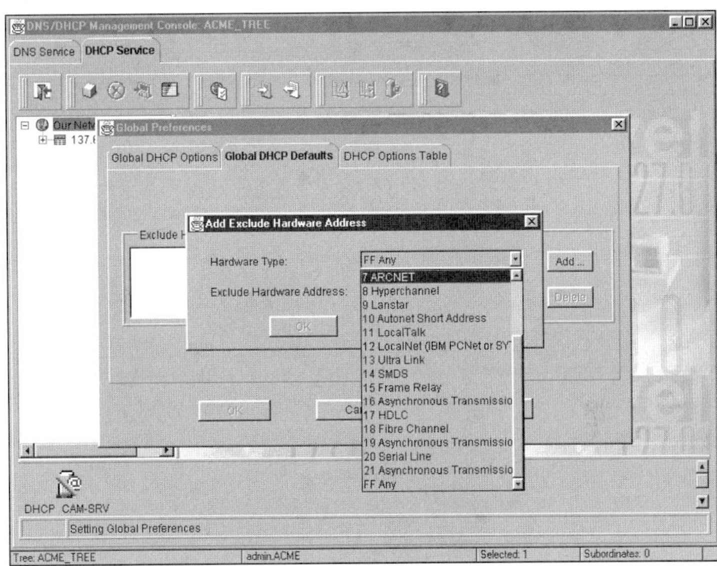

5. Click the DHCP Options Table tab. A list of DHCP options is displayed, listing all available DHCP options including codes, data syntax, and the option name.

6. Select a desired option from those listed and then click Add. When you select a DHCP option, if any additional information is required to support the option, you are prompted to provide that information. For example, if you select option 85 for NDS Server, you are prompted to supply the IP address of the NDS Server.

7. Provide any requested information specific to the selected option (as in Figure 23.34) and then click OK. The Global Preferences dialog box is redisplayed, listing the global options that have been set.

8. When you have completed selecting global DHCP options, click OK.

FIGURE 23.34

Selecting DHCP options from the Options table

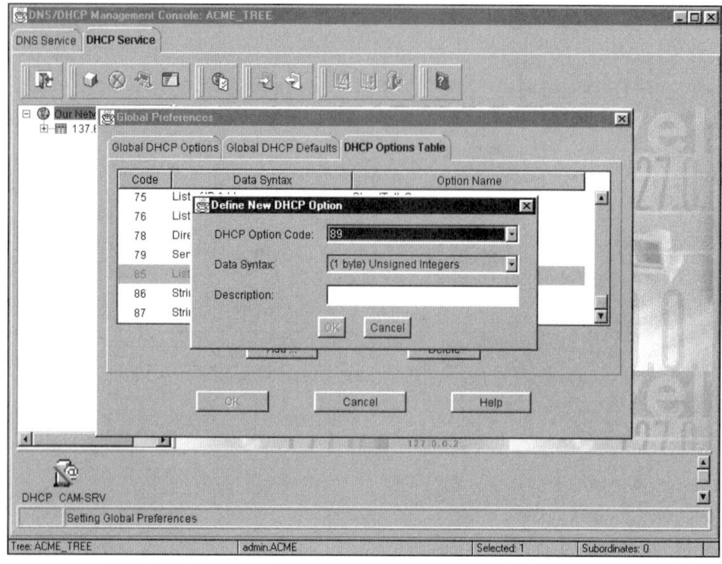

Creating a DHCP Server Object

You use the DNS/DHCP Management Console to create and set up a DHCP server object. A DHCP server object can be created or located under any of the following objects:

- Organization (O)
- Organization unit (OU)
- Country (C)
- Locality (L)

To create and set up a DHCP server object, complete the following steps:

1. Click the DHCP Service tab of the DNS/DHCP Management Console. The Our Network object is the only object displayed on the DNS/DHCP Management Console's left pane.

2. Click Create on the toolbar. The Create New DHCP Object dialog box is displayed, enabling you to create a DHCP server object, a subnet object, or a subnet pool object. An example of this dialog box is shown in Figure 23.35.

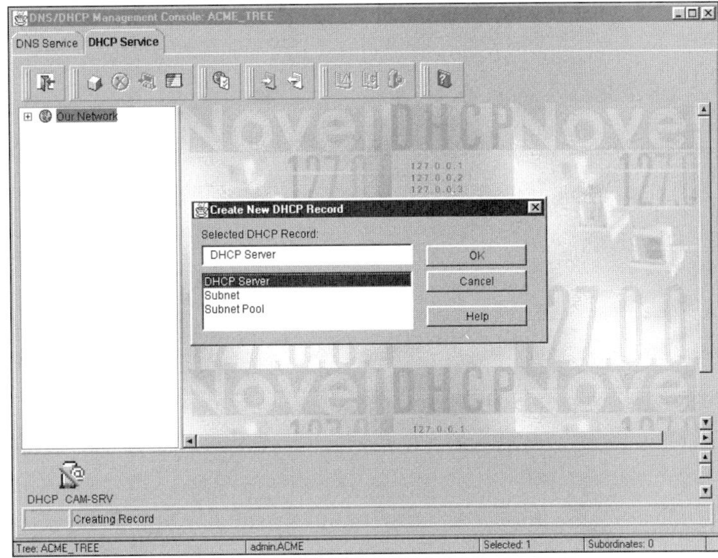

FIGURE 23.35

Creating a DHCP server object

3. Select DHCP Server and click OK. The Create DHCP Server dialog box is displayed, prompting you to select a server object.

4. Use the Browse button to select a server within the context and then click Create. The DHCP server object is created and displayed in the lower pane of the DNS/DHCP Management Console. An example of selecting a DHCP server is shown in Figure 23.36.

FIGURE 23.36

Selecting a DHCP server object to be created

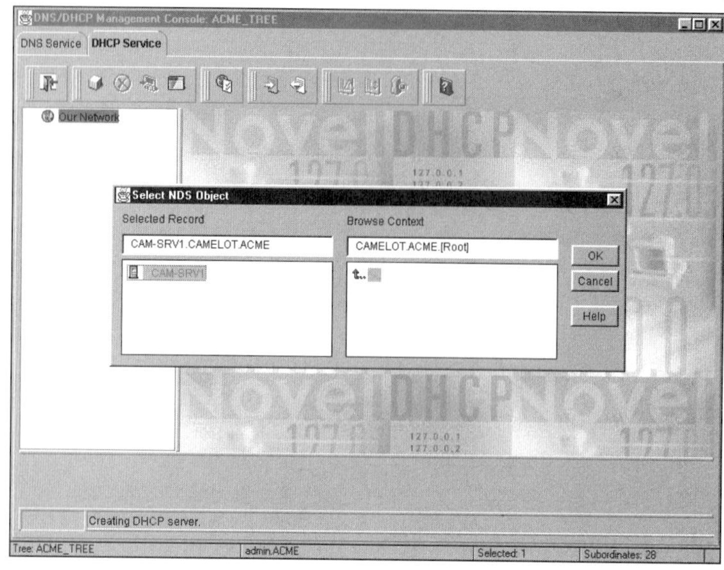

Creating a Subnet Object

You use the DNS/DHCP Management Console to create and set up a DHCP subnet object for each of the subnets to which you will assign addresses. To create and set up a subnet object, complete the following steps:

1. Click the DHCP Service tab of the DNS/DHCP Management Console. The Our Network object will be the only object displayed on the DNS/DHCP Management Console's left pane.

2. Click Create on the toolbar. The Create New DHCP Object dialog box is displayed, enabling you to create a DHCP server, a subnet, or a subnet pool object.

3. Select Subnet and click OK. The Create Subnet dialog box is displayed. For each subnet you create, enter the following information in the fields provided: subnet name, NDS context, subnet address, and subnet mask. If you have set up a default DHCP server, its name is displayed and can be changed. You can click the Define Additional Properties check box to provide more detailed configuration, including DHCP options specific to each subnet. An example of this dialog box is shown in Figure 23.37.

Creating a new subnet for DHCP

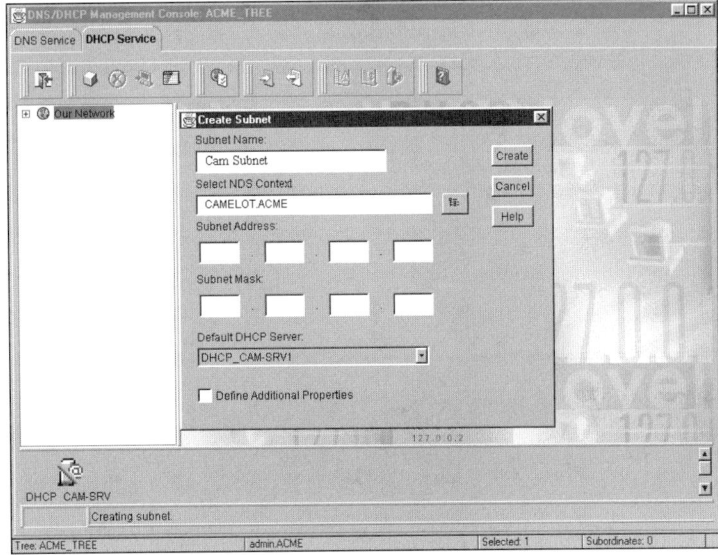

4. Enter the required information and then click Create. The DHCP subnet object is created and displayed in the left pane of the DNS/DHCP Management Console.

Creating Subnet Address Ranges

You also use the DNS/DHCP Management Console to create and set up subnet address range objects for each pool of addresses you want to be dynamically assigned by DHCP. To create and set up a subnet address range object, complete the following steps:

1. Click the DHCP Service tab of the DNS/DHCP Management Console.

2. Select the subnet object under which you want to create the subnet address range object, and then click Create. The Create New DHCP Record dialog box is displayed, as shown in Figure 23.38.

FIGURE 23.38

Creating a subnet range in the DNS/DHCP utility

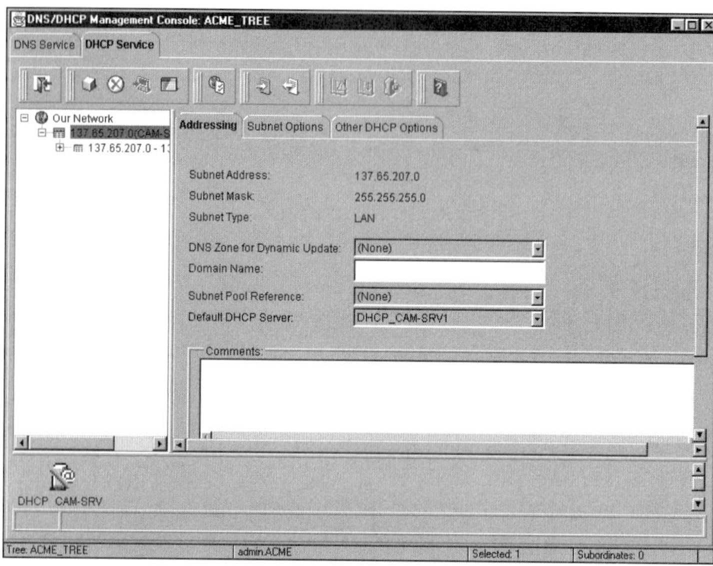

3. Select Subnet Address Range and click OK. The Create New Subnet Address Range dialog box is displayed.

4. Enter a name for the subnet address range, specify the range's starting and ending address, and then click Create. If you click the Define Additional Properties check box, the range's detailed information dialog box is displayed, enabling you to provide more detailed configuration information. An example of the Create Subnet Address Range dialog box is shown in Figure 23.39.

Creating IP Address Objects

You use the DNS/DHCP Management Console to create and set up any IP address objects to be assigned to specific devices or to be excluded from dynamic assignment. Create an IP address object for each such device or address. Assigning a specific address to a client requires you to specify the client's media-access control (MAC) address or Client ID.

FIGURE 23.39

Specifying a subnet address range

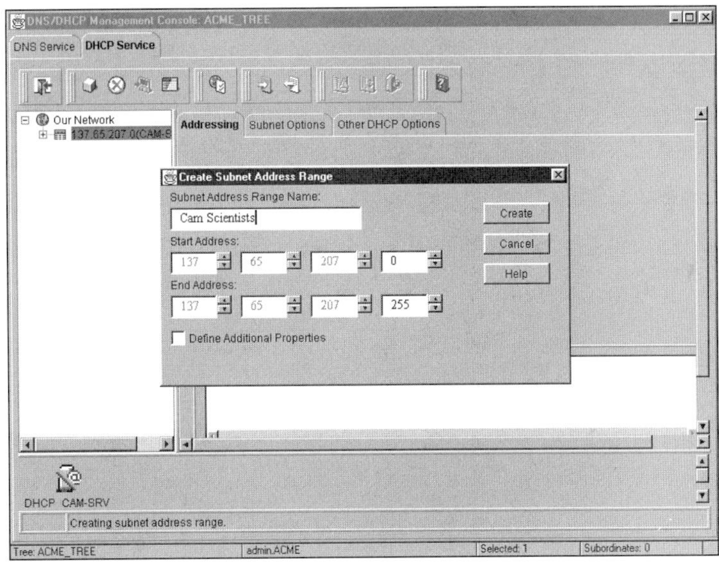

If you have set up subnets and subnet address ranges, you are not required to set up individual IP addresses unless you want to perform manual address assignment or exclude addresses from assignment. To create and set up an IP address object, complete the following steps:

1. Click the DHCP Service tab of the DNS/DHCP Management Console.
2. Select the subnet object of the target IP address and then click Create on the toolbar. The Create New DHCP Object dialog box is displayed.
3. Select IP Address and click OK. The Create IP Address dialog box is displayed.
4. Enter the IP address to be assigned or excluded, select the assignment type, and then click Create as shown in Figure 23.40.

FIGURE 23.40

Creating an IP address for a single user

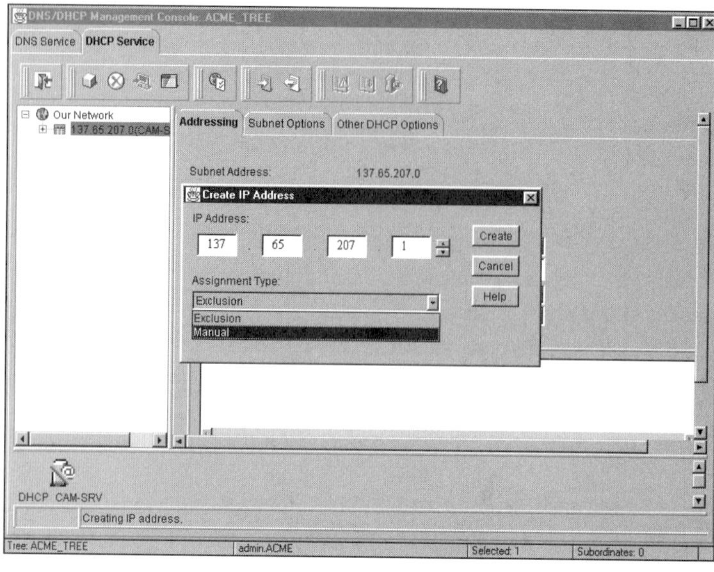

If you choose Manual Assignment Type, you must provide information for either the Client Identifier or MAC Address fields. You can also specify the MAC type by clicking in the field; the default is FF, Any.

Starting the DHCP Server

After you have created and set up a DHCP server and configured the NDS objects required for DHCP, enter the following command at the DHCP server console:

```
LOAD DHCPSRVR
```

After you load DHCPSRVR.NLM, the DHCP server can respond to client requests and assign IP addresses.

Configuring Clients to Use DHCP

Configuring clients to use DHCP is performed at the client workstation. To configure Windows 95/98 and Windows NT client workstations to use DHCP, complete the following steps:

1. At the client desktop, select Start → Settings → Control Panel, and then double-click Network. The Network dialog box is displayed, listing the network components installed on the client workstation.

2. Select TCP/IP for this adapter card and click Properties. The TCP/IP Properties dialog box is displayed, usually showing the IP Address tab page.

3. Select Obtain an IP Address Automatically, and then click OK. The next time the client starts up, it will send a request to the DHCP server for an IP address.

NOTE

Any client configuration settings override the configuration received from a DHCP server. The only exception is the hostname parameter set on the DNS Configuration tab of TCP/IP Properties dialog box.

Detailed DHCP Configuration

This section provides detailed information about configuring DHCP objects using the DNS/DHCP Management Console. All the procedures in this section assume that you have already launched the utility and that you have selected the DHCP Service tab.

Modifying a DHCP Server Object After a DHCP server object has been created, you can double-click the server icon to display and modify detailed information about the DHCP server object. The DHCP server object's detailed information dialog box displays two tab pages, Server and Options.

On the Server tab page, you can view the Subnet Address Ranges Serviced by This Server and Subnets Serviced by This Server. You can enter comments (up to 256 characters) about the server in the comments field.

On the Options tab page, you can configure policies specific to this DHCP server. You can configure the Set SNMP Traps Option parameter for None (default), Major Events, or All. You can configure the Set Audit Trail and Alerts Option parameter for None (default), Major Events, or All. You can also set the Enable Audit Trail Log on this page (the default is not enabled).

You can also configure the Mobile User Options parameter on the Options tab page to the following:

- No mobile users allowed
- Allow mobile users, but delete a previously assigned address (default)
- Allow mobile users, but do not delete a previously assigned address

Another option available on the DHCP Server Options tab page is Ping Enable. Click this check box to have the server ping an address before the address is assigned to a device. Doing so ensures that the address is not already in use; however, pinging the address also increases network traffic.

Modifying an Existing Subnet Object

After a subnet object has been created, you can use the DNS/DHCP Management Console to display three tab pages of detailed information about the subnet object that include Address, Subnet Options, and Other DHCP Options.

The Address tab page displays Subnet Address, Mask, and Type attributes from information entered when the object was created. If changes are required to these attributes, you must delete the subnet object and recreate it. If you are going to use Dynamic DNS, this is the page where you configure the DNS zone for dynamic updating (DDNS) and domain name.

You can modify the subnet pool reference from the default (none) to the subnet pool to which this subnet object is assigned. You can also modify the subnet's default DHCP server on the Address tab page and enter up to 256 characters of information in the Comments field.

You can configure lease types on the Subnet Options tab page. A lease type can be permanent or timed. If you specify leases to be timed, specify the lease duration in days, hours, and minutes. You can also specify the settings for Set Boot Parameter Options on the Subnet Options tab page.

DHCP options can be configured from the Other DHCP Options tab page. Any options that are set for this subnet are displayed here. You can set additional DHCP options by clicking Modify, which displays the Modify DHCP Options dialog box. You pick a DHCP option from the Available DHCP Options list and then click Add.

Click Default to display the Default DHCP Options dialog box listing all DHCP options and values configured for a subnet.

Modifying a Subnet Address Range Object

To modify a subnet address range object, you must first select the object, which displays in the left pane of the DHCP Service dialog box. Clicking on the subnet address range object displays its detailed information in the right pane and enables modifications. The following range type options are available:

- Dynamic BOOTP
- Dynamic DHCP with Automatic Host Name Generation
- Dynamic DHCP
- Dynamic BOOTP and DHCP (the default)
- Excluded

You can also specify a DHCP server other than the default server for this subnet address range object.

Modifying an Existing IP Address Object

After an IP address object has been created, its detailed information dialog box displays three tab pages:

- Address
- Usage
- Other DHCP Options

On the Address tab page, the IP address field of the object is displayed in read-only format. You can set the Assignment Type parameter to Manual or Excluded, and you can specify a client identifier. You can change the MAC type from the default FF, Any to any of the following:

- 15, Frame Relay
- 16, Asynchronous Transfer Mode (ATM)
- 17, HDLC
- 18, Fibre Channel
- 19, Asynchronous Transfer Mode (ATM)
- 20, Serial Line
- 21, Asynchronous Transfer Mode (ATM)

You can enter the IP address's MAC address, hostname, and DNS domain suffix, and you can identify an NDS object to use a specific IP address on the Address tab page. The Usage tab page displays the IP Address Lease Expiration option, which can be either Permanent or Timed. If Timed is selected, the year, month, day, hour, and minute that the lease expires are displayed.

DHCP options can be configured from the Other DHCP Options tab page. Any options that are set for this IP address object are displayed here. You can set additional DHCP options by clicking Modify.

Creating a Subnet Pool Object

A subnet pool object is a logical group of related subnet objects of the same type. A subnet pool object can be created or located under any of the following objects:

- Organization (O)
- Organization unit (OU)
- Country (C)
- Locality (L)

To create a new subnet pool object, complete the following steps:

1. Click Create on the toolbar.
2. Select Subnet Pool and click OK.
3. Enter a unique name for the subnet pool object.
4. Use the Browse button to select the NDS context in which to create the subnet pool object.

After a subnet pool object has been created, you can select it and check the Define Additional Properties check box to display the detailed information dialog box and to add subnet objects to and remove them from the subnet pool object. Only subnet objects with the same range type can be added to a subnet pool object.

Modifying a Subnet Pool Object

Click Add to bring up a dialog box with a list of available subnet objects (either LAN or WAN) to be added to the list. After a subnet object has been added to the subnet pool object, its NDS distinguished name is updated in the subnet object's subnet pool list attribute.

Using DNS

Plan to install and operate a primary name server and at least one secondary name server on your NDS tree. The secondary name servers provide load balancing and fault tolerance to your DNS implementation.

When you configure your zone, the primary name server is considered authoritative for the zone, meaning that it contains the most up-to-date information about the zone and all the hosts within it.

A secondary name server receives its zone data from the primary name server. When it starts up and at periodic intervals, the secondary name server queries the primary name server to determine whether the information it contains has been changed. If the zone information in the secondary name server is older than the zone information in the primary name server, a zone transfer occurs and the secondary name server receives the zone information from the primary name server.

Planning and Implementing Zones

If you are running a primary name server and providing DNS service for a zone, the size or geography of your network might require creating subzones within the zone. Keep the zone data as a separate partition, and replicate the partition to all places on your network where you have a name server for the zone. Doing so enables independent replication of the zone data and also provides a degree of fault tolerance in the case of server downtime.

The Novell DNS Server as a Primary Name Server

You must install the Novell DNS server as a primary name server to have authoritative control over your zone and to take advantage of Dynamic DNS (DDNS), the dynamic updating of DNS by DHCP.

When operating the Novell DNS server as a primary name server, you use the DNS/DHCP Management Console to make configuration changes. When you operate a primary name server, the zone data can receive dynamic updates from DHCP servers. Non-Novell secondary name servers can transfer data in from the Novell primary name server.

Configuring DNS

The DNS/DHCP Management Console provides similar interfaces for configuring both DNS and DHCP. The left pane of the DNS Service dialog box displays all DNS resources, the right pane displays detailed information about the object selected in the left pane, and the lower pane displays all DNS servers.

The view in the left pane of the DNS Service dialog box is similar to the DNS hierarchical structure, with the virtual All Zones object as the root of the three hierarchical levels shown. The first level contains the zone objects, the second level contains the Resource Record Set (RRSet) objects, and the third level contains the individual resource records. An example of this is shown in Figure 23.41.

The view in the right pane of the DNS Service dialog box provides detailed information about DNS objects selected in the left pane. The detailed information varies, depending on the type of object selected. For example, a zone object's detailed information includes tab pages for Attributes and Start of Authority, whereas the detailed information for resource records provides only an Attributes page.

The lower pane of the DNS Service dialog box displays all currently existing DNS server objects in the NDS tree and a description of their operational status.

FIGURE 23.41

A view of the attributes for the DNS Service window

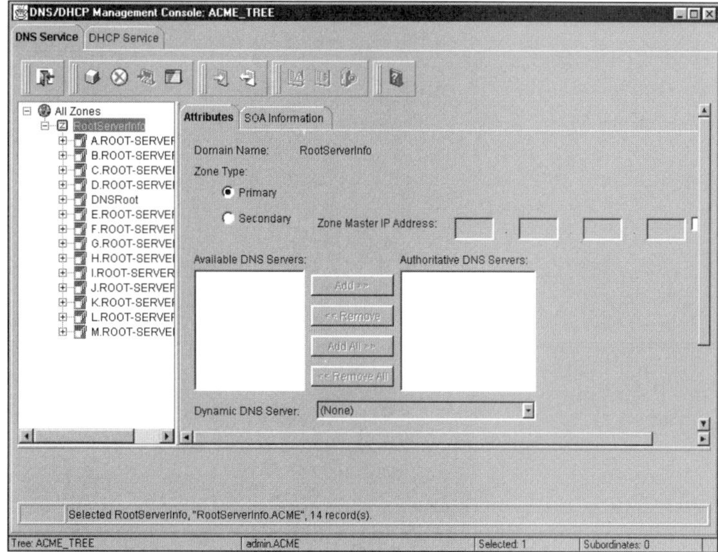

Importing DNS Configuration Information

You can use the Novell DNS/DHCP Management Console to import existing DNS configuration information. The DNS information should be in DNS BIND Master file format. To import existing DNS configuration information using the Management Console, complete the following steps:

1. Launch the DNS/DHCP Management Console by double-clicking the icon, or load it through NWADMIN.

2. Click the DNS Service tab.

3. Click Import DNS Database. The Import-File Input dialog box is displayed, requesting the location of the DNS BIND Master file as shown in Figure 23.42.

FIGURE 23.42

Importing an existing DNS configuration information file

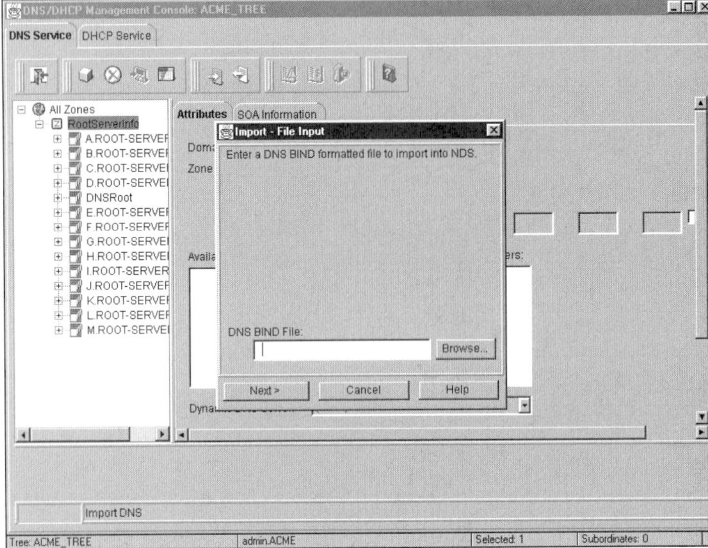

4. Enter the drive and path to the DNS database file, or click the Browse button to navigate your way to the file. After you select the file to import, the path to that file is displayed in the DNS File dialog box.

5. Click Next. The Import DNS - Zone List dialog box is displayed, listing each zone found in the configuration file.

6. Select the Zone Context and click Next.

7. The Import dialog box is displayed, indicating the zone context and the zones to import. The subnet address and name are displayed in the list.

8. Click Import.

9. The Server Input dialog box is displayed, prompting you to select a default NetWare server to manage the newly imported zone.

10. Use the Browse button to select the target server, and then click OK.

Setting Up DNS

This section describes how to set up DNS for a common environment. Your situation may vary from this description depending on your network configuration. The following steps must be completed before setting up DNS:

1. Install Novell NetWare 5 on the selected server or servers.

2. Load the Novell Client software delivered with NetWare 5 on client computers that will be used to administer DNS and DHCP.

3. Install the DNS/DHCP Management Console on client computers that will be used to administer DNS and DHCP.

Creating a DNS Server Object

Use the DNS/DHCP Management Console to create and set up a DNS server object for each DNS server you plan to operate. To create and set up a DNS server object, complete the following steps:

1. Click the DNS Service tab of the DNS/DHCP Management Console, if necessary. The All Zones object is the only object displayed on the DNS/DHCP Management Console's left pane.

2. Click Create on the toolbar. The Create New DNS Object dialog box shown in Figure 23.43 is displayed, enabling you to create a DNS server object or a zone object.

3. Select DNS Server and click OK. The Create New DNS Server dialog box is displayed, prompting you to select a DNS server object.

4. Enter the desired server's name or use the Browse button to select the server.

5. Enter the server's domain name and then click Create. The DNS server object is created and displayed in the lower pane of the DNS/DHCP Management Console.

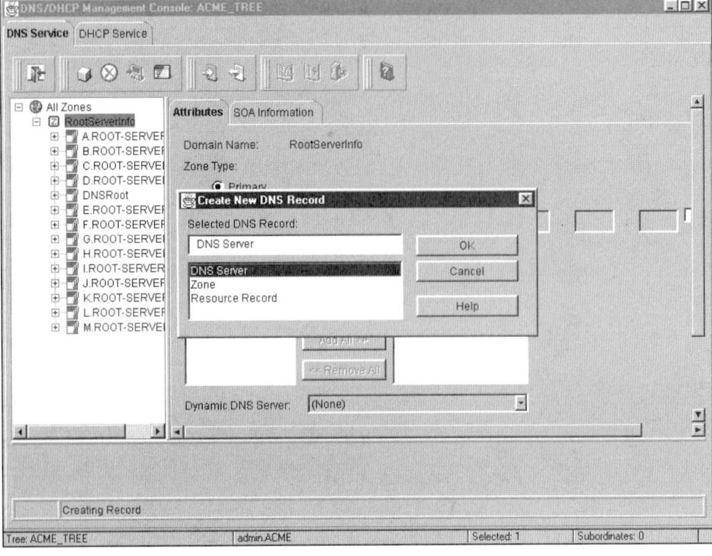

Creating a DNS server object

Creating a Primary DNS Zone Object

After you create a DNS server object, use the DNS/DHCP Management Console to create and set up a primary DNS zone. To create a primary DNS zone object, complete the following steps:

1. Click the DNS Service tab of the DNS/DHCP Management Console. The All Zones object and the Root Server Info zone object are displayed in the DNS/DHCP Management Console's left pane.

2. Click Create on the toolbar, select Zone, and then click OK. The Create Zone dialog box is displayed. The default setting is to create a new, primary zone. An example of this dialog box is shown in Figure 23.44.

FIGURE 23.44

Creating a new primary DNS Zone

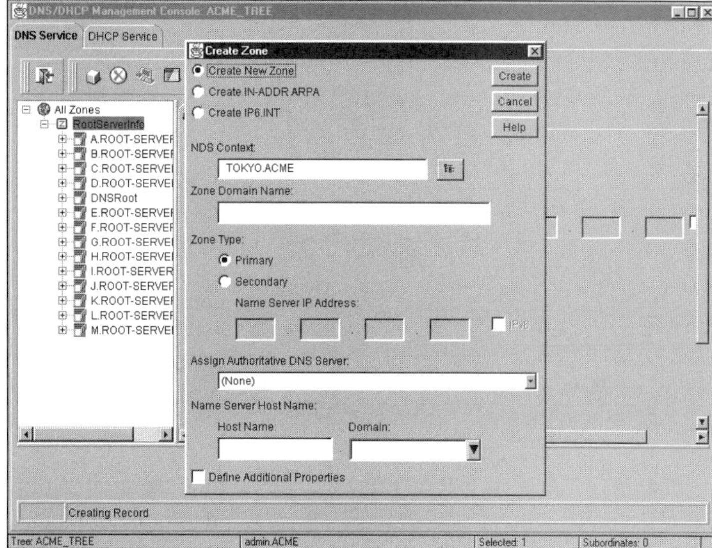

3. Use the Browse button to select the NDS context for the zone.

4. Enter a name for the zone object in the Zone Domain Name field.

5. In the Assign Authoritative DNS Server field, select a DNS server. Once you have selected an authoritative DNS server, the Name Server Host Name field is filled with the name of the authoritative DNS server.

6. Click Create. A message is displayed indicating that the new zone has been created, and you are reminded to create the Address record for the host server domain name and corresponding Pointer record in the IN-ADDR.ARPA zone (if you have not already done so).

Starting the DNS Server

After you have created and set up a DNS server object and a DNS zone object, enter the following command at the DNS server console:

```
LOAD NAMED
```

After NAMED.NLM is loaded, the DNS server can respond to queries for the zone.

Configuring Clients to Use DNS

Clients are configured to use DNS at the client workstation. To configure Windows NT or Windows 95/98 client workstations to use DNS, complete the following steps:

1. At the client desktop, select Start → Settings → Control Panel, and then double-click Network. The Network dialog box is displayed, listing the network components installed on the client workstation.
2. Select TCP/IP, and then click Properties. The TCP/IP Properties dialog box is displayed, usually showing the IP Address tab page.
3. Click the DNS Configuration tab.
4. Provide a hostname and domain name for each client.
5. Enter the IP address of DNS servers for this client in the search order of preference, and then click OK. The client can now send DNS queries to the DNS name server.

Creating a Zone Object

The DNS zone object is an NDS container object that comprises Resource Record Set (RRSet) objects and resource records. This section provides information about how to create a Secondary DNS zone object and an IN-ADDR.ARPA zone object.

Creating a Secondary DNS Zone Object

After you create a DNS server object, you can use the DNS/DHCP Management Console to create and set up a Secondary DNS zone object. To create a Secondary DNS zone object, you must provide the IP address of the DNS server that will perform zone in transfers for the secondary zone.

1. Click the DNS Service tab of the DNS/DHCP Management Console.
2. Click Create on the toolbar, select Zone, and then click OK.
3. Use the Browse button to select the NDS context for the zone.

4. Enter a name for the zone object in the Zone Domain Name field.

5. Under Zone Type, select Secondary. When you select a secondary type zone, the Assign Authoritative DNS Server field and the Name Server Host Name field entries are optional.

6. Enter the IP address of the DNS server that will provide zone out transfers for this secondary zone. You can optionally select to assign an authoritative DNS server.

7. Click Create. A message is displayed indicating that the new zone has been created, and you are reminded to create the Address record for the host server domain name and corresponding Pointer record in the IN-ADDR.ARPA zone (if you have not already done so).

Creating an IN-ADDR.ARPA Zone Object

After you create a DNS server object, you can use the DNS/DHCP Management Console to create and set up an IN-ADDR.ARPA zone object. To create an IN-ADDR.ARPA zone object, complete the following steps:

1. Click the DNS Service tab of the DNS/DHCP Management Console.

2. Click Create on the toolbar, select Zone, and then click OK. The Create Zone dialog box is displayed. The default setting is to create a new, primary zone.

3. Select Create IN-ADDR.ARPA.

4. Use the Browse button to select the NDS context for the zone.

5. Enter an IP address in the Zone Domain Name field. After you enter the IP address, it is reversed and prepended to .IN-ADDR.ARPA and reflected in the box below the Zone Domain Name field.

6. Under Zone Type, select Primary or Secondary. If you select Secondary, you must enter the IP address of the DNS Name Server that will provide zone out transfers to this zone.

7. In the Assign Authoritative DNS Server field, select a DNS server. Once you have selected an authoritative DNS server, the Name Server Host Name field is filled with the name of the authoritative DNS server.

8. Click Create, and then click Save.

Creating an IP6.INT Zone Object

After you create a DNS server object, you can use the DNS/DHCP Management Console to create and set up an IP6.INT zone object. Only one IP6.INT DNS zone object can exist in an NDS tree. To create an IP6.INT zone object, complete the following steps:

1. Click the DNS Service tab of the DNS/DHCP Management Console.

2. Click Create on the toolbar, select Zone, and then click OK. The Create Zone dialog box is displayed. The default setting is to create a new, primary zone.

3. Select Create IP6.INT.

4. Use the Browse button to select the NDS context for the zone.

5. Under Zone Type, select Primary or Secondary. If you select Secondary, you must enter the IP address of the DNS Name Server that will provide zone out transfers to this zone.

6. For a Primary zone, click in the Assign Authoritative DNS Server field to select a DNS server to service the zone.

7. Click Create, and then click Save.

Modifying a Zone Object

After you have created a zone object, you can modify it and provide more detailed configuration information. To modify a new zone object's attributes, complete the following steps:

1. Select the zone object you want to modify.

2. To change a Primary zone to a Secondary zone, click the Secondary check box and provide the Primary DNS Server's IP address in the Zone Master IP Address field.

3. To designate a DNS name server to be an Authoritative DNS Server, select one or more entries from the Available DNS Servers list and click Add. The selected DNS name server's name is moved from the list of Available DNS Servers to the list of Authoritative DNS Servers. If only one server is available, that server automatically becomes the designated server.

4. To select a server from the list of Authoritative DNS Servers to become the designated server, click the Dynamic DNS Server field.

5. Type any relevant comments about the zone directly into the Comments field.

To view or modify a new zone object's Start of Authority information, click the SOA Information tab. The following information is displayed:

- Zone master
- E-mail address
- Serial number
- Interval values:
  - Refresh (default is 180 minutes)
  - Retry (default is 60 minutes)
  - Expire (default is 168 hours)
  - Minimal caching (default is 24 hours)

Creating Resource Records

A *resource record* is a piece of information about a domain name. Each resource record contains information about a particular piece of data within the domain. To create a new resource record, complete the following steps:

1. Select the zone object under which you want to create a new resource record. The Create New DNS Object dialog box is displayed.

2. Select Resource Record and click OK. The Create Resource Record dialog box is displayed, prompting you for the domain name of the resource record you want to create. You can select the A record (the default) to create an Address record or the CNAME record to create a canonical name, or you can check the Others box to create a resource record from the displayed list of supported resource record types.

3. Enter the domain name you want to associate with this resource record. The name you select is prepended to the domain name of the zone under which the resource record will be created.

4. Enter any additional information required for the resource record type, and then click Create. After you have created a resource record, its type cannot be modified. If changes are required, you must delete the resource record and create a new one.

NOTE

Start of Authority (SOA) is defined as part of a zone object's attributes, and a Pointer (PTR) record is created automatically when any new A resource record or IPv6 (AAAA) resource record is created if the IN-ADDR.ARPA zone exists.

If you are creating a new resource record within an existing RRSet object, the Domain Name field is displayed in read-only format in the Create Resource Record dialog box. The domain name was defined for the RRSet object and must be the same for subordinate resource record objects.

Summary

One of the notable new features in NetWare 5 is pure IP. Pure IP enables you to run the TCP/IP protocol stack on both the client and the server. NetWare 5 offers several options to help you migrate your company's network from IPX to pure IP. The Compatibility Mode processes allow you to run IPX-dependent NLMs and applications on a pure IP network. The migration agent translates protocols between a pure IP network and an IPX network. As a result, you can continue to use IPX-dependent NLMs and applications, and you can migrate some segments of your company's network to pure IP while maintaining IPX on other segments. Users on the IPX network can then continue to use services on the pure IP network, and vice versa.

Appendixes

APPENDIX A

The CD-ROM Set Included with This Book

This appendix includes information and installation instructions for the contents of the three CD-ROMs included with this book. The CD-ROMs contain:

Disc 1:

- NetWare 5 Operating System — 3-User Demo

Disc 2:

- Client Software (including Z.E.N.works Starter Pack)

Disc 3:

- Complete NetWare 5 Online Documentation
- Visio Solution Pack for NDS (30-day trial version)
- Visio Professional 5.0 Test Drive (30-day trial version)

NetWare 5 Operating System — 3-User Version

The NetWare 5 Operating System CD-ROM (Disc 1) that comes with this book contains a 3-user version with the NetWare 5 license embedded in the NetWare 5 code. No separate license disk is required to install this software. During installation, the license will be loaded from the CD itself. Additionally, this software has no expiration date, so you can install it at any time.

NetWare 5 Minimum Requirements

Here are the minimum requirements for server hardware in order to run NetWare 5:

- Server-class PC with a Pentium processor
- VGA display adapter

- 64MB of RAM
- 600MB available disk space (50MB for the boot partition, 550MB for the NetWare partition)
- Network board
- CD-ROM drive
- PS/2 or serial mouse recommended

Installing NetWare 5

The following steps guide you through the installation of NetWare 5 on your system:

1. Create a 50MB DOS boot partition.
2. Install a CD-ROM drive and drivers according to your hardware vendor's instructions.
3. Insert the NetWare 5 Operating System CD-ROM (Disc 1) and type **INSTALL**.
4. Accept the License Agreement.
5. Choose the server language, if prompted.
6. Select New Server.
7. Confirm computer settings.
8. When prompted for the License Diskette, select the license located in the \LICENSE directory on the NetWare 5 Operating System CD-ROM. *Please note that there is no separate license diskette.*
9. Complete the installation by following the on-screen instructions.

For more in-depth instructions on the installation of NetWare 5, refer to Chapter 2.

Client Software

Disk 2 of the CD-ROM set contains the Client Software from Novell, which includes the Z.E.N.works Starter Pack.

Installing Client Software

Follow these steps to install the Client Software:

1. On a computer running Windows, insert the Client Software CD-ROM (Disc 2) and run WINSETUP.EXE.
2. Select a language for the installation.
3. Select a platform for the installation.
4. Select the software to install.
5. Complete the installation by following the on-screen instructions.

For more detailed information on the installation of Novell Clients, refer to Chapter 17.

NetWare 5 Online Documentation

Complete NetWare 5 Online Documentation is included on Disc 3 of the CD-ROM set that accompanies this book. To install the documentation on your hard drive:

1. Insert Disc 3 of the CD-ROM set included with this book.

2. Go to Start → Run → Browse. Select the D drive.

3. Go to the NOVDOCS directory, select SETUP.EXE, and select OK.

4. Follow the on-screen instructions to complete the installation.

The Visio Solution Pack for NDS

The Visio Solution Pack for NDS (Novell Directory Services) is a powerful add-on tool for use with Visio Professional 5.0 (a Test Drive trial version is included on Disc 3 of the CD-ROM set) to design and document Novell directory trees. The Solution Pack for NDS will minimize the time network managers spend implementing and upgrading directory-enabled networks by providing a clear, hierarchical, and graphical view of those networks. The Visio Solution Pack for NDS is a 30-day demonstration CD and expires 30 days from the time you first install the CD.

This product contains the following key features:

- **Over 40 predrawn SmartShapes symbols for container and leaf objects** — Each shape includes the custom properties, such as login name and network address, that you need when creating new objects in the NDS database.

- **Automatic diagramming of existing NDS trees** — Visio Professional and the SolutionPack automatically diagram existing directory trees by reading a text file exported from NDS using Novell's VExport utility, available from `www.visio.com`. The diagram will include the standard schema, without extensions, complete with selected attributes populating custom properties data fields.

- **Capability to export Visio diagrams to the NDS database** — You can create diagrams of new trees using Visio Professional and the Solution Pack and then use Novell's VImport utility to write the new and updated objects from a Visio diagram to the NDS database.

- **Automatic diagramming of top and bottom levels of the directory tree** — Wizard-style dialog boxes guide you through diagram creation, speeding the process and ensuring proper line routing.
- **Online Help and SmartShapes Help that follow Novell standards** — More than a collection of shapes, the Solution Pack for NDS includes part of Novell's NDS design principles, ensuring correct and efficient structures for new and updated directory trees.
- **Easy integration with Microsoft Office and the Internet** — You can embed NDS tree diagrams in Microsoft Office documents or save the drawings as HTML pages for communication over the Web.

NOTE

To download Novell's VImport and VExport Utilities free of charge, please read and agree to the License Agreement at `www.visio.com`. These utilities are subutilities derived from Novell's OImport and OExport utilities. The complete versions of these tools and technical support information can be obtained from Novell Consulting at `www/novell.com/consulting`.

System Requirements

You must have the installed version of Visio Professional 5.0 or higher, full license, or Test Drive version (included on Disc 3). Your system must meet these requirements:

- Microsoft Windows 95/98 or Windows NT 4.0
- 486/66 processor (minimum); Pentium processor or higher (recommended)
- 16MB of RAM (Windows 95/98); 24MB of RAM (Windows NT)
- 5MB of free hard-disk space
- A CD-ROM drive (for installation only)

Installation of Professional 5.0 Test Drive

1. Insert Disc 3 of the CD-ROM set included with this book.
2. Go to Start → Run → Browse. Select the D drive.
3. Go the VISTDPRO directory, select SETUP.EXE, and press OK.
4. Follow the on-screen instructions to complete the installation.

Installation of the Solution Pack for NDS

1. Insert Disc 3 of the CD-ROM set included with this book.
2. Go to Start → Run → Browse. Select the D drive.
3. Next, go to the NDS directory, then select SETUP.EXE and press OK.
4. Follow the on-screen instructions to complete the installation.

For additional information about Visio products and features, plus installation hints, please refer to the GUIDETOVISIONDS.HTML file on the root of Disc 3 of the CD-ROM set, and to the README.TXT files contained within the Visio directories.

APPENDIX B

NDS Error Codes and Definitions

This appendix provides a list of the NDS error codes and, where appropriate, any action that should be taken to resolve each error condition. You can use this appendix as a reference when troubleshooting NDS or other operating system problems on your NetWare 5 servers. For more information on troubleshooting NDS and related problems, refer to Chapter 10, "NetWare 5 Features," in conjunction with this appendix.

Novell Directory Services Error Codes

This section provides information on the NDS error codes and provides a description of the error and any client action that needs to be taken to remedy the problem. In some cases you will not see an explanation or action. This is because the error is internal to NDS and in most cases you will not see it, nor can you take any action on it. We include them, though, to provide you with a complete listing.

NO_SUCH_ENTRY —601 0xFFFFFDA7 FDA7

Explanation: This error on an NetWare 5 server during DSTRACE usually means that an entry is missing from the entry record table on the source server.

Client Action: Check the context specified for the object name entered. If the command line input was the object name, check the workstation's context. Make sure that it points to the correct level of the Directory for the object name specified. If the input includes the object's full or partial context, make sure that the leading and trailing dots are specified appropriately and that the types are correct. This error is common if you are trying to delete bindery type objects through NWADMIN or the 4.02 version of NETADMIN. Use the 4.01 version of NETADMIN to delete bindery type objects from a 4.0*x* server. This error should not occur in NetWare 5.

Server Action: Do a SET DSTRACE=+SYNC on both the source and the target server (and any other servers in the replica list) to see which object is returning the –601 error and what errors the target server is getting in return. If the object is not a server object, try deleting it. If the object with the error is a server object, see if DSTRACE returns any other errors besides –601 and attempt to resolve them. If there are no additional errors, do a Send All Objects from the server reporting the error (the source server), or Receive All Objects from the target server using DSREPAIR. (This method will help only if the source server is the master.) Send All Objects causes a lot of network traffic!

NO_SUCH_VALUE –602 0xFFFFFDA6 FDA6

Explanation: The requested property value could not be found. If this error is encountered during the login or authentication process, it usually means that either the user's or the server's public keys could not be located. If this is the case, regenerate the user's key pair by changing the password with utilities.

An occurrence of this error during the synchronization process between servers means that a value of an object being synchronized is missing from the target server. This error may be a temporary condition that exists because of the loosely consistent nature of Directory Services.

Server Action: What error are you seeing on the target server? You may see one of the following messages without an error code:

- **Error unable to communicate** — Look in DSTRACE for the object with the problem (SET DSTRACE=+SYNC). The problem is either the public key or the remote ID. Run DSREPAIR to verify remote server IDs. If errors appear there, run this same option once more to verify remote server IDs. If you get a –602 or –603 in DSREPAIR when verifying remote server IDs, call your Novell Authorized Service Center for support. Be aware, however, that a public key cannot be repaired unless at least one server in the tree is authenticating without problems to the target server. The server authenticating OK to the target server must also have a real copy of the target server object, so it must have a replica (other than a subordinate reference) of the partition holding the target server object. If this is only a two-server tree, the target server will need to be removed from the tree and reinstalled.

- **Error sending updates** — Look in DSTRACE for the object with the problem (SET DSTRACE=+SYNC) and try deleting the object.

NO_SUCH_ATTRIBUTE –603 0xFFFFFDA5 FDA5

Explanation: The requested property could not be found. In the Directory, if a property does not contain a value, then the property does not exist for the specific object.

Client Action: Ensure that the property being requested is a valid DS property (check spelling and syntax). Use NLIST.EXE to determine if the property exists for the specified object. For example, NLIST *user=username* /d will show all of the properties and their values for the specified user name. (To see all of the properties associated with the object requires supervisor rights to the object in question. Browse rights are given by default.) We have seen this error occur when users try to edit properties that are grayed out in the utilities (properties that are not supported in the current DS schema). This error can also occur when there are schema synchronization problems in a mixed tree (4.0*x* and NetWare 5 servers in the same tree).

Server Action: This error is basically the same as a –602 error except that you get a –602 on a multivalued property and a –603 on a single-valued property. What error are you seeing on the target server? You may see one of the following messages without an error code:

- **Error unable to communicate** — Look in DSTRACE for the object with the problem (SET DSTRACE−+SYNC). This problem is either the public key or the remote ID. Run DSREPAIR to verify remote server IDs. If errors appear there, run this same option once more to verify remote server IDs. If you get a –602 or –603 in DSREPAIR when verifying remote server IDs, call your Novell Authorized Service Center for support. Be aware, however, that a public key cannot be repaired unless at least one server in the tree is authenticating without problems to the target server. The server authenticating OK to the target server must also have a real copy of the target server object, so it must have a replica (other than a subordinate reference) of the partition holding the target server object. If this tree is only a two-server tree, the target server will need to be removed from the tree and reinstalled.

- **Error sending updates** — Look in DSTRACE for the object with the problem (SET DSTRACE=+SYNC) and try deleting the object. If there is currently a mixed environment in the tree or if there ever were NetWare 5 servers in a now completely 4.0*x* tree, this could be a schema problem. Run the Global Schema Update option in DSREPAIR on a NetWare 5 server. If there are no longer any NetWare 5 servers in the tree, or if the Global Schema Update does not fix the problem, bring the server down with the master replica of the partition returning the error and then bring the server back up. Upon startup, the server will force a schema update. The schema problem should now be resolved.

NO_SUCH_CLASS -604 0xFFFFFDA4 FDA4

Explanation: An object class that does not exist in the Directory is being referenced by a utility. An object class in NDS is similar to the object type in the bindery. For example, object type 1 in the bindery is a user object and in the Directory the object class is USER. The class indicates the kind of object to be created.

Action: NetWare 4 utilities access only Novell's base schema, which must be present for the Directory to operate. Determine what utility is being used to create the object. This utility is attempting to use an object class that is currently not defined in NDS. The NetWare 4.0 utilities only display valid object classes. NetWare 5 allows the schema to be extended, so this error in NetWare 5 may point to schema synchronization problems.

NO_SUCH_PARTITION -605 0xFFFFFDA3 FDA3

Explanation: A partition with the specified name does not exist.

Action: Ensure that the partition name requested is valid and is a valid object name.

ENTRY_ALREADY_EXISTS -606 0xFFFFFDA2 FDA2

Explanation: An attempt was made to add an object at the same level as a preexisting object of the same name but not necessarily the same class.

Action: Specify a different name for the object being added or rename the existing object.

NOT_EFFECTIVE_CLASS -607 0xFFFFFDA1 FDA1

Explanation: This error indicates that the class being used to create the specified object is a noneffective class and cannot be used when creating an object. There are two types of object classes in the Directory — effective and noneffective. All effective classes can be used to create objects. (The class being used to create the specified object is referred to as the "base class" of the object.) User would be one example of an effective class. Noneffective classes are used as superclasses to define information associated with various effective classes.

Action: The standard Novell utilities that ship with NetWare 4 only allow effective classes to be used when creating objects. Find out what utility is being used to create the object. This may mean that your non-Novell utility is not following the rules of the specified object.

ILLEGAL_ATTRIBUTE -608 0xFFFFFDA0 FDA0

Explanation: An attempt was made to add a property that is illegal to an object. The NDS schema determines which properties can be inherited by an object class. (Refer to the Directory Services Schema documentation in Chapter 3, "Novell Directory Services Objects and Properties.") This error can also occur in mixed trees (4.0*x* and NetWare 5 servers in the same tree) or in upgraded trees (4.0*x* servers that have been upgraded to NetWare 5) when a server does not have the correct schema.

Client Action: You cannot add the specified property to the specified object.

Server Action: Do a SET DSTRACE=+SYNC and then SET DSTRACE=*H to see the object causing the error. If the object is not a server object, try deleting it. In the case of a schema problem, run Global Schema Update in DSREPAIR from a NetWare 5 server. If there are no longer any NetWare 5 servers in the tree or if Global Schema Update does not correct the problem, bring the server down containing the master replica of the partition showing errors and then bring the server back up. Upon startup, the server will force a schema update, which usually corrects these schema problems. If the problem persists, call your Novell Authorized Service Center for support.

MISSING_MANDATORY -609 0xFFFFFD9F FD9F

Explanation: This error indicates that one or more of the mandatory properties for the object being created are missing. Each object class in the Directory has a set of mandatory properties (properties that must contain a value before the object can be created). For example, a USER object in the Directory is required to have a Common Name (CN) and a Surname. Without these properties the object will not be created. A property exists only if there is a value supplied for the given property. This error can also occur in mixed trees (4.0*x* and NetWare 5 servers in the same tree) when a server does not have the correct schema.

Client Action: Input the required information when creating the object.

Server Action: Do a SET DSTRACE=+SYNC and then SET DSTRACE=*H to see the object causing the error. If the object is not a server object, try deleting it.

In the case of a schema problem, run Global Schema Update in DSREPAIR from a NetWare 5 server. If there are no longer any NetWare 5 servers in the tree or if Global Schema Update does not correct the problem, bring the server down with the master replica of the partition showing errors and then bring the server back up. Upon startup, the server will force a schema update, which usually corrects these schema problems. If the problem persists, call your Novell Authorized Service Center for support.

ILLEGAL_DS_NAME -610 0xFFFFFD9E FD9E

Explanation: Illegal Directory Names are those that are too long (more than 255 characters) or ones that contain illegal character combinations. The '\' character may be followed only by a '.' or '=' or '+' or '\'.

ILLEGAL_CONTAINMENT -611 0xFFFFFD9D FD9D

Explanation: The containment rules of the Directory specify where an object class may appear in relation to other objects in the Directory tree. For example, the object class Country can only be created at the top of the Directory, and the object class User can only be created under Organizations and Organizational Units. The Schema enforces the containment rules for NDS.

Action: Go to the appropriate container to create the object.

CANT_HAVE_MULTIPLE_VALUES -612 0xFFFFFD9C FD9C

Explanation: This error indicates that the specified property is single valued. All properties are either single or multivalued. For example, the Group Membership property is multivalued. A user can be a member of multiple groups. The Group Membership property exists once and contains multiple group names (values).

Action: For this property (information category in the utility), only one value (piece of information) can be supplied.

SYNTAX_VIOLATION -613 0xFFFFFD9B FD9B

Explanation: An attribute value being added to an object is incorrect. This error is most often encountered if that value is the name of another object that does not exist. This error is also seen during the installation or upgrade to NetWare 5.

Client Action: For most cases, verify that the object name being added as a value is correct.

Server Action: If a new NetWare 5 server being installed hangs while copying over the Directory Services objects, check the DSTRACE screen of the server with the master replica of the partition where the new NetWare 5 server is being installed. If the master is giving errors, run DSREPAIR on the master. If problems persist, do a SET DSTRACE=+SYNC to find the object returning the error and check the description field (and any other field that accepts a string) for any unusual ASCII characters. Correct the corruption or delete the object, and the replica should complete copying to the new server.

We have also seen this error occur when a bindery-type object (usually created by a third-party program) becomes corrupt. If the –613 errors are on these objects, delete all objects created by the program and then reinstall the program.

DUPLICATE_VALUE –614 0xFFFFFD9A FD9A

Explanation: An attempt was made to add a duplicate value to the specified property.

Action: Enter a different value.

ATTRIBUTE_ALREADY_EXISTS –615 0xFFFFFD99 FD99

Explanation: An attempt was made to add a property that already exists.

Action: If the attribute is multivalued, just add the specified value to the existing property. If the property is single valued, you will need to delete the property in order to create it again with the new value.

MAXIMUM_ENTRIES_EXIST –616 0xFFFFFD98 FD98

Explanation: This error indicates that the maximum number of entries (objects) exists in the Directory tree. The maximum number of objects that can be created in the Directory is FFFFFF (3 bytes of FF), which equal 16,777,215 decimal. Some of these entries are used by the Directory itself.

Action: For the current version of the Directory, you have reached the maximum number of objects that can be created. You will need to delete objects that are no longer needed.

DATABASE_FORMAT –617 0xFFFFFD97 FD97
INCONSISTENT_DATABASE –618 0xFFFFFD96 FD96

Explanation: This error indicates that an error has been encountered in the database itself. Usually this error means that the number of entries in a container does not match the number stored in the container's entry. When this error occurs during synchronization, the target server has a corrupted database.

Action: Run DSREPAIR only once.

TIP

If you run DSREPAIR a second time, the original .OLD database files will be overwritten after 72 hours, and it will not be possible to restore their former Directory Information Base (DIB).

If the error persists after running DSREPAIR the first time, consult your Novell Authorized Service Center.

INVALID_COMPARISON −619 0xFFFFFD95 FD95

Explanation: An attempt was made either to compare two properties that are not comparable or to use an invalid compare syntax.

Action: Check the syntax and verify that the properties are comparable.

COMPARISON_FAILED −620 0xFFFFFD94 FD94
TRANSACTIONS_DISABLED −621 0xFFFFFD93 FD93

Explanation: This error indicates that Transaction Tracking (TTS) has been disabled for the server on which the Directory operation is taking place. When TTS is disabled, NDS operations, which require modifying the database on that server, are disabled as well.

Action: At the console prompt of the file server type **ENABLE TTS**. If TTS was disabled because the SYS volume is full, log into the file server, delete unnecessary files from the SYS volume, and type **ENABLE TTS** at the file server. If you are unable to log into the file server, try running VREPAIR on volume SYS and selecting Purge Deleted Files from the VREPAIR menu. If there still is not enough space, put another drive into the server and span the SYS volume across both drives to give SYS more space.

INVALID_TRANSPORT −622 0xFFFFFD92 FD92
SYNTAX_INVALID_IN_NAME −623 0xFFFFFD91 FD91
REPLICA_ALREADY_EXISTS −624 0xFFFFFD90 FD90

Explanation: This error indicates that a replica of the specified partition already exists on the server.

Action: Select a different server.

TRANSPORT_FAILURE -625 0xFFFFFD8F FD8F

Explanation: This error occurs when either a client and a server or two servers cannot communicate with each other across the network.

Action: Check for SAP filtering of the DS SAP types of 26B and 278. Check cabling, the LAN card, and the LAN driver. Make sure they can RCONSOLE to the target server. Does typing **DISPLAY SERVERS** on the source server show the target server? Are other servers also showing this –625 error to the same target server? Can workstations attach and log into the target server from the same segment as the source server? Type **RESET ROUTERS** and then type **SET DSTRACE=*U** at the source server to flag all servers as UP and retry communicating with them. This error is almost always a LAN communication issue. Occasionally a change of the server's name, a move of the server object, or a change to the internal IPX number can also cause this error to occur. Run DSREPAIR with the option to Repair Network Addresses on the Source Server to check the internal IPX number of the target server. The change may not complete successfully. This error can also occur when trying to communicate with servers that have locked databases (that is, with DSREPAIR).

ALL_REFERRALS_FAILED -626 0xFFFFFD8E FD8E

Explanation: The object could not be found. It is still possible that the object does exist but that a server could not communicate with the server holding a copy of the object. The target server tried to walk the tree by contacting all other servers in the replica ring and was unable to do so. This error commonly occurs when partition management is requested and the requested operation cannot take place because a key server is inaccessible. Invalid creation timestamps can also return this error.

Server Action: Run DSREPAIR with the options to Repair Network Addresses and verify remote server IDs. Check the replica rings to verify that there is one master replica for the partition in question. Check the replica states and make sure they are all ON. Resolve whatever problems you find in the DSREPAIR.LOG file. Look in DISPLAY SERVERS to see if the tree name is present. If not, check the issues with –625 errors (including SAP filtering). If creation timestamps are invalid, running the NetWare 5 DSREPAIR with the option to Check External References under Advanced Options (only available in newer DSREPAIRs) should repair this problem.

CANT_REMOVE_NAMING_VALUE −627 0xFFFFFD8D FD8D

Explanation: This error indicates that an attempt was made to delete the naming property, but the naming value cannot be removed.

Action: Rename the object, then delete the property.

OBJECT_CLASS_VIOLATION −628 0xFFFFFD8C FD8C

Explanation: An object class violation has occurred.

Server Action: This error can occur when the source server's objects are unknown but are fine on the target server. Isolate the bad replica by either locking the databases with DSREPAIR and then running NETADMIN or NWADMIN to view the objects or by using DSVIEW (available on NetWire). Then delete the bad replica and add it back again through Partition Manager (verifying first that the master is a good copy).

A schema synchronization problem can also generate this error. Run the Global Schema Update option in DSREPAIR on a NetWare 5 server. If there are no longer any NetWare 5 servers in the tree, or if the Global Schema Update does not fix the problem, bring the server down with the master replica of the partition returning the error and then bring the server back up. Upon startup, the server will force a schema update, which usually corrects a schema problem.

ENTRY_IS_NOT_LEAF −629 0xFFFFFD8B FD8B

Explanation: This error indicates that the object being deleted or modified is not a leaf object. A container object that does not contain any objects is considered a leaf object and therefore can be deleted. If you attempt to delete a container object that does contain objects of any class, the following error message is returned: "The utility can't delete <object class>=<object name> because it is not a leaf object." A container object that is a partition root cannot be deleted.

Action: Delete all objects under the container object that is being deleted or modified. If the object is a partition root, merge the partition with the parent partition and then delete the object.

DIFFERENT_TREE −630 0xFFFFFD8A FD8A

ILLEGAL_REPLICA_TYPE −631 0xFFFFFD89 FD89

Explanation: This error indicates that a request was made of a replica, but the replica was the wrong type and therefore the request could not complete.

Server Action: This is usually seen at the file server console when attempting to set the bindery context. The bindery context requires a writable replica (either a read/write or a master) in order to be set. Verify that the server has a writable replica of the partition containing the container to which you are attempting to set the bindery context.

SYSTEM_FAILURE **–632 0xFFFFFD88 FD88**

Explanation: This error indicates that unexpected results have occurred. For example, the client requested that the Directory return a network address attribute and the Directory actually returned a public key attribute. This condition may be temporary. While the client usually returns errors in the –301 to –399 range, the client as well as the server returns this error during the authentication process. A server may return a –632 during synchronization because authentication could not complete due to an error in the public key—the key is the right key, but it is corrupt (not the right format). This error can also be returned in DSTRACE when the server is unable to open the local database. However, –632 is just a general error, which means that the process being attempted failed because the server(s) being contacted was busy or down, or the source server could not authenticate to it.

Symptom: After upgrading a server, the DS is unable to open the database. SET DSTRACE=ON and then SET DSTRACE=+MISC. Then dismount and remount the SYS volume. Check the DSTRACE screen and confirm that a –632 error is returned when DS tries to open the database. If so, the database is corrupted. DS will need to be removed from the server and reinstalled (either from another replica in the tree or, if a single-server environment, from backup).

Server Action: Run DSREPAIR with the option to verify remote server IDs on every server in the replica list. Then go back and run DSREPAIR a second time with the option to verify remote server IDs on every server in the replica list. If the remote server ID check returns a –632 after running it the second time, call your Novell Authorized Service Center. Otherwise, try to resolve the process that failed.

INVALID_ENTRY_FOR_ROOT **–633 0xFFFFFD87 FD87**

Explanation: An attempt was made to either restore or move an object that is flagged as a partition root but whose base class is not a container, or to perform a split at an object whose base class is not a container.

NO_REFERRALS -634 0xFFFFFD86 FD86

Explanation: This means that the target server does not have a copy of what the source server is requesting. In other words, the source server has no objects that match the request and no referrals to search for the object.

Action: None required. This is not a serious error, just a response.

REMOTE_FAILURE -635 0xFFFFFD85 FD85

Explanation: In order to complete some operations, a server will need to contact another server. If this is not possible (because of a link being down, for example), this error will be returned.

Action: The target server does not have the correct information about the source server. This error is often caused by a problem with local to remote IDs or the server object. Run DSREPAIR with the option to verify remote server IDs on every server in the replica list. Then go back and run DSREPAIR a second time with the option to verify remote server IDs on all servers in the replica list. Resolve any errors found after the second run of DSREPAIR.

UNREACHABLE_SERVER -636 0XFFFFFD84 FD84
PREVIOUS_MOVE_IN_PROGRESS -637 0XFFFFFD83 FD83

Explanation: Once an object has been moved from one context in the Directory to another, the Directory will not allow that object to be moved again until all replicas of that object have been updated. The length of time for a move to complete will vary depending on the size of the replica, the number of replicas, and condition of the communication links between all the servers holding the replicas. This error can be caused by a moved object that lost the original object (the primary obituary) or by a broken partition.

Action: Leave the object in its current context until it can be moved again. This may require that the object be left in its new context for several minutes. If the object still cannot be moved, load the NetWare 5 DSREPAIR with –m (LOAD DSREPAIR –M) and then run Repair Local Database. (For 4.0*x* DSREPAIR, type **LOAD DSREPAIR –A**, Select Options, and toggle A until it reads "Find obituaries for move and move-inhibit.") View the DSREPAIR.LOG file, which will display objects that have move obituaries. Verify that the problem objects and all their attributes have been successfully moved to the new location by running NWADMIN or NETADMIN and viewing the objects. If the objects have been moved, load the NetWare 5 DSREPAIR with –MR (load the 4.0x DSREPAIR with –A, Select Options, then toggle A until it reads "Purge obituaries for move and move-inhibit"), which will delete the move obituaries for those problem objects. Use SET DSTRACE=+J and SET DSTRACE=*F to verify that the purger ran successfully.

NO_CHARACTER_MAPPING –638 0xFFFFFD82 FD82
INCOMPLETE_AUTHENTICATION –639 0xFFFFFD81 FD81
INVALID_CERTIFICATE –640 0xFFFFFD80 FD80
INVALID_REQUEST –641 0xFFFFFD7F FD7F

Explanation: The server did not understand the request. For example, a client workstation could have sent an incorrect verb.

Server Action: This error can be caused by a nonsynchronized schema. Run the NetWare 5 DSREPAIR and do a Global Schema Update. This error can also be a response error, so check for errors on the target server and resolve any that you may find there first.

INVALID_ITERATION –642 0xFFFFFD7E FD7E

Explanation: A client workstation sent an invalid iteration handle.

SCHEMA_IS_NONREMOVABLE –643 0xFFFFFD7D FD7D

Explanation: An attempt was made to delete an NDS structure or configuration.

SCHEMA_IS_IN_USE –644 0xFFFFFD7C FD7C

Explanation: An attempt was made to delete an NDS configuration or structure (such as a container object) that still contains an object using that structure.

Action: First delete the object or property, then delete the structure.

CLASS_ALREADY_EXISTS –645 0xFFFFFD7B FD7B

Explanation: This error indicates that the object class being created already exists as a class in the schema of the Directory. (See also NO_SUCH_CLASS –604 0xFFFFFDA4.)

Action: This error should occur only in a utility that updates the schema of the Directory. Determine the utility that is causing the error.

BAD_NAMING_ATTRIBUTES **–646** **0xFFFFFD7A** **FD7A**
NOT_ROOT_PARTITION **–647** **0xFFFFFD79** **FD79**

Explanation: An attempt was made to execute a function that is required on the root partition. Either the client did not pass on the root partition name or the client attempted to perform the function somewhere other than the root partition.

INSUFFICIENT_STACK **–648** **0xFFFFFD78** **FD78**
INSUFFICIENT_BUFFER **–649** **0xFFFFFD77** **FD77**

Explanation: The server ran out of memory. The operating system will self-correct this error.

Action: Be patient. See Novell's manual *Supervising the Network* under the category "Resolving Server Memory Problems."

AMBIGUOUS_CONTAINMENT **–650** **0xFFFFFD76** **FD76**
AMBIGUOUS_NAMING **–651** **0xFFFFFD75** **FD75**
DUPLICATE_MANDATORY **–652** **0xFFFFFD74** **FD74**
DUPLICATE_OPTIONAL **–653** **0xFFFFFD73** **FD73**
PARTITION_BUSY **–654** **0xFFFFFD72** **FD72**

Explanation: Another partition operation is currently taking place. For example, if a request has previously been issued to split a partition, a second request for a split (even at another point in the same partition) will result in this error.

Server Action: This is a normal error immediately after a partition operation has been initiated. If this error does not go away, in the 310 build of the DS this error can indicate that the target server does not think that the source server has a copy of that partition. Confirm this through DSREPAIR.LOG or by watching DSTRACE. Try running PTEST (4.0*x*) or Cancel Partition Operation (NetWare 5) to abort the partition operation on the source server. You can also remove the source server from the tree or call your Novell Authorized Service Center for support.

MULTIPLE_REPLICAS **–655** **0xFFFFFD71** **FD71**

Explanation: This error is an internal error that appears as a result of a programming discrepancy, not a system inconsistency.

CRUCIAL_REPLICA –656 0xFFFFFD70 FD70

Explanation: An attempt was made to perform one of the following illegal operations on a master replica: remove it, change its replica type (the correct way to change a replica type is to change the replica type of another server's replica to the master, which will indirectly force the master to become a read/write), or request that it receive all updates from the master. This error can also be caused by trying to add a replica to the server where the master of that replica already exists.

SCHEMA_SYNC_IN_PROGRESS –657 0xFFFFFD6F FD6F

Explanation: The function could not be completed because Directory synchronization is in progress.

Action: Wait a while and try again.

SKULK_IN_PROGRESS –658 0xFFFFFD6E FD6E

Explanation: The function could not be completed because replica synchronization is in progress.

Action: Wait a while and try again.

TIME_NOT_SYNCHRONIZED –659 0xFFFFFD6D FD6D

Explanation: NDS uses timestamps to determine the order of events that take place in the Directory. Time Synchronization services have been implemented to maintain a consistent time across the network. Modification operations require the issuance of a timestamp. If a replica on a server has issued a timestamp and the time on that server is set back, in 4.0*x* no further modification operations may take place until the time on the server moves past the last modification time on the partition. This applies only to operations that modify, not to those that just read information. In other words, users will be able to log into the Directory, but no objects can be edited through the utilities. In NetWare 5, the Directory will issue synthetic timestamps on objects, enabling those objects to be modified, yet still not allow illegal timestamps. The server console will display a synthetic time error when the server time is behind the NDS time.

Action: Check DSTRACE for other errors first and resolve any you find. Then run Repair Timestamps (found in the NetWare 5 DSREPAIR), which will reset the timestamps to the current server time. The 4.0*x* equivalent of Repair Timestamps is Rebuild Replicas and is performed from the Partition Manager. This action will delete the objects from all replicas except the Master and then recopy all objects from the Master copy to all other replicas. BEWARE! If the Master copy was corrupt in any way, the other replicas will also be corrupt when a Repair Timestamps or Rebuild Replicas action is performed. Repair Timestamps or Rebuild Replicas can also cause considerable traffic on the network. You may have to perform this action on a partition by partition basis.

RECORD_IN_USE	**–660**	**0xFFFFFD6C**	**FD6C**
DS_VOLUME_NOT_MOUNTED	**–661**	**0xFFFFFD6B**	**FD6B**
DS_VOLUME_IO_FAILURE	**–662**	**0xFFFFFD6A**	**FD6A**
DS_LOCKED	**–663**	**0xFFFFFD69**	**FD69**

Explanation: The Directory database is locked on the server. This error will be seen in DSTRACE when the source server is trying to synchronize with the target server, which has a locked database. There will be no activity in the TRACE screen on the server with the locked database. The server with the problem will often get an error when it tries to open the Directory while mounting the SYS volume. We have seen this error occur when DSREPAIR is loaded on the server, when DSDUMP has the Directory locked, when the hard drive on the server is going bad, and when a new 4.02 server installation does not complete properly.

Action: Try running DSREPAIR on the server.

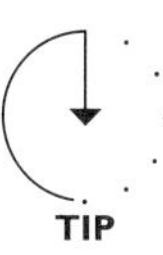
TIP

Run DSREPAIR. If DSREPAIR is run more than once, keep in mind that the .OLD database files will be overwritten after 72 hours. If DSREPAIR doesn't fix the problem, try bringing the server down and bringing it back up again. If running DSREPAIR and bringing the server down do not fix this error, the server may need to be removed from the tree. If this is a new server with no replicas on it, remove DS from the server. If you don't want to remove DS from the server, escalate the call. When the DS is locked, the normal removal of DS on a 4.02 server may not complete properly. You may need to load install with the –dsremove switch (LOAD INSTALL -DSREMOVE) and then try to remove DS through install. This will most likely return an error about being unable to remove DS but will perform the removal anyway. Try loading install with the –dsremove switch again and try the removal a second time. DSI should report that DS was already removed from the server. Don't use –DSREMOVE unless the normal removal process won't work! The –dsremove switch will ignore errors and warnings and may not perform all the steps necessary to do a clean removal.

OLD_EPOCH **–664 0xFFFFFD68 FD68**

Explanation: This is an NDS timestamp error.

NEW_EPOCH **–665 0xFFFFFD67 FD67**

Explanation: This is an NDS timestamp error.

INCOMPATIBLE_DS_VERSION **–666 0xFFFFFD66 FD66**

Explanation: This error occurs when performing operations that require the same schema, but there are servers involved in the operation with dissimilar schemas.

Symptom: Partition Manager returns this error when a partition operation is requested and the server with the Master replica is a NetWare 5 server, but there are other 4.0 servers on the replica list (including servers holding subordinate reference replicas). DSREPAIR for NetWare 5 may also return this error during a remote to local ID check.

Server Action: Most partition operations involving a NetWare 5 server as the server holding the Master will not be able to complete to 4.0*x* servers. The 4.0*x* servers on the replica list must be upgraded to NetWare 5 before the partition operation can be completed. If the Master replica were on a 4.02 server, you would not have this particular problem. If this error is seen in DSREPAIR during a remote to local ID check, do a SET DSTRACE=!V on the NetWare 5 server. This check will reset the list of restricted versions (DS versions that are restricted from synchronization) to the default, which is DS 290 and above.

PARTITION_ROOT **–667 0xFFFFFD65 FD65**

Explanation: This error indicates that the object being manipulated is the root of a Directory Services partition. This error would most commonly occur when you attempt to delete a container object that is a partition root.

Action: Using the partition management tools, merge this partition into the parent partition.

ENTRY_NOT_CONTAINER **–668 0xFFFFFD64 FD64**

Explanation: An illegal function was attempted on a leaf object.

FAILED_AUTHENTICATION **–669 0xFFFFFD63 FD63**

Explanation: An invalid password was sent. Authentication failed. This error is seen in DSTRACE when one server tries to synchronize with another server. The most likely problems are either the remote ID or the public key.

Server Action: Try running DSREPAIR with the option to verify remote server IDs on the source server and all other servers on the replica list. If there are errors in the DSREPAIR.LOG file, run DSREPAIR with the option to verify remote server IDs once more on every server in the replica list. This should resolve the problem with incorrect remote IDs. The other scenario is when the source server is either using or looking at the wrong public key (the key is the right format, but is for the wrong object). If the problem is the public key and if the source server has a REAL copy of the target server object (a Master, R/W, or R/O replica of the partition containing the target server object), check to see if the other servers on that replica list (for the partition containing the target server object) are able to authenticate to the target server. If another server can authenticate, do a Send All Objects from the good server, or a Receive All Objects on the target server (but only if the server with the "good" copy has the Master).

Also, remember that Send All Objects generates a lot of traffic. If no servers can authenticate to the target server, remove DS from the target server and reinstall it back into the tree or call your Novell Authorized Service Center for support.

If the source server has a subordinate reference replica or no replica of the partition containing the target server object, the external reference to that object will need to be re-backlinked. Call your Novell Authorized Service Center for support.

INVALID_CONTEXT	**–670**	**0xFFFFFD62**	**FD62**
NO_SUCH_PARENT	**–671**	**0xFFFFFD61**	**FD61**
NO_ACCESS	**–672**	**0xFFFFFD60**	**FD60**

Explanation: The client does not have sufficient results to complete the requested operation. This error in DSTRACE means that the target server's replica list doesn't match the source server's replica list.

Server Action: Compare the replica ring information for all the servers on the replica list (available though Display Replica Information). If you confirm that the target server doesn't have the source server on its replica list, then either remove DS from the target server or call your Novell Authorized Service Center for support.

REPLICA_NOT_ON	**–673**	**0xFFFFFD5F**	**FD5F**

Explanation: The replica is in the process of being created on a server. Until all the object information has been received on that server, the replica is "off" (not available for use by Directory clients).

Server Action: Wait. If the replica is stuck, look for the error that is preventing the replica from turning "on" and address that problem.

INVALID_NAME_SERVICE	**–674**	**0xFFFFFD5E**	**FD5E**
INVALID_TASK	**–675**	**0xFFFFFD5D**	**FD5D**
INVALID_CONN_HANDLE	**–676**	**0xFFFFFD5C**	**FD5C**
INVALID_IDENTITY	**–677**	**0xFFFFFD5B**	**FD5B**
DUPLICATE_ACL	**–678**	**0xFFFFFD5A**	**FD5A**
PARTITION_ALREADY_EXISTS	**–679**	**0xFFFFFD59**	**FD59**
TRANSPORT_MODIFIED	**–680**	**0xFFFFFD58**	**FD58**
ALIAS_OF_AN_ALIAS	**–681**	**0xFFFFFD57**	**FD57**
AUDITING_FAILED	**–682**	**0xFFFFFD56**	**FD56**
INVALID_API_VERSION	**–683**	**0xFFFFFD55**	**FD55**
SECURE_NCP_VIOLATION	**–684**	**0xFFFFFD54**	**FD54**
MOVE_IN_PROGRESS	**–685**	**0xFFFFFD53**	**FD53**
NOT_LEAF_PARTITION	**–686**	**0xFFFFFD52**	**FD52**
CANNOT_ABORT	**–687**	**0xFFFFFD51**	**FD51**
CACHE_OVERFLOW	**–688**	**0xFFFFFD50**	**FD50**
INVALID_SUBORDINATE_COUNT	**–689**	**0xFFFFFD4F**	**FD4F**
INVALID_RDN	**–690**	**0xFFFFFD4E**	**FD4E**
MOD_TIME_NOT_CURRENT	**–691**	**0xFFFFFD4D**	**FD4D**
INCORRECT_BASE_CLASS	**–692**	**0xFFFFFD4C**	**FD4C**
MISSING_REFERENCE	**–693**	**0xFFFFFD4B**	**FD4B**

Explanation: A required reference is missing from the object. This error is frequently seen in the NetWare 5 utilities if you are trying to delete an object with a zero creation timestamp.

Server Action: Run the latest version of the NetWare 5 DSREPAIR on the server. This will give objects with missing creation timestamps a valid timestamp. If the object continues to give a –693 error during deletion, there is still a server in that partition's replica list with a zero creation timestamp for that object. Run the latest DSREPAIR on each server on that partition's replica list.

LOST_ENTRY	**–694**	**0xFFFFFD4A**	**FD4A**
AGENT_ALREADY_REGISTERED	**–695**	**0xFFFFFD49**	**FD49**
DS_LOADER_BUSY	**–696**	**0xFFFFFD48**	**FD48**
DS_CANNOT_RELOAD	**–697**	**0xFFFFFD47**	**FD47**
REPLICA_IN_SKULK	**–698**	**0xFFFFFD46**	**FD46**

Explanation: The replica is busy skulking, and no other replica processes will be done until the skulk has completed.

Server Action: Usually this error occurs as a normal part of a partition operation and will resolve itself. If this error does not go away, check for other errors that may be preventing the partition operation from completing. Remember that the master replica is controlling all partition operations.

FATAL **–699 0xFFFFFD45 FD45**

Explanation: An unrecoverable error has occurred and the operation cannot be completed. This error can be caused by a variety of problems.

Server Action: Go to the target server and look for a response TRACE error. (Turn off the DSTRACE filters by using a setting like FFFF6FF7 or 8164B19 in 4.0x or an 8164B91 in NetWare 5.) Sometimes you will see an error without an error code (such as "skulk lost entry"), which can also be important. Resolve the error on the target server. Treat a "skulk lost entry" error the same as a –601 error.

Error –709 (Hex: FFFFFD3B)

Explanation: Invalid response. A DS client makes an invalid request and receives an invalid response.

Error –715 (Hex: FFFFFD35)

Explanation: A checksum error has occurred.

Error –716 (Hex: FFFFFD34)

Explanation: An error was received because checksumming is not supported.

Other Error Codes

This section describes additional error codes that, for the most part, are internal to NDS and would not be seen by a network administrator unless they are coding to NDS.

–1	**FFFFFFFF**	**"DSERR_INSUFFICIENT_SPACE"**
–19	**FFFFFF89**	**"DSERR_BUFFER_TOO_SMALL"**
–120	**FFFFFF88**	**"DSERR_VOLUME_FLAG_NOT_SET"**

–121	FFFFFF87	"DSERR_NO_ITEMS_FOUND"
–122	FFFFFF86	"DSERR_CONN_ALREADY_TEMPORARY"
–123	FFFFFF85	"DSERR_CONN_ALREADY_LOGGED_IN"
–124	FFFFFF84	"DSERR_CONN_NOT_AUTHENTICATED"
–125	FFFFFF83	"DSERR_CONN_NOT_LOGGED_IN"
–126	FFFFFF82	"DSERR_NCP_BOUNDARY_CHECK_FAILED"
–127	FFFFFF81	"DSERR_LOCK_WAITING"
–128	FFFFFF80	"DSERR_LOCK_FAIL"
–129	FFFFFF7F	"DSERR_OUT_OF_HANDLES"
–130	FFFFFF7E	"DSERR_NO_OPEN_PRIVILEGE"
–131	FFFFFF7D	"DSERR_HARD_IO_ERROR"
–132	FFFFFF7C	"DSERR_NO_CREATE_PRIVILEGE"
–133	FFFFFF7B	"DSERR_NO_CREATE_DELETE_PRIV"
–134	FFFFFF7A	"DSERR_R_O_CREATE_FILE"
–135	FFFFFF79	"DSERR_CREATE_FILE_INVALID_NAME"
–136	FFFFFF78	"DSERR_INVALID_FILE_HANDLE"
–137	FFFFFF77	"DSERR_NO_SEARCH_PRIVILEGE"
–138	FFFFFF76	"DSERR_NO_DELETE_PRIVILEGE"
–139	FFFFFF75	"DSERR_NO_RENAME_PRIVILEGE"
–140	FFFFFF74	"DSERR_NO_SET_PRIVILEGE"
–141	FFFFFF73	"DSERR_SOME_FILES_IN_USE"
–142	FFFFFF72	"DSERR_ALL_FILES_IN_USE"
–143	FFFFFF71	"DSERR_SOME_READ_ONLY"
–144	FFFFFF70	"DSERR_ALL_READ_ONLY"
–145	FFFFFF6F	"DSERR_SOME_NAMES_EXIST"
–146	FFFFFF6E	"DSERR_ALL_NAMES_EXIST"
–147	FFFFFF6D	"DSERR_NO_READ_PRIVILEGE"
–148	FFFFFF6C	"DSERR_NO_WRITE_PRIVILEGE"
–149	FFFFFF6B	"DSERR_FILE_DETACHED"
–150	FFFFFF6A	"DSERR_NO_ALLOC_SPACE"
–150	FFFFFF6A	"DSERR_TARGET_NOT_A_SUBDIR"
–150	FFFFFF6A	"ERR_INSUFFICIENT_MEMORY"
–151	FFFFFF69	"DSERR_NO_SPOOL_SPACE"
–152	FFFFFF68	"DSERR_INVALID_VOLUME"
–153	FFFFFF67	"DSERR_DIRECTORY_FULL"
–154	FFFFFF66	"DSERR_RENAME_ACROSS_VOLUME"
–155	FFFFFF65	"DSERR_BAD_DIR_HANDLE"
–156	FFFFFF64	"DSERR_INVALID_PATH"
–156	FFFFFF64	"DSERR_NO_SUCH_EXTENSION"

–157	FFFFFF63	"DSERR_NO_DIR_HANDLES"
–158	FFFFFF62	"DSERR_BAD_FILE_NAME"
–159	FFFFFF61	"DSERR_DIRECTORY_ACTIVE"
–160	FFFFFF60	"DSERR_DIRECTORY_NOT_EMPTY"
–161	FFFFFF5F	"DSERR_DIRECTORY_IO_ERROR"
–162	FFFFFF5E	"DSERR_IO_LOCKED"
–163	FFFFFF5D	"DSERR_TRANSACTION_RESTARTED"
–164	FFFFFF5C	"DSERR_RENAME_DIR_INVALID"
–165	FFFFFF5B	"DSERR_INVALID_OPENCREATE_MODE"
–166	FFFFFF5A	"DSERR_ALREADY_IN_USE"
–167	FFFFFF59	"DSERR_INVALID_RESOURCE_TAG"
–168	FFFFFF58	"DSERR_ACCESS_DENIED"
–190	FFFFFF42	"DSERR_INVALID_DATA_STREAM"
–191	FFFFFF41	"DSERR_INVALID_NAME_SPACE"
–192	FFFFFF40	"DSERR_NO_ACCOUNTING_PRIVILEGES"
–193	FFFFFF3F	"DSERR_NO_ACCOUNT_BALANCE"
–194	FFFFFF3E	"DSERR_CREDIT_LIMIT_EXCEEDED"
–195	FFFFFF3D	"DSERR_TOO_MANY_HOLDS"
–196	FFFFFF3C	"DSERR_ACCOUNTING_DISABLED"
–197	FFFFFF3B	"DSERR_LOGIN_LOCKOUT"
–198	FFFFFF3A	"DSERR_NO_CONSOLE_RIGHTS"
–208	FFFFFF30	"DSERR_Q_IO_FAILURE"
–209	FFFFFF2F	"DSERR_NO_QUEUE"
–210	FFFFFF2E	"DSERR_NO_Q_SERVER"
–211	FFFFFF2D	"DSERR_NO_Q_RIGHTS"
–212	FFFFFF2C	"DSERR_Q_FULL"
–213	FFFFFF2B	"DSERR_NO_Q_JOB"
–214	FFFFFF2A	"DSERR_NO_Q_JOB_RIGHTS"
–214	FFFFFF2A	"DSERR_UNENCRYPTED_NOT_ALLOWED"
–215	FFFFFF29	"DSERR_Q_IN_SERVICE"
–215	FFFFFF29	"DSERR_DUPLICATE_PASSWORD"
–216	FFFFFF28	"DSERR_Q_NOT_ACTIVE"
–216	FFFFFF28	"DSERR_PASSWORD_TOO_SHORT"
–217	FFFFFF27	"DSERR_Q_STN_NOT_SERVER"
–217	FFFFFF27	"DSERR_MAXIMUM_LOGINS_EXCEEDED"
–218	FFFFFF26	"DSERR_Q_HALTED"
–218	FFFFFF26	"DSERR_BAD_LOGIN_TIME"
–219	FFFFFF25	"DSERR_Q_MAX_SERVERS"

–219	FFFFFF25	"DSERR_NODE_ADDRESS_VIOLATION"
–220	FFFFFF24	"DSERR_LOG_ACCOUNT_EXPIRED"
–222	FFFFFF22	"DSERR_BAD_PASSWORD"
–223	FFFFFF21	"DSERR_PASSWORD_EXPIRED"
–224	FFFFFF20	"DSERR_NO_LOGIN_CONN_AVAILABLE"
–232	FFFFFF18	"DSERR_WRITE_TO_GROUP_PROPERTY"
–233	FFFFFF17	"DSERR_MEMBER_ALREADY_EXISTS"
–234	FFFFFF16	"DSERR_NO_SUCH_MEMBER"
–235	FFFFFF15	"DSERR_PROPERTY_NOT_GROUP"
–236	FFFFFF14	"DSERR_NO_SUCH_VALUE_SET"
–237	FFFFFF13	"DSERR_PROPERTY_ALREADY_EXISTS"
–238	FFFFFF12	"DSERR_OBJECT_ALREADY_EXISTS"
–239	FFFFFF11	"DSERR_ILLEGAL_NAME"
–240	FFFFFF10	"DSERR_ILLEGAL_WILDCARD"
–241	FFFFFF0F	"DSERR_BINDERY_SECURITY"
–242	FFFFFF0E	"DSERR_NO_OBJECT_READ_RIGHTS"
–243	FFFFFF0D	"DSERR_NO_OBJECT_RENAME_RIGHTS"
–244	FFFFFF0C	"DSERR_NO_OBJECT_DELETE_RIGHTS"
–245	FFFFFF0B	"DSERR_NO_OBJECT_CREATE_RIGHTS"
–246	FFFFFF0A	"DSERR_NO_PROPERTY_DELETE_RIGHTS"
–247	FFFFFF09	"DSERR_NO_PROPERTY_CREATE_RIGHTS"
–248	FFFFFF08	"DSERR_NO_PROPERTY_WRITE_RIGHTS"
–249	FFFFFF07	"DSERR_NO_PROPERTY_READ_RIGHTS"
–250	FFFFFF06	"DSERR_TEMP_REMAP"
–251	FFFFFF05	"DSERR_UNKNOWN_REQUEST"
–251	FFFFFF05	"DSERR_NO_SUCH_PROPERTY"
–251	FFFFFF05	"ERR_REQUEST_UNKNOWN"
–252	FFFFFF04	"DSERR_MESSAGE_QUEUE_FULL"
–252	FFFFFF04	"DSERR_TARGET_ALREADY_HAS_MSG"
–252	FFFFFF04	"DSERR_NO_SUCH_OBJECT"
–253	FFFFFF03	"DSERR_BAD_STATION_NUMBER"
–254	FFFFFF02	"DSERR_BINDERY_LOCKED"
–254	FFFFFF02	"DSERR_DIR_LOCKED"
–254	FFFFFF02	"DSERR_SPOOL_DELETE"
–254	FFFFFF02	"DSERR_TRUSTEE_NOT_FOUND"
–255	FFFFFF01	"DSERR_HARD_FAILURE"
–255	FFFFFF01	"DSERR_FILE_NAME"
–255	FFFFFF01	"DSERR_FILE_EXISTS"

–255	FFFFFF01	"DSERR_CLOSE_FCB"
–255	FFFFFF01	"DSERR_IO_BOUND"
–255	FFFFFF01	"DSERR_NO_SPOOL_FILE"
–255	FFFFFF01	"DSERR_BAD_SPOOL_PRINTER"
–255	FFFFFF01	"DSERR_BAD_PARAMETER"
–255	FFFFFF01	"DSERR_NO_FILES_FOUND"
–255	FFFFFF01	"DSERR_NO_TRUSTEE_CHANGE_PRIV"
–255	FFFFFF01	"DSERR_TARGET_NOT_LOGGED_IN"
–255	FFFFFF01	"DSERR_TARGET_NOT_ACCEPTING_MSGS"
–255	FFFFFF01	"DSERR_MUST_FORCE_DOWN"
–255	FFFFFF01	"ERR_OF_SOME_SORT"
–301	FFFFFED3	"ERR_NOT_ENOUGH_MEMORY"
–302	FFFFFED2	"ERR_BAD_KEY"
–303	FFFFFED1	"ERR_BAD_CONTEXT"
–304	FFFFFED0	"ERR_BUFFER_FULL"
–305	FFFFFECF	"ERR_LIST_EMPTY"
–306	FFFFFECE	"ERR_BAD_SYNTAX"
–307	FFFFFECD	"ERR_BUFFER_EMPTY"
–308	FFFFFECC	"ERR_BAD_VERB"
–309	FFFFFECB	"ERR_EXPECTED_IDENTIFIER"
–310	FFFFFECA	"ERR_EXPECTED_EQUALS"
–311	FFFFFEC9	"ERR_ATTR_TYPE_EXPECTED"
–312	FFFFFEC8	"ERR_ATTR_TYPE_NOT_EXPECTED"
–313	FFFFFEC7	"ERR_FILTER_TREE_EMPTY"
–314	FFFFFEC6	"ERR_INVALID_OBJECT_NAME"
–315	FFFFFEC5	"ERR_EXPECTED_RDN_DELIMITER"
–316	FFFFFEC4	"ERR_TOO_MANY_TOKENS"
–317	FFFFFEC3	"ERR_INCONSISTENT_MULTIAVA"
–318	FFFFFEC2	"ERR_COUNTRY_NAME_TOO_LONG"
–319	FFFFFEC1	"ERR_SYSTEM_ERROR"
–320	FFFFFEC0	"ERR_CANT_ADD_ROOT"
–321	FFFFFEBF	"ERR_UNABLE_TO_ATTACH"
–322	FFFFFEBE	"ERR_INVALID_HANDLE"
–323	FFFFFEBD	"ERR_BUFFER_ZERO_LENGTH"
–324	FFFFFEBC	"ERR_INVALID_REPLICA_TYPE"
–325	FFFFFEBB	"ERR_INVALID_ATTR_SYNTAX"
–326	FFFFFEBA	"ERR_INVALID_FILTER_SYNTAX"
–328	FFFFFEB8	"ERR_CONTEXT_CREATION"

–329	FFFFFEB7	"ERR_INVALID_UNION_TAG"
–330	FFFFFEB6	"ERR_INVALID_SERVER_RESPONSE"
–331	FFFFFEB5	"ERR_NULL_POINTER"
–332	FFFFFEB4	"ERR_NO_SERVER_FOUND"
–333	FFFFFEB3	"ERR_NO_CONNECTION"
–334	FFFFFEB2	"ERR_RDN_TOO_LONG"
–335	FFFFFEB1	"ERR_DUPLICATE_TYPE"
–336	FFFFFEB0	"ERR_DATA_STORE_FAILURE"
–337	FFFFFEAF	"ERR_NOT_LOGGED_IN"
–338	FFFFFEAE	"ERR_INVALID_PASSWORD_CHARS"
–339	FFFFFEAD	"ERR_FAILED_SERVER_AUTHENT"
–340	FFFFFEAC	"ERR_TRANSPORT"
–341	FFFFFEAB	"ERR_NO_SUCH_SYNTAX"
–342	FFFFFEAA	"ERR_INVALID_DS_NAME"
–343	FFFFFEA9	"ERR_ATTR_NAME_TOO_LONG"
–344	FFFFFEA8	"ERR_INVALID_TDS"
–345	FFFFFEA7	"ERR_INVALID_DS_VERSION"
–346	FFFFFEA6	"ERR_UNICODE_TRANSLATION"
–347	FFFFFEA5	"ERR_SCHEMA_NAME_TOO_LONG"
–348	FFFFFEA4	"ERR_UNICODE_FILE_NOT_FOUND"
–349	FFFFFEA3	"ERR_UNICODE_ALREADY_LOADED"
–350	FFFFFEA2	"ERR_NOT_CONTEXT_OWNER"
–351	FFFFFEA1	"ERR_ATTEMPT_TO_AUTHENTICATE_0"
–352	FFFFFEA0	"ERR_NO_WRITABLE_REPLICAS"
–353	FFFFFE9F	"ERR_DN_TOO_LONG"
–354	FFFFFE9E	"ERR_RENAME_NOT_ALLOWED"

APPENDIX C

NetWare 5 Server Console Commands

Server console commands and utilities enable you to change server parameters, monitor the load on the server, and control its allocation of resources. This appendix lists and describes each of the server console commands for NetWare 5. The online help screen will list each of the commands for your use. You can access the help screen at the server prompt by typing:

```
HELP
```

The SFT III server console commands are not included in this appendix. If you need information about these commands you should refer to the documentation that comes with the intraNetWare SFT III product.

You can enter the server console commands only at the server prompt or command line. These commands can also be used in the AUTOEXEC.NCF file but not in the STARTUP.NCF file. A few commands are available only in the AUTOEXEC.NCF file and will not function at the server prompt. For example, the commands FILE SERVER NAME and IPX INTERNAL NET are available only in the AUTOEXEC.NCF file.

The server console commands can also be placed in NetWare command files other than the AUTOEXEC.NCF file. The NetWare command files have .NCF file extensions and are used to group the server console commands together to perform specific tasks. The command files should be stored in the SYS:SYSTEM directory. You can execute a command file by typing the command filename (without the .NCF extension) at the server prompt.

Server Console Commands

The following section presents each NetWare 5 server console command, gives its syntax, and provides examples.

ABORT REMIRROR

This command stops the remirroring of a NetWare file system partition. By default NetWare will automatically begin remirroring a mirrored partition that is out of synchronization. The partition can fall out of synchronization if one-half of the mirror is disabled or damaged. The remirror process will start automatically after the pair is back up and running. The syntax for this command is:

```
ABORT REMIRROR partition_number
```

You can selectively stop the remirroring process for any of the NetWare partitions.

Example: abort remirror 3

See also: REMIRROR PARTITION

ADD NAME SPACE

This command enables you to add and support non-DOS files, such as Macintosh, NFS (UNIX), OS/2 HPFS, and FTAM on the NetWare volume. The command is executed only once for each name space on each NetWare volume. The syntax for this command is:

```
ADD NAME SPACE name [TO [volume_name]]
```

The name parameter can be replaced with one of these terms:

- **Macintosh** — used for Apple Macintosh files
- **NFS** — used for UNIX files
- **OS/2** — used for IBM OS/2 HPFS files

The name space support module (file with .NAM file extension) must be loaded on the server before you can execute this command. For example, to support the Macintosh files the MAC.NAM name space module must be loaded first.

Once a volume is configured for name space support, the appropriate name space NLMs must be loaded prior to mounting the volume. Therefore, you must copy the .NAM name space file to the DOS partition of the server and include the statement to load the file in the STARTUP.NCF file. Once a volume is set to store a non-DOS file system, the setting cannot be reversed unless the volume is deleted.

To display the name space support currently loaded on the server, you can enter the ADD NAME SPACE command without the other parameters. A list of all the loaded name spaces is displayed.

Example: add name space mac to sys
See also: VMVOLUMES

Alert

This command allows you to specify what form an event should generate. For example, you can have the event sent to a log file or to the console or to everyone, and so on. For more information and help, type HELP ALERT at the server console prompt.

Syntax: ALERT nmID {Commands} {ON | OFF}, ALERT #50019 ALL OFF
Commands:

EVENT	Description: Generate Event BIT(s)
LOG	Description: Log to File BIT(s)
EVERYONE	Description: Send to Everyone BIT(s)
CONSOLE	Description: Display on Console BIT(s)
BELL	Description: No Ring the Bell BIT(s)
ID	Description: Display ID BIT(s)
LOCUS	Description: Display LOCUS BIT(s)
ALERT	Description: No Alert BIT(s)
NMID	Description: No Display nmID BIT(s)
ALL	Description: Toggle (LOG, CONSOLE, EVERYONE,BELL)

ALIAS

This command creates an alias command that is used in place of an original command. For example you can type ALIAS V VOLUME. Typing V is now equivalent to typing the whole command VOLUME at the server prompt.

After you type ALIASES, a list of current aliases will be displayed on the server. Here is an example of an alias displayed on the server:

```
1. V alias for <VOLUME>
```

BIND

This command assigns or connects a specific communication protocol to a LAN driver loaded on the server. A communication protocol must be linked to the network board, or it will not be able to send and receive packets to and from the network. The syntax to connect a protocol to the network board is:

```
BIND protocol [TO] board_name [protocol_parameter . . .]
```

or

```
BIND protocol [TO] LAN_driver [driver parameters . . .]
      [protocol_parameter . . .]
```

NetWare supports multiple communication protocol stacks in the server. The LAN driver and protocol stack modules must be loaded before this command can be used. The BIND command can be used to connect multiple protocol stacks to a single LAN adapter, or a single protocol can use multiple LAN adapters.

Example: bind ipx to ne3200 slot=3 frame=ethernet_802.2 net=12345678

See also: UNBIND

BINDERY

This command adds or removes a bindery context to or from the list of all bindery contexts for this server.

Examples:

bindery add context = OU=Department OU=Division O=Corporation

bindery delete context = OU=Department OU=Division O=Corporation

BROADCAST

This command enables you to send a message to all the users that are currently logged in or attached to the server. You can also broadcast to a list of users or connection numbers. The syntax for the broadcast message is as follows:

```
BROADCAST "message" [[TO] user_name | connection_number]
      [[and | ,] username | connection_number . . .]
```

Example: broadcast "Please log out of the server. Server going down in 5 minutes" or "Hello to supervisor 5 10 11 23."

See also: SEND

CLEAR STATION

This command clears the connection for a specific connection number. After this command is issued against the user, the workstation will no longer be attached to the server and all the allocated resources at the server are removed. The syntax for this command is:

```
CLEAR STATION station_number
```

You can use the MONITOR program to determine connection numbers or match the connection number with the user.

Example: clear station 5

CLS

This command clears the console screen.

Example: cls

See also: OFF

CONFIG

This command displays the current status of the following information:

- File server name
- Internal network number for the server
- NDS tree name
- Hardware settings on all the network boards installed
- Network address for each network board
- LAN drivers loaded
- Communication protocol bound to the network board
- Frame type assigned to the protocol

- Board name assigned
- Effective bindery services context

Example: config

CSET

Category SET allows you to view or set SET parameters by a particular category. For example, cset MEMORY. Hitting any key other than ESC will cause you to scroll down through all the memory SET parameters. Hitting Y will allow you to change a parameter as you scroll through them.

DISABLE LOGIN

This command prevents additional clients from logging into the server but does not log out the clients that are already logged in. This command applies to all clients of the server whether they are users trying to connect to the server or another NetWare 5 server authenticating to support replica synchronization for NDS.

Example: disable login
See also: ENABLE LOGIN

DISABLE TTS

This command manually turns off the transaction tracking system (TTS) feature. During normal operation there is no reason for you ever to turn TTS off. NDS depends on TTS, and you should not disable it. TTS will automatically become disabled when the TTS backout volume is full or when server memory is insufficient.

The DISABLE TTS command is primarily a tool for application developers who need to test transactional applications with TTS disabled.

After you have manually disabled TTS, you should enable TTS using the ENABLE TTS command or reboot the server.

Example: disable tts
See also: ENABLE TTS

DISMOUNT

This command causes the selected volume to be dismounted. If you have open files on that volume, the server prints a warning on the server console screen and prompts you for confirmation before it dismounts the volume. The syntax for this command is:

```
DISMOUNT volume_name
```

You can use DISMOUNT to make a volume unavailable to your users. This allows you to do maintenance on the volume while the server is up.

If you have a volume that is not used very often, such as a CD-ROM, you can dismount it until you need to use it again. Mounted volumes take up memory.

If the volume being dismounted is the SYS: volume, which contains the NDS files, then the NDS is closed for that server. All requests that require NDS will be directed to another server in the network, which has another copy of the same NDS partition information.

Example: dismount sys

See also: MOUNT

DISPLAY ENVIRONMENT

This command displays the current search paths and the current values of the set parameters for the server. The name of the set parameter will be highlighted in white with the current value in yellow. This command will only display set parameters that are not marked as hidden. When each set parameter is displayed, it will include the limits (min and max) values, as well as the default setting of the set parameter, if applicable. For more information about this command, type HELP DISPLAY ENVIRONMENT at the server console prompt.

Example: DISPLAY ENVIRONMENT

DISPLAY INTERRUPTS

This command displays the interrupt handler and interrupt statistics information. This command will show you the current hardware interrupts that have been assigned. For more information about this command you can type HELP DISPLAY INTERRUPTS.

Examples:

DISPLAY INTERRUPTS	(Displays interrupts currently in use)
DISPLAY INTERRUPTS 3 10	(Displays interrupts 3 and 10)
DISPLAY INTERRUPTS ALL	(Displays all system interrupts)
DISPLAY INTERRUPTS PROC	(Displays per processor interrupt information)

DISPLAY MODIFIED ENVIRONMENT

This command will display only the persistent set parameters that have been changed from their default value. It will display the current setting and the default setting. For more information about this command you can type HELP DISPLAY MODIFIED at the server console prompt.

Example: Display Modified Environment

DISPLAY NETWORKS

This command displays the server's list of all the network numbers that the internal router is aware of. The list shows the IPX network number (which includes the internal network number of the server), the number of hops (networks that must be crossed) to reach the network, and the estimated time in ticks for a packet to reach the network. A tick is 1/18th of a second. The total number of networks is displayed at the end of the list.

Example: display networks

See also: DISPLAY SERVERS

DISPLAY PROCESSORS

The command displays the processor status for any or all processors you have running in your server. For more information about this command, you can type HELP DISPLAY PROCESSORS at the server console prompt.

Examples:

DISPLAY PROCESSORS [P# P# P#]

DISPLAY PROCESSORS (Displays the status of all processors)

DISPLAY PROCESSORS 1 3 (Displays the status of processors 1 and 3)

DISPLAY SERVERS

This command displays the list of all the devices that send out a Service Advertising Protocol that the internal router is aware of. This command shows all servers regardless of type; for example, print servers, queue servers, and others are displayed.

The list shows the advertising name (typically a server) and the number of hops (networks that must be crossed) to reach the server. The total number of servers is displayed at the bottom of the list.

Example: display servers

See also: DISPLAY NETWORKS

DOWN

This command brings down the server. The server going down means that all the connections are cleared, all volumes will be dismounted, and IPX packet routing is suspended. If there are files in use by a workstation when the DOWN command is issued, the server will display a warning on the console screen and ask for confirmation before it goes down.

You should always type the DOWN command before turning the power to the server off. The DOWN command ensures data integrity by writing all cache buffers to disk, closing all files, and updating the appropriate directory and file allocation table.

Example: down

See also: EXIT, and RESTART SERVER

ECHO OFF

This command tells the server not to echo or display the commands in the NetWare Command File to the screen when they are executed. This command is only valid for use in the .NCF files. ECHO OFF is the default.

Example: echo on

See also: ECHO ON

ECHO ON

This command tells the server to echo the commands in the NetWare Command File to the screen as they are executed. This command is only valid for use in the .NCF files. The default is not to echo.

Example: echo off

See also: ECHO OFF

ENABLE LOGIN

This command allows clients to connect and log into the server. This command is the default when the server is booted. You should use this command only if you have disabled login using the DISABLE LOGIN command. This command does not affect users that are already connected.

The ENABLE LOGIN command prevents the supervisor account from being locked out by the intruder detection.

Example: enable login

See also: DISABLE LOGIN

ENABLE TTS

This command manually turns on the transaction tracking system feature of NetWare 5. During normal operation TTS is always enabled.

When volume SYS is mounted, TTS is automatically enabled if there is enough disk space and memory to allow transaction tracking. NDS depends on TTS, and you should always leave it enabled. If a problem occurs that disables TTS automatically, you must fix the problem before you can enable TTS.

The server will automatically disable TTS if one of the following events occurs:

- Volume SYS becomes full
- Insufficient memory to operate TTS

Example: enable tts

See also: DISABLE TTS

EXIT

After the server has been taken down, the EXIT command leaves the server program and returns to DOS. This allows you to access the DOS files or rerun the SERVER.EXE program.

The DOWN command must always be issued before the EXIT command. If the REMOVE DOS command was issued, the server will perform a reboot.

After you bring down the server, it is still connected to the network and receiving packets. You can still execute console commands that deal with packets such as TRACK ON and TRACK OFF.

Example: exit

See also: DOWN, and RESTART SERVER

FILE SERVER NAME

This command sets the server name when the server boots up. The file server name is used to identify the server on the network. The file server name is distributed throughout the network using the SAP. The name chosen should be a unique value on the network because it does have the SAP. The syntax for this command is:

```
FILE SERVER NAME server_name
```

The clients find the server by knowing the name of the server. The file server name for NetWare 5 is also widely used in NDS.

This command is available only in the AUTOEXEC.NCF file and cannot be used at the server prompt.

Example: file server name CAM-SRV1

HELP

This command displays the help screen at the file server console. The help screen lists all the server console commands with examples of how to use them. You can specify an individual command with HELP. The HELP ALL command will list all the server console commands in alphabetical order and pause in between each command.

Example: help, help bind, or help all

IPX INTERNAL NET

This command sets the internal network number that the router uses to identify all services/clients that reside in the same machine as the router. For NetWare 5, the internal network number is very important and is used in NDS. The syntax for this command is:

```
IPX INTERNAL NET network_address
```

The internal IPX network number chosen should be a unique number on the network. This command is available only in the AUTOEXEC.NCF file.

Example: ipx internal net 370DC321

LANGUAGE

This command sets the server console to use the language specified. The server console command and server utilities or NLM programs will use the appropriate language message files. The syntax for this command has several options:

- **Language** — displays current NLM language
- **Language list** — displays list of available languages
- **Language name|number** — sets language by name or number
- **Language add number name** — adds a new language name and number
- **Language rename number new_name** — renames the language specified

Example: language spanish

LIST DEVICES

This command displays all the physical device information for the server.

Example: List Devices

LOAD

This command executes a NetWare Loadable Module file and links it to the operating system. The file executed is named with one of the following extensions: .NLM (server utilities), .DSK (disk driver), and .LAN (LAN driver). The LOAD command searches the SYS:SYSTEM directory by default for the files. The SYS volume must be mounted. The syntax for the LOAD command is:

```
LOAD [path] load_module [parameter . . .]
```

You can also specify a complete path name for the file to be loaded or set up additional paths to search for the file by using the SEARCH command.

Example: load monitor

Note: Typing load before loading an NLM is no longer necessary in NetWare 5.

See also: UNLOAD, SEARCH

MAGAZINE INSERTED

This command acknowledges the insertion of the specified media magazine in response to the "Insert Magazine" console alert.

Example: magazine inserted

MAGAZINE NOT INSERTED

This command acknowledges that the insertion of the specified media magazine was not performed.

Example: magazine not inserted

MAGAZINE NOT REMOVED

This command acknowledges that the removal of the magazine was not performed.

Example: magazine not removed

MAGAZINE REMOVED

This command acknowledges the removal of a magazine from the specified device in response to the "Remove Magazine" console alert.

Example: remove magazine

MEDIA INSERTED

This command acknowledges insertion of the specified media in response to the "Insert Media" console alert.

Example: media inserted

MEDIA NOT INSERTED

This command acknowledges that insertion of the specified media was not performed.

Example: media not inserted

MEDIA NOT REMOVED

This command acknowledges that removal of the media was not performed.

Example: media not removed

MEDIA REMOVED

This command acknowledges removal of the media from the specified device in response to the "Remove Magazine" console alert.

Example: remove media

MEMORY MAP

This command displays a map of server RAM.

Example: memory map

MEMORY

This command displays the total memory installed that the NetWare operating system can address.

Example: memory

See also: REGISTER MEMORY

MIRROR STATUS

This command displays all mirrored logical disk partitions and the status of each.

Example: mirror status

MODULES

This command displays names and descriptions for all the NetWare Loadable Modules currently loaded on the server.

Example: modules

MOUNT

This command causes the specified volume to be mounted as a NetWare volume. The syntax for the MOUNT command is:

```
MOUNT volume_name or MOUNT ALL
```

Example: mount sys, MOUNT ALL

NAME

This command displays the server's name. The NAME command is still supported in NetWare 5 but is not very useful because the server prompt includes the server name.

Example: name

See also: FILE SERVER NAME

NCP ADDRESSES

This command will display the currently registered NCP service addresses. For more information about this command, type HELP NCP ADDRESSES at the server console prompt.

Example: NCP ADDRESSES

NCP DUMP

This command dumps the NCP standard deviation statistics to a specified file.

Example: NCP DUMP filename.ext

NCP STATS

This command displays the NCP statistics on incoming NCP requests. The command can also be used to reset counters.

Example: NCP STATS {RESET}

NCP TRACE

This command decodes the incoming NCP packets to the screen or to a file if specified. The syntax for this command is as follows:

```
NCP TRACE ON {filename.ext}

NCP TRACE OFF
```

OFF

This command clears the server console screen and is equivalent to the CLS command.

Example: off

See also: CLS

PAUSE

This command causes the screen and processing to stop and waits for a key to be pressed while in a NetWare Control File (NCF).

Example: pause

PROTECT

This command is used when you have an NCF file that is used to load NLM(s) and you would like to load them in a protected address space.

Example: PROTECT (NCF file name); for example, PROTECT Grpwise

PROTECTION

This command will display the information about the protected memory address spaces in the system. It also provides the ability to enable and disable the restart feature for a protected address space. For more information about this command, type HELP PROTECTION at the server console prompt.

Examples:

Protection

Protection ADDRESS_SPACE1

Protection restart ADDRESS_SPACE1

Protection no restart ADDRESS_SPACE1

PROTOCOL

This command displays the protocol identification numbers registered with the server. These numbers are based on the server's communication protocol and media type. The PROTOCOL command can also be used to register new protocol IDs and numbers with the server. The proper syntax for this command is:

```
PROTOCOL or PROTOCOL REGISTER protocol_name frame id_number
```

If you load a communication protocol module and try to bind it, you may get an error message stating that the module is not loaded. The error message probably means that the communication protocol or the media type contained in the driver is not registered with NetWare. In this case, you should use the PROTOCOL REGISTER to register the new protocol.

Example: protocol register ip ethernet_ii 800

PROTOCOL REGISTER or PROTOCOL

This command allows you to view registered protocols or register additional protocols and frame types.

Example: PROTOCOL REGISTER IP ETHERNET_II 800

PSM

This command will execute a Platform Support Module (PSM) console command. To display a list of supported PSM commands, you can type **PSM ?**. For more information you can type **HELP PSM** at the server console prompt.

Example: PSM ?

REGISTER MEMORY

For some hardware systems, NetWare 5 does not recognize more than 16MB of RAM. In these situations, you must use the REGISTER MEMORY command at the console. This command uses the following syntax:

```
REGISTER MEMORY memory_start memory_length
```

You can replace the memory_start with a value in hexadecimal representing a memory address beyond 16MB. In most cases, this is the value 0x1000000 (which equates to 16MB). The memory_length is the value of the memory installed that is beyond 16MB. This number must be an even paragraph boundary that is divisible by 0x10. For example, to add 4MB of memory above 16MB (for a total of 20MB RAM), you need to enter the following command:

```
REGISTER MEMORY 1000000 1250000
```

This command can be added to the AUTOEXEC.NCF file for automatic registration of memory when the server is booted. For EISA-based machines, memory above 16MB is registered automatically.

See also: MEMORY

REM or ; or

Each of these commands is used to specify a comment line or a remark in the AUTOEXEC.NCF, or NCF.

Example: REM This line will load the LAN driver for the NE3200 network board.

REMIRROR PARTITION

This command starts the remirroring of a logical disk partition. Partition remirroring typically consumes upward of 70 percent of the CPU's time, so you might want to delay the remirroring process until activity on the server is reduced. The syntax for this command is:

```
REMIRROR PARTITION partition_number
```

Example: remirror partition 4

REMOVE DOS

After the server is running, the memory being used by DOS can be released and given to the server cache memory. Once this command is issued and the server is brought down, the EXIT command will not be able to return to DOS. You must power off the machine to reboot.

By removing DOS from the server's memory, you are providing an additional 1MB of memory for the server cache memory. However, since DOS is no longer residing in memory of the server, the files located on the DOS drives are no longer accessible. This can be implemented as a security step because the NLMs cannot then be loaded from the DOS drivers.

You can also use the REMOVE DOS command to enable warm booting of the server using the EXIT command.

Example: remove dos

See also: EXIT

RESET ENVIRONMENT

This command will display and prompt for every set parameter that has been changed from its default value, querying the console user whether to change the value back to its default value or to skip to the next modified set parameter. For more information about this command, type HELP RESET ENVIRONMENT at the server console prompt.

Example: RESET ENVIRONMENT

RESET ROUTER

This command clears the information stored in the internal router tables of the server. The RESET ROUTER command erases all known servers and networks. The router will automatically rebuild the tables as SAP and RIP advertising information is received.

This command is useful when you want to debug communication problems you may have in the network or the server itself. By resetting the router, you can tell whether the server is receiving the routing information.

For example, if several servers or bridges on your network go down, any packets sent to or through their routers will be lost. If you reset routers in the server that are still up, the router sends a request to the nearest server to verify any other networks or routes it knows about. From this information, the router builds a new, accurate router table.

Example: reset router

RESTART SERVER

This command reloads the SERVER.EXE software after the DOWN command has been issued. This command is valid only if the server has not been exited. The following options are available with the RESTART SERVER command:

- **-ns** — Do not use the STARTUP.NCF file.
- **-na** — Do not use the AUTOEXEC.NCF file.
- **-d** — Break into the internal debugger.

Example: restart server

SCAN FOR NEW DEVICES

This command checks for storage devices and hardware that have been added since the server was last booted. This command causes the operating system to look for and add new devices on the system.

Example: scan for new devices

SEARCH

This command dictates where the server should automatically search for the NetWare Loadable Module (.NLM) files and the NetWare Command File (.NCF). The directory that the server searches by default is SYS:SYSTEM. You can use this command to add additional search paths and to display the current setting for the search paths on the server. The proper syntax for the SEARCH command is:

```
SEARCH [ADD [number]] path
```

or

```
SEARCH DEL [number]
```

Example: search add 4 c:\nwserver\nlms or search del 1

SECURE CONSOLE

This command enables you to restrict access to the server console by:

- Restricting the loading of NLMs from every place but the current search path
- Preventing keyboard entry into the internal NetWare debugger
- Preventing anyone except the console operator from changing the date and time
- Removing DOS from the server

Example: secure console

SEND

This command enables you to send a message to all users logged in or attached to the server or a list of users or connection numbers. The syntax for the SEND command is:

```
SEND "message" [[TO] user_name | connection_number] [[and |,]
   username | connection_number . . .]
```

Example: send "Please delete some files" to jack and jill

SET

This command displays and changes the server's configuration information. Many configuration parameters can be adjusted by using this command. Typing the SET command without a configuration parameter name displays a small menu of configuration parameters. The display shows the configuration parameter name, its current setting, the limits that it can be set to, and a description of what the configuration parameter controls. The syntax for this command is:

```
SET [parameter_name] [=parameter_value]
```

The SET command can be used in the STARTUP.NCF and AUTOEXEC.NCF files. The following three configuration parameters can be set in the STARTUP.NCF (they cannot be set from the server console command line):

- Minimum Packet Receive Buffers
- Maximum Physical Receive Packet Size
- Cache Buffer Size

Example: set bindery context = OU=NORAD.O=ACME

SET TIME

This command sets the server date and time; accepting a variety of formats. You can set just the date, just the time, or both. The syntax for the SET TIME command is:

```
SET TIME [month/day/year] [hour:minute:second]
```

This command assumes that if the time is specified, a colon will separate the hours and minutes. If "am" or "pm" is not specified, the server will assume the time has been entered during working hours. Working hours are 7:00 to 12:00 A.M. and 1:00 to 6:00 P.M.

The month can be entered as a number or a name. If the month is entered as a number, the command assumes that the month precedes the day or year number.

Example: set time April 6 1999 3:45:00 pm

See also: TIME, and SET

SET TIME ZONE

This command sets the server time zone using the specific time zone strings in NetWare 5. The SET TIME ZONE command is also used to display the current setting of the time zone on the server. The syntax for this command is:

```
SET TIME ZONE zone [hour[daylight]]
```

Example: set time zone MST7MDT

SPEED

This command displays the CPU speed rating for the server hardware. The speed is a processor-relative value in which a 386-based machine has a slower rating than a 486-based machine. The Pentium class of machines is faster or has a higher speed rating for the processor.

Example: speed

SPOOL

This command allows you to create, change, or display spooler mappings. These mappings are needed to set up default print queues for NPRINT and CAPTURE. They also support applications that make calls to printer numbers rather than to queues. The syntax for the SPOOL command is:

```
SPOOL
```

or

```
SPOOL number [TO] [QUEUE] queue_name
```

Example: spool 1 to queue hp4si

START PROCESSORS

This command will start all secondary processors on your server.

Examples:

START PROCESSORS [P# P# P#...]

START PROCESSORS (Starts all secondary processors)

START PROCESSORS 1 3 (Starts secondary processors 1 and 3)

STOP PROCESSORS

This command will stop all secondary processors on your server.

Examples:

STOP PROCESSORS [P# P# P#...]

STOP PROCESSORS (Starts all secondary processors)

STOP PROCESSORS 1 3 (Starts secondary processors 1 and 3)

SWAP

This command adds or removes the swap file from a volume and set MIN, MAX, and MIN Free. If no parameters are given, then all swap file information is displayed. The following constraints apply:

- All values are in millions of bytes.
- MIN or MINIMUM = Minimum swap file size, with a default of 2
- MAX or MAXIMUM = Maximum swap file size with a default = Free volume space
- MIN FREE or MINIMUM FREE = Minimum free space to be left on volume not occupying the swap file, with a default of 5

Examples:

Swap

Swap add vol2

Swap add vol3 min = 5 max = 100 min free = 10

Swap delete vol3

Swap parameter vol1 min = 2 max = 1000 min free = 100

TIME

This command displays the current server date, time, and time synchronization status.

Example: time

See also: SET TIME

TRACK OFF

This command closes the Router Tracking Screen on the server that views the activity on the server caused by sending and receiving advertising packets from the Service Advertising Protocol and Routing Information Protocol.

Example: track off

See also: TRACK ON

TRACK ON

This command starts the Router Tracking Screen and makes it active on the server console. The screen displays the activity caused by sending and receiving advertising packets from the Service Advertising Protocol and Routing Information Protocol.

Example: track on

See also: TRACK OFF

UNBIND

This command disconnects the specified communication protocol stack from a LAN adapter. The LAN adapter is specified by the LAN driver name if the driver is only servicing one adapter. If the LAN driver is servicing more than one adapter, the optional parameters indicate the hardware settings of the adapter to be unbound. If either the LAN driver or the protocol stack is unloaded using the command, the protocol stack will automatically be unbound from the LAN adapter. The syntax for the UNBIND command is:

```
UNBIND protocol [FROM] LAN_driver [driver parameters . . .]
```

or

```
UNBIND protocol [FROM] board_name
```

Example: unbind ipx from ne3200 slot=3 frame=ethernet_802.2
See also: BIND

UNLOAD

This command removes or unlinks the NetWare Loadable Module from the operating system. The NLM, which was previously loaded, is removed from the server memory. You can use the UNLOAD command to upgrade or change any of the NLMs loaded on the server.

Example: unload pserver
See also: LOAD

VERSION

This command displays the server's version information and copyright notice.
Example: version

VOLUME

This command displays a list of all the volumes currently mounted on the server.

Example: volume
See also: MOUNT

VMDISMOUNT

This command allows volume maintenance or repairs while the file server is up by making a volume unavailable to the users temporarily.

Example: vmdismount sys or vmdismount 0

VMMOUNT

This command makes a volume available to users.
Example: vmmount sys or vmmount 0

VMVOLUMES

This command displays a list of the currently mounted volumes including the number, status, and name.

Example: vmvolumes

APPENDIX D

NetWare 5 Debugger Commands

The NetWare 5 operating system includes an internal assembly language debug utility. This debugger enables you to execute the commands listed in this appendix. You can use the debugger to help determine the cause of a server abend or simply to become more familiar with the internal structure of NetWare 5. The NetWare 5 debugger features color-coded data that will help you more easily identify the more important information and make it quicker and easier to use.

When the debugger is entered, it will display the following: a screen with a "#" as the prompt; default information, including the location in code at which the server abended or was manually interrupted; and the cause of the abend or trap. The general registers and flags are also presented.

Invoking the NetWare 5 Debugger

Four methods are available to invoke the debugger: two from the server console, one from a program, and one from hardware.

From the Server Console

- Press Alt+Left Shift+Right Shift+Esc simultaneously at the server keyboard. You can supply this key combination either while the server is running or after an abend. This will not work if the server is hung in a tight infinite loop (some infinite loops are not too tight), if it has interrupts disabled, or if the server console has been locked.

- If the server abends or GPIs (General Power Interrupts), you can type **386debug** to invoke the debugger. The characters you type are not echoed to the screen, but the "#" prompt will immediately appear. Remember, the "#" prompt indicates that you are in the debugger.

From an NLM Program

- If the NLM program supplies an INT 3 in the desired code segment, the program will invoke the debugger. If the programmer is using C and the CLIB interface, he or she can call a `Breakpoint()` function.

With Hardware or Manually

- You can break into a server by using an NMI board. After the server has abended, you can use either of the steps for the Server Console to enter the debugger. This method seems abrupt but may be required if the software program being debugged is in a tight infinite loop with interrupts disabled.

Debugger Commands

Once you have entered the debugger, you can display a great deal of information. The debugger commands and their functions are listed in Tables D.1 through D.4.

TABLE D.1

Debugger Commands

COMMAND	FUNCTION
Q	Quits the debugger and returns to DOS.
G	Continues server execution (go) from the current position.
G [address(es)]	Begins execution at the current position and then sets a temporary breakpoint at the address or several temporary breakpoints at the addresses.
P	Proceeds with the next instruction. Using this command, you can trace or single-step each of the following instructions. One limitation is that this command will not single-step through loops in the code or trace into a subroutine call. You can repeat this command by simply pressing Enter at the prompt.
T or S	Enables you to trace or single-step through the program code, through loops, and into subroutine calls.
U address	Enables you to unassemble instructions from a specific address, which can be done for count instructions. You can repeat this command by simply pressing Enter at the prompt.

Continued

TABLE D.1

Continued

COMMAND	FUNCTION
V	Enables you to switch over and view the server console screens. You will be able to step through the screens sequentially.
? address	Displays the closest symbols to the address if symbolic information has been loaded. By default, this command is the EIP register.
N symbol	Enables you to assign a symbol name to a specific name address.
N –symbolname	Removes the specific symbol name.
N—	Removes all defined symbols.
Z expression	Evaluates the expression. This command is useful as a calculator in the debugger. Zd will evaluate the expression in decimal.

TABLE D.2

Help Commands

COMMAND	FUNCTION
H	Displays help for general commands.
.H	Displays help for the "." commands.
HB	Displays help for breakpoints.
HE	Displays help for expressions.
H3	Displays help for SFT III commands.

TABLE D.3

Dot "." Commands

COMMAND	FUNCTION
.a	Displays the reason for an abend or a break.
.c	Does a diagnostic memory dump to floppy or hard disk.
.d	Displays a page directory map for the current debugger domain.
.d	Displays a page entry map for the current debugger domain.
.f	Toggles the developer option flag ON/OFF.
.g	Displays the GDT.

COMMAND	FUNCTION
.h	Displays help for the "." commands.
.I	Displays the IDT.
.I2	Displays the IDT for Processor 2. This command defaults to the math coprocessor on a single-processor system.
.l offset[offset]	Displays the linear address given to page map offsets.
.la[linear address] [<cr3>]	Finds all aliases of a linear address.
.lp[physical address] [<cr3>]	Finds all linear mappings of a physical address.
.lx address	Displays page offsets and values used for translation.
.m	Displays loaded module names and addresses.
.p	Displays all process names and addresses.
.p address	Displays *address* as a process control block.
.r	Displays the running process control block.
.s	Displays all screen names and addresses.
.?	Displays the server state.
.s address	Displays *address* as a screen structure. If no address is specified, this command displays all screen names and addresses.
.t address	Displays *address* as a TSS structure.
.ts [segnum]	Displays GDT *[segnum]* as a TSS structure.
.v	Displays the server version.

TABLE D.4 Memory Commands

COMMAND	FUNCTION
C address	Interactively changes the contents of a memory location.
C address = number(s)	Changes the memory contents beginning at *address* to the specified number(s). *Number* is a hexadecimal value.
C address = "text string"	Changes the memory contents starting at *address* to the text string value.
D address [count]	Dumps the contents of memory, starting at *address*, for *count* number of bytes. The address and count are in hexadecimal values. *Count* is an optional value; if it is not supplied, one page (100h bytes) will be displayed. This command can be repeated continually by pressing Enter after each dump of contents.
M address [L length] bytepattern(s)	Searches memory for a byte pattern match, starting at the location *address* and continuing until *L length* is reached. If a match is found, 128 bytes (starting with the pattern) are displayed. This command can be repeated by pressing Enter at the # prompt.

Registers

Tables D.5 through D.7 list the NetWare 5 debugger commands used on the microprocessor's internal registers. These registers are both the general and flag registers.

TABLE D.5

NetWare 5 Debugger Commands Used on the Microprocessor's Internal Registers

COMMAND	FUNCTION
R	Displays the EAX, EBX, ECX, EDX, ESI, EDI, ESP, EBP, EIP, and flag registers.
Name of Register = value	Enables you to change a specific register to a new value. This command affects the EAX, EBX, ECX, EDX, ESI, EDI, ESP, EBP, EFL, and EIP registers.
Name of F flag = value	Enables you to change a specific flag register to a new value. The value has to be 0 or 1, since these are the only values the flag register can hold. This command affects the CF, AF, ZF, SF, IF, TF, PF, DF, and OF flag registers.

TABLE D.6

Input/Output Commands

COMMAND	FUNCTION
I[B,W,D] port	Inputs a (B)yte, (W)ord, or (D)ouble word from a port. The default is byte O[B,W,D] port = value. Outputs a (B)yte, (W)ord, or (D)ouble word value to a port.

TABLE D.7

Breakpoints Commands

COMMAND	FUNCTION
B	Displays all breakpoints that are currently set.
B = address	Sets an execution breakpoint at *address*. The break will occur if EIP = address is changed and the condition evaluates to TRUE.
BC number	Clears the breakpoint specified by *number*.
BCA	Clears all breakpoints.
BI = address	Sets an I/O read/write breakpoint at address. This breakpoint will occur when the specified I/O port address is accessed with either a read or a write.
BR = address {condition}	Sets a read/write breakpoint at the address specified when the indicated condition is true.
BW = address {condition}	Sets a write breakpoint at the address specified when the indicated condition is true.

Debug Expressions

In Table D.8, all the numbers in the debug expressions are entered and shown in hex format. In addition to the numbers, the following registers, flags, and operators can be used in the debug expressions:

Registers: EAX, EBX, ECX, EDX, ESI, EDI, ESP, EBP, EIP

Flags: FLCF, FLAF, FLZF, FLSF, FLIF, FLTF, FLPF, FLDF, FLOF

TABLE D.8

Debug Expressions and Their Numbers

SYMBOL	DESCRIPTION	PRECEDENCE
|		e
( )	(Expression) Causes the expression to be evaluated at a higher level.	0
[ ]	[Size Expression] Causes the expression to be evaluated at a higher precedence and then uses the value of the expression as a memory address.	0
{ }	{Size Expression} Causes the expression to be evaluated at a higher precedence and then uses the value of the expression as a port address.	0
!	Logical Not	1
-	2's Complement	1
~	1's Complement	1
*	Multiply	2
/	Divide	2
%	Mod	2
+	Add	3
-	Subtract	3
>	Bit Shift Right	4
<<	Bit Shift Left	4

<table>
<tr><th>SYMBOL</th><th>DESCRIPTION</th><th>PRECEDENCE</th></tr>
<tr><td>></td><td>Greater Than</td><td>5</td></tr>
<tr><td><</td><td>Less Than</td><td>5</td></tr>
<tr><td>>=</td><td>Greater Than or Equal To</td><td>5</td></tr>
<tr><td><=</td><td>Less Than Or Equal To</td><td>5</td></tr>
<tr><td>==</td><td>Equal To</td><td>6</td></tr>
<tr><td>!=</td><td>Not Equal To</td><td>6</td></tr>
<tr><td>&</td><td>Bitwise AND</td><td>7</td></tr>
<tr><td>^</td><td>Bitwise XOR</td><td>8</td></tr>
<tr><td>|</td><td>Bitwise OR</td><td>9</td></tr>
<tr><td>&&</td><td>Logical AND</td><td>10</td></tr>
<tr><td>||</td><td>Logical OR</td><td>11</td></tr>
</table>

Conditional Evaluation

`expression1 ? expression2, expression3`

If `expression1` is true, then the result is the value of `expression2`. Otherwise (if expression1 is not true) the result is the value of `expression3`.

Index

Symbols & Numbers

A

(continued)

C

(continued)

D

E

(continued)

(continued)

N

(continued)

(continued)

(continued)

(continued)

Q

R

S

(continued)

(continued)

U

V

W

X

Y

Z

IDG Books Worldwide, Inc.
End-User License Agreement

READ THIS. You should carefully read these terms and conditions before opening the software packet(s) included with this book ("Book"). This is a license agreement ("Agreement") between you and IDG Books Worldwide, Inc. ("IDGB"). By opening the accompanying software packet(s), you acknowledge that you have read and accept the following terms and conditions. If you do not agree and do not want to be bound by such terms and conditions, promptly return the Book and the unopened software packet(s) to the place you obtained them for a full refund.

1. **License Grant.** IDGB grants to you (either an individual or entity) a nonexclusive license to use one copy of the enclosed software program(s) (collectively, the "Software") solely for your own personal or business purposes on a single computer (whether a standard computer or a workstation component of a multiuser network). The Software is in use on a computer when it is loaded into temporary memory (RAM) or installed into permanent memory (hard disk, CD-ROM, or other storage device). IDGB reserves all rights not expressly granted herein.

2. **Ownership.** IDGB is the owner of all right, title, and interest, including copyright, in and to the compilation of the Software recorded on the disk(s) or CD-ROM ("Software Media"). Copyright to the individual programs recorded on the Software Media is owned by the author or other authorized copyright owner of each program. Ownership of the Software and all proprietary rights relating thereto remain with IDGB and its licensers.

3. **Restrictions On Use and Transfer.**

   (a) You may only (i) make one copy of the Software for backup or archival purposes, or (ii) transfer the Software to a single hard disk, provided that you keep the original for backup or archival purposes. You may not (i) rent or lease the Software, (ii) copy or reproduce the Software through a LAN or other network system or through any computer subscriber system or bulletin-board system, or (iii) modify, adapt, or create derivative works based on the Software.

   (b) You may not reverse engineer, decompile, or disassemble the Software. You may transfer the Software and user documentation on a permanent basis, provided that the transferee agrees to accept the terms and conditions of this Agreement and you retain no copies. If the Software is an update or has been updated, any transfer must include the most recent update and all prior versions.

4. **Restrictions On Use of Individual Programs.** You must follow the individual requirements and restrictions detailed for each individual program in Appendix A of this Book. These limitations are also contained in the individual license agreements recorded on the Software Media. These limitations may include a requirement that after using the program for a specified period of time, the user must pay a registration fee or discontinue use. By opening the Software packet(s), you will be agreeing to abide by the licenses and restrictions for these individual programs that are detailed in Appendix A and on the Software Media. None of the material on this Software Media or listed in this Book may ever be redistributed, in original or modified form, for commercial purposes.

5. **Limited Warranty.**

(a) IDGB warrants that the Software and Software Media are free from defects in materials and workmanship under normal use for a period of sixty (60) days from the date of purchase of this Book. If IDGB receives notification within the warranty period of defects in materials or workmanship, IDGB will replace the defective Software Media.

(b) **IDGB AND THE AUTHORS OF THE BOOK DISCLAIM ALL OTHER WARRANTIES, EXPRESS OR IMPLIED, INCLUDING WITHOUT LIMITATION IMPLIED WARRANTIES OF MERCHANTABILITY AND FITNESS FOR A PARTICULAR PURPOSE, WITH RESPECT TO THE SOFTWARE, THE PROGRAMS, THE SOURCE CODE CONTAINED THEREIN, AND/OR THE TECHNIQUES DESCRIBED IN THIS BOOK. IDGB DOES NOT WARRANT THAT THE FUNCTIONS CONTAINED IN THE SOFTWARE WILL MEET YOUR REQUIREMENTS OR THAT THE OPERATION OF THE SOFTWARE WILL BE ERROR FREE.**

(c) This limited warranty gives you specific legal rights, and you may have other rights that vary from jurisdiction to jurisdiction.

6. **Remedies.**

(a) IDGB's entire liability and your exclusive remedy for defects in materials and workmanship shall be limited to replacement of the Software Media, which may be returned to IDGB with a copy of your receipt at the following address: Software Media Fulfillment Department, Attn.: *Novell's Guide to NetWare® 5 Networks*, IDG Books Worldwide, Inc., 7260 Shadeland Station, Ste. 100, Indianapolis, IN 46256, or call 1-800-762-2974. Please allow three to four weeks for delivery. This Limited Warranty is void if failure of the Software Media has resulted from accident, abuse, or misapplication. Any replacement Software Media will be warranted for the remainder of the original warranty period or thirty (30) days, whichever is longer.

(b) In no event shall IDGB or the authors be liable for any damages whatsoever (including without limitation damages for loss of business profits, business interruption, loss of business information, or any other pecuniary loss) arising from the use of or inability to use the Book or the Software, even if IDGB has been advised of the possibility of such damages.

(c) Because some jurisdictions do not allow the exclusion or limitation of liability for consequential or incidental damages, the above limitation or exclusion may not apply to you.

7. **U.S. Government Restricted Rights.** Use, duplication, or disclosure of the Software by the U.S. Government is subject to restrictions stated in paragraph (c)(1)(ii) of the Rights in Technical Data and Computer Software clause of DFARS 252.227-7013, and in subparagraphs (a) through (d) of the Commercial Computer—Restricted Rights clause at FAR 52.227-19, and in similar clauses in the NASA FAR supplement, when applicable.

8. **General.** This Agreement constitutes the entire understanding of the parties and revokes and supersedes all prior agreements, oral or written, between them and may not be modified or amended except in a writing signed by both parties hereto that specifically refers to this Agreement. This Agreement shall take precedence over any other documents that may be in conflict herewith. If any one or more provisions contained in this Agreement are held by any court or tribunal to be invalid, illegal, or otherwise unenforceable, each and every other provision shall remain in full force and effect.

CD-ROM Installation Instructions

For complete contents and descriptions of the software included on the three CD-ROMs that accompany *Novell's Guide to NetWare 5 Networks*, please see Appendix A, "The CD-ROM Set Included with This Book." Detailed installation instructions and system requirements are also provided for all included programs.

To install the software on any of the three CD-ROMs included with this book with Windows 95, 98, or NT 4.0, follow these steps:

1. Place the desired CD-ROM disc in your CD-ROM drive.

2. Click the Start button and select Run.

3. Type the letter of your CD-ROM drive with a colon and backslash (for instance, **D:**) and the directory name that contains the program you wish to run, followed by the name of the appropriate executable installation file. For example, to install the Visio Solution Pack for NDS (Disc 3), you would type the following:

   ```
   D:\nds\setup.exe
   ```

4. Click OK and follow the on-screen installation instructions.